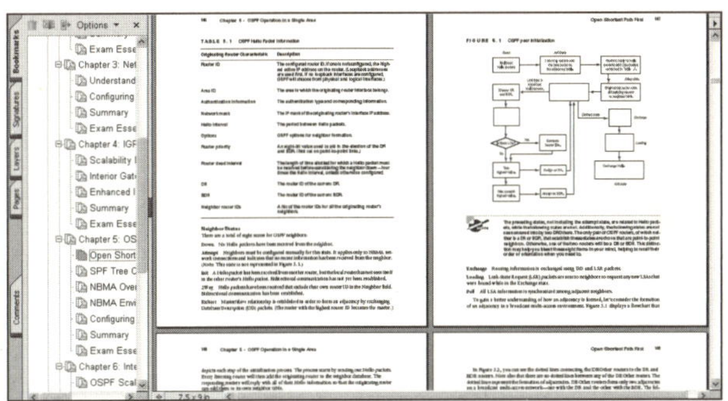

Access the

in PDF!

- Full search capabilities let you quickly find the information you need.
- Complete with tables and illustrations.
- Adobe Acrobat Reader with Search included.

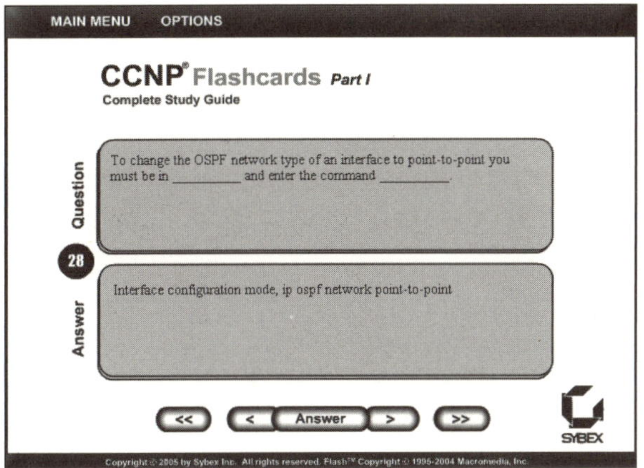

Reinforce understanding of key topics with flashcards for your PC, Pocket PC, or Palm handheld!

- Contains over 600 flashcard questions.
- Runs on multiple platforms for usability and portability.
- Quiz yourself anytime, anywhere!

CCNP® Complete Study Guide

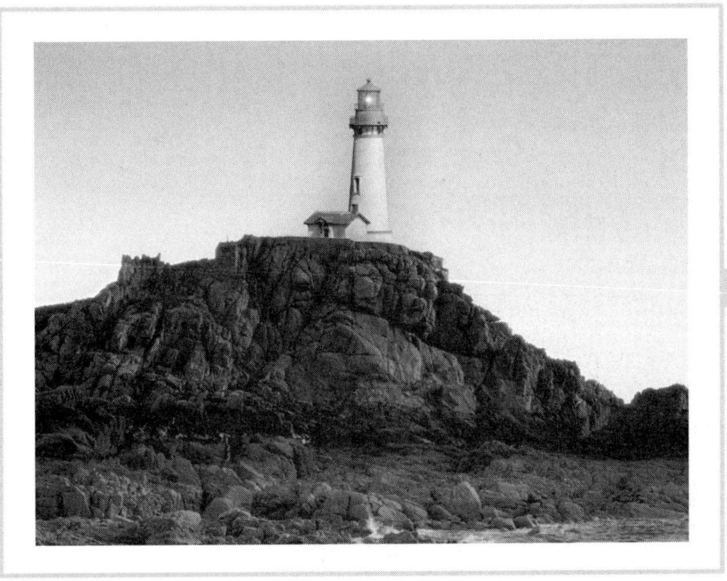

Wade Edwards, CCIE, Terry Jack, CCIE,
Todd Lammle, CCNP, Robert Padjen, CCNP,
Arthur Pfund, CCIE, Toby Skandier, CCNP,
Carl Timm, CCIE

San Francisco • London

SYBEX

Associate Publisher: Neil Edde
Acquisitions and Developmental Editor: Maureen Adams
Production Editor: Mae Lum
Technical Editor: Craig Vazquez
Copyeditor: Sarah Lemaire
Compositor: Craig J. Woods, Happenstance Type-O-Rama
Graphic Illustrator: Happenstance Type-O-Rama
CD Coordinator: Dan Mummert
CD Technician: Kevin Ly
Proofreaders: Jim Brook, Candace English, Jennifer Larsen, Nancy Riddiough
Indexer: Nancy Guenther
Book Designers: Bill Gibson, Judy Fung
Cover Designer: Archer Design
Cover Illustrator/Photographer: Photodisc and Victor Arre

Library of Congress Card Number: 2005920775

ISBN: 0-7821-4421-7

Manufactured in the United States of America

10 9 8 7 6 5 4 3 2 1

To Our Valued Readers:

Thank you for looking to Sybex for your CCNP exam prep needs. Cisco developed the CCNP certification to validate expertise in implementing and managing Cisco internetworking solutions, and it is currently one of the most highly sought after IT certifications. Just as Cisco is committed to establishing measurable standards for certifying those professionals who work in the field of internetworking, Sybex is committed to providing those professionals with the information they need to excel.

We at Sybex are proud of our reputation for providing certification candidates with the practical knowledge and skills needed to succeed in the highly competitive IT marketplace. This four-in-one CCNP Complete Study Guide reflects our commitment to provide CCNP candidates with the most up-to-date, accurate, and economical instructional material on the market.

The authors and the editors have worked hard to ensure that the book you hold in your hands is comprehensive, in-depth, and pedagogically sound. We're confident that this book will exceed the demanding standards of the certification marketplace and help you, the CCNP certification candidate, succeed in your endeavors.

As always, your feedback is important to us. If you believe you've identified an error in the book, please send a detailed e-mail to support@sybex.com. And if you have general comments or suggestions, feel free to drop me a line directly at nedde@sybex.com. At Sybex, we're continually striving to meet the needs of individuals preparing for certification exams.

Good luck in pursuit of your CCNP certification!

Neil Edde
Publisher—Certification
Sybex, Inc.

Software License Agreement: Terms and Conditions

The media and/or any online materials accompanying this book that are available now or in the future contain programs and/or text files (the "Software") to be used in connection with the book. SYBEX hereby grants to you a license to use the Software, subject to the terms that follow. Your purchase, acceptance, or use of the Software will constitute your acceptance of such terms.

The Software compilation is the property of SYBEX unless otherwise indicated and is protected by copyright to SYBEX or other copyright owner(s) as indicated in the media files (the "Owner(s)"). You are hereby granted a single-user license to use the Software for your personal, noncommercial use only. You may not reproduce, sell, distribute, publish, circulate, or commercially exploit the Software, or any portion thereof, without the written consent of SYBEX and the specific copyright owner(s) of any component software included on this media.

In the event that the Software or components include specific license requirements or end-user agreements, statements of condition, disclaimers, limitations or warranties ("End-User License"), those End-User Licenses supersede the terms and conditions herein as to that particular Software component. Your purchase, acceptance, or use of the Software will constitute your acceptance of such End-User Licenses.

By purchase, use or acceptance of the Software you further agree to comply with all export laws and regulations of the United States as such laws and regulations may exist from time to time.

Software Support

Components of the supplemental Software and any offers associated with them may be supported by the specific Owner(s) of that material, but they are not supported by SYBEX. Information regarding any available support may be obtained from the Owner(s) using the information provided in the appropriate read.me files or listed elsewhere on the media.

Should the manufacturer(s) or other Owner(s) cease to offer support or decline to honor any offer, SYBEX bears no responsibility. This notice concerning support for the Software is provided for your information only. SYBEX is not the agent or principal of the Owner(s), and SYBEX is in no way responsible for providing any support for the Software, nor is it liable or responsible for any support provided, or not provided, by the Owner(s).

Warranty

SYBEX warrants the enclosed media to be free of physical defects for a period of ninety (90) days after purchase. The Software is not available from SYBEX in any other form or media than that enclosed herein or posted to `www.sybex.com`. If you discover a defect in the media during this warranty period, you may obtain a replacement of identical format at no charge by sending the defective media, postage prepaid, with proof of purchase to:

SYBEX Inc.
Product Support Department
1151 Marina Village Parkway
Alameda, CA 94501
Web: `http://www.sybex.com`

After the 90-day period, you can obtain replacement media of identical format by sending us the defective disk, proof of purchase, and a check or money order for $10, payable to SYBEX.

Disclaimer

SYBEX makes no warranty or representation, either expressed or implied, with respect to the Software or its contents, quality, performance, merchantability, or fitness for a particular purpose. In no event will SYBEX, its distributors, or dealers be liable to you or any other party for direct, indirect, special, incidental, consequential, or other damages arising out of the use of or inability to use the Software or its contents even if advised of the possibility of such damage. In the event that the Software includes an online update feature, SYBEX further disclaims any obligation to provide this feature for any specific duration other than the initial posting.

The exclusion of implied warranties is not permitted by some states. Therefore, the above exclusion may not apply to you. This warranty provides you with specific legal rights; there may be other rights that you may have that vary from state to state. The pricing of the book with the Software by SYBEX reflects the allocation of risk and limitations on liability contained in this agreement of Terms and Conditions.

Shareware Distribution

This Software may contain various programs that are distributed as shareware. Copyright laws apply to both shareware and ordinary commercial software, and the copyright Owner(s) retains all rights. If you try a shareware program and continue using it, you are expected to register it. Individual programs differ on details of trial periods, registration, and payment. Please observe the requirements stated in appropriate files.

Copy Protection

The Software in whole or in part may or may not be copy-protected or encrypted. However, in all cases, reselling or redistributing these files without authorization is expressly forbidden except as specifically provided for by the Owner(s) therein.

Acknowledgments

We would like to thank Neil Edde and Maureen Adams for giving us the opportunity to update this Study Guide. We would also like to take a moment to thank everyone else involved in the creation of this book, including Production Editor Mae Lum; Technical Editor Craig Vazquez; Copyeditor Sarah Lemaire; Proofreaders Jim Brook, Candace English, Jennifer Larsen, and Nancy Riddiough; Indexer Nancy Guenther; and Dan Mummert and Kevin Ly of the CD group.

Contents at a Glance

Contents

Introduction

This book is intended to help you continue on your exciting new path toward obtaining your CCNP certification. Before reading this book, it is important to have at least read the *CCNA: Cisco Certified Network Associate Study Guide, 5th Edition* (Sybex, 2005). You can take the CCNP tests in any order, but you should have passed the CCNA exam before pursuing your CCNP. Many questions in the Building Cisco Remote Access Networks (BCRAN) exam are built on the CCNA material. However, we have done everything possible to make sure that you can pass the BCRAN exam by reading this book and practicing with Cisco routers.

Cisco Systems' Place in Networking

Cisco Systems has become an unrivaled worldwide leader in networking for the Internet. Its networking solutions can easily connect users who work from diverse devices on disparate networks. Cisco products make it simple for people to access and transfer information without regard to differences in time, place, or platform.

Cisco Systems' big picture is that it provides end-to-end networking solutions that customers can use to build an efficient, unified information infrastructure of their own or to connect to someone else's. This is an important piece in the Internet/networking-industry puzzle because a common architecture that delivers consistent network services to all users is now a functional imperative. Because Cisco Systems offers such a broad range of networking and Internet services and capabilities, users needing regular access to their local network or the Internet can do so unhindered, making Cisco's wares indispensable.

Cisco answers this need with a wide range of hardware products that form information networks using the Cisco Internetwork Operating System (IOS) software. This software provides network services, paving the way for networked technical support and professional services to maintain and optimize all network operations.

Along with the Cisco IOS, one of the services Cisco created to help support the vast amount of hardware it has engineered is the Cisco Certified Internetworking Expert (CCIE) program, which was designed specifically to equip people to effectively manage the vast quantity of installed Cisco networks. The business plan is simple: If you want to sell more Cisco equipment and have more Cisco networks installed, ensure that the networks you installed run properly.

However, having a fabulous product line isn't all it takes to guarantee the huge success that Cisco enjoys—lots of companies with great products are now defunct. If you have complicated products designed to solve complicated problems, you need knowledgeable people who are fully capable of installing, managing, and troubleshooting them. That part isn't easy, so Cisco began the CCIE program to equip people to support these complicated networks. This program, known colloquially as the Doctorate of Networking, has also been very successful, primarily due to its extreme difficulty. Cisco continuously monitors the program, changing it as it sees fit, to make sure that it remains pertinent and accurately reflects the demands of today's internetworking business environments.

Building on the highly successful CCIE program, Cisco Career Certifications permit you to become certified at various levels of technical proficiency, spanning the disciplines of network design and support. So, whether you're beginning a career, changing careers, securing your present position, or seeking to refine and promote your position, this is the book for you!

Cisco Certified Network Professional (CCNP)

The Cisco Certified Network Professional (CCNP) certification has opened up many opportunities for the individual wishing to become Cisco-certified but who is lacking the training, the expertise, or the bucks to pass the notorious and often failed two-day Cisco torture lab. The new Cisco certifications will truly provide exciting new opportunities for the CNE and MCSE who just don't know how to advance to a higher level.

So, you're thinking, "Great, what do I do after I pass the CCNA exam?" Well, if you want to become a CCIE in Routing and Switching (the most popular certification), understand that there's more than one path to the CCIE certification. The first way is to continue studying and become a Cisco Certified Network Professional (CCNP). That means taking four more tests in addition to obtaining the CCNA certification.

We'll discuss requirements for the CCIE exams later in this introduction.

The CCNP program will prepare you to understand and comprehensively tackle the internetworking issues of today and beyond—not limited to the Cisco world. You will undergo an immense metamorphosis, vastly increasing your knowledge and skills through the process of obtaining these certifications.

Remember that you don't need to be a CCNP or even a CCNA to take the CCIE lab, but to accomplish that, it's extremely helpful if you already have these certifications.

What Are the CCNP Certification Skills?

Cisco demands a certain level of proficiency for its CCNP certification. In addition to those required for the CCNA, these skills include the following:

- Installing, configuring, operating, and troubleshooting complex routed LAN, routed WAN, and switched LAN networks, and Dial Access Services.
- Understanding complex networks, such as IP, IGRP, IPX, Async Routing, extended access lists, IP RIP, route redistribution, route summarization, OSPF, VLSM, BGP, Serial, IGRP, Frame Relay, ISDN, ISL, DDR, PSTN, PPP, VLANs, Ethernet, access lists, and transparent and translational bridging.

To meet the Cisco Certified Network Professional requirements, you must be able to perform the following:

- Install and/or configure a network to increase bandwidth, quicken network response times, and improve reliability and quality of service.
- Maximize performance through campus LANs, routed WANs, and remote access.
- Improve network security.
- Create a global intranet.

- Provide access security to campus switches and routers.
- Provide increased switching and routing bandwidth—end-to-end resiliency services.
- Provide custom queuing and routed priority services.

How Do You Become a CCNP?

After becoming a CCNA, the four exams you must take to get your CCNP are as follows:

Exam 642-801: Building Scalable Cisco Internetworks (BSCI) A while back, Cisco retired the Routing (640-603) exam and now uses this exam to build on the fundamentals of the CCNA exam. BSCI focuses on large multiprotocol internetworks and how to manage them. Among other topics, you'll be tested on IS-IS, OSFP, and BGP. This book covers all the objectives you need to understand for passing the BSCI exam. The BSCI exam is also a required exam for the CCIP and CCDP certifications, which will be discussed later in this introduction.

Exam 642-811: Building Cisco Multilayer Switched Networks (BCMSN) The Building Cisco Multilayer Switched Networks exam tests your knowledge of the 1900 and 5000 series of Catalyst switches.

Exam 642-821: Building Cisco Remote Access Networks (BCRAN) The Building Cisco Remote Access Networks (BCRAN) exam tests your knowledge of installing, configuring, monitoring, and troubleshooting Cisco ISDN and dial-up access products. You must understand PPP, ISDN, Frame Relay, and authentication.

Exam 642-831: Cisco Internetwork Troubleshooting (CIT) The Cisco Internetwork Troubleshooting (CIT) exam tests you on troubleshooting information. You must be able to troubleshoot Ethernet and Token Ring LANS, IP, IPX, and AppleTalk networks, as well as ISDN, PPP, and Frame Relay networks.

CCNP Exam Objectives

At the beginning of each chapter in this book, we have included the listing of the exam objectives covered in the chapter. These are provided for easy reference and to assure you that you are on track with the objectives. Exam objectives are subject to change at any time without prior notice and at Cisco's sole discretion. Please visit the CCNP page of Cisco's website (`http://www.cisco.com/en/US/learning/le3/le2/le37/le10/learning_certification_type_home.html`) for the most current listing of exam objectives.

Building Scalable Cisco Internetworks (BSCI)

To pass the BSCI exam, you'll need to master the following subject areas:

Technology

List the key information routers needs to route data.

Describe classful and classless routing protocols.

Describe link-state router protocol operation.

Compare classful and classless routing protocols.

Compare distance vector and link-state routing protocols.

Describe concepts relating to extending IP addresses and the use of VLSMs to extend IP addresses.

Describe the features and operation of EIGRP.

Describe the features and operation of single-area OSPF.

Describe the features and operation of multi-area OSPF.

Explain basic OSI terminology and Network layer protocols used in OSI.

Identify similarities and differences between Integrated IS-IS and OSPF.

List the types of IS-IS routers and their role in IS-IS area design.

Describe the hierarchical structure of IS-IS areas.

Describe the concept of establishing adjacencies.

Describe the features and operation of BGP.

Explain how BGP policy-based routing functions within an autonomous system.

Explain the use of redistribution between BGP and Interior Gateway Protocols (IGPs).

Implementation and Configuration

Given a set of network requirements, identify the steps to configure an Enhanced IGRP environment and verify proper operation (within described guidelines) of your routers.

Given an addressing scheme and other laboratory parameters, identify the steps to configure a single-area OSPF environment and verify proper operation (within described guidelines) of your routers.

Given an addressing scheme and other laboratory parameters, identify the steps to configure a multiple-area OSPF environment and verify proper operation (within described guidelines) of your routers.

Given an addressing scheme and other laboratory parameters, identify the steps to configure Cisco routers for proper Integrated IS-IS operation.

Identify the steps to select and configure the different ways to control routing update traffic.

Identify the steps to configure router redistribution in a network.

Identify the steps to configure policy-based routing using route maps.

Given a set of network requirements, identify the steps to configure a BGP environment and verify proper operation (within described guidelines) of your routers.

Identify the steps to configure a router for Network Address Translation with overload, static translations, and route maps.

Design

Describe the three-layer hierarchical design model and explain the function of each layer: Access, Distribution and Core.

Given specific requirements, choose the correct routing protocol to meet the requirements.

Identify the correct IP addressing scheme, including features of IPv6.

Describe the concepts relating to route summarization and apply them to hypothetical scenarios.

Troubleshooting

Identify the steps to verify OSPF operation in a single area.

Identify the steps to verify OSPF operation in multiple areas.

Identify verification methods that ensure proper operation of Integrated IS-IS on Cisco routers.

Identify the steps to verify route redistribution.

Describe the scalability problems associated with internal BGP.

Interpret the output of various `show` and `debug` commands to determine the cause of route selection errors and configuration problems.

Identify the steps to verify Enhanced IGRP operation.

Building Cisco Multilayer Switched Networks (BCMSN)

To pass the BCMSN exam, you'll need to master the following subject areas:

Technology

Describe the Enterprise Composite Model used for designing networks and explain how it addresses enterprise network needs for performance, scalability, and availability.

Describe the Physical, Data Link and Network layer technologies used in a switched network, and identify when to use each.

Explain the role of switches in the various modules of the Enterprise Composite Model (Campus Infrastructure, Server Farm, Enterprise Edge, and Network Management).

Explain the function of the Switching Database Manager [specifically Content Addressable Memory (CAM) and Ternary Content Addressable Memory (TCAM)] within a Catalyst switch.

Describe the features and operation of VLANs on a switched network.

Describe the features of the VLAN trunking protocols, including 802.1Q, ISL (emphasis on 802.1Q), and dynamic trunking protocol.

Describe the features and operation of 802.1Q Tunneling (802.1QinQ) within a service provider network.

Describe the operation and purpose of managed VLAN services.

Describe how VTP versions 1 and 2 operate, including domains, modes, advertisements, and pruning.

Explain the operation and purpose of the Spanning Tree Protocol (STP) on a switched network.

Identify the specific types of Cisco route switch processors, and provide implementation details.

List and describe the operation of the key components required to implement inter-VLAN routing.

Explain the types of redundancy in a multilayer switched network including hardware and software redundancy.

Explain how IP multicast operates on a multilayer switched network, including PIM, CGMP, and IGMP.

Describe the quality issues with voice traffic on a switched data network, including jitter and delay.

Describe the QoS solutions that address voice quality issues.

Describe the features and operation of network analysis modules on Catalyst switches to improve network traffic management.

Describe Transparent LAN Services and how they are implemented in a service provider network.

Implementation and Operation

Convert CatOS to native IOS on Catalyst switches and manage native IOS images according to best practices.

Configure access ports for static and multi-VLAN membership.

Configure and verify 802.1Q trunks.

Configure and verify ISL trunks.

Configure VTP domains in server, client, and transparent modes.

Enable spanning tree on ports and VLANs.

Configure Spanning Tree parameters, including port priority, VLAN priority, root bridge, BPDU guard, PortFast and UplinkFast.

Implement IP technology on a switched network with auxiliary VLANs.

Configure and verify router redundancy using HSRP, VRRP, GLBP, SRM, and SLB.

Configure QoS features on multilayer switched networks to provide optimal quality and bandwidth utilization for applications and data.

Configure Fast EtherChannel and Gigabit EtherChannel to increase bandwidth for interswitch connections.

Planning and Design

Compare end-to-end and local VLANs, and determine when to use each.

Design a VLAN configuration with VTP to work for a given specific scenario.

Select multilayer switching architectures, given specific multilayer switching needs.

Describe the general design models when implementing IP telephony in a switched network environment.

Plan QoS implementation within a multilayer switched network.

Troubleshooting

Troubleshoot common VLAN problems on a switched network.

Tune and troubleshoot Spanning Tree Protocol on a multilayer switched network to enhance network performance, prevent network loops, and minimize downtime.

Identify inter-VLAN routing performance and scalability issues, and propose solutions.

Verify and troubleshoot inter-VLAN routing on a switched network

Identify QoS implementation issues at the network Access layer.

Identify QoS implementation issues at the network Distribution and Core layers.

Building Cisco Remote Access Networks (BCRAN)

To pass the BCRAN exam, you'll need to master the following subject areas:

General Knowledge

Describe how different WAN technologies can be used to provide remote access to a network, including asynchronous dial-in, Frame Relay, ISDN, cable modem, and DSL.

Describe traffic control methods used to manage traffic flow on WAN links.

Explain the operation of remote network access control methods.

Identify PPP components, and explain the use of PPP as an access and encapsulation method.

Describe the structure and operation of virtual private network technologies

Describe the process of Network Address Translation (NAT).

Implementation and Operation

Configure asynchronous modems and router interfaces to provide network access.

Configure an ISDN solution for remote access.

Configure Frame Relay operation and traffic control on WAN links.

Configure access control to manage and limit remote access.

Configure DSL operation using Cisco IOS.

Configure VPN operation using Cisco IOS.

Configure Network Address Translation (NAT).

Planning and Design

Design a Cisco remote access solution using asynchronous dial-up technology.

Plan a Cisco ISDN solution for remote access or primary link backup.

Design a Cisco Frame Relay infrastructure to provide access between remote network components.

Design a solution of access control to meet required specifications.

Plan traffic shaping to meet required quality of service on access links.

Troubleshooting

Troubleshoot non-functional remote access systems.

Troubleshoot a VPN system.

Troubleshoot traffic control problems on a WAN link.

Cisco Internetwork Troubleshooting (CIT)

To pass the CIT exam, you'll need to master the following subject areas:

Technology

Identify troubleshooting methods.

Explain documentation standards and the requirements for document control.

Implementation and Operation

Establish an optimal system baseline.

Diagram and document system topology.

Document end-system configuration.

Verify connectivity at all layers.

Select an optimal troubleshooting approach.

Planning and Design

Plan a network documentation system.

Plan a baseline monitoring scheme.

Plan an approach to troubleshooting that minimizes system downtime.

Troubleshooting

Use Cisco IOS commands and applications to identify system problems at all layers.

Isolate system problems to one or more specific layers.

Resolve sub-optimal system performance problems at layers 2 through 7.

Resolve local connectivity problems at layer 1.

Restore optimal baseline service.

Work with external providers to resolve service provision problems.

Work with system users to resolve network related end-use problems.

How to Use This Book

If you want a solid foundation for the serious effort of preparing for the CCNP, then look no further. We've put this book together in a way that will thoroughly equip you with everything you need to pass all four CCNP exams as well as teach you networking on Cisco platforms.

This book is loaded with valuable information. You'll get the most out of your study time if you tackle it like this:

1. Take the assessment tests on the accompanying CD. It's okay if you don't know any of the answers—that's why you bought this book! But you do need to carefully read over the

explanations for any question you get wrong and make note of which chapters the material is covered in. This will help you plan your study strategy. Again, don't be disheartened if you don't know any answers—just think instead of how much you're about to learn.

2. Study each chapter carefully, making sure that you fully understand the information and the test objectives listed at the beginning of each chapter. Zero in on any chapter or part of a chapter that deals with areas where you missed questions in the assessment tests.
3. Take the time to complete the Written Labs for each exam, which are also available on the accompanying CD. Do *not* skip this! It directly relates to the exams and the relevant information you must glean from the chapter you just read. So, no skimming! Make sure you really, *really* understand the reason for each answer.
4. Answer all the review questions related to each chapter, also found on the CD. While you're going through the questions, jot down any questions that trouble you and study those sections of the book again. Don't throw away your notes; go over the questions that were difficult for you again before you take the exam. Seriously: Don't just skim these questions! Make sure you completely understand the reason for each answer, because the questions were written strategically to help you master the material that you must know before taking the exams.
5. Complete all the Hands-on Labs on the CD, referring to the relevant chapter material so that you understand the reason for each step you take. If you don't happen to have a bunch of Cisco equipment lying around to practice on, be sure to study the examples extra carefully.
6. Try your hand at the bonus exams on the CD. Testing yourself will give you a clear overview of what you can expect to see on the real thing.
7. Answer all the flashcard questions on the CD. The flashcard program will help you prepare completely for the exams.

The electronic flashcards can be used on your Windows computer, Pocket PC, or Palm device.

8. Make sure you read the Exam Essentials at the end of the chapters and are intimately familiar with the information in those sections.

Try to set aside the same time every day to study, and select a comfortable, quiet place to do so. Pick a distraction-free time and place where you can be sharp and focused. If you work hard, you'll get it all down, probably faster than you expect.

This book covers everything you need to know to pass the CCNP exams. If you follow the preceding eight steps; really study; and practice the review questions, bonus exams, electronic flashcards, Written Labs and Hands-on Labs; and practice with routers and switches, or simulators for these devices, it will be diamond-hard to fail the CCNP exams.

What's on the CD?

We've provided some cool tools to help you with your certification process. All the following gear should be loaded on your workstation when you're studying for the test:

The Sybex test engine The test preparation software, developed by the experts at Sybex, prepares you to pass the CCNP exams. In this test engine, you'll find review and assessment questions from each chapter of the book, plus eight bonus exams. You can take the assessment tests, test yourself by chapter, or take the bonus exams. Your scores will show how well you did on each exam objective.

Electronic flashcards for PC and Palm devices We've included more than 600 flashcard questions that can be read on your PC, Palm, or Pocket PC device. These are short questions and answers designed to test you on the most important topics needed to pass the exams.

Glossary of terms Knowing the definitions of key terms is important in your studies. Therefore, we have provided an exhaustive list of terms and their definitions.

Written labs In addition to review questions, we feel it's important to be able to answer questions on your own. The Written Labs are short question/answers. If you can answer these with no problem, you are very familiar with the contents of this book.

Hands-on labs These are designed to give you the hands-on practice that you need not only to prepare for the exams, but also to prepare you for the real world. Ideally, you should have your own home lab, or access to the Cisco technologies on which you are being tested. With these at your fingertips and the labs we provide, you should be able to perform tasks that Cisco expects its CCNPs to perform.

Commands used in this book This section lists the syntax, parameters, and variables for the Cisco IOS commands that were discussed in the body of this book. Each command is accompanied by a brief description of its purpose. If you need more information about a specific command, the index in the book can point you to the page that describes the command in detail.

***CCNP Complete Study Guide* in PDF** Sybex offers the *CCNP Complete Study Guide* in PDF format on the CD so you can read the book on your PC or laptop if you travel and don't want to carry a book, or if you just like to read from the computer screen. Adobe Acrobat Reader is also included on the CD.

Where Do You Take the Exams?

You may take the exams at any of the more than 800 Thomson Prometric Authorized Testing Centers around the world; find out more at `www.2test.com` or (800) 204-EXAM (3926). You can also register and take the exams at a Pearson VUE authorized center—`www.vue.com`; (877) 404-EXAM (3926).

To register for a Cisco certification exam:

1. Determine the number of the exam you want to take. The exams discussed in this book are numbered as follows:
   - Exam 642-801: Building Scalable Cisco Internetworks (BSCI)

- Exam 642-811: Building Cisco Multilayer Switched Networks (BCMSN)
- Exam 642-821: Building Cisco Remote Access Networks (BCRAN)
- Exam 642-831: Cisco Internetwork Troubleshooting Support (CIT)

2. Register with the nearest Thomson Prometric Registration Center or Pearson VUE testing center. You'll be asked to pay in advance for the exam. At the time of this writing, the exams are $125 each and must be taken within one year of payment. You may schedule an exam up to six weeks in advance or as late as the same day you want to take it. If you fail a Cisco exam, you must wait 72 hours before you get another shot at taking it. If something comes up and you need to cancel or reschedule your exam appointment, contact Thomson Prometric or Pearson VUE at least 24 hours in advance.
3. When you schedule the exam, you'll get instructions regarding all appointment and cancellation procedures, the ID requirements, and information about the testing-center location.

Tips for Taking Your Exams

The CCNP exams are multiple choice, and depending on which exam you take, they contain between 55 and 75 questions and must be completed in 75 or 90 minutes.

Many questions on the exam have answer choices that at first glance look a lot alike, especially the syntax questions (see the sidebar). Remember to read through the choices carefully, because close doesn't cut it. If you get commands in the incorrect order or forget one measly character, you'll get the question wrong. So, to practice, do the Hands-on Labs provided on the CD over and over again until they feel natural to you.

Watch That Syntax!

Unlike Microsoft or other IT certification tests, the Cisco exams have answer choices that are syntactically similar. Although some syntax is dead wrong, it's usually just *subtly* wrong. Some other choices might be syntactically correct, but they're shown in the wrong order. Cisco does split hairs, and it's not at all averse to giving you classic trick questions. Here's an example:

True or False: `access-list 101 deny ip any any eq 23` denies Telnet access to all systems.

This statement looks correct because most people refer to the port number (`23`) and think, "Yes, that's the port used for Telnet." The catch is that you can't filter IP on port numbers (only TCP and UDP).

Also, never forget that the right answer is the Cisco answer. In many cases, more than one appropriate answer is presented, but the *correct* answer is the one that Cisco recommends.

Here are some general tips for exam success:

- Arrive early at the exam center so you can relax and review your study materials.
- Read the questions *carefully*. Don't jump to conclusions. Make sure you're clear about *exactly* what each question asks.

- When answering multiple-choice questions that you're not sure about, use the process of elimination to discard the obviously incorrect answers first. Doing this greatly improves your odds if you need to make an educated guess.
- You can no longer move forward and backward through the Cisco exams. Double-check your answer before pressing Next, because you can't change your mind.

After you complete an exam, you'll get immediate, online notification—a printed Examination Score Report that indicates your pass or fail status and your exam results by section. The test administrator will give you that report. Test scores are automatically forwarded to Cisco within five working days after you take the test, so you don't need to send in your score. If you pass the exam, you'll usually receive confirmation from Cisco within four weeks.

How to Contact the Authors

You can reach Wade Edwards at `ccie7009@hotmail.com`, where you can ask questions relating to his books. You can reach Terry Jack at `terry@globalnettraining.co.uk`. You can reach Todd Lammle through Globalnet Training Solutions, Inc. (`www.globalnettraining.com`), his training company in Dallas, or at RouterSim, LLC (`www.routersim.com`), his software company in Denver. You can reach Robert Padjen at `robpadjen@comcast.net`, Arthur Pfund at `apfund@qwest.net`, Toby Skandier at `tskandier@hotmail.com`, and Carl Timm at `carl_timm@hotmail.com`. They are interested in delivering the best product possible to their readers. If you have any suggestions that could make this book better serve the technical community, please do not hesitate to send them your ideas.

Building Scalable Cisco Internetworks (BSCI)

Routing Principles

THE CCNP EXAM TOPICS COVERED IN THIS CHAPTER INCLUDE THE FOLLOWING:

- ✓ Understand how routers route data.
- ✓ Know the difference between classful and classless routing.
- ✓ Know how link-state routing protocols operate.
- ✓ Know the difference between distance-vector and link-state routing protocols.

In this chapter, you will learn the fundamentals of what is required to move a packet, or route a packet, across an internetwork. This chapter gives you an overview of the fundamentals of routing and the factors that affect routing. It also takes a look at how distance-vector routing protocols stack up to link-state routing protocols.

This is an important chapter that will provide you with a solid understanding of the covered topics before attempting the more advanced topics covered later in this book. As in sports, if you don't know the fundamentals of how to play the game, you will never be able to attain the level of excellence you could have if you had learned the fundamentals. With that in mind, let's get started!

Components of Routing Data

You may be thinking at this point, "What is routing and how does it work?" The "What is routing?" part is easy to answer. Routing is the process of forwarding a packet from one place on an internetwork to another. As for the second portion of the question, "How does it work?" that will take a little more explanation.

The first thing you will need to understand is logical addressing. Logical addressing is used to provide identification for each host on a network as well as for the network itself. Logical addressing is very similar to the way addressing works for your own home. The state, city, and zip code portion of an address is similar to the network portion of a logical address. It tells the postal service, or in this case, the router, in what general area to find your home, or the network. Your street address, or in this case the host address, tells the postal service, or router, exactly where you are. Upon receiving a packet from a host, the router will need to make a routing decision. After the decision has been made, the router will switch the packet to the appropriate interface on the router to forward it out. You heard me right; the router actually switches packets as well as routes them.

Let's take a look at the three obstacles a router must clear in order to make an accurate routing decision:

- Does the router that is sending and receiving the traffic know the protocol being used? The protocols that are most widely used are IP and IPX. Other protocols, such as AppleTalk and DECnet, may also be used.
- The router then checks to see if the destination network address exists in its routing table. The router will look for a route that matches the destination network address with the longest matching network mask. If the router does not find a route to the destination network, the router will discard the packet and send an ICMP destination network unreachable message to the source of the packet.

- A matching route must have been found or the packet will not reach this third step. From the routing table, the router determines which interface to use to forward the packet. If the routing table entry points to an IP address, the router will perform a recursive lookup on that next-hop address until the router finds an interface to use. The router switches the packet to the outbound interface's buffer. The router then determines the layer 2 address—MAC, DLCI, and so on—that maps to the layer 3 address. The packet is then encapsulated in a layer 2 frame appropriate for the type of encapsulation used by the outbound interface. The outbound interface then places the packet on the medium and forwards it to the next hop.

The packet continues this process until it reaches its destination.

Routing Tables

At this point you may be wondering, "What is a routing table?" The first thing you need to understand is what a route is. The easiest way to explain a route is to think of using an online map. You are required to enter your current location, or source location, and your destination. After you enter this information, the online map will do its nice little calculation and print the best route to take you from your source location to the destination. A route in the world of internetworking is essentially the same, with each router keeping track of the next hop in the route between itself and the next downstream router toward the destination. Once a router has learned a route, it places it in a repository for future use, assuming it has not already learned a route that it considers to be better. This repository is known as a *routing table*.

In order to view the IP routing table on your router, you need to use the command `show ip route`. Let's take a look at an actual routing table:

```
2501A#sh ip route
Codes: C - connected, S - static, I - IGRP, R - RIP, M - mobile, B - BGP D -
EIGRP, EX - EIGRP external, O - OSPF, IA - OSPF inter area N1 - OSPF NSSA
external type 1, N2 - OSPF NSSA external type 2 E1 - OSPF external type 1, E2 -
OSPF external type 2, E - EGP i - IS-IS, L1 - IS-IS level-1, L2 - IS-IS level-2,
* - candidate default U - per-user static route, o - ODR, P - periodic
downloaded static route T - traffic engineered route

Gateway of last resort is not set

     172.16.0.0/16 is subnetted, 1 subnets
C       172.16.50.0 is directly connected, FastEthernet0/0
C       192.168.24.0 is directly connected, FastEthernet0/0
     10.0.0.0/8 is subnetted, 1 subnets
C       10.10.10.0 is directly connected, Serial0/0
R       175.21.0.0/16 [120/1] via 10.10.10.1, 00:00:18, Serial0/0
2501A#
```

Now you may be wondering what all of this means. So, let's break it down.

The Codes section at the very top tells you how the route was learned. As you may have noticed, there are many different ways a route can be learned. It's not important for you to memorize all of the possible codes. What is important is for you to know how to use the Codes section to find out how a route was learned.

Next, note the line Gateway of last resort is not set. The gateway of last resort, also known as a default route, is where your router will send IP packets if there isn't a match in the routing table. In this example, the gateway of last resort has not been set. This means if the router receives a packet destined for an unknown network, it will drop the packet and send an ICMP destination network unreachable message to the originator of the packet.

The next items in the routing table are the routes the router knows about. Let's go ahead and break down a route into its components. We will use the following example:

```
R        175.21.0.0/16 [120/1] via 10.10.10.1, 00:00:18, Serial0
```

R The means by which the route entry was learned on this router. In this case, the R stands for RIP. From this, you can deduce that the entry you are looking at was learned by the RIP routing protocol.

175.21.0.0/16 The network address and prefix length (number of bits set to 1 in the subnet mask) of the destination network.

[120 The administrative distance of the route. (We will explain administrative distance a little later in this chapter.)

/1] The metric of the route specific to the routing protocol used to determine the route. RIP uses hops as its metric. A *hop* is how many routers away—excluding this router—the destination network is. In this example, there is one router between this router and the destination.

via 10.10.10.1 The next-hop address for the route. This is the address that the packet will need to be sent to in order for the packet to reach its destination.

00:00:18 The length of time since the route has been updated in the routing table. In this example, the route was updated 18 seconds ago.

Serial0 The interface the route was learned through. This is also the interface the packet will be switched to in order for the packet to be forwarded toward its destination. If you see another IP address here, at least one additional lookup will have to occur within the same routing table, which is defined as a recursive lookup, until a route is finally encountered that does list an exit interface in this position.

Populating the Routing Table

Now that you know what's in a routing table, you may be wondering how those routes get there. Before a route can populate a routing table, the router has to learn about the route. There are two ways a router can learn about a route:

- Static definition by an administrator
- Dynamic learning through routing protocols

Statically Defined Routes

A statically defined route is one in which a route is manually entered into the router. A static route can be entered into the router with the following command in global configuration mode:

```
ip route prefix mask {address|interface} [distance]
```

The parts of this command are as follows:

- *prefix* is the IP route prefix for the destination.
- *mask* is the prefix mask for the destination.
- *address* represents the IP address of the next hop that can be used to reach the destination.
- *interface* is the network interface to use.
- *distance* is an optional parameter that represents the administrative distance.

As you can see, with the static route you can choose to either set the next-hop address or use a connected interface on the router. You can also set the administrative distance of the static route. (We will explain administrative distance a little later in this chapter.) When a static route has the administrative distance set to a value other than the default value, it is generally done to create what is known as a floating static route. Here is an example of a configured static route:

```
2501A(config)#ip route 192.168.20.0 255.255.255.0 172.16.50.1
```

If you want to configure a default route, all you need to do for the destination prefix is set it to 0.0.0.0 and set the mask to 0.0.0.0. ANDing with a mask of all 0s turns any intended destination address into all 0s. Comparing this to the configured destination prefix of all 0s always gets a match. The mask length, however, is the shortest possible, with no 1s set, so any other match will always be chosen. When no other matches exist, this default route will be used, hence its name.

You then need to decide what to set your next hop to. This default route will send any packets that do not have a match in the routing table to the next hop defined.

The advantages to using static routes in an internetwork are that the administrator has total control of what is in the router's routing table and there is no network overhead for a routing protocol. Using static routes for a small network is fine. It's not going to be hard to implement, and you have total control in the network.

The downfall of using only static routes is they do not scale well. What do we mean by that? Let's look at an example of how many routes you would need to enter for the number of routers in these different internetworks, where the routers are daisy-chained with one link between each pair of neighbors and the two end routers have stub Ethernets, resulting in each router being connected to two network segments:

- A network with two routers would require two static routes.
- A network with three routers would require six static routes.
- A network with 100 routers would require 9,900 static routes.

The generic equation is the same one used to determine the number of full-mesh links in WAN networking: $n(n-1)$ or $n^2 - n$, where n represents the total number of routers in the internetwork. As you can see, as an internetwork grows, the number of static routes the administrator needs to control becomes unmanageable. Keep in mind that any static route you add, edit, or delete will need to be propagated across all devices. What is the alternative? The alternative is to use a routing protocol to dynamically learn routes.

Dynamically Learned Routes

What is dynamic routing? *Dynamic routing* is a process in which a routing protocol will find the best path in a network and maintain that route. Think about the online map scenario I used earlier. There are multiple ways to get from where you are to your destination. The online map takes all those routes into consideration and uses a predefined set of rules to discover the best route to the destination.

A routing protocol works the same way. It will discover all the possible routes to one destination, implement its predefined rules, and come up with the best route to the destination. One thing a routing protocol will take into consideration that an online map will not is what happens when a portion of the route to the destination has been closed. The routing protocol will automatically find an alternate route to the destination.

Routing protocols are easier to use than static routes. This comes at a cost, though. We're not talking about a monetary cost either. A routing protocol consumes more CPU cycles and network bandwidth than a static route. For a large network, the cost is worth it.

There are two types of dynamic routing protocols in use today: Interior Gateway Protocols (IGPs) and External Gateway Protocols (EGPs). IGPs are used to exchange routing information within the same *routing domain*. A routing domain is the collection of routers and end systems that operate under a common set of administrative rules. Barring hierarchical design with areas or route filtering, two routers can be said to be in the same routing domain if each router's noncommon, directly connected networks can be expected to appear in the other router's routing table, all learned via the same dynamic routing protocol. Areas and filters make the routing domain boundary a bit more difficult to define without closer investigation.

An *autonomous system (AS)* is a collection of routing domains under the same administrative control. An EGP is used to exchange routing information between different ASs. An example of an EGP is the Border Gateway Protocol (BGP). BGP will be covered in detail in Chapter 8, "Border Gateway Protocol," and Chapter 9, "Advanced Border Gateway Protocol."

IGPs can be broken into two classes: distance-vector and link-state. IGPs can also be broken into two categories: classful routing protocols and classless routing protocols. We will first take a look at the different classes of routing protocols.

An important term to understand is *convergence*. Convergence is the process in which all routers update their routing tables and create a consistent view of the network. It will be covered in detail later in this chapter.

Distance-Vector Routing

Distance-vector routing is broken down into two parts: distance and vector. Distance is the measure of how far it is to reach the destination, or the metric to reach the destination. Vector, or direction, is the direction the packet must travel to reach that destination. This is determined by the next hop of the path.

Distance-vector routing protocols are known to *route by rumor*. What this means is that a router will learn routes from its neighbors. Those neighbors learned the routes from their neighbors. It reminds me of my old high school days when one person would tell another person something and by the end of the day the entire school knew.

So, what routing protocols are distance-vector routing protocols? The only ones we are concerned about in this book are Routing Information Protocol (RIP), Interior Gateway Routing Protocol (IGRP), and Enhanced Interior Gateway Routing Protocol (EIGRP). Because IGRP and EIGRP are covered in great detail in Chapter 4, "IGRP and EIGRP," we will not spend much time on them here.

EIGRP is what is known as an advanced distance-vector routing protocol, or hybrid. For the BSCI course, Cisco considers EIGRP in the distance-vector routing protocol class.

Table 1.1 compares the different distance-vector routing protocols covered in this study guide.

TABLE 1.1 Distance-Vector Comparisons

Characteristic	RIPv1	RIPv2	IGRP	EIGRP
Count to infinity	✓	✓	✓	
Split horizon with poison reverse	✓	✓	✓	✓
Holddown timer	✓	✓	✓	
Triggered updates with route poisoning	✓	✓	✓	✓
Load balancing with equal paths	✓	✓	✓	✓
Load balancing with unequal paths			✓	✓
VLSM support		✓		✓

TABLE 1.1 Distance-Vector Comparisons *(continued)*

Characteristic	RIPv1	RIPv2	IGRP	EIGRP
Automatic summarization	✓	✓	✓	✓
Manual summarization		✓		✓
Metric	Hops	Hops	Composite	Composite
Hop count limit	15	15	255 (100 by default)	255 (100 by default)
Support for size of network	Small	Small	Medium	Large
Method of advertisement	Broadcast	Multicast	Broadcast	Multicast

The algorithm Cisco supports for RIP and IGRP is known as Bellman-Ford. For EIGRP, Cisco supports the Diffusing Update Algorithm (DUAL).

EIGRP and IGRP are Cisco proprietary routing protocols.

Most distance-vector routing protocols have common characteristics:

Periodic updates The length of time before a router will send out an update. For RIP, this time is 30 seconds. For IGRP, the time is 90 seconds. This means that once the periodic update timer expires, a broadcast or multicast (in the case of RIPv2) of the entire routing table is sent out. Uncharacteristic of distance-vector routing protocols, EIGRP does not send periodic updates, but ironically, OSPF can be said to do so every 30 minutes, in the form of link-state advertisement (LSA) refreshes.

Neighbors Other routers on the same logical, or data-link, connection. In a distance-vector routing protocol, a router will send its routing table to its connected neighbors. Those neighbors will send their updated routing tables to their connected neighbors. This continues until all the routers participating in the selected routing domain have updated routing tables.

Broadcast or multicast updates When a router becomes active, it will send out a routing advertisement or Hello packet to the broadcast or designated multicast address, stating that it is alive. In return, neighboring routers in the same routing domain will respond to this broadcast or multicast.

Full routing table updates Most distance-vector routing protocols will send their entire routing table to their neighbors. This occurs when the periodic update timer expires.

Routing by rumor A router will send its routing table to all of its directly connected neighbors. In return, all of the neighboring routers send their routing tables to all of their directly connected neighbors. This continues until all routers in the same distance-vector routing domain converge upon the same information.

Triggered updates and route poisoning One way to speed up convergence on a network is with the use of *triggered updates* and *route poisoning*. Instead of the router's having to wait until the periodic update timer expires to send out an update, a triggered update sends out an update as soon as a significant event occurs. An example would be if a router notices that one of its connected networks went down. The router will then send out an update stating that the downed network was unreachable, thus speeding up convergence and cutting down on the risk of network loops due to convergence issues.

Route poisoning is the immediate removal of a route from the local router's routing table, once it is determined that the route is no longer valid and subsequently advertises this fact to neighbors. Because this determination can be almost immediate in RIP, through direct connection to the failed link or through receipt of triggered updates, there is little opportunity in RIP networks these days for routes to enter a holddown state and slowly age out. Even RIP, as an example of a distance-vector routing protocol, converges in less than 30 seconds in modern networks due to route poisoning and triggered updates. IGRP still takes the long way home, as discussed in the IGRP convergence section coming up in this chapter.

Holddown timer The holddown timer is used when information about a route changes for the worse (greater metric or unreachable). When the new information is received or a route is removed, the router will place that route in a holddown state. This means that the router will advertise but will not accept worse advertisements about this route from any neighbor, other than the one from which the route was originally learned, for the time period specified by the holddown timer. After the time period expires, the router will start considering all advertisements about the route.

The benefit of using holddown timers is that, if used properly, they will cut down on the amount of wrong information being advertised about routes. The disadvantage is that convergence times may increase.

Invalid and flush timers These timers solve the problem of what happens when a router goes down. Because the router isn't sending out updates, the other routers in the network don't know that a router has gone down and that the routes are unreachable. So, the routers continue to send packets to the routes connected to the missing router. This means the packets never make it to their destination. The way an invalid timer solves this issue is by associating a period of time with a route. If the route is not updated in the routing table in this set period of time, the route is marked as unreachable, and the router will send this new information in a triggered update and in its periodic updates. Depending on the routing protocol, the default invalid timer is set at three or six times the periodic update timer and is reset for a particular route upon receipt of an update for that route.

The invalid timer should not be confused with the flush timer. Although both the invalid and flush timers are somewhat tied to when an update is received, the flush timer is set for a longer period of time, after which the route is stripped from the local routing table and no longer advertised.

Cisco suggests that you leave all timers at their default settings, but that if you must change them, for IGRP, make sure that the flush timer is equal to or greater than the sum of the invalid and holddown timers, as it is by default. Otherwise, without the route kept in holddown in the routing table, the routing table is unprotected from the routing protocol's acceptance of worse routes that are actually invalid, but may still be circulating on the network and could be accepted sooner than the holddown timer would have permitted. It's likely that the invalid routes would have been purged from the routing domain before the routing protocol resumes, if the holddown timer is permitted to run its course. While this same argument makes sense for RIP, the default timer settings do not follow this rule of thumb. For RIP, when no router actually goes down, but a route does go away and triggered updates are able to perform their duty, these timers are basically academic in nature. For IGRP, however, they work exactly as described. The upcoming discussions on RIP and IGRP convergence will clarify this point.

Split horizon with poison reverse *Split horizon* with *poison reverse* helps prevent what is known as a routing loop. A routing loop occurs when a router learns a route from a neighbor and the router turns around and sends that route back to the neighbor that the router learned it from, causing an infinite loop.

Split horizon Consider an example: Router A learns about route 10.10.10.0 from Router B, which is two hops away from 10.10.10.0. Router B tells Router A that Router A is three hops away from network 10.10.10.0. Router A, after populating its routing table with the route, sends an advertisement back to Router B stating that Router A has a route to 10.10.10.0. In this advertisement, Router A tells Router B that Router B is four hops away from network 10.10.10.0. Of course, Router B already knows of a path to network 10.10.10.0 that puts it only two hops away. So, Router B wisely ignores the less desirable route advertised by Router A.

The problem arises if network 10.10.10.0 goes down. Router B would learn that the route is down. In turn, Router B would mark the network as unreachable and pass the information to Router A at Router B's next update interval. Theoretically, before this can happen, Router A could send an update to Router B, stating, as it has all along, that Router A can reach network 10.10.10.0; remember, Router B has not informed Router A that network 10.10.10.0 is unreachable. So, Router B receives the update from Router A about being able to reach network 10.10.10.0. Router B at this point, no longer aware of a better path to network 10.10.10.0, will update its routing table with the new information. When Router B receives a packet destined for network 10.10.10.0, it will look in its routing table and see that the next hop is Router A. So, it forwards the packet to Router A. When Router A receives this packet, it looks in its routing table and notices that Router B is the next hop; remember that Router B initially sent the route to Router A in an update. This causes an infinite loop.

The only thing that stops this process from running indefinitely is the fact that distance-vector routing protocols define infinity in finite terms. Once one router increments the metric to the established infinite value, the neighbor receiving this infinite advertisement realizes that the route is unreachable and advertises the same back to its confused neighbor. This can take a bit of time, though. Split horizon prevents this by establishing a rule that a route cannot be advertised out the same interface on which it was learned.

Poison reverse Poison reverse is related to split horizon, as it uses the same "keep track of who advertised it to you" philosophy. With IGRP, poison reverse comes into play when a neighbor router tells the local router about a downed network that the neighbor has been advertising as active, and for which the neighbor represents the only next hop to that network. In future updates sent back to the neighbor, the local router will bend the split horizon rule by advertising the route back to the neighbor from which it was learned, but by using an infinite metric to imply its inaccessibility through the local router. For IGRP, infinity is the value 4,294,967,295, which represents a 32-bit field of all 1s in binary. This is just to make sure there is no misunderstanding about the fact that the local router most certainly cannot help with an alternate route to the network. It is RIP, not IGRP, that employs what is known as local route poisoning by immediately removing the route from the local routing table. So IGRP must deal with the protracted presence of the route until it can be flushed, and poison reverse is its coping mechanism.

The other interesting issue you may notice is that IGRP keeps suspected bad routes in the routing table until after the holddown timer expires, and labels them as such. So it's your position, as the administrator or technician, to cope with the fact that a route appears to be down in the routing table but still passes traffic to the listed next-hop address. If the network comes back up, the entry will not change until after the holddown timer expires, but each router in line to the destination will operate the same way, passing the traffic until it makes it to the final destination, barring any other unforeseen circumstances. So, verification and faith and a little trick to be mentioned soon (look for the `clear` command) will have to tide you over.

Make sure you realize there is a difference between route poisoning and poison reverse. Route poisoning is explained earlier in this section.

Counting to infinity In networks where split horizon, triggered updates, and holddowns are not implemented, the phenomenon outlined in the previous split-horizon discussion, known as counting to infinity, occurs. When the destination network goes down, the updates about the destination being unreachable can arrive between scheduled update times. If an upstream (away from the downed route) neighbor's update timer expires before ours does, the local router will receive an update about the route that leads it to believe that the network is once again reachable. Any combination of split horizon, triggered updates, and holddown timers would mitigate the effects of this situation. Without any of these mechanisms, the bad route will be volleyed back and forth between the neighbors—with an incrementing metric—until the predefined maximum routing domain diameter (16 for RIP and 100, by default, for IGRP) is reached for the number of hops by each router.

Without enforcing maximum hop counts, this situation could literally go on forever. When a route reaches the maximum hop count (infinity), the route is marked as unreachable and removed from the router's routing table. Even IGRP and EIGRP report the number of hops to a destination network in their routing updates and enforce a configured maximum diameter. They just don't use hop count in the calculation of their metrics.

Now that you have an understanding of how distance-vector routing protocols function, let's take a look at them. We will cover only RIP in this chapter because IGRP and EIGRP are covered in detail in Chapter 3, "Network Address Translation."

ROUTING INFORMATION PROTOCOL (RIP)

This section is going to hit only the key areas of RIP, because that's all that is really pertinent to the BSCI exam. There are currently two versions of RIP in existence: RIP version 1 and RIP version 2. Let's take a brief look at the major differences between them.

RIP version 1 (RIPv1) is considered a classful routing protocol, whereas RIP version 2 (RIPv2) is a classless routing protocol. The key difference between a classful and classless routing protocol is that a classful routing protocol does not send a subnet mask in the update and a classless routing protocol does. Classful versus classless routing is covered in more detail later in this chapter. Other attributes RIPv2 has that RIPv1 doesn't are as follows:

- Authentication of routing updates through the use of cleartext or MD5 (optional)
- Multicast route updates
- Next-hop addresses carried with each advertised route entry

In order to activate RIPv2 you must first enter the `router rip` command in global configuration mode. After RIP has been activated on the router you must enter the command `version 2` in router configuration mode.

Real World Scenario

RIP Migration

John is the network engineer for company XYZ. Currently, XYZ has only 14 routers and is running RIPv1. Recently XYZ purchased company ABC. Company ABC had 10 routers that were also running RIP. John has been tasked with merging the two companies' networks. John remembers back when he was studying for the BSCI that RIP has a maximum consecutive device count of 15. Well, he now has 24 routers and will exceed this limit for a number of paths. Noticing the dilemma, he decides to implement EIGRP to replace the RIP network. In order to make sure the company doesn't lose connectivity, John decides he will implement EIGRP and leave RIP on the devices until EIGRP is completely implemented. By choosing to do it this way, John will be able to migrate the two networks together without losing connectivity.

What you need to concentrate on at this point is the commonality among the two versions of RIP, such as updates and timers:

- They are considered distance-vector routing protocols.
- They use the Bellman-Ford algorithm.

- The metric used to determine the best route is hop count. A route can extend through 15 routers—or hops—and then will be marked as unreachable.
- The route update timer for periodic updates is set to 30 seconds.
- The route invalid timer is set to 180 seconds. This is the time the router will wait for an update before a route will be marked as unreachable and the holddown timer will be started, which is also 180 seconds.
- The route flush timer is set to 240 seconds. This is the time between the route's last received update and the route being removed from the routing table. In the time period between the invalid timer and the flush timer, neighboring routers will be notified about the route's being unreachable, unless the holddown timer expires before the flush timer does and updates come in for the route. In that case, business resumes as usual, possibly through a path less desirable than the original, but one that's valid and the best known one.

Now that you have a good understanding of how distance-vector routing works, let's take a look at link-state routing and its functionality.

If you need to view real-time information about the operation of RIPv1 or RIPv2, you can use the `debug ip rip` command.

The `ip default-network` command can be used with RIPv1 or RIPv2 to advertise a default network to your neighboring devices.

Link-State Routing

Remember how with a distance-vector routing protocol, the router knew only the direction in which to send the packet and the distance to get there? *Link-state routing* is different in that each router knows the exact topology of the network. This in turn limits the number of bad routing decisions that can be made. Link-state routing can accomplish this because every router in the routing domain or area has a similar view of the network, placing itself at the root of a hierarchical tree. Each router in the network will report on the state of each directly connected link. Each router then plays a part in propagating this learned information until all routers in the network have it. Each router that receives this information will take a snapshot of it.

It's important to realize that the other routers do not make any change to the updates received. This in turn ensures that all routers in the process have the same relative view of the network, allowing each router to make its own routing decisions based upon the same information.

Another key difference of link-state routing is that each router does not send its entire routing table. The only information that is sent are the changes that have occurred or a message stating that nothing has changed after a given period of time has passed. This is known as a link-state advertisement (LSA). An LSA is generated for each link on a router. Each LSA includes an identifier for the link, the state of the link, and a metric for the link. With the use of LSAs, link-state protocols cut down on the amount of bandwidth utilized. The disadvantage of a link-state routing protocol is that it is more complex to configure than a distance-vector routing protocol.

The link-state routing protocols that are covered in this book are as follows:

- Open Shortest Path First (OSPF)
- Integrated Intermediate System to Intermediate System (Integrated IS-IS)

Keep in mind these are not the only link-state routing protocols. These are the ones that are covered by the BSCI exam, though.

Because we will cover link-state routing in more detail in Chapter 4, Chapter 5, "OSPF Operation in a Single Area," and Chapter 6, "Interconnecting OSPF Areas," we will give you only a brief introduction to the operation of link-state routing here.

The basic functionality of link-state routing is broken down into the following steps:

1. The first thing each router does, as it becomes active, is form an adjacency with its directly connected neighbors.
2. After forming adjacencies, the router then sends out link-state advertisements (LSAs) to each of its neighbors. After receiving and copying the information from the LSA, the router forwards—or floods—the LSA to each of its neighbors.
3. All of the routers then store the LSAs in their own database. This means that all routers have the same view of the network topology.
4. Each router then uses the Dijkstra algorithm to compute its best route to a destination.

As stated previously, this is a brief introduction to link-state routing. Link-state routing will be covered in greater detail later in this book. Table 1.2 compares the link-state routing protocols covered in this study guide. Remember that EIGRP is considered a hybrid protocol, meaning that it contains traits of both distance-vector and link-state routing protocols. Also remember that if you are forced to consider EIGRP to be one or the other only, consider it a distance-vector routing protocol.

TABLE 1.2 Link-State Comparisons

Characteristic	OSPF	IS-IS	EIGRP
Hierarchical topology supported through areas	✓	✓	
Retains knowledge of all possible routes	✓	✓	✓
Manual route summarization	✓	✓	✓
Automatic route summarization			✓
Event-triggered announcements	✓	✓	✓
Load balancing with unequal-cost paths			✓
Load balancing with equal-cost paths	✓	✓	✓
VLSM support	✓	✓	✓

TABLE 1.2 Link-State Comparisons *(continued)*

Characteristic	OSPF	IS-IS	EIGRP
Metric	Cost	Cost	Composite
Hop count limit	Unlimited	1024	100 by default
Support for size of network	Very large	Very large	Large

Now that we've discussed the different classes of routing protocols, let's focus on the two different categories of routing protocols.

Classful Routing

What is classful routing? Classful routing is used to route packets based upon the default major network boundary, derived from the class of the IP address. In order to fully understand this concept, let's review the defaults for the different classes of IP addresses.

Class A networks reserve the first octet for the network portion of the IP address, and the remaining three octets are available for host addressing. The value of the first octet of a Class A network will always be between 1 and 127, inclusive. There are a total of 126 Class A networks; 127 is reserved for diagnostic testing and thus cannot be used. There are various other reserved Class A networks, such as the 10 network, but the majority are usable and already allocated. There are 16,777,214 unsubnetted hosts available per Class A network.

Class B networks reserve the first and second octets for the network portion of the IP address, and the remaining two octets are available for host addressing. The value of the first octet of a Class B network will always be between 128 and 191, inclusive. There are a total of 16,384 Class B networks with 65,534 hosts per network.

Class C networks reserve the first, second, and third octets for the network portion of the IP address and the remaining octet for host addressing. The value of the first octet of a Class C network will always be between 192 and 223, inclusive. There are a total of 2,097,152 available Class C networks with 254 hosts per network.

Class D IP addresses have no network/host structure, as they are used solely for multicasting and, like broadcast addresses, multicast addresses can be only destination addresses, never source addresses. As a result, there is no need or way to split Class D addresses up into smaller subnets, because no device will ever be configured with a Class D address as its interface address. Furthermore, there is no subnet mask associated with Class D addresses. The value of the first octet of a Class D address will always be between 224 and 239, inclusive. There are theoretically 268,435,456 Class D addresses, which are not split into networks and hosts.

Class E networks are regarded as experimental, and, like Class D addresses, they have no network/host structure nor will they ever be assigned to a device's interface. The value of the first octet of a Class E address is always between 240 and 255, inclusive.

It's not necessary to convert an IP address in binary form to decimal in order to determine its class. When faced with such a task, the quickest way to determine the class of an IP address in binary form is to label the first four bits A, B, C, and D, after the classes of addresses. Wherever the first 0 falls, that is the class of address you are dealing with. If all four bits are 1s, the class of address is E. For example, a first octet of 10101010 would represent a Class B address, due to the first 0 being in the B position. 10101010 converts to decimal 170, so you can see that the trick worked in this case. Trust me, it always does.

Classful routing therefore bases all of its routing decisions upon the default major network boundary derived from each of the first three classes of IP address. The major drawback to the use of classful addressing and routing is that a tremendous number of IP addresses can be wasted. We will explain this in more detail in Chapter 3.

The routing protocols covered in this book that are considered classful routing protocols are as follows:

- RIPv1
- IGRP

With all of this in mind, let's take a look at what is known as classless routing.

Classless Routing

Classless routing, also known as classless interdomain routing (CIDR), is not dependent on the default boundaries of the different classes of IP addresses. Classless routing actually allows each route's subnet mask to be sent in the routing update with the route. Classless routing also opens the door for variable-length subnet masking (VLSM), which extends IP addressing beyond the limitations of using fixed-length subnet masks (FLSMs) by allowing you to specify the most efficient subnet mask to use for the size of network in question. This allows you to conserve IP addresses, extending the use of IP address space. This topic is covered in more detail in Chapter 3.

To simplify the difference between classless and classful routing, let's use an example of a college campus. The college campus is built with buildings of identical size. It doesn't matter how many offices in each building will be occupied; all buildings are the same size and every office has to have a number. This is analogous to a classful network design, where every host has a host ID and participates in the same size network, regardless of how many hosts will ever really be on that network. The addresses that are not used on a network cannot be used on a different network that is running short of addresses. All networks will have to grow the same amount to be able to cover the largest need. All buildings have to remain identical in size, even if those that are not full must grow to keep up with the growth of the fullest building. All of the wasted office space is just that. Each group in a building is confined to that building and cannot grow into the less-populated buildings.

Introducing classless routing would be like allowing each building to be only as large as the group within the building, wasting no office space and having only enough empty offices to cover projected growth. In other words, classless routing leads to the ability to use not only subnet masks that are not the default masks, but also to use VLSM—subnet masks of different sizes—so that address waste is minimized.

The routing protocols we cover in this book that are considered classless routing protocols are the following:

- RIPv2
- EIGRP
- OSPF

- IS-IS
- BGP

So far, we have described how routes are learned, the different classes of routing protocols, and the different categories of routing protocols. Now that you have a firm grasp on these concepts, it's time to move on to how these routes you've learned actually get placed in a routing table.

The Final Decision on What Routes Populate the Routing Table

There are a couple of different factors that make the final decision on what routes will be placed in the routing table, namely, administrative distance and metric, assuming that no route filtering is in place that would specifically prevent a route from being placed in the routing table. The first factor to be taken into consideration when making the decision of what route to place in the routing table is administrative distance.

What is administrative distance? *Administrative distance (AD)* is the trustworthiness of the routing protocol that produced the route. Administrative distance can be any value between 0 and 255. The lower the number, the more trustworthy the source of the route.

Table 1.3 shows the default administrative distance that a Cisco router will use to decide the best route to a destination.

TABLE 1.3 Default Administrative Distance

Source of Route	Default Administrative Distance
Connected Interface	0
Static Route	1
EIGRP Summary	5
External BGP	20
EIGRP	90
IGRP	100
OSPF	110
IS-IS	115
RIP	120
EGP	140
External EIGRP	170

TABLE 1.3 Default Administrative Distance *(continued)*

Source of Route	Default Administrative Distance
Internal BGP	200
Unknown	255

If more than one route exists to a given destination, the route with lowest administrative distance will be placed in the routing table. You may be wondering what happens if multiple routes to a given destination have the same administrative distance. This is when the second factor—metric—comes into play.

If you establish a static route by supplying the exit interface instead of the next-hop address, it will have a metric of 0, just like a directly connected network would, making it preferable to next hop-based static routes. This is useful with the `ip unnumbered` command or whenever you want a static route based not on the availability of the remote next-hop address but instead on the availability of the local interface.

A *metric* is the value of a route specific to a routing protocol. If multiple routes have the same administrative distance, then the metric is used as the tiebreaker. Here's a simple way to think about it: The router first looks to see which route can be trusted the most. If the router has multiple routes that are equally trustworthy, the router will then look to see which route has the lowest metric, which is the one it finds to be the most desirable. That is the route that will populate the routing table. Depending on the routing protocol and its configuration, multiple routes with the same AD and metric could be placed into the routing table simultaneously.

Let's summarize everything you've learned so far about routing tables and how they are populated. At this point, you know that routes are learned either dynamically or statically. Those routes are then placed in the routing table based on which one is the most trusted. If multiple routes exist that are equally trusted, the one that is the most desirable is placed in the routing table.

Let's revisit the life of a packet. When a packet is sent to a destination, if the destination is not on the same network as the source, the packet will be sent to a local router for the immediate network. The router then looks in its routing table to see if it has a route to the destination network. If the router does not have a route and a default gateway doesn't exist, the packet is discarded and an ICMP error message is sent to the packet's source. In fact, any router along the path to the destination network could run into this same problem and discard the packet, notifying the original source device of the execution. So, if a route exists, how does the packet reach the destination? We're going to explore getting a packet to its destination in the next section.

Reaching the Destination

After a router receives a packet, the router removes the data-link framing, or the layer 2 header and trailer, if one exists, in order to find the layer 3 destination address. Once the destination address is read, the router looks in its routing table for a route to the destination address. Assuming a match for the destination is in the routing table, the router reads the next-hop address or exit interface to reach the destination from the entry. If the router reads a next-hop address, it will perform a recursive lookup on the address. This means that the router looks at the network portion of the next-hop address and then looks in its own routing table for an entry matching this destination address.

The router continues this process until it arrives upon an entry that designates a connected exit interface instead of a next-hop address. Once this is accomplished, the router switches the packet to the outbound interface's buffer. The router discovers the type of connection between the outbound interface and the next-hop address. After the connection type has been discovered, the packet is encapsulated in the appropriate layer 2 encapsulation for the connection. The packet will now be placed on the medium and forwarded to the next hop. This continues until the packet reaches its destination.

The entire process of how a packet gets forwarded toward the destination can be broken down into five steps:

1. As the frame's header arrives at the router's inbound interface, the MAC process checks the hardware destination address against the burned-in MAC address of the interface, the broadcast address, and any multicast addresses that the interface may be listening for. If the MAC process finds that the hardware destination address is applicable, a cyclic redundancy check (CRC) is performed on the frame to make sure it's not corrupt. If the frame passes CRC, the packet is pulled from the frame. The frame is discarded, and the packet is stored in the router's main memory.

2. The router searches the routing table for the longest match to the destination address found in the packet's header. If the router finds no match, and a default gateway does not exist, the router will discard the packet and send an ICMP destination unreachable message to the originating device. If the router does find a match, it will discover the next-hop address or the connected interface for this route. If the route points to a connected interface, a recursive lookup doesn't need to be performed and the next step can be skipped.

3. Once the next-hop address is known, the router performs a recursive lookup. This is performed to locate the directly connected interface on the router to forward the packet out; it may take multiple iterations before an entry with an exit interface is found. If any of the recursive lookups points to an IP address that the routing table has no entry for and the default gateway is not set, the router will discard the packet and notify the packet's source via ICMP.

4. The packet is now switched to the outbound interface's buffer. Assuming that the outbound interface uses layer 2 addressing, the router attempts to learn the MAC address or layer 2 identifier of the next-hop interface in order to map the layer 3 address to a layer 2 address. The router looks in the appropriate local table such as an ARP cache. In the case of ARP, if the layer 2 mapping is not found, the router will broadcast an ARP request through the outbound interface to the locally connected segment to request the MAC address of the interface associated with the local segment of the next-hop device, which may be another router or the final destination. Under normal circumstances, the next-hop device sends an ARP reply with its MAC address. All other devices hearing the broadcast

will realize that the ARP request is not for them based on layer 3 address information in the ARP header; they will not reply to the request, but instead quietly discard the ARP request packet. No layer 2 information is necessary for many point-to-point media. If a frame is placed on the wire, only the intended recipient will receive it, because it is the only other device on the wire.

5. At this point, the type of connection between the directly connected interface and the next-hop interface is known. The router encapsulates the packet in the appropriate data-link frame for the type of connection. The outbound interface places the frame with the layer 2 address of the next-hop device on the wire. This process continues at each router that the packet encounters until it reaches its destination.

Figure 1.1 gives you a visual example of the life of a packet:

1. The packet is encapsulated with the layer 2 frame structure of the local network and sent from the originator to its default gateway.
2. The frame is received by R1; the data-link frame is removed; the destination address is found in the routing table; the next hop is discovered; the outbound interface is discovered; and the packet is switched to the outbound interface buffer.
3. The outbound interface receives the packet and resolves the layer 3 address to the layer 2 address of the next-hop router, and the packet is framed in the data-link framing of the outbound interface. The frame, with the layer 2 address of the next-hop router, is then placed on the medium.
4. The frame is received and dismantled by R2. The destination Network layer address is found in the routing table, which points to a directly connected interface. The packet is switched to the outbound interface buffer.
5. The outbound interface maps the layer 3 address to a layer 2 address that is needed to reach the destination. The packet is framed according to the interface's layer 2 technology and is then placed on the medium.
6. The packet arrives at its destination.

So far, you have followed the life of a packet. You should have a grasp on what a routing table is, how that table is populated, and how a packet reaches its destination. You now need to focus on verifying what routes are in a routing table and what tools are used to test and troubleshoot actual connectivity to the destinations they represent.

FIGURE 1.1 The life of a packet

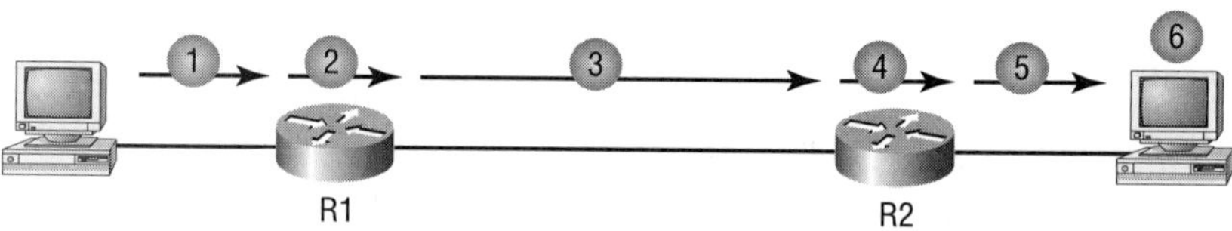

Convergence

Convergence time is the time it takes for all routers to agree on the network topology after a change in the network. The routers have synchronized their routing tables.

There are at least two different detection methods used by all routing protocols. The first method is used by the Physical and Data Link layer protocols. When the network interface on the router does not receive three consecutive keepalives, the link will be considered down.

The second detection method is that when the routing protocol at the Network and Transport layers fails to receive three consecutive Hello messages, the link will be considered down.

After the link is considered down is when the routing protocols differ. Routing protocols have timers that are used to stop network loops from occurring on a network when a link failure has been detected. Holddown timers are used to give the network stability while new route calculations are being performed. They also allow all the routers a chance to learn about the failed route to avoid routing loops and counting to infinity problems. Because a routing domain cannot converge during this holddown period, this can cause a delay in the routing process of the domain. Because of this slow convergence penalty, link-state routing protocols do not use holddown timers.

The following section describes the convergence process for RIP, IGRP, EIGRP, and link-state protocols when a link failure occurs in a network.

RIP Convergence

Convergence time is one of the problems associated with distance-vector routing protocols. This section details the convergence process of the RIP protocol. We'll use Figure 1.2 to help describe the RIP convergence process.

The following list describes the RIP convergence events when a problem occurs. In Figure 1.2, the WAN between Routers D and F goes down. This link was along the path from Routers A through D, when delivering packets to the Ethernet segment off of Router F. Now, these four routers, in particular Router D, must learn the path through Router E, but each of the four routers will notice an additional hop to this network. Here's what happens:

1. Router D poisons this directly connected route in its own routing table, removes it, and sends a triggered update to Routers E and C. Any routes with Router D's interface in that downed link or Router F's address on that link as a next hop will also be poisoned. This will almost definitely include the Ethernet segment off of Router F.

FIGURE 1.2 Convergence

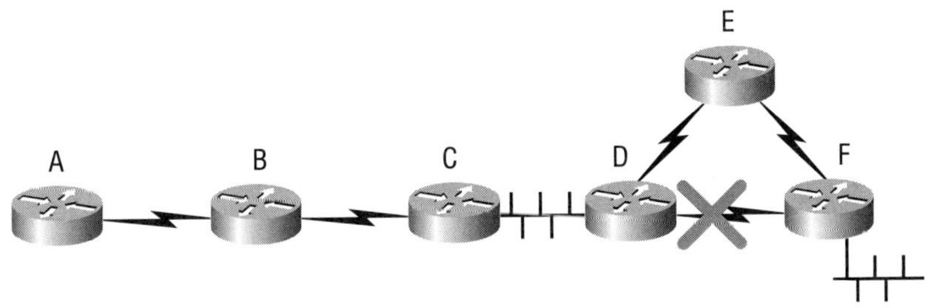

2. Router C was using this path to access Router F's Ethernet, but Router E goes directly through Router F. So the only effect on Router E is the poisoning and removal of the WAN link from its routing table. Router C, however, poisons both routes, removing both of them from its routing table. Router C sends a triggered update to Router B, which in turn sends a triggered update to Router A, each router poisoning and removing the route locally. Router F also sends a triggered update to Router E.
3. The triggered updates that Router E received from Router D and Router F prompt it to send out its own triggered updates in each direction. These updates tell both of its neighbors that all of the routes they used to have access to are still accessible through Router E. Router D enters the new route for Router F's Ethernet—through Router E—into its routing table.
4. Router D accepts this new route to the destination network, as it did not have it in holddown because it was just purged; a route must be in the routing table in order to be in a holddown state. Because route poisoning is in use, the same situation exists on the other routers, as well. Very quickly, they will be ready to accept the new metric.
5. Router D advertises the new metric to Router C, and even if Router C had not poisoned and removed the route from its routing table, but instead had this route in holddown, it would accept the new metric, because it is from the source of the original advertisement—Router D.
6. The same effect trickles down to Routers C, B, and A in that triggered updates cause route poisoning and subsequent triggered updates. So none of them have the failed route in their routing table, nor do they have any of the routes that were accessible through the failed link, including Router F's Ethernet network, which allows their routing table entries to be updated almost immediately by the less desirable metrics. In other words, even if the advertiser of the original route was not advertising a worse metric, which itself is grounds for believing the worse metric, the fact that poisoning removed the routes from their routing tables makes these new updates look like routes they never heard of, causing them to be learned without incident.

Without triggered updates and route poisoning, the time required for Router A to converge would be the detection time, plus the holddown time, two update times, and another update time. The complete convergence to Router A could be over 240 seconds. With these mechanisms working for you, however, convergence will occur in an internetwork of this size in about 15 seconds. It will benefit you, though, to understand the logic behind the scenario that results in the convergence time of roughly 240 seconds.

If the network comes back up, both Routers D and F would immediately broadcast RIP requests for the neighbor's entire routing table, toward each other across the link between them in order to try to speed up convergence without taking a chance on waiting for the other device to start advertising across the link on its own. Instead of the normal broadcast or multicast, the response is a unicast back to the requesting interface. The industrious reader could model this scenario in a lab environment, if available. You could intentionally administratively shut down an interface, while watching the results of the `debug ip rip` command, and then bring the interface back up, allowing all that has been presented here to be observed.

IGRP Convergence

Despite the leaps and bounds Cisco has taken in improving RIP convergence, IGRP still converges according to the standard theory, by default, taking quite a bit of time if left to its own devices, but resulting in an environment that is more resistant to some forms of network instability. IGRP resets its invalid and holddown timers each time an update is received, including triggered updates, but IGRP does not immediately reset its flush timer when it receives a triggered update that a route is down. It waits until the next scheduled update time to start the flush timer. What this means is that the flush time could be as much as 90 seconds longer than configured, when measured from the triggered update that advertises the route as unreachable. A well-placed `clear ip route *` command will speed things along, though.

The following process can be modeled in the lab by issuing the `shutdown` command on the interface of Router D that faces Router F. Using Figure 1.2 as an example, let's take a look at IGRP convergence, keeping in mind that the following enumerated list is not necessarily in chronological order, nor could an exact order be guaranteed:

1. Router D detects the failure on the link to Router F. Router D poisons this directly connected route in its own routing table by removing it, as well as the route for the Ethernet segment off of Router F, because this link was in the path to get there. Router D sends a triggered update to Routers C and E.
2. Router F detects the failure on the same link and poisons the route locally, as well as any routes with Router D's nearest interface address or Router F's interface on that link as a next hop. Router F sends out a triggered update to Router E, detailing these lost routes.
3. Router C sends a triggered update to Router B, and Router B sends one to Router A. Routers A, B, C, and E all start invalid and holddown timers for each of the inaccessible routes, unless there was one or more equal-cost paths (or unequal, with use of the `variance` command) to one or more of them, in which case the downed route will be removed and all traffic will use the remaining route or routes. At the next scheduled update time for each route, the routers will start the routes' flush timers, unless the original source notifies the routers that the links are back up, in which case the route is reinstated as an operational routing table entry.

One tricky point of contention here is that the routing table will likely say "`is possibly down`" next to the destination network, even when the route has been re-established. Attempts at verifying connectivity through `ping` or `traceroute` should meet with success, regardless. Some nominal amount of time after the holddown timer expires, you'll be able to observe the route entry returning to its normal state. Issuing the `clear ip route *` command will speed the process along.

4. Router D broadcasts a request to Router C. Both Router D and Router F broadcast a request to Router E, basically to all remaining active interfaces, asking for the entire routing table of each router in hopes of jump-starting new methods of access to the lost networks. Router C sends back a poison-reverse response to Router D for those routes it originally learned through Router D that are affected by the outage. Router E does the same for Router F.

5. It's where Router D and its downed WAN link are concerned that Router E could create a slight mess initially. The good news is that Router D will learn the alternate—and currently the only—route to the Ethernet segment off of Router F. Router D's request may well arrive at Router E before Router F's triggered update, as three keepalives must be missed before Router F will consider the link down and you manually shut the link down on Router D's side. In such a case, Router E will unicast its reply to Router D that the downed link is available through Router E. This is because Router E had an equal-cost alternative path to the downed network that it learned through Router F. So, to advertise Router E's alternative path to Router D as accessible is not a violation of the poison-reverse rule. That's only for affected routes that Router E learned through Router D, of which there are none. Router E is content to advertise only a single route for each unique destination, and the route through Router F will do nicely—or will it? Because Router D removed its own directly connected route entry, there is nothing stopping it from using this new advertisement that once looked suboptimal when Router D itself had direct access to this network. The triggered update from Router F initiates a triggered update from Router E, and a subsequent resetting of all the appropriate timers, which serves to set Router D straight that the network is truly down.
6. At this point, it appears that the route is possibly down, but the path through Router E apparently has become engraved in the routing table, while attempts to ping an interface on the downed network will no doubt fail. This is only IGRP's optimism showing through, erring on the side of too much information. Remember, even after the link has been re-established, this confusing entry will remain, and the holddown timer will have to expire before the entry is cleaned up and joined by its equal-cost partner. Again, `clear ip route *` works like a charm here to get you back to where you feel you should be. Additionally, watching the festivities through `debug ip igrp transactions` will clarify this process and reassure you that Router D has been informed that the route truly is down, in any direction. Still, Router D is confused enough to return alternating destination unreachable messages, instead of the usual timing out, during ping, as long as the network remains down.
7. Router D then sends a triggered update out all active interfaces participating in the IGRP routing process for the appropriate autonomous system, which includes this new entry.
8. Routers A, B, and C receive this update in turn. They would ignore the new route since it is in holddown, but because each one receives the update from the source of the original route, they each implement the new route, although the entry in the table will not appear to change until after the holddown timer expires. Because they point to the previous next hop still, connectivity will tend to be maintained. While in holddown, each router will continue to use poison reverse for the affected routes, back toward their respective advertising router.
9. Once all holddown timers expire, respective routing tables are then updated with an accurate routing table entry.

Without triggered updates and dumb luck or the smart design of the IGRP protocol that gets these routers to continue to use suspect routes to successfully pass traffic, the time it could take for Router A to converge could be the detection time, plus the holddown time, plus two update times, plus another update time, which is over 490 seconds.

EIGRP Convergence

Let's take a look at the convergence time of Enhanced IGRP (EIGRP). We will again use Figure 1.2 to help describe the convergence process:

1. Router D detects the link failure between Routers D and F and immediately checks its topology table for a feasible successor. We will assume Router D does not find an alternate route in the topology table and puts the route into active convergence state. In reality, taking bandwidth and delay into account, all that must be true for the path through Router E to be a feasible successor and for the process to stop right here is for the metric from Router E to the Ethernet segment off of Router F (the reported distance, RD, from Router E for this route) to be less than Router D's metric of the route that just went down (the feasible distance, FD). If this is the case, this path will be in the topology table, and convergence will already be over. I give you the beauty of EIGRP. Beware the ugliness, of which being a proprietary protocol is a good example.
2. Router D sends a QUERY message advertising the routes that it lost with infinite metrics (4,294,967,295, same as for IGRP) out all active interfaces looking for a route to the failed link and affected networks. Routers C and E acknowledge the QUERY.
3. Router C sends back a REPLY message advertising the routes requested with infinite metrics. Router D acknowledges the REPLY.
4. Router E sends back a REPLY message with routes to the networks that Router D lost, including to the downed network, thinking that it still has the alternate, equal-cost route to offer, not yet having been informed by Router F of its demise. Router D acknowledges the REPLY.
5. Router D places the new routes in the topology table, which then updates the routing table, due to their unopposed selection as successors.
6. Because both neighbors sent back REPLY messages, Router D sends both of them UPDATE messages, thinking that its local routing table has settled down with the changes. Because Router C has been using poison reverse, Router D updates it with the two new routes it learned. But because it learned these from Router E and has nothing new from Router C, the UPDATE to Router E is blank. Return UPDATE messages are often considered acknowledgments for earlier UPDATE messages, with no separate acknowledgment messages necessary.
7. Router C responds with an UPDATE, which Router D acknowledges. Router E sends an UPDATE with the link between Router D and Router F, which it still thinks is accessible through Router F. The reason Router E includes it in an UPDATE message is because it once thought there were two equal-cost paths to get there. Any such changes are eventually sent in an UPDATE message, because these are the messages that suggest the dust has settled and these are the results.
8. However, shortly thereafter, Router E learns from Router F that the network between Router D and Router F is truly down, and immediately sends out a QUERY to Router D looking for another path to the downed network, which also serves to notify Router D that the network is inaccessible through Router E now, as well. Router D acknowledges the QUERY.

9. Router D sends a REPLY, which is acknowledged by Router E, advertising that it too has an infinite metric to that network. Router D and Router E now consider themselves synchronized. Router D also updates its own EIGRP tables with the fact that the network is lost, but it still knows that the Ethernet segment off of Router F is accessible through Router E.
10. In response to this latest news from Router E, Router D sends a QUERY to Router C, just to make sure that it hasn't learned of this network in the meantime. Router C acknowledges this QUERY and sends back a REPLY message that confirms to Router D that no path exists to the downed network. After acknowledging this REPLY, Router D and Router C consider themselves synchronized. The EIGRP routing domain has converged.

Router A convergence time is the total time of detection, plus the query and reply time, plus the update propagation time—about two seconds total. However, the time can be slightly longer.

In case it was not apparent from the foregoing discussion, EIGRP employs various message types, including UPDATE, QUERY, and REPLY. It makes sense that UPDATE and REPLY messages can carry new routing information that could alter the receiving router's EIGRP tables. More subtly, QUERY messages also carry route information that the receiving router treats as new, with respect to the sending router. The QUERY/REPLY pair is invaluable to EIGRP to make sure that one or more specific routes are synchronized between the pair of routers exchanging these messages, especially when there was an earlier discrepancy. For example, in step 8 in the preceding description, Router E used a QUERY message, not an UPDATE message, to inform Router D that it agreed that the link between Router D and Router F was down.

Link-State Convergence

Using Figure 1.2 as a reference, let's now take a look at the convergence cycle used in link-state routing protocols within a single area:

1. Router D detects the link failure between Routers D and F. The route entry for that link and any dependent links are removed from Router D. A link-state advertisement (LSA) for OSPF, or a link-state PDU (LSP) for IS-IS, is sent out all eligible OSPF or IS-IS interfaces on Router D.
2. Routers C and E receive the LSA or LSP and forward it out to all eligible interfaces, which are normally all active interfaces except for the interface where the LSA was received, unless Router C is the OSPF-designated router of the Ethernet network it shares with Router D and Router D is not the backup designated router. If that's the case, then Router C will flood the LSA back out that interface also, as part of its duties as a designated router.
3. All routers wait five seconds, by default, and then run the shortest path first (SPF) algorithm. After the algorithm is run, Router D adds the route through Router E, and Routers C, B, and A update the metric in their routing table to that route.

4. After what could be another 30 seconds, Router F sends out an LSA or LSP to all eligible OSPF or IS-IS interfaces after timing out the link to Router D. All routers wait five seconds after receipt of the advertisement and then run the SPF algorithm, and all routers now know that the route to the Ethernet segment off of Router F is through Router E.

Router A convergence time is the time of detection, plus the LSA forwarding time, plus five seconds. This is about six seconds. However, if Router F's time to converge is considered, then the time can be about 36 seconds.

RFC 2328 is suggested reading for those interested in learning just about all they ever wanted to know about how OSPF operates at the nuts-and-bolts level.

Verifying and Testing a Route

Verifying and testing routes are very important topics to understand. If you understand all of the details that go into making a map, but you do not understand how to read that map and drive a car, you will be lost.

We start this section with an explanation of how to verify what routes are in a routing table and conclude the section with a way to test the connectivity to the routes.

Verifying Routes

Verifying routes is actually a simple item to understand. No matter what routing protocol or, for that matter, routing protocols the router has in use, the process is the same.

You will first log into the router, which will be in user EXEC mode. You will know you're in this mode because the router name will be followed with a > symbol:

```
2501A>
2501A>show ip route
```

After you enter the command, the routing table will be displayed:

```
2501A>sh ip route
Codes: C - connected, S - static, I - IGRP, R - RIP, M - mobile, B - BGP D -
EIGRP, EX - EIGRP external, O - OSPF, IA - OSPF inter area N1 - OSPF NSSA
external type 1, N2 - OSPF NSSA external type 2 E1 - OSPF external type 1, E2 -
OSPF external type 2, E - EGP i - IS-IS, L1 - IS-IS level-1, L2 - IS-IS level-2,
* - candidate default U - per-user static route, o - ODR, P - periodic
downloaded static route T - traffic engineered route

Gateway of last resort is not set
```

```
     172.16.0.0/24 is subnetted, 1 subnets
C       172.16.50.0 is directly connected, FastEthernet0/0
C       192.168.24.0 is directly connected, FastEthernet0/0
R       175.21.0.0/16 [120/1] via 10.10.10.1, 00:00:18, Serial0
2501A#
```

You will now be able to verify all connected, statically defined, and dynamically learned routes.

As you can see, it's easy to verify the routes the router knows. After discovering the routes on the router, you can start testing the connectivity to a route.

Remember, if you ever want to clear all the routes in your routing table, use the command `clear ip route *`. This will cause your router to purge its routing table and relearn all active routes. As you've seen, this is very useful in case you want to get the most up-to-date routing information.

Testing and Troubleshooting Routes

What you need to understand at this point is that the tools you will use to test connectivity will also be used to troubleshoot connectivity issues.

There are two tools that can be used for these tasks:

- Ping
- Traceroute

One of the tools you should use in the testing and troubleshooting phase is Ping. The `ping` command is used to test IP connectivity to a destination. Ping uses ICMP to accomplish this task. With debugging turned on for ICMP packets, let's take a look at how Ping accomplishes this:

```
3640#debug ip icmp
ICMP packet debugging is on
3640#ping 10.10.10.1

Type escape sequence to abort.
Sending 5, 100-byte ICMP Echos to 10.10.10.1, timeout is 2 seconds:
!!!!!
Success rate is 100 percent (5/5), round-trip min/avg/max = 28/28/28 ms
3640#
2d01h: ICMP: echo reply rcvd, src 10.10.10.1, dst 10.10.10.2
2d01h: ICMP: echo reply rcvd, src 10.10.10.1, dst 10.10.10.2
2d01h: ICMP: echo reply rcvd, src 10.10.10.1, dst 10.10.10.2
2d01h: ICMP: echo reply rcvd, src 10.10.10.1, dst 10.10.10.2
2d01h: ICMP: echo reply rcvd, src 10.10.10.1, dst 10.10.10.2
```

So, what happened? Router 3640 sent an ICMP echo to 10.10.10.1 on router 2501. Router 2501 received the ICMP echo from router 3640 and sent an ICMP echo reply telling router 3640 the packet has reached its destination of 10.10.10.1 on router 2501, signifying a successful ping. If the destination network were unreachable, when router 2501 received the ICMP echo from router 3640, it would have dropped the packet and returned an ICMP destination unreachable message.

Now that you understand the concept of Ping and how it works, you need to learn how to implement it. Using Ping is relatively simple. All you need to do is enter the command **ping** followed by the address or host name of the device you want to ping (omitting the address/host name parameter from the command will begin the extended ping dialog, allowing you to alter the default settings and have more control over the process):

```
3640#ping 10.10.10.1

Type escape sequence to abort.
Sending 5, 100-byte ICMP Echos to 10.10.10.1, timeout is 2 seconds:
!!!!!
Success rate is 100 percent (5/5), round-trip min/avg/max = 28/28/28 ms
```

Let's examine the information you receive back:

```
Sending 5, 100-byte ICMP Echos to 10.10.10.1, timeout is 2 seconds:
```

Sending 5 This means you are sending five packets.

100-byte The size of each packet.

ICMP Echos The type of packet sent.

10.10.10.1 The destination address.

timeout is 2 seconds The packet will be deemed dropped if an echo reply is not received within two seconds.

The ! symbol represents a successful ping. A ping that has timed out would be represented by a period, such as:

```
.....
```

Let's examine the last line of the sequence:

```
Success rate is 100 percent (5/5), round-trip min/avg/max = 28/28/28 ms
```

Success rate The percentage of successful packets sent and received.

(5/5) This means five packets were sent and five packets were received back.

round-trip min/avg/max These values represent the shortest, average, and longest times it took to receive an ICMP echo reply.

Ping may be an easy concept to grasp, but it is the one tool you will use the most as a network engineer.

The other tool that will be used for testing and troubleshooting a route is Traceroute. The `traceroute` command gives you a router-by-router account of the path a packet takes to get to a destination. It does not, however, supply information on the return path of user or ICMP packets, which could be different, depending on reverse-route selection among the routers in the internetwork. Traceroute is best used when you need to discover the location where the packet is being dropped or a routing loop occurs.

Traceroute takes advantage of the time to live (TTL) field of an IP packet. The value of the TTL field represents how many layer 3 devices (hops) a packet can enter before it is dropped. Traceroute exploits this by setting the TTL to a value of 1 in the IP header of a UDP port 33434 packet that it sends toward the destination.

IANA reserves this TCP/UDP port number for traceroute use. There are also about 800 additional port numbers following this value that are unassigned and possibly available for traceroute use. The key is to use a port number that will not be active on the destination device.

The packet will reach the first router in the path, which will, as one of its first layer 3 tasks, decrease the TTL by 1 to 0 and drop the packet with no further processing. The executing router sends an ICMP time exceeded message to the traceroute originator. The originator then increases the TTL by 1 to a value of 2 and sends the packet toward the destination. The packet reaches the first router in the path and the TTL is decreased by 1 to a value of 1. That router then forwards the packet toward the second router in the path to the destination. The second router then decreases the TTL by 1 to a value of 0.

At this point, the packet is dropped and an ICMP time exceeded message is sent to the originator. This process continues until the destination is reached or the maximum TTL (30, by default) has been used. The originator displays the identity of the executioner upon receipt of each time exceeded message, creating a sequenced list of devices between the traceroute originator and target. The originator knows the trace is over when it receives an ICMP destination port unreachable message from the traceroute target, indicating that the packet made it all the way to the intended recipient, and there are no more intermediate devices to discover. Cisco devices offer an extended `traceroute` command, while in privileged EXEC mode, that can be used to adjust defaults, like maximum TTL and source IP address.

All you need to do in order to use the basic `traceroute` command is to enter **`traceroute`** followed by the destination address. Just entering **`traceroute`** will begin the dialog for the extended `traceroute` command. Here's an example of a successful traceroute from router R1 in Figure 1.3:

```
R1#traceroute 11.11.11.1

Type escape sequence to abort.
Tracing the route to 11.11.11.1

  1 12.12.12.2 12 msec 12 msec 12 msec
  2 10.10.10.2 24 msec 24 msec *
R1#
```

FIGURE 1.3 Traceroute

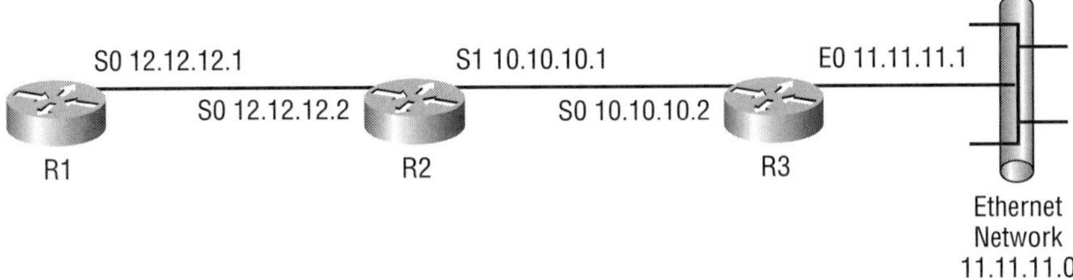

Here's what's going on in Figure 1.3:

1. R1 sends a packet toward the destination with the TTL set to a value of 1.
2. R2 receives the packet, decreases the TTL by 1 to a value of 0, and sends an ICMP time exceeded message back to R1.
3. R1 sends another packet toward the destination with the TTL set to a value of 2.
4. R2 receives the packet, decreases the TTL by 1 to a value of 1, and forwards to packet to R3.
5. R3 receives the packet, realizes that the destination of the packet is itself, looks in the protocol field of the IP header, and finds that UDP is the next protocol to get the datagram. Once R3's UDP process sees that the destination port of 33434 is not an active application, R3 triggers an ICMP destination port unreachable message back to R1, which ends the trace.

From this, you learn there are two hops to the destination. The numbers preceding the lines correspond to the value of the TTL for that series of three packets (by default). You can change the minimum and maximum TTL values in the extended Traceroute utility, which will cause a value other than 1 in the first column of the first line to be reported. Tracing to a non-existent address on a network known to the originator can cause multiple lines of asterisks to display until the maximum TTL value is reached, at which point the trace ends (just in case you want to see that happen in a production environment without establishing a career-limiting routing loop).

If the packet had made it through the first hop and not the second, you would have then been able to locate where the break in the connection occurred. If there had been a routing loop, the traceroute would have shown the path bouncing between two or more routers multiple times before the TTL expired. Asterisks (*) represent packets that went out but were unanswered before timing out, which is a period of three seconds, by default.

As you can tell, Ping and Traceroute are two valuable tools for testing and troubleshooting routes. Trust me, you will come to love these two commands in your production environment.

This is a very important chapter to understand. You need to have a strong understanding of the information covered to be able to grasp the concepts that will be covered from here on out. If you don't feel you have fully grasped the concepts covered, please review this chapter until you feel comfortable with it.

Summary

Routing allows information from one network to be shared with a different network. In order for this to be accomplished, a router must understand how to reach the destination. This is accomplished through static or dynamic routing. Static routing requires you to manually configure the router paths to remote destinations. Static routing works well in a small network but doesn't scale well.

When the network you are on is a larger one, it's a better idea to use dynamic routing. Dynamic routing allows routers to dynamically discover the available paths to a destination. Using the metrics associated with the various advertised routes, the router is able to determine the best path to a destination.

Dynamic routing comes in two forms: distance-vector routing and link-state routing. Distance-vector routing protocols share their entire routing table with their directly connected neighbors; this means that a distance-vector routing protocol sees the network only from the perspective of its neighbor. These routing tables are broadcast or multicast out at fixed intervals. Distance-vector routing protocols work well for small networks but do not scale well to larger networks.

Link-state routing protocols work extremely well for large networks. They are less bandwidth intensive than distance-vector routing protocols and also provide a view of the entire network. Link-state routing protocols accomplish this by keeping a link-state database. The link-state database is a list of all possible routes to all destinations. Link-state routing protocols are less bandwidth intensive than distance-vector routing protocols because they send out routing updates only when a change has occurred to the network, unlike distance-vector routing protocols that send out their entire routing table at fixed intervals.

EIGRP is a Cisco-proprietary advanced distance-vector or distance-vector/link-state hybrid routing protocol. It routes by rumor and sees the network only from the perspective of its neighbors, just as distance-vector routing protocols do. But in addition, EIGRP sends Hello packets for neighbor discovery and as connectivity keepalives, builds tables other than the routing table, and does not send out periodic updates containing the entire routing table, just as link-state routing protocols do.

Exam Essentials

Understand how routers route data. Routers receive frames that should be, under normal circumstances with no special configuration, addressed to the router. The frame is discarded after CRC comparison passes. The router examines the layer 3 packet header information to determine the layer 3 address of the destination device. Armed with this information, the router performs a lookup in its own protocol-based (such as IP) routing table for the protocol that formatted the packet. If it finds a suitable entry in its table, it switches the packet to the outbound buffer of the exit interface for encapsulation in a frame suitable for the media for which that interface is configured. The match may be in the form of a default route, which will be used, as long as no longer prefix matches exist. If the router fails to find an entry that matches the destination address and no default route is known, then the router drops the packet and sends an ICMP destination unreachable message back to the source of the packet, as determined by another examination of the layer 3 header.

Describe classful and classless routing protocols. RIPv1 and IGRP are classful routing protocols; RIPv2, EIGRP, OSPF, IS-IS, and BGP are classless routing protocols. Classful routing protocols do not send a subnet mask in routing updates; classless routing protocols do. This means that a classful routing protocol assumes classful IP boundaries when it does have enough information about the true subnet mask, resulting in the inability to have more than one subnet mask per classful IP network (no VLSM) or to separate subnets even of the same mask length by a different classful network (discontiguous subnets). A classless protocol does not have these restrictions, as long as automatic summarization is turned off.

Understand a routing table and how it is populated. A router's routing table contains the routes that the router will use to send packets to their destinations. When populating the routing table, the router first looks at the administrative distance of the route. A router will select the routes with the lowest administrative distance. If multiple routes exist to a destination with the same administrative distance, the route with the lowest metric will then be selected to populate the routing table.

Know the difference between distance-vector and link-state routing protocols. RIPv1, RIPv2, and IGRP are all distance-vector routing protocols. These protocols send their entire routing table to neighbors at fixed intervals. OSPF and IS-IS are link-state routing protocols. These routing protocols will send out an update only when a change has occurred to the network. EIGRP is known as a hybrid, or advanced distance-vector, routing protocol. It has characteristics of both a distance-vector and a link-state routing protocol.

Understand what convergence time is. Convergence time is the amount of time that is required for all the routers within a routing domain to have the same relative understanding of a network from their individual viewpoints. Because distance-vector routing protocols send their entire routing table at fixed intervals, they require more time to converge than link-state routing protocols.

IP Addressing

THE CCNP EXAM TOPICS COVERED IN THIS CHAPTER INCLUDE THE FOLLOWING:

- ✓ Review the fundamental concepts of IPv4 and IPv6 addressing.
- ✓ Understand the benefits of extending IP addresses.
- ✓ Learn how VLSM can be used to extend IP addresses.
- ✓ Become familiar with CIDR (classless interdomain routing).
- ✓ Recognize the benefits of route summarization.
- ✓ Examine the features of IPv6.

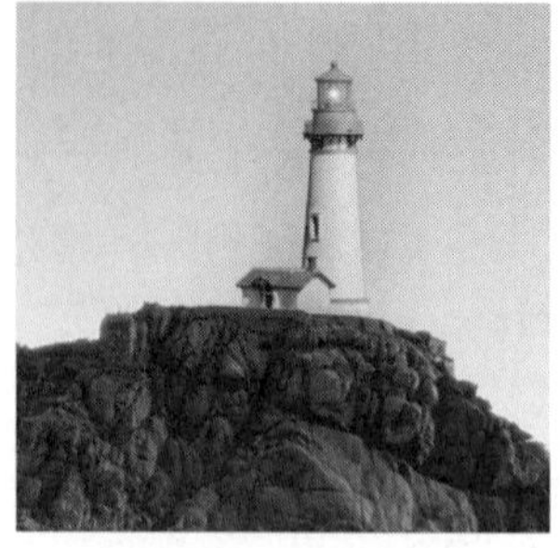

In this chapter, we will discuss both IPv4 and IPv6 addressing. However, we assume that you have a basic understanding of IPv4 addressing and subnetting.

Even though this chapter does review IP addressing, you must have a fundamental understanding of IP subnetting before reading this chapter. The *CCNA Study Guide, 4th Edition,* by Todd Lammle (Sybex, 2004) has a complete chapter on IP addressing and subnetting. Please read that chapter prior to reading this chapter, if you are not already familiar with the topic.

After we review IPv4 addressing, we will provide detailed descriptions and examples of advanced IPv4 addressing techniques that you can use on your production networks to extend IPv4 addresses. First, we'll discuss variable-length subnet masks (VLSMs) and provide an example to show how VLSMs can be used to help save precious address space on your network.

After discussing VLSMs, we will provide an understanding of classless interdomain routing (CIDR), as well as summarization techniques. Finally, we will explain the next generation of IP addressing known as IPv6 and show how this can alleviate the shortage of IP addresses on the global Internet. We will also discuss how IPv6 provides some enhanced networking features.

After you have read the chapter, you can use both the written and hands-on labs on the accompanying CD to help you better prepare for using the advanced IP addressing techniques found in this chapter. Also, to help you study for the Building Scalable Cisco Internetworks (BSCI) exam, be sure to read the review questions on the CD.

Review of IPv4 Addressing

One of the most important topics in any discussion of TCP/IP is IP addressing. An *IP address* is a numeric identifier assigned to each interface on an IP network. It designates the location of a device on the network. An IP address is a software address, not a hardware address. A hardware address is hard-coded on a network interface card (NIC) and used for finding hosts on a local network. The hardware address is also known as the MAC, or Media Access Control, address. In Cisco terms, the hardware address is known as the burned-in address (BIA). IP addressing was designed to allow a host on one network to communicate with a host on a different network, regardless of the type of LANs in which the hosts are participating.

Before we get into the more difficult aspects of IPv4 addressing, let's look at some of the basics.

IP Terminology

In this chapter, we'll introduce you to a number of terms that are fundamental to an understanding of TCP/IP. We'll start by defining a few terms that are the most important:

Bit Either a 1 (on) or a 0 (off).

Byte Traditionally, eight bits, but if parity is used, user information will only be able to occupy the high order seven bits. The use of the word *byte* in certain literature has also degraded the meaning by referring to the most elemental number of bits as a byte. For example, the technical documentation of a 64-bit processor may refer to a 64-bit byte. For the rest of this chapter, always assume that a byte is eight bits.

Octet Always eight bits.

Prefix length The *prefix* is the part of the IP address that represents either the network address, when the default subnet mask is used, or the network address and subnet number combined. In other words, the prefix is everything in the IP address except the host ID. The *prefix length* is the number of bits that the prefix extends from the highest order bit to the end of the prefix, often presented in CIDR notation (a slash followed by the number of mask bits that are set to 1). Subtracting the prefix length from 32 yields the length of the host ID.

A more advanced use of the term *prefix* is to describe the number of bits common to all networks in an administrative superset (supernet) of networks or subnets of some standard prefix length or set of prefix lengths in order to collectively refer to all of the smaller networks with one entry. In this sense, a prefix is neither the network address nor the combination of the network address and subnet number, but rather the number of bits that a larger group of such networks and subnets have in common. The context of the discussion should reveal the exact intent of the use of the term prefix.

Network address The numeric designation used by IP devices to determine if packets should be routed to a remote network or if they should remain on the immediate link, for example, 172.16.0.0/16 and 10.0.0.0/8. The network address identifies the segment that all hosts with the same network address share. Although not necessarily technically accurate, it's common to refer to both a default prefix and the prefix of a subnetted address as the network address.

Subnet address Also known as the *subnet number*, the numeric portion of an IP address that was part of the host ID, by default, but which is taken over for network identification in order to more efficiently use address space by customizing the number of networks under our administrative control and the number of hosts on any and all such networks.

Host address or identifier (ID) The numeric portion of an IP address that uniquely identifies a router or host on an IP network. It's sometimes necessary to consider the binary representation of the host ID in order to truly understand it, especially when its boundary does not coincide with that of an octet. Examples of host IDs are 1.1 in 172.16.1.1/16 and 1.1.1 in 10.1.1.1/8.

Broadcast address Used by applications and hosts to send information to all nodes on a network and characterized by all binary 1s in the host ID portion of the IP address, for example, 172.16.255.255/16 and 10.255.255.255/8.

The Hierarchical IP Addressing Scheme

An IPv4 address is made up of 32 bits of information. These are divided into four sections, referred to as *octets* or *bytes*, containing one byte (eight bits) each. You can depict an IP address using three methods:

- Dotted-decimal, as in 172.16.30.56
- Binary, as in 10101100.00010000.00011110.00111000
- Hexadecimal, as in AC 10 1E 38

All of these examples represent the same IP address. Although hexadecimal is not used as often as dotted-decimal or binary when IP version 4 addressing is discussed, you might find an IP address stored as hexadecimal in some programs. The 32-bit IP address is a structured, or hierarchical, address. Although an unstructured type of addressing scheme, like that of MAC addresses, could have been used, the structured variety was chosen for a good reason.

The advantage of the hierarchical scheme is that it can, in a single address, represent both the network on which a device resides and a unique identity for that device on that network. Unstructured addresses can only hope to be unique throughout the network, but not to represent where on the network they reside. With an unstructured address scheme, all routers on the Internet would need to store the address of each and every interface on the Internet. This would make efficient routing impossible, even if only a fraction of the possible addresses were used. The use of a network portion that can be tracked separately from the host portion allows smaller routing tables than would be possible by tracking each individual address in its entirety.

The solution to this unstructured address dilemma is to use a two- or three-level hierarchical addressing scheme that is structured by network and host or by network, subnet, and host. An unstructured address is similar to how a Social Security number works in that you may know when the number was issued and where the individual resided when that unique number was assigned to them, but the number is no help, by itself, in locating them today.

A two- or three-level hierarchical address is comparable to the sections of a telephone number. The first section, the area code, designates a very large area. The second section, the prefix, narrows the scope to a local calling area. The final segment, the customer number, zooms in on the specific subscriber. IPv4 addresses use the same type of layered structure. Rather than all 32 bits being treated as a unique identifier, as in MAC addressing, one part of the address is designated as the network address, and the other part is designated as either the subnet and host addresses or just the host address, if the default mask is used. Note that in some literature, the *host address* may be referred to as the *node address*.

In the following sections, we will discuss network addressing and the three different address classes:

- Class A addresses
- Class B addresses
- Class C addresses

Network Addressing

The network address collectively identifies each network. Every interface on the same network shares that network address as part of its IP address. In the IP address 172.16.30.56, for example, 172.16.0.0 is the network address, by default, because of the classful boundary.

The host address singularly identifies each interface on a network segment. This part of the address must be unique because it identifies a particular interface—an individual—as opposed to a network, which is a group. Of course, host addresses may be duplicated across subnet boundaries. Otherwise, IP address space would be grossly limited. Nevertheless, when the entire 32-bit IP address is taken as a unit, by combining the network and host portions, it becomes unique across the accessible internetwork.

In the sample IP address 172.16.30.56, 30.56 is the host address because of the default Class B boundary.

The designers of the Internet decided to create classes of networks based on network size. For the small number of networks possessing a very large number of nodes, they created the Class A network. At the other extreme is the Class C network, reserved for the numerous networks with a small number of nodes. The class distinction for networks between very large and very small is predictably called a Class B network. The default division of an IP address into a network and node address is determined by the class designation of a network. Table 2.1 provides a summary of the three classes of networks, which will be described in much more detail throughout this chapter, plus special classes D and E.

TABLE 2.1 The Three Classes of IP Addresses Used in Networks Today

Class	Leading Bit Pattern	Default Subnet Mask	Address Range	Number of Addresses per Network
A	0	255.0.0.0	1.0.0.0–126.255.255.255	16,777,214
B	10	255.255.0.0	128.0.0.0–191.255.255.255	65,534
C	110	255.255.255.0	192.0.0.0–223.255.255.255	254
D	1110	None	224.0.0.0–239.255.255.255	Multicast
E	1111	None	240.0.0.0–255.255.255.255	Experimental

To ensure efficient routing, Internet designers defined a mandate for the leading bits section of the address for each network class. For example, because a router knows that a Class A network address always starts with 0, the router can determine the default boundary between network and host portions after reading only the first bit of its address. This capability is invaluable when the router has no way of determining the actual prefix length of an address. It allows at least a minimum level of functionality and reachability.

This is where the address schemes define the difference between a Class A, a Class B, a Class C, a Class D, and a Class E address. Class D is used for multicast addresses and Class E is reserved for experimental uses. Recall from Chapter 1, "Routing Principles," that a neat trick that you can use to almost immediately determine the class of an IP address in binary form is to label the first four bits A, B, C, and D. Wherever the first zero lies is the class of address you are dealing with. No 0s in the first four bits signify a Class E address. Try it.

Some IP addresses are reserved for special purposes, and network administrators shouldn't assign them to nodes. Table 2.2 lists some of the members of this exclusive little club and explains why they're included in it. For a more complete list of special-use addresses, consult RFC 3330, "Special-Use IPv4 Addresses," and RFCs 1700 (page 3) and 3232, "Assigned Numbers."

TABLE 2.2 Reserved IP Addresses

Address	Function
Network address 0 with node address of all 0s (0.0.0.0/8)	Original Unix general broadcast. Interpreted to mean "this network or segment." Source address only.
Network address 0 with node address of all 0s (0.0.0.0/32)	Interpreted to mean "this host on this network." Source address only.
Network address 0 with specific node address (0.*x*.*x*.*x*/8)	Interpreted to mean "specified host on this network." Source address only.
Entire IP address set to all 0s (0.0.0.0/0)	Used by devices to generate the default route.
Network 127	Reserved for loopback tests. Designates the local node and allows that node to send a test packet to itself without generating network traffic. Should never appear outside a host.
Node address of all 0s	Interpreted to mean "this network." Mainly appears in routing tables and engineering documents to refer to the entire network in general, but to no particular node. Should never appear as a source or destination address in a packet header.
Node address of all 1s	A directed broadcast. Interpreted to mean "all nodes" on the specified network; for example, 128.2.255.255/16 means "all nodes on network 128.2" (Class B address). Destination address only.
Entire IP address set to all 1s (same as 255.255.255.255)	Broadcast to all nodes on the current network; sometimes called a limited broadcast or an "all ones broadcast." Destination address only, not to appear outside local segment.

Let's now take a look at the different network address classes, which can be assigned to an individual host.

Class A Addresses

In a Class A address, the first byte—or octet—is assigned to the network address, and the three remaining bytes are used for the node addresses, by default. The Class A format is

Network.Node.Node.Node

For example, in the IP address 49.22.102.70, 49 is the network address and 22.102.70 is the node address. Every machine on this particular network would have the distinctive network address of 49.

Class A network addresses have the first bit of the first byte set to 0 by definition, and the seven remaining bits are available for IANA manipulation. Thus, the maximum number of Class A networks that can be created is 128. Why? Because each of the seven bit positions can either be 0 or 1, thus 2^7 or 128. But to complicate things further, it was also decided that the network address of all 0s (0000 0000) would be reserved to designate the default route and other special-use addresses (see Table 2.2 earlier in this chapter). Thus, the actual number of usable Class A network addresses is 128 minus 1, or 127. However, the address 127 is reserved for diagnostics, so that can't be used, which means that you can use only numbers 1 through 126 in the first octet to designate Class A networks.

It can also be argued that the total number is 125, because Class A network 10 is reserved for private (intranet) use by RFC 1918. RFCs 1700 and 3330 expose still other reserved Class A networks. Still others, visible as reserved via a brute-force journey through the American Registry for Internet Numbers' (ARIN—`arin.net`) whois service, reveal why there are precious few Class A addresses in the wild, all of which have been spoken for.

Each Class A address has three bytes (24 bit positions) for the host address of a machine. Thus, there are 2^{24}—or 16,777,216—unique combinations and, therefore, precisely that many possible unique node addresses for each Class A network. Because addresses with the two patterns of all 0s and all 1s in the host ID are reserved, the actual maximum usable number of nodes for a Class A network is 2^{24} minus 2, which equals 16,777,214.

Here's an example of how to figure out the valid host IDs in a Class A network:

10.0.0.0 All host bits off is the network address.

10.255.255.255 All host bits on is the broadcast address.

The valid hosts are the numbers in between the network address and the broadcast address: 10.0.0.1 through 10.255.255.254. Note that 0s and 255s are valid in the second, third, or even last octet of the IP address. All you need to remember when trying to find valid host addresses is that the host bits cannot all be turned off or on at the same time.

As alluded to earlier, when you request a network number from ARIN, don't expect to be assigned a Class A address. These have all been taken for quite some time. Big names such as HP and IBM got in the game early enough to have their own Class A network. However, a check of the Internet Assigned Numbers Authority (IANA) records shows that several corporations were handed Class A addresses back in 1995, and that Stanford University's Class A was given back to IANA in

July 2000. The records also indicate that the IANA has control of many Class A addresses, ones that have not been allocated to regional ISPs. A company can also buy another company to get a Class A network ID. For example, Compaq got the 16 network by acquiring Digital.

Class B Addresses

In a Class B address, the first two bytes are assigned to the network address, and the remaining two bytes are used for host addresses, by default. The format is

Network.Network.Node.Node

For example, in the IP address 172.16.30.56, the network address is 172.16, and the host address is 30.56.

With a network address being two bytes of eight bits each, there would be 65,536 unique combinations. But the Internet designers decided that all Class B addresses should start with the two binary digits 10. This leaves 14 bit positions for IANA to manipulate; therefore, there are 16,384 unique Class B addresses.

A Class B address uses two bytes for node addresses. This is 2 to the power of 16 minus the two reserved patterns (all 0s and all 1s in the host portion), for a total of 65,534 possible node addresses for each Class B network.

Here is an example of how to find the valid hosts in a Class B network:

172.16.0.0 All host bits turned off is the network address.

172.16.255.255 All host bits turned on is the broadcast address.

The valid hosts would be the numbers in between the network address and the broadcast address: 172.16.0.1 through 172.16.255.254.

Just as you saw with Class A addresses, all Class B addresses have also been assigned. Many universities, which were connected to the Internet in the early 1990s, in addition to many big-name organizations such as Microsoft, Cisco, Sprint, Xerox, Novell, and Sun Microsystems, have all of these addresses consumed. However, they are available under the right circumstances.

Class C Addresses

The first three bytes of a Class C address are dedicated to the network portion of the address, with only one measly byte remaining for the host address, by default. The format is

Network.Network.Network.Node

Using the example IP address 192.168.100.102, the network address is 192.168.100, and the host address is 102.

In a Class C address, the first three bit positions are always the binary 110. The calculation is as follows: 3 bytes, or 24 bits, minus 3 reserved positions, equals 21 positions left for IANA manipulation. There are, therefore, 2 to the power of 21, or 2,097,152, possible Class C networks.

Each unique Class C network uses one byte for node addresses. This leads to 2 to the power of 8, or 256, minus the two reserved patterns of all 0s and all 1s in the host portion, for a total of 254 node addresses for each Class C network.

Here's an example of how to find a valid host ID in a Class C network:

192.168.100.0 All host bits turned off is the network ID.

192.168.100.1 The first host.

192.168.100.254 The last host.

192.168.100.255 All host bits turned on is the broadcast address.

Extending IP Addresses

In the "old days," when the Network Information Center (InterNIC) assigned a network number to an organization, it assigned either the first octet (a Class A network), the first two octets (a Class B network), or the first three octets (a Class C network). The organization could take this one network number and further subdivide it into smaller networks through a process called *subnetting*.

To illustrate, let's say that our organization has been assigned the Class B network 172.16.0.0. We have several different network segments, each of which needs a unique network number. So, we decide to subnet our network. We use a subnet mask of 255.255.255.0. The *subnet mask* determines where in our IP address is the boundary between the subnet number and the host ID. If we write our IP address and subnet mask out in binary, as illustrated in the following IP address example, the 1s in the mask correspond to the network portion of the address, and the 0s correspond to the node portion of the address.

Decimal	172	16	0	0
Binary	10101100	00010000	00000000	00000000
Decimal	255	255	255	0
Binary	11111111	11111111	11111111	00000000

So, in this case, instead of having one network (172.16.0.0) with 65,534 available host numbers, we have 256 networks (172.16.0.0–172.16.255.0) with 254 available host numbers in each subnet.

We can calculate the number of hosts available on a subnet by using the formula $2n - 2 =$ *number of available host IPs*, where n is the number of host bits (in our example, 8). The minus 2 (– 2) represents our not being able to assign all host bits on and all host bits off, which are reserved to an interface as an IP address.

Similarly, the number of networks (or subnets) can be calculated with nearly the same formula: $2n =$ *number of available networks*, where n is the number of subnet bits (in our example, 8). As long as we use the `ip subnet-zero` global configuration command, we no longer need to subtract 2 from this result and may use the all 0s and all 1s subnets. Without this command configured, we must also subtract 2 from this result, leaving only 254 subnets, not including subnet 0 and subnet 255. So, with subnetting we have balanced our need for available network and host numbers. However, there may be instances where we need fewer host numbers on a particular subnet and more host numbers on another.

Let's extend our example to include a serial link between two routers, as shown in Figure 2.1.

FIGURE 2.1 IP address example

Because these are routers and not switches, each interface on the same router belongs to a different network. The facing interfaces on opposing routers need to share a network to talk. How many IP numbers do we really need on the network interconnecting the two routers? Because a point-to-point link will never have anything but two devices, we need only two IP numbers, one for each serial interface, as shown in Figure 2.1. Unfortunately, we have an eight-bit subnet mask (i.e., 255.255.255.0), so we are wasting 252 of the 254 available numbers on the subnet. One possible solution to this dilemma is to use VLSMs.

Variable-Length Subnet Masks

As the name suggests, with *variable-length subnet masks (VLSMs)* we can have different subnet masks for different subnets of the same classful network. So, for the serial link in the preceding example, we could have a subnet mask of 255.255.255.252. If we do the math and look at our subnet in binary, we see that we have only two host bits, as shown in our first VLSM example.

Decimal	255	255	255	252
Binary	11111111	11111111	11111111	11111100

Therefore, this subnet mask will give us only two valid IP addresses ($2^2 - 2 = 2$), which is exactly what we need for our serial link.

As another example, consider what would happen if we were running out of IP numbers on a particular subnet. Perhaps we have several web servers on network 172.16.10.0, with a subnet mask of 255.255.255.0 (which we could also write in CIDR notation as 172.16.10.0/24, due to there being 24 bits turned on in our subnet mask). With only eight bits left over for host identification, we have only 254 available host addresses.

However, in our web server implementation, each URL needs its own IP number, and our need for unique IP numbers is about to grow beyond the 254 numbers that we have available. It is possible to support several URLs to an IP address, but for this example we'll use only one address per URL.

Yet again, VLSMs can provide a solution. Instead of making our subnet mask longer, as in the previous example, we can make our subnet mask shorter. This is called *route aggregation*, in general, or *supernetting* when dealing with a prefix length shorter than the default for the class in question.

Our second VLSM example demonstrates would happen if we reduced our prefix length from 24 bits to 23 bits.

Decimal	255	255	254	0
Binary	11111111	11111111	11111110	00000000

We now have a network of 172.16.10.0 with a subnet mask of 255.255.254.0, which can also be written as 172.16.10.0/23. Again, by doing the math ($2^9 - 2 = 510$, because we have nine host bits), we see that we now have 510 available IP addresses instead of 254.

Let's work through a VLSM design example, as depicted in Figure 2.2.

FIGURE 2.2 VLSM design example

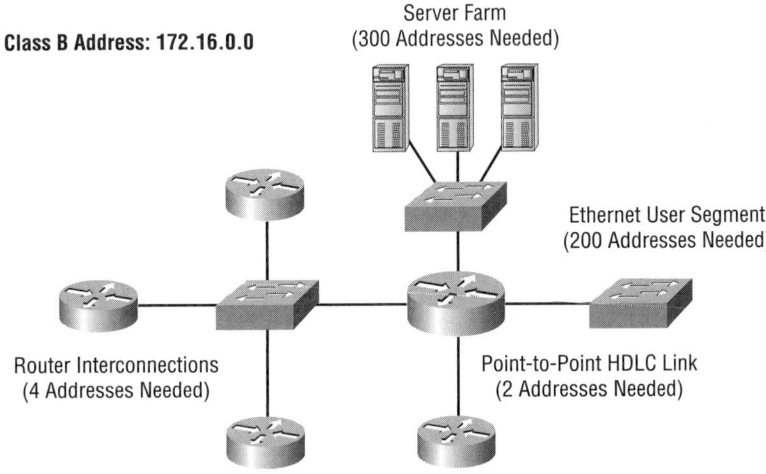

In this example, we have the following set of requirements for our network addressing:

- A server farm requires 300 IP addresses.
- A user segment requires 200 IP addresses.
- A serial link between two routers requires two IP addresses.
- A switched subnet interconnecting four routers requires four IP addresses.
- We have been assigned the Class B network of 172.16.0.0.

We will now go through a simple three-step process for efficiently calculating the IP address ranges to be assigned to each segment. We say "efficiently," because we will be using the minimum number of IP addresses required to accomplish our goal with a few extra to account for expected growth. Changing addresses once they've been implemented can be time-consuming, costly, and may require significant down time.

1. Create a table detailing the segments and the number of hosts required on each segment, as shown in Table 2.3.

TABLE 2.3 Number of IP Addresses Used in Figure 2.2

Description of Segment	Number of IP Addresses Required
Server farm	300
Ethernet user segment	200
Serial link	2
Router interconnection switched subnet	4

2. Determine the subnet mask required to support the requirements defined in step 1, and expand the table to list the subnet masks.

We can use our formula 2*n* – 2 = *number of hosts* to create a handy reference chart to quickly determine how many hosts can be supported for any given subnet mask, as shown in Table 2.4. The table goes up to only 1022 hosts, because Cisco has a design recommendation that you should not have a non-routed network segment with more than 500 hosts (due to performance problems caused by broadcast traffic). To confuse you further, understand that some Cisco documentation states that the number of hosts on a segment can be up to 800! Just keep in mind the amount of traffic when making this decision.

TABLE 2.4 Number of Hosts Needed in Figure 2.2

Maximum Number of Hosts	Bits in Subnet Mask	Subnet Mask
2	30	255.255.255.252
6	29	255.255.255.248
14	28	255.255.255.240
30	27	255.255.255.224
62	26	255.255.255.192
126	25	255.255.255.128
254	24	255.255.255.0

TABLE 2.4 Number of Hosts Needed in Figure 2.2 *(continued)*

Maximum Number of Hosts	Bits in Subnet Mask	Subnet Mask
510	23	255.255.254.0
1022	22	255.255.252.0

Referring to Table 2.4, we can easily determine the subnet mask required for each segment in our example by looking for the closest subnet size greater than or equal to the number of hosts needed, as shown in Table 2.5.

TABLE 2.5 Subnet Masks for Figure 2.2

Description of Segment	Number of IP Addresses Required	Subnet Mask (Number of Subnet Bits)
Server farm	300	255.255.254.0 (23)
Ethernet user segment	200	255.255.255.0 (24)
Serial link	2	255.255.255.252 (30)
Router interconnection switched subnet	4	255.255.255.248 (29)

3. Starting with the segment requiring the greatest prefix length, begin allocating addresses.

Let's begin with the serial link, which has a prefix length of 30 bits. Because all of our addresses are going to start with 172.16, we will examine only the last 16 bits of the IP address. In Table 2.6, we see the binary representations of the last two octets of the subnet mask, the subnet address, the first and last valid IP addresses in the subnet, and the broadcast address. Remember that the host portion of an assigned address cannot be all 1s, which is the broadcast address, or all 0s, which is the address of the network, or *wire*.

TABLE 2.6 Networks, Hosts, and Subnets for Figure 2.2

	3rd Octet 128 64 32 16 8 4 2 1	4th Octet 128 64 32 16 8 4 2 1	Decimal IP Address (Last 16 bits in bold)
Subnet Mask	1 1 1 1 1 1 1 1	1 1 1 1 1 1 0 0	255.255.**255.252**
Subnet	0 0 0 0 0 0 0 0	0 0 0 0 0 0 0 0	172.16.**0.0**

TABLE 2.6 Networks, Hosts, and Subnets for Figure 2.2 *(continued)*

	3rd Octet 128 64 32 16 8 4 2 1	4th Octet 128 64 32 16 8 4 2 1	Decimal IP Address (Last 16 bits in bold)
First IP in range	0 0 0 0 0 0 0 0	0 0 0 0 0 0 0 1	172.16.**0.1**
Last IP in range	0 0 0 0 0 0 0 0	0 0 0 0 0 1 1 0	172.16.**0.2**
Broadcast	0 0 0 0 0 0 0 0	0 0 0 0 0 1 1 1	172.16.**0.3**

By simply subtracting the non-0, non-255 (interesting) octet value in our mask (252, in this case, and there will be only one such value, in any case—all other octet values will be 0 or 255) from 256 (call 256 "the magic number"), we get the increment size that takes us from one subnet boundary to the next in the octet that we found interesting. Always start with 0 in the interesting octet; that will be the first valid subnet and will look exactly like the network we started subnetting from.

The next subnet can always be determined by adding the increment to the current value, yielding 4 in the fourth octet, for the second subnet. This continues until the sum equals the original value of the interesting octet of the subnet mask (252, in this case), and no octets to the left of the interesting octet are within your authority to make any larger. Practicing with this shortcut method is the only way to truly understand each of these nuances.

After picking the first available network number (172.16.0.0), given our 30-bit subnet mask and eliminating host IP addresses that are all 1s and all 0s, we have the following range of numbers: 172.16.0.1–172.16.0.2. The broadcast address is all host bits on, or 172.16.0.3, which is also the address right before the next subnet address. We can take one of these numbers and assign it to one side of the serial link. The other number can be assigned to the other end of the serial link.

Next, we will calculate the range of IP addresses to use for our switched subnet, containing four router interfaces. We pick the first available network address, given our 29-bit subnet mask and previous choices. In this case, the first available network is 172.16.0.8, as shown in Table 2.7.

TABLE 2.7 IP Address Range for Switched Subnet in Figure 2.2

	3rd Octet 128 64 32 16 8 4 2 1	4th Octet 128 64 32 16 8 4 2 1	Decimal IP Address (Last 16 bits in bold)
Subnet mask	1 1 1 1 1 1 1 1	1 1 1 1 1 0 0 0	255.255.**255.248**
Subnet	0 0 0 0 0 0 0 0	0 0 0 0 1 0 0 0	172.16.**0.8**
First IP in range	0 0 0 0 0 0 0 0	0 0 0 0 1 0 0 1	172.16.**0.9**
Last IP in range	0 0 0 0 0 0 0 0	0 0 0 0 1 1 1 0	172.16.**0.14**
Broadcast	0 0 0 0 0 0 0 0	0 0 0 0 1 1 1 1	172.16.**0.15**

Again, subtracting 248 from 256 leaves a value of 8, our increment. The first valid value of the fourth octet, as always, is 0, but that's already taken. Add 8, and the next subnet boundary is 8. Because the 0 subnet was based on an increment of 4, we are fine placing this subnet at 8. In fact, there is another two-host subnet at 4, which we had to skip—that can be used in the future.

Eliminating host IP addresses that contain all 1s and all 0s, as before, we discover that our valid IP address range for this segment is 172.16.0.9–172.16.0.14. The broadcast address is all host bits on, or 172.16.0.15, which is also one less than the next subnet boundary of 172.16.0.16, found by using our increment of 8.

Now we will perform the same steps on the Ethernet user segment, as shown in Table 2.8, and the server farm segment, as shown in Table 2.9.

TABLE 2.8 Valid Addresses for Ethernet Segment in Figure 2.2

	3rd Octet **128 64 32 16 8 4 2 1**	**4th Octet** **128 64 32 16 8 4 2 1**	**Decimal IP Address** **(Last 16 bits in bold)**
Subnet mask	1 1 1 1 1 1 1 1	0 0 0 0 0 0 0 0	255.255.**255.0**
Subnet	0 0 0 0 0 0 0 1	0 0 0 0 0 0 0 0	172.16.**1.0**
First IP in range	0 0 0 0 0 0 0 1	0 0 0 0 0 0 0 1	172.16.**1.1**
Last IP in range	0 0 0 0 0 0 0 1	1 1 1 1 1 1 1 0	172.16.**1.254**
Broadcast	0 0 0 0 0 0 0 1	1 1 1 1 1 1 1 1	172.16.**1.255**

TABLE 2.9 Valid Addresses for Server Farm Segment in Figure 2.2

	3rd Octet **128 64 32 16 8 4 2 1**	**4th Octet** **128 64 32 16 8 4 2 1**	**Decimal IP Address** **(Last 16 bits in bold)**
Subnet mask	1 1 1 1 1 1 1 0	0 0 0 0 0 0 0 0	255.255.**254.0**
Subnet	0 0 0 0 0 0 1 0	0 0 0 0 0 0 0 0	172.16.**2.0**
First IP in range	0 0 0 0 0 0 1 0	0 0 0 0 0 0 0 1	172.16.**2.1**
Last IP in range	0 0 0 0 0 0 1 1	1 1 1 1 1 1 1 0	172.16.**3.254**
Broadcast	0 0 0 0 0 0 1 1	1 1 1 1 1 1 1 1	172.16.**3.255**

From these tables, we see that our IP address range for the Ethernet user segment is 172.16.1.1–172.16.1.254. This is because we have no interesting octet. However, by realizing we have complete control over the third octet, which has a mask value of 255, we can see that we have an increment of 1 when 255 is subtracted from 256, which is how default subnets work. Because the previous two subnets have a third-octet value of 0, we must start in the third octet with at least a value of 1, and the subnet gets the entire range of addresses with 1 in the third octet.

In addition, notice that the IP address range for the server farm segment is 172.16.2.1–172.16.3.254. This is because the interesting octet is now the third octet, with a value of 254. Subtracting this from 256 leaves us with an increment of 2. Remembering to apply this to only the third octet, we determine we can have values of 0, 2, 4, 6, and so on, in the third octet, but we already have subnets with 0 and 1 in that octet, so 2 is the first available value. Because the increment is 2, we get the entire range up to, but not including, the next subnet boundary, which is 4 in the third octet.

In summary, we have defined the following address ranges for our four segments, as detailed in Table 2.10.

TABLE 2.10 Valid IP Addresses for All Four Segments Used in Figure 2.2

Description of Segment	Address Range
Server farm	172.16.2.1–172.16.3.254
Ethernet user segment	172.16.1.1–172.16.1.254
Serial link	172.16.0.1–172.16.0.2
Router interconnection switched segment	172.16.0.9–172.16.0.14

We can now take our VLSM address ranges and apply them to our network diagram, as shown in Figure 2.3.

FIGURE 2.3 VLSM example with IP addresses

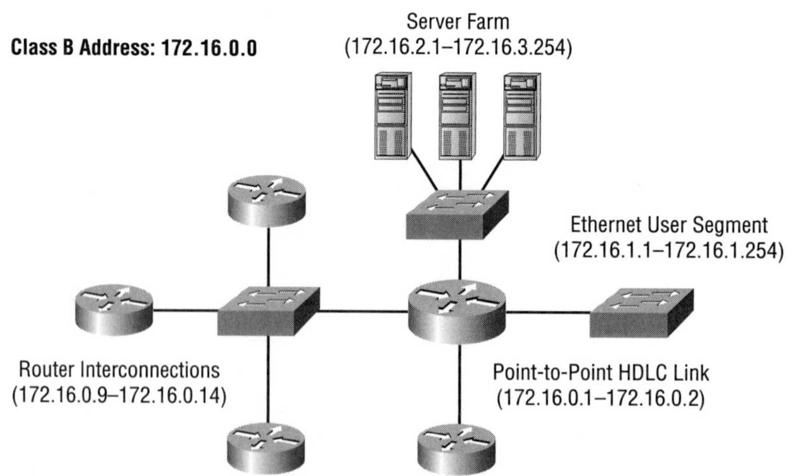

Design Considerations with VLSM

Now that we've seen how valuable VLSMs can be in preserving those precious IP addresses, be aware that there's a catch. Specifically, if you use a classful routing protocol (a protocol that doesn't send a subnet mask) such as RIPv1 or IGRP, then VLSMs are not going to work.

RIPv1 and IGRP routing protocols do not have a field in their update packets for subnet information. Therefore, subnet information does not get communicated. This makes for some fairly interesting, although inefficient, scenarios. A router running RIPv1or IGRP will adhere to the following main points when sending updates:

- If the subnet to be advertised is not part of the same classful network as the interface over which the update is to be sent, then the router automatically summarizes the subnet, advertising the classful network instead. This, coupled with the receive behavior detailed in the next bulleted list, prohibits the implementation of discontiguous subnets.
- If the subnet to be advertised is a different subnet of the same classful network as the interface over which the update is to be sent, it will be sent out only if the subnet mask is identical to that of the interface, which is how the router makes certain that it does not advertise an overlapping address range. In other words, if the classful networks are the same but the subnet masks are not, the router will simply refuse to advertise the subnet.

A router running RIPv1 or IGRP will adhere to the following main points when receiving updates:

- For any routing updates received on an interface, in the same classful network, the router will apply the same subnet mask as the interface to the route. With the mask applied, if no host bits are set to 1, then the route is already in the table and the update is ignored. Note that under normal circumstances, the neighboring router would never advertise such a route. More likely, if any of the host bits are set, the router will place a /32 route for the exact address in its table, hardly efficient. Furthermore, only RIPv1, not IGRP, will further propagate this host route to additional routers.
- For any routing updates received on an interface, not in the same classful network, the router will determine if any other of its interfaces have addresses in the same classful network. If so, the router will ignore the update so as not to create potentially conflicting entries. This is what breaks the routing domain when using discontiguous subnets and classful routing protocols. Without specific subnet mask information, the receiving router has no idea that the advertisement intends to offer something it is not already aware of. Otherwise, if no other interfaces are in this classful network, the router will apply the classful mask to the update and create an entry in its routing table.

Classless routing protocols, however, do support the advertisement of subnet information in the packet. So, you can use VLSM with routing protocols such as RIPv2, EIGRP, OSPF, or IS-IS.

As mention in the bulleted lists earlier, another important point to consider when assigning addresses is to not have discontiguous networks. Specifically, if you have two subnets of the same classful network separated by a different classful network, some of your hosts could become unreachable. Consider the network shown in Figure 2.4.

FIGURE 2.4 Discontiguous networking example

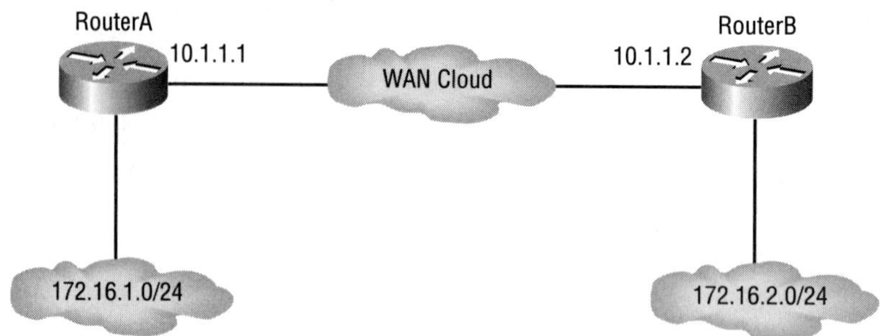

If *automatic route summarization* is configured (with classful routing protocols, it is, and it cannot be disabled), then both RouterA and RouterB in Figure 2.4 will be advertising to the WAN cloud that they are the route to network 172.16.0.0/16. While there are techniques and alternate routing protocols to overcome this behavior that will be discussed in the "Route Summarization" section later in this chapter, it makes for better network design to not separate a network's subnets by another network when using classful routing protocols.

Classless Interdomain Routing

Classless interdomain routing (CIDR) is an industry standard for displaying the number of subnet bits used with the IP address of a host or a network. Let's say you have a 172.16.10.1 address with a 255.255.255.0 mask. Instead of writing the IP address and subnet mask separately, you can combine them. For example, 172.16.10.1/24 means that the subnet mask has 24 out of 32 bits on.

The following list shows all the possible CIDRs:

0.0.0.0 = /0	255.255.128.0 = /17
128.0.0.0 = /1	255.255.192.0 = /18
192.0.0.0 = /2	255.255.224.0 = /19
224.0.0.0 = /3	255.255.240.0 = /20
240.0.0.0 = /4	255.255.248.0 = /21
248.0.0.0 = /5	255.255.252.0 = /22
252.0.0.0 = /6	255.255.254.0 = /23
254.0.0.0 = /7	255.255.255.0 = /24
255.0.0.0 = /8	255.255.255.128 = /25
255.128.0.0 = /9	255.255.255.192 = /26
255.192.0.0 = /10	255.255.255.224 = /27

255.224.0.0 = /11

255.240.0.0 = /12

255.248.0.0 = /13

255.252.0.0 = /14

255.254.0.0 = /15

255.255.0.0 = /16

255.255.255.240 = /28

255.255.255.248 = /29

255.255.255.252 = /30

255.255.255.254 = /31

255.255.255.255 = /32

Notice that the CIDR list starts at /0 and goes up to /32. With the release of RFC 3021, a /31 can be used on a point-to-point link instead of a /30, which will reduce the number of addresses used by half. Because a point-to-point connection connects only two systems, there is no reason to have one address dedicated to the network and one to the broadcast address. Cisco introduced RFC 3021 support with IOS version 12.0(14)S. You must remember to disable directed broadcasts with the `no ip directed-broadcast` global configuration command when using this feature. A /32 address is designated as a host route and is usually assigned to the loopback interface on a router.

Let's now examine how Cisco handles CIDR.

Cisco and CIDR

Cisco has not always followed the CIDR standard. Take a look at the way a Cisco 2500 series router with a legacy version of IOS asks you to put the subnet mask in the configuration when using the Setup mode:

```
Configuring interface Ethernet0:
  Is this interface in use? [yes]: <Enter>
  Configure IP on this interface? [yes]: <Enter>
    IP address for this interface: 1.1.1.1
    Number of bits in subnet field [0]: 8
    Class A network is 1.0.0.0, 8 subnet bits; mask is /16
```

Notice that the router asks for the number of bits used only for subnetting, which does not include the default mask bits. When dealing with these questions, remember that your answers involve the number of bits used for creating subnets, not the number of bits in the subnet mask. The industry standard is that you count all bits used in the subnet mask and then display that number as a CIDR; for example, the /16 the 2500 reported back to you takes into account all 16 bits that are set to 1.

The newer IOS that runs on Cisco routers, however, runs a Setup script that no longer asks you to enter the number of bits used only for subnetting. Here's an example of a new 1700 series router in Setup mode:

```
Configure IP on this interface? [no]: y
IP address for this interface: 1.1.1.1
```

```
Subnet mask for this interface [255.0.0.0]: 255.255.0.0
Class A network is 1.0.0.0, 16 subnet bits; mask is /16
```

Notice that the Setup mode asks you to enter the subnet mask address. It then displays the mask using the CIDR slash notation format. Much better.

Route Summarization

In the "Design Considerations with VLSM" section earlier in this chapter, we briefly mentioned the concept of route summarization. So what is it, and why do we need it? On very large networks, there may be hundreds or even thousands of individual networks and subnetworks being advertised. All these routes can be very taxing on a router's memory and processor. For example, routers on the Internet were starting to be overwhelmed with a couple of hundred thousand routes. After summarizing routes and using CIDR, the number of routes has been dramatically reduced.

In many cases, the router doesn't even need specific routes to each and every subnet (for example, 172.16.1.0/24). It would be just as happy if it knew how to get to the major network (for example, 172.16.0.0/16) and let another router take it from there. In our telephone network example, the local telephone switch should only need to know to route a phone call to the switch for the called area code. Similarly, a router's ability to take a group of subnetworks and summarize them as one network (in other words, one advertisement) is called *route summarization*, as illustrated in Figure 2.5.

FIGURE 2.5 Route summarization

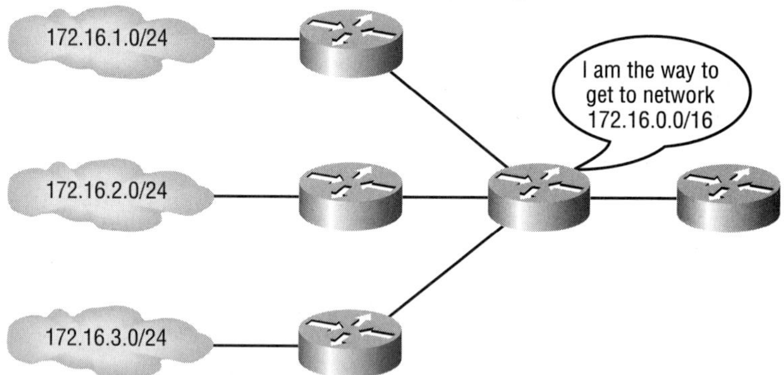

In some of the literature, you may find route summarization referred to as *route aggregation.*

Besides reducing the number of routing entries that a router must keep track of, route summarization can also help protect an external router from making multiple changes to its routing table due to instability within a particular subnet. For example, let's say that we were working on a router that connected to 172.16.2.0/24. As we were working on the router, we rebooted it several times. If we were not summarizing our routes, an external router would see each time 172.16.2.0/24 went away and came back. Each time, it would have to modify its own routing table. However, if our external router were receiving only a summary route (i.e., 172.16.0.0/16), then it wouldn't have to be concerned with our work on one particular subnet. This is especially a problem for EIGRP, which can create stuck in active (SIA) routes that can lead to a network melt-down.

We will get the most benefit from route summarization when the networks or subnetworks that we're summarizing are numerically and physically contiguous. To illustrate this point, let's look at an example.

Route Summarization Example 1

We have the following networks that we want to advertise as a single summary route:

172.16.100.0/24
172.16.101.0/24
172.16.102.0/24
172.16.103.0/24
172.16.104.0/24
172.16.105.0/24
172.16.106.0/24

To determine what the summary route would be for these networks, we can follow a simple two-step process:

1. Write out each of the numbers in binary, as shown in Table 2.11.

TABLE 2.11 Summary Example

IP Network Address	Binary Equivalent
172.16.100.0	**10101100.0001000.01100**100.0
172.16.101.0	**10101100.0001000.01100**101.0
172.16.102.0	**10101100.0001000.01100**110.0
172.16.103.0	**10101100.0001000.01100**111.0
172.16.104.0	**10101100.0001000.01101**000.0
172.16.105.0	**10101100.0001000.01101**001.0
172.16.106.0	**10101100.0001000.01101**010.0

2. Examine the table to determine the maximum number of bits (starting from the left) that all of the addresses have in common. (Where they are lined up, we boldfaced them to make them easier for you to see.) The number of common bits is the prefix length for the summarized address (/20).

In this example, we can see from the table that all of the addresses have the first 20 bits in common. The decimal equivalent of these first 20 bits is 172.16.96.0. So, we can write our new summarized address as 172.16.96.0/20. If we were to later add a network 172.16.98.0, it would need to be behind the router summarizing this address space. If we didn't, it could cause problems.

Another way that works more quickly, once you get it down, is to avoid binary and do just about everything in decimal, as outlined in the following steps:

1. Count the number of networks you're trying to summarize, calling the first octet that changes value among the networks the interesting octet. Make sure you include any networks that are skipped, just in case you're not dealing with a continuous run of networks. Often, the quickest way to accomplish this step is to subtract the value of the interesting octet of the first network from that of the last network and add 1 to the result, just to make sure both the first and last networks are counted.
2. Recalling the series of numbers that stems from the powers of 2 (0, 2, 4, 8, and so on), see if there is a value that matches the number of networks you are trying to summarize. Otherwise, choose the next highest block size. In this case, we are trying to summarize seven subnets, so we need to look at the block size of 8.
3. Starting with 0, count up by the block size until you reach or exceed the starting value in the interesting octet. Alternatively, divide the starting value of the interesting octet by the block size and ignore the remainder. Then, multiply the result by the block size. In this case, we get (100 div 8) × 8 = 96, where *div* is the operand for integer division, which ignores any remainder from the operation. This result is the closest block boundary in the interesting octet without going over.
4. Confirm that starting with the boundary from the previous step will include all networks that we need to summarize. In our case, a block size of 8 starting with 96 will extend only to a value of 103 in the interesting octet, not enough to cover the end of our run of networks. Simply increasing the block size to the next power of two, or 16, in this case, will always cover our needs. The thing we must confirm is that 96 is still a power of 16, as it was for 8. In this case it is, but if our starting point from step 3 had been 88 or 104, we would have had to adjust down to 80 or 96, respectively, to accommodate a block size of 16.
5. Subtract the block size from our magic number, 256, and get 240, in this case. Combine this information with the result of step 3, and we have our summary address and mask. The 96 contributes to the value of the interesting octet of the summary address, 172.16.96.0, and the 240 is the value of the same octet in the mask, 255.255.240.0, or /20.

Okay, this is confusing, we know. This is why we're going to give you three more examples. The preceding five steps of the "faster" method may take a while to read, but once you get them down, the process of finding an answer without breaking out the binary is incredibly efficient.

Route Summarization Example 2

In this example, we will summarize 10.1.0.0 through 10.7.0.0. First, put everything into binary and then follow the bits, starting on the left and stopping when the bits do not match in each and every network. Notice where we stopped boldfacing the following:

10.1.0.0	**00001010.00000**001.00000000.00000000
10.2.0.0	**00001010.00000**010.00000000.00000000
10.3.0.0	**00001010.00000**011.00000000.00000000
10.4.0.0	**00001010.00000**100.00000000.00000000
10.5.0.0	**00001010.00000**101.00000000.00000000
10.6.0.0	**00001010.00000**110.00000000.00000000
10.7.0.0	**00001010.00000**111.00000000.00000000

Now, create the network number using only the boldfaced bits. Set all the bits that are not in boldface to 0. As a result, the second octet has no bits on (bits in the boldfaced section), so we get this:

```
10.0.0.0
```

To come up with the summary mask, consider all the boldfaced bits as 1s. Because eight bits are boldfaced in the first octet and five bits in the second, we'll get this:

```
255.248.0.0 or /13
```

The answer written in CIDR format is 10.0.0.0/13. Now let's see it with trimmed-down steps the non-binary way:

1. The interesting octet is the second octet. There are seven networks that need to be included in the summary.
2. The block size we should start with is 8.
3. (1 div 8) × 8 = 0. So the value of the interesting octet in the summary address might be 0.
4. This starting point with a block size of 8 will cover from the values 0 through 7, inclusive, so we're fine. Our summary address is 10.0.0.0.
5. 256 – 8 = 248, so this is the value of the mask in the second octet, all others being 0 and/or 255. Our mask for our summary address is 255.248.0.0, or /13.

Route Summarization Example 3

This example will show you how to summarize 172.16.16.0 through 172.16.31.0. First, let's put the network addresses into binary and then line up the bits:

172.16.16.0	**10101100.0001000.0001**0000.00000000
172.16.17.0	**10101100.0001000.0001**0001.00000000

172.16.18.0 **10101100.0001000.0001**0010.00000000

172.16.19.0 **10101100.0001000.0001**0011.00000000

172.16.20.0 **10101100.0001000.0001**0100.00000000

172.16.21.0 **10101100.0001000.0001**0101.00000000

172.16.22.0 **10101100.0001000.0001**0110.00000000

172.16.23.0 **10101100.0001000.0001**0111.00000000

172.16.24.0 **10101100.0001000.0001**1000.00000000

172.16.25.0 **10101100.0001000.0001**1001.00000000

172.16.26.0 **10101100.0001000.0001**1010.00000000

172.16.27.0 **10101100.0001000.0001**1011.00000000

172.16.28.0 **10101100.0001000.0001**1100.00000000

172.16.29.0 **10101100.0001000.0001**1101.00000000

172.16.30.0 **10101100.0001000.0001**1110.00000000

172.16.31.0 **10101100.0001000.0001**1111.00000000

Notice where the bits stop matching throughout—after the boldface. Consider only the bits that are the same to get the network address, setting all other bits to 0:

```
172.16.16.0
```

Now, create the summary mask by counting all the bits that are in boldface up to the point where they stop matching. We have eight bits in the first octet, eight bits in the second octet, and four bits in the third octet. That is a /20 or

```
255.255.240.0
```

Using the non-binary shortcut, the following is true:

1. The interesting octet is the third octet. There are (31 – 16) + 1 = 16 networks that need to be included in the summary.
2. The block size we should start with is 16.
3. (16 div 16) × 16 = 16. So, the value of the interesting octet in the summary address might be 16.
4. This starting point with a block size of 16 will cover from the values 16 through 31, inclusive, so we are fine. Our summary address is 172.16.16.0.
5. 256 – 16 = 240, so this is the value of the mask in the third octet, all others being 0 and/or 255. Our mask for our summary address is 255.255.240.0, or /20.

The answer written in CIDR format is 172.16.16.0/20. Boy, the longer binary method sure seems like a pain in the pencil, huh? Try this as a shortcut, without completely leaving the binary method. Take the first number and the very last number, and put them into binary:

172.16.16.0	**10101100.0001000.0001**0000.00000000
172.16.31.0	**10101100.0001000.0001**1111.00000000

Can you see that we actually came up with the same numbers? It is a lot easier than writing out possibly dozens of addresses. Now, you have three ways to choose from in order to find your comfort zone. Let's do another example, but let's use both of our shortcuts.

Route Summarization Example 4

In this example, we will show you how to summarize 192.168.32.0 through 192.168.63.0. By using only the first network number and the last, we'll save a lot of time and come up with the same network address and subnet mask:

First number: 192.168.32.0 = **11000000.10101000.001**00000.00000000

Last number: 192.168.63.0 = **11000000.10101000.001**11111.00000000

Network address: 192.168.32.0

Subnet mask: 255.255.224.0 or /19

But this still involves binary-to-decimal conversion, which can take a bit of precious time that we may not have, depending on when the question is asked, if you know what I mean. The non-binary method produces the same results:

1. The interesting octet is the third octet. There are (63 – 32) + 1 = 32 networks that need to be included in the summary.
2. The block size we should start with is 32.
3. (32 div 32) × 32 = 32. So, the value of the interesting octet in the summary address might be 32.
4. This starting point with a block size of 32 will cover from the values 32 through 63, inclusive, so we are fine. Our summary address is 192.168.32.0.
5. 256 – 32 = 224, so this is the value of the mask in the third octet, all others being 0 and/or 255. Our mask for our summary address is 255.255.224.0, or /19.

Route Summarization Example 5

Sometimes you just cannot easily summarize a set of routes to one summary address. If might be more advantageous to summarize them into more than one summary address. In this example, we will show you how to determine when you should use more than one summary address. The addresses are 169.254.100.0 through 169.254.200.0 and 167.1.200.0 through 167.4.2.0. We'll break it down like we did before into binary:

Number 1: 169.254.100.0= **10101001.11111110.**01100100.00000000

Number 2: 169.254.200.0= **10101001.11111110.**11001000.00000000

Number 3: 167.1.200.0= **10100111.00000**100.00000010.00000000

Number 4: 167.4.2.0= **10100111.00000**001.11001000.00000000

If you wanted to try and summarize the above addresses into single aggregate address, it would be 160.0.0.0/4, because only the first four bits match among all four addresses, which is a very large address range. We will need to use two separate addresses, which are 169.254.0.0/16 and 167.0.0.0/13. Here's the non-binary way:

1. The interesting octet is the third octet for the first range. There are (200 – 100) + 1 = 101 networks that need to be included in the summary.
2. The block size we should start with is 128.
3. (101 div 128) × 128 = 0. So, the value of the interesting octet in the summary address might be 0.
4. This starting point with a block size of 128 will cover from the values 0 through 127, inclusive, so we have a problem. Increasing the block size to 256 and confirming that our starting point is still valid makes our summary address 169.254.0.0.
5. 256 – 256 = 0, so this is the value of the mask in the third octet, all others being 0 and/or 255. Our mask for our summary address is 255.255.0.0, or /16.

For the second range, the following is true:

1. The interesting octet is the second octet. There are (4 – 1) + 1 = 4 networks that need to be included in the summary.
2. The block size we should start with is 4.
3. (1 div 4) × 4 = 0. So, the value of the interesting octet in the summary address might be 0.
4. This starting point with a block size of 4 will cover from the values 0 through 3, inclusive, so we have a problem. Increasing the block size to 8 and confirming that our starting point is still valid makes our summary address 167.0.0.0.
5. 256 – 8 = 248, so this is the value of the mask in the second octet, all others being 0 and/or 255. Our mask for our summary address is 255.248.0.0, or /13.

Design Considerations for Route Summarization

Keep the following information in mind when designing your network summarization points:

- Only classless routing protocols support manual route summarization. Examples of classless routing protocols include RIPv2, EIGRP, OSPF, BGP4, and IS-IS. Therefore, if you are working in a RIPv1 or IGRP environment, manual route summarization is not going to work for you.

Classless and classful protocols were discussed in Chapter 1.

- Route summarization is most effective when the addresses have been organized in a hierarchy (i.e., "hierarchical addressing"). When we speak of addresses being hierarchical, we mean that the IP subnets at the "bottom of the tree" (in other words, the ones with the longest subnet masks) are subsets of the subnets at the "top of the tree" (i.e., the ones with the shortest subnet masks). Figure 2.6 will be used to illustrate hierarchical versus non-hierarchical addressing.

FIGURE 2.6 Discontiguous networking example

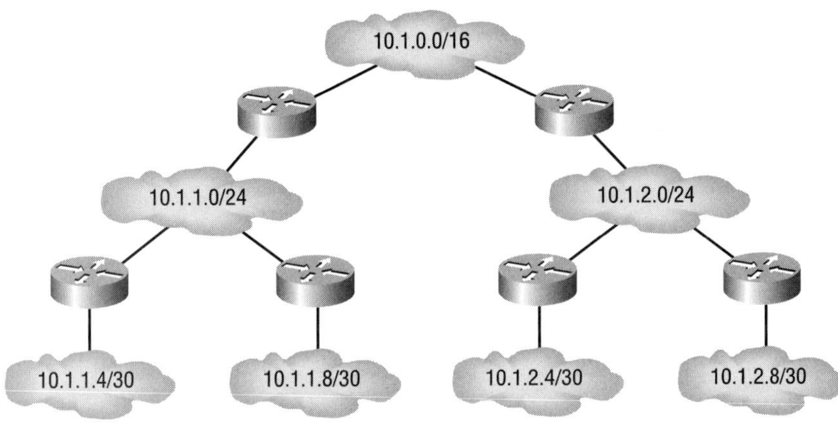

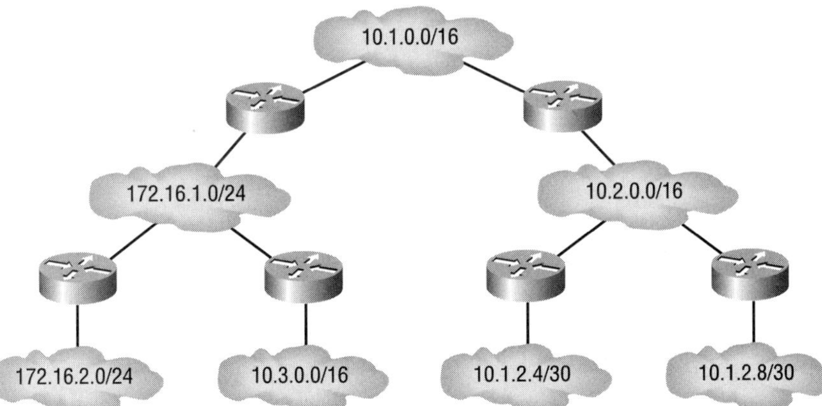

In the VLSM section of this chapter, we discussed how route summarization in discontiguous networks could cause some hosts to become unreachable, as we saw in Figure 2.4. If both RouterA and RouterB are sending out advertisements to the WAN cloud advertising that they are the path to network 172.16.0.0/16, then devices in the WAN cloud equidistant from each will enter both paths in their routing table, causing intermittent functionality, because half of the traffic goes in one direction and the other half goes in the other direction, without regard to which way is the correct way. Others will enter the route with the least cost in their routing table, which will have only a 50/50 chance of working for any given packet.

Remember that you can avoid this situation by proper address planning ahead of time. However, you may find yourself in a situation where you are dealing with a legacy installation, and you need to overcome this issue of discontiguous networks.

One solution is to turn off automatic route summarization for the classless routing protocols. To keep routing protocols such as RIPv2 and EIGRP from automatically summarizing routes, we can explicitly disable route summarization in the Cisco IOS. Following are examples of IOS configurations where we are disabling automatic route summarization. As the OSPF chapters will show, OSPF does not automatically summarize.

To turn off auto-summarization for RIP version 2 routing domains, use a router configuration similar to the following:

```
router rip
 version 2
 network classful_network_number
 network classful_network_number
 no auto-summary
```

To turn off auto-summarization for EIGRP routing domains, use a router configuration similar to the following:

```
router eigrp AS_number
 network classful_network_number
 network classful_network_number
 no auto-summary
```

Another way to allow discontiguous networks to be interconnected over a serial link is to use Cisco's IOS feature called IP unnumbered. We'll look at this next.

IP Unnumbered

With *IP unnumbered*, a serial interface is not on a separate network, as most router interfaces tend to be. Instead, the serial port "borrows" an IP address from another interface. In the following router configuration example, interface Serial 0 is using a borrowed IP address from interface Ethernet 0:

```
interface serial 0
 ip unnumbered ethernet 0
```

Therefore, by using IP unnumbered, the apparently discontiguous subnets, shown in Figure 2.4, are actually supported. Because the unnumbered interface shares another local interface's IP address, it is advised that a loopback interface be used, because virtual interfaces never go down and the unnumbered interface will become inoperative should the associated numbered interface go down.

IP unnumbered is compatible with point-to-point links only. An error will be returned if an interface on a non-point-to-point segment, such as Ethernet, is attempted to be configured as unnumbered.

There are a few things to be aware of before using IP unnumbered interfaces. Because the serial interface has no unique IP address, you will not be able to ping the interface to see if it is up, because the numbered interface will source the echo reply, although you can determine the interface status with Simple Network Management Protocol (SNMP). Nevertheless, pinging through the unnumbered interface to one on the remote side from the echo source leads us to believe the configuration is operational. In addition, IP security options are not supported on an IP unnumbered interface. Due to the difficulty with troubleshooting IP unnumbered interfaces, it is a practice that should be avoided.

IP Helper Address

IP helper addresses are needed when the forwarding of UDP broadcast packets is required. Such instances would be when you need to forward DHCP or DNS requests. In order to enable the use of IP helper addresses, you need to enter the following command in interface configuration mode on the interface from which the unicasts should be sourced:

```
ip helper-address address
      address - the address you need to forward the UDP packets to.
```

You can have multiple IP helper addresses on an interface. By default, the router will unicast the following UDP broadcast packets to the helper address specified as long as the helper address is not associated with the interface on which the broadcast was received:

- Trivial File Transfer Protocol (TFTP—port 69)
- Domain Naming System (DNS—port 53)
- Time service (port 37)
- NetBIOS Name Server (port 137)
- NetBIOS Datagram Server (port 138)
- Bootstrap Protocol (BootP) client and server datagrams (ports 67 and 68)
- TACACS service via the login host protocol (port 49)
- IEN-116 Name Service (port 42—obsolete)

You can add UDP ports to the list of broadcast packets that will be forwarded by using the following command:

```
ip forward-protocol udp port
    port - the destination UDP port number
```

You can add additional UDP broadcast packets that will be unicast-forwarded by using the `ip forward-protocol udp` *port* command in global configuration mode, where *port* is the UDP port number or related keyword for which to enable forwarding. You can also turn off the default and additionally configured UDP broadcast packets that will be sent by using the no version of the command. The following is an example of turning off the TFTP and TACACS service from being forwarded to the helper address, turning on the Citrix client locator service, and configuring the IP address of 182.16.45.9 as the helper address reachable through interface Ethernet0:

```
Router#conf t
Router(config)#no ip forward-protocol udp tftp
Router(config)#no ip forward-protocol udp 49
Router(config)#ip forward-protocol udp 1604
Router(config)#interface Ethernet0
Router(config-if)#ip helper-address 182.16.45.9
Router(config-if)#exit
Router(config)#exit
Router#
```

Decimal-to-Binary Conversion Chart

For your convenience, Table 2.12 provides a decimal-to-binary chart to help you with your IP addressing. The vertical column of four digits is the leftmost binary digits, and the horizontal row of four digits is the rightmost bits of each octet.

An Overview of IPv6 Addressing

The IPv6 addressing scheme has been developed to be compatible with the current IPv4 addressing standard, which allows the new IPv6 networks to coexist with IPv4 networks. IPv6 increases the size of the address space from 32 bits to 128 bits, which provides 340,282,366,920,938,463,463,374,607,431,768,211,456, or 3.4×10^{38}, addresses. IPv6 also improves routing, security, and quality of service (QoS) features, while simplifying the IP header. The IPv6 addressing architecture is described in RFC 3513, which defines how the address space will be utilized.

Let's talk about how IPv6 addresses are represented.

TABLE 2.12 Decimal-to-Binary Chart

	0000	0001	0010	0011	0100	0101	0110	0111	1000	1001	1010	1011	1100	1101	1110	1111
0000	0	1	2	3	4	5	6	7	8	9	10	11	12	13	14	15
0001	16	17	18	19	20	21	22	23	24	25	26	27	28	29	30	31
0010	32	33	34	35	36	37	38	39	40	41	42	43	44	45	46	47
0011	48	49	50	51	52	53	54	55	56	57	58	59	60	61	62	63
0100	64	65	66	67	68	69	70	71	72	73	74	75	76	77	78	79
0101	80	81	82	83	84	85	86	87	88	89	90	91	92	93	94	95
0110	96	97	98	99	100	101	102	103	104	105	106	107	108	109	110	111
0111	112	113	114	115	116	117	118	119	120	121	122	123	124	125	126	127
1000	128	129	130	131	132	133	134	135	136	137	138	139	140	141	142	143
1001	144	145	146	147	148	149	150	151	152	153	154	155	156	157	158	159
1010	160	161	162	163	164	165	166	167	168	169	170	171	172	173	174	175
1011	176	177	178	179	180	181	182	183	184	185	186	187	188	189	190	191
1100	192	193	194	195	196	197	198	199	200	201	202	203	204	205	206	207
1101	208	209	210	211	212	213	214	215	216	217	218	219	220	221	222	223
1110	224	225	226	227	228	229	230	231	232	233	234	235	236	237	238	239
1111	240	241	242	243	244	245	246	247	248	249	250	251	252	253	254	255

IPv6 Address Format

Unlike the usual dotted-decimal format of the IPv4 address, IPv6 is represented by hexadecimal numbers. A hexadecimal number is equivalent to four bits, also known as a nibble because it is half a byte, and is numbered 0–9 and A–F. A represents 10 and F represents 15, and they are not case-sensitive. The IPv6 address is a 32-digit hexadecimal numeric value, in eight four-digit clusters, known as fields, separated by colons (:), representing the 128-bit address. Here is an example of a valid IPv6 address: 1041:0000:130B:0000:0000:09C0:586C:1305.

There are some techniques used to shorten the IPv6 address. One of these techniques is to omit leading 0s in the address field, so 0000 can be compressed to just 0 and 09C0 can be compressed to 9C0. You can omit leading 0s but not trailing 0s. The previous IPv6 address example could be shortened to 1041:0:130B:0:0:9C0:586C:1305. Another technique is to use double colons (::) to represent a contiguous block of 0s. Again, the previous IPv6 address can be further shortened to 1041:0:130B::9C0:586C:1305.

For some IPv6 addresses, this technique can really shorten the address. For example, the IPv6 address FF01:0:0:0:0:0:1 can be compressed to FF01::1. There is a limitation in using double colons on the address. You can use it only once in any address, because if two double colons are placed in the same address, there will be no way to identify the size of each block of 0s.

Let's not forget about what is called the subnet mask in IPv4 terms but in the IPv6 world is called the address prefix. The IPv6 prefix is used to distinguish which portion of the address represents the network identifier. The slash (/) followed by the prefix length is the format used for IPv6 and is the same format used by CIDR for IPv4 addresses. The prefix length is a decimal value that indicates the number of high-order contiguous bits that comprise the network portion of the IPv6 address. An example of using the prefix is 1041:0:130B::9C0:586C:1305/64. If the IPv6 address ends in a double colon, it can be omitted. For example, the IPv6 address 8010:968:8680:265::/64 can be written as 8010:968:8680:265/64.

Now let's talk about the three types of IPv6 addresses.

IPv6 Address Types

IPv6 defines three types of addresses: unicast, anycast, and multicast. A unicast address is used to represent a single interface on a device. A packet that is sent to a unicast address is delivered to the interface identified by that address.

An anycast address is used to identify multiple different interfaces. A packet that is sent to an anycast address will be delivered to the closest interface that has that anycast address assigned. The routing protocol will determine which device will get the packet, based on shortest distance.

A multicast address is used to address a set of interfaces (within a certain scope) that will receive the same packet. This is not unlike the way multicast works in the IPv4 world, except that there are a lot more multicast addresses available. Let's discuss each of these address types in greater detail.

IPv6 Unicast Address

There are different types of unicast addresses:

- Global unicast address
- Site-local unicast address
- Link-local unicast address
- IPv4-mapped IPv6 address
- IPv4-compatible IPv6 address
- Unspecified address

The other type of unicast address, 0:0:0:0:0:0:0:1, or ::1, is the loopback address and performs the same function as 127.0.0.1 does in IPv4. It is used to identify a transmission sent by a node back to itself, usually for testing purposes, and should never leave the sending node. This cannot be assigned to a physical interface, and IPv6 routers do not forward traffic either sourced from or destined to this address.

Global Unicast Address

The IPv6 aggregatable global unicast address is the equivalent to the Class A, B, or C IPv4 address. Theoretically, a global unicast address is any address that is not one of the other named types, which accounts for 85 percent of the IPv6 address space. But IANA has been limited to allocating only aggregatable global unicast addresses, which begin with binary 001, a portion of the address known as the global unicast format prefix, which is 2000::/3 in IPv6 hexadecimal notation. This is still the largest block of assigned IPv6 addresses and represents ⅛ of the total address space.

The structure of global unicast addresses enables aggregation of the routing prefixes that will limit the number of routing table entries in the global routing table. Global unicast addresses are aggregated upward through an organization and eventually to the Internet service providers (ISPs). Figure 2.7 shows that global unicast addresses, which start with binary 001, are made up of a global routing prefix, followed by a subnet ID, and finally an interface ID.

FIGURE 2.7 IPv6 global unicast address format

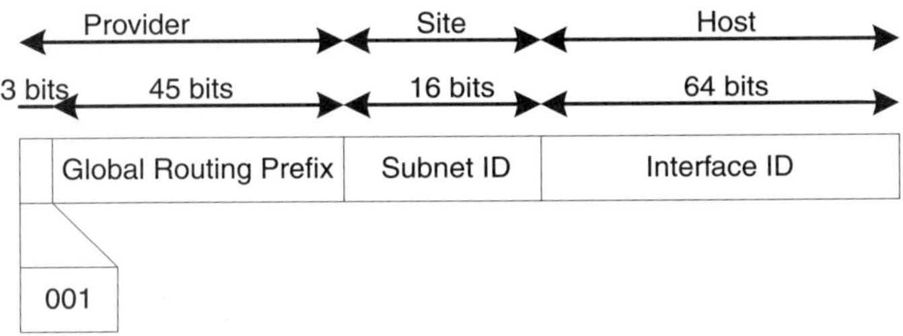

Global unicast addresses are required to have 64-bit interface identities in the extended universal identifier (EUI-64) format. IPv6 uses a modified EUI-64 format to identify a unique interface on a network segment. This modified EUI-64 is based on the Data Link layer (MAC) address of an interface. It usually inserts the 16-bit value of 0xFFFE between the 24-bit vendor ID and the 24-bit vendor-supplied unique extension identifier of the MAC address. Also the modified EUI-64 format says that the u-bit, which is usually set to 0 by the manufacturer to signify a globally unique value of the address, must be inverted, or set to 1, which indicates that the address may have a less official value that must only be unique on a local level. This gives the administrator the freedom and flexibility to design a locally significant addressing scheme for links, such as serial links and tunnel endpoints, which do not have burned-in hardware addresses from which to create an interface ID. Figure 2.8 shows how this modification would take place.

A MAC address of 0060.08D2.7B4B will be converted to the 64-bit identifier of 0260.08FF.FED2.7B4B. This identifier is then used to create an IPv6 address such as 205B:8B:CC16:6E:260:8FF:FED2:7B4B.

Site-Local Unicast Address

Site-local unicast addresses are similar in concept to the RFC 1918 Intranet address space for IPv4 networks. These addresses can be used to restrict communication to a specific portion of the network or to assign addresses for a network that is not connected to the global Internet without requiring a globally unique address space. IPv6 routers will not forward traffic with site-local source or destination addresses outside the boundary of the site's network.

FIGURE 2.8 Converting a MAC address to an EUI-64 address

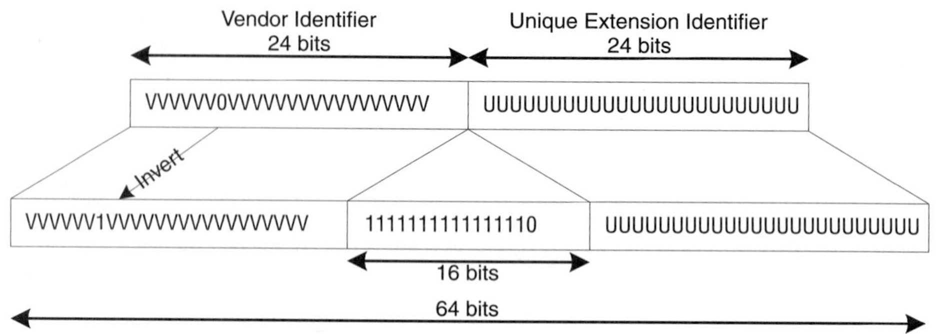

The site-local unicast addresses use the prefix range FEC0::/10, which is padded with 38 0s and then appends the 16-bit subnet identifier, followed by the 64-bit interface ID. Figure 2.9 shows the format of the site-local unicast address.

FIGURE 2.9 Site-local unicast address

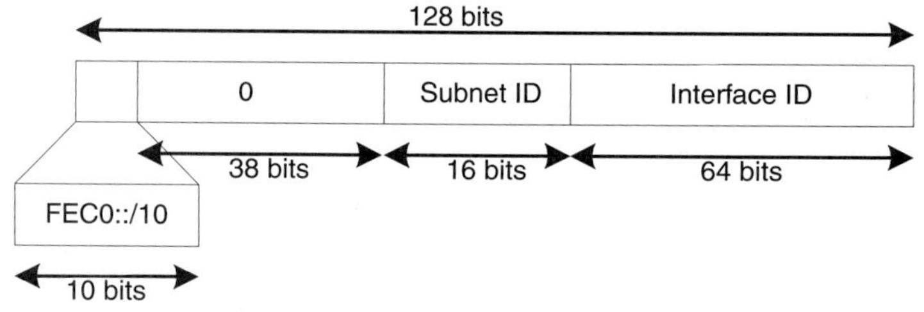

Link-Local Unicast Address

A link-local unicast address is used in the neighbor discovery protocol and is used only on the local link network. This is used by the stateless auto-configuration process for devices to discover the Data Link layer address of the network and to find and keep track of neighbors. A link-local unicast address uses the prefix range FE80::/10, which is padded with 54 0s, followed by the 64-bit interface ID. Figure 2.10 shows the format of the link-local unicast address.

FIGURE 2.10 Link-local unicast address

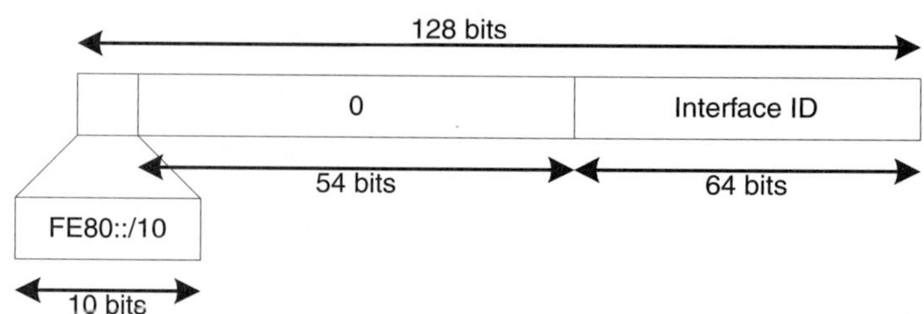

IPv4-Compatible IPv6 Address

As a transition mechanism, the IPv4-compatible IPv6 address is used to tunnel IPv6 packets over an IPv4 infrastructure, without the need to preconfigure tunnels through the IPv4 network. This address type embeds an IPv4 address in the low-order 32 bits. It pads all 96 high-order bits with 0s. It is used between two interfaces that support both the IPv4 and IPv6 protocol stacks, but are separated by devices that support only IPv4, and the format is 0:0:0:0:0:0:A.B.C.D, or ::A.B.C.D, where A.B.C.D is the IPv4 unicast address. Nodes that are assigned IPv4-compatible IPv6 addresses perform *automatic tunneling*. Whenever a node with one of these addresses sources or receives an IPv6 packet whose next hop is over an IPv4 interface, it must encapsulate the IPv6 packet within an IPv4 packet before sending it out. Conversely, these nodes must be prepared to accept IPv4 packets with IPv6 packets encapsulated within. In addition to the information found in RFC 3513, RFC 2893 gives additional details concerning IPv4-compatible IPv6 addresses.

IPv4-Mapped IPv6 Address

This type of address also embeds an IPv4 address in the low-order 32-bits, but with 0s in only the first 80 high-order bits and 1s in the next 16 bits—bits 81 to 96. This address type is used by devices that support both IPv4 and IPv6 protocol stacks in order that they may communicate with devices that support only IPv4. On the dual-stack device, an IPv6 application that is sending traffic to the IPv4 device's IPv4-mapped IPv6 address will recognize the meaning of this type of address and send IPv4 packets—not IPv6 packets—to that destination. In other words, this type of addressing mechanism does not encapsulate IPv6 packets within IPv4 packets. Conversely, if such a node receives a pure IPv4 packet that must be forwarded into the IPv6 domain, the dual-stack node will create the IPv4-mapped IPv6 address, to be used as the IPv6-header source address, from the incoming packet's original IPv4 source address. So any return traffic will be known by the dual-stack node to be destined for an IPv4-only interface, and will be forwarded as such. IPv4-mapped IPv6 addresses are even more of a transition mechanism, and their address format is ::FFFF:A.B.C.D, where A.B.C.D is the IPv4 unicast address. A common use for this type of address is when an IPv6-enabled DNS server responds to the request of a dual IPv6/IPv4 node with the IP address of an IPv4-only node. The DNS server returns the IPv4-mapped IPv6 address, and the dual node knows what to do from there.

Unspecified Address

An unspecified IPv6 address is a special address that is used as a placeholder by a device that does not have an IPv6 address. This might happen when the node requests an address from a DHCP server or when the duplicate address detection packet is sent. The format is 0:0:0:0:0:0:0:0 but can be represented by 0::0 or just ::/128. This IPv6 address cannot be assigned to any interface and should not be used as a destination address.

IPv6 Anycast Address

An IPv6 anycast address is a global unicast address that is assigned to many interfaces in different devices on the network. This means that this same network address is assigned to more than one interface on the network. A packet that is sent to an anycast address will be delivered to the closest interface with that anycast address. The closest interface is determined by the routing protocol being used. Because anycast addresses are global unicast addresses, there is no way to tell that a global unicast address is also an anycast address.

Therefore, any device configured with an anycast address will have to be configured explicitly to recognize the address as an anycast address. You will never see traffic from an anycast address because you cannot source IPv6 traffic using an anycast address; it is used only for destination traffic. In fact, RFC 3513 suggested using anycast addresses only for routers—not end nodes—until the complexities of their use could be determined in the real world.

IPv6 Multicast Address

In the IPv6 world, there is no such thing as broadcast traffic because it is all multicast traffic—no more broadcast storms. IPv6 multicast traffic has a prefix of FF00::/8 and is used as an identifier for a set of interfaces that want to receive the same packets. This is very similar to the way multicast works in the IPv4 world, with one exception. IPv6 multicast traffic can be limited to a certain scope. The octet after the initial 0xFF prefix defines the public/private nature and scope of the multicast address. The first nibble of the octet determines if this is a transient (0001) or permanent (0000) multicast address, with the first three bits always set to 0. A permanent multicast address is a well-known or IANA-assigned address. A transient address is locally assigned. The second nibble determines the scope of the multicast address and can be one of the following:

- Interface-local, for loopback multicast transmissions only (0001–1)
- Link-local (0010–2)
- Subnet-local (0011–3)
- Admin-local (0100–4)
- Site-local (0101–5)
- Organization-local (1000–8)
- Global (1110–E)

The remaining 112 bits are used for the multicast group ID. This means that you can have millions of multicast groups. The following are the special reserved multicast addresses used to identify specific functions:

- FF01::1—All nodes within the interface-local scope (only within this device)
- FF02::1—All nodes on a local link (link-local scope)
- FF01::2—All routers within the interface-local scope
- FF02::2—All routers on a local link
- FF05::2—All routers in the site (site-local scope)
- FF02::1:FF*XX*:*XXXX*—Solicited-node multicast address, where *XX*:*XXXX* is the lower-order 24 bits of the IPv6 address of an interface.

The TTL—time to live—value is not used in IPv6 multicast to define scope.

The solicited-node multicast addresses are used in neighbor solicitation messages to assist with neighbor discovery. An IPv6 node must join the associated solicited-node multicast group for every unicast or anycast address assigned. Neighbor solicitation messages are not covered because they are beyond the scope of this study guide.

Summary

IP addresses can be separated into Classes A, B, C, D, and E. Class D is used for multicast traffic, and Class E is currently not being used. The first octet identifies to which class it belongs: Class A addresses have first octets in the range from 0 to 127, Class B addresses have first octets from 128 to 191, and Class C addresses have first octets from 192 to 223. CIDR is used to easily identify the subnet mask of an IP address with slash notation, as well as to allow ISPs to assign non-classful address space to customers, thus reducing wasted addresses. VLSM is used to allow a network to be variably subnetted to make more efficient use of the IP addresses available. Some routing protocols allow for VLSM (e.g., RIPv2 and EIGRP) because they transmit the mask of the network within the routing update.

Route summarization reduces the number of routes needed to represent a set of networks. This preserves the resources, such as memory and processor cycles, on the routers in the network. When two or more subnets of the same classful network are separated by a different classful network, this makes the separated network discontiguous and will result in the inability to reduce the number of advertisements and subsequent routing table entries. For some routing protocols that automatically summarize routes, this can cause reachability problems, so you need to use a classless routing protocol and disable automatic summarization, if it is currently enabled.

With the global shortage of IPv4 address space, a new protocol has been introduced that will alleviate this problem without affecting end-to-end functionality. IPv6 not only greatly increases the number of IP addresses available, but it also brings improvements and new features to the IP protocol. These features are an expanded number of multicast addresses, the ability to natively support IPSec and QoS, and automatically determining the local subnet address without using DHCP by using the stateless auto-configuration process. IPv6 brings new features and concepts to networking that you will need to know.

Exam Essentials

Understand VLSM. Variable-length subnet masks enable a classful network to contain subnetworks of varying sizes. This allows a more efficient use of the network address space. For point-to-point links you can use a 30-bit or the new 31-bit mask, both of which allow for only two hosts, without requiring the same mask used on a LAN segment.

Understand decimal-to-binary conversions. Decimal-to-binary conversion takes a base 10 number, the ones we are used to seeing, and converts it into a base 2 number, which is a series of 1s and 0s. This is important to know, because this base 2 number is the electronic basis for the network, subnet, and host portions of an IP address.

Understand CIDR notation. Classless interdomain routing started out as a way for service providers to offer customers address space more suited to their business needs without the constraints of classful boundaries. This process leads to less waste of IP addresses and allows continued use of IPv4, long after experts predicted we would have to convert to IPv6. A handy side-effect of the CIDR movement is the CIDR notation that allows us to represent the subnet mask in a one- or two-character shorthand (/*xx*).

Know how to implement VLSM. In implementing VLSM, you take a given address space—usually a classful network—and break it up to allow networks of different sizes. You should be able to determine the correct subnet mask for each network according to the number of addresses needed and allocate it in such a way as to allow the most flexibility for future growth.

Understand the concept of route summarization. Route summarization is the process of combining multiple network advertisements into a single advertisement that can represent the combined networks. This technique allows the upstream routers to carry fewer network advertisements and reduces the size of the routing tables. This promotes stability and reduces memory and processor overhead in the backbone routers.

Know the three types of IPv6 addresses. The three types of IPv6 addresses are unicast, anycast, and multicast. Although unicast and anycast addresses are indistinguishable from each other (because they are allocated from the same range 2000::/3), multicast addresses are allocated from the FF00::/8 address range. The format of IPv6 addresses is different from the quad-octet dotted-decimal IPv4 format, because each 16-bit field is represented by four hexadecimal numbers separated by a colon (:). There are eight of these fields in the 128-bit IPv6 address, and they can be compressed by deleting leading 0s. You can further compress an IPv6 address by substituting double colons (::) for a consecutive series of leading 0s, but this can appear only once in the address.

Understand the types of unicast and multicast addresses. Site-local addresses are a type of IPv6 unicast address, and they are used when you are not going to be connecting the network to the global Internet. Link-local addresses are another type of IPv6 unicast address, but unlike site-local addresses, link-local addresses are significant only to the local subnet. There are millions of IPv6 multicast addresses, and they can be scoped to limit the range the packets will travel. The following are the available scopes listed from the smallest to the largest ranges: interface-local, link-local, subnet-local, admin-local, site-local, organization-local, and global.

Network Address Translation

THE CCNP EXAM TOPICS COVERED IN THIS CHAPTER INCLUDE THE FOLLOWING:

- ✓ Understand how NAT and PAT work.
- ✓ Learn how to configure static and dynamic NAT and PAT.
- ✓ Learn how to use route maps to control NAT functions.

In the previous chapter, we discussed how to extend the life of the IP address space and how VLSM and CIDR helped when using IPv4. We also talked about IPv6 and how it will create more address space in the future. In this chapter we will find out how *NAT (Network Address Translation)* and *PAT (Port Address Translation)* can also be used to extend the current address space by translating one address to another and how this might help to alleviate shortage. We will also talk about how to configure both dynamic and static NAT and PAT.

While Cisco doesn't specifically mention NAT and PAT in their exam objectives, it's still very important that you learn the topics covered in this chapter.

Understanding Network Address Translation

Let's talk about the history behind NAT. It was first implemented in Cisco IOS release 11.2 and is defined in RFC 1631 and RFC 3022 as a way to alleviate the depletion of the IPv4 address space. It is a temporary workaround to the immediate problem of too many hosts and not enough IP addresses. It is a kludge that breaks the rules of IP, which creates other problems. For example, when you used IPSec to protect your traffic, it was incompatible with NAT until Cisco found a workaround, but even this has its problems. This is what I call a kludge to fix another kludge.

RFC 1918 was created to set aside a number of IP addresses for people to use inside their networks. It set aside the following ranges of IP addresses:

- 10.0.0.0 to 10.255.255.255 or 10.0.0.0/8
- 172.16.0.0 to 172.31.255.255 or 172.16.0.0/12
- 192.168.0.0 to 192.168.255.255 or 192.168.0.0/16

These IP addresses will never appear in the global routing table, and so they can be used by organizations for their private internal intranets. Multiple companies can use the 10.0.0.0/8 address space within their own networks, so theoretically, there's an unlimited supply of IP addresses. If these IP addresses are not going to be globally unique, how can hosts from these networks communicate across the Internet? They must be translated, and this is where NAT comes into play. NAT also can be used when two networks are merged and they both use the same address space.

NAT Terminology

NAT is often associated with the translation of a private IP address into a registered IP address, although this is not always the case, as you will see. As an example of private-to-registered translation, a private IP address of 10.12.2.10 might be translated into the registered IP address of 135.167.12.2. Cisco uses the following terms to distinguish which IP addresses get translated into which:

Inside local The *inside local* address is the IP address used by a host on the private side of the network. In our example, this would be 10.12.2.10.

Inside global The *inside global* address is the public, often registered IP address into which the inside local address will be translated. This is typically a globally unique and globally routable IP address, which hosts on the outside network would use to communicate with the inside host. In our example, this is 135.167.12.2.

Obviously, all IP addresses are *routable* in the usual definition of the term, which is in the context of the OSI model. In this section, by *routable* we specifically mean that the appropriate hosts on the network have a route to this address. For example, the Internet backbone routers do not know how to get to the 10 addresses because they don't have a route entry. So we say that address isn't globally routable, although it may be locally routable inside your intranet. *Registered* is also sometimes used in place of globally routable.

Outside global The *outside global* address is the actual IP address of a host that resides on the outside public network and is usually a globally unique and globally routable IP address. Our example did not use an outside global address, but one was assumed to exist as a destination address, which would be known to our transmitting host as long as no inbound translation of outside addresses is being performed.

Outside local The *outside local* address is the IP address used to translate an outside global IP address. This may or may not be a registered IP address, but it must be routable on the inside of your network. Our example did not use an outside local address, because our assumption remains that no inbound translation of outside addresses is being performed.

NAT can be broken into two broad types—NAT and PAT. NAT is the one-to-one translation of IP addresses from an inside local IP address, usually one from the RFC 1918 space, to an inside global IP address that is unique and routable on the Internet. However, if NAT is being performed between two private networks, perhaps to overcome duplicated address space, there would not have to be any registered addresses involved. As you can see, we need terms other than private and registered to describe where these address spaces have their domain, which is why we have defined inside, outside, local, and global.

PAT, which is sometimes referred to as *NAPT (Network Address and Port Translation)*, can be viewed as a many-to-one translation, because it can take multiple inside local IP addresses and translate them to one inside global IP address.

The Elusive Terminology of NAT

After swimming through the easily confused terms that NAT brings to the table, you can probably see how easy it is, for example, to call an address an outside global address when what you really mean is inside global. We all think of the private address space as being reserved for the inside network, which is where the "inside" NAT reference gets its name, but many of us erroneously extend this idea to the addresses themselves, equating all addresses associated with inside hosts as local. It's important to understand that the location of the host defines the inside/outside characteristic, while the original/translated address spaces define the local/global characteristic, respectively, with each inside host generally having one of each. If the inside network natively uses private addresses, then the private addresses are the local addresses. If these addresses get translated to registered addresses on their way out to the public site of the NAT server, then the registered translation is the global address, but both of them refer to the same *inside* host. It's important to note that no host will ever be both inside and outside for the same translation. Which hosts are inside hosts and which ones are outside hosts will be contingent upon which router interfaces get the `ip nat inside` and `ip nat outside` commands applied to them. More about those commands later in this chapter.

Let's talk about the NAT process; that may help clear up any questions you might have from the preceding definitions. We'll talk about how NAT processes packets from the inside to the outside, and then we'll discuss the reverse.

How NAT Works

Traffic that is sourced on the inside of the network, coming to an interface marked as inside, will have an inside local address as its source IP address and an outside global address as the destination IP address, assuming that no inbound translation of outside addresses is being performed.

Notice we said outside *global*. The destination would be considered outside local only if bidirectional NAT is being performed. Remember to ask where the source device thinks is the location of the address it is sending to—on the local network or on the other side of the router that is transparently acting as the NAT server. If the source host thinks it's talking to a local device, and the NAT server must step in and provide the smoke and mirrors to make the communication occur with a device that is actually not local, then and only then is the address referred to as an outside *local* address.

When that traffic reaches the NAT process and is switched to the outside network, going out an interface marked as outside, the source IP address will be translated to an inside global address, and the destination IP address will still be known as the outside global address, as it has not changed. Figure 3.1 shows the inside/outside and local/global relationship.

When traffic is sourced on the outside of the network, coming to an interface marked as outside, the source IP address is known as the outside global address, while the destination IP address is known as the inside global address. When that traffic reaches the NAT process and is switched to the inside network, going out an interface marked as inside, the source IP address will still be known as the outside global address, assuming that it was not translated coming in, and the translated destination IP address will be known as the inside local address. Let's talk about some of the advantages to using NAT.

Which Camp Are You From?

To further the NAT terminology debate, let's cover an issue that has the NAT-speaking world firmly divided into two different camps, with most campers completely unaware that there's another camp! While it is not technically inaccurate, on a basic level, to consider the outside local and outside global addresses to be the same when translation of the outside address space is not being performed, such a habit generally serves only to muddy the waters. Until you truly have a grasp on the terminology, stick with the more distilled concepts outlined here. Your ability to keep these terms in their proper context will benefit, and you won't miss any questions along the way as a result. Furthermore, one camp maintains that it is simply wrong to make reference to an outside local address when the outside global address has not been translated. If you take the basic definition of an outside local address, you'll find that the outside local address space, indeed any local address space, must be routable on the inside network. With that basic tenet in mind, calling the outside global address—which, as a global address, must be routable on the outside network, not necessarily on the inside network—an outside local address simply makes no sense. As mentioned earlier, it also muddies the waters. Does this remind you of high school geometry proofs? Do yourself a favor. Because the converse cannot be proven quite so easily, run as fast as you can to the camp that believes the outside global address—by definition, an address of a node on the outside network that is routable on the outside network—can never be called a local address of any kind.

FIGURE 3.1 NAT inside/outside and local/global relationship

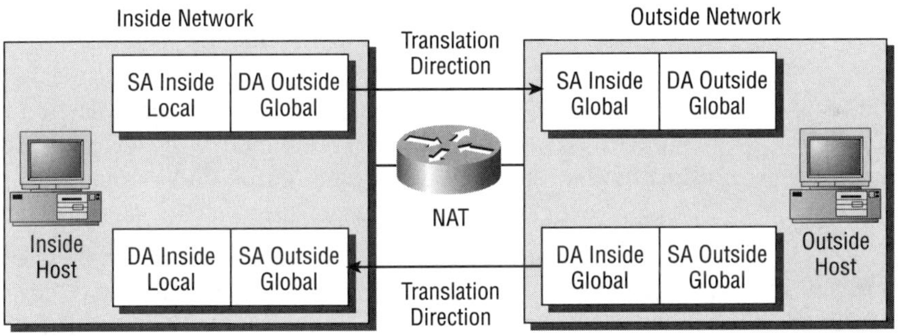

The Advantages of NAT

There are many advantages to using NAT. In this section, you will learn about some of the more important benefits, including the following:

- NAT allows you to incrementally increase or decrease the number of registered IP addresses without changing devices (hosts, switches, routers, and so on) in the network. You still need to change the device doing the NAT but not every other device.

- NAT can be used either statically or dynamically:
  - Static translations are manually configured to translate a single local IP address to a single global IP address, and vice versa. This translation always exists in the NAT table until it is manually removed. Optionally, this translation could be configured between a single local IP address and port pair to a single global IP address and port pair using either TCP or UDP. These port values needn't be the same value.
  - Dynamic mappings are configured on the NAT border router by using a pool of one or more registered IP addresses. Devices on the inside network that wish to communicate with a host on the outside network can use these addresses in the pool. This allows multiple internal devices to utilize a single pool of IP addresses. You can go even further and use a single IP address by configuring overloading, which will translate both the IP address and port number.
- NAT can be configured to allow the basic load sharing of packets among multiple servers using the TCP load distribution feature. TCP load distribution uses a single virtual global IP address, which is mapped to multiple real local IP addresses. Incoming connections are distributed in a round-robin fashion among the IP addresses in the local pool. The packets for each individual connection, or flow, are sent to the same local IP address to ensure proper session communications.

There is no artificial limit to the number of NAT connections that can be active on a router at any given time. The limit is determined by the amount of DRAM available on the NAT router. Each NAT translation is stored in RAM and uses approximately 160 bytes. This means that about 1.53MB of RAM (often rounded to 1.6MB in Cisco documentation) is required for 10,000 NAT translations, which is far more than the average router needs to provide.

- If you switch Internet service providers (ISPs) and need to change the registered IP addresses you are using, NAT makes it so you don't have to renumber every device in your network. The only change is the addresses that are being used in the NAT pool.
- NAT also helps if you have merged with another company and you're both using the same RFC 1918 address space. You can configure NAT on the border router between your routing domains to translate the address from one network to the other, and vice versa, with each side spoofed into believing the other side is in a different, non-conflicting network.

The Disadvantages of NAT

Now that we've sold you on using NAT in your network, you should be aware of the disadvantages as well. The following is a list of some of the disadvantages of using NAT compared to using individually registered IP addresses on each internal network host:

- NAT increases latency (delay). Delays are introduced into the packet-switching process because of the processor overhead needed to translate each IP address contained in the packet header. The router's CPU must be used to process every packet to decide if the router needs to translate the IP addresses in the IP header. Depending upon the type of traffic, NAT will change the IP addresses inside the payload, but this is on an application-by-application basis.

- NAT hides end-to-end IP addresses that render some applications unusable. Some applications that use the IP address of the host computer inside the payload of the packet will break when NAT translates the addresses in the IP header and not inside the packet's payload. As noted in the last bullet, this has been fixed somewhat, but this is on an application-by-application basis and is not scalable in the long term.
- Because NAT changes IP addresses, there is a loss in the ability to track an IP flow end-to-end. This does provide an advantage from a security standpoint by eliminating a hacker's ability to identify the packet's true source. However, this slight increase in security is at the expense of end-to-end accountability.
- NAT also makes troubleshooting or tracking down where malicious traffic is coming from more troublesome. This is because the traffic could be coming from a single user who is using a different IP address depending on when the traffic passes through the NAT router. This makes tracing back a malicious connection and making that person accountable much more difficult.
- Because a host that needs to be accessed from the outside network will have two IP addresses—one inside local and one inside global—this creates a problem called split DNS. You need to set up two DNS servers, one for global addresses and one for local addresses. This can lead to administrative nightmares and problems if inside hosts are pointing to the DNS server with the global addresses, because the host's local peers are not accessible to it by those addresses. Also, problems arise whenever outside hosts query the DNS server with the local addresses, the latter case requiring additional translation or configuration before it can be possible.

NAT Traffic Types

NAT supports many traffic types. The BSCI exam may include questions on both the supported and unsupported traffic types. The following two sections take a look at these traffic types.

Supported Traffic Types

NAT supports the following traffic types:

- TCP traffic that does not carry source and destination IP addresses inside the application stream
- UDP traffic that does not carry source and destination IP addresses inside the application stream
- Hypertext Transfer Protocol (HTTP)
- Trivial File Transfer Protocol (TFTP)
- File Transfer Protocol (FTP `PORT` and `PASV` command)
- Archie, which provides lists of anonymous FTP archives
- Finger, a tool that determines whether a person has an account on a particular computer

- Network Time Protocol (NTP)
- Network File System (NFS)
- Many of the r* Unix utilities (rlogin, rsh, rcp)
- Internet Control Message Protocol (ICMP)
- NetBIOS over TCP (datagram, name, and session services)
- Progressive Networks' RealAudio
- White Pines' CuSeeMe
- Xing Technologies' StreamWorks
- DNS A and PTR queries
- H.323 (IOS releases 12.0(1)/12.0(1)T or later)
- Session Initiation Protocol (SIP)
- NetMeeting (IOS releases 12.0(1)/12.0(1)T or later)
- VDOLive (IOS releases 11.3(4)/11.3(4)T or later)
- Vxtreme (IOS releases 11.2(4)/11.3(4)T or later)
- IP Multicast—source address translation only (IOS releases 12.0(1)T or later)
- PPTP support with Port Address Translation (PAT) (IOS release 12.1(2)T or later)
- Skinny Client Protocol, IP Phone to Cisco CallManager (IOS release 12.1(5)T or later)

Unsupported Traffic Types

NAT does not support the following traffic types:

- Routing protocols
- DNS zone transfers
- BOOTP/DHCP
- Talk
- Ntalk
- Simple Network Management Protocol (SNMP)
- Netshow

NAT Operations

Understanding how NAT functions will assist you in making better configuration decisions. In this section we will cover the operations of NAT when it is configured to provide the following functions:

- Translating inside local addresses
- Overloading inside global addresses
- Using TCP load distribution
- Overlapping networks

Translating Inside Local Addresses

A router running the NAT process usually connects two networks and translates the local non-registered IP addresses into global registered IP addresses, which are routable on the Internet. NAT follows a six-step process, as shown in Figure 3.2.

FIGURE 3.2 The process of translating inside local addresses

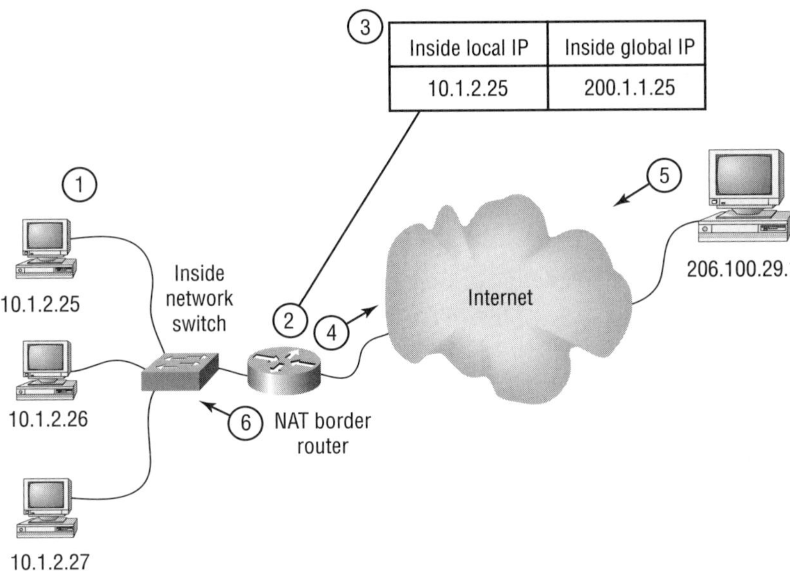

The six-step process illustrated in Figure 3.2 is as follows:

1. Device at IP address 10.1.2.25 sends a packet and attempts to open a connection to 206.100.29.1.
2. When the first packet arrives at the NAT border router, it first checks to see if there is an entry for the source address that matches one in the NAT table.
3. If a match is found in the NAT table, it continues to step 4. If a match is not found, the NAT router uses an address from its pool of available IP addresses. A simple entry is created that associates an inside IP address to an outside IP address. In this example, the NAT router will associate the address of 10.1.2.25 to 200.1.1.25.
4. The NAT border router then replaces the inside IP address of 10.1.2.25 with the global IP address 200.1.1.25. This makes the destination host send returning traffic back to 200.1.1.25, which is a registered IP address on the Internet.
5. When the host on the Internet with the IP address 206.100.29.1 replies to the packet, it uses the IP address assigned by the NAT router as the destination IP address, which is 200.1.1.25.

6. When the NAT border router receives the reply from 206.100.29.1 with a packet destined for 200.1.1.25, the NAT router again checks its NAT table. The NAT table will show that the inside local IP address of 10.1.2.25 should receive this packet and will replace the inside global destination IP address in the header and forward the packet to the inside local destination IP address.

Steps 2 through 6 are repeated for each individual packet. The destination host could also be behind a NAT device and might be actually using the same address space as the host that initiated the traffic. The source will never know because NAT is transparent to the hosts involved.

Overloading Inside Global Addresses

You can reduce the number of IP addresses in the inside global IP address pool by allowing the NAT border router to use a single inside global IP address for many inside local IP addresses; this is called PAT or *overloading*. When NAT overloading is enabled, the router maintains additional information in the NAT table to keep track of the layer 4 protocol information. When multiple inside local IP addresses map to one inside global IP address, NAT uses the protocol and TCP/UDP port number of each inside host to make a unique and distinguishable inside global IP address/port combination, or *socket*. For the rest of this chapter, the word *address* will imply socket when referring to PAT.

Because you are using a pool of IP addresses, the pool can contain more than one IP address. This allows a very large number of hosts' inside local addresses to be translated to a small pool of inside global IP addresses when using overloading.

Figure 3.3 shows the NAT operation when one inside global IP address represents multiple inside local IP addresses. The TCP port number represents the unique portion of the inside global IP address that makes it capable of distinguishing between the two local IP addresses on the inside of the network.

FIGURE 3.3 NAT overloading inside global IP addresses

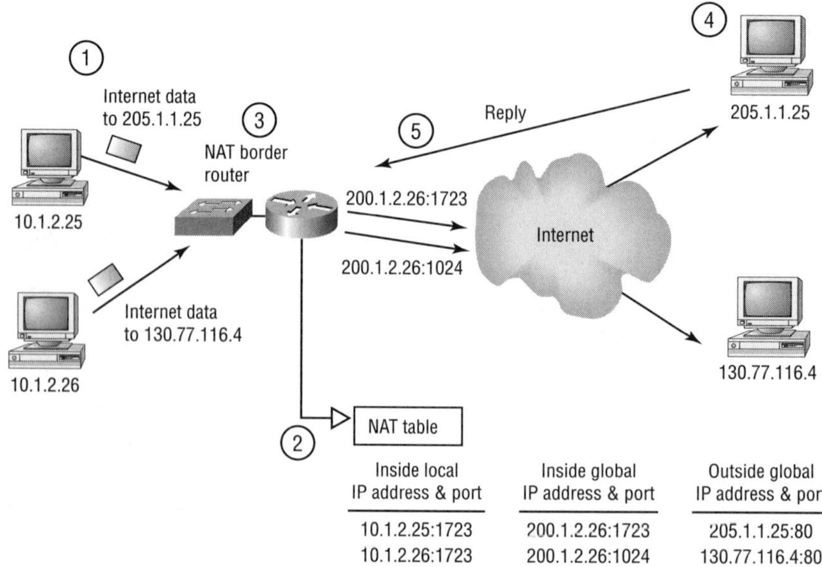

Inside local IP address & port	Inside global IP address & port	Outside global IP address & port
10.1.2.25:1723	200.1.2.26:1723	205.1.1.25:80
10.1.2.26:1723	200.1.2.26:1024	130.77.116.4:80

When the router processes multiple inside local IP addresses to a single globally routable inside IP address, it performs the following steps to overload the inside global IP address:

1. The device with the inside local IP address of 10.1.2.25 attempts to open a connection to a host with outside global IP address 205.1.1.25 on an outside network.
2. The first packet that the NAT border router receives from the host at 10.1.2.25 causes the router to check the NAT table. Because no translation entries exist for this source, the router creates an entry in the NAT table. Since overloading is enabled and other translations are active, the router reuses the inside global IP address and saves enough information to translate returning packets. This type of entry is called an extended entry because it contains additional information, specifically the layer 4 protocol and TCP or UDP port number.
3. The router replaces the inside local source IP address of 10.1.2.25 with the selected inside globally routable IP address and a unique port number and then forwards the packet. In this example, the source IP address is shown as the inside global address 200.1.2.26:1723 in the NAT table.
4. The host at 205.1.1.25 receives the packets and responds to the host at 10.1.2.25 by using the inside global IP address and port in the source field of the original packet (200.1.2.26:1723).
5. The NAT border router receives the packet from 205.1.1.25 destined for 200.1.2.26. It performs a NAT table lookup using the layer 4 protocol, inside global IP address, and port as the key. The router then translates the address back to the inside local destination IP address of 10.1.2.25, keeping the port number of 1723, and forwards the packet.

Steps 2 through 5 are continued for all subsequent communications until the TCP connection is closed. Once the TCP connection is closed, the NAT router deletes the entry in the NAT table. UDP connections don't contain state information so they are deleted after a set time of inactivity.

Both hosts at IP address 205.1.1.25 and 130.77.116.4 think they are talking to a single host at IP address 200.1.2.26. They are actually talking end-to-end to different hosts, with the port number being the differentiator the NAT border router uses to forward the packets to the correct host on the inside network. In fact, you could allow approximately 64,000 different hosts using a single layer 4 protocol to share a single inside global IP address by using the many available TCP and UDP port numbers.

Using TCP Load Distribution

TCP load distribution is a dynamic form of inside global destination IP address translation that can be configured to distribute the load of incoming connections among a pool of inside local IP addresses. Once the mapping scheme is created, an inside global destination IP address matching an access list is replaced with an IP address from a rotary pool of IP addresses in a round-robin fashion.

When new connections are established from the outside network to the inside network, all non-TCP traffic is passed without being translated, unless another translation type is applied to the interface. Figure 3.4 illustrates the TCP load distribution feature, so let's look at the process NAT uses to map one virtual IP address to several real IP addresses.

FIGURE 3.4 TCP load distribution steps

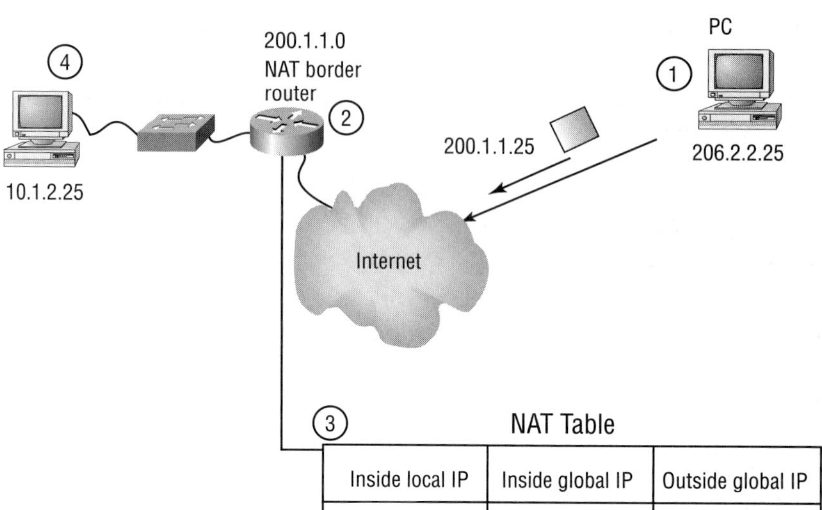

Inside local IP	Inside global IP	Outside global IP
10.1.2.25:80	200.1.1.25:80	206.2.2.25:3058

1. In Figure 3.4, the PC using outside global IP address 206.2.2.25 attempts to open a TCP connection to the virtual host at inside global IP address 200.1.1.25.
2. The NAT border router receives this new connection request and creates a new translation, because one didn't exist in the NAT table. This allocates the next real inside local IP address of 10.1.2.25 as the inside local IP address and adds this information to the NAT table using the same destination port number as the original layer 4 header, port 80.

Note that this example shows only a single inside host, 10.1.2.25, which is not a practical use for this feature. In production, two or more hosts on the same inside network would be configured into the rotary pool to service the incoming requests, with the NAT border router using a round-robin approach to establishing new connections with these multiple devices running the same network-accessible applications and data.

3. The NAT border router then replaces the virtual inside global destination IP address with the selected real inside local IP address and then forwards the packet.
4. The host at the real inside local IP address of 10.1.2.25 receives the packets and responds to the Internet host through the NAT border router.
5. The NAT border router receives the packet from the server and performs another NAT table lookup using the inside local IP address and port number as the key. The NAT border router then translates the source inside local address to the virtual inside global IP address and

forwards the packet. Packets will flow from that real inside local IP address to the Internet host as long as the TCP session is established, meaning that the translation entry still exists.

6. Assuming there were additional inside hosts with consecutive inside local addresses assigned to them and entered into the rotary pool on the NAT border router, the next connection request to the virtual inside global IP address would cause the NAT border router to allocate 10.1.2.26 for the inside local IP address. This continues until all IP addresses in the pool are used; then the router starts at the beginning of the pool.

Overlapping Networks

We'll start with a couple of examples to define an overlapping network. Let's say your internal network uses an IP address range that is owned by another company and is being used by that company on the Internet. Another possibility might be that you have merged with a company and you are both using the same RFC 1918 address space and do not want to renumber. Figure 3.5 shows an example of NAT translating overlapping addresses.

FIGURE 3.5 NAT translating overlapping addresses

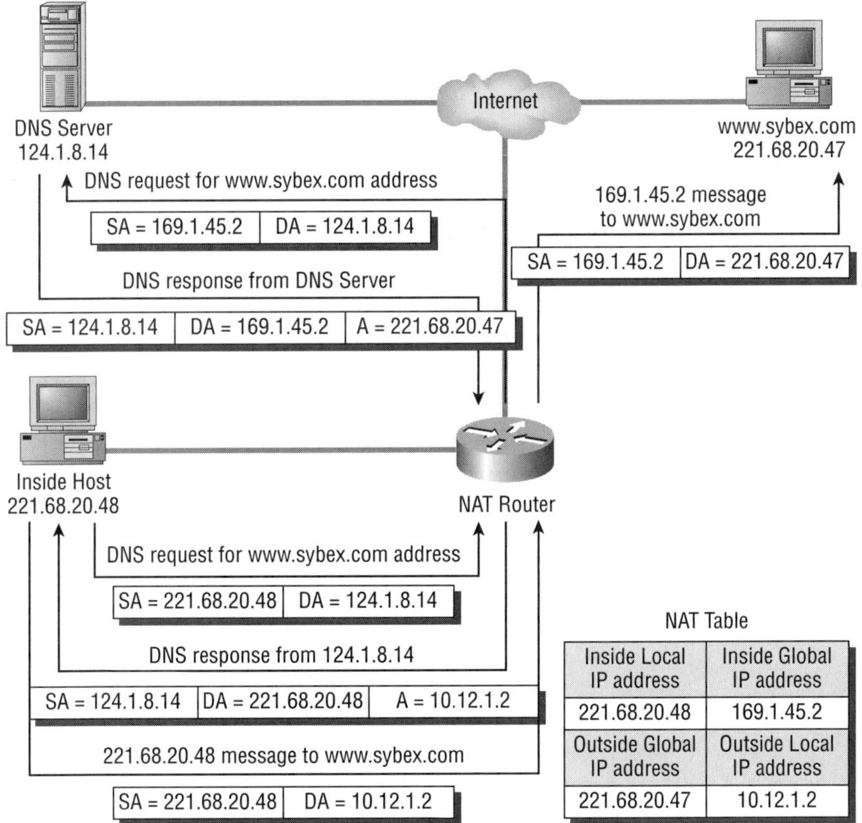

The following steps are performed when translating overlapping addresses:

1. The host on the inside network at IP address 221.68.20.48 tries to open a connection to a web server on the outside network by using its fully qualified domain name. This request triggers a name-to-address lookup query from the host to a domain name server (DNS) at IP address 124.1.8.14.
2. The NAT border router translates the outgoing request to a pool of outbound IP addresses; in this case, it chooses 169.1.45.2. The router then intercepts the returning DNS reply and detects that the resolved IP address inside the reply (221.68.20.47) matches the inside range of IP addresses for which it is translating traffic. This address would appear local to the inside host that requested the address. So it's not the appropriate address for the inside host to try to communicate with. It is a potentially overlapping IP address with another host on the inside of the network.
3. To allow the inside host to communicate with the host on the outside network and not accidentally put it in touch with the incorrect host on the inside, the NAT border router creates a simple translation entry that maps the overlapping IP address to an address from a pool of outside local IP addresses. In this case, it is IP address 10.12.1.2.
4. The NAT border router replaces the IP address inside the DNS reply with this outside local address allocated from the pool and forwards the reply to the original requester at inside local IP address 221.68.20.48.
5. The host on the inside of the network initiates a connection to the web server on the outside using outside local IP address 10.12.1.2. The router translates the inside local source IP address to the inside global address 169.1.45.2 and the outside local destination IP address to the outside global address 221.68.20.47, which receives the packet and continues the conversation.
6. For each packet sent from the inside host to the outside host, the router performs a NAT table lookup, replaces the destination address with 221.68.20.47, and replaces the source address with 169.1.45.2. The replies go through the reverse process.

There are two pools involved here—one for the inside-to-outside traffic and one for the outside-to-inside traffic. The inside device must use the DNS-supplied outside local IP address of the outside device—10.12.1.2—for the overlapping NAT to work. The inside device cannot use the outside global IP address of the outside device—221.68.20.47—because it is potentially the same address as another host on the inside network, and the inside device would ARP to find that device's MAC address, believing that they share the local subnet. This would result in the incorrect association of the outside global IP address with the MAC address of an inside device. The intended recipient would never be reached, because the router would not receive packets to be routed.

Configuring NAT

In this section, we will talk about the commands needed for the following NAT configurations:

- Static NAT
- Dynamic NAT

- Using overloading for NAT
- TCP load distribution
- Translation of overlapping addresses

We will also cover how to verify NAT operations, troubleshoot NAT problems, and clear NAT translation entries. First, let's talk about what all these configurations have in common.

Each interface involved in the NAT process must be designated either an inside or outside interface, but not both at the same time. There must be at least one interface on the router configured as inside and at least one configured as outside. This way the router knows how to handle inbound and outbound traffic on an interface. In this example, the Ethernet0 interface is the inside and the Serial0 interface is the outside. The `ip nat inside` and `ip nat outside` commands must be used from interface configuration mode to tell the router which interface is performing which role in the NAT process. The following commands show how to configure our example router:

```
Border(config)#interface ethernet0
Border(config-if)#ip nat inside
Border(config-if)#exit
Border(config)#interface serial0
Border(config-if)#ip nat outside
Border(config-if)#exit
Border(config)#
```

As you can see from the following excerpt from the router configuration, the interfaces have been designated as inside and outside:

```
!
interface Ethernet0
  ip address 10.1.2.254 255.255.255.0
  ip nat inside
!
interface Serial0
  ip address 200.1.1.1 255.255.255.0
  ip nat outside
!
```

Configuring Static NAT

Static NAT is used to map a single inside global IP address to a single inside local IP address. Usually the inside local IP address is one from the RFC 1918 address space and the inside global IP address is an Internet-routable address. IP addresses must be assigned to interfaces on the router that will be participating in NAT in order for proper processing of IP traffic on those interfaces. You must be in global configuration mode in order to configure NAT. The command to use is `ip nat inside source static` *`local-ip global-ip`*.

The *local-ip* is the local IP address of the host on the inside of the network to translate, and the *global-ip* is the global IP address this inside host will be known as to the outside world. In this example, a host on the inside network needs to access the Internet. Its IP address is 10.1.2.25 and is not routable on the Internet. When the NAT border router receives a packet from 10.1.2.25 destined for the Internet, the router must be configured to translate that IP address to one that is globally routable. In this case it is 200.1.1.25 and the following command is used:

```
Border(config)#ip nat inside source static 10.1.2.25 200.1.1.25
Border(config)#
```

This creates a permanent entry in the NAT table. Now when traffic arrives for IP address 200.1.1.25 from the outside network, it will be translated to 10.1.2.25 and forwarded to the inside network, and vice versa. This allows a device on the inside network using a non-Internet-routable IP address to be accessible from the outside network. You can use this to make your internal DNS, web, etc. servers accessible from the Internet. Optionally, you can configure just a certain port to be translated. Adding a protocol and port numbers to the `ip nat inside source static` NAT command does this. The following is an example of using an IP address and port combination:

```
Border(config)#ip nat inside source static tcp 10.1.2.25 80 200.1.1.25 80
Border(config)#ip nat inside source static tcp 10.1.2.24 80 200.1.1.25 81
Border(config)#
```

As you can see, the two port numbers do not need to match on both sides. I have translated requests for port 81 from the outside to port 80 on the inside, which is commonly referred to as port redirection. Now let's discuss dynamic NAT.

Real World Scenario

Using Static NAT to Assist with Network Changes

Company XYZ needs to move a server from its old data center to its new data center. During this transition, both the old and new data centers will be operational. The problem is that at the remote warehouses they are using handheld scanners to process orders. The server they are connecting to will be moving to the new data center, but the subnet it currently is connected to is not going to move, so it will need to have a new IP address. There are about 1,000 of these handheld scanners that need to have the server IP address changed in their configuration. The IT staff estimates that it would take about 10 minutes to change each scanner, and they don't have the personnel to make this change overnight.

Static NAT can be used here to allow these handheld scanners at the remote warehouses to communicate to the new server IP address without touching every device. You configure NAT on each router at the remote locations to change the old IP address of the server to the new IP address. This way they can still communicate, and the IT staff can take more time to change the handheld units at one warehouse at a time.

Let's see how this configuration would look from a remote location. The old server IP address is 17.1.1.60 and the new server IP address is 192.168.235.80. On the remote router you would need to configure the LAN interface as the outside NAT interface and the WAN interface as the inside NAT interface. Then you would configure the static NAT entry using the `ip nat inside source static` command. The following is an example of how to configure a remote router:

```
Warehouse1#conf t
Warehouse1(config)#interface ethernet0
Warehouse1(config-if)#ip nat outside
Warehouse1(config-if)#interface serial0.35
Warehouse1(config-if)#ip nat inside
Warehouse1(config-if)#exit
Warehouse1(config)#ip nat inside source static 192.168.235.80 17.1.1.60
Warehouse1(config)#exit
Warehouse1#
```

Now we can look at the translations taking place with the show `ip nat translations` command:

```
Warehouse1#show ip nat translations
Pro Inside global  Inside local        Outside local       Outside global
tcp 17.1.1.60:2001 192.168.235.80:2001 192.100.110.176:2004 192.100.110.176:2004
tcp 17.1.1.60:2001 192.168.235.80:2001 192.100.110.175:2008 192.100.110.175:2008
tcp 17.1.1.60:2001 192.168.235.80:2001 192.100.110.182:2002 192.100.110.182:2002
tcp 17.1.1.60:2001 192.168.235.80:2001 192.100.110.186:2009 192.100.110.186:2009
tcp 17.1.1.60:2001 192.168.235.80:2001 192.100.110.177:2023 192.100.110.177:2023
tcp 17.1.1.60:2001 192.168.235.80:2001 192.100.110.192:2013 192.100.110.192:2013
Warehouse1#
```

Configuring Dynamic NAT

Dynamic NAT is used to map inside local IP addresses to inside global IP addresses on the fly from a pool of available IP addresses. Again, you must have IP addresses assigned to the interfaces on the router that will be participating in the NAT process in order for IP processing on those interfaces to occur.

The dynamic NAT configuration starts in global configuration mode. In our example network, we will use one interface connected to the inside network (Ethernet0) and one interface connected to the Internet (Serial0). When a host on the inside of the network wants to communicate with a host on the Internet, the NAT border router receives a packet from an interface marked as NAT inside. The outbound interface is marked as NAT outside, and so the router will choose an available IP address from the pool and assign it to the NAT table entry. Once an IP address is allocated, it cannot be allocated to another translation entry until that entry times out or is manually removed.

When traffic goes from inside to outside, NAT translations happen after routing has taken place. Therefore, any access lists or policy routing will have been applied before the NAT translation happens. An access list will need to be created to inform the NAT process what traffic will be translated and what traffic will not. The next step is to configure a pool of IP addresses that will be allocated to outbound sessions. This is done with the `ip nat pool` command. The syntax of this command is as follows:

```
ip nat pool pool-name start-ip end-ip netmask net-mask
```

or

```
ip nat pool pool-name start-ip end-ip prefix-length length
```

The *pool-name* is any unique string that identifies this address pool. The *start-ip* and *end-ip* are the starting and ending IP addresses within the pool. The *net-mask* is the network mask in dotted-decimal format that will be used with the addresses in the pool. Optionally, you can use the `prefix-length` keyword followed by the *length* of the CIDR prefix instead of using a network mask. Finally, you need to tie the access list and pool together with the `ip nat inside source` command. The following is the syntax of this command:

```
ip nat inside source list acc-list pool pool-name
```

The *acc-list* is the number or name of the access list you created that specifies the traffic to NAT, and the *pool-name* is the unique string used when you created the pool of IP addresses. The following is an example of configuring dynamic NAT using a pool:

```
Border(config)#interface ethernet0
Border(config-if)#ip nat inside
Border(config-if)#interface serial0
Border(config-if)#ip nat outside
Border(config-if)#exit
Border(config)#access-list 12 permit 10.1.2.0 0.0.0.255
Border(config)#ip nat pool OUTBOUND 200.1.1.2 200.1.1.254 prefix-length 24
Border(config)#ip nat inside source list 12 pool OUTBOUND
Border(config)#
```

Configuring NAT Using Overloading

Once all IP addresses in a pool have been allocated, any new connection attempts will fail. So if your ISP allocated you only 13 IP addresses, then only the first 13 users will be able to access the Internet. Once a NAT entry has expired, the IP address is released back to the pool and the next user will be able to access the Internet. This doesn't sound like a very efficient use of the IP addresses.

Configuring overloading allows the router to reuse each IP address in the pool. It can do this because it changes not only the IP address but also the port number. This is what is called Port Address Translation (PAT) or Network Address and Port Translation (NAPT). The router will add the layer 4 protocol and port information for each translation entry, which allows more inside IP addresses to access the outside network than there are IP addresses in the pool.

When tying the access list to the NAT pool with the `ip nat inside source list` command, the `overload` keyword is added to configure the overloading feature. The pool of addresses can even be just one IP address in size, but it can support approximately 64,000 inside users using a single layer 4 protocol by varying the outbound port numbers. The following example shows the commands used for the overloading feature:

```
Border(config)#ip nat inside source list 12 pool OUTBOUND overload
Border(config)#
```

What happens if you're using DHCP on the outbound interface and you don't know what the IP address is going to be? You can't configure a pool of IP addresses if you don't know the outside IP address. You can configure the router to use the IP address of the outside interface as the outgoing NAT address by using the same `ip nat inside source` command but with slightly different parameters. You still need to specify the traffic to NAT with the `list` keyword, followed by the access list number. But instead of specifying a pool name, you use the `interface` keyword followed by the interface name and the `overload` parameter. The router will then use the IP address of the interface specified. This can be a static IP address or one that is acquired from DHCP. The following example uses the IP address of the Ethernet1 interface instead of a pool of IP addresses:

```
Border(config)#ip nat inside source list 12 interface ethernet1 overload
Border(config)#
```

Now let's talk about a pretty cool feature of NAT called TCP load distribution.

Configuring TCP Load Distribution

NAT has a feature that is really unrelated to getting hosts using RFC 1918 address space to be able to communicate on the Internet. Using this feature in NAT, you can establish a virtual host on the inside network that coordinates basic load sharing among real inside hosts. This allows a host that is heavily used, such as a web server, to be able to handle the load of incoming requests by spreading the load among several mirrored servers. Destination addresses that match an access list are replaced with addresses from a pool that has been designated as a rotary pool by adding the `type rotary` keywords to the end of the `ip nat pool` command. Allocation of the IP addresses from this pool is done in a round-robin fashion and only when a new connection is opened from the outside to the inside.

The router performs the following steps when translating a rotary pool:

1. Let's say a host on the outside network at IP address 155.1.3.2 sends a request to open a connection to the virtual host at IP address 20.1.1.254.

2. The router receives the connection request and creates a new translation. It will allocate the next IP address from the pool of inside local IP addresses. This is, for example, the real host at IP address 20.1.1.1.
3. The router then replaces the destination address (20.1.1.254) with the selected real host IP address (20.1.1.1) from the pool and forward the packet.
4. The host at 20.1.1.1 receives the packet and sends a response packet back to continue the communication.
5. The router receives the packet and performs a NAT table lookup. The router finds the appropriate entry in the table and translates the source address to the IP address of the virtual host (20.1.1.254) and forwards the packet to the outside host at 155.1.3.2.

When a new connection request is received, it causes the router to allocate the next available IP address from the rotary pool (20.1.1.2) and the whole process starts again with the new real host. The following example shows how to create and use a rotary pool:

```
Border(config)#interface ethernet0
Border(config-if)#ip nat inside
Border(config-if)#interface serial0
Border(config-if)#ip nat outside
Border(config-if)#exit
Border(config)#ip nat pool WEB-HOSTS 20.1.1.1 20.1.1.9 netmask 255.255.255.0
  ➥type rotary
Border(config)#access-list 12 permit 20.1.1.254
Border(config)#ip nat inside destination list 12 pool WEB-HOSTS
Border(config)#
```

Configuring NAT for Overlapping Addresses

Configuring NAT for *overlapping address translation* is similar to configuring dynamic NAT. The difference is you must create and apply a pool of IP addresses for the traffic to the inside of the network, as well as a pool for the outbound traffic.

You still need to create an access list to identify the traffic to NAT, but you need to create a second pool. Then you need to use the `ip nat outside source` command to tie the access list and second pool to NAT traffic coming from the outside interface. The syntax is the same for `ip nat outside source` as it is for `ip nat inside source`:

```
ip nat outside source list acc-list pool pool-name
```

The following illustrates the commands used for configuring NAT for overlapping addresses:

```
Border(config)#access-list 12 permit 10.1.1.0 0.0.0.255
Border(config)#ip nat pool INSIDEPOOL 200.1.1.2 200.1.1.254 netmask
  ➥255.255.255.0
Border(config)#ip nat pool OUTSIDEPOOL 10.1.2.1 10.1.2.254 prefix-length 24
```

```
Border(config)#ip nat inside source list 12 pool INSIDEPOOL
Border(config)#ip nat outside source list 12 pool OUTSIDEPOOL
Border(config)#
```

The effect of this configuration is that any outbound packet with an inside local address in the 10.1.1.0 subnet will be translated to an address from the inside global range of 200.1.1.2 to 200.1.1.254. This will make sure that no 10.1.1.0 addresses make it off of the inside network, thus avoiding any conflicts with the outside overlapping network. Conversely, any inbound packet with an outside global address that is found to be a duplicate of the inside local subnet 10.1.1.0 will be translated to an outside local address in the range 10.1.2.1 to 10.1.2.254, thus avoiding any conflict with inside local address space.

Verifying and Troubleshooting the NAT Configuration

There are two commands used to verify the NAT configuration on a router. The `show ip nat translations` command shows the translations in the NAT table: The following is an example of its output:

```
Border#show ip nat translations
Pro Inside global   Inside local    Outside local   Outside global
--- 200.1.1.25      10.1.1.25       ---             ---
--- 200.1.1.26      10.1.1.25       ---             ---
tcp 200.1.1.50:25   10.1.1.50:25    206.1.1.25:25   206.1.1.25:25
tcp 200.1.1.51:514  10.1.1.51:514   155.1.9.6:1021  155.1.9.6:1021
Border#
```

Adding the `verbose` keyword at the end of the command will display more information about each NAT table entry. These items include how long ago the entry was created, when it was last used, and how long before the entry will expire. The following is the output from adding the `verbose` keyword:

```
Border#show ip nat translations verbose
Pro Inside global   Inside local    Outside local   Outside global
--- 200.1.1.25      10.1.1.25       ---             ---
    create 2d18h, use 2d18h, flags: static, use_count: 0
--- 200.1.1.26      10.1.1.26       ---                 ---
    create 2d18h, use 2d18h, flags: static, use_count: 0
tcp 200.1.1.50:25   10.1.1.50:25    206.1.1.25:25   206.1.1.25:25
    create 05:53:05, use 05:53:05, left 18:06:54, flags: extended,
      ➥use_count: 0
tcp 200.1.1.51:514 10.1.1.51:514  155.1.9.6:1021 155.1.9.6:1021
    create 02:22:51, use 00:22:28, left 23:37:31, flags: extended,
      ➥use_count: 0
Border#
```

The second command is used to display the statistics and configuration information for NAT. The `show ip nat statistics` command displays the following information about the NAT table and statistics:

```
Border#show ip nat statistics
Total active translations: 4 (2 static, 2 dynamic; 2 extended)
Outside interfaces:
  Serial0
Inside interfaces:
  Ethernet0
Hits: 13654693  Misses: 42
Expired translations: 1202
Dynamic mappings:
-- Inside Source
[Id: 1] access-list 12 pool outbound refcount 5
 pool outbound: netmask 255.255.255.0
        start 200.1.1.2 end 200.1.1.254
        type generic, total addresses 252, allocated 4 (2%), misses 0
Border#
```

The `debug ip nat` command is used to troubleshoot NAT problems on the router. In the following output you will notice that the inside local source address of 10.1.1.25, which gets translated to an inside global source address of 200.1.1.25, is sending a packet to the destination address 206.1.1.25. An arrow (–>) symbol indicates that the packet was translated, and an asterisk (*) symbol indicates that the packet is traveling through the fast path. The first packet in a conversation will be processed through a process-switched or slow path, and additional packets will be able to be switched faster through the fast path. The following example shows the output from the `debug ip nat` command:

```
Border#debug ip nat
IP NAT debugging is on
Border#
NAT: s=10.1.1.25->200.1.1.25, d=206.1.1.25 [0]
NAT: s=206.1.1.25, d=200.1.1.25->10.1.1.25 [0]
NAT: s=10.1.1.25->200.1.1.25, d=206.1.1.25 [1]
NAT: s=10.1.1.25->200.1.1.25, d=206.1.1.25 [2]
NAT: s=10.1.1.25->200.1.1.25, d=206.1.1.25 [3]
NAT*: s=206.1.1.25, d=200.1.1.25->10.1.1.25 [1]
NAT: s=10.1.1.25->200.1.1.25, d=206.1.1.25 [4]
NAT: s=10.1.1.25->200.1.1.25, d=206.1.1.25 [5]
NAT: s=10.1.1.25->200.1.1.25, d=206.1.1.25 [6]
NAT*: s=206.1.1.25, d=200.1.1.25->10.1.1.25 [2]
Border#
```

Once debugging is enabled, it remains in effect until you turn it off with the `no debug ip nat` command; to turn off all debugging, use the `undebug all` command.

Turning on debugging information in a production router can have a significant impact on performance.

Occasionally, you will need to delete a NAT translation from the NAT table. Sometimes NAT is configured properly, but translations need to be cleared and reset to resolve a problem. Table 3.1 shows the commands used to clear the NAT table.

TABLE 3.1 Commands to Clear the NAT Table

Command	Meaning
`clear ip nat translation *`	Clears all NAT table entries.
`clear ip nat translation inside` *global-ip*	Clears the inside NAT translation table entry for the specified IP address.
`clear ip nat translation outside` *local-ip*	Clears the outside NAT translation table entry for the specified IP address.
`clear ip nat translation` *protocol inside global-ip global-port local-ip local-port [outside local-ip local-port global-ip global-port]*	Clears the specific extended NAT table entry represented by the global and local IP addresses and ports.

Often, the router will not allow you to remove or change the NAT configuration because dynamic translations have been created. When this occurs, you need to remove the inside or outside designation from an interface so translations cannot be created. When this happens, all NAT translations stop on the router. Then you can clear the translations and reconfigure or remove the NAT configuration.

Summary

As the Internet grows and companies need more and more IP addresses, the number of available IP addresses diminishes. This is one of the main reasons for the implementation of NAT and PAT. You need to understand how NAT and PAT work and how to configure each technology. NAT and PAT enable a private IP network using non-registered IP addresses to access outside networks such as the Internet. NAT also can translate the addresses of two overlapping networks, such as when two companies merge that are using the same IP address space.

There are some disadvantages of using NAT and PAT in a network. Specifically, they don't allow for full end-to-end communications between two hosts using their configured addresses, making troubleshooting a challenge at times. Some protocols and applications carry IP address information in the payload of the packet, and the embedded IP addresses might not get translated by the NAT border router.

There are many IOS commands used for viewing NAT configuration and troubleshooting NAT problems. The show `ip nat translation` command is one of the most useful, in addition to `debug ip nat`.

Exam Essentials

Understand how NAT and PAT operate. NAT is a technology, specified in RFC 1631 and RFC 3022, used to hide network addresses behind one or more IP addresses. A company can use IP addresses set aside by RFC 1918 on their internal networks and use a pool of Internet-routable IP addresses to connect their company to the Internet. PAT is similar to NAT but with a single IP address, and the port numbers are changed to make each connection unique.

Know the advantages of NAT and PAT. The advantages of NAT and PAT are that they allow an entire network to hide behind one or more IP addresses and that they allow a certain level of security and allow a company to change ISPs without having to renumber their entire network. NAT also allows a basic level of load-balancing between multiple hosts performing the same function.

Know the disadvantages of NAT and PAT. The disadvantages of NAT and PAT are that there are some protocols and applications that will not work because they carry IP address information in the payload of the packets they send and they do not provide end-to-end significance for the IP address. Cisco IOS corrects some of these problems with the more popular protocols and applications, but it cannot cover them all. There also can be a significant delay in translating IP addresses, which introduces latency in the communications path and causes application performance problems.

Understand how to configure NAT and PAT using Cisco IOS. One option when configuring NAT is to use dynamic NAT using a pool of IP addresses or by using the IP address of the outbound interface. You can also reuse those IP addresses by using the overload feature, which sometimes is called PAT. You can also configure a static NAT translation from an inside local IP address to an inside global IP address. A static translation can also be configured based upon both the IP address and port values.

Know the troubleshooting commands for NAT and PAT. The commands used to troubleshoot NAT are `show ip nat translations` with the optional `verbose` keyword and `debug ip nat`. The latter command will log NAT events as they occur on the router. The `show ip nat statistics` command is used to not only display how many translations are active but also to see the NAT configuration on the router.

IGRP and EIGRP

THE CCNP EXAM TOPICS COVERED IN THIS CHAPTER INCLUDE THE FOLLOWING:

- ✓ Understand how EIGRP operates.
- ✓ Understand how to configure EIGRP and verify proper operation.
- ✓ When route selection and configuration problems occur, understand how to use the various show and debug commands to determine the cause of the problem.

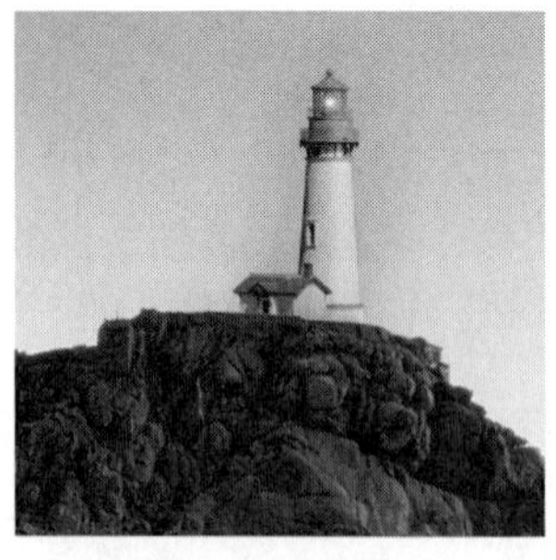

So far in this book, you have learned how routing protocols are used to exchange IP address information between routers in an enterprise network. IP addressing schemes establish a hierarchy that makes path information both distinct and efficient. A router receives this routing information via a given interface. It then advertises the information it knows to the other physical interfaces. This routing process occurs at layer 3 of the OSI model. In this chapter, in order to decide on the best routing protocol or protocols to use, we'll take a look at both the Interior Gateway Routing Protocol (IGRP) and its big brother, the Enhanced Interior Gateway Routing Protocol (EIGRP).

Unlike link-state routing protocols IS-IS and OSPF, IGRP and EIGRP are proprietary Cisco protocols and run on Cisco routers and internal route processors found in the Cisco Distribution and Core layer switches. (We need to note here that Cisco has licensed IGRP to be used on other vendors' equipment such as Compaq and Nokia.) Each of these routing protocols also has its own identifiable functions, so we'll discuss each routing protocol's features and differences. Once you understand how these protocols differ from OSPF and how they calculate routes, you will learn how to configure these protocols and fine-tune them with configuration changes to make each perform at peak efficiency.

Scalability Features of Routing Protocols

Several times in this book as we look at the different routing protocols—IS-IS, OSPF, IGRP, EIGRP, and BGP—we will refer back to distance-vector and link-state routing protocol differences. It is important to understand how these protocols differ from one another.

As networks grow and administrators implement or use Cisco-powered networks, IS-IS and OSPF might not be the most efficient or recommended protocols to use. IS-IS and OSPF do have some advantages over IGRP and EIGRP, including the following:

- They are versatile.
- They use a very scalable routing algorithm.
- They allow the use of a routing protocol that is compatible with non-Cisco routers.

Cisco provides two proprietary solutions that allow better scaling and convergence, which can be very critical issues. These are the Interior Gateway Routing Protocol (IGRP) and Enhanced IGRP (EIGRP), with EIGRP offering, by far, the better scaling and convergence of the two. Network growth imposes a great number of changes on the network environment and takes into consideration the following factors:

- The number of hops between end systems
- The number of routes in the routing table

- The different ways a route was learned
- Route convergence

IGRP and EIGRP can be used to maintain a very stable routing environment, which is absolutely crucial in larger networks.

As the effects of network growth start to manifest themselves, whether your network's routers can meet the challenges faced in a larger scaled network is completely up to the routing protocol the routers are running. If you use a protocol that's limited by the number of hops it can traverse, the number of routes it can store in its table, or even the inability to communicate with other protocols, then you have a protocol that will likely hinder the growth of your network.

All the issues we've discussed so far are general scalability considerations. Before we look at IGRP and EIGRP, let's take another look at the differences between link-state routing protocols and distance-vector protocols and the scalability issues of each.

Link-state routing and distance-vector protocols are discussed in detail in Chapter 1, "Routing Principles."

Distance-Vector Protocol Scalability Issues

In small networks—meaning those with fewer than 100 routers and an environment that's much more forgiving of routing updates and calculations—distance-vector protocols perform fairly well. However, you'll run into several problems when attempting to scale a distance-vector protocol to a larger network—convergence time, router overhead (CPU and memory utilization), and bandwidth utilization all become factors that hinder scalability.

A network's convergence time is determined by the ability of the protocol to propagate changes within the network topology. Distance-vector protocols don't use formal neighbor relationships between routers. A router using distance-vector algorithms becomes aware of a topology change in two ways:

- When a router fails to receive a routing update from a directly connected router
- When a router receives an update from a neighbor notifying it of a topology change somewhere in the network

Routing updates are sent out on a default or specified time interval. When a topology change occurs, it could take up to 90 seconds before a neighboring router realizes the change. When the router finally recognizes the change, it recalculates its routing table and sends the whole routing table out all physical interfaces.

Not only does this cause significant network convergence delay, it also devours bandwidth—just think about 100 routers all sending out their entire routing table and imagine the impact on your bandwidth. It's not exactly a sweet scenario, and the larger the network, the worse it gets, because a greater percentage of bandwidth is needed for routing updates.

As the size of the routing table increases, so does CPU utilization, because it takes more processing power to calculate the effects of topology changes and then converge using the new information. Also, as more routes populate a routing table, it becomes increasingly complex to determine the best path and next hop for a given destination. The following list summarizes the scalability limitations inherent in distance-vector algorithms:

- Network convergence delay
- Increased CPU utilization
- Increased bandwidth utilization

Scalability Limitations of Link-State Routing Protocols

Link-state routing protocols alleviate the scalability issues faced by distance-vector protocols, because the algorithm uses a different procedure for route calculation and advertisement. This enables them to scale along with the growth of the network.

Addressing distance-vector protocols' problem with network convergence, link-state routing protocols maintain a formal neighbor relationship with directly connected routers that allows for faster route convergence. They establish peering by exchanging Hello packets during a session, which cements the neighbor relationship between two directly connected routers. This relationship expedites network convergence because neighbors are immediately notified of topology changes. Hello packets are sent at short intervals (typically every 10 seconds), and if an interface fails to receive Hello packets from a neighbor within a predetermined hold time—usually three or four times the Hello time—the neighbor is considered down, and the router will then flood the update to its neighbors. This occurs before the new routing table is calculated, so it saves time. Neighbors receive the update, copy it, flood it to their neighbors, and *then* calculate the new routing table. This procedure is followed until the topology change has been propagated throughout the network.

It's noteworthy that the router sends an update concerning only the *new* information—not the entire routing table. As a result, the update is much smaller, which saves both bandwidth and CPU utilization. Plus, if there are no network changes, updates are sent out only at specified or default intervals, which differ among specific routing protocols and can range from 30 minutes to two hours. These are often called paranoid updates.

These key differences permit link-state routing protocols to function well in large networks—they really have little to no limitations when it comes to scaling, other than the fact that they're a bit more complex to configure than distance-vector protocols.

Interior Gateway Routing Protocol

Interior Gateway Routing Protocol (IGRP) was developed by Cisco in the mid-1980s to overcome the distance limitations of the Routing Information Protocol (RIP). Instead of using the hop count metric like RIP, IGRP uses a composite metric to overcome the distance limitations of RIPv1. The composite metric is made up of the following four elements; by default, only bandwidth and delay are used:

- Bandwidth
- Delay

- Load
- Reliability

Maximum transmission unit (MTU) information is included in routing updates but cannot be configured to be part of the composite metric.

IGRP does not use hop count as a variable in the composite metric; it does, however, track hop count. IGRP can traverse 100 hops but can be configured to accommodate up to 255 hops.

Although IGRP does overcome the distance limitations of RIP, it still has its own limitations. IGRP is a Cisco-proprietary routing protocol. This means IGRP cannot be used with other vendors' products. The other limitation is that IGRP is a classful distance-vector routing protocol, which means it doesn't scale well for large internetworks.

In the next few sections, we will explore how IGRP operates and how to implement IGRP in an internetwork.

While RIP depends on UDP for transport, utilizing port 520, IGRP, EIGRP, and OSPF interface with the Internet layer directly, utilizing IP protocol numbers 9, 88, and 89, respectively.

IGRP Features and Operation

IGRP sends out periodic broadcasts of its entire routing table. Upon initialization, IGRP broadcasts a request out all IGRP-enabled interfaces. IGRP then performs a check on the received updates to validate that the source address of the update belongs to the same subnet that the update was received on. Each router then uses the learned routes to determine the best routes to every destination network.

Like RIPv1, IGRP is a classful routing protocol. IGRP does not send out subnet masks with its routing updates. This means that IGRP cannot be used on a network that has employed VLSM.

IGRP employs the use of autonomous systems (ASs). If you remember, an AS is a collection of routing domains under the same administrative control. An IGRP AS is actually a routing domain and not a true AS. An AS can have multiple instances of IGRP and other routing protocols running concurrently. An IGRP AS is a set of routers running the IGRP routing protocol with the same AS number.

Allowing multiple IGRP ASs to exist under a single AS means an administrator can better segment an internetwork. The administrator will be able to create an IGRP AS for each routing domain, which means better control of communications throughout the internetwork and between routing domains through redistribution.

IGRP recognizes three types of routes within its updates:

Interior Networks directly connected to a router interface.

System Routes advertised by other IGRP neighbors within the same IGRP AS.

Exterior Routes learned via IGRP from a different IGRP AS, which provides information used by the router to set the gateway of last resort. The *gateway of last resort* is the path a packet will take if a specific route isn't found on the router.

IGRP has other features that are briefly described in Table 4.1. Most of these features were added to make IGRP more stable; a few were created to deal with routing updates and make network convergence faster.

TABLE 4.1 IGRP Features

Feature	Description
Configurable metrics	The user can configure metrics involved in the algorithm responsible for calculating route information.
Triggered update	Updates are sent out prior to the update interval timer expiring. This occurs when the metrics for a route change.
Holddown timer	Implemented to prevent routing loops. When inferior updates are received, IGRP places a route in *holddown*. Holddown means that the router won't accept any new information on a given route for a certain period of time, except from the source of the original route.
Unequal-cost load-balancing	Allows packets to be shared or distributed across multiple unequal-cost paths.

IGRP Timers

The update interval for IGRP is 90 seconds by default. IGRP uses a random factor of 20 percent to stagger updates, so the update interval is actually between 72 and 90 seconds.

By default, when a route is first learned, its associated invalid timer is set to three times the update interval, or 270 seconds, and its associated flush timer is set to seven times the update interval, or 630 seconds. If for some reason the invalid timer expires, the route will be marked as unreachable. The route will continue to exist in the routing table and be advertised to neighbors as unreachable until the flush timer expires. Once the flush timer has expired, the route will be deleted from the routing table.

When an advertising router marks a route as unreachable, the receiving routers will place the route in a holddown state. During the period a route is in holddown, the router will ignore all updates about the route. This prevents routing loops when routes become unreachable. A holddown timer is set to 280 seconds, or three times the update interval plus 10 seconds.

As noted in the "IGRP Convergence" section in Chapter 1, each time a route is received in a periodic update, the associated timers are reset for that route. For triggered updates received off-schedule, the invalid and holddown timers are reset, just as they would be for a periodic update, but the flush timer is reset at the next periodic update time, whether or not an update is received. From then on, the flush timer continues to increment, as long as no valid updates for that route are received from that neighbor or until the flush timer expires, and the route is removed from the routing table.

Timers can be adjusted, and the holddown timer can be turned off. Remember that holddown timers are used to prevent loops in an internetwork. To adjust the timers, you need to go into router configuration mode for the IGRP AS to which you want to make these adjustments. Once there, you can enter the following command:

```
timers basic update invalid holddown flush [sleeptime]
```

In order to disable the holddown timer, enter the following command in router configuration mode:

```
no metric holddown
```

Setting the sleeptime allows you to control when a triggered update will be sent. The triggered update will not be sent until the sleeptime expires. An important note to remember is not to adjust any timers without proper reason to do so. Incorrectly adjusting timers can use excess bandwidth and increase convergence time, just to mention a few of the problems that can occur. If you do adjust any timers on a router, be sure to adjust the timers accordingly for all the other routers participating in the same IGRP AS. Failing to do so can cause unexpected results from your internetwork.

IGRP Metrics

Metrics are the mathematics used to select a route. The higher the metric associated with a route, the less desirable it is. For IGRP, the Bellman-Ford algorithm uses the following equation and creates the overall 24-bit metric assigned to a route:

$$\text{metric} = [(K1 \times \text{bandwidth}) + [(K2 \times \text{bandwidth}) \div (256 - \text{load})] + (K3 \times \text{delay})] \times [K5 \div (\text{reliability} + K4)]$$

The elements in this equation are as follows:

- By default, K1 = K3 = 1, K2 = K4 = K5 = 0. Therefore, by default, the metric formula reduces to:

  $$\text{metric} = (1 \times \text{bandwidth}) + (1 \times \text{delay})$$

  $$\text{metric} = \text{bandwidth} + \text{delay}$$

- The `show ip protocols` command shows you the configured K-values for all IGRP and EIGRP autonomous systems. Notice from the following output that the default values are set for IGRP AS 100:

```
Router#show ip protocols
Routing Protocol is "igrp 100"
  Sending updates every 90 seconds, next due in 71 seconds
  Invalid after 270 seconds, hold down 280, flushed after 630
  Outgoing update filter list for all interfaces is
  Incoming update filter list for all interfaces is
  Default networks flagged in outgoing updates
```

```
Default networks accepted from incoming updates
IGRP metric weight K1=1, K2=0, K3=1, K4=0, K5=0
IGRP maximum hopcount 100
IGRP maximum metric variance 1
Redistributing: igrp 100
Routing for Networks:
  10.0.0.0
  192.168.24.0
Routing Information Sources:
  Gateway         Distance      Last Update
  10.10.10.1           100      00:00:49
Distance: (default is 100)
```

- Delay is computed as one-tenth the sum of all the measured delays, in microseconds, of the outbound interfaces of the links along the path, which is to say, the cumulative delay along the path in tens of microseconds.
- Bandwidth = [10000000/(BW in Kbps)]. BW is the lowest bandwidth of the links along the path.
- You can compute delay yourself and find the lowest bandwidth in the path by issuing the command `show interface` *`interface_type interface_number`* on each outbound interface along the path, adding up the `DLY` values and comparing bandwidths to determine the lowest. Here's a sample of the output for the Serial 0/0 interface, with all but the first four lines of output removed:

```
Router#sh int s0/0
Serial0/0 is up, line protocol is up
  Hardware is PowerQUICC Serial
  MTU 1500 bytes, BW 1544 Kbit, DLY 20000 usec,
     reliability 255/255, txload 1/255, rxload 1/255
```

Here you can see this interface is showing an MTU of 1,500 bytes, a bandwidth of 1,544 Kbps (1.544 Mbps, or the T-1 rate), a delay of 20,000 microseconds, reliability of 100 percent, and the lowest possible transmit and receive loads (1/255). The actual metric computation, based on cumulative measured values, is demonstrated in the section "Verifying and Troubleshooting IGRP" later in this chapter.

The preceding formula is used for the non-default values of K5, when K5 does not equal 0. If K5 equals the default value of 0, then that part of the formula is not used at all. This formula is used instead: metric = [(K1 × bandwidth) + [(K2 × bandwidth) ÷ (256 – load)] + (K3 × delay)]. The important point is that the final term—[K5 ÷ (reliability + K4)]—would evaluate to 0 when K5 is set to 0, making the entire metric 0. This would be unacceptable, which is why the term is omitted when K5 equals the default value of 0.

If necessary, you can adjust metric constants in router configuration mode. Metrics are used to change the manner in which routes are calculated. After you enable IGRP on a router, metric weights can be changed using the following command:

```
metric weights tos K1 K2 K3 K4 K5
```

Note that the no version of this command returns the constants to their default values, and that the type of service parameter (`tos`) must always be 0, as shown in the following router output:

```
Router(config)#router igrp AS_number
Router(config-router)#metric weights ?
  <0-8>  Type Of Service (Only TOS 0 supported)
```

Table 4.2 shows the relationship between the constant and the metric it affects.

TABLE 4.2 Metric Association of K-Values

Value	Metric
K1	Bandwidth
K2	Loading of the link (effective bandwidth percentage used)
K3	Delay
K4, *K5*	Reliability

Each constant is used to assign a weight to a specific variable. This means that when the metric is calculated, the algorithm will assign a greater importance to the specified metric. By assigning a weight, you are able to specify what is more important. If bandwidth were of greatest concern to a network administrator, then a greater weight would be assigned to *K1*. If delay is unacceptable, then the *K3* value should be assigned a greater weight.

Cisco suggests leaving all K-values at their default, due to the likelihood of unexpected results that might compromise your network's stability. Consider, for instance, the case where you might be inclined to adjust the default value of *K2* in order to include load as a variable included in routing decisions. Because load is updated every five seconds, based on a rolling five-minute average, the IGRP metric is now subject to change every five seconds. This can cause links over which a new application process is initiated to go into hold-down due to the increased load causing the metric to rise more than 110 percent. Conversely, a plummeting load can initiate flash updates to neighbors. As you can see, either scenario is unacceptable and leads directly to route instability. Take Cisco's advice—leave these constants at their defaults.

Note that MTU is not actually represented by any of the K-value constants. This is because MTU is never used in the calculation of the composite metric. The use of MTU is discussed more in the EIGRP section later in this chapter.

As well as tuning the actual metric weights, you can do other tuning. All routing protocols have an administrative distance associated with the protocol type. If multiple protocols are running on a router, the administrative distance value helps the router decide which route was learned by the most trusted method. The route learned by the method with the lowest administrative distance will be chosen. IGRP has a default administrative distance of 100. The tuning of this value is accomplished with the `distance` command, like this:

```
Router(config-router)#distance ?
  <1-255>  Administrative distance
```

Valid values for the administrative distance range from 1 to 255; the lower the value, the better. A route with an administrative distance of 255 will not be used.

When redistributing static routes or other protocol types within IGRP, there are two options on how you can enter the metric for the redistributed routes. The first option you have is to set the metric for each instance of redistribution; the command will be covered in Chapter 10, "Route Optimization." The second option is to set a default metric for all redistributed routes. This gives you less granularity when setting metrics but is faster to configure. The following command, when entered in router configuration mode, will set the default metric:

```
default-metric bandwidth delay reliability loading MTU
      bandwidth = a value between 0 and 4,294,967,295 (in Kbps)
      delay = a value between 0 and 4,294,967,295 (in 10-microsecond units)
      reliability = a range from 0 to 255 (255 is the most reliable)
      loading = range from 0 to 255 (255 means the link is completely loaded)
      MTU = a value between 0 and 4,294,967,295
```

The bandwidth and delay that you enter should be "ready to use." This means no adjustment will be made before using them in the metric calculation formula. Bandwidth is expected to be the minimum bandwidth of all the links along the path to the destination network, and the value you enter for delay is considered to be already one-tenth the actual cumulative delay along the path to the destination.

When a router receives multiple routes for a specific network, one of the routes must be chosen as the best route from all of the advertisements. While the router is told that it's possible to get to a given network over multiple interfaces, it forgets about all but the best and all traffic will be sent over the best route.

Load Balancing

Load balancing is a way that a router can send traffic over multiple paths to the same destination. It is used to cut down on the amount of traffic passing over a single path to a destination. IGRP, by default, is set to load-balance across four equal-cost paths, meaning four paths with equal metrics. IGRP can be configured to support a single path or simultaneous use of two to six equal- or unequal-cost paths. In order to change the number of paths for load-balancing IGRP, the `maximum-paths` *`number_of_paths`* command must be entered in router configuration mode:

```
Router(config-router)#maximum-paths ?
  <1-6>  Number of paths
```

Load balancing for IGRP and EIGRP differs from other routing protocols. IGRP and EIGRP can load-balance across unequal-cost paths, where other routing protocols require load balancing across equal-cost paths. This means that multiple paths that do not have the same metric can be used for load balancing. Unequal-cost load balancing is made possible through the concept of route *variance*. The variance is a multiplier that is used to determine what the acceptable metric for a route is for it to be included in the routing table. In order to configure the variance, enter the `variance` *`multiplier`* command in router configuration mode:

```
Router(config-router)#variance ?
  <1-128>  Metric variance multiplier
```

The path with the lowest metric is entered into the routing table, as always. The variance is then applied to the lowest metric to determine what other routes can be included in the routing table. If the variance is set to 1, as it is by default, then only equal-cost routes will be accepted. There are actually two requirements that must be satisfied, in order for alternate routes to be admitted into the routing table:

- The first requirement is the obvious one. The metric for the route through the neighboring router must be less than or equal to the product of the variance times the lowest local metric for the same destination network.
- The second requirement is not known by most, but is no less imperative. Unlike RIP which adds a hop to its own metric in an advertisement for a route, an IGRP or EIGRP router advertises its own metric to its neighbor, leaving the calculation of the additional metric value to the receiving neighbor. This behavior is due to the fact that only the receiving neighbor knows of the outbound variables that contribute to the final composite metric, from its point of view, for any given route. The advertised metric is actually the metric used by the advertising router in its routing table. That brings us to the second requirement. This advertised metric must be less than the lowest metric that the local router currently uses for the same destination network.

All this means it's possible that, even though an alternate route's metric is less than or equal to the product of the variance and the best local route, a route would not be used for unequal-cost load balancing if the advertising neighbor is farther away from the destination network than the local router is. This is a safeguard to avoid routing loops. If the neighboring router is farther from the destination than the local router is, perhaps the local router is the next hop for the neighbor. We definitely wouldn't want to perpetuate such a loop by sending a portion of our traffic through such a path.

The other ramification of all of this is that if a neighbor is used by the local router as the next hop of an alternate route to a destination network, then conversely the local router will not be selected by that neighbor as the next hop for the same destination network. This is because the rule does not allow for the advertised metric to be equal to the local metric. It must be better, meaning the local metric is worse, which would not satisfy this requirement for the neighbor.

Once the paths have been selected, the traffic is then divided up according to the actual metric of each path. For example, let's imagine that the path with the highest metric for load balancing is four times greater than the path with the lowest metric. For every one packet that is sent across the higher metric path, four packets will have been sent across the lower metric path.

IGRP Redistribution

At this point, we will only briefly cover redistribution for IGRP. Redistribution will be covered in greater detail in Chapter 10. You may be wondering what redistribution is. Redistribution is the process in which routes learned by one routing method or protocol—whether static or dynamic—are shared with a dynamic routing protocol. For routing protocols that use AS numbers to distinguish routing instances on the same router, these methods could actually be the exact same dynamic routing protocol, with redistribution occurring between the different AS numbers. IGRP and EIGRP certainly qualify as examples of these routing protocols. Let's look at Figure 4.1.

As you can see in this example, we have Router2, which has IGRP 100 and EIGRP 150 running on it. Router2 knows about all the routes in both IGRP 100 and EIGRP 150. Router1 knows only about the routes in IGRP 100, and Router3 knows only about routes in EIGRP 150.

So what can we do in order for Router1 and Router3 to know about the same routes? We can redistribute IGRP 100 into EIGRP 150 on Router2. This will give Router3 the same routes as Router2. If we stopped here, this would be known as one-way redistribution. One-way redistribution means that redistribution occurred in only one direction between the two routing protocols.

If we want all routers in this network to have the same routes, we must set up what is known as mutual redistribution. Mutual redistribution is when redistribution occurs in both directions between the routing protocols involved. In this case, we would need to redistribute IGRP 100 into EIGRP 150 and EIGRP 150 into IGRP 100 on Router2. Once converged, all the routers on this network will know the same routes.

FIGURE 4.1 IGRP redistribution example

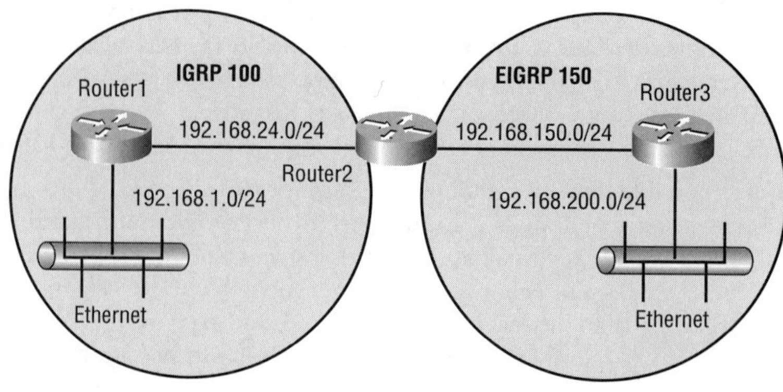

Here are some special features of redistribution for IGRP and EIGRP that you won't find in other routing protocols. Redistribution will automatically occur between IGRP and EIGRP with the same AS number. Take a look at Figure 4.2.

FIGURE 4.2 Automatic redistribution example

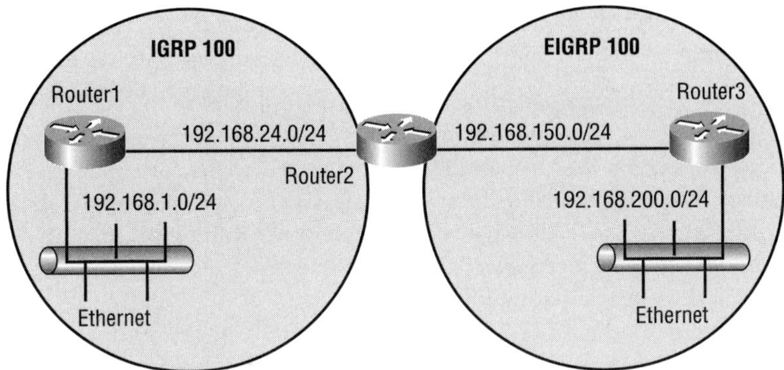

In this example, redistribution will not need to be configured. Because both IGRP and EIGRP have AS number 100, redistribution will automatically occur. If they had different AS numbers, then redistribution would have needed to be configured on Router2. (The actual configuration of redistribution will be covered in detail in Chapter 10.)

Now that you have a good grasp on how IGRP operates, let's take a look at how to configure it on a router.

IGRP Configuration

The basic configuration of IGRP is very straightforward. In order to initialize IGRP on a router, enter the `router igrp` *`AS#`* command in global configuration mode:

```
Router(config)#router igrp ?
  <1-65535>  Autonomous system number
```

Once you've initialized IGRP on the router, you need to specify the interfaces that you want to include in the IGRP AS process, through the use of the classful network. In order to accomplish this, enter the `network` *`A.B.C.D`* command in router configuration mode:

```
Router(config-router)#network ?
  A.B.C.D  Network number
```

IGRP expects classful network addresses, so entering subnet addresses has no additional effect. In fact, it would be considered incorrect to do so. IGRP watches out for you, however, by converting the classless entry to a classful one, as can be seen with the `show run` or `show ip protocols` commands.

That's all that is needed to configure basic IGRP.

You can also configure IGRP so it will send unicast updates to its neighbors. A unicast update is sent directly to the specified neighbor instead of being broadcast, cutting down on the amount of bandwidth utilized for updates. In order to configure unicast updates, enter the `neighbor` *`A.B.C.D`* command in router configuration mode:

```
Router(config-router)#neighbor ?
  A.B.C.D  Neighbor address
```

As noted earlier, IGRP's `network` command pays attention only to the classful portion of the address you enter. So when you use the `network` statement, any interface on the router that falls into the classful network range will be included in the IGRP routing domain. This causes a problem when you don't want one of the interfaces in the classful range to participate in the IGRP AS. This type of scenario could arise when you are running another routing protocol over one of your WAN connections and the interface participating in that connection is in the same classful network range as an interface participating in the IGRP AS.

Without the `neighbor` command to force unicasts to the WAN neighbor, the interface will broadcast updates over the WAN link. The router on the other end of the link receives the update packet and drops it, because that router's interface isn't participating in the IGRP AS. This will not break anything, but it wastes bandwidth.

The way to overcome this is to use the `passive-interface` command. The `passive-interface` command allows an interface's associated network—and possibly subnet—to be advertised in the IGRP routing domain, but the interface will not listen to or send IGRP updates itself. You need to enter the `passive-interface` *`interface_type interface_number`* command under the IGRP process in router configuration mode to configure an interface as a passive-interface (interface Serial 0/0 shown):

```
Router(config-router)#passive-interface s0/0
```

Now that you have a basic understanding of how to configure IGRP, let's walk through an actual configuration. Take a look at Figure 4.3.

Let's assume for the given network that the layer 3 interface addresses are already configured. We're going to concentrate only on the routing protocol for this example.

The configuration for the network would occur as follows:

```
Router1>enable
Router1#configure terminal
Router1(config)#router igrp 100
Router1(config-router)#network 172.16.0.0
Router1(config-router)#network 192.168.100.0

Router2>enable
Router2#configure terminal
Router2(config)#router igrp 100
Router2(config-router)#network 192.168.100.0
```

```
Router2(config-router)#network 192.168.21.0

Router3>enable
Router3#configure terminal
Router3(config)#router igrp 100
Router3(config-router)#network 172.16.0.0
Router3(config-router)#network 192.168.21.0
```

FIGURE 4.3 IGRP configuration example

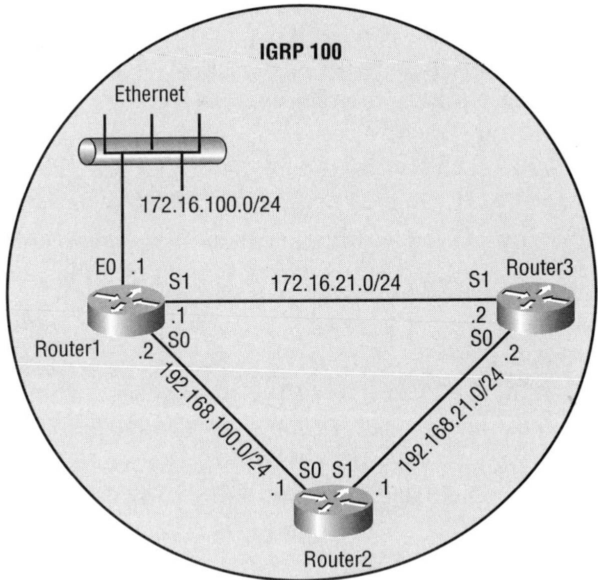

This would configure IGRP for the network. If you decide to cut down on excess bandwidth usage on the Ethernet segment of Router1, you will make interface Ethernet 0 passive. Here is the configuration that would accomplish this:

```
Router1>enable
Router1#configure terminal
Router1(config)#router igrp 100
Router1(config-router)#passive-interface e0
```

That's all there is to it. As you can see, configuring IGRP is a straightforward process. From personal experience, I ask you to remember one thing about IGRP, or any other routing protocol for that matter: Do not adjust timers or K-values unless it is for an important reason and you thoroughly understand the consequences. Adjusting these parameters in a production network can cause serious problems, and you will not want to deal with the repercussions.

Verifying and Troubleshooting IGRP

Now that you know how to configure IGRP, we need to focus on how to verify that it is operating correctly and, if IGRP is not operating correctly, how to troubleshoot it.

There are two important items to keep in mind when working with IGRP:

- Remember that IGRP is a standard distance-vector routing protocol. What this means to you as the engineer is that IGRP does not keep a topology table. So you need to look at the routing table to verify most information.
- IGRP is a classful routing protocol. If you have implemented redistribution, or if IGRP is automatically redistributing with EIGRP, the routes being redistributed must be on classful boundaries or on the same non-classful boundary as a prefix of the exact same length and value as configured on one or more of its own interfaces. If they are not, IGRP will not accept the routes into its routing table. If you have implemented VLSM in another routing protocol, you will want to make sure that you summarize the routes to the classful or similar non-classful boundary that you want advertised into IGRP.

Route Information

As stated earlier, you will receive most of your information about the operation of IGRP from the routing table. In order to view the routing table, you need to enter the following command in privileged EXEC mode:

```
Router#show ip route
Codes: C - connected, S - static, I - IGRP, R - RIP, M - mobile, B - BGP
       D - EIGRP, EX - EIGRP external, O - OSPF, IA - OSPF inter area
       N1 - OSPF NSSA external type 1, N2 - OSPF NSSA external type 2
       E1 - OSPF external type 1, E2 - OSPF external type 2, E - EGP
       i - IS-IS, L1 - IS-IS level-1, L2 - IS-IS level-2, ia - IS-IS inter area
       * - candidate default, U - per-user static route, o - ODR
       P - periodic downloaded static route

Gateway of last resort is not set

C    192.168.24.0/24 is directly connected, Loopback0
I    20.0.0.0/8 [100/7382] via 10.10.10.1, 00:00:43, Serial2/0.1
     10.0.0.0/24 is subnetted, 1 subnets
C       10.10.10.0 is directly connected, Serial2/0.1
```

As you can see from the routing table, we have one route learned via IGRP. You will know the routes learned via IGRP from the code of I in front of the route entry. The routing table is a very important verification and troubleshooting tool, because it informs you of all the routes that have been learned via IGRP that were considered the best for their respective destination network. If a route is not there that you believe should be there, you need to start troubleshooting.

Once you have viewed the routing table, you can enter the following command, using the appropriate routing entry, to view more detailed information about a particular route:

```
Router#show ip route 20.0.0.0
Routing entry for 20.0.0.0/8
  Known via "igrp 100", distance 100, metric 7382
  Redistributing via igrp 100
  Advertised by igrp 100 (self originated)
  Last update from 10.10.10.1 on Serial2/0.1, 00:00:03 ago
  Routing Descriptor Blocks:
  * 10.10.10.1, from 10.10.10.1, 00:00:03 ago, via Serial2/0.1
      Route metric is 7382, traffic share count is 1
      Total delay is 25000 microseconds, minimum bandwidth is 2048 Kbit
      Reliability 255/255, minimum MTU 1500 bytes
      Loading 1/255, Hops 0
```

This command can give you details about a particular route. The most important information you can learn from this command is the details of the composite metric for the particular route. The command informs you what the minimum bandwidth, cumulative delay, reliability, load, and minimum MTU are for the particular routing entry's path to the destination network. Recall that the metric is computed as

$$[(10000000 \div \text{minimum bandwidth}) + (\text{cumulative delay} \div 10)] = [(10000000 \div 2048) + (25000 \div 10)] = 4882.8125 + 2500 = 7382$$

Note that fractional values are truncated, not rounded.

Routing Protocol Information

You can also view information that is specific to routing protocols. There are two ways in which to view this information. The first way to view this information is at the global level of the router. Entering the following command, in privileged EXEC mode, provides you with specific information about all routing protocols on the router:

```
Router#show ip protocols
Routing Protocol is "igrp 100"
  Sending updates every 90 seconds, next due in 71 seconds
  Invalid after 270 seconds, hold down 280, flushed after 630
  Outgoing update filter list for all interfaces is
  Incoming update filter list for all interfaces is
  Default networks flagged in outgoing updates
  Default networks accepted from incoming updates
  IGRP metric weight K1=1, K2=0, K3=1, K4=0, K5=0
  IGRP maximum hopcount 100
  IGRP maximum metric variance 1
  Redistributing: igrp 100
```

```
  Routing for Networks:
    10.0.0.0
    192.168.24.0
  Routing Information Sources:
    Gateway         Distance      Last Update
    10.10.10.1           100      00:00:49
  Distance: (default is 100)
```

As you can see, the router in this example is running only IGRP. If it had been running other routing protocols, you would have seen information about each of the routing protocols on the router. This command gives you the values set for all of your timers and shows what routes this particular router is advertising to its neighbors. For IGRP and EIGRP, it also gives you the values for maximum hop count and variance.

As seen earlier in this chapter, the other way to view specific routing protocol information is at the interface level. The most important information you will receive from the following command, entered in privileged EXEC mode, is what the bandwidth, delay, reliability, load, and MTU are for that particular interface:

```
Router#show interface serial 2/0.1
Serial2/0.1 is up, line protocol is up
  Hardware is DSCC4 Serial
  Internet address is 10.10.10.2/24
  MTU 1500 bytes, BW 2048 Kbit, DLY 20000 usec,
     reliability 255/255, txload 1/255, rxload 1/255
  Encapsulation FRAME-RELAY
```

All of the commands covered so far give information about IGRP on the particular router. This is important information, but if a route is not there that should be, it might not give you all the information you need. The next section covers how to monitor what your router is sending to its neighbors and also what it is receiving from its neighbors.

Viewing Route Updates

Viewing the routing updates that your router is sending and receiving is an invaluable tool. The following debug commands give you a step-by-step account of what is happening between your router and its neighbors:

```
Router#debug ip igrp events
IGRP event debugging is on
Router#
15:34:08: IGRP: received update from 10.10.10.1 on Serial2/0.1
15:34:08: IGRP: Update contains 0 interior, 1 system, and 0 exterior routes.
15:34:08: IGRP: Total routes in update: 1
15:34:55: IGRP: sending update to 255.255.255.255 via Serial2/0.1 (10.10.10.2)
15:34:55: IGRP: Update contains 0 interior, 1 system, and 0 exterior routes.
```

```
15:34:55: IGRP: Total routes in update: 1
15:34:55: IGRP: sending update to 255.255.255.255 via Loopback0 (192.168.24.1)
15:34:55: IGRP: Update contains 0 interior, 2 system, and 0 exterior routes.
15:34:55: IGRP: Total routes in update: 2
```

The `debug ip igrp events` command allows you to view the routing updates sent to the router every 90 seconds by its neighbors. It also allows you to view the routing updates that the router sends to its neighbors every 90 seconds. The routing updates sent by the router to its neighbors contain the destination address (the broadcast address 255.255.255.255 or a unicast address, due to the use of the `neighbor` command), interface, a summary of the types of routes, and the number of routes sent. The routing updates received by the router from its neighbors include the same information, except the destination address is replaced with the source address.

If the data contained in the `debug ip igrp events` doesn't give you enough information, there is another `debug` command that will provide you with more information about the routes contained in the routing update. Enter the following command in privileged EXEC mode:

```
Router#debug ip igrp transactions
IGRP protocol debugging is on
Router#
15:36:21: IGRP: sending update to 255.255.255.255 via Serial2/0.1 (10.10.10.2)
15:36:21:       network 192.168.24.0, metric=501
15:36:21: IGRP: sending update to 255.255.255.255 via Loopback0 (192.168.24.1)
15:36:21:       network 20.0.0.0, metric=7382
15:36:21:       network 10.0.0.0, metric=6882
15:37:07: IGRP: received update from 10.10.10.1 on Serial2/0.1
15:37:07:       network 20.0.0.0, metric 7382 (neighbor 501)
```

The `debug ip igrp transactions` command provides detailed information about the routes contained in the routing update. As you can see in the debug output, the debugging of IGRP transactions contains all networks that were in the update, as well as their metrics. Updates received by the router also contain the neighbor's metric. Recall that the neighbor's advertised metric is used in conjunction with the variance command to avoid the trap of load balancing by using a potential routing loop.

Both of the `debug` commands discussed in this section can be entered to display the detailed information about the routes, as well as display a summary of the types of routes. This makes it convenient to view all the information about the updates that the router is sending and receiving.

In order for you to be able to view debug output, you must have logging enabled. Logging will send the debug messages to the destination that you state in the `logging` command. In order to enable logging, you may need to enter the `logging on` command in global configuration mode. After enabling logging, you can specify where to send the messages. The following is a list of some of the most common destinations for a message to be sent:

- Using a host name or IP address will send the messages to a Syslog server.
- `buffered` will send the messages to the router's buffer.
- `console` will send the messages to the router's console.

These destinations are not the only places logging can be set up for. In order to configure the router to send messages to one of these destinations, you will need to enter the `logging` command followed by one of the destinations in global configuration mode.

After enabling debugging, you will need to be able to turn it off. In privileged EXEC mode, enter the command `undebug all` to turn off all debugging.

With all these tools in hand, you should be able to verify and troubleshoot IGRP operation accurately. With practice, you should be able to troubleshoot IGRP in no time. Now that you have a full understanding of how IGRP functions, how to configure IGRP, and how to verify and troubleshoot IGRP operation, let's move on to the big brother of IGRP: EIGRP.

Enhanced Interior Gateway Routing Protocol

Enhanced Interior Gateway Routing Protocol (EIGRP) is better than its little brother, IGRP. EIGRP allows for incremental routing updates and formal neighbor relationships, which overcome some of the limitations of IGRP. The enhanced version uses the same type of information as IGRP, obtained by distance-vector methods, yet with a different algorithm, and scaled for a 32-bit metric, as opposed to IGRP's 24-bit metric. EIGRP uses DUAL (Diffusing Update Algorithm) for metric calculation, which permits rapid convergence. This algorithm allows for the following:

- Automatic backup route determination, if one is available
- Sending out queries for an alternate route if no route can be found
- Support of variable-length subnet masks (VLSMs)
- Reliable communication with neighbors

EIGRP fixes many of the problems associated with IGRP, such as the propagation of the entire routing table, which IGRP sends when changes occur in the network topology, as well as periodically, even in the absence of change.

One unique characteristic of EIGRP is that it is both a link-state routing and a distance-vector protocol. How can this be? Let's look at how this protocol combines the best from both routing protocol types.

Along with rapid convergence discussed earlier, EIGRP reduces bandwidth usage. It does this not by making scheduled updates, but by sending updates only when a topology change occurs. When EIGRP does send an update, the update contains information only on the change in the topology, which requires a path or metric change. Another plus is the fact that only the routers that need to know about the change receive the update.

Basically, EIGRP establishes neighbor relationships and keeps tables in addition to the routing table, just like link-state protocols. However, just like distance-vector routing protocols, EIGRP still routes by rumor and trusts whatever it hears from its adjacent neighbors. Related to this behavior, unlike link-state routing protocols, EIGRP does not build a hierarchical view of the entire routing domain with itself as the root of the inverted tree.

One of the most attractive features of EIGRP is its support of all the major layer 3 routed protocols using protocol-dependent modules (PDMs), those being IP, IPX, and AppleTalk. At the same time, EIGRP can maintain a completely loop-free routing topology and very predictable behavior, even when using all three routed protocols over multiple redundant links. Besides the protocol-dependent modules, EIGRP has three other components that make up the four components of EIGRP:

- Reliable Transport Protocol (RTP)
- Neighbor discovery/recovery
- Diffusing Update Algorithm (DUAL)

With all these features, EIGRP must be hard to configure, right? Guess again. Cisco has made this part easy as well and allows you to implement load balancing over equal- or unequal-cost links. So why would you use anything else? Well, I guess you might if all your routers weren't Cisco routers. Remember, EIGRP is proprietary and runs only on Cisco routers and route switch processors.

Now that we have mentioned all this, we've sold you on EIGRP, right? Well, if we stopped right here, you'd miss out on many other important details of the route-tagging process, neighbor relationships, route calculation, and the metrics used by EIGRP, which will be discussed in the next few sections. Following that discussion, we will look at how to configure EIGRP, tune EIGRP, load-balance, and troubleshoot. We will also briefly cover redistributing routes. This topic will be covered in greater detail in Chapter 10.

Route Tagging

Route tagging is used to distinguish routes learned by the different EIGRP sessions. By defining a different AS number, EIGRP can run multiple sessions on a single router. Routers using the same AS number speak to each other and share routing information, which includes the routes learned and the advertisement of topology changes.

Route redistribution, which is covered in its own section later in this chapter, allows routes learned by one EIGRP AS session to be shared with another session. When route redistribution occurs, the routes are tagged as being learned from an external EIGRP session. Internal EIGRP routes have an administrative distance of 90, while external EIGRP routes have a less trusted administrative distance of 170.

Neighbor Relationships

Using Hello messages, EIGRP establishes and maintains neighbor relationships with neighboring routers. This is a quality of a link-state routing protocol. EIGRP uses the Hello protocol, just like OSPF, to establish and maintain the peering relationships with directly connected routers. OSPF will be discussed in Chapter 5, "OSPF Operation in a Single Area," and Chapter 6, "Interconnecting OSPF Areas." The Hello packets sent between EIGRP neighboring routers determine the state of the connection between them. Once the neighbor relationship is established, the routers then exchange route information.

Each EIGRP session running on a router maintains a neighbor table in which each router stores information on all the routers known to be directly connected neighbors. The neighboring router's IP address, hold time interval, smooth round-trip timer (SRTT), and queue information are all kept in this table, which is used to help determine when a neighbor is acquired or lost, resulting in topology changes that need to be propagated to neighboring routers.

The only time EIGRP advertises its entire routing table is when two neighbors initiate communication. When this happens, both neighbors advertise their entire routing tables to each other. After each has learned its neighbor's directly connected or known routes, only changes to the routing table are propagated.

One thing to keep in mind about EIGRP is that it doesn't broadcast Hello packets. Instead, EIGRP will send multicast Hellos to the well-known multicast address of 224.0.0.10. Sending a multicast Hello instead of a broadcast allows any device not running EIGRP to filter the packet on the network interface card (NIC). Doing this cuts down on needless processing of packets. Remember, if this had been a broadcast packet, all of the devices on the network would need to process the packet, causing undue CPU load on end stations attached to this network.

Hello packets are multicast at intervals of five seconds. For multipoint interfaces of X.25, Frame Relay, and ATM, as well as non-packet-switched networks like BRI ISDN that have access speeds equal to or less than the speed of a T1, the Hello packet will be unicast every 60 seconds.

Each Hello packet sent contains the EIGRP version number, the AS number, the K-values, and the hold time. In order for neighboring routers to form adjacencies, they must be using the same AS number and K-values.

When initial Hello messages are sent out, replies to the Hello packets are sent with the neighboring router's topology table (which is different from the routing table) and include each route's metric information, with the exception of any routes that were already advertised by the router receiving the reply. As soon as the reply is received, the receiving router sends out what is called an ACK (acknowledgment) packet to acknowledge receipt, and the routing table is updated if any new information is received from the neighboring router. Once the topology table has been updated, the originating router will then advertise its entire table to any new neighbors that come online. Then when the originating router receives information from its neighbors, the route calculation process begins.

Now that you have a good understanding of how EIGRP neighbors form adjacencies, let's take a look at how EIGRP chooses the best routes.

Route Calculation

EIGRP uses multicasts instead of broadcasts. Therefore, only devices running EIGRP are affected by routing updates or queries. Where IGRP updates use a 24-bit format, EIGRP uses a 32-bit format for greater granularity. The default IGRP metric, which includes only bandwidth and delay, can simply be multiplied by 256 to obtain the corresponding EIGRP metric. Only changes in the network topology are advertised, instead of the entire topology table.

EIGRP is called an advanced distance-vector protocol, because it contains properties of both distance-vector and link-state routing protocols when calculating routes. DUAL is much faster and calculates the shortest path to a destination when updates or Hello messages, or the lack thereof, cause a change in the routing table. Recalculation occurs only when the changes directly affect the routes contained in the topology table.

This last statement may be confusing. If a change occurs to a network that is directly connected to a router, all of the relevant information is used to calculate a new metric and route entry for it. If a link between two EIGRP peers becomes congested, both routers would have to calculate a new route metric and then advertise the change to any other directly connected routers.

Now that you understand the difference between a route update and a route calculation, we can summarize the steps that a router takes to calculate, learn, and propagate route update information.

Redundant Link Calculation

The topology database stores all known routes to a destination and the metrics used to calculate the least-cost path. Once the best routes have been calculated, they are moved to the routing table. The topology table can store up to six routes to a destination network, meaning that EIGRP can calculate the best path for up to six redundant paths. Using the known metrics to the destination, the router must make a decision as to which path to make its primary path and which path to use as a standby or secondary path to a destination network. Once the decision is made, the primary route—the one with the lowest metric—will become the *successor* and be added to the routing table. Any route that has an advertised distance lower than the successor's feasible distance will become a feasible successor route.

The path-cost calculation decisions are made from information contained in the routing table using the bandwidth and delay from both the local and adjacent routers. Using this information, a composite metric is calculated. The local router adds its cost to the cost advertised by the adjacent router. The total cost is the metric. Figure 4.4 shows how cost is used to select the best route (successor) and the backup route (feasible successor).

FIGURE 4.4 The best-route selection process

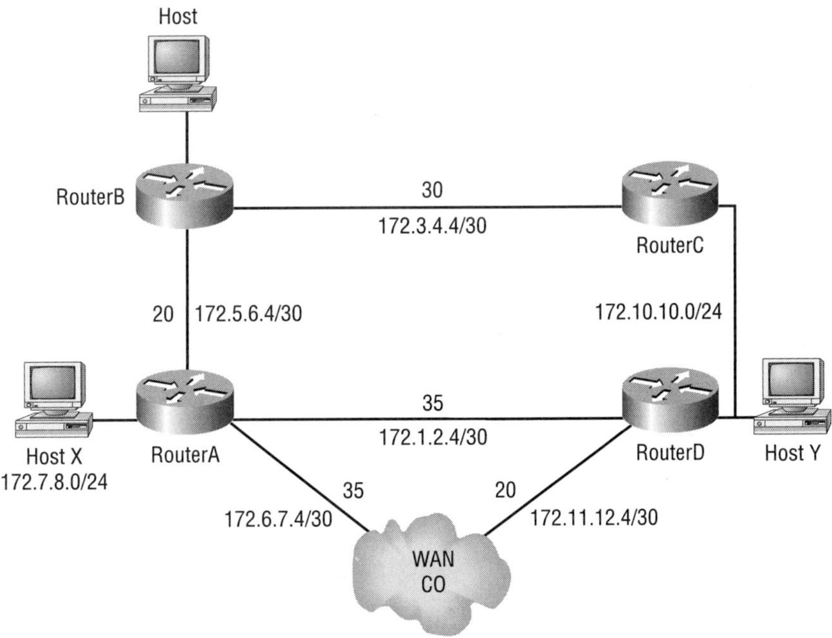

Using RouterA as a starting point, we see that there are three different routes to Host Y. Each link has been assigned a cost. In this example, RouterD and the WAN all have advertised costs to Host Y that they send to RouterA. This is known as the advertised distance. To calculate the advertised distance, add together the metrics between the advertising router and the destination and multiply by 256. In order to determine the feasible distance, you need to add the metric to reach a neighbor to the calculated metric from the advertising router to the destination and then multiply by 256. The lowest calculated metric becomes the feasible distance, and that route becomes the successor. Any route with advertised distance less than the feasible distance becomes a feasible successor route.

Let's calculate the lowest metric for Host X to get to Host Y. We'll use the path from Host X to RouterA to RouterB to RouterC and finally to Host Y for our first path calculation. To calculate the total metric, we add 20 (RouterA to RouterB) to 30 (RouterB to RouterC) and multiply it by 256 for a final value of 12,800.

Now let's calculate the metric for the path from Host X to RouterA to the WAN to RouterD and then to Host Y. Add the metric from the WAN to RouterD, 20, to the metric from the WAN to RouterA, 35; the total is 55. Multiplying 55 by 256 gives us a value of 14,080.

Finally, we will calculate the total metric from Host X to RouterA to RouterD to Host Y. Take the metric 35 and multiply it by 256 for a value of 8,960. The value 8,960 becomes the feasible distance, and the path to RouterD becomes the successor.

In order to calculate the feasible successor routes, we need to look at the advertised distance to the destination from each neighbor. The neighbors with an advertised distance lower than the feasible distance will become feasible successors. In this case, all of the routes will become feasible successors.

Information given in Table 4.3 closely, though not exactly, represents what is contained in an actual topology table. The Status field shows whether a new route is being calculated or if a primary route has been selected. In our example, the route is in passive state because it has already selected the primary route.

TABLE 4.3 Topology Table Information

Status	Route—Adjacent Router's Address (Metrics)	Number of Successors	Feasible Distance
P	172.10.10.0/24 via 172.1.2.6 (3611648/3609600) via 172.5.6.6 (4121600/3609600) via 172.6.7.6 (5031234/3609600)	1 (RouterC)	3611648

The route with the best metric contains the lowest metric value and is chosen as the primary route. If there is more than one route to a destination, the route with the second-lowest metric will be chosen as the feasible successor, as long as the advertised distance of the potential feasible successor is not greater than the feasible distance of the successor. Primary routes are moved to the routing table after selection. More than one route can be made a primary route in order to load-balance.

EIGRP uses the same metrics as IGRP (by default, bandwidth and delay). Those metrics are:

- Bandwidth
- Delay
- Reliability
- Load

Just as with IGRP, there is no specific calculation for the maximum transmission unit (MTU) as a metric. The MTU, however, is used as a tiebreaker for equal metric paths.

Bandwidth and delay are the two metrics used by default. The other metrics can be configured manually. When you configure reliability, load, and MTU, this can cause the topology table to be calculated more often.

Updates and Changes

EIGRP also has link-state properties. One of these properties is that it propagates only changes in the routing table instead of sending an entire new routing table to its neighbors. EIGRP relies on IP to deliver updates to its neighbors, as shown in a breakdown of an EIGRP packet in Figure 4.5. When changes occur in the network, a regular distance-vector routing protocol will send the entire routing table to its neighbors. By avoiding sending the entire routing table, less bandwidth is consumed and less CPU overhead is achieved. Neighboring routers don't have to reinitialize the entire routing table; all the routers need to do is insert the new route changes. This is one of the big advantages that EIGRP has over IGRP.

FIGURE 4.5 An IP frame showing the protocol type to be EIGRP

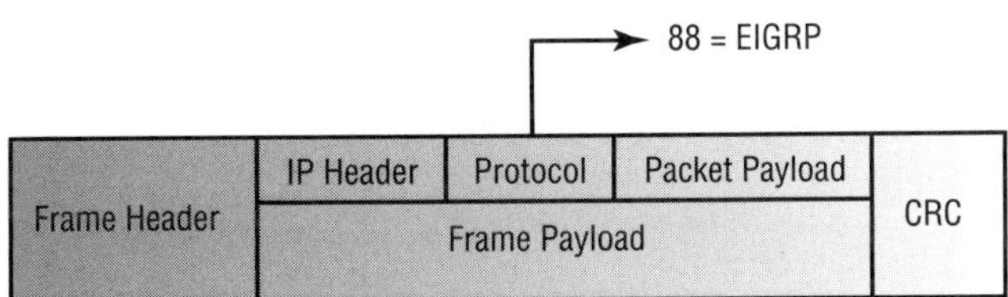

Updates can follow two paths. If a route update contains a better metric or a new route, the routers simply exchange the information. If the update contains information that a network is unavailable or that the metric is worse than before, an alternate path might need to be found. If the new metric is still better than the metric of the feasible successor, the entry will remain, and its metric will be adjusted. When a new path must be found, the router first searches the topology database for feasible successors. If no feasible successors are found, a query is multicast to all adjacent routers. Each router then responds to the query. Depending on how the router responds, different paths will be taken. After the intermediate steps are taken, either of two final actions can occur:

- If route information is eventually found, the route is added to the routing table, and an update is sent.
- If the responses from the adjacent routers do not contain route information, the route is removed from the topology and routing tables.

After the routing table has been updated, the new information is sent to all adjacent routers via multicast.

Reliable Transport Protocol (RTP) is the key to EIGRP routing updates. RTP allows for guaranteed delivery in sequential order of EIGRP routing updates.

EIGRP RTP multicasts Hello packets, queries, and update packets whenever possible. These multicast packets are sent to the well-known multicast address of 224.0.0.10. Unicast packets are always used for acknowledgments (ACKs), which are basically empty Hello packets, and replies. Unicast packets will also be used to send Hello packets for multipoint interfaces on X.25, Frame Relay, and ATM that have access speeds equal to or less than the speed of a T1. Hello packets are sent unreliably and never acknowledged.

EIGRP implements a unique mechanism known as *pacing* in order to prevent routing updates from consuming too much bandwidth on lower speed links. Pacing allows EIGRP to regulate the amount of traffic it sends to a portion of the interface's bandwidth. The traffic we're referring to is Hello packets, routing updates, queries, replies, and acknowledgments.

The default setting for pacing in EIGRP is 50 percent of the bandwidth on any given interface. This default setting can be adjusted with the following command in interface configuration mode:

```
ip bandwidth-percent eigrp as-number percent
      as-number = Autonomous System Number
      percent = percent of bandwidth EIGRP may use
```

This is an important command to configure if you have manipulated routing by changing the bandwidth statement. Note also that EIGRP will not sustain such utilization, but bursts could occasionally consume 100 percent of a link's bandwidth. This limitation is a safeguard against such occurrences.

Diffusing Update Algorithm

One last topic must be discussed in order for us to fully understand the EIGRP route calculation. That topic is the Diffusing Update Algorithm (DUAL). DUAL is the algorithm by which all computation of routes for EIGRP occurs. A full understanding of DUAL is beyond the scope of the BSCI exam, so we're only going to briefly discuss it here.

One of the biggest advantages of DUAL is how it speeds up convergence. It accomplishes this by not recalculating routes when it doesn't need to. Let's take a look at the way DUAL operates.

An EIGRP neighbor sends an update to a router informing the router that the metric for a route has changed or that there has been a topology change. At this point, the router looks for a better route. The router looks for a feasible successor to the destination that has a better metric than the new metric for the route. If a feasible successor is found, the router will immediately choose it as the new successor. The router will now increase its own metric and advertise it to its neighbors. If a feasible successor is not found, then DUAL will start recalculating to find a new successor.

There are three instances that causes DUAL to recalculate:

- An alternate route is not found.
- The new best route is still the original successor.
- The new best route is not a feasible successor.

When the recalculation begins, the router queries all its neighbors about the destination. The router then tracks the queries it has sent so it knows when all neighbors have replied.

When a neighbor receives a query, it first marks the route as unreachable and queries each of its neighbors—this is what is meant by *diffusing*. The neighbor then replies with one of the following six responses:

- The neighbor will reply with an infinite metric if it doesn't have any information about the destination.
- The neighbor will reply with its current best route if the route is already active.
- If the query is not from the neighbor in the path of a successor, the neighbor will reply with its current best route and the route will remain passive.
- If the neighbor in the path of a successor sent the query and the replying router doesn't have any other neighbors, it will reply with an infinite metric.
- The neighbor will reply with the new best route if it has multiple routes to the destination.
- If the neighbor has other neighbors besides the querying router, it will propagate the query to its other neighbors. When it doesn't have an alternate route, then the route is through the router that sent the query, or the route is not through a neighbor in the path of a feasible successor. The process then occurs on each of the routers receiving the propagated query.

Once the original querying router receives all replies from its neighbors, the router selects the new best route. The router then sends out a routing update with the new information.

An issue will occur if any of the neighbors do not reply to the query. If the active timer expires—which is set to three minutes by default—the router will declare the route stuck in active (SIA).

With all this in mind, you can now see how DUAL can cut down on the number of times it must recalculate routes. What this means for you is a faster converging network.

EIGRP Metrics

EIGRP utilizes several databases or tables of information to calculate routes. These databases are as follows:

- The route database (routing table) where the best routes are stored
- The topology database (topology table) where all route information resides
- A neighbor table that is used to house information concerning other EIGRP neighbors

Each of these databases exists separately for each routed protocol configured for EIGRP:

- The IP session is called IP-EIGRP.
- The IPX session is called IPX-EIGRP.
- The AppleTalk session is called AT-EIGRP.

Therefore, it is possible for EIGRP to have nine active databases when all three protocols are configured on the router, even more for multiple concurrently configured autonomous systems.

As stated previously, the metrics used by EIGRP are the same as those used by IGRP. As with IGRP, metrics decide how routes are selected. The higher the metric associated with a route, the less desirable the route is. The following equation is used by EIGRP to calculate the composite metric:

$$\text{metric} = [(K1 \times \text{bandwidth}) + [(K2 \times \text{bandwidth}) \div (256 - \text{load})] + (K3 \times \text{delay})] \times [K5 \div (\text{reliability} + K4)] \times 256$$

The elements in this equation are as follows:

- By default, K1 = K3 = 1, K2 = K4 = K5 = 0. Therefore, by default, the metric formula reduces to:

  $\text{metric} = (1 \times \text{bandwidth}) + (1 \times \text{delay}) \times 256$

  $\text{metric} = (\text{bandwidth} + \text{delay}) \times 256$
- Delay is computed as one-tenth the sum of all the measured delays, in microseconds, of the outbound interfaces of the links along the path, which is to say, the cumulative delay along the path in tens of microseconds.
- Bandwidth = [10000000 ÷ (BW in Kbps)]. BW is the lowest bandwidth of the links along the path.

Alternatively, the metric can be described as (bandwidth + delay) as long as

- Delay = [Delay in 10s of microseconds] × 256
- Bandwidth = [10000000 ÷ (BW in Kbps)] × 256

Just as with IGRP, you can set the metrics manually from within the configuration mode. One important thing to keep in mind when manually setting metrics is that in order for EIGRP routers to form neighbors, they must have the same K-values in the Hello packet. If the K-values are different, the routers will not form adjacencies with each other. With that in mind, let's take a look at how to tune these settings.

EIGRP Tuning

The metrics used with EIGRP are tuned in the same manner as the metrics for IGRP. Metrics are tuned to change the manner in which routes are calculated. The same command is used for IGRP and EIGRP. In order to enter the following command, you must be in router configuration mode:

```
metric weights tos K1 K2 K3 K4 K5
```

Each constant is used to assign a weight to a specific variable. This means that when the metric is calculated, the algorithm will assign a greater importance to the specified metric. By assigning a weight, you are able to specify what is most important. If bandwidth is of greatest concern to a network administrator, a greater weight should be assigned to *K1*. If delay is unacceptable, the *K2* constant should be assigned a greater weight. The `tos` variable is the type of service. Refer back to Table 4.2 for the relationship between the constant and the metric it affects. Also, remember that EIGRP uses only bandwidth and delay, by default, when calculating routes.

Other tuning is possible. All routing protocols have an administrative distance associated with the protocol type. If multiple protocols are running on one router, the administrative distance value helps the router decide which path is best. The protocol with the lower administrative distance will be chosen. EIGRP has a default administrative distance of 90 for internal routes and 170 for external routes. Use the following command, in router configuration mode, to make changes:

```
distance 1-255
```

Valid values for the administrative distance range from 1 to 255. Again, the lower the value, the better. If an administrative distance of 255 is chosen, routes will be considered unreachable and will be ignored.

When redistributing static routes or routes from other routing protocols into EIGRP, there are two options on how you can enter the metric for the redistributed routes. The first option is to set the metric for each instance of redistribution; that command will be covered in Chapter 10. The second option is to set a default metric for all redistributed routes. This gives you less granularity when setting metrics, but it is faster. The following command, when entered in router configuration mode, sets the default metric:

```
default-metric bandwidth delay reliability load MTU
    bandwidth = a value between 0 and 4,294,967,295 (in Kbps)
    delay = a value between 0 and 4,294,967,295 (in 10-microsecond units)
    reliability = a range from 0 to 255 (255 is the most reliable)
    load = range from 0 to 255 (255 means the link is completely loaded)
    MTU = a value between 0 and 4,294,967,295
```

EIGRP allows you to set the value for Hello intervals and holddown timers on a per-interface basis. Remember, it's safer to leave the default settings for the timers. Adjusting timers can cause your internetwork to react in unexpected ways. In order to set the Hello interval, you must first decide which interface to set it on. After navigating to interface configuration mode for the selected interface, the following command needs to be entered:

```
ip hello-interval eigrp AS# seconds
    AS# = the EIGRP autonomous system number
    seconds = the amount of time, in seconds, for the Hello interval.
```

The default setting for the Hello interval is 60 seconds for low-speed NBMA networks and 5 seconds for all other networks.

The hold time is the amount of time a router will wait to receive a Hello packet before it marks all of the routes from the neighbor as unavailable. The hold time default is three times the Hello interval. As a rule of thumb, the hold time should always be set to three times the Hello interval.

As in setting the Hello interval, you must set it on an interface. After you have selected the interface and navigated to interface configuration mode, enter the following command:

```
ip hold-time eigrp AS# seconds
    AS# = the EIGRP autonomous system number
    seconds = the amount of time, in seconds, for the hold time.
```

In this section, we explained EIGRP metrics and how to fine-tune EIGRP. We will now take a look at redistribution for EIGRP at a high level.

Redistribution for EIGRP

This section briefly covers redistribution for EIGRP. Redistribution is covered in depth in Chapter 10. At a high level, there are really only a few concepts that you need to keep in mind about redistributing EIGRP.

The first concept you need to know about redistributing EIGRP is that EIGRP is a classless routing protocol. What this means is that if another routing protocol is being redistributed into EIGRP, you don't need to worry about the issue of VLSM. EIGRP accepts routes that have implemented VLSM and routes that haven't implemented VLSM.

The problem arises when EIGRP is redistributed into a classful routing protocol. If VLSM has been implemented in the EIGRP domain, routes utilizing VLSM will not be redistributed to the classful routing protocol. The way to overcome this issue is to summarize the routes you want to redistribute at the classful IP address boundaries, or at least at boundaries known to the receiving router.

The other concept you need to be familiar with is that of automatic redistribution between EIGRP and IGRP. The only time this will occur is when both EIGRP and IGRP reference the same AS number and have at least one router on which both are running. With any other routing protocol, whether it be IGRP with a different AS number or another EIGRP AS, manual configuration of redistribution will be required.

Let's put all this new understanding of EIGRP to use and learn how to implement it.

Configuring EIGRP

The basic configuration of EIGRP is very similar to IGRP. To initialize EIGRP on the router, you need to enter the following command in global configuration mode:

```
router eigrp AS#
    AS# = any value between 1 and 65,535
```

Once you have initialized EIGRP on the router, you need to specify the interfaces you want to include in the EIGRP AS process. In order to accomplish this, the following command needs to be entered in router configuration mode:

```
network A.B.C.D
    A.B.C.D = network number
```

In IOS version 12.0(4)T, Cisco started allowing the wildcard mask to be entered along with the network address. A wildcard mask is an inverted subnet mask. In other words, for every value of 1 in a subnet mask, the value for the same bit in the wildcard mask would be 0.

This may get a little confusing since EIGRP is a classless routing protocol. In IOS versions that do not allow you to enter the wildcard mask with the `network` command, the network address entered must be of classful boundaries. This can cause a problem. When entering a classful network address, you could possibly end up adding interfaces to EIGRP that you do not want participating in EIGRP.

This type of scenario could arise when you are running another routing protocol over one of your WAN connections and the interface participating in that connection is in the same classful network range as an interface participating in the EIGRP AS. What happens is that the interface on the WAN connection will send unneeded routing updates over the WAN connection. This will not break anything, but it will use bandwidth.

The way to overcome this is to use the `passive-interface` command. This command allows an interface's subnet to be advertised in EIGRP updates but does not allow the interface to send or receive them. You need to enter the following command under the routing protocol process in router configuration mode to configure an interface as a passive-interface:

```
passive-interface interface
   interface = the interface you don't want to send or receive EIGRP updates.
```

One important concept you must be aware of is that EIGRP by default automatically summarizes routes at the classful network boundary when the route crosses the classful network boundaries. This enables EIGRP to easily work in conjunction with RIPv1 and IGRP. There are times when you would prefer to have all subnets from classful networks advertised. The following command needs to be entered in router configuration mode to disable automatic summarization of routes:

```
no auto-summary
```

If you ever desire to turn automatic summarization back on, you just need to enter this command without the `no` in front of it.

Now that we have an understanding of how to configure basic EIGRP, let's take a look at Figure 4.6.

For this exercise, you can assume that none of the routers are running a version of IOS that supports the wildcard mask's addition to the network statement. Also, the layer 2 technology has already been configured. With that in mind, let's walk through the configuration of these devices.

The configuration for the network would occur as follows:

```
Dallas>enable
Dallas#configure terminal
Dallas(config)#router eigrp 100
```

```
Dallas(config-router)#network 172.20.0.0
Dallas(config-router)#network 192.168.24.0

Richardson>enable
Richardson#configure terminal
Richardson(config)#router eigrp 100
Richardson(config-router)#network 192.168.24.0

Ft_Worth>enable
Ft_Worth#configure terminal
Ft_Worth(config)#router eigrp 100
Ft_Worth(config-router)#network 172.20.0.0

Plano>enable
Plano#configure terminal
Plano(config)#router eigrp 100
Plano(config-router)#network 172.20.0.0
```

FIGURE 4.6 Configuring basic EIGRP operation

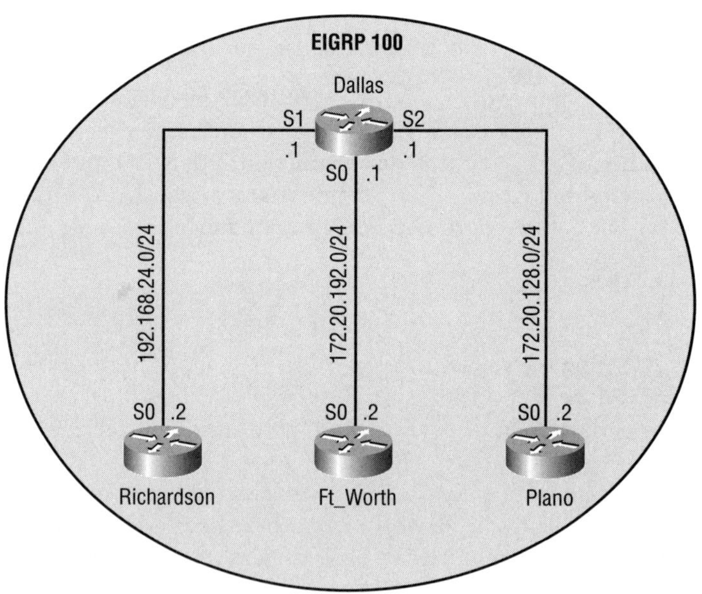

Now that we have configured the network for EIGRP, let's take a look at the routing table to verify it has all the routes it needs:

```
Richardson#show ip route
Codes: C - connected, S - static, I - IGRP, R - RIP, M - mobile, B - BGP
       D - EIGRP, EX - EIGRP external, O - OSPF, IA - OSPF inter area
       N1 - OSPF NSSA external type 1, N2 - OSPF NSSA external type 2
       E1 - OSPF external type 1, E2 - OSPF external type 2, E - EGP
       i - IS-IS, L1 - IS-IS level-1, L2 - IS-IS level-2, * - candidate default
       U - per-user static route, o - ODR

Gateway of last resort is not set

C     192.168.24.0/24 is directly connected, Serial0
D     172.20.0.0/16 [90/2297856] via 192.168.24.1, 00:00:02, Serial0
```

Richardson is displaying one route to network 172.20.0.0. The reason Richardson is displaying one route for the network, and you know the network has been broken down into two subnets, is because of default automatic summarization. In order for Richardson to see two routes advertised, we need to disable automatic summarization on Dallas:

```
Dallas>enable
Dallas#configure terminal
Dallas(config)#router eigrp 100
Dallas(config-router)#no auto-summary
```

Now that we have disabled automatic summarization, let's take a look at Richardson's routing table:

```
Richardson#show ip route
Codes: C - connected, S - static, I - IGRP, R - RIP, M - mobile, B - BGP
       D - EIGRP, EX - EIGRP external, O - OSPF, IA - OSPF inter area
       N1 - OSPF NSSA external type 1, N2 - OSPF NSSA external type 2
       E1 - OSPF external type 1, E2 - OSPF external type 2, E - EGP
       i - IS-IS, L1 - IS-IS level-1, L2 - IS-IS level-2, * - candidate default
       U - per-user static route, o - ODR

Gateway of last resort is not set

C     192.168.24.0/24 is directly connected, Serial0
      172.20.0.0/24 is subnetted, 2 subnets
D        172.20.128.0 [90/2297856] via 192.168.24.1, 00:00:02, Serial0
D        172.20.192.0 [90/2297856] via 192.168.24.1, 00:00:02, Serial0
```

There is one other way you can handle summarizing ranges in EIGRP. You can use the following command, in interface configuration mode, to create summary addresses that are not at the classful boundary. This is a very useful tool in large internetworks:

```
ip summary-address eigrp AS# address mask
     AS# = the eigrp autonomous system number.
     address = the summary aggregate address to apply to an interface.
     mask = subnet mask
```

With this in mind, we will summarize 172.20.128.0/24 and 172.20.192.0/24 on Dallas into the summary address of 172.20.128.0/17. We need to enter the summary command on interface S1 of Dallas:

```
Dallas>enable
Dallas#configure terminal
Dallas(config)#interface S1
Dallas(config-if)#ip summary-address eigrp 100 172.20.128.0 255.255.128.0
```

Now let's take a look at the routing table on Richardson to verify the summary address:

```
Richardson#show ip route
Codes: C - connected, S - static, I - IGRP, R - RIP, M - mobile, B - BGP
      D - EIGRP, EX - EIGRP external, O - OSPF, IA - OSPF inter area
      N1 - OSPF NSSA external type 1, N2 - OSPF NSSA external type 2
      E1 - OSPF external type 1, E2 - OSPF external type 2, E - EGP
      i - IS-IS, L1 - IS-IS level-1, L2 - IS-IS level-2, * - candidate default
      U - per-user static route, o - ODR

Gateway of last resort is not set

C     192.168.24.0/24 is directly connected, Serial0
      172.20.0.0/17 is subnetted, 1 subnets
D        172.20.128.0 [90/2297856] via 192.168.24.1, 00:01:04, Serial0
```

As you can see, configuration of EIGRP is a straightforward process. Now that you know how to configure EIGRP, we need to take a look at how to verify proper operation of EIGRP and how to troubleshoot it if it isn't operating properly.

Unlike IGRP, EIGRP supports update authentication. This topic is not covered in this study guide because it is beyond the scope of the BSCI exam. However, it's something we believe you need to be aware of.

Verifying and Troubleshooting EIGRP

Now that you know how to configure EIGRP, let's focus on how to verify that it is operating correctly and, if not, how to troubleshoot it. Unlike IGRP, EIGRP has more tools available for verification and troubleshooting.

Route Information

The routing table provides you with information about how the router is routing. In order to view the routing table, you need to enter the following command in privileged EXEC mode:

```
Dallas#show ip route
Codes: C - connected, S - static, I - IGRP, R - RIP, M - mobile, B - BGP
       D - EIGRP, EX - EIGRP external, O - OSPF, IA - OSPF inter area
       N1 - OSPF NSSA external type 1, N2 - OSPF NSSA external type 2
       E1 - OSPF external type 1, E2 - OSPF external type 2, E - EGP
       i - IS-IS, L1 - IS-IS level-1, L2 - IS-IS level-2, ia - IS-IS inter area
       * - candidate default, U - per-user static route, o - ODR
       P - periodic downloaded static route

Gateway of last resort is not set

C    192.168.24.0/24 is directly connected, Loopback0
     20.0.0.0/24 is subnetted, 1 subnets
D       20.20.20.0 [90/1889792] via 10.10.10.1, 00:00:08, Serial2/0.1
     10.0.0.0/24 is subnetted, 1 subnets
C       10.10.10.0 is directly connected, Serial2/0.1
```

As can be seen from the routing table, you have one route that you've learned from EIGRP. You will know the routes learned from EIGRP from the code of `D` in front of the route line. If you would like to only view routes learned by EIGRP, the following command may be used:

```
Dallas#sh ip route eigrp
     20.0.0.0/24 is subnetted, 1 subnets
D       20.20.20.0 [90/1889792] via 10.10.10.1, 00:07:31, Serial2/0.1
```

The routing table doesn't give you detailed information about the routes the router has learned. To view detailed information about a route, the following command, with the appropriate destination attached, needs to be entered in privileged EXEC mode:

```
Dallas#show ip route 20.20.20.0
Routing entry for 20.20.20.0/24
  Known via "eigrp 100", distance 90, metric 1889792, type internal
  Redistributing via eigrp 100
  Last update from 10.10.10.1 on Serial2/0.1, 00:02:41 ago
```

```
  Routing Descriptor Blocks:
  * 10.10.10.1, from 10.10.10.1, 00:02:41 ago, via Serial2/0.1
      Route metric is 1889792, traffic share count is 1
      Total delay is 25000 microseconds, minimum bandwidth is 2048 Kbit
      Reliability 255/255, minimum MTU 1500 bytes
      Loading 1/255, Hops 1
```

This command can give you quite a bit of detail about a particular route. The most important information you can learn from this command is the details of the composite metric for the particular route. The command informs you what the bandwidth, delay, reliability, and load are for the particular route.

The routing table displays only the best routes to a destination. In order to view all routes to a destination, you need to view the EIGRP topology table.

In order to view the EIGRP topology table, the following command can be entered to list all successors and feasible successors for destinations:

```
Dallas#show ip eigrp topology
IP-EIGRP Topology Table for AS(100)/ID(192.168.24.1)

Codes: P - Passive, A - Active, U - Update, Q - Query, R - Reply,
       r - reply Status, s - sia Status

P 10.10.10.0/24, 1 successors, FD is 1761792
         via Connected, Serial2/0.1
P 20.20.20.0/24, 1 successors, FD is 1889792
         via 10.10.10.1 (1889792/128256), Serial2/0.1
P 192.168.24.0/24, 1 successors, FD is 128256
         via Connected, Loopback0
```

Numerous qualifiers can be added to the end of this command in order to list different information about the EIGRP topology table. For example, you would enter the `show ip eigrp topology` command, with the appropriate route attached, in order to view detailed topology information about a route:

```
Dallas#show ip eigrp topology 192.168.24.0
IP-EIGRP topology entry for 192.168.24.0/24
  State is Passive, Query origin flag is 1, 1 Successor(s), FD is 128256
  Routing Descriptor Blocks:
  0.0.0.0 (Loopback0), from Connected, Send flag is 0x0
      Composite metric is (128256/0), Route is Internal
      Vector metric:
        Minimum bandwidth is 10000000 Kbit
        Total delay is 5000 microseconds
        Reliability is 255/255
```

```
    Load is 1/255
    Minimum MTU is 1514
    Hop count is 0
```

This command gives you detailed information about the composite metric of a route. Knowing this information helps you understand why one particular route is preferred over another.

Routing Protocol Information

In order to view how particular routing protocols are configured on the router, the following command can be entered in privileged EXEC mode:

```
Dallas#show ip protocols
Routing Protocol is "eigrp 100"
  Outgoing update filter list for all interfaces is
  Incoming update filter list for all interfaces is
  Default networks flagged in outgoing updates
  Default networks accepted from incoming updates
  EIGRP metric weight K1=1, K2=0, K3=1, K4=0, K5=0
  EIGRP maximum hopcount 100
  EIGRP maximum metric variance 1
  Redistributing: eigrp 100
  Automatic network summarization is not in effect
  Routing for Networks:
    10.0.0.0
    192.168.24.0
  Routing Information Sources:
    Gateway         Distance      Last Update
    10.10.10.1            90      00:01:07
  Distance: internal 90 external 170
```

The preceding output informs you that EIGRP 100 is configured on the router; that no incoming or outgoing filters have been set; what the K-values, the maximum hop count for EIGRP, and the variance are; that automatic summarization is not in use; and the routes that the router is advertising for EIGRP 100.

The following command allows you to view a summary of all the interfaces on the routers that are participating in EIGRP:

```
Dallas#show ip eigrp interfaces
IP-EIGRP interfaces for process 100

                    Xmit Queue   Mean   Pacing Time   Multicast    Pending
Interface    Peers  Un/Reliable  SRTT   Un/Reliable   Flow Timer   Routes
Se2/0.1        1        0/0       717       0/11         3559         0
Lo0            0        0/0         0       0/10            0         0
```

In this output, you see that on the Dallas router, both interface Serial 2/0.1 and interface Loopback 0 are participating in EIGRP 100.

Viewing Neighbor Information

Knowing what's going on between the router and its neighbor can be a very useful tool in verifying and troubleshooting the operation of EIGRP. The following command displays all of the routers with which the router has formed neighbor relationships:

```
Dallas#show ip eigrp neighbor
IP-EIGRP neighbors for process 100
H   Address                 Interface   Hold Uptime   SRTT   RTO  Q  Seq Type
                                        (sec)         (ms)       Cnt Num
0   10.10.10.1              Se2/0.1       13 00:09:36  717  4302  0  2
```

The show ip eigrp neighbor command lists only a summary of the router's neighbors. In order to view more detailed information about the neighbors, you can add the detail keyword to the end of the command line:

```
Dallas#show ip eigrp neighbor detail
IP-EIGRP neighbors for process 100
H   Address                 Interface   Hold Uptime   SRTT   RTO  Q  Seq Type
                                        (sec)         (ms)       Cnt Num
0   10.10.10.1              Se2/0.1       12 00:10:05  717  4302  0  2
   Version 12.0/1.0, Retrans: 0, Retries: 0
```

As you can see, this command also displays the number of retransmissions that have occurred and the number of retries for a packet currently being sent to the neighbor.

You can also enter a command that will allow any changes that occur to a neighbor to be logged. The command to accomplish this is eigrp log-neighbor-changes and it must be entered in router configuration mode. With this command, the following logs are generated:

```
16:01:31: %DUAL-5-NBRCHANGE: IP-EIGRP 100: Neighbor 10.10.10.1 (Serial2/0.1) is
  up: new adjacency
```

The preceding log informs you that the router has formed a new adjacency with 10.10.10.1.

```
16:02:33: %DUAL-5-NBRCHANGE: IP-EIGRP 100: Neighbor 10.10.10.1 (Serial2/0.1) is
  down: holding time expired
```

The preceding log informs you that the router has lost the adjacency with 10.10.10.1.

You can also view neighbor information with the debug eigrp neighbors command. This command also informs you when new neighbors are discovered and when current neighbors are lost. As with IGRP, in order to view debug information, you must configure logging. Note, however, that `logging console debugging` is enabled by default. Here is an example of the output of the `debug eigrp neighbors` command:

```
Dallas#debug eigrp neighbors
EIGRP Neighbors debugging is on
15:54:10: EIGRP: Holdtime expired
15:54:10: EIGRP: Neighbor 10.10.10.1 went down on Serial2/0.1
15:54:13: EIGRP: New peer 10.10.10.1
```

All of the commands described so far give information about EIGRP on the particular router and information about its neighbors. This is important information, but if a route is not there that should be or a neighbor relationship hasn't been formed that you believe should have, all the commands covered so far might not give you the detailed information needed to resolve the issue. The next section explains how to view and interpret the EIGRP information being sent between routers.

Viewing EIGRP Packets

Viewing the routing updates your router is sending and receiving is an invaluable tool. The following `debug` commands will give you a step-by-step account of what is happening between your router and its neighbors.

```
Dallas#debug ip eigrp
IP-EIGRP Route Events debugging is on
16:04:19: IP-EIGRP: 10.10.10.0/24 - do advertise out Serial2/0.1
16:04:19: IP-EIGRP: 192.168.24.0/24 - do advertise out Serial2/0.1
16:04:19: IP-EIGRP: Int 192.168.24.0/24 metric 128256 - 256 128000
16:04:19: IP-EIGRP: Processing incoming UPDATE packet
16:04:19: IP-EIGRP: Int 20.20.20.0/24 M 1889792 - 1249792 640000 SM 128256 -
  ➥256 128000
16:04:19: IP-EIGRP: Int 20.20.20.0/24 metric 1889792 - 1249792 640000
16:04:19: IP-EIGRP: Processing incoming UPDATE packet
16:04:19: IP-EIGRP: Int 192.168.24.0/24 M 4294967295 - 1657856 4294967295
  ➥SM 429 4967295 - 1657856 4294967295
```

The `debug ip eigrp` command allows you to view the routing updates sent between the router and its neighbors. The information contained is the routes and their corresponding metric the router has received along with what routes the router is going to send out and the interface that will advertise the route. Recall that the value 4,294,967,295 represents infinity for IGRP and EIGRP, thus an unreachable advertisement.

The `debug eigrp packets` command can be used to view the following types of packets sent between the router and its neighbors:

- Hello
- Update
- Request

- Query
- Reply

The update and query messages are all considered reliable EIGRP messages. This means that the receiving router must send back an acknowledgment to the message.

Here's an example of the output of the `debug eigrp packets` command:

```
Dallas#debug eigrp packets
EIGRP Packets debugging is on
   (UPDATE, REQUEST, QUERY, REPLY, HELLO, IPXSAP, PROBE, ACK, STUB,
     ➥SIAQUERY, SIAREPLY)
Dallas#
16:07:43: EIGRP: Received HELLO on Serial2/0.1 nbr 10.10.10.1
16:07:43:   AS 100, Flags 0x0, Seq 0/0 idbQ 0/0 iidbQ un/rely 0/0 peerQ
  ➥un/rely 0/0
16:07:43: EIGRP: Sending HELLO on Loopback0
16:07:43:   AS 100, Flags 0x0, Seq 0/0 idbQ 0/0 iidbQ un/rely 0/0
16:07:43: EIGRP: Received HELLO on Loopback0 nbr 192.168.24.1
16:07:43:   AS 100, Flags 0x0, Seq 0/0 idbQ 0/0
16:07:43: EIGRP: Packet from ourselves ignored
16:07:44: EIGRP: Sending HELLO on Serial2/0.1
16:07:44:   AS 100, Flags 0x0, Seq 0/0 idbQ 0/0 iidbQ un/rely 0/0
16:07:47: EIGRP: Received HELLO on Serial2/0.1 nbr 10.10.10.1
16:07:47:   AS 100, Flags 0x0, Seq 0/0 idbQ 0/0 iidbQ un/rely 0/0 peerQ
  ➥un/rely 0/0
```

You can also view the number of EIGRP packets sent and received on the router. The `show ip eigrp traffic` command displays the number of packets sent and received for each of these packet types:

- Hello
- Update
- Query
- Reply
- ACKs

The next example shows the output for the `show ip eigrp traffic` command:

```
Dallas#show ip eigrp traffic
IP-EIGRP Traffic Statistics for process 100
  Hellos sent/received: 632/622
  Updates sent/received: 19/18
```

```
Queries sent/received: 0/0
Replies sent/received: 0/0
Acks sent/received: 8/11
```

There is one more command I'm going to explain. The `show ip eigrp events` command is an undocumented command. This command displays a log of every EIGRP event—when routes are injected and removed from the routing table and when EIGRP adjacencies reset or fail. This information can be used to see if there are routing instabilities in the network. Here's an example of the output from this command:

```
Dallas#show ip eigrp events
Event information for AS 100:
1    16:14:45.007 Poison squashed: 192.168.24.0/24 reverse
2    16:14:44.967 Change queue emptied, entries: 1
3    16:14:44.967 Metric set: 20.20.20.0/24 1889792
4    16:14:44.967 Update reason, delay: new if 4294967295
5    16:14:44.967 Update sent, RD: 20.20.20.0/24 4294967295
6    16:14:44.967 Update reason, delay: metric chg 4294967295
7    16:14:44.967 Update sent, RD: 20.20.20.0/24 4294967295
8    16:14:44.967 Route install: 20.20.20.0/24 10.10.10.1
9    16:14:44.967 Find FS: 20.20.20.0/24 4294967295
10   16:14:44.967 Rcv update met/succmet: 1889792 128256
11   16:14:44.967 Rcv update dest/nh: 20.20.20.0/24 10.10.10.1
12   16:14:44.967 Metric set: 20.20.20.0/24 4294967295
13   16:14:42.059 Peer up: 10.10.10.1 Serial2/0.1
14   16:14:39.963 Peer down end, handle: 0
15   16:14:39.963 NDB delete: 20.20.20.0/24 1
16   16:14:39.963 Poison squashed: 20.20.20.0/24 rt gone
17   16:14:39.963 RDB delete: 20.20.20.0/24 10.10.10.1
18   16:14:39.963 Not active net/1=SH: 20.20.20.0/24 0
19   16:14:39.963 FC not sat Dmin/met: 4294967295 1889792
20   16:14:39.963 Find FS: 20.20.20.0/24 1889792
21   16:14:39.963 Peer down: 10.10.10.1 Serial2/0.1
```

As I stated at the beginning of this section, there are many tools available for verifying and troubleshooting EIGRP. Remember, the tools covered here are not the only ones. I know all this information can be overwhelming at first, but with time and practice it will become second nature.

Summary

Was that some cool information or what? EIGRP is a Cisco proprietary routing protocol. Guess what that means? It means if you have a multi-vendor network, you're probably not going to want to use EIGRP.

So if you can't use it in a multi-vendor environment, why would you want to use it at all? EIGRP provides the best of both distance-vector and link-state routing protocols. That's right—EIGRP is a hybrid routing protocol. EIGRP, unlike other routing protocols, allows for unequal-cost load balancing. That means that EIGRP can use multiple links to load balance information across, even if the links do not have the same cost.

Another big draw to EIGRP is its ease of configuration. When using EIGRP, you need to determine what autonomous system number you want to use. This number needs to be the same on all the routers you want sharing the routing information. Once you've made this determination, you are ready to start configuring EIGRP.

In order to configure EIGRP, you first need to enable it on the device. Once you've enabled EIGRP on the device, you then need to specify the networks on the router you want participating in EIGRP. It's important to remember that the network statement in EIGRP doesn't tell EIGRP which network to advertise. What the network statement does do is to tell EIGRP which interfaces to allow to participate in EIGRP. EIGRP then looks at the network address and mask that the interface belongs to and advertises that network address and mask.

Congratulations! You have now made it through EIGRP. EIGRP will be on the BSCI exam; however, IGRP will not. Even though IGRP is not covered on the exam, it is still important to know in order to understand EIGRP. Remember, EIGRP is simply an enhancement to IGRP.

Exam Essentials

Know the key differences between IGRP and EIGRP. There are two key differences between IGRP and EIGRP: IGRP is a classful pure distance-vector routing protocol and EIGRP is a classless hybrid distance-vector routing protocol. Classful routing protocols do not send subnet mask information in their routing updates, whereas classless routing protocols do send subnet mask information.

Understand how DUAL operates. When EIGRP learns the network topology, it will run the DUAL algorithm to determine the best route to a destination. This best route becomes the successor route. Other routes to the same destination that have an advertised distance less than the feasible distance of the successor route will become feasible successor routes. DUAL will not run again until all the routes to the destination are lost.

Understand how to configure EIGRP. One of the most attractive features of EIGRP is its ease of configuration. To configure EIGRP, you first need to enable it on the device with the `router eigrp` *`as#`* command. Next you need to specify the interfaces to participate in EIGRP with the `network` command. That's all there is to basic EIGRP configuration.

Understand how to verify and troubleshoot proper operation of EIGRP. After the configuration of the network, you should be able to verify proper operation of EIGRP. You can still use the standard verification commands such as `show ip route` and `show ip protocols`. In addition to those commands, such EIGRP specific commands as `show ip eigrp traffic` and `show ip egrp events` can be used.

OSPF Operation in a Single Area

THE CCNP EXAM TOPICS COVERED IN THIS CHAPTER INCLUDE THE FOLLOWING:

- ✓ Understand how OSPF operates in a single area.
- ✓ Understand how to configure OSPF in a single area.
- ✓ Identify the steps to verify OSPF operation in a single area.
- ✓ When route selection and configuration problems occur, understand how to use the various show and debug commands to determine the cause of the problem.

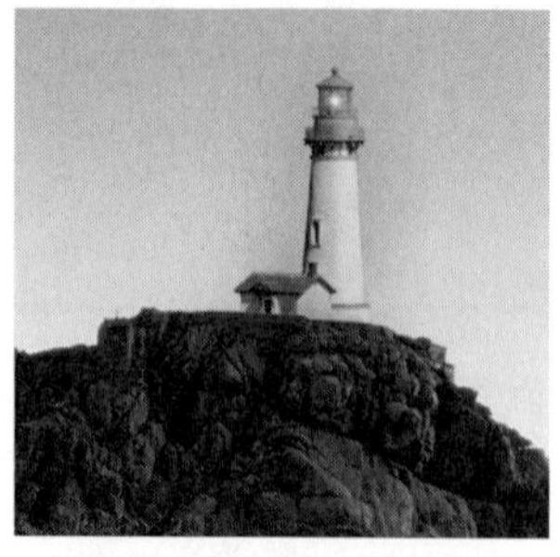

This chapter is the introduction to Open Shortest Path First (OSPF) areas. It introduces the term *OSPF areas* and discusses the role of OSPF areas in OSPF routing. It's very important that you take the time to learn the terminology used in OSPF. Without this knowledge, the remaining sections of the chapter will be difficult to follow.

Open Shortest Path First

Open Shortest Path First (OSPF) is an open standards routing protocol. It is important to recognize that Cisco's implementation of OSPF is a standards-based version. This means that Cisco based its version of OSPF on the open standards. While doing so, Cisco has also added features to its version of OSPF that may not be found in other implementations of OSPF. This becomes important when interoperability is needed.

OSPF has become one of the most widely used routing protocols in existence today because of the ability to implement it across multi-vendor platforms. OSPF utilizes Dijkstra's Shortest Path First (SPF) algorithm, which allows for faster network convergence. The popularity of OSPF is continuing to grow with the advent of Multi-Protocol Label Switching (MPLS). Currently, the only routing protocols MPLS traffic engineering has extensions for are OSPF and IS-IS.

John Moy heads up the working group of OSPF. Two RFCs define OSPF: Version 1 is defined by RFC 1131, and Version 2 is defined by RFC 2328. Version 2 is the only version to make it to an operational status. However, many vendors modify OSPF. OSPF is known as a link-state routing protocol (link-state routing protocols were discussed in Chapter 1, "Routing Principles"). The Dijkstra algorithm is used to calculate the shortest path through the network. Within OSPF, links become synonymous with interfaces.

Some of the advantages of OSPF are as follows:

- Support of hierarchical network design through the use of areas.
- The use of link-state databases reduces the chances of routing loops.
- Full support of classless routing behavior.
- Decreased size in routing tables through the use of manual route summarization. Automatic route summarization is not supported by OSPF.
- Routing updates are sent only when the information is needed, decreasing the use of network bandwidth for routing updates.
- Utilization of multicast packets decreases the impact on routers not running OSPF and end stations.
- Support of authentication, which allows the user to implement more secure networks.

OSPF is a robust protocol, and due to its robustness, you must learn many terms in order to understand the operation of OSPF. The next section covers the terminology necessary to enable you to understand the many operations and procedures performed by the OSPF process.

OSPF Terminology

The most basic of terms that are related to OSPF are related to many routing protocols. We begin by defining relationships among routers. From there, we will move on to defining terms relating to OSPF operations.

Neighbor A neighbor refers to a connected (physically adjacent) router that is running an OSPF process with the adjoining interface assigned to the same area. Neighbors are found via Hello packets. No routing information is exchanged with neighbors unless adjacencies are formed.

Adjacency An adjacency refers to the logical connection between a router and its corresponding designated routers and backup designated routers or its point-to-point neighbor. The formation of this type of relationship depends heavily on the type of network that connects the OSPF routers. On point-to-point connections, the two routers will form adjacencies with each other without requiring a designated router. Not all neighbors become adjacent.

Link In OSPF, a link refers to a network or router interface assigned to any given network. Within OSPF, link is synonymous with interface.

Interface The interface is a physical or logical interface on a router. When an interface is added to the OSPF process, it is considered by OSPF as a link. If the interface is up, then the link is up. OSPF uses this association to build its link database.

Link-state advertisement *Link-state advertisement (LSA)* is an OSPF data packet containing link-state and routing information that is shared among OSPF routers. LSAs are covered in detail in Chapter 6, "Interconnecting OSPF Areas."

Designated router A *designated router (DR)* is used only when the OSPF router is connected to a broadcast (multi-access) network. To minimize the number of adjacencies formed, a DR is chosen to disseminate/receive routing information to/from the remaining routers on the broadcast network or link.

Backup designated router A *backup designated router (BDR)* is a hot standby for the DR on broadcast (multi-access) networks. The BDR receives all routing updates from OSPF adjacent routers but does not flood LSA updates.

OSPF areas *OSPF areas* often map to network or subnet boundaries. Areas are used to establish a hierarchical network. OSPF uses four types of areas, all of which are discussed later in this chapter.

Internal router An internal router is a router that has all of its interfaces participating in one area.

Area border router An *area border router (ABR)* is a router that has multiple area assignments. An interface may belong to only one area. If a router has multiple interfaces and if any of these interfaces belong to different areas, the router is considered an ABR.

Autonomous system boundary router An *autonomous system boundary router (ASBR)* is a router with an interface connected to an external network or to a different AS. An external network or autonomous system refers to an interface belonging to a different routing protocol such as EIGRP. An ASBR is responsible for injecting route information learned by other routing protocols into OSPF.

Non-broadcast multi-access *Non-broadcast multi-access (NBMA)* networks are networks such as Frame Relay, X.25, and ATM. This type of network is one of two NBMA network types, along with point-to-multipoint. NBMA networks allow for multi-access but have no broadcast ability, unlike Ethernet. They require special OSPF configuration to function properly. Specifically, you must manually define neighbors, due to the non-broadcast characteristic, but a DR and a BDR will be elected, due to the multi-access nature of the network. In order for such elections to work, however, the network must be arranged in a full-mesh configuration.

Broadcast (multi-access) Networks such as Ethernet allow concurrent access, as well as provide broadcast ability. A DR and BDR will be elected for multi-access networks, and neighbors will be discovered automatically for broadcast networks. This network type is a Cisco-proprietary implementation.

Be aware that Cisco often uses the stand-alone, standards-based term *broadcast* to refer to a *broadcast multi-access* network. It is imperative that you realize this fact in order to understand the properties of the broadcast network type discussed here and later in this chapter, because some of the characteristics are due to the multi-access—not broadcast—nature of these networks. For example, the ability to automatically discover neighbors and the propensity to multicast Hellos and updates ties to the broadcast properties, but it is the multi-access characteristic that leads to the election of a DR. This latter behavior exists for non-broadcast multi-access (NBMA) networks, as well. Note that the two network types share the multi-access characteristic, not the ability to send broadcasts.

Point-to-point Leased-line circuits are examples of OSPF point-to-point networks, by default. For NBMA networks, this type of network connection consists of a Cisco-proprietary configuration. The network can be configured on Frame Relay and ATM circuits to allow point-to-point connectivity. This configuration eliminates the need for a DR and BDR.

Point-to-multipoint This type of connection is the other type of NBMA network and treats each of the router interconnections as point-to-point links, not electing a DR and BDR and not requiring a full-mesh configuration. Cisco offers both a proprietary broadcast and standards-based non-broadcast option for this type of network. As a result, automatic neighbor detection relies on which of these you choose. Alternatively, Inverse ARP may be used for neighbor discovery, which is outside of the responsibility of OSPF.

Router ID The router ID is an IP address that is used to identify the router. Cisco chooses the configured router ID, if one is configured. If a router ID is not configured, the router ID will be the highest IP address of all configured loopback interfaces. If no loopback addresses are configured, OSPF will choose the highest IP address of all configured physical interfaces on the router.

All of these terms play an important part in understanding the operation of OSPF. You must know and understand each of these terms. As you read through this chapter, you will be able to place the terms in their proper context.

OSPF Operation

OSPF operation can be divided into three categories:

- Neighbor and adjacency initialization
- LSA flooding
- SPF tree calculation

We will discuss each in the following sections. Before we discuss these three categories in more detail, let's first take a look at the basic step-by-step operation of OSPF:

- OSPF routers send Hello packets out all interfaces participating in the OSPF process. If the router and the router on the other side of the connection agree on the parameters set forth in the Hello packet, the routers will form neighbor relationships.
- Some of the neighbors will form adjacencies. Forming adjacencies is dependent upon the type of network the Hello packet is being sent across and the types of routers exchanging the Hello packets.
- The routers will send link-state advertisements (LSAs), which contain descriptions of the router's links and the state of each link to the adjacent router.
- The routers that receive the LSAs will then record the information into their link-state database and forward the LSAs on to their respective neighbors. This allows all routers participating in the OSPF process to have the same view of the network, although from their own perspective.
- After learning all LSAs, each router will run the Dijkstra SPF algorithm to learn the shortest path to all the known destinations. Each router uses this information to create its SPF tree. The information contained in the SPF tree is then used to populate the routing table.

Now that you have a basic understanding of how OSPF operates, let's take a more in-depth look at each of the three categories previously mentioned.

Neighbor and Adjacency Initialization

Neighbor/adjacency formation is a very big part of OSPF operation. These relationships are often easily formed over point-to-point connections, but much more complex procedures are required when multiple OSPF routers are connected via a broadcast multi-access medium.

The Hello protocol is used to discover neighbors and establish adjacencies. Hello packets contain a great deal of information regarding the originating router. Hello packets are multicast or unicast out every interface on a 10-second interval for point-to-point and broadcast multi-access interfaces and on a 30-second interval for NBMA interfaces, by default. The data contained in the Hello packet can be seen in Table 5.1. It is important to remember that the router ID, area ID, and authentication information are carried in the common OSPF header. The Hello packet uses the common OSPF header.

TABLE 5.1 OSPF Hello Packet Information

Originating Router Characteristic	Description
Router ID	The configured router ID. If one is not configured, the highest active IP address on the router. (Loopback addresses are used first. If no loopback interfaces are configured, OSPF will choose from physical and logical interfaces.)
Area ID	The area to which the originating router interface belongs.
Authentication information	The authentication type and corresponding information.
Network mask	The IP mask of the originating router's interface IP address.
Hello interval	The period between Hello packets.
Options	OSPF options for neighbor formation.
Router priority	An eight-bit value used to aid in the election of the DR and BDR. (Not set on point-to-point links.)
Router dead interval	The length of time allotted for which a Hello packet must be received before considering the neighbor down—four times the Hello interval, unless otherwise configured.
DR	The router ID of the current DR.
BDR	The router ID of the current BDR.
Neighbor router IDs	A list of the router IDs for all the originating router's neighbors.

Neighbor States

There are a total of eight states for OSPF neighbors:

Down No Hello packets have been received from the neighbor.

Attempt Neighbors must be configured manually for this state. It applies only to NBMA network connections and indicates that no recent information has been received from the neighbor. (Note: This state is not represented in Figure 5.1.)

Init A Hello packet has been received from another router, but the local router has not seen itself in the other router's Hello packet. Bidirectional communication has not yet been established.

2Way Hello packets have been received that include their own router ID in the Neighbor field. Bidirectional communication has been established.

ExStart Master/slave relationship is established in order to form an adjacency by exchanging Database Description (DD) packets. (The router with the highest router ID becomes the master.)

FIGURE 5.1 OSPF peer initialization

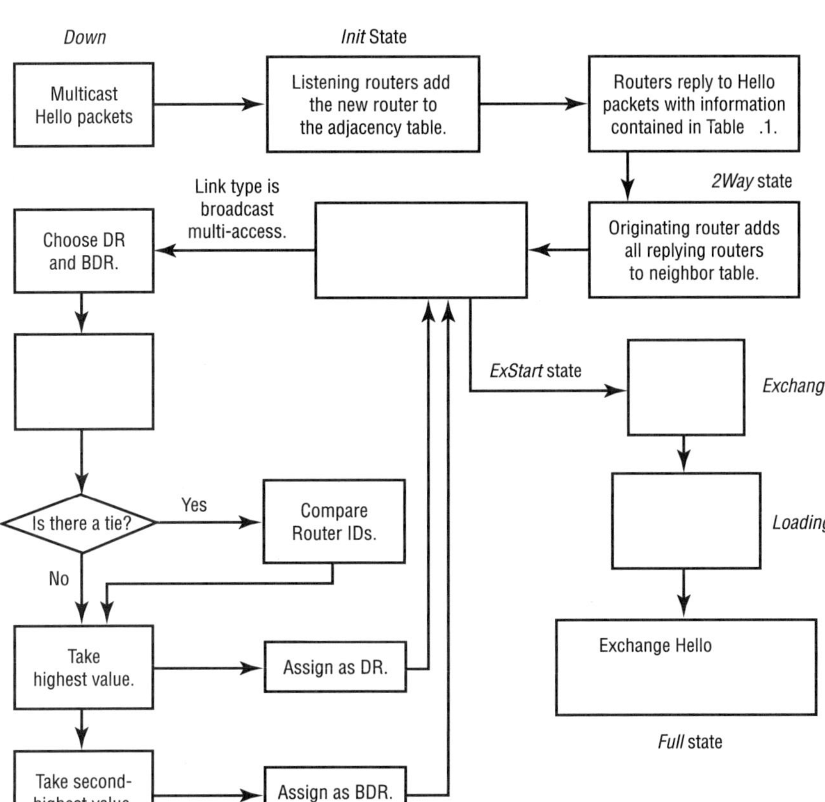

The preceding states, not including the attempt state, are related to Hello packets, while the following states are not. Additionally, the following states are not seen entered into by two DROthers. The only pair of OSPF routers, of which neither is a DR or BDR, that establish these states are those that are point-to-point neighbors. Otherwise, one of the two routers will be a DR or BDR. This distinction may help you bisect these eight items in your mind, helping to recall their order or orientation when you need to.

Exchange Routing information is exchanged using DD and LSR packets.

Loading Link-State Request (LSR) packets are sent to neighbors to request any new LSAs that were found while in the Exchange state.

Full All LSA information is synchronized among adjacent neighbors.

To gain a better understanding of how an adjacency is formed, let's consider the formation of an adjacency in a broadcast multi-access environment. Figure 5.1 displays a flowchart that depicts each step of the initialization process. The process starts by sending out Hello packets. Every listening router will then add the originating router to the neighbor database. The responding routers will reply with all of their Hello information so that the originating router can add them to its own neighbor table.

Adjacency Requirements

Once neighbors have been identified, adjacencies must be established so that routing (LSA) information can be exchanged. There are two steps required to change a neighboring OSPF router into an adjacent OSPF router:

1. Establish two-way communication (achieved via the Hello protocol).
2. Establish database synchronization—this consists of three packet types being exchanged between routers:
   - Database Description (DD) packets
   - Link-State Request (LSR) packets
   - Link-State Update (LSU) packets

Once the database synchronization has taken place, the two routers are considered adjacent. This is how adjacency is achieved, but you must also know when an adjacency will occur.

When adjacencies form depends on the network type. If the link is point-to-point, the two neighbors will become adjacent if the Hello packet information for both routers is configured properly.

On broadcast multi-access networks, adjacencies are formed only between the OSPF routers on the network and the DR and BDR, as well as between the DR and BDR. Figure 5.2 illustrates an example. Three types of routers are pictured: DR, BDR, and DROther. DROther routers are routers that have interfaces on the same network as the DR and BDR but only represent their own router links, not the network, via LSAs.

FIGURE 5.2 OSPF adjacencies for multi-access networks

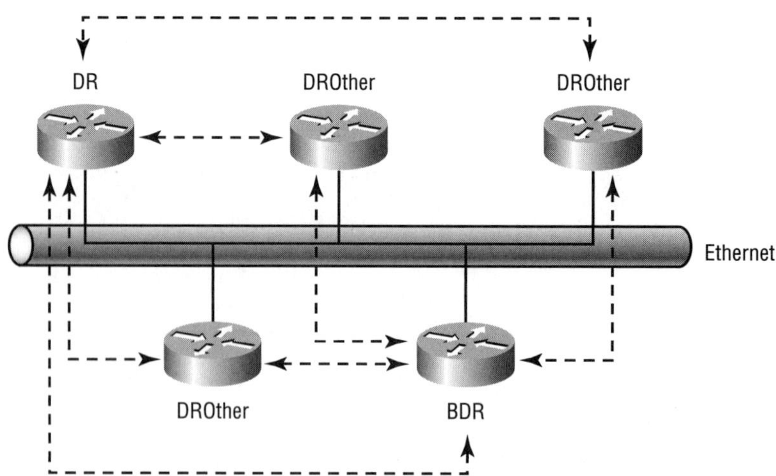

In Figure 5.2, you can see the dotted lines connecting the DROther routers to the DR and BDR routers. Note also that there are no dotted lines between any of the DROther routers. The dotted lines represent the formation of adjacencies. DROther routers form only two adjacencies on a broadcast multi-access network—one with the DR and the other with the BDR. The following router output indicates the assignments of routers connected via a broadcast multi-access network as well as three point-to-point network connections.

Note that the serial interface and subinterface connections displayed next do not have DR/BDR/DROther assignments, because point-to-point and point-to-multipoint links do not elect a DR and BDR. DR/BDR roles and election are covered more fully in the following section, "DR and BDR Election Procedure."

```
RouterA#show ip ospf neighbor

Neighbor ID     Pri State          Dead Time   Address         Interface
172.16.22.101   1   FULL/DROTHER   00:00:32    172.16.22.101   FastEthernet0/0
172.16.247.1    1   FULL/DR        00:00:34    172.16.22.9     FastEthernet0/0
172.16.245.1    1   2WAY/DROTHER   00:00:32    172.16.12.8     FastEthernet1/0
172.16.244.1    1   2WAY/DROTHER   00:00:37    172.16.12.13    FastEthernet1/0
172.16.247.1    1   FULL/BDR       00:00:34    172.16.12.9     FastEthernet1/0
172.16.249.1    1   FULL/DR        00:00:34    172.16.12.15    FastEthernet1/0
172.16.248.1    1   2WAY/DROTHER   00:00:36    172.16.12.12    FastEthernet1/0
172.16.245.1    1   FULL/  -       00:00:34    172.16.1.105    Serial3/0.1
172.16.241.1    1   FULL/  -       00:00:34    172.16.202.2    Serial3/1
172.16.248.1    1   FULL/  -       00:00:35    172.16.1.41     Serial3/3.1
RouterA#
```

We need to bring up a few important points about this output. Notice that five different interfaces are configured to use OSPF.

Interface FastEthernet 0/0 shows only a DROther and a DR. You know that there must always be a DR and a BDR for each multi-access segment with two or more router interfaces. Deductively, you can ascertain that RouterA must be the BDR for this segment. Furthermore, interface FastEthernet 1/0 shows neighboring DROthers, a DR, and a BDR, meaning that RouterA is also a DROther on this network segment. What further proves this point is RouterA's relationship with the other DROthers. Remember that adjacencies are formed only by DRs and BDRs and their neighbors on multi-access networks. Two DROthers will only go as far as the 2Way state with one another.

It's also important to recognize that this command displays all OSPF neighbors and not specific adjacencies. To learn adjacency formations, study the following summarization:

- Valid point-to-point broadcast neighbors form adjacencies.
- Non-broadcast neighbors require special configuration (for example, neighbors on NBMA or point-to-multipoint non-broadcast interfaces) for adjacency formation.
- Broadcast multi-access neighbors require the election of a DR and a BDR. All other routers form adjacencies with only the DR and BDR.

DR and BDR Election Procedure

Each OSPF interface (multi-access networks only) possesses a configurable router priority. The Cisco default is 1. If you don't want a router interface to participate in the DR/BDR election, set the router priority to 0 using the `ip ospf priority` command in interface configuration mode. Here is a sample (the priority field is highlighted for ease of identification):

```
RouterA#show ip ospf interface
FastEthernet0/0 is up, line protocol is up
  Internet Address 172.16.22.14/24, Area 0
  Process ID 100, Router ID 172.16.246.1, Network Type BROADCAST, Cost: 1
  Transmit Delay is 1 sec, State BDR, Priority 1
  Designated Router (ID) 172.16.247.1, Interface address 172.16.22.9
  Backup Designated router (ID) 172.16.246.1, Interface address 172.16.22.14
  Timer intervals configured, Hello 10, Dead 40, Wait 40, Retransmit 5
    Hello due in 00:00:08
  Neighbor Count is 2, Adjacent neighbor count is 2
    Adjacent with neighbor 172.16.22.101
    Adjacent with neighbor 172.16.247.1 (Designated Router)
  Suppress hello for 0 neighbor(s)
  Message digest authentication enabled
    Youngest key id is 10
RouterA#
```

This value is key when electing the DR and BDR. Let's go through the steps that occur in any given router when the DR and BDR are elected for a specific multi-access network of which it is a member:

1. The local router creates a list of eligible neighbors. The eligible neighbors are those with which the local router has entered at least a 2Way state. The local router adds itself to this list and to all lists that are formed from this list in subsequent steps, for which it qualifies.
2. From this list, all routers whose participating interfaces have a router priority of 0 are removed. These routers will be among the DROthers on this network.
3. The local router makes note of the current DR and BDR values for later comparison.
4. A list of all routers not claiming to be the DR (their own Hello packets do not list them as the DR) is compiled from the list resulting from step 2.
5. The local router will select the BDR from the list in step 4, based on the following criteria in order:
   - If one or more of the routers in the list have declared themselves the BDR, then the one of these with the highest priority is selected to be the BDR.
   - If all router priorities are equal, the router with the highest router ID becomes the BDR.
   - If no router in the resulting list from step 4 has declared itself the BDR, then the router with the highest router priority is selected to be the BDR.

- If all routers have the same router priority, then the router with the highest router ID is selected to be the BDR.

6. A list of all routers claiming to be the DR (their own Hello packets list them as the DR) is compiled from the list resulting from step 2.
7. The local router will select the DR from the list in step 6, based on the following criteria in order:
   - The router with the highest router priority is selected to be the DR.
   - If all router priorities are equal, the router with the highest router ID is selected to be the DR.
   - If the resulting list from step 6 is empty, meaning that no router has declared itself the DR, then the BDR that was selected in step 5 becomes the DR.
8. If the local router's DR status has been altered by the preceding steps, either causing it to become, or cease to be, the DR, based on a comparison to the results of step 3, then it will repeat steps 4 through 7. This serves to make sure that the local router does not declare itself both the DR and the BDR, because both may be declared by default. If selected to be the DR, the local router will definitely not make the BDR list the next time around in step 4. Conversely, if dethroned as the DR, the local router can become eligible to be the BDR the next time around, by making the list in step 4.

You should remember that the previous process occurs independently for each router interface when a router becomes active on a segment for which it does not detect a current DR. If a DR and BDR already exist on the segment, any new interfaces accept the DR and BDR regardless of their own router ID or router priority. This minimizes changes on the segment, which can otherwise generate new router and network LSAs, causing a need for the entire routing domain to reconverge, which leads to temporary instability.

To further the example, if initially there is only one OSPF router interface active on the segment, it becomes the DR. The next router would become the BDR. Barring some event that causes a router's interface state machine to trigger a new election, all subsequent initializing interfaces on the multi-access network would accept the existing DR and BDR and form adjacencies with them. In other words, OSPF does not allow preempting for the DR even if another router becomes active that has a higher router priority or router ID. This allows for greater network stability because a router with a higher priority, oscillating from up to down, will not affect the router selected as the DR.

LSA Flooding

LSA flooding is the method by which OSPF shares routing information. Via LSU packets, LSA information containing link-state data is shared with all OSPF routers. The network topology is created from the LSA updates. Flooding is used so that all OSPF routers have the topology map from which SPF calculations may be made.

Efficient flooding is achieved through the use of a reserved multicast address, 224.0.0.5 (AllSPF-Routers). LSA updates (indicating that something in the topology changed) are handled somewhat differently. The network type determines the multicast address used for sending updates. Table 5.2 contains the multicast address associated with LSA flooding. Networks that do not natively support broadcasts, such as point-to-multipoint non-broadcast networks, use the adjacent router's unicast IP address. Figure 5.3 depicts a simple update and flood scenario on a broadcast multi-access network.

TABLE 5.2 LSA Update Multicast Addresses

Multicast Address	Description
224.0.0.5	AllSPFRouters
224.0.0.6	AllDRouters

Once the LSA updates have been flooded throughout the network, each recipient must acknowledge that the flooded update was received. It is also important that the recipient validate the LSA update.

FIGURE 5.3 LSA updates and flooding

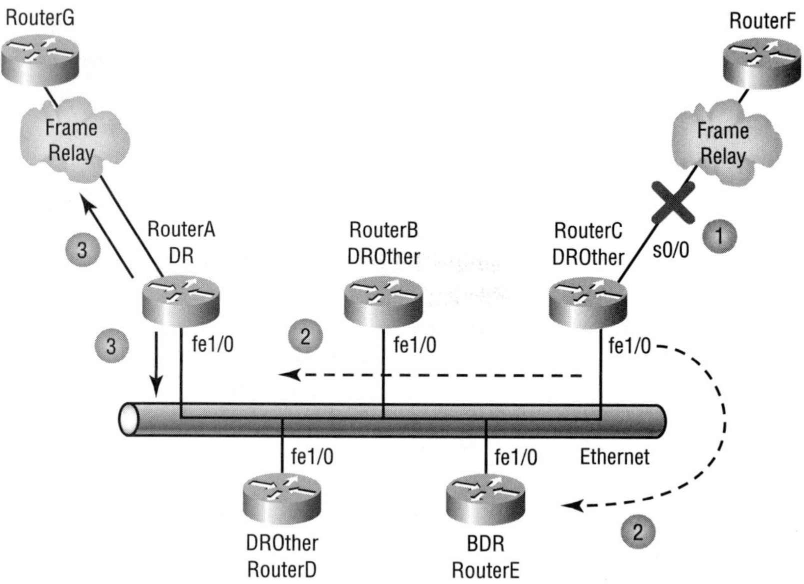

LSA Acknowledgment and Validation

LSA acknowledgments are sent from a router to the originating router to acknowledge the receipt of a LSA. There are two different methods routers can use to acknowledge receipt of LSAs:

Explicit acknowledgment The recipient sends a link-state acknowledgment packet to the originating interface.

Implicit acknowledgment A duplicate of the flooded LSA is sent back to the originator.

Here is a packet decode of an explicit acknowledgment:

```
IP Header - Internet Protocol Datagram
  Version:              4
  Header Length:        5
  Precedence:           6
  Type of Service:      %000
  Unused:               %00
  Total Length:         84
  Identifier:           1285
  Fragmentation Flags:  %000
  Fragment Offset:      0
  Time To Live:         1
IP Type:              0x59  OSPF (Hex value for protocol number)
  Header Checksum:      0x8dda
  Source IP Address:    131.31.194.140
  Dest. IP Address:     224.0.0.6
  No Internet Datagram Options
OSPF - Open Shortest Path First Routing Protocol
  Version:                  2
  Type:                     5  Link State Acknowledgement
  Packet Length:            64
  Router IP Address:        142.42.193.1
  Area ID:                  1
  Checksum:                 0x6699
  Authentication Type:      0  No Authentication
  Authentication Data:
  ........            00 00 00 00 00 00 00 00
Link State Advertisement Header
  Age:                      3600   seconds
  Options:                  %00100010
        No AS External Link State Advertisements
  Type:                     3  Summary Link (IP Network)
```

```
  ID:                         0x90fb6400
  Advertising Router:         153.53.193.1
  Sequence Number:            2147483708
  Checksum:                   0x3946
  Link State Length:          28
Link State Advertisement Header
  Age:                        3600  seconds
  Options:                    %00100010
        No AS External Link State Advertisements
  Type:                       3  Summary Link (IP Network)
  ID:                         0x90fb6400
  Advertising Router:         131.31.193.1
  Sequence Number:            2147483650
  Checksum:                   0x25c0
  Link State Length:          28
Frame Check Sequence:    0x00000000
```

You can tell that this is a link-state acknowledgment packet based on the OSPF header information. You will see that it is a type 5 OSPF packet, or a link-state acknowledgment packet.

There are two methods by which an implicit acknowledgment may be made:

Direct method The acknowledgment, either explicit or implicit, is sent immediately. The following criteria must be met before the Direct method is used:

- A duplicate flooded LSA is received.
- LSA age equals MaxAge (one hour).

Delayed method The recipient waits to send the LSA acknowledgment with other LSA acknowledgments that need to be sent.

Validation occurs through the use of the sequencing, checksum, and aging data contained in the LSA update packet. This information is used to make sure that the router possesses the most recent copy of the link-state database. One important item to know about LSAs is that there are multiple types of LSAs. We discuss the different types of LSAs in more detail in the next chapter.

SPF Tree Calculation

Shortest Path First (SPF) trees are paths through the network to any given destination. A separate path exists for each known destination. Chapter 6 goes into complete detail about the types of destinations and their advertisements.

Once all of the OSPF routers have synchronized link-state databases, each router is responsible for calculating the SPF tree for each known destination. This calculation is done using the Dijkstra algorithm. In order to do calculations, metrics for each link are required.

OSPF Metrics

OSPF uses a metric referred to as *cost*. A cost is associated with every outgoing interface along an SPF tree. The cost of the entire path is the sum of costs of the outgoing interfaces along the path. Because cost is an arbitrary value as defined in RFC 2328, Cisco had to implement its own method of calculating the cost for each OSPF-enabled interface. Cisco uses a simple equation of 10^8/bandwidth. The bandwidth is the configured bandwidth for the interface.

This value may be overridden by using the `ip ospf cost` command. The cost is manipulated by changing the value to a number within the range of 1 to 65,535. Because the cost is assigned to each link, the value must be changed on each interface.

Cisco bases link cost on bandwidth. Other vendors may use other metrics to calculate the link's cost. When connecting links between routers from different vendors, you may have to adjust the cost to match the other router. If both routers do not assign the same cost to a link, it can result in suboptimal routing.

NBMA Overview

Non-broadcast multi-access networks (for example, Frame Relay and ATM) present a special challenge for OSPF. As you know, multi-access networks use an election process to select a DR and a BDR to represent all OSPF routers on the network. This election process requires the participation of all routers on the multi-access network. However, Hello packets are used to facilitate the communication for the election process. This works fine on broadcast multi-access because the connected devices on the network can hear the AllSPFRouters multicast address for the subnet.

When you move to a non-broadcast form of multi-access network, you lose the assurance that all connected devices are receiving the Hello packets and are participating in the DR/BDR election.

Because of the difficulty in running OSPF on NBMA networks, it's important to know which configuration, or environment, will be the most effective solution. The next section discusses some possible solutions for implementing OSPF over NBMA networks.

NBMA Environments

Earlier, we mentioned that there are three types of networks: broadcast multi-access, non-broadcast multi-access, and point-to-point. Although NBMA requires somewhat more configuration to make OSPF operational, it also gives you the option of deciding how you want it to behave.

With extended configurations on NBMA interfaces, an administrator can cause OSPF to behave as if it were running on one of the following five network types:

- Broadcast
- Non-broadcast

- Point-to-point
- Point-to-multipoint
- Point-to-multipoint non-broadcast

It is important for you to know what the Hello and Dead intervals are for each of the five network types as well as whether the network type will elect a designated router (DR) and a backup designated router (BDR). If you change the network type, you must make sure all other interfaces on that particular network segment have at least the same Hello and Dead interval, or they will not communicate. It's a good idea if you change the network type on one interface on the network segment to change all the other network types on all the other interfaces to match. This is suggested but not required. You could just change the Hello and Dead intervals for the interfaces to the same as the interface with the different network type. The only issue with this solution is dependent upon the network type—a DR/BDR may be elected or not.

Table 5.3 summarizes the important differences between the five configurable OSPF network types.

TABLE 5.3 Network Types

Network Type	Hello/Dead Intervals (seconds)	Elects DR/BDR	Neighbor Discovery	OSPF Packet Addressing	Cisco Proprietary
Broadcast (multi-access)	10/40	Yes	Automatic	Multicast	Yes
Non-broadcast multi-access	30/120	Yes	Manual	Unicast	No
Point-to-point (with broadcasts)	10/40	No	Automatic	Multicast	Yes
Point-to-multipoint (with broadcasts)	30/120	No	Automatic	Multicast	Yes
Point-to-multipoint non-broadcast	30/120	No	Manual	Unicast	No

Broadcast

The default Hello interval for a broadcast network is 10 seconds and the Dead interval is four times the Hello interval, or 40 seconds. A broadcast network will elect a DR and BDR. In order to achieve a broadcast implementation of OSPF on an NBMA network, a full mesh must exist among the routers. Figure 5.4 depicts what the NBMA network would have to look like. You can see that each router has a permanent virtual circuit (PVC) configured with all of the other routers.

FIGURE 5.4 NBMA broadcast implementation

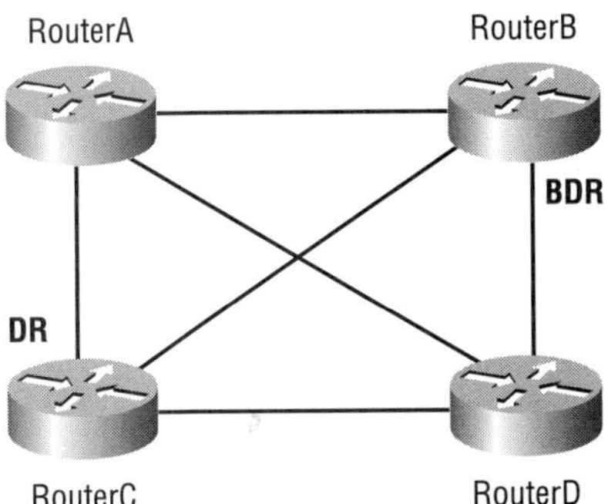

This configuration guarantees that all routers have connectivity and that all are able to participate in the DR/BDR election process. Once the DR and BDR have been chosen, the meshed networks act as a broadcast network. All LSA updates are sent to the DR and BDR, and the DR floods the updates out every active OSPF interface.

One of the major weaknesses with this configuration is that if one of the PVCs fails (especially if it is a PVC between a DROther and the DR), then communication is also halted between the two adjacent peers, and the OSPF routing domain no longer functions properly.

It is also important to note that non-broadcast is the default network type on physical NBMA interfaces. Remember, you are able to change the network type on any interface in an OSPF process. In order to configure broadcast as the network type for an interface, you must enter the `ip ospf network broadcast` command in interface configuration mode.

Non-Broadcast

A non-broadcast environment requires that all OSPF neighbors be manually configured. This is the default setting for physical interfaces with Frame Relay encapsulation, as well as for their point-to-multipoint subinterfaces. By manually configuring each neighbor, OSPF knows exactly which neighbors need to participate and which neighbor is identified as the DR. Also, communication between neighbors is done via unicast instead of multicast. This configuration also requires a full mesh and has the same weakness as the broadcast environment.

For non-broadcast networks the default Hello interval is 30 seconds and the Dead interval is four times the Hello interval, 120 seconds. Non-broadcast multi-access networks do elect a DR and BDR, due to their multi-access nature. In order to set which router you want as the DR, you must set the priority in the `neighbor` statement to elect the neighbor as the DR. In order to manually configure who your neighbors are, the following command must be entered in router configuration mode for the selected OSPF process:

```
neighbor ip_address
    ip_address = the ip address of the neighbor.
```

If you would like to set the priority of this router to become the DR, you will need to append the priority of the neighbor:

```
neighbor ip_address priority value
    ip_address = the ip address of the neighbor.
    value = the priority value of the neighbor. The value will range
    from 0 to 255, with 0 meaning a router will never become the DR
    and 255 being the best setting for a router to become the DR.
```

To manually configure a network type of non-broadcast, you need to enter the `ip ospf network non-broadcast` command in interface configuration mode for the selected interface.

Point-to-Point

A point-to-point environment uses subinterfaces on the physical interface to create point-to-point connections with other OSPF neighbors. No DR or BDR is elected because the link is treated as a point-to-point circuit. This allows for faster convergence.

A full mesh is not required when implementing this environment. PVCs on the subinterface may fail, but there is still OSPF connectivity to other PVCs on the same physical interface.

The drawback of a point-to-point environment is inefficient flooding. Because of multiple PVCs per interface and depending on the mesh of the PVCs, one LSA update can be flooded multiple times.

The default Hello interval for point-to-point networks is 10 seconds and the Dead interval is four times the Hello interval, 40 seconds. To change a network type to point-to-point, enter the command `ip ospf network point-to-point` in interface configuration mode for the selected interface.

Point-to-Multipoint

A point-to-multipoint environment is very similar to the point-to-point environment. No DR or BDR is chosen. All PVCs are treated as point-to-point links. The only difference is that all the PVCs go back to a single router. Figure 5.5 depicts the difference between a true point-to-point environment and a point-to-multipoint deployment.

A point-to-multipoint network will send Hello packets every 30 seconds and the Dead interval is four times the Hello interval, 120 seconds. The `ip ospf network point-to-multipoint` command can be used in interface configuration mode to set the network type as point-to-multipoint. The default behavior of simulating broadcasts is assumed, unless the command is followed by the `non-broadcast` parameter. OSPF also implements host routes to ensure spoke-to-spoke reachability in a point-to-multipoint network environment.

Now that you understand the basics of OSPF, we're going to show you how to configure OSPF in a single area environment.

FIGURE 5.5 Point-to-point vs. point-to-multipoint

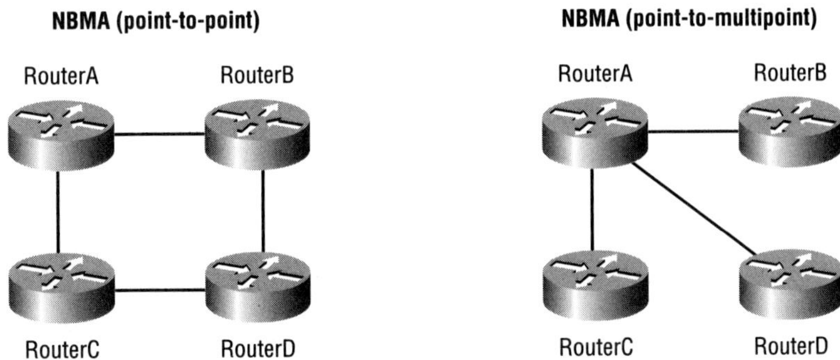

Configuring OSPF

Configuring OSPF is a simple task. There are many options that are allowed within OSPF, such as statically configuring neighbors, creating a virtual link between an area that is not physically connected to Area 0, neighbor/adjacency encryption, and many more. The following sections describe how to configure OSPF in different environments.

Enabling OSPF is common for all implementations of OSPF; the difference comes when you configure parameters to make OSPF behave in the desired fashion. We'll cover parameters for NBMA as well.

The basic elements of OSPF configuration are:

- Enabling OSPF
- Configuring OSPF for different network types
- Configuring the OSPF area
- Route summarization
- Route redistribution (covered in detail in Chapter 10, "Route Optimization")
- Interface parameters

We'll start with basic configuration of OSPF and then introduce commands relating to NBMA, as well as the methods and commands used to verify proper configuration and operation of OSPF.

Discovering the Network with OSPF

The moment OSPF is enabled on a router and networks are added to the OSPF process, the router will try to discover the OSPF neighbors on the connected links that support or simulate broadcasts. Here is a sample of which OSPF events transpire when the interface is added to an OSPF process:

```
RouterA(config-router)#network 172.16.10.5 0.0.0.0 area 0
RouterA(config-router)#
OSPF: Interface Serial0 going Up
OSPF: Tried to build Router LSA within MinLSInterval
OSPF: Tried to build Router LSA within MinLSInterval^Z
RouterA#
OSPF: rcv. v:2 t:1 l:44 rid:172.16.20.1
      aid:0.0.0.0 chk:3B91 aut:0 auk: from Serial0
OSPF: rcv. v:2 t:2 l:32 rid:172.16.20.1
      aid:0.0.0.0 chk:2ECF aut:0 auk: from Serial0
OSPF: Rcv DBD from 172.16.20.1 on Serial0 seq 0x71A opt 0x2      flag
  ➥0x7 len 32 state INIT
OSPF: 2 Way Communication to 172.16.20.1 on Serial0, state 2WAY
OSPF: Send DBD to 172.16.20.1 on Serial0 seq 0x2E opt 0x2      flag 0x7 len 32
OSPF: First DBD and we are not SLAVE
OSPF: rcv. v:2 t:2 l:52 rid:172.16.20.1
      aid:0.0.0.0 chk:A641 aut:0 auk: from Serial0
OSPF: Rcv DBD from 172.16.20.1 on Serial0 seq 0x2E opt 0x2      flag
  ➥0x2 len 52 state EXSTART
OSPF: NBR Negotiation Done. We are the MASTER
OSPF: Send DBD to 172.16.20.1 on Serial0 seq 0x2F opt 0x2      flag 0x3 len 52
OSPF: Database request to 172.16.20.1
OSPF: rcv. v:2 t:2 l:32 rid:172.16.20.1
      aid:0.0.0.0 chk:35C1 aut:0 auk: from Serial0
OSPF: rcv. v:2 t:3 l:36 rid:172.16.20.1
      aid:0.0.0.0 chk:5A1 aut:0 auk: from Serial0
OSPF: Rcv DBD from 172.16.20.1 on Serial0 seq 0x2F opt 0x2      flag
  ➥0x0 len 32 state EXCHANGE
OSPF: Send DBD to 172.16.20.1 on Serial0 seq 0x30 opt 0x2      flag 0x1 len 32
OSPF: rcv. v:2 t:4 l:64 rid:172.16.20.1
      aid:0.0.0.0 chk:F4EA aut:0 auk: from Serial0
OSPF: rcv. v:2 t:2 l:32 rid:172.16.20.1
      aid:0.0.0.0 chk:35C0 aut:0 auk: from Serial0
OSPF: Rcv DBD from 172.16.20.1 on Serial0 seq 0x30 opt 0x2      flag
  0x0 len 32 state EXCHANGE
OSPF: Exchange Done with 172.16.20.1 on Serial0
OSPF: Synchronized with 172.16.20.1 on Serial0, state FULL
```

This simple **debug** output describes exactly what we talked about earlier in this chapter regarding LSA exchanges and the state of adjacent OSPF neighbors. The state information was underlined for your convenience.

We used the OSPF debugging commands to produce this output. The configuration commands consisted of two simple OSPF commands:

router ospf 1 This command starts the OSPF process on RouterA. The number 1 indicates the OSPF process ID. The OSPF process ID is significant only to the router on which it is configured. Using a different process ID on the same router generates a separate OSPF routing process, which does not share routing information with any other OSPF process. This is not desirable for basic router configurations, but is invaluable for VPN service providers in keeping customer traffic separated.

network 172.16.10.5 0.0.0.0 area 0 This command adds the link or links associated with 172.16.10.5 to the OSPF routing process. The wildcard mask indicates that only this single IP address is going to be included in the routing process. Area 0 indicates that the interface with the address 172.16.10.5 is assigned to Area 0.

The generic IOS syntax for the commands is `router ospf` *`process-id`* and `network` *`ip-address wildcard-mask`* `area` *`area-id`*, respectively.

This would be a good time to explain what a wildcard mask is. The wildcard mask used for OSPF is the same type of wildcard mask used in access lists. The 0 bits signify the bits that must be an exact match and the 1 bit represents the "don't care" bits. For instance, if I entered the command `network 172.168.24.0 0.0.0.3 area 0`, the interface on the router with the IP address of 172.168.24.1 or 172.168.24.2 would have OSPF started on it, and the network attached to this interface, in this case 172.168.24.0/30, would be advertised in this router's LSA to its neighbors.

Be aware that entering the mask in standard subnet mask format will result in OSPF's converting what you enter into the corresponding wildcard mask by subtracting each octet's value from 255. While this works in the real world, it is technically incorrect when you are asked to implement the correct syntax. To help get used to inverted wildcard masks, you can use this technique to begin with a standard mask and convert it to a wildcard mask by subtracting each octet's value from 255. Note that due to the flexibility of the wildcard mask and the lack of restriction from mixing 1s and 0s (unlike with subnet masks), this technique may yield only a starting point, but it's still helpful until you become more familiar with wildcard masks.

Point-to-Point

Because the link described by the previous output is point-to-point, no DR/BDR election occurred; instead, each router decided which would be the master and which would be the slave. Once the master/slave roles had been established, DBD (another acronym for database description) packets containing LSA information for each router were exchanged.

LSA exchanges continue until the link-state databases for each router are synchronized. Once that happens, the OSPF state changes to Full.

Broadcast

Discovering the neighbors on a broadcast network is done somewhat differently. Here you will see what happens on a broadcast multi-access network:

```
RouterA(config-if)#router ospf 1
RouterA(config-router)#network 172.16.230.0 0.0.0.255 area 0
OSPF: Interface Ethernet0 going Up
OSPF: Tried to build Router LSA within MinLSInterval
OSPF: Tried to build Router LSA within MinLSInterval
RouterA(config-router)#
OSPF: end of Wait on interface Ethernet0
OSPF: DR/BDR election on Ethernet0
OSPF: Elect BDR 172.16.240.1
OSPF: Elect DR 172.16.240.1
OSPF: Elect BDR 0.0.0.0
OSPF: Elect DR 172.16.240.1
      DR: 172.16.240.1 (Id)   BDR: none
OSPF: Build router LSA for area 0, router ID 172.16.240.1
```

We end the output here, because we know that once adjacencies have been established, the link-state databases must synchronize during the Exchange state and the transfer of DBD packets containing LSA updates.

Of interest in this output is the election of the DR and BDR. Recall from the earlier series of steps outlining the election process that the BDR is elected first and the local router will throw its hat in the ring unless configured not to. Additionally, recall that the router considers the DR and BDR both to be 0.0.0.0, initially, a value shown in this output, only if it is not replaced by a valid address. This was the first router on the network to become active. Therefore, because Ethernet 0 is the only active OSPF interface on the multi-access network, at the moment, the local router with a router ID of 172.16.240.1 (the loopback 0 IP address) is chosen to be the BDR, without contest.

When the process goes on to elect the DR, the only router capable is the local router. The role of DR is also taken by 172.16.240.1, without contest. According to the election rules, because the local router changed state with respect to DR status, the selection process is repeated in order to make sure the same router is not both DR and BDR. Because the local router is on the list of routers claiming to be the DR, it is no longer eligible to be the BDR, so the BDR is reset to 0.0.0.0 before the next round of elections, which is where it remains. You can see this in the output, because there are no other routers active on this multiaccess network and the BDR eligibility list is empty. The local router again wins the DR election and the final result is that this router is the DR and there is no BDR.

No new commands were used to create this output. The only difference was that the network 172.16.230.0 was configured on a broadcast multi-access network.

Configuring OSPF—Single Area

The easiest (and least scalable) way to configure OSPF is to simply use Area 0. If all you want to configure is one area, we recommend that you use Area 0, but you can use any area number. However, once a second area is added, either the original area must be converted to Area 0 or the new area must be numbered Area 0, because in multi-area configurations, there must be an Area 0. Creating a single backbone area makes it easy to understand what OSPF is doing, but once you get a number of routers in the area with all the interfaces assigned to Area 0, processing time is going to be much greater and convergence slower.

To start learning, however, a single area is the perfect place to start. You have already seen the command that is used for assigning an interface to an area. Let's look at the configuration of a few routers to get a good feeling for how it is done. Figure 5.6 depicts the physical layout of a test network.

FIGURE 5.6 OSPF area topology

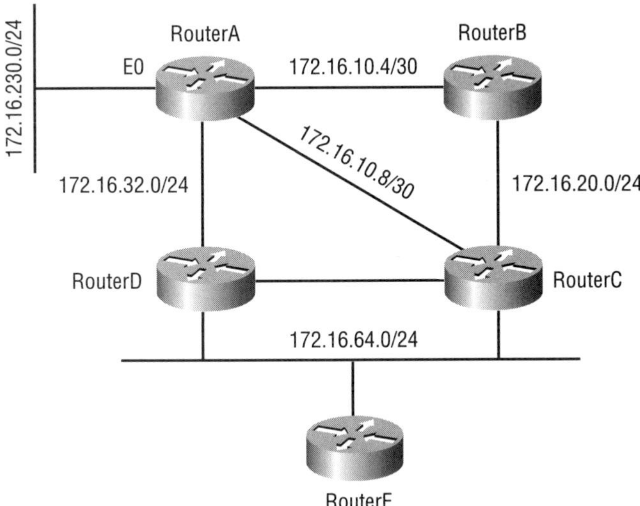

Only two of the five configurations are shown—otherwise you would just see a lot of redundant information. Notice the very specific wildcard masks in the network statements. These facilitate the removal or addition of specific links when troubleshooting. If you have a link that is flapping, you can easily remove it so that it does not cause LSA flooding within the area. After the link has stabilized, it will be very easy to add the interface back in.

For example, if all of the router's interfaces could be summarized by a network statement of 172.16.0.0 0.0.255.255, then you would need only one network statement to add all interfaces to the OSPF process. However, if one out of the many interfaces was flapping, you could not easily isolate that interface so that it would not cause unnecessary LSA flooding. Let's examine the IOS configuration for this topology:

```
RouterA#show running-config
Building configuration...
```

```
Current configuration:
!
version 11.2
no service password-encryption
no service udp-small-servers
no service tcp-small-servers
!
hostname RouterA
!
enable password cisco
!
!
interface Loopback0
 ip address 172.16.240.1 255.255.255.0
!
interface Ethernet0
 ip address 172.16.230.20 255.255.255.0
!
interface Serial0
 ip address 172.16.10.5 255.255.255.252
 clockrate 2000000
 dce-terminal-timing-enable
!
interface Serial1
 ip address 172.16.10.9 255.255.255.252
 clockrate 2000000
 dce-terminal-timing-enable
!
interface Serial2
 ip address 172.16.32.1 255.255.255.0
 clockrate 2000000
 dce-terminal-timing-enable
!
interface Serial3
 no ip address
 shutdown
!
interface BRI0
 no ip address
 shutdown
```

```
!
router ospf 1
 network 172.16.230.0 0.0.0.255 area 0
 network 172.16.32.0 0.0.0.255 area 0
 network 172.16.10.5 0.0.0.0 area 0
 network 172.16.10.9 0.0.0.0 area 0
!

RouterB#show running-config
Building configuration...

Current configuration:
!
version 12.0
service timestamps debug uptime
service timestamps log uptime
no service password-encryption
!
hostname RouterB
!
enable password cisco
!
ip subnet-zero
!
!
!
interface Loopback0
 ip address 172.16.241.1 255.255.255.0
 no ip directed-broadcast
!
interface Ethernet0
 no ip address
 no ip directed-broadcast
 shutdown
!
interface Serial0
 ip address 172.16.10.6 255.255.255.252
 no ip directed-broadcast
 no ip mroute-cache
 no fair-queue
!
```

```
interface Serial1
 ip address 172.16.20.1 255.255.255.0
 no ip directed-broadcast
 clockrate 2000000
 dce-terminal-timing-enable
!
interface Serial2
 no ip address
 no ip directed-broadcast
 shutdown
!
interface Serial3
 no ip address
 no ip directed-broadcast
 shutdown
!
interface BRI0
 no ip address
 no ip directed-broadcast
 shutdown
!
router ospf 1
 network 172.16.10.6 0.0.0.0 area 0
 network 172.16.20.0 0.0.0.255 area 0
!
```

As you can see, these are very simple, straightforward configurations. All interfaces are assigned to Area 0. The use of a host wildcard mask (0.0.0.0) has the distinct advantage of making troubleshooting a bit easier, because affected interfaces are immediately identifiable.

An interesting fact about creating a single area is that there are no ABRs. It is possible to have an ASBR in a single-area configuration, even without having an ABR. If external routes are injected into the area, the router injecting them will be considered an ASBR. On the other hand, in order to activate an ABR, any interface on the router must be assigned to a different area.

It is also important to recognize that the neighbor discovery was automatic in this particular single-area configuration. Now let's move on to an environment where sometimes neighbors must be configured manually.

Configuring OSPF—Single Area (NBMA Environment)

Previously, we mentioned five different possible ways to configure NBMA network interfaces. They are as follows:

- Broadcast
- Non-broadcast multi-access

- Point-to-point
- Point-to-multipoint broadcast
- Point-to-multipoint non-broadcast

We'll outline three of these methods in this section. The IOS senses the media type for all interfaces and assigns the default network type accordingly. When changing from the default, the key that is common to all five configuration methods is the `ip ospf network` command.

This command has the options of specifying broadcast, non-broadcast, point-to-point, point-to-multipoint (with broadcast emulation) and point-to-multipoint non-broadcast network types.

Broadcast Configuration

A full mesh among all OSPF routers is required for this environment to be configured and work properly. A full explanation of the PVC configuration is beyond the scope of this chapter, but here is a sample configuration:

```
RouterA#conf t
Enter configuration commands, one per line. End with CNTL/Z.
RouterA(config)#int serial 1
RouterA(config-if)#ip address 172.16.11.1 255.255.255.0
RouterA(config-if)#ip ospf network broadcast
RouterA(config-if)#encapsulation frame-relay
RouterA(config-if)#frame-relay map ip 172.16.11.2 102 broadcast
RouterA(config-if)#frame-relay map ip 172.16.11.3 103 broadcast
RouterA(config-if)#frame-relay map ip 172.16.11.4 104 broadcast
RouterA(config-if)#router ospf 1
RouterA(config-router)#network 172.16.11.0 0.0.0.255 area 0
RouterA(config-router)#^Z
RouterA#show running-config
Building configuration...

Current configuration:
!
version 11.2
no service password-encryption
no service udp-small-servers
no service tcp-small-servers
!
hostname RouterA
!
enable password cisco
!
!
```

```
interface Loopback0
 ip address 172.16.240.1 255.255.255.0
!
interface Ethernet0
 ip address 172.16.230.20 255.255.255.0
!
interface Serial0
 ip address 172.16.10.5 255.255.255.252
 clockrate 2000000
 dce-terminal-timing-enable
!
interface Serial1
 ip address 172.16.11.1 255.255.255.0
 encapsulation frame-relay
 ip ospf network broadcast
 frame-relay map ip 172.16.11.2 102 broadcast
 frame-relay map ip 172.16.11.3 103 broadcast
 frame-relay map ip 172.16.11.4 104 broadcast
!
interface Serial2
 no ip address
 shutdown
!
interface Serial3
 no ip address
 shutdown
!
interface BRI0
 no ip address
 shutdown
!
router ospf 1
 network 172.16.10.5 0.0.0.0 area 0
 network 172.16.11.0 0.0.0.255 area 0
!
```

Connected routers would have similar configurations. The key to this configuration is to override the default network type by using the `ip ospf network broadcast` command.

Non-Broadcast Configuration

This environment requires all neighbors to be statically configured so that a DR may be chosen from the attached routers on the network segment. We use the same commands as for the configuration of a broadcast network, with the exception of the `neighbor` statements used under the OSPF routing process. Here is a sample configuration:

```
RouterB#conf t
Enter configuration commands, one per line. End with CNTL/Z.
RouterB(config)#interface serial1
RouterB(config-if)#ip address 172.16.25.1 255.255.255.0
RouterB(config-if)#ip ospf network non-broadcast
RouterB(config-if)#encapsulation frame-relay ietf
RouterB(config-if)#frame-relay map ip 172.16.25.10 210 broadcast
RouterB(config-if)#frame-relay map ip 172.16.25.11 211 broadcast
RouterB(config-if)#frame-relay map ip 172.16.25.12 212 broadcast
RouterB(config-if)#router ospf 1
RouterB(config-router)#neighbor 172.16.25.10 priority 1
RouterB(config-router)#neighbor 172.16.25.11 priority 1
RouterB(config-router)#neighbor 172.16.25.12 priority 1
RouterB(config-router)#network 172.16.25.0 0.0.0.255 area 0
RouterB(config-router)#^Z
RouterB#
```

Note the parameters `priority 1` at the end of the neighbor statements. The value of 1 overrides the default of 0. If left at the default value, the neighbor would be considered ineligible to become the DR by the local router, and the local router would not initially send Hello statements to the neighbor. For NBMA networks, a DR eligible router initially only sends Hello packets to and enters the ATTEMPT state with other routers that also have DR potential. A priority value greater than 0 causes the local router to consider the neighbor to have DR potential. Only if the local router is elected DR will it start sending Hello packets to all other routers.

Point-to-Multipoint

This configuration does away with the assumption that there are PVCs configured for all routers creating a full mesh. The same `ip ospf network` command is used to specify that the network type is `point-to-multipoint non-broadcast`. This tells the router that no DR/BDR needs to be elected and that the interface should be treated as multiple point-to-point links. Alternatively, the `non-broadcast` parameter may be left off for the default simulated broadcast behavior over the multiple links. Here is a sample configuration:

```
RouterC#conf t
Enter configuration commands, one per line. End with CNTL/Z.
RouterC(config)#interface serial2
RouterC(config-if)#ip address 172.16.26.1 255.255.255.0
RouterC(config-if)#ip ospf network point-to-multipoint non-broadcast
RouterC(config-if)#encapsulation frame-relay ietf
RouterC(config-if)#frame-relay local dlci 300
```

```
RouterC(config-if)#frame-relay map ip 172.16.26.12 312 broadcast
RouterC(config-if)#frame-relay map ip 172.16.26.13 313 broadcast
RouterC(config-if)#router ospf 1
RouterC(config-router)#neighbor 172.16.26.12 cost 1
RouterC(config-router)#neighbor 172.16.26.13 cost 5
RouterC(config-router)#network 172.16.26.0 0.0.0.255 area 0
RouterC(config-router)#^Z
RouterC#
```

Note that the `priority` parameter is valid only on NBMA networks, not on point-to-multipoint interfaces. Conversely, the cost parameter is not valid on NBMA networks, only point-to-multipoint interfaces. We suggest that the `cost` parameter be specified for neighbors on point-to-multipoint networks. Otherwise, the default cost will be used, which may result in suboptimal routing.

Once the configuration has been created, it's time to test it and make sure it works. There are several `show` commands that facilitate this task, and we discuss them in the following section.

Verifying OSPF Configuration

This section describes several ways in which to verify proper OSPF configuration and operation. Table 5.4 contains a list of OSPF `show` commands.

TABLE 5.4 OSPF *show* Commands

Command	Description
`show ip ospf`	Summarizes all relative OSPF information such as OSPF processes, router ID, area assignments, authentication, and SPF statistics.
`show ip ospf process-id`	Shows the same information as the `show ip ospf` command but only for the specified process.
`show ip ospf border-routers`	Displays the router IDs of all ABRs and ASBRs within the autonomous system.
`show ip ospf database`	Displays the link-state database.
`show ip ospf interface`	Displays interface OSPF parameters and other OSPF information specific to the interface.
`show ip ospf neighbor`	Displays each OSPF neighbor and adjacency status.

show ip ospf

The `show ip ospf` command is used to display OSPF information for one or all OSPF processes running on the router. Information contained therein includes the router ID, area information, SPF statistics, and LSA timer information. Here is a sample output:

```
RouterA#sho ip ospf
 Routing Process "ospf 1" with ID 172.16.240.1
 Supports only single TOS(TOS0) routes
 SPF schedule delay 5 secs, Hold time between two SPFs 10 secs
 Number of DCbitless external LSA 0
 Number of DoNotAge external LSA 0
 Number of areas in this router is 1. 1 normal 0 stub 0 nssa
    Area BACKBONE(0)
        Number of interfaces in this area is 3
        Area has no authentication
        SPF algorithm executed 17 times
        Area ranges are
        Link State Update Interval is 00:30:00 and due in 00:17:52
        Link State Age Interval is 00:20:00 and due in 00:07:52
        Number of DCbitless LSA 0
        Number of indication LSA 0
        Number of DoNotAge LSA 0

RouterA#
```

show ip ospf border-routers

The `show ip ospf border-routers` command displays the process ID on the router, the route to the ABR or ASBR, and the SPF information. Here is a sample output:

```
RouterC#show ip ospf border-routers

OSPF Process 1 internal Routing Table

Codes: i - Intra-area route, I - Inter-area route

i 172.16.240.1 [65] via 172.16.1.106, Serial1, ABR,  Area 0, SPF 582
i 172.16.241.1 [65] via 172.16.1.94, Serial11, ASBR,  Area 0, SPF 582
RouterC#
```

This is a simple output that shows only one ABR and one ASBR. In order to have an ABR, you must have multiple areas configured. In order to have an ASBR, external routes on an external autonomous system must be connected to the router and redistributed from another routing protocol into OSPF.

show ip ospf database

The information displayed by the `show ip ospf database` command indicates the number of links and the neighboring router ID. The output is broken down by area. Greater detail will be given for this command and its output in Chapter 6. Here is a sample output:

```
RouterA#show ip ospf database

       OSPF Router with ID (172.16.240.1) (Process ID 1)


                Router Link States (Area 0)

Link ID         ADV Router      Age         Seq#        Checksum Link count
172.16.240.1    172.16.240.1    1530        0x80000016  0x9C7C   4
172.16.241.1    172.16.241.1    667         0x80000008  0x3AFF   3
RouterA#
```

show ip ospf interface

The `show ip ospf interface` command displays all interface-related OSPF information. Data is displayed about OSPF information for all interfaces or for specified interfaces. Information includes the interface IP address, area assignment, Process ID, router ID, network type, cost, priority, DR/BDR (if applicable), timer intervals, and adjacent neighbor information. Here is a sample output:

```
RouterA#show ip ospf interface
BRI0 is administratively down, line protocol is down
   OSPF not enabled on this interface
BRI0:1 is administratively down, line protocol is down
   OSPF not enabled on this interface
BRI0:2 is administratively down, line protocol is down
   OSPF not enabled on this interface
Ethernet0 is up, line protocol is up
  Internet Address 10.11.230.20/24, Area 0
  Process ID 1, Router ID 172.16.240.1, Network Type BROADCAST, Cost: 10
  Transmit Delay is 1 sec, State DR, Priority 1
  Designated Router (ID) 172.16.240.1, Interface address 10.11.230.20
  No backup designated router on this network
  Timer intervals configured, Hello 10, Dead 40, Wait 40, Retransmit 5
    Hello due in 00:00:08
  Neighbor Count is 0, Adjacent neighbor count is 0
```

```
  Suppress hello for 0 neighbor(s)
Loopback0 is up, line protocol is up
  Internet Address 172.16.240.1/24, Area 0
  Process ID 1, Router ID 172.16.240.1, Network Type LOOPBACK, Cost: 1
  Loopback interface is treated as a stub Host
Serial0 is up, line protocol is up
  Internet Address 172.16.10.5/30, Area 0
  Process ID 1, Router ID 172.16.240.1, Network Type POINT_TO_POINT, Cost: 64
  Transmit Delay is 1 sec, State POINT_TO_POINT,
  Timer intervals configured, Hello 10, Dead 40, Wait 40, Retransmit 5
    Hello due in 00:00:02
  Neighbor Count is 1, Adjacent neighbor count is 1
    Adjacent with neighbor 172.16.241.1
  Suppress hello for 0 neighbor(s)
Serial1 is administratively down, line protocol is down
   OSPF not enabled on this interface
```

show ip ospf neighbor

`show ip ospf neighbor` is a very useful command. It summarizes the pertinent OSPF information regarding neighbors and the adjacency state. If a DR or BDR exists, that information is also displayed. Here is a sample:

```
RouterA#show ip ospf neighbor

Neighbor ID   Pri  State     Dead Time  Address      Interface
172.16.241.1    1  FULL/  -  00:00:39   172.16.10.6   Serial0
RouterA#
```

Summary

OSPF is one of the most widely used routing protocols in existence today. OSPF is a link-state routing protocol. This means that OSPF will send routing updates only when a change occurs to the network. By sending routing updates only as changes occur, OSPF is able to better utilize bandwidth than a distance-vector routing protocol.

OSPF supports a hierarchical network topology. OSPF is able to accomplish this topology through the use of areas. By using areas, OSPF can segment off different parts of the network for better routing control. In this chapter, we concerned ourselves with only a single OSPF area; in the next chapter, we will take a look at hierarchical design using multiple OSPF areas.

To configure OSPF, you first need to determine the process ID to use. The process ID is local to the device and allows you to configure more than one OSPF process on a device. Once the process ID has been determined, you are ready to start configuring OSPF.

In order to configure OSPF, you need to enable it on the device. Then you need to specify which networks on the router you want to participate in OSPF. It's important to remember that the `network` statement in OSPF doesn't tell OSPF which network to advertise. What the network statement does do is tell OSPF which interfaces to allow to participate in OSPF. OSPF then looks at the network address and mask to which the interface belongs and advertises that network address and mask.

Now that you have an understanding of OSPF in a single area, it's time to take it to the next level. Let's learn how to configure OSPF in multiple areas in the next chapter.

Exam Essentials

Know the advantages of OSPF. OSPF is a link-state routing protocol. It sends updates only when a change has occurred to a network. Therefore, OSPF utilizes less bandwidth and has faster convergence than a distance-vector routing protocol. OSPF also utilizes the concept of areas in support of a hierarchical topology.

Understand the operation of OSPF. During the neighbor and adjacency initialization phase of OSPF, a router learns of its neighbors and forms adjacencies. Once this phase has been completed, OSPF enters the LSA flooding phase. During this phase, OSPF learns the topology of the network. The final phase of OSPF is the SPF tree calculation. Once OSPF has learned the topology of a network, it runs an SPF calculation to determine which routes to use.

Know the different network types. OSPF consists of five different network types: broadcast (multi-access), non-broadcast multi-access, point-to-point (broadcast), and point-to-multipoint (both broadcast and non-broadcast). The multi-access network types elect a DR/BDR, with the broadcast variety having default Hello/Dead intervals of 10/40, automatic neighbor discovery, and using multicasts. The non-broadcast multi-access (NBMA) network type also elects a DR/BDR, but has a default Hello/Dead interval of 30/120 and unicasts to neighbors that must be manually configured with DR election priorities greater than 0. The point-to-point network type does not elect a DR/BDR, has a default Hello/Dead interval of 10/40, and uses multicasts to send OSPF packets and automatically discover neighbors. Finally, the point-to-multipoint network type does not elect a DR/BDR and has a default Hello/Dead interval of 30/120. If the point-to-multipoint interface is configured to support broadcasts, it will also use multicasts and automatically discover neighbors. Otherwise, it uses unicasts and must be told of its neighbors and their cost.

Configure OSPF in a single area. When configuring OSPF in a single area, you first need to determine what area you will utilize. Then you need to determine the devices and interfaces that will participate in the area. After all the planning has been completed, all that's left is to configure OSPF on the devices.

Verify the proper operation of OSPF. Without verifying the operation of OSPF, there isn't a way for us to know if OSPF is actually running correctly or not. So the first thing that should be done after configuring OSPF is to verify its operation. The commands discussed in this chapter are the best way of verifying OSPF operation. Keep in mind that these same commands can be used for troubleshooting OSPF operation as well.

Interconnecting OSPF Areas

THE CCNP EXAM TOPICS COVERED IN THIS CHAPTER INCLUDE THE FOLLOWING:

- ✓ **Understand how OSPF operates in multiple areas.**
- ✓ **Understand how to configure OSPF in multiple areas.**
- ✓ **Identify the steps to verify OSPF operation in multiple areas.**
- ✓ **When route selection and configuration problems occur, understand how to use the various show and debug commands to determine the cause of the problem.**

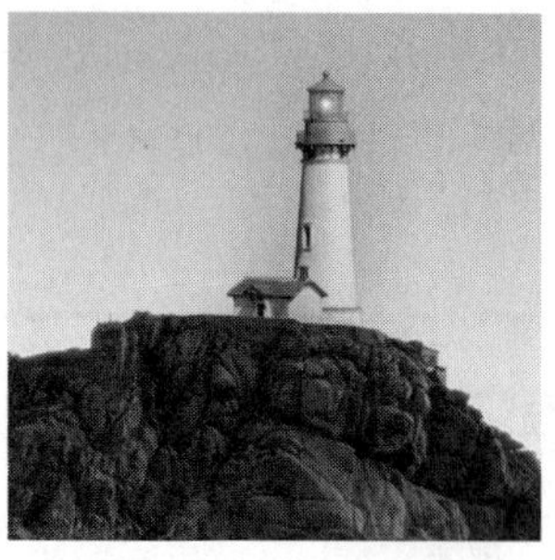

In this chapter, we will illustrate the scalability constraints of an OSPF network with a single area. The concept of multi-area OSPF will be introduced as a solution to these scalability limitations. This chapter also identifies the various categories of routers used in multi-area configurations. These router categories include a backbone router, internal router, area border router (ABR), and autonomous system boundary router (ASBR). We'll explore how these routers can use summarization and default routes to reduce the amount of route information that is injected into an area, thus reducing a router's memory and processor overhead.

The functions of different OSPF link-state advertisements (LSAs) are very important to understand for the BSCI exam, and we will detail the types of LSAs used by OSPF. We will show how these LSAs can be minimized through the effective implementation of specific OSPF area types.

Specifically, we will examine stub areas, totally stubby areas, and not-so-stubby areas and show how these areas can be used to minimize the number of LSAs advertised into an area. We'll also provide a set of design guidelines and configuration examples, as well as the syntax required to configure route summarization at both area border routers and autonomous system boundary routers.

You'll learn that all areas need to have a link to Area 0. If an area is not attached to Area 0, *virtual links* can be used to span *transit areas* in OSPF networks where all areas are not physically adjacent to the backbone area. We will conclude with a collection of `debug` and `show` commands that can be used to effectively monitor and troubleshoot a multi-area OSPF implementation.

OSPF Scalability

In the previous chapter, we examined the configuration of OSPF networks that contained a single area. We saw that OSPF had significant advantages over distance-vector protocols, such as RIP, due to OSPF's ability to represent an entire network within its link-state database, thus vastly reducing the time required for convergence.

However, let's consider what the router does in order to give us such great performance. Each router recalculates its database every time there is a topology change, requiring CPU overhead. Each router has to hold the entire link-state database, which represents the topology of the entire network, requiring memory overhead. Furthermore, each router contains a complete copy of the routing table, requiring more memory overhead. Keep in mind that the number of entries in the routing table may be significantly greater than the number of networks in the routing table, because we may have multiple routes to multiple networks.

With these OSPF behavioral characteristics in mind, it becomes obvious that in very large networks, single-area OSPF has some serious scalability considerations. Fortunately, OSPF gives us the ability to take a large OSPF topology and break it down into multiple, more manageable areas, as illustrated in Figure 6.1.

Consider the advantages of this hierarchical approach. First of all, routers that are internal to a defined area need not worry about having a link-state database for the entire network, only their own areas, thus reducing memory overhead. Second, routers that are internal to a defined area now only have to recalculate their link-state database when there is a topology change within their particular area. Topology changes in one area will not cause global OSPF recalculations, thus reducing processor overhead. Finally, because routes can be summarized at area boundaries, the routing tables on each router need not be as large as they would be in a single-area environment.

Of course, as we start subdividing our OSPF topology into multiple areas, we introduce some complexity into our configuration. Therefore, in this chapter we will examine these various configuration subtleties, in addition to learning strategies for effectively troubleshooting multi-area OSPF networks.

FIGURE 6.1 OSPF areas

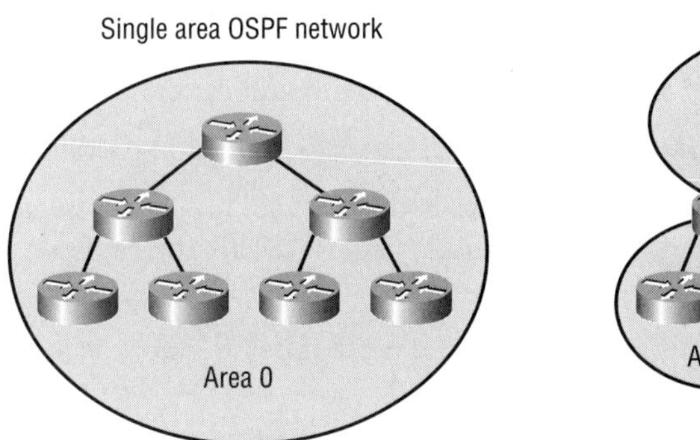

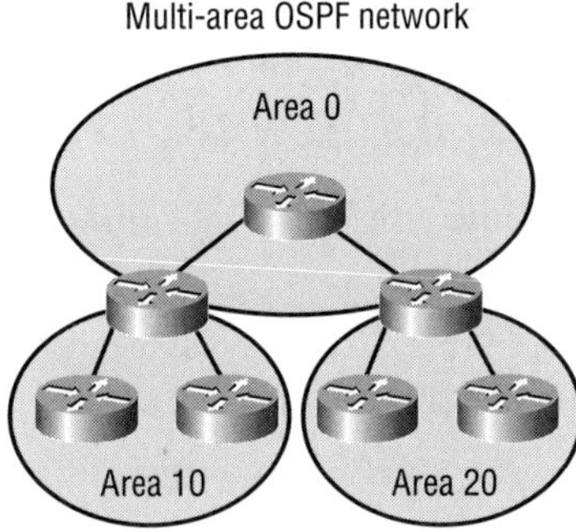

Categories of Multi-Area Components

This section covers the various roles that routers play in a large OSPF network. These include backbone routers, internal routers, area border routers, and autonomous system boundary routers. We'll also discuss the different types of advertisements that are used in an OSPF network and the different types of areas that can be configured.

OSPF Router Roles

As we alluded to earlier, routers within a multi-area OSPF network fall into different categories. To gain an understanding of the various roles that our routers can play, let's consider Figure 6.2.

FIGURE 6.2 Router roles

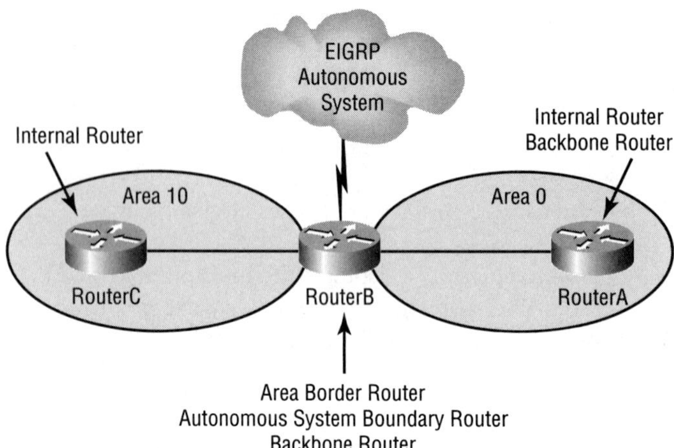

Starting at the core of the given network and working our way outward, consider RouterA. Notice that RouterA is part of Area 0. As we learned in the previous chapter, Area 0 is referred to as the *backbone area*. Therefore, we can make the following definition:

Backbone router A backbone router is any router that exists (wholly or in part) in OSPF Area 0.

Another distinction we can make about RouterA is that it is contained completely within a single area, in this case Area 0. Because all of RouterA's interfaces are internal to a single area, we can make the following definition:

Internal router An internal router is any router that has all of its interfaces as members of the same area.

Remember that a router can play more than one role. In our example, RouterA is both a backbone router and an internal router.

Now consider RouterB. Notice that RouterB meets the requirement to be classified as a backbone router (in other words, RouterB has one or more interfaces that are part of Area 0). However, unlike RouterA, RouterB is partially in Area 0 and partially in Area 10. There is yet another term used to define routers that have interfaces in more than one area:

Area border router (ABR) An area border router is any router that is connected to multiple OSPF areas. Cisco recommends that an ABR belong to only one OSPF process and that no router belong to more than three areas.

Recall that the topology of an OSPF area is contained in a link-state database. Therefore, if a router is connected to multiple areas, it will contain multiple link-state databases.

This should be a design consideration when sizing a router that will function as an area border router.

Notice also that RouterB is connected to an EIGRP network. Whether an OSPF network is connected to an EIGRP network, a BGP network, an OSPF network with a different Process ID, or a network running any other such external routing process, this external network may be referred to as an *autonomous system*. The scenario of an OSPF router sitting at the boundary of an external routing process leads us to a fourth category of OSPF router:

Autonomous system boundary router (ASBR) An autonomous system boundary router is any OSPF router that is also connected to an external routing process and exchanges routing information between the OSPF routing process and the external routing process.

The ability of an ASBR to exchange routing information between its OSPF routing process and the external routing process to which the router is connected is not an automatic process. Such routes are exchanged through a process called *route redistribution*, which is the focus of Chapter 10, "Route Optimization."

Link-State Advertisements

Recall that a router's link-state database is made up of link-state advertisements (LSAs). However, just as we had multiple OSPF router categories to consider, we also have multiple types of LSAs to consider. While the importance of LSA classification may not be immediately apparent, you will see its application when we examine the various types of OSPF areas. Table 6.1 lists all of the possible types of LSAs.

TABLE 6.1 LSA Types

Type Code	Description
1	Router LSA
2	Network LSA
3	Network Summary LSA
4	ASBR Summary LSA
5	AS External LSA
6	Group Membership LSA
7	NSSA External LSA
8	External Attributes LSA

TABLE 6.1 LSA Types *(continued)*

Type Code	Description
9	Opaque LSA (link-local scope)
10	Opaque LSA (area-local scope)
11	Opaque LSA (AS scope)

There are a total of 11 LSA types in existence. For the BSCI exam, you should be concerned with only the first five types and Type 7. We will now drill down into each of these LSA types to give you a better understanding of each. Keep in mind that it is very important to understand the different LSA types, not only for the exam but also for the real world.

Type 1 LSA Referred to as a *router link advertisement (RLA)*, the Type 1 LSA is an advertisement sent by a router to all other routers in its area. The Type 1 LSA contains information about all of the router's links in the area, the status of each link, and the cost for each link. A router, which has connections to multiple areas, will send a Type 1 LSA to each of the areas the router is connected to, but only describing links it has in each respective area, not sharing this information across area boundaries.

Type 2 LSA Referred to as a *network link advertisement (NLA)*, the Type 2 LSA is generated only on multi-access networks, and then only by designated routers (DRs) when they are fully adjacent with at least one other router on the network. Recall that a designated router is elected to represent other routers in its network, and it has established adjacencies with each of the routers within its network. The DR uses the Type 2 LSA to send out information about the state of other routers that are part of the same network, information it has learned through receipt of Type 1 LSAs from these routers. The Type 2 LSA describes each of the routers on the DR's network, including the DR. Note that the Type 2 LSA is sent only to routers that are in the area containing the network for which the advertising router is the DR.

Type 3 and Type 4 LSAs Referred to as *summary link advertisements (SLAs)*, the Type 3 and Type 4 LSAs are generated by area border routers. These ABRs send Type 3 and Type 4 LSAs to all routers within a single area only. These LSAs advertise non-backbone intra-area routes, routes within an area, into the backbone area (Area 0) and both intra-area and inter-area routes, routes to other areas, to non-backbone areas. The only real difference between Type 3 and Type 4 LSAs is that a Type 3 will advertise networks outside of an area into an area and a Type 4 will advertise routes to ASBRs into an area. A special example of a Type 3 LSA is created by the `default information originate` command.

Type 5 LSA Referred to as *AS external link advertisements*, Type 5 LSAs are sent by autonomous system boundary routers. These ASBRs use Type 5 LSAs to advertise routes that are external to the OSPF autonomous system or a default route external to the OSPF autonomous system that is reachable through them.

Type 7 LSA To overcome the limitations of an ASBR not being able to belong to a stub area, LSA Type 7, *NSSA external LSA*, was created. Type 7 LSAs are generated only by an ASBR in a not-so-stubby area (NSSA). The Type 7 LSA will propagate across the area to the NSSA ABR. Once the Type 7 LSA reaches the ABR, the ABR will convert the Type 7 LSA into a Type 5 LSA and propagate it to the backbone. The Type 7 LSA advertises routes that are external to the OSPF autonomous system.

OSPF Area Types

One of our main motivations for subdividing a single OSPF area into multiple areas was to reduce router overhead. We decided that all routers didn't need to have the entire network topology in their link-state databases. Let's now examine the types of areas that can reduce router overhead:

Stub area Whenever a route external to an AS is learned, the ASBR generates a Type 5 LSA and floods throughout the OSPF autonomous system. Also, an ABR will generate a Type 4 LSA for ASBRs and flood them throughout an area. In some cases all of the routers in an area don't need to know this information. For example, take a look at Figure 6.3.

As you can see in this figure, all routers in Area 1 must send their packets through the ABR in order for the packets to reach a network external to the AS. In this case, the routers in Area 1 do not need to know about the Type 4 and 5 LSAs, since the ABR handles the forwarding of packets to networks external to the AS. All the flooding of the Type 4 and 5 LSAs would do is use up CPU power and memory on the internal routers of Area 1. A better idea would be to make Area 1 a stub area. That way, the ABR will block the flooding of Type 4 and 5 LSAs, and instead the ABR will generate a Type 3 LSA with a default route for all networks external to the AS. The ABR would then flood that and any intra-area Type 3 LSA to all internal routers in Area 1. Now all of the internal routers for Area 1 would know that if a packet is to be sent to a network not contained within Area 1, they will forward the packet to the ABR and let it handle the packet. Important items to keep in mind about stub areas are that if you need to configure a virtual link, the virtual link cannot traverse a stub area and ASBRs cannot exist in a stub area. Virtual links is covered in more detail later in this chapter.

Totally stubby area To further reduce the number of LSAs that an internal router will need to process, the router can be configured as a totally stubby area. In addition to not propagating Types 4 and 5 LSAs, a totally stubby area does not propagate Type 3 LSAs, except for one Type 3 LSA that advertises a default route out of the area. The only way an internal router of a totally stubby area knows how to reach any destination not contained within the local area is through a default route to the ABR. The function of a totally stubby area is Cisco-specific, which is an important concept to remember when designing an OSPF network in a multi-vendor routing environment.

Not-so-stubby area (NSSA) Like a stub area, a not-so-stubby area does not propagate Type 5 LSAs, which means an ASBR cannot be part of a stub area. However, sometimes there is a need, on a limited basis, to import external routes to an area. Such a situation is where NSSAs, which will allow an ASBR to participate in the area, are useful. Instead of the ASBR sending out Type 5 LSAs, it will send out Type 7 NSSA External LSAs. The Type 7 LSAs cannot be advertised into another OSPF area. So what happens is that the ABR for the NSSA receives the Type 7 LSA and translates it into a Type 5 LSA. The Type 5 LSA is then allowed to be flooded throughout the OSPF autonomous system.

FIGURE 6.3 Stub area

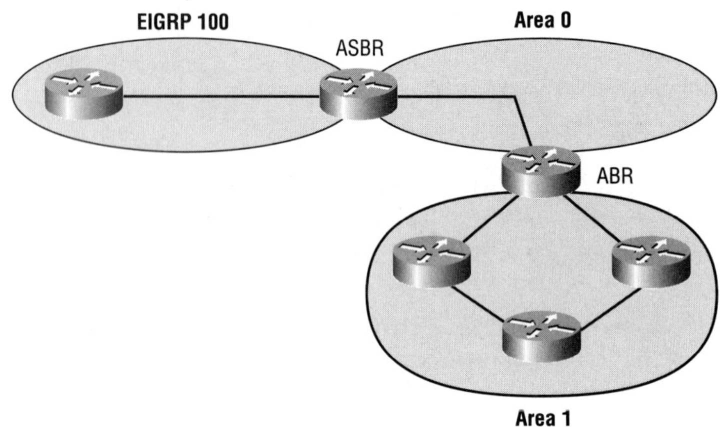

Basic Multi-Area Configuration

Consider the multi-area OSPF network shown in Figure 6.4. To review some of the router classifications that we previously discussed, notice that RouterA would be classified as both an internal router and a backbone router. Also, RouterB would be classified as both a backbone router and an area border router. Finally, RouterC would be classified as an internal router.

FIGURE 6.4 Sample multi-area configuration

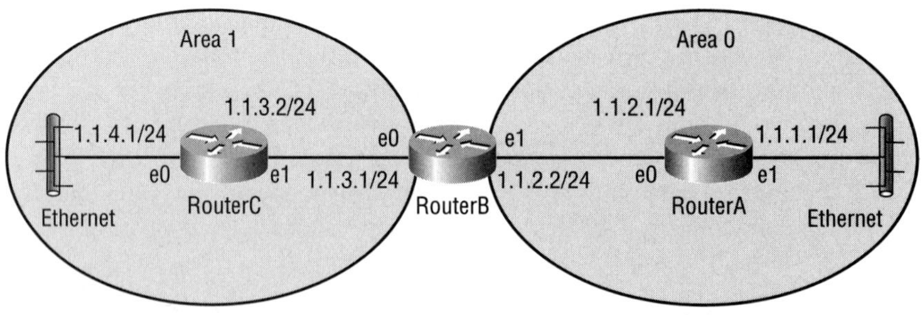

RouterA

```
interface Ethernet0
  ip address 1.1.2.1 255.255.255.0
!
interface Ethernet1
  ip address 1.1.1.1 255.255.255.0
!
router ospf 70
  network 1.1.1.0 0.0.0.255 area 0
  network 1.1.2.0 0.0.0.255 area 0
```

RouterB

```
interface Ethernet0
  ip address 1.1.3.1 255.255.255.0
!
interface Ethernet1
  ip address 1.1.2.2 255.255.255.0
!
router ospf 70
  network 1.1.2.0 0.0.0.255 area 0
  network 1.1.3.0 0.0.0.255 area 1
```

RouterC

```
interface Ethernet0
  ip address 1.1.4.1 255.255.255.0
!
interface Ethernet1
  ip address 1.1.3.2 255.255.255.0
!
router ospf 70
  network 1.1.3.0 0.0.0.255 area 1
  network 1.1.4.0 0.0.0.255 area 1
```

Configuring Multi-Area OSPF

Let's examine the syntax to configure OSPF on RouterA. First, we need to enable the OSPF process on the router:

```
RouterA (config)#router ospf 70
```

where 70 is the Process ID.

Next, we need to identify each of the networks connected to the router that we want to participate in the OSPF process. The `network` statement will actually add interfaces that have an IP address that falls within the range specified in the network statement. In this example, we have two networks connected to RouterA (1.1.1.0/24 and 1.1.2.0/24):

```
RouterA(config-router)#network 1.1.1.0 0.0.0.255 area 0
```

where `1.1.1.0 0.0.0.255` is the network and wildcard mask of a network connected to RouterA and where 0 is the area that network 1.1.1.0/24 is a member of.

```
RouterA(config-router)#network 1.1.2.0 0.0.0.255 area 0
```

Note that the previous two statements could be consolidated into a single statement, such as the following, because both interfaces are members of the same area. The same goes for the two statements shown later for RouterC.

```
RouterA(config-router)#network 1.1.0.0 0.0.255.255 area 0
```

The syntax for RouterB is similar to that used for RouterA. The primary difference is that RouterB is connected to two areas, for which individual `network` statements are necessary:

```
RouterB(config)#router ospf 70
RouterB(config-router)#network 1.1.2.0 0.0.0.255 area 0
RouterB(config-router)#network 1.1.3.0 0.0.0.255 area 1
```

The syntax for RouterC is very similar to that of RouterA. The difference is that RouterA is internal to Area 0, thereby classifying it as a backbone router:

```
RouterC(config)#router ospf 70
RouterC(config-router)#network 1.1.3.0 0.0.0.255 area 1
RouterC(config-router)#network 1.1.4.0 0.0.0.255 area 1
```

Stub Area Configuration

Because the main purpose of having stub areas is to keep such areas from carrying external routes, we need to review some design guidelines before configuring a stub area or a totally stubby area:

- Area 0 (the backbone area) cannot be made a stub area.
- More than one area must exist.

- Because autonomous system boundary routers inject external routes, do not make any area containing an ASBR a stub area. (However, see the discussion of NSSAs in this chapter.)
- Because routers within a stub area use a default route to get out of the stub area, typically there is only one route out of the stub area. Therefore, a stub area should usually contain only a single area border router. Keep in mind that since a default route is being used, if a stub area contains more than one ABR, a non-optimal path may be used.
- If you decide to make a particular area a stub area, be sure to configure *all* the routers in the area as stubby. If a router within a stub area has not been configured as stubby, it will not be able to correctly form adjacencies and exchange OSPF routes.

With these guidelines in mind, let's examine a sample configuration for a stub area. Consider the network shown in Figure 6.5. We're going to make Area 25 a stub area. In this example, we won't be concerned with the configuration of RouterA, because it does not participate in Area 25. We will then examine the syntax for RouterB, RouterC, and RouterD.

FIGURE 6.5 OPSF configuration example continued—stub area configuration

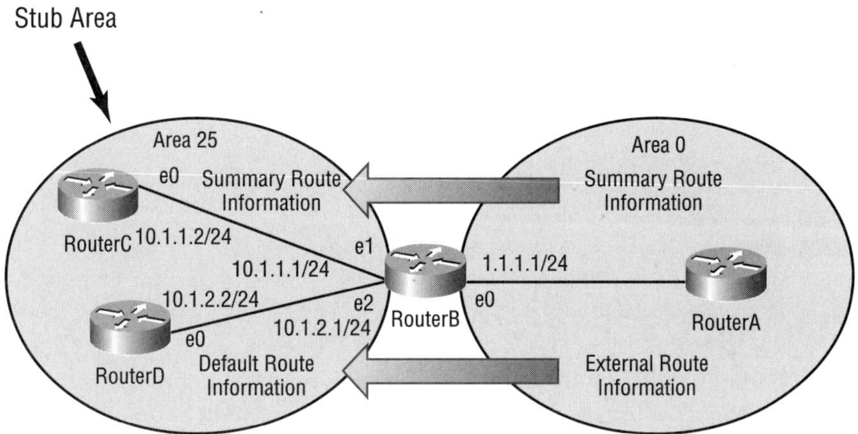

RouterB

```
interface Ethernet0
  ip address 1.1.1.1 255.255.255.0
!
interface Ethernet1
  ip address 10.1.1.1 255.255.255.0
!
interface Ethernet2
  ip address 10.1.2.1 255.255.255.0
!
```

```
router ospf 10
  network 1.0.0.0 0.255.255.255 area 0
  network 10.0.0.0 0.255.255.255 area 25
  area 25 stub
```

RouterC

```
interface Ethernet0
  ip address 10.1.1.2 255.255.255.0
!
router ospf 1
  network 10.0.0.0 0.255.255.255 area 25
  area 25 stub
```

RouterD

```
interface Ethernet0
  ip address 10.1.2.2 255.255.255.0
!
router ospf 100
  network 10.0.0.0 0.255.255.255 area 25
  area 25 stub
```

Configuring OSPF for a Stub Area

First, we'll configure RouterB. Notice that RouterB is an ABR and that it is the only ABR in Area 25, as recommended in our stub area design guidelines. When configuring an ABR that is a member of a stub area, be cautious to configure only the stub area as stubby:

`RouterB(config)#`**`router ospf 10`**

where 10 is the Process ID.

`RouterB(config-router)#`**`network 1.0.0.0 0.255.255.255 area 0`**

where `1.0.0.0 0.255.255.255` is the network and wildcard mask of a network connected to RouterB and where 0 is the area that network 1.1.1.0/24 is a member of.

`RouterB(config-router)#`**`network 10.0.0.0 0.255.255.255 area 25`**

where `10.0.0.0 0.255.255.255` is a summary network and wildcard mask of networks connected to RouterB and where 25 is the area that networks 10.1.1.0/24 and 10.1.2.0/24 are members of.

`RouterB(config-router)#`**`area 25 stub`**

where 25 is the area that we have designated as stubby.

Notice that instead of using two `network` statements to represent networks 10.1.1.0/24 and 10.1.2.0/24, we used a single `network` statement specifying network 10.0.0.0/8, which will include all the interfaces contained in these two networks. Using a summarized `network` statement like this will by no means alter any routes that will be advertised. In other words, advertisements will still be sent for both networks and a summary address of the two networks will not be sent.

We will also use the 10.0.0.0/8 summary when we configure RouterC and RouterD. Remember that it's critical that all routers that are members of a stub area be configured as stubby for that area. Therefore, RouterC and RouterD will have identical OSPF configurations:

```
RouterC(config)#router ospf 1
RouterC(config-router)#network 10.0.0.0 0.255.255.255 area 25
RouterC(config-router)#area 25 stub

RouterD(config)#router ospf 100
RouterD(config-router)#network 10.0.0.0 0.255.255.255 area 25
RouterD(config-router)#area 25 stub
```

Let's review some key elements of our stub area configuration example:

- The syntax to make a router stubby is `area` *`area-id`* `stub`.
- All routers that are part of Area 25 are configured as stubby.
- Area 25 has only one ABR (i.e., only one path out of the area).
- The ABR used the `area` *`area-id`* `stub` command only for Area 25, not for Area 0, which is not stubby.

Totally Stubby Area Configuration

Using the same network topology as we had for the stub area configuration, let's examine how to make Area 25 a totally stubby area. Remembering that the difference between a stub area and a totally stubby area is that a totally stubby area doesn't allow summary routes to be injected into it; we need only change the configuration of RouterB. Because RouterB is the ABR, it will be the router that will have the responsibility for blocking summary routes from entering the totally stubby area. So, again consider our network, as illustrated in Figure 6.6.

RouterB

```
interface Ethernet0
  ip address 1.1.1.1 255.255.255.0
!
interface Ethernet1
  ip address 10.1.1.1 255.255.255.0
!
interface Ethernet2
```

```
  ip address 10.1.2.1 255.255.255.0
!
router ospf 10
  network 1.0.0.0 0.255.255.255 area 0
  network 10.0.0.0 0.255.255.255 area 25
  area 25 stub no-summary
```

FIGURE 6.6 OPSF configuration example continued—totally stubby area configuration

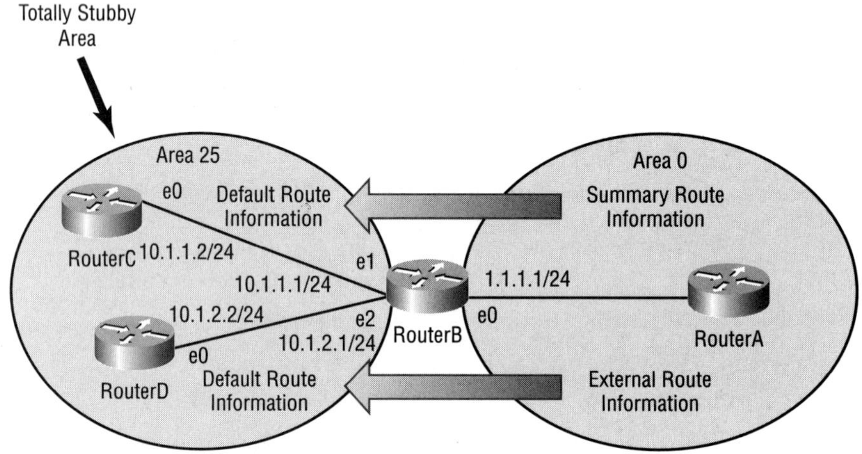

RouterC

```
interface Ethernet0
  ip address 10.1.1.2 255.255.255.0
!
router ospf 1
  network 10.0.0.0 0.255.255.255 area 25
  area 25 stub
```

RouterD

```
interface Ethernet0
  ip address 10.1.2.2 255.255.255.0
!
router ospf 100
  network 10.0.0.0 0.255.255.255 area 25
  area 25 stub
```

Configuring OSPF for a Totally Stubby Area

Notice that we have to change, from the previous example, only the configuration of RouterB. We simply add the `no-summary` argument to the `area` *area-id* `stub` command:

```
RouterB(config)#router ospf 10
```

where 10 is the Process ID.

```
RouterB(config-router)#network 1.0.0.0 0.255.255.255 area 0
```

where `1.0.0.0 0.255.255.255` is the network and wildcard mask of a network connected to RouterB and where 0 is the area that network 1.1.1.0/24 is a member of.

```
RouterB(config-router)#network 10.0.0.0 0.255.255.255 area 25
```

where `10.0.0.0 0.255.255.255` is a summary network and wildcard mask of networks connected to RouterB and where 25 is the area that networks 10.1.1.0/24 and 10.1.2.0/24 are members of.

```
RouterB(config-router)#area 25 stub no-summary
```

where the `no-summary` argument makes Area 25 totally stubby.

Not-So-Stubby Area Configuration

Recall that a not-so-stubby area (NSSA) is useful when there is an area that requires the injection of external routes from an ASBR, but we still want to eliminate the injection of Type 5 LSAs from the ABR. Figure 6.7 presents such a scenario. We want to prevent Area 0 from injecting Type 5 LSAs into Area 1, which can be assumed to originate to the right of Area 0 from an unseen ASBR, yet we still need external routes from the RIP routing process to be injected into Area 1 and propagated to other OSPF areas. The solution to these requirements is to make Area 1 an NSSA.

FIGURE 6.7 OPSF configuration example continued—not-so-stubby area configuration

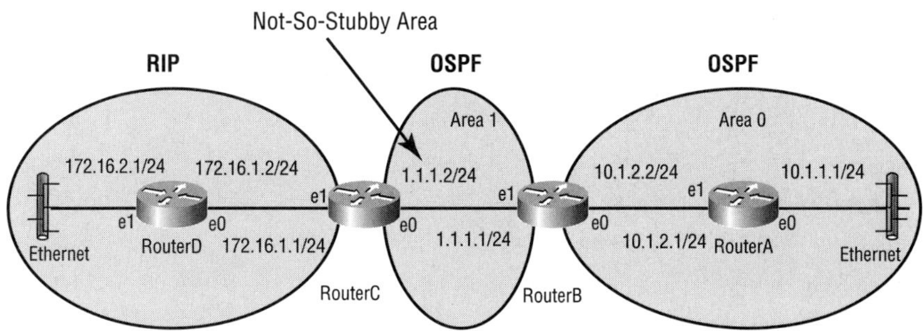

RouterA

```
interface Ethernet0
  ip address 10.1.1.1 255.255.255.0
!
interface Ethernet1
  ip address 10.1.2.1 255.255.255.0
!
router ospf 24
  network 10.0.0.0 0.255.255.255 area 0
```

RouterB

```
interface Ethernet0
  ip address 10.1.2.2 255.255.255.0
!
interface Ethernet1
  ip address 1.1.1.1 255.255.255.0
!
router ospf 24
  network 10.0.0.0 0.255.255.255 area 0
  network 1.0.0.0 0.255.255.255 area 1
  area 0 range 10.0.0.0 255.0.0.0
  area 1 nssa
```

RouterC

```
interface Ethernet0
  ip address 1.1.1.2 255.255.255.0
!
interface Ethernet1
  ip address 172.16.1.1 255.255.255.0
!
router ospf 24
  redistribute rip
  network 1.0.0.0 0.255.255.255 area 1
  default-metric 128
  area 1 nssa
!
router rip
```

```
  redistribute ospf 24
  network 172.16.0.0
  default-metric 3
```

RouterD

```
interface Ethernet0
  ip address 172.16.1.2 255.255.255.0
!
interface Ethernet1
  ip address 172.16.2.1 255.255.255.0
!
router rip
  network 172.16.0.0
```

Configuring OSPF for a Not-So-Stubby Area

Let's examine the configuration of each of these routers, beginning with RouterA. RouterA is a backbone router (and an internal router), which does not participate in our NSSA (Area 1). Therefore, RouterA doesn't need any special NSSA configuration. However, by way of review, we will still examine its syntax:

```
RouterA(config)#router ospf 24
```

where 24 is the Process ID.

```
RouterA(config-router)#network 10.0.0.0 0.255.255.255 area 0
```

where `10.0.0.0 0.255.255.255` is a network and wildcard mask summarization of the networks connected to RouterA and where 0 is the area that networks 10.1.1.0/24 and 10.1.2.0/24 are members of.

RouterB does participate in the NSSA. Therefore, it will require a special configuration:

```
RouterB(config)#router ospf 24
RouterB(config-router)#network 10.0.0.0 0.255.255.255 area 0
RouterB(config-router)#network 1.0.0.0 0.255.255.255 area 1
RouterB(config-router)#area 0 range 10.0.0.0 255.0.0.0
```

where `10.0.0.0 255.0.0.0` is the network number and subnet mask of a network that summarizes the individual networks within Area 0, thus reducing the number of a router's routing table entries.

```
RouterB(config-router)#area 1 nssa
```

where `1` is the area that is being designated as a not-so-stubby area.

Notice that the configuration for RouterB included the command `area` *`area-id`* `range` *`network_address network_mask`*, which can be used on area border routers to summarize the IP address space being used by routers within a given area to other areas.

Notice also the `area` *`area-id`* `nssa` command. This command tells the router that the specified area the router is connected to is a not-so-stubby area. As we saw when configuring stub areas, all routers within a not-so-stubby area must agree that they are connected to a NSSA (in other words, be configured with the `area` *`area-id`* `nssa` command).

To expand upon the idea of advertising summarized routes, the `area` *`area-id`* `range` *`network_address network_mask`* command is used to summarize inter-area routes on an ABR. Similarly, we can summarize external routes on an autonomous system boundary router (ASBR) with the command `summary-address` *`network_address network_mask`*. Proper use of these summarization tools can greatly reduce the number of routes that have to be maintained by a router, thus reducing memory and processor overhead.

RouterC will be an even more complex configuration. Not only is RouterC part of an NSSA, it also participates in an RIP routing process. In order to exchange its OSPF and RIP routes, RouterC must perform route redistribution (route redistribution is the focus of Chapter 10):

```
RouterC(config)#router ospf 24
RouterC(config-router)#redistribute rip
```

where `rip` is the routing protocol whose routes are being injected into the OSPF routing process.

```
RouterC(config-router)#network 1.0.0.0 0.255.255.255 area 1
RouterC(config-router)#default-metric 128
```

where `128` is the OSPF metric value to be assigned to routes being redistributed into the OSPF routing process.

```
RouterC(config-router)#area 1 nssa
RouterC(config-router)#router rip
```

This enables the RIP routing process on the router.

```
RouterC(config-router)#redistribute ospf 24
```

where `ospf 24` is the routing process whose routes are being injected into the RIP routing process.

```
RouterC(config-router)#network 172.16.0.0
RouterC(config-router)#default-metric 3
```

where 3 is the RIP metric value (hop count) to be assigned to OSPF routes being redistributed into the RIP routing process.

RouterD is internal to the RIP routing process. Therefore, RouterD does not require any NSSA-specific configuration:

```
RouterD(config)#router rip
RouterD(config-router)#network 172.16.0.0
```

OSPF Virtual Links

When designing a multi-area OSPF network, all areas should be connected to the backbone area. However, there may be instances when an area will need to cross another area to reach the backbone area, as shown in Figure 6.8. Because, in this example, Area 20 does not have a direct link to Area 0, we need to create a virtual link.

FIGURE 6.8 OSPF virtual link

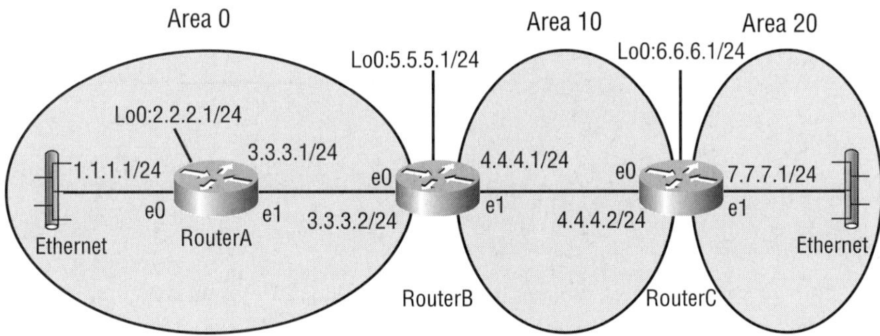

The syntax for creating a virtual link across an area is

```
area area-id virtual-link router-id
```

where *area-id* is the number of the transit area, in this example Area 10, and *router-id* is the IP address of the highest loopback interface configured on a router or can be manually set.

To manually set the *router-id*, you need to enter the command `router-id` *id-in-IP-address-format* in router configuration mode. If you do not manually set the *router-id* and a loopback interface has not been configured on the router, then the *router-id* is the highest IP address configured on the router.

Note that a virtual link has area border routers as the end points of the link. Virtual links will be used, in the real world, to merge corporate networks during transition phases. When two companies merge and the companies both have OSPF networks, both companies will have their own Area 0. In this instance, a virtual link would be created between the discontiguous Area 0s until the networks could be fully merged.

As shown in Figure 6.9, we are going to create a virtual link from Area 20 to Area 0, with Area 10 acting as the transit area. Let's examine the configuration of RouterB and RouterC, because RouterA does not have any virtual-link-specific configuration.

Here are the configurations of RouterB and RouterC:

```
RouterB(config)#router ospf 10
RouterB(config-router)#network 3.0.0.0 0.255.255.255 area 0
RouterB(config-router)#network 4.0.0.0 0.255.255.255 area 10
RouterB(config-router)#area 10 virtual-link 6.6.6.1
```

FIGURE 6.9 OSPF virtual link

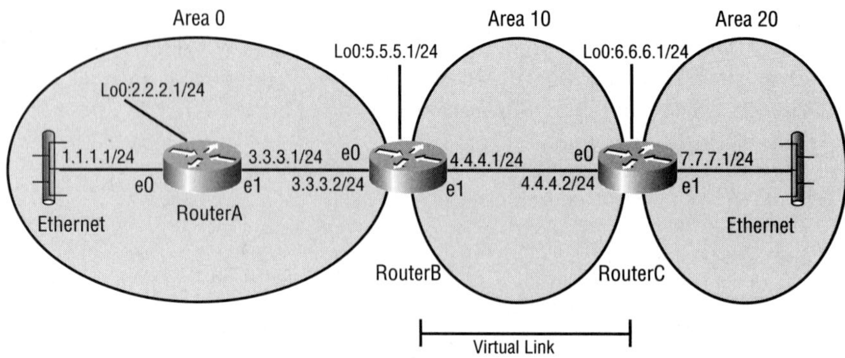

where 10 is the Area ID of the transit area and `6.6.6.1` is the highest loopback address of the ABR joining the transit area to Area 20.

```
RouterC(config)#router ospf 10
RouterC(config-router)#network 4.0.0.0 0.255.255.255 area 10
RouterC(config-router)#network 7.0.0.0 0.255.255.255 area 20
RouterC(config-router)#area 10 virtual-link 5.5.5.1
```

where 10 is the Area ID of the transit area and `5.5.5.1` is the highest loopback address of the ABR joining the transit area to the backbone area.

It would not have mattered if there had been one or more routers between the ABRs of Area 10. The configuration of the ABRs would have been the same, with each one pointing to the other.

RouterA

```
interface Loopback0
  ip address 2.2.2.1 255.255.255.0
!
internet Ethernet0
  ip address 1.1.1.1 255.255.255.0
!
interface Ethernet1
  ip address 3.3.3.1 255.255.255.0
```

```
!
router ospf 10
  network 1.0.0.0 0.255.255.255 area 0
  network 3.0.0.0 0.255.255.255 area 0
```

RouterB

```
interface Loopback0
  ip address 5.5.5.1 255.255.255.0
!
interface Ethernet0
  ip address 3.3.3.2 255.255.255.0
!
interface Ethernet1
  ip address 4.4.4.1 255.255.255.0
!
router ospf 10
  network 3.0.0.0 0.255.255.255 area 0
  network 4.0.0.0 0.255.255.255 area 10
  area 10 virtual-link 6.6.6.1
```

RouterC

```
interface Loopback0
  ip address 6.6.6.1 255.255.255.0
!
interface Ethernet0
  ip address 4.4.4.2 255.255.255.0
!
interface Ethernet1
  ip address 7.7.7.1 255.255.255.0
!
router ospf 10
  network 4.0.0.0 0.255.255.255 area 10
  network 7.0.0.0 0.255.255.255 area 20
  area 10 virtual-link 5.5.5.1
```

Verifying and Troubleshooting OSPF

Now that you know how to configure OSPF in a multiple area network, we need to focus on how to verify that it is operating correctly and, if not, how to troubleshoot it.

Route Information

Just like with other routing protocols, you should always verify that the correct information is in the routing table:

```
plano#show ip route
Codes: C - connected, S - static, I - IGRP, R - RIP, M - mobile, B - BGP
       D - EIGRP, EX - EIGRP external, O - OSPF, IA - OSPF inter area
       N1 - OSPF NSSA external type 1, N2 - OSPF NSSA external type 2
       E1 - OSPF external type 1, E2 - OSPF external type 2, E - EGP
       i - IS-IS, L1 - IS-IS level-1, L2 - IS-IS level-2, ia - IS-IS inter area
       * - candidate default, U - per-user static route, o - ODR
       P - periodic downloaded static route

Gateway of last resort is not set

O IA 192.168.24.0/24 [110/112] via 10.10.10.1, 00:00:02, Serial2/0.1
     20.0.0.0/24 is subnetted, 1 subnets
C       20.20.20.0 is directly connected, FastEthernet2/0
     172.16.0.0/24 is subnetted, 1 subnets
O IA    172.16.20.0 [110/113] via 10.10.10.1, 00:00:02, Serial2/0.1
     172.20.0.0/24 is subnetted, 2 subnets
C       172.20.128.0 is directly connected, Loopback0
C       172.20.192.0 is directly connected, Loopback1
     10.0.0.0/24 is subnetted, 1 subnets
C       10.10.10.0 is directly connected, Serial2/0.1
```

As can be seen from this routing table, there are two routes that were learned through OSPF. You will know the routes learned from OSPF by the code O in front of the route line. The code IA after the O means the routes are inter-area routes. If you would like to view only routes learned by OSPF, the following command may be used:

```
plano#show ip route ospf
O IA 192.168.24.0/24 [110/112] via 10.10.10.1, 00:01:07, Serial2/0.1
     172.16.0.0/24 is subnetted, 1 subnets
O IA    172.16.20.0 [110/113] via 10.10.10.1, 00:01:07, Serial2/0.1
```

To view detailed information about a particular route, the following command, with the appropriate destination attached, needs to be entered in privileged EXEC mode:

```
plano#show ip route 192.168.24.0
Routing entry for 192.168.24.0/24
  Known via "ospf 1", distance 110, metric 112, type inter area
  Last update from 10.10.10.1 on Serial2/0.1, 00:01:36 ago
  Routing Descriptor Blocks:
  * 10.10.10.1, from 192.168.24.1, 00:01:36 ago, via Serial2/0.1
      Route metric is 112, traffic share count is 1
```

By viewing the detailed route information in the preceding example, you can discern that the route was learned from OSPF process 1, the distance is 110, the metric is 112, and the route is an inter-area route.

To view the OSPF routing information known by an ABR or ASBR, you can enter the `show ip ospf border-routers` command to view the internal routing table. The following is a sample output from this command:

```
plano#show ip ospf border-routers

OSPF Process 1 internal Routing Table

Codes: i - Intra-area route, I - Inter-area route

i 192.168.24.1 [48] via 10.10.10.1, Serial2/0.1, ABR, Area 0, SPF 6
```

Link-State Database Information

The command `show ip ospf database` will give you information about the all the LSA data stored in the router's OSPF link-state database. Here is a sample output from Plano's OSPF link-state database:

```
plano#show ip ospf database

            OSPF Router with ID (172.20.192.1) (Process ID 1)

                Router Link States (Area 0)

Link ID         ADV Router      Age         Seq#       Checksum Link count
172.20.192.1    172.20.192.1    315         0x80000003 0x8972   2
192.168.24.1    192.168.24.1    316         0x80000003 0xC11B   2
```

```
                Summary Net Link States (Area 0)

Link ID         ADV Router      Age         Seq#       Checksum
20.20.20.0      172.20.192.1    424         0x80000001 0xC2BA
172.16.20.0     192.168.24.1    473         0x80000001 0xF8AF
192.168.24.0    192.168.24.1    530         0x80000001 0x9662

                Router Link States (Area 2)

Link ID         ADV Router      Age         Seq#       Checksum Link count
172.20.192.1    172.20.192.1    433         0x80000001 0xD916   1

                Summary Net Link States (Area 2)

Link ID         ADV Router      Age         Seq#       Checksum
10.10.10.0      172.20.192.1    189         0x80000004 0xFD6B
172.16.20.0     172.20.192.1    304         0x80000001 0x97E0
192.168.24.0    172.20.192.1    304         0x80000001 0x3593
```

This command allows you to view the entire OSPF link-state database for the router. If you just want to view specific LSA information stored in the database, there are parameters that can be used with the command. Note that the `ADV Router` column lists the router ID of the advertising router.

Routing Protocol Information

In order to view detailed information about OSPF configured on the router, use the following command:

```
plano#show ip ospf
 Routing Process "ospf 1" with ID 172.20.192.1 and Domain ID 0.0.0.1
 Supports only single TOS(TOS0) routes
 Supports opaque LSA
 It is an area border router
 SPF schedule delay 5 secs, Hold time between two SPFs 10 secs
 Minimum LSA interval 5 secs. Minimum LSA arrival 1 secs
 Number of external LSA 0. Checksum Sum 0x0
 Number of opaque AS LSA 0. Checksum Sum 0x0
 Number of DCbitless external and opaque AS LSA 0
 Number of DoNotAge external and opaque AS LSA 0
 Number of areas in this router is 2. 2 normal 0 stub 0 nssa
 External flood list length 0
```

```
    Area BACKBONE(0)
        Number of interfaces in this area is 1
        Area has no authentication
        SPF algorithm executed 6 times
        Area ranges are
        Number of LSA 5. Checksum Sum 0x39C58
        Number of opaque link LSA 0. Checksum Sum 0x0
        Number of DCbitless LSA 0
        Number of indication LSA 0
        Number of DoNotAge LSA 0
        Flood list length 0
    Area 2
        Number of interfaces in this area is 2
        It is a stub area
          generates stub default route with cost 1
        Area has no authentication
        SPF algorithm executed 4 times
        Area ranges are
        Number of LSA 4. Checksum Sum 0x2A3F4
        Number of opaque link LSA 0. Checksum Sum 0x0
        Number of DCbitless LSA 0
        Number of indication LSA 0
        Number of DoNotAge LSA 0
        Flood list length 0
```

The `show ip OSPF` command gives detailed information on how OSPF is configured on the router. What we can learn from the preceding output is that the router is participating in OSPF process 1, the router ID is 172.20.192.1, it is an area border router, it has one interface configured in Area 0 and two interfaces configured in Area 2, which is a stub area, and none of the areas are using authentication. This command also informs you of the configured area type.

The following command provides you with information about the interfaces on the router configured for OSPF:

```
plano#show ip ospf interface
Serial2/0.1 is up, line protocol is up
  Internet Address 10.10.10.2/24, Area 0
  Process ID 1, Router ID 172.20.192.1, Network Type POINT_TO_POINT, Cost: 48
  Transmit Delay is 1 sec, State POINT_TO_POINT,
  Timer intervals configured, Hello 10, Dead 40, Wait 40, Retransmit 5
    Hello due in 00:00:07
  Index 1/1, flood queue length 0
  Next 0x0(0)/0x0(0)
```

```
  Last flood scan length is 1, maximum is 1
  Last flood scan time is 0 msec, maximum is 0 msec
  Neighbor Count is 1, Adjacent neighbor count is 1
    Adjacent with neighbor 192.168.24.1
  Suppress hello for 0 neighbor(s)
FastEthernet2/0 is up, line protocol is up
  Internet Address 20.20.20.1/24, Area 2
  Process ID 1, Router ID 172.20.192.1, Network Type BROADCAST, Cost: 1
  Transmit Delay is 1 sec, State DR, Priority 1
  Designated Router (ID) 172.20.192.1, Interface address 20.20.20.1
  No backup designated router on this network
  Timer intervals configured, Hello 10, Dead 40, Wait 40, Retransmit 5
    Hello due in 00:00:07
  Index 1/2, flood queue length 0
  Next 0x0(0)/0x0(0)
  Last flood scan length is 0, maximum is 0
  Last flood scan time is 0 msec, maximum is 0 msec
  Neighbor Count is 0, Adjacent neighbor count is 0
  Suppress hello for 0 neighbor(s)
```

For each interface configured for OSPF, this command informs you of the OSPF process ID, the router ID, the OSPF network type, the cost, the number of neighbors, the number of adjacent neighbors, and the neighbor the router is adjacent with.

Viewing Neighbor Information

In OSPF, knowing who your neighbors are is very important. Many times, routing information not being received by a router could mean that the state of the neighbor relationship hasn't reached full. To view who a router's neighbors are and the state of each neighbor relationship, use the following command:

```
plano#show ip ospf neighbor

Neighbor ID     Pri   State           Dead Time   Address         Interface
192.168.24.1      1   FULL/  -        00:00:39    10.10.10.1      Serial2/0.1
```

In the preceding example, the router has one neighbor and the state is full. This command would also inform you if the state were something different. The `detail` parameter can be added to the end of the command line to view more detailed information:

```
plano#show ip ospf neighbor detail
 Neighbor 192.168.24.1, interface address 10.10.10.1
    In the area 0 via interface Serial2/0.1
```

```
Neighbor priority is 1, State is FULL, 6 state changes
DR is 0.0.0.0 BDR is 0.0.0.0
Options is 0x2
Dead timer due in 00:00:39
Neighbor is up for 00:04:42
Index 1/1, retransmission queue length 0, number of retransmission 1
First 0x0(0)/0x0(0) Next 0x0(0)/0x0(0)
Last retransmission scan length is 1, maximum is 1
Last retransmission scan time is 0 msec, maximum is 0 msec
```

The `show ip ospf neighbor detail` command provides you with detailed information about a neighbor, such as how long the router will wait for a Hello packet before declaring the neighbor as Dead.

If you would like to see the states routers go through when forming adjacencies, the `debug ip ospf adj` command can be used.

```
plano#debug ip ospf adj
OSPF adjacency events debugging is on
plano#
 len 32
3d02h: OSPF: Rcv DBD from 192.168.24.1 on Serial2/0.1 seq 0x1BED opt
  ➥0x2 flag 0x
7 len 32  mtu 1500 state EXSTART
3d02h: OSPF: NBR Negotiation Done. We are the SLAVE
3d02h: OSPF: Send DBD to 192.168.24.1 on Serial2/0.1 seq 0x1BED opt
  ➥0x42 flag 0x
2 len 132
3d02h: OSPF: Rcv DBD from 192.168.24.1 on Serial2/0.1 seq 0x1BEE opt
  ➥0x2 flag 0x
3 len 132  mtu 1500 state EXCHANGE
3d02h: OSPF: Send DBD to 192.168.24.1 on Serial2/0.1 seq 0x1BEE opt
  ➥0x42 flag 0x
0 len 32
3d02h: OSPF: Database request to 192.168.24.1
3d02h: OSPF: sent LS REQ packet to 10.10.10.1, length 24
3d02h: OSPF: Rcv DBD from 192.168.24.1 on Serial2/0.1 seq 0x1BEF opt
  ➥0x2 flag 0x
1 len 32  mtu 1500 state EXCHANGE
3d02h: OSPF: Exchange Done with 192.168.24.1 on Serial2/0.1
3d02h: OSPF: Send DBD to 192.168.24.1 on Serial2/0.1 seq 0x1BEF opt
  ➥0x42 flag 0x
0 len 32
```

```
3d02h: OSPF: Synchronized with 192.168.24.1 on Serial2/0.1, state FULL
3d02h: %OSPF-5-ADJCHG: Process 1, Nbr 192.168.24.1 on Serial2/0.1 from LOADING
to FULL, Loading Done
3d02h: OSPF: Build router LSA for area 0, router ID 172.20.192.1, seq
  ➥0x80000006
```

As you can see, this particular debug command gives you step-by-step information about the forming of adjacencies as they occur. This command is great for troubleshooting problems with forming adjacencies. For instance, it will inform you if the Hello times are different between two routers. Another way to view the events occurring while forming adjacencies would be the debug ip ospf events command.

Viewing OSPF Packets

The debug ip ospf packet command provides you with information contained within each OSPF packet, including the version of OSPF, the router ID, and the area ID:

```
plano#debug ip ospf packet
OSPF packet debugging is on
plano#
3d02h: OSPF: rcv. v:2 t:1 l:48 rid:192.168.24.1
      aid:0.0.0.0 chk:B7DA aut:0 auk: from Serial2/0.1
3d02h: OSPF: rcv. v:2 t:1 l:48 rid:192.168.24.1
      aid:0.0.0.0 chk:B7DA aut:0 auk: from Serial2/0.1
3d02h: OSPF: rcv. v:2 t:1 l:48 rid:192.168.24.1
      aid:0.0.0.0 chk:B7DA aut:0 auk: from Serial2/0.1
```

The commands covered in this section provide you with great detail about OSPF and its operation. In order to become proficient with them, you will need to practice, but I don't suggest doing this on your company network. Issuing the debug ip ospf packet command on a production network will cause high CPU utilization and could crash the router. So set up a lab and start playing around with these commands, and before you know it, you'll be able to troubleshoot any OSPF issues out there.

Summary

When dealing with OSPF in multiple areas, you need to understand the OSPF router types. These router types include backbone router, internal router, area border router, and autonomous system boundary router. A backbone router is a router that belongs to Area 0; an internal router fully belongs to one area; an area border router is a router that belongs to more than one area; and an autonomous system boundary router is a router that is redistributing into OSPF.

When using OSPF in multiple areas, one area must be Area 0. Area 0 is the backbone area for OSPF. The other areas can be of multiple area types: normal areas, stub areas, totally stubby areas, and not-so-stubby areas. A normal area supports all LSA types except LSA Type 7. Normal areas are the default area type for OSPF. A stub area doesn't support Type 5 LSAs. A totally stubby area doesn't support LSA Types 3/4 and 5. Because stub and totally stubby areas don't support Type 5 LSAs, an ASBR cannot belong to one of these areas. To overcome this limitation, not-so-stubby areas were created.

The configuration of OSPF in multiple areas is almost the same as the configuration of OSPF in a single area. The only difference is that you will have multiple areas assigned to at least one device.

Guess what? That's it for OSPF. OSPF is a protocol that requires some practice and study. Trust me, you will encounter OSPF in the real world often enough that you should dedicate some time to it. Now we're going to move on to the other link-state routing protocol: IS-IS.

Exam Essentials

Understand the different types of routers for OSPF. OSPF routers consist of internal, backbone, ABR, and ASBR. An internal router is one whose interfaces belong to only one area. A backbone router is one in which the router has at least one interface in Area 0. An ABR has one interface in Area 0 and at least one other interface in a different area. An ASBR is a router that has one interface in OSPF and is redistributing into OSPF.

Know the different types of LSAs. There are six types of LSAs that you need to know: Types 1, 2, 3/4, 5, and 7. Type 1 and 2 LSAs are generated and propagated within an area. Type 3/4 LSAs are summary LSAs generated by an ABR. Type 5 LSAs are generated by an ASBR to advertise routes outside of OSPF. Type 7 LSAs are generated by an ASBR contained within an NSSA.

Know the different types of areas. There are four types of areas that you need to know: normal, stub, totally stubby, and not-so-stubby (NSSA). A normal area allows all LSA types into it (except Type 7 LSAs, technically). A stub area doesn't allow Type 5 LSAs but still allows Type 1, 2, and 3/4 LSAs. A totally stubby area allows only Type 1 and 2 LSAs. An NSSA allows an ASBR to be added to a stub area. The ASBR will generate a Type 7 LSA that will be converted to a Type 5 LSA at the ABR.

Know which area must be configured if multiple areas are used. When a single OSPF area is configured, it can be any number. If multiple OSPF areas are configured, one of the areas must be Area 0, which is the backbone area.

Understand what a virtual link is used for. In OSPF, all areas should be connected to the backbone area, Area 0. However, sometimes this is not possible or desirable. When an area is not connected to Area 0, you must create a virtual link, which will connect the discontiguous area to Area 0.

Integrated IS-IS

THE CCNP EXAM TOPICS COVERED IN THIS CHAPTER INCLUDE THE FOLLOWING:

- ✓ Understand OSI terminology and Network layer protocols used in OSI.
- ✓ Be able to compare IS-IS and OSPF.
- ✓ Know the different types of IS-IS routers and their role in IS-IS area design.
- ✓ Understand why IS-IS uses a hierarchical topology.
- ✓ Know how IS-IS establishes adjacencies.
- ✓ Understand how to configure and verify IS-IS.

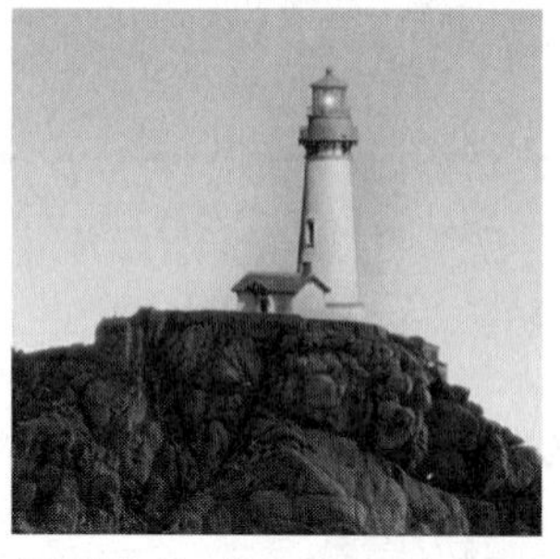

You may be interested to learn that there are other link-state routing protocols in existence besides OSPF. One of these routing protocols is known as Intermediate System to Intermediate System (IS-IS). In fact, IS-IS is based on yet another link-state routing protocol from Novell—the Netware Link Services Protocol (NLSP).

The goal of this chapter is to raise your knowledge of IS-IS to the level of knowledge you have for OSPF. This chapter begins with a brief history of IS-IS, followed by a description of the operation of IS-IS. After you feel comfortable with the operation of IS-IS, we will move on to the configuration of IS-IS in an internetwork. This chapter concludes by exploring the methods available to verify proper operation of IS-IS and how to troubleshoot it if it is not operating properly.

By the time you complete this chapter, you should have a thorough understanding of the fundamentals behind IS-IS. You will also be able to implement it in a real-world network. Pay attention to the details covered in this chapter, because IS-IS will introduce new concepts that you may not be familiar with, such as Connectionless Network Services (CLNS).

Integrated Intermediate System to Intermediate System

Typically when a link-state routing protocol is talked about, OSPF is the routing protocol that is being referred to. There is another link-state routing protocol, known as *Intermediate System to Intermediate System (IS-IS)*. IS-IS was developed by Digital Equipment Corporation as an International Standards Organization (ISO) protocol to route *Connectionless Network Services (CLNS)*, which is a Network layer protocol of the Open Systems Interconnection (OSI) suite of protocols.

IS-IS was being developed by ISO at roughly the same time OSPF was being developed by the Internet Architecture Board (IAB). Many years ago, industry experts believed that the OSI suite would eventually replace TCP/IP. With this in mind, it was proposed that IS-IS become the Internet Engineering Task Force (IETF) recommended standard for routing TCP/IP. An extension was added to IS-IS to allow the simultaneous routing of both IP and CLNS. This extension became known as Integrated IS-IS. Integrated IS-IS can route in either a CLNS environment, an IP environment, or an environment made up of both.

Numerous battles were fought over whether OSPF or Integrated IS-IS would become the recommended standard routing protocol for IP. When the war was over and the smoke had cleared, OSPF had won.

So you may be wondering why you need to learn IS-IS if OSPF became the recommended standard for IP. IS-IS is still implemented in numerous service provider backbones. With MPLS starting to make a presence, it is certain that at some point in your career you will encounter IS-IS. Remember that the only routing protocols that can be used for MPLS traffic engineering are IS-IS and OSPF.

Because you have a good understanding of OSPF, learning IS-IS shouldn't be that much of a challenge. The two routing protocols share many of the same basic concepts:

- Both of them are link-state routing protocols.
- To maintain their link-state databases, both routing protocols use the Dijkstra SPF algorithm.
- Both, through the use of areas, support a hierarchical network topology.
- They both use Hello packets to form adjacencies with their neighbors.
- For broadcast multi-access networks, they both elect a designated router (DR).
- They both support VLSM and the summarization of areas.
- Both allow the use of authentication to ensure a more secure network.
- Both allow multiple instances per device, OSPF with the process ID and IS-IS with a tag after the `router isis` command.

Although IS-IS and OSPF share many common features, they do have quite a few differences:

- Whereas OSPF routers can be part of multiple areas, an IS-IS router belongs to only one area per routing process.
- In OSPF, the boundaries of areas are set in the router. The boundaries of areas are on the network connections between routers for IS-IS, reiterating that each router is in only one area per routing process.
- IS-IS utilizes CLNS protocol data units (PDUs) to send information between routers instead of using IP packets, like OSPF does.
- IS-IS allows for the preempting of DRs, where OSPF does not.
- OSPF DROthers do not form adjacencies with other DROthers on broadcast multi-access networks, while in the same environment, all IS-IS intermediate systems form adjacencies with one another.
- The backbone of an IS-IS network is designated by the type of routers in it instead of being designated by an area number (0, in the case of OSPF).

Now that you know a little about the history of IS-IS and how IS-IS compares to OSPF, let's focus on its operation.

Integrated IS-IS Operation

OSI uses terms that you may not currently be familiar with. Before we delve into the operation of IS-IS, we'll discuss the terms you need to know.

IS-IS Terminology

This section discusses some of the terms that are used when referring to IS-IS that you may not be familiar with.

ES An end system (ES) is a non-routing network device, such as a host.

IS An intermediate system (IS) is a routing device, in our case a router.

ES-IS End System to Intermediate System (ES-IS) is the protocol that is used to enable end systems to discover intermediate systems and vice versa.

SNPA The subnetwork point of attachment (SNPA) is the point at which subnetwork services are provided.

PDUs Protocol data units (PDUs) are the data passed between an OSI layer of one node to the peer OSI layer of another node.

DLPDU A data link frame is referred to as a data link PDU (DLPDU).

NPDU A packet is referred to as a network PDU (NPDU).

LSP The *link-state PDU (LSP)* is the IS-IS equivalent of the OSPF LSA. The main difference between the two is that the LSA is encapsulated behind the OSPF header and the IP packet, whereas the LSP is a packet all its own.

Level 1 intermediate systems Level 1 intermediate systems route within an area. When the destination is outside an area, they route toward a Level 2 system.

Level 2 intermediate systems Level 2 intermediate systems route between areas and toward other ASs.

NET The *network entity title (NET)* uniquely defines each router on the network. The NET is a network address, which contains a system ID and an area ID.

All of these terms play an important part in understanding the operation of IS-IS. You must come to know and understand each of these terms. As you read through this chapter, you'll be able to place the terms in their proper context.

IS-IS Areas

In order for you to better understand the use of areas for IS-IS, let's first have a quick review of how areas are used for OSPF. Refer to Figure 7.1.

FIGURE 7.1 OSPF areas

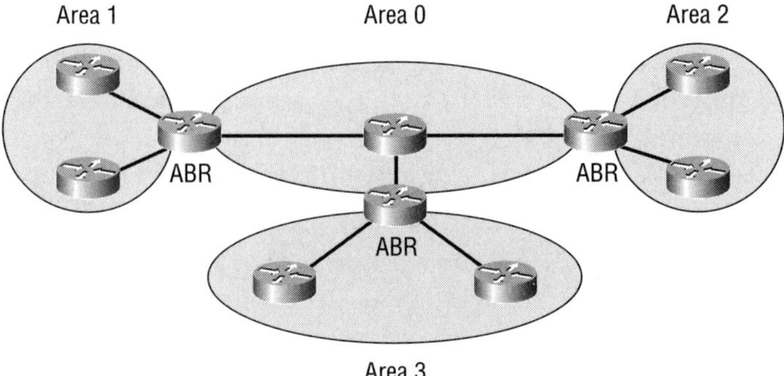

OSPF area boundaries fall within a router. These routers are known as ABRs. OPSF ABRs are allowed to have multiple interfaces in different areas. Also notice that the backbone area for OSPF must be numbered as Area 0. One last item to remember about OSPF is that if an area is not set up as a totally stubby area, summary LSAs will be sent into the area. This means that all routers in that particular area will know about inter-area routes. With all of this in mind, let's take a look at the same topology, except this time it's running IS-IS as the routing protocol. Refer to Figure 7.2.

FIGURE 7.2 IS-IS areas

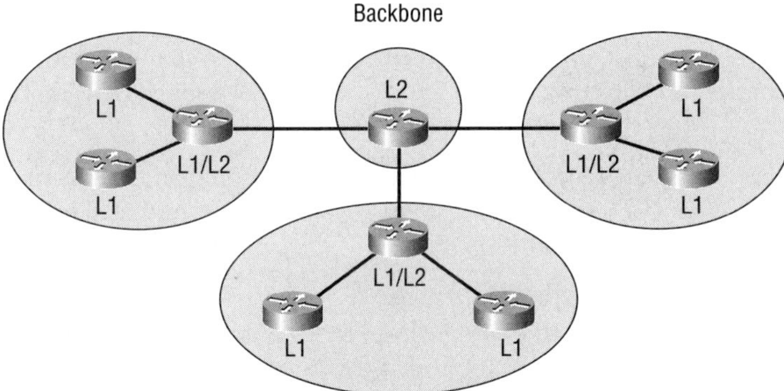

The first difference you should have noticed between the OSPF network and the IS-IS network is that the area boundaries for IS-IS are on the connections, not the routers. You should have also noticed that the routers are all completely within an area; the routers do not have some interfaces in one area and other interfaces in another area. Another important item to note about IS-IS is that the backbone can have any area ID. It is not limited to Area 0 like OSPF.

Now you may be wondering what all the L1, L2, and L1/L2 routers are. This would be a good time to explain these different types of routers:

L1 routers A *Level 1 (L1) router* is a router in a non-backbone area. L1 routers know only about intra-area routes. All they know about inter-area routes is a default route to the L1/L2 router for the area. All routers within a Level 1 area contain the same link-state database. These routers receive link-state PDUs (LSPs) only from within the area. They will not receive LSPs from other areas. L1 routers will not receive any information from an L2 router. The L1 router would be the equivalent of an internal router for OSPF.

L2 routers *Level 2 (L2) routers* are the *backbone routers*. They handle all of the inter-area traffic. An L2 router can belong only to the backbone area. L2 routers will send LSPs to all other L2 routers and to all L1/L2 routers, regardless of the area the L1/L2 router belongs to. The L2 router can be compared to a backbone router for OSPF.

L1/L2 routers *Level 1/Level 2 (L1/L2) routers* are similar in function to an OSPF ABR. L1/L2 routers will send LSPs to both L1 and L2 routers. The LSPs that the L1/L2 router sends to L1 routers help it to maintain its Level 1 link-state database. The LSPs that the L1/L2 router sends to L2 routers help it to maintain its Level 2 link-state database. The L1/L2 router contains two link-state databases, and information stored in the Level 2 link-state database is not shared with any L1 routers.

An IS-IS Level 1 area is very similar to an OSPF totally stubby area. This is because all the L1 routers within the area know only about each other. If they need to reach a network not contained within the area, they must communicate through the L1/L2 router.

Now that we've covered the routers, it's a good time to talk about the three different levels of routing for IS-IS:

Level 1 routing *Level 1 routing* is routing between intermediate systems within the same area. Basically, Level 1 routing is intra-area routing, and it occurs between all routers contained within the same area.

Level 2 routing *Level 2 routing* occurs between intermediate systems in different areas. All Level 2 routing will cross the backbone at some point. You can think of Level 2 routing as inter-area routing, and it occurs between routers in different IS-IS areas.

Level 3 routing *Level 3 routing* is routing between different routing domains. This type of routing will occur when traffic needs to leave the IS-IS routing domain to reach another routing domain. Level 3 routing is also known as internetwork routing.

Because IS-IS routers are totally contained in one area, the area ID is associated with the entire router, per routing process, instead of with an interface as is the case with OSPF. IS-IS allows for up to three area IDs to be associated with one routing process. The main use of multiple areas being configured on a device is for migrating from one area to another.

You now need to learn how to create an area and how to uniquely identify a router in that area. This is accomplished through what is known as the network entity title (NET).

Network Entity Titles

So far, we've discussed the commonalities and differences between IS-IS and OSPF. The main focus of Integrated IS-IS is how it can route IP packets. What we need to remember is that IS-IS is a CLNP protocol, not a TCP/IP protocol. This means that even though routing IP is supported, IS-IS still communicates with CLNS PDUs. An ISO addressing scheme must be implemented for IS-IS to function. The ISO address is known as a network entity title (NET). The NET is used just like an IP address to uniquely identify a router on the internetwork. The NET on Cisco devices may take the form of a variety of standard Network Service Access Point (NSAP) formats. Each of these formats has three common values:

Area ID The area ID is typically a one- or two-octet field that precedes the system ID. The area ID is used to signify the area the router belongs to. The area ID can span up to two octets if need be. For the BSCI, we will concentrate on a one-octet area ID. For the NSAP addressing scheme used with IS-IS, the area ID is everything to the left of the system ID.

System ID The system ID is used to identify the router. It is similar to the router ID in OSPF. The system ID can be up to eight octets in length. Cisco supports only a six-octet field for the system ID. Whether or not the vendor you are using supports more than six octets, the number of octets used must be the same throughout the IS-IS routing domain. Normally, the system ID will be set to one of the MAC addresses on the router. This is not a rule, and the system ID can be represented in a number of ways. The system ID that is used for a router must be unique throughout the IS-IS routing domain. There must be only one system ID set per router, regardless of the number of routing processes. The system ID must be common across all routing processes on the same router.

SEL The NSAP selector byte (SEL) is a one-octet field that represents the service being offered at the network level of the device. For our implementation of IS-IS, the SEL will always be set to 00. 00 represents the router. A good comparison to the SEL is the TCP or UDP port number being associated with an IP address, forming a socket that identifies a unique application instance on the internetwork. Basically, it tells you what service is being referenced for the particular address.

As previously mentioned, the NET can come in and be entered in a variety of NSAP formats, the last eight bytes of each serving the same function. Let's go ahead and take a look at the three most common formats, as shown in Figure 7.3.

As you can see, there are three common NSAP formats that the NET may be in:

- Standard eight-octet format
- OSI NSAP format
- GOSIP format

It is important that you know these three formats exist. The BSCI exam concentrates mainly on the standard eight-octet format. So that will be the one we will focus on in this chapter.

FIGURE 7.3 Network entity title formats

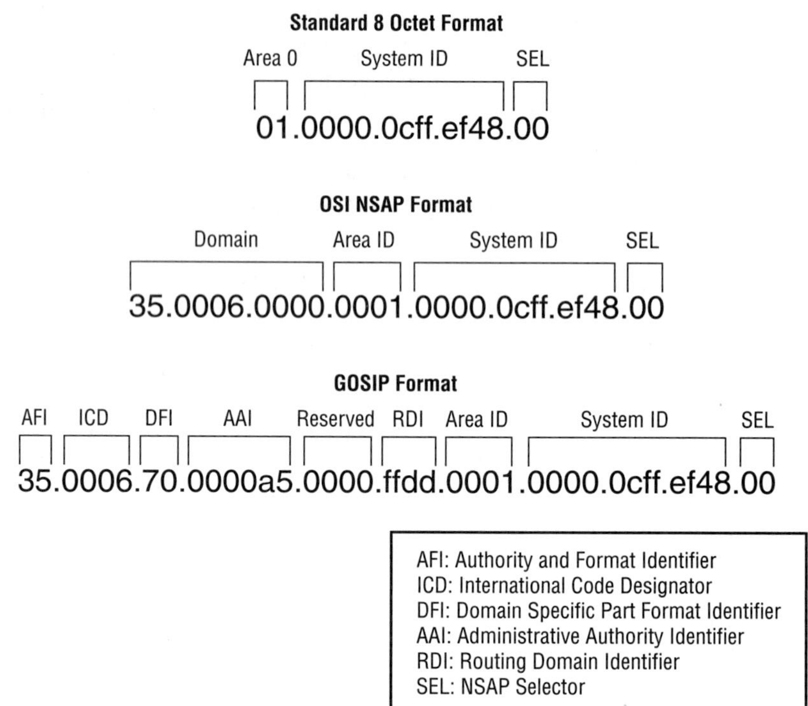

Neighbor and Adjacency Initialization

IS-IS utilizes Hello PDUs to discover its neighbors and to form adjacencies with them. After the formation of adjacencies, Hello PDUs are sent out every 10 seconds by default to maintain the adjacencies. The *Hello PDU* contains information about the router, the router's capabilities, and certain parameters about the interface sending the Hello PDU. Once the two routers agree on their respective capabilities and the parameters set forth, the routers will form an adjacency.

Sounds similar to OSPF, doesn't it? There is one major difference you need to be aware of. In OSPF, it is required that all routers forming adjacencies have the same Hello and Dead intervals. This is not true for IS-IS. The Hello PDU contains the hold time set by the neighboring router. The receiving router then uses this specific hold time for the neighbor. So the neighbor is never considered dead until the hold time associated with the neighbor is exhausted. This allows for different Hello and Dead intervals to be used by neighboring routers.

Adjacencies for IS-IS are broken down into Level 1 adjacencies and Level 2 adjacencies. *Level 1 adjacencies* are formed between L1 routers and neighboring L1 and L1/L2 routers in the same area. *Level 2 adjacencies* are formed between L2 routers and neighboring L2 and L1/L2 routers. If two L1/L2 routers are neighboring, then both a Level 1 and a Level 2 adjacency will be formed between the two routers. Adjacencies are never formed between an L1 router and an L2 router.

Because there are two different types of adjacencies that can be formed in an IS-IS network, there are separate Hello PDUs for Level 1 and Level 2. An L1 router sends only a Level 1 type of Hello PDU, an L2 router sends only a Level 2 type of Hello PDU, and an L1/L2 router needs to send both types of Hello PDUs in a broadcast multi-access network. If two L1/L2 routers are neighbors on a point-to-point network, only one Hello PDU will be sent that contains information for both the Level 1 and Level 2. So the L1/L2 routers will still form a Level 1 adjacency and a Level 2 adjacency with each other.

Remember, the standards and Cisco refer to these networks as simply broadcast networks, which is how you need to be able to recognize them, but it's the multi-access nature of these networks that leads to DR election.

Designated Router

For broadcast multi-access networks, IS-IS, like OSPF, supports the election of a designated router. The difference is that in IS-IS this designated router is known as a *designated IS (DIS)*. The DIS reduces the amount of traffic required for all routers to advertise their links over broadcast multi-access networks and the amount of traffic required to flood LSPs. The DIS advertises a pseudonode. The pseudonode is a representation of the network all the routers are connected to. The DIS appears in the link-state database as another router. Each router on that network will then form one adjacency with the pseudonode.

The DIS assigns a one-octet pseudonode ID to the broadcast multi-access network, which is then added to the system ID of the DIS to create the LAN ID. The LAN ID will be the source of the LSPs for the pseudonode in the link-state database. Even though the DIS has its own set of LSPs, it still generates the LSPs for the pseudonode.

One of the key differences between the OSPF DR and the IS-IS DIS is how they handle the flooding of the LSPs. In OSPF, a router will form an adjacency only with a DR and a BDR, which are then responsible for making sure all of the routers get the LSAs from the DR. The BDR is there in case this goal cannot be achieved.

This is not true with the IS-IS DIS. Routers in an area will form an adjacency with the DIS, but the routers will still form adjacencies with each other. Each router will multicast LSPs to its neighbors. The main function of the DIS is to make sure the routers receive all the LSPs. This is accomplished through the use of sequence number PDUs (SNPs). The use of SNPs will be covered in detail in the upcoming section, "LSP Flooding."

Another important concept for you to understand about the DIS's use in IS-IS is the fact that there can be more than one DIS. Remember how there are Level 1 and Level 2 adjacencies? Well, there are Level 1 and Level 2 DISs also. If Level 1 and Level 2 areas exist in the same broadcast multi-access network, a DIS will be elected for each level. A DIS is not elected if it is a point-to-point network. To make it even more interesting, the same router could end up filling the role as both the L1 DIS and the L2 DIS. Each of the pseudonodes created would be independent of each other.

Like OSPF, IS-IS has a process for electing the DIS. The first item taken into consideration when electing the DIS is the router priority. The router priority can be manually set to any value between 0 and 127. A router with the priority of 0 will never be elected. The default priority for Cisco devices is 64. The router with the highest router priority will win. Also, if a router is an L1/L2, you can manually set the router priority for the L1 portion to a value different than the router's L2 priority. If more than one router is found with the highest router ID, the highest system ID will be used to break the tie. In order to manually set the router priority for Level 1, you need to enter the following command in interface configuration mode:

```
isis priority value level-1
```

If you wanted to set the router priority for Level 2, you would use the same command but replace the `Level-1` keyword with the `Level-2` keyword.

In order to see what the current router priority setting is for an IS-IS interface, use the `show clns interface` command. Here's a sample output:

```
plano#show clns interface
FastEthernet2/0 is up, line protocol is up
  CLNS protocol processing disabled
Serial2/0 is up, line protocol is down
  CLNS protocol processing disabled
Serial2/0.1 is down, line protocol is down
  Checksums enabled, MTU 1500, Encapsulation FRAME-RELAY
  ERPDUs enabled, min. interval 10 msec.
  CLNS fast switching disabled
  CLNS SSE switching disabled
  DEC compatibility mode OFF for this interface
  Next ESH/ISH in 33 seconds
  Routing Protocol: IS-IS
    Circuit Type: level-1-2
    Interface number 0x0, local circuit ID 0x100
    Level-1 Metric: 10, Priority: 127, Circuit ID: plano.00
    Number of active level-1 adjacencies: 0
    Level-2 Metric: 10, Priority: 0, Circuit ID: plano.00
    Number of active level-2 adjacencies: 0
    Next IS-IS Hello in 5 seconds
Serial2/0.16 is down, line protocol is down
  CLNS protocol processing disabled
Serial2/0.17 is down, line protocol is down
  CLNS protocol processing disabled
FastEthernet2/1 is up, line protocol is up
  CLNS protocol processing disabled
Serial2/1 is administratively down, line protocol is down
  CLNS protocol processing disabled
Loopback0 is up, line protocol is up
  CLNS protocol processing disabled
Loopback1 is up, line protocol is up
  CLNS protocol processing disabled
```

As you can deduce from the preceding output, Plano has only one interface configured for IS-IS. The Level 1 priority is set to 127. This means that more than likely this interface will become the DIS for the Level 1 area. The Level 2 priority is set to 0, which means this interface will never become the DIS for the Level 2 area.

There are a couple of notes you should make about the differences between OSPF DRs and IS-IS DISs. The first is the fact that IS-IS does not elect a backup designated router like OSPF does. The second, and in my opinion the most interesting, is the difference in the way IS-IS and OSPF handle the situation when a router comes online with a higher router priority than the current designated router. If this occurs in OSPF, nothing will happen. However, IS-IS will allow for pre-empting the DIS. This means that if a router comes online that has a higher router priority than the current DIS, the new router will become the DIS. A new LAN ID will be created, and new LSPs reflecting the new DIS will be generated.

IS-IS PDUs

Before we move on to the way routers flood LSPs, now would be a good time to have an overview of the nine different types of IS-IS PDUs. There are three main categories that IS-IS PDUs fall into:

- Hello PDU
- Link-state PDU (LSP)
- Sequence number PDU (SNP)

Each of the three main categories can be broken down into the actual PDUs used for that category. Let's look at each of these categories in more detail.

Hello PDU

Hello PDUs, as we've previously discussed, are used to initialize and maintain router adjacencies. There are actually three types of Hello PDUs:

Level 1 LAN IS-IS Hello PDU The Level 1 LAN IS-IS Hello PDU is used by Level 1 routers to form adjacencies on broadcast multi-access networks. These PDUs are passed only between Level 1 routers and L1/L2 routers to form Level 1 adjacencies.

Level 2 LAN IS-IS Hello PDU As you can probably guess from the name, the Level 2 LAN IS-IS Hello PDUs are used to form Level 2 adjacencies on broadcast multi-access networks. Level 2 and L1/L2 routers use these PDUs to form Level 2 adjacencies.

Point-to-Point IS-IS Hello PDU The point-to-point IS-IS Hello PDU is used on point-to-point connections to form adjacencies. The point-to-point IS-IS Hello PDU can be used to form a Level 1 or Level 2 adjacency.

If you remember from our earlier discussion, an L1/L2 router could use a combination of these Hello PDUs to form its Level 1 and Level 2 adjacencies.

Link-State PDU (LSP)

The link-state PDU (LSP) is used in much the same way that an OSPF router uses its LSA packets. The LSP is used to advertise routing information. There are two possible types of LSPs available:

Level 1 LSP The Level 1 LSP is used to advertise Level 1 link-state routing information between Level 1 routers. It contains data about the routing information that the advertising Level 1 router knows. Level 1 LSPs are used to form the Level 1 link-state database.

Level 2 LSP Level 2 LSPs are used to advertise the link-state routing information a Level 2 router knows about. This information is used to help form the Level 2 link-state database.

It is very possible that a router will utilize both types of LSPs. If a router is an L1/L2 router, it will use the Level 1 LSP to help it form its Level 1 link-state database, and it will use the Level 2 LSP to help it form its Level 2 link-state database. After a router receives all of the LSPs, it utilizes the SPF algorithm to select the routes to populate its routing table.

In a broadcast multi-access network, routers will multicast LSPs. Level 1 LSPs are multicast to the MAC address 0180.C200.0014. This MAC address is known as AllL1ISs. MAC address 0180.C200.0015, known as AllL2ISs, is where routers will multicast all Level 2 LSPs on a broadcast multi-access network. Routers use unicast instead of multicast on point-to-point networks, because only one unicast will ever be necessary for each LSP.

Sequence Number PDU (SNP)

Sequence number PDUs (SNP) are used primarily to ensure that routers have the most up-to-date LSPs. If you think about it, the operation of SNPs is very similar to the use of acknowledgment packets. There are four different types of SNPs available:

Complete sequence number PDU (CSNP) *Complete sequence number PDUs (CSNPs)* contain the most up-to-date list of all LSPs. When a link first comes up, CSNPs are used to ensure the routers have the latest LSPs to form their link-state databases. CSNPs are also used periodically to ensure that routers have the latest information. Level 1 and Level 2 adjacencies have their own CSNPs. In other words, a Level 1 CSNP is used only for Level 1 information, and a Level 2 CSNP is used only for Level 2 information. CSNPs are sent out only by DISs, so you will not find CSNPs on point-to-point connections.

Partial sequence number PDU (PSNP) A *partial sequence number PDU (PSNP)* contains only the latest sequence number information for a few LSPs. Point-to-point connections do not use CSNPs, but broadcast multi-access networks use both CSNPs and PSNPs, as outlined in the next section, "LSP Flooding." PSNPs can be used to request missing LSP information after receiving CSNPs in broadcast multi-access networks. In the absence of CSNPs, point-to-point networks use PSNPs to acknowledge the receipt of LSP routing updates. Like CSNPs, PSNPs are also specific to the level they are representing.

Now that we have covered the different types of PDUs used in IS-IS networks, let's take a look at how these different PDUs are used to create a router's link-state database.

LSP Flooding

In order to construct the router's link-state databases, LSP flooding is utilized. In order to create the Level 1 link-state database, Level 1 LSPs are flooded throughout the Level 1 area. Flooding Level 2 LSPs over all Level 2 adjacencies creates a Level 2 link-state database. The creation of these link-state databases would not be possible without the use of SNPs.

All routers on a broadcast multi-access network will receive multicast LSPs from their neighbors. The designated IS router for Level 1 will multicast a CSNP, which contains information about all Level 1 LSPs in its link-state database, to the multicast address AllL1ISs. A Level 2 DIS will do the same except it will multicast the CSNP to the AllL2ISs multicast address. The default time the CSNP will be multicast is 10 seconds for Cisco devices.

After the DIS has multicast the CSNP, all of the routers on that broadcast multi-access network will compare the CSNP to all the LSPs stored in their link-state database. If a router detects that it has an LSP that is missing from the CNSP or if the router has an LSP that is newer than the CSNP, the router will multicast the LSP to all of its neighbors. It's feasible that the neighbors could detect the missing LSP in the CSNP but do nothing, because they already received the missing LSP from their neighbor. Remember that all routers—even so-called DROthers in OSPF parlance—form adjacencies with all other routers. Recall that there are no DROther-to-DROther adjacencies in OSPF.

A PSNP will be multicast by a router if the router notices that an LSP contained in the CSNP is missing from its link-state database. The DIS will then send the LSP to the router that requested it.

LSP flooding on point-to-point networks functions differently from LSP flooding on broadcast multi-access networks. A router sends an LSP to its neighbor on the point-to-point network. The router then waits for a PSNP to be sent from the neighbor acknowledging the receipt of the LSP. If the router doesn't receive the PSNP in a specified period of time, it will retransmit the LSP to the neighbor. The default time period the router will wait is five seconds for Cisco devices.

Once a router receives all of the LSPs, it runs the SPF algorithm to select the routes to populate its routing table.

SPF Algorithm

Once a router's link-state database has been created, the router needs to create the shortest path tree. The shortest path tree is then used to select the routes to populate the router's routing table. The IS-IS metrics that can be used to create the shortest path tree are default, delay, expense, and error. We're going to concentrate on default, because it's the only IS-IS metric that is supported by Cisco devices.

The default metric can be any value between 0 and 63, inclusive; Cisco defaults it to 10. The default metric can be set to a different value for every IS-IS interface on the router and for the different levels in which the interface may be participating. If you do not specify the level of routing in which the metric should be used for SPF calculation for that interface, it will be used for both L1 and L2 calculations, if applicable.

You can specify a different metric for each level by issuing the `isis metric` *`default_metric`* `[level-1|level-2]` command twice, once for each level. The metric for an IS-IS route is the sum of all outgoing interfaces involved in the path. Like OSPF, the route that IS-IS will choose is the route with the lowest metric. The maximum value IS-IS supports for a route is 1023.

IS-IS classifies routes based on whether they are L1 routes or L2 routes. L1 routes are always internal to an IS-IS routing domain. L2 routes can be further classified as internal or external. An L2 external route is a route that is external to the IS-IS routing domain, whereas an L2 internal route is internal to the IS-IS routing domain. An L1 route is always preferred over an L2 route.

If multiple routes are found to a destination, the route with the best metric will be selected. If multiple routes with the same metric are found, IS-IS will use all of the routes. For load balancing, IS-IS supports up to six paths of equal cost.

There's one last topic we need to cover before moving on to configuring IS-IS. That topic is the type of networks supported by IS-IS.

Network Types

One item that makes IS-IS configuration easier than OSPF is that IS-IS supports only two types of networks instead of four. The supported network types for IS-IS are broadcast multi-access and point-to-point. Unlike OSPF, the network types for IS-IS are non-configurable. This means that you're stuck with whatever network type is assigned to the interface by default.

In order for routers to form adjacencies on broadcast multi-access networks, the router sends out either a Level 1 LAN Hello PDU or a Level 2 LAN Hello PDU, depending on whether the router is an L1, L2, or L1/L2 router. On point-to-point networks, the routers send out a point-to-point Hello PDU.

The network type of broadcast is assigned to all broadcast multi-access interfaces on a router. For NBMA networks, broadcast is assigned to multipoint subinterfaces and point-to-point is assigned to all point-to-point subinterfaces. Physical interfaces, which are connected to NBMA networks, are considered by IS-IS to be multipoint interfaces, so the network type of broadcast is assigned to them also. It may seem a little confusing, but multipoint WAN connections are actually treated by IS-IS the same as a broadcast multi-access LAN connection. The same type of Hello PDUs are used, and a DIS is elected.

There is a serious problem you'll need to watch for when IS-IS is used over NBMA networks. That problem is Hello PDU mismatches. This occurs when two devices on the same connection are sending different types of Hello PDUs. For instance, this problem could arise when you connect a point-to-point subinterface of one router to a physical interface on another router. If you remember correctly, the default network type for a physical interface connected to a NBMA network is broadcast. So what happens in this instance is that you have one router sending Level 1 or 2 LAN Hello PDUs and the other router sending point-to-point Hello PDUs. The two routers will not form an adjacency.

The way to overcome this issue is to make sure that both sides of the connection are either point-to-point or multipoint. Here is a list you can memorize so you will not encounter this situation on NBMA networks:

- Physical interfaces can connect to other physical interfaces or to multipoint subinterfaces.
- Multipoint subinterfaces can connect to other multipoint subinterfaces or to physical interfaces.
- Point-to-point subinterfaces can connect only to other point-to-point subinterfaces.

Now that you have a good understanding of how IS-IS operates, we'll show you how to configure IS-IS.

Configuring IS-IS

An important item for you to note is to make sure the IOS your routers are running supports CLNS. Remember, even in an IP-only environment, IS-IS still sends CLNS PDUs. If your routers are not running an IOS that supports CLNS, you will not be able to configure IS-IS.

Figure 7.4 displays a network with three areas and five routers.

FIGURE 7.4 Multiple area IS-IS network

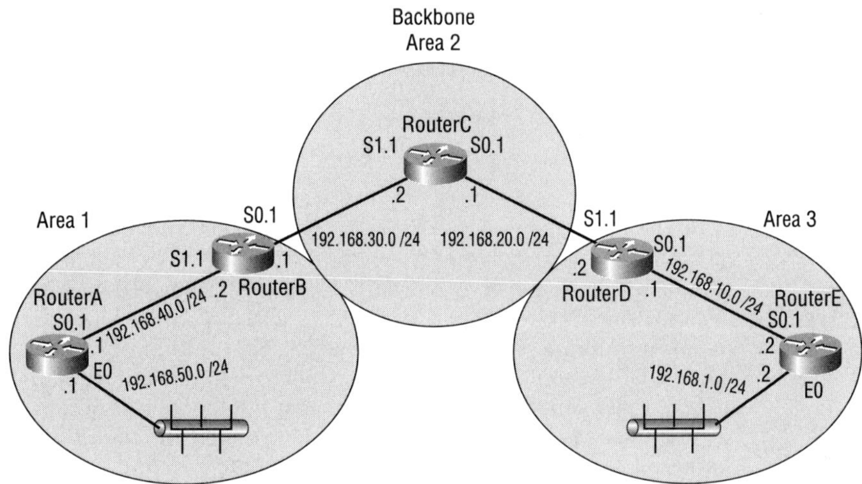

We're going to configure just Area 1 to start with. The first step is to enable IS-IS on the routers and to assign the NET. You enable IS-IS on a router with the `router isis` command. The NET is set with the command `net` *`areaID.systemID.SEL`*:

```
RouterA#conf t
Enter configuration commands, one per line. End with CNTL/Z.
RouterA(config)#router isis
RouterA(config-router)#net 01.0000.0000.0001.00
RouterA(config-router)#^Z
RouterA#

RouterB#conf t
Enter configuration commands, one per line. End with CNTL/Z.
```

```
RouterB(config)#router isis
RouterB(config-router)#net 01.0000.0000.0002.00
RouterB(config-router)#^Z
RouterB#
```

One item you should be aware of is that Cisco routers running a single instance of IS-IS are, by default, L1/L2 routers. With that in mind, look at Figure 7.4 again. What you needed to notice is that RouterA is an L1 router. The level of a router can be set with the `is-type` *`type`* command, where *`type`* is the level of the router, either `level-1`, `level-1-2`, or `level-2-only`.

As an alternative, you might issue the interface command `isis circuit-type` *`type`* so you can set the majority of the interfaces to one level, using the `is-type` command, while an individual interface or two can be set differently.

So we need to go back to RouterA and configure it as an L1 router before we move on:

```
RouterA#conf t
Enter configuration commands, one per line. End with CNTL/Z.
RouterA(config)#router isis
RouterA(config-router)#is-type level-1
RouterA(config-router)#^Z
RouterA#
```

While not an objective of the BSCI exam, the following information is helpful to know. IS-IS routers can participate in multiple areas, much like OSPF can run multiple routing processes to keep routing information separate. Unlike OSPF, multiple IS-IS areas cannot intercommunicate, because they are actually separate routing processes, but the `redistribute` command cannot be used to combine routing information from multiple processes, as is supported by OSPF. While the area ID of each routing process must be different, the system ID must be the same across all processes, much like the router ID of an OSPF router is the same across all areas in which it is a member, but the area number varies.

Now that we have enabled IS-IS, configured the NET, and set the proper level of the router, we need to enable IS-IS on the appropriate interfaces. Enabling IS-IS on the interface is different from the other routing protocols we've covered so far. In order to enable IS-IS on an interface, enter the `ip router isis` command on the appropriate interfaces:

```
RouterA#conf t
Enter configuration commands, one per line. End with CNTL/Z.
RouterA(config)#interface e0
RouterA(config-if)#ip router isis
RouterA(config-if)#exit
RouterA(config)#interface s0.1
```

```
RouterA(config-if)#ip router isis
RouterA(config-if)#^Z
RouterA#

RouterB#conf t
Enter configuration commands, one per line. End with CNTL/Z.
RouterB(config)#interface s0.1
RouterB(config-if)#ip router isis
RouterB(config-if)#exit
RouterB(config)#interface s1.1
RouterB(config-if)#ip router isis
RouterB(config-if)#^Z
RouterB#
```

That's all there is to it. Configuring IS-IS is a straightforward task.

To enable IS-IS for CLNS, enter the `clns router isis` command in interface configuration mode.

Now that we have it configured, let's take a look at the routing table of RouterB:

```
RouterB#sh ip route
Codes: C - connected, S - static, I - IGRP, R - RIP, M - mobile, B - BGP
       D - EIGRP, EX - EIGRP external, O - OSPF, IA - OSPF inter area
       N1 - OSPF NSSA external type 1, N2 - OSPF NSSA external type 2
       E1 - OSPF external type 1, E2 - OSPF external type 2, E - EGP
       i - IS-IS, L1 - IS-IS level-1, L2 - IS-IS level-2, * - candidate default
       U - per-user static route, o - ODR

Gateway of last resort is not set

i L1    192.168.50.0/24 [115/20] via 192.168.40.1, Serial1.1
C    192.168.40.0/24 is directly connected, Serial1.1
C    192.168.30.0/24 is directly connected, Serial0.1
```

Notice from the preceding output that the route RouterB learned from RouterA was an internal Level 1 route.

Now that you have a feeling for how to configure IS-IS in a single area, let's enable IS-IS on the rest of the routers:

```
RouterC#conf t
Enter configuration commands, one per line. End with CNTL/Z.
```

```
RouterC(config)#router isis
RouterC(config-router)#net 02.0000.0000.0003.00
RouterC(config-router)#is-type level-2-only
RouterC(config-router)#^Z
RouterC#

RouterD#conf t
Enter configuration commands, one per line. End with CNTL/Z.
RouterD(config)#router isis
RouterD(config-router)#net 03.0000.0000.0004.00
RouterD(config-router)#^Z
RouterD#

RouterE#conf t
Enter configuration commands, one per line. End with CNTL/Z.
RouterE(config)#router isis
RouterE(config-router)#net 03.0000.0000.0005.00
RouterE(config-router)#is-type level-1
RouterE(config-router)#^Z
RouterE#
```

Now that we have IS-IS enabled on all of the routers, let's add the interfaces:

```
RouterC#conf t
Enter configuration commands, one per line. End with CNTL/Z.
RouterC(config)#interface s0.1
RouterC(config-if)#ip router isis
RouterC(config-if)#exit
RouterC(config)#interface s1.1
RouterC(config-if)#ip router isis
RouterC(config-if)#^Z
RouterC#

RouterD#conf t
Enter configuration commands, one per line. End with CNTL/Z.
RouterD(config)#interface s0.1
RouterD(config-if)#ip router isis
RouterD(config-if)#exit
RouterD(config)#interface s1.1
RouterD(config-if)#ip router isis
RouterD(config-if)#^Z
```

```
RouterD#

RouterE#conf t
Enter configuration commands, one per line. End with CNTL/Z.
RouterE(config)#interface s0.1
RouterE(config-if)#ip router isis
RouterE(config-if)#exit
RouterE(config)#interface e0
RouterE(config-if)#ip router isis
RouterE(config-if)#^Z
RouterE#
```

After configuring all the routers for IS-IS, let's look at the differences between the L1, L2, and L1/L2 routing tables. We'll start by taking a look at the routing table of RouterA:

```
RouterA#sh ip route
Codes: C - connected, S - static, I - IGRP, R - RIP, M - mobile, B - BGP
       D - EIGRP, EX - EIGRP external, O - OSPF, IA - OSPF inter area
       N1 - OSPF NSSA external type 1, N2 - OSPF NSSA external type 2
       E1 - OSPF external type 1, E2 - OSPF external type 2, E - EGP
       i - IS-IS, L1 - IS-IS level-1, L2 - IS-IS level-2, * - candidate default
       U - per-user static route, o - ODR

Gateway of last resort is not set

i L1 192.168.30.0/24 [115/20] via 192.168.40.1, Serial0.1
C    192.168.40.0/24 is directly connected, Serial0.1
C    192.168.50.0/24 is directly connected, Ethernet0
i*L1 0.0.0.0/0 [115/10] via 192.168.40.2, Serial0.1
```

The first item you should notice is that only two routes are learned from IS-IS, and one of the routes is a default route. Remember that an L1 IS-IS area is similar to an OSPF totally stubby area in that routes external to the area are not advertised into the area. The L1/L2 router, RouterB, advertises only a default route to RouterA for all of the other networks outside the area. RouterB knows about all of the other routes. The other internal L1 route RouterA knows about is a directly connected interface on RouterB. Since we keep mentioning RouterB, let's go ahead and take a look at its routing table:

```
RouterB#sh ip route
Codes: C - connected, S - static, I - IGRP, R - RIP, M - mobile, B - BGP
       D - EIGRP, EX - EIGRP external, O - OSPF, IA - OSPF inter area
       N1 - OSPF NSSA external type 1, N2 - OSPF NSSA external type 2
       E1 - OSPF external type 1, E2 - OSPF external type 2, E - EGP
```

```
      i - IS-IS, L1 - IS-IS level-1, L2 - IS-IS level-2, * - candidate default
      U - per-user static route, o - ODR

Gateway of last resort is not set

i L1    192.168.50.0/24 [115/20] via 192.168.40.1, Serial1.1
i L2    192.168.1.0/24 [115/40] via 192.168.30.2, Serial0.1
i L2    192.168.10.0/24 [115/30] via 192.168.30.2, Serial0.1
i L2    192.168.20.0/24 [115/20] via 192.168.30.2, Serial0.1
C    192.168.40.0/24 is directly connected, Serial1.1
C    192.168.30.0/24 is directly connected, Serial0.1
```

The main difference you should notice about RouterB's routing table is that it doesn't have the default route in it. The reason RouterB doesn't have a default route is that it is an L1/L2 router. Being an L1/L2 router, RouterB forms adjacencies with the L1 routers in its area and the backbone L2 router. That is why you see the L2 routes in the routing table. Now that you understand the differences between the routes that an L1 router knows and the routes that an L1/L2 router knows, we need to examine the routing table of an L2 router. With that in mind, let's take a look at RouterC's routing table:

```
RouterC#sh ip route
Codes: C - connected, S - static, I - IGRP, R - RIP, M - mobile, B - BGP
      D - EIGRP, EX - EIGRP external, O - OSPF, IA - OSPF inter area
      N1 - OSPF NSSA external type 1, N2 - OSPF NSSA external type 2
      E1 - OSPF external type 1, E2 - OSPF external type 2, E - EGP
      i - IS-IS, L1 - IS-IS level-1, L2 - IS-IS level-2, * - candidate default
      U - per-user static route, o - ODR

Gateway of last resort is not set

i L2    192.168.50.0/24 [115/30] via 192.168.30.1, Serial1.1
i L2    192.168.40.0/24 [115/20] via 192.168.30.1, Serial0.1
i L2    192.168.1.0/24 [115/30] via 192.168.20.2, Serial0.1
i L2    192.168.10.0/24 [115/20] via 192.168.20.2, Serial0.1
C    192.168.30.0/24 is directly connected, Serial1.1
C    192.168.20.0/24 is directly connected, Serial0.1
```

As you probably expected, an L2 router has only L2 routes in its routing table. This is because an L2 router forms adjacencies only with other L2 routers and L1/L2 routers. If you remember back to when we were discussing how LSPs are flooded through a network, you will recall that an L1/L2 route advertises L2 LSPs to its L2 neighbors and advertises L1 LSPs to its

L1 neighbors. Because this occurs, all RouterC knows about the routes sent to it is that they are L2 LSPs, even if the routes originated as L1 routes.

Theoretically, IS-IS supports the creation of virtual links. Cisco's implementation of IS-IS does not allow for the creation of virtual links.

By now, you should have a good understanding of how to configure IS-IS. What we need to focus on now is how to make sure IS-IS is operating properly and what tools to use to troubleshoot it if it's not operating properly.

Verifying and Troubleshooting IS-IS

Now that you know how to configure IS-IS in a multiple area network, we need to focus on how to verify that it is operating correctly and, if not, how to troubleshoot it.

Route Information

Just like with other routing protocols, you should always verify that the correct information is in the routing table:

```
RouterB#show ip route
Codes: C - connected, S - static, I - IGRP, R - RIP, M - mobile, B - BGP
       D - EIGRP, EX - EIGRP external, O - OSPF, IA - OSPF inter area
       N1 - OSPF NSSA external type 1, N2 - OSPF NSSA external type 2
       E1 - OSPF external type 1, E2 - OSPF external type 2, E - EGP
       i - IS-IS, L1 - IS-IS level-1, L2 - IS-IS level-2, * - candidate default
       U - per-user static route, o - ODR

Gateway of last resort is not set

i L1    192.168.50.0/24 [115/20] via 192.168.40.1, Serial1.1
i L2    192.168.1.0/24  [115/40] via 192.168.30.2, Serial0.1
i L2    192.168.10.0/24 [115/30] via 192.168.30.2, Serial0.1
i L2    192.168.20.0/24 [115/20] via 192.168.30.2, Serial0.1
C    192.168.40.0/24 is directly connected, Serial1.1
C    192.168.30.0/24 is directly connected, Serial0.1
```

As can be seen from this routing table, there is one Level 1 route and three Level 2 routes that were learned through IS-IS. You know that a route is a Level 1 IS-IS route by the code `L1`, and you recognize a Level 2 IS-IS route by the code `L2`. The code `I` at the beginning of the line means that the route is an IS-IS route. If you would like to view only routes learned by IS-IS, the following command may be used:

```
RouterB#show ip route isis
i L1     192.168.50.0/24 [115/20] via 192.168.40.1, Serial1.1
i L2     192.168.1.0/24  [115/40] via 192.168.30.2, Serial0.1
i L2     192.168.10.0/24 [115/30] via 192.168.30.2, Serial0.1
i L2     192.168.20.0/24 [115/20] via 192.168.30.2, Serial0.1
```

Link-State Database Information

The command `show isis database` gives you information about all the LSP information stored in the router's IS-IS link-state database. Here is a sample output from Houston's IS-IS link-state database:

```
Houston#show isis database

IS-IS Level-1 Link State Database
LSPID                  LSP Seq Num  LSP Checksum  LSP Holdtime  ATT/P/OL
0000.0C00.0C35.00-00   0x0000000C   0x5696        792           0/0/0
0000.0C00.40AF.00-00*  0x00000009   0x8452        1077          1/0/0
0000.0C00.62E6.00-00   0x0000000A   0x38E7        383           0/0/0
0000.0C00.62E6.03-00   0x00000006   0x82BC        384           0/0/0
0800.2B16.24EA.00-00   0x00001D9F   0x8864        1188          1/0/0
0800.2B16.24EA.01-00   0x00001E36   0x0935        1198          1/0/0

IS-IS Level-2 Link State Database
LSPID                  LSP Seq Num  LSP Checksum  LSP Holdtime  ATT/P/OL
0000.0C00.0C35.03-00   0x00000005   0x04C8        792           0/0/0
0000.0C00.3E51.00-00   0x00000007   0xAF96        758           0/0/0
0000.0C00.40AF.00-00*  0x0000000A   0x3AA         1077          0/0/0
```

The `show isis database` command allows you to view the entire IS-IS link-state database for the router. It lists all of the LSPs the router knows about. If you see an asterisk next to an LSP ID, that means the LSP was generated locally.

If you just want to view specific information stored in the Level 1 or Level 2 database, there are parameters that can be used with the command. Here's an example of viewing detailed information about a Level 2 link-state database:

```
Dallas#show isis database detail level-2

IS-IS Level-2 Link State Database
LSPID                  LSP Seq Num  LSP Checksum  LSP Holdtime  ATT/P/OL
```

```
0000.0C00.1111.00-00*  0x00000006    0x4DB3        1194          0/0/0
  Area Address: 01
  NLPID:        0xCC
  IP Address:   160.89.64.17
  Metric: 10    IS 0000.0C00.1111.09
  Metric: 10    IS 0000.0C00.1111.08
  Metric: 10    IP 160.89.65.0 255.255.255.0
  Metric: 10    IP 160.89.64.0 255.255.255.0
  Metric: 0     IP-External 10.0.0.0 255.0.0.0
```

The `show isis database detail level-2` command allows you to view the area and routing information for each LSP stored in the particular level's link-state database.

Viewing the database may not always help you solve an issue. If an LSP is missing from the database, you need a way to find out why that LSP is missing. The `debug isis update-packets` command can do that for you:

```
Austin#debug isis update-packets
ISIS-Update: Sending L1 CSNP on Ethernet0
ISIS-Update: Sending L2 CSNP on Ethernet0
ISIS-Update: Updating L2 LSP
ISIS-Update: Delete link 888.8800.0181.00 from
    L2 LSP 1600.8906.4022.00-00, seq E
ISIS-Update: Updating L1 LSP
ISIS-Update: Sending L1 CSNP on Ethernet0
ISIS-Update: Sending L2 CSNP on Ethernet0
ISIS-Update: Add link 8888.8800.0181.00 to
    L2 LSP 1600.8906.4022.00-00, new seq 10, len 91
ISIS-Update: Sending L2 LSP 1600.8906.4022.00-00,
    seq 10, ht 1198 on Tunnel0
ISIS-Update: Sending L2 CSNP on Tunnel0
ISIS-Update: Updating L2 LSP
ISIS-Update: Rate limiting L2 LSP 1600.8906.4022.00-00,
    seq 11 (Tunnel0)
ISIS-Update: Updating L1 LSP
ISIS-Update: Rec L2 LSP 888.8800.0181.00.00-00 (Tunnel0)
ISIS-Update: PSNP entry 1600.8906.4022.00-00,
    seq 10, ht 1196
```

The `debug isis update-packets` command gives you the details of all LSPs that the router is sending and receiving. It also informs you of all SNPs being sent and received.

A situation can arise when authentication has been configured and neighboring routers have conflicting passwords set. When this occurs, the routers will still form adjacencies, but neither will receive LSPs from the other. By using this **debug** command, you will be informed that an LSP didn't pass authentication. That's a good indicator to check how authentication is configured on each device. IS-IS authentication is beyond the scope of the BSCI exam, so we will not cover it here.

Routing Protocol Information

In order to view detailed information about IS-IS configured on the router, use the following command:

```
Austin#show clns protocol

 IS-IS Router: <Null Tag>
         System Id: 0000.0C00.224D.00 IS-Type: level-1-2
    Manual area address(es):
            01
      Routing for area address(es):
            01
      Interfaces supported by IS-IS:
          Serial1 - IP
          Serial0 - IP
      Next global update in 530 seconds
      Redistributing:
      static
      Distance: 10
```

The show clns protocol command gives detailed information of how IS-IS is configured on the router. What you can learn from the preceding output is the router's system ID, the level of the router, the area it is participating in, the areas the router is routing, the interfaces configured for IS-IS, what's being redistributed into IS-IS, and the IS-IS cost.

The following command provides you with information about the interfaces on the router configured for IS-IS:

```
plano#show clns interface
FastEthernet2/0 is up, line protocol is up
  CLNS protocol processing disabled
Serial2/0 is up, line protocol is down
  CLNS protocol processing disabled
Serial2/0.1 is down, line protocol is down
  Checksums enabled, MTU 1500, Encapsulation FRAME-RELAY
  ERPDUs enabled, min. interval 10 msec.
  CLNS fast switching disabled
  CLNS SSE switching disabled
  DEC compatibility mode OFF for this interface
```

```
    Next ESH/ISH in 33 seconds
    Routing Protocol: IS-IS
      Circuit Type: level-1-2
      Interface number 0x0, local circuit ID 0x100
      Level-1 Metric: 10, Priority: 127, Circuit ID: plano.00
      Number of active level-1 adjacencies: 0
      Level-2 Metric: 10, Priority: 0, Circuit ID: plano.00
      Number of active level-2 adjacencies: 0
      Next IS-IS Hello in 5 seconds
Serial2/0.16 is down, line protocol is down
  CLNS protocol processing disabled
Serial2/0.17 is down, line protocol is down
  CLNS protocol processing disabled
FastEthernet2/1 is up, line protocol is up
  CLNS protocol processing disabled
Serial2/1 is administratively down, line protocol is down
  CLNS protocol processing disabled
Loopback0 is up, line protocol is up
  CLNS protocol processing disabled
Loopback1 is up, line protocol is up
  CLNS protocol processing disabled
```

For each interface configured for IS-IS, the `show clns interface` command informs you of the circuit type, the IS-IS priority, the metric, and the number of active adjacencies.

Viewing Neighbor Information

For IS-IS, it is important to know who your neighbors are. Many times routing information not being received by a router could be caused by neighbor adjacencies not being formed. To view who a router's neighbors are, use the following command:

```
Austin#show clns is-neighbors

System Id       Interface  State Type  Priority        Circuit Id
  ➥Format
0000.0C00.0C35  Ethernet1  Up    L1    64          0000.0C00.62E6.03  Phase V
0800.2B16.24EA  Ethernet0  Up    L1L2  64/64       0800.2B16.24EA.01  Phase V
0000.0C00.3E51  Serial1    Up    L2    0           04                 Phase V
0000.0C00.62E6  Ethernet1  Up    L1    64          0000.0C00.62E6.03  Phase V
```

In the preceding example, the router has three Level 1 neighbors and two Level 2 neighbors. If you noticed, one of the neighbors is an L1/L2 router, which means this router will form a Level 1 and a Level 2 adjacency with the router. The command also informs you if the state were something different. The `detail` parameter can be added to the end of the command line to view the area address for each of the neighbors. You can also use the command **`show clns neighbors`** to find out IS-IS and ES-IS neighbors.

If you would like to view the Hello PDUs a router is sending and receiving, the **`debug isis adj-packets`** command can be used:

```
Austin#debug isis adj-packets

ISIS-Adj: Rec L1 IIH from 0000.0c00.40af (Ethernet0), cir type 3, cir id
BBBB.BBBB.BBBB.01
ISIS-Adj: Rec L2 IIH from 0000.0c00.40af (Ethernet0), cir type 3, cir id
BBBB.BBBB.BBBB.01
ISIS-Adj: Rec L1 IIH from 0000.0c00.0c36 (Ethernet1), cir type 3, cir id
CCCC.CCCC.CCCC.03
ISIS-Adj: Area mismatch, level 1 IIH on Ethernet1
ISIS-Adj: Sending L1 IIH on Ethernet1
ISIS-Adj: Sending L2 IIH on Ethernet1
ISIS-Adj: Rec L2 IIH from 0000.0c00.0c36 (Ethernet1), cir type 3, cir id
BBBB.BBBB.BBBB.03
```

Debugging IS-IS adjacency packets provides you with knowledge of what Hello PDUs the router is sending and receiving. (IIH is an abbreviation for IS-IS Hello.) This can be a powerful tool when you're trying to find out why routers aren't forming adjacencies. For instance, if you had two routers that weren't forming adjacencies with each other and one router had a physical interface connected to the NBMA network and the other router had a subinterface connected to the NBMA network, it might be hard to figure out why they weren't forming adjacencies. With the `debug isis adj-packets` command, you would be informed of a Hello PDU mismatch. That was just one example of how the command can help you out with adjacency issues.

Viewing SPF Information

Frequent SPF calculations can indicate a problem in your network. Periodic SPF calculations occur every 15 minutes. If you are encountering more frequent calculations than the periodic calculations, you could have a problem in your network. You can view SPF calculations with the command `show isis spf-log`:

```
Austin#show isis spf-log
                   Level 1 SPF log
  When    Duration  Nodes  Count Last trigger LSP   Triggers
00:36:38    3124     40      1       Austin.00-00   TLVCODE
00:33:25    3216     41      5       Austin.00-00   TLVCODE NEWLSP
00:31:40    3096     41      1       Dallas.00-00   TLVCODE
00:29:01    3004     41      2       Austin.00-00   ATTACHFLAG LSPHEADER
```

```
00:29:46    3384    41    1    Austin.00-01  TLVCODE
00:28:01    2932    41    3    Austin.00-00  TLVCODE
00:27:30    3140    41    1                  PERIODIC
00:24:30    3144    41    1    Austin.01-00  TLVCODE
00:21:45    2908    41    1    Austin.01-00  TLVCODE
00:20:57    3148    41    3    Plano.00-00   TLVCODE TLVCONTENT
00:17:46    3054    41    1    Austin.00-00  TLVCODE
00:14:35    2958    41    1    Houston.00-00 TLVCODE
00:12:30    3632    41    1                  PERIODIC
00:10:31    2988    41    1    Austin.00-01  TLVCODE
00:09:44    3016    41    1    ElPaso.00-00  TLVCODE
00:06:02    2932    41    1    Plano.00-00   TLVCONTENT
00:04:29    2988    41    2    Plano.00-00   TLVCONTENT
00:02:58    3228    41    1    Austin.00-00  TLVCODE
00:01:29    3120    41    3    Waco.03-00    TLVCONTENT
```

This command informs you how long it was between SPF calculations, how long they took, how many devices were involved, how many triggers caused the calculation, the last LSP that caused the trigger, and what the triggers were. Note the timing of the periodic triggers—separated by 15 minutes—down to the second. It really is like clockwork.

There are a number of `debug` commands that can be used to help you better understand what is happening with the SPF calculations. The following is a list of some of the more common `debug` commands with an explanation of each:

debug isis spf-events The `debug isis spf-events` command is best used when you want to see the IS-IS routes that will be placed in the routing table. The command also informs you if a route was rejected from being added to the routing table. This could occur if the route already exists in the routing table with a lower administrative distance than IS-IS.

debug isis spf-triggers The `debug isis spf-triggers` command is best used when you need to find out what is triggering a SPF calculation. The command informs you what level the SPF calculation was done for and what the cause of the calculation was.

debug isis spf-statistics The `debug isis spf-statistics` command informs you how long it took to perform an SPF calculation.

Before diving too deep into IS-IS troubleshooting, try the `clear isis *` command. It clears up a number of adjacency issues (and others) caused by various inconsistencies that are simply "ghosts in the machine."

By now, you should have the proper tools at hand to configure, verify, and troubleshoot an IS-IS network. My suggestion would be to spend time in a lab practicing configuring, breaking, and troubleshooting IS-IS. Once you've done that, you'll have the necessary knowledge to work on IS-IS in a production network.

Summary

See, I told you IS-IS isn't that bad. By now, you should understand how IS-IS operates and how to configure it.

We began by learning the different levels of IS-IS routers and what they are used for. IS-IS routers can be categorized into one of three categories: Level 1 (L1), Level 2 (L2), or Level 1/Level 2 (L1/L2). A Level 1 IS-IS router belongs to a non-backbone IS-IS area and forms adjacencies with other neighboring Level 1 and Level 1/2 routers in the same area. A Level 2 router belongs only to the IS-IS backbone area and will form Level 2 adjacencies with all neighboring Level 2 routers in its area and all neighboring Level 1/2 routers. An L1/L2 router belongs to a non-backbone IS-IS area and will form Level 1 adjacencies with all neighboring Level 1 routers in its area and will form Level 2 adjacencies with all neighboring Level 2 and L1/L2 routers.

IS-IS utilizes LSPs to populate the link-state database. SNPs are utilized to make sure LSPs are received. IS-IS supports a designated IS (DIS) in broadcast multi-access networks. The DIS is similar to the OSPF DR. The DIS is responsible for making sure all of the routers on the broadcast multi-access network receive the LSPs they should.

Configuring IS-IS requires you to first enable IS-IS on the device. Once you have enabled it, you will enter into router configuration mode. Then you need to specify the NET for the device. In router configuration mode, you can also specify which type of IS-IS router the device is; by default, a device is a Level 1/2 router. The last step in configuring IS-IS is to enable it on the interfaces you want to participate in IS-IS.

IS-IS is the last of the Interior Gateway Protocols (IGPs) we will cover in the BSCI part of the book. We will now change our focus to the Exterior Gateway Protocols (EGPs), with an emphasis on the Border Gateway Protocol (BGP). If you don't feel comfortable with the information covered so far, now would be a good time to stop and go back to those areas. It's very important that you have a good grasp on IGPs before moving onto EGPs.

Exam Essentials

Know the similarities and differences between OSPF and IS-IS. OSPF and IS-IS share many characteristics; both of them are link-state routing protocols, use the Dijkstra SPF algorithm, use a hierarchical network topology, use Hello packets to form adjacencies, utilize DRs, support VLSM, and support authentication. They also have a few differences; an IS-IS router's area boundaries are on the link, IS-IS utilizes CLNS PDUs, and IS-IS supports DR pre-empting.

Understand the different router types used in IS-IS. There are three different types of IS-IS routers: L1, L2, and L1/2. L1 routers are in a non-backbone area, know only about intra-area routes, know about inter-area routes through a default route to the L1/L2 router for the area, and contain the same link-state database as other L1 routers in the same area. L2 routers are the backbone routers, handle all of the inter-area traffic, can belong only to the backbone area, and will send LSPs to all other L2 routers and to all L1/L2 routers, regardless of the area the L1/L2 router belongs to. L1/2 routers are similar to OSPF ABRs, contain an L1 link-state database, and contain an L2 link-state database.

Understand the adjacencies that different IS-IS routers form. L1 routers will form adjacencies with all neighboring L1 routers and L1/2 routers in the same area. L1/2 routers will form L1 adjacencies with all neighboring L1 and L1/2 routers in the same area. L1/2 routers will form L2 adjacencies with all neighboring L1/2 and L2 routers regardless of area. L2 routers will form L2 adjacencies with all neighboring L2 routers in the same area and all neighboring L1/2 routers regardless of area.

Know what LSPs are and what they are used for. LSPs are used to advertise routing information. An L1 LSP is used to advertise L1 link-state routing information between L1 routers and to form the L1 link-state database. An L2 LSP is used to advertise L2 link-state routing information between L2 routers and to form the L2 link-state database.

Know how to configure an IS-IS network. Configuring IS-IS is pretty simple. To configure IS-IS to route only IP traffic, you need to issue the `router isis` command in global configuration mode, the `net` command in router configuration mode, and the `ip router isis` command in interface configuration mode. To configure IS-IS in a mixed IP/CLNS environment to route both IP and CLNS traffic, you need to enter the previously discussed commands for enabling IS-IS in an IP environment and also add the `clns router isis` command in interface configuration mode.

Border Gateway Protocol

THE CCNP EXAM TOPICS COVERED IN THIS CHAPTER INCLUDE THE FOLLOWING:

- ✓ **Understand how BGP operates.**
- ✓ **Understand how to configure and verify BGP.**

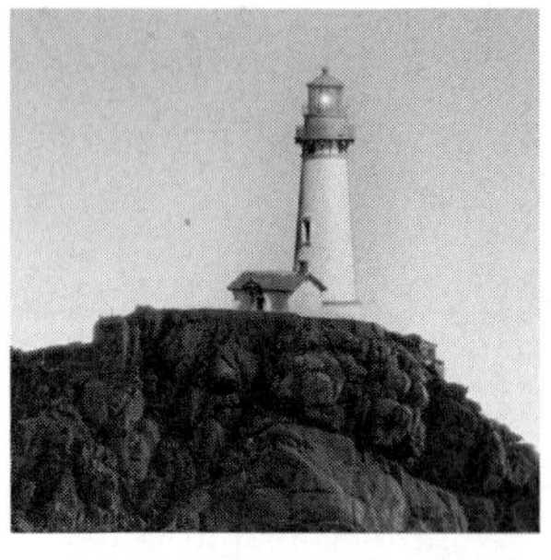

Up to this point we've covered how routing occurs within an autonomous system (intra-AS routing). We have yet to cover how routing occurs between different autonomous systems (inter-AS routing). That is the focus of the next two chapters.

In this chapter, you'll be introduced to the concept of *Exterior Gateway Protocols (EGPs)*. We're going to concentrate our focus on the Border Gateway Protocol. The early part of this chapter primarily consists of the theory of BGP operation such as the history, the difference between iBGP and eBGP, neighbor relationships, and route selection. We'll then show how to implement BGP in its most basic form. Enabling BGP, configuring neighbors, and injecting routes are all explained. We also cover how to verify BGP's operation and troubleshoot it if it isn't operating properly. You will learn the `show` commands and the `debug` commands that can be used to verify and troubleshoot BGP operation. Chapter 9, "Advanced Border Gateway Protocol," covers the more in-depth concepts of BGP.

Border Gateway Protocol

Border Gateway Protocol (BGP) is known as the routing protocol for the Internet. The Internet is made up of numerous autonomous systems. BGP is used to share routing information between the different autonomous systems.

BGP has been around for quite some time. The first implementation of BGP occurred in 1989 and was known as BGP version 1. BGPv1 was a classful routing protocol and didn't allow for aggregation of routes. To overcome the limitations of BGPv3, a new form of BGP was created, known as BGP version 4. BGPv4 was first implemented in 1993. It introduced the use of classless interdomain routing (CIDR) and allowed for the aggregation of routes.

BGP utilizes a reliable transport protocol for transmission. Transmission Control Protocol (TCP) was the reliable transport protocol decided on for BGP transmissions. BGP uses port 179 of TCP for establishing connections. Because TCP is considered a reliable transport protocol at layer 4, BGP is able to eliminate the need to implement explicit update fragmentation, retransmission, acknowledgment, and sequencing.

An important item to note about BGP is that it doesn't worry about intra-AS routing. BGP trusts that the IGP or IGPs being utilized in the AS will take care of the intra-AS routing. BGP concerns itself with inter-AS routing. A BGP speaker will share network reachability information with neighboring BGP speakers. The network reachability information contains data on all of the different autonomous systems it has traversed. This information is then used by the BGP speaker to create a graph, or tree, of all the autonomous systems in use. The tree then allows BGP to remove routing loops and to enforce certain policies for its autonomous system.

Before we dive into the operation of BGP, it is important to understand the terms that are used by BGP.

BGP is defined in many Requests for Comments (RFCs), which include 1771–1774, 1863, 1965–1966, 1997–1998, 2042, 2283, 2385, and 2439, to mention a few. BGPv4, the latest version, and autonomous systems are defined in RFC 1771.

BGP Terminology

Make sure you're familiar with the following BGP terminology for the BSCI exam:

Autonomous system An autonomous system was originally defined as a set of devices under the same administrative control that used a single IGP for intra-AS routing and an EGP for inter-AS routing. With the rapid changes that have occurred over the years, the definition of an autonomous system has changed. An *autonomous system (AS)* is now considered to be a set of devices under the same administrative control with one or more IGPs controlling intra-AS routing and an EGP for inter-AS routing. Even though an autonomous system may have multiple IGPs operating at the same time, the autonomous system will appear to other autonomous systems as having one coherent interior routing plan. This allows the existence of multiple IGP autonomous systems (EIGRP 100 and EIGRP 200, for example), which are really not the same as EGP autonomous systems, within the same EGP AS.

BGP speaker Any routing device that is running a BGP routing process is known as a *BGP speaker.*

Peers When two BGP speakers form a TCP connection between them they are known as *peers.* The term neighbor is the same as the term peer.

eBGP *External Border Gateway Protocol (eBGP)* is the routing protocol used to exchange routing information between BGP peers in different autonomous systems.

iBGP *Internal Border Gateway Protocol (iBGP)* is the routing protocol used to exchange routing information between BGP peers in the same autonomous system.

Inter-AS routing *Inter-AS routing* is routing that occurs between different autonomous systems.

Intra-AS routing *Intra-AS routing* is routing that occurs within the same autonomous system.

The terms defined in this section will appear throughout the next two chapters.

Now that you have some of the BGP terminology down, we can focus on how BGP operates.

BGP Operation

BGP is known as the routing protocol of the Internet. BGP allows for the communication of routing information between different autonomous systems spread throughout the world.

Figure 8.1 shows numerous autonomous systems, which will utilize BGP to share routing information. There are two forms of BGP used: internal BGP (iBGP) and external BGP (eBGP).

All BGP speakers contained within the same autonomous system use internal BGP (iBGP) to communicate with one another. There are a couple of important items to note about multiple BGP speakers within the same autonomous system. First, all of the BGP speakers must peer with one another. This means that you must configure a full mesh for iBGP to operate properly. This doesn't mean all devices must be connected to one another—just that all of the BGP speakers must have layer 3 reachability. iBGP will utilize the TCP protocol to form the peering sessions between the iBGP peers. There are ways to overcome the full mesh limitations, but they will be explained in Chapter 9.

Another important characteristic of iBGP peers is that they will not advertise iBGP-learned routes to one another. Then how do these internal routes get distributed within the AS, you ask? By the IGP, of course. BGP is not meant to replace the IGP, and there is no comparison between iBGP and an IGP, so don't get caught by that common fallacy. When an iBGP speaker advertises an eBGP-learned route to its iBGP peers, which should be all BGP speakers in its AS, there is no need for them to advertise this route to other iBGP peers, because all of them have been informed of the route already by the original iBGP peer. If any of these iBGP speakers also speak eBGP, it is perfectly acceptable for them to advertise this iBGP-learned route to their eBGP peer.

External BGP (eBGP) is utilized between BGP speakers in different autonomous systems. Like iBGP, eBGP peering sessions require the BGP speakers participating to have layer 3 connectivity among themselves. TCP is then utilized by eBGP to form the peering sessions.

After forming peers, the BGP speakers use the peering information to create a loop-free map of the autonomous systems involved. This is also known as a BGP tree.

FIGURE 8.1 Multiple autonomous systems

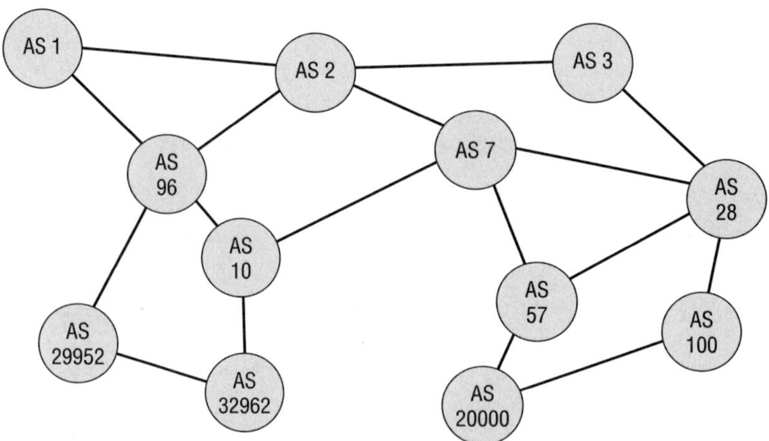

Once BGP speakers have formed peers and created their BGP tree, they will start exchanging routing information. The BGP speakers will first exchange their entire BGP routing tables. From that point forward, the peers will exchange incremental updates of their BGP routing tables and KEEPALIVE messages to keep the connection up.

Understand that the BGP routing table is actually a new structure. It is not the IP routing table, now that BGP entries are found in it. Instead, the BGP routing table is much like a topology database, and it contains entries that may never make it into the IP routing table for one reason or another. While the command `show ip route bgp` will display any BGP-learned routes that make it into the IP routing table, the command `show ip bgp` is required to display the contents of the actual BGP routing table.

From a bird's-eye view, that's all there is to BGP. Sounds a little too easy, right? That would be a good assumption. BGP is a very complex routing protocol. That's why we have dedicated two chapters to it. We will now dive into the different components that make up the way BGP operates.

Message Header Format

BGP will process a message only when the entire message has been received. BGP requires that a message be a minimum of 19 octets to a maximum of 4,096 octets. The basic message header format is broken down into these fields:

- 16-byte Marker field
- 2-byte Length field
- 1-byte Type field

Figure 8.2 gives the layout for the BGP message header.

Marker The Marker field is 16 bytes long. The Marker field is used to detect a loss of synchronization between a set of BGP peers and also to authenticate incoming BGP messages. The value of the Marker field depends on the type of message. If an OPEN message does not contain authentication information, the Marker must be set to all 1s.

Length The Length field is 2 bytes long and indicates the length of the entire message including the Marker field. The value for the Length field must be at least 19 and no more than 4,096.

FIGURE 8.2 Message header format

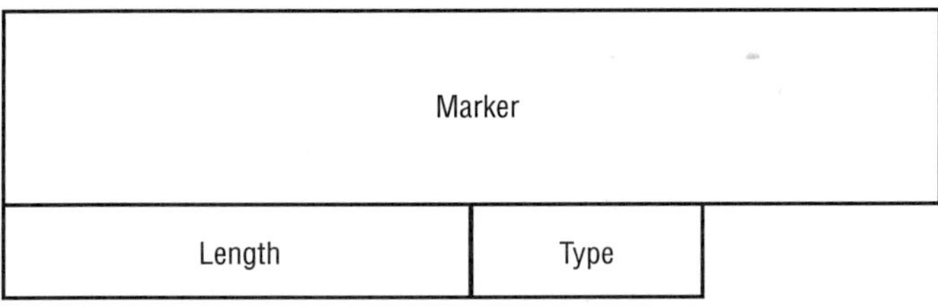

Type The Type field is 1 byte long and indicates the type code of the message. There are four possible values for this field, as listed in Table 8.1.

TABLE 8.1 Type Field Values

Type Value	Message Type
1	OPEN message
2	UPDATE message
3	NOTIFICATION message
4	KEEPALIVE message

Let's take a more in-depth look at each of these different message types.

OPEN Message

The OPEN message is the first type of message sent after a TCP session has been formed. When the OPEN message is accepted, a KEEPALIVE message confirming the OPEN message is returned. After the KEEPALIVE is sent to confirm the OPEN message, incremental UPDATE messages, NOTIFICATION messages, and KEEPALIVE messages will be exchanged between the BGP peers.

The OPEN message contains the fixed-size BGP header and the following fields, as depicted in Figure 8.3.

FIGURE 8.3 OPEN message format

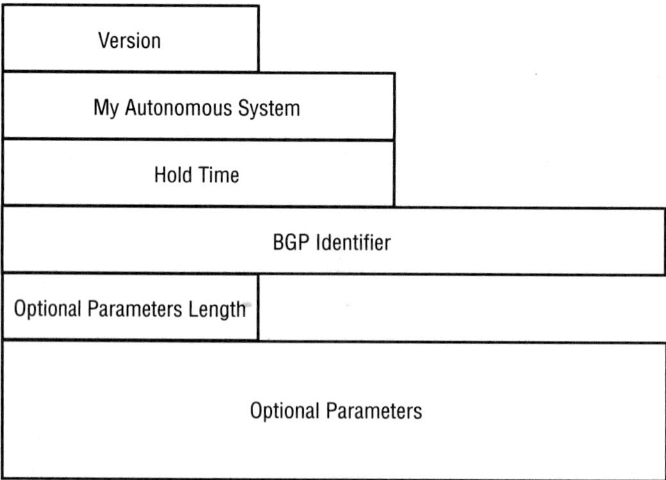

Version The Version field is 1 byte long and is used in determining the version of BGP for the neighbors to use. BGP speakers will attempt to negotiate the highest version number that both BGP speakers support. If a version number is specified in the version field that the other BGP speaker does not support, an error message will be returned to the sender and the TCP session will be torn down. The TCP session is then established again, and the version number is lowered. This process continues until a common version number is reached.

My Autonomous System The My Autonomous System field is 2 bytes long and contains the autonomous system number of the sending BGP speaker. This field lets the receiving BGP speaker know the autonomous system of its neighbor and is eventually used in the creation of the BGP speaker's BGP tree.

Hold Time The Hold Time field is 2 bytes long and informs the receiving BGP speaker of the proposed value for the holdtime by the sending BGP speaker. The receiving BGP speaker calculates the lowest of its configured holdtime and the value in the Hold Time field. This will determine the number of seconds the BGP speaker will allow between the receipt of KEEPALIVE and/or UPDATE messages. If one of these messages is not received in the time specified by the holdtime, the neighbor is considered dead. Each time one of the messages is received, the holdtime is reset to 0.

Unlike the negotiation for the BGP version, where a connection is reset to negotiate a common version number, the negotiation for the holdtime does not reset the connection.

The BGP speakers can set the value for the holdtime to 0. If this occurs, no KEEPALIVE messages are sent. This means that the connection will always be up. Having a holdtime of 0 could cause problems if one side of the connection has a loss of communications. Because KEEPALIVE messages are not being exchanged, the other side of the connection would never know the loss of communication occurred. If the value of the Hold Time field is not 0, it must then be at least 3.

BGP Identifier The BGP Identifier field is 4 bytes long and contains the BGP identifier of the sending BGP speaker. The *BGP identifier* is similar to the router ID (RID) for OSPF. It identifies the particular BGP speaker. Like the OSPF RID, the BGP identifier will be the highest loopback IP address on the router. If a loopback doesn't exist on the router, it will be the highest IP address configured for any interface on the router. The BGP identifier is set during the startup process of BGP. In other words, once the BGP identifier is set, it will not change unless you restart the BGP process. It is a good idea when using BGP to configure a loopback interface to set the BGP identifier.

Optional Parameters Length The Optional Parameters Length field is 1 byte in length and represents the total length of the Optional Parameters field. A value of 0 for the Optional Parameters Length field indicates that no optional parameters have been set.

Optional Parameters The Optional Parameters field is a variable-length field containing a list of optional parameters that will be used in the BGP neighbor negotiation. Each optional parameter is represented by a <*parameter type*, *parameter length*, *parameter value*> triplet. Figure 8.4 illustrates the format of the Optional Parameters field.

Parameter Type The Parameter Type field is 1 byte long and identifies the individual parameter.

Parameter Length The Parameter Length field is 1 byte long and contains the length of the Parameter Value field.

Parameter Value The Parameter Value field is of variable length and is interpreted based on the value of the Parameter Type field.

FIGURE 8.4 Optional Parameters field format

Parameter Type	Parameter Length	Parameter Value (variable)

UPDATE Message

After BGP speakers have become peers, they will exchange incremental UPDATE messages. UPDATE messages contain the routing information for BGP. The information contained in the UPDATE message is used to construct a loop-free routing environment.

Not only does the UPDATE message contain a feasible route to use, it also contains any unfeasible routes to withdraw. A single UPDATE message can contain at most one feasible route to use but may contain multiple unfeasible routes to withdraw.

It's important to understand the distinction between a route and a prefix. Each UPDATE message may advertise only a single feasible route, but it may advertise multiple prefixes in its NLRI field. Said a different way, each UPDATE message can advertise a single way to get to multiple networks. It makes sense, then, that any network that is not accessible at the end of the advertised route would not be in the Network Layer Reachability Information (NLRI) field of the same UPDATE message.

The UPDATE message contains the fixed-size BGP header and the following fields, as depicted in Figure 8.5.

FIGURE 8.5 UPDATE message format

Unfeasible Routes Length (2 bytes)
Withdrawn Routes (variable)
Total Path Attributes Length (2 bytes)
Path Attributes (variable)
Network Layer Reachability Information (variable)

Unfeasible Routes Length Field

The Unfeasible Routes Length field is 2 bytes long and contains the length of the Withdrawn Routes field. A value of 0 signifies that the Withdrawn Routes field is not present in this UPDATE message.

Withdrawn Routes Field

The Withdrawn Routes field is of variable length and contains a list of IP address prefixes that will be withdrawn. Each of the IP address prefixes is in the following format and is illustrated in Figure 8.6.

FIGURE 8.6 IP address prefix formats

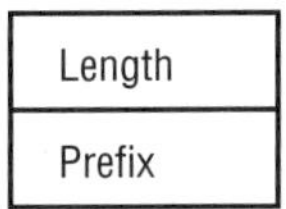

Length The Length field is 1 byte long and contains the length, in bits, of the IP address prefix. If this field is set to 0, it means all IP address prefixes.

Prefix The Prefix field is of variable length and contains the IP address prefix.

Total Path Attributes Length Field

The Total Path Attributes Length (TPAL) field is 2 bytes long and contains the length of the Path Attributes field. A value of 0 in this field signifies that there is no NLRI information in this UPDATE message.

Path Attributes Field

The Path Attributes field is of variable length and contains a sequence of attributes about a path. The Path Attributes field is present in every UPDATE message. Of course, it may be empty, which will be indicated by a TPAL of 0.

The information contained in the Path Attributes field is used to track specific route information and is also used for routing decisions and filtering. Each path attribute is broken down into an *<attribute type, attribute length, attribute value>* triple.

The Attribute Type field is 2 bytes in length and consists of the Attribute Flags byte followed by the Attribute Type Code byte.

Attribute Flags The attribute flags state whether path attributes are one of the following:

- Well-known mandatory—This attribute must be recognized by all implementations of BGP and be present in the UPDATE message. A BGP session will be terminated if a well-known attribute is not present in the UPDATE message.
- Well-known discretionary—This attribute must be recognized by all implementations of BGP but doesn't need to be present in the UPDATE message.

- Optional transitive—This attribute allows for optional attributes that are not recognized by an implementation of BGP to be passed along to a BGP speaker's peers.
- Optional non-transitive—If an optional attribute is not recognized by an implementation of BGP and the transitive flag is not set, the optional attribute will not be passed on to the BGP speaker's peers.

The attribute's flag sets which category a path attribute belongs to through the use of its bits:

- The first high order bit (bit 0) is the optional bit. If the bit is set to 1, the path attribute is optional. If the bit is set to 0, the path attribute is well-known.
- The second high order bit (bit 1) is the transitive bit. This bit defines whether an optional attribute is transitive or not. An optional transitive attribute will have the bit set to 1 and an optional non-transitive attribute will have the bit set to 0. If an attribute is well-known, the transitive bit will always be set to 1.
- The third high order bit (bit 2) is the partial bit. The partial bit will state whether the optional transitive attribute is partial or complete. A complete optional transitive attribute will have the bit set to 0, and a partial will have the bit set to 1. All well-known and optional non-transitive attributes will have the partial bit set to 0.
- The fourth high order bit (bit 3) is the extended length bit. The extended length bit is used to specify whether the attribute length is 1 or 2 bytes. An attribute length of 1 byte will have the bit set to 0, and for an attribute length of 2 bytes, the bit will be set to 1.
- The four lower order bits (bits 4–7) are unused. They will be set to 0 and ignored.

Attribute Type Code The Attribute Type Code field specifies the type of path attribute. Table 8.2 lists the possibilities for the attribute type code.

TABLE 8.2 Attribute Type Codes

Type Code	Attribute Name	Category
1	ORIGIN	Well-known mandatory
2	AS_PATH	Well-known mandatory
3	NEXT_HOP	Well-known mandatory
4	MULTI_EXIT_DISC	Optional non-transitive
5	LOCAL_PREF	Well-known discretionary
6	ATOMIC_AGGREGATE	Well-known discretionary
7	AGGREGATOR	Optional transitive

TABLE 8.2 Attribute Type Codes *(continued)*

Type Code	Attribute Name	Category
8	COMMUNITY	Optional transitive
9	ORIGINATOR_ID	Optional non-transitive
10	CLUSTER_LIST	Optional non-transitive
11	DPA	Destination point attribute for BGP
12	Advertiser	BGP/IDRP route server
13	RCID_PATH/CLUSTER_ID	BGP/IDRP route server
14	Multiprotocol Reachable NLRI	Optional non-transitive
15	Multiprotocol Unreachable NLRI	Optional non-transitive
16	Extended Communities	N/A
256	Reserved for development	N/A

We are going to focus on only the first 10 attribute type codes. The others are beyond the scope of the information needed for the BSCI exam. Let's take a more in-depth look at each of the first 10 attribute type codes:

- *ORIGIN* is a well-known mandatory attribute. The autonomous system that originates the routing information creates the ORIGIN attribute. It is contained in all UPDATE messages that propagate the routing information.
- *AS_PATH* is a well-known mandatory attribute that contains a list of all the autonomous systems the routing information has transited. The AS_PATH component is composed of a sequence of AS path segments. Each AS path segment is represented by the triplet of *<path segment type, path segment length, path segment value>*. When a BGP speaker advertises a learned route to other BGP speakers in its AS, the BGP speaker will not modify the AS_PATH attribute. When a BGP speaker advertises a learned route to other BGP speakers outside of its AS, it modifies the AS_PATH in the following ways:
  - For AS_PATH with the first path segment of AS_SEQUENCE, the BGP speaker will append its AS number as the last part of the sequence.
  - For AS_PATH with the first path segment of AS_SET, the BGP speaker will add a new path segment with the type of AS_SEQUENCE with its AS number in the sequence.

  When a BGP speaker originates the route, it includes an empty AS_PATH attribute when advertising to BGP speakers in its own AS, iBGP peers. The BGP speaker includes its AS number in the AS_PATH attribute when advertising to BGP speakers outside of its AS, eBGP peers.

- *NEXT_HOP* is a well-known mandatory attribute that specifies the IP address of the border router that should be used as the next hop to the destination specified. Following are the rules for how the next hop is determined for the various cases that may arise:
  - In eBGP, the next hop is the IP address of the external neighbor that announced the route.
  - In iBGP:

    Internal routes (from inside the AS) use as a next hop the IP address of the internal neighbor that announced the route. Because iBGP peers will not re-advertise these routes to each other, the next hop will be the iBGP peer that brought the route into the AS, the logical exit point to get to the prefixes advertised with the route. Because we will have a full mesh of TCP connections or the equivalent, all iBGP speakers will simultaneously converge on this same next hop for the route.

    External routes use the same next hop address as was originally injected into the AS by eBGP. These next hop addresses remain unaltered, by default, within the AS.
  - In a multi-access network, the next hop will generally be the IP address of the interface on the same multi-access media that advertised the route, very much like an IGP.
- *MULTI_EXIT_DISC* is an optional non-transitive attribute. If multiple entry or exit points exist to the same AS, it can be used to determine which one to use. The entry or exit point with the lowest metric is used.
- *LOCAL_PREF* is a well-known discretionary attribute. This attribute is used by a BGP speaker in setting the degree of preference of a route, which is used to indicate the preferred path to exit the AS. The BGP speaker includes this attribute in advertisements to its iBGP peers.
- *ATOMIC_AGGREGATE* is a well-known discretionary attribute. When a BGP speaker receives overlapping routes from its peers, it may set the ATOMIC_AGGREGATE attribute. The attribute is set if the BGP speaker chooses a less specific route to a destination over a more specific route—meaning the router chose a route with a shorter subnet mask rather than one with a longer mask.
- *AGGREGATOR* is an optional transitive attribute. When a BGP speaker performs route aggregation, it includes in the AGGREGATOR attribute its AS number and BGP identifier.
- *COMMUNITY* is an optional transitive attribute. The COMMUNITY attribute specifies the communities a route belongs to. Communities are covered in more detail in Chapter 9.
- *ORIGINATOR_ID* is an optional non-transitive attribute. A BGP speaker performing the role of a route reflector creates this attribute. The BGP identifier of the originating route reflector is included in the ORIGINATOR_ID attribute. This attribute is specific only to the local AS. Route reflectors are covered in more detail in Chapter 9.
- *CLUSTER_LIST* is an optional non-transitive attribute. The CLUSTER_LIST attribute is composed of a list of CLUSTER_ID values. When a route reflector reflects a route, it appends its CLUSTER_ID to the CLUSTER_LIST. Cluster IDs and route reflectors are covered in more detail in Chapter 9.

Network Layer Reachability Information (NLRI) Field

With BGP version 4 came the support for classless interdomain routing (CIDR). BGPv4 is able to advertise routes regardless of classful boundaries. BGPv4 accomplishes this through the use of the *Network Layer Reachability Information (NLRI)* field.

The NLRI field is a variable-length field, which contains the IP address prefix of the route. The NLRI field consists of a 1-byte Length field and a variable-length Prefix field:

Length The Length field indicates the length of the IP address prefix. You can think of the Length field as being similar to a subnet mask. By knowing the subnet mask, you are able to determine what the network address is. The same is true for the Length field. If the value for the Length field is set to 0, this indicates that all IP addresses are included.

Prefix The Prefix field is of variable length and contains the actual IP address prefix.

KEEPALIVE Message

KEEPALIVE messages are used to ensure that connectivity still exists between peers. The *KEEPALIVE* message is made up of only the fixed-size BGP message header. A KEEPALIVE message will be sent in order to restart the hold timer. The interval at which a KEEPALIVE message is sent is recommended to be one-third the holdtime value. This is why the holdtime must be at least 3 seconds if it is not 0. A KEEPALIVE message will not be sent if an UPDATE message was sent during this period of time. If the holdtime is set to 0, a KEEPALIVE message will never be sent.

NOTIFICATION Message

Whenever an error occurs during a BGP session, the BGP speaker generates a NOTIFICATION message. As soon as the BGP speaker generates the NOTIFICATION message, the session is terminated. The NOTIFICATION message contains error codes and error sub-codes that allow network administrators to more efficiently troubleshoot the problem. Figure 8.7 lays out the format of the NOTIFICATION message.

The Error Codes field is 1 byte in length and has six possible error codes. The Error Subcodes field is 1 byte in length and contains the error sub-code. Only the first three error codes have error sub-codes. Table 8.3 lists the possible error codes and their related error sub-codes.

FIGURE 8.7 NOTIFICATION message format

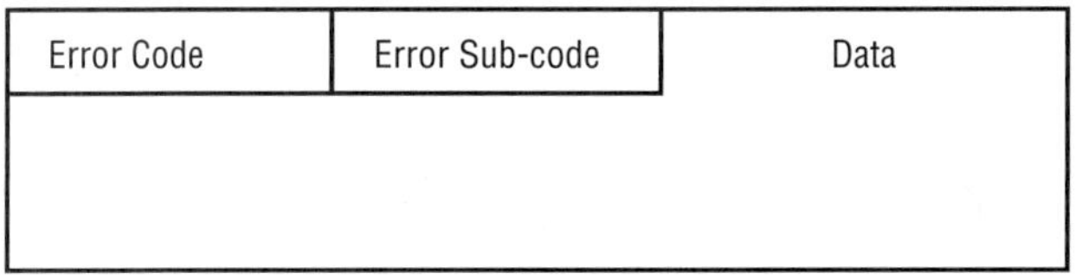

Error Code	Error Sub-code	Data

TABLE 8.3 Error Codes and Related Error Sub-codes

Error Code Number	Type	Error Sub-code Number	Type
1	Message header error		
		1	Connection Not Synchronized
		2	Bad Message Length
		3	Bad Message Type
2	OPENmessage error		
		1	Unsupported Version Number
		2	Bad Peer AS
		3	Bad BGP Identifier
		4	Unsupported Optional Parameter
		5	Authentication Failure
		6	Unacceptable Hold Timer
		7	Unsupported Capability
3	UPDATEmessage error		
		1	Malformed Attribute List
		2	Unrecognized Well-known Attribute
		3	Missing Well-known Attribute
		4	Attribute Flags Error
		5	Attribute Length Error
		6	Invalid ORIGIN Attribute
		7	AS Routing Loop

TABLE 8.3 Error Codes and Related Error Sub-codes *(continued)*

Error Code Number	Type	Error Sub-code Number	Type
		8	Invalid NEXT_HOP Attribute
		9	Optional Attribute Error
		10	Invalid Network Field
		11	Malformed AS_PATH
4	Hold Timer expired		
5	Finite State Machine error		
6	Cease		

The Cease error is simply any other error than the ones listed.

Now that you have a thorough understanding of the different message types BGP uses, let's go ahead and take a look at how all of this comes together.

Neighbor Negotiation

Before BGP communications can occur, BGP speakers must become neighbors, or peers. The first step in forming a peer is for the BGP speakers to form a TCP session with each other using TCP port 179. If this does not occur, the BGP speakers will never become peers. After the TCP session has been established, the BGP speakers send an OPEN message to each other. From that point forward, the BGP speakers send incremental UPDATE messages, NOTIFICATION messages, and KEEPALIVE messages.

The process through which the forming of neighbors occurs is known as the finite state machine.

Finite State Machine

The BGP finite state machine (FSM) dictates which states the peer relationship must traverse. There are six possible states that the forming of the peers can go through. We will cover each of the different states in this section. Figure 8.8 shows the functional relationships among the six states in the BGP FSM.

FIGURE 8.8 The BGP finite state machine

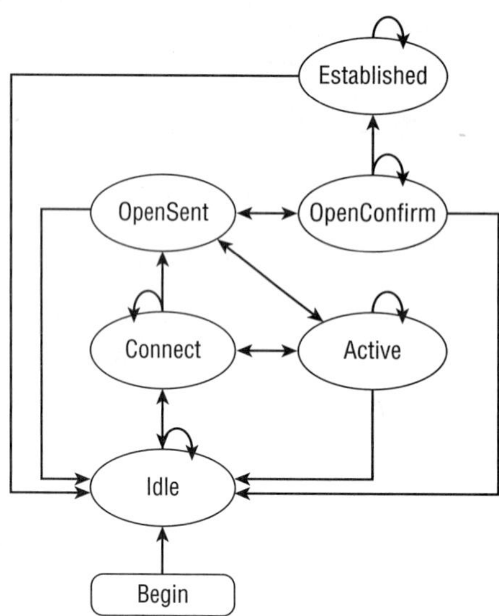

Idle state The *Idle state* is the first state that a BGP speaker enters when starting a BGP session. In this state, the BGP speaker is waiting for a BGP start event, refuses all incoming BGP connections, and does not initiate any BGP connections. The start event can be initiated by either the BGP speaker or the system administrator. Once a start event has occurred, the BGP speaker will initialize all of its BGP resources. The BGP speaker then starts the ConnectRetry timer, initiates a TCP connection to the BGP speaker that it wants to peer with, and also listens for any connection attempt started by the other BGP speaker. The BGP speaker then changes its BGP state to Connect. If any errors occur during this process, the TCP session is ended and the BGP speaker's state transitions back to Idle. A new start event needs to occur for the BGP speaker to attempt the connection again. If the start events are being automatically generated, the BGP speaker will wait 60 seconds before it retries the connection. For each successive retry from then on, the time will double. This helps alleviate persistent flapping of the BGP speaker.

Connect state In the *Connect state*, BGP is waiting for the TCP connection to be formed. Once the connection is successfully completed, the BGP speaker clears the ConnectRetry timer, completes initialization, sends an OPEN message to the remote BGP speaker, and transitions its state to OpenSent. If the TCP connection is not successfully formed, the BGP speaker restarts the ConnectRetry timer, continues to listen for an attempted connection from the remote BGP speaker, and transitions its state to Active. If the ConnectRetry timer expires, the BGP speaker resets the timer, initiates a TCP session, continues to listen for an attempted connection from the remote BGP speaker, and stays in the Connect state. If any other type of events causes an error, the BGP speaker closes the TCP connection and transitions its state to Idle. All BGP start events are ignored in the Connect state.

Active state In the *Active state*, the BGP speaker is attempting to initiate a TCP session with the BGP speaker it wants to peer with. Once the connection is successfully completed, the BGP speaker clears the ConnectRetry timer, completes initialization, sends an OPEN message to the remote BGP speaker, and transitions its state to OpenSent. If the ConnectRetry timer expires, the BGP speaker resets the timer, initiates a TCP session, continues to listen for an attempted connection from the remote BGP speaker, and transitions to the Connect state. If the BGP speaker detects another BGP speaker trying to form a TCP session with it and the remote BGP speaker's IP address is not the expected IP address, the BGP speaker rejects the connection, resets the ConnectRetry timer, continues to listen for an attempted connection from the remote BGP speaker, and stays in the Active state. If any other types of events cause an error, the BGP speaker closes the TCP connection and transitions its state to Idle. All BGP start events are ignored in the Active state.

OpenSent state In the *OpenSent state*, the BGP speaker is waiting to receive an OPEN message from the remote BGP speaker. Once the BGP speaker receives the OPEN message, all of the fields are checked. If an error is detected by the BGP speaker, it sends a NOTIFICATION message to the remote BGP speaker and terminates the TCP, and the state of the BGP speaker transitions to Idle. If no errors are found with the OPEN message, the BGP speaker sends a KEEPALIVE message to the remote BGP speaker, sets the keepalive timer, and sets the hold timer to the negotiated value. The BGP speakers then negotiate the holdtime. A negotiated value of 0 means that the keepalive timer and the hold timer will never be reset. After the holdtime has been negotiated, the BGP speaker determines whether the connection will be iBGP or eBGP, because this will affect the UPDATE processing discussed shortly. If the two BGP speakers are in the same autonomous system, the BGP type will be iBGP. If they are in different autonomous systems, the BGP type will be eBGP. Once the type of BGP has been determined, the state transitions to OpenConfirm. During this state, it is possible that the BGP speaker may receive a TCP disconnect message. If this should occur, the BGP speaker transitions to the Active state. If any other types of events cause an error, the BGP speaker closes the TCP connection and transitions its state to Idle. All BGP start events are ignored in the OpenSent state.

OpenConfirm state In the *OpenConfirm state*, the BGP speaker is waiting to receive a KEEPALIVE message from the remote BGP speaker. Once the KEEPALIVE message is received, the BGP speaker resets the hold timer and transitions to the Established state. At this point, the peer relationship has been formed. If a NOTIFICATION message is received instead of a KEEPALIVE message, the BGP speaker changes its state to Idle. In the case of the hold timer expiring before the KEEPALIVE message is received, the BGP speaker sends a NOTIFICATION message to the remote BGP speaker, ends the TCP session, and changes its state to Idle. The BGP speaker may receive a disconnect message from TCP. If this happens, the BGP speaker will change its state to Idle. The BGP speaker will also change its state to Idle if a stop event is initiated automatically or by the system administrator. If any other types of events cause an error, the BGP speaker closes the TCP connection and transitions its state to Idle. All BGP start events are ignored in the OpenConfirm state.

Established state Once a BGP speaker reaches the *Established state*, all of the neighbor negotiations are complete. As long as everything goes right, the BGP peers exchange UPDATE messages and KEEPALIVE messages. Each time a BGP speaker receives an UPDATE message or KEEPALIVE message, it resets its hold timer. If the hold timer ever expires before an UPDATE message or KEEP-ALIVE message is received, the BGP speaker sends a NOTIFICATION message to its peer, terminates the TCP session, and changes its state to Idle. The other events that will cause a BGP speaker to change its state to Idle are if it receives a NOTIFICATION message from its peer, an error is detected in the UPDATE message, a disconnect message is received from TCP, a stop event is initiated, or any other event occurs that causes the BGP speaker to generate a NOTIFICATION message. All BGP start events are ignored in the Established state.

Once BGP peers have reached the Established state, they will start exchanging routing information. Now would be a good time for us to take a look at how a BGP speaker copes with the exchange of routing information.

Route Selection

By this point, you should have a good understanding of how BGP speakers exchange routing information. What you may not know is the process the routing information goes through when a BGP speaker receives it and how the BGP speaker decides which routes it will accept for local use and which of those routes it will advertise to its peers.

In order to fully understand the process the route will go through, you first need to understand what the Routing Information Bases are and what they are used for.

Routing Information Bases

When a BGP speaker learns a route, that route needs to pass through the BGP speaker's Routing Information Base (RIB). All BGP speakers contain a RIB. A RIB is broken down into three parts:

- Adj-RIBs-In
- Loc-RIB
- Adj-RIBs-Out

Adj-RIBs-In One *Adj-RIB-In* exists for each peer a BGP speaker has. This RIB is where incoming BGP routes are stored. After BGP routes have been placed, they are then put through the inbound policy engine. The *inbound policy engine* is where the routes are filtered or have their attributes manipulated, based on a predefined policy set by the router's administrator. If a BGP route makes it through the inbound policy filter, it is then sent to the Loc-RIB.

Loc-RIB The *Loc-RIB* is what the router uses to make its own BGP routing decisions. The router then sends all of the BGP routes contained in the Loc-RIB to the outbound policy engine. The *outbound policy engine* is a predefined policy set by the router's administrator for the purpose of filtering and manipulating BGP routes before placing them in the Adj-RIBs-Out.

Adj-RIBs-Out If a BGP route makes it through the outbound policy engine, the route is placed in the Adj-RIBs-Out. An *Adj-RIB-Out* exists for each peer of a BGP speaker. The routes that are placed in the Adj-RIBs-Out will be advertised to the BGP speaker's peers.

A BGP route will continue this routine for each BGP speaker it is advertised to. Figure 8.9 and the following list will give you a step-by-step look at how all of this occurs.

FIGURE 8.9 BGP route processing

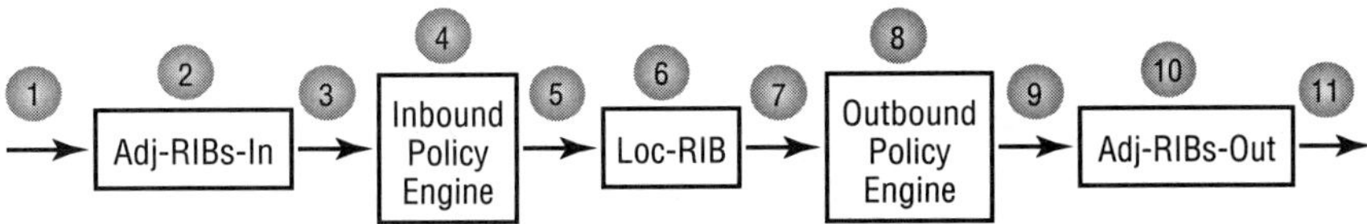

1. The BGP speaker receives the BGP routes.
2. The received BGP routes are placed in the Adj-RIBs-In.
3. The BGP routes are sent to the inbound policy engine.
4. The inbound policy engine filters and manipulates routes based on the policy set by the router's administrator. BGP routes that are filtered out by the inbound policy engine are dropped at this point.
5. The remaining BGP routes are then forwarded to the Loc-RIB.
6. The BGP speaker stores the routes in the Loc-RIB. The router uses these routes to make BGP routing decisions.
7. The BGP routes are then forwarded to the outbound policy engine.
8. The outbound policy engine filters and manipulates routes based on the policy set by the router's administrator. BGP routes that are filtered out by the outbound policy engine are dropped at this point.
9. The BGP routes that make it through the outbound policy engine are then forwarded to the Adj-RIBs-Out.
10. The received BGP routes are then stored in the Adj-RIBs-Out.
11. All BGP routes stored in the Adj-RIBs-Out are then advertised to all of the BGP speaker's peers.

With an understanding of the function of all the different RIBs, let's take a look at how all of this fits into the decision process of a BGP speaker.

Decision Process

The decision process is the actual process that decides what routes the BGP speaker will accept, the routes it will use locally, and the routes it will advertise to its peers. The decision process is broken down into three distinct phases:

- Phase 1 is responsible for calculating the degree of preference for a route learned from a neighboring AS. This phase is also responsible for advertising the routes with the highest degree of preference to the BGP speakers in the local AS.
- Phase 2 occurs after the completion of phase 1. Phase 2's responsibilities include deciding which route to a specified destination is the best. It then stores this route in the BGP speaker's Loc-RIB. The BGP speaker uses the routes installed during this phase for making BGP routing decisions.

- Phase 3 begins once the Loc-RIB of the BGP speaker is updated. Phase 3 is when a BGP speaker will determine, based on the policies set in the outbound policy engine, which routes it will advertise to peers in neighboring autonomous systems. Route aggregation can also be performed during this phase.

This is a high-level view of the decision process. We will now take a more in-depth look at what actually occurs during each of the three phases.

Phase 1

Phase 1 is also known as the Calculation of Degree Preference phase. Whenever a BGP speaker receives an UPDATE message from a peer in a neighboring AS, phase 1 will begin. Once the BGP speaker receives the UPDATE message, it locks the Adj-RIB-In used for that peer. The BGP speaker leaves the Adj-RIB-In locked until the completion of phase 1. For each feasible route the BGP speaker receives, it calculates the degree of preference. The degree of preference is the attractiveness of a route. The BGP speaker calculates the degree of preference based on the locally preconfigured policy.

Phase 2

Phase 2 is also known as the Route Selection phase. As soon as phase 1 is complete, phase 2 will initiate. During phase 2, the BGP speaker will lock all of its Adj-RIBs-In and unlock them once the phase is complete. At this point, any routes that have a NEXT_HOP attribute set to an address the BGP speaker doesn't have a route to should be excluded. The BGP speaker will select a route that is the only route to a destination to put in the Loc-RIB. If multiple routes exist to the same destination, the BGP speaker will select the route with the highest degree of preference. This route will then be inserted into the BGP speaker's Loc-RIB. In the case that multiple routes exist to the same destination and they have the same degree of preference, the following tiebreaking rules will apply, in order:

- If the BGP speaker is configured to use the MULTI_EXIT_DISC (MED) and the MEDs of the routes differ, the BGP speaker will select the route with the lowest MED.
- If the BGP speaker is not configured to use the MED or the MEDs do not differ, the BGP speaker will select the route with the lowest cost to the next-hop address.
- If the cost of the routes does not differ, the BGP speaker will select the route that was advertised by a BGP speaker in a neighboring AS with the lowest BGP identifier.
- If the route was not advertised by a BGP speaker in a neighboring AS, the BGP speaker will select the route advertised by the iBGP peer with the lowest BGP identifier.

Phase 3

Phase 3 is also known as the Route Dissemination phase. Phase 3 will initiate when any of the following four events occur:

- When phase 2 completes.
- When routes, stored in the Loc-RIB, to local destinations change.
- When any locally generated routes, not learned by BGP, change.
- When a new BGP connection has been established.

During phase 3, the routes stored in the Loc-RIB will be passed through the outbound policy engine. The routes that make it through the outbound policy engine are then placed in the Adj-RIBs-Out. These are the routes that the BGP speaker advertises to its peers. The BGP speaker can optionally perform route aggregation during this phase.

Cisco's implementation of BGP uses the following steps, in order, for route selection, assuming that BGP Multipath for load sharing is not enabled:

1. If the route specifies a next hop that is inaccessible, drop the update.
2. Prefer the route with the largest weight.
3. If the weights are the same, prefer the route with the largest local preference.
4. If the local preferences are the same, prefer the route that was originated by BGP running on this router, with those produced by the `network` or `redistribute` commands preferred over those produced by the `aggregate-address` command.
5. If no route was locally originated, prefer the route that has the shortest AS_PATH. For purposes of making this choice, all AS_SETs count as one, regardless of the size of the set. Additionally, confederation AS counts are not included.
6. If all routes have the same AS_PATH length, prefer the route with the lowest origin type, where IGP is lower than EGP, and EGP is lower than INCOMPLETE. INCOMPLETE routes generally come from redistribution.
7. If the origin codes are the same, prefer the route with the lowest MED attribute.
8. If the routes have the same MED, prefer the eBGP-learned route over the iBGP-learned route.
9. If the routes are still the same, prefer the route through the lowest IGP metric to the BGP next hop.
10. Prefer the route advertised by the BGP router with the lowest BGP router ID.
11. Prefer the path with the shortest cluster list length. (Refer to Chapter 9 for discussions on route reflection.)
12. Prefer the path advertised by the neighbor with the lowest IP address, as determined by the address used in the `neighbor` command for the remote TCP peer connection.

The system administrator can affect the routing decisions a BGP speaker makes. The way this is done is through route filtering.

Route Filtering

Route filtering for BGP can be used for many different reasons. It can be used to manipulate the attributes of a BGP, which in turn affects the way that the BGP speaker will view the route. Route filtering can also be used to permit or deny certain routes from being accepted by the BGP speaker or from being advertised by the speaker. BGP route filtering can occur as either ingress filtering or egress filtering:

Ingress filtering *Ingress filtering* occurs when a route is received by the BGP speaker and passed to the inbound policy engine. At this point, the system administrator can create a policy, which will either permit or deny certain routes. The system administrator can also set up certain policies, which will manipulate the BGP attributes of a route. For example, the system administrator can manipulate the local preference of a route. By doing this, the system administrator can better control which routes are stored in the BGP speaker Loc-RIB.

Egress filtering *Egress filtering* occurs when a route is passed into the outbound policy engine. Egress filtering functions the same as ingress filtering. The only difference is that the BGP speaker is making the decisions on the routes being advertised to its peers and manipulating those routes' BGP attributes.

There are different ways to implement BGP route filtering. The three filtering techniques that are most commonly used are route maps, distribute lists, and prefix lists. We will take a brief look at each of these different filtering techniques here. These filtering techniques are covered in more detail in Chapter 9.

Route maps Out of all the filtering techniques available, route maps give the user the most control over routing decisions. Route maps are a sequence of `set` and `match` statements. A `match` statement is used to decide which IP routes to permit or deny. If the particular sequence of the route map is permitting the IP routes, the `set` statement can be used to manipulate the attributes of the path. Route maps can be implemented as either ingress or egress filters.

Distribute lists Distribute lists are filters that can be implemented as either an ingress or egress filter. Unlike route maps where you can actually manipulate the attributes of a route, distribute lists allow you only to permit or deny a route. A distribute list is tied to either an access list or a prefix list. The access list or prefix list actually states which particular routes to permit or deny.

Prefix lists Prefix lists are similar to access lists. A prefix list can be used to limit the information advertised into a router or advertised by the router. Prefix lists give you a little more control than access lists. The major benefit of a prefix list over an access list is that a prefix list contains a sequence number for each line of the prefix list. This allows you to add, remove, and modify lines in a prefix list without having to delete it and re-create it as you would an access list.

The use of ingress and egress filters gives the system administrator tremendous control over the BGP routing decisions a BGP speaker will make. The various filtering techniques introduced here are not limited to BGP. These filtering techniques can be used for all the other routing protocols we've covered so far. We will take a more detailed look at these filtering techniques in regard to the other routing protocols covered in Chapter 10, "Route Optimization."

BGP Synchronization

BGP synchronization seems to be a sticking point for numerous people in their study of BGP. To fully understand BGP synchronization, you must first understand the difference between a transit AS and a stub AS.

Transit AS A *transit AS* is an autonomous system connected to multiple autonomous systems, allowing the routes learned from one autonomous system to be passed along to another autonomous system. Refer to Figure 8.10.

FIGURE 8.10 Transit and stub ASs

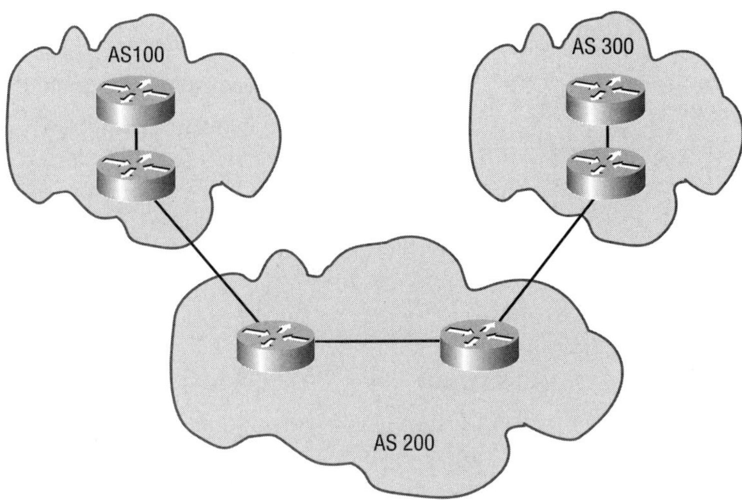

In this example, AS 200 would be a transit AS. The routes the AS learns from AS 300 will transit AS 200 and be received by AS 100. The same is true for AS 100. The routes AS 200 learns from AS 100 will transit the AS and be passed on to AS 300. In other words, a transit AS is an AS that allows information learned from another AS to transit through to another AS.

Stub AS A *stub AS* is an AS that does not allow information to transit through it to another AS. If you refer back to Figure 8.10, notice that both AS 100 and AS 300 are stub ASs. AS 100 and AS 300 are single-homed autonomous systems. A single-homed AS is an autonomous system that has only one entry and exit point. All single-homed autonomous systems are stub ASs.

BGP synchronization requires that BGP be synchronized with the IGP before any transit information can be advertised. In other words, the eBGP speaker will wait to hear an advertisement of the route it learned via iBGP from the IGP running in the AS, before advertising the route to an eBGP neighbor. To better understand this concept, refer to Figure 8.11.

In this example, R1 and R2 are eBGP peers, R2 and R4 are iBGP peers, R4 and R5 are eBGP peers, and R3 is not running BGP. What will happen when R1 sends a packet destined for R5 is that the packet is received by R2, which in turn forwards the packet to R3, because R3 is the IGP next hop for R2 to reach R4, the BGP next hop. Because R3 is not running BGP and the BGP routes have not been redistributed into the IGP, R3 doesn't know how to get to R5. So R3 will drop the packet. There are a couple of ways to overcome this:

- You could redistribute the BGP routes into the IGP. This would seem like the most logical thing to do. However, redistributing BGP routes into an IGP is not a good idea. In 1994, there were under 20,000 routes in the Internet's BGP routing tables. At the start of 2005, there were over 180,000 routes in the default-free Internet, so an IGP would have a meltdown if required to carry that many routes. Never mind the continued growth that is expected.

- You could run iBGP on R3, which would allow you to disable BGP synchronization. By doing this, R3 will know that to reach R5 it must forward the packet on to R4, and the route to R5 will not need to be synchronized with the IGP. Being an iBGP speaker in a full-mesh configuration, R3 would be informed by R4 that R4 is the BGP next hop to R5 at the same time that R2 would learn that fact. Therefore, there is no need to wait for the IGP to learn this.

In general, there are two conditions that would enable synchronization to be turned off, if either or both are true. The first is that the AS is a stub and carries no transit traffic. The second is if all routers in the AS speak iBGP and are configured in a TCP full mesh with one another.

Because full-mesh iBGP is highly recommended and often configured, most implementations of BGP you see in the real world will have BGP synchronization turned off. By default, BGP synchronization is on. In order to turn off BGP synchronization, you need to enter the following command in router configuration mode:

```
no synchronization
```

The information covered in this section should give you a good understanding of how BGP synchronization occurs. In the next section, we will take a look at the use of route aggregation in BGP.

Synchronization with a partial mesh is not a substitute for running iBGP on all routers in the AS and configuring a full mesh with no synchronization, because black holes are still likely to develop due to a discrepancy between BGP-learned routes and IGP-learned routes. Just because the AS will not advertise these black holes to neighboring ASs does not mean that their existence is not a problem.

FIGURE 8.11 BGP synchronization

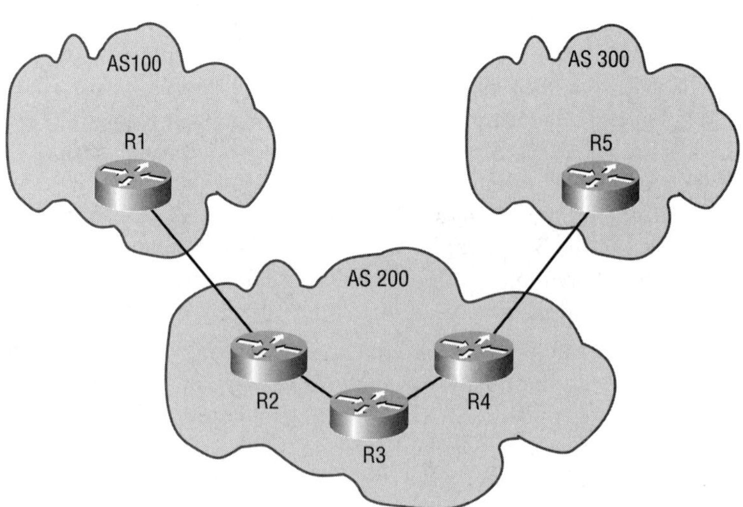

Route Aggregation

Route aggregation, also known as route summarization, is a means by which multiple routes can be combined into a single route. By utilizing route aggregation, the number of routes in a routing table will shrink, thus consuming less memory. BGP route aggregation can occur during phase 3 of the BGP decision process.

There are some rules you must be familiar with concerning BGP route aggregation:

- If routes contain the MED and NEXT_HOP attributes, these attributes must be identical in order for the routes to be aggregated.
- Paths with different attribute type codes cannot be aggregated together.
- Paths with the same attribute type codes can be aggregated together.

Computing the summary route to use was covered in detail in Chapter 2, "IP Addressing." If you need further practice on computing aggregate routes, refer back to Chapter 2. The configuration of aggregate routes is covered later in this chapter. Now that you know what BGP is and how it functions, you need to understand when to implement BGP and when not to implement it.

When and When Not to Use BGP

BGP is a very complex routing protocol and doesn't always need to be implemented in order to route to different autonomous systems. The use of static and default routes is an alternative to use in place of BGP. The question is, When should you use BGP and when should you use static or default routes? The answer to that question: It depends on the scenario. Here are a few instances when static or default routes could be used instead of BGP:

- The routers in your network don't have much memory and/or processing power. The number of routes contained in the Internet is huge. If a router doesn't have enough memory and/or processing power, it can cause undue delays in your network.
- Your AS is connected to only one other AS, and you do not need to enforce any policies.
- Your network doesn't have enough bandwidth to support the amount of traffic that BGP must pass.

Here are a few instances when you would need to implement BGP:

- When you need to enforce inbound and/or outbound policies on information entering or leaving your network.
- When your network has multiple connections to different autonomous systems, and you want your autonomous system to pass information from one autonomous system to another autonomous system. In other words, you want your AS to be a transit AS.
- When connecting different Internet service providers to one another.

These are only a few of the reasons to (or not to) implement BGP. The longer you spend working with BGP in the real world, the better you will be at spotting when and when not to use BGP. It's like anything in life: The more you practice it, the better you will become.

A tremendous amount of material has been covered so far in this chapter. It is very important for you to have a good understanding of the operation of BGP before moving on to the configuration section of this chapter. If you do not feel comfortable with all of the information covered so far, stop and review the material. Once you feel comfortable with this information, move on to the configuration section.

Configuring BGP

In this section, we're going to take a step-by-step approach to configuring BGP. We will start off with the minimal information required to configure BGP and move on to more complex configurations.

Minimal BGP Configuration

We are going to start this section with the minimal information needed to configure BGP. Take a look at Figure 8.12.

FIGURE 8.12 Basic BGP implementation

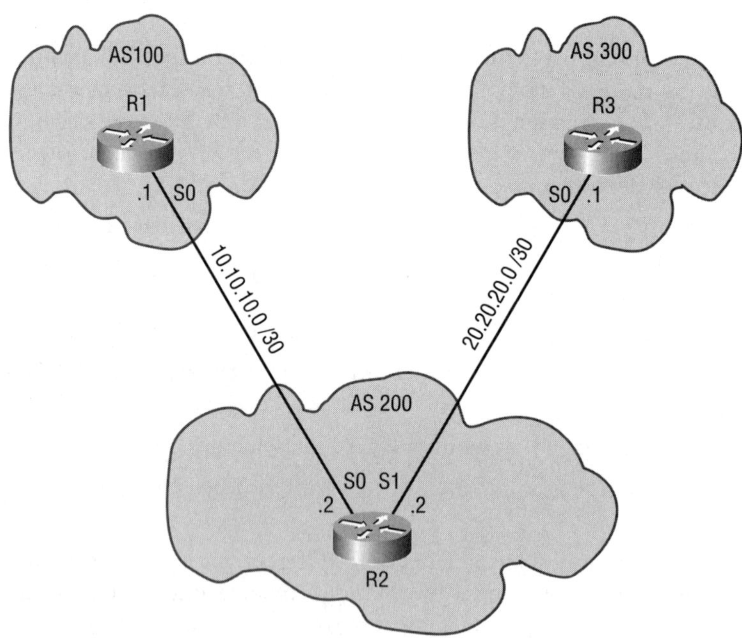

In order to enable BGP on a device, the following command needs to be entered in global configuration mode:

```
router bgp autonomous-system-number
   autonomous-system-number - the AS number of the local AS.
```

Now that you know the relevant command, let's go ahead and enable BGP on each of the devices in Figure 8.12:

```
R1#conf t
Enter configuration commands, one per line. End with CNTL/Z.
R1(config)#router bgp 100
R1(config-router)#^Z
R1#

R2#conf t
Enter configuration commands, one per line. End with CNTL/Z.
R2(config)#router bgp 200
R2(config-router)#^Z
R2#

R3#conf t
Enter configuration commands, one per line. End with CNTL/Z.
R3(config)#router bgp 300
R3(config-router)#^Z
R3#
```

Now that we have enabled BGP on the router, we need to tell the BGP process which routers we want to form peer relationships with. It's important to note that BGP requires you to manually set who your neighbors will be. This is accomplished through the use of the following command:

```
neighbor address remote-as autonomous-system-number
   address - the IP address of the remote device.
   autonomous-system-number - the AS number of the remote device.
```

Be aware that because every bidirectional peering requires a complementary neighbor statement on each peer, and because the formula for determining the number of relationships in a full-mesh environment is $n(n-1)/2$, the total number of neighbor commands is twice that, or $n(n-1)$. That can be quite a few neighbor commands.

With this in mind, let's go ahead and set up our peer relationships for each device:

```
R1#conf t
Enter configuration commands, one per line. End with CNTL/Z.
R1(config)#router bgp 100
R1(config-router)#neighbor 10.10.10.2 remote-as 200
R1(config-router)#^Z
R1#

R2#conf t
Enter configuration commands, one per line. End with CNTL/Z.
R2(config)#router bgp 200
R2(config-router)#neighbor 10.10.10.1 remote-as 100
R2(config-router)#neighbor 20.20.20.1 remote-as 300
R2(config-router)#^Z
R2#

R3#conf t
Enter configuration commands, one per line. End with CNTL/Z.
R3(config)#router bgp 300
R3(config-router)#neighbor 20.20.20.2 remote-as 200
R3(config-router)#^Z
R3#
```

That's all there is to a basic BGP configuration. Now that you have the basics down, we're going to incorporate configuring iBGP with eBGP.

iBGP and eBGP Configuration

In this network, we will configure iBGP and eBGP. The loopback address of each router participating in iBGP is used in the `neighbor` statement when referring to the router. The directly connected interface addresses are used for the eBGP connections.

Using a loopback address for an iBGP session is a good idea. A loopback interface is always up and will never go down unless administratively shut down. This way, if an iBGP speaker has more than one path to its iBGP neighbor and one of the paths goes down, the connection will stay up. The reason the TCP connection stays up is because of the existence of another route to the same destination. When using loopback interfaces for BGP sessions, the following additional command needs to be entered in router configuration mode:

```
neighbor address update-source interface
   address - IP address of the remote device.
   interface - the interface to use as the source for the BGP session.
```

Without this command, the BGP speakers will never become peers with one another. The reason is because the remote BGP speaker expects to receive the packet from the BGP speaker's loopback address, but without the `update-source` keyword, the BGP packet will use the address of the outbound interface of the BGP speaker. The remote BGP speaker will receive the packet and ignore it because that is not the address it is expecting to see. With the `update-source` keyword, the packet will contain the address of the loopback interface and not the outbound interface.

Now that you understand how this works, take a look at Figure 8.13.

We're now going to do a step-by-step configuration of the network in Figure 8.13. When configuring this network, we do not want BGP to be synchronized with the IGP. In order to disable synchronization, you will need to enter the command `no synchronization` on each router in AS 200. The loopback addresses for routers R2, R3, and R4 are as follows:

R2 Lo0-2.2.2.2

R3 Lo0-3.3.3.3

R4 Lo0-4.4.4.4

FIGURE 8.13 iBGP and eBGP network

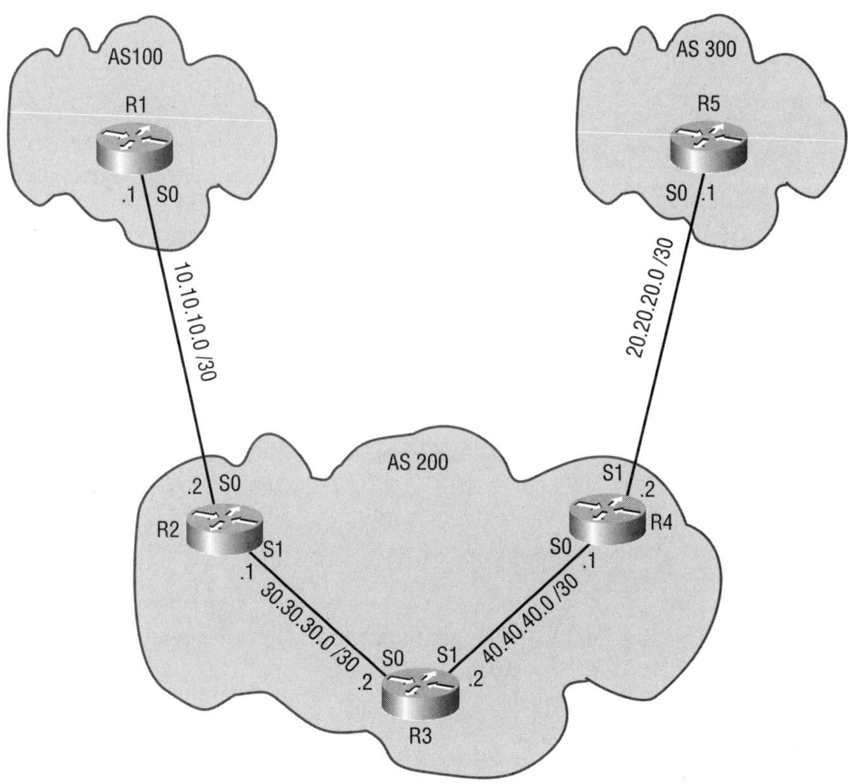

Armed with this information, let's go ahead and enable BGP on all of the devices and disable synchronization on the devices that will be running iBGP:

```
R1#conf t
Enter configuration commands, one per line. End with CNTL/Z.
R1(config)#router bgp 100
R1(config-router)#^Z
R1#

R2#conf t
Enter configuration commands, one per line. End with CNTL/Z.
R2(config)#router bgp 200
R2(config-router)#no synchronization
R2(config-router)#^Z
R2#

R3#conf t
Enter configuration commands, one per line. End with CNTL/Z.
R3(config)#router bgp 200
R3(config-router)#no synchronization
R3(config-router)#^Z
R3#

R4#conf t
Enter configuration commands, one per line. End with CNTL/Z.
R4(config)#router bgp 200
R4(config-router)#no synchronization
R4(config-router)#^Z
R4#

R5#conf t
Enter configuration commands, one per line. End with CNTL/Z.
R5(config)#router bgp 300
R5(config-router)#^Z
R5#
```

Now that we have BGP enabled, let's go ahead and assign the neighbors. Don't forget the `update-source` command for the iBGP connections:

```
R1#conf t
Enter configuration commands, one per line. End with CNTL/Z.
R1(config)#router bgp 100
R1(config-router)#neighbor 10.10.10.2 remote-as 200
```

```
R1(config-router)#^Z
R1#

R2#conf t
Enter configuration commands, one per line. End with CNTL/Z.
R2(config)#router bgp 200
R2(config-router)#neighbor 10.10.10.1 remote-as 100
R2(config-router)#neighbor 3.3.3.3 remote-as 200
R2(config-router)#neighbor 4.4.4.4 remote-as 200
R2(config-router)#neighbor 3.3.3.3 update-source Lo0
R2(config-router)#neighbor 4.4.4.4 update-source Lo0
R2(config-router)#^Z
R2#

R3#conf t
Enter configuration commands, one per line. End with CNTL/Z.
R3(config)#router bgp 200
R3(config-router)#neighbor 2.2.2.2 remote-as 200
R3(config-router)#neighbor 4.4.4.4 remote-as 200
R3(config-router)#neighbor 2.2.2.2 update-source Lo0
R3(config-router)#neighbor 4.4.4.4 update-source Lo0
R3(config-router)#^Z
R3#

R4#conf t
Enter configuration commands, one per line. End with CNTL/Z.
R4(config)#router bgp 200
R4(config-router)#neighbor 20.20.20.1 remote-as 300
R4(config-router)#neighbor 3.3.3.3 remote-as 200
R4(config-router)#neighbor 2.2.2.2 remote-as 200
R4(config-router)#neighbor 3.3.3.3 update-source Lo0
R4(config-router)#neighbor 2.2.2.2 update-source Lo0
R4(config-router)#^Z
R4#

R5#conf t
Enter configuration commands, one per line. End with CNTL/Z.
R5(config)#router bgp 300
R4(config-router)#neighbor 20.20.20.2 remote-as 200
R5(config-router)#^Z
R5#
```

As you can see, the configuration of iBGP compared to eBGP isn't different. What determines whether the connection is iBGP or eBGP is whether the remote BGP speaker is in the same AS or not.

eBGP Multihop Configuration

Situations do exist where the remote BGP speaker you are going to communicate with is not directly connected. When this occurs, it's known as an eBGP multihop. An eBGP multihop will occur when the connection to the remote BGP speaker is not a direct connection between the local BGP speaker's egress interface and the remote BGP speaker's ingress interface. There are a couple of different reasons why this could occur:

- There is another router in between the local BGP speaker and the remote BGP speaker that cannot run BGP.
- You are sourcing the BGP connection from a loopback interface on at least one of the BGP speakers involved.

There is one important item that you must take note of when implementing eBGP multihop. The two BGP speakers participating must have a route between them. This route can be learned utilizing one of the different IGPs. The route cannot be a default route. If this route does not exist, the BGP speakers will never form a peer relationship because they don't know how to find each other. In order to configure eBGP multihop, you must enter the following command on both BGP speakers involved in router configuration mode:

```
neighbor address ebgp-multihop [ttl]
    address - IP address of the remote device.
    ttl - an optional parameter that can be set to inform the device the maximum
number of hops away the neighbor is. The default value is 1.
```

With this in mind, take a look at Figure 8.14.

In this figure, R2 will not be participating in BGP. We will also be using the loopback interfaces of R1 and R3 as the address of each BGP speaker. Remember from the previous example, if loopback interfaces are used, the `update-source` keyword must also be used. The IP addresses for R1 and R3 are as follows:

R1 Lo0-1.1.1.1

R3 Lo0-3.3.3.3

For this configuration, we will assume that R1 and R3 know how to reach each other. Let's go ahead and enable BGP and set the peers on this network:

```
R1#conf t
Enter configuration commands, one per line. End with CNTL/Z.
R1(config)#router bgp 100
R1(config-router)#neighbor 3.3.3.3 remote-as 200
R1(config-router)#^Z
R1#
```

```
R3#conf t
Enter configuration commands, one per line. End with CNTL/Z.
R3(config)#router bgp 200
R3(config-router)#neighbor 1.1.1.1 remote-as 100
R3(config-router)#^Z
R3#
```

FIGURE 8.14 eBGP multihop

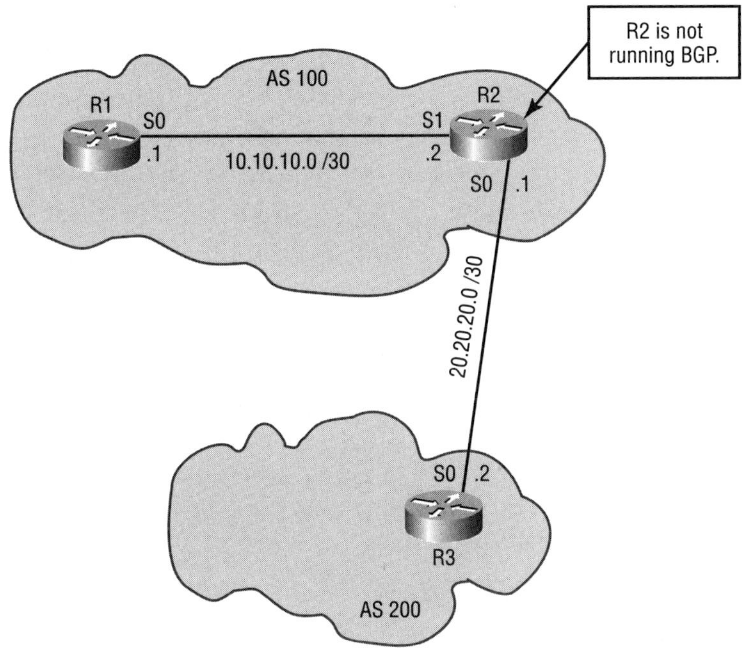

This configuration will not work as it is set up currently. We need to set the update source on R1 and R3. We also need to set up eBGP multihop on each of those devices:

```
R1#conf t
Enter configuration commands, one per line. End with CNTL/Z.
R1(config)#router bgp 100
R1(config-router)#neighbor 3.3.3.3 update-source Lo0
R1(config-router)#neighbor 3.3.3.3 ebgp-multihop
R1(config-router)#^Z
R1#

R3#conf t
Enter configuration commands, one per line. End with CNTL/Z.
```

```
R3(config)#router bgp 200
R3(config-router)#neighbor 1.1.1.1 update-source Lo0
R3(config-router)#neighbor 1.1.1.1 ebgp-multihop
R3(config-router)#^Z
R3#
```

With the addition of the `update-source` and `ebgp-multihop` keywords, this BGP configuration will now work. Now that you've configured a BGP network, we need to turn our focus to injecting routes into BGP.

Injecting Routes into BGP

There are a couple of different ways to inject routes into BGP for advertisement:

- You could redistribute the IGP into BGP. Redistribution is the process of injecting the routing information known by one routing protocol into another routing protocol.
- You can manually configure the routes for BGP to advertise.

Each of these ways of injecting routes will work equally successfully. Making the decision on which form to use depends on the number of routes you want to inject into BGP. If you want to inject only a few routes into BGP, your best choice would be to manually configure BGP with the routes to advertise. On the other hand, if you want BGP to advertise numerous routes contained in your IGP, you need to redistribute the IGP into BGP. The preferred method of injecting routes into BGP is through manual configuration and not through redistribution. The reason is if you have a route that flaps, that is, appears and then disappears continuously, routers on the Internet will penalize that route and the route could get dampened or temporarily removed from their routing tables.

Let's look at how to configure each of these different forms of injecting routes into BGP.

Manually Injecting Routes into BGP

Manually injecting routes into BGP enables you to decide the exact routes you want a BGP speaker to advertise to its peers. The following command needs to be entered in router configuration mode:

```
network network-address mask subnet-mask
   network-address - the address of the network you want to advertise.
   subnet-mask - the subnet mask of the network you want to advertise.
```

Refer to Figure 8.15.

In this scenario, we will configure eBGP between routers R2 and R3. The loopback addresses of R2 and R3 will be used for the BGP session. R2 and R3 are running an IGP between them containing only the loopback addresses. R1 and R2 are running an IGP between them. So R2 knows about the Ethernet segment on R1. R1 will not run BGP. We want R2 to advertise its connection to R1, and we also want R2 to advertise the Ethernet segment on R1 to R3. We want R3 to advertise its Ethernet segment to R2. At this point, we will go ahead and enable BGP on

R2 and R3. We will also set the update source and eBGP multihop information on R2 and R3. R2's loopback interface number is 0, and the address is 2.2.2.2. R3's loopback interface number is 0, and the address is 3.3.3.3:

```
R2#conf t
Enter configuration commands, one per line. End with CNTL/Z.
R2(config)#router bgp 100
R2(config-router)#neighbor 3.3.3.3 remote-as 200
R2(config-router)#neighbor 3.3.3.3 update-source Lo0
R2(config-router)#neighbor 3.3.3.3 ebg-multihop
R2(config-router)#^Z
R2#

R3#conf t
Enter configuration commands, one per line. End with CNTL/Z.
R3(config)#router bgp 200
R3(config-router)#neighbor 2.2.2.2 remote-as 100
R3(config-router)#neighbor 2.2.2.2 update-source Lo0
R3(config-router)#neighbor 2.2.2.2 ebg-multihop
R3(config-router)#^Z
R3#
```

FIGURE 8.15 Manually injecting routes into BGP

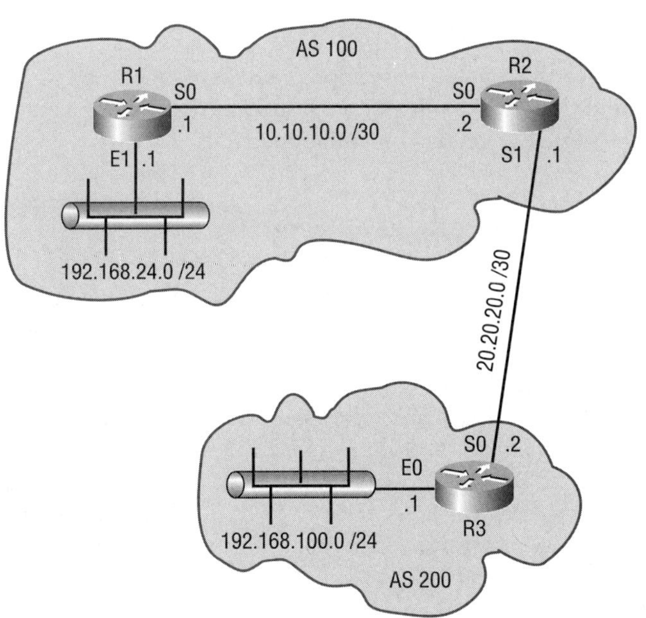

Now that we have BGP running on each device, and they have formed peer relationships with each other, we will go ahead and inject the routes into BGP:

```
R2#conf t
Enter configuration commands, one per line. End with CNTL/Z.
R2(config)#router bgp 100
R2(config-router)#network 10.10.10.0 mask 255.255.255.252
R2(config-router)#network 192.168.24.0 mask 255.255.255.0
R2(config-router)#^Z
R2#

R3#conf t
Enter configuration commands, one per line. End with CNTL/Z.
R3(config)#router bgp 200
R3(config-router)#network 192.168.100.0 mask 255.255.255.0
R3(config-router)#^Z
R3#
```

That's all there is to it. As you can see, manually injecting routes into BGP is not a complicated task. You must make sure that the route you want to inject into BGP is in the BGP speaker's routing table. If the route is not there, BGP will not advertise it. The major drawback with manually injecting routes into BGP occurs when there are numerous routes you want to inject. You would need to manually enter all of the networks into the BGP configuration, which can become very time-consuming. The way around that is by using redistribution.

Redistributing Routes into BGP

Redistributing routes into BGP can save you a tremendous amount of time when you need BGP to advertise numerous routes from your network. In order to configure redistribution into BGP, the following command needs to be entered in router configuration mode:

```
redistribute protocol process-id
   protocol - the routing protocol to redistribute.
   process-id - if protocol is IGRP or EIGRP this the AS number.
              - if protocol is OSPF this is the process-id.
              - if protocol is RIP or IS-IS the process-id is not needed.
```

In Figure 8.16, eBGP will need to be configured between routers R2 and R3. R1 will not have BGP configured. We will use the loopback interfaces on R2 and R3 for the BGP session. R2's loopback interface number is 0, and the address is 2.2.2.2. R3's loopback interface number is 0, and the address is 3.3.3.3. R1 and R2 are running an EIGRP AS 100 as their IGP. We will want to redistribute all of the routes R2 knows into BGP. We will also want to redistribute the Ethernet segment on R3 into BGP. The Ethernet segment on R3 does not have a routing protocol running.

FIGURE 8.16 Redistributing routes into BGP

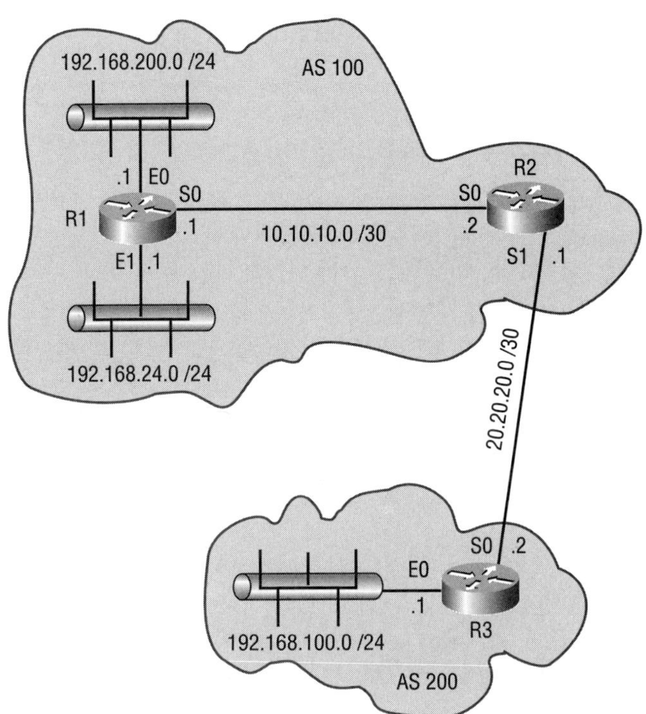

In order to redistribute this segment, we will need to use connected as the protocol for redistribution. This will redistribute all of the connected interfaces on R3 into BGP. With all of this in mind, let's enable BGP on R2 and R3 and configure their peer relationships with each other:

```
R2#conf t
Enter configuration commands, one per line. End with CNTL/Z.
R2(config)#router bgp 100
R2(config-router)#neighbor 3.3.3.3 remote-as 200
R2(config-router)#neighbor 3.3.3.3 update-source Lo0
R2(config-router)#neighbor 3.3.3.3 ebg-multihop
R2(config-router)#^Z
R2#

R3#conf t
Enter configuration commands, one per line. End with CNTL/Z.
R3(config)#router bgp 200
```

```
R3(config-router)#neighbor 2.2.2.2 remote-as 100
R3(config-router)#neighbor 2.2.2.2 update-source Lo0
R3(config-router)#neighbor 2.2.2.2 ebg-multihop
R3(config-router)#^Z
R3#
```

We now need to configure redistribution on R2 and R3:

```
R2#conf t
Enter configuration commands, one per line. End with CNTL/Z.
R2(config)#router bgp 100
R2(config-router)#redistribute eigrp 100
R2(config-router)#^Z
R2#

R3#conf t
Enter configuration commands, one per line. End with CNTL/Z.
R3(config)#router bgp 200
R3(config-router)#redistribute connected
R3(config-router)#^Z
R3#
```

By using the `redistribute` command, we have injected all of the EIGRP routes that R2 knows about into BGP. We have also injected the connected interface addresses from R3 into BGP. The problem you will encounter by just redistributing routes into BGP is that there may be some routes you do not want BGP to know about. Filtering could be used to filter out the routes that you do not want BGP to know about. We cover this concept in detail in Chapter 9.

You should now have a good understanding of how to configure the basic components of BGP. We will cover the configurations of the more advanced topics of BGP in Chapter 9. Now that we have BGP configured, we need to be able to verify that it is working properly and, if any issues occur, be able to troubleshoot them.

Verifying and Troubleshooting the Operation of BGP

After configuring BGP, you're going to have to be able to verify that it is operating properly and, if it isn't operating correctly, know how to troubleshoot it.

Route Information

The first item you will want to check is the router's routing table to make sure that all the routes that should appear do appear:

```
R3#sh ip route
Codes: C - connected, S - static, I - IGRP, R - RIP, M - mobile, B - BGP
       D - EIGRP, EX - EIGRP external, O - OSPF, IA - OSPF inter area
       N1 - OSPF NSSA external type 1, N2 - OSPF NSSA external type 2
       E1 - OSPF external type 1, E2 - OSPF external type 2, E - EGP
       i - IS-IS, L1 - IS-IS level-1, L2 - IS-IS level-2, * - candidate default
       U - per-user static route, o - ODR

Gateway of last resort is not set

R    2.0.0.0/8 [120/1] via 20.20.20.1, 00:00:03, Serial0
     3.0.0.0/32 is subnetted, 1 subnets
C       3.3.3.3 is directly connected, Loopback0
     4.0.0.0/32 is subnetted, 1 subnets
D       4.4.4.4 [90/2297856] via 30.30.30.2, 00:08:25, Serial1
B    192.168.24.0/24 [20/2172416] via 2.2.2.2, 00:08:25
     20.0.0.0/30 is subnetted, 1 subnets
C       20.20.20.0 is directly connected, Serial0
     5.0.0.0/32 is subnetted, 1 subnets
D       5.5.5.5 [90/2809856] via 30.30.30.2, 00:08:25, Serial1
D    192.168.200.0/24 [90/2684416] via 30.30.30.2, 00:08:25, Serial1
     40.0.0.0/30 is subnetted, 1 subnets
D       40.40.40.0 [90/2681856] via 30.30.30.2, 00:08:25, Serial1
     10.0.0.0/30 is subnetted, 1 subnets
B       10.10.10.0 [20/0] via 2.2.2.2, 00:08:26
D    192.168.100.0/24 [90/2195456] via 30.30.30.2, 00:08:26, Serial1
     30.0.0.0/30 is subnetted, 1 subnets
C       30.30.30.0 is directly connected, Serial1
```

In the preceding example, the router has learned two routes from BGP. The way you will know a route has been learned from BGP is by the code `B` at the front of the line. The `show ip route` command displays only the routes that have been placed in the router's routing table.

A router could know more BGP routes than the ones in the routing table. For one reason or another, the routes were not placed in the routing table. Some reasons for this may be a synchronization issue or a route manipulation issue. If you would like to view all of the routes the router has learned from BGP, use the following command (note this output is not from the same router):

```
R5#show ip bgp
BGP table version is 3, local router ID is 5.5.5.5
Status codes: s suppressed, d damped, h history, * valid, > best, i - internal
Origin codes: i - IGP, e - EGP, ? - incomplete

   Network          Next Hop            Metric LocPrf Weight Path
* i3.0.0.0          3.3.3.3                  0    100      0 ?
* i4.0.0.0          3.3.3.3                  0    100      0 ?
* i5.0.0.0          3.3.3.3                  0    100      0 ?
* i10.10.10.0/30    2.2.2.2                  0    100      0 100 i
* i20.20.20.0/30    2.2.2.2                  0    100      0 100 i
* i30.0.0.0         3.3.3.3                  0    100      0 ?
* i40.0.0.0         3.3.3.3                  0    100      0 ?
* i192.168.24.0     2.2.2.2            2172416    100      0 100 i
*>i192.168.100.0    30.30.30.2         2195456    100      0 ?
*>i192.168.200.0    30.30.30.2         2684416    100      0 ?
```

The `show ip bgp` command lists all of the routes that a router has learned from BGP. The * at the beginning of a line informs you that the route is a valid BGP route. If a route has been placed in the routing table, a > will follow the asterisk. If the route will not appear in the routing table, nothing appears there. The `i` indicates that the route was learned via an internal BGP session. The network address of the route follows. The Next Hop field is the router ID of the router that the local router will send packets to in order to reach the destination. If a router doesn't have a route to the next-hop address, the route will not be placed in the routing table. The Metric field is the cost associated with a route. The LocPrf field is the local preference of the route. The default value for this field is 100. The Weight field is the weight of the route and does not get passed to other routers because it is specific to the local router. The Path field is the autonomous systems a route has traversed.

Viewing Neighbor Information

It is important with BGP to know the status of a router's BGP peering sessions. The following command gives you a summary of the routers a router is peering with:

```
R3#show ip bgp summary
BGP router identifier 3.3.3.3, local AS number 200
BGP table version is 13, main routing table version 13
10 network entries and 10 paths using 1210 bytes of memory
5 BGP path attribute entries using 528 bytes of memory
BGP activity 31/21 prefixes, 34/24 paths
```

```
Neighbor  V    AS MsgRcvd MsgSent   TblVer  InQ OutQ Up/Down  State/PfxRcd
2.2.2.2   4   100     114     139       13    0    0 01:05:50         3
4.4.4.4   4   200     108     135       13    0    0 01:05:51         0
5.5.5.5   4   200     111     148       13    0    0 00:42:32         0
```

As you can tell, there is more information here than just who the router's peers are. The first line of output informs you of the router's BGP identifier and the local AS number. The next line that's underlined above tells you how many routes the router has learned from BGP. As for the peer information contained, the command will inform you of the BGP identifier of the peer, the negotiated BGP version between the peers, the autonomous system number of the peer, how many messages have been sent and received, the BGP table version, how long the connection has been in the current state, and the state of the connection. Get familiar with using the `show ip bgp summary` command. It is a command you will find yourself using time and time again.

If you would like to find out more detailed information about a peer connection, you can use the `show ip bgp neighbors` command:

```
R3#show ip bgp neighbors
BGP neighbor is 2.2.2.2,  remote AS 100, external link
 Index 3, Offset 0, Mask 0x8
  BGP version 4, remote router ID 2.2.2.2
  BGP state = Established, table version = 13, up for 01:20:55
  Last read 00:00:55, hold time is 180, keepalive interval is 60 seconds
  Minimum time between advertisement runs is 30 seconds
  Received 129 messages, 0 notifications, 0 in queue
  Sent 154 messages, 4 notifications, 0 in queue
  Prefix advertised 51, suppressed 0, withdrawn 1
  Connections established 7; dropped 6
  Last reset 01:21:05, due to User reset
  3 accepted prefixes consume 96 bytes
  0 history paths consume 0 bytes
  External BGP neighbor may be up to 255 hops away.
Connection state is ESTAB, I/O status: 1, unread input bytes: 0
Local host: 20.20.20.2, Local port: 179
Foreign host: 2.2.2.2, Foreign port: 11005

Enqueued packets for retransmit: 0, input: 0  mis-ordered: 0 (0 bytes)

Event Timers (current time is 0xBC4458):
Timer          Starts    Wakeups            Next
Retrans            86          0             0x0
TimeWait            0          0             0x0
AckHold            86         42             0x0
SendWnd             0          0             0x0
```

```
KeepAlive          0          0            0x0
GiveUp             0          0            0x0
PmtuAger           0          0            0x0
DeadWait           0          0            0x0

iss: 3793881560  snduna: 3793883310  sndnxt: 3793883310     sndwnd:  16289
irs:  852054893  rcvnxt:  852056670  rcvwnd:      16251  delrcvwnd:    133

SRTT: 300 ms, RTTO: 607 ms, RTV: 3 ms, KRTT: 0 ms
minRTT: 32 ms, maxRTT: 300 ms, ACK hold: 200 ms
Flags: passive open, nagle, gen tcbs

Datagrams (max data segment is 536 bytes):
Rcvd: 134 (out of order: 0), with data: 86, total data bytes: 1776
Sent: 131 (retransmit: 0), with data: 85, total data bytes: 1749
```

The `show ip bgp neighbors` command provides you with the same information provided by the `show ip bgp summary` command but with more detail about each of the BGP peering connections.

If you would like to restart a BGP peering session, you can use the `clear ip bgp` *`peer-address`* command, where the *`peer-address`* is the address of the peer you would like to restart the connection with. You can also use the `clear ip bgp` *`autonomous-system-number`* command, where the *`autonomous-system-number`* is the autonomous system number of the peers that you want to restart the peering connections with. If you use the `clear ip bgp *` command, you will restart all peering connections on the router.

With the `show` commands covered in this section, you should be able to determine whether BGP is operating correctly or not. These commands can also aid you in the troubleshooting of BGP. If you are not able to determine what is causing the issue, you will need to obtain more detailed information about the information that is being passed between the BGP peers. That is where the `debug` commands come into play.

Debugging BGP Information

Using the `debug` commands with BGP will provide you with real-time feedback of the BGP operation. An important item to note is that the `debug` commands can use a tremendous amount of the router's processing power. When using the `debug` commands, use them wisely.

Below is a list of the possible `debug` commands for BGP:

```
R3#debug ip bgp ?
  A.B.C.D     BGP neighbor address
  dampening   BGP dampening
  events      BGP events
  keepalives  BGP keepalives
  updates     BGP updates
  <cr>
```

We will take a look at each of these commands and what information they can provide.

The `debug ip bgp` command can be used to view the sending and receiving of OPEN messages between a local router and the routers that it is trying to peer with. This command can help you locate a problem in the sending or receiving of an OPEN message:

```
R3#debug ip bgp
BGP debugging is on
03:53:28: BGP: 2.2.2.2 closing
03:53:28: BGP: 4.4.4.4 closing
03:53:28: BGP: 5.5.5.5 closing
03:53:29: BGP: 2.2.2.2 open active, delay 24384ms
03:53:29: BGP: 4.4.4.4 open active, delay 7660ms
03:53:29: BGP: 5.5.5.5 open active, delay 7192ms
03:53:36: BGP: 5.5.5.5 open active, local address 3.3.3.3
03:53:36: BGP: 5.5.5.5 sending OPEN, version 4
03:53:36: BGP: 5.5.5.5 OPEN rcvd, version 4
03:53:36: BGP: 5.5.5.5 unrecognized OPEN parameter (0x2/0x6)
03:53:36: BGP: 5.5.5.5 unrecognized OPEN parameter (0x2/0x2)
03:53:36: BGP: 5.5.5.5 unrecognized OPEN parameter (0x2/0x2)
03:53:37: BGP: 4.4.4.4 open active, local address 3.3.3.3
03:53:37: BGP: 4.4.4.4 sending OPEN, version 4
03:53:37: BGP: 4.4.4.4 OPEN rcvd, version 4
03:53:53: BGP: 2.2.2.2 open active, local address 3.3.3.3
03:53:53: BGP: 2.2.2.2 open failed: Connection refused by remote host
03:54:10: BGP: 2.2.2.2 passive open
03:54:10: BGP: 2.2.2.2 OPEN rcvd, version 4
03:54:10: BGP: 2.2.2.2 sending OPEN, version 4
```

The `debug ip bgp` *`peer-address`* `updates` command is used to view information about the UPDATE messages being sent between BGP peers. The command lets you view all of the routes contained in the UPDATE message. This command can aid in locating a route being withdrawn or added that shouldn't be. It's also useful in locating where a route is not being added or withdrawn that should be:

```
R3#debug ip bgp 2.2.2.2 updates
BGP updates debugging is on for neighbor 2.2.2.2
03:57:48: BGP: 2.2.2.2 computing updates, neighbor version 0, table
  ➥version 14, starting at 0.0.0.0
03:57:48: BGP: 2.2.2.2 send UPDATE 3.0.0.0/8, next 20.20.20.2, metric
  ➥0, path 200
03:57:48: BGP: 2.2.2.2 send UPDATE 4.0.0.0/8 (chgflags: 0x0), next
  ➥20.20.20.2, path  (before routemap/aspath update)
```

```
03:57:48: BGP: 2.2.2.2 send UPDATE 5.0.0.0/8 (chgflags: 0x0), next
  ➥20.20.20.2, path  (before routemap/aspath update)
03:57:48: BGP: 2.2.2.2 send UPDATE 30.0.0.0/8 (chgflags: 0x0), next
  ➥20.20.20.2, path  (before routemap/aspath update)
03:57:48: BGP: 2.2.2.2 send UPDATE 40.0.0.0/8 (chgflags: 0x0), next
  ➥20.20.20.2, path  (before routemap/aspath update)
03:57:48: BGP: 2.2.2.2 send UPDATE 192.168.100.0/24, next 20.20.20.2,
  ➥metric 2195456, path 200
03:57:48: BGP: 2.2.2.2 send UPDATE 192.168.200.0/24, next 20.20.20.2,
  ➥metric 2684416, path 200
03:57:48: BGP: 2.2.2.2 3 updates enqueued (average=54, maximum=58)
03:57:48: BGP: 2.2.2.2 update run completed, ran for 40ms, neighbor
  ➥version 0, start version 14, throttled to 14, check point net 0.0.0.0
03:57:48: BGP: 2.2.2.2 rcv UPDATE w/ attr: nexthop 2.2.2.2, origin i,
  ➥metric 2172416, path 100
03:57:48: BGP: 2.2.2.2 rcv UPDATE about 192.168.24.0/24
03:57:48: BGP: 2.2.2.2 rcv UPDATE w/ attr: nexthop 2.2.2.2, origin i,
  ➥metric 0, path 100
03:57:48: BGP: 2.2.2.2 rcv UPDATE about 10.10.10.0/30
03:57:48: BGP: 2.2.2.2 rcv UPDATE about 20.20.20.0/30
```

The `debug ip bgp dampening` command is used to display information about routes being dampened. This command can aid in locating a routing loop.

To view the state transitions of routers attempting to become BGP peers, use the `debug ip bgp events` command. This command can be useful in locating an attempted peering session that is stuck in a state or oscillating between states:

```
R3#debug ip bgp events
BGP events debugging is on
04:02:56: BGP: 2.2.2.2 went from Active to Idle
04:02:56: BGP: 2.2.2.2 went from Idle to Connect
04:02:56: BGP: 2.2.2.2 went from Connect to OpenSent
04:02:56: BGP: 2.2.2.2 went from OpenSent to OpenConfirm
04:02:57: BGP: 2.2.2.2 went from OpenConfirm to Established
04:02:57: BGP: 2.2.2.2 computing updates, neighbor version 0, table
  ➥version 26, starting at 0.0.0.0
04:02:57: BGP: 2.2.2.2 update run completed, ran for 4ms, neighbor version 0,
  ➥ start version 26, throttled to 26, check point net 0.0.0.0
04:02:58: BGP: 4.4.4.4 computing updates, neighbor version 26, table
  ➥version 29, starting at 0.0.0.0
04:02:58: BGP: 4.4.4.4 update run completed, ran for 0ms, neighbor version 26,
  ➥start version 29, throttled to 29, check point net 0.0.0.0
```

```
04:02:58: BGP: 5.5.5.5 computing updates, neighbor version 26, table
  ➥version 29, starting at 0.0.0.0
04:02:58: BGP: 5.5.5.5 update run completed, ran for 4ms, neighbor version 26,
  ➥start version 29, throttled to 29, check point net 0.0.0.0
```

If you would like to view the KEEPALIVE messages a router is sending and receiving, you can use the `debug ip bgp keepalives` command. This command can help you locate a connection where the potential peer is encountering communication problems:

```
R3#debug ip bgp keepalives
BGP keepalives debugging is on
04:06:44: BGP: 5.5.5.5 sending KEEPALIVE
04:06:44: BGP: 5.5.5.5 KEEPALIVE rcvd
04:06:44: BGP: 5.5.5.5 sending KEEPALIVE
04:06:44: BGP: 5.5.5.5 KEEPALIVE rcvd
04:06:45: BGP: 4.4.4.4 sending KEEPALIVE
04:06:46: BGP: 4.4.4.4 KEEPALIVE rcvd
04:06:46: BGP: 4.4.4.4 sending KEEPALIVE
04:06:46: BGP: 4.4.4.4 KEEPALIVE rcvd
04:07:25: BGP: 2.2.2.2 sending KEEPALIVE
04:07:26: BGP: 2.2.2.2 KEEPALIVE rcvd
04:07:26: BGP: 2.2.2.2 sending KEEPALIVE
04:07:26: BGP: 2.2.2.2 KEEPALIVE rcvd
```

The `debug ip bgp updates` command provides you with information on all UPDATE messages your router is sending and receiving. With this command, you are able to view all of the BGP routes that are being added or withdrawn:

```
R3#debug ip bgp updates
BGP updates debugging is on
04:08:33: BGP: 5.5.5.5 computing updates, neighbor version 0, table version 8,
  ➥starting at 0.0.0.0
04:08:33: BGP: 5.5.5.5 send UPDATE 3.0.0.0/8, next 3.3.3.3, metric 0, path
04:08:33: BGP: 5.5.5.5 send UPDATE 4.0.0.0/8 (chgflags: 0x8), next 3.3.3.3,
  ➥path (before routemap/aspath update)
04:08:33: BGP: 5.5.5.5 send UPDATE 5.0.0.0/8 (chgflags: 0x8), next 3.3.3.3,
  ➥path (before routemap/aspath update)
04:08:33: BGP: 5.5.5.5 send UPDATE 30.0.0.0/8 (chgflags: 0x8), next 3.3.3.3,
  ➥path (before routemap/aspath update)
04:08:33: BGP: 5.5.5.5 send UPDATE 40.0.0.0/8 (chgflags: 0x8), next 3.3.3.3,
  ➥path (before routemap/aspath update)
04:08:33: BGP: 5.5.5.5 NEXT_HOP part 1 net 192.168.100.0/24, next 30.30.30.2
04:08:33: BGP: 5.5.5.5 send UPDATE 192.168.100.0/24, next 30.30.30.2,
  ➥metric 219 5456, path
```

```
04:08:33: BGP: 5.5.5.5 NEXT_HOP part 1 net 192.168.200.0/24, next 30.30.30.2
04:08:33: BGP: 5.5.5.5 send UPDATE 192.168.200.0/24, next 30.30.30.2,
  ➥metric 268 4416, path
04:08:33: BGP: 5.5.5.5 3 updates enqueued (average=57, maximum=61)
04:08:33: BGP: 5.5.5.5 update run completed, ran for 44ms, neighbor version 0,
  ➥start version 8, throttled to 8, check point net 0.0.0.0
04:08:34: BGP: 4.4.4.4 computing updates, neighbor version 0, table version 8,
  ➥starting at 0.0.0.0
04:08:34: BGP: 4.4.4.4 send UPDATE 3.0.0.0/8, next 3.3.3.3, metric 0, path
04:08:34: BGP: 4.4.4.4 send UPDATE 4.0.0.0/8 (chgflags: 0x8), next 3.3.3.3,
  ➥path (before routemap/aspath update)
04:08:34: BGP: 4.4.4.4 send UPDATE 5.0.0.0/8 (chgflags: 0x8), next 3.3.3.3,
  ➥path (before routemap/aspath update)
04:08:34: BGP: 4.4.4.4 send UPDATE 30.0.0.0/8 (chgflags: 0x8), next 3.3.3.3,
  ➥path (before routemap/aspath update)
04:08:34: BGP: 4.4.4.4 send UPDATE 40.0.0.0/8 (chgflags: 0x8), next 3.3.3.3,
  ➥path (before routemap/aspath update)
04:08:34: BGP: 4.4.4.4 NEXT_HOP part 1 net 192.168.100.0/24, next 30.30.30.2
04:08:34: BGP: 4.4.4.4 send UPDATE 192.168.100.0/24, next 30.30.30.2,
  ➥metric 219 5456, path
04:08:34: BGP: 4.4.4.4 NEXT_HOP part 1 net 192.168.200.0/24, next 30.30.30.2
04:08:34: BGP: 4.4.4.4 send UPDATE 192.168.200.0/24, next 30.30.30.2,
  ➥metric 268 4416, path
04:08:34: BGP: 4.4.4.4 3 updates enqueued (average=57, maximum=61)
04:08:34: BGP: 4.4.4.4 update run completed, ran for 48ms, neighbor version 0,
  ➥start version 8, throttled to 8, check point net 0.0.0.0
```

Don't forget that once you have issued a `debug` command, you need to enter the `undebug all` or `no debug all` command to turn off debugging. In order to become familiar with the `debug` commands, I suggest setting up a lab environment where you can practice them. Do not attempt to practice `debug` commands in a live environment. The use of `debug` commands in a live environment can cause processing issues with a router. You should use them for troubleshooting in a live environment only once you have sufficient experience in a lab.

Summary

We have covered a tremendous amount of material in this chapter. BGP is an Exterior Gateway Protocol. This means that BGP is used to route between different autonomous systems. The Internet relies heavily on BGP.

BGP utilizes the TCP protocol and runs over port 179. Because BGP uses TCP, its traffic is transmitted reliably. All iBGP devices must have a logical TCP connection with one another, forming a full mesh, in order for BGP to operate smoothly.

When a BGP route is received, it is placed into the Adj-RIBs-In. From here, it is then run through the inbound policy engine. The inbound policy engine is where BGP policies can be implemented on incoming routes. Next, the route is run through the decision process. The decision process determines whether a route will be placed into the BGP routing table. After routes have been placed into routing table, they are then run through the outbound policy engine. The outbound policy engine is where BGP policies can be implemented on outbound routes. Once the outbound routes are run through the outbound policy engine, they are then placed into the Adj-RIBs-Out.

Simple BGP configuration is not too difficult. You need to determine the autonomous system number to use. If you're doing this in the real world, the autonomous system number will be assigned to you by ARIN, or you can use a private AS. Next, you need to enable BGP and configure your iBGP neighbors. Remember that iBGP neighbors should be fully meshed. Finally, you need to configure your eBGP neighbors.

BGP is a very complex routing protocol and should not be taken lightly. We have covered only what is needed to configure a basic BGP network. Chapter 9 expands on the information contained in this chapter and introduces you to the more advanced topics of BGP. If you do not have a good understanding of BGP at this point, you need to stop and revisit the information contained in this chapter. Having a good understanding of the operation of BGP and how to configure basic BGP networks is essential to the understanding of the material that will be covered in Chapter 9.

Exam Essentials

Know the different message types. You need to be able to list the four different message types utilized by BGP. BGP uses the OPEN, UPDATE, NOTIFICATION, and KEEPALIVE messages. The OPEN message is the first type of message sent after a TCP session has been formed. When the OPEN message is accepted, a KEEPALIVE message confirming the OPEN message is returned. After the KEEPALIVE is sent to confirm the OPEN message, incremental UPDATE messages, NOTIFICATION messages, and KEEPALIVE messages will be exchanged between the BGP peers.

Know the different attribute type codes. Well-known attributes must be supported by all BGP implementations, whereas optional attributes do not have to be supported by all BGP implementations. Mandatory attributes must be present in all UPDATE messages, whereas discretionary attributes do not need to be present in UPDATE messages. If an attribute is transitive, it is passed along, even if a BGP speaker doesn't recognize it. If an attribute is non-transitive and a BGP speaker doesn't recognize it, the attribute is not passed along.

Explain the difference between iBGP and eBGP. iBGP is used for routing within an autonomous system. All devices within an autonomous system speaking iBGP should be fully meshed or using one of the alternatives to a full-mesh configuration discussed in Chapter 9. eBGP is used to provide routing between different autonomous systems.

Understand BGP synchronization. BGP synchronization requires that a route be present in the eBGP router's IGP routing table before it will be advertised to an eBGP peer. Synchronization ensures that a destination can be reached through IGP routing, in case there isn't full iBGP interconnectivity in the AS. If all of the devices within an autonomous system are running iBGP and are configured as a full mesh, synchronization can be disabled. Synchronization with a partial mesh is not a substitute for a full-mesh iBGP network with no synchronization, because black holes are still likely to develop. Just because the AS will not advertise these black holes to neighboring ASs does not mean that their existence is not a problem.

Know how to configure BGP. Basic BGP configuration is relatively simple. All you need to do is enable BGP on a device and specify who your neighbors will be. Remember that all iBGP peers should be fully meshed unless you are using an alternative.

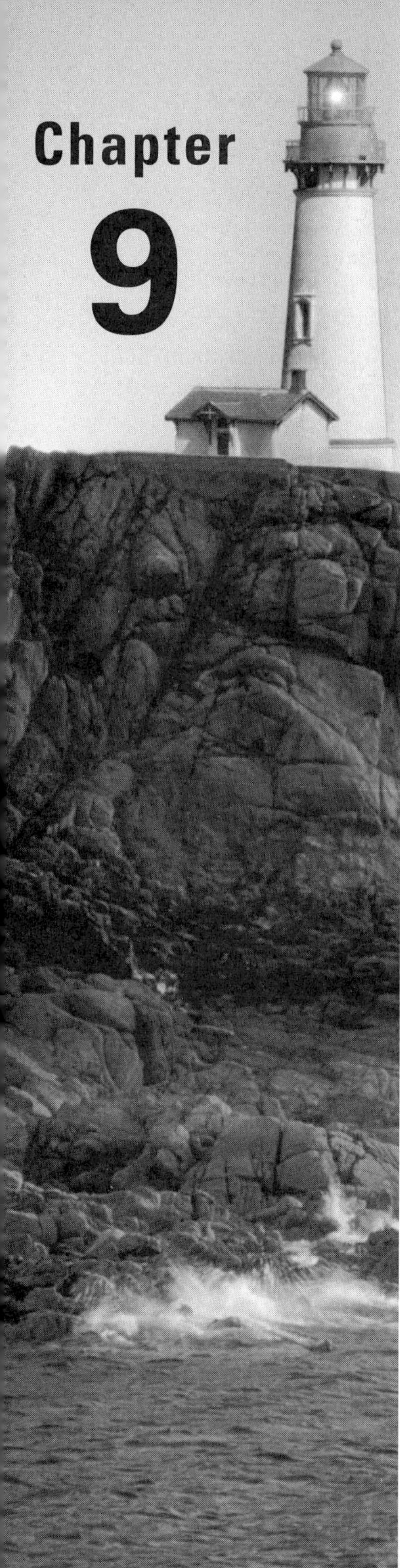

Advanced Border Gateway Protocol

THE CCNP EXAM TOPICS COVERED IN THIS CHAPTER INCLUDE THE FOLLOWING:

- ✓ Understand how BGP policy-based routing functions.
- ✓ Understand how redistribution works between BGP and Interior Gateway Protocols (IGPs).
- ✓ Understand how to configure and verify BGP.
- ✓ Know the scalability problems associated with iBGP.
- ✓ When route selection and configuration problems occur, understand how to use the various show and debug commands to determine the cause of the problem.

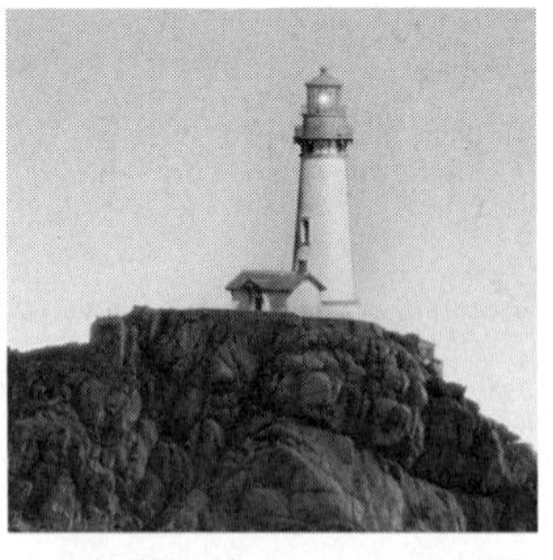

Chapter 8, "Border Gateway Protocol," introduced you to BGP and how to configure a basic BGP network. This chapter builds on what you learned in that chapter.

In this chapter, we will address the scalability issues associated with internal BGP. You will learn the BGP technologies available to overcome the limitations of internal BGP. We will also delve more deeply into the creation and enforcement of BGP policies.

By the end of this chapter, you should have the necessary knowledge and tools to begin practicing the implementation of more advanced BGP networks. We will begin this chapter with a look at the scalability limitations of internal BGP and what is available to overcome these limitations.

Overcoming Scalability Limitations of iBGP

As a network grows in size, iBGP can cause scalability issues. The main issue of concern is fully meshing BGP inside an AS. iBGP devices will not advertise a route they have learned from an iBGP neighbor to another iBGP neighbor, which is why iBGP requires a fully meshed network. In small networks, this doesn't cause any scalability issues, but as a network grows into a large network, scalability can become a real problem. The reason fully meshing an iBGP network causes a problem is the number of sessions needed to fully mesh the network.

Think of it like this: For n BGP speakers, the number of sessions needed would be $n(n - 1)/2$. For a network with only four BGP speakers, you would need only six sessions. That's not too bad, but if you double the number of BGP speakers, you would need 28 sessions, and if you double that number of BGP speakers, you would need 120 sessions. As you can see, the more BGP speakers that are added, the harder it becomes to manage the number of sessions required. Not only that, but to establish $n(n - 1)/2$ sessions, you must enter twice as many configuration commands (one at each of the two ends of the session), or $n(n - 1)$.

There are a couple of alternatives to fully meshed iBGP networks in use today:

- Route reflection
- Confederations

Each of these alternatives can be used by itself or together to overcome the iBGP scalability issue.

Route Reflection

Route reflection was first defined in RFC 1966 and was later revised by RFC 2796. Route reflection allows a BGP speaker—known as a route reflector—to advertise iBGP-learned routes to certain other iBGP peers. This overcomes the limitation of a BGP speaker's not being able to re-advertise iBGP learned routes to other iBGP peers, alleviating the need for a fully meshed iBGP network. Before we dive too deeply into route reflection, there are some basic terms you need to understand:

- *Route reflection* is the operation of a BGP speaker advertising an iBGP-learned route to other iBGP peers.
- *Route reflector* is the BGP speaker that advertises the iBGP-learned route to other iBGP peers.
- *Reflected route* is a route that has been through the route reflection operation.
- *Client peers* are BGP speakers, which will receive reflected routes from a route reflector and participate in that route reflector's cluster.
- *Non-client peer* is a BGP speaker that must be fully meshed and doesn't participate in a route reflector's cluster.
- *Cluster* is a route reflector and all of its client peers.

There are three specific criteria set forth that route reflection needs to meet.

Simplicity An alternative to fully meshed iBGP must be simple to understand and configure.

Easy transition When transitioning from a fully meshed iBGP network, the alternative must not cause a change to the topology or AS. This allows for easy migration from fully meshed iBGP to route reflection.

Compatibility A non-compliant BGP peer must continue to participate in the AS without any loss of BGP routing information.

In order to fully understand route reflection, we must revisit what happens to an iBGP network that is not fully meshed. Refer to Figure 9.1.

In this example, the following is what happens when a route is learned by R2 from R1:

1. R1 sends the route to R2.
2. R2 receives the route and stores it locally.
3. R2 sends the route to R3.
4. R3 receives the route and stores it locally.
5. R4 never learns the new route.

This same scenario would hold true if a route was sent from R5 to R4. In this case, R2 would never learn the route. That is why iBGP requires a full mesh—so that R4 would advertise R5's routes to both R3 and R2, in which case, all iBGP speakers synchronize on this same route information. We will now look at how route reflection overcomes this limitation in the same type of scenario.

FIGURE 9.1 Non–fully meshed iBGP

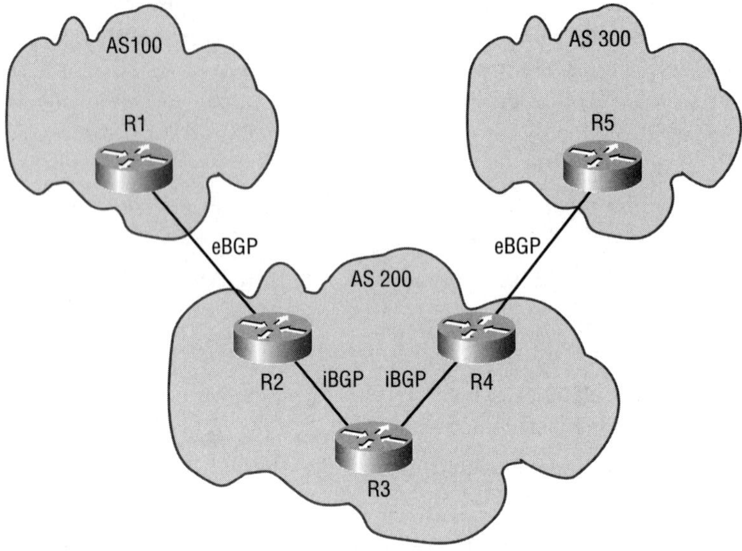

The following list describes the three distinct cases that a route reflector may be called upon to handle. Each case describes what the route reflector will do in response:

- Reflector receives a route from a non-client iBGP peer.

  The route reflector would reflect to all clients. This behavior intentionally violates the normal iBGP behavior, which would be to not advertise the route to any iBGP peers.

- Reflector receives a route from a client peer.

  The route reflector would reflect to all non-client peers and also to the client peers other than the originator. Hence, the client peers are not required to be fully meshed. iBGP traffic from a client to the reflector is treated the same as eBGP traffic would be.

- Route from an eBGP peer.

  The route reflector would send the update to all client and non-client peers. This behavior is no different from behavior in a non-reflection environment.

Figure 9.2 depicts the use of route reflectors. When a route is sent from R1 to R2, the sequence of events that will occur is as follows:

1. R1 sends the route to R2.
2. R2 receives the route and stores it locally.
3. R2 sends the route to R3.
4. R3 receives the route and stores it locally.
5. R3 reflects the route to R4.
6. R4 receives the route and stores it locally.

Depending on the policies in place for the AS, R4 could have sent the route to R5.

FIGURE 9.2 Route reflection

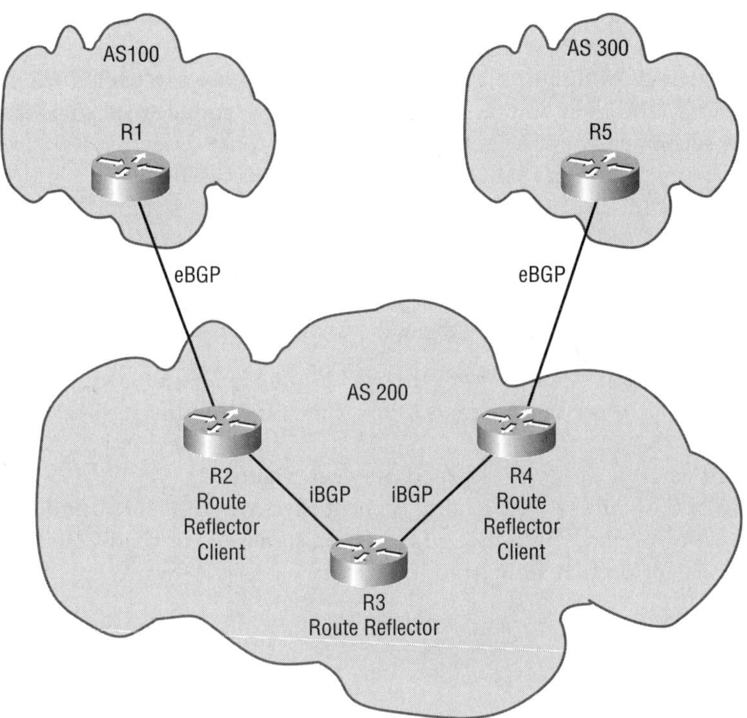

There is one major disadvantage with route reflection. Using route reflectors instead of a fully meshed iBGP can create single points of failure. A single point of failure is a point that if it fails will cause all information for the devices below it not to reach them. A route reflector can be a single point of failure.

To overcome this limitation, you can implement multiple reflectors in the same cluster. Implementing redundant route reflectors for a cluster will eliminate the single point of failure. Both route reflectors will reflect routes to all of the clients in the cluster, to each other, and to all other iBGP peers. When one route reflector in a cluster receives a route from another route reflector in the same cluster, it will ignore the route. This is accomplished by assigning all route reflectors in the same cluster the same *cluster ID*. That way, when a route reflector receives a route from a route reflector with the same cluster ID, it knows to ignore the route. This aids in avoiding routing loops. If you don't configure the cluster ID, the route reflector's router ID will be used. This is fine in most cases, except when multiple route reflectors are part of the same cluster. In this case, not setting the cluster ID can cause routing loops. For best practices, you should always configure a cluster ID.

Route reflectors can help in maintaining the scalability of iBGP. The next section takes a look at how to configure iBGP for route reflection.

Configuring Route Reflection for iBGP

In this section, you will learn to configure basic route reflection. After that, we will turn our focus to multiple route reflectors within a single cluster.

Basic route reflection configuration is pretty simple. You need to decide what device will be the route reflector, and then you need to set up the iBGP connections appropriately. The configuration for setting up route reflection occurs on the route reflector. The client needs no special configuration, nor does it realize anything different is taking place, nor does it behave any differently. The following additional command is the only command that is needed to configure a route reflector:

```
neighbor peer-address route-reflector-client
  peer-address - the IP address of the BGP speaker you want to peer with.
```

The `neighbor` *`peer_address`* `route-reflector-client` command needs to be entered for each peer that you want to become a client of this route reflector and receive other iBGP originated routes.

Let's implement what we have just learned. Refer to Figure 9.3.

We will use R1 as the route reflector, and the client peers will be R2, R3, and R4. When configuring iBGP, use the loopback interface address of each device for the BGP session and turn off synchronization. The loopback interface information is as follows:

R1 Lo0-1.1.1.1

R2 Lo0-2.2.2.2

R3 Lo0-3.3.3.3

R4 Lo0-4.4.4.4

FIGURE 9.3 Basic route reflection

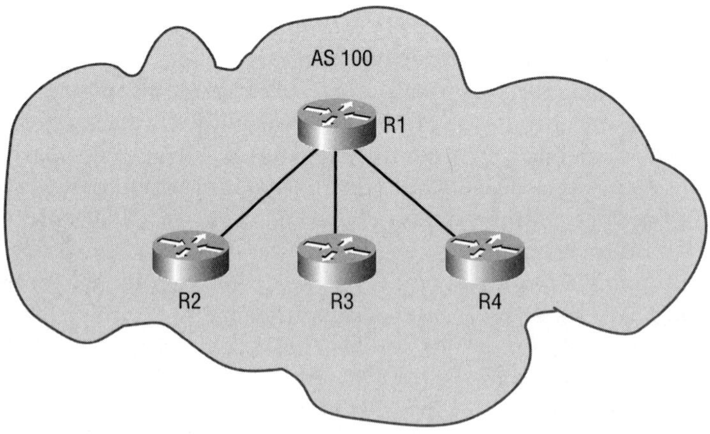

The first task is to configure iBGP on each of the routers:

```
R1#conf t
Enter configuration commands, one per line. End with CNTL/Z.
R1(config)#router bgp 100
R1(config-router)#no synchronization
R1(config-router)#neighbor 2.2.2.2 remote-as 100
R1(config-router)#neighbor 2.2.2.2 update-source Lo0
R1(config-router)#neighbor 3.3.3.3 remote-as 100
R1(config-router)#neighbor 3.3.3.3 update-source Lo0
R1(config-router)#neighbor 4.4.4.4 remote-as 100
R1(config-router)#neighbor 4.4.4.4 update-source Lo0
R1(config-router)#^Z
R1#

R2#conf t
Enter configuration commands, one per line. End with CNTL/Z.
R2(config)#router bgp 100
R2(config-router)#no synchronization
R2(config-router)#neighbor 1.1.1.1 remote-as 100
R2(config-router)#neighbor 1.1.1.1 update-source Lo0
R2(config-router)#^Z
R2#

R3#conf t
Enter configuration commands, one per line. End with CNTL/Z.
R3(config)#router bgp 100
R3(config-router)#no synchronization
R3(config-router)#neighbor 1.1.1.1 remote-as 100
R3(config-router)#neighbor 1.1.1.1 update-source Lo0
R3(config-router)#^Z
R3#

R4#conf t
Enter configuration commands, one per line. End with CNTL/Z.
R4(config)#router bgp 100
R4(config-router)#no synchronization
R4(config-router)#neighbor 1.1.1.1 remote-as 100
R4(config-router)#neighbor 1.1.1.1 update-source Lo0
R4(config-router)#^Z
R4#
```

At this point, this network will not work. We need to configure the route reflector:

```
R1#conf t
Enter configuration commands, one per line. End with CNTL/Z.
R1(config)#router bgp 100
R1(config-router)#neighbor 2.2.2.2 route-reflector-client
R1(config-router)#neighbor 3.3.3.3 route-reflector-client
R1(config-router)#neighbor 4.4.4.4 route-reflector-client
R1(config-router)#^Z
R1#
```

That's all there is to configuring basic iBGP route reflection. It's important to note that additional configuration takes place only on the server. The client's configuration actually tends to undergo a reduction in its configuration, because `neighbor` statements to other clients in the cluster are no longer used. When configuring multiple route reflectors in a cluster, we need to assign each of the route reflectors the cluster ID for the cluster. The cluster ID can be assigned by issuing the following command in router configuration mode:

```
bgp cluster-id cluster-ID
  cluster-ID - The ID for the cluster.
```

We're now going to implement a cluster with multiple route reflectors. Refer to Figure 9.4.

FIGURE 9.4 Multiple route reflector cluster

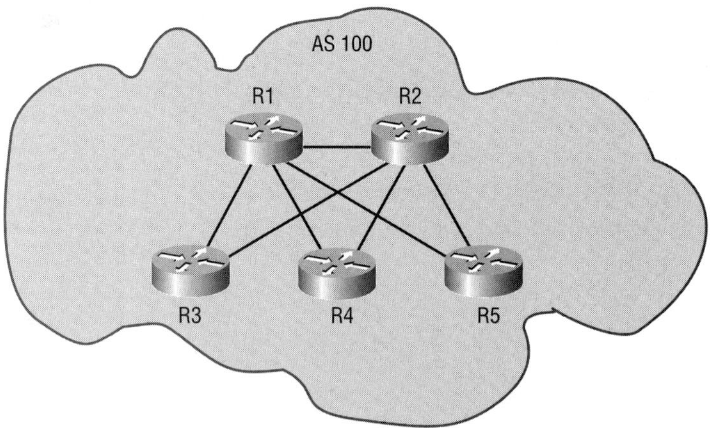

We will use R1 and R2 as the route reflectors, and the client peers will be R3, R4, and R5. Each of the route reflectors needs a peering session with each of the clients. The cluster ID we will use is 1. When configuring iBGP, use the loopback interface address of each device for the BGP session and turn off synchronization. The loopback interface information is as follows:

R1 Lo0-1.1.1.1

R2 Lo0-2.2.2.2

R3 Lo0-3.3.3.3

R4 Lo0-4.4.4.4

R5 Lo0-5.5.5.5

The first task is to configure iBGP on each of the routers:

```
R1#conf t
Enter configuration commands, one per line. End with CNTL/Z.
R1(config)#router bgp 100
R1(config-router)#no synchronization
R1(config-router)#neighbor 2.2.2.2 remote-as 100
R1(config-router)#neighbor 2.2.2.2 update-source Lo0
R1(config-router)#neighbor 3.3.3.3 remote-as 100
R1(config-router)#neighbor 3.3.3.3 update-source Lo0
R1(config-router)#neighbor 4.4.4.4 remote-as 100
R1(config-router)#neighbor 4.4.4.4 update-source Lo0
R1(config-router)#neighbor 5.5.5.5 remote-as 100
R1(config-router)#neighbor 5.5.5.5 update-source Lo0
R1(config-router)#^Z
R1#

R2#conf t
Enter configuration commands, one per line. End with CNTL/Z.
R2(config)#router bgp 100
R2(config-router)#no synchronization
R2(config-router)#neighbor 1.1.1.1 remote-as 100
R2(config-router)#neighbor 1.1.1.1 update-source Lo0
R2(config-router)#neighbor 3.3.3.3 remote-as 100
R2(config-router)#neighbor 3.3.3.3 update-source Lo0
R2(config-router)#neighbor 4.4.4.4 remote-as 100
R2(config-router)#neighbor 4.4.4.4 update-source Lo0
R2(config-router)#neighbor 5.5.5.5 remote-as 100
R2(config-router)#neighbor 5.5.5.5 update-source Lo0
R2(config-router)#^Z
R2#

R3#conf t
Enter configuration commands, one per line. End with CNTL/Z.
R3(config)#router bgp 100
R3(config-router)#no synchronization
R3(config-router)#neighbor 1.1.1.1 remote-as 100
R3(config-router)#neighbor 1.1.1.1 update-source Lo0
```

```
R3(config-router)#neighbor 2.2.2.2 remote-as 100
R3(config-router)#neighbor 2.2.2.2 update-source Lo0
R3(config-router)#^Z
R3#

R4#conf t
Enter configuration commands, one per line. End with CNTL/Z.
R4(config)#router bgp 100
R4(config-router)#no synchronization
R4(config-router)#neighbor 1.1.1.1 remote-as 100
R4(config-router)#neighbor 1.1.1.1 update-source Lo0
R4(config-router)#neighbor 2.2.2.2 remote-as 100
R4(config-router)#neighbor 2.2.2.2 update-source Lo0
R4(config-router)#^Z
R4#

R5#conf t
Enter configuration commands, one per line. End with CNTL/Z.
R5(config)#router bgp 100
R5(config-router)#no synchronization
R5(config-router)#neighbor 1.1.1.1 remote-as 100
R5(config-router)#neighbor 1.1.1.1 update-source Lo0
R5(config-router)#neighbor 2.2.2.2 remote-as 100
R5(config-router)#neighbor 2.2.2.2 update-source Lo0
R5(config-router)#^Z
R5#
```

The route reflectors with the appropriate cluster ID need to be configured:

```
R1#conf t
Enter configuration commands, one per line. End with CNTL/Z.
R1(config)#router bgp 100
R1(config-router)#bgp cluster-id 1
R1(config-router)#neighbor 3.3.3.3 route-reflector-client
R1(config-router)#neighbor 4.4.4.4 route-reflector-client
R1(config-router)#neighbor 5.5.5.5 route-reflector-client
R1(config-router)#^Z
R1#

R2#conf t
Enter configuration commands, one per line. End with CNTL/Z.
```

```
R2(config)#router bgp 100
R2(config-router)#bgp cluster-id 1
R2(config-router)#neighbor 3.3.3.3 route-reflector-client
R2(config-router)#neighbor 4.4.4.4 route-reflector-client
R2(config-router)#neighbor 5.5.5.5 route-reflector-client
R2(config-router)#^Z
R2#
```

That's all there is to route reflectors. They are not the hardest technology to implement, but they can save you a tremendous amount of time when configuring a large iBGP network, not to mention reducing the amount of network traffic, memory, and processor overhead needed for BGP.

Let's turn our focus to the other alternative to a fully meshed iBGP network: confederations.

Confederations

Confederations were initially laid out in RFC 1965, which was later made obsolete by RFC 3065. Confederations allow you to break one autonomous system into multiple mini-autonomous systems. Think of it this way: I have one AS for all of Texas. I decide that the number of iBGP connections needed for this region is going to be tremendous. So I decide to segment the AS into major city locations. I would create a mini-AS each for Dallas, Austin, and Houston. These three areas will consider each of the others to be a different autonomous system, even though they are part of the same AS. Any AS external to the AS for Texas will not even know that the Texas AS has been segmented into mini-autonomous systems. This allows iBGP to run only within each mini-AS. The sessions between the mini-autonomous systems will be eBGP sessions. The outside world knows about only the AS for Texas.

This allows the administrator to cut down on the number of iBGP connections within the AS and, if need be, administer policies between the mini-autonomous systems. Before we get too deep into confederations, there are a few terms that should first be explained:

- *AS confederation* is a collection of autonomous systems that appear to the outside world as one autonomous system.
- *AS confederation identifier (ID)* is an AS number that represents the confederation as a whole and is advertised to other autonomous systems.
- *Member-AS* is an AS that is contained within the confederation.
- *Member-AS number* is an AS number that represents the particular member-AS.
- *Mini-AS* is also known as the member-AS.
- *Private AS* is an AS number that should not be advertised to the outside world. The AS numbers reserved for private autonomous systems are 64512 to 65534, with 65535 the absolute last AS value being officially reserved and not part of the private AS space.
- *Public AS* is an AS number that must be assigned. The public AS number range is 1 to 64,511 and is assigned by ARIN.

When implementing confederations, it's important to note that all BGP speakers participating in a mini-AS must be fully meshed for iBGP. In other words, the rules that apply for iBGP within a normal AS still apply to the mini-AS. This means that routing within the mini-AS will perform the same as iBGP routing in a normal AS. So we could use route reflectors within the mini-AS to further reduce the full-mesh issue. The NEXT_HOP, MED, and LOCAL_PREF attributes will be retained when crossing mini-AS boundaries.

Figure 9.5 depicts the use of confederations. The following is the sequence of events that occur when a route is sent from R1 to R2:

1. R1 sends the route to R2. R1 knows only about AS 200; it doesn't know about the mini-ASs.
2. R2 receives the route from R2 and stores it locally.
3. R2 sends the route to its iBGP peers, R3 and R4.
4. R3 and R4 receive the route and store it locally.
5. R4 sends the route to R5. This is an eBGP session. R5 will see the route as coming from the mini-AS.
6. R5 receives the route and stores it locally.
7. R5 sends the route to iBGP peers, R6 and R7.
8. R6 and R7 receive the route and store it locally.
9. R7 sends the route to R8. This is an eBGP session. R8 sees the route as coming from AS 200. R8 does not know anything about the mini-ASs.

FIGURE 9.5 Confederation

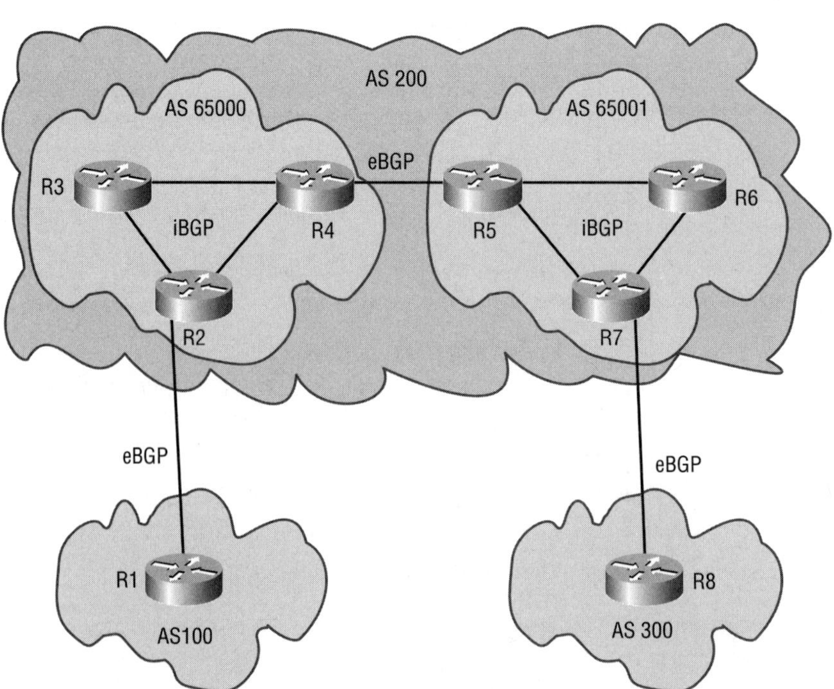

How is this able to happen? When confederations were developed, two new AS_PATH segment types were also created (you may remember the segment types of AS_SEQUENCE and AS_SET from the AS_PATH attribute discussion in Chapter 8):

- *AS_CONFED_SEQUENCE* is an ordered set of member-AS numbers in the local confederation that the UPDATE message has traversed. This is an AS_PATH segment Type 3.
- *AS_CONFED_SET* is an unordered set of member-AS numbers in the local confederation that the UPDATE message has traversed. This is an AS_PATH segment Type 4.

To understand how this works, refer back to Figure 9.5. We will take a step-by-step look at what happens to the AS_PATH as it traverses the confederation.

1. R2 receives the route from R1.
2. R2 does nothing to the AS_PATH, because it doesn't have any eBGP peers to send the route to.
3. R2 sends the route to both of its iBGP peers in the member-AS.
4. R3 and R4 receive the route from R2.
5. R3 does nothing to the AS_PATH because it doesn't have any eBGP peers to send the route to.
6. R4 checks to see if its eBGP peer is part of the same confederation. In this case, it is.
7. R4 then checks the AS_PATH to see if the first segment is of type AS_CONFED_SEQUENCE. In this case, it is not. So R4 appends an AS_CONFED_SEQUENCE type with its member-AS number. If the first segment had been of type AS_CONFED_SEQUENCE, R4 would have just added its member-AS number to the sequence.
8. R4 sends the route to R5.
9. R5 receives the route from R4.
10. R5 does nothing to the AS_PATH, because it doesn't have any eBGP peers to send the route to.
11. R5 sends the route to its iBGP peers.
12. R6 and R7 receive the route from R5.
13. R6 does nothing to the AS_PATH, because it doesn't have any eBGP peers to send the route to.
14. R7 checks to see if its eBGP peer is part of the same confederation. In this case, it is not part of the same confederation.
15. R7 removes the segment of type AS_CONFED_SEQUENCE from the AS_PATH. R7 then adds the confederation ID to the end of the AS_SEQUENCE. If an AS_SEQUENCE had not existed, R7 would have added a segment of type AS_SEQUENCE to the AS_PATH, including its own confederation ID.
16. R7 sends the route to R8.
17. R8 receives the packet. When R8 looks at the AS_PATH, it never sees the member-AS numbers because the AS_CONFED_SEQUENCE was removed from the AS_PATH by R7. R8 sees the confederation ID, which is understood to be the neighboring non-confederation AS, in the AS_SEQUENCE segment.

That's really all there is to the operation of confederations. With all this information in hand, we can start to configure confederations.

Configuring Confederations

When configuring confederations, you first need to enable BGP on the devices. The `router bgp` *`member-AS-number`* command will accomplish this. After BGP has been enabled, you will be required to configure all BGP speakers participating in the confederation with the confederation ID. The following command can be used in router configuration mode for BGP to accomplish this:

`bgp confederation identifier` ***`confederation-ID`***

> *`confederation-ID`* `- the AS number you want advertised to all BGP peers outside of the confederation.`

After successfully configuring the confederation ID on all BGP speakers participating in the confederation, you need to specify on each of these BGP speakers what the member-AS numbers are to all member-ASs in the confederation. This is done so the BGP speaker can determine whether its BGP peer is part of the confederation. The following command needs to be entered in router configuration mode:

`bgp confederation peers` ***`AS-number`*** **`[...`*****`AS-number`*****`]`**

> *`AS-number`* `[...AS-number] - all of the member-AS numbers of all of the member-ASes participating in the confederation. This does not include the local member-AS the BGP speaker is part of.`

This command, along with the normal commands used to configure BGP, is all that's needed to configure confederations. There are a couple of rules you need to keep in mind when configuring confederations:

- When configuring `neighbor` statements for BGP peers in the confederation, use their respective member-AS numbers.
- When configuring a BGP speaker in a neighboring AS to a peer with a BGP speaker in the confederation, use the confederation ID in the `neighbor` statement.
- When enabling BGP on a BGP speaker in a member-AS, use the member-AS number.

We will configure the BGP network depicted in Figure 9.6. You need to use the loopback interfaces of all routers for the BGP sessions. You do not need to take care of the IGP. We will assume it is already configured correctly and includes the loopback interfaces:

R1 Lo0-1.1.1.1

R2 Lo0-2.2.2.2

R3 Lo0-3.3.3.3

R4 Lo0-4.4.4.4

R5 Lo0-5.5.5.5

R6 Lo0-6.6.6.6

R7 Lo0-7.7.7.7

FIGURE 9.6 Configuring confederations

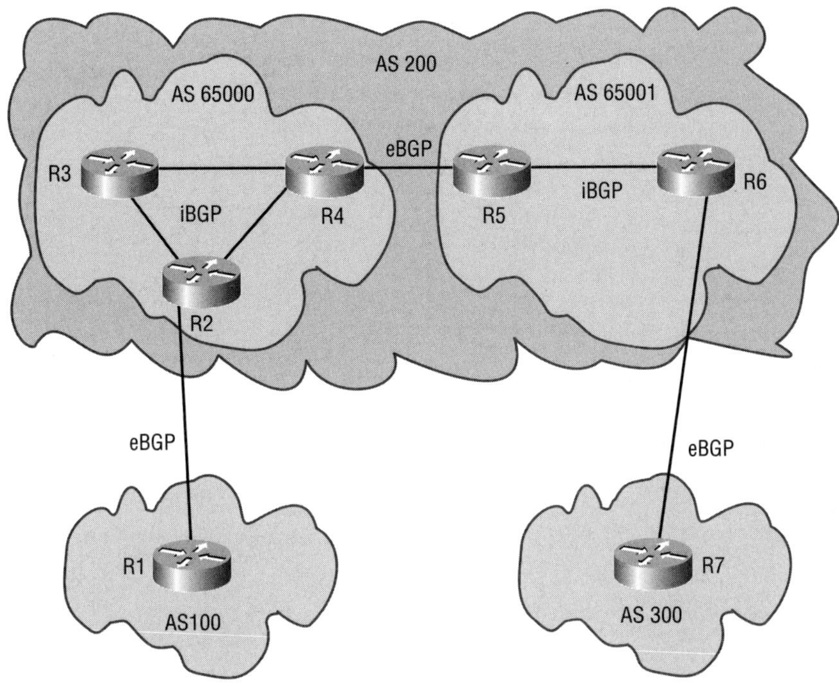

We will start by configuring the member-AS 65000:

```
R2#conf t
Enter configuration commands, one per line. End with CNTL/Z.
R2(config)#router bgp 65000
R2(config-router)#no synchronization
R2(config-router)#bgp confederation identifier 200
R2(config-router)#bgp confederation peers 65001
R2(config-router)#neighbor 3.3.3.3 remote-as 65000
R2(config-router)#neighbor 3.3.3.3 update-source Lo0
R2(config-router)#neighbor 4.4.4.4 remote-as 65000
R2(config-router)#neighbor 4.4.4.4 update-source Lo0
R2(config-router)#^Z
R2#

R3#conf t
Enter configuration commands, one per line. End with CNTL/Z.
R3(config)#router bgp 65000
```

```
R3(config-router)#no synchronization
R3(config-router)#bgp confederation identifier 200
R3(config-router)#bgp confederation peers 65001
R3(config-router)#neighbor 2.2.2.2 remote-as 65000
R3(config-router)#neighbor 2.2.2.2 update-source Lo0
R3(config-router)#neighbor 4.4.4.4 remote-as 65000
R3(config-router)#neighbor 4.4.4.4 update-source Lo0
R3(config-router)#^Z
R3#

R4#conf t
Enter configuration commands, one per line. End with CNTL/Z.
R4(config)#router bgp 65000
R4(config-router)#no synchronization
R4(config-router)#bgp confederation identifier 200
R4(config-router)#bgp confederation peers 65001
R4(config-router)#neighbor 2.2.2.2 remote-as 65000
R4(config-router)#neighbor 2.2.2.2 update-source Lo0
R4(config-router)#neighbor 3.3.3.3 remote-as 65000
R4(config-router)#neighbor 3.3.3.3 update-source Lo0
R4(config-router)#^Z
R4#
```

Now that we have iBGP configured for member-AS 65000, let's go ahead and configure iBGP for member-AS 65001:

```
R5#conf t
Enter configuration commands, one per line. End with CNTL/Z.
R5(config)#router bgp 65001
R5(config-router)#no synchronization
R5(config-router)#bgp confederation identifier 200
R5(config-router)#bgp confederation peers 65000
R5(config-router)#neighbor 6.6.6.6 remote-as 65001
R5(config-router)#neighbor 6.6.6.6 update-source Lo0
R5(config-router)#^Z
R5#

R6#conf t
Enter configuration commands, one per line. End with CNTL/Z.
R6(config)#router bgp 65001
R6(config-router)#no synchronization
R6(config-router)#bgp confederation identifier 200
```

```
R6(config-router)#bgp confederation peers 65000
R6(config-router)#neighbor 5.5.5.5 remote-as 65001
R6(config-router)#neighbor 5.5.5.5 update-source Lo0
R6(config-router)#^Z
R6#
```

At this point, we have iBGP configured for each of the member-ASs in AS 200. We now need to configure eBGP between the two:

```
R4#conf t
Enter configuration commands, one per line. End with CNTL/Z.
R4(config)#router bgp 65000
R4(config-router)#neighbor 5.5.5.5 remote-as 65001
R4(config-router)#neighbor 5.5.5.5 update-source Lo0
R4(config-router)#neighbor 5.5.5.5 ebgp-multihop
R4(config-router)#^Z
R4#

R5#conf t
Enter configuration commands, one per line. End with CNTL/Z.
R5(config)#router bgp 65001
R5(config-router)#neighbor 4.4.4.4 remote-as 65000
R5(config-router)#neighbor 4.4.4.4 update-source Lo0
R5(config-router)#neighbor 4.4.4.4 ebgp-multihop
R5(config-router)#^Z
R5#
```

Recall from the section in Chapter 8 on eBGP multihop that we must utilize the `ebgp-multihop` parameter of the `neighbor` command whenever we establish an eBGP peering relationship with an interface on a router that the router being configured is not directly connected to. This includes loopback interfaces, to which nothing is ever directly connected. They're logical interfaces, not physical ones.

The last item we need to configure is the connections to the neighboring AS:

```
R1#conf t
Enter configuration commands, one per line. End with CNTL/Z.
R1(config)#router bgp 100
R1(config-router)#no synchronization
R1(config-router)#neighbor 2.2.2.2 remote-as 200
R1(config-router)#neighbor 2.2.2.2 update-source Lo0
R1(config-router)#neighbor 2.2.2.2 ebgp-multihop
R1(config-router)#^Z
R1#
```

```
R2#conf t
Enter configuration commands, one per line. End with CNTL/Z.
R2(config)#router bgp 65000
R2(config-router)#neighbor 1.1.1.1 remote-as 100
R2(config-router)#neighbor 1.1.1.1 update-source Lo0
R2(config-router)#neighbor 1.1.1.1 ebgp-multihop
R2(config-router)#^Z
R2#

R7#conf t
Enter configuration commands, one per line. End with CNTL/Z.
R7(config)#router bgp 300
R7(config-router)#no synchronization
R7(config-router)#neighbor 6.6.6.6 remote-as 200
R7(config-router)#neighbor 6.6.6.6 update-source Lo0
R7(config-router)#neighbor 6.6.6.6 ebgp-multihop
R7(config-router)#^Z
R7#

R6#conf t
Enter configuration commands, one per line. End with CNTL/Z.
R6(config)#router bgp 65001
R6(config-router)#neighbor 7.7.7.7 remote-as 300
R6(config-router)#neighbor 7.7.7.7 update-source Lo0
R6(config-router)#neighbor 7.7.7.7 ebgp-multihop
R6(config-router)#^Z
R6#
```

That's all there is to configuring confederations. An important item to remember is that route reflectors and confederations can be used together to better scale iBGP. In some cases, you may be required to implement a route reflector inside of a member-AS. This is a totally legitimate solution. You would just need to configure the confederation and route reflector the same as you normally would. No extra commands are needed.

BGP Filters

Filters are a means by which BGP routes can be blocked, permitted, or manipulated. All of these concepts help in creating a BGP policy. Chapter 8 briefly discussed the use of filters to block or permit traffic. In this section, we will discuss those concepts in more detail and also take a look at how filters can be used to manipulate BGP routes.

We will also take an in-depth look at distribute lists, prefix lists, and route maps. We conclude this section with a discussion of how to manipulate BGP routes.

Distribute Lists

Distribute lists can be used to filter inbound or outbound advertisements for a BGP session to a peer. Distribute lists are an effective tool in deciding which routes the router will accept or send out.

Distribute lists rely on either a standard access list or an extended access list to decide which routes to permit or deny. In order to create a distribute list, you need to follow the following process:

1. Decide the routes that need to be blocked from and/or accepted by the router.
2. Determine whether an inbound filter on the router or an outbound filter on another device would be better to use.
3. Create an access list to deny the routes to be blocked and to permit the routes that need to be advertised.
4. Add the distribute list to the appropriate BGP sessions.

The command you need to use to implement the distribute list is as follows:

```
neighbor peer-address distribute-list access-list-number [in | out]
  peer-address - address of the BGP peer you want to apply the filter to.
  access-list-number - the number of the access list you created for
  the distribute list.
```

After taking a look at Figure 9.7, we will utilize a distribute list to filter a route. We will start by going through the four steps previously mentioned.

FIGURE 9.7 Distribute list

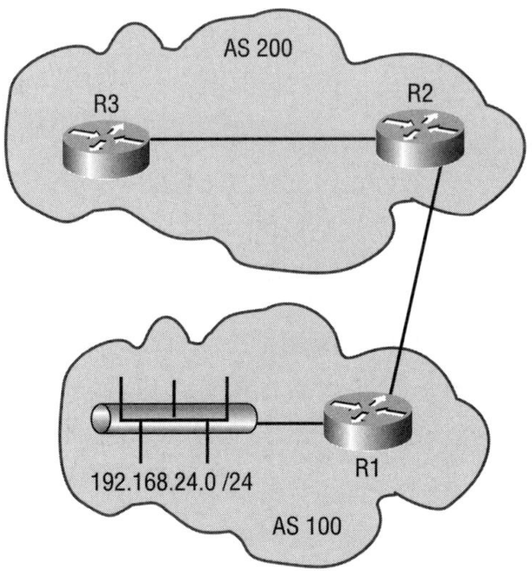

1. The route to R1's Ethernet segment needs to be blocked from R3.
2. In order to prevent unnecessary UPDATE messages for the route, it would be a better choice to put an outbound filter on R2.
3. Create the access list on R2:

```
R2#conf t
Enter configuration commands, one per line. End with CNTL/Z.
R2(config)#access-list 1 deny 192.168.24.0 0.0.0.255
R2(config)#access-list 1 permit any
R2(config)#^Z
R2#
```

When creating an access list, there is an implicit deny all at the end of the access list. If a permit any had not been added to the access list, all routes would have been denied.

4. Add the distribute list to the BGP session on R2 for R3. The address used by R3 for the BGP session is 3.3.3.3:

```
R2#conf t
Enter configuration commands, one per line. End with CNTL/Z.
R2(config)#router bgp 200
R2(config-router)#neighbor 3.3.3.3 distribute-list 1 out
R2(config-router)#^Z
R2#
```

That's all there is to configuring distribute lists. The major drawback of distribute lists for BGP filtering is that they rely on an access list. Access lists are not flexible. If you need to deny a new route or permit a new route, you need to delete the access list and reconfigure it with the new information. That is where prefix lists can help.

Prefix Lists

Prefix lists were first introduced in IOS 12.0. They operate in much the same way as distribute lists. *Prefix lists* are generally used to filter routes. Prefix lists can be combined with route maps. We will discuss that in more detail in the next section.

The first two steps covered for distribute lists are the same for prefix lists:

1. Decide which routes need to be blocked from and/or accepted by the router.
2. Determine whether an inbound filter on the router or an outbound filter on another device would be better to use.

Where the processes differ is in the last two steps. Instead of creating an access list, you need to create a prefix list. Instead of attaching the `distribute-list` keyword to the `neighbor` statement, you need to attach the `prefix-list` keyword to the `neighbor` statement. Thus, the third and fourth steps for prefix lists would be as follows:

3. Create a prefix list.
4. Attach the `prefix-list` keyword to the `neighbor` statement.

You may be wondering, if distribute lists and prefix lists are so similar, why not use distribute lists and forget about prefix lists? Remember: Distribute lists rely on an access list. An access list reads from top to bottom, and any new line of the access list you add is placed at the end of the access list. The problem occurs if you need to permit or deny a new route closer to the beginning of the access list after the access list has been created. In order to accomplish this, you would need to remove the access list and configure a new access list. Prefix lists overcome this limitation with the use of sequence numbers. For instance, if you had a prefix list that had sequence 10 and sequence 15 and you decided you needed to enter a new prefix list line before sequence 15, you could use sequence 11, 12, 13, or 14 to accomplish this. Prefix lists are easier to manage as a network grows in size. An important item to remember about prefix lists is that they have an implicit `deny all` at the end of them.

When configuring a prefix list, if you do not specify a sequence number, the first line of the prefix list will start at 5 and each additional line added increments by 5. To configure a prefix list, the following command needs to be used in global configuration mode:

```
ip prefix-list list-name [seq seq-value] {permit | deny} network/len
➥[ge ge-value] [le le-value]
list-name - the name to use for the prefix list.
seq-value - the numeric value of the sequence. seq is an optional paramater.
network - the network address.
len - the length of the subnet mask.
ge-value - the from value of the range.
le-value - the to value of the range.
```

The *`le-value`* and the *`ge-value`* can be used to create a range of addresses to permit or deny for the network address entered. You can also use the values independently of each other. For instance, if the network address of 192.168.24.0 /24 was entered and the *`ge-value`* of 28 was used, any addresses within the network address with a subnet mask equal to or greater than /28 would be the addresses that would be matched. If the *`le-value`* of 28 had been used instead of the *`ge-value`*, any addresses within the network address with a mask between /24 and /28 would be the addresses that were matched.

Now that you know the syntax, we will walk through the configuration of a line for a prefix list:

```
R1#conf t
Enter configuration commands, one per line. End with CNTL/Z.
R1(config)#ip prefix-list ?
```

```
  WORD             Name of a prefix list
  sequence-number  Include/exclude sequence numbers in NVGEN

R1(config)#ip prefix-list 1 ?
  deny         Specify packets to reject
  description  Prefix-list specific description
  permit       Specify packets to forward
  seq          sequence number of an entry

R1(config)#ip prefix-list 1 seq ?
  <1-4294967294>  Sequence number

R1(config)#ip prefix-list 1 seq 10 ?
  deny    Specify packets to reject
  permit  Specify packets to forward

R1(config)#ip prefix-list 1 seq 10 permit ?
  A.B.C.D  IP prefix <network>/<length>, e.g., 35.0.0.0/8

R1(config)#ip prefix-list 1 seq 10 permit 192.168.24.0/24 ?
  ge  Minimum prefix length to be matched
  le  Maximum prefix length to be matched
  <cr>
```

To permit all or deny all routes, the following prefix list lines can be used:

```
ip prefix-list name permit 0.0.0.0/0 le 32
ip prefix-list name deny 0.0.0.0/0 le 32
```

Name is the name of the prefix list. You can optionally specify the sequence number.

After the prefix list has been created, you need to apply it to the appropriate BGP session. The command to associate a prefix list with a BGP session is as follows:

```
neighbor peer-address prefix-list name {in | out}
  peer-address - address of the BGP peer you want to apply the filter to.
  name - the name of the prefix list to associate.
```

Now that you understand how to create and apply prefix lists, let's put that knowledge to work. Refer to Figure 9.8.

FIGURE 9.8 Prefix lists

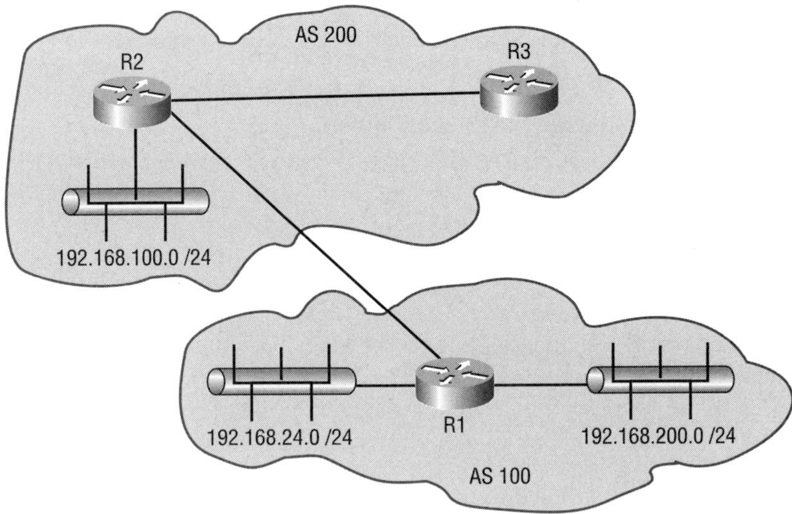

We will now apply the four steps:

1. R1's Ethernet segment 192.168.24.0 /24 and R2's Ethernet segment 192.168.100.0 /24 should not be advertised to R3. All other BGP routes should.
2. In order to prevent unneeded UPDATE messages for the routes, it would be a better choice to put an outbound filter on R2.
3. Create the prefix list on R2:

```
R2#conf t
Enter configuration commands, one per line. End with CNTL/Z.
R2(config)#ip prefix-list TEST seq 10 deny 192.168.24.0/24
R2(config)#ip prefix-list TEST seq 15 deny 192.168.100.0/24
R2(config)#ip prefix-list TEST seq 20 permit 0.0.0.0/0 le 32
R2(config)#^Z
R2#
```

4. Add a prefix list to the BGP session on R2 for R3. The address used by R3 for the BGP session is 3.3.3.3:

```
R2#conf t
Enter configuration commands, one per line. End with CNTL/Z.
R2(config)#router bgp 200
R2(config-router)#neighbor 3.3.3.3 prefix-list TEST out
R2(Config-router)#^Z
R2#
```

Route Maps

Route maps can be used to filter as well as manipulate BGP routes. A *route map* is made up of a sequence of conditions. A sequence in a route map is composed of the following command:

route-map *name* {**permit** | **deny**} [***sequence-number***]

name - the name of the route map. All sequences in a route map must have the same value for the name.

sequence-number - specifies the position of the condition.

After this command is entered, you will enter route map configuration mode. This may be a mode of the router that you have not experienced. In this mode, you will configure the specific conditions for the particular sequence of the route map. The conditions consist of `match` and `set` commands. The `match` command is used to specify the criteria for the sequence. The `set` command specifies the action that will occur if the condition defined by the `match` statement is met. A route map can match on any of the following `match` statements:

`match as-path`	Used to match a BGP autonomous system path access list.
`match community-list`	Used to match a BGP community.
`match interface`	Used to distribute any routes that have their next hop out one of the interfaces specified.
`match ip address`	Used to match any routes that have a destination network address that is permitted by the specified standard access list, extended access list, or prefix list.
`match ip next-hop`	Used to match any routes that have a next-hop address permitted by the specified standard access list, extended access list, or prefix list.
`match ip route-source`	Used to match any routes that have been advertised by any address in the range referenced by the specified standard access list, extended access list, or prefix list.
`match metric`	Used to match any routes with the specified metric.
`match route-type`	Used to match any routes with the specified type.
`match tag`	Used to match any routes with the specified tag.

As you can probably tell, there are quite a few conditions that can be matched. Covering all of these different match conditions is beyond the scope of this study guide. We will visit the most relevant throughout the rest of this section and in Chapter 10, "Route Optimization."

The actions that can be specified with the `set` command are as numerous as those for the `match` command:

`set as-path`	Used to modify the AS_PATH attribute.
`set automatic-tag`	Used to automatically compute the tag value.
`set comm-list`	Used to set the BGP community list for deletion.
`set community`	Used to set the BGP COMMUNITY attribute.
`set dampening`	Used to set the parameters for BGP route flap dampening.
`set default interface`	Used to set the default output interface.
`set interface`	Used to set the output interface.
`set ip default next-hop`	Used to set the default next-hop address along the path.
`set ip next-hop`	Used to set the next-hop address.
`set ip precedence`	Used to set the IP Precedence field.
`set ip qos-group`	Used to set a group ID that can be used later to classify packets into groups for collective QoS treatment.
`set ip tos`	Used to set the IP Type of Service field.
`set level`	Used to set where to import the route.
`set local-preference`	Used to set the BGP LOCAL_PREF path attribute.
`set metric`	Used to set the metric value for the destination routing protocol.
`set metric-type`	Used to set the type of metric for the destination routing protocol.
`set origin`	Used to set the BGP origin code.
`set tag`	Used to set the tag value for the destination routing protocol.
`set weight`	Used to set the BGP weight for the routing table.

After configuring the route map using the `set` and `match` statements, you need to apply the route map to the neighbor session that you would like to apply the filter to. This can be accomplished with the following command:

`neighbor` ***`peer-address`*** **`route-map`** ***`name`*** `[in |out]`

  `peer-address` `- the address used by the peer for the BGP session.`

  `name` `- the name of the route map.`

Let's take a look at Figure 9.9.

FIGURE 9.9 Route map

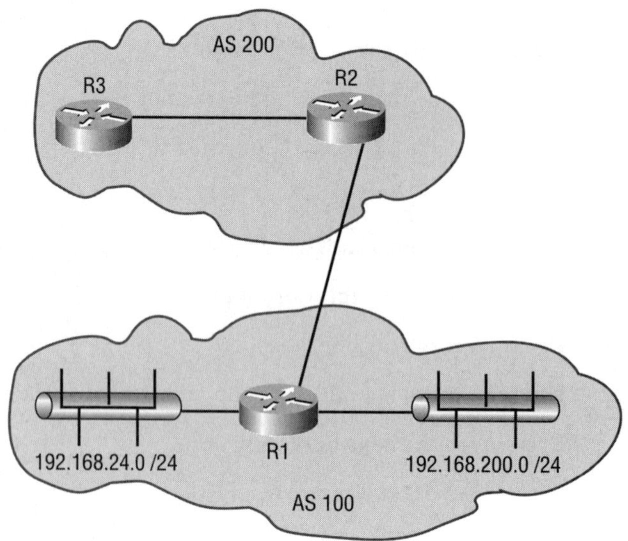

What we want to do is deny network 192.168.24.0 /24 from being advertised to R3. We do want R2 to know the route. The address used by R3 for the BGP session is 3.3.3.3:

```
R2#conf t
Enter configuration commands, one per line. End with CNTL/Z.
R2(config)#access-list 1 permit 192.168.24.0 0.0.0.255
R2(config)#route-map FILTER1 deny 10
R2(config-route-map)#match ip address 1
R2(config-route-map)#route-map FILTER1 permit 20
R2(config-route-map)#exit
R2(config)#router bgp 200
R2(config-router)#neighbor 3.3.3.3 route-map FILTER1 out
R2(config-router)#^Z
R2#
```

That's really all there is to using route maps to filter.

A route map can also be used with the `redistribute` command to affect routes that are being redistributed into the routing protocol.

Configuring route maps to manipulate routes is basically the same as configuring them to filter traffic. We will use the same example as in Figure 9.9. This time, instead of blocking network 192.168.24.0 /24, we will permit it, but we will manipulate its local preference:

```
R2#conf t
Enter configuration commands, one per line. End with CNTL/Z.
R2(config)#access-list 1 permit 192.168.24.0 0.0.0.255
R2(config)#route-map FILTER1 permit 10
R2(config-route-map)#match ip address 1
R2(config-route-map)#set local-preference 200
R2(config-route-map)#route-map FILTER1 permit 20
R2(config-route-map)#exit
R2(config)#router bgp 200
R2(config-router)#neighbor 3.3.3.3 route-map FILTER1 out
R2(config-router)#^Z
R2#
```

What we did in this example was adjust the LOCAL_PREF of the route to 200 for R3.

Route maps are a very powerful tool and can be used to manipulate routes as well as filter them. To become proficient with route maps, you need to practice using them. I would suggest trying them with different conditions, such as using a prefix list instead of an access list, or manipulating the different BGP attributes. It is well worth your time to learn route maps extremely well, because they are used for most complex routing scenarios.

There is one other filter that can be used for filtering routes. This is a filter list, and it uses AS path lists to filter routes. An AS path list allows you to filter routes based on the ASs they have traversed. Configuring AS path filters is beyond the scope of this study guide and is not covered here. You can visit Cisco's website for more information on configuring AS path filters.

Communities

Filtering information based on the IP prefix can become tedious in large networks because of the number of potential routes. There is a way to overcome this and it's known as communities. A *community* is a group of destinations that have some common attribute. Destinations can be added to a community by setting their COMMUNITY attribute. Routing policies can then be enforced based on using the COMMUNITY attribute to affect routing decisions. Destinations can be grouped into a single community or multiple communities regardless of their physical location and autonomous system. By default, all routes belong to the Internet, a well-known community.

There are other well-known communities, besides the Internet, that a destination can belong to:

- *NO_EXPORT*—A route belonging to this community will not be advertised to an eBGP peer. This includes member-ASs within a confederated AS.
- *NO_ADVERTISE*—A route belonging to this community will not be advertised to any BGP peer, whether it's iBGP or eBGP.
- *LOCAL_AS*—This community was first introduced in Cisco IOS 12.0. Routes belonging to this community will be advertised to other mini-ASs belonging to the same confederation. The routes are not be advertised outside of the confederation.
- *Internet*—This is the default community all BGP speakers belong to. No type of route filtering is used.

In order to add a route to a community, you need to create a route map and use the `set community` command to add the route to the community. This can occur for routes being advertised to the BGP speaker from a peer, routes being advertised from the BGP speaker to a peer, and routes being redistributed into BGP.

For example, we want to add route 192.168.200.0 /24 to community 200, and we want to add all other routes to the NO_EXPORT community. EIGRP 100 is redistributing the routes into BGP. This is the configuration that needs to occur:

```
R2#conf t
Enter configuration commands, one per line. End with CNTL/Z.
R2(config)#access-list 1 permit 192.168.200.0 0.0.0.255
R2(config)#route-map COMMUNITY1 permit 10
R2(config-route-map)#match ip address 1
R2(config-route-map)#set community 200
R2(config-route-map)#route-map COMMUNITY1 permit 20
R2(config-route-map)#set community no-export
R2(config-route-map)#exit
R2(config)#router bgp 200
R2(config-router)#neighbor 3.3.3.3 route-map COMMUNITY1 in
R2(config-router)#^Z
R2#
```

If community 200 already existed, the keyword `additive` would have needed to be added to the end of the `set community` command. In order to remove routes from a community, the command `set community none` would need to be used.

The previously mentioned commands will not fully configure a community. The COMMUNITY attribute is stripped from outgoing BGP updates. In order to enable the propagating of community information to a peer, the following command needs to be entered in BGP configuration mode:

```
neighbor peer-address send-community
  peer-address - the address used by a BGP peer for the BGP session.
```

Once communities have been configured for a network, you can use the communities to filter and manipulate the routes belonging to the community. In order to accomplish this, you first need to create a community list. The *community list* contains all of the communities that you want the policy to affect. In order to create a community list, use the following command in global configuration mode:

```
ip community-list number {permit | deny} community-number
number - the number of the community list. For a standard community
  list it will be from 1 - 99. For an extended community list it will
  be from 100-500. We will only look at standard.
community-number - one or more community numbers configured by the set
  community command. If entering multiple communities, separate them
  with a space.
```

Once you have created your community list, you can then use it within a route map. In order to use community list to perform the matches for a route map, you need to use the `match community` *`number`* command within the route map, where the *`number`* is the community list number.

In the real world, you need to check with your ISP to ensure that they will accept communities.

Peer Groups

It is quite common for a BGP speaker to use the same update policies for its peers. An update policy consists of the same outbound route maps, distribute lists, filter lists, update source, and so on. Having to configure the same update policy on a BGP speaker for all of its neighbors can become strenuous, and more important, when making modifications to the update policy, there is room for errors. There is a way around this, and it's known as peer groups. *Peer groups* allow you to group all of a BGP speaker's neighbors that need to use the same policy into one group. The update policy is then applied to all members of that peer group.

A peer group update policy can contain any of the options listed in Table 9.1.

TABLE 9.1 Update Policy Options

Option	Description
`advertise-map`	Specifies the route map for conditional advertisement.
`advertisement-interval`	Sets the minimum interval between sending eBGP routing updates.

TABLE 9.1 Update Policy Options *(continued)*

Option	Description
`default-originate`	Originates the default route to this neighbor.
`description`	Creates a neighbor-specific description.
`inbound/outbound distribute-list`	Filters updates to/from this neighbor.
`ebgp-multihop`	Allows eBGP neighbors not on directly connected networks.
`inbound/outbound filter-list`	Establishes BGP filters.
`maximum-prefix`	Sets the maximum number of prefixes accepted from this peer.
`next-hop-self`	Disables the next-hop calculation for this neighbor.
`password`	Sets a password.
`inbound/outbound prefix-list`	Applies a prefix list to a neighbor.
`remote-as`	Specifies a BGP neighbor.
`remove-private-AS`	Removes a private AS number from outbound updates.
`inbound/outbound route-map`	Applies a route map to a neighbor.
`route-reflector-client`	Configures a neighbor as a route reflector client.
`send-community`	Sends the COMMUNITY attribute to this neighbor.
`soft-reconfiguration`	Per neighbor soft reconfiguration.
`timers`	Sets BGP per neighbor timers.
`unsuppress-map`	Route map to selectively unsuppress suppressed routes.
`update-source`	Source of routing updates.
`version`	Sets the BGP version to match a neighbor.
`weight`	Sets the default weight for routes from this neighbor.

The network depicted in Figure 9.10 would be a good candidate for peer groups.

FIGURE 9.10 Peer groups

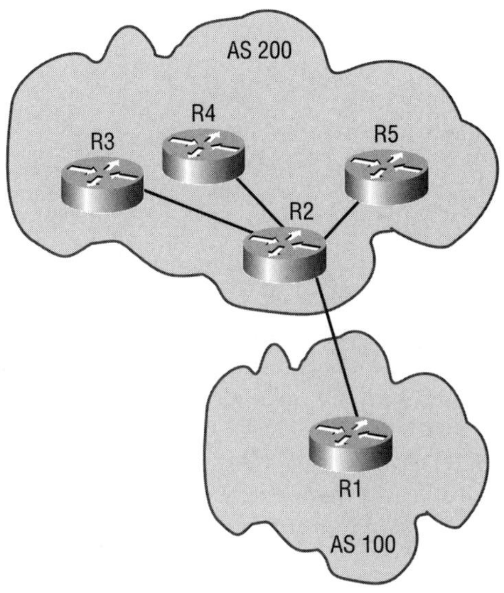

Routers R3, R4, and R5 would be a good choice for a peer group on R2. That is, they'd be a good choice as long as the update policies for all of them are the same. In this example, all you would need to do is set up one update policy and apply it to BGP sessions for R3, R4, and R5.

An important item to note about peer groups is that the peers do not all need to belong to the same AS. You can have a peer group that contains eBGP peers and iBGP peers.

So you may be wondering how to configure peer groups. It's actually a three-step process.

1. Create the peer group.
2. Assign the options to the peer group.
3. Assign the respective peers to the peer group.

First, we're going to look at creating the peer group. In order to create a peer group, the following command needs to be entered in router configuration mode for BGP:

```
neighbor name peer-group
  name - the name of the peer group.
```

Once this command has been entered, the peer group has been created.

After creating the peer group, you need to assign the options for the peer group. The options that are available for the update policy were listed in Table 9.1. The command to use is as follows:

```
neighbor name option
  name - the name of the peer group.
```

option - the option to use in the update policy.

It's important to note that an update policy can be made up of numerous options.

Once the update policy has been configured, you need to assign the respective peers to the peer group. This can be accomplished with the following command in router configuration mode:

neighbor *peer-address* peer-group *name*

peer-address - the address of the peer used for the BGP session.

name - the name of the peer group.

That's all there is to it. If you ever need to make a modification to the peer group update policy, you can make the modification once and it will take effect on all of the BGP sessions with the peers in the peer group. For peers that need more options than are in the update policy for the peer group, all you need to do is specify the other options needed. Those peers will still participate in the peer group. The easiest way to think of a peer group is to think of it as a template of the most common update policy options among a group of peers.

In order for updated peer group information to take effect, you need to clear the BGP sessions that belong to the peer group.

Now that you have an understanding of how peer groups work and the basic components required to configure them, we will walk through putting all of the steps together. Refer to Figure 9.11.

FIGURE 9.11 Peer group configuration

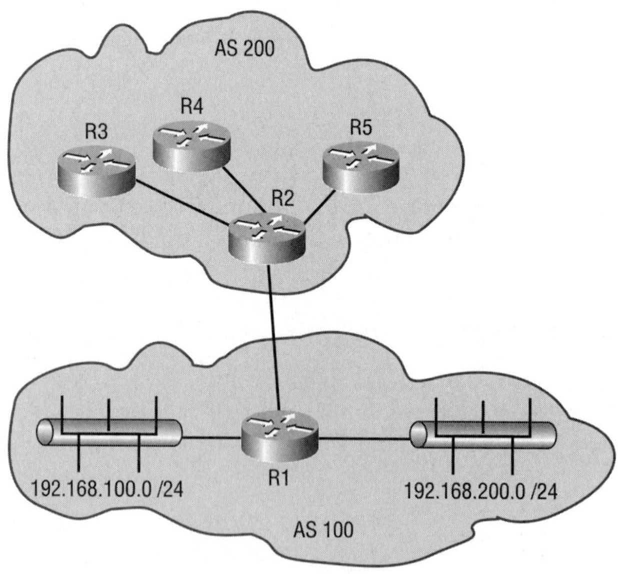

In this example, eBGP has already been configured between R1 and R2. What we need to do is configure iBGP for AS 200. We will use a peer group on R2 for R3, R4, and R5. R2 will perform as a route reflector for the AS. Lo0 on routers R3, R4, and R5 will be used as the source interface for the BGP session to R2. R2 will use its Lo0 interface as the source for the BGP sessions to all iBGP devices. The addresses for each of the device's Lo0 interfaces are as follows:

R2-2.2.2.2

R3-3.3.3.3

R4-4.4.4.4

R5-5.5.5.5

The Ethernet segment on R1 with the address of 192.168.100.0 /24 should not be advertised to R3, R4, and R5. All other routes should be known.

We will start by configuring the route map to block the network 192.168.100.0 /24:

```
R2#conf t
Enter configuration commands, one per line. End with CNTL/Z.
R2(config)#access-list 1 permit 192.168.100.0 0.0.0.255
R2(config)#route-map PEERGROUPFILTER deny 10
R2(config-route-map)#match ip address 1
R2(config-route-map)#route-map PEERGROUPFILTER permit 20
R2(config-route-map)#exit
R2(config)#
```

Now that we have configured the route map, we need to create the peer group on R2:

```
R2(config)#router bgp 200
R2(config-router)#neighbor PEERGROUP1 peer-group
R2(config-router)#
```

After creating the peer group, we need to configure the update policy:

```
R2(config-router)#neighbor PEERGROUP1 remote-as 200
R2(config-router)#neighbor PEERGROUP1 route-reflector-client
R2(config-router)#neighbor PEERGROUP1 update-source lo0
R2(config-router)#neighbor PEERGROUP1 route-map PEERGROUPFILTER out
```

Finally, we need to add the respective peers to the peer group:

```
R2(config-router)#neighbor 3.3.3.3 peer-group PEERGROUP1
R2(config-router)#neighbor 4.4.4.4 peer-group PEERGROUP1
R2(config-router)#neighbor 5.5.5.5 peer-group PEERGROUP1
R2(config-router)#^Z
R2#
```

That is all that is needed for the configuration on R2. The configuration on the peers isn't any different from a normal BGP configuration:

```
R3#conf t
Enter configuration commands, one per line. End with CNTL/Z.
R3(config)#router bgp 200
R3(config-router)#neighbor 2.2.2.2 remote-as 200
R3(config-router)#neighbor 2.2.2.2 update-source lo0
R3(config-router)#^Z
R3#

R4#conf t
Enter configuration commands, one per line. End with CNTL/Z.
R4(config)#router bgp 200
R4(config-router)#neighbor 2.2.2.2 remote-as 200
R4(config-router)#neighbor 2.2.2.2 update-source lo0
R4(config-router)#^Z
R4#

R5#conf t
Enter configuration commands, one per line. End with CNTL/Z.
R5(config)#router bgp 200
R5(config-router)#neighbor 2.2.2.2 remote-as 200
R5(config-router)#neighbor 2.2.2.2 update-source lo0
R5(config-router)#^Z
R5#
```

Peer groups can be used to cut down on the amount of configuration needed in large BGP networks. They can also help to eliminate errors that occur when attempting to configure multiple update policies that are supposed to contain the same information.

Multi-homing

Multi-homing is the process of having more than one connection to one or more service providers. We are going to take a look at two different types of multi-homing: multi-homing to a single service provider and multi-homing to multiple service providers.

Single service provider Multi-homing to a single service provider provides redundancy for your network in case one of the connections to the service provider goes down. There are a couple of different ways you can accomplish this. The first would be to use the same router in your network for both connections to the service provider. This is probably the easiest way. It does introduce a single point of failure to the service provider. The other way would be to use different routers in your network to make separate connections to the service provider. This is the more complicated way. The advantage is you don't have a single point of failure to the service provider. When multi-homing to a single service provider, you don't need to use BGP unless routing policies are required.

Multiple service providers Even with different types of multi-homing that can occur to a single service provider, there is still the limitation of the service provider itself being a single point of failure. Multi-homing to multiple service providers overcomes this limitation. With multi-homing to multiple service providers, you still have the same options of connecting to it as you do with multi-homing to a single service provider. There is an item that you need to take note of when connecting to multiple service providers: If you are using BGP to connect to the multiple service providers and your eBGP devices are running iBGP between themselves, there is the possibility of your AS becoming a transit AS. This means that the service providers could end up passing traffic through your AS. This could consume part of your bandwidth and cause congestion in your network. If you don't want the service providers to use your network, you need to implement BGP policies that do not allow it. For instance, you could use the NO_EXPORT community on routes coming in from each of the providers. This would allow your local BGP speakers to learn the routes, but the routes would not be propagated to the other service provider. Another way would be to create an AS path filter that allows only routes originated from your AS to be advertised out. You would then need to apply the filters to each of the outgoing BGP sessions. These are only a couple of ways of preventing your AS from becoming a transit AS.

So, how can you create a multi-homed environment? Actually, there are a few ways:

Default static routes Default static routes are the easiest way to configure multi-homing. All they require are the configuration of two default routes: one pointing to each of the service provider's devices. You would then need to add a metric to the end of each of the static routes. Give the lower metric to the route you want to be your primary connection. Give the higher metric to the route you want to back up the primary. That way, if the primary connection encounters trouble, the backup will take effect. When the primary line becomes the backup, it will resume the role of transporting the data to the service provider. The limitation to this is that traffic may end up taking a less optimal path to the destination.

Common IGP Another means of communicating with the provider is to use a common agreed-upon IGP. The service provider can then inject any routes into the IGP. You would then redistribute these routes into your local IGP. By doing this, you are better able to make routing decisions based on the best metric of the routes. The problem with this method is that you do not want too many routes being advertised into your local IGP. Too many routes in a routing table can cause latency in your network. Another problem with using this method is that you will still receive a default route for all of the other routes that have not been injected into the IGP. That in turn means that the traffic you are sending still may not take the best path to the destination.

BGP BGP allows for the greatest control of the routing decisions by your local devices. By enabling BGP to the service provider, you are able to enforce policies on the routes you are receiving. This enables you to better state which paths to take, ensuring that your traffic is taking the best path to the destination. This is true only when you are accepting the full routing table from the service provider. There are times when you will be accepting only a partial routing table from the service provider. In this case, you are still able to enforce BGP policies on the routes you are receiving. There isn't a guarantee when accepting partial routing tables that your traffic is taking the best path to the destination. The control you have over the BGP policies that you're able to enforce still makes the use of BGP a better choice than using a common IGP with the service provider.

Resolving Next-Hop Issues

In Chapter 8, we discussed how a BGP speaker must know how to reach the next hop of a route before that route can be used. In many cases, iBGP devices will not know how to reach the eBGP speaker of a neighboring AS. The reason is that the remote eBGP speaker is not participating in the IGP of the local AS. If this occurs, there is a way around it. The `next-hop-self` command can be used to manipulate the NEXT_HOP attribute of a route.

In Figure 9.12, R2 and R3 are running an IGP for AS 200, and R2 is not including its direct connection to R1 in the IGP. This would cause an issue. Any BGP routes from R1 that R3 learned would not be used by R3. The reason is that any route leaving AS 100 destined for AS 200 would have its NEXT_HOP attribute set to R1, but R3 doesn't know how to get to R1. One way to overcome that would be to use the `neighbor` *`peer-address`* `next-hop-self` command on R2, where the *`peer-address`* is the address used by R3 for the BGP session. What would happen at this point is that any route being passed from R2 to R3 would have the NEXT_HOP attribute set to R2. In this case, R3 would be able to use the routes from AS 100 because it knows how to reach R2 and R2 knows how to reach R1.

FIGURE 9.12 Next-hop issues

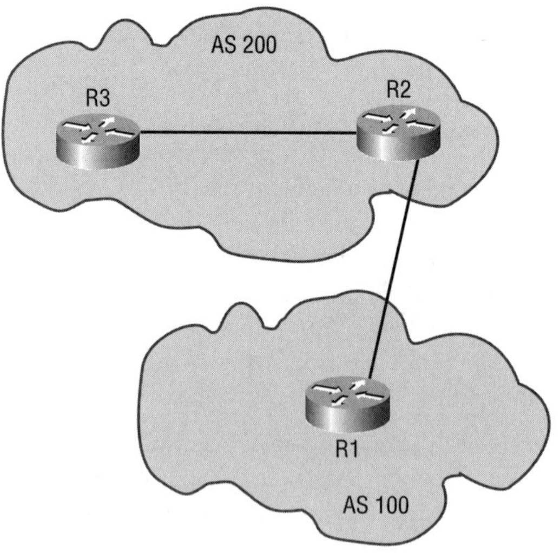

Route Aggregation

Route aggregation, or route summarization, is the process of advertising a single route for multiple routes. This is useful in limiting the number of routes that will be stored in a routing table, thus cutting down on the amount of memory and processing power required.

In small networks, route aggregation may not be an important item to implement, but in large networks it can be very important. By default, BGP has route summarization enabled. This means in BGP that when a route is redistributed from an IGP into BGP, only the classful portion of the address is accepted. This may not always be the most desired situation. The problem that can arise is that the most optimal path is not selected. In order to disable automatic route summarization for BGP, you need to enter the following command in router configuration mode for BGP:

```
no auto-summary
```

If you want to summarize information contained in BGP, you can accomplish this by manually configuring aggregate routes. In order to configure an aggregate address, you need to enter the following command in router configuration mode:

```
aggregate-address address mask
```

This command creates a summary address in the BGP routing table, if at least one more specific route exists. The summarized route will have the ATOMIC_AGGREGATE attribute set to show that some information may be missing. Also, the summarized route will appear as coming from the AS that it was created in. Creating a summary address in this manner will not stop the advertisement of more specific routes.

If you would like to suppress more specific routes from being advertised, you need to enter the following command in router configuration mode for BGP:

```
aggregate-address address mask summary-only
```

Appending the `summary-only` parameter to the end of the `aggregate-address` command suppresses the advertisement of more specific routes. This command can be useful when you need to limit the size of the routing tables.

There is one last way to create a summarized route. The following command creates a summarized route, and instead of setting the ATOMIC_AGGREGATE attribute, it adds a segment of type AS_SET to the AS_PATH attribute:

```
aggregate-address address mask as-set
```

The `as-set` parameter is used chiefly to keep track of the complete series of autonomous systems that originated the aggregate's component routes so that they're included in subsequent updates. This feature helps reduce loops in the case of the aggregate making its way into any of the originating autonomous systems. A potential downside is that the BGP routing table's entry of the aggregate might change every time one of the component routes goes down, thereby removing the associated AS from the AS set.

Summarized routes can be used to limit the size of a routing table. Limiting the size of the routing table cuts down on the amount of memory and processing power required. If you need a refresher on how to determine what the summarized route should be, refer back to Chapter 2, "IP Addressing."

Summary

This chapter covered the more advanced topics of BGP. Because of iBGP requiring a full mesh, it introduces scalability limitations. To overcome these scalability limitations, route reflectors and/or confederations can be used.

A cluster consists of a route reflector and its clients. In the cluster, all of the clients must have a logical connection to the route reflector. However, clients are not required to have a logical connection to each other. When a client advertises a route to the route reflector, the route reflector will send, or reflect, that route to all of the other clients in the cluster. By doing this, route reflectors eliminate the need for a fully meshed iBGP network.

Confederations allow for the creation of mini-autonomous systems within an autonomous system. To the outside world, these mini-autonomous systems look as if they are just one autonomous system, but to each other they appear as different autonomous systems. This helps to decrease the size of the iBGP network that must be fully meshed.

One of the most powerful features of BGP is its ability to implement policies. Policies are rules that will be applied to certain routes. These policies can be implemented through the use of route maps, distribute lists, and prefix lists. When the same policy needs to be applied to multiple peers, you should use peer groups. Peer groups allow the creation of a single outbound policy that can then be applied to multiple peers. This decreases the number of configuration errors by decreasing the amount of configuration required.

As you can probably tell by now, BGP is a very complex routing protocol. The topics covered in this chapter are complex BGP configurations. You will need to spend time in a lab environment to fully understand the different advanced features of BGP. Do not try to implement any of these features in a live production environment until you have spent time in a test environment mastering them.

Exam Essentials

Explain the alternatives to fully meshed iBGP networks. One of the problems with iBGP is that it must be fully meshed. There are two alternatives to using a fully meshed iBGP network: route reflectors and confederations or a combination of the two.

Explain the operation of route reflectors. A route reflector is an alternative to using a fully meshed iBGP network. A route reflector cluster consists of a route reflector and route reflector clients. The route reflector learns routes from route reflector clients. The route reflector then sends these routes to the other route reflector clients in the cluster.

Explain the operation of a confederation. A confederation is another alternative to a fully meshed iBGP network. When using confederations, you're able to break your autonomous system down into mini-autonomous systems. These mini-autonomous systems look at each other as if they are different autonomous systems; however, other autonomous systems regard the mini-autonomous systems as one autonomous system.

Explain the purpose of communities. BGP routes can be grouped into communities. These communities can then have policies applied to them. Communities allow you to be more granular in the creation of BGP policies.

Explain multi-homing. When an autonomous system has more than one eBGP connection to one or more autonomous systems, it is known as multi-homing. When using multi-homing, you need to decide whether you want your autonomous system to allow information from one remote autonomous system to transit to another. If you do not want information transiting your autonomous system, you need to create BGP policies to disallow this action.

Route Optimization

THE CCNP EXAM TOPICS COVERED IN THIS CHAPTER INCLUDE THE FOLLOWING:

- ✓ Understand how to select and configure the different methods for controlling route updates.
- ✓ Know how to configure and verify route redistribution.
- ✓ Know how to configure policy-based routing using route maps.
- ✓ Understand the concepts relating to route summarization.

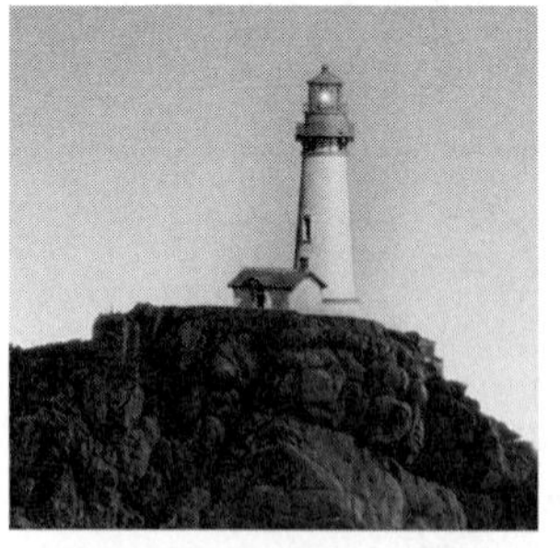

In this chapter, we are going to take the information you learned about filtering in the last chapter and show how it can be applied to the different IGPs. We will also explain policy-based routing and the need for it in networks. We conclude this chapter with a look at networks running multiple IGPs and how to share routing information between them. We also look at route summarization and how it can be used with the different IGPs.

Companies are no longer able to use bandwidth as a resolution for issues. Most companies are going to be looking for the engineer who can optimize their current network. This will help companies to better use the resources they currently have and provide a more reliable network. The engineer who can optimize a company's current network and provide better uptime will be in high demand.

Filtering

Like BGP filtering, *filtering* for IGPs can provide a means of controlling the routing information that is being passed throughout the network. In this section, we will look at three technologies that can aid in the control of routing information and traffic:

- Access groups
- Distribute lists
- Route maps

Access Groups

Access groups do not filter routes; they are used to filter packets traversing a device. An access group is applied to an interface in order to allow and/or deny certain information from entering or leaving a device. You can actually think of access groups as a security measure.

Access groups apply standard or extended IP access lists to an interface. In order to configure an access group, the following command needs to be entered on the interface you want the access group to apply to:

```
ip access-group number [in | out]
  number - the number of the access list to apply to the access group.
```

Now would be a good time to look at Figure 10.1.

FIGURE 10.1 Access groups

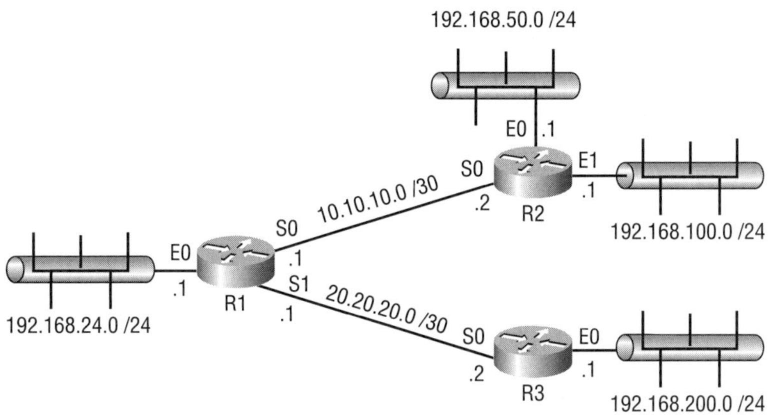

In this example, it has been decided that no host on 192.168.24.0 /24 should be able to contact any host on 192.168.50.0 /24. You can accomplish this with the use of access groups. You have two options at this point: The first option would be to create a standard access list on R2 denying information from 192.168.24.0 /24 and permitting all other traffic. You would then need to apply the access group to R2's E0 interface as either inbound or outbound—in this case, it would be outbound. The problem with this is that the traffic from R1 that is going to be denied is still going to pass over the link, using up extra bandwidth. The best choice, and your second option, would be to create an extended access group on R1, denying traffic from 192.168.24.0 /24 destined for 192.168.50.0 /24. You would then need to apply the access group to R1's E0 interface as either inbound or outbound—in this case, it would be inbound. By doing this, no extra bandwidth on the connection would be used. This solution would better optimize your network.

Now that you understand the concept behind access groups, let's go ahead and configure the more optimized solution described in the preceding paragraph:

```
R1#conf t
Enter configuration commands, one per line. End with CNTL/Z.
R1(config)#access-list 100 deny ip 192.168.24.0 0.0.0.255 192.168.50.0
  ➥0.0.0.255
R1(config)#access-list 100 permit ip any any
R1(config)#interface e0
R1(config-if)#ip access-group 100 in
R1(config-if)#^Z
R1#
```

That's all there is to access groups. Remember that access groups do not filter routes; they filter traffic.

Distribute Lists

Distribute lists for IGPs function the same as distribute lists used for BGP. The implementation of distribute lists is a little different than for BGP. In BGP, you specified the distribute list on the session that you wanted to enforce it on. With the IGP routing protocols, you need to specify the distribute list as either inbound or outbound for the entire routing protocol, which means it will affect all interfaces on the device participating in the selected routing protocol. You are able to overcome this by specifying at the end of the distribute list the interfaces that you want to apply it to.

You need to enter the following command in router configuration mode for the selected routing protocol in order to configure the distribute list:

```
distribute-list {number | prefix name} {in | out}[interface]
  number | prefix name - the number of the access list to use or the
    name of the prefix list to use.
  interface - this is optional. If you specify interfaces the
    distribute list will only affect the interfaces entered for the
    selected routing protocol. If you do not specify an interface the
    distribute list will apply to all interfaces on the device
    participating in the selected routing protocol.
```

One difference that you may have noticed between the IGP distribute list and the BGP distribute list is that you can use prefix lists with the IGP distribute list.

Remember: In order to use prefix lists, you must be running Cisco IOS 12.0 or greater.

So let's take a look at configuring distribute lists with IGP. Refer to Figure 10.2.

What we want to do here is set up two distribute lists on R1. The first distribute list will block the network 192.168.50.0 /24 from being advertised to R3. The second will need to block the network 192.168.88.0 /24 from being advertised to R2 and R3:

```
R1#conf t
Enter configuration commands, one per line. End with CNTL/Z.
R1(config)#access-list 1 deny 192.168.50.0 0.0.0.255
R1(config)#access-list 1 permit any
R1(config)#access-list 2 deny 192.168.88.0 0.0.0.255
R1(config)#access-list 2 permit any
R1(config)#router eigrp 100
R1(config-router)#distribute-list 1 out s1
R1(config-router)#distribute-list 2 out
R1(config-router)#^Z
R1#
```

FIGURE 10.2 IGP distribute list

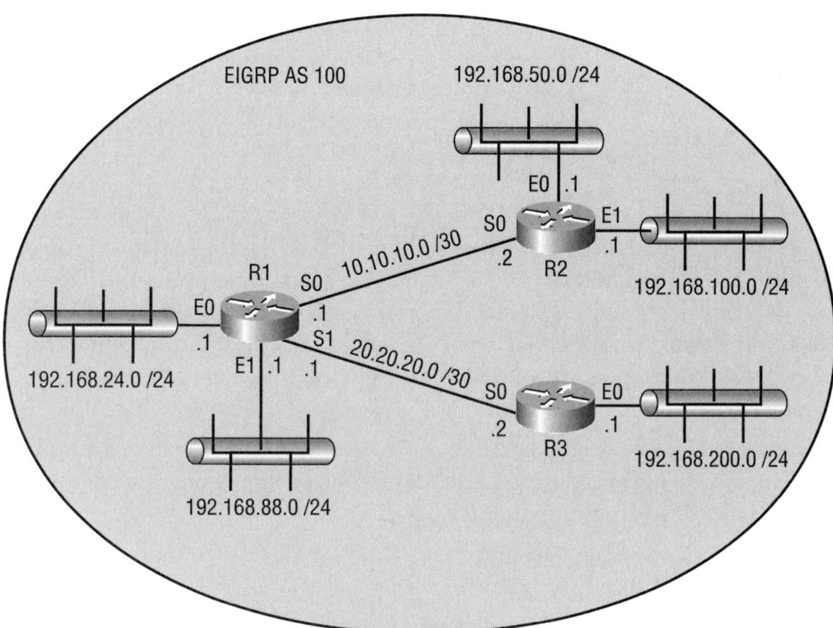

That'll do it. The distribute list that we have put in place will block the necessary routes from being advertised.

Route Maps

Route maps for IGPs allow you to filter and/or manipulate routes during redistribution or policy-based routing. Because policy-based routing and redistribution are covered in detail later in this chapter, we're just going to have a quick review of route maps.

Route maps are broken up into sequences. Each sequence has its own conditions. If the sequence of a route map is permit and the condition laid forth in the `match` statement is met, the sequence can apply the conditions in the `set` statements. The `set` statements allow the user to specify what actions to perform on any route that has met the condition in the `match` statement. If the sequence is of type deny, no `set` statements will be able to be used.

Remember: A list of `match` statements in a sequence has an implicit deny all at the end of it.

By using sequences, you're able to manipulate the route map without having to delete it and reconfigure the modified route map.

You cannot directly use a route map as you can with BGP. BGP allows you to attach a route map to a BGP session for filtering and/or manipulation of the routing information passing over the session. IGPs do not allow you to do this. You must use a route map with either redistribution or policy-based routing.

Policy-Based Routing

Policy-based routing is a means by which administrators can implement routing that strays from the standard routing laid out in destination-based routing protocols. Destination-based routing protocols will route based on the shortest path to a destination. Policy-based routing allows an administrator to determine where they want to route traffic. Some reasons to implement policy-based routing are as follows. Keep in mind, these are not the only reasons administrators might base their decisions on:

- Traffic may need to be routed based on the type of traffic. For instance, non-interactive traffic, such as e-mail, may need to be routed over slower connections, and interactive traffic may need to be routed over faster connections.
- Traffic may need to be load-balanced in a way that differs from how the standard routing protocols would handle load balancing.
- Traffic may need to be prioritized based on the type of traffic it is.
- Traffic may need to be classified based on the source network or based on some other method. You would need to implement this type of policy-based routing when traffic from one network needs precedence over another network's traffic.

Policy-based routing is enabled on the inbound interface of the policy router that the traffic will be coming in on. You specify a route map, which will control enforcing the policies. The route map is then associated with the interface on which the policy needs to be enforced.

In order to enable policy-based routing, you need to configure a route map to enforce the policies. You then need to enable policy-based routing on the interface where these policies need to be enforced. In order to enable policy-based routing, you need to enter the following command on the appropriate interface:

```
ip policy route-map name
  name - the name of the route map.
```

Let's look at some of the different policies that can be enforced and how to configure them.

Policy-based routing can also be applied so that it takes into account the traffic generated on the device it is applied to. To do this, enter the `ip local policy route-map` *name* command in global configuration mode.

Source-Based Policies

Source-based policy routing allows you to make the routing decisions based on where the traffic originates. Refer to Figure 10.3.

FIGURE 10.3 Source-based policies

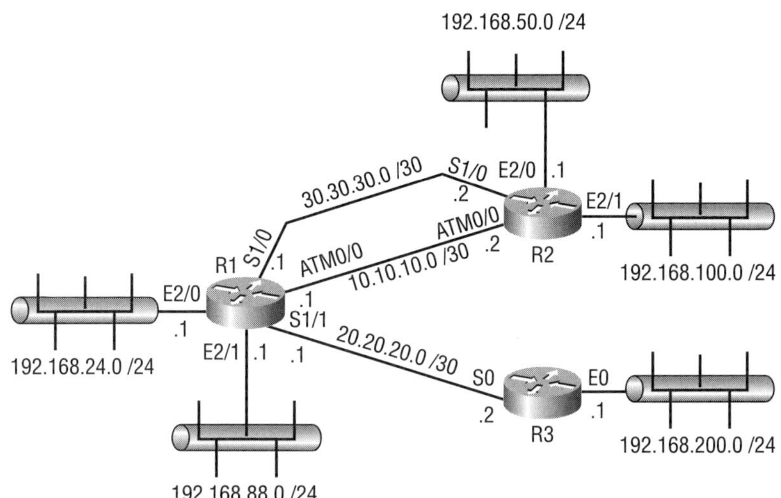

We need to create a policy on R1 that will send the traffic from network 192.168.200.0 /24 destined for network 192.168.50.0 /24 and network 192.168.100.0 /24 out R1's ATM0/0 interface. All other traffic destined for these networks needs to be routed across R1's S1/0 interface.

```
R1#conf t
Enter configuration commands, one per line. End with CNTL/Z.
R1(config)#access-list 100 permit ip 192.168.200.0 0.0.0.255
  ➥192.168.50.0 0.0.0.255
R1(config)#access-list 100 permit ip 192.168.200.0 0.0.0.255
  ➥192.168.100.0 0.0.0.255
R1(config)#access-list 110 permit ip any 192.168.50.0 0.0.0.255
R1(config)#access-list 110 permit ip any 192.168.100.0 0.0.0.255
R1(config)#route-map POLICY1 permit 10
R1(config-route-map)#match ip address 100
R1(config-route-map)#set interface atm0/0
R1(config-route-map)#route-map POLICY1 permit 20
R1(config-route-map)#match ip address 110
R1(config-route-map)#set interface s1/0
R1(config-route-map)#exit
R1(config)#interface s1/1
```

```
R1(config-if)#ip policy route-map POLICY1
R1(config-if)#exit
R1(config)#interface e2/0
R1(config-if)#ip policy route-map POLICY1
R1(config-if)#exit
R1(config)#interface e2/1
R1(config-if)#ip policy route-map POLICY1
R1(config-if)#^Z
R1#
```

By using the keyword `default` before `interface` or `next-hop` (to be illustrated next) in the `set` clause, you can allow the interfaces and next hops of explicit routes to take precedence, with these settings coming into play only when such explicit routes do not exist. The examples here override any explicit routes, which may not be what you intend in every situation.

Type of Traffic Policies

Type of traffic policy routing allows you to make routing decisions based on the type of traffic that is crossing the policy router. Refer to Figure 10.4.

In this scenario, we need to create a policy on R1 so that all traffic entering R1 from R2 and R3 will be routed based on the type of traffic. In this case, we need to send all SMTP traffic over the connection to ISP 2 and all other traffic over the connection to ISP 1. This time, we will set the next hop instead of the exit interface:

```
R1#conf t
Enter configuration commands, one per line. End with CNTL/Z.
R1(config)#access-list 100 permit tcp any any eq smtp
R1(config)#route-map TRAFFICPOLICY1 permit 10
R1(config-route-map)#match ip address 100
R1(config-route-map)#set ip next-hop 172.16.80.1
R1(config-route-map)#route-map TRAFFICPOLICY1 permit 20
R1(config-route-map)#set ip next-hop 172.16.90.1
R1(config-route-map)#exit
R1(config)#interface s1/0
R1(config-if)#ip policy route-map TRAFFICPOLICY1
R1(config-if)#exit
R1(config)#interface S1/1
```

```
R1(config-if)#ip policy route-map TRAFFICPOLICY1
R1(config-if)#^Z
R1#
```

FIGURE 10.4 Type of traffic policies

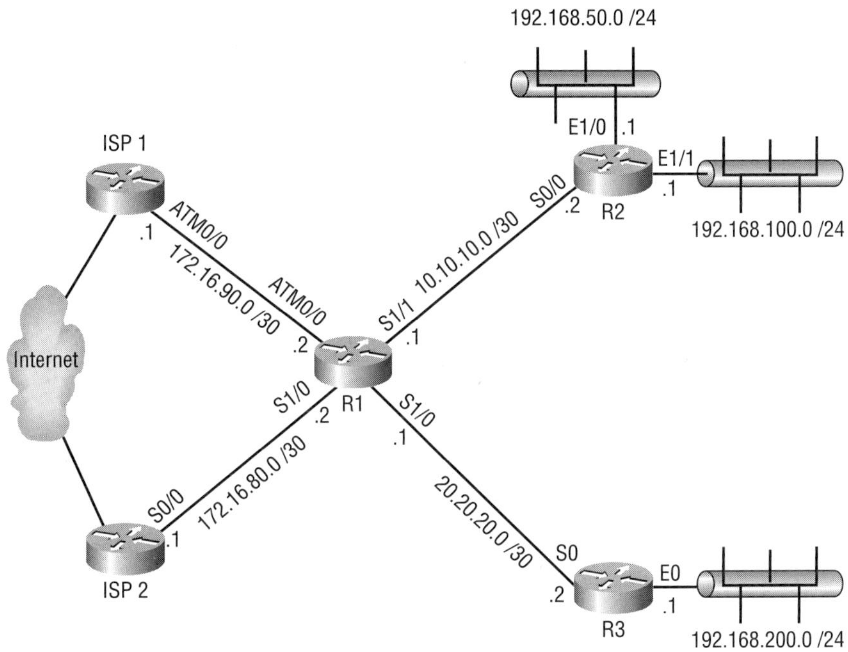

Type of Service Policies

Type of service policies allow the tagging of a packet with the defined classification by setting the IP precedence or type of service (ToS) values. By allowing the packets to be tagged with the defined classification, the administrator is able to define the different classes of service at the perimeter of the network and implement quality of service (QoS), defined for each class of service in the core of the network. The QoS can be implemented through the use of priority, custom, and weighted fair-queuing techniques. Using QoS eliminates the need to define the class of service at every WAN interface in the core of the network.

We are going to explore configuring only the ToS policies. We will not look at setting up queuing. If you would like more information on queuing, please refer to Cisco's website. Figure 10.5 depicts a network that could use ToS policies.

FIGURE 10.5 Type of service policies

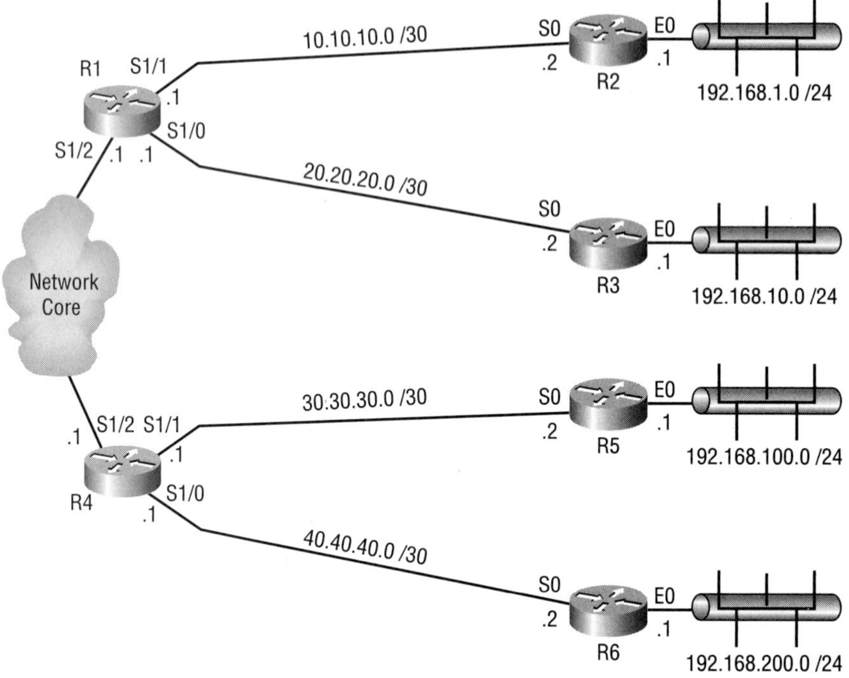

In this scenario, we will configure ToS policies on R1 and R4. The policy on R1 needs to set the ToS for network 192.168.1.0 /24 for maximum reliability and network 192.168.10.0 /24 for minimum delay, and all other traffic needs to be set to normal. The policy on R4 needs to set the ToS for network 192.168.100.0 /24 for maximum throughput and network 192.168.200.0 /24 for minimum monetary cost, and all other traffic needs to be set to normal.

```
R1#conf t
Enter configuration commands, one per line. End with CNTL/Z.
R1(config)#access-list 1 permit 192.168.1.0 0.0.0.255
R1(config)#access-list 2 permit 192.168.10.0 0.0.0.255
R1(config)#route-map TOSPOLICY1 permit 10
R1(config-route-map)#match ip address 1
R1(config-route-map)#set ip tos max-reliability
R1(config-route-map)#route-map TOSPOLICY1 permit 20
R1(config-route-map)#match ip address 2
R1(config-route-map)#set ip tos min-delay
R1(config-route-map)#route-map TOSPOLICY1 permit 30
R1(config-route-map)#set ip tos normal
```

```
R1(config-route-map)#exit
R1(config)#interface s1/0
R1(config-if)#ip policy route-map TOSPOLICY1
R1(config-if)#exit
R1(config)#interface S1/1
R1(config-if)#ip policy route-map TOSPOLICY1
R1(config-if)#^Z
R1#

R4#conf t
Enter configuration commands, one per line. End with CNTL/Z.
R4(config)#access-list 1 permit 192.168.100.0 0.0.0.255
R4(config)#access-list 2 permit 192.168.200.0 0.0.0.255
R4(config)#route-map TOSPOLICY1 permit 10
R4(config-route-map)#match ip address 1
R4(config-route-map)#set ip tos max-throughput
R4(config-route-map)#route-map TOSPOLICY1 permit 20
R4(config-route-map)#match ip address 2
R4(config-route-map)#set ip tos min-monetary-cost
R4(config-route-map)#route-map TOSPOLICY1 permit 30
R4(config-route-map)#set ip tos normal
R4(config-route-map)#exit
R4(config)#interface s1/0
R4(config-if)#ip policy route-map TOSPOLICY1
R4(config-if)#exit
R4(config)#interface S1/1
R4(config-if)#ip policy route-map TOSPOLICY1
R4(config-if)#^Z
R4#
```

Through the use of policy-based routing, the administrator will have better control of the path that a packet follows. Policy-based routing also allows the administrator to overcome the shortest path limitations put in place by standard destination-based routing protocols.

Verifying and Troubleshooting Policy-Based Routing Operation

After implementing policy-based routing, you need a way to verify that it is operating properly, and if it is not, then you need to be able to troubleshoot it. That's what will be covered in this section.

The `show ip policy` command lists all the interfaces configured for policy-based routing and their associated route maps:

```
R1#show ip policy
Interface         Route map
FastEthernet0/0policy3
Serial0/0.1       policy2
Serial0/0.2       policy1
Serial0/0.3       policy2
```

From the preceding output, you can determine which interfaces have policy-based routing enabled and which route map is enforcing the policy. After you have determined the interfaces that have policy-based routing enabled, you can view the contents of the route map that is enforcing the policy. You can view all the route maps on the router with the command `show route-map`:

```
R1#show route-map
route-map policy1, permit, sequence 10
  Match clauses:
    ip address (access-lists): 1
  Set clauses:
    ip next-hop 192.168.10.1
  Policy routing matches: 0 packets, 0 bytes
route-map policy1, permit, sequence 20
  Match clauses:
  Set clauses:
  Policy routing matches: 0 packets, 0 bytes
route-map policy2, permit, sequence 10
  Match clauses:
    ip address (access-lists): 2
  Set clauses:
    ip next-hop 192.168.20.1
  Policy routing matches: 0 packets, 0 bytes
route-map policy2, permit, sequence 20
  Match clauses:
  Set clauses:
  Policy routing matches: 0 packets, 0 bytes
route-map policy3, permit, sequence 10
  Match clauses:
    ip address (access-lists): 3
  Set clauses:
    ip next-hop 192.168.30.1
```

```
  Policy routing matches: 253 packets, 27965 bytes
route-map policy3, permit, sequence 20
  Match clauses:
  Set clauses:
  Policy routing matches: 0 packets, 0 bytes
```

The preceding output informs you what is being used as the `match` condition and, if a match is made, what the `set` condition is. The output also provides you the number of matches for a sequence of the route map.

The **debug ip policy** command can be used to determine what policy-based routing is doing. This command provides you with information on the packets that were matched and the related routing information. It also informs you when a packet doesn't match.

Consider the network in Figure 10.6.

FIGURE 10.6 Debugging policy-based routing

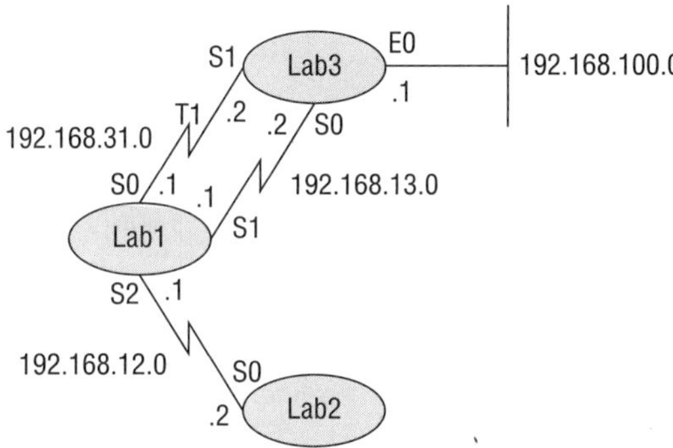

Below is the configuration and output from an exchange between the routers LAB1 and LAB2, regarding LAB3:

```
LAB1#conf t
Enter configuration commands, one per line. End with CNTL/Z.
LAB1(config)#access-list 100 permit ip any 192.168.100.0 0.0.0.255
LAB1(config)#route-map Sendtotl permit 10
LAB1(config-route-map)#match ip address 100
LAB1(config-route-map)#set interface s0
LAB1(config-route-map)#exit
LAB1(config)#interface s2
LAB1(config-if)#ip policy route-map Sendtotl
LAB1(config-if)#^Z
LAB1#debug ip policy
Policy routing debugging is on
```

```
LAB2#ping 192.168.100.1

LAB1#
8w4d: IP: s=192.168.12.2 (Serial2), d=192.168.100.1, len 100, policy match
8w4d: IP: route map SENDTOT1, item 10, permit
8w4d: IP: s=192.168.12.2 (Serial2), d=192.168.100.1 (Serial0), len 100,
  ➥policy routed
8w4d: IP: Serial2 to Serial0 192.168.100.1
LAB1#

LAB2#ping 10.0.0.1

LAB1#
8w4d: IP: s=192.168.12.2 (Serial2), d=10.0.0.1 (Serial0), len 100,
  ➥policy rejected -- normal forwarding
LAB1#
```

Notice how the 56K link on LAB1's interface S1 is not used in this exchange. This policy may have been necessary because a protocol such as RIP was load-balancing across the two links, as if they were equal. The result of the PBR configuration is that traffic coming in LAB1's S2 interface, bound for the 192.168.100.0 network, is forced over the T1, making traffic flow much faster overall.

Redistribution

We briefly discussed redistribution in Chapter 8, "Border Gateway Protocol." To refresh you, *redistribution* is the process of allowing routing information known in one routing protocol to be shared with another routing protocol. It should be noted here that routing protocols are the only items that can be redistributed into. You can redistribute such items as connected interfaces, static routes, and default routes into a routing protocol.

There are two types of redistribution available: *one-way redistribution* and *mutual redistribution*. One-way redistribution occurs when routing information contained in a routing protocol is shared with another routing protocol, but the other routing protocol doesn't share its routing information with the sharing protocol. Mutual redistribution is the process of two routing protocols sharing their routing information with each other.

Before we get too far into redistribution, we should revisit some of the topics discussed earlier in this study guide. If you can remember back to the first chapter, we discussed how routes were selected for the routing table. Administrative distance is the first deciding factor in selecting which route to place in the routing table. The route with the lowest administrative distance is the route that will be selected. If you do not remember the administrative distance values, this would be a good time to go back and review. There is a chance that more than one route to the same destination will have the same administrative distance. When this occurs, the route with the lowest metric is the route that will be selected; if load balancing is in use multiple routes may be selected. Each routing protocol calculates the metric in its own way.

Another topic that's important to review is the difference between classful and classless routing protocols. Classful routing protocols do not advertise the subnet mask of a route. So either received routes are handled as classful routes, meaning that they are assumed at the classful boundaries, or they take the subnet mask of the subnet they were received on, if they share the same major network number. Classless routing protocols send the subnet mask with the route. This allows for better use of addressing. One of the problems you will run into with redistribution occurs when you need to redistribute from a classless routing protocol to a classful routing protocol. We will cover this topic in more detail later in this chapter.

Now would be a good time to go back and briefly revisit all of the IGPs that we have discussed thus far:

RIP If you remember from our earlier discussion, there are actually two versions of RIP: RIPv1 and RIPv2. RIPv1 is a classful routing protocol, whereas RIPv2 is a classless routing protocol. Both versions of RIP use a metric known as hop count. Hop count is the number of routers that a packet must pass through to reach its destination.

IGRP and EIGRP IGRP and EIGRP are Cisco proprietary routing protocols. Both use a composite metric made up of the following:

- Bandwidth
- Delay
- Reliability
- Load

IGRP is a classful routing protocol, whereas EIGRP is a classless routing protocol. Remember: If IGRP and EIGRP are running on the same router and both of them are using the same autonomous system number, they will automatically redistribute with each other. If they do not have the same autonomous system number, you will need to manually redistribute between them. These are the only IGPs we will discuss in this study guide that behave in this manner.

Although redistribution occurs automatically from IGRP to EIGRP when identical AS numbers are used, the resulting route entries in EIGRP do not have the same administrative distance as EIGRP routes originated within the EIGRP AS. While native routes carry an administrative distance of 90, routes redistributed into EIGRP, even those from the same AS in IGRP, carry an administrative distance of 170, far less trustworthy or desirable. The converse is not true, because IGRP has no default mechanism for favoring native routes over redistributed routes to the same destination network. As you will see in this chapter, however, you can influence the use of redistributed routes by how you set their metrics.

OSPF and IS-IS OSPF and IS-IS are both classless routing protocols. Both of these protocols also use the Dijkstra algorithm to calculate the cost of a link.

Classless to Classful Redistribution

The problem with classless to classful redistribution lies in the fact that a route that you are attempting to redistribute to the classful routing protocol isn't of classful boundaries. So how do you overcome this? Careful planning. Summarization is the best means of resolving this issue.

You need to first determine which of the routes that are going to be redistributed do not fall on a classful boundary. Once you have determined this, you can summarize the routes. An important item to note is if you are going to manually summarize a route, the route must be summarized before it reaches the router that it will be redistributed on. If this does not occur, the route will not be redistributed.

Filtering with Redistribution

When redistributing, it may not always be desirable to redistribute all of the routes contained in the routing protocol. If this is the case, you can filter the routes that you are going to redistribute. You can accomplish this through the use of a route map.

Another time you may need to use filtering is when performing mutual redistribution in multiple places between the same routing protocols. The reason for this is you may not find it desirable to have the same route redistributed into the other protocol from multiple routers.

Configuring Redistribution

This section takes a look at how to configure redistribution for RIPv1 and RIPv2, IGRP, EIGRP, OSPF, and IS-IS. We conclude this section with the use of filters with redistribution.

RIP

When redistributing routes into RIP, you need to configure two items:

- The routing protocol to redistribute into RIP
- The metric to use for the routes from the other routing protocol

These items can be configured in one of two ways:

- Add the metric to the redistribution line. This will provide the same metric for all of the routes that are being redistributed with the redistribution line.
- Use the `default-metric` command with the simple metric to specify the metric for all routes being redistributed into RIP. You can then configure the redistribution line without the metric attached to it. The issue with this method is that all routes from all redistributions occurring on this router into RIP will have the same metric.

So let's take a look at how to configure these two different scenarios. We will start with including the metric with the redistribution line. Refer to Figure 10.7.

We will configure one-way redistribution from IGRP AS 100 into RIP on R1:

```
R1#conf t
Enter configuration commands, one per line. End with CNTL/Z.
R1(config)#router rip
R1(config-router)#redistribute igrp 100 metric 1
R1(config-router)#^Z
R1#
```

Now we will configure the same type of redistribution, but this time we will use the `default-metric` command:

```
R1#conf t
Enter configuration commands, one per line. End with CNTL/Z.
R1(config)#router rip
R1(config-router)#default-metric 1
R1(config-router)#redistribute igrp 100
R1(config-router)#^Z
R1#
```

That's all there is to configuring basic redistribution into RIPv1 and RIPv2. If you do not specify a metric when redistributing into RIP, the default will be 0. Because RIP doesn't understand a metric of 0, the routes will not be used. So you must specify a metric. We will cover the classless to classful redistribution issues a little later in this section.

FIGURE 10.7 Redistribution into RIP

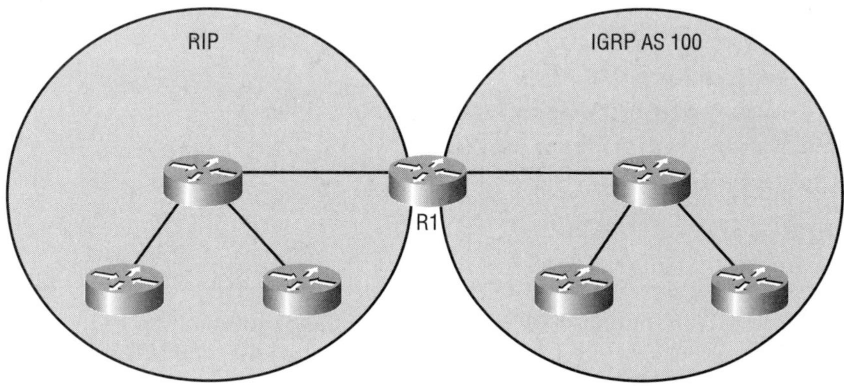

IGRP

Redistribution into IGRP is very similar to redistribution into RIP. When redistributing routes into IGRP, you need to configure two items:

- The routing protocol to redistribute into IGRP
- The metric to use for the routes from the other routing protocol

These items can be configured in one of two ways:

- Add the metric to the redistribution line. This will provide the same metric for all of the routes that are being redistributed with the redistribution line.
- Use the `default-metric` command with the composite metric to specify the metric for all routes being redistributed into IGRP. You can then configure the redistribution line without the metric attached to it. The issue with this method is that all routes from all redistributions occurring on this router into IGRP will have the same metric.

So let's take a look at how to configure these two different scenarios. We will start with including the metric with the redistribution line. Refer to Figure 10.8.

We will configure one-way redistribution from RIP into IGRP AS 100 on R1:

```
R1#conf t
Enter configuration commands, one per line. End with CNTL/Z.
R1(config)#router igrp 100
R1(config-router)#redistribute rip metric 100 100 200 1 1500
R1(config-router)#^Z
R1#
```

Now we will configure the same type of redistribution, but this time we will use the `default-metric` command:

```
R1#conf t
Enter configuration commands, one per line. End with CNTL/Z.
R1(config)#router igrp 100
R1(config-router)#default-metric 100 100 200 1 1500
R1(config-router)#redistribute rip
R1(config-router)#^Z
R1#
```

Even though IGRP and EIGRP use bandwidth and delay by default, you must enter bandwidth, delay, reliability, load, and MTU when redistributing into them.

FIGURE 10.8 Redistribution into IGRP

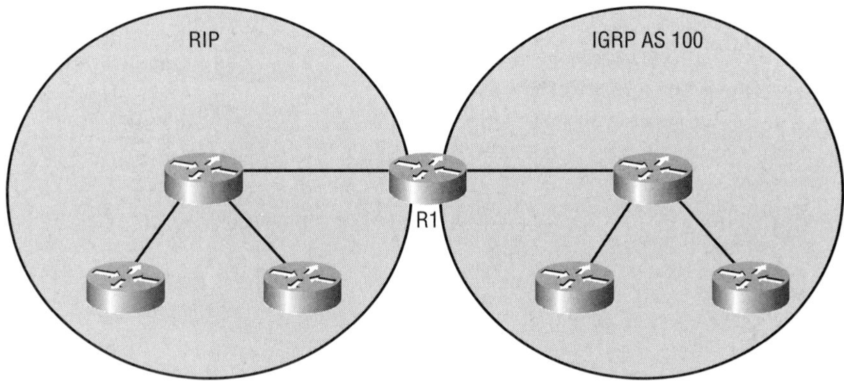

As we said at the beginning of this section, basic IGRP redistribution is almost the same as basic RIP redistribution. IGRP requires you to specify a metric, except when the redistribution occurs with another instance of IGRP or EIGRP. All instances of IGRP and EIGRP use the same composite style of metrics. This means that the metric will carry across the redistribution. Redistributing any other routing protocol, except IGRP or EIGRP, into IGRP requires you to set the metric. If a metric is not specified, the metric value defaults to 0. Because IGRP uses a composite metric, it will not understand a metric of 0 and the routes will not be used. So you must specify a metric.

EIGRP

Basic EIGRP redistribution is exactly the same as basic IGRP redistribution. EIGRP, however, is a classless routing protocol. Like IGRP, EIGRP requires you to specify a metric except when the redistribution occurs with another instance of EIGRP or IGRP. All instances of EIGRP and IGRP use the same composite style of metrics, meaning that the metric will carry across the redistribution. Redistributing any other routing protocol, except EIGRP or IGRP, into EIGRP will require you to set the metric. If a metric is not specified, the metric value defaults to 0. Because EIGRP uses a composite metric, it will not understand a metric of 0 and the routes will not be used. Be smart and always supply a metric for routes being redistributed into EIGRP.

OSPF

When redistributing into OSPF, it is not required to set a metric. If a metric is not stated, the default will be 20. It is a good idea to set the metric so all of the redistributed routes do not have the same metric.

Because OSPF is a classless routing protocol, it accepts routes that are not of classful boundaries. In order for OSPF to accomplish this, you need to append the keyword `subnets` to the end of the redistribution line. The `subnets` keyword allows for classless routes to be redistributed into OSPF. Without the `subnets` keyword, OSPF will accept only classful routes and will reject classless routes. Refer to Figure 10.9.

FIGURE 10.9 OSPF redistribution

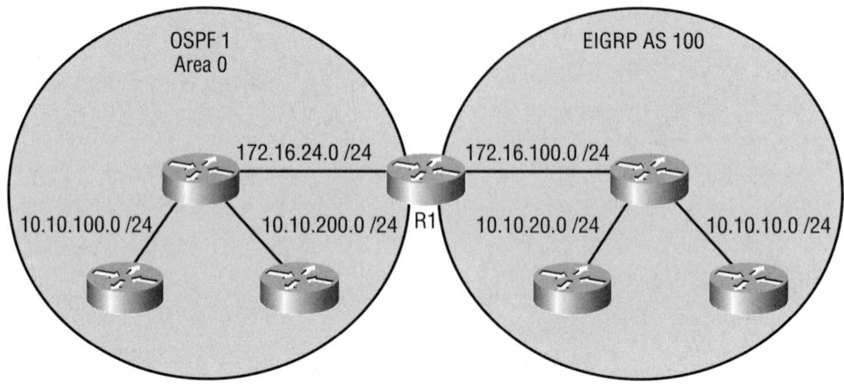

We will need to configure redistribution from EIGRP AS 100 into OSPF 1 on R1. We will assign the metric of 100 to the redistributed routes. We also need to make sure that the redistributed routes are in their classless form:

```
R1#conf t
Enter configuration commands, one per line. End with CNTL/Z.
R1(config)#router ospf 1
R1(config-router)#redistribute eigrp 100 metric 100 subnets
R1(config-router)#^Z
R1#
```

OSPF also allows you to define what type of external routes the redistributed routes are: Type 1 or Type 2. To accomplish this, you need to add the `metric-type` keyword to the redistribution line specifying the type of route.

Refer back to the network in Figure 10.9. The same redistribution needs to occur, except this time we need to make sure that all routes coming from EIGRP AS 100 are marked as Type 2 external routes:

```
R1#conf t
Enter configuration commands, one per line. End with CNTL/Z.
R1(config)#router ospf 1
R1(config-router)#redistribute eigrp 100 metric 100 subnets metric-type 2
R1(config-router)#^Z
R1#
```

If you would like to set a default metric for all routes redistributed into OSPF, you would use the `default-metric` command with the value of the metric.

An important item to note is that you can run multiple OSPF processes on the same router. These different OSPF processes do not automatically redistribute between themselves. You need to configure redistribution in order for the different OSPF processes to share routing information with one another.

The Two Metric Types of OSPF

As mentioned in this section, OSPF defines two external metric types: Type 1 and Type 2. By default, routes are redistributed into OSPF as Type 2. From the perspective of the router computing the cost to a route external to the OSPF autonomous system, a Type 1 external route (marked with `E1` in the IP routing table) has a metric that is the sum of the internal OSPF cost, all the way back to the ASBR, and the external redistributed cost. From the viewpoint of the same router, a Type 2 external route (marked with `E2` in the IP routing table) has a metric equal only to the redistributed cost that the ASBR originally advertised, with no premium for pathways back internal to the ASBR.

IS-IS

Like OSPF, IS-IS does not require you to set a metric. If a metric is not defined, the default will be 0. IS-IS does understand 0 as a valid metric. You should still define a metric, however. Unlike the other routing protocols, IS-IS does not support the `default-metric` command, which requires you to set the metric on the redistribution line.

When redistributing into IS-IS, it is suggested that you specify whether the routes are internal or external and the level of the routes being redistributed. If you do not specify these things, IS-IS will default redistributed routes to internal Level 2 routes. This in turn will represent the metrics of these connections the same way it would represent the metrics of any internal IS-IS route. So it is advisable if you are redistributing routes into IS-IS to set them as external routes. This way, the metric will be higher and will better represent that the route is not an internal route to the IS-IS process.

It is important to note that IS-IS is a classless routing protocol and doesn't require extra configuration in order to redistribute classless routes. Let's refer to Figure 10.10.

In this example, we're going to configure R1 so that the routes from EIGRP AS 100 are redistributed into IS-IS. We will set the metric of these routes to 10 and set them to external Level 2 routes:

```
R1#conf t
Enter configuration commands, one per line. End with CNTL/Z.
R1(config)#router isis
R1(config-router)#redistribute eigrp 100 metric 10 metric-type external
R1(config-router)#^Z
R1#
```

Other routing protocols do not require you to specify anything about them when redistributing their routes into another routing protocol, but IS-IS does. When redistributing IS-IS into another routing protocol, you must specify whether the routes you want to redistribute are Level 1 (`level-1` keyword), Level 2 (`level-2` keyword), or Level 1/Level 2 (`level-1-2` keyword) routes. If you specify Level 1 routes, no Level 2 routes will be redistributed, and vice versa. So in order to redistribute all routes from IS-IS into another routing protocol, you must specify Level 1 and Level 2 routes.

FIGURE 10.10 IS-IS redistribution

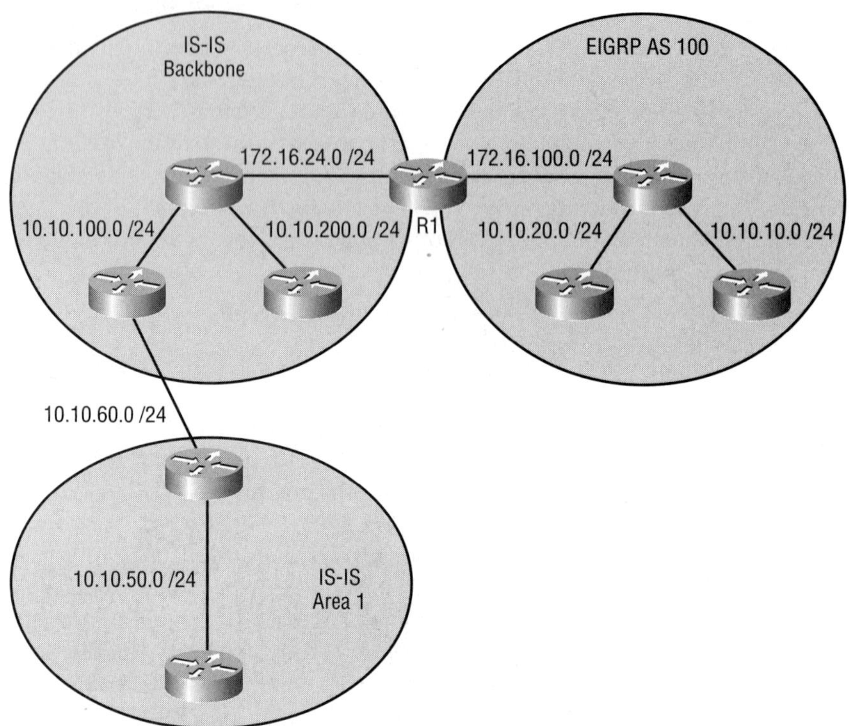

In the previous example, we redistributed routes from EIGRP AS 100 into IS-IS. This time, let's reverse the process, and in doing so, redistribute only the Level 2 routes from IS-IS into EIGRP AS 100:

```
R1#conf t
Enter configuration commands, one per line. End with CNTL/Z.
R1(config)#router eigrp 100
R1(config-router)#redistribute isis level-2 metric 100 100 200 1 1500
R1(config-router)#^Z
R1#
```

This configuration will redistribute only the IS-IS Level 2 routes into EIGRP AS 100. If we wanted all IS-IS routes to redistribute into EIGRP AS 100, we would need to use the following configuration:

```
R1#conf t
Enter configuration commands, one per line. End with CNTL/Z.
R1(config)#router eigrp 100
```

```
R1(config-router)#redistribute isis level-1-2 metric 100 100 200 1 1500
R1(config-router)#^Z
R1#
```

That's really all there is to basic IS-IS redistribution. So far, we have described basic redistribution into all of the IGPs covered in this study guide. We're now going to look at redistributing connected interfaces, static routes, and default routes into the different routing protocols. We will then conclude the redistribution section with a look at VLSM to FLSM redistribution and incorporating filters into redistribution.

Connected Interfaces, Static Routes, and Default Routes

There are instances when you will find it important to redistribute your static and default routes and your connected interfaces into a routing protocol. You may be thinking, "Okay, I understand the static and default route redistribution, but when would I ever need to redistribute a connected interface?" That is a legitimate question. There are instances when you will have an interface participating in a routing protocol, but you still need to redistribute that interface into the routing protocol. This is probably a little confusing.

Remember back to when I briefly mentioned VLSM to FLSM redistribution and how you may need to summarize routes to be able to redistribute them? The routes must be summarized before they reach the redistributing router, because a router has no way of redistributing a summary route that it created. The redistributed route must come from its own routing table. In the case one of the routes that need to be summarized is directly connected to the redistributing router, you cannot summarize the route at that point. The only option you may have is to redistribute the connected interface on the neighboring router on the other side of the link into the routing protocol. You could then create a summary route including that route, which the neighboring router would advertise to the redistributing router, and the redistributing router would be able to redistribute the summary route into the classful routing protocol. Redistributing routes based on connected networks also comes in handy when you do not wish to include the network in the routing process, but you would like the route based on that network in the routing process.

In addition to illustrating the redistribution of connected interfaces, we're going to take a look at how to redistribute static and default routes into each of the different IGPs.

Connected Interfaces

Redistributing connected interfaces is pretty simple. For all of the routing protocols we've discussed, all you need to do is use the keyword `connected` instead of another routing protocol. Let's take a look at redistributing connected interfaces into RIP, IGRP, EIGRP, OSPF, and IS-IS.

RIP

```
R1#conf t
Enter configuration commands, one per line. End with CNTL/Z.
R1(config)#router rip
```

```
R1(config-router)#redistribute connected metric 1
R1(config-router)#^Z
R1#
```

IGRP

```
R1#conf t
Enter configuration commands, one per line. End with CNTL/Z.
R1(config)#router igrp 100
R1(config-router)#redistribute connected metric 100 100 200 1 1500
R1(config-router)#^Z
R1#
```

EIGRP

```
R1#conf t
Enter configuration commands, one per line. End with CNTL/Z.
R1(config)#router eigrp 100
R1(config-router)#redistribute connected metric 100 100 200 1 1500
R1(config-router)#^Z
R1#
```

OSPF

```
R1#conf t
Enter configuration commands, one per line. End with CNTL/Z.
R1(config)#router ospf 1
R1(config-router)#redistribute connected metric 100 subnets
R1(config-router)#^Z
R1#
```

IS-IS

```
R1#conf t
Enter configuration commands, one per line. End with CNTL/Z.
R1(config)#router isis
R1(config-router)#redistribute connected metric 0 metric-type external
R1(config-router)#^Z
R1#
```

As you can see, redistributing connected interfaces into the routing protocols is really no different from redistributing another routing protocol into them.

Static Routes

Redistributing static routes is just as simple as redistributing connected interfaces. All you need to do is use the `static` keyword instead of a routing protocol. The following are examples for each of the routing protocols discussed.

RIP

```
R1#conf t
Enter configuration commands, one per line. End with CNTL/Z.
R1(config)#router rip
R1(config-router)#redistribute static metric 1
R1(config-router)#^Z
R1#
```

IGRP

```
R1#conf t
Enter configuration commands, one per line. End with CNTL/Z.
R1(config)#router igrp 100
R1(config-router)#redistribute static metric 100 100 200 1 1500
R1(config-router)#^Z
R1#
```

EIGRP

```
R1#conf t
Enter configuration commands, one per line. End with CNTL/Z.
R1(config)#router eigrp 100
R1(config-router)#redistribute static metric 100 100 200 1 1500
R1(config-router)#^Z
R1#
```

OSPF

```
R1#conf t
Enter configuration commands, one per line. End with CNTL/Z.
R1(config)#router ospf 1
R1(config-router)#redistribute static metric 100 subnets
R1(config-router)#^Z
R1#
```

IS-IS

```
R1#conf t
Enter configuration commands, one per line. End with CNTL/Z.
R1(config)#router isis
R1(config-router)#redistribute static ip metric 0 metric-type external
R1(config-router)#^Z
R1#
```

Default Routes

When redistributing default routes into RIP, IGRP, and EIGRP, you redistribute them the same way you redistribute static routes. Redistributing default routes into IS-IS and OSPF differs from the way you do it for their counterpart static routes.

OSPF

OSPF ASBRs do not by default advertise default routes. In order to enable the advertising of a default route, the `default-information originate` command needs to be used. Whatever OSPF router you enter this command on, even if the router is not currently an ASBR, will become an ASBR. It's just like issuing the `redistribute` command. The command makes the router become an ASBR in software.

The `default-information originate` command advertises default routes to the other routers participating in the OSPF process if the ASBR has a default route of its own. So if the default route were to be removed from the ASBR's routing table, the ASBR would cease originating the default information and OSPF would declare that route unreachable. In order to overcome the issue of the ASBR requiring its own default route before originating the default route, OSPF allows for the keyword `always` to be appended to the `default-information originate` command. With the use of the `always` keyword, the ASBR always sends a default route into OSPF, even if there is not a default route available in its own routing table. If the OSPF process has only one default, this is a good approach. If there is more than one router originating a default route, you should not use the `always` keyword. The following is an example of a default route being redistributed into OSPF:

```
R1#conf t
Enter configuration commands, one per line. End with CNTL/Z.
R1(config)#ip route 0.0.0.0 0.0.0.0 10.10.10.1
R1(config)#router ospf 1
R1(config-router)#default-information originate
R1(config-router)#^Z
R1#
```

IS-IS

Like OSPF, IS-IS uses the `default-information originate` command to redistribute default routes into IS-IS. IS-IS, however, does not support the use of the `always` keyword. Default routes redistributed into IS-IS are advertised only to the Level 2 area. The default route is not advertised into a Level 1 area. Level 1 areas have their own way of discovering default gateways. The following is a sample of a default route being redistributed into IS-IS:

```
R1#conf t
Enter configuration commands, one per line. End with CNTL/Z.
R1(config)#ip route 0.0.0.0 0.0.0.0 10.10.10.1
R1(config)#router isis
R1(config-router)#default-information originate
R1(config-router)#^Z
R1#
```

OSPF allows you to set a metric value and a metric type for the default route. IS-IS does not allow you to set these values for a default route.

Classless to Classful Redistribution

There are only two routing protocols we've covered for which we really need to worry about classless to classful redistribution: RIPv1 and IGRP. The problem is these two routing protocols are still used in networks today.

So what causes the problem with redistribution between classless and classful routing protocols? The problem arises because classful routing protocols do not send a subnet mask with a route. Because classless routing protocols do send the subnet mask with the route, you will encounter situations where you need to redistribute routes into the classful routing protocol that do not fall within the classful boundaries.

How do we overcome these instances? There are actually two ways you can overcome the classless to classful redistribution limitation:

- Make sure you have summarized all networks to their classful boundaries that need to be redistributed before they reach the redistributing router.
- On the redistributing router, create a static route with the classful variant of the classless route and point it to interface null0. Redistribute the static route into the classful routing protocol.

Null0 is an interface that doesn't exist. The null0 interface can be used with static routes to route a packet into a black hole of sorts. In other words, if you have traffic that you do not want to reach a particular destination, you can create the static route for that destination with the next-hop interface pointing to null0. Any traffic that enters the router destined for the network specified in the static route is sent to the null0 interface and dropped. In other words, the traffic will not reach that destination.

So if static routes to null0 keep packets from reaching a destination, why would we ever want to use that type of static route for classless to classful redistribution? The reason we would do this is the route will be advertised into the classful routing protocol. All of the traffic destined for that network is forwarded back to the router that originated the classful advertisement from its static route. Because the originating router has more specific routes for the destination, it will use those routes and will never use the route to null0, hence solving the redistribution limitation.

To better understand these two methods, we will walk through a couple of examples. We'll start with the summarization solution. Refer to Figure 10.11.

FIGURE 10.11 Summarization solution

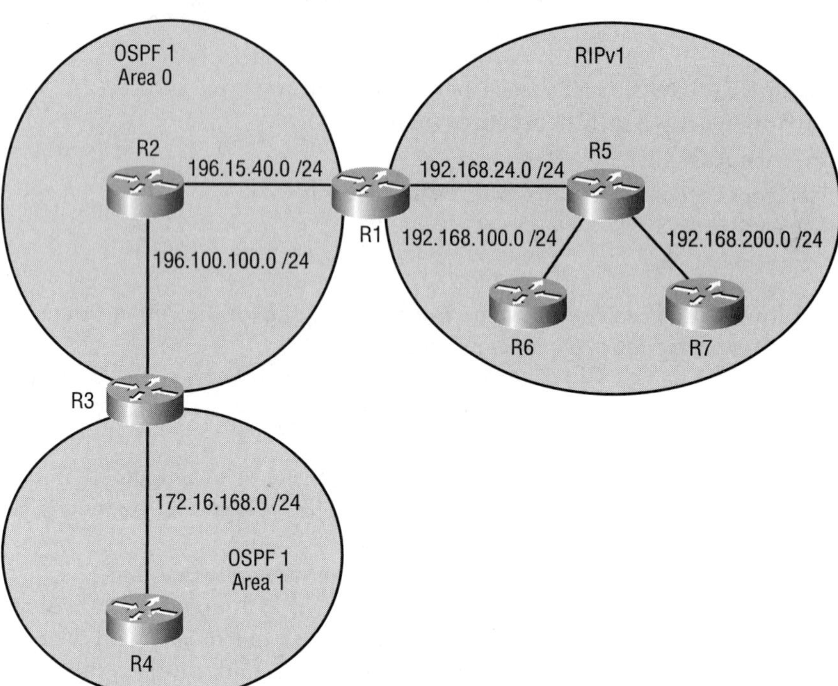

You should've noticed in Figure 10.11 that Area 1 has the address 172.16.168.0 /24. If you just set up normal redistribution between OSPF 1 and RIPv1, that route would not be redistributed. So what we need to do is create an area range on R3 to summarize Area 1 to 172.16.0.0 /16. Once the area range is set up, then redistribution can be configured and the route will be redistributed. Here's the configuration that would accomplish this:

```
R3#conf t
Enter configuration commands, one per line. End with CNTL/Z.
R3(config)#router ospf 1
R3(config-router)#area 1 range 172.16.0.0 255.255.0.0
R3(config-router)#^Z
R3#

R1#conf t
Enter configuration commands, one per line. End with CNTL/Z.
R1(config)#router rip
R1(config-router)#redistribute ospf 1 metric 1
R1(config-router)#^Z
R1#
```

Now let's look at the option of creating a static route pointing to null0. We will first need to configure on R1 a static route for 172.16.0.0 255.255.0.0 pointing to null0. We would then redistribute the static route into RIP. The following is the configuration to accomplish this:

```
R1#conf t
Enter configuration commands, one per line. End with CNTL/Z.
R1(config)#ip route 172.16.0.0 255.255.0.0 null0
R1(config)#router rip
R1(config-router)#redistribute static metric 1
R1(config-router)#^Z
R1#
```

This scenario would accomplish the same task as the first. The method you use is up to you. Either one will accomplish the task.

Filtering with Redistribution

Using route maps to filter and/or manipulate routes for redistribution is a very powerful tool. When redistributing routes, you may not want all of the routes contained within a routing protocol to be shared with another routing protocol. The way to accomplish this would be to set up a route map to block the routes.

Route maps can also be used to manipulate routes during redistribution. You may ask yourself, "When would you want to do that?" One of the reasons to manipulate the routes is when all of the routes being redistributed shouldn't have the same metric. Remember that using a `default-metric` command will set all routes being redistributed into the routing protocol on that router to the same metric. If you use the `metric` keyword on the redistribution line, you will set all routes being redistributed during that particular instance to the same metric. If you do not want all of the routes being redistributed during an instance of redistribution, you can create a route map to filter the routes based on the IP prefix and then set the metric for those particular routes.

Let's go ahead and take a look at a couple of these examples. Refer to Figure 10.12.

FIGURE 10.12 Filtering during redistribution

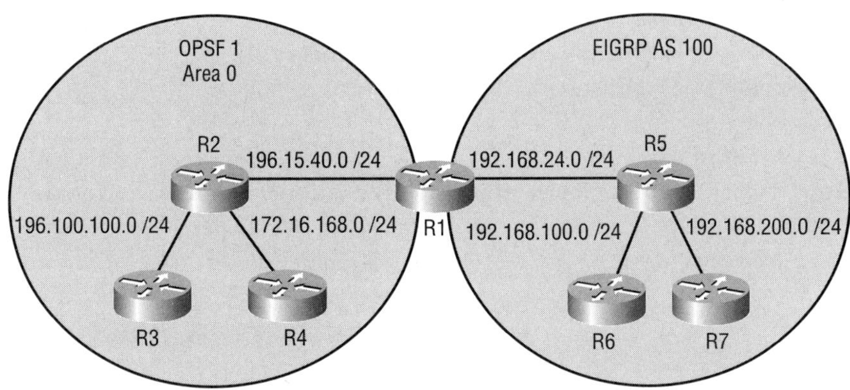

In this example, we will redistribute the routes contained in EIGRP AS 100 into OSPF 1. However, we do not want the route 192.168.200.0 /24 redistributed into OSPF 1. We do want all other routes and any future routes to be redistributed. First, we need to create a route map that will deny that route and permit all other routes. We will then configure the redistribution and include the route map:

```
R1#conf t
Enter configuration commands, one per line. End with CNTL/Z.
R1(config)#access-list 1 permit 192.168.200.0 0.0.0.255
R1(config)#route-map EIGRPTOOSPF deny 10
R1(config-route-map)#match ip address 1
R1(config-route-map)#route-map EIGRPTOOSPF permit 20
R1(config-route-map)#exit
R1(config)#router ospf 1
R1(config-router)#redistribute eigrp 100 metric 100 subnets route-map
  ➥EIGRPTOOSPF
R1(config-router)#^Z
R1#
```

That will do it. All other routes will be permitted, and 192.168.200.0 /24 will be denied. Now that you understand how to filter routes with route maps for redistribution, let's build on it. This time, we still want to block route 192.168.200.0 /24 and set the metric of route 192.168.100.0 /24 to 150, and for any future routes, we want their metric to be set to 100:

```
R1#conf t
Enter configuration commands, one per line. End with CNTL/Z.
R1(config)#access-list 1 permit 192.168.200.0 0.0.0.255
R1(config)#access-list 2 permit 192.168.100.0 0.0.0.255
R1(config)#route-map EIGRPTOOSPF deny 10
R1(config-route-map)#match ip address 1
R1(config-route-map)#route-map EIGRPTOOSPF permit 20
R1(config-route-map)#match ip address 2
R1(config-route-map)#set metric 150
R1(config-route-map)#route-map EIGRPTOOSPF permit 30
R1(config-route-map)#set metric 100
R1(config-route-map)#exit
R1(config)#router ospf 1
R1(config-router)#redistribute eigrp 100 metric 100 subnets route-map
  ➥EIGRPTOOSPF
R1(config-router)#^Z
R1#
```

Here's a breakdown of what will occur:

1. 192.168.200.0 /24 will match the statement contained in sequence 10. Because sequence 10 is a deny sequence, the route will not be redistributed.
2. 192.168.100.0 /24 will match the statement contained in sequence 20. Since the condition says to set the metric to 150, the route's metric will be set to 150. The route is redistributed because the sequence is a permit.
3. All other routes will be accepted by sequence 30 since no `match` statement was specified. The metric of all the routes will be set to 100 as specified by the `set metric` action, and then all routes will be redistributed because the sequence is a permit.

Using route maps with redistribution is an important concept to grasp. They are used frequently in the real world. In order to master the concepts of redistribution and redistribution with route maps, you need to spend time practicing using them. It will help you in the long run.

Summarization

We would like to revisit the topic of route summarization here. *Route summarization* is the process of combining multiple network ranges into one network range. We have briefly discussed the use of route summarization for most of the IGPs we've covered in this study guide and BGP. We'd like to take a minute to go over those again and also show you how to use summarization for routes being redistributed into a routing protocol. We will look at each of the routing protocols individually.

Routing protocols such as RIPv1, RIPv2, IGRP, EIGRP, and BGP support automatic summarization. Automatic summarization will occur when routing information crosses a classful network boundary. Manual summarization is supported by RIPv2, EIGRP, IS-IS, OSPF, and BGP. RIPv1 and IGRP do not support the concept of manual summarization, because they are classful routing protocols. They do, however, automatically summarize on classful network boundaries, leading to their lack of support for discontiguous subnets.

EIGRP

EIGRP uses summarization the same way, whether it's for a route originating in EIGRP or a route being redistributed into EIGRP. In order to summarize a route, you need to use the `ip summary-address eigrp` *AS#* command on the interface you want to perform the summarization. The following is an example of an EIGRP summary route being placed on interface Serial 0:

```
R1#conf t
Enter configuration commands, one per line. End with CNTL/Z.
R1(config)#interface s0
```

```
R1(config-if)#ip summary-address eigrp 100 172.16.0.0 255.255.0.0
R1(config-if)#^Z
R1#
```

This configuration creates a summary address of 172.16.0.0 /16 for EIGRP AS 100 that will be advertised to the neighbor on interface S0.

OSPF

The way you would configure a summary address for internal OSPF routes is different from the way you would configure a summary address for a route being redistributed into OSPF.

To configure summary addresses for internal OSPF routes, you use area ranges. For instance, Area 1 has the following network addresses in it:

- 172.16.16.0 /24
- 172.16.32.0 /24
- 172.16.48.0 /24

We want to be able to send out one route for all of the routes contained in Area 1. We would need to create a summary address of 172.16.0.0 /18. If you do not remember how to summarize addresses, refer back to Chapter 2, "IP Addressing." In order to implement this, you would need to create an area range for this summary address on the ABR for Area 1. Here's the configuration required:

```
R1#conf t
Enter configuration commands, one per line. End with CNTL/Z.
R1(config)#router ospf 1
R1(config-router)#area 1 range 172.16.0.0 255.255.192.0
R1(config-router)#^Z
R1#
```

If the same addresses in the preceding example that we needed to summarize were redistributed into OSPF, we would need to use the command `summary-address` *`address mask`* on the ASBR that was performing the redistribution. The following is the needed configuration:

```
R1#conf t
Enter configuration commands, one per line. End with CNTL/Z.
R1(config)#router ospf 1
R1(config-router)#summary-address 172.16.0.0 255.255.192.0
R1(config-router)#^Z
R1#
```

It's important to note that this command can be used only on an ASBR, and it must be used for routes being redistributed into OSPF.

IS-IS

IS-IS summarizes internal routes and redistributed routes in the same way as in the previous section about OSPF. In order to summarize routes for IS-IS, you must use the `summary-address` command with one of the following keywords:

- `level-1` will summarize routes redistributed into the Level 1 area.
- `level-2` will summarize Level 1 routes that are going into the Level 2 backbone. It will also summarize routes that are being redistributed into the Level 2 backbone.
- `level-1-2` will perform both Level 1 and Level 2 summarization.

The following routes are contained in a Level 1 area:

- 172.16.126.0 /24
- 172.16.4.0 /24
- 172.16.48.0 /24

In order to configure summarization, you would first need to figure out the summary address for these routes. In this case, the summary address would be 172.16.0.0 /17. Then you would configure the summary address on the Level 1/2 router attached to the area. Here's the configuration that needs to be entered on the Level 1/2 router:

```
R1#conf t
Enter configuration commands, one per line. End with CNTL/Z.
R1(config)#router isis
R1(config-router)#summary-address 172.16.0.0 255.255.128.0 level-2
R1(config-router)#^Z
R1#
```

This configuration summarizes the three routes into one route, and the Level 2 backbone would know of only this one route.

Summary

When all of these techniques are used together, they can help optimize a network's performance. In turn, they can help you better perform your job.

There are many methods to use for filtering routing information. These methods include access groups, distribute lists, and route maps. Access groups are used to filter traffic crossing a router, distribute lists are used to filter routing updates, and route maps are used to filter routes being redistributed.

Policy-based routing allows for routing to occur in a method that differs from the rules established by dynamic routing protocols. This is accomplished by creating a policy that will define how certain traffic should be routed for certain destinations.

Route information is not shared between different routing domains, by default (except between IGRP and EIGRP using the same AS number). In certain situations, you may want to share route information between these different routing domains. When this is the case, you need to configure redistribution.

The larger a routing table is, the more CPU cycles are required to route information. In an effort to reduce the size of routing tables, you can use summarization. Routing protocols such as RIPv1, RIPv2, IGRP, EIGRP, and BGP support automatic summarization. Automatic summarization will occur when routing information crosses a classful network boundary. Manual summarization is supported by RIPv2, EIGRP, IS-IS, OSPF, and BGP.

We've covered a tremendous amount of information in this part of the study guide. You should feel a sense of accomplishment in making it this far. The topics covered here are intended not only to help you pass the BSCI exam but to help you succeed in the networking field. Take time to practice and solidify your understanding of these topics so that you may better perform your job and take the next step up the ladder of networking knowledge.

Exam Essentials

Explain the use of filters. There are many methods to use for filtering routing information. These methods include access groups, distribute lists, and route maps. Access groups are used to filter traffic crossing a router, distribute lists are used to filter routing updates, and route maps are used to filter routes being redistributed.

Explain why policy-based routing is used and when it should be used. Policy-based routing allows routing to occur in a method that differs from the rules established by dynamic routing protocols. This is accomplished by creating a policy that defines how certain traffic should be routed for certain destinations.

Understand the concept of redistribution. Route information is not shared between different routing domains by default (except between IGRP and EIGRP using the same AS number). In certain situations, you may want to share route information between these different routing domains. When this is the case, you need to configure redistribution.

Understand why summarization is needed. The larger a routing table is, the more CPU cycles are required to route information. In an effort to reduce the size of routing tables, you can use summarization. Routing protocols such as RIPv1, RIPv2, IGRP, EIGRP, and BGP support automatic summarization. Automatic summarization will occur when routing information crosses a classful boundary. Manual summarization is supported by RIPv2, EIGRP, IS-IS, OSPF, and BGP.

Design Considerations

THE CCNP EXAM TOPICS COVERED IN THIS CHAPTER INCLUDE THE FOLLOWING:

- ✓ Understand the three-layer hierarchical design model and know the function of each of the three layers: Access, Distribution, and Core.
- ✓ Choose the correct routing protocol given specific design requirements.
- ✓ Recognize the benefits of route summarization and apply proper route summarization to a hypothetical scenario.

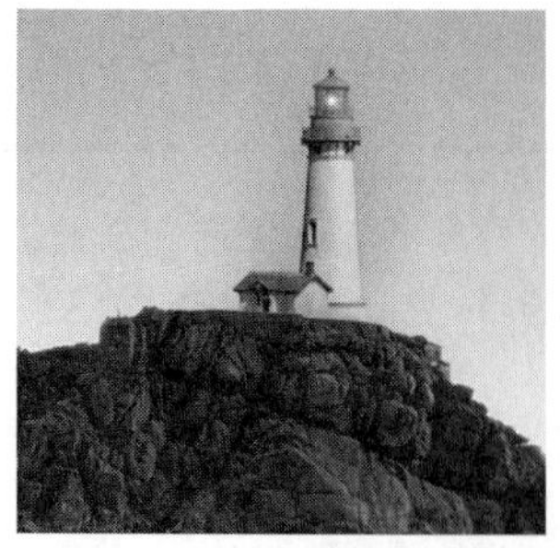

This chapter covers the Cisco three-layer hierarchical design model and talks about the proper layout of IP addressing to allow route aggregation through summarization. We will also discuss how these design considerations are affected by the routing protocol selected and why one routing protocol is more desirable given a set of circumstances. Network design is very subjective, and some people have strong views on the topic. Mainly, good network design is a function of experience and planning. We will try to help you understand the considerations for good network design.

Three-Layer Hierarchical Design Model

You'll likely use the Cisco three-layer hierarchical design model as a guideline when designing a network using the three-layer network design method. It consists of the Access, Distribution, and Core layers. The Access layer is where end users gain access to the network. The Distribution layer is a point where multiple Access layer devices are aggregated to the next layer. The last layer—the Core layer—is where all distribution devices are connected, and it also connects to other Core layer devices.

These are not hard and fast rules. You can even have a more hierarchical design in your network by hanging another Access layer below the first Access layer. This way, the higher Access layer takes on a partial role of the Distribution layer for the lower level Access layer, which is why it is sometimes called an N-tier design approach. The advantages to using this design model are improved fault isolation, ease of understanding for new engineers, easy network growth, and the cost savings that come from a more efficient network.

Because this is a design guideline, you can also think of the three-layer hierarchy from a WAN or campus network perspective. Both have three layers and both perform aggregation at each level, but there are some distinct differences. In the WAN, the three layers are all routers, and the aggregation is mainly for routes and secondarily for bandwidth. The campus network is usually a LAN where the three layers are a combination of routers or layer 3 switches and layer 2 switches. It is used mainly for bandwidth aggregation and secondarily for route summarization. Figure 11.1 shows a three-layer WAN hierarchy, and Figure 11.2 shows a three-layer campus hierarchy. We will discuss the WAN and campus considerations for each layer in detail.

Access Layer

The *Access layer* is the first layer that users encounter, and it's where some access control can be performed and packets can be marked.. Now we'll look at the WAN and campus network hierarchies of the Access layer and demonstrate how the Access layer is utilized for each.

FIGURE 11.1 Three-layer WAN hierarchy

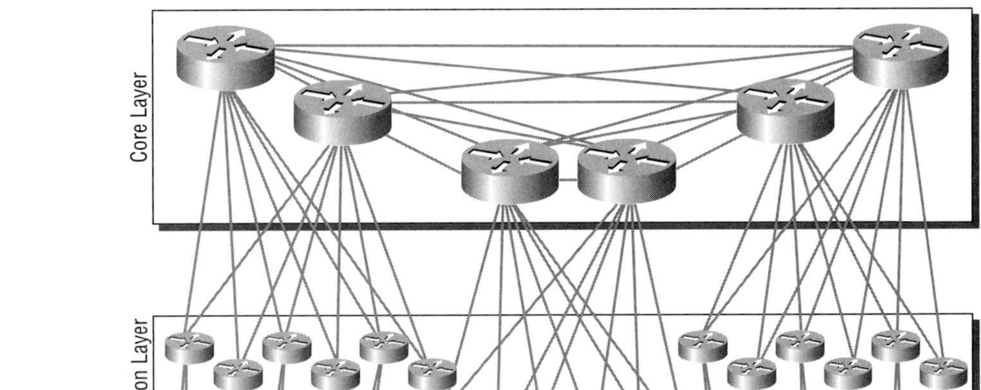

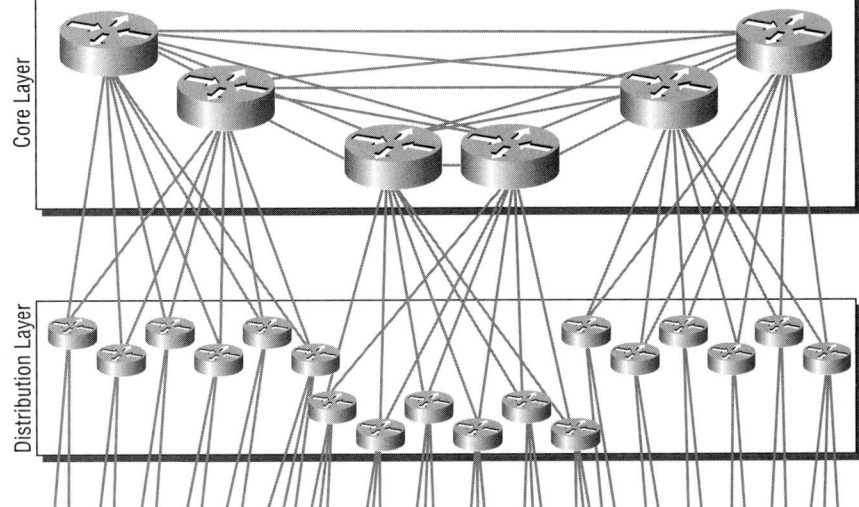

Access Layer for the WAN Network

In the WAN hierarchy, the Access layer consists of mainly lower speed routers that connect a remote site to a Distribution layer router within the same geographic region. The speed of the router depends upon the bandwidth requirements at the remote site. Layer 3 access control is provided at this layer, as is the optional marking of packets.

There can be a backup connection to a second Distribution layer router within the same region, which allows redundancy from the remote site in case a circuit is disrupted. To further enhance redundancy, a second Access layer router can be deployed at the remote site, which is connected to a second Distribution layer router in case the router or circuit is disrupted. In this case, a protocol such as HSRP, VRRP, or GLBP is used to allow these routers to appear as a single router to make the failover transparent to the end users. These protocols allow two or more routers to appear as one to back each other up in case one fails or to distribute the routing load among a number of routers. The level of redundancy needed depends upon the number of users that will be affected and the business importance of this remote site.

FIGURE 11.2 Three-layer campus hierarchy

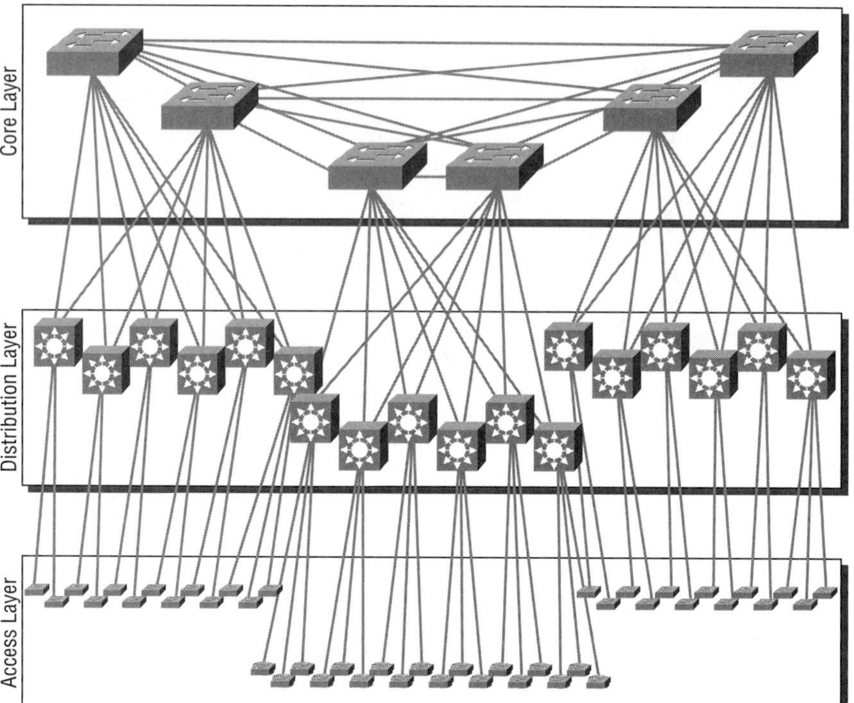

Because the Access layer provides access to the rest of the network through slower WAN links, congestion can occur. The Access layer can perform a traffic shaping function to ensure that congestion is left in check using *Random Early Detection (RED)*, *Weighted Random Early Detection (WRED)*, or *Distributed Weighted Random Early Detection (DWRED)* technologies. These technologies randomly drop packets in TCP flows when a buffer starts to become too full. This will avoid the buffer filling to capacity and the router needing to drop every packet.

If this is a large remote site, the Access layer router will also need to aggregate routes from the remote site to reduce the number of routes sent to the Distribution layer. This is usually not the case since remote sites generally have small networks.

Access Layer for the Campus Network

In a campus network, the Access layer is where users gain access to the network, and it is the first device they connect to. This is usually a layer 2 switch with high port density that connects users on a floor, or part of a floor, to a Distribution layer switch. This is where layer 2 access control using VLAN access control lists (VACLs) is performed and optionally packets can be marked.

The marking or coloring of packets is used to identify traffic flows and give that traffic the required priority or level of service that it needs. For example, FTP packets can be marked as the lowest priority and voice packets as the highest priority. This way, the FTP or other lower priority packets on congested links will not delay the voice packets.

Cisco does not suggest access controls be used at this level of the campus network, but this information has been included to let you know that VACLs can be configured at this layer. In Cisco's opinion, the Access layer is not a legitimate place for access control.

The Access layer can also implement VLANs to allow hosts to be on the same subnet without requiring that they be connected to the same switch. The VLAN can span multiple Access layer switches if you trunk it to the Distribution layer. The Distribution layer will allow intra-VLAN traffic to be switched to the appropriate Access layer switch. Figure 11.3 shows how hosts on different switches can belong to the same local VLAN.

With Cisco's adoption of 802.1*x*, used to authenticate both wireless and wire line users, the Access layer in the campus network can also offer authentication services for devices connecting to the network. This requires the user to enter a username and password, which are checked against an authentication server such as RADIUS or TACACS+, to gain access to the network. You no longer need to worry about exposing your network to intruders who might connect their laptops to the corporate network in the lobby or a training room, and it's very useful for keeping rogue wireless access points off the network.

FIGURE 11.3 Local VLANs

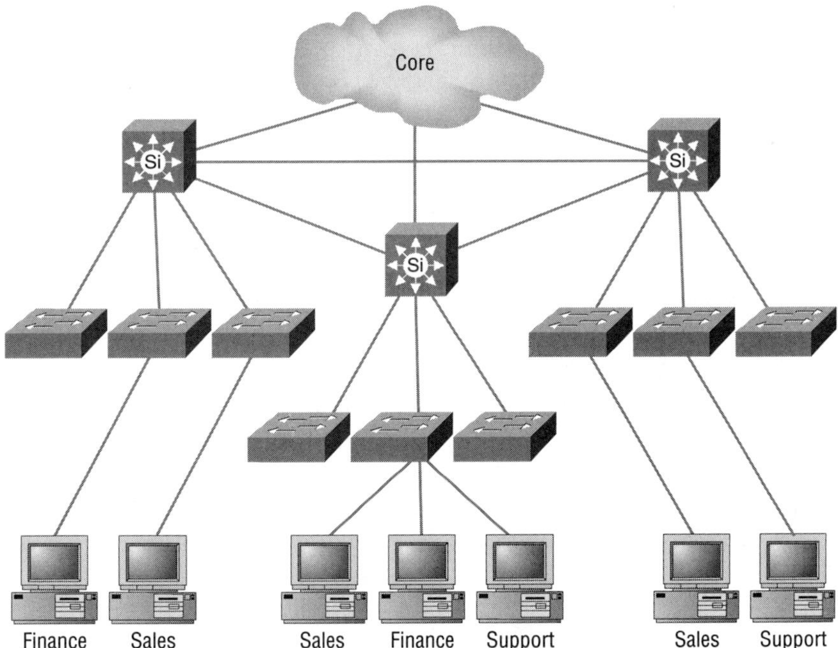

Redundancy is one of the key aspects of this design model. The Spanning Tree Protocol (STP) is used to ensure a loop-free layer 2 network. This allows multiple links between an Access layer switch and the Distribution layer, where STP will block all but one connection between them. It can take up to 30 seconds for a redundant connection to start forwarding packets, and so because of this delay, enhancements have been made to the STP algorithm. These enhancements include Cisco's uplink-fast and 802.1w, or Rapid Spanning Tree Protocol (RSTP), and can achieve sub-second failover to a redundant link. Sometimes the Access layer utilizes a layer 3 switch and provides for smaller broadcast domains, which takes some of the pressure from the Distribution layer.

Distribution Layer

The middle layer of the hierarchical model is the *Distribution layer,* and it is the glue that holds the Access and Core layers together. It is used for both IP address and bandwidth aggregation, plus it is where additional access control and queuing can be configured.

Distribution Layer for the WAN Network

In a WAN network, the Distribution layer routers will take in many lower speed links from the Access layer and aggregate them to a higher speed link to the Core layer. The distribution routers will also be connected to one another to reduce congestion on the links to the core. This will also eliminate the need to send traffic to the core that is destined for the same region it was sourced from.

Because aggregation is the mantra for this layer of the hierarchy, it is very important that you assign IP addresses correctly or this layer can become a bottleneck in your network. The distribution router will aggregate routes into the core for all access networks in its region. The routing tables on these routers can become quite large because they need to know how to reach all access networks in their region, plus all aggregated networks in the core.

Redundancy can be achieved by using multiple circuits from the distribution routers to the core. Because there are usually no client devices at this layer of the hierarchy, using a redundancy protocol such as HSRP, VRRP, or GLBP is not necessary. A dynamic routing protocol will provide route redundancy from the Access layer and to the Core layer.

Distribution Layer for the Campus Network

Within a campus network, the Distribution layer is the workhorse that will take all Access layer layer 2 switches and aggregate their bandwidth to the Core layer. The Distribution layer is either a large router or a layer 3 switch. Because this is the first layer 3 device the traffic has encountered, layer 3 access controls are applied at this layer.

When using a layer 3 switch, VLANs can be utilized to allow hosts on multiple Access layer switches to use the same layer 3 network address space. This can enhance security by allowing only the hosts on the VLAN to communicate directly with one another. Communications between subnets can then be subject to layer 3 access control.

You can optionally configure the marking of packets for quality of service (QoS) at this layer, but it is not advised because the Access layer is a better place for this service. Instead, you can configure queuing to ensure that higher priority traffic will be processed first if there is congestion on the links.

Redundancy is achieved by using a layer 2 redundancy technology such as STP on both the Core and the Access layers. Multiple interfaces can be aggregated through inverse multiplexing if greater bandwidth is needed to the core of the network.

Core Layer

The *Core layer* is a high-speed data pump that is the backbone of the network and should not be burdened by additional services. It receives traffic on one interface and quickly switches it to the appropriate outbound interface to provide increased packet switching and an optimized transport. The Core layer should not be marking or filtering any traffic but can use information in the packets to enqueue traffic to ensure QoS across the backbone. The keys to a good Core layer are redundancy, fast convergence, and independence from the connection technology (for example, SONET, GigE, and ATM). The core in a WAN network looks different from the core in a campus network because the first operates at layer 3 and the second operates at layer 2.

Core Layer for the WAN Network

The devices in the core of a WAN network are usually very-high-speed routers that can sustain operating at very high bandwidths. They look at the layer 3 address within each packet and switch the packet to the outbound interface based upon that address. High-speed switching techniques, such as Cisco Express Forwarding (CEF), are utilized to increase packet-switching speed and ensure that packets are not delayed.

Like the distribution routers, they are connected to one another to ensure an optimum path through the backbone. With route summarization, the routing tables in the core routers should be pretty small to ensure a shorter lookup time and conserve system resources.

Core Layer for the Campus Network

The devices in the core of a campus network are usually layer 2 switches that have high-speed links from the Distribution layer. Sometimes multiple interfaces are aggregated to increase the bandwidth from the Distribution layer to the core. The Core layer can optionally have layer 3 switches to provide for greater segmentation of the network and reduce the workload for the Distribution layer. If layer 3 switches are used, then the core looks more like the WAN network and functions very much the same.

This is the layer where WAN and Internet routers reside for traffic exiting the local area network. Redundancy is achieved by utilizing a layer 2 redundancy technology such as STP, and trunking between core devices is used to increase bandwidth. When you add layer 3 switches on every layer of the campus network, it looks and acts like the WAN network design but with higher bandwidths. Next, we will talk about allocating IP addresses within your network and what design considerations you need to watch out for.

IP Address Assignment

IP address assignment is a crucial aspect of network design. If you assign IP addresses to the network arbitrarily, there will be no way that *route summarization* can take place. Your network will not scale because the routing tables on all the routers in your network will become very large and will have performance problems. As the number of routes grows, the amount of memory needed to store and manipulate those routes increases. There is also increased CPU and network utilization. When you design a network with summarization in mind, you will reduce the size of the routing tables in all routers in your network, which allows them to do their job more efficiently. Plus, readdressing a network to resolve these problems can be very difficult, costly, and time-consuming.

If you are using RFC 1918 address space within your network, then it's a little easier because you have such a huge block of address space to allocate from. If you don't have the luxury of a large address space and you need to allocate from a smaller block, then you need to plan very well. You also need to leave plenty of address space for growth.

We will be using the 10.0.0.0/8 IP address space from RFC 1918 in our examples of a large national network. Figure 11.4 illustrates the sample network that we will be allocating addresses for.

You can see that there are four major regions at the core of the network and that each region has two core routers. Each core router is connected to a core router in each other region, which allows redundant connections among all regions. Each region is going to be allocated ¼ of the total address space available within that region. Instead of seeing thousands of routes for each network within a given region, the other core routers will see only a single aggregate route from that region. Table 11.1 shows the breakdown of the address space and which regions it is allocated to.

FIGURE 11.4 Sample network

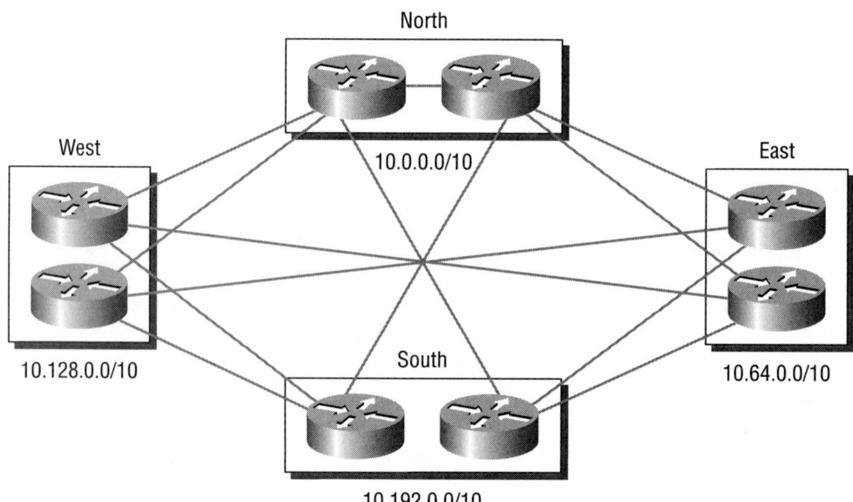

TABLE 11.1 Address Space and Regional Allocation

Region	Address Space
North	10.0.0.0/10
East	10.64.0.0/10
West	10.128.0.0/10
South	10.192.0.0/10

If one region needs more addresses, then you would need to change the allocations. You don't always have an even 1/4 split, but you may have a 1/2, 1/4, 1/8, 1/8 split. This is fine, but you should try to allocate each region from address space that can be aggregated to a small number of prefixes.

Now we will look at a single region and see how these addresses are further divided to accommodate the number of devices within a zone. Each zone represents a single geographical area and acts as an aggregation point for that area. Figure 11.5 shows the West region and the zones within that region.

There are 10 zones in the West region, and each zone is allocated 1⁄16 of the address space allocated to the entire region. The region was allocated 10.128.0.0/10. Table 11.2 shows the 10 zones and their address space allocation.

FIGURE 11.5 West region network

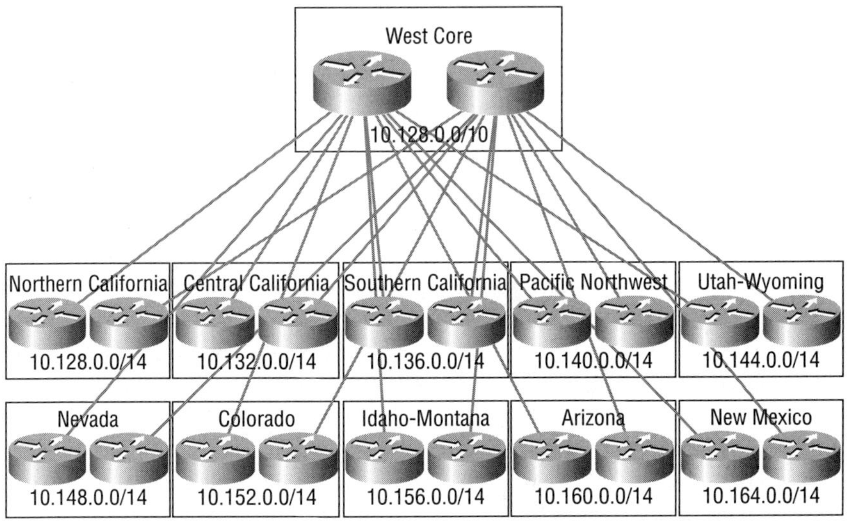

TABLE 11.2 The 10 Zones and Their Address Space Allocation

Zone	Address Space
Northern California	10.128.0.0/14
Central California	10.132.0.0/14
Southern California	10.136.0.0/14
Pacific Northwest	10.140.0.0/14
Utah-Wyoming	10.144.0.0/14
Nevada	10.148.0.0/14
Colorado	10.152.0.0/14
Idaho-Montana	10.156.0.0/14
Arizona	10.160.0.0/14
New Mexico	10.164.0.0/14

Each one of these zones contains two distribution routers for redundancy, and each distribution router has a connection to one of the core routers for its region. California, as you can see, has three zones because there are so many sites that need connectivity in that state.

Each distribution router also has a connection to two other zones so it can have a fast path to other portions of the network. Usually these inter-region connections are engineered to accommodate patterns of heavy traffic between two zones within a region. They also act as backups in case the connection to the core is disrupted.

Let's now look at a single zone and see how its address space is further subdivided to meet the need of the sites within that geographical region. This is where a site is connected to the rest of the network and where the access routers reside. Figure 11.6 shows the Utah-Wyoming zone and all its sites.

You can see that access routers connect a single site to the distribution router within the zone. There can be multiple sites within a single city, but they usually have connections only back to the distribution routers and not to each other. Address space at this point is allocated on an as-needed basis. If you are using RFC 1918 addresses, then you can be a little generous, but if you're using address space you've paid for, then you need to be stingier and allocate only those addresses needed. You should allocate the number of addresses that you predict will be needed in about two years. This will allow you enough for growth but will not allocate too many. Because we are using RFC 1918 address space, each site is allocated at least one Class C address, with some needing two or four Class C addresses. We are allocating the 10.144.0.0/24 address space for WAN links.

FIGURE 11.6 Utah-Wyoming network

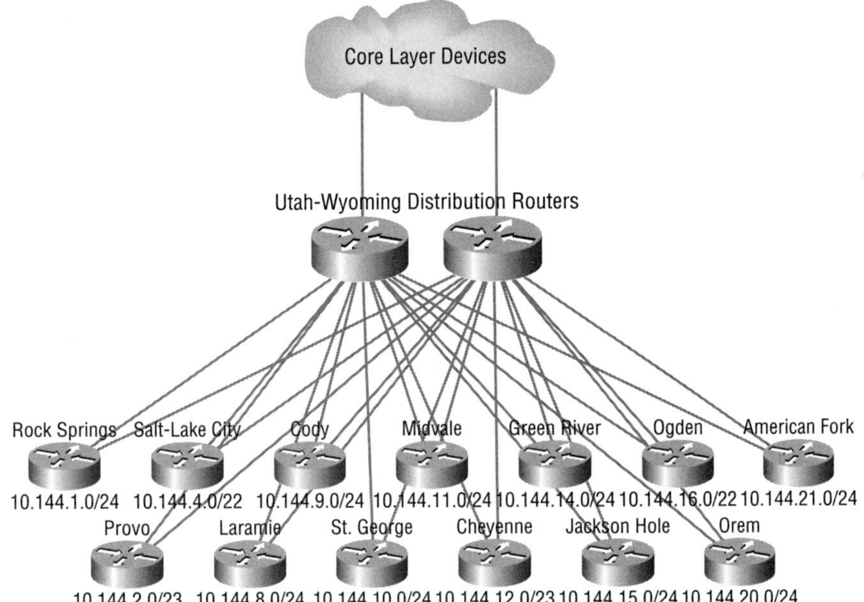

Table 11.3 shows how we have allocated addresses to the remote sites.

TABLE 11.3 Sites and Their Address Space Allocation

Site	Address Space
Rock Springs	10.144.1.0/24
Provo	10.144.2.0/23
Salt Lake City	10.144.4.0/22
Laramie	10.144.8.0/24
Cody	10.144.9.0/24
St. George	10.144.10.0/24
Midvale	10.144.11.0/24
Cheyenne	10.144.12.0/23
Green River	10.144.14.0/24

TABLE 11.3 Sites and Their Address Space Allocation *(continued)*

Site	Address Space
Jackson Hole	10.144.15.0/24
Ogden	10.144.16.0/22
Orem	10.144.20.0/24
American Fork	10.144.21.0/24

We have used only three percent of the addresses available in the zone. This allows us to increase the number of sites within the zone without needing to allocate more address space. The distribution routers for the Utah-Wyoming zone will need to advertise only a single aggregate route (10.144.0.0/14) to the core and to the other distribution routers, which will reduce the size of the routing table.

We hope this helps you understand why IP address allocation and assignment are very important in a good network design. We also hope this gives you a good understanding of how this allocation is accomplished. For more information about summarization, look back at Chapter 2, "IP Addressing." Now let's talk about how routing protocols can work with you or against you when designing a network.

Considering Routing Protocols in Network Design

In the previous section, you learned how to allocate IP addresses to allow for aggregation through summarization. In this section, we will discuss the different routing protocols and how they can be configured to meet the network design requirements. When designing a network, one routing protocol can meet certain requirements, while another one cannot. These requirements usually include one or more of the following:

- Summarize network route advertisements.
- Support a large number of devices within a network.
- Offer speedy convergence to promote network stability.
- Use a hierarchical network design.

There are many routing protocols available, but to facilitate the summarization requirement, the protocol needs to be a classless routing protocol. This means that it must send the subnet mask in its routing updates. Supporting a large number of devices and offering speedy convergence can be seen as mutually exclusive, but some protocols have features to make both possible.

Other routing protocols such as Routing Information Protocol version 1 (RIPv1) and Interior Gateway Routing Protocol (IGRP) are classful, so they do not support these requirements. RIP version 2 (RIPv2) is a classless routing protocol but does not scale in a large network because of slow convergence. Because of these limitations, we will look at *Open Shortest Path First (OSPF)*, *Enhanced Interior Gateway Routing Protocol (EIGRP)*, *Integrated Intermediate System to Intermediate System (IS-IS)*, and *Border Gateway Protocol (BGP)*, in that order.

OSPF

OSPF is an industry-standard classless IP routing protocol available on most networking hardware that switches packets at layer 3. It is a link-state routing protocol used to route traffic within a routing domain, and we assume that you know how OSPF operates. OSPF allows for aggregation of addresses but only at *area border routers (ABRs)* or *autonomous system boundary routers (ASBRs)*. Routes within a single area cannot be aggregated. OSPF in multiple areas requires a hierarchical network addressing design because it uses one backbone area, with individual areas directly connected to the backbone area, and ABRs advertise summary routes, at best. Not designing hierarchically for multiple areas tends to break the OSPF routing domain.

Because of the way OSPF operates, you need to make sure that the borders of your OSPF areas correspond to the transition points from one layer to another. For example, Figure 11.7 shows how the border between Areas 0 and 1 and Areas 2 and 0 occurs at the distribution router where summaries are sent into Area 0.

FIGURE 11.7 OSPF summarization

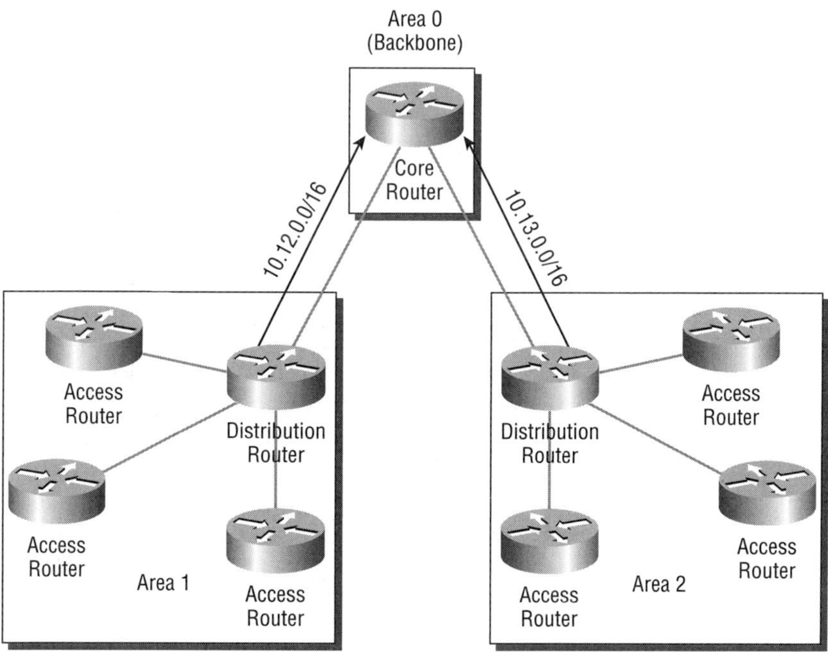

This way, all the routes under each distribution router in Area 1 can be aggregated to a single route—10.12.0.0/16—into Area 0 and from Area 2 using 10.13.0.0/16. Area 0 routers will see only two aggregate routes and not the individual routes that make up Areas 1 and 2. This is done by configuring the range of IP addresses that will be found in that area.

If you are also looking to aggregate routes between core routers, then OSPF will not be your routing protocol of choice. This is because there is no border between two OSPF areas that corresponds to the connection between the two core routers. You would need to have a third area configured between the core routers, but this would break how OSPF operates and is not a good design practice.

OSPF has a feature called a stub area, which allows a lower end router to operate in a larger OSPF network without using a lot of system resources. No external routes are carried into the stub area. A default route is the only way a router within a stub area can know how to get to any external network. This router knows how to get to other networks within the same area and knows the summary routes from other areas, but all external routes are filtered out at the ABR. This makes it possible for a large number of devices to be supported within a network.

Cisco has added another feature to the concept of stub areas called the totally stubby area. This area type filters out not only external routes at the ABR but also summary advertisements from other areas. Only a default route and routes within that area are shown in the routing table.

These two features assist with your design considerations because if you have an area where the routers are having problems running the SPF, or Dijkstra, algorithm because of insufficient system resources, you can make that area a stub or totally stubby area. You can also increase the number of routers within an area without affecting the entire network. This will also decrease the time needed for the network to converge when a change occurs. Only those changes needed are advertised into the area that needs that information.

EIGRP

EIGRP is a Cisco proprietary classless IP routing protocol used for routing inside an autonomous system (AS). EIGRP does not have the concept of areas. EIGRP is an advanced distance-vector routing protocol due to its basis in distance-vector principles with simultaneous link-state features. EIGRP automatically summarizes at classful boundaries, but allows you to turn this feature off and manually summarize at any interface. This means that you can advertise one summary route out one interface and another summary route out another interface. Figure 11.8 illustrates the summary routes that would be advertised.

This is a very powerful feature that allows you to summarize not only up to the Core layer of the network but also down to the Access layer and over to other devices in the same layer of the network. You don't need to summarize everywhere, but it's a nice feature to have.

For example, EIGRP does not have a concept like an OSPF totally stubby area, but you can emulate this by advertising a default summary route out all interfaces connected to lower layer routers. This way, they see only one route to the outside world in their routing table. You will be able to run EIGRP on a lower end router. This technique does not work if the lower layer routers have multiple connections to the upper layer routers. The router would get two default routes and would attempt to load-balance between them, which might not be the desired result.

FIGURE 11.8 EIGRP summarization

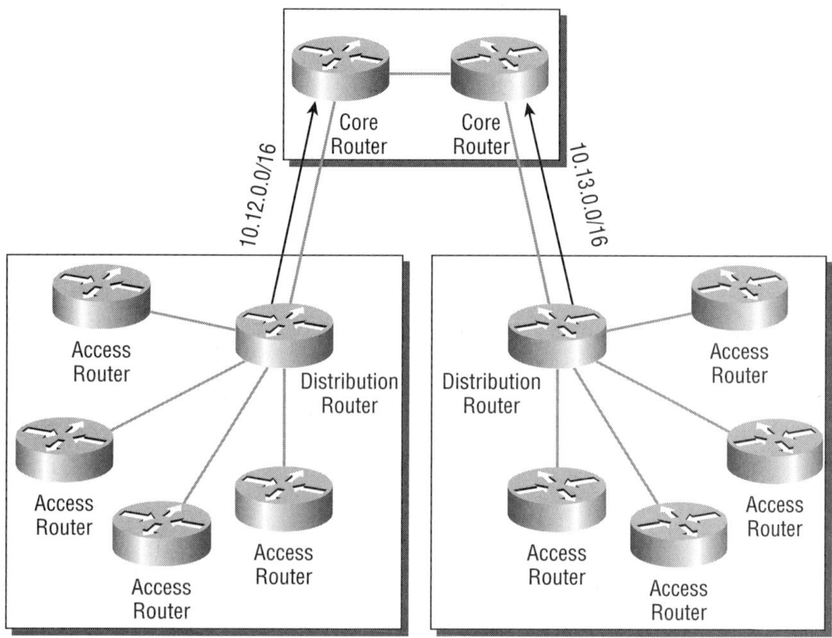

The time needed for convergence can be decreased for EIGRP by reducing the number of routing advertisements within a portion of your network, which promotes network stability. EIGRP has added the concept of stub routing, but it is different than an OSPF stub area. This feature is used to limit the number of query packets that need to be sent and tracked when a route is removed from the topology table. When a route goes missing from the topology table, EIGRP marks it as active and sends out query messages to its neighbors to see if they have a route to the network. This continues until every router is contacted, and if a query packet gets lost or a neighbor is unreachable, the route can become stuck in active (SIA), which is a bad thing to happen. An EIGRP router does not send these messages to neighbors on networks when the router is configured as a stub, which decreases the amount of time needed to reconcile an active route.

Multi-access interfaces, such as Ethernet and frame relay, are supported by EIGRP stub routing only when all routers on that interface's segment, except the central distribution hub router to which all the stub routers direct their traffic, are configured as stub routers.

IS-IS

Integrated Intermediate System to Intermediate System (IS-IS) is a classless IP routing protocol that is similar to OSPF because both use the Dijkstra algorithm. It is a link-state routing protocol with areas just like OSPF has and so also requires a hierarchical network design to support multiple areas. Because it is like OSPF, it has the same restrictions that OSPF has with regard to needing to summarize only at the borders of areas. Figure 11.9 shows how you would summarize using IS-IS.

FIGURE 11.9 IS-IS summarization

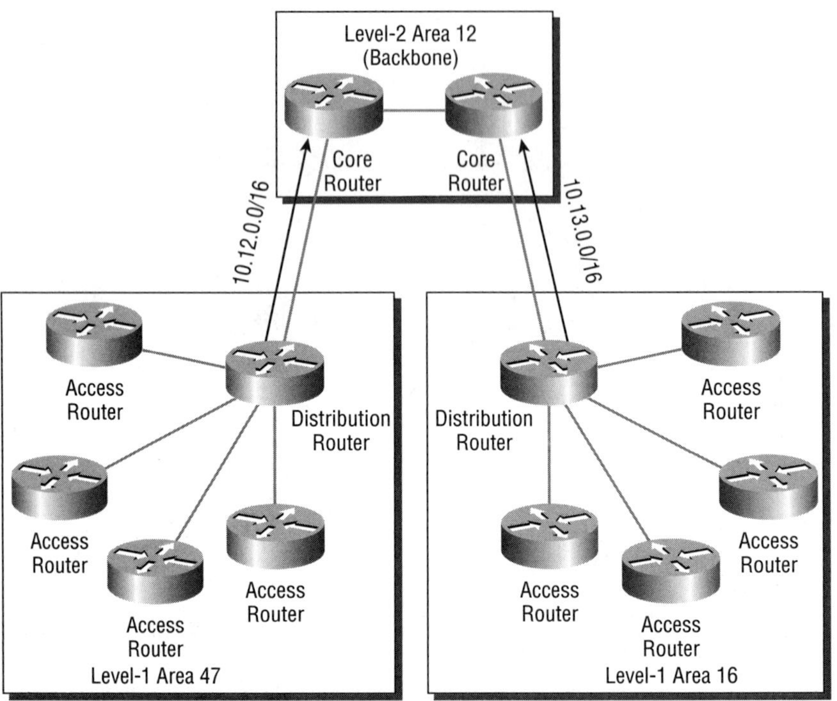

You can see from Figure 11.9 that IS-IS is summarizing into the Level 2, or backbone, area from the Level 1 area. You might notice that in OSPF a router can be in two areas, but in IS-IS a router can be in only one area. The transition from one area to another happens on the link between routers and not within the router itself.

Areas in IS-IS are what we call in OSPF totally stubby, meaning that the only routes within an area are routes contained in the area and a default route. Because IS-IS has natural totally stubby areas, the amount of system resources needed for a Level 1 router is smaller and can mean that you can have many routers within a single Level 1 area. This is a good thing, but it could lead to suboptimal routing because each Level 1 router will send traffic to the nearest Level 2 router to exit the area. This router may not be the closest to the traffic's final destination.

To attempt to combat the suboptimal routing problem, IS-IS has a feature called route leaking. Route leaking occurs when Level 2 routes are sent, or leaked, into a Level 1 area from the Level 2 router. This allows the Level 1 router to make a more informed routing decision regarding the leaked routes. It will send traffic to the Level 2 router that is closest to the destination, and not the closest Level 2 router.

BGP

BGPv4 is a classless IP routing protocol that is used to route traffic on the global Internet. BGP is considered a path-vector routing protocol and is used to route between routing domains or autonomous systems. If you are connecting your network to the global Internet from two different Internet service providers (ISPs), you must run BGP between your autonomous system and your ISPs' ASs.

Like EIGRP, you can summarize at any time, but unlike EIGRP, which summarizes at the interface level, you can summarize at the neighbor level, to each neighbor differently. Recall that BGP establishes TCP connections to its neighbors, which do not have to be physically attached, meaning multiple neighbors of a particular BGP speaker could be found out the same interface. We assume that you know how BGP works, so let's see how BGP can summarize by looking at Figure 11.10.

Because we're using BGP between neighboring routers—called peers—you can see from Figure 11.10 that we are summarizing to upstream neighbors, going from AS 200 to AS 100 and from AS 300 to AS 100 at the transition points between the layers of our network. In addition to summarizing routing advertisements, you can advertise the more specific routes as well. This allows you to route a section of your network differently than the rest of the network.

To promote stability within a BGP network, the protocol has a feature called dampening. This feature sets a penalty value for a route that was in the routing table and was recently withdrawn. If this cycle of advertisements and withdrawals continues, the route will be suppressed. This means that it will not make it into the routing table and will not be propagated to other BGP peers. Once a period of stability has been established for this route, it will be reinstated into the routing table and will be advertised to its BGP peers. This is so that instability in one portion of the network will not cause instability in the entire network.

FIGURE 11.10 BGP summarization

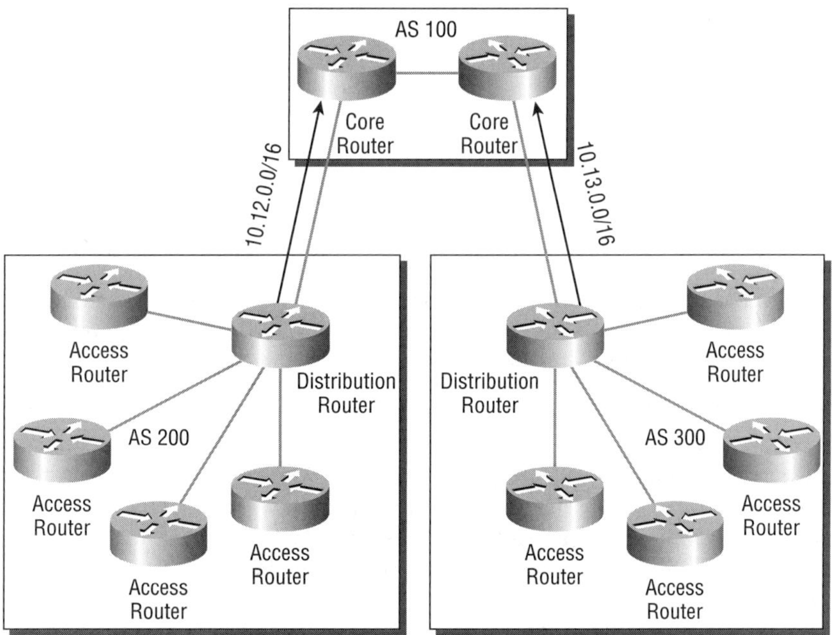

Summary

While the Cisco three-layer hierarchical design model is just a guideline and not a set of strict rules, you'll still want to follow it pretty closely when designing your own networks. Because there are many networks and no two are identical, this model can be tailored to fit your particular requirements.

The Access layer is where everything starts. Here the user gains access to the network through high port density layer 2 switches, and local VLANs can be used. Local VLANs can also provide a level of flexibility by allowing a VLAN to span many Access layer switches, allowing all ports within the VLAN to be protected from the rest of the network by layer 3 access control lists.

The Distribution layer is the workhorse of the model and where layer 3 is terminated. Aggregation and summarization take place here, and connections into the core are fast, so they do not become a bottleneck in the network.

The Core layer is primarily made up of fast layer 2 switches or high-end routers. The Core layer should be able to provide for fast packet switching and optimized transport through the backbone of the network. No filtering or access control should be configured at this level because it would slow the switching of the devices in this layer.

Proper IP address allocation should be a top priority when designing a network. Without it, you will not be able to summarize your network advertisements and thus slow down the Distribution layer, causing the Distribution layer to become the bottleneck in the network.

While IGRP, RIPv1, and RIPv2 are good routing protocols, they are not well suited for larger networks with a complicated network design. OSPF, IS-IS, EIGRP, and even BGP can be used within your large network to accomplish almost any network design requirement. They allow summarization and allow each routing protocol to scale in a large network. OSPF and IS-IS are the only protocols that require a hierarchical topology, but EIGRP and BGP can certainly work in that kind of environment.

Exam Essentials

Understand the three-layer network design model. The three layers are the Access, Distribution, and Core layers. You also need to know that the Core and Access layers consist mainly of layer 2 switches, and the Distribution layer has either a high-speed router or a layer 3 switch.

Know what happens at each layer of the three-layer model. In a campus network, the Access layer is a high port density layer 2 switch that can use VLANs to allow hosts on different switches to belong to the same layer 3 subnet. The Distribution layer in a campus network is the workhorse where layer 3 is terminated and summarized, plus it is where access lists are configured. In a campus network, the Core layer is used for packet switching and optimized transport across the backbone of the network.

Understand where you can summarize using each routing protocol. OSPF and IS-IS can be configured to summarize only at the border of each area, but EIGRP and BGP can summarize at the interface and neighbor levels, respectively.

Know which routing protocols require a hierarchical network design. Both OSPF and IS-IS require a hierarchical network design because both have a single backbone area, with other areas directly connected to the backbone area.

Building Cisco Multilayer Switched Networks (BCMSN)

The Campus Network

THE CCNP EXAM TOPICS COVERED IN THIS CHAPTER INCLUDE THE FOLLOWING:

- ✓ Identify the correct Cisco Systems product solution given a set of network switching requirements.
- ✓ Describe the Enterprise Composite Model (Campus Infrastructure, Server Farm, Enterprise Edge, Network Management) used for designing networks.
- ✓ Identify enterprise network needs for performance, scalability, and availability.
- ✓ Understand the physical, data-link, and network layer technologies used in a multilayer switched network.
- ✓ Describe the Enterprise Composite Model components and explain how switches fit into these roles.

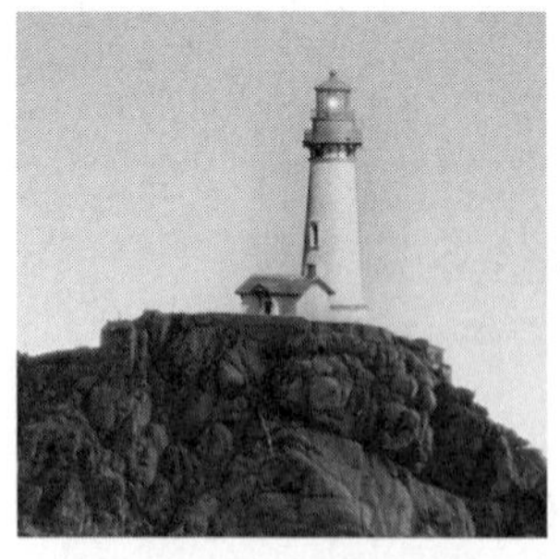

The definition of a campus network has never been straightforward, but the common description is a group of LAN segments within a building or group of buildings that connect to form one network. Typically, one company owns the entire network, including the wiring between buildings. This local area network (LAN) typically uses Ethernet, Token Ring, Fiber Distributed Data Interface (FDDI), or Asynchronous Transfer Mode (ATM) technologies. The size of the campus network is not defined, as it may be inside a single large building or spread across something as large as a distributed university campus. In fact, with the advent of Metro Ethernet, it may even be dispersed across different towns.

An Enterprise network connects all shared services and data within an enterprise. Some enterprises are global, and some are very self-contained. An Enterprise network may consist of several campus networks as well as possible WAN cores—that really depends on the size of the enterprise.

The main challenge for network administrators is to make the campus network run efficiently and effectively. To do this, they must understand current campus networks as well as the new emerging campus networks. Therefore, in this chapter, you will learn about current and future requirements of campus internetworks (the connecting of several campuses). We'll explain the limitations of traditional campus networks as well as the benefits of the emerging campus designs. You will learn how to choose from among the new generation of Cisco switches to maximize the performance of your networks. Understanding how to design for the emerging campus networks is not only critical to your success on the Switching exam, it's also critical for implementing production networks.

As part of the instruction in network design, we'll discuss the specifics of technologies, including how to implement Ethernet and the differences between layer 2, layer 3, and layer 4 switching technologies. In particular, you will learn how to implement FastEthernet, Gigabit Ethernet, Fast EtherChannel, and multilayer switching (MLS) in the emerging campus designs. This will help you learn how to design, implement, and maintain an efficient and effective internetwork.

You will learn about the Cisco hierarchical model, which is covered in all the Cisco courses. In particular, you will learn which Catalyst switches can—and should—be implemented at each layer of the Cisco model. You will also learn how to design networks based on switch and core blocks. Finally, you will learn about SAFE, the Cisco secure blueprint for enterprise networks, including a description of the network in terms of modules and how they are constructed and interact.

This chapter provides you with a thorough overview of campus network design (past, present, and future) and teaches you how, as a network administrator, to choose the most appropriate technology for particular network needs. This will enable you to configure and design your network now, with the future in mind.

Understanding Campus Internetworks

The history of networking is a history of ebbs and flows. From the initial networks, which were designed to provide access to simple central, shared resources on the mainframe computer, we moved to the distributed architecture of networks in the 1990s. This has been followed by a move toward server farms, which in many ways appear to be a return to the old centralized networking from the past.

Mainframes were not always discarded; some still carry out huge batch processing tasks in banks and insurance companies, but many just became storage areas for data and databases. The NetWare or NT server took over as a file/print server and soon started running most other programs and applications as well. Groups of servers running sympathetic applications were clustered together in domains, or other administrative groups, and new directory services emerged to allow easy discovery of domain services. Networks were developed to find the simplest, cheapest, and most reliable mechanisms to establish and maintain connectivity with the resources.

Over the last 20 years, we have witnessed the birth of the LAN and the growth of WANs (wide area networks) and the Internet. More than anything else, the Internet is changing our lives daily, with ever-increasing numbers of online transactions taking place, education and entertainment services becoming available, and people just plain having fun communicating with each other in exciting new ways.

So how will networks evolve in the 21st century? Are we still going to see file and print servers at all branch locations, or will servers migrate to common locations? Are all workstations going to connect to the Internet with ISPs to separate the data, voice, and other multimedia applications? I wish I had a crystal ball.

Looking Back at Traditional Campus Networks

In the 1990s, the traditional campus network started as one LAN and grew and grew until segmentation needed to take place just to keep the network up and running. In this era of rapid expansion, response time was secondary to just making sure the network was functioning. Besides, the majority of applications were store-and-forward, such as e-mail, and there was little need for advanced quality of service options.

By looking at the technology, you can see why keeping the network running was such a challenge. Typical campus networks ran on 10BaseT or 10Base2 (thinnet). As a result, the network was one large collision domain—not to mention even one large broadcast domain. Despite these limitations, Ethernet was used because it was scalable, effective, and somewhat inexpensive compared to other options. (IBM "owned" Token Ring, and getting it installed frequently meant getting in IBM to do it—sometimes expensive and often impractical.) ARCnet was used in some networks, but Ethernet and ARCnet are not compatible, and the networks became two separate entities. ARCnet soon became history. Token Ring became marginalized. Ethernet became king.

Because a campus network can easily span many buildings, bridges were used to connect the buildings; this broke up the collision domains, but the network was still one large broadcast domain. More and more users were attached to the hubs used in the network, and soon the performance of the network was considered extremely slow.

Performance Problems and Solutions

Availability and performance are the major problems with traditional campus networks. Availability is affected by the number of users attempting to access the network at any one time, plus the reliability of the network itself. The performance problems in traditional campus networks include collisions, bandwidth, broadcasts, and multicasts.

Collisions

A campus network typically started as one large collision domain, so all devices could see and also collide with each other. If a host had to broadcast, then all other devices had to listen, even though they themselves were trying to transmit. And if a device were to exhibit a jabber (malfunction by continually transmitting), it could bring down the entire network.

Because routers didn't really become cost effective until the late 1980s, bridges were used to break up collision domains. That created smaller collision domains and was therefore an improvement, but the network was still one large broadcast domain and the same old broadcast problems still existed. Bridges also solved distance-limitation problems because they usually had repeater functions built into the electronics and/or they could break up the physical segment.

Bandwidth

The *bandwidth* of a segment is measured by the amount of data that can be transmitted at any given time. Think of bandwidth as a water hose; the amount of water that can go through the hose depends on two elements:

- Pressure
- Distance

The pressure is the current, and the bandwidth is the size of the hose. If you have a hose that is only ¼-inch in diameter, you won't get much water through it regardless of the current or the size of the pump on the transmitting end.

Another issue is distance. The longer the hose, the more the water pressure drops. You can put a repeater in the middle of the hose and re-amplify the pressure of the line, which would help, but you need to understand that all lines (and hoses) have degradation of the signal, which means that the pressure drops off the further the signal goes down the line. For the remote end to understand digital signaling, the pressure must stay at a minimum value. If it drops below this minimum value, the remote end will not be able to receive the data. In other words, the far end of the hose would just drip water instead of flow. You can't water your crops with drips of water; you need a constant water flow.

The solution to bandwidth issues is maintaining your distance limitations and designing your network with proper segmentation of switches and routers. Congestion on a segment happens when too many devices are trying to use the same bandwidth. By properly segmenting the network, you can eliminate some of the bandwidth issues. You never will have enough bandwidth for your users; you'll just have to accept that fact. However, you can always make it better.

Broadcasts and Multicasts

Remember that all protocols have broadcasts built in as a feature, but some protocols can really cause problems if not configured correctly. Some protocols that, by default, can cause problems if they are not correctly implemented are Internet Protocol (IP), Address Resolution Protocol (ARP), Network Basic Input/Output System (NetBIOS), Internetwork Packet Exchange (IPX), Service Advertising Protocol (SAP), and Routing Information Protocol (RIP). However, remember that there are features built into the Cisco router Internetworking Operating System (IOS) that, if correctly designed and implemented, can alleviate these problems. Packet filtering, queuing, and choosing the correct routing protocols are some examples of how Cisco routers can eliminate some broadcast problems.

Multicast traffic can also cause problems if not configured correctly. Multicasts are broadcasts that are destined for a specific or defined group of users. If you have large multicast groups or a bandwidth-intensive application such as Cisco's IPTV application, multicast traffic can consume most of the network bandwidth and resources.

To solve broadcast issues, create network segmentation with bridges, routers, and switches. However, understand that you'll move the bottleneck to the routers, which break up the broadcast domains. Routers process each packet that is transmitted on the network, which can cause a bottleneck if an enormous amount of traffic is generated.

Understanding Broadcast Effects

Just in case anyone is still confused about broadcasts, consider this analogy: Suppose you worked in an office where there was a telephone system that included a broadcast capability. Every time the phone rang, everyone would have to answer it and listen to who the broadcast transmission was aimed at—"Hello, is that the Domain Name Server?" How long would it be before all these interruptions caused you to throw the phone out of the window? That's what broadcasts do to PCs. Each interruption causes single-tasking operating systems to stop what they are doing—writing to the hard drive, processing, and so on—and answer the phone.

Virtual LANs (VLANs) are a solution as well, but VLANs are just broadcast domains with artificial boundaries. A VLAN is a group of devices on different network segments defined as a broadcast domain by the network administrator. The benefit of VLANs is that physical location is no longer a factor for determining the port into which you would plug a device into the network. You can plug a device into any switch port, and the network administrator gives that port a VLAN assignment. Remember that routers or layer 3 switches must be used for different VLANs to intercommunicate.

The 80/20 Rule

The traditional campus network placed users and groups in the same physical location. If a new salesperson was hired, they had to sit in the same physical location as the other sales personnel and be connected to the same physical network segment in order to share network resources. Any deviation from this caused major headaches for the network administrators.

The rule that needed to be followed in this type of network was called the *80/20 rule* because 80 percent of the users' traffic was supposed to remain on the local network segment and only 20 percent or less was supposed to cross the routers or bridges to the other network segments. If more than 20 percent of the traffic crossed the network segmentation devices, performance issues arose. Figure 12.1 shows a traditional 80/20 network.

Because network administrators are responsible for network design and implementation, they improved network performance in the 80/20 network by making sure that all the network resources for the users were contained within the local network segment. The resources included network servers, printers, shared directories, software programs, and applications.

FIGURE 12.1 A traditional 80/20 network

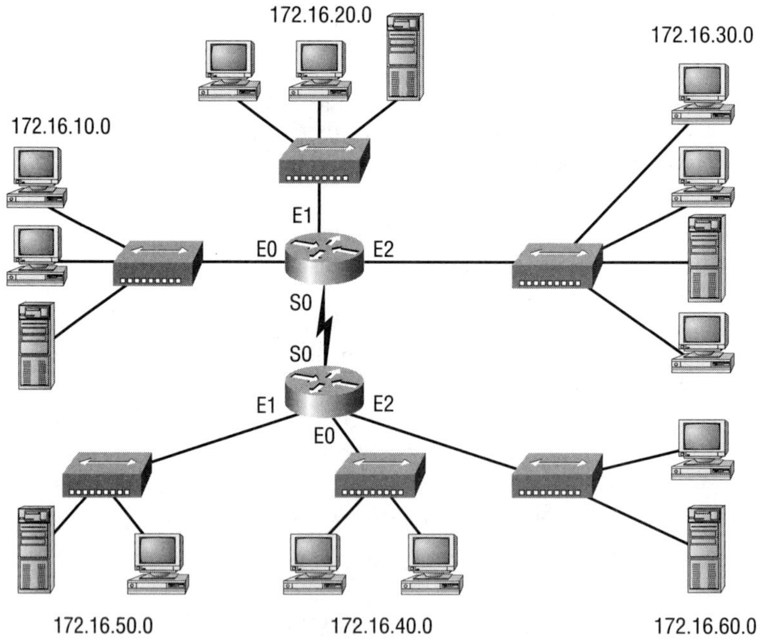

The New 20/80 Rule

With new web-based applications and computing, any PC can be a subscriber or publisher at any time. Also, because businesses are pulling servers from remote locations and creating server farms (sounds like a mainframe, doesn't it?) to centralize network services for security, reduced cost, and administration, the old 80/20 rule is obsolete and could not possibly work in this environment. All traffic must now traverse the campus backbone, which means we now have a *20/80 rule* in effect. 20 percent of what the user performs on the network is local, whereas up to 80 percent crosses the network segmentation points to get to network services. Figure 12.2 shows the new 20/80 network.

FIGURE 12.2 A 20/80 network

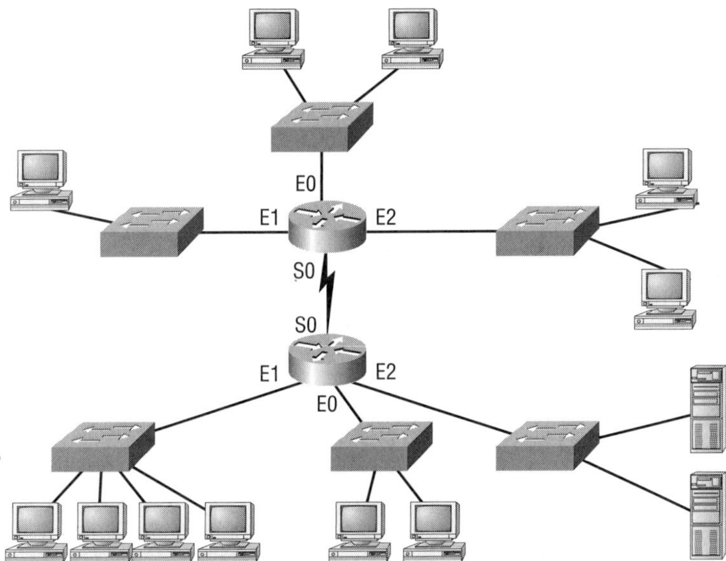

The problem with the 20/80 rule is not the network wiring and topology as much as it is the routers themselves. They must be able to handle an enormous number of packets quickly and efficiently at wire speed. This is probably where I should be talking about how great Cisco routers are and how our networks would be nothing without them. I'll get to that later in this chapter—trust me.

Virtual LANs

With this new 20/80 rule, more and more users need to cross broadcast domains (VLANs), and this puts the burden on routing, or layer 3 switching. By using VLANs within the new campus model, you can control traffic patterns and control user access easier than in the traditional campus network. Virtual LANs break up broadcast domains by using either a router or a switch that can perform layer 3 functions. Figure 12.3 shows how VLANs are created and might look in an internetwork.

FIGURE 12.3 VLANs break up broadcast domains in a switched internetwork.

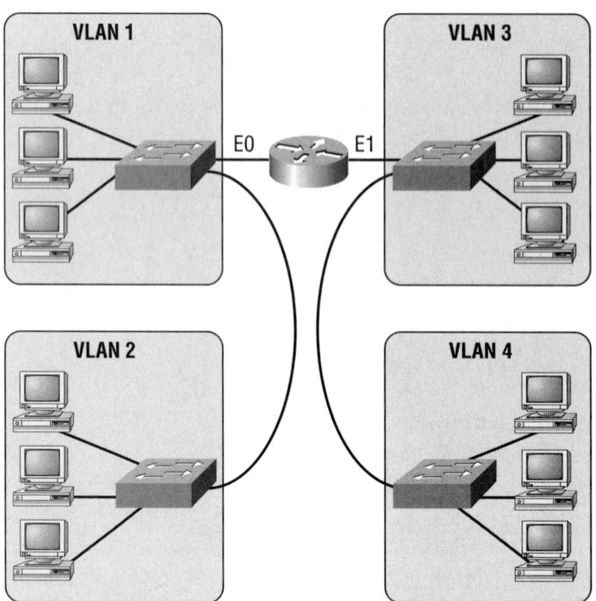

Chapter 14, "VLANs, Trunks, and VTP," includes detailed information about VLANs and how to configure them in an internetwork. It is imperative that you understand VLANs, because the traditional way of building the campus network is being redesigned and VLANs are a large factor in building the new campus model.

Introducing the New Campus Model

The changes in customer network requirements—in combination with the problems with collision, bandwidth, and broadcasts—have necessitated a new network campus design. Higher user demands and complex applications force the network designers to think more about traffic patterns instead of solving a typical isolated department issue. We can no longer just think about creating subnets and putting different departments into each subnet. We need to create a network that makes everyone capable of reaching all network services easily. Server farms, where all enterprise servers are located in one physical location, really take a toll on the existing network infrastructure and make the way we used to design networks obsolete. We must pay attention to traffic patterns and how to solve bandwidth issues. This can be accomplished with higher end routing and switching techniques.

Because of the new bandwidth-intensive applications, video and audio being delivered to the desktop, as well as more and more work being performed on the Internet, the new campus model must be able to provide the following:

Fast convergence When a network change takes place, the network must be able to adapt very quickly to the change and keep data moving swiftly.

Deterministic paths Users must be able to gain access to a certain area of the network without fail.

Deterministic failover The network design must have provisions that make sure the network stays up and running even if a link fails.

Scalable size and throughput As users and new devices are added to the network, the network infrastructure must be able to handle the new increase in traffic.

Centralized applications Enterprise applications accessed by all users must be available to support all users on the internetwork.

The new 20/80 rule Instead of 80 percent of the users' traffic staying on the local network, 80 percent of the traffic now crosses the backbone and only 20 percent stays on the local network.

Multiprotocol support Campus networks must support multiple protocols, both routed and routing protocols. Routed protocols are used to send user data through the internetwork (for example, IP or IPX). Routing protocols are used to send network updates between routers, which will in turn update their routing tables. Examples of routing protocols include RIP, Enhanced Interior Gateway Routing Protocol (EIGRP), and Open Shortest Path First (OSPF).

Multicasting Multicasting is sending a broadcast to a defined subnet or group of users. Users can be placed in multicast groups, for example, for videoconferencing.

QoS We need to be able to prioritize different traffic types.

Network Services

The new campus model provides remote services quickly and easily to all users. The users have no idea where the resources are located in the internetwork, nor should they care. There are three types of network services, which are created and defined by the administrator and should appear to the users as local services:

- Local services
- Remote services
- Enterprise services

Local Services

Local services are network services that are located on the same subnet or network as the users accessing them. Users do not cross layer 3 devices, and the network services are in the same broadcast domain as the users. This type of traffic never crosses the backbone.

Remote Services

Remote services are close to users but not on the same network or subnet as the users. The users would have to cross a layer 3 device to communicate with the network services. However, they might not have to cross the backbone.

Enterprise Services

Enterprise services are defined as services that are provided to all users on the internetwork. Layer 3 switches or routers are required in this scenario because an enterprise service must be close to the core and would probably be based in its own subnet. Examples of these services include Internet access, e-mail, and possibly videoconferencing. When servers that host enterprise services are placed close to the backbone, all users would be the same distance from the servers, but all user data would have to cross the backbone to get to the services.

Using Switching Technologies

Switching technologies are crucial to the new network design. Because the prices on layer 2 switching have been dropping dramatically, it is easier to justify the cost of buying switches for your entire network. This doesn't mean that every business can afford switch ports for all users, but it does allow for a cost-effective upgrade solution when the time comes.

To understand switching technologies and how routers and switches work together, you must understand the Open Systems Interconnection (OSI) model. This section will give you a general overview of the OSI model and the devices that are specified at each layer.

You'll need a basic understanding of the OSI model to fully understand discussions in which it is included throughout the rest of this book. For more detailed information about the OSI model, please see *CCNA: Cisco Certified Network Associate Study Guide, 4th edition,* by Todd Lammle (Sybex, 2004).

Open Systems Interconnection (OSI) Model

As you probably already know, the *Open Systems Interconnection (OSI) model* has seven layers, each of which specifies functions that enable data to be transmitted from host to host on an internetwork. Figure 12.4 shows the OSI model and the functions of each layer.

The OSI model is the cornerstone for application developers to write and create networked applications that run on an internetwork. What is important to network engineers and technicians is the encapsulation of data as it is transmitted on a network.

FIGURE 12.4 The OSI model and the layer functions

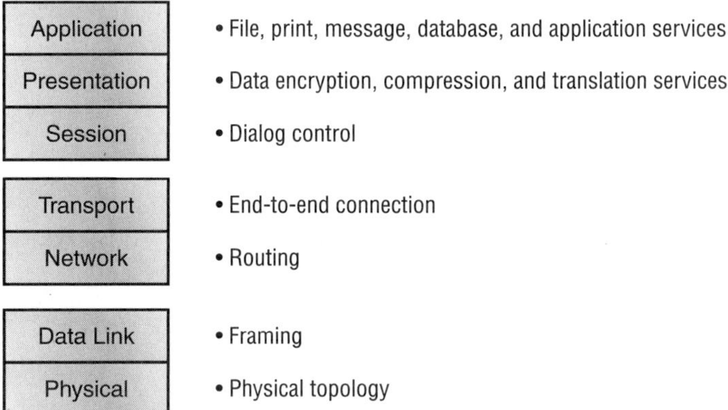

Data Encapsulation

Data encapsulation is the process by which the information in a protocol is wrapped, or contained, in the data section of another protocol. In the OSI reference model, each layer encapsulates the layer immediately above it as the data flows down the protocol stack.

The logical communication that happens at each layer of the OSI reference model doesn't involve many physical connections, because the information each protocol needs to send is encapsulated in the layer of protocol information beneath it. This encapsulation produces a set of data called a packet (see Figure 12.5).

FIGURE 12.5 Data encapsulation at each layer of the OSI reference model

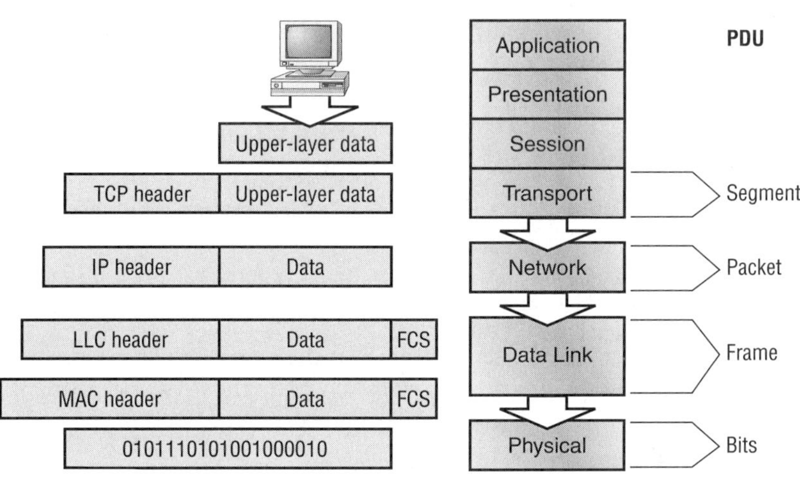

Looking at Figure 12.5, you can follow the data down through the OSI reference model as it's encapsulated at each layer. Cisco courses typically focus only on layers 2 through 4.

Each layer communicates only with its peer layer on the receiving host, and they exchange protocol data units (PDUs). The PDUs are attached to the data at each layer as it traverses down the model and is read only by its peer on the receiving side. Each layer has a specific name for the PDU, as shown in Table 12.1.

TABLE 12.1 OSI Encapsulation

OSI Layer	Name of Protocol Data Units (PDUs)
Transport	Segments/Datagram
Network	Packets
Data Link	Frames
Physical	Bits

Starting at the Application layer, data is converted for transmission on the network and then encapsulated in Presentation layer information. When the Presentation layer receives this information, it looks like generic data. The Presentation layer hands the data to the Session layer, which is responsible for synchronizing the session with the destination host.

The Session layer then passes this data to the Transport layer, which transports the data from the source host to the destination host in a reliable fashion. But before this happens, the Network layer adds routing information to the packet. It then passes the packet on to the Data Link layer for framing and for connection to the Physical layer. The Physical layer sends the data as 1s and 0s to the destination host. Finally, when the destination host receives the 1s and 0s, the data passes back up through the model, one layer at a time. The data is de-encapsulated at each of the OSI model's peer layers.

At a transmitting device, the data encapsulation method is as follows:

1. User information is converted to data for transmission on the network.
2. Data is converted to segments at the Transport layer, and any reliability parameters required are set up.
3. Segments are converted to packets or datagrams at the Network layer, and routing information is added to the PDU.
4. Packets or datagrams are converted to frames at the Data Link layer, and hardware addresses are used to communicate with local hosts on the network medium.
5. Frames are converted to bits, and 1s and 0s are encoded within the digital signal.

Now that you have a sense of the OSI model and how routers and switches work together, it is time to turn your attention to the specifics of each layer of switching technology.

Layer 2 Switching

Layer 2 switching is hardware based, which means it uses the *Media Access Control (MAC)* address from the host's network interface cards (NICs) to filter the network. Switches use *application-specific integrated circuits (ASICs)* to build and maintain filter tables. It is okay to think of a layer 2 switch as a multiport bridge.

Layer 2 switching provides the following:

- Hardware-based bridging (MAC)
- Wire speed
- High speed
- Low latency
- Low cost

Layer 2 switching is so efficient because there is no modification to the data packet, only to the frame encapsulation of the packet, and only when the data packet is passing through dissimilar media (such as from Ethernet to FDDI).

Use layer 2 switching for workgroup connectivity and network segmentation (breaking up collision domains). This enables you to create a flatter network design and one with more network segments than traditional 10BaseT shared networks.

Layer 2 switching has helped develop new components in the network infrastructure:

Server farms Servers are no longer distributed to physical locations, because virtual LANs can be used to create broadcast domains in a switched internetwork. This means that all servers can be placed in a central location, yet a certain server can still be part of a workgroup in a remote branch, for example.

Intranets These enable organization-wide client/server communications based on a web technology.

These new technologies are enabling more data to flow off local subnets and onto a routed network, where a router's performance can become the bottleneck.

Limitations of Layer 2 Switching

Layer 2 switches have the same limitations as bridge networks. Remember that bridges are good if you design the network by the 80/20 rule: users spend 80 percent of their time on their local segment.

Bridged networks break up collision domains, but the network is still one large broadcast domain. Similarly, layer 2 switches (bridges) cannot break up broadcast domains, which can cause performance issues and limit the size of your network. Broadcasts and multicasts, along with the slow convergence of spanning tree, can cause major problems as the network grows. Because of these problems, layer 2 switches cannot completely replace routers in the internetwork.

Routing

We want to explain how routing works and how routers work in an internetwork before discussing layer 3 switching next. Routers and layer 3 switches are similar in concept but not design. In this section, we'll discuss routers and what they provide in an internetwork today.

Routers break up collision domains as bridges do. In addition, routers also break up broadcast/multicast domains.

The benefits of routing include:

- Breakup of broadcast domains
- Multicast control
- Optimal path determination
- Traffic management
- Logical (layer 3) addressing
- Security

Routers provide optimal path determination because the router examines each and every packet that enters an interface and improves network segmentation by forwarding data packets to only a known destination network. Routers are not interested in hosts, only networks. If a router does not know about a remote network to which a packet is destined, it will just drop the packet and not forward it. Because of this packet examination, traffic management is obtained.

The Network layer of the OSI model defines a virtual—or logical—network address. Hosts and routers use these addresses to send information from host to host within an internetwork. Every network interface must have a logical address, typically an IP address.

Security can be obtained by a router reading the packet header information and reading filters defined by the network administrator (access control lists).

Layer 3 Switching

The only difference between a layer 3 switch and a router is the way the administrator creates the physical implementation. Also, traditional routers use microprocessors to make forwarding decisions, and the switch performs only hardware-based packet switching. However, some traditional routers can have other hardware functions as well in some of the higher end models. Layer 3 switches can be placed anywhere in the network because they handle high-performance LAN traffic and can cost-effectively replace routers.

Layer 3 switching is all hardware-based packet forwarding, and all packet forwarding is handled by hardware ASICs. Layer 3 switches really are no different functionally from a traditional router and perform the same functions, which are listed here:

- Determine paths based on logical addressing
- Run layer 3 checksums (on header only)
- Use time to live (TTL)
- Process and respond to any option information
- Can update Simple Network Management Protocol (SNMP) managers with Management Information Base (MIB) information
- Provide security

The benefits of layer 3 switching include the following:

- Hardware-based packet forwarding
- High-performance packet switching
- High-speed scalability
- Low latency
- Lower per-port cost
- Flow accounting
- Security
- Quality of service (QoS)

Layer 4 Switching

Layer 4 switching is considered a hardware-based layer 3 switching technology that can also consider the application used (for example, Telnet or FTP). Layer 4 switching provides additional routing above layer 3 by using the port numbers found in the Transport layer header to make routing decisions. These port numbers are found in Request for Comments (RFC) 1700 and reference the upper layer protocol, program, or application.

Layer 4 information has been used to help make routing decisions for quite a while. For example, extended access lists can filter packets based on layer 4 port numbers. Another example is accounting information gathered by NetFlow switching in Cisco's higher end routers.

The largest benefit of layer 4 switching is that the network administrator can configure a layer 4 switch to prioritize data traffic by application, which means a QoS can be defined for each user. For example, a number of users can be defined as a Video group and be assigned more priority, or bandwidth, based on the need for videoconferencing.

However, because users can be part of many groups and run many applications, the layer 4 switches must be able to provide a huge filter table or response time would suffer. This filter table must be much larger than any layer 2 or 3 switch. A layer 2 switch might have a filter table only as large as the number of users connected to the network, maybe even smaller if some hubs are used within the switched fabric. However, a layer 4 switch might have five or six entries for each and every device connected to the network! If the layer 4 switch does not have a filter table that includes all the information, the switch will not be able to produce wire-speed results.

Multilayer Switching (MLS)

Multilayer switching (MLS) combines layer 2, 3, and 4 switching technologies and provides high-speed scalability with low latency. It accomplishes this combination of high-speed scalability with low latency by using huge filter tables based on the criteria designed by the network administrator.

Multilayer switching can move traffic at wire speed and also provide layer 3 routing, which can remove the bottleneck from the network routers. This technology is based on the concept of route once, switch many.

Multilayer switching can make routing/switching decisions based on the following:

- MAC source/destination address in a Data Link frame
- IP source/destination address in the Network layer header
- Protocol field in the Network layer header
- Port source/destination numbers in the Transport layer header

There is no performance difference between a layer 3 and a layer 4 switch because the routing/switching is all hardware based.

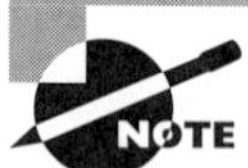

MLS will be discussed in more detail in Chapter 18, "Multilayer Switching."

It is important that you have an understanding of the different OSI layers and what they provide before continuing on to the Cisco three-layer hierarchical model.

Understanding the Cisco Hierarchical Model

Most of us learned about hierarchy early in life. Anyone with older siblings learned what it was like to be at the bottom of the hierarchy! Regardless of where we were first exposed to hierarchy, most of us experience it in many aspects of our lives. *Hierarchy* helps us to understand where things belong, how things fit together, and what functions go where. It brings order and understandability to otherwise complex models. If you want a pay raise, hierarchy dictates that you ask your boss, not your subordinate. That is the person whose role it is to grant (or deny) your request.

Hierarchy has many of the same benefits in network design that it has in other areas. When used properly in network design, it makes networks more predictable. It helps us to define and expect at which levels of the hierarchy we should perform certain functions. You would ask your boss, not your subordinate, for a raise because of their respective positions in the business hierarchy. The hierarchy requires that you ask someone at a higher level than yours. Likewise, you can use tools such as access lists at certain levels in hierarchical networks and you must avoid them at others.

Let's face it, large networks can be extremely complicated, with multiple protocols, detailed configurations, and diverse technologies. Hierarchy helps us to summarize a complex collection of details into an understandable model. Then, as specific configurations are needed, the model dictates the appropriate manner for them to be applied.

The *Cisco hierarchical model* is used to help you design a scalable, reliable, cost-effective hierarchical internetwork. Cisco defines three layers of hierarchy, as shown in Figure 12.6, each with specific functionality.

FIGURE 12.6 The Cisco hierarchical model

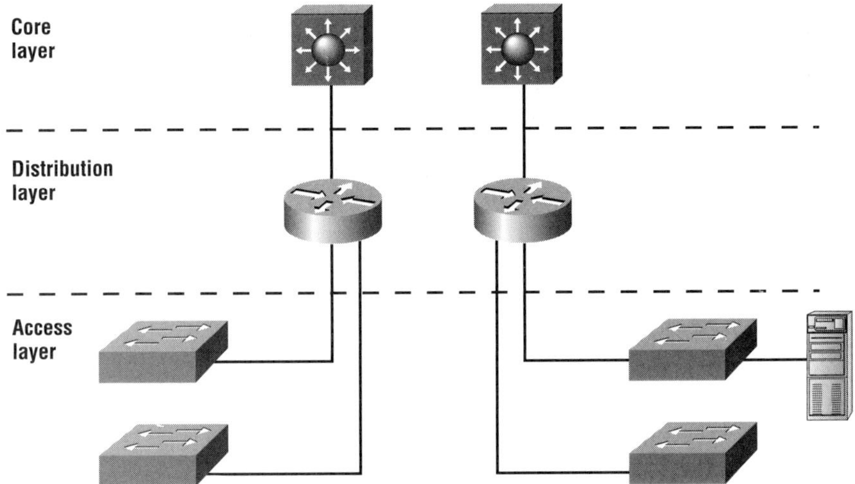

The three layers are as follows:

- Core
- Distribution
- Access

Each layer has specific responsibilities. Remember, however, that the three layers are logical and not necessarily physical. "Three layers" does not necessarily mean "three separate devices." Consider the OSI model, another logical hierarchy. The seven layers describe functions but not necessarily protocols, right? Sometimes a protocol maps to more than one layer of the OSI model, and sometimes multiple protocols communicate within a single layer. In the same way, when you build physical implementations of hierarchical networks, you might have many devices in a single layer, or you might have a single device performing functions at two layers. The definition of the layers is logical, not physical.

Before we examine these layers and their functions, consider a common hierarchical design, as shown in Figure 12.7. The phrase "keep local traffic local" has almost become a cliché in the networking world. However, the underlying concept has merit. Hierarchical design lends itself perfectly to fulfilling this concept. Now, let's take a closer look at each of the layers.

FIGURE 12.7 A hierarchical network design

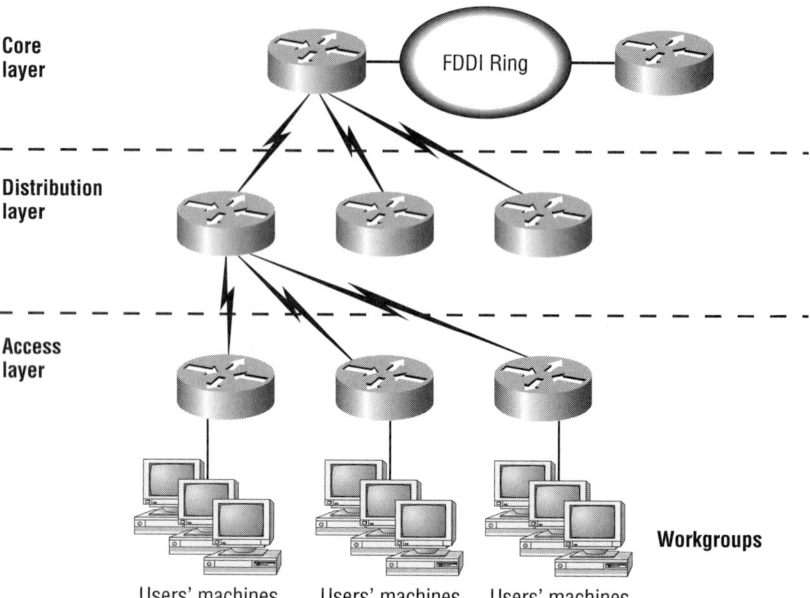

Core Layer

The *core layer* is literally the core of the network. At the top of the hierarchy, the core layer is responsible for transporting large amounts of traffic both reliably and quickly. The only purpose of the core layer of the network is to switch traffic as quickly as possible. The traffic transported across the core is common to a majority of users. However, remember that user data is processed at the distribution layer, and the distribution layer forwards the requests to the core, if needed.

If there is a failure in the core, *every single* user can be affected. Therefore, fault tolerance at this layer is an issue. The core is likely to see large volumes of traffic, so speed and latency are driving concerns here. Given the function of the core, we can now look at some design specifics to consider. Let's start with some things you know you don't want to do:

- Don't do anything to slow down traffic. This includes using access lists, routing between VLANs, and packet filtering.
- Don't support workgroup access here.
- Avoid expanding the core when the internetwork grows (that is, adding routers). If performance becomes an issue in the core, give preference to upgrades over expansion.

There are a few things that you want to make sure to get done as you design the core:

- Design the core for high reliability. Consider Data Link technologies that facilitate both speed and redundancy, such as FDDI, FastEthernet (with redundant links), Gigabit Ethernet, or even ATM.

- Design with speed in mind. The core should have very little latency.
- Select routing protocols with lower convergence times. Fast and redundant Data Link connectivity is no help if your routing tables are shot!

Distribution Layer

The *distribution layer* is sometimes referred to as the workgroup layer and is the communication point between the access layer and the core. The primary function of the distribution layer is to provide routing, filtering, and WAN access and to determine how packets can access the core, if needed. The distribution layer must determine the fastest way that user requests are serviced (for example, how a file request is forwarded to a server). After the distribution layer determines the best path, it forwards the request to the core layer. The core layer is then responsible for quickly transporting the request to the correct service.

The distribution layer is the place to implement policies for the network. Here, you can exercise considerable flexibility in defining network operation. Generally, the following should be done at the distribution layer:

- Implement tools such as access lists, packet filtering, and queuing.
- Implement security and network policies, including address translation and firewalls.
- Redistribute between routing protocols, including static routing.
- Route between VLANs and other workgroup support functions.
- Define broadcast and multicast domains.

Things to avoid at the distribution layer are limited to those functions that exclusively belong to one of the other layers.

Access Layer

The *access layer* controls user and workgroup access to internetwork resources. The access layer is sometimes referred to as the desktop layer. The network resources that most users need are available locally. Any traffic for remote services is handled by the distribution layer. The following functions should be included at this layer:

- Continued (from distribution layer) access control and policies.
- Creation of separate collision domains (segmentation).
- Workgroup connectivity to the distribution layer.
- Technologies such as dial-on-demand routing (DDR) and Ethernet switching are frequently seen in the access layer. Static routing (instead of dynamic routing protocols) is seen here as well.

As already noted, having three separate levels does not have to imply having three separate routers. It could be fewer, or it could be more. Remember that this is a *layered* approach.

Using Cisco Catalyst Products

Understanding the campus size and traffic is an important factor in network design. A large campus is defined as several or many colocated buildings, and a medium campus is one or more colocated buildings. Small campus networks have only one building.

By understanding your campus size, you can choose Cisco products that will fit your business needs and grow with your company. Cisco switches are produced to fit neatly within its three-layer model. This helps you decide which equipment to use for your network efficiently and quickly.

It should be noted that the Cisco range of switches is in a transitional phase between two operating systems. The Catalyst Operating System (CatOS) is the traditional method and is often referred to as using `set` commands because when configuring, the command often begins with the word "set." Switches in this line include the 4000 and the 6000/6500.

The switches based on the IOS are called Catalyst IOS (CatIOS) switches. The interface to configure these switches resembles that of the IOS router but isn't entirely the same. Anyone familiar with configuring a router, though, will be comfortable configuring one of these switches. The switches that use this include the 2950, the 3550, and the 8500 series.

With some switches—for instance, the 6000/6500 series—you have a choice between the two types of operating systems. When this occurs, the CatOS is the default OS. This is liable to change as Cisco promotes the transition to IOS-based offerings.

Cisco Express Forwarding (CEF) allows for real layer 3 switches to forward traffic based on a complete layer 3 topology map. This map is shared with the ASICs at each port, enabling each port to know which port a packet should be forwarded to. Rather than forwarding based on MAC address, forwarding is done by layer 3 address. Only switches that have true layer 3 capabilities can do this type of switching. These devices include the 3550 series, the 4000 series, the 6000/6500 series with PFC2, and the 8500 series.

There are two general rules when it comes to Cisco switches: The lower model numbers usually cost less, and purchasing a device with more ports drives down the per-port cost. In addition, the model number may typically be split into two sections: For slot-based switches, the second number usually refers to the number of physical slots it has. The 6509 is a nine-slot device in the 6500 family of switches.

Access Layer Switches

The access layer, as you already know, is where users gain access to the internetwork. The switches deployed at this layer must be able to handle connecting individual desktop devices to the internetwork. The switches here are usually characterized as having a large number of ports and being low cost. Most access switches don't have a lot of frills.

The Cisco solutions at the access layer include the following:

2950 Provides switched 10/100 Mbps to the desktop. All ports are capable of full duplex, and options include Gigabit Ethernet interfaces. The standard Cisco IOS means that the switch supports functionality for basic data, video, and voice services. All Catalyst 2950 and 2955 switches also support the Cisco Cluster Management Suite (CMS) software, which allows users to use a standard web browser to simultaneously configure and troubleshoot multiple Catalyst desktop switches.

3550 Provides a range of stackable selections that can be used as access switches with the Standard Multilayer Software Image (SMI). Many options are available, including 24 and 48 ports, inline power for IP telephony, and a range of 10/100/1000Mbps ports.

If power for IP phones is required but a switch with inline power is not available, Cisco also has a product called the Inline Power Patch Panel that adds inline power to an existing Catalyst switch.

4000 Provides a 10/100/1000Mbps advanced high-performance enterprise solution for up to 96 users and up to 36 Gigabit Ethernet ports for servers. Some models also support the delivery of inline power for IP telephones.

Distribution Layer Switches

As discussed earlier, the primary function of the distribution layer is to provide routing, filtering, and WAN access and to determine how packets can access the core, if needed.

Distribution layer switches are the aggregation point for multiple access switches and must be capable of handling large amounts of traffic from these access layer devices. The distribution layer switches must also be able to participate in MLS and be able to handle a route processor.

The Cisco switches that provide these functions are as follows:

3550 series This range includes a variety of stackable switches supporting a huge range of features. Full IOS operation complete with MLS is available, and this makes the switch suitable for both access layer and distribution layer switching.

4000 series One of the most scalable switches, the 4000 can be used as a distribution switch if the supervisor IV engine supporting MLS is installed. The 4000 series switches support advanced QoS, security, and flexibility, achieved with a range of modules. Numerous chassis are available, providing advanced features such as non-blocking architecture and resilience through redundant supervisors. This range has been given a real boost by Cisco.

6000 The Catalyst 6000 can provide up to 384 10/100Mbps Ethernet connections, 192 100FX FastEthernet connections, or 130 Gigabit Ethernet ports. (With the recent release of the 10/100/1000 card, the 6500 can now support up to 384 10/100/1000 Ethernet connections.) In addition to regular connections, IP telephone connections with inline power are also supported. The 6000 can be outfitted with a Multilayer Switch Feature Card (MSFC) to provide router functionality as well as a Policy Feature Card (PFC) for layer 3 switching functionality.

Core Layer Switches

The core layer must be efficient and do nothing to slow down packets as they traverse the backbone. The following switches are recommended for use in the core:

6500 The Catalyst 6500 series switches are designed to address the need for gigabit port density, high availability, and multilayer switching for the core layer backbone and server-aggregation environments. These switches use the Cisco IOS to utilize the high speeds of the ASICs, which allows the delivery of wire-speed traffic management services end to end.

8500 The Cisco Catalyst 8500 is a core layer switch that provides high-performance switching. The Catalyst 8500 uses ASICs to provide multiple-layer protocol support, including IP, IP multicast, bridging, ATM switching, and policy-enabled QoS.

All these switches provide wire-speed multicast forwarding, routing, and Protocol Independent Multicast (PIM) for scalable multicast routing. These switches are perfect for providing the high bandwidth and performance needed for a core router. The 6500 and 8500 switches can aggregate multiprotocol traffic from multiple remote wiring closets and workgroup switches.

Applying the Building Blocks

Remember the saying, "Everything I need to know I learned in kindergarten?" Well, it appears to be true. Cisco has determined that following the hierarchical mode they have created promotes a building-block approach to network design. If you did well with building blocks in your younger years, you can just apply that same technique to building large, multimillion-dollar networks. Kind of makes you glad it's someone else's money you're playing with, doesn't it?

In all seriousness, Cisco has determined some fundamental campus elements that help you build network building blocks:

Switch blocks Access layer switches connected to the distribution layer devices

Core blocks Support of multiple switch blocks connected together with 4000, 6500, or 8500 switches

Within these fundamental elements, there are three contributing variables:

Server blocks Groups of network servers on a single subnet

WAN blocks Multiple connections to an ISP or multiple ISPs

Mainframe blocks Centralized services to which the enterprise network is responsible for providing complete access

By understanding how these work, you can build large, expensive networks with confidence (using someone else's money). After the network has been built, you need to allow the switches to talk to each other to allow for redundancy and to route around outages. We will cover these topics later in this section after the blocks are discussed.

Switch Block

The *switch block* is a combination of layer 2 switches and layer 3 routers. The layer 2 switches connect users in the wiring closet into the access layer and provide 10Mbps or 100Mbps dedicated connections; 2950 Catalyst switches can be used in the switch block.

From here, the access layer switches connect into one or more distribution layer switches, which will be the central connection point for all switches coming from the wiring closets. The distribution layer device is either a switch with an external router or a multilayer switch. The distribution layer switch then provides layer 3 routing functions, if needed.

The distribution layer router prevents broadcast storms that could happen on an access layer switch from propagating throughout the entire internetwork. The broadcast storm would be isolated to only the access layer switch in which the problem exists.

Switch Block Size

To understand how large a switch block can be, you must understand the traffic types and the size and number of workgroups that will be using them. The number of switches that can collapse from the access layer to the distribution layer depends on the following:

- Traffic patterns
- Routers at the distribution layer
- Number of users connected to the access layer switches
- Distance VLANs must traverse the network
- Spanning tree domain size

If routers at the distribution layer become the bottleneck in the network (which means the CPU processing is too intensive), the switch block has grown too large. Also, if too many broadcasts or multicast traffic slow down the switches and routers, your switch blocks have grown too large.

Having a large number of users does not necessarily indicate that the switch block is too large; too much traffic going across the network does.

Core Block

If you have two or more switch blocks, the Cisco rule of thumb states that you need a *core block*. No routing is performed at the core, only transferring of data. It is a pass-through for the switch block, the server block, and the Internet. Figure 12.8 shows one example of a core block.

The core is responsible for transferring data to and from the switch blocks as quickly as possible. You can build a fast core with a frame, packet, or cell (ATM) network technology. The Switching exam is based on an Ethernet core network.

FIGURE 12.8 The core block

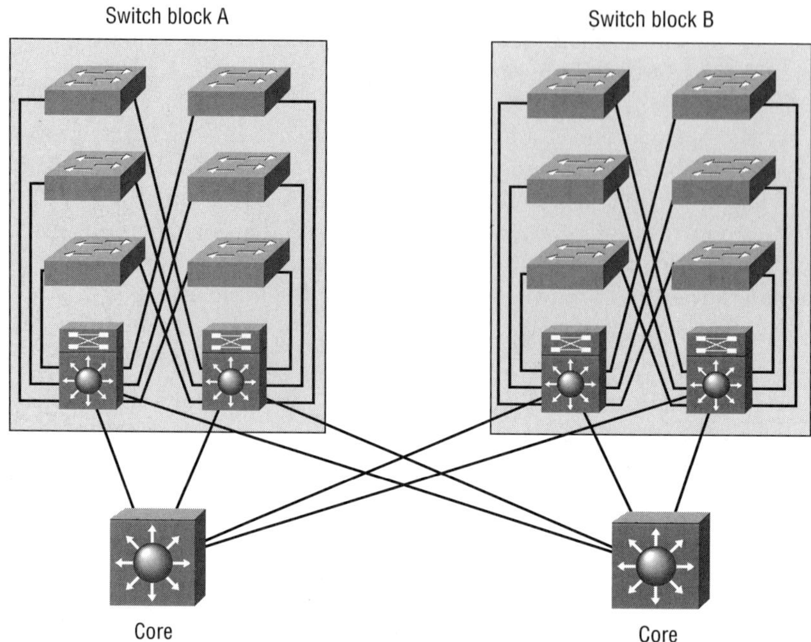

Typically, you would have only one subnet configured on the core network. However, for redundancy and load balancing, you could have two or more subnets configured.

Switches can trunk on a certain port or ports. This means that a port on a switch can be a member of more than one VLAN at the same time. However, the distribution layer will handle the routing and trunking for VLANs, and the core is only a pass-through after the routing has been performed. Because of this, core links do not carry multiple subnets per link; the distribution layer does.

A Cisco 6500 or 8500 switch is recommended at the core, and even though only one of those switches might be sufficient to handle the traffic, Cisco recommends two switches for redundancy and load balancing. You could consider a 4000 or 3550 Catalyst switch if you don't need the power of the 6500 or the 8500.

Collapsed Core

A *collapsed core* is defined as one switch performing both core and distribution layer functions; however, the functions of the core and distribution layer are still distinct. The collapsed core is typically found in a small network.

Redundant links between the distribution layer and the access layer switches, and between each access layer switch, can support more than one VLAN. The distribution layer routing is the termination for all ports. Figure 12.9 shows a collapsed core network design.

FIGURE 12.9 Collapsed core

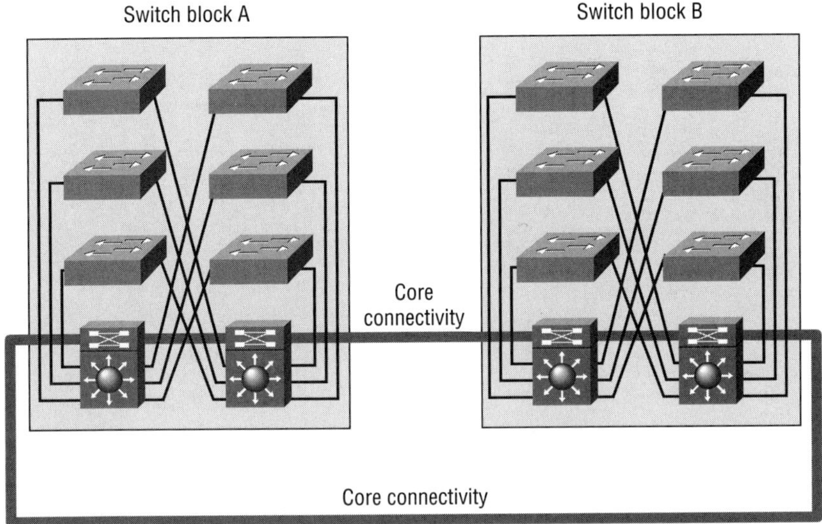

In a collapsed core network, the Spanning Tree Protocol (STP) blocks the redundant links to prevent loops. Hot Standby Routing Protocol (HSRP) can provide redundancy in the distribution layer routing. It can keep core connectivity if the primary routing process fails.

Dual Core

If you have more than two switch blocks and need redundant connections between the core and distribution layer, you need to create a dual core. Figure 12.10 shows an example of a dual-core configuration. Each connection would be a separate subnet.

In Figure 12.10, you can see that each switch block is redundantly connected to each of the two core blocks. The distribution layer routers already have links to each subnet in the routing tables, provided by the layer 3 routing protocols. If a failure on a core switch takes place, convergence time will not be an issue. HSRP can be used to provide quick cutover between the cores. (HSRP is covered in Chapter 20, "Quality of Service (QoS).")

Core Size

Routing protocols are the main factor in determining the size of your core. This is because routers, or any layer 3 device, isolate the core. Routers send updates to other routers, and as the network grows, so do these updates, so it takes longer to converge or to have all the routers update. Because at least one of the routers will connect to the Internet, it's possible that there will be more updates throughout the internetwork.

The routing protocol dictates the size of the distribution layer devices that can communicate with the core. Table 12.2 shows a few of the more popular routing protocols and the number of blocks each routing protocol supports. Remember that this includes all blocks, including server, mainframe, and WAN.

FIGURE 12.10 Dual-core configuration

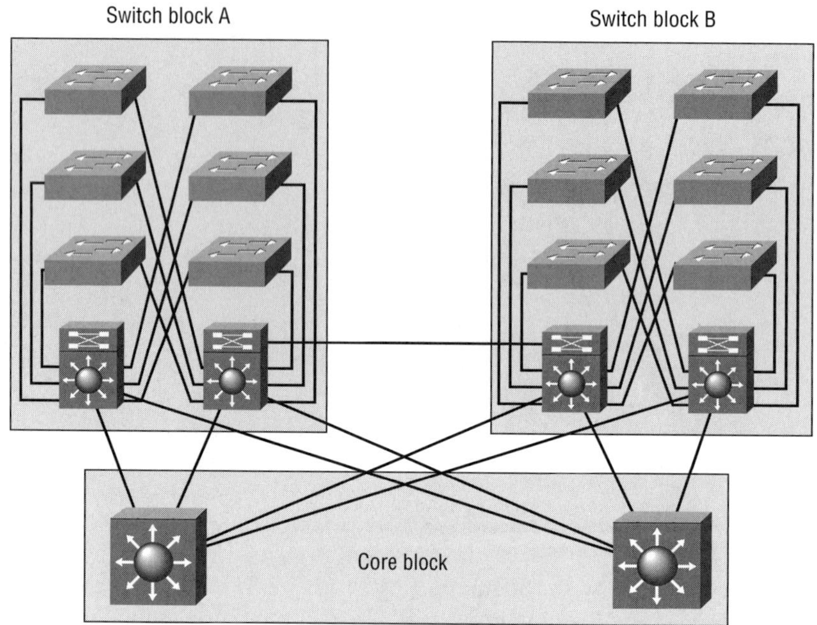

TABLE 12.2 Blocks Supported by Routing Protocols

Routing Protocol	Maximum Number of Peers	Number of Subnet Links to the Core	Maximum Number of Supported Blocks
OSPF	50	2	25
EIGRP	50	2	25
RIP	30	2	15

Scaling Layer 2 Backbones

Typically, layer 2 switches are in the remote closets and represent the access layer, the layer where users gain access to the internetwork. Ethernet switched networks scale well in this environment, where the layer 2 switches then connect into a larger, more robust layer 3 switch representing the distribution layer. The layer 3 device is then connected into a layer 2 device representing the core. Because routing is not necessarily recommended in a classic design model at the core, the model then looks like this:

Access	Distribution	Core
Layer 2 switch	Layer 3 switch	Layer 2 switch

Spanning Tree Protocol (STP)

Chapter 15, "Layer 2 Switching and the Spanning Tree Protocol (STP)," and Chapter 16, "Using Spanning Tree with VLANs," detail the STP, but some discussion is necessary here. STP is used by layer 2 bridges to stop network loops in networks that have more than one physical link to the same network. There is a limit to the number of links in a layer 2 switched backbone that needs to be taken into account. As you increase the number of core switches, the problem becomes that the number of links to distribution links must increase also, for redundancy reasons. If the core is running the Spanning Tree Protocol, then it can compromise the high-performance connectivity between switch blocks. The best design on the core is to have two switches without STP running. You can do this only by having a core without links between the core switches. This is demonstrated in Figure 12.11.

Figure 12.11 shows redundancy between the core and distribution layer without spanning tree loops. This is accomplished by not having the two core switches linked together. However, each distribution layer 3 switch has a connection to each core switch. This means that each layer 3 switch has two equal-cost paths to every other router in the campus network.

FIGURE 12.11 Layer 2 backbone scaling without STP

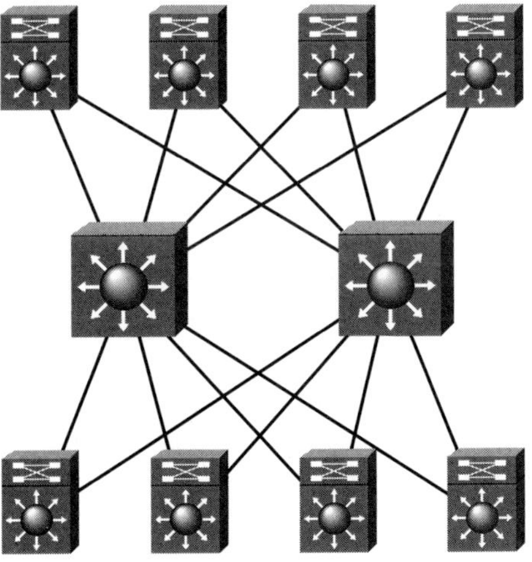

Scaling Layer 3 Backbones

As discussed in the previous section, "Scaling Layer 2 Backbones," you'll typically find layer 2 switches connecting to layer 3 switches, which connect to the core with the layer 2 switches. However, it is possible that some networks might have layer 2/layer 3/layer 3 designs (layer 2 connecting to layer 3 connecting to layer 3). But this is not cheap, even if you're using someone else's money. There is always some type of network budget, and you need to have good reason to spend the type of money needed to build layer 3 switches into the core.

There are three reasons you would implement layer 3 switches into the core:

- Fast convergence
- Automatic load balancing
- Elimination of peering problems

Fast Convergence

If you have only layer 2 devices at the core layer, the STP will be used to stop network loops if there is more than one connection between core devices. The STP has a convergence time of more than 50 seconds, and if the network is large, this can cause an enormous number of problems if it has just one link failure.

STP is not implemented in the core if you have layer 3 devices. Routing protocols, which can have a much faster convergence time than STP, are used to maintain the network.

Automatic Load Balancing

If you provide layer 3 devices in the core, the routing protocols can load-balance with multiple equal-cost links. This is not possible with layer 3 devices only at the distribution layer, because you would have to selectively choose the root for utilizing more than one path.

Elimination of Peering Problems

Because routing is typically performed in the distribution layer devices, each distribution layer device must have "reachability" information about each of the other distribution layer devices. These layer 3 devices use routing protocols to maintain the state and reachability information about neighbor routers. This means that each distribution device becomes a peer with every other distribution layer device, and scalability becomes an issue because every device has to keep information for every other device.

If your layer 3 devices are located in the core, you can create a hierarchy, and the distribution layer devices will no longer be peers to each other's distribution device. This is typical in an environment in which there are more than 100 switch blocks.

SAFE

SAFE is Cisco's Secure Blueprint for Enterprise Networks, the stated aim of which is to provide information on the best practice for designing and implementing secure networks. Recently, the issue of security in networking has been receiving a huge amount of attention. As part of this attention, Cisco has been at the forefront of developing this process, which is based upon the products of Cisco and its partners.

The SAFE methodology involves creating a layered approach to security, such that a failure at one layer does not compromise the whole network. Instead, it operates like a military "defense in depth."

Defense in depth is a concept that explains how it is expected that an enemy will be able to penetrate your defensive perimeter, but that it will take time and effort. Multiple lines of defense slow down an attacker and give you more time to discover and stop them. Additionally, each line of defense can have its own procedures, in the hope that the attacker may not be skilled in all countermeasures.

One of the main features of this new set of principles is that it defines a slightly different modular concept from the original core, distribution, and access layers. That is not to say that these original layers are no longer used in design; rather, the SAFE approach is to use an alternative. In practice, designers see both methods as useful and may appropriate features from each. The basis for the new modular design concept is shown in Figure 12.12.

FIGURE 12.12 Enterprise Composite Module

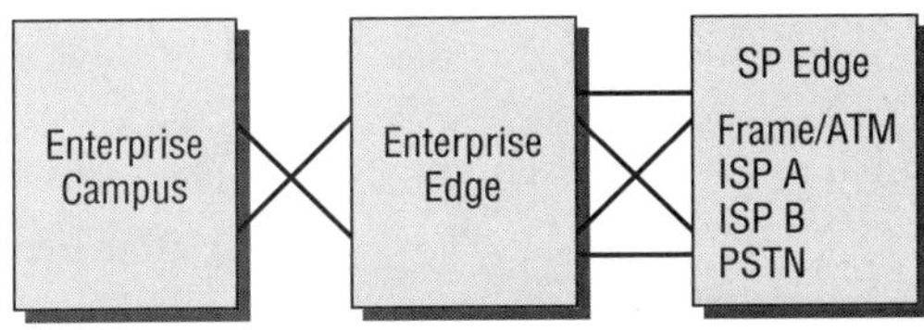

This high-level diagram shows only three blocks. Each block represents a different functional area, providing a modular understanding of the security issues. From our perspective, we need to focus in a little more on the detail, and this is expanded in the main SAFE block diagram, shown in Figure 12.13.

FIGURE 12.13 Enterprise SAFE block diagram

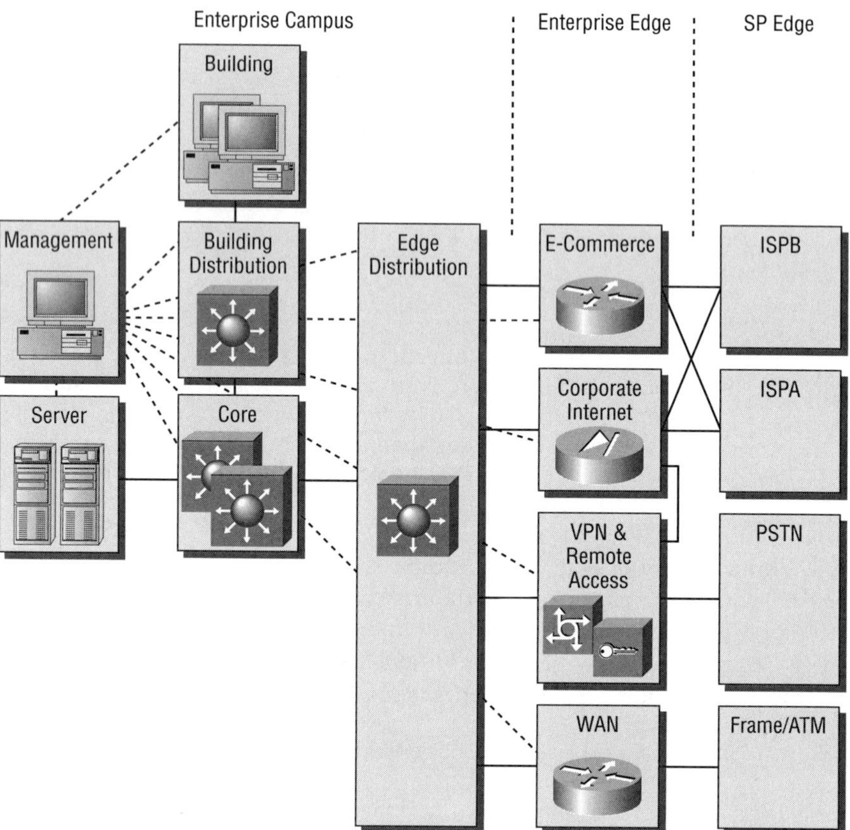

Figure 12.13 shows a much clearer breakout of the actual modules inside SAFE that need to be managed and secured. Each module has its own threats and protection issues. It is not expected that every network would be built using all modules, but rather that this provides a framework for understanding the security issues involved and isolating them.

From the perspective of the Cisco CCNP training program, we need to focus in again, this time looking in a little more detail at the Campus Module, as shown in Figure 12.14.

Note that the Campus Module contains a number of smaller modules, each of which is associated with a specific function:

Management Module Designed to facilitate all management within the campus network as defined by the SAFE architecture. The Management Module must be separated from the managed devices and areas by a firewall, by separate VLANs, and by separate IP addresses and subnet allocation.

Building Module SAFE defines the Building Module as the part of the network that contains end-user workstations and devices plus the layer 2 access points. Included in this are the Building Distribution Module and Building Access Module.

Building Distribution Module This module provides standard distribution layer services to the building switches, including routing, access control, and, more recently, QoS (quality of service) support.

Building Access Module The Building Access Module defines the devices at the access layer, including layer 2 switches, user workstations, and, more recently, IP telephones.

Core Module This module follows the principles of the core part of the standard Cisco three-layer module, focusing on transporting large amounts of traffic both reliably and quickly.

Server Module The main goal of the Server Module is to provide access to the application services by end users and devices.

FIGURE 12.14 Enterprise Campus Module detailed diagram

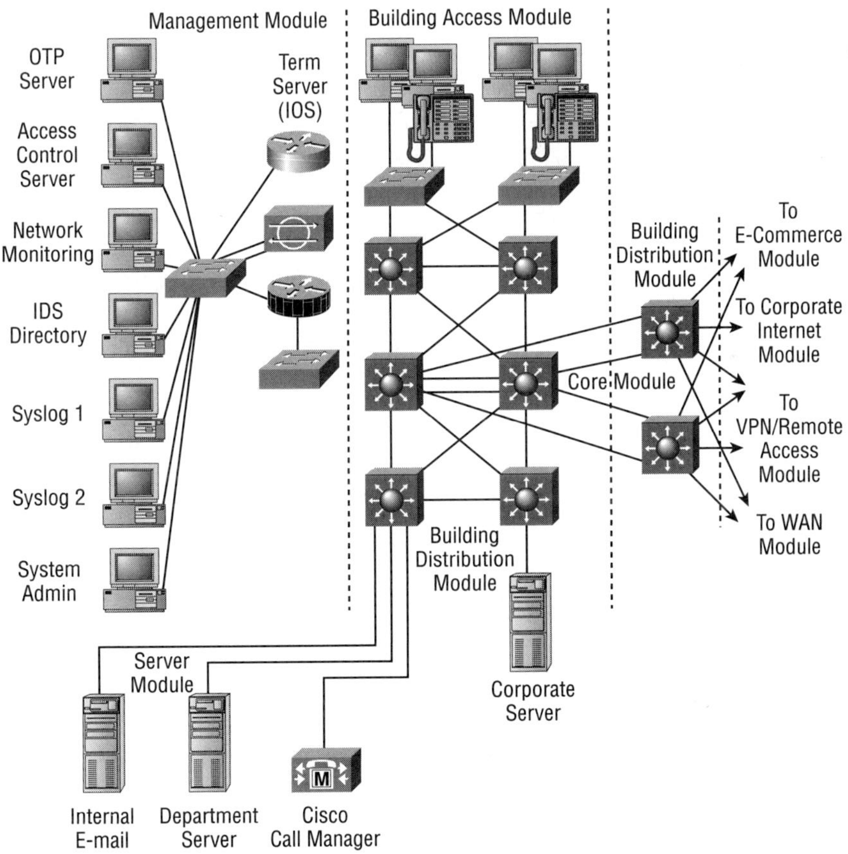

Summary

Cisco Systems manufactures a large, varied, and ever-changing range of equipment. Over the years, the acquisition of a number of companies producing switches has meant that the range has not always appeared entirely consistent, but as time marches on, some of the differences in the underlying basics of the equipment are beginning to disappear. The most obvious differences in switch models now comes down to two factors: Are the switches modular (4000, 6500) or fixed footprint (2950, 3550), and do they support just layer 2 (2950) or can you buy a layer 3 capability (4000, 6500, 3550)?

Of course, the next question that arises is, "Which switch should I choose?" Naturally there are issues of cost and size (in terms of ports and so on), but that may not be sufficient to help you design a complex network. So Cisco has pioneered some design guidelines that will help you put a specific Cisco box into a "location" in your internetwork, dependent upon the technologies required at that network point.

In order to understand all of this, there are two specific areas that we had to focus on. The first was how Cisco defines the network design model, in terms of redundancy, QoS, throughput, security, and so on, and how the Cisco models explain that to us. Cisco uses a three-layer model in which the access layer is used to provide redundant access to end users, the distribution layer manages policy, and the core layer provides fast access to the network backbone. Cisco also has a second model, related to its Secure Blueprint for Enterprise Networks (SAFE) guidelines, called the Enterprise Composite Module, which allows easy identification of modules such as the Management, Campus, Enterprise Edge, and SP Edge modules.

The second area we focused on was what technologies are available. Switches have traditionally been layer 2 devices, operating by forwarding data using MAC address tables. This is fast, but not very scalable, which means that routers, operating at layer 3, have been used. Modern devices can commonly combine the switching and routing processes, resulting in layer 3 switching. Layer 4 switching is an extension of that process, using the port fields inside TCP and UDP to assist with forwarding decisions. The total effect is commonly referred to as multilayer switching—MLS.

Exam Essentials

Understand the concept behind the three-layer model. In order to provide some framework to the design process, Cisco has designed the three-layer model, with the built-in principles that functionality can be assigned to a specific layer. This allows easier equipment selection and configuration, as long as you remember which layer does what! The access layer is used to provide access for most users into the rest of the network. The distribution layer is used for routing, filtering, and for some access tasks. Finally, the core layer is used to link switch blocks, and nothing that slows traffic down should be run here.

Understand the reasoning behind each of the switch block types. A switch block is a collection of switching devices that provide access and distribution layer functions. Each of the block models has specific needs, and the Cisco range of equipment is designed to carry out the appropriate tasks. The result is that different switches perform optimally at different layers. Servers may benefit from duplex connectivity and larger bandwidth than clients, due to the aggregated traffic, and because SAFE planning demands that the network be protected in depth, blocks must be clearly defined.

Understand the different product lines and the individual products that Cisco has available for switching tasks. Some Cisco devices are standard layer 2 switches and use just the MAC address for forwarding. This is simple, cheap, and pretty fast. But the limits of scalability mean that such devices cannot be used throughout the network, so Cisco also manufactures switches that provide real layer 3 services. Understanding the needs of different layers assists with the selection of the correct switch and the planning of the appropriate configuration, which might be simple layer 2 switching, or possibly MLS.

Connecting the Switch Block

THE CCNP EXAM TOPICS COVERED IN THIS CHAPTER INCLUDE THE FOLLOWING:

- ✓ Describe LAN segmentation with VLANs.
- ✓ Provide physical connectivity between two devices within a switch block.
- ✓ Provide connectivity from an end user station to an access layer device.
- ✓ Configure a switch for initial operation.
- ✓ Apply IOS command set to diagnose and troubleshoot a switched network.
- ✓ Configure Fast EtherChannel and Gigabit EtherChannel on inter-switch links.

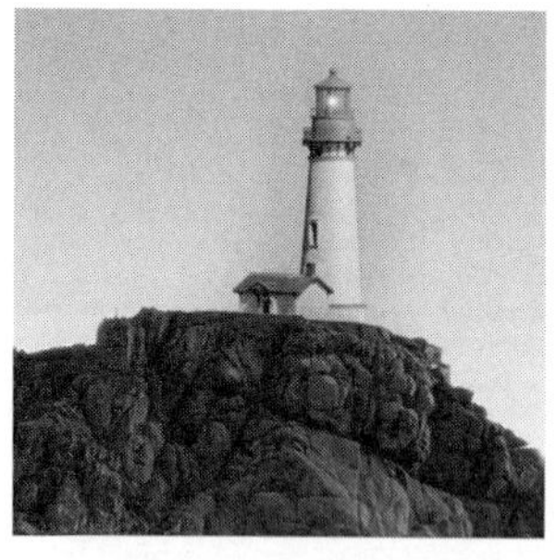

We have come a long way since the beginning of networking. We have lived through several mini-revolutions, and now we find ourselves at a time when Ethernet is king. Gaining ground over all rivals until most of them are left only in memory, this simple protocol has grown to support data transfer at 10, 100, 1000 and (almost) 10,000 Mbits/second (Mbps). What a happy life being a network manager, knowing that your favorite protocol has expansion capability for the future.

This inherent growth capability, combined with the creation of a sound hierarchical network that follows the Cisco three-layer model, means that you too can be a LAN top gun.

This chapter helps you understand the different *contention media* available. Contention is the media access process used by Ethernet. This book covers only contention media because it is the most widely used; for the pragmatic reasons of cost, simplicity, and ease of implementation, Ethernet (or its variations) runs on most of the networks in the world.

But the development of faster Ethernets has changed many of the original concepts along the way. The full-duplex connectivity option has removed the need for the contention algorithm, because each transmitting station has access to its own pair of wires. Some Gigabit Ethernet implementations may demand a larger minimum frame size, and switched Ethernet removes the need for the collision algorithm by using micro-segmentation to create mini-collision domains. So, first we'll review the basics of Ethernet networking and then move on to how to use the various flavors of Ethernet networking in your access, distribution, and core networks.

After you have learned about the different Ethernet cable media types, you'll learn how to log in and configure both a set-based switch and an IOS-based switch. The set-based switch we will focus on is the modular 4000 series, and the IOS switches are the new 2950 and the excellent 3550, which supports several bells and whistles. Those old hands among you will notice the retirement of the 1900 series switches, which ran both a version of the IOS and a menu interface. You will also see that the 5000 series has gone as the same way. So long, old friend.

On the accompanying CD, there's a hands-on lab in which you'll connect the switches together and configure them.

Understanding Cable Media

To know when and how to use the different kinds of cable media, you need to understand what users *do* on the corporate network. The way to find this information is to ask questions. After that, you can use monitoring equipment to really see what is going on inside the network cabling. Before you deploy an application on a corporate network, carefully consider bandwidth requirements as well as latency issues. More and more users need to compete for bandwidth on the network because of bandwidth-consuming applications. Although layer 2 switches break up collision domains and certainly help a congested network if correctly designed and installed, you must also understand the different cable media types available and where to use each type for maximum efficiency. That's where this chapter comes in.

The Background of IEEE Ethernet

In 1980, the Digital Equipment Corporation, Intel, and Xerox (DIX) consortium created the original Ethernet. Predictably, Ethernet_II followed and was released in 1984. The standards-setting organization, the Institute of Electrical and Electronics Engineers (IEEE), termed this the 802.*x* project. The 802.*x* project was initially divided into three groups:

- The High Level Interface (HILI) group became the 802.1 committee and was responsible for high-level internetworking protocols and management.
- The Logical Link Control (LLC) group became the 802.2 committee and focused on end-to-end link connectivity and the interface between the higher layers and the medium-access-dependent layers.
- The Data Link and Medium Access Control (DLMAC) group became responsible for the medium-access protocols. The DLMAC ended up splitting into three committees:
  - 802.3 for Ethernet
  - 802.4 for Token Bus
  - 802.5 for Token Ring

DEC, Intel, and Xerox pushed Ethernet, while Burroughs, Concord Data Systems, Honeywell, Western Digital—and later, General Motors and Boeing—pushed 802.4. IBM took on 802.5.

The IEEE then created the 802.3 subcommittee, which came up with an Ethernet standard that happens to be almost identical to the earlier Ethernet_II version of the protocol. The two differ only in their descriptions of the Data Link layer. Ethernet_II has a Type field, whereas 802.3 has a Length field. Even so, they're both common in their Physical layer specifications, MAC addressing, and understanding of the LLC layer's responsibilities.

See *CCNA: Cisco Certified Network Associate Study Guide, 4th edition*, by Todd Lammle (Sybex, 2004) for a detailed explanation of Ethernet frame types.

Ethernet_II and 802.3 both define a bus-topology LAN at 10Mbps, and the cabling defined in these standards is identical:

10Base2/Thinnet Segments up to 185 meters using RG58 coax at 50 ohms.

10Base5/Thicknet Segments up to 500 meters using RG8 or RG11 at 50 ohms.

10BaseT/UTP All hosts connect by using unshielded twisted-pair (UTP) cable with a central device (a hub or switch). Category 3 UTP is specified to support up to 10Mbps, Category 5 to 100Mbps, Category 5e to 1000Mbps, and Category 6 to 1000Mbps.

Category 5e and Category 6 cables are relatively new. While both are designed to support data running at up to 1000 Mbits/second, the quality of the cables differs in that Category 5e still has performance specified at 100MHz and Category 6 has the performance specified at speeds of up to 250MHz. Category 6, if installed to the correct standard, provides better quality signal transfer.

LAN Segmentation Using Switches

Ethernet is the most popular type of network in the world and will continue to be so, ensured by the low cost of implementation coupled with the huge installed base of equipment. It is therefore important for you to understand how hubs and switches work within an Ethernet network.

By using *switched Ethernet* in layer 2 of your network, you no longer have to share bandwidth with the different departments in the corporation. With hubs, all devices have to share the same bandwidth (collision domain), which can cause havoc in today's networks. This makes a switched Ethernet LAN much more scalable than one based on shared Ethernet.

Hubs are layer 1 devices. The best way to think of them is as multi-port repeaters, repeating everything that comes their way, including runt frames, giant frames, and frames failing the frame check sequence at the end.

Even though layer 2 switches break the network into smaller collision domains, the network is still one large broadcast domain. Nowadays, switched Ethernet has largely replaced shared hubs in the networking world because each connection from a host to the switch is in its own collision domain. This is often referred to as *micro-segmentation* (as opposed to *segmentation*, where a legacy bridge may have created only two LAN segments). Remember that, with shared hubs, the network was one large collision domain and one large broadcast domain, whereas layer 2 switches break up collision domains on each port, but all ports are still considered, by default, to be in one large broadcast domain. Only virtual LANs, covered in Chapter 14, "VLANs, Trunks, and VTP," break up broadcast domains in a layer 2 switched network.

Switched Ethernet is a good way to allocate dedicated 10Mbps, 100Mbps, or 1000Mbps connections to each user. By also running full-duplex Ethernet, you can theoretically double the throughput on each link. In the next sections, we'll discuss how Ethernet is used in your network, the differences between the Ethernet types, and the half- and full-duplex options.

Using Ethernet Media in Your Network

In this section, you'll learn the difference between the Ethernet media types and how to use them in your networks. We'll cover the following Ethernet types:

- 10BaseT
- FastEthernet
- Gigabit Ethernet

10BaseT

10BaseT stands for 10 million bits per second (Mbps), baseband technology, twisted-pair. This Ethernet technology has the highest installed base of any network in the world. It runs the carrier sense multiple access collision detection (CSMA/CD) protocol and, if correctly installed, is an efficient network. However, if it gets too large and the network is not segmented correctly, problems occur. It is important to understand collision and broadcast domains and how to correctly design the network with switches and routers.

Using 10BaseT at the Access Layer

10BaseT Ethernet is typically used only at the access layer, and even then, FastEthernet (100BaseT) is quickly replacing it as the prices for 100BaseT continue to drop. It would be poor design to place 10BaseT at the distribution or core layers. You need transits that are much faster than 10BaseT at these layers to aggregate user traffic.

Distance

The distance that 10BaseT can run and be within specification is 100 meters (330 feet). The 100 meters includes the following:

- 5 meters from the switch to the patch panel
- 90 meters from the patch panel to the office punch-down block
- 5 meters from the punch-down block to the desktop connection

This doesn't mean that you can't run more than 100 meters on a cable run; it just is not guaranteed to work.

FastEthernet

FastEthernet is 10 times faster than 10Mbps Ethernet. The great thing about FastEthernet is that, like 10BaseT, it is still based on the CSMA/CD signaling. This means that you can run 10BaseT and 100BaseT on the same network without any problems. What a nice upgrade path this type of network can give you. You can put all your clients on 10BaseT and upgrade only the servers to 100BaseT if you need to. However, you can't even buy a PC that doesn't have a 10/100 Ethernet card in it anymore, so you really don't need to worry about compatibility and speed issues from the user's perspective.

Using FastEthernet at All Three Layers

FastEthernet works great at all layers of the hierarchical model. It can be used to give high performance to PCs and other hosts at the access layer, provide connectivity from the access layer to the distribution layer switches, and connect the distribution layer switches to the core network. Connecting a server block to the core layer would need, at a minimum, FastEthernet or maybe even Gigabit Ethernet.

IEEE Specifications for FastEthernet

There are two different specifications for FastEthernet, but the IEEE 802.3u is the most popular. The 802.3u specification is 100Mbps over Category 5, twisted-pair (typically just Category 5 or 5-plus is used for FastEthernet). The second Ethernet specification, called 802.12, used a different signaling technique, called Demand Priority Access Method (DPAM), which was more efficient than the CSMA/CD access method. The IEEE passed both methods in June 1995, but because 802.3 Ethernet had such a strong name in the industry, 802.12—also called 100VG-AnyLAN—has virtually disappeared from the market. As with the Macintosh and NetWare operating systems, it doesn't mean anything if you have a better product; it matters only how you market it.

The IEEE 802.3u committee's goals can be summarized as follows:

- Provide seamless integration with the installed base.
- Provide 100BaseT at only two times (or less) the cost of 10BaseT.
- Increase aggregate bandwidth.
- Provide multiple-vendor standardization and operability.
- Provide time-bounded delivery.

Precisely speaking, 802.12 is usually referred to as 100VG-AnyLAN. 100 is for 100Mbps, VG is for voice-grade cable, and AnyLAN is because it was supposed to be able to use either Ethernet or token-ring frame formats. The main selling point—the use of all four pairs of voice-grade cable—was also its main drawback. This feature is useful if all you have is VG, but it's overshadowed completely by 100BaseT if you have Category 5 cable or better. Developed at the time that Category 5 was becoming popular, wide-scale implementations of new cabling systems just completely sidelined 802.12.

Media Independent Interface (MII)

FastEthernet requires a different interface than 10BaseT Ethernet. 10Mbps Ethernet used the attachment unit interface (AUI) to connect Ethernet segments. This provided a decoupling of the MAC layer from the different requirements of the various Physical layer topologies, which allowed the MAC to remain constant but meant the Physical layer could support any existing and new technologies. However, the AUI interface could not support 100Mbps Ethernet because of the high frequencies involved. 100BaseT needed a new interface, and the media independent interface (MII) provides it.

100BaseT actually created a new subinterface between the Physical layer and the Data Link layer, called the Reconciliation Sublayer (RS). The RS maps the 1s and 0s to the MII interface. The MII uses a nibble, which is defined as 4 bits. AUI used only 1 bit at a time. Data transfers across the MII at one nibble per clock cycle, which is 25MHz. 10Mbps uses a 2.5MHz clock.

Full-Duplex Ethernet and FastEthernet

Full-duplex Ethernet can both transmit and receive simultaneously and uses point-to-point connections. It is typically referred to as "collision free" because it doesn't share bandwidth with any other devices. Frames sent by two nodes cannot collide because physically separate transmit and receive circuits are between the nodes.

Both 10Mbps and 100Mbps Ethernet use four of the eight pins available in standard Category 5 UTP cable. Pin 1 on one side and pin 3 on the other are linked, as are pins 2 and 6. When the connection is configured for half duplex, the data can flow in only one direction at a time, while with full duplex, data can come and go without collisions because the receive and send channels are separate.

Full duplex is available when connected to a switch but not to a hub. Full duplex is also available on 10Mbps, 100Mbps, and Gigabit Ethernet. Because it eliminates collisions, a full-duplex connection will disable the collision detection function on the port.

Using Full-Duplex Ethernet in the Distribution Layer

Full-duplex Ethernet provides equal bandwidth in both directions. But because users typically work with client/server applications using read/write asymmetrical traffic, arguably the best performance increase gained by full-duplex connectivity would be in the distribution layer, not necessarily in the access layer. Nonetheless, the ease with which it can be implemented and the increase in throughput—no matter how incremental—means that many networks run full duplex throughout the network.

Full duplex with flow control was created to avoid packets being dropped if the buffers on an interface fill up before all packets can be processed. However, some vendors might not interoperate, and the buffering might have to be handled by upper-layer protocols instead.

Auto-Negotiation

Auto-negotiation is a process that enables clients and switches to agree on a link capability. This is used to determine the link speed as well as the duplex being used. The auto-negotiation process uses priorities to set the link configuration. Obviously, if both a client and a switch port can use 100Mbps, full-duplex connectivity, that would be the highest priority ranking, whereas half-duplex, 10Mbps Ethernet would be the lowest ranking.

Auto-negotiation uses Fast Link Pulse (FLP), which is an extension to the Normal Link Pulse (NLP) standard used to verify link integrity. NLP is part of the original 10BaseT standard. Commonly, these auto-negotiation protocols do not work that well, and you would be better off to configure the switch and NICs to run in a dedicated mode instead of letting the clients and switches auto-negotiate. Later in this chapter, we'll show you how to configure your switches with both the speed and duplex options.

Auto-negotiation is one of the most common causes of frame check sequence (FCS) and alignment errors. If two devices are connected and one is set to full-duplex and the other to half-duplex, one is sending and receiving on the same two wires while the other is using two wires to send and two wires to receive. Statically configuring the duplex on the ports eliminates this problem.

Intermittent connectivity issues can often be traced to auto-negotiation problems. If a single user occasionally has long connectivity outages, statically setting speed and duplex on both ends often helps.

Distance

FastEthernet does have some drawbacks. It uses the same signaling techniques as 10Mbps Ethernet, so it has the same distance constraints. In addition, 10Mbps Ethernet can use up to four repeaters, whereas FastEthernet can use only one or two, depending on the type of repeater. Table 13.1 shows a comparison of FastEthernet technologies.

Of course, the issue of the number of Ethernet repeaters in use is really only of concern when using a hub-based half-duplex system. Once we move to a switched Ethernet environment, the collision domains are considerably reduced in size and we don't need repeaters, and the use of full-duplex Ethernet removes the need to detect collisions entirely, changing the CSMA/CD operation to just CSMA.

TABLE 13.1 Comparison of FastEthernet Technologies

Technology	Wiring Category	Distance
100BaseTX	Category 5 UTP wiring; Categories 6 and 7 are now available. Category 6 is sometimes referred to as Cat 5 plus. Two-pair wiring.	100 meters
100BaseT4	Four-pair wiring, using UTP Category 3, 4, or 5.	100 meters
100BaseFX	Multimode fiber (MMF) with 62.5-micron fiber-optic core with a 125-micron outer cladding (62.5/125).	400 meters

Gigabit Ethernet

In the corporate market, *Gigabit Ethernet* is the new hot thing. What is so great about Gigabit is that it can use the same network that your 10Mbps and 100Mbps Ethernet now use. You certainly do have to worry about distance constraints, but what a difference it can make in just a server farm alone!

Just think how nice it would be to have all your servers connected to Ethernet switches with Gigabit Ethernet and all your users using 100BaseT-switched connections. Of course, all your switches would connect with Gigabit links as well. Add xDSL and cable to connect to the Internet, and you have more bandwidth than you ever could have imagined just a few years ago. Will it be enough bandwidth a few years from now? Probably not. If you have the bandwidth, users will find a way to use it.

Parkinson's Law states that data expands to fill the space available for storage, but experience shows that this law can be equally applied to bandwidth.

Using Gigabit Ethernet in the Enterprise

Cisco's Enterprise model shows a number of different blocks, as defined in Chapter 12, "The Campus Network." Gigabit Ethernet has value in a number of these different blocks.

The Server Module is a natural choice, because the high demand placed on the network bandwidth by some modern applications would certainly be able to utilize gigabit availability.

The Building Distribution Module carries large amounts of inter-VLAN traffic, and as the 20/80 rule kicks in even more, this additional traffic would benefit from gigabit-speed data transfer.

The Core Module is responsible for connecting all other modules, and it is certain that gigabit throughput would suit the three general principles of core data requirements: speed, speed, and more speed!

The Management Module, Building Module, and Edge Distribution Module are less likely at the moment to need gigabit speeds. Most management machines have less data to transfer than applications, most users would be more than satisfied with 100Mbps full duplex, and the slower WAN speeds at the edge of the network does not need serving by gigabit transfer. Nonetheless, there is rarely such a thing as an average network, and you would be well advised to consider carefully where you might get the best from this exciting technology.

Protocol Architecture

Gigabit Ethernet became an IEEE 802.3 standard in the summer of 1998. The standard was called 802.3z. Gigabit is a combination of Ethernet 802.3 and Fiber Channel and uses Ethernet framing the same way 10BaseT and FastEthernet do. This means that not only is it fast, but it can run on the same network as older Ethernet technology, which provides a nice migration plan. The goal of the IEEE 802.3z was to maintain compatibility with the 10Mbps and 100Mbps existing Ethernet network. They needed to provide a seamless operation to forward frames between segments running at different speeds. The committee kept the minimum and maximum frame lengths the same. However, they needed to change the CSMA/CD for half-duplex operation from its 512-bit times to help the distance that Gigabit Ethernet could run.

Will Gigabit ever run to the desktop? Maybe. Probably. People said that FastEthernet would never run to the desktop when it came out, but it's now common. If Gigabit is run to the desktop, however, it's hard to imagine what we'll need to run the backbone with. 10000BaseT to the rescue! Yes, 10 Gigabit Ethernet is out!

In fact, there is now a 10 Gigabit Ethernet Alliance—a group of vendors and other interested parties who together have created the technology behind IEEE 802.3ae, the 10 Gigabit Ethernet standard.

Comparing 10BaseT, FastEthernet, and Gigabit Ethernet

There are some major differences between FastEthernet and Gigabit Ethernet. FastEthernet uses the MII, and Gigabit uses the gigabit media independent interface (GMII). 10BaseT used the AUI. A new interface was designed to help FastEthernet scale to 100Mbps, and this interface was redesigned for Gigabit Ethernet. The GMII uses an eight-bit data path instead of the four-bit path that FastEthernet MII uses. The clocking must operate at 125MHz to achieve the 1Gbps data rate.

Time Slots

Because Ethernet networks are sensitive to the round-trip-delay constraint of CSMA/CD, time slots are extremely important. Remember that in 10BaseT and 100BaseT, the time slots were 512-bit times. However, this is not feasible for Gigabit because the time slot would be only 20 meters in length. To make Gigabit usable on a network, the time slots were extended to 512 bytes (4096-bit times!). However, the operation of full-duplex Ethernet was not changed at all. Table 13.2 compares the new Gigabit Ethernet technologies.

TABLE 13.2 Comparison of Gigabit Ethernet Technologies

Technology	Wiring Category	Cable Distance
1000BaseCX	Copper-shielded twisted-pair	25 meters
1000BaseT	Copper Category 5, four-pair wiring, UTP	100 meters
1000BaseSX	MMF using 62.5 and 50-micron core, uses a 780-nanometer laser	260 meters
1000BaseLX	Single-mode fiber that uses a 9-micron core, 1300-nanometer laser	From 3 kilometers up to 10 kilometers
1000BaseZX	9-micron single-mode fiber or disposition-shifted fiber	Up to 100 kilometers

Real World Scenario

Jumbo Frames

If Gigabit Ethernet is used from source to destination, you might consider using jumbo frames. These are Ethernet frames that are 9000 bytes long. Jumbo frames don't work well if Gigabit is not used from end to end because fragmentation will take place, causing a small amount of latency. Although jumbo frames aren't likely to be used to the desktop, they can speed up the process of data transfer between servers. An e-commerce web server that makes a lot of calls to a database and gets large amounts of data at once would be a good candidate.

Connecting and Logging In to a Switch

The new range of Cisco switches—the 2950 and 3550—run a version of IOS. This makes configuring the switch very similar to configuring a router. The 4000 series is still set based, which means you use the command `set` to configure the router. Throughout the rest of this book, we'll show you commands for these switches.

As a general guideline, you would be expected to use the 2950 as an access layer switch (because of its cheap per-port cost) and then utilize the more powerful 3550 at the distribution layer. Although these are only rough guidelines, the 3550 does support an internal routing option, which gives it the additional features essential in a modern distribution switch, and the 2950 has a number of different port types and densities, which provide relatively cheap connections for desktop PCs.

There are two types of operating systems that run on Cisco switches:

IOS based You can configure the Catalyst 2950 and 3550 switches from a command-line interface (CLI) that is almost identical to the one used on Cisco routers. The only differences are some of the commands, which are switch-specific.

Set based Uses older, set-based CLI configuration commands. The current Cisco switches that use the set-based commands are the 4000 and the 6000 series.

The shelf life of CatOS—the set-based operating system installed on older switches such as the 4000, 5000, and 6000 series—is now very short. Although Cisco has not publicly stated that it is *not* included in the current exam, my feeling is that questions on CatOS will become fewer until they gradually disappear. I have left CatOS configuration examples and questions in this revision of the book because you may come across them either during the exam or "in the wild," but I would advise you to check the Cisco website regularly for information regarding its demise.

Cabling the Switch Block Devices

You can physically connect to a Cisco Catalyst switch by connecting either to the console port or to an Ethernet port, just as you would with a router.

Connecting to the Console Port

The 2950, 3550, and 4000 series switches all have a console port on the back, which is an RJ-45 port. The console cables for these switches are rolled cables. (Older 5000 series switches have a console connector that uses only an RS-232-type connector, which comes with the switch when purchased.)

After you connect to the console port, you need to start a terminal emulation program, such as HyperTerminal in Windows. The settings are as follows:

- 9600bps
- 8 data bits
- No parity
- 1 stop bit
- No flow control

Do not connect an Ethernet cable, ISDN, or live telephone line into the console port. The voltage levels are higher, and the result may well be a burned-out console port.

Connecting to an Ethernet Port

The Catalyst 2950 and 3550 series switches have a number of different arrangements of ports. They are not modular in the sense that the 4000 series switches are. All ports are at least 10/100Mbps, and some also support 1000Mbps. Connecting hosts to any of these ports requires a straight-through cable, but to connect the ports to another switch as an uplink, you must use a crossover cable.

The Catalyst 4000 switches can run either 10Mbps or 100Mbps on any port, depending on the type of cards you buy. Gigabit cards are also available. The supervisor cards always take the first slot and have two FastEthernet or Gigabit Ethernet ports for uplinks using either copper or fiber. All devices connected into either the 2950/3550 or 4000 series switches must be within 100 meters (330 feet) of the switch port.

When connecting devices such as workstations, servers, printers, and routers to the switch, you must use a straight-through cable. Use a crossover cable to connect between switches.

When a device is connected to a port, the port status light-emitting diode (LED) light (also called the port link LED or link state LED) on the switching module panel comes on and stays on. If the light does not come on, the other end might be off or there might be a cable problem.

Also, if a light comes on and off, a speed matching or duplex problem may exist. I'll show you how to check that in the next section.

4000 Switch Startup

The 4000 series switch loads the software image from flash and then asks you to enter a password, even if there isn't one set. Press Enter, and you will see a `Console>` prompt. At this point, you can enter Enable mode and configure the switch by using **set** commands:

```
BOOTROM Version 5.1(2), Dated Apr 26 1999 10:41:04
BOOT date: 08/02/02 BOOT time: 08:49:03
Uncompressing NMP image.  This will take a minute...
Downloading epld sram device please wait ...
Programming successful for Altera 10K10 SRAM EPLD
Updating epld flash version from 0000 to 0600

Cisco Systems Console

Enter password: [Press return here]
2001 Mar 22 22:22:56 %SYS-5-MOD_OK:Module 1 is online
2001 Mar 22 22:23:06 %SYS-5-MOD_OK:Module 2 is online

Console>
```

2950 Switch Startup

When you connect to the 2950 console, the IOS is booted. As the switch boots, it will show diagnostics on the screen. It displays the version of code, information about the flash storage, various part and serial numbers, and so on. If there is no saved configuration file, you are presented with an option to enter the basic configuration using a process called setup:

```
System serial number: FOC0650W11A
         --- System Configuration Dialog ---
Would you like to enter the initial configuration dialog? [yes/no]:
```

If you enter **yes**, then the following menu is displayed:

```
Would you like to enter the initial configuration dialog? [yes/no]: yes

At any point you may enter a question mark '?' for help.
Use ctrl-c to abort configuration dialog at any prompt.
Default settings are in square brackets '[]'.


Basic management setup configures only enough connectivity
```

```
for management of the system, extended setup will ask you
to configure each interface on the system

Would you like to enter basic management setup? [yes/no]:
```

The menu is self-explanatory, but quite limited. You can set the switch name, enter passwords, set up vlan1, and assign IP addresses to interfaces. The rest of the configurations are defaults, and to be honest, it is rare for anyone to use this method of configuration.

You can exit the setup mode at any time by pressing Ctrl+C, and you can enter the setup mode from the privileged mode by entering the command `setup`.

The alternative is to answer **no** to the option to enter setup, and then you are presented with the user-mode switch prompt:

```
Switch>
```

No passwords are set, and entering the command `enable` will take you to the privileged prompt:

```
Switch#
```

Cisco IOS- and Set-Based Commands

In this section, you'll learn how to configure the basics on both types of switches. Specifically, you'll learn how to do the following:

- Set the passwords.
- Set the host name.
- Configure the IP address and subnet mask.
- Identify the interfaces.
- Set a description on the interfaces.
- Configure the port speed and duplex.
- Verify the configuration.
- Erase the switch configuration.

Setting the Passwords

The first thing you should do is configure the passwords. You don't want unauthorized users connecting to the switch. You can set both the user-mode and privileged-mode passwords, just as you can with a router. However, you use different commands.

As with any Cisco router, the login (user-mode) password can be used to verify authorization of the switch, including Telnet and the console port. The enable password is used to allow access to the switch so the configuration can be viewed or changed.

4000 Series Set-Based Switch

To configure the two passwords on a 4000 series switch, use the command `set password` for the user-mode password and the command `set enablepass` for the enable password:

```
2001 Mar 21 06:31:54 %SYS-5-MOD_OK:Module 1 is online
2001 Mar 21 06:31:54 %SYS-5-MOD_OK:Module 2 is online

Console> en

Enter password:
Console> (enable) set password ?
Usage: set password
Console> (enable) set password [Press enter]
Enter old password:
Enter new password:
Retype new password:
Password changed.
```

When you see the `Enter old password` prompt, you can leave it blank and press Enter if you don't have a password set. The output for the `Enter new password` prompt doesn't show on the console screen. If you want to clear the user-mode (login) password, type in the old password and then just press Enter when you're asked for a new password.

To set the enable password, type the command **`set enablepass`** and then press Enter:

```
Console> (enable) set enablepass
Enter old password:
Enter new password:
Retype new password:
Password changed.
Console> (enable)
```

You can type **`exit`** at this point to log out of the switch completely, which will enable you to test your new passwords.

2950 and 3550 Switches

The commands for setting the passwords are the same as for a router. Those of you used to configuring the password levels on a 1900 switch will find that they are optional on an IOS-based device. The enable secret password supersedes the enable password and automatically encrypts the displayed password by default.

```
Switch>enable
Switch#conf t
Enter configuration commands, one per line.  End with CNTL/Z.
Switch(config)#enable ?
```

```
  last-resort  Define enable action if no TACACS servers respond
  password     Assign the privileged level password
  secret       Assign the privileged level secret
  use-tacacs   Use TACACS to check enable passwords
```

As you can see from the script, the password can be set locally or can be assigned using a protocol called TACACS.

```
Switch(config)#enable secret ?
  0      Specifies an UNENCRYPTED password will follow
  5      Specifies an ENCRYPTED secret will follow
  LINE   The UNENCRYPTED (cleartext) 'enable' secret
  level  Set exec level password
```

Entering the password with no additional options causes the password to be encrypted automatically, thus preventing it from being read by unauthorized viewers. You can see that `san-fran` has become `$1$dytq$1j7l6VJbtocypNs1DgW2X.`

```
Switch(config)#enable secret san-fran
Switch(config)#^Z
Switch#show running-config

Building configuration...

Current configuration : 1404 bytes
!
version 12.1
no service pad
service timestamps debug uptime
service timestamps log uptime
no service password-encryption
!
hostname Switch
!
enable secret 5 $1$dytq$1j7l6VJbtocypNs1DgW2X.
!
```

Because the enable secret password takes precedence over the standard enable password, it is common practice for many users to set only the enable secret. More complex security is commonly obtained using TACACS.

The remote access Telnet (vty) password prevents unauthorized access by other network users. By default, this is disabled, and the `show running-config` command will display no vty numbers. The passwords are set using the line mode, after which they will appear, as in the following example:

```
Switch#conf t
Enter configuration commands, one per line.  End with CNTL/Z.
Switch(config)#line vty 0 4
Switch(config-line)#login
% Login disabled on line 1, until 'password' is set
% Login disabled on line 2, until 'password' is set
% Login disabled on line 3, until 'password' is set
% Login disabled on line 4, until 'password' is set
% Login disabled on line 5, until 'password' is set
Switch(config-line)#password telnet
Switch(config-line)#^Z
Switch#
```

Now the running configuration displays both the lines configured for access and the password:

```
Switch#show running-config
Building configuration...

Current configuration : 1448 bytes

[output omitted]

line con 0
line vty 0 4
 password telnet
 login
line vty 5 15
 login
!
end
```

Setting the Host Name

The host name on a switch, as well as on a router, is only locally significant. A good rule of thumb is to name the switch after the location it is serving.

In this case, this means that the switch's host name doesn't have any function whatsoever on the network or for name resolution. However, it is helpful to set a host name on a switch so you can identify the switch when connecting to it.

Management applications such as Cisco Works, and processes such as the Cisco Discovery Protocol (CDP), use the host name of a device to differentiate it from other devices. Not changing the host name can lead to some confusion and cause more work to find out just which "switch" is having problems.

2950 and 3550 Switches

The switch command to set the host name is exactly as it is with any router. The 2950 and 3550 begin life with a device name of "Switch." Setting the host name is simple:

```
switch#
switch#conf t
Enter configuration commands, one per line.  End with CNTL/Z.
switch(config)#hostname Terry_2950
Terry_2950(config)#^Z
Terry_2950#
```

Setting the IP Information

You do not have to set any IP configuration on the switch to make it work. You can just plug in devices, and they should start working, as they do on a hub. IP address information is set so that you can either manage the switch via Telnet or other management software, or configure the switch with different VLANs and other network functions.

4000 Series Set-Based Switch

To set the IP address information on a 4000 series switch, configure the supervisor engine that is plugged into slot 1 of every switch. This is called the in-band logical interface. Use the command `set interface sc0`:

```
Terry_4000> (enable) set interface sc0 172.16.10.17 255.255.255.0
Interface sc0 IP address and netmask set.
```

By default, the switch is configured for VLAN 1, which can be seen by using the `show interface` command. Notice also that the broadcast address for the subnet shows up and that you can change it by entering it with the `set interface sc0` command (but we can think of only one reason that you would want to change it—to mess with the people in your MIS department):

```
Terry_4000> (enable) show interface
sl0: flags=51<UP,POINTOPOINT,RUNNING>
slip 0.0.0.0 dest 0.0.0.0
sc0: flags=63<UP,BROADCAST,RUNNING>
vlan 1 inet 172.16.10.17 netmask 255.255.255.0 broadcast 172.16.10.255
Terry_4000> (enable)
```

The command `set interface sl0 ip_address mask` would be used for modem access to the switch. This enables addressing on the Serial Line Internet Protocol (SLIP) process. Before accessing the switch via a modem, the modem process must be enabled on the switch by using the `set system modem enable` command. The modem operates at a speed of 9600bps by default.

Real World Scenario

Remote Management

Many organizations have a large number of switches that need to be managed, and administrators often need access directly to the console port for remote management. A setup that allows remote access direct to the console port is desirable because some problems will prevent Telnet or management access, which means you have to physically be there. Not something you want to do at 3 A.M.!

Rather than installing several modems and telephone lines, consider an access server. A 3600 with asynchronous modules, for example, can have over 100 such connections for up to 16 devices at a time and also allow for security features such as a RADIUS or TACACS+ authentication server or an IOS firewall configuration.

2950 and 3550 Switches

Cisco recommends that you use VLAN 1 for management of the switch device and then create other VLANs for users. By default, all interfaces are in VLAN 1, supporting the plug-and-play operation of switches. To set the IP configuration, you should use the command `ip address` in interface mode, as shown here:

```
Terry_2950#conf t
Enter configuration commands, one per line.  End with CNTL/Z.
Terry_2950 (config)#int vlan 1
Terry_2950 (config-if)#ip address 172.16.1.1 255.255.255.0
Terry_2950(config-if)#no shut
Terry_2950 (config-if)#^Z
Terry_2950#
```

Don't worry just yet what a VLAN is; we will be covering that in Chapter 15, "Layer 2 Switching and the Spanning Tree Protocol (STP)." For the moment, just concentrate on getting the switch up and running, using as many defaults as possible.

Remember that as far as IP is concerned, the switch is simply another host. This means that the default gateway should also be set, and the command is `ip default-gateway`, which is a global-mode command:

```
Terry_2950(config)#ip default-gateway 172.16.1.254
Terry_2950(config)#^Z
Terry_2950#

Terry_2950#sho run
Building configuration...

[output cut]

interface Vlan1
 ip address 172.16.1.1 255.255.255.0
 no ip route-cache
!
ip default-gateway 172.16.1.254
ip http server
!
Terry_2950#
```

It is possible to assign the IP address to any VLAN, but if you assign another IP address to a different VLAN on a 2950, the original IP address is immediately stripped off VLAN 1 and the VLAN is shut. If you are connected to the switch via a Telnet connection, you will be cut off from the switch. So reassigning the IP address to a different VLAN on a 2950 switch should only be carried out when connected to the console port.

Identifying Switch Interfaces

It is important to understand how to access switch ports. The 4000 series uses the `slot/port` command. The IOS-based switches use the `type slot/port` command.

4000 Series Set-Based Switch

You can use the `show` command to view port statistics on a 4000 switch. Notice that, by default, the duplex and speed of the port are both set to `auto`. Also, typically the ports on a 4000 and 6000 series switch can be enabled, but it might be necessary to configure the ports so that they can be enabled with the `set port enable` command. You can turn off any port with the `set port disable` command as follows:

```
Terry_4000> (enable) show port ?
Usage: show port
```

```
       show port <mod_num>
       show port <mod_num/port_num>
Terry_4000> (enable) show port 2/1
Port  Name   Status  Vlan  Level  Duplex Speed  Type
----- -------------- ----------- ------- ------------
 2/1        connect   2    normal  auto  auto 10/100BaseTX

Terry_4000> (enable) set port disable 2/1
Port 2/1 disabled.
Terry_4000> (enable) show port 2/1
Port  Name    Status     Vlan    Level  Duplex Speed  Type
----- ---------------- -------- ------- ------ ------------
 2/1          disabled    1      normal  auto  auto 10/100BaseTX

Terry_4000> (enable) set port enable 2/1
Port 2/1 enabled.
Terry_4000> (enable) show port 2/1
Port  Name   Status     Vlan      Level  Duplex  Speed Type
---- ------ --------- ---------- ----- ------- ------------
 2/1        connect     1        normal  auto    auto 10/100BaseTX
```

The command `show config` displays the complete current configuration of the set-based switch.

2950 and 3550 Switches

These switches take the *`type slot/port`* command with either the `interface` command or the `show` command. The `interface` command enables you to set interface-specific configurations. As the range of 2950 and 3550 switches increases, it may be that several slots are available. The following example demonstrates a 2950:

```
Terry_2950#config t
Enter configuration commands, one per line.  End with CNTL/Z
Terry_2950(config)#interface fastEthernet ?
   <0-2>  FastEthernet interface number
Terry_2950(config)#interface fastEthernet 0/?
   <1-24>  FastEthernet interface number
Terry_2950(config)#interface fastEthernet 0/1
Terry_2950(config-if)#?
Interface configuration commands:
  arp                  Set arp type (arpa, probe, snap) or timeout
```

```
  bandwidth           Set bandwidth informational parameter
  carrier-delay       Specify delay for interface transitions
  cdp                 CDP interface subcommands

[output cut]

  spanning-tree       Spanning Tree Subsystem
  speed               Configure speed operation.
  storm-control       storm configuration
  switchport          Set switching mode characteristics
  timeout             Define timeout values for this interface
```

To configure the FastEthernet ports, the command is `interface fastethernet 0/#`:

You can switch between interfaces by using the `interface fa 0/#` command. Notice that we demonstrate the following commands with spaces or without—it makes no difference.

```
Terry_2950(config-if)#interface fa 0/2
Terry_2950(config-if)#interface fa0/3
Terry_2950(config-if)#exit
```

You can view the ports with the `show interface` command:

```
Terry_2950#show interface fa0/1
FastEthernet0/1 is down, line protocol is down
  Hardware is Fast Ethernet, address is 000b.be53.2c01 (bia 000b.be53.2c01)
  MTU 1500 bytes, BW 10000 Kbit, DLY 1000 usec,
     reliability 255/255, txload 1/255, rxload 1/255
  Encapsulation ARPA, loopback not set
  Keepalive set (10 sec)
  Auto-duplex, Auto-speed
  input flow-control is off, output flow-control is off

[output cut]
```

Configuring Interface Descriptions

You can set a description on an interface, which will enable you to administratively set a name for each interface. As with the host name, the descriptions are only locally significant.

4000 Series Set-Based Switch

To set a description for the 4000 switch, use the `set port name` *`slot/port`* command. Spaces are allowed. You can set a name up to 21 characters long:

```
Terry_4000> (enable) set port name 2/1 Sales Printer
Port 2/1 name set.
Terry_4000> (enable) show port 2/1
Port  Name          Status   Vlan Level  Duplex Speed  Type
----- ------------- -------- ---- ----- ------- ------ -----
2/1  Sales Printer  notconnect 2  normal  auto  auto 10/100BaseTX
```

2950 and 3550 Switches

For the 2950 and 3550 series switches, use the `description` command. You cannot use spaces with the `description` command, but you can use underscores if you need to:

```
Terry_2950#config t
Enter configuration commands, one per line.  End with CNTL/Z.
Terry_2950(config)#interface fa0/1
Terry_2950(config-if)#description Finance_VLAN
Terry_2950(config-if)#interface fa0/2
Terry_2950(config-if)#description trunk_to_Building_4
Terry_2950(config-if)#
```

You can view the descriptions with either the `show interface` command or the `show running-config` command:

```
Terry_2950#sho run
Building configuration...

Current configuration : 1387 bytes
!
version 12.1
no service pad
service timestamps debug uptime
service timestamps log uptime
no service password-encryption
!
hostname Terry_2950
!
ip subnet-zero
!
spanning-tree extend system-id
```

```
!
interface FastEthernet0/1
 description Finance_VLAN
 no ip address
!
interface FastEthernet0/1
 description trunk_to_Building_4
 no ip address
[output cut]
```

Configuring the Port Speed and Duplex

By default, all 10/100 ports on the 2950, 3550, and 4000 are set to auto-detect the speed and duplex of the port.

4000 Series Set-Based Switch

Because the ports on a 10/100 card are auto-detect, you don't necessarily have to set the speed and duplex. However, there are situations where the auto-detect does not work correctly, and by setting the speed and duplex, you can stabilize the link:

```
Terry_4000> (enable) set port speed 2/1 ?
Usage: set port speed <mod_num/port_num>  <4|10|16|100|auto>
Terry_4000> (enable) set port speed 2/1 100
Port(s) 2/1 speed set to 100Mbps.
```

If you set the port speed to `auto`, both the speed and duplex are set to auto-negotiate the link. You can't set the duplex without first setting the speed:

```
Terry_4000> (enable) set port duplex 2/1 ?
Usage: set port duplex <mod_num/port_num> <full|half>
Terry_4000> (enable) set port duplex 2/1 full
Port(s) 2/1 set to full-duplex.
Terry_4000> (enable) ^C
```

Notice that the command Ctrl+C was used in the preceding code. This is a break sequence used on both types of switches.

You can view the duplex and speed with the `show port` command:

```
Terry_4000> (enable) show port 2/1
Port  Name          Status     Vlan   Level  Duplex Speed Type
----- ------------- ---------- ----- ------ ------- ----- -----
 2/1  Sales Printer notconnect  2    normal  full    100 10/100BaseTX
```

2950 and 3550 Switches

You can configure multiple options on any port. Speed can be set to 10, 100, or auto, and duplex can be set to half, full, or auto. You cannot configure duplex to full if the speed is set to `auto`. Here is an example from a 2950:

```
Terry_2950(config)#int fa0/1
Terry_2950(config-if)#speed ?
  10    Force 10 Mbps operation
  100   Force 100 Mbps operation
  auto  Enable AUTO speed configuration

Terry_2950(config-if)#speed 100
Terry_2950(config-if)#duplex ?
  auto  Enable AUTO duplex configuration
  full  Force full duplex operation
  half  Force half-duplex operation

Terry_2950(config-if)#duplex full
Terry_2950(config-if)#^Z
Terry_2950#

Terry_2950#sho int fa0/1
FastEthernet0/1 is down, line protocol is down
  Hardware is Fast Ethernet, address is 000b.be53.2c01 (bia 000b.be53.2c01)
  Description: Finance_VLAN
  MTU 1500 bytes, BW 10000 Kbit, DLY 1000 usec,
     reliability 255/255, txload 1/255, rxload 1/255
  Encapsulation ARPA, loopback not set
  Keepalive set (10 sec)
  Full-duplex, 100Mb/s
```

Verifying Connectivity

It is important to test the switch IP configuration. You can use the "big three" tests of Ping, Traceroute, and Telnet on all IOS-based switches and the 4000 and 6000 as well.

4000 Series Set-Based Switch

Use the IP utilities Ping, Telnet, and Traceroute to test the switch in the network as follows:

```
Terry_4000> (enable) ping 172.16.10.10
172.16.10.10 is alive
Terry_4000> (enable) telnet ?
```

```
Usage: telnet <host> [port]
       (host is IP alias or IP address in dot notation: a.b.c.d)
Terry_4000> (enable) traceroute
Usage: traceroute [-n] [-w wait] [-i initial_ttl] [-m max_ttl] [-p dest_port]
   [-q nqueries] [-t tos] host
   [data_size]
(wait = 1..300, initial_ttl = 1..255, max_ttl = 1..255
dest_port = 1..65535, nqueries = 1..1000, tos = 0..255
data_size = 0..1420, host is IP alias or IP address in
dot notation: a.b.c.d)
```

You can use the keystrokes Ctrl+Shift+**6**, then **X**, as an escape sequence.

2950 and 3550 Switches

You can use the Ping and Traceroute programs, and you can telnet into and out of any of the switches, as long as a password has been set up:

```
Terry_2950#ping 172.16.10.10
Sending 5, 100-byte ICMP Echos to 172.16.10.10, time out is 2 seconds:
!!!!!
Success rate is 100 percent (5/5), round-trip min/avg/max 0/2/10/ ms
```

You can omit the word `telnet` and just enter the host name or IP address of the target host, if you wish.

```
Terry_2950#conf t
Terry_2950(config)#ip host jack 172.16.10.10
Terry_2950(config)#^Z
Terry_2950#ping jack
Sending 5, 100-byte ICMP Echos to 172.16.10.10, time out is 2 seconds:
!!!!!
Success rate is 100 percent (5/5), round-trip min/avg/max 0/2/10/ms
```

Physical Troubleshooting

If the ping test doesn't work, make sure IP addressing and gateways are set up correctly. If they are, and no other part of the network is having problems, there is a good chance that the problem has to do with the Physical layer.

When testing Physical layer connectivity, it is important to focus the tests on the cabling and on the interfaces. In those instances when it is possible, test the port on the switch by plugging in a laptop directly. Plugging the patch cord into a different port can test the cable inside the wall. Finally, test the NIC by plugging the PC into a different cable run and port.

Saving and Erasing the Switch Configuration

The IOS-based switches hold their configuration in the `running-config` file. Using the command `copy running-config startup-config` copies this file to nonvolatile RAM (NVRAM), where it is saved as the `startup-config` file. The 4000 series switches automatically copy their configuration to NVRAM. You can delete the configurations if you want to start over.

It is also common to back up the configuration files on a Trivial File Transfer Protocol (TFTP) server, but despite your best efforts, things will go wrong at some time in any network. First, make sure that the TFTP server is available using the `ping` command. Ensure that access to the server directory is authorized and then enter the command **`copy running-config`** (or **`copy startup-config`**) **`tftp`**. A small menu follows, prompting you for the server IP address and filename to be stored. The router indicates a successful (or unsuccessful) file transfer.

2950 and 3550 Switches

The command `show running-config` (abbreviated here to `show run`), displays the configuration file the switch is currently implementing:

```
Terry_2950#show run
Building configuration...

Current configuration : 1411 bytes
!
version 12.1
no service pad
service timestamps debug uptime
service timestamps log uptime
no service password-encryption
!
hostname Terry_2950
!
[output cut]
```

The command `show startup-config` (abbreviated here to `show star`), displays the configuration file the switch has saved in NVRAM. It follows that this is the file that will be implemented when the switch is next started. Note that the two displays are slightly different:

```
Terry_2950#show star
Using 1411 out of 32768 bytes
!
version 12.1
no service pad
service timestamps debug uptime
service timestamps log uptime
no service password-encryption
!
hostname Terry_2950
!
[output cut]
```

To delete the startup configuration file, use the command `erase startup-config`. This will require a reboot of the switch to arrive at an empty configuration file. You can not erase the `running-config` file.

```
Terry_2950#erase ?
  flash:          Filesystem to be erased
  nvram:          Filesystem to be erased
  startup-config  Erase contents of configuration memory
```

4000 Series Set-Based Switch

To delete the configurations stored in NVRAM on the 4000 series switch, use the `clear config all` command. The `erase all` command deletes the contents of flash without warning. Be careful! Here is the code:

```
Terry_4000> (enable) clear config ?
Usage: clear config all
       clear config <mod_num>
       clear config rmon
       clear config extendedrmon
Terry_4000> (enable) clear config all
This command will clear all configuration in NVRAM.
This command will cause ifIndex to be reassigned on the next system startup.
Do you want to continue (y/n) [n]? y


System configuration cleared.
```

To delete the contents of flash, use the `erase all` command:

```
Terry_4000> (enable) erase all
FLASH on Catalyst:
Type              Address                  Location
Intel 28F016      20000000                 NMP (P3) 8MB SIM

Erasing flash sector...
Terry_4000> (enable)
Terry_4000> (enable) show flash
File      Version          Sector   Size    Built
--------- -------------- -------- ------- -------
```

Notice that when you type **`erase all`** and press Enter, the switch just starts erasing the flash and you can't break out of it. By using a `show flash` command, you can see that the contents of flash are now empty. You might not want to try this on your production switches. You can use the `copy tftp flash` command to reload the software.

Cisco has recently announced that all of their examinations now have simulation questions. It seems likely that these will become ever more sophisticated, with more complex configurations being required as time moves on, and there will be greater emphasis placed upon such questions. Make sure that you understand and are able to reproduce all of the commands in every chapter, because they could crop up in any one of several simulation questions. The hands-on labs on the accompanying CD will provide invaluable help if you carry them out honestly.

Summary

You can use several different types of Ethernet in a network, and it's very important that you remember the distance each type of Ethernet media can run. For instance, the distance that 10BaseT can run is 100 meters, or 330 feet. The 100 meters includes 5 meters from the switch to the patch panel, 90 meters from the patch panel to the office punch-down block, and 5 meters from the punch-down block to the desktop connection.

For FastEthernet, there are various specifications for each type. For 100BaseTX, Category 5 UTP wiring, Categories 5e, 6, and 7 are now available. Category 5e is sometimes referred to as Cat 5 plus. 100BaseTX requires two-pair wiring and a distance of 100 meters. 100BaseT4 requires four-pair wiring, using UTP Category 3, 4, or 5. The distance for 100BaseT4 is 100 meters. 100BaseFX requires multimode fiber (MMF) with 62.5-micron fiber-optic core and a 125-micron outer cladding (62.5/125). The distance for the 100BaseFX is 400 meters.

For Gigabit Ethernet, the specifications for each type also vary. For instance, the 1000BaseCX requires a copper-shielded twisted-pair and a distance of 25 meters. The 1000BaseT requires copper Category 5, four-pair wiring, UTP, and 100 meters distance. The 1000BaseSX requires MMF using 62.5 and 50-micron core, uses a 780-nanometer laser, and requires a distance of up to 260 meters. 1000BaseLX uses single-mode fiber with a 9-micron core and uses a 1300-nanometer laser. The distance for a 1000BaseLX is anywhere from 3 kilometers to 10 kilometers. Finally, the 1000BaseZX uses single-mode fiber with a 9-micron core or disposition-shifted fiber. The distance for a1000BaseZX is up to 100 kilometers.

You need to understand how to connect to and how to configure both a set-based switch and an IOS-based switch. It is not enough to just be able to copy down these commands and move on to the next section. The defaults, which are set on all Cisco switches, are there for the benefit of the plug-and-play kiddies—as a CCNP, you are expected to go far beyond that! You need to understand why these configurations are needed, so that you can make knowledge-based judgments on when to use the command options to move away from the default.

You can set host names and descriptions to identify your switch and the interfaces, enabling you to administer the network more efficiently. And you can control access to the switch in several ways, using console, Telnet, and enable passwords to protect against unauthorized users. You should also be able to configure an IP address and default gateway on each switch so that you can make remote connections, which allows you to manage your switch without having to stand next to it. Finally, you should be able to verify the configuration by performing connectivity tests around the network using the standard IP tools of Ping, Traceroute, and Telnet.

Exam Essentials

Understand how the set-based and IOS-based command lines are different. Set-based commands belong to a legacy operating system purchased by Cisco when they bought the original switching company, so they bear no resemblance to the Cisco IOS at all. The only three commands in use—`set`, `clear`, and `show`—are used for all purposes. Interface/port configurations, passwords, and all VLAN and trunking options are changed from the defaults using `set` commands. Configurations are removed using `clear` commands, and `show` commands are used to display configurations, interfaces, memory, and so on.

Newer switches, such as the 3550 and 2950, use the familiar Cisco router IOS command set. Password, host name, and other administrative commands are the same as for the router, and the only real difference is that because this is a switch, the command options may be reduced, omitting router specifics, such as routing, on the 2950 switches. The 3550 switches, which support native routing, and the 4000 and 6500 series running the native IOS upgrade actually support routing as well, and so they have a full set of IOS commands.

Understand physical network connectivity. Some cables are suitable for some tasks but not for others, and the characteristics of each cable help determine which tasks they should be used for. For instance, Ethernet cables can be straight-through, as used with PCs to switch connections, or crossover, as used for switch-to-switch links. You need to know the characteristics and limitations of each type of cable.

Understand logical network connectivity. There are several issues to confront with connectivity at layers 1 and 2. We know that hubs operate at layer 1 and switches operate at layer 2, which immediately identifies some major differences. For instance, a switch allows for full-duplex connectivity, but a hub does not. Also, turning on auto-detection for speed forces duplex into auto-detect mode.

VLANs, Trunks, and VTP

THE CCNP EXAM TOPICS COVERED IN THIS CHAPTER INCLUDE THE FOLLOWING:

- ✓ Describe LAN segmentation with VLANs.
- ✓ Ensure broadcast domain integrity by establishing VLANs.
- ✓ Configure access ports for static membership of single and multiple VLANs.
- ✓ Describe the different Trunking Protocols.
- ✓ Configure ports as 802.1Q trunks and verify their operation.
- ✓ Configure ports as ISL trunks and verify their operation.
- ✓ Understand the operation of VTPv1 and VTPv2, including the functions of domains, modes, advertisements, and pruning.
- ✓ Configure switches in VTP domains in server, client, and transparent modes.
- ✓ Understand local VLANs and end-to-end VLANs, and determine which to use.
- ✓ Design VLAN configurations with VTP for operation in a specific scenario.
- ✓ Understand managed VLAN services.
- ✓ Know the features and functionality of 802.1Q Tunneling (802.1QinQ) in service provider networks.
- ✓ Configure auxiliary VLANs with IP technology.

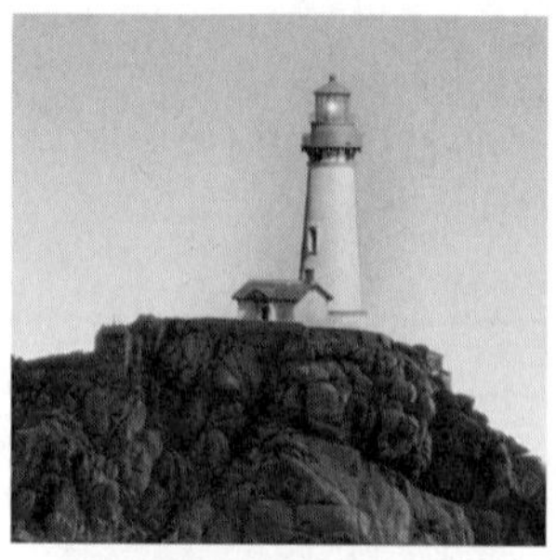

You likely already know that a LAN is a group of stations that use broadcast frames to share common services. Most legacy protocols use broadcasts to carry out simple administrative functions such as finding a server, advertising their services, and even acquiring naming and addressing information. These days, we can go much further using a virtual local area network (VLAN).

A VLAN is a logical grouping of network users and resources connected to administratively defined ports on a layer 2 switch. By creating these administrative groupings, you are able to create smaller broadcast domains within a switch by assigning different ports in the switch to different subnetworks. A VLAN is treated as its own subnet or broadcast domain. This means that when frames are broadcast, they are switched between ports only within the same VLAN.

By using VLANs, you're no longer confined to creating workgroups based on physical locations. VLANs can be organized by location, function, department, or even the application or protocol used, regardless of where the resources or users are located. VLANs can be created locally on a single switch, or they can be extended across many switches in a LAN, using special trunk protocols to carry the additional VLAN header information. This technique is called *frame tagging*, and it uses special identification methods that either encapsulate a frame or insert a new field in a frame, to identify it as belonging to a particular VLAN as it traverses a switched internetwork fabric.

One of the real problems facing network administrators managing large switched networks is that of consistency. With VLAN numbers and names requiring unique configuration, it is easy to lose control of the process, resulting in conflicting information about the same VLAN.

VTP—the VLAN Trunking Protocol—was developed to deal precisely with this problem. By creating a process where one switch can act as a server, updating other switches in the same domain, consistency of VLAN description can easily be achieved.

Understanding the Design Benefits of Virtual LANs

Remember that layer 2 switches break up collision domains and that only routers can break up broadcast domains. However, virtual LANs can be used to break up broadcast domains in layer 2 switched networks. Routers are still needed in a layer 2 virtual LAN switched internetwork to enable the different VLANs to communicate with each other.

There are many benefits to creating VLANs in your internetwork. Remember that in a layer 2 switched network, the network is a *flat network*, as shown in Figure 14.1. Every broadcast packet transmitted is seen by every device on the network, regardless of whether the device needs to receive the data.

FIGURE 14.1 A flat network structure

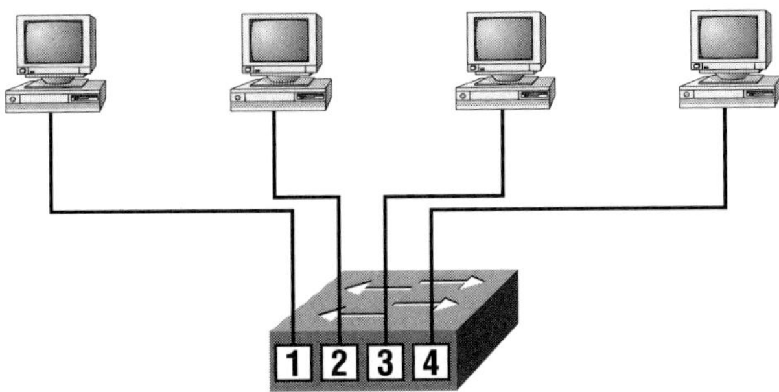
1
2
3
4
• Each segment has its own collision domain.
• All segments are in the same broadcast domain.

In a flat network, all users can see all devices. You cannot stop devices from broadcasting or users from trying to respond to broadcasts. Your only security consists of passwords on the servers and other devices.

By creating VLANs, you can solve many of the problems associated with layer 2 switching.

Broadcast Control

Broadcasts occur in every protocol, but how often they occur depends on the protocol, the application(s) running on the network, and how these services are used. VLANs can define smaller broadcast domains, which means that it is possible to stop application broadcasts to segments that do not use the application.

Although some older applications have been rewritten to reduce their bandwidth needs, there is a new generation of applications that are bandwidth greedy, consuming all they can find. These are multimedia applications that use broadcasts and multicasts extensively. Faulty equipment, inadequate segmentation, and poorly designed firewalls can also add to the problems of broadcast-intensive applications.

NOTE

For the moment, you should consider multicast traffic to be the same as broadcast traffic. The switch has no default knowledge of multicast groups, and forwards it out of every port. We deal with this issue in detail in Chapter 18, "Multilayer Switching."

These bandwidth-gobbling applications have added a new factor to network design because broadcasts can propagate through the switched network. Routers, by default, send broadcasts only within the originating network, but layer 2 switches forward broadcasts to all segments. This is called a *flat network* because it is one broadcast domain.

As an administrator, you must make sure the network is properly segmented to keep problems on one segment from propagating through the internetwork. The most effective way of doing this is through switching and routing. Because switches have become more cost-effective, a lot of companies are replacing the hub-and-router network with a pure switched network and VLANs. The largest benefit gained from switches with defined VLANs is that all devices in a VLAN are members of the same broadcast domain and receive all broadcasts. The broadcasts, by default, are filtered from all ports that are on a switch and are not members of the same VLAN.

Every time a VLAN is created, a new broadcast domain is created. VLANs are used to stop broadcasts from propagating through the entire internetwork. Some sort of internal route processor or an external router must be used in conjunction with switches to provide connections between networks (VLANs).

Security

In a simple internetwork, host connectivity is achieved by connecting hosts to hubs and switches that are linked together with routers. Security is then maintained at the router, but this causes three serious security problems:

- Anyone connecting to the physical network has access to the network resources on that physical LAN.
- A user can plug a network analyzer into the hub and see all the traffic in that network.
- Users can join a workgroup just by plugging their workstation into the existing hub.

By using VLANs and creating multiple broadcast groups, administrators now have control over each port and user. Users can no longer just plug their workstation into any switch port and have access to network resources. The administrator controls each port and whatever resources it is allowed to use.

Because groups can be created according to the network resources a user requires, switches can be configured to inform a network management station of any unauthorized access to network resources. If inter-VLAN communication needs to take place, restrictions on a router can also be implemented. Restrictions can also be placed on hardware addresses, protocols, and applications.

Flexibility and Scalability

VLANs also add more flexibility to your network by allowing only the users you want in the broadcast domain regardless of their physical location. Layer 2 switches read frames only for filtering; they do not look at the network-layer protocol. This can cause a switch to forward all broadcasts. However, by creating VLANs, you are essentially creating separate broadcast domains. Broadcasts sent out from a node in one VLAN will not be forwarded to ports configured in a different VLAN. By assigning switch ports or users to VLAN groups on a switch—or a group of connected switches (called a *switch fabric*)—you have the flexibility to add only the users you want in the broadcast domain regardless of their physical location. This can stop broadcast storms caused by a faulty network interface card (NIC) or stop an application from propagating throughout the entire internetwork.

When a VLAN gets too big, you can create more VLANs to keep the broadcasts from consuming too much bandwidth. The fewer users in a VLAN, the fewer users are affected by broadcasts.

The Collapsed Backbone and the VLAN

To understand how a VLAN looks to a switch, it's helpful to begin by first looking at a traditional collapsed backbone. Figure 14.2 shows a collapsed backbone created by connecting physical LANs to a router.

Each network is attached to the router, and each network has its own logical network number. Each node attached to a particular physical network must match that network number to be able to communicate on the internetwork. Now let's look at what a switch accomplishes. Figure 14.3 shows how switches remove the physical boundary.

FIGURE 14.2 Switches remove the physical boundary.

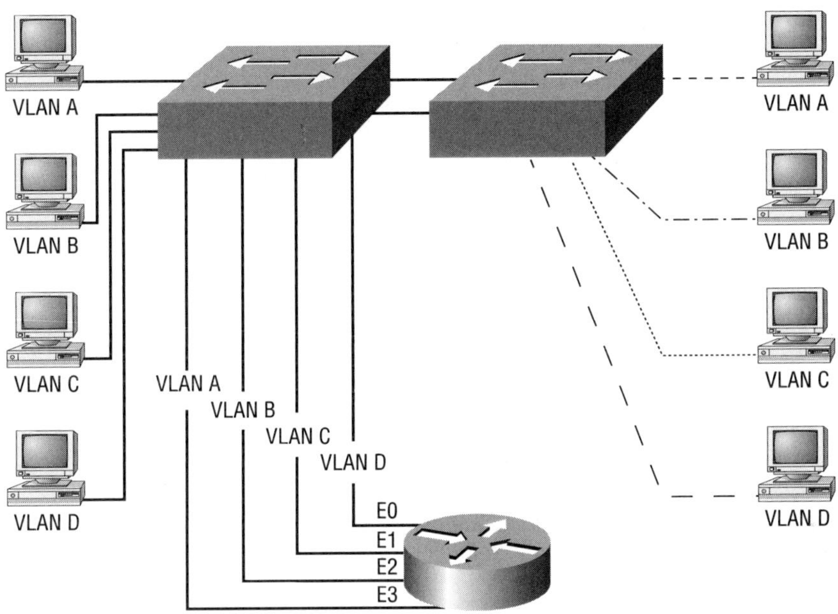

FIGURE 14.3 Physical LANs connected to a router

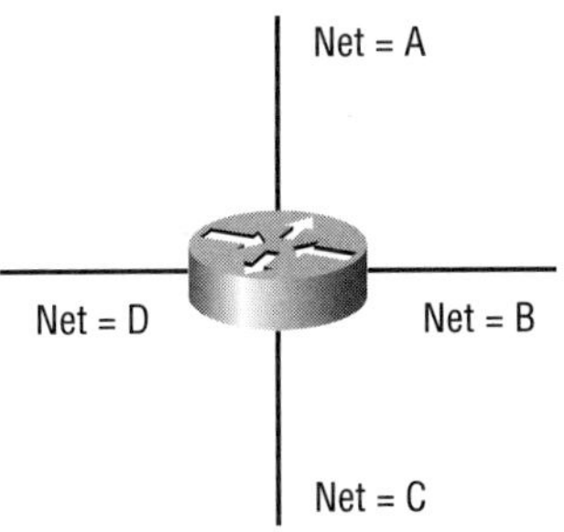

Switches create greater flexibility and scalability than routers can by themselves because switches define the network VLANs and VLAN port assignments. You can group users into communities of interest, which are known as VLAN organizations.

Because of switches, we don't need routers anymore, right? Wrong. In Figure 14.3, notice that there are four VLANs, or broadcast domains. The nodes within each VLAN can communicate with each other but not with any other VLAN or node in another VLAN. When configured in a VLAN, the nodes think they are actually in a collapsed backbone, as in Figure 14.2. What do these hosts in Figure 14.2 need to do in order to communicate to a node or host on a different network? They need to go through the router, or other layer 3 device, just as they do when they are configured for VLAN communication, as shown in Figure 14.3. Communication between VLANs, just as in physical networks, must go through a layer 3 device.

If the creation of VLANs using the existing addressing scheme does not produce the segmentation that you need, you may have to bite the bullet and renumber your network. But it's not all bad news. Creating a new IP addressing scheme from the ground up may seem like a huge task, but it is greatly simplified by using an automatic addressing process such as Dynamic Host Configuration Protocol (DHCP).

Scaling the Switch Block

First introduced in Chapter 12, "The Campus Network," switch blocks represent a switch or group of switches providing access to users. These switches then connect to distribution layer switches, which in turn handle routing issues and VLAN distribution.

To understand how many VLANs can be configured in a switch block, you must understand the following factors:

- Traffic patterns
- Applications used
- Network management
- Group commonality
- IP addressing scheme

Cisco recommends a one-to-one ratio between VLANs and subnets. For example, if you have 2000 users in a building, then you must understand how they are broken up by subnets to create your VLANs. If you had 1000 users in a subnet—which is ridiculous—you would create only two VLANs. If you had only 100 users in a subnet, you would create about 20 VLANs or more.

It is actually better to create your broadcast domain groups (VLANs) and then create a subnet mask that fits the need. That is not always possible, and you usually have to create VLANs around an already-configured network.

VLANs should not extend past the distribution switch on to the core.

Defining VLAN Boundaries

When building the switch block, you need to understand two basic methods for defining the VLAN boundaries:

- End-to-end VLANs
- Local VLANs

End-to-End VLANs

An *end-to-end VLAN* spans the switch fabric from end to end; all switches with ports configured in end-to-end VLANs understand about any and all VLANs that may be configured on the network. End-to-end VLANs are configured to allow membership based on function, project, department, and so on.

The best feature of end-to-end VLANs is that users can be placed in a VLAN regardless of their physical location. The administrator defines the port the user is connected to as a VLAN member. If the user moves, the administrator defines their new port as a member of their existing VLAN. In accordance with the 80/20 rule, the goal of an administrator in defining end-to-end VLANs is to maintain 80 percent of the network traffic as local, or within the VLAN. Only 20 percent or less should extend outside the VLAN.

Local VLANs

Unlike an end-to-end VLAN, a *local VLAN* is configured by physical location and not by function, project, department, and so on. Local VLANs are used in corporations that have centralized server and mainframe blocks because end-to-end VLANs are difficult to maintain in this situation. In other words, when the 80/20 rule becomes the 20/80 rule, end-to-end VLANs are more difficult to maintain, so you will want to use a local VLAN.

In contrast to end-to-end VLANs, local VLANs are configured by geographic location; these locations can be a building or just a closet in a building, depending on switch size. Geographically configured VLANs are designed around the fact that the business or corporation is using centralized resources, such as a server farm. The users will spend most of their time utilizing these centralized resources and 20 percent or less on the local VLAN. From what you have read in this book so far, you must be thinking that 80 percent of the traffic is crossing a layer 3 device. That doesn't sound efficient, does it?

Because many modern applications are not very tolerant of delay (a bit like users), you must design a geographic VLAN with a fast layer 3 device (or devices) for interconnecting your VLANs and for general site-to-site connectivity. Fortunately, layer 3 devices themselves are becoming faster. The benefit of this design is that it will give the users a predetermined, consistent method of getting to resources. But you cannot create this design with a lower end layer 3 model. In the past, these network types were only possible in large corporations with plenty of spending power, but as technology develops, the price is going down.

Assigning VLAN Memberships

After your VLANs are created, you need to assign switch ports to them. There are two types of VLAN port configurations: static and dynamic. A static VLAN requires less work initially but is more difficult for an administrator to maintain. A dynamic VLAN, on the other hand, takes more work up front but is easier to maintain.

Static VLANs

In a *static VLAN*, the administrator creates a VLAN and then assigns switch ports to it. The association does not change until the administrator changes the port assignment. This is the typical way of creating VLANs, and it is the most secure. This type of VLAN configuration is easy to set up and monitor, working well in a network where the movement of users within the network is maintained by basically just locking the network closet doors. Using network management software to configure the ports can be helpful but is not mandatory.

Dynamic VLANs

If the administrator wants to do a little more work up front and add all devices' hardware addresses to a database, hosts in an internetwork can be assigned VLAN assignments dynamically. By using intelligent management software, you can enable hardware (MAC) addresses, protocols, or even applications to create dynamic VLANs. A *dynamic VLAN* will tell the switch port which VLAN it belongs to, based on the MAC address of the device that connects to the port.

For example, suppose MAC addresses have been entered into a centralized VLAN management application. If a node is then attached to an unassigned switch port, the VLAN management database can look up the hardware address and assign and configure the switch port to the correct VLAN. This can make management and configuration easier for the administrator. If a user moves, the switch automatically assigns them to the correct VLAN. However, more administration is needed initially to set up the database than to set up static VLANs, and additional administration is required for upkeep of the database.

Cisco administrators can use the VLAN Management Policy Server (VMPS) service to set up a database of MAC addresses that can be used for the dynamic addressing of VLANs. VMPS is a MAC-address-to-VLAN mapping database.

Configuring Static VLANs

For the Switching exam, Cisco is primarily interested in static VLAN configuration. We'll show you how to configure VLANs on a Catalyst 4000 switch and on a range of Catalyst IOS-based switches.

It is important to understand the difference between the Catalyst 4000 series VLAN configuration and the IOS-based VLAN configuration.

Catalyst 4000 Series

To configure VLANs on a Catalyst 4000 switch, use the `set vlan` *`vlan#`* `name` *`vlan_name`* command. Then, after your VLANs are configured, assign the ports to each VLAN:

```
Terry_4000> (enable) set vlan 2 name Sales
Vlan 2 configuration successful
```

After the VLAN is configured, use the `set vlan` *`vlan# slot/ports`* command:

```
Terry_4000> (enable) set vlan 2 2/1-2
VLAN  Mod/Ports
----  -----------------------
2     1/1-2
      2/1-2

Please configure additional information for VLAN 2.
Terry_4000> (enable)
```

The additional information the switch wants you to configure is the VLAN Trunk Protocol (VTP) information. (VTP and trunking are covered in more detail at the end of this chapter, where we will continue with the 4000 switch VLAN configuration.) The 4000 series switch enables you to configure as many ports as you wish to a VLAN at one time.

Catalyst 2950 and 3550 Series

To configure VLANs on an IOS-based switch, first you need to enter the *VLAN database*. This mode is entered by typing the command **`vlan database`**. This command changes the prompt, as can be seen from the next example. Once in this new privileged mode, use `vlan` *`vlan#`* `name` *`vlan_name`*. Note that you do not enter the standard configuration mode to enter this configuration:

```
Terry_2950#vlan database
Terry_2950(vlan)#vlan ?
  <1-1005>  ISL VLAN index

Terry_2950(vlan)#vlan 2 ?
  are         Maximum number of All Route Explorer hops for this VLAN
  backupcrf   Backup CRF mode of the VLAN
  bridge      Bridging characteristics of the VLAN
  media       Media type of the VLAN
  mtu         VLAN Maximum Transmission Unit
  name        Ascii name of the VLAN
  parent      ID number of the Parent VLAN of FDDI or Token Ring type VLANs
  ring        Ring number of FDDI or Token Ring type VLANs
  said        IEEE 802.10 SAID
```

```
  state       Operational state of the VLAN
  ste         Maximum number of Spanning Tree Explorer hops for this VLAN
  stp         Spanning tree characteristics of the VLAN
  tb-vlan1    ID number of the first translational VLAN for this VLAN (or zero
              if none)
  tb-vlan2    ID number of the second translational VLAN for this VLAN (or zero
              if none)
  <cr>

Terry_2950(vlan)#vlan 2 name ?
  WORD  The ascii name for the VLAN

Terry_2950(vlan)#vlan 2 name marketing
VLAN 2 added:
    Name: marketing
Terry_2950(vlan)#vlan 3 name production
VLAN 3 added:
    Name: production
Terry_2950(vlan)#exit
APPLY completed.
Exiting....
```

Remember that a created VLAN is unused until it is mapped to a switch port or ports, and that all ports are always in VLAN 1 unless set otherwise.

After you create the VLANs that you want, you use the `show vlan` command to see the configured VLANs. However, notice that, by default, all ports on the switch are in VLAN 1. To change that, you need to go to each interface and tell it what VLAN to be a part of:

```
Terry_2950#show vlan

VLAN Name                             Status    Ports
---- -------------------------------- --------- -------------------------------
1    default                          active    Fa0/1, Fa0/2, Fa0/3, Fa0/4
                                                Fa0/5, Fa0/6, Fa0/7, Fa0/8
                                                Fa0/9, Fa0/10, Fa0/11, Fa0/12
                                                Fa0/13, Fa0/14, Fa0/15, Fa0/16
                                                Fa0/17, Fa0/18, Fa0/19, Fa0/20
                                                Fa0/21, Fa0/22, Fa0/23, Fa0/24
2    marketing                        active
```

```
3    production                     active
1002 fddi-default                   active
1003 token-ring-default             active
1004 fddinet-default                active
1005 trnet-default                  active

VLAN Type  SAID       MTU   Parent RingNo BridgeNo Stp  BrdgMode Trans1 Trans2
---- ----- ---------- ----- ------ ------ -------- ---- -------- ------ ------
1    enet  100001     1500  -      -      -        -    -        0      0
2    enet  100002     1500  -      -      -        -    -        0      0
3    enet  100003     1500  -      -      -        -    -        0      0
1002 fddi  101002     1500  -      -      -        -    -        0      0
1003 tr    101003     1500  -      -      -        -    -        0      0

VLAN Type  SAID       MTU   Parent RingNo BridgeNo Stp  BrdgMode Trans1 Trans2
---- ----- ---------- ----- ------ ------ -------- ---- -------- ------ ------
1004 fdnet 101004     1500  -      -      -        ieee -        0      0
1005 trnet 101005     1500  -      -      -        ibm  -        0      0

Remote SPAN VLANs
------------------------------------------------------------------------------

Primary Secondary Type              Ports
------- --------- ----------------- ------------------------------------------
```

Configuring the interfaces on the 2950 and 3550 is very different. After the VLANs have been created, the interface needs to be made a member of the appropriate VLAN. The command `switchport mode access` is used to tell the port that it will be a member of a single VLAN. It is told what VLAN it is a member of with the command `switchport access vlan` *`vlan#`*.

```
Terry_2950(config-if)#switchport ?
  access          Set access mode characteristics of the interface
  host            Set port host
  mode            Set trunking mode of the interface
  nonegotiate     Device will not engage in negotiation protocol on this
                  interface
  port-security   Security related command
  priority        Set appliance 802.1p priority
  protected       Configure an interface to be a protected port
  trunk           Set trunking characteristics of the interface
  voice           Voice appliance attributes
```

```
Terry_2950(config-if)#switchport access ?
  vlan  Set VLAN when interface is in access mode

Terry_2950(config-if)#switchport mode access
Terry_2950(config-if)#^Z
Terry_2950#conf t

Enter configuration commands, one per line.  End with CNTL/Z.
Terry_2950(config)#int fa 0/2
Terry_2950(config-if)#switchport ?
  access         Set access mode characteristics of the interface
  host           Set port host
  mode           Set trunking mode of the interface
  nonegotiate    Device will not engage in negotiation protocol on this
                 interface
  port-security  Security related command
  priority       Set appliance 802.1p priority
  protected      Configure an interface to be a protected port
  trunk          Set trunking characteristics of the interface
  voice          Voice appliance attributes

Terry_2950(config-if)#switchport mode ?
  access   Set trunking mode to ACCESS unconditionally
  dynamic  Set trunking mode to dynamically negotiate access or trunk mode
  trunk    Set trunking mode to TRUNK unconditionally

Terry_2950(config-if)#switchport mode access
Terry_2950(config-if)#switchport access ?
  vlan  Set VLAN when interface is in access mode

Terry_2950(config-if)#switchport access vlan 2
Terry_2950(config-if)#^Z
```

Now you need to confirm that the configuration has been accepted and the port to VLAN relationship has been established. You can use the `show vlan` command we used earlier, but the VLANs will also be shown in the running configuration:

```
Terry_2950#show run
00:49:36: %SYS-5-CONFIG_I: Configured from console by consolesho run
Building configuration...
```

```
Current configuration : 1512 bytes
version 12.1

[output cut]

interface FastEthernet0/2
 switchport access vlan 2
 switchport mode access
 no ip address
```

Now, type **show vlan** to see the ports assigned to each VLAN:

```
Terry_2950#show vlan

VLAN Name                             Status    Ports
---- -------------------------------- --------- -------------------------------
1    default                          active    Fa0/1, Fa0/3, Fa0/4, Fa0/5
                                                Fa0/6, Fa0/7, Fa0/8, Fa0/9
                                                Fa0/10, Fa0/11, Fa0/12, Fa0/13
                                                Fa0/14, Fa0/15, Fa0/16, Fa0/17
                                                Fa0/18, Fa0/19, Fa0/20, Fa0/21
                                                Fa0/22, Fa0/23, Fa0/24
2    marketing                        active    Fa0/2
3    production                       active
1002 fddi-default                     active
1003 token-ring-default               active
1004 fddinet-default                  active
1005 trnet-default                    active

[output truncated]

Terry_2950#
```

Identifying VLANs

VLANs can span multiple connected switches, which (as we stated earlier) Cisco calls a switch fabric. Switches within the switch fabric must keep track of frames as they are received on the switch ports, and they must keep track of the VLAN they belong to as the frames traverse the switch fabric. Switches use frame tagging to perform this function. Switches can then direct frames to the appropriate port.

There are two types of links in a switched environment:

Access link An *access link* is a link that is part of only one VLAN, which is referred to as the native VLAN of the port. Any device attached to an access link is unaware of a VLAN membership. This device just assumes it is part of a broadcast domain, with no understanding of the physical network. Switches remove any VLAN information from the frame before it is sent to an access-link device. Access-link devices cannot communicate with devices outside of their VLAN unless the packet is routed through a router.

Trunk link Trunks can carry multiple VLANs. Originally named after the trunks of the telephone system, which carry multiple telephone conversations, a *trunk link* is used to connect switches to other switches, to routers, or even to servers. Trunk links are supported on FastEthernet or Gigabit Ethernet only. To identify the VLAN that a frame belongs to, Cisco switches support two identification techniques: Inter-Switch Link (ISL) and 802.1Q. Trunk links are used to transport VLANs between devices and can be configured to transport all VLANs or just a few VLANs. Trunk links still have a native VLAN, and that VLAN is used if the trunk link fails.

Frame Tagging

The switch in an internetwork needs a way to keep track of users and frames as they travel the switch fabric and VLANs. Frame identification, called *frame tagging*, uniquely assigns a user-defined ID to each frame. This is sometimes referred to as a VLAN ID or color.

Frame tagging is used to identify the VLAN that the packet belongs to. The tag is placed on the frame as it enters the first switch it runs into. As long as the frame does not exit out a non-trunk port, the frame keeps the identifying tag. This enables each switch to see what VLAN the frame belongs to, and each switch that the frame reaches must identify the VLAN ID and then determine what to do with the frame based on the filter table. If the frame reaches a switch that has another trunk link, the frame can be forwarded out the trunk-link port. After the frame reaches an exit to an access link, the switch removes the VLAN identifier. The end device receives the frames without having to understand the VLAN identification.

If you are using NetFlow switching hardware on your Cisco switches, this enables devices on different VLANs to communicate after taking just the first packet through the router. This means that communication can occur from port to port on a switch, instead of from port to router to port, when traversing VLANs.

VLAN Identification Methods

To keep track of frames traversing a switch fabric, VLAN identification is used to identify which frames belong to which VLAN. There are multiple trunking methods:

Inter-Switch Link (ISL) Proprietary to Cisco switches, ISL is used for FastEthernet and Gigabit Ethernet links only. It can be used on switch ports and router interfaces as well as server interface cards to trunk a server. Server trunking is good if you are creating functional VLANs and don't want to break the 80/20 rule. The server that is trunked is part of all VLANs (broadcast domains) simultaneously. The users do not have to cross a layer 3 device to access a company-shared server.

IEEE 802.1Q Created by the IEEE as a standard method of frame tagging. It actually inserts a field into the frame to identify the VLAN.

LAN Emulation (LANE) Used to communicate with multiple VLANs over ATM.

802.10 (FDDI) Used to send VLAN information over Fiber Distributed Data Interface (FDDI). Uses a SAID field in the frame header to identify the VLAN. This is proprietary to Cisco devices.

The Cisco Switching exam now covers only the ISL and 802.1Q methods of VLAN identification, and the fact that the 2950, 3550, etc. series support only 802.1Q means that there should only be a small chance of ISL coming up on the exam.

It is possible for a packet to move from one type of network, such as FDDI, to another, such as Ethernet. Ethernet, FDDI, Token Ring, and ATM have standards enabling the switch to translate one type into a different type. The configuration on the switch requires specifically stating that VLAN 53 is the same thing as ATM ELAN 953, for example. The code for this is derived from translational bridging.

Inter-Switch Link Protocol (ISL)

Inter-Switch Link Protocol (ISL) is a way of explicitly tagging VLAN information onto an Ethernet frame. This tagging information enables VLANs to be multiplexed over a trunk link through an external encapsulation method. By running ISL, you can interconnect multiple switches and still maintain VLAN information as traffic travels between switches on trunk links.

Cisco created the ISL protocol, and therefore ISL is proprietary to Cisco devices only. If you need a nonproprietary VLAN protocol, use the 802.1Q, which is covered next in this chapter.

ISL is an external tagging process, which means that the original frame is not altered but instead is encapsulated with a new 26-byte ISL header and a 4-byte frame check sequence (FCS) field at the end of the frame. Because the frame is encapsulated with information, only ISL-aware devices can read the frame. Token Ring devices can also be connected with the appropriate ports, if VTP version 2 is being used. The size of the frame can be up to 1548 bytes long for Ethernet and 17,878 bytes for Token Ring.

On multi-VLAN (trunk) ports, each frame is tagged as it enters the switch. ISL NICs enable servers to send and receive frames tagged with multiple VLANs, so the frames can traverse multiple VLANs without going though a router, which reduces latency. This technology can also be used with probes and certain network analyzers. In addition, it enables users to attach to servers quickly and efficiently without going through a router every time they need to communicate with a resource. Administrators can use the ISL technology to simultaneously include file servers in multiple VLANs, for example.

It is important to understand that ISL VLAN information is added to a frame as soon as that frame enters the switch. The ISL encapsulation is removed from the frame if the frame is forwarded out an access link.

Preventing communication from one VLAN to another might be desirable, but the network design might still require that some devices have access to all VLANs. In addition to configuring a filter on a router, you can install a network card that is ISL- or 802.1Q-capable. This enables an e-mail server or database server to be directly connected to all VLANs without a router being involved.

Standard for Virtual Bridged Local Area Networks (IEEE 802.1Q)

Unlike ISL, which uses an external tagging process and encapsulates a frame with a new ISL encapsulation, 802.1Q uses an internal tagging process by modifying the existing internal Ethernet frame. To access both links and trunk links, the frame looks as if it is just a standard Ethernet frame because it is not encapsulated with VLAN information. The VLAN information is added to a field within the frame itself.

Like ISL, the purpose of 802.1Q is to carry the traffic of more than one subnet down a single cable. 802.1Q tags the frame in a standard VLAN format, which allows for the VLAN implementations of multiple vendors. The standard tag allows for an open architecture and standard services for VLANs and a standard for protocols in the provision of these services. Because adding VLAN information to a frame affects the frame length, two committees were created to deal with this issue: 802.3ac and 802.1Q.

The VLAN frame format defined in both the 802.1Q and 802.3ac is a four-byte field that is inserted between the original Ethernet frame Source address field and the Type or Length field. The CRC of the frame must be recomputed whenever the VLAN information is inserted or removed from the frame. The Ethernet frame size can now be up to 1522 bytes if a tag is inserted.

The VLAN Tag Protocol Identifier (TPID) is globally assigned and uses an EtherType field value of 0x81-00. The Tag Control Information (TCI) is a 16-bit value and has three fields contained within:

User Priority A three-bit field used to assign up to eight layers of priority. The highest priority is 0, and the lowest is 7 (specified in 802.1Q).

Canonical Format Indicator (CFI) A one-bit field that is always a 0 if running an 802.3 frame. This field was originally designed to be used for Token Ring VLANs, but it was never implemented except for some proprietary Token Ring LANs.

VLAN ID (VID) The actual VLAN number that the frame is assigned upon entering the switch (12 bits). The reserved VLAN IDs are as follows:

0x0-00 Null, or no VLAN ID, which is used when only priority information is sent

0x0-01 Default VLAN value of all switches

0x-F-FF Reserved

Because Ethernet frames can not exceed 1518 bytes, and ISL and 802.1Q frames can exceed 1518 bytes, the switch might record the frame as a baby giant frame.

Trunking

Trunk links are point-to-point, 100Mbps, or 1000Mbps links between two switches, between a switch and a router, or between a switch and a server. Trunk links carry the traffic of multiple VLANs, from 1 to 1005 at a time. You cannot run trunk links on 10Mbps links.

Cisco switches use the Dynamic Trunking Protocol (DTP) to manage trunk negation in the Catalyst switch engine software release 4.2 or later, using either ISL or 802.1Q. DTP is a point-to-point protocol and was created to send trunk information across 802.1Q trunks. Dynamic ISL (DISL) was used to support trunk negation on ISL links only before DTP was released in software release 4.1; and before DISL, auto-negotiation of trunk links was not allowed.

A *trunk* is a port that supports multiple VLANs, but before it became a trunk, it was the member of a single VLAN. The VLAN it is a member of when it becomes a trunk is called a native VLAN. If the port were to lose the trunking ability, it would revert to membership in its native VLAN.

Configuring Trunk Ports

This section shows you how to configure trunk links on the 4000 series and the 2950/3550 series IOS-based switches.

4000 Switch

To configure a trunk on a 4000 series switch, use the `set trunk` command, and on the IOS-based switch, use the `trunk on` command:

```
Terry_4000> (enable) set trunk 2/12 ?
Usage: set trunk <mod_num/port_num>
[on|off|desirable|auto|nonegotiate] [vlans] [trunk_type]
(vlans = 1..1005 An example of vlans is 2-10,1005)
       (trunk_type = isl,dot1q,dot10,lane,negotiate)

Terry_4000> (enable) set trunk 2/12 on isl
Port(s) 2/12 trunk mode set to on.
Port(s) 2/12 trunk type set to isl.
Terry_4000> (enable) 2003 Mar 21 06:31:54
%DTP-5-TRUNKPORTON:Port 2/12 has become isl trunk
```

Port 2/12 has become a trunk port that uses ISL encapsulation. Notice that we did not specify the VLANs to trunk. By default, all VLANs would be trunked. Take a look at a configuration in which we specified the VLANs to use:

```
Terry_4000> (enable) set trunk 2/12 on 1-5 isl
Adding vlans 1-5 to allowed list.
```

```
Please use the 'clear trunk' command to remove
vlans from allowed list.
Port(s) 2/12 allowed vlans modified to 1-1005.
Port(s) 2/12 trunk mode set to on.
Port(s) 2/12 trunk type set to isl.
```

Notice that, even though we told the switch to use VLANs 1–5, it added 1–1005 by default. To remove VLANs from a trunk port, use the `clear vlan` command. We'll do that in a minute.

We need to explain the different options for turning up a trunk port:

on The switch port is a permanent trunk port regardless of the other end. If you use the `on` state, you must specify the frame-tagging method because it will not negotiate with the other end.

off The port becomes a permanent non-trunk link.

desirable The port you want to trunk becomes a trunk port only if the neighbor port is a trunk port set to `on`, `desirable`, or `auto`.

auto The port wants to become a trunk port but becomes a trunk only if the neighbor port asked the port to be a trunk. This is the default for all ports. However, because `auto` switch ports will never ask (they respond only to trunk requests), two ports will never become a trunk if both of them are set to `auto`.

nonegotiate Makes a port a permanent trunk port, but because the port does not use DTP frames for communication, there is no negotiation. If you're having DTP problems with a switch port connected to a non-switch device, then use the `nonegotiate` command when using the `set trunk` command. This enables the port to be trunked, but you won't be sent any DTP frames.

Be careful when using the `nonegotiate` option. It is not unusual to set up switches initially with `auto` or `desirable` trunks and then lock them down with `on`, after the switch fabric has settled down. If two trunk ports are configured with `auto` or `desirable`, they need to receive the negotiate packets to tell that there is another trunk-capable device on the other side. If both trunk ports are set to `desirable` but `nonegotiate`, no trunk will come up.

2950 and 3550 Series

The 2950 switches support the same options but with different commands, as in the next example. The 2950 series supports only IEEE 802.1Q VLANs, whereas the 3550 support ISL as well:

```
Terry_2950(config-if)#switchport trunk ?
  allowed  Set allowed VLAN characteristics when interface is in trunking mode
  native   Set trunking native characteristics when interface is in trunking
           mode
  pruning  Set pruning VLAN characteristics when interface is in trunking mode
```

```
Terry_2950(config-if)#switchport mode ?
  access    Set trunking mode to ACCESS unconditionally
  dynamic   Set trunking mode to dynamically negotiate access or trunk mode
  trunk     Set trunking mode to TRUNK unconditionally

Terry_2950(config-if)#switchport mode dynamic ?
  auto       Set trunking mode dynamic negotiation parameter to AUTO
  desirable  Set trunking mode dynamic negotiation parameter to DESIRABLE

Terry_2950(config-if)#switchport mode dynamic auto
Terry_2950(config-if)#^Z
Terry_2950#
```

Clearing VLANs from Trunk Links

As demonstrated in the preceding sections, all VLANs are configured on a trunk link unless cleared by an administrator. If you do not want a trunk link to carry VLAN information because you want to stop broadcasts on a certain VLAN from traversing the trunk link, or because you want to stop topology change information from being sent across a link where a VLAN is not supported, use the `clear trunk` command.

This section shows you how to clear VLANs from trunk links on both the 4000 and IOS-based series of switches.

4000 Series

The command to clear a VLAN from a trunk link is `clear trunk` *`slot/port vlans`*. Here is an example:

```
Terry_4000> (enable) clear trunk 2/12 5-1005
Removing Vlan(s) 5-1005 from allowed list.
Port 1/2 allowed vlans modified to 1-4
```

2950 and 3550 Series Switches

The command `switchport trunk allowed vlan remove` *`vlan-list`* is used to limit which VLANs can use a particular trunk:

```
Terry_2950(config)# interface fa 0/10
Terry_2950(config-if)# switchport trunk allowed vlan remove 2-10,12,15
```

Use a hyphen to show a contiguous range of VLANs that are to be excluded and use a comma to separate VLANs that are not contiguous. Do not leave spaces. From the configuration, you can see that the specified VLANs have been removed from the supported list:

```
Terry_2950#show run
Building configuration...
```

```
version 12.1

[output cut]

interface FastEthernet0/10
 switchport trunk allowed vlan 1,11,13,14,16-1005
 switchport mode trunk
 no ip address
```

Verifying Trunk Links

On the 4000 series, you can verify your trunk ports using the `show trunk` command. If you have more than one port trunking and want to see statistics on only one trunk port, you can use the `show trunk` *`port_number`* command:

```
Terry_4000> (enable) show trunk 2/12
Port      Mode         Encapsulation  Status        Native vlan
--------  -----------  -------------  ------------  -----------
 2/12     on           isl            trunking      1

Port      Vlans allowed on trunk
--------  ---------------------------------------------------------
 2/12     1-4

Port      Vlans allowed and active in management domain
--------  ---------------------------------------------------------
 2/12     1

Port      Vlans in spanning tree forwarding state and not pruned
--------  ---------------------------------------------------------
 2/12     1
Terry_4000> (enable)
```

The 2950/3550 series of Catalyst switches continue to do it differently than the 4000. To view the trunk status of a port on one of these switches, the command `show interface` *`interface_id`* `switchport` needs to be used:

```
Terry_2950#show interface fa0/10 switchport
Name: Fa0/10
Switchport: Enabled
Administrative Mode: trunk
Operational Mode: down
```

```
Administrative Trunking Encapsulation: dot1q
Negotiation of Trunking: On
Access Mode VLAN: 1 (default)
Trunking Native Mode VLAN: 1 (default)
Administrative private-vlan host-association: none
Administrative private-vlan mapping: none
Operational private-vlan: none
Trunking VLANs Enabled: 1,11,13,14,16-1005
Pruning VLANs Enabled: 2-1001

Protected: false

Voice VLAN: none (Inactive)
Appliance trust: none
Terry_2950#
```

A VLAN that is enabled on the switch is one that the switch has learned exists in the switch fabric of the LAN. Somewhere out there, a device needs that particular VLAN, or it might be configured for future use. An active VLAN is a VLAN in which one or more ports on this switch are members.

Using VLAN Trunk Protocol (VTP)

VLAN Trunk Protocol (VTP) was created by Cisco to manage all the configured VLANs across a switched internetwork and to maintain consistency throughout the network. VTP enables an administrator to add, delete, and rename VLANs. These changes are then propagated to all switches.

VTP provides the following benefits to a switched network:

- Consistent configuration of global VLANs across all switches in the network
- Enabling VLANs to be trunked over mixed networks—for example, Ethernet to ATM LANE or FDDI
- Accurate tracking and monitoring of VLANs
- Dynamic reporting when VLANs are added to all switches
- Plug-and-play VLAN adding to the switched network

To enable VTP to manage your VLANs across the network, you must first create a VTP server. All servers that need to share VLAN information must use the same domain name, and a switch can be in only one domain at a time. This means that a switch can share VTP domain information only with switches configured in the same VTP domain.

A VTP domain can be used if you have more than one switch connected in a network. If all switches in your network are in only one VLAN, then VTP doesn't need to be used. VTP information is sent between switches via a trunk port between the switches.

Switches advertise VTP management domain information, such as the name, as well as a configuration revision number and all known VLANs with any specific parameters.

You can configure switches to receive and forward VTP information through trunk ports but not process information updates nor update their VTP database. This is called VTP transparent mode.

You can set up a VTP domain with security by adding passwords, but remember that every switch must be set up with the same password, which might be difficult. However, if you are having problems with users adding switches to your VTP domain, then a password can be used.

Switches detect the additional VLANs within a VTP advertisement and then prepare to receive information on their trunk ports with the newly defined VLAN in tow. The information would be VLAN ID, 802.10 SAID fields, or LANE information. Updates are sent out as revision numbers that are notification +1. Any time a switch sees a higher revision number, it knows the information it receives is more current and will overwrite the current database with the new one.

Do you remember the `clear config all` command we talked about in Chapter 13, "Connecting the Switch Block"? Well, guess what? It really doesn't "clear all" after all. It seems that VTP has its own NVRAM, which means that VTP information as well as the revision number would still be present if you perform a `clear config all`. You can clear the revision number by power-cycling the switch.

VTP Modes of Operation

There are three modes of operation within a VTP domain: server, client, and transparent. Figure 14.4 shows the three *VTP modes*.

Real World Scenario

The Threat of High Revision Numbers

Many organizations have discovered the need for physical security when a device with only VLAN 1 but a high configuration revision number is added to the network. If a switch is a part of a test lab and then needs to be placed into production, it is best to clear everything and then power-cycle it. There have been instances of wiped switches erasing the VLAN setup of large organizations because the new device had a higher configuration revision number but had only VLAN 1. If a port belongs to a VLAN and that VLAN is removed, the port shuts down until the VLAN exists again. Adding the VLANs back and propagating them is a snap. The hassle and stress occur with discovering the problem. Using a VTP password is encouraged to prevent people from accidentally causing problems.

FIGURE 14.4 VTP modes

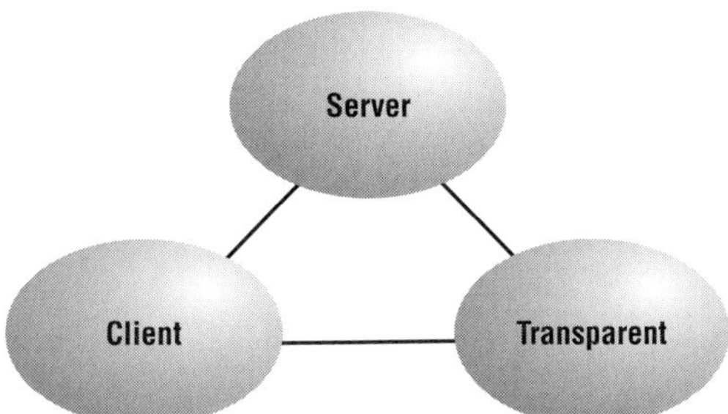

Server

VTP server mode is the default for all Catalyst switches. You need at least one server in your VTP domain to propagate VLAN information throughout the domain. The following must be completed within server mode:

- Create, add, or delete VLANs on a VTP domain.
- Change VTP information. Any change made to a switch in server mode is advertised to the entire VTP domain.

Global VLANs must be configured on a server. The server adds the VLANs to the switch configuration, so every time the switch boots up, the VLAN knowledge is propagated.

Client

VTP clients receive information from VTP servers and send and receive updates, but they cannot make any changes to the VTP configuration as long as they are clients. No ports on a client switch can be added to a new VLAN before the VTP server notifies the client switch about the new VLAN. If you want a switch to become a server, first make it a client so that it receives all the correct VLAN information, and then change it to a server. No global VTP information is kept if the switch loses power.

Transparent

VTP transparent switches do not participate in the VTP domain, but they still receive and forward VTP advertisements through the configured trunk links. However, for a transparent switch to advertise the VLAN information out the configured trunk links, VTP version 2 must be used. If not, the switch does not forward anything. VTP transparent switches can add and delete VLANs because they keep their own database and do not share it with other switches. Transparent switches are considered locally significant.

VTP Advertisements

After the different types of VTP switches are defined, the switches can start advertising VTP information between them. VTP switches advertise information they know about only on their trunk ports. They advertise the following:

- Management domain name
- Configuration revision number
- VLANs the switch knows about
- Parameters for each VLAN

The switches use multicast MAC addresses, so all neighbor devices receive the frames. A VTP server creates new VLANs, and that information is propagated through the VTP domain.

Figure 14.5 shows the three VTP advertisements: client, summary, and subset.

The three types of messages are as follows:

Client requests Clients can send requests for VLAN information to a server. Servers respond with both summary and subset advertisements.

Summary These advertisements are sent out every 300 seconds on VLAN 1 and every time a change occurs.

Subset These advertisements are VLAN-specific and contain details about each VLAN.

FIGURE 14.5 VTP advertisement content

Client Advertisement Request
Version
Code
Rsvd
Mgmt D Len
Management domain name
Start value

Summary Advertisement
Version code follows mgmt D Len
Management domain name
Config revision number
Updater identity
Updater timestamp
MD5

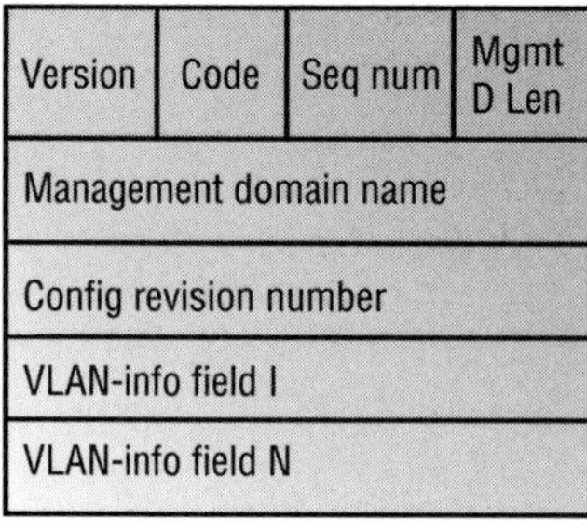

The summary advertisements can contain the following information:

Management domain name The switch that receives this advertisement must have the name that is in this field, or the update is ignored.

Configuration revision number Receiving switches use this to identify whether the update is newer than the one they have in their database.

Updater identity The name of the switch from which the update is sent.

Updater timestamp Might or might not be used.

MD5Digest The key sent with the update when a password is assigned to the domain. If the key doesn't match, the update is ignored.

Subset Advertisements

The subset advertisements contain specific information about a VLAN. After an administrator adds, deletes, or renames a VLAN, the switches are notified that they are about to receive a VLAN update on their trunk links via the VLAN-info field 1. Figure 14.6 shows the VTP subset advertisement inside this field.

FIGURE 14.6 Subset advertisement

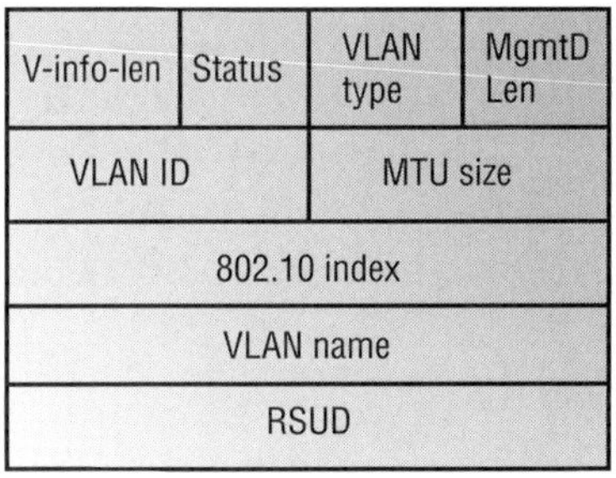

V-info-len
Status
VLAN type
MgmtD Len
VLAN ID
MTU size
802.10 index
VLAN name
RSUD

The following list includes some of the information that is advertised and distributed in the VLAN-info field 1:

VLAN ID Either ISL or 802.1Q

802.10 SAID field that identifies the VLAN ID in FDDI

VTP VTP domain name and revision number

MTU Maximum transmission size for each VLAN

Configuration Revision Number

The revision number is the most important piece in the VTP advertisement. Figure 14.7 shows an example of how a revision number is used in an advertisement.

FIGURE 14.7 VTP revision number

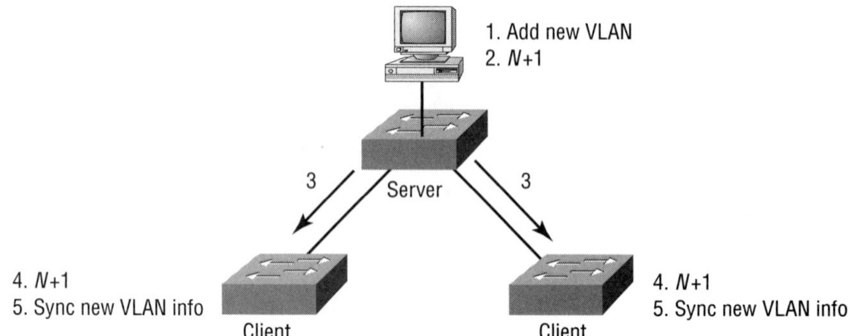

Figure 14.7 shows a configuration revision number as *N*. As a database is modified, the VTP server increments the revision number by 1. The VTP server then advertises the database with the new configuration revision number.

When a switch receives an advertisement that has a higher revision number, then the switch overwrites the database in NVRAM with the new database being advertised.

Configuring VTP

There are several options that you need to be aware of before attempting to configure the VTP domain:

1. Consider the version number of the VTP you will run.
2. Decide if the switch is going to be a member of an already existing domain or if you are creating a new one. To add it to an existing domain, find the domain name and password, if used.
3. Choose the VTP mode for each switch in the internetwork.

After everything is configured, the new setup should be verified to ensure that the connections work properly.

Configuring the VTP Version

There are two versions of VTP that are configurable on Cisco switches. Version 1 is the default VTP version on all switches and is typically used. No VTP version configuration is needed if you will be running version 1. Version 1 and version 2 are not compatible, so it is an all-or-nothing configuration for your switches. However, if all your switches are VTP version 2 compatible, changing one switch changes all of them. Be careful if you are not sure whether all your switches are version 2 compatible.

You would configure version 2 for the following reasons:

Token Ring VLAN support To run Token Ring, you must run version 2 of the VTP protocol. This means that all switches must be capable of running version 2.

TLV support Unrecognized type-length-value (TLV) support. If a VTP advertisement is received and has an unrecognized type-length-value, the version 2 VTP switches will still propagate the changes through their trunk links.

Transparent mode Switches can run in transparent mode, which means that they only forward messages and advertisements, not add them to their own database. In version 1, the switch checks the domain name and version before forwarding, but in version 2, the switches forward VTP messages without checking the version.

Consistency checks Consistency checks are run when an administrator enters new information in the switches, either with the CLI or other management software. If information is received by an advertisement or read from NVRAM, a consistency check is not run. A switch checks the digest on a VTP message, and if it is correct, no consistency check is made.

To configure VTP version 2 on a 4000 series, use the `set vtp v2 enable` command:

```
Terry_4000> (enable) set vtp v2 enable
This command will enable the version 2 function
in the entire management domain.
All devices in the management domain should
be version2-capable before enabling.
Do you want to continue (y/n) [n]? y
VTP domain  modified
Terry_4000> (enable)
```

The IOS-based switches once again demand that you access the VLAN database in order to configure VTP. Both versions are supported, as shown next:

```
Terry_2950#vlan database
Terry_2950(vlan)#?
VLAN database editing buffer manipulation commands:
  abort  Exit mode without applying the changes
  apply  Apply current changes and bump revision number
  exit   Apply changes, bump revision number, and exit mode
  no     Negate a command or set its defaults
  reset  Abandon current changes and reread current database
  show   Show database information
  vlan   Add, delete, or modify values associated with a single VLAN
  vtp    Perform VTP administrative functions.

Terry_2950(vlan)#vtp ?
  client       Set the device to client mode.
```

```
domain       Set the name of the VTP administrative domain.
password     Set the password for the VTP administrative domain.
pruning      Set the administrative domain to permit pruning.
server       Set the device to server mode.
transparent  Set the device to transparent mode.
v2-mode      Set the administrative domain to V2 mode.
```

Configuring the Domain

After you decide which version to run, set the VTP domain name and password on the first switch. The VTP name can be up to 32 characters long. On both the 4000 and the IOS-based switches, you can set the VTP domain password. The password is a minimum of 8 characters and a maximum of 64 on the 4000, and although truncated to 64 characters on the IOS-based switches, it has no minimum value.

```
Terry_4000> (enable) set vtp domain ?
Usage: set vtp [domain <name>] [mode <mode>]
[passwd <passwd>]
[pruning <enable|disable>]
[v2 <enable|disable>
       (mode = client|server|transparent
        Use passwd '0' to clear vtp password)
Usage: set vtp pruneeligible <vlans>
       (vlans = 2..1000
        An example of vlans is 2-10,1000)
Terry_4000> (enable) set vtp domain Globalnet
VTP domain Globalnet modified
Terry_4000> (enable)

Terry_2950(vlan)#vtp password ?
  WORD  The ascii password for the VTP administrative domain.

Terry_2950(vlan)#vtp password globalnet
Setting device VLAN database password to globalnet.
Terry_2950(vlan)#
```

Configuring the VTP Mode

Create your first switch as a server and then create the connected switches as clients, or whatever you decided to configure them as. You don't have to do this as a separate command as we did; you can configure the VTP information in one line, including passwords, modes, and versions:

```
Terry_4000> (enable) set vtp domain
Usage: set vtp [domain <name>] [mode <mode>]
```

```
[passwd <passwd>]pruning <enable|disable>]
[v2 <enable|disable>
(mode = client|server|transparent
        Use passwd '0' to clear vtp password)
Usage: set vtp pruneeligible <vlans>
       (vlans = 2..1000
        An example of vlans is 2-10,1000)
Terry_4000> (enable) set vtp domain Globalnet mode server
VTP domain Globalnet modified
```

On the 2950 and 3550 switches, the commands are as follows:

```
Terry_2950#conf t
Enter configuration commands, one per line.  End with CNTL/Z.
Terry_2950(config)#vtp ?
  domain     Set the name of the VTP administrative domain.
  file       Configure IFS filesystem file where VTP configuration is stored.
  interface  Configure interface as the preferred source for the VTP IP updater
             address.
  mode       Configure VTP device mode.
  password   Set the password for the VTP administrative domain.
  pruning    Set the adminstrative domain to permit pruning.
  version    Set the adminstrative domain to VTP version.

Terry_2950(config)#vtp mode ?
  client       Set the device to client mode.
  server       Set the device to server mode.
  transparent  Set the device to transparent mode.
```

Verifying the VTP Configuration

You can verify the VTP domain information by using the commands `show vtp domain` and `show vtp statistics`.

The `show vtp domain` command shows you the domain name, mode, and pruning information:

```
Terry_4000> (enable) show vtp domain
Domain Name           Domain Index VTP Version Local Mode  Password
--------------------- ------------ ----------- -----------------------
Globalnet       1            2           server
Vlan-count Max-vlan-storage Config Revision Notifications
---------- ---------------- --------------- --------------------------
5          1023             1               disabled
```

```
Last Updater    V2 Mode  Pruning  PruneEligible on Vlans
--------------- -------- -------- -------------------------------------
172.16.10.14    disabled disabled 2-1000
Terry_4000> (enable)
```

4000 Series

The `show vtp statistics` command shows a summary of VTP advertisement messages sent and received. It also shows configuration errors if any were detected:

```
Terry_4000> (enable) show vtp statistics
VTP statistics:
summary advts received         0
subset  advts received         0
request advts received         0
summary advts transmitted      5
subset  advts transmitted      2
request advts transmitted      0
No of config revision errors   0
No of config digest errors     0
VTP pruning statistics:
Trunk     Join Transmitted  Join Received  Summary advts received from
                                           non-pruning-capable device
--------  ----------------  -------------  ---------------------------
 2/12     0                 0              0
Terry_4000> (enable)
```

2950 and 3550 Series Switches

On the IOS-based switches, you have to use the `show vtp counters` command to achieve the same result:

```
Terry_2950#show vtp counters
VTP statistics:
Summary advertisements received    : 0
Subset advertisements received     : 0
Request advertisements received    : 0
Summary advertisements transmitted : 0
Subset advertisements transmitted  : 0
Request advertisements transmitted : 0
Number of config revision errors   : 0
Number of config digest errors     : 0
Number of V1 summary errors        : 0
```

```
VTP pruning statistics:

Trunk      Join Transmitted Join Received    Summary advts received from
                                             non-pruning-capable device
--------   ---------------- ---------------- ---------------------------
```

Adding to a VTP Domain

You need to be careful when adding a new switch into an existing domain. If a switch is inserted into the domain and has incorrect VLAN information, the result could be a VTP database propagated throughout the internetwork with false information.

Before inserting a switch, make sure that you follow these three steps:

1. Perform a `clear config all` to remove any existing VLAN configuration on a set-based switch. On the IOS-based switches, you must ensure that the new switch has no VTP configuration. If it has, you should erase the startup-config (after saving it to a TFTP server or as a text file).
2. Power-cycle the switch to clear the VTP NVRAM.
3. Configure the switch to perform the mode of VTP that it will participate in. Cisco's rule of thumb is that you create several VTP servers in the domain, with all the other switches set to client mode.

VTP Pruning

To preserve bandwidth, you can configure the VTP to reduce the number of broadcasts, multicasts, and other unicast packets. This is called *VTP pruning*. VTP restricts broadcasts to only trunk links that must have the information. If a trunk link does not need the broadcasts, the information is not sent. VTP pruning is disabled by default on all switches.

Figure 14.8 shows that if a switch does not have any ports configured for VLAN 5 and a broadcast is sent throughout VLAN 5, the broadcast would not traverse the trunk link going to the switch without any VLAN 5 members.

Enabling pruning on a VTP server enables pruning for the entire domain, and by default, VLANs 2 through 1005 are eligible for pruning. VLAN 1 can never prune.

Use the following command to set VLANs to be eligible for pruning:

```
Terry_4000> (enable) set vtp pruneeligible ?
Usage: set vtp [domain <name>] [mode <mode>]
[passwd <passwd>] [pruning <enable|disable>]
[v2 <enable|disable> (mode = client|server|transparent
        Use passwd '0' to clear vtp password)
Usage: set vtp pruneeligible <vlans>
       (vlans = 2..1000
        An example of vlans is 2-10,1000)
Terry_4000> (enable) set vtp pruneeligible 2
Vlans 2-1000 eligible for pruning on this device.
VTP domain Globalnet modified.
```

FIGURE 14.8 VTP pruning

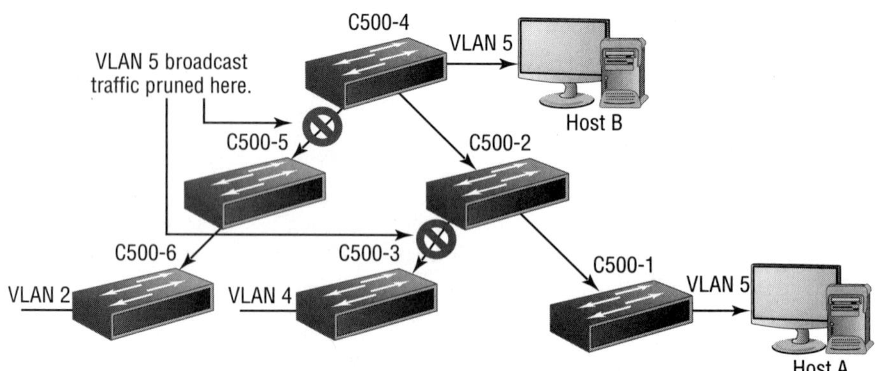

Notice once again that when you enable a VLAN for pruning, by default, it configures all the VLANs. Use the following command to clear the unwanted VLANs:

```
Terry_4000> (enable) clear vtp pruneeligible 3-1005
Vlans 1,3-1005 will not be pruned on this device.
VTP domain Globalnet modified.
Terry_4000> (enable)
```

To verify the pruned state of a trunk port, use the `show trunk` command.

To set pruning on the 2950 and 3550, head into VLAN database mode. The command `vtp pruning` enables the pruning process while the command `switchport trunk pruning vlan remove` *`vlan-id`* removes VLANs from the list of pruning-eligible VLANs:

```
Terry_2950#vlan database
Terry_2950(vlan)#vtp ?
  client       Set the device to client mode.
  domain       Set the name of the VTP administrative domain.
  password     Set the password for the VTP administrative domain.
  pruning      Set the administrative domain to permit pruning.
  server       Set the device to server mode.
  transparent  Set the device to transparent mode.
  v2-mode      Set the administrative domain to V2 mode.

Terry_2950(vlan)#vtp pruning ?
  v2-mode  Set the administrative domain to V2 mode.
  <cr>
```

```
Terry_2950(vlan)#vtp pruning
Pruning switched ON
Terry_2950(vlan)#
Terry_2950#

Terry_2950#configure terminal
Terry_2950 (config)#interface fa 0/10
Terry_2950 (config-if)#switchport trunk pruning vlan remove 2-5,10
```

Auxiliary VLANs

IP telephony involves the use of an IP-based network to replace the legacy telephony services provided by PBX (private branch exchange) systems. This involves the use of an IP telephone, a call manager, and gateway services for the access to the main telephone network. The call manager will probably be located in a network server, and many of the gateway functions will be provided inside the networking equipment. Cisco's 6500 series switches support many gateway functions.

IP packets traveling to and from the PC and to and from the phone share the same physical link to the same port of the switch. If the switch is already configured on a subnet-per-VLAN basis, this can cause problems if insufficient IP addresses are available.

One way of meeting the demands of mixed services, such as voice and data, is to allocate a VLAN specifically for the purpose of carrying voice traffic. These special VLANs are known as *auxiliary VLANs*. One advantage of auxiliary VLANs is that they can be used to ensure that data traveling across the shared link does not reduce the quality of service demanded by the IP phones. Another is that they allow the creation of a new VLAN with a new range of IP addresses just for the phones.

The IEEE 802.1p protocol is used to define quality of service (QoS) at the MAC layer. Priorities are appended to the frame and these are regenerated at each layer 2 forwarding interface, based upon priorities established in the switches. This is covered in greater detail later in this book, but I just wanted to point out how QoS can be achieved with auxiliary VLANs.

802.1Q Tunneling

Modern networks are increasingly more complex, with new requirements being developed as new applications and ways of working appear. Sometimes there is a need for ISP customers to have their VLANs extended across the service provider network. The technique that supports this is called 802.1Q in Q, or more simply, 802.1Q tunneling. This is supported in the Catalyst 3550 series.

As you have read in this chapter, the 802.1Q protocol provides for a tag to be inserted inside the standard Ethernet frame carrying VLAN information. When 802.1Q tunneling is implemented, this happens twice. The first time it is implemented by the customer, and the second time it is implemented by the service provider.

At the tunnel boundary, the second tag—called the *metro tag*—is added, containing a VLAN ID unique to that customer. The frames are switched across the service provider network, and at the egress point, the metro tag is stripped and the exposed customer-specific 802.1Q frame is forwarded to the customer.

There are some restrictions to this technology, both in terms of the configuration options and the protocol operation. For example, these metro frames must be switched, not routed, and only layer 2 QoS is supported. Nonetheless, as more service providers offer switched networks across metropolitan areas, this is likely to become increasingly common.

Summary

Broadcast domains exist as layer 2 switched networks, but they can be broken up by creating virtual LANs. When you create VLANs, you are able to create smaller broadcast domains within a switch by assigning different ports in the switch to different subnetworks.

VLANs can be configured on both set-based and IOS-based switches, and it is still important to understand how to configure VLANs on both types as well as how to set the configuration of VLANs on individual interfaces.

Trunking enables you to send information about multiple VLANs down one link, in contrast to an access link that can send information about only one VLAN. Trunking is configured between switches, often between the access and distribution layer switches, but could be between any switches depending upon your particular topology. Trunking could be configured between a switch and a router, or a switch and a host, where special demands exist, such as the remote device needing to know about multiple VLANs.

The VLAN Trunk Protocol (VTP) is used to maintain consistency of VLAN information across a domain. This doesn't really have much to do with trunking except that VTP information is only sent down trunk links. VTP is used to update all switches in the internetwork with VLAN information.

Exam Essentials

Understand what a trunk is. A trunk is a link between a switch and another device that allows the traffic from multiple VLANs to cross it. Special trunk protocols are used to carry the additional information needed, which cannot be incorporated into the standard Ethernet frame. Two protocols—the Cisco proprietary ISL and the standards-based IEEE 802.1Q—have been developed for this purpose. When a packet crosses a trunk, it retains any ISL or dot1q information detailing what VLAN the packet belongs to.

Understand the difference between ISL and 802.1Q. ISL is a Cisco proprietary VLAN format, whereas 802.1Q is a standard. Network cards are made to support both types, which enables PCs and servers to receive and send VLAN-specific traffic. The big difference between the two is that ISL encapsulates the original packet in a new 30-byte frame, whereas 802.1Q just inserts a 4-byte additional field into the existing Ethernet frame.

Know the configuration differences between the different switches. The 4000 series uses the standard `set` commands, whereas the 2950 and 3550 series use IOS commands. The IOS-based switches configure VLAN and VTP configurations in VLAN database configuration mode, but assign interfaces to VLANs in interface configuration mode. Using CatOS, the 4000 makes no such distinctions. But remember that the 4000 series switches, along with the 6500 and 8500, can be upgraded to use IOS, in which case the configuration commands are standard IOS-based.

Understand when a VLAN should be used. VLANs are used to separate broadcast traffic into different groupings. If a switch has ports 1–10 in VLAN 1 and ports 11–20 in VLAN 2, a packet arriving from a device connected to port 5 can't talk to a device connected to port 15 without some sort of routing engine participating. Know that VLANs can be used for security as well as to break up existing large broadcast domains.

Understand what VTP is and how it is used. VTP carries VLAN information between switches, which can be configured to be servers, clients, or transparent. VTP information is contained within a domain, and it ensures that VLAN naming and numbering is consistent within a domain, as well as reducing configuration overhead.

Layer 2 Switching and the Spanning Tree Protocol (STP)

THE CCNP EXAM TOPICS COVERED IN THIS CHAPTER INCLUDE THE FOLLOWING:

- ✓ Understand the Physical, Data Link, and Network layer technologies used in a multilayer switched network.
- ✓ Describe Spanning Tree (STP), and explain the operation of common and per-VLAN STP implementations.
- ✓ Configure Spanning Tree in both Common Spanning Tree (CST) and per-VLAN modes.

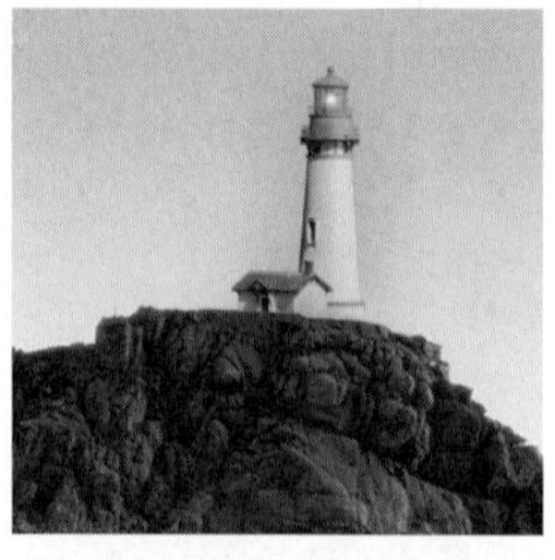

In this chapter, we'll explore the three distinct functions of layer 2 switching: address filtering, forward/filter decision-making, and loop avoidance. We will probe the issue of loop avoidance in depth and discuss how the Spanning Tree Protocol (STP) works to stop network loops from occurring on your layer 2 network.

This chapter continues the discussion of layer 2 switching started in Chapter 12, "The Campus Network." We will consider the different modes of switching that may be employed, move on to see how network loops occur in a layer 2 network, and then provide an introduction to STP, including the different components of STP and how to configure STP on layer 2 switched networks. It is necessary for networking professionals to have a clear understanding of the STP, so by the end of this chapter, you will know how to use STP to stop network loops, broadcast storms, and multiple frame copies. In Chapter 16, "Using Spanning Tree with VLANs," we'll continue discussing STP and provide the more complex and advanced configurations used with it.

It is typical these days to create a network with redundant links; this provides consistent network availability when a network outage occurs on one link. STP provides the necessary loop-avoidance function, but there are several additional features that can be utilized. For example, it is possible to load-balance over the redundant links as well, and VLANs have a special part to play, so we will continue the discussion in Chapter 16.

Layer 2 LAN Switching

You can think of layer 2 switches as bridges with more ports. Remember from Chapter 12 that layer 2 switching is hardware based, which means that it uses the Media Access Control (MAC) address from the hosts' network interface cards (NICs) to filter the network. You should also remember how switches use application-specific integrated circuits (ASICs) to build and maintain filter tables.

However, there are some differences between bridges and switches that you should be aware of. This section outlines those differences and then discusses the three functions of layer 2 switching.

Comparing Bridges to Switches

The following list describes the differences between bridges and switches. Table 15.1 provides an overview of that comparison.

- Bridges are software based because the program runs in RAM. Switches are hardware based because they use ASIC chips to help make filtering decisions.

- Bridges can have only one spanning tree instance per bridge. Switches can have many. (Spanning tree is covered later in this chapter.)
- Bridges can have up to only 16 ports. A switch can have hundreds.

You probably won't go out and buy a bridge, but it's important to understand how bridges are designed and maintained because layer 2 switches function in a similar fashion.

TABLE 15.1 A Comparison of Bridges and Switches

	Bridges	Switches
Filtering	Software based	Hardware based
Spanning tree numbers	One spanning tree instance	Many spanning tree instances
Ports	16 ports maximum	Hundreds of ports available

Three Switch Functions at Layer 2

There are three distinct functions of layer 2 switching:

Address learning Layer 2 switches and bridges remember the source hardware address of each frame received on an interface and enter it into a MAC database.

The forwarding and filtering decision When a frame is received on an interface, the switch looks at the destination hardware address and looks up the exit interface in the MAC database.

Loop avoidance If multiple connections between switches are created for redundancy, network loops can occur. STP is used to stop network loops and allow redundancy.

These functions of the layer 2 switch—address learning, forward and filtering decisions, and loop avoidance—are discussed in detail in the following sections.

Address Learning

The layer 2 switch is responsible for *address learning*. When a switch is powered on, the MAC filtering table is empty. When a device transmits and a frame is received on an interface, the switch takes the source address and places it in the MAC filter table. It remembers what interface the device is located on. The switch has no choice but to flood the network with this frame because it has no idea where the destination device is located.

If a device answers and sends a frame back, then the switch takes the source address from that frame, places the MAC address in the database, and associates this address with the interface on which the frame was received. Because the switch now has two MAC addresses in the filtering table, the devices can now make a point-to-point connection and the frames are forwarded only between the two devices. This is what makes layer 2 switches better than hubs. In a hub network, all frames are forwarded out all ports every time.

Figure 15.1 shows the procedures for building a MAC database.

FIGURE 15.1 How switches learn hosts' locations

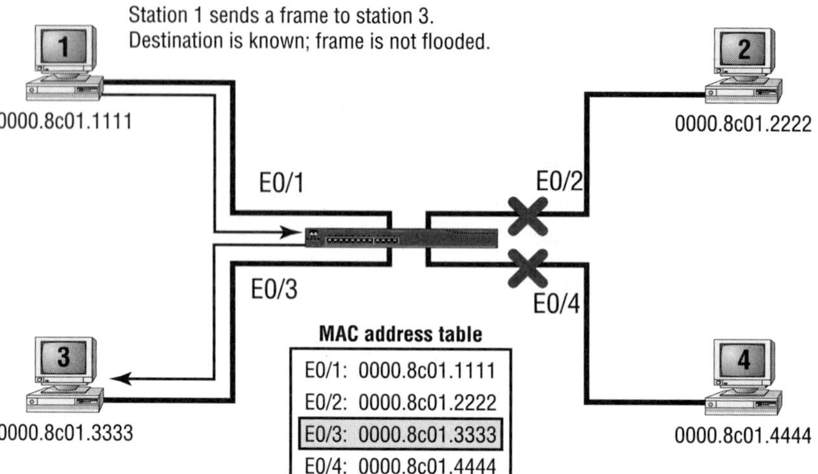

In the figure, four hosts are attached to a switch. The switch has nothing in the MAC address table when it is powered on. The figure shows the switch's MAC filter table after each device has communicated with the switch. The following steps show how the table is populated:

1. Station 1 sends a frame to station 3. Station 1 has a MAC address of 0000.8c01.1111. Station 3 has a MAC address of 0000.8c01.3333.
2. The switch receives the frame on Ethernet interface 0/1, examines the source and destination MAC addresses, and places the source address in the MAC address table.
3. Because the destination address is not in the MAC database, the frame is forwarded out of all interfaces; this is called flooding.
4. Station 3 receives the frame and responds to station 1. The switch receives this frame on interface E0/3 and places the source hardware address in the MAC database.
5. The switch knows the interface associated with station 1's MAC address and forwards the frame only out of that interface. Effectively, station 1 and station 3 now have a point-to-point connection, and only those two devices will receive the frames. Stations 2 and 4 do not see the frames.

If the two devices do not communicate with the switch again within a certain time limit, the switch flushes the entries from the database to keep the database as current as possible.

Forwarding/Filtering Decision

The layer 2 switch also uses the MAC filter table to both forward and filter frames received on the switch. This is called the *forwarding and filtering decision*. When a frame arrives at a switch interface, the destination hardware address is compared to the forward/filter MAC database. If the destination hardware address is known and listed in the database, the frame is sent out only on the correct exit interface. The switch does not transmit the frame out of any interface except for the destination interface, thus preserving bandwidth on the other network segments. This is called frame filtering.

If the destination hardware address is not listed in the MAC database, the frame is flooded out all active interfaces except the interface on which the frame was received. If a device answers, the MAC database is updated with the device location (interface).

In modern switches, the switching or bridging table is known as the CAM or TCM table. I will cover these in detail in Chapter 21, "Catalyst Switch Technologies." For the moment, please accept that these are just tables, optimized for pretty fast lookup.

Broadcast and Multicast Frames

Remember, layer 2 switches forward all broadcasts and multicasts by default. The forwarding/filtering decision is not made because broadcast packets are designed to go to every device on the segment and multicasts are destined for every device listening for a particular type of packet. Whereas the MAC address of a given device is normally determined by the MAC address that is burned into the network card, broadcasts and multicasts are a way of targeting multiple devices.

A broadcast targets every device on the subnet by setting all the bits in the destination MAC address to 1. Thus, the 48-bit destination MAC address, which uses hexadecimal notation, is FFFF.FFFF.FFFF. Every device is trained to look for frames addressed to its own unicast MAC address and frames addressed to the broadcast MAC address. An example of a packet that every device needs to hear is an ARP request.

A multicast is a frame that needs to be forwarded to every device that is participating in a certain process. This process is usually defined at layer 3, so if five routers are using the EIGRP routing protocol and one sends out an update, it sends the update to the multicast IP address 224.0.0.10. Each router is listening for any packet with that IP address as its destination, but switches don't look at the IP address when the frame is received—they only look at the MAC address. There is a special format that hosts use when the packet is part of a multicast process, creating a MAC address for the frame from a reserved range. Hosts that have joined the multicast group look out for frames addressed to the multicast MAC address. Switches don't join the group, so they must treat multicast frames as broadcasts, flooding them out of every interface. This process is covered in detail in Chapter 19, "Understanding and Configuring Multicast Operation."

When a switch receives either of these types of frames, the frames are then quickly flooded out of all active ports of the switch by default. To have broadcasts and multicasts forwarded out of only a limited number of administratively assigned ports, you can create virtual LANs, which were discussed in Chapter 14, "VLANs, Trunks, and VTP."

Loop Avoidance

Finally, the layer 2 switch is responsible for *loop avoidance*. Now obviously, it's a good idea to use redundant links between switches, because they help stop complete network failures if one link fails. Redundant links are extremely helpful, but they can cause more problems than they solve. The more redundancy built into a network, the more loops will occur, causing loops within loops and exacerbating any problems caused. In this section, we'll discuss some of the most serious problems:

- Broadcast storms
- Multiple frame copies
- MAC table instability

Broadcast Storms

Without a loop-avoidance scheme, switches will flood broadcasts endlessly throughout the internetwork. This can lead to a broadcast storm. Figure 15.2 shows how a broadcast might be propagated throughout the network. As each broadcast reaches a network segment where multiple switch ports are connected, the frame will be duplicated as it is forwarded by all switches, thus increasing the frame count. Broadcasts are processed by each host, and the resultant overhead to all attached devices rapidly becomes unacceptable.

FIGURE 15.2 Broadcast storms

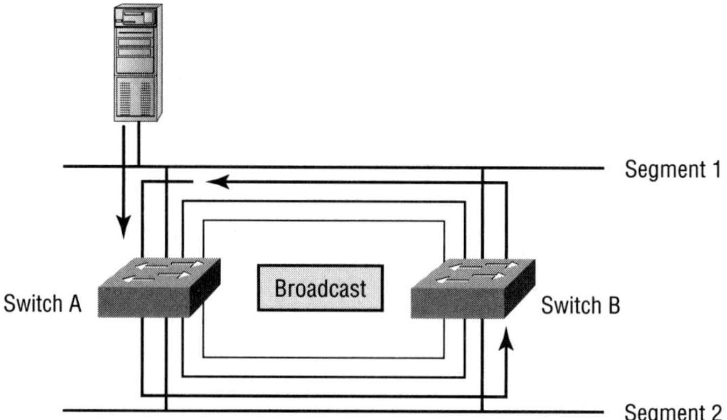

Multiple Frame Copies

Another problem is that a device can receive multiple copies of the same frame because the frame can arrive from different segments at the same time. Figure 15.3 shows how multiple frames can arrive from multiple segments simultaneously.

All frames addressed to a host are processed, and although upper layer protocols such as TCP may be able to easily identify that frames are duplicated, there is still an unnecessary processing overhead. Additionally, some connectionless protocols may not realize that frames contain duplicate information and may become confused.

FIGURE 15.3 Multiple frame copies

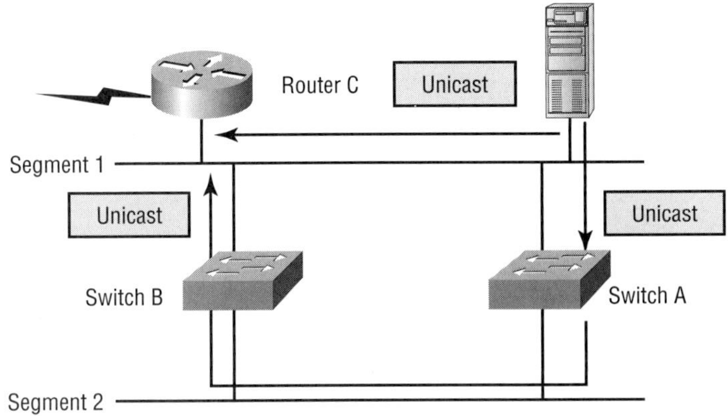

MAC Table Instability

Another problem is that of MAC table instability. Because the switch can receive frames from a single MAC address on different ports (due to frames looping), the MAC table is constantly being updated to reflect the new "location" of the course host. The result is that frames may not be forwarded out of the correct interface, causing data to be lost, resulting in retransmission and extra load on the network.

To solve these three problems, the Spanning Tree Protocol (STP) was developed.

Spanning Tree Operation

In layer 3 devices, which are typically routers, the routing protocols are responsible for making sure routing loops do not occur in the network. What is used to make sure network loops do not occur in layer 2 switched networks? That is the job of the *Spanning Tree Protocol (STP)*.

Digital Equipment Corporation (DEC), which was purchased by Compaq before the merger with Hewlett-Packard, was the original creator of STP. Actually, Radia Perlman is credited with the main development of STP and should get the credit. The IEEE created its version of STP, called 802.1D, using the DEC version as the basis. By default, all Cisco switches run the IEEE 802.1D version of STP, which is not compatible with the DEC version.

The big difference between the two types of STP from an administrative point of view is the range of values that can be set for the priority. A bridge using DEC STP can be set as high as 255, and a switch using IEEE STP can be set as high as 65535. If the two could be used together, a bridge set as a very low priority on DEC would stand a good chance of becoming the root in an IEEE STP network.

The big picture is that STP stops network loops from occurring on your layer 2 network (bridges or switches). STP switches constantly monitor the network to find all links and to make sure loops do not occur by shutting down redundant links.

The Spanning Tree Protocol executes an algorithm called the spanning tree algorithm. Switches choose a reference point in the network and calculate the redundant paths to that reference point. After a loop in the network is discovered, the spanning tree algorithm chooses one path on which to forward frames and shuts down the other redundant links to stop any frames from being forwarded along looped paths. The reference point is called the root bridge.

There can be only one *root bridge* in any given network. The root bridge ports are called designated ports, and designated ports operate in what is called forwarding state. Forwarding state ports send and receive traffic.

If you have other switches in your network, as shown in Figure 15.4, they are called non-root bridges. However, the port that has the lowest cumulative cost to the root bridge is called a root port, and it sends and receives traffic. The cost is determined by the bandwidth of a link.

FIGURE 15.4 Spanning tree operations

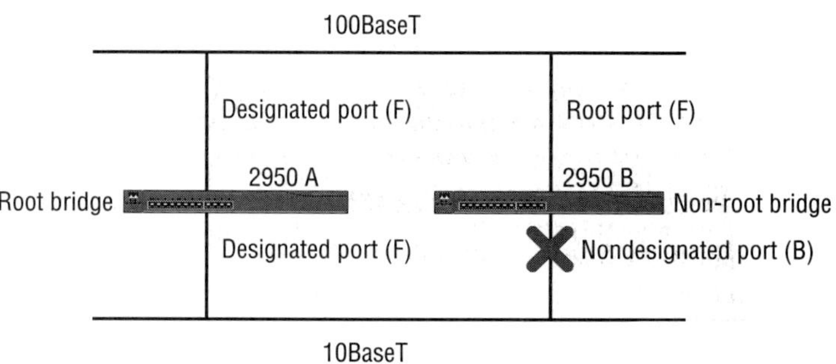

Ports that forward traffic away from the root bridge are called the *designated ports*. Because the root can forward traffic only away from itself, all its ports are designated ports. The other port or ports on the bridge are considered *nondesignated ports* and will not send or receive traffic. This is called blocking mode.

This section covers exactly how a group of switches determines the best path throughout the network and how you can modify the results. This section covers port selection and link cost values as well as the different spanning tree states that a particular port might be in.

Selecting the Best Path

Using spanning tree, a group of switches determines the best path from any point A to any point B. To do this, all the switches need to communicate, and each switch needs to know what the network looks like. In order to know what links should be dynamically disabled, a root bridge must be selected and each switch needs to determine the type of each port.

Selecting the Root Bridge

Switches or bridges running STP exchange information with what are called *Bridge Protocol Data Units (BPDUs)*. BPDUs multicast frames containing port cost and other information. The bridge ID of each device is sent to other devices using BPDUs.

The *bridge ID* is used to determine the root bridge in the network and to determine the root port. The bridge ID is eight bytes long and includes the priority and the MAC address of the device. The priority on all devices running the IEEE STP version is 32768 by default. The lower the bridge ID, the more likely a device is to become the root bridge.

At startup, switches multicast their ID inside BPDUs. To determine the root bridge, switches in the network compare the bridge IDs they receive via the BPDUs and their own ID. Whichever switch has the lowest bridge ID becomes the root bridge. If two switches or bridges have the same priority value, then the MAC address is used to determine which has the lowest ID.

For example, if two switches—A and B—both use the default priority of 32768, the MAC address will be used. If switch A's MAC address is 0000.0c00.1111 and switch B's MAC address is 0000.0c00.2222, switch A would become the root bridge.

Because each switch comes with a burned-in MAC address, if the switches use the default priority, then the one with the lowest MAC address becomes the root bridge. This means that this device will have a large number of packets passing through it. If you have a 6509 and have spent lots of money on the fabric upgrades to a 256GB backplane, the last thing you want is for an old switch in a closet to become the root bridge. For this reason, it is strongly recommended that you lower the number on the priority for core switches. Chapter 16 gives more information on dealing with designs.

The following network analyzer output shows a BPDU broadcasted on a network. BPDUs are sent out every two seconds by default. That might seem like a lot of overhead, but remember that this is only a layer 2 frame, with no layer 3 information in the packet:

```
Flags:         0x80  802.3
Status:        0x00
Packet Length:64
Timestamp:     19:33:18.726314 02/28/2003
802.3 Header
  Destination:  01:80:c2:00:00:00
  Source:       00:b0:64:75:6b:c3
  LLC Length:   38
802.2 Logical Link Control (LLC) Header
  Dest. SAP:    0x42  802.1 Bridge Spanning Tree
  Source SAP:   0x42  802.1 Bridge Spanning Tree
  Command:      0x03  Unnumbered Information
802.1 - Bridge Spanning Tree
```

```
  Protocol Identifier:  0
  Protocol Version ID:  0
  Message Type:         0  Configuration Message
  Flags:                %00000000
  Root Priority/ID:     0x8000  /  00:b0:64:75:6b:c0
  Cost Of Path To Root: 0x00000000  (0)
  Bridge Priority/ID:   0x8000  / 00:b0:64:75:6b:c0
  Port Priority/ID:     0x80  /  0x03
  Message Age:                    0/256 seconds     (exactly 0seconds)
  Maximum Age:                    5120/256 seconds   (exactly 20seconds)
  Hello Time:                    512/256 seconds     (exactly 2seconds)
  Forward Delay:                    3840/256 seconds    (exactly 15seconds)
Extra bytes (Padding):
  ........              00 00 00 00 00 00 00 00
Frame Check Sequence:  0x2e006400
```

Notice the cost of path to root. It is 0 because this switch is actually the root bridge. We'll discuss path costs in more detail later in this chapter in the section, "Selecting the Designated Port."

The preceding network analyzer output also shows the BPDU timers, which are used to prevent bridging loops, because the timers determine how long it will take the spanning tree to converge after a failure.

BPDUs are susceptible to propagation delays, which can happen because of packet length, switch processing, bandwidth, and switch utilization problems. These delays can lead to instability in a network, because temporary loops might occur when BPDUs are not received in time for remote switches in the network to include their information in the STP "plan." The STP uses timers to force ports to wait for the correct topology information.

As you can see in the output, the hello time is 2 seconds, the maximum age is 20 seconds, and the forward delay is 15 seconds. These are the defaults.

When a switch first boots up, the only MAC address it knows is its own, so it advertises itself as the root. As it collects BPDUs, it will acknowledge another device as the root, if necessary. When a switch receives a BPDU advertising a device as root, with a better bridge ID than the current root is using, the switch caches this information and waits. It will wait the duration of the MaxAge timer before using the new root, allowing other switches in the network to also receive the BPDU. This reduces the possibility of loops.

Selecting the Root Port

After the root bridge selection process is complete, all switches must calculate their cumulative costs to the root bridge. Each switch listens to BPDUs on all active ports, and if BPDUs advertising cost from the root are received on more than one port, the switch knows it has a redundant link to the root bridge. Eventually, one switch in the loop has to determine which port will become the root port and which port will be put into blocking state.

To determine the port that will be used to communicate with the root bridge, the path cost is determined. The path cost is an accumulated total cost based on the bandwidth of the links. The IEEE 802.1D specification proved to be unworkable with the introduction of higher speed Ethernets, and the values were recently revised to handle the new higher speed links. Both cost values are shown in Table 15.2.

TABLE 15.2 STP Link Cost

Speed	New IEEE Cost	Original IEEE Cost
10Gbps	2	1
1Gbps	4	1
100Mbps	19	10
10Mbps	100	100

Included in the BPDUs that a switch sends out is the cost of getting a frame to the root bridge. A neighboring device receives this information and adds the cost of the link the BPDU arrived on, and that becomes the cost for the neighboring device. For example, switch A sends out a BPDU to switch B saying that A can reach the root with a path cost of 38. The BPDU travels across a gigabit link between switch A and B. B receives the BPDU, giving the cost of 38, and adds the cost of the link the BPDU arrived on, which is 4. Switch B knows that it can reach the root by sending frames through switch A with a total path cost of 42.

After the cost is determined for all links to the root bridge, the switch decides which port has the lowest cost. The lowest cost port is put into forwarding mode, and the other ports are placed in blocking mode. If there are equal-cost paths, the port with the lowest port ID is put into the forwarding state. In the previous example, if switch B had two paths to the root, both with a cost of 42, the switch needs some other way of figuring out which single path will be used. If switch A is accessed via gigabit port 0/3 and switch C is accessed via gigabit port 0/7, switch B will send frames via switch A because it is attached to the lower numerical port number.

Selecting the Designated Port

A designated port is one that is active and forwarding traffic, but doesn't lead to the root. Often, a designated port on one switch connects to the root port on another switch, but it doesn't have to. Because the root bridge doesn't have any ports that lead to itself, and because its ports are never dynamically turned off, all its ports are labeled as designated ports.

The selection of a designated port is fairly easy. If there are two switches that have equal-cost paths to get to the root and are connected to each other, there must be some way of resolving the topological loop that exists. The switches simply examine the bridge IDs, and whichever device has the lower bridge ID is the one that will be responsible for forwarding traffic from that segment. Figure 15.4, shown earlier, illustrates this point.

Spanning Tree Port States

The ports on a bridge or switch running the STP will go through four transitional states:

Blocking Won't forward frames; listens to BPDUs. All ports are in blocking state by default when the switch is powered on.

Listening Listens to BPDUs to make sure no loops occur on the network before passing data frames.

Learning Learns MAC addresses and builds a filter table, but does not forward frames.

Forwarding Bridge port is able to send and receive data. A port is never placed in forwarding state unless there are no redundant links or the port determines that it has the best path to the root bridge.

An administrator can put a port in disabled state, or if a failure with the port occurs, the switch puts it into disabled state.

Typically, switch ports are in either blocking or forwarding state. A forwarding port is a port that has been determined to have the lowest cost to the root bridge. However, if the network has a topology change because of a failed link, or the administrator adds a new switch to the network, the ports on a switch will be in listening and learning states.

Blocking ports are used to prevent network loops. After a switch determines the best path to the root bridge, all other ports may be placed in the blocking state. Blocked ports will still receive BPDUs.

If a switch determines that a blocked port should now be the designated port, it will go to listening state. It checks all BPDUs heard to make sure that it won't create a loop after the port goes to forwarding state.

Figure 15.5 shows the default STP timers and their operation within STP.

FIGURE 15.5 STP default timers

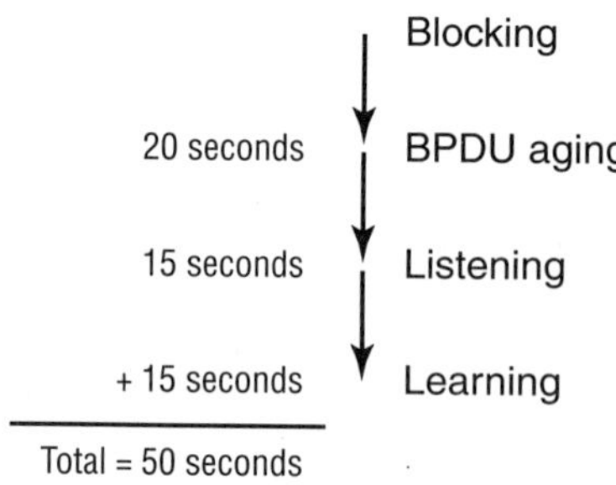

Notice the time from blocking to forwarding. Blocking to listening is 20 seconds (BPDU aging). Listening to learning is another 15 seconds (listening). Learning to forwarding is 15 seconds (learning), for a total of 50 seconds. However, the switch could go to disabled if the port is administratively shut down or the port has a failure.

Convergence

Convergence occurs when bridges and switches have transitioned to either the forwarding or blocking state. No data is forwarded until convergence occurs. Convergence is important in making sure that all devices have the same database.

The problem with convergence is the time it takes for all devices to update. Before data can start to be forwarded, all devices must be updated. The time it usually takes to go from blocking to forwarding state is 50 seconds. Changing the default STP timers is not recommended, but the timers can be adjusted if they need to be. The time it takes to transition a port from the listening state to the learning state or from the learning state to the forwarding state is called the forward delay.

Real World Scenario

Sizing the Network

Each device uses the timers configured on the root bridge. If the timers need to be changed, Cisco recommends that they not be changed directly. Instead, first experiment with the `spantree diameter` option. It will set the timers based on the size of the switched network. The larger the network, the more time is allowed for propagation, which increases the timers. The default diameter is seven switches across. Setting the diameter smaller than your actual network size increases the chance of broadcast storms.

Spanning Tree Example

In Figure 15.6, the three switches all have the same priority of 32768. However, notice the MAC address of each switch. By looking at the priority and MAC addresses of each switch, you should be able to determine the root bridge.

Because 2950A has the lowest MAC address and all three switches use the default priority, 2950A will be the root bridge.

To determine the root ports on switches 2950B and 2950C, you need to look at the cost of the link connecting the switches. Because the connection from both switches to the root switch is from port 0 using a 100Mbps link, that has the best cost and both switches' root port will then be port 0.

Use the bridge ID to determine the designated ports on the switches. The root bridge always has all ports as designated. However, because both 2950B and 2950C have the same cost to the root bridge and because switch 2950B has the lowest bridge ID, the designated port will be on switch 2950B. Because 2950B has been determined to have the designated port, switch 2950C will put port 1 in blocking state to stop any network loop from occurring.

FIGURE 15.6 Spanning tree example

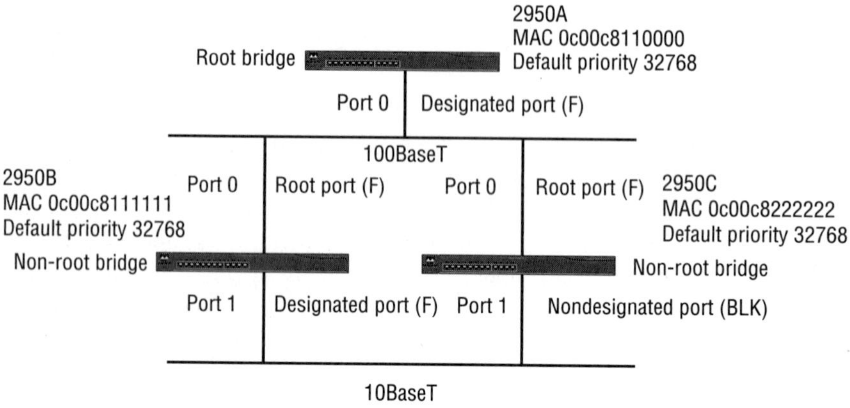

The STP algorithm is often referred to after the name of its creator, Edsger W. Dijkstra, as in Dijkstra's Algorithm. It's not as descriptive as the STP algorithm, but I still like to use it.

LAN Switch Types

One last thing we need to cover before we can move on—the actual forwarding techniques used by switches. LAN switching forwards (or filters) frames based on their hardware destination—the MAC address. There are three methods by which frames can be forwarded or filtered. Each method has its advantages and disadvantages, and by understanding the different LAN switch methods available, you can configure your switches to make smarter switching decisions.

Here are the three switching modes:

Store-and-forward With the *store-and-forward* mode, the complete data frame is received on the switch's buffer, a cyclic redundancy check (CRC) is performed on the frame, and then the destination address is looked up in the MAC filter table.

Cut-through With the *cut-through* mode, the switch waits for only the destination hardware address to be received and then looks up the destination address in the MAC filter table.

FragmentFree *FragmentFree* is the default mode for the Catalyst 1900 switch; it is sometimes referred to as modified cut-through. The switch checks the first 64 bytes of a frame for fragmentation (because of possible collisions) before forwarding the frame.

Figure 15.7 shows the different points where the switching mode takes place in the frame. The different switching modes are discussed in detail next.

FIGURE 15.7 Different switching modes within a frame

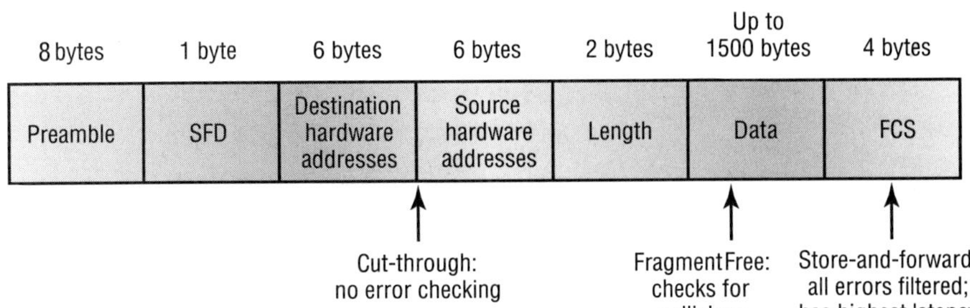

Store-and-Forward

With the store-and-forward switching method, the LAN switch copies the entire frame onto its onboard buffers and computes the CRC. Because it copies the entire frame, latency through the switch varies with frame length.

The frame is discarded if it contains a CRC error, if it's too short (fewer than 64 bytes including the CRC), or if it's too long (more than 1518 bytes including the CRC). If the frame doesn't contain any errors, the LAN switch looks up the destination hardware address in its forwarding or switching table and determines the outgoing interface. It then forwards the frame to its destination.

This is the mode used by modern Catalyst switches, and it further allows for quality of service (QoS) to be applied to the frame by reading additional data. QoS is covered in detail in Chapter 20, "Quality of Service (QoS)."

Cut-Through (Real Time)

With the cut-through switching method, the LAN switch copies only the destination address (the first six bytes following the preamble) onto its onboard buffers. It then looks up the hardware destination address in the MAC switching table, determines the outgoing interface, and forwards the frame toward its destination. A cut-through switch provides reduced latency because it begins to forward the frame as soon as it reads the destination address and determines the outgoing interface.

Some switches can be configured to perform cut-through switching on a per-port basis until a user-defined error threshold is reached. At that point, they automatically change over to store-and-forward mode so they will stop forwarding the errors. When the error rate on the port falls below the threshold, the port automatically changes back to cut-through mode.

FragmentFree (Modified Cut-Through)

FragmentFree is a modified form of cut-through switching. In FragmentFree mode, the switch waits for the collision window (64 bytes) to pass before forwarding. If a packet has an error, it almost always occurs within the first 64 bytes. FragmentFree mode provides better error checking than the cut-through mode, with practically no increase in latency.

Configuring Spanning Tree

The configuration of spanning tree is pretty simple unless you want to change your timers or add multiple spanning tree instances—then it can get complex. The timers and more advanced configurations are covered in Chapter 16.

STP is enabled on all Cisco switches by default. However, you might want to change your spanning tree configuration to have many spanning tree instances. This means that each VLAN can be its own spanning tree. This is known as Per-VLAN spanning tree.

To enable or disable spanning tree on a set-based switch, use the `set spantree` *`parameter`* command. This is performed on a VLAN-by-VLAN basis rather than a port-by-port configuration:

```
Terry_4000> (enable) set spantree disable 1-1005
Spantrees 1-1005 disabled.

Terry_4000> (enable) set spantree enable 1-1005
Spantrees 1-1005 enabled.
```

The preceding configuration shows the disabling of spanning tree on an individual VLAN basis. To enable spanning tree on an individual VLAN basis, use `set spantree enable` *`VLAN(s)`*. Cisco recommends that you do not disable spanning tree on a switch, particularly on uplinks where a loop can occur.

Real World Scenario

Detecting Loops

On switches that have a CPU usage indicator, this is sometimes also called "the spanning tree loop indicator." It's relatively rare to see the CPU usage indicator get much past 20 percent utilization for more than a few seconds at a time. If network connectivity has been lost and you suspect a spanning tree loop is the culprit, take a look at the CPU usage indicator. If utilization reaches 70 percent or higher, when the switch never sees that level of usage during normal operation, that's a good indicator of a spanning tree loop.

Spanning tree is enabled by default on modern switches, but you can enable or disable the protocol as needed. To enable or disable spanning tree on an IOS-based switch, use the `spanning-tree vlan` *`vlan_number`* command or the `no spanning-tree vlan` *`vlan_number`* command. Use the `show spanning-tree` command to view the spanning tree status. The following configuration shows how to enable and disable spanning tree on a 2950 switch:

```
Terry_2950#conf t
Terry_2950(config)#no spanning-tree vlan 1
Terry_2950(config)#^Z

Terry_2950#show spanning-tree

No spanning tree instances exist.

Terry_2950#conf t
Terry_2950(config)#spanning-tree vlan 1
Terry_2950(config)#^Z

Terry_2950#show spanning-tree

VLAN0001
  Spanning tree enabled protocol ieee
  Root ID     Priority     0
              Address      00b0.6414.1180
              Cost         100
              Port         1 (FastEthernet0/1)
              Hello Time    2 sec   Max Age 20 sec   Forward Delay 15 sec

  Bridge ID   Priority     32769  (priority 32768 sys-id-ext 1)
              Address      000b.be53.2c00
              Hello Time    2 sec   Max Age 20 sec   Forward Delay 15 sec
              Aging Time 300

Interface        Port ID                       Designated                 Port ID
Name             Prio.Nbr      Cost Sts       Cost Bridge ID              Prio.Nbr
---------------- -------- --------- --- --------- -------------------- --------
Fa0/1            128.1          100 LIS         0      0 00b0.6414.1180 128.1
Fa0/24           128.24         100 LIS       100 32769 000b.be53.2c00 128.24

Terry_2950#
```

Notice that the commands include mandatory references to the VLANs. You will remember that all ports are in VLAN 1 by default. In the next chapter we will be considering the use of different spanning trees for each VLAN, and these commands will make a little more sense then. In the meantime, just trust me and accept that the Cisco IOS demands that you enter a VLAN number at this time.

To see the spanning tree configuration and whether it is active on a Catalyst 4000 set-based switch, use the `show spantree` command as shown here:

```
Terry_4000> (enable) show spantree
VLAN 1
Spanning tree enabled
Spanning tree type          ieee

Designated Root             00-e0-34-88-fc-00
Designated Root Priority    32768
Designated Root Cost        0
Designated Root Port        1/0
Root Max Age   20 sec    Hello Time 2  sec   Forward Delay 15 sec

Bridge ID MAC ADDR          00-e0-34-88-fc-00
Bridge ID Priority          32768
Bridge Max Age 20 sec    Hello Time 2  sec   Forward Delay 15 sec

Port  Vlan  Port-State     Cost   Priority Fast-Start Group-Method
----  ----  -------------- -----  -------- ---------- ------------
 1/1   1    forwarding       19   32       disabled
 1/2   1    not-connected    19   32       disabled
 2/1   1    not-connected   100   32       disabled
 2/2   1    not-connected   100   32       disabled
 2/3   1    not-connected   100   32       disabled
 2/4   1    not-connected   100   32       disabled
 2/5   1    not-connected   100   32       disabled
<Output truncated>
```

By default, the `show spantree` command provides information about VLAN 1. You can gather spanning tree information about other VLANs by using the `show spantree` *`vlan#`* command.

The `show spantree` command provides you the following information:

Designated root The MAC address of the root bridge.

Designated root priority The priority of the root bridge. All bridges have a default of 32768.

Designated root cost The cost of the shortest path to the root bridge.

Designated root port The port that is chosen as the lowest cost to the root bridge.

Root timers The timers received from the root bridge.

Bridge ID MAC address This bridge's ID. This plus the bridge priority make up the bridge ID.

Bridge ID priority The priority set; the preceding bridge output is using the default of 32768.

Bridge timers The timers used by this bridge.

Ports in the spanning tree Not all available ports are displayed in the preceding output. However, this field does show all ports participating in this spanning tree. It also shows whether they are forwarding.

Although the command abbreviation `show span` works on all the switches, you will get much different output if you use it on the 4000 series. This is because a SPAN (Switch Port Analyzer) is the port used to connect to a sniffer. On the 4000, abbreviate `spantree` to no less than `spant` to avoid this.

Summary

At layer 2 of the OSI model, you have very little information to work with when it comes to forwarding data—essentially just the MAC address. And yet in layer 2 switching, functions including address learning, forwarding versus filtering, and loop avoidance can be taken. Obviously, there are some clever things going on.

Forwarding and filtering is, of course, managed using the bridging (switching) table, constructed by reading source MAC addresses as frames are passed through the switch. This is very similar to legacy bridging, apart from the fact that multi-port switches support micro-segmentation, and have several ways of forwarding frames, including store-and-forward, cut-through, and FragmentFree switching.

Additional links can be implemented to provide redundancy in a network; however, these redundant links can introduce problems such as broadcast storms, multiple frame copies, and multiple loops. The Spanning Tree Protocol (STP) can be used to break network loops by forcing some switches to place some of their ports into a blocking mode. This is done by having one bridge assume a sort of control—the root—and other switches calculating the shortest distance to the root, thus allowing the loop to be seen and broken.

Exam Essentials

Understand that the Spanning Tree Protocol (STP) controls the switched network topology. Redundancy is essential in modern networks, and without STP, switches would often have multiple paths to get to a given destination. Frame duplication due to the multiple paths, plus nonstop broadcast forwarding, would lead to broadcast storms and general instability.

Understand the importance of the root bridge. The root bridge is the center of the spanning tree universe; all STP calculations are based on which device is the root. You need to know how the root is selected and how to influence the process. Switches calculate which is the shortest path to the root and disable ports that promote redundancy.

Know the different types of ports. The root port is the port on a switch that has the least-cost path to the root bridge. A designated port is a port that is active but does not lead to the root. All the ports on the root bridge are active and are designated ports. You need to know how switches decide what state their ports will be in.

Understand the method of breaking ties. Whenever there is a tie, there is always a method of breaking it. Remember that a lower number is usually better. The bridge ID is a combination of the configured priority and the MAC address, so if two switches have the same priority value, the lowest MAC address will break the tie. If two ports on a single switch can reach the root with paths of the same cost, then the lowest numbered one is used.

Using Spanning Tree with VLANs

THE CCNP EXAM TOPICS COVERED IN THIS CHAPTER INCLUDE THE FOLLOWING:

- ✓ Describe LAN segmentation with VLANs.
- ✓ Describe Spanning Tree (STP), and explain the operation of common and per-VLAN STP implementations.
- ✓ Configure Spanning Tree in both Common Spanning Tree (CST) and per-VLAN modes.
- ✓ Configure Spanning Tree parameters including: port priority, VLAN priority, and root bridge selection.
- ✓ Enable advanced Spanning Tree features such as BPDU guard, PortFast and UplinkFast and BackboneFast.
- ✓ Configure Fast EtherChannel and Gigabit EtherChannel on inter-switch links.

Redundancy is the ability to provide an immediate backup solution to a fault in the network that might otherwise cause a network or component service outage. When you're building a redundant network—which is a network with redundant power, hardware, links, and other network-critical components—network loops can occur. The Spanning Tree Protocol (STP) was created to overcome the problems associated with transparent bridging at layer 2.

Unfortunately, STP is a far from optimal protocol. We can hardly blame the designers for this—all they had to work with was a forwarding system designed to transmit broadcasts out of every port, and the option of adding a little intelligence with Bridge Protocol Data Units (BPDUs). So legacy STP leaves us with suboptimal forwarding paths, unused spare links, and the possibility (probability, even) of very slow convergence after a network failure.

This chapter extends our coverage of STP by focusing on providing link redundancy by using STP and the IEEE 802.1D algorithm used to support STP on a per-VLAN basis. The Spanning Tree Protocol uses timers to make the network stable. You'll also learn how to manage the different STP timers to maximize the efficiency of your network, and how to implement specific additions to STP to decrease convergence times.

Creating VLAN Standards

The history of using STP with VLANs is interesting, because it acts as a macro for how many standards have been developed. In the past, Cisco and the IEEE have differed in their approaches to the use of these two protocols together.

As you discovered in Chapter 15, "Layer 2 Switching and the Spanning Tree Protocol (STP)," STP has some well-understood problems. First, convergence will be relatively slow because of the forwarding delays. This is unacceptable in modern networks where users and applications expect immediate recovery from equipment failures. Additionally, it is likely that a general spanning tree topology applied to all VLANs will result in suboptimal paths for some users. The result has been a spate of developments, some proprietary and some standards-based, to overcome these problems.

Per-VLAN Spanning Tree (PVST) is a Cisco proprietary implementation of STP. PVST uses Inter-Switch Link (ISL) routing and runs a separate instance of STP for each and every VLAN.

The IEEE uses Common Spanning Tree (CST), which is defined with IEEE 802.1Q. The IEEE 802.1Q defines one spanning tree instance for all VLANs. A new mechanism, recently standardized as 802.1s, allows multiple spanning tree instances but in a more complex fashion;

it runs multiple instances of STP on a one-to-one basis with VLANs. There is one more implementation of STP, and that is called PVST+. Because it ends with a plus sign, it must be better, right? Well, maybe. What it does is allow CST information to be passed into PVST. Cisco thinks it would be easier if you simply had all Cisco switches; then you wouldn't even have to think about this issue.

This chapter covers the current protocols supported by Cisco and compares the options. The following list includes a brief explanation of each STP implementation:

Per-VLAN Spanning Tree (PVST) Default for Cisco switches; runs a separate instance of spanning tree for each VLAN. Makes smaller STP implementations for easier convergence.

Common Spanning Tree (CST) The 802.1Q standard; runs one large STP on the entire network regardless of the number of VLANs. Problems with convergence can occur in large networks.

Per-VLAN Spanning Tree+ (PVST+) Allows Cisco switches to communicate with CST switches.

Multiple Spanning Tree (MST) The 802.1s standard, supported by Cisco on IOS-based switches since versions of 12.1. Allows multiple instances of STP and group VLAN mapping.

In the rest of this section, we'll go into more detail about each type of STP implementation and its use with VLANs.

Per-VLAN Spanning Tree (PVST)

The Spanning Tree Protocol does not scale well with large switched networks. In such networks, delays can occur in receiving BPDUs. These delays can cause instability in the STP database and convergence delay problems, which means that the network will not be forwarding frames.

To solve problems associated with late BPDUs and convergence delays, Cisco created a concept entitled *Per-VLAN Spanning Tree (PVST)*. This creates smaller STP implementations, which are easier for the switches to manage. Each VLAN has a unique Spanning Tree Protocol topology for its root, port cost, path cost, and priority.

When running PVST, you still provide a loop-free network, but it is based within each VLAN. Each switch has a spanning tree process running for each VLAN. If a switch has five VLANs that it knows about, then it will have five instances of spanning tree running. The benefits of having a PVST are as follows:

- The spanning tree topology is smaller because all links will not necessarily support all VLANs.
- The STP recalculation time is reduced when the switched network is converging.
- The switched network is easier to scale.
- Recovery is faster than with a large network that has one STP instance.
- Administrative control of forwarding paths is permitted on a subnet basis.
- Load balancing over redundant links is permitted when VLAN priorities are established for those links.

There are, however, some disadvantages of using a spanning-tree-per-instance implementation:

- The utilization on the switch is a factor because it needs to manage all the STP instances.
- You must take into consideration that the trunk links have to support all the VLAN STP information as well.
- It requires ISL.
- PVST is a Cisco proprietary protocol.

Common Spanning Tree (CST)

The IEEE 802.1Q is referred to as the *Common Spanning Tree (CST)*. It is also called the Mono-Spanning Tree because it uses only one spanning tree instance regardless of the size of the switched layer 2 network.

The CST runs on all VLANs by default, and all switches are involved in the election process to find the root bridge. The switches then form an association with that root bridge. Typically, using CST does not allow for the optimization of the root bridge placement.

There are some advantages to CST. With one STP instance, there are fewer BPDUs consuming bandwidth. Because there is only one instance of STP in the network, there is less STP processing performed by the switches.

Normally, the disadvantages outweigh the advantages in a larger network. With a single root bridge, the path that has been calculated as the best cost to the root bridge might not be the most efficient for some users to send their data. Another disadvantage of CST is that the STP topology increases in size to make sure all ports in the network are found. This can cause delays in the update and convergence times if the network topology is too large.

Per-VLAN Spanning Tree+ (PVST+)

Per-VLAN Spanning Tree+ (PVST+) is an extension of the PVST standard. Starting with the Catalyst software 4.1 or later, PVST+ is supported on Cisco Catalyst switches. This enables Cisco switches to support the IEEE 802.1Q standard. Basically, the PVST+ extension of the PVST protocol provides support for links across an IEEE 802.1Q CST region.

PVST+ also supports the Cisco default PVST and adds checking mechanisms to make sure there are no configuration problems on trunked ports and VLAN IDs across switches. PVST+ is plug-and-play compatible with PVST with no configuration necessary. To provide support for the IEEE 802.1Q standard, Cisco's existing PVST has been modified with additional features, enabling it to support a link across the IEEE 802.1Q Common Spanning Tree region.

PVST+ includes the following features:

- Provides notification of inconsistencies related to port trunking or VLAN identification across the switches.
- Adds mechanisms to ensure that there is no unknown configuration.
- Tunnels PVST BPDUs through the 802.1Q VLAN region as multicast data.
- Provides compatibility with IEEE 802.1Q's CST and Cisco's PVST protocols.

- Interoperates with 802.1Q-compliant switches using CST through 802.1Q trunking. A CST BPDU is transmitted or received with an IEEE standard bridge group MAC address.
- Blocks ports that receive inconsistent BPDUs in order to prevent forwarding loops.
- Notifies users via Syslog messages about all inconsistencies.

Multiple Spanning Tree (MST)

Multiple Spanning Tree (MST) builds upon the proprietary PVST+ standard. With MST, a number of spanning tree instances can be created, but they are not mapped one-to-one to VLANs. The reason for this is that in most networks—even those supporting hundreds of VLANs—there are a small number of optimal topologies. As each instance of STP demands its own root and all the associated BPDU activity, the processing overhead can be unnecessarily high if you allow each VLAN to have its own spanning tree. Better to create the STP instances and then map VLANs to those instances.

MST features include switches that are grouped together in MST "regions"—interconnected bridges that have the same MST configuration. Each switch in an MST region maintains three attributes: a configuration name, a revision number, and a table associating each of the VLANs supported per MST instance (up to the 4096 maximum). These attributes are common across a domain and must be shared by all switches. Different attributes signify a different domain, which changes the switch-to-switch relationship. Finally, different instances of STP have several VLANs mapped to them, creating the opportunity for VLANs to operate with optimal topology, but reducing the overhead associated with PVST.

MST was approved by the IEEE as 802.1s in June 2003, so a standards-based implementation of this protocol is likely to figure extensively in the future.

Readers wishing to know more about 802.1s than is covered in the CCNP program should visit `www.cisco.com/warp/public/473/147.html`.

Scaling the Spanning Tree Protocol

The STP prevents loops in layer 2 switched networks and is basically plug-and-play. It might be advantageous nonetheless, to change some of the default timers and settings to attempt to create a more stable environment.

In this section, we'll discuss how to scale the STP protocol on a large, switched internetwork. It is important to understand how to provide proper placement of the root bridge to create an optimal topology. If the root bridge is automatically chosen through an election, which is the default, the actual path that the frames can take might not be the most efficient. As the administrator, you can then change the root placement to create a more optimal path. However, it's possible that your changes could cause more damage instead, so you want to think through your network design before making any changes.

To change the root placement, you need to do the following:

- Determine the root device.
- Configure the device.
- Set the port cost.
- Set the port priorities.
- Change the STP timers.

Determining the Root

Determining the root device is the most important decision that you make when configuring STP on your network. If you place the root in the wrong place, it will be difficult to scale the network, and, really, that is what you are trying to do: create a scalable layer 2 switched internetwork.

However, by placing the root switch as close as possible to the center of your network, more optimal and deterministic paths can be easily chosen. You can choose the root bridge and secondary and backup bridges as well. Secondary bridges are very important for network stability in case the root bridge fails. Choosing the root is typically the best thing to do, but if that root goes down for maintenance, spanning tree will select a new root—and because all other switches have the same priority, it might be a switch you wouldn't usually want to be the root bridge.

Because the root bridge should be close to the center of the network, the device will typically be a switch that a lot of traffic passes through such as a distribution layer switch, a core layer switch, or one that does routing or multilayer switching. An access layer switch would not usually be chosen.

After the root bridge has been chosen and configured, all the connected switches must determine the best path to the root bridge. The STP uses several different factors in determining the best path to the root bridge:

- Port cost
- Path cost
- Port priority

When a BPDU is sent out a switch port, the BPDU is assigned a port cost. The path cost, which is the sum of all the port costs, is then determined. The STP first looks at the path cost to calculate the forwarding and blocking ports. If the path costs are equal on two or more links to the root bridge, the port ID is used to determine the root port. The port with the lowest port ID is determined to be the forwarding port. You can change the port used by changing the port priority, but Cisco doesn't recommend this. However, we'll show you how to do it later in this section (so you can have some fun on a rainy Saturday).

Configuring the Root

After you choose the best switch to become your root bridge, you can use the Cisco command-line interface (CLI) to configure the STP parameters in a switched network.

The command to configure the STP is `set spantree`. The following switch output (from our Catalyst 4000) shows the different command parameters you can use when configuring the STP. We are interested in the `set spantree root` and `set spantree root secondary` commands at this point:

```
Terry_4000(enable) set spantree ?
Set spantree commands:
----------------------------------------------------------------------------
set spantree disable         Disable spanning tree
set spantree enable          Enable spanning tree
set spantree fwddelay        Set spantree forward delay
set spantree hello           Set spantree hello interval
set spantree help            Show this message
set spantree maxage          Set spantree max aging time
set spantree portcost        Set spantree port cost
set spantree portfast        Set spantree port fast start
set spantree portpri         Set spantree port priority
set spantree portvlancost    Set spantree port cost per vlan
set spantree portvlanpri     Set spantree port vlan priority
set spantree priority        Set spantree priority
set spantree root            Set switch as primary or secondary root
set spantree uplinkfast      Enable or disable uplinkfast groups
set spantree backbonefast    Enable or disable fast convergence
Terry_4000 (enable)
```

The `set spantree root` command sets the primary root bridge for a specific VLAN, or even for all your VLANs. The `set spantree root secondary` command enables you to configure a backup root bridge.

In the following switch output, notice the options that are available with the `set spantree root` command:

```
Terry_4000> (enable) set spantree root ?
Usage: set spantree root [secondary] <vlans> [dia <network_diameter>]
                         [hello <hello_time>]
       (vlans = 1..1005, network_diameter = 2..7, hello_time = 1..10)
```

Table 16.1 shows the parameters available with the `set spantree` command and their definitions.

TABLE 16.1 *set spantree root* Parameters

Parameter	Definition
root	Designation to change the switch to the root switch. The `set spantree root` command changes the bridge priority from 32768 to 8192.

TABLE 16.1 *set spantree root* Parameters *(continued)*

Parameter	Definition
`secondary`	Designation to change the switch to a secondary root switch if the primary fails. This automatically changes the bridge priority from a default of 32768 to 16384.
`vlan_list`	An optional command that changes the STP parameters on a specified VLAN. If no VLAN is specified, then it changes only VLAN 1 by default. You can change the parameters for VLANs 1–1005.
`dia` *`network diameter`*	Another optional command that specifies the maximum number of bridges between any two points where end stations attach. You can set these parameters from 2 to 7. Figure the network diameter by starting at the root bridge and counting the number of bridges in the VLAN. The root bridge is 1, so if you have only one more switch, set the network diameter to 2. This changes the timers in the VLAN to reflect the new diameter.
`hello` *`hello_time`*	An optional command that specifies in seconds the duration between configuration messages from the root switch. You can set this anywhere from 1 to 10 seconds (2 is the default).

The following switch output is an example of using the `set spantree root` command:

```
Terry_4000> (enable) set spantree root 1-4 dia 2
VLANs 1-2 bridge priority set to 8192.
VLANs 1-2 bridge max aging time set to 10.
VLANs 1-2 bridge hello time set to 2.
VLANs 1-2 bridge forward delay set to 7.
Switch is now the root switch for active VLANs 1-4.
Terry_4000> (enable)
```

The `set spantree root` command tells the switch to change the bridge priority to 8192, which automatically changes the switch to the root bridge. The `1-4` represents the VLANs for which the STP will change the parameters, and the `dia` 2 is the network diameter. To figure the network diameter, we simply counted the number of switches from the root, including the root bridge, which in our example equals 2.

Notice the output after the command. The bridge priority was changed to 8192, the maximum age time was changed to 10, hello time is still 2 seconds, and the forward delay was set to 7 seconds. If the network diameter is set, the STP sets the timers to what it would consider efficient for that size network.

You can verify your STP configuration with the `show spantree` command. If you type the command **`show spantree`** with no parameters, it will show you the spanning tree configuration

Real World Scenario

When a Root Isn't the Root

Using the `set spantree root` command is great when the organization is very centralized. But in a decentralized environment, you might use this command only to find that a coworker set the priority of a different switch to a lower value by using the `set spantree priority` command. This will result in the switch you configured being no more than the backup root bridge. When setting a particular switch to become the root, always make sure that the switch you configured knows it's the root and that other switches know it as well. I find it useful to check one last time as I finish, just to make sure everything is well.

for all VLANs. You can type **show spantree *vlan*** to see the parameters for just a particular VLAN. The following switch output shows the spanning tree information for VLAN 1:

```
Terry_4000> (enable) show spantree 1
VLAN 1
Spanning tree enabled
Spanning tree type          ieee

Designated Root             00-e0-34-88-fc-00
Designated Root Priority    8192
Designated Root Cost        0
Designated Root Port        1/0
Root Max Age   10 sec    Hello Time 2  sec   Forward Delay 7  sec

Bridge ID MAC ADDR          00-e0-34-88-fc-00
Bridge ID Priority          8192
Bridge Max Age 10 sec    Hello Time 2  sec   Forward Delay 7  sec

Port      Vlan  Port-State     Cost   Priority  Fast-Start
--------- ----  -------------  -----  --------  ----------
 1/1      1     forwarding      19       32     disabled
 1/2      1     forwarding      19       32     disabled
 2/1      1     not-connected   100      32     disabled
 2/2      1     not-connected   100      32     disabled
 2/3      1     not-connected   100      32     disabled
 2/4      1     not-connected   100      32     disabled
 2/5      1     not-connected   100      32     disabled
<output truncated>
```

Notice that the bridge ID priority is set to 8192; the designated root and bridge ID MAC address are the same because this is the root bridge. The port states are both 19, which is the default for 100Mbps. Because both ports are in forwarding state, the 2950 switch must have one of its FastEthernet ports in blocking mode. Let's take a look by using the `show spanning-tree` command on the 2950:

```
Terry_2950# show spanning-tree

VLAN0001
  Spanning tree enabled protocol ieee
  Root ID    Priority    8192
             Address     00e0.3488.fc00
             Cost        5
             Port        1 (FastEthernet0/1)
             Hello Time   2 sec  Max Age 10 sec  Forward Delay 7 sec

  Bridge ID  Priority    32769  (priority 32768 sys-id-ext 1)
             Address     000b.be53.2c00
             Hello Time   2 sec  Max Age 10 sec  Forward Delay 7 sec
             Aging Time 300

Interface        Port ID                     Designated           Port ID
Name             Prio.Nbr    Cost Sts        Cost Bridge ID       Prio.Nbr
---------------- -------- --------------- -------------------- --------
Fa0/1            128.1      100 FWD          0       1 00b0.6414.1180 128.1
Fa0/24           128.24     100 BLK          0       1 00b0.6414.1180 128.12
```

Notice that port fa0/24 is in blocking mode and port fa0/1 is in forwarding mode. If we want port fa0/24 to be in forwarding mode and fa0/21 to be in blocking mode, we can set the port costs to help the switch determine the best path to use. Note that we are not saying you should do this; we just want to show you how.

Setting the Port Cost

The parameters in this next set are used to enable the network administrator to influence the path that spanning tree chooses when setting the port priority, port cost, and path cost.

Cisco does not recommend changing these settings unless it's absolutely necessary. However, the best way to get a good understanding of how the STP works is by changing the defaults. We do not recommend trying any of this on a production network unless you have permission from the network manager, who understands that you can bring the network down by doing so.

By changing the port cost, you can change the port ID, which means it can be a more desirable port to STP. Remember that STP uses the port ID only if there is more than one path to the root bridge and they are of equal cost. Path cost is the sum of the costs between a switch and the root bridge. The STP calculates the path cost based on the media speed of the links between the switch and the port cost of each port forwarding the frames. In the hands-on lab on the accompanying CD, both links are 100Mbps, so the port ID is important and will be used.

To change the path used between a switch and the root bridge, first calculate the current path cost. Then change the port cost of the port you want to use, making sure that you keep in mind the alternate paths if the primary path fails before making any changes to your switch. Remember that ports with a lower port cost are more likely to be chosen; this doesn't mean they always will be chosen.

To change the port cost of a port on a 4000 series switch, use the `set spantree portcost` command:

```
Terry_4000> (enable) set spantree portcost ?
Usage: set spantree portcost <mod_num/port_num> <cost>
       set spantree portcost <trcrf> <cost>
       (cost = 1..65535)
```

The parameters to set the cost of a port are the module and port number and the cost you want to configure. The following example shows how to set the port cost on port 1/1 from the default of 19 to 10:

```
Terry_4000> (enable) set spantree portcost 1/1 10
Spantree port 1/1 path cost set to 10.
```

You would verify the change with the `show spantree` command. However, because both ports are in forwarding mode, the preceding command will not change the switch's STP parameters. Notice in the following switch output that both ports are forwarding, but the costs of the ports are different:

```
Port      Vlan Port-State    Cost  Priority Fast-Start
--------- ---- ------------- ----- -------- ----------
 1/1        1  forwarding      10       32  disabled
 1/2        1  forwarding      19       32  disabled
```

Remember that a root switch will be forwarding on all active ports, so the port IDs are irrelevant to the switch. However, the 2950 must then choose a port to perform blocking on the interface with the lowest cost.

To change the port cost on an IOS-based switch, use the `spanning-tree cost` interface command. The cost value can be any number from 1 to 200000000; however, you cannot make it less than the path cost of both links. What you need to do is to raise the port priority of the port that we don't want STP to use for forwarding. Notice in the following example that we change the cost of port fa0/24 to 20. This should make the fa0/24 port a more desirable path:

```
Terry_2950#conf t
Enter configuration commands, one per line.  End with CNTL/Z.
```

```
Terry_2950(config)#interface fa0/24
Terry_2950(config-if)#spanning-tree ?
  bpdufilter      Don't send or receive BPDUs on this interface
  bpduguard       Don't accept BPDUs on this interface
  cost            Change an interface's spanning tree port path cost
  guard           Change an interface's spanning tree guard mode
  link-type       Specify a link type for spanning tree protocol use
  port-priority   Change an interface's spanning tree port priority
  portfast        Enable an interface to move directly to forwarding on link up
  stack-port      Enable stack port
  vlan            VLAN Switch Spanning Tree

Terry_2950(config-if)#spanning-tree cost ?
  <1-200000000>   port path cost

Terry_2950(config-if)#spanning-tree cost 20
Terry_2950(config-if)#^Z
```

To verify the port priorities, use the `show spanning-tree` command:

```
Terry_2950#show spanning-tree

VLAN0001
  Spanning tree enabled protocol ieee

[Output cut]

Interface        Port ID                   Designated            Port ID
Name             Prio.Nbr   Cost Sts       Cost Bridge ID        Prio.Nbr
---------------- -------- --------------- -------------------- --------
Fa0/1            128.1         5 FWD        0      1 00b0.6414.1180 128.1
Fa0/24           128.24       20 BLK        0      1 00b0.6414.1180 128.12
```

In the preceding switch output, notice that port fa0/1 is forwarding and port fa0/24 is now blocking. In the output, the port path cost is 5 for port fa0/1 and 20 for port fa0/24. This is a pretty simple and straightforward configuration and worked fine, but the network suffered downtime due to convergence, so caution should be used when changing the port costs in a real production network. Also, you need to plan your final topology, because you can cause havoc in a network if the configuration is not thought out carefully. The port costs are propagated in the BPDUs, so a small change on one switch can affect how spanning tree chooses the various ports on a switch a few cable segments away.

You can get a good idea of the delays associated with spanning tree convergence if you try this out for yourself. Immediately after making the changes to the port cost, enter the **show spanning-tree** command on the 2950 switch. If you keep repeating the command, you will see the switch going through the blocking, listening, and learning modes on the way to forwarding. You can time the process with your watch.

Setting the Port Priority

Another option you can use to help the switch determine the path selection that STP uses in your network is to set the port priorities. Remember, this only influences STP; it doesn't demand that STP do anything. However, between setting the port cost and priority, STP should always make your path selection.

The port priority and port cost configurations work similarly. The port with the lowest port priority will forward frames for all VLANs. The command to set a port priority is `set spantree portpri`:

```
Terry_4000> (enable) set spantree portpri ?
Usage: set spantree portpri <mod_num/port_num> <priority>
       set spantree portpri <trcrf> <trcrf_priority>
       (priority = 0..63, trcrf_priority = 0..7)
Terry_4000> (enable)
```

The possible port priority range is from 0 to 63, and the default is 32. If all ports have the same priority, then the port with the lowest port number will forward frames. For example, 2/1 is lower than 2/2. In the following example, the 4000 switch priority for port 1/1 is set to 20:

```
Terry_4000> (enable) set spantree portpri 1/1 20
Bridge port 1/1 port priority set to 20.
Terry_4000> (enable)
```

After you change your port priority, you can verify the configuration with the `show spantree 1/1` command:

```
Terry_4000> (enable) show spantree 1/1
Port      Vlan Port-State    Cost  Priority Fast-Start
--------- ---- ------------- ----- -------- ----------
 1/1      1    forwarding       10       20  disabled
 1/1      2    forwarding       10       20  disabled
 1/1      3    forwarding       10       20  disabled
 1/1      4    forwarding       10       20  disabled
 1/1      1003 not-connected    10       20  disabled
```

```
 1/1       1005  not-connected     10         4   disabled
Terry_4000> (enable)
```

Notice that because port 1/1 is a trunked port, all VLAN priorities were changed on that port. Also notice in the following output that the priority is 20 for 1/1, but the default of 32 is set for 1/2:

```
Terry_4000> (enable)show spantree
[output cut]
Port      Vlan  Port-State     Cost   Priority  Fast-Start
--------- ----  -------------  -----  --------  ----------
 1/1        1   forwarding      10       20     disabled
 1/2        1   forwarding      19       32     disabled
```

You can go one step further and set the port priority on a per-VLAN basis. The port with the lowest priority will forward frames for the VLAN for which you've set the priority. Again, if all the ports have the same priority, the lowest port number wins and begins forwarding frames.

There is an advantage to setting the port priority per VLAN. If you have a network with parallel paths, STP stops at least one link from forwarding frames so a network loop will not occur. All traffic would then have to travel over only the one link. However, by changing the port priority for a specific group of VLANs, you can distribute the VLANs across the two links. This isn't quite as good as load sharing, but at least you get to use both links as opposed to having one sit idle.

To change the priority of STP for a certain VLAN or group of VLANs, use the `set spantree portvlanpri` command:

```
Terry_4000> (enable) set spantree portvlanpri ?
Usage: set spantree portvlanpri <mod_num/port_num>   <priority> [vlans]
(priority = 0..63)
Terry_4000> (enable)
```

The priority can be set for each VLAN from 0 to 63. In the following example, we'll set port 1/1 to forward only VLANs 1 and 2 and set port 1/2 to forward VLANs 3 and 4. Figure 16.1 shows the physical topology involved.

FIGURE 16.1 Prioritizing traffic by VLAN

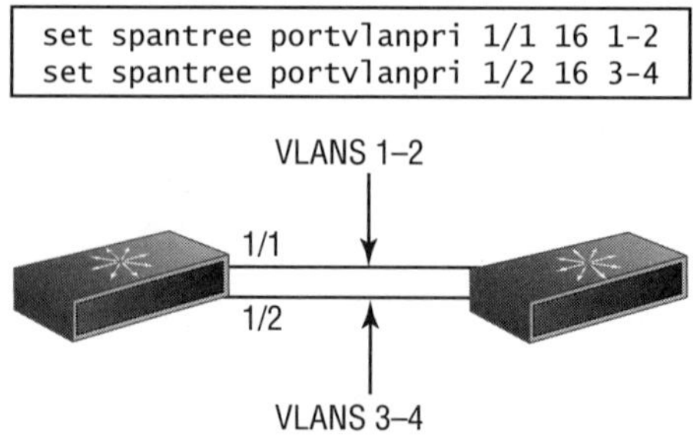
set spantree portvlanpri 1/1 16 1-2
set spantree portvlanpri 1/2 16 3-4
VLANS 1–2
1/1
1/2
VLANS 3–4

```
Terry_4000> (enable) set spantree portvlanpri 1/1 16 1-2
Port 1/1 vlans 1-2 using portpri 16.
Port 1/1 vlans 3-1004 using portpri 20.
Port 1/1 vlans 1005 using portpri 4.

Terry_4000> (enable) set spantree portvlanpri 1/2 16 3-4
Port 1/2 vlans 1-2,5-1004 using portpri 32.
Port 1/2 vlans 3-4 using portpri 16.
Port 1/2 vlans 1005 using portpri 4.
Terry_4000> (enable)
```

The preceding switch output displays the VLAN priority information. We set both VLAN port priorities to 16. Notice that for VLANs 1–4, the priority is 16. However, on port 1/1, all the other VLANs are listed as having a port priority of 20 because that is what we set the port priority to earlier in this chapter. On port 1/2, the switch thinks all the other ports have a port priority of 32, except for VLAN 1005, which becomes a default priority of 4.

You can view the changes by using the `show spantree` *`slot/port`* command, as shown here:

```
Terry_4000> (enable) show spantree 1/1
Port      Vlan Port-State    Cost  Priority Fast-Start
--------- ---- ------------- ----- -------- ----------
 1/1      1    forwarding      10      16   disabled
 1/1      2    forwarding      10      16   disabled
 1/1      3    forwarding      10      20   disabled
 1/1      4    forwarding      10      20   disabled
 1/1      1003 not-connected   10      20   disabled
 1/1      1005 not-connected   10       4   disabled

Terry_4000> (enable) show spantree 1/2
Port      Vlan Port-State    Cost  Priority Fast-Start
--------- ---- ------------- ----- -------- ----------
 1/2      1    forwarding      19      32   disabled
 1/2      2    forwarding      19      32   disabled
 1/2      3    forwarding      19      16   disabled
 1/2      4    forwarding      19      16   disabled
 1/2      1003 not-connected   19      32   disabled
 1/2      1005 not-connected   19       4   disabled
Terry_4000> (enable)
```

Setting the VLAN priority on the IOS-based switches is carried out using the interface command `spanning-tree vlan` *`vlan_number`* `port-priority` *`priority`*. Looking at the default configuration, we can see that the port priority is set to 128.

```
Terry_2950#show spanning-tree

VLAN0001
  Spanning tree enabled protocol ieee

[Output cut]

Interface        Port ID                      Designated          Port ID
Name             Prio.Nbr   Cost Sts      Cost Bridge ID      Prio.Nbr
---------------- -------- --------------- -------------------- --------
Fa0/1            128.1      100 BLK         0       1 00b0.6414.1180 128.1
Fa0/24           128.24      20 FWD         0       1 00b0.6414.1180 128.12
```

If we want to change the VLAN port priority on the 2950 switch to make the port more desirable, then we can reduce the priority as follows:

```
Terry_2950#conf t
Terry_2950(config)#interface fa0/1
Terry_2950(config-if)#spanning-tree vlan 1 port-priority 20
Terry_2950(config-if)#^Z
Terry_2950#sho span

VLAN0001
  Spanning tree enabled protocol ieee
  Root ID    Priority    1
             Address     00b0.6414.1180
             Cost        20
             Port        24 (FastEthernet0/24)
             Hello Time   2 sec  Max Age 20 sec  Forward Delay 15 sec

  Bridge ID  Priority    32769  (priority 32768 sys-id-ext 1)
             Address     000b.be53.2c00
             Hello Time   2 sec  Max Age 20 sec  Forward Delay 15 sec
             Aging Time 300

Interface        Port ID                      Designated              Port ID
Name             Prio.Nbr   Cost  Sts     Cost Bridge ID           Prio.Nbr
---------------- -------- ------------- --------- --------------------
Fa0/1             20.1        20   FWD      0       1 00b0.6414.1180 128.1
Fa0/24           128.24       20   BLK      0       1 00b0.6414.1180 128.12
```

By changing either the port priority or the port cost, you can persuade the switch to use your chosen paths. However, there are some miscellaneous other STP variables that you can change. We'll discuss those next.

Changing the STP Timers

The timers are important in an STP network to stop network loops from occurring. The different timers are used to give the network time to update the correct topology information to all the switches and also to determine the whereabouts of all the redundant links.

The problem with the STP timers is that, if a link goes down, it takes up to 50 seconds for the backup link to take over forwarding frames. This is a convergence problem that can be addressed when instability is occurring in the network. The following timers can be changed:

fwddelay This interval indicates how long it takes for a port to move from listening to learning state and then from learning to forwarding state. The default is 15 seconds, but it can be changed to anywhere from 4 to 30 seconds. If you set this too low, the switch won't be allowed ample time to make sure no loops will occur before setting a port in forwarding mode. The following switch output shows how to set the `fwddelay` to 10 seconds:

```
Terry_4000> (enable) set spantree fwddelay ?
Usage: set spantree fwddelay <delay> [vlans]
       (delay = 4..30 seconds, vlan = 1..1005)
Terry_4000> (enable) set spantree fwddelay 10
Spantree 1 forward delay set to 10 seconds.
```

hello This is the time interval for sending BPDUs from the root switch. It is set to 2 seconds by default; you would think it couldn't be set any lower, but it can be increased or decreased. You can set it to 1 second to actually double the amount of BPDUs sent out that must be lost before triggering an unwanted convergence in the network. However, it doubles the CPU load and processing load as well. The following switch output shows how to change the BPDU timers to 1 second:

```
Terry_4000> (enable) set spantree hello ?
Usage: set spantree hello <interval> [vlans]
       (interval = 1..10, vlan = 1..1005)
Terry_4000> (enable) set spantree hello 1
Spantree 1 hello time set to 1 seconds.
```

maxage The max age is the amount of time that a switch will hold BPDU information. If a new BPDU is not received before the max age expires, then the BPDU is discarded and is considered invalid. The default is 20 seconds; it can be set to as low as 6 seconds. However, network instability will happen if too many BPDUs are discarded because this timer is set too low. The following output shows how to change the max age of a BPDU to 30 seconds:

```
Terry_4000> (enable) set spantree maxage ?
Usage: set spantree maxage <agingtime> [vlans]
```

```
        (agingtime = 6..40, vlan = 1..1005)
Terry_4000> (enable) set spantree maxage 30
Spantree 1 max aging time set to 30 seconds.
Terry_4000> (enable)
```

Rather than directly modifying the timers, it is usually better to modify the size of the network. Table 16.1 referred to a "diameter" value that can be set when selecting the spanning tree root. The diameter used is the width of the network from one side to the other. Three switches daisy-chained together would have a diameter of 3, whereas three configured in a triangle would have a diameter of 2.

The diameter automatically sets the timers to a value appropriate to the size of your network. Setting the timers yourself to low values in a large network risks topological loops because the delay might not be long enough to account for BPDU propagation delay. The best thing to do is to use the diameter option when setting the root and then modify the timers from there, if necessary.

We have been discussing redundant links and STP, but most of the discussion has been about how to make STP run efficiently, and that is by making the non-root port a blocking port. We discussed load balancing only when we showed you how to set the port priority on a per-VLAN basis. However, that really wasn't load balancing to the degree that is possible with a Cisco switched network. In the next section, we'll cover the most efficient ways of using redundant links in a large, switched internetwork.

To set similar parameters on the IOS-based switches, use the global command `spanning-tree vlan` *`vlan_number options`* as follows:

```
Terry_2950(config)#spanning-tree ?
  backbonefast   Enable BackboneFast Feature
  etherchannel   Spanning tree etherchannel specific configuration
  extend         Spanning Tree 802.1t extensions
  loopguard      Spanning tree loopguard options
  mode           Spanning tree operating mode
  pathcost       Spanning tree pathcost options
  pathcost       Spanning tree pathcost options
  uplinkfast     Enable UplinkFast Feature
  vlan           VLAN Switch Spanning Tree

Terry_2950(config)#spanning-tree vlan 1 ?
  forward-time   Set the forward delay for the spanning tree
  hello-time     Set the hello interval for the spanning tree
  max-age        Set the max age interval for the spanning tree
  priority       Set the bridge priority for the spanning tree
  root           Configure switch as root
  <cr>

Terry_2950(config)#spanning-tree vlan 1 forward-time ?
  <4-30>  number of seconds for the forward delay timer
```

```
Terry_2950(config)#spanning-tree vlan 1 hello-time ?
  <1-10>  number of seconds between generation of config BPDUs

Terry_2950(config)#spanning-tree vlan 1 max-age ?
  <6-40>  maximum number of seconds the information in a BPDU is valid
```

Using Redundant Links with STP

Fast EtherChannel and *Gigabit EtherChannel* allow high-speed redundant links in a spanning tree environment by allowing dual parallel links to be treated as though they were one link. Cisco Fast EtherChannel technology uses the standards-based 802.3 Full-Duplex Fast Ethernet to provide a reliable high-speed solution for the campus network backbone. Fast EtherChannel can scale bandwidth within the campus, providing full-duplex bandwidth at wire speeds of 200Mbps to 800Mbps. It provides high bandwidth, load sharing, and redundancy of links in a switched internetwork.

Broadcast traffic, as well as unicast and multicast traffic, is distributed equally across the links in the channel. Fast EtherChannel also provides redundancy in the event of a link failure. If a link is lost in a Fast EtherChannel network, traffic is rerouted to one of the other links in just a few milliseconds, making the convergence transparent to the user.

Gigabit EtherChannel works in the same fashion that Fast EtherChannel does, except that it's faster. Each device has a limit to the number of ports that can participate, but it's in the range of two to eight, giving a potential channel size of 16Gbps.

Modifications to EtherChannel

EtherChannel has undergone some changes in the last four years on Cisco switches. It used to be that you had to group the ports together in order to use them in a channel. Ports 1–4 had to be used together, 5–8 had to be used together, and so on. If you were using only two, then they had to be the first two ports in the group of four. Of course, they all had to be on the same blade as well. The first thing an administrator would do when troubleshooting was to make sure the correct ports were being used.

The restrictions aren't quite as difficult now, though. For example, CatOS version 5.3 or higher system enables you to use whatever ports you want to, as long as they are configured the same.

Different devices will also forward frames across the channel in different ways, and some can be set up to apply rules based on layer 3 or layer 4 headers. The secret to setting up an effective EtherChannel topology is to understand the limitations of your equipment and software.

This section will introduce you to the several ways of configuring redundant links. In the part about EtherChannel, you'll learn about the communication protocol that switches use and how load balancing takes place. You will then learn how the switch can violate the usual rules that spanning tree lives by, to create a network that responds faster when there is a problem.

Parallel Fast EtherChannel Links

Fast EtherChannel uses load distribution to share the links in a bundle. A bundle is a group of FastEthernet or Gigabit Ethernet links managed by the Fast EtherChannel process. Should one link in the bundle fail, the Ethernet Bundle Controller (EBC) informs the Enhanced Address Recognition Logic (EARL) ASIC of the failure, and the EARL in turn ages out all addresses learned on that link. The EBC and the EARL use hardware to recalculate the source and destination address pair on a different link.

The convergence time is sometimes referred to as the failover time, which is the time it takes for the new address to be relearned—about 10 microseconds. Windowing flow control techniques can make this process a touch longer, but that depends on the particular application in use. The key is not having the application time out, and the failover time is fast enough to stop the timeout from happening.

EtherChannel Guidelines

EtherChannel does not work under certain circumstances. This is to ensure that no network loops will occur if the bundle comes up. There are certain guidelines to follow when configuring EtherChannel technology:

- All ports must be in the same VLAN, or they must all be trunk ports that belong to the same native VLAN.
- All ports must be configured as the same trunk mode—if trunking is used.
- When trunking is used, all ports must be configured with the same VLAN range. If it is not the same, packets will be dropped and the ports will not form a channel when set to the `auto` or `desirable` mode.
- All ports must be configured with the same speed and duplex settings.
- If broadcast limits are configured on the ports, configure the limits for all the ports or packets might be dropped.
- The ports cannot be configured in a channel as dynamic VLAN ports.
- Port security must be disabled on channeled ports.
- All ports must be enabled in the channel before the channel can come up. If you disable a port, a link failure occurs.

Configuring EtherChannel

To create an EtherChannel bundle, use the `set port channel` command. You must first make sure that all the conditions for EtherChannel have been met.

Notice the switch output when we try to configure the ports on our 4000 switch as a bundle to the 2950 switch:

```
Terry_4000> (enable) set port channel 1/1-2 on
Mismatch in trunk mode.
Mismatch in port duplex.
Mismatch in STP port priority.
Failed to set port(s) 1/1-2 channel mode to on.
Terry_4000> (enable)
```

There is a mismatch in trunking, duplex, and STP port priority. All the ports must be configured the same for EtherChannel to work.

To view the configuration of a port, use the `show port capabilities` *`slot/port`* command:

```
Terry_4000> (enable) show port capabilities 1/1
Model                       WS-X5509
Port                        1/1
Type                        100BaseTX
Speed                       100
Duplex                      half,full
Trunk encap type            ISL
Trunk mode                  on,off,desirable,auto,nonegotiate
Channel                     1/1-2
Broadcast suppression       percentage(0-100)
Flow control                no
Security                    yes
Membership                  static,dynamic
Fast start                  yes
Rewrite                     no
Terry_4000> (enable)
```

The preceding output shows the card model number and the configuration of the port. The easiest way for us to make sure all the ports we want to channel are configured the same is to just clear the configuration. We're not suggesting that you just clear your config whenever any problems come up, but the configuration we created in this chapter is pretty extensive, and it's easier to simply clear it out of the switch to perform the next function:

```
Terry_4000> (enable) clear config all
This command will clear all configuration in NVRAM.
This command will cause ifIndex to be reassigned on the next system startup.
Do you want to continue (y/n) [n]? y
........
.................
System configuration cleared.
Console> (enable)
```

Remember that you need to reset the switch after erasing the configuration to clear the configuration. We need to reconfigure the switch with an IP address and trunking on ports 1/1 and 1/2. We're also going to delete the configuration on the 2950, so then we will have both switches back to our STP default:

```
Terry_2950#erase startup-config
Erasing the nvram filesystem will remove all files! Continue? [confirm]
```

Now that we have both the switches back to their default configurations, we'll just configure the host names and IP addresses and turn on trunking on ports 1/1 and 1/2 of the 4000 and ports fa0/1 and fa0/24 of the 2950:

```
#configure terminal
(config)#hostname Terry_2950
Terry_2950(config)#int vlan 1
Terry_2950(config-if)#ip address 172.16.10.2 255.255.255.0
Terry_2950(config-if)#exit
Terry_2950(config)#ip default-gateway 172.16.10.1
Terry_2950(config)#int fa 0/1
Terry_2950(config-if)#switchport ?
  access         Set access mode characteristics of the interface
  host           Set port host
  mode           Set trunking mode of the interface
  nonegotiate    Device will not engage in negotiation protocol on this
                 interface
  port-security  Security related command
  priority       Set appliance 802.1p priority
  protected      Configure an interface to be a protected port
  trunk          Set trunking characteristics of the interface
  voice          Voice appliance attributes

Terry_2950(config-if)#switchport mode trunk
Terry_2950(config-if)#int fa 0/24
Terry_2950(config-if)#switchport mode trunk
Terry_2950(config-if)#^Z

Console> (enable) set prompt Terry_4000>
Terry_4000> (enable) set interface sc0 172.16.10.4 255.255.255.0
Interface sc0 IP address and netmask set.
Terry_4000> (enable) set trunk 1/1 on
Port(s) 1/1 trunk mode set to on.
Terry_4000> (enable) set trunk 1/2 on
Port(s) 1/2 trunk mode set to on.
Terry_4000> (enable)
```

To verify that the ports are trunking, use the show trunk command:

```
Terry_4000> (enable) show trunk
Port      Mode         Encapsulation  Status     Native vlan
--------  -----------  -------------  ---------- -----------
  1/1     on           isl            trunking   1
  1/2     on           isl            trunking   1
```

Let's try to configure EtherChannel between the switches again:

```
Terry_4000> (enable) set port channel 1/1-2 on
Port(s) 1/1-2 channel mode set to on.
Terry_4000> (enable) 2003 Jul 25 23:08:20 %PAGP-5
PORTFROMSTP:Port 1/1 left bridge  port 1/1
2003 Jul 25 23:08:20 %PAGP-5-PORTFROMSTP:Port 1/2 left   bridge port 1/2
2003 Jul 25 23:08:20 %PAGP-5-PORTTOSTP:Port 1/1 joined   bridge port 1/1-2
2003 Jul 25 23:08:21 %PAGP-5-PORTTOSTP:Port 1/2 joined   bridge port 1/1-2
```

To verify the EtherChannel bundle, use the show port channel command:

```
Terry_4000> (enable) show port channel
Port  Status     Channel   Channel     Neighbor  Neighbor
                 mode      status      device    port
----- ---------- --------- ----------- --------- -------
 1/1  errdisable on        channel
 1/2  errdisable on        channel
----- ---------- --------- ----------- --------- -------
Terry_4000> (enable)
```

You can see that the status is error disabled and that no neighbors are found. This is because we still need to configure Fast EtherChannel on the 2950 switch. If this were a remote switch, you would lose contact with the switch and have to go to the site and console into the switch to configure EtherChannel. You should configure the remote site first; then you will lose contact with it until you configure the local switch bundle.

To configure the EtherChannel bundle on a 2950 switch, use the interface command channel-group *group_number* mode *mode_type*:

```
Terry_2950(config)#int fa 0/1
Terry_2950(config-if)#channel-group ?
  <1-6>  Channel group number

Terry_2950(config-if)#channel-group 1 ?
  mode  Etherchannel Mode of the interface
```

```
Terry_2950(config-if)#channel-group 1 mode ?
  auto       Enable PAgP only if a PAgP device is detected
  desirable  Enable PAgP unconditionally
  on         Enable Etherchannel only

Terry_2950(config-if)#channel-group 1 mode on
Terry_2950(config-if)#int fa 0/24
Terry_2950(config-if)#channel-group 1 mode on
Terry_2950(config-if)#exit
```

To view the channel status on the IOS-based switch, use the `show etherchannel` *`options`* command.

```
Terry_2950#show etherchannel ?
  <1-6>         Channel group number
  brief         Brief information
  detail        Detail information
  load-balance  Load-balance/frame-distribution scheme among ports in
                port-channel
  port          Port information
  port-channel  Port-channel information
  summary       One-line summary per channel-group

Terry_2950#show etherchannel det
                Channel-group listing:
                -----------------------

Group: 1
----------
Group state = L2
Ports: 3   Maxports = 8
Port-channels: 1 Max Port-channels = 1
                Ports in the group:
                -------------------
Port: Fa0/1
------------

Port state    = Up Mstr In-Bndl
Channel group = 1           Mode = On/FEC     Gcchange = 0
Port-channel  = Po1         GC   = 0x00010001    Pseudo port-channel = Po1
Port index    = 0           Load = 0x00
```

```
Age of the port in the current state: 00d:00h:10m:25s

Port: Fa0/24
------------

Port state    = Up Mstr In-Bndl
Channel group = 1           Mode = On/FEC     Gcchange = 0
Port-channel  = Po1         GC   = 0x00010001    Pseudo port-channel = Po1
Port index    = 0           Load = 0x00

Age of the port in the current state: 00d:00h:05m:45s
                Port-channels in the group:
                ----------------------

Port-channel: Po1
------------

Age of the Port-channel    = 00d:00h:10m:26s
Logical slot/port    = 1/0          Number of ports = 2
GC                   = 0x00010001     HotStandBy port = null
Port state           = Port-channel Ag-Inuse

Ports in the Port-channel:

Index   Load   Port    EC state
------+------+------+------------
  0      00     Fa0/1    on
  0      00     Fa0/24   on

Time since last port bundled:    00d:00h:05m:45s    Fa0/24
```

To verify the EtherChannel on the 4000 series switch, use the `show port channel` command:

```
Terry_4000> (enable) show port channel
Port  Status     Channel   Channel     Neighbor                Neighbor
                 mode      status      device                  port
----- ---------- --------- ----------- ------------------ ----------
 1/1  connected  on        channel     cisco 2950  Terry_2950     A
 1/2  connected  on        channel     cisco 2950  Terry_2950     B
----- ---------- --------- ----------- ------------------ ----------
Terry_4000> (enable)
```

The preceding switch output shows the port numbers, status, mode, channel status, neighbor device, and neighbor port ID. Our EtherChannel is working!

Port Aggregation Protocol (PAgP)

The *Port Aggregation Protocol (PAgP)* is used to add more features to the EtherChannel technology. This protocol is used to learn the capabilities of the neighbors' EtherChannel ports. By doing this, it allows the switches to connect via Fast EtherChannel automatically. PAgP has four options when configuring the channel: `on`, `off`, `desirable`, and `auto`. The first two—`on` and `off`—are self-explanatory. A `desirable` link wants to become a channel, whereas a link set to `auto` doesn't want to but will if it has to. A channel will form if one of the following combinations is used:

- `on-on`
- `on-desirable`
- `on-auto`
- `desirable-desirable`
- `desirable-auto`

The PAgP protocol groups the ports that have the same neighbor device ID and neighbor group capability into a channel. This channel is then added to the Spanning Tree Protocol as a single bridge port.

For PAgP to work, all the ports must be configured with static, not dynamic, VLANs, and all the ports must also be in the same VLAN or be configured as trunk ports. All ports must be the same speed and duplex as well. In other words, all the ports must be configured the same or PAgP will not work.

If an EtherChannel bundle is already working and you make a change on a port, all ports in that bundle are changed to match the port. If you change the speed or duplex of one port, all ports will then run that speed or duplex.

Load Balancing and Redundancy

Each switch operates a channel in a different fashion, but there are two main issues that all the switches must face:

- How they forward traffic across the bundle of physical links
- What happens if a link fails

This section will cover the basics. Cisco provides a guide at `www.cisco.com/warp/public/473/4.html`, detailing how each of the switches deals with these two topics.

Load Balancing

A channel is nothing more than a bundle of circuits that pretend to act like a single cable. Although this is convenient for increasing bandwidth without causing problems with spanning tree, it leaves us wondering which link gets used when a frame wants to cross the channel. The following list shows how each switch approach this task:

The 4000 Will send frames across the channel in a fashion that depends on the source and destination MAC addresses. An X-OR process is run on the last bit in the MAC addresses. The output will be one of 0.0, 0.1, 1.0, or 1.1. All frames where the source and destination MAC addresses end in 1 will use the same circuit. All frames where the last bit in the source is 0 and the last bit in the destination is 1 will use a different circuit. There is no load balancing between the circuits.

The 2950 and 3550 Will also send frames across the channel in a fashion that depends on the source and destination MAC addresses, but with the following caveats: If source-MAC address forwarding is used, frames are sent to hosts across the ports the source MAC address is associated with. If destination-MAC address forwarding is implemented, frames are forwarded according to the destination host's MAC address/port association. In either case, there is symmetry in the frame transfer, with frames following predictable paths according to entries in the bridging tables. Source-based forwarding is enabled by default.

Layer 3+ switches A switch that can recognize layer 3 or higher information can be configured to forward frames based on higher layer header information. For example, the 6000 series can be configured with hardware that enables it to choose what circuit to use based on source, destination, or both. For addressing, it can use MAC addressing, IP addressing, or port values.

Redundancy

Because of the dynamic, load-balancing nature of 2950 and 3550 switches, redundancy and the management of traffic after a port failure are almost transparent. Frames previously carried over the port that fails are transferred to the port with the least traffic load at the moment of failure.

The 4000 works in a similar fashion, in that frames previously carried over the failed link are switched to the remaining segments within the EtherChannel.

PortFast

By default, the Spanning Tree Protocol (STP) runs on all ports on a switch. Because most of the ports connect to workstations, printers, servers, routers, and so on, it's basically a waste of resources for these point-to-point ports to be running the Spanning Tree Protocol. When a device—let's say, a workstation—powers up, it takes up to 50 seconds before the switch forwards data on the port, because the STP is making sure no loops are going to occur when the port is in forwarding mode. Not only is this a waste of time (because a loop does not occur with point-to-point links), but some protocols or applications could time out.

PortFast is used to make a point-to-point port almost immediately enter into forwarding state by decreasing the time of the listening and learning states. This is very helpful for switch ports that have workstations or servers attached, because these devices will connect immediately instead of waiting for the STP to converge. If you connect a hub to a port configured with PortFast and then accidentally connect another port into the switch from the hub, you will have a network loop, and STP will not stop it. It is important to make sure that PortFast is used only on point-to-point links connected only to workstations or servers.

Configuring PortFast

To configure PortFast on a switch, use the `set spantree portfast` command. The following switch output shows how to configure ports 2/1–12 with PortFast:

```
Terry_4000> (enable) set spantree portfast ?
Usage: set spantree portfast <mod_num/port_num>   <enable|disable>
       set spantree portfast <trcrf> <enable|disable>

Terry_4000> (enable) set spantree portfast 2/1-12 enable
Warning: Spantree port fast start should only be enabled on ports connected
to a single host. Connecting hubs, concentrators, switches, bridges, etc. to a
fast start port can cause temporary spanning tree loops. Use with caution.
Spantree ports 2/1-12 fast start enabled.
Terry_4000> (enable)
```

Notice the nice warning received on the switch console when PortFast was turned on. Also notice that we were able to turn on all 12 ports of our 10/100 card.

To configure PortFast on an IOS-based switch, use the `spanning-tree portfast` interface command:

```
Terry_2950(config)#int fa 0/12
Terry_2950(config-if)#switchport mode access

Terry_2950(config-if)#spanning-tree ?
  bpdufilter     Don't send or receive BPDUs on this interface
  bpduguard      Don't accept BPDUs on this interface
  cost           Change an interface's spanning tree port path cost
  guard          Change an interface's spanning tree guard mode
  link-type      Specify a link type for spanning tree protocol use
  port-priority  Change an interface's spanning tree port priority
  portfast       Enable an interface to move directly to forwarding on link up
  stack-port     Enable stack port
  vlan           VLAN Switch Spanning Tree

Terry_2950(config-if)#spanning-tree port

Terry_2950(config-if)#spanning-tree portfast ?
  disable  Disable portfast for this interface
  trunk    Enable portfast on the interface even in trunk mode
  <cr>

Terry_2950(config-if)#spanning-tree portfast
```

```
%Warning: portfast should only be enabled on ports connected to a single host.
Connecting hubs, concentrators, switches, bridges, etc. to this interface
when portfast is enabled, can cause temporary bridging loops.

Use with CAUTION

%Portfast has been configured on FastEthernet0/12 but will only have effect
when the interface is in a non-trunking mode.
Terry_2950(config-if)
```

This parameter must be configured on each port you want to run PortFast. Note the words of caution associated with this command.

PortFast and BPDUs

Some switches support an addition to PortFast called BPDUGuard. There is never a guarantee that someone won't add a switch at their desk. Then, for redundancy, they also connect that switch to the LAN drop at their neighbor's desk. Now assume that you enable PortFast on that port. Congratulations, you now have a spanning tree loop!

BPDUGuard is a feature that can be set on many switches that enable PortFast. It monitors for BPDUs on that port. If a BPDU arrives, the switch shuts down the port, placing it in the `errdisable` state, and generates a status message.

UplinkFast

UplinkFast is used to minimize network downtime by ensuring that network loops do not occur when the network topology changes. STP convergence time is very time-consuming, so network loops can occur temporarily when the convergence is taking place. Additionally, some hosts will not be available for communication during the convergence time because STP has disabled ports on a switch during convergence. The key to both problems is decreased convergence time, which UplinkFast was developed to provide.

UplinkFast enables a blocked port on a switch to begin forwarding frames immediately when a link failure is detected on the root port. For the switch to change a port from blocking to forwarding mode, UplinkFast must have direct knowledge of the link failure; otherwise a loop might occur.

To utilize UplinkFast, several criteria must be met. First, UplinkFast must obviously be enabled on the switch. The switch must have at least one blocked port, and the failure must be on the root port. If the failure is not on a root port, UplinkFast ignores it and normal STP functions will occur.

When a link fault occurs on the primary root link, UplinkFast transitions the blocked port to a forwarding state. UplinkFast changes the port without passing through the listening and learning phases, which enables the switch to skip the normal convergence time and start forwarding in about 3 to 4 seconds instead of the usual 50 seconds.

UplinkFast was designed to work with access layer switches, not core switches, because the switch running UplinkFast must not be the root bridge.

Configuring UplinkFast

When configuring UplinkFast, remember that all VLANs on the switch are affected and that you cannot configure UplinkFast on individual VLANs.

To configure UplinkFast on a set-based switch, use the `set spantree uplinkfast` command:

```
Terry_4000> (enable) set spantree uplinkfast ?
Usage: set spantree uplinkfast <enable> [rate <station_   update_rate>]
[all-protocols <off|on>]
       set spantree uplinkfast <disable>
```

The options are really just `enable` or `disable`. The station update rate value is the number of multicast packets transmitted per 100 milliseconds (by default, it is set to 15 packets per millisecond). It is not recommended that you change this value.

The switch provides an output describing what the command changed on the switch, as shown here:

```
Terry_4000> (enable) set spantree uplinkfast enable
VLANs 1-1005 bridge priority set to 49152.
The port cost and portvlancost of all ports set to above 3000.
Station update rate set to 15 packets/100ms.
uplinkfast all-protocols field set to off.
uplinkfast enabled for bridge.
Terry_4000> (enable)
```

The VLAN priorities are automatically changed to 49152, and the port costs are set to above 3000. These are changed to make it unlikely that the switch will become the root switch.

You can verify the UplinkFast configuration with the `show spantree uplinkfast` command:

```
Terry_4000> (enable) show spantree uplinkfast
Station update rate set to 15 packets/100ms.
uplinkfast all-protocols field set to off.

VLAN           port list
-----------------------------------------------
1              1/1(fwd)
2              1/1(fwd)
3              1/1(fwd)
4              1/1(fwd)
Terry_4000> (enable)
```

Notice that all four VLANs are changed and that we were not asked which VLANs to run UplinkFast on.

To configure UplinkFast on an IOS-based switch, use the command `spanning-tree uplinkfast` in global configuration mode:

```
Terry_2950(config)#spanning-tree ?
  backbonefast   Enable BackboneFast Feature
  etherchannel   Spanning tree etherchannel specific configuration
  extend         Spanning Tree 802.1t extensions
  loopguard      Spanning tree loopguard options
  mode           Spanning tree operating mode
  pathcost       Spanning tree pathcost options
  portfast       Spanning tree portfast options
  uplinkfast     Enable UplinkFast Feature
  vlan           VLAN Switch Spanning Tree

Terry_2950(config)#spanning-tree uplinkfast ?
  max-update-rate  Rate at which station address updates are sent
  <cr>

Terry_2950(config)#spanning-tree uplinkfast
Terry_2950(config)#
```

To verify that UplinkFast is configured and running, use the command `show spanning-tree uplinkfast`:

```
Terry_2950#show spanning-tree uplinkfast
UplinkFast is enabled

Station update rate set to 150 packets/sec.

UplinkFast statistics
-----------------------
Number of transitions via uplinkFast (all VLANs)            : 0
Number of proxy multicast addresses transmitted (all VLANs) : 0

Name                 Interface List
-------------------- ------------------------------------
VLAN0001
VLAN0002
VLAN0003

Terry_2950
```

The default frame generation rate is 150pps, which is displayed with the `show uplink-fast` command. The next command used to help STP maintain a consistent network is BackboneFast.

BackboneFast

Sometimes a switch might receive a BPDU from another switch that identifies the second switch as the root bridge when a root bridge already exists. This shouldn't happen, except when a new switch comes online and the BPDU is considered "inferior."

BPDUs are considered inferior when a switch has lost its link to the root bridge. The switch transmits the BPDUs with the information that it is now the root bridge as well as the designated bridge. The receiving switch ignores the inferior BPDU for the max age time, to prevent spanning tree loops.

After receiving inferior BPDUs, the receiving switch tries to determine whether there is an alternate path to the root bridge. If the port that the inferior BPDUs are received on is already in blocking mode, then the root port and other blocked ports on the switch become alternate paths to the root bridge. However, if the inferior BPDUs are received on a root port, then all presently blocking ports become the alternate paths to the root bridge. Also, if the inferior BPDUs are received on a root port and there are no other blocking ports on the switch, the receiving switch assumes that the link to the root bridge is down and the max age time expires, which turns the switch into the root switch.

If the switch finds an alternate path to the root bridge, it uses this new alternate path. This new path, and any other alternate paths, will be used to send a Root Link Query BPDU. By turning on *BackboneFast*, the Root Link Query BPDUs are sent out as soon as an inferior BPDU is received. This can enable faster convergence in the event of a backbone link failure. To ensure proper operation, BackboneFast should be enabled on all switches, including the root, if it is enabled at all.

Configuring and Verifying BackboneFast

Configuring BackboneFast sounds difficult, but it is really quite easy. You enable it with the `set spantree backbonefast` command, as you can see in the following example:

```
Terry_4000> (enable) set spantree backbonefast
Usage: set spantree backbonefast <enable|disable>

Terry_4000> (enable) set spantree backbonefast enable
Backbonefast enabled for all VLANs
```

Notice in the preceding switch output that BackboneFast is enabled for all VLANs, and it must be enabled on all switches in your network to function. To verify that it is running on a switch, use the `show spantree backbonefast` command:

```
Terry_4000> (enable) show spantree backbonefast
Backbonefast is enabled.
Terry_4000> (enable)
```

The preceding command shows that BackboneFast is enabled. That's all there is to it. It is a little different with the IOS-based switches:

```
Terry_2950(config)#spanning-tree ?
  backbonefast  Enable BackboneFast Feature
```

```
  etherchannel  Spanning tree etherchannel specific configuration
  extend        Spanning Tree 802.1t extensions
  loopguard     Spanning tree loopguard options
  mode          Spanning tree operating mode
  pathcost      Spanning tree pathcost options
  portfast      Spanning tree portfast options
  uplinkfast    Enable UplinkFast Feature
  vlan          VLAN Switch Spanning Tree

Terry_2950(config)#spanning-tree backbonefast ?
  <cr>
```

Rapid Spanning Tree Protocol

In the beginning, all bridges were inherently slow and it was accepted by users and applications developers alike that convergence would be slow. Cisco engineers have worked to develop solutions that overcame the basic flaws in STP that became obvious only when switching matured and took over from legacy bridging. All of the previous enhancements to the STP, such as PortFast, UplinkFast, and BackboneFast, have been proprietary.

Rapid Spanning Tree Protocol (RSTP), which has been standardized as 802.1w, can be regarded as a replacement for the proprietary extensions. Recalling the two core concepts of the 802.1D STP from Chapter 15, let's compare the old with the new.

First, 802.1D specifies that there are five different states that a port can be in. Each state is accompanied by a port mode, so a blocking port, for example, cannot be a root or designated port.

RSTP assumes that three of these states can be regarded as essentially the same from the perspective of other switches. Listening, blocking, and disabled modes are all characterized by the facts that they do not forward frames and they do not learn MAC addresses, so RSTP places them all into a new mode: discarding. Learning and forwarding ports remain more or less the same. The effect of this change is to decouple the port states from the port roles.

The second big difference is the timing operation. In 802.1D STP, bridges would only send out a BPDU when they received one on their root port. These legacy bridges essentially act as forwarding agents for BPDUs that are generated by the root. In contrast, 802.1w-enabled switches send out BPDUs every hello time, containing current information.

The combination of these two changes forces spanning tree to operate in a much faster mode, with convergence being achieved in just a few seconds (typically about three times the two-second update timer), largely because if a switch fails to receive BPDUs on an interface for seconds, it presumes that the port at the other end of the link is down.

This rapid transition to the forwarding state, caused by switches no longer having to wait for the timer mechanism, is similar in concept to the proprietary PortFast mechanism, and only operates on edge ports and point-to-point links. Other enhancements in RSTP, such as the synchronization of root port information and the explicit forwarding authorization granted by switches to other switches, have parallels with the UplinkFast and BackboneFast extensions.

It is likely that as time passes, greater emphasis will be placed by Cisco on the standardized mechanisms of 802.1w rather than the proprietary extensions to 802.1D.

Those wishing to learn more about RSTP than is covered in the CCNP program should visit `www.cisco.com/warp/public/473/146.html`.

Summary

The Spanning Tree Protocol (STP) was originally designed to work on bridged networks, which in turn were designed to segment LANs to allow for additional growth. Remember that collision domains have some upper limits, largely based upon the back-off algorithm inside Ethernet, which gradually nibbles away at the available bandwidth. These networks carried slow applications data—often FTP or e-mail—and although redundancy was planned to cover for bridge failures, slow convergence was readily accepted.

Modern-day switches have replaced bridges, and the design criteria have shifted dramatically. Now we have expectations of almost instant recovery from network failures because the applications themselves place those demands on the network. With so many applications having an interactive or multimedia component, and with business relying so heavily on the LAN infrastructure, slow legacy STP no longer meets our needs and expectations.

You should now be familiar with all of the bells and whistles that bring STP into the 21st century. Whether they be proprietary implementations of PortFast, UplinkFast, or BackboneFast, or their soon-to-happen replacement by standards-based alternatives such as 802.1s and 802.1w, we need their help to get STP to work the way we want. Related to this, you have several configuration options for changing the STP timers to speed up convergence in a legacy network.

These days it's possible to configure separate spanning trees on different VLANs, giving us the multiple benefits of planning optimal topologies while also creating faster converging and smaller (hence more efficient) spanning trees. Finally, it is often advantageous to increase bandwidth at certain places in the network using port aggregation protocols such as EtherChannel. These "channelizing" protocols provide an inexpensive and simple mechanism for increasing bandwidth on point-to-point links using existing interfaces.

Exam Essentials

Know the types of spanning tree available. STP comes in a variety of different flavors, and you need to be sure which one to configure. It's not necessarily a case of which one is best, because not every switch supports every option, but you do need to understand the different types of spanning tree and know what their limitations and benefits are. ISL is Cisco proprietary and allows for one spanning tree instance per VLAN (PVST), whereas the standards-based 802.1Q supports only Common Spanning Tree (CST), unless you also implement 802.1s and the MST option.

Know what can be configured to reduce the delay a port must go through with a topology change. A perennial STP problem is slow convergence. The Cisco proprietary options of PortFast, BackboneFast, and UplinkFast are capable of speeding up the process, and you need to understand what they are doing and under what circumstances you can use them. At the time this book went to press, these are the main players, but the recent standardization of 802.1w—RSTP—means that they may be used less in the future.

Understand how an EtherChannel works. An EtherChannel is formed from bonding together between two and eight ports connecting the same two switches. A single command on each switch logically binds the circuits together, but only if each circuit is configured in an identical fashion.

Inter-VLAN Routing

THE CCNP EXAM TOPICS COVERED IN THIS CHAPTER INCLUDE THE FOLLOWING:

- ✓ Understand VLAN trunking protocols including 802.1Q, ISL, and the dynamic trunking protocol.
- ✓ Describe inter-VLAN routing and name the components.
- ✓ Configure access ports for static membership of single and multiple VLANs.
- ✓ Configure ports as 802.1Q trunks and verify their operation.
- ✓ Configure ports as ISL trunks and verify their operation.
- ✓ Identify the Cisco Route Switch processors and explain how they are implemented.

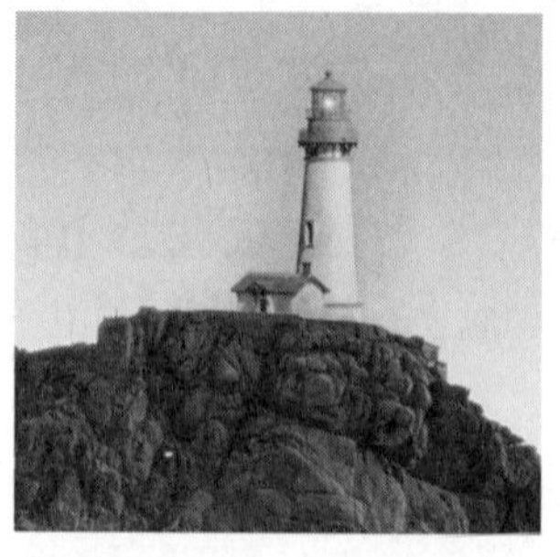

First, let's have a quick review. Routers break up broadcast domains, and layer 2 switches are used to break up collision domains. If you connect all your switches together, they will be in one broadcast domain. You can break up broadcast domains in layer 2 switched networks by creating virtual LANs (VLANs). However, the hosts within a VLAN can communicate only within the same VLAN by default.

Obviously you cannot bridge together VLANs, because that would allow the forwarding of broadcasts across the VLAN boundary and would just create a larger single VLAN. For devices in one VLAN to communicate with devices in a different VLAN, they must be routed through a layer 3 device. This is called *inter-VLAN routing*. You can perform inter-VLAN routing with internal route processors in a layer 2 switch or with an external router called an *external route processor*.

In this chapter, we cover both internal route processors and external route processors and explain how to configure them for inter-VLAN configuration.

The term *route processor* is used commonly when discussing the device used for inter-VLAN communications, but we should be clear. This is really just a router, either running externally or as firmware or software in a switch. Modern implementations of route processors run IOS and support routing protocols in common with routers.

Routing Between VLANs

The main reason for the creation of a VLAN is to keep traffic within local workgroups. We have already mentioned in this book that you cannot communicate between VLANs without a router (layer 3 device), so understanding the configuration of VLANs and understanding routing need to go hand in hand in order to understand the full process of inter-VLAN communications.

Route processors provide the communication that hosts need between VLANs. However, if you are using local VLANs (see Chapter 14, "VLANs, Trunks, and VTP" for a thorough explanation), a good rule of thumb is to design your networks so at least 80 percent of the users' traffic does not cross over into another VLAN. Therefore, you should design the network so that the users have access to local servers and other needed resources to prevent excessive packets from crossing the route processor.

Real World Scenario

ISL Network Cards

It is worth repeating that many network card vendors nowadays make NICs that can understand ISL and 802.1Q encapsulated packets. When attempting to keep a large percentage of traffic from straying from the local VLAN, these cards can be very useful. Fitting a server with an ISL or 802.1Q-aware NIC means that the server can be a member of multiple VLANs and connect to a switch via a trunk link.

Example scenarios include installing one of these NICs in an e-mail server or a database server. Anything that a large number of people, across several VLANs, need to access is a candidate for this type of connection. It often makes more fiscal sense to upgrade a server NIC than to upgrade an entire router.

Cisco recommends that VLANs should be configured one for one with IP subnet designs. This means that you need to create a subnet design for your network, taking into account the needs of the various VLANs. If you are using variable-length subnet masking (VLSM), this is pretty straightforward, but if for some reason you are constrained to a single subnet mask, you may need to select the mask first and then design your VLANs around the subnet design. For example, if you have engineering, marketing, sales, and support departments, you will typically—not always, but typically—create a subnet for each department, making sure you have room for growth. You would then create a VLAN for each department. In Chapter 14, we discussed the differences between local and end-to-end VLANs. Regardless of the type of VLAN you configure, each of these types would be associated with a subnet.

The route processor managing the inter-VLAN routing would have multiple interfaces (real or virtual), and each would have an IP address in the subnet associated with the interface VLAN. Each device within a VLAN would have a default gateway of the IP address of the inter-VLAN device connected to its VLAN. The inter-VLAN device would then route any packets with a destination not on the local network.

Before configuring routing between your VLANs, you need to understand the type of data sharing that is needed. By understanding the user and business needs, you can design the network with load balancing and/or redundant links if needed.

When configuring routing, you can choose from three options:

- Multiple links
- A single trunk link
- An internal or external route processor

VLSM (variable-length subnet masking) is a technique designed to create flexible subnets and get the most from your available IP address space. It is covered in detail in Part I of this book.

Multiple Links

You can configure your VLANs to inter-communicate by connecting a separate router interface into separate switch ports that are configured for each VLAN. Each workstation in the VLAN would have its default gateway configured for the physical router interface's own VLAN/subnet. Figure 17.1 shows how this might look in an internetwork.

FIGURE 17.1 Routers with multiple links

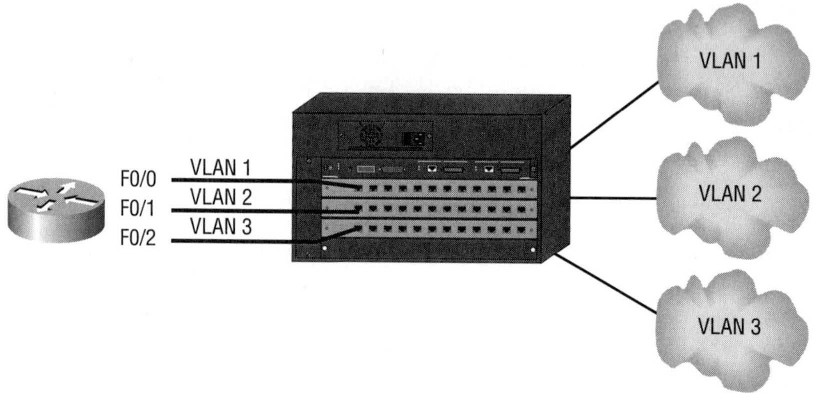

This is a perfectly workable solution for small networks, but it does not scale well when you have more than a few VLANs. It depends on the type of router you have. For every VLAN, you need to have a router interface (typically FastEthernet or Gigabit Ethernet), so a larger, more expensive router can have more interfaces without being saturated. But sooner rather than later, you will run out of physical interfaces.

The more VLANs you have, the more router interfaces you have to purchase with the router. Also, you should have a fast router such as a high-end (at least a 4700 or 7200 series) router that can route quickly so the router does not become a bottleneck. Cost then becomes the issue with multiple links, and the possible requirement for multiple or redundant route processors doubles the cost.

Real World Scenario

Using Legacy Equipment

Using multiple links is not a desirable thing to do in most cases, but there are times when it might be the only solution. The alternate solutions—using a trunk, for example—require Fast Ethernet at the least. Trunks do not run over 10Mbits/second Ethernet. So if you have some routers with only slower Ethernet interfaces, such as the obsolete 2500 series, then you would be able to effect inter-VLAN routing with one of those—albeit quite slowly.

A Single Trunk Link

Another possible solution to routing between VLANs is creating a trunk link on a switch and then using a frame-tagging protocol such as ISL or 802.1Q (which are used to identify VLAN/ frame relationships as they traverse FastEthernet and Gigabit Ethernet links) on the router. Cisco calls this solution "router on a stick."

Figure 17.2 shows how the internetwork might look with a single trunk link for all VLANs.

FIGURE 17.2 Single trunk link for all VLANs

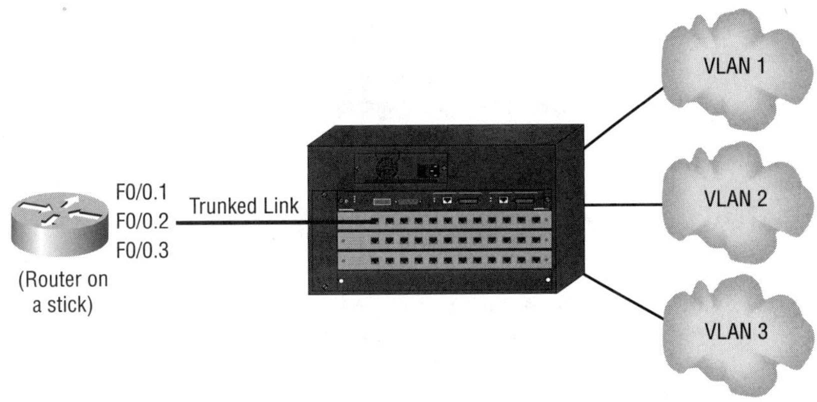

This solution uses only one router interface on the router, but it also puts all the traffic on one interface. You really have to have a fast router to do this. Also, to even perform this function, you need, at minimum, a FastEthernet interface on a 2600 series router. ISL does not work on 10BaseT interfaces, nor would you want to run this on 10BaseT because it is processor- and bandwidth-intensive.

An Internal Route Processor

An *internal route processor* is a router on a card that fits inside the switch. This enables a switch to route packets without having the packets leave the box that the switch resides in. You need to add an internal route processor to a layer 2 device—for example, a 4000 Catalyst switch—to be able to provide forwarding of layer 3 packets without an external router.

Adding an internal route processor makes a layer 2 switch into a multilayer switch and can integrate layer 2 and layer 3 (and possibly layer 4) functionality in a single box. The 4000 series uses a *Layer 3 Switching Module (L3SM)*, and the 6000 series uses the *Multilayer Switch Module (MSM)* and the *Multilayer Switch Feature Card (MSFC)* to perform this function. The MSM and MSFC—and older Route Switch Modules (RSMs) and Route Switch Feature Cards (RSFCs)—are configured in exactly the same way on older switches.

The 4000 series router module (WS-X4232-L3) consists of a 4GB routing switch fabric with 4GB interfaces. Two of these gigabit connections appear on the front panel, making externally accessible gigabit router ports, while the two remaining ports are connected internally to the switch backplane. (There are also 32 10/100M ports, which are standard layer 2 ports and not linked into the routing fabric.)

Most of the time, ports 3 and 4 are configured as part of the same channel, and subinterfaces are added as needed using either ISL or 802.1Q encapsulation. The configuration of gigabit ports 3 and 4 on the router module must be consistent with the configuration of port slot/1 and slot/2 on the switch.

The traffic flow between the module and the switch can be seen using the global commands `show interface port-channel` or `show interface gigabit`.

The L3SM is plugged directly into the switch and runs the Cisco IOS in order to perform inter-VLAN communication. The 4000 series switch sees the RSM as a single trunked port with a single MAC address. In other words, it appears as a router on a stick to the switch.

Internal Routing on an IOS-Based Switch

More recently, an entirely new method for inter-VLAN switching has emerged. The migration of Cisco switches over to IOS has meant that a new generation of switches is equipped with native routing capabilities. Not only are these faster than those switches with additional daughter boards or routing cards, but they support a variety of enhanced features that we will examine later in the book such as QoS (quality of service) and layer 3 switching.

Using ISL and 802.1Q Routing

The best solution to inter-VLAN routing might be to provide a Gigabit Ethernet router interface for each VLAN. Obviously this can be cost prohibitive, as well as stretching the physical limitations of router options. What if you have 200 VLANs? Can you really afford a router with 200 Gigabit Ethernet ports? That would be an interesting configuration.

Well, there are some other options open to you, because you can use just one interface for all your VLANs. Using either the Cisco proprietary Inter-Switch Link (ISL) or the standards-based 802.1Q protocol, you can configure routing between VLANs with only one FastEthernet or one Gigabit Ethernet interface. To run either ISL or 802.1Q, you need to have two VLAN-capable FastEthernet or Gigabit Ethernet devices such as a Cisco 4000 or 6500 switch and a 7000 (or larger) series router. (We will be using a 2600 router in the hands-on lab, but that is a little low-powered for larger networks.)

Remember from Chapter 14 that both ISL and 802.1Q are trunking protocols, ways of explicitly tagging VLAN information onto an Ethernet frame. This tagging information enables VLANs to be multiplexed over a trunk link through an external encapsulation method. By running a trunking protocol on the switch and router interfaces, you can interconnect both devices and maintain VLAN information end to end.

You can configure inter-VLAN routing with either an external router or an internal route processor that can be placed in a slot of a modular Catalyst switch such as the 4000 and 6500 series (as well as the old 5000 series). In this section, we take a look at both options.

Configuring ISL/802.1Q with an External Router

An external layer 3 device can be used to provide routing between VLANs. You can use almost any router to perform the function of external routing between VLANs, but if trunking is being used, the selected router must support the VLAN tagging method used, whether it's ISL or 802.1Q; then the FastEthernet or Gigabit Ethernet interface would be your choice.

If you have a few small VLANs that perform 80 percent or more of their network function on the local VLAN, then you can probably get away with a 10Mbps Ethernet connection into each VLAN. Just remember that 10Mb interfaces do not support trunking, so the configuration would be one VLAN per interface. You should get FastEthernet if you can.

The external router interface needs to be configured with a trunking protocol encapsulation such as ISL or 802.1Q, thus allowing different VLANs to be assigned to different subinterfaces. These subinterfaces give you an extremely flexible solution for providing routing between VLANs. To perform ISL routing on a single interface, the interface must be at least a FastEthernet interface that supports ISL routing. The Cisco 1750 is the least expensive router that can perform this function.

To configure ISL/802.1Q routing on a single interface, you must first configure the subinterfaces. These are configured by using the *`int.subinterface_number`* global command. Here is an example on a 2600 router with a FastEthernet interface:

```
Terry_2620#configure terminal
Enter configuration commands, one per line.  End with CNTL/Z.
Terry_2620(config)#interface fa0/0.?
  <0-4294967295>  FastEthernet interface number

Terry_2620(config)#interface fa0/0.1
Terry_2620(config-subif)#
```

Notice the number of subinterfaces available (4.2 billion). You can choose any number that feels good because the subinterfaces are only locally significant to the router. However, we usually like to choose the VLAN number for ease of administration. Notice that the prompt on the router is now telling you that you are configuring a subinterface (`config-subif`).

After you configure the subinterface number you want, you then need to define the type of encapsulation you are going to use. Here is an example of the different types of trunking protocols you can use:

```
Terry_2620(config-subif)#encapsulation ?
  dot1Q   IEEE 802.1Q Virtual LAN
```

```
  isl     Inter Switch Link - Virtual LAN encapsulation
  sde     IEEE 802.10 Virtual LAN - Secure Data Exchange
  tr-isl  Token Ring Inter Switch Link - Virtual LAN encapsulation
```

You're not done yet. You need to tell the subinterface which VLAN it is a member of, and you provide this information on the same line as the encapsulation command. Here is an example:

```
Terry_2620(config-subif)#encapsulation isl ?
  <1-1000>  Virtual LAN Identifier.
```

Notice that you can configure the subinterface to be a part of any VLAN up to 1000. The `dot1Q` encapsulation is for the IEEE standard 802.1Q trunking, and `isl` is for ISL encapsulation.

After you choose the interface and encapsulation type and VLAN number, configure the IP address that this subinterface is a member of. The complete configuration looks like this:

```
Terry_2620#configure terminal
Enter configuration commands, one per line.  End with CNTL/Z.
Terry_2620(config)#interface fa0/0.1
Terry_2620(config-subif)#encapsulation isl 1
Terry_2620(config-subif)#ip address 172.16.10.1 255.255.255.0
```

The preceding configuration is for subinterface fa0/0.1 to VLAN 1. You would create a subinterface for each VLAN. You can verify your configuration with the `show running-config` command:

```
!
interface FastEthernet0/0.1
 encapsulation isl 1
 ip address 172.16.10.1 255.255.255.0
```

If you had elected the 802.1Q encapsulation, the complete router configuration would look like this:

```
Terry_2620#configure terminal
Enter configuration commands, one per line.  End with CNTL/Z.
Terry_2620(config)#interface fa0/0.1
Terry_2620(config-subif)#encapsulation dot1Q 1
Terry_2620(config-subif)#ip address 172.16.10.1 255.255.255.0
```

Once again, you can verify your configuration with the `show running-config` command:

```
!
interface FastEthernet0/0.1
 encapsulation dot1Q 1
 ip address 172.16.10.1 255.255.255.0
!
```

Configuring ISL/802.1Q on an Internal Route Processor

Up until recently, the situation was that if you did not have an external router or if you had many VLANs, you would use a Layer 3 Services Module (L3SM) to provide the layer 3 routing for your 4000/6500 series switch.

The introduction of the Supervisor III and IV engines for the Catalyst 4000 and above changes all this. These new Supervisor engines run IOS, and this means that they can route natively without the need for additional hardware. Obviously, Cisco might recommend an upgrade if you are planning much inter-VLAN routing, which is probably a good idea. The faster switching available with these native IOS devices will certainly improve packet forwarding.

First, however, we will look at the configuration of the older design switches, which have a native switching fabric supplemented by some sort of routing module. We will look at a 4000 series switch that has an L3SM in slot 3. Let's first confirm the hardware configuration of the switch:

```
Terry_4000> (enable) show module
Mod Slot Ports Module-Type               Model               Sub Status
--- ---- ----- ------------------------- ------------------- --- --------
1   1    0     Switching Supervisor      WS-X4012            no  ok
2   2    34    10/100/1000 Ethernet      WS-X4232            no  ok
3   3          Router Switch Card        WS-X4232-L3         no  ok

Mod Module-Name         Serial-Num
--- ------------------- --------------------
1                       JAE044001T8
2                       JAE04271V1N
3                       JAE0427155N

Mod MAC-Address(es)                        Hw     Fw         Sw
--- -------------------------------------- ------ ---------- -----------------
1   00-03-e3-7a-6b-00 to 00-03-e3-7a-6e-ff 2.1    5.4(1)     4.5(2)
2   00-02-b9-61-89-e0 to 00-02-b9-61-8a-0f 2.3
3   00-03-4a-a0-d3-ab to 00-02-4b-a0-d0-cf 1.0    12.0(7)W5( 12.0(7)
```

Now that we have confirmed that the switch sees the router module in port 3, we need to access the L3SM using the `session` command:

```
Terry_4000> (enable) session 3
Trying Router...
Connected to Router.
Escape character is \Q^]'.
Router>
```

You are now connected to the internal route processor, and you should continue to configure the device as you would any other router. Notice in the following router output that we set the host name and routing protocol as well:

```
Router>
Router>enable
Router#
Router#configure terminal
Enter configuration commands, one per line.  End with CNTL/Z.
Router(config)#hostname Terry_L3SM
Terry_L3SM(config)#router eigrp 10
Terry_L3SM (config-router)#network 172.16.0.0
```

As we mentioned, the route processor looks like any Cisco router, because it is running IOS. Remember that it's just as important to configure the routing protocols on this device as it is to configure them on any other router. The route processor is able to handle most of the routing protocols that a traditional router can. Be careful of large routing tables, though.

Configuring VLANs on an Internal Route Processor

First, it would be common practice to set up the internal gigabit interfaces to act as Gigabit EtherChannel trunks. This needs to be done at both the L3SM and switch parts of the internal link. On the L3SM, the configuration looks like this:

```
Terry_L3SM#configure terminal
Terry_L3SM(config)#interface GigabitEthernet3
Terry_L3SM(config-if)#channel-group 1
Terry_L3SM(config)#interface GigabitEthernet4
Terry_L3SM(config-if)#channel-group 1
```

And on the Catalyst, it looks like this:

```
Terry_4000> (enable)set port channel 3/1-2 mode on
Terry_4000> (enable)set trunk 3/1  nonegotiate dotlq 1-1005
Terry_4000> (enable)set trunk 3/2  nonegotiate dotlq 1-1005
```

Next, instead of creating subinterfaces as you would with an external router, you need to configure each VLAN with the `interface vlan #` command. This establishes a direct virtual connection between the switch backplane and the routing module, and what you are actually doing is associating each VLAN with a virtual interface. Here is an example of how to configure the processor to route between three VLANs:

```
Terry_L3SM#configure terminal
Terry_L3SM(config)#interface vlan 1
Terry_L3SM(config-if)#ip address 172.16.1.1 255.255.255.0
Terry_L3SM(config-if)#interface vlan 2
```

```
Terry_L3SM(config-if)#ip address 172.16.2.1 255.255.255.0
Terry_L3SM(config-if)#interface vlan 3
Terry_L3SM(config-if)#ip address 172.16.3.1 255.255.255.0
Terry_L3SM(config-if)#no shutdown
```

The interesting part of the configuration is the necessary `no shutdown` command for each VLAN interface. Notice in the preceding configuration that we performed a `no shutdown` only on interface VLAN 3. Take a look at the output of interface VLAN 2:

```
Terry_L3SM#show interface vlan 2
Vlan2 is administratively down, line protocol is down
```

It is important to think of each VLAN interface as a separate interface that needs an `ip address` and a `no shutdown` performed, just as with any other router interface.

You can then verify your configuration with the `show running-config` command:

```
Terry_L3SM#show running-config
Current configuration:
!
version 12.0
service timestamps debug uptime
service timestamps log uptime
no service password-encryption
!
hostname Terry_L3SM
!
interface Vlan1
 ip address 172.16.1.1 255.255.255.0
!
interface Vlan2
 ip address 172.16.2.1 255.255.255.0
!
interface Vlan3
 ip address 172.16.3.1 255.255.255.0
!
router eigrp 10
 network 172.16.0.0
```

To view the routing table on the internal processor, use the `show ip route` command:

```
Terry_L3SM#show ip route
Codes: C - connected, S - static, I - IGRP, R - RIP,   M - [output cut]
Gateway of last resort is not set
```

```
     172.16.0.0/24 is subnetted, 3 subnets
C       172.16.3.0 is directly connected, Vlan3
C       172.16.2.0 is directly connected, Vlan2
C       172.16.1.0 is directly connected, Vlan1

Terry_L3SM#
```

Assigning MAC Addresses to VLAN Interfaces

The RSM uses only one global MAC address for all VLAN interfaces on the device. This is the burned-in address (BIA), which can be viewed using the `show interface vlan` command. If you want to assign a specific MAC address to a VLAN interface, use the `mac-address` interface command. You might want to configure this option to enhance the operation of the RSM interface. Here is an example:

```
Terry_L3SM#configure terminal
Terry_L3SM(config)#interface vlan 2
Terry_L3SM(config-if)#mac-address 4004.0144.0011
Terry_L3SM(config-if)#exit
Terry_L3SM(config)#exit
Terry_L3SM#show running-config
[output cut]
interface Vlan2
 mac-address 4004.0144.0011
 ip address 172.16.2.1 255.255.255.0
```

Defining a Default Gateway

One thing to keep in mind before configuring ISL on your switches is that the switches must be configured correctly with an IP address, subnet mask, and default gateway. Understand that this has nothing to do with routing, because the switches work only at layer 2. However, the switches need to communicate with IP through the network. Remember that this will not affect data that is passing through the switch. You can think of layer 2 switches as being just like any host on the network. To be able to send packets off the local network, you need to have a default gateway configured.

To configure a default gateway on a 4000 series switch, use the `set ip route` command:

```
Terry_4000> (enable) set ip route 0.0.0.0 172.16.1.1
Route added.
```

You can also use the command `set ip route default 172.16.1.1`, which configures the route the same as the `set ip route 0.0.0.0 172.16.1.1` command does.

The IOS switch `default-gateway` command was covered in Chapter 13, "Connecting the Switch Block."

Configuring Internal Routing on an IOS-Based Switch

At this stage of learning, it is a simple matter to configure internal routing. The configuration on the modular L3SM is just about identical to that on the modern IOS-based layer 3 switches. This example shows a 3550 configured as a VTP server, and with two VLANs configured. In addition, two interfaces are placed into the created VLANs. No routing protocols are needed unless the requirement exists to route outside the connected VLAN table.

```
Terry_3550# configure terminal
Terry_3550(config)#vtp domain globalnet
Terry_3550(config)#vtp mode server
Terry_3550(config)#vlan 2
Terry_3550(config-vlan)#name PRODUCTION
Terry_3550(config-vlan)#ip address 172.16.2.1 255.255.255.0
Terry_3550(config-vlan)#exit
Terry_3550(config)#vlan 3
Terry_3550(config-vlan)#name SALES
Terry_3550(config-vlan)#ip address 172.16.3.1 255.255.255.0
Terry_3550(config-vlan)#exit
Terry_3550(config)#vlan 1
Terry_3550(config-vlan)#ip address 172.16.1.1 255.255.255.0
Terry_3550(config-vlan)#exit

Terry_3550(config)#interface FastEthernet0/1
Terry_3550(config-if)#description PRODUCTION MANAGER
Terry_3550(config-if)#switchport access vlan 2
Terry_3550(config-if)#switchport mode access

Terry_3550(config)#interface FastEthernet0/2
Terry_3550(config-if)#description SALES MANAGER
Terry_3550(config-if)#switchport access vlan 3
Terry_3550(config-if)#switchport mode access
```

This gives rise to the following running configuration, viewed with the IOS standard `show running-config` statement:

```
Terry_3550#show run
!
[output cut]
!
interface FastEthernet0/1
 description PRODUCTION MANAGER
 switchport access vlan 2
```

```
 switchport mode access
 no ip address
!
interface FastEthernet0/2
 description SALES MANAGER
 switchport access vlan 3
 switchport mode access
 no ip address
!
[output cut]
!
interface Vlan1
 ip address 172.16.1.1 255.255.255.0
!
interface Vlan2
 ip address 172.16.2.1 255.255.255.0
!
interface Vlan3
 ip address 172.16.3.1 255.255.255.0
!
[output truncated]
!
Terry_3550#
```

The only other thing we need to do is make sure that the routing table is properly populated. By default, IP routing is not enabled on a layer 3 switch, so we need to configure that with the global command `ip routing`. After this is done, you can view the routing table in the normal way:

```
Terry_3550#
Terry_3550#conf t
Terry_3550(config)#ip routing
Terry_3550(config)#exit
Terry_3550#

Terry_3550#show ip route
Codes: C - connected, S - static, I - IGRP, R - RIP, M - mobile, B - BGP
       D - EIGRP, EX - EIGRP external, O - OSPF, IA - OSPF inter area
       N1 - OSPF NSSA external type 1, N2 - OSPF NSSA external type 2
       E1 - OSPF external type 1, E2 - OSPF external type 2, E - EGP
       i - IS-IS, L1 - IS-IS level-1, L2 - IS-IS level-2, ia - IS-IS inter area
       * - candidate default, U - per-user static route, o - ODR
       P - periodic downloaded static route
```

```
Gateway of last resort is not set

     172.16.0.0/24 is subnetted, 2 subnets
C       172.16.1.0 is directly connected, Vlan1
C       172.16.2.0 is directly connected, Vlan2
C       172.16.3.0 is directly connected, Vlan3
Terry_3550#
```

Notice that the complete range of routing protocols is available for use. This immensely powerful piece of equipment can be used for full multilayer switching and routing as needed. So far we have not needed to configure a routing protocol, as all of our subnets are directly attached, but as the internetwork grows we shall undoubtedly need to configure dynamic routing.

Summary

VLANs are designed to keep broadcasts within artificial limits, and this makes them a useful design tool. But nobody can expect that all of the data in one VLAN will remain there. Users will need to communicate with services and hosts on other VLANs, and that means going through a router.

Question: What do you get when you bridge two VLANs together?

Answer: A bigger VLAN!

So, to get from one VLAN to another, data needs to be forwarded across a router! Routers are needed to enable hosts on different networks to communicate, and also for inter-VLAN communication. The router in question can be either an external router or an internal route processor, or it can run in the IOS in native mode. All are suitable and can do the task, but the advantages of internal processing is clear—cost, simplicity, and speed of link to the router fabric are all factors.

You can use both internal routers and external routers to configure an ISL/802.1Q. You can also use them for inter-VLAN configuration. Further, both ISL and 802.1Q are able to differentiate between VLANs at the router interface.

Exam Essentials

Know the difference between an internal and an external route processor. An external route processor is a standard router that is routing between VLANs. An external router can accept packets across a trunk terminating at a single Ethernet interface, or it can have several connections, one per VLAN. The second method is required if there are only 10Mb Ethernet interfaces available, because you cannot configure trunks on standard Ethernet.

An internal route processor is a special card inside the switch that routes between VLANs. Once connected internally to the route processor, you can configure it in a similar fashion to the external processor/router, as it will run IOS. Modern layer 3 switches with an intelligent matrix run IOS and can be configured in the same way.

Know how to configure VLANs on each of the routers. On an internal route processor, the router has VLAN interfaces as opposed to the Ethernet or serial interfaces found on an external router. The interfaces are accessed in the same fashion, but on an internal router, each VLAN interface gets an IP address and the `no shutdown` command must be issued to activate the interface.

On an external router, you must select the appropriate FastEthernet or Gigabit Ethernet interface and create subinterfaces, preferably labeling them the same as the VLAN that will reside there. Configure each subinterface with the appropriate encapsulation and IP address and then issue the `no shutdown` command on the physical interface.

Know how to configure routing on the router and on the switch. Both internal and external route processors can be configured to route packets from one network to another based on routing protocol information. To configure a dynamic routing protocol, you must enter global configuration mode and use the `router` command followed by routing protocol–specific information. No routing protocol may be needed if all VLANs in your network have an interface on the route processor and there are no external links.

To configure routing on a switch, you must configure a default gateway on the switch. Use the command `set ip route` to accomplish this, pointing to an IP address that can forward packets to other networks, something like a router interface.

Chapter 18

Multilayer Switching (MLS)

THE CCNP EXAM TOPICS COVERED IN THIS CHAPTER INCLUDE THE FOLLOWING:

- ✓ Identify the components necessary to effect multilayer switching.
- ✓ Apply flow masks to influence the type of MLS cache.
- ✓ Describe layers 2, 3, 4 and multilayer switching.
- ✓ Verify existing flow entries in the MLS cache.
- ✓ Describe how MLS functions on a switch.
- ✓ Configure a switch to participate in multilayer switching.
- ✓ Determine appropriate multilayer switching architectures for specific needs.

The expression *multilayer switching (MLS)* can be very confusing. If you ask 10 different vendors what it means, you will probably get 11 different answers! After all, you already know that switching is a layer 2 function, where frames are forwarded using just the MAC address and a dynamic table. You may also recall that routing, a layer 3 function where packets are forwarded using IP addresses, sometimes also uses some layer 4 information.

Some people will argue that there is really no such thing as layer 3 switching and that this is all vendor-speak, just smoke and mirrors to confuse poor buyers into selecting a product. This is rather harsh, but it is true that defining layer 3 switching can be problematical.

So let's get down to business. Why do you need layer 3 switching when you have layer 3 routing? The answer to this question is simple: enhanced performance. Why do you implement any features on any piece of Cisco equipment? To improve performance and to take advantage of the robust feature set provided by Cisco. Routers, by their nature, need to analyze packets in great detail before forwarding them. This takes time, and anything that we can do to reduce the time is of benefit, especially in the modern world of QoS-hungry applications.

MLS can be implemented using more than one technology, because it really is just a vendor description for how routing can be speeded up. Cisco has two separate techniques. One involves the use of a route processor (either external or internal) that communicates specific information to a Cisco switch. The other technique is called Cisco Express Forwarding (CEF), and this requires that the switch have a routing function such as the 3550 series or the 4000 series running native IOS. In this chapter, you'll learn about both.

Understanding the Fundamentals of MLS

The first of the Cisco MLS implementations involves the use of a *router on a stick*. Figure 18.1 depicts the router-on-a-stick architecture. As you can see from the diagram, there are multiple hosts using two separate VLAN assignments. One segment is running on VLAN 10 and the other is running on VLAN 50. Both VLANs are connected to the same switch. The switch is then connected to a router. This figure illustrates an external router, but an RSM provides the same functionality, just internally.

By now you understand that for Host A on VLAN 10 to communicate to Host D on VLAN 50, packets must be routed through Router A. Because of the VLAN assignments, the switch must send the packet to the router on interface FE0/0.10. The router knows that the route to the network assigned to VLAN 50 is through interface FE0/0.50. The packet is then sent back to the switch and forwarded to Host D.

FIGURE 18.1 Router-on-a-stick diagram

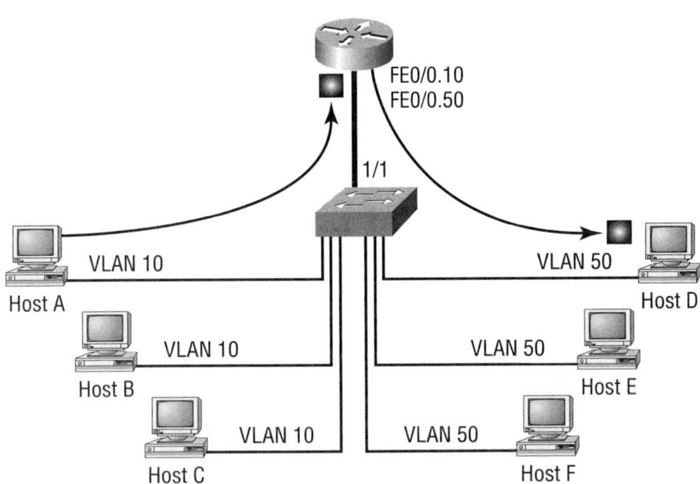

Now back to our original question. Why use layer 3 switching? You can see in Figure 18.1 that it is very inefficient to have to use a router to move a packet from Host A to Host D when they are connected to the same switch. MLS is used to bypass the router on subsequent packets of the same flow. A *flow* is a table entry for a specific conversation, created by using source and destination header information for layers 3 and 4. The switch caches the routing information for that particular flow to make changes to future frames. Several fields within a frame make it unique:

- Source and destination IP addresses
- Source and destination MAC addresses
- Type of service (ToS)
- Protocol type (for example, HTTP, FTP, ICMP, and so on)

These are just some of the characteristics of a frame that can be used to establish a flow. A switch can be configured to support simple flows, such as IP address to IP address, or the switch can support complex flows dealing with port and protocol information.

Don't allow the regular changing of descriptions between packets and frames confuse you. Remember first that packets are what makes an IP flow, and in general, flows are described using layer 3 and above information. But remember also that packets are encapsulated inside frames and that local delivery across a switch is carried out using the MAC addresses. So, while packets are delivered end-to-end without changing, it is common for frames to be modified by routers when the source and destination MAC addresses are changed.

To summarize, we use MLS to enable the switch to forward the first packet in the flow to the router and then learn what should be done with the rest of the packets in the flow so the router doesn't need to route them. In Figure 18.1, the switch makes the necessary VLAN and destination MAC address changes in the subsequent frames.

Large Packet Streams

MLS tends to work better when the packet stream is fairly large. If a user is browsing the corporate intranet, they might be getting information from multiple servers located in various areas. This is a common problem associated with all forms of caching. But if that same user is downloading a file via FTP, it is easy to see that the hundreds of fragments are all coming from the same place and going to the same place. Only the initial fragment needs to be routed; the rest of them are layer 3 switched.

So for the best results, use MLS when large files are accessed or when the same type of information is accessed on a frequent basis. Users checking their e-mail every minute is an example of an application that generates small but frequent packets.

MLS Requirements

Some Cisco Catalyst switches require additional hardware to make use of the packet header information. While the 3550 series and the 4000 series with the Supervisor IV card have on-board processing, Catalyst 6000 series switches use the *Multilayer Switch Feature Card (MSFC)* and the *Policy Feature Card (PFC)* to gather and cache header information. (You may remember that the old Catalyst 5000 switches used the *NetFlow Feature Card (NFFC)* to gather this information and cache it.) A detailed process, which will be discussed later in this chapter, enables switches to establish flows.

MLS requires three components to function in any network (we have already briefly discussed two of them):

- *Multilayer Switching Route Processor (MLS-RP)* is a directly attached router. This can be an MLS-capable external router or an RSM installed in the switch.
- *Multilayer Switching Switch Engine (MLS-SE)* is an MLS-capable switch (a 6000 with an MSFC and PFC).
- *Multilayer Switching Protocol (MLSP)* is a protocol that runs on the router and enables it to communicate to the MLS-SE regarding topology or security changes.

Now that you have a basic understanding of what MLS does and what is required for MLS to function in a network, let's get into the nitty-gritty of how it works. Throughout the rest of the chapter, you will see the preceding abbreviations many times.

MLS Procedures

We discussed the three required components of MLS. It is important to understand how they work together to enable layer 3 switching. Let's look at a sample network topology that supports MLS.

Figure 18.2 shows a simple architecture of a router and a switch with two connected hosts on the switch. Again, the hosts have different VLAN assignments, requiring the router's intervention to route packets. Notice that the figure depicts the main interface with two subinterfaces: FE0/0.2 and FE0/0.3. As it stands, the current topology requires that all packets sent from the client on VLAN 3 to the client on VLAN 2 be routed by the external router. If there are a large number of packets, this creates a lot of unnecessary work.

FIGURE 18.2 MLS example topology

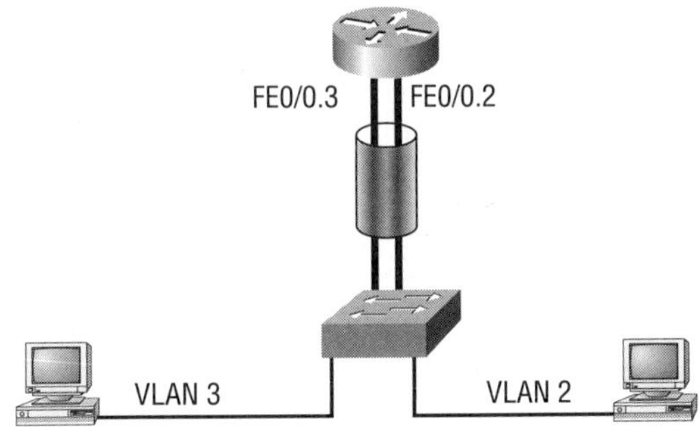

MLS follows a four-step process to establish the layer 3 switching functionality. These four steps can then be broken down into more detailed processes, which will be discussed shortly. Don't panic if these first descriptions leave you a bit confused; the detailed explanation should clear things up. The four steps required to enable MLS are as follows:

MLSP discovery The MLS-RP uses MLSP to send hello packets out all interfaces to discover any MLS-SE devices and establish the MLS-RP/MLS-SE neighbor relationships.

Identification of candidate packets The NFFC or PFC watches incoming packets and as it forwards the packets to the router, it creates partial cache entries for them, thus identifying the packets as potential candidates for a flow. A candidate packet is one that has yet to return from the router.

Identification of enable packets The NFFC or PFC watches packets coming from the MLS-RP and tries to match them with candidate packet entries. If matches are made, the packets are tagged as enable packets and a shortcut forwarding entry is made in the CAM table. This shortcut tells the switch how to duplicate the effect of routing. Everything that the router did to the packet, the switch is now able to do.

Layer 3 switching of subsequent flow packets Incoming packets are compared against CAM table entries. If the packets match the flow criteria, the switch will take the shortcut information and make any necessary changes, and the packet is directly forwarded to the appropriate exit port for the flow.

As we said, the preceding list is an overview of the steps that must take place before packets can be switched at layer 3. We'll discuss each step in detail next.

MLSP Discovery

Switches need routers to perform the initial route table lookup and the packet rewrite. This dependency requires that MLS adjacencies are established between the switch and the router. This is accomplished by using MLSP.

Initially, the router, or MLS-RP, sends hello packets containing all the MAC addresses and VLANs configured for use on the router. These messages are sent every 15 seconds to a layer 2 multicast address of 01-00-0C-DD-DD-DD. This is the address for the CGMP process on a Cisco switch. The intended recipients of these hello packets are the MLS-SE devices on the network.

CGMP is covered in detail in Chapter 19, "Understanding and Configuring Multicast Operation," and Chapter 20, "Quality of Service (QoS)."

When an MLS-SE receives the information, it makes an entry in the CAM table of all the MLS-RP devices in the layer 2 network. Layer 2 is mentioned because MLS-SE devices are not concerned with devices that are not directly connected to layer 2 devices, such as switches. Figure 18.3 depicts the MLSP discovery process.

Part of the information that is stored in the CAM table after an MLSP hello packet is received is an ID called an XTAG. The following is a description of the significance and purpose of the XTAG.

FIGURE 18.3 MLSP discovery

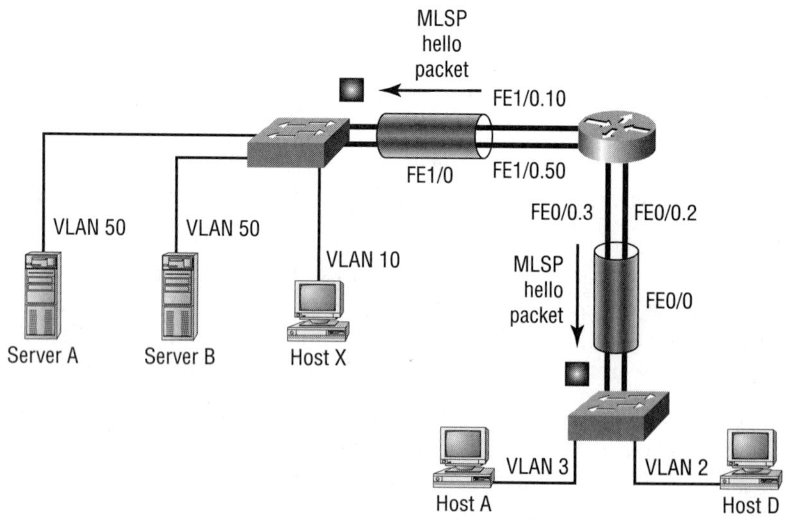

XTAGs

An *XTAG* is a unique identifier that MLS switches use to keep track of the MLS routers in the network. All the MAC addresses and VLANs in use on the MLS-RP are associated with the XTAG value in the CAM table.

The following output is from a Catalyst 6509 with an MSFC and PFC. The `show mls` command was issued to provide the output:

```
Terry_6509> (enable) show mls
Total packets switched = 4294967295
Total Active MLS entries = 85
IP Multilayer switching aging time = 256 seconds
IP Multilayer switching fast aging time = 0 seconds,  packet
threshold = 0
IP Current flow mask is Destination flow
Active IP MLS entries = 85
Netflow Data Export version: 7
Netflow Data Export disabled
Netflow Data Export port/host is not configured.
Total packets exported = 0

IP MSFC ID      Module XTAG MAC               Vlans
--------------- ------ ---- ----------------- ----------
172.16.100.5    15     1    00-d0-bc-e3-70-b1 2,3

IPX Multilayer switching aging time = 256 seconds
IPX flow mask is Destination flow
IPX max hop is 0
Active IPX MLS entries = 0

IPX MSFC ID     Module XTAG MAC               Vlans
--------------- ------ ---- ----------------- ----------
172.16.100.5    15     1    -                 -

Terry_6509> (enable)
```

You can clearly see that the MSFC has been assigned the XTAG value of 1. The MSFC is a daughter card residing on the Supervisor card, which is why it uses module 15. The MSFC receives the assignment because the MSFC was configured as the MLS-RP. In this example, only one MAC address is associated with XTAG 1. However, two VLANs are associated with it.

MLS Cache

After MLS-SEs have established CAM entries for MLS-RPs, the switch is ready to start scanning packets and creating cache entries. This was described previously as the identification of candidate and enable packets.

The cache entries are made in order to maintain flow data. Flow data enables the MLS-SE to rewrite the packets with the new source and destination MAC address and then forward the packets. All of this is done without sending the packets to the router for a route lookup and to be rewritten.

Cache entries happen in two steps:

- Candidate packet entries
- Enable packet entries

After these entries have been made in the MLS-SE, subsequent packets are matched against existing flow entries and dealt with accordingly.

Identifying Candidate Packets

The process of identifying *candidate packets* is quite simple. As has already been established, the MLS-SE has MAC address entries for any and all interfaces that come from the MLS-RP. Using this information, the MLS-SE starts watching for incoming frames destined for any MLS-RP-related MAC addresses.

An incoming frame will match one of the following three criteria:

- Not destined for an MLS-RP MAC address.
- Destined for an MLS-RP MAC address, and a cache entry already exists for this flow.
- Destined for an MLS-RP MAC address, but no cache entry exists for this flow.

Different actions will be taken by the MLS-SE, depending on which criteria match.

Destination Other Than the MLS-RP

If the incoming frame is not destined for a MAC address associated with the MLS-RP, no cache entry is made. No cache entry is made because MLS is used to avoid additional route lookups. If the frame is destined for another MAC address in the CAM table, the frame is layer 2 switched.

Figure 18.4 depicts the occurrence of a candidate packet.

Cache Entry Exists

When frames destined for an MLS-RP MAC address enter the switch, the switch checks whether a cache entry has been made that matches the attributes of the current packet.

As was previously mentioned, each frame has distinguishing characteristics or attributes that enable the MLS-SE to categorize a packet into a flow. For instance, all packets from a particular IP address and destined for a different IP address can be placed by a switch into a flow. A flow entry can use IP addresses as well as, optionally, layer 4 information. The MLS-SE uses these cache attributes to match header information in future incoming packets. If an incoming packet has the same attributes as an established flow cache entry, the packet is layer 3- or shortcut-switched.

No Cache Entry

When an incoming frame destined for the MLS-RP is compared against the cache and no existing flow entry is found, a new cache entry is made. At this point, the packet is tagged as a candidate packet.

After the cache entry is made, the packet is forwarded to the router (MLS-RP) for normal processing. Here the router performs the route lookup, rewrites the layer 2 header, and sends the packet out the next-hop interface, whichever it might be.

FIGURE 18.4 Candidate packet

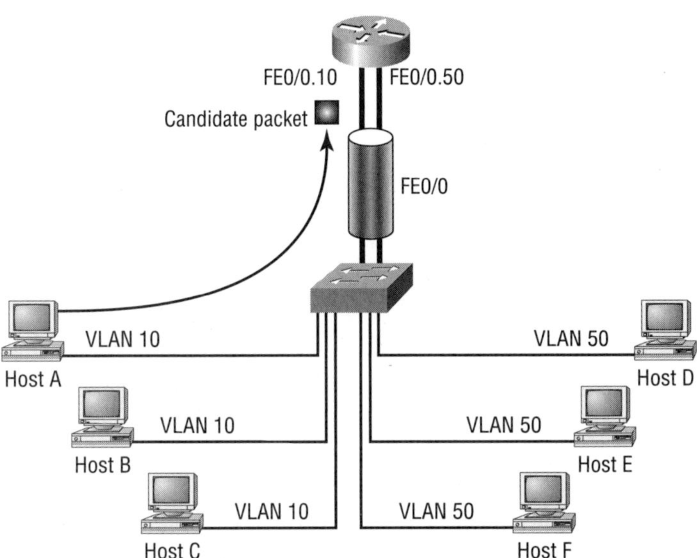

The state of the MLS cache is only partial at this stage. A complete flow cache has not been established because the MLS-SE has only seen a packet come in and be forwarded to the router. It still needs to see the packet come back from the router before the flow is complete.

Identifying Enable Packets

Enable packets are the missing piece of the flow cache puzzle. Just as the MLS switch watches all incoming frames destined for the MLS router's MAC addresses, it also watches all the packets coming from the MLS router.

It watches these packets, hoping for a match with the candidate packet cache entry. If it can make the match, the packet is tagged as an enable packet and the remaining elements of the flow cache are completed in the CAM table. Figure 18.5 depicts the occurrence of an enable packet.

The match is made by using the following criteria:

- The source MAC address is from an MLS-RP.
- The destination IP address matches the source IP address of a candidate packet.
- The source MAC address is associated with the same XTAG value as the candidate packet's destination MAC address.

If all three of these criteria are met, the MLS-SE completes the shortcut cache entry.

Frame Modification

It is important to understand that this shortcut switching occurs at layer 3. The layer 2 frame addresses (that are a part of the conversation) coming after the first frame are rewritten by the switch. Normally, a router (layer 3 device) would rewrite the frame with the necessary information. A rewrite consists of changing the VLAN assignment, the source and destination MAC addresses, and the checksums. The MLS-SE can also modify the TTL, TOS, and encapsulation.

FIGURE 18.5 Enable packet

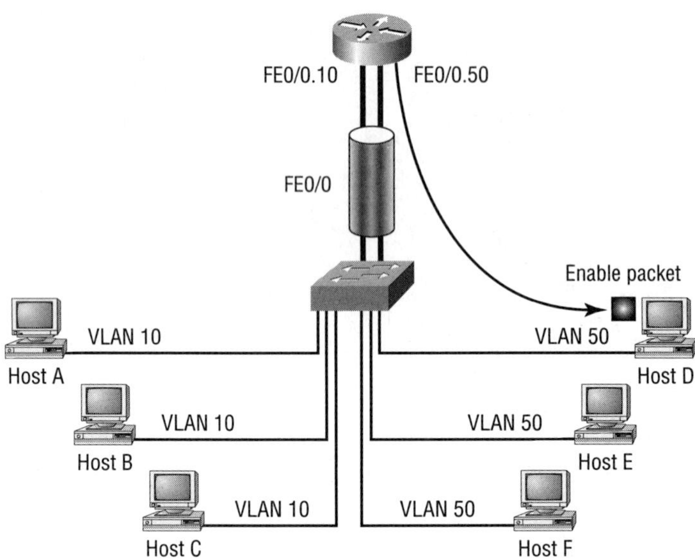

Because these packets are no longer sent to the router, the MLS-SE must perform the rewrite function. When the switch changes the source and destination MAC addresses, the MLS-SE uses the MAC address of the MLS-RP for the source, and it changes the destination MAC to the MAC of the directly connected host. Through this procedure, the frame appears to the destination host as if it had come through the router. Figure 18.6 depicts the differences between the incoming frame and the exiting frame.

Subsequent Packets

After the candidate and enable packets have been identified and a shortcut, or flow cache, has been established, subsequent packets are forwarded by the switch to the destination without the use of the router. Because the MLS-SE has the capability to rewrite the frames, it can make the necessary modifications and forward the frame directly to the destination host.

The MLS-SE caches the necessary information such as the source and destination IP addresses, the source and destination MAC addresses, and the MLS-RP-related MAC addresses. Using this information, the MLS-SE is then capable of identifying packets belonging to a specific flow, rewriting the frame, and forwarding the packets to the proper destination.

Disabling MLS

There is a right way and a wrong way to disable MLS on a router or switch. Both methods are discussed in this section.

FIGURE 18.6 Frame modification

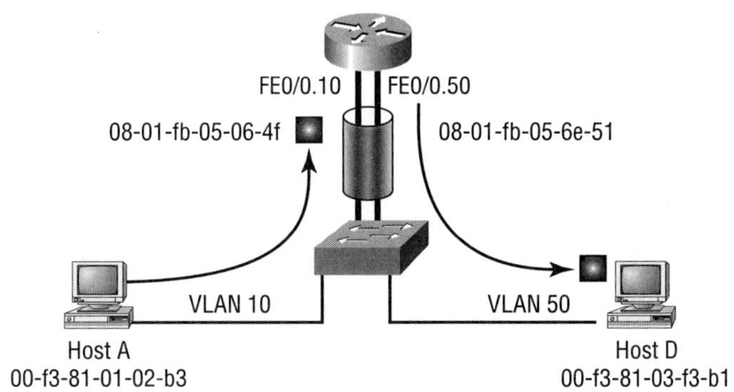

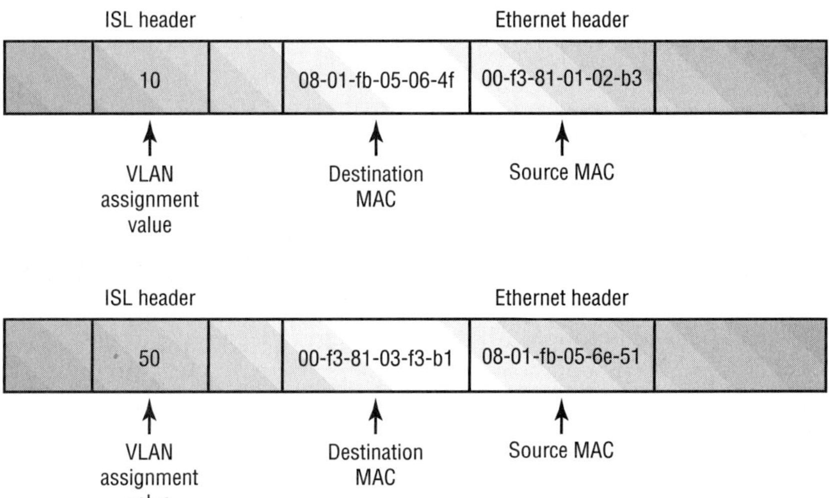

The Right Way to Disable MLS

The correct way to disable MLS depends on the equipment that you are using. Disabling MLS on a router can be paralleled with disabling MLS on an MSFC for a 6500 series switch. The command is similar: `no mls rp ip` issued from the interface. To disable MLS completely, you can issue the same command from global configuration mode. The consequences of this action vary depending on the system on which it is issued. When the command is issued on the router, the router alone disables MLS. When it's issued on an MSFC, MLS is disabled on the MSFC and the switch itself.

MLS is enabled by default for IP traffic and disabled for IPX. To disable MLS on a 6000/6500 series switch, MLS should be disabled by issuing the `no mls ip` command on the MSFC.

The Wrong Way to Disable MLS

There are several ways to inadvertently disable MLS on switches. Some are temporary, and others are permanent. Here is a list of MSFC/router commands that can disable MLS:

- `no ip routing`
- `ip security`
- `ip tcp compression-connections`
- `ip tcp header-compression`
- `clear ip route`

By disabling IP routing on the MSFC or router, you automatically disable MLS. The `ip security` command disables MLS on the interface to which the command is applied. The same results occur with the `ip tcp` compression commands. The `clear ip route` command simply clears the MLS cache entries, and the flow caches must be reestablished.

Configuring MLS-RP

To fully enable MLS, you must properly configure all participating devices. This section will describe the different configurations and settings that must be executed on the MLS-RP. Remember, the MLS-RP can be an external router or an MSFC on a 6000 series switch.

We will discuss optional configuration settings. These options depend on the existing layer 2 network and configuration. All the remaining subsections, except for "Verifying the MLS Configuration," apply only to external routers. We will start with the most basic and essential commands and then move on to management commands that can be used for verification and troubleshooting if necessary.

Enabling MLS

Although MLS is enabled on an MSFC, other routers may or may not need MLS enabled before it can be used. To enable MLS on a route processor, type the command **`mls rp ip`** while in global configuration mode. Much like the `ip routing` command, enabling MLS on a router just begins the process; you still need to configure more. Here is an example:

```
Terry_2620#configure terminal
Enter configuration commands, one per line.  End with CNTL/Z.
Terry_2620(config)#mls rp ip
Terry_2620(config)#^Z
Terry_2620#
```

```
!
ip subnet-zero
mls rp ip
!
```

Enabling MLS on the router is just the tip of the iceberg as far as required configuration tasks are concerned. We'll continue with the domain information that is needed.

VTP Domain Assignments

If a router interface is connected to a switch that is a VTP server or client, assigning the VLAN Trunk Protocol (VTP) domain is also a necessary step for MLS to work properly. It is very important to note that this step should be executed before any further MLS interface-specific commands are entered.

Failing to assign the VTP domain before configuring interfaces will place interfaces into a "null domain" rather than the proper one. Fixing this requires disabling MLS on the interfaces, and then fixing the domain and adding the interfaces back in.

Verifying the VTP Domain

First, you should verify which VTP domain the interface belongs to. This is done with the `show vtp domain` command from the switch. You can also obtain this information by looking at the switch configuration. Here are the two examples:

```
Terry_6509> show vtp domain
Domain Name  Domain Index VTP Version Local Mode  Password
-----------  ------------ ----------- ----------  --------
test         1            2           server      -

Vlan-count Max-vlan-storage Config Revision Notifications
---------- ---------------- --------------- -------------
7          1023             2               disabled

Last Updater   V2 Mode  Pruning  PruneEligible on Vlans
-------------- -------- -------- -------------------------
172.16.10.1    disabled disabled 2-1000
Terry_6509>

Terry_6509> (enable) show running-config
```

```
.....
.........
.........
.........
.........
..
-- omitted text --
!
#vtp
set vtp domain test
set vtp mode server
```

VTP Interface Configuration

After you have the VTP domain name, you're ready to assign the router interface to that VTP domain. This is done with the execution of the command `mls rp vtp-domain` *`domain_name`* on the specified interface, as in the following example:

```
Terry_2620#configure terminal
Enter configuration commands, one per line.  End with CNTL/Z.
Terry_2620(config)#interface fastethernet 4/0
Terry_2620(config-if)#mls rp vtp-domain test
Terry_2620(config-if)#^Z
Terry_2620#

!
interface FastEthernet4/0
 ip address 172.16.10.1 255.255.255.0
 no ip directed-broadcast
 no ip route-cache
 no ip mroute-cache
 mls rp vtp-domain test
!
```

VLAN Assignments

The command to establish a VLAN is used only if an external router's interface is not using ISL or 802.1Q encapsulation. (RSMs and MSFCs use logical VLAN interfaces.) An example is a router that has two physical interfaces connected to the same switch, each to a different VLAN. This scenario doesn't require that the router be aware of VLAN assignments and would typically be found on routers that have only 10Mb interfaces.

If you wish to enable MLS on interfaces that don't use VLANs, you can issue the `mls rp vlan-id` *`vlan_id_number`* command to assign a VLAN to the interface. Here's an example:

```
Terry_2620#configure terminal
Enter configuration commands, one per line.  End with CNTL/Z.
Terry_2620(config)#interface fastethernet 4/0
Terry_2620(config-if)#mls rp vlan-id 10
Terry_2620(config-if)#^Z
Terry_2620#

!
interface FastEthernet4/0
 ip address 172.16.10.1 255.255.255.0
 no ip directed-broadcast
 no ip route-cache
 no ip mroute-cache
 mls rp vtp-domain test
 mls rp vlan-id 10
!
```

Interface Configurations

After VTP and VLAN assignments have been made, you can finally enable MLS on the interface. This is done with the same command that was used to globally enable MLS: `mls rp ip`, as in this example:

```
Terry_2620#configure terminal
Enter configuration commands, one per line.  End with CNTL/Z.
Terry_2620(config)#interface fastethernet 4/0
Terry_2620(config-if)#mls rp ip
Terry_2620(config-if)#^Z
Terry_2620#

!
interface FastEthernet4/0
 ip address 172.16.10.1 255.255.255.0
 no ip directed-broadcast
 no ip route-cache
 no ip mroute-cache
 mls rp vtp-domain test
 mls rp vlan-id 10
 mls rp ip
!
```

MSA Management Interface

As you may remember, MLS has three components. The third component is MLSP, the communication protocol itself. Well, in order for MLS to function between a switch and a router, MLSP must be able to communicate between both devices.

This requirement makes this next configuration step essential for MLS functionality. At least one interface on the router that is connected to the same switch must be enabled as the management interface. This indicates which interface is going to participate in MLSP exchanges.

Another requirement is that there be at least one management interface per VLAN on the switch. To specify a router interface as a management interface, issue the `mls rp management-interface` command on the specified interface. Here's an example of the syntax for the command:

```
Terry_2620#configure terminal
Enter configuration commands, one per line.  End with CNTL/Z.
Terry_2620(config)#interface fastethernet 4/0
Terry_2620(config-if)#mls rp management-interface
Terry_2620(config-if)#^Z
Terry_2620#
```

Verifying the MLS Configuration

After all the pieces have been configured, you can issue the `show mls rp` command to view the MLS status and information on the router. There are two options in correlation with the main command. All three commands are shown here:

show mls rp This command displays global MLS information.

show mls rp interface **interface** This command displays interface-specific MLS information.

show mls rp vtp-domain **domain_name** This command displays MLS information for the VTP domain.

Here is an example of the global command:

```
Terry_2620#show mls rp
multilayer switching is globally enabled
mls id is 0010.a6a9.3400
mls ip address 172.16.21.4
mls flow mask is destination-ip
number of domains configured for mls 1

vlan domain name: test
   current flow mask: destination-ip
   current sequence number: 3041454903
   current/maximum retry count: 0/10
```

```
   current domain state: no-change
   current/next global purge: false/false
   current/next purge count: 0/0
   domain uptime: 00:34:35
   keepalive timer expires in 4 seconds
   retry timer not running
   change timer not running
   fcp subblock count = 1

   1 management interface(s) currently defined:
      vlan 10 on FastEthernet4/0

   1 mac-vlan(s) configured for multi-layer switching:

      mac 0010.a6a9.3470
         vlan id(s)
         10

   router currently aware of following 1 switch(es):
      switch id 00-e0-4e-2d-43-ef

Terry_2620#
```

Here's an example of the interface option:

```
Terry_2620#show mls rp interface fastethernet 4/0
mls active on FastEthernet4/0, domain test
interface FastEthernet4/0 is a management interface
Terry_2620#
```

These are the `show` commands, and as with any IOS, there are debugging opportunities. Table 18.1 provides a summary of the debug commands available for MLS troubleshooting.

TABLE 18.1 MLS Debug Command Summary

Command	Description
`all`	Performs all MLS debugging
`error`	Displays information about MLS errors
`events`	Displays information from MLS events

TABLE 18.1 MLS Debug Command Summary *(continued)*

Command	Description
`ip`	Displays IP MLS events
`locator`	Displays MLS locator information
`packets`	Displays information for all MLS packets
`verbose packets`	Displays information on all MLS verbose packets

Access Control Lists (ACLs)

It's not unusual to want to use an access control list (ACL) to filter traffic from one VLAN to another, especially if one VLAN needs higher security than the others do. The problem is that you usually want all the packets to be examined by the access control list, and the switch is forwarding only the first one.

Until IOS release 12.0(2), inbound access control lists were not supported. If a router interface had an inbound access control list applied, MLS was disabled. With versions after 12.0(2), inbound access control lists are supported, but the support is not enabled by default. Use the command `mls rp ip input-acl` from global configuration mode to enable the router to use MLS with inbound access control lists.

Outbound access control lists are a little more problematic. Although they have always been supported, applying the access control list to an interface will clear the MLS cache information for connections passing through that interface. Another packet needs to be forwarded to the router to start the MLS process again. Also, outbound lists utilizing the following functions will disable MLS on the interface to which they are applied:

- TOS
- Established
- Log
- Precedence
- Reflexive

This is because these features require the router to examine every packet. Because these features tend to be more security related than a simple access control list often is, using these features disables MLS on the interface in question.

Configuring the MLS Switch Engine

The configuration of MLS on a switch is very simple. MLS is on by default for the 6000. The only time when it is necessary to perform configuration tasks on the MLS-SE is when you want to change specific MLS attributes or when the device requires configuration. Here are some examples:

- Using an external router
- Establishing flows
- Changing the MLS cache aging timers
- Enabling NetFlow Data Export (NDE)

Each of these topics are addressed in this section.

Enabling MLS on the MLS-SE

As mentioned, the only time you need to actually enable MLS on the switch is when it has been disabled or on a system on which MLS is off by default.

To enable MLS on the MLS-SE, issue the command `set mls enable`. Here's an example:

```
Terry_6506> (enable) set mls enable
Multilayer switching is enabled
Terry_6506> (enable)
```

If the MLS route processor being used is an external router, the switch needs to be told to send MLSP packets to the appropriate IP address. Use the command `set mls include` *`rp_ip_address`* to tell the switch which IP address that is. The command `show mls include` displays the list of IP addresses of external route processors.

Configuring Flow Masks

A flow is the cache entry on the switch that is used for layer 3 switching. The switch learns the appropriate information from the MLS router and the switch caches the information for subsequent packets in the stream. Typically, flow information is received from a router based on what type of access control list is configured on the outbound interface.

There are three ways of configuring flow masks:

Destination-IP This is the default mask and is the least specific. A flow is created for each destination IP address, and all packets—no matter the source—get layer 3 switched if they match the destination. This mask is used if no outbound access control list is used.

Source-Destination-IP The switch engine will have a flow entry for each source/destination pair of addresses. No matter what applications are used between the two addresses, all traffic that matches the source and destination IP addresses will be switched according to this flow. This mask is used if there is a standard access control list used on the outbound interface.

IP-Flow This mask builds flows that have a specific source and destination port in addition to specific source and destination IP addresses. Two different processes—for example, HTTP and Telnet—from one client to a single server will create two different masks because the port numbers are different. This mask is used if the outbound access control list is extended.

If no outbound access control list is configured on the router but either IP-Flow or Source-Destination-IP is desired, it is possible to configure the switch to build flows in a more specific fashion. The command `set mls flow [destination|destination-source|full]` can be used to tell the MLS switch what information to cache with candidate packets.

Using Cache Entries

MLS entry or shortcut cache exists on the PFC for 6000 series switches. The purpose of the cache is consistent across all platforms: The cache is a layer 3 switching table. It maintains the flow information that facilitates MLS.

Here is a sample of a layer 3 cache table:

```
Terry_6509> (enable) show mls entry
Dest-IP  Source-IP Prot DstPrt SrcPrt Dest-Mac Vlan
  ➥EDst   ESrc DPort SPort  Stat-Pkts  Stat-Bytes  Uptime   Age
--------------- --------------- ----- ------ ------ ----------------- ----
  ➥---- ---- ------ ------ ---------- ----------- -------- --------
MSFC 10.10.100.5 (Module 15):
172.16.10.1 -               -     -      -      00-30-96-2d-24-20   188
  ➥ARPA ARPA 2/7     2/6    870         157785      00:05:29 00:00:27
172.16.55.115    -               -     -      -      00-30-96-2d-24-20  188
  ➥ARPA ARPA 2/7     2/6    2407       642886      00:00:39  00:00:00
172.16.96.101    -             -     -      -     00-d0-bc-f3-69-44  4
  ➥ARPA ARPA 2/2     2/7    2710       2200670     00:12:23  00:00:00
172.16.8.35    -             -     -      -     00-d0-bc-f3-66-9c  180
  ➥ARPA ARPA 3/7     3/3    76634      24951932    00:24:31  00:00:00
172.16.8.17    -             -     -      -     00-30-96-2d-24-20  188
  ➥ARPA ARPA 2/7     2/6    81752      26599352    00:18:32  00:00:00
172.16.8.102   -             -     -      -     00-30-96-2d-24-20  188
  ➥ARPA ARPA 2/7     2/6    313        148298      00:00:24  00:00:22
```

This command has many options, but the most basic ones involve viewing cache information based on the source and destination IP addresses. The syntax of the command is `show mls entry [rp|destination|source]` *`ip_address`*. Also, be aware that the display has room for many pieces of information, but you won't see them unless the flow is based on that information. For example, when using the preceding Destination-IP flow, the source IP address isn't displayed. You will always be able to see the destination IP address and the destination MAC address.

Cache entries are kept while the flow is active. After the flow no longer receives traffic, the cache entry gets aged out and removed from the layer 3 cache on the NFFC or PFC. This attribute can be modified and adjusted. You'll learn how to do that next.

A candidate entry is cached for five seconds to allow for an enable packet to arrive from the router. If the enable packet doesn't arrive in that time, the switch assumes that the best path is not through itself and removes the entry.

Modifying the Cache Aging Time

A layer 3 cache entry remains in cache for 256 seconds after the last packet for the flow has passed through the switch. This is the default value. The value can be changed to different values depending on your needs as a network administrator.

The syntax is `set mls agingtime` *`agingtime`*, where *`agingtime`* is a value of seconds. The value is a multiple of 8. The valid range is from 8 to 2032. If the value specified is not a multiple of 8, the nearest multiple is used. Here is an example:

```
Terry_6506> (enable) set mls agingtime 125
Multilayer switching aging time set to 128
Terry_6506> (enable)
```

Modifying Fast Aging Time

When the layer 3 cache grows greater than 32KB in size, the possibility increases that the PFC or NFFC will not be able to perform all layer 3 switching, causing some packets to be forwarded to the router. To aid in maintaining a layer 3 cache smaller than 32KB, you can enable and adjust fast aging times.

Because some flows can be very short—a DNS query, for example—you can enable packet thresholds that can be used in correlation with the fast aging time to quickly age out these entries. Both of these attributes are thresholds. When you set the fast aging time, you specify the amount of time for which *n* number of packets (defined by the packet threshold) must have used the cache entry.

When a flow is initialized, the switch must see a number of packets equal to or greater than the packet threshold set within the time specified by the fast aging time. If this criterion isn't met, the cache entry is aged out immediately.

Valid values for the fast aging time are 32, 64, 96, and 128. Valid values for the packet threshold are 0, 1, 3, 7, 15, 31, and 63. Let's try an example to illustrate how this works.

Suppose you configured a fast aging time of 64 seconds and set the packet threshold to 31 packets by using the `set mls agingtime fast 64 31` command on the switch. This is telling the MLS-SE that a layer 3 cache entry has 64 seconds in which 31 packets or more must utilize the entry. If this doesn't happen, the cache entry is removed.

The actual syntax for the command is `set mls agingtime fast` *`fastagingtime pkt_threshold`*. An example configuration follows:

```
Terry_6506> (enable) set mls agingtime fast 64 31
Multilayer switching fast aging time set to 64 seconds for
   entries with no more than 31 packets switched.
Terry_6506> (enable)
```

Verifying the Configuration

MLS-SE configuration settings can be seen by using the `show mls ip` command. This command provides information regarding the aging time, the fast aging time, and the packet threshold values. In addition, it gives summary statistics for the type of flow mask and MLS entries. Finally, it provides details about the MLS-RP, including XTAG, MAC, and VLAN values. Here's an example:

```
Terry_6509> show mls ip
IP Multilayer switching aging time = 256 seconds
IP Multilayer switching fast aging time = 64 seconds,  packet threshold = 31
IP Current flow mask is Destination flow
Active IP MLS entries = 87
Netflow Data Export version: 7
Netflow Data Export disabled
Netflow Data Export port/host is not configured.
Total packets exported = 0

IP MSFC ID      Module XTAG MAC               Vlans
--------------- ------ ---- ----------------- ------------
172.16.10.1     15     1    00-d0-bc-f4-81-c0 10,100
Terry_6509>
```

Displaying the MLS Cache Entries

There are several methods of viewing MLS cache entries. The base command is `show mls entry`. However, many options are available to customize the output of this basic command.

If you are on a switch and issue the help command for `show mls entry`, this is what you get:

```
Terry_6509> (enable) show mls entry ?
Usage: show mls entry [mod] [long|short]
       show mls entry ip [mod] [destination <ip_addr_spec>]
       [source <ip_addr_spec>] [protocol <protocol>]
       [src-port <src_port>] [dst-port <dst_port>]
       [short|long]
    show mls entry ipx [mod] [destination <ipx_addr_spec>]        [short|long]
     (mod = 15 or 16
ip_addr_spec = ip_addr|ip_addr/netmask|ip_addr/maskbit (maskbit: 0..32)
     protocol = 1..255|ip|ipinip|icmp|igmp|tcp|udp
     src_port, dst_port = 1..65535|dns|ftp|smtp|telnet|x|www
     ipx_addr_spec = dest_net.dest_node|dest_net/mask)
Terry_6509> (enable)
```

As you can see, there are quite a few options. This command, with the options shown, enables the administrator to view very general information or very specific information. To get an idea of what can be generated from this command, let's review the options.

You can show MLS entries based on the module. The `long` and `short` options modify the output in different ways. `Long` displays the information all on one line, and `short` displays the information by using carriage returns. It is impossible to give an example due to the formatting limitations in this book.

More specific information can be obtained by specifying an IP address or port information. By specifying options, you can refine your output. Instead of getting pages and pages of cache entries, you get entries that match your criteria.

Removing MLS Cache Entries

If you do not want to wait for aging times to expire, or if you want to clear the cache immediately, you can issue the `clear mls entry` command. This command also has options that enable the network administrator to clear specific cache entries instead of the entire table.

The syntax of this command is as follows:

```
clear mls entry destination ip_addr_spec source ip_addr_spec flow
   protocol src_port dst_port [all]
```

The use of the `all` optional keyword causes all MLS cache entries to be removed. If you use specific IP addresses, ports, or protocols, specific cache entries can be removed.

The `clear mls entry all` command must be used with care, because all flows will revert to being routed with an immediate impact upon performance

Using Acceptable MLS Topologies

Few topologies support MLS. Due to the nature of MLS, only certain system topologies allow candidate and enable packets to transit the router and switch properly. If both candidate and enable packets cannot be identified, no complete flow cache entry can be made. Acceptable topologies include the following:

Router on a stick This includes one router (internal RSM/MSFC or external) and one switch. The router has a single connection to the network, which is the stick (see Figure 18.7).

Multiple switches, one router This is acceptable if only one switch connects to the router and the switches are connected via an ISL trunk (see Figure 18.8).

The second of the Cisco MLS implementations involves a process called Cisco Express Forwarding (CEF), which we will discuss in the next section.

FIGURE 18.7 Router on a stick

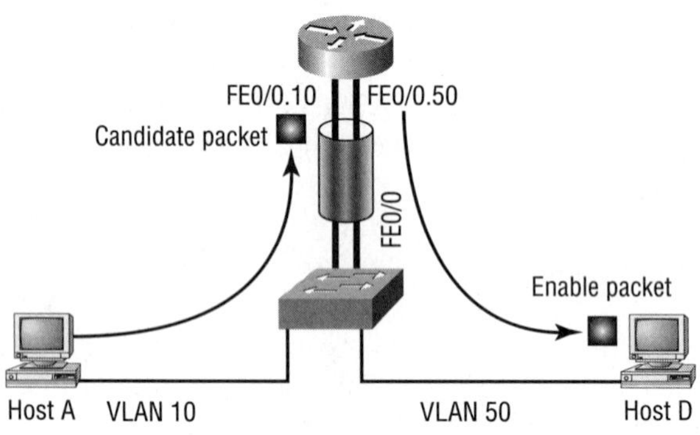

FIGURE 18.8 Multiple switches, one router

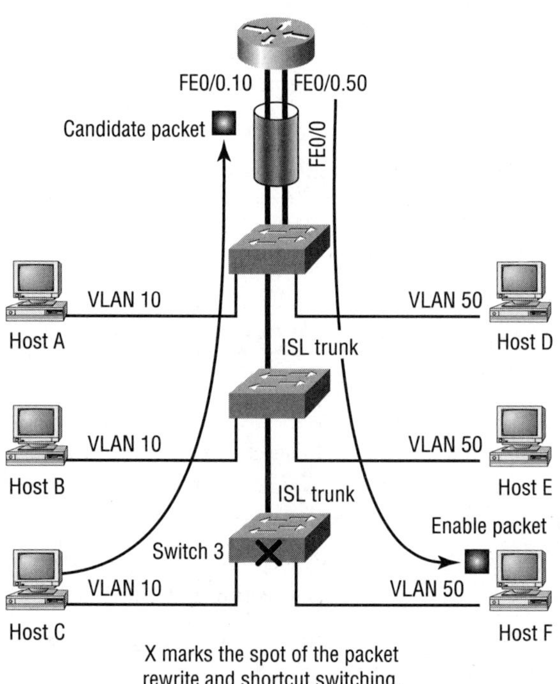

Cisco Express Forwarding (CEF)

Two of the newer additions to the Cisco range (the 3550 and 4000 series) are sometimes described as multilayer switches, with the obvious inference that something beyond legacy routing is going on. With respect to the 3550 series and both the 4000 and 6500 series using the Supervisor IV engine, that something is *Cisco Express Forwarding (CEF)*. In fact, the 3550 is advertised as supporting CEF-based multilayer switching.

CEF differs from other MLS implementations, in that there is no caching in the traditional sense. Caching introduces a number of issues that need to be addressed. For example, how long should a cache stay valid? How big should a cache be permitted to grow? And how do we deal with routing topology changes that invalidate cache entries?

Well, Cisco has constantly worked to try to optimize cache behavior, but the problems remain. It seems that the only good way to do layer 3 data forwarding is to use a routing table. But that slows everything down again, right? Actually no, not necessarily. You see, if you create a stripped-down version of the routing table and a separate adjacency table (which is similar to a separate ARP cache), then you can get the best of both worlds. The table resides close to the interfaces (figuratively speaking), keeping data away from the busy route processor and its buses. And because the table is in communication with the main routing table, it is always as up-to-date as the main table.

The Trouble with CEF and Layer 3 Switching

It may seem wrong to refer to CEF as layer 3 switching, but layer 3 switching is so poorly defined that it is easy to see how someone could become confused. Remember, though, that the CEF process has much in common with the way we have previously described layer 3 switching.

The routing decision is taken for the first packet at the route processor, and the frame address is rewritten to allow the packet to be properly forwarded. This is true in both CEF and layer 3 switching. It is also true to say that subsequent frames are forwarded (and the MAC address rewritten) according to cached information, and that they never get to the route processor.

I guess that, arguably, the story of layer 3 switching began a long time ago with the introduction of fast switching, and it has just progressed to caches further away from the route processor. Sometimes the cache is moved all the way to a separate box, namely the switch. But once modern switches incorporate IOS and the associated routing capability, the cache would naturally move back into the same housing.

The point here is that layer 3 switching really is vendor-speak, and in an ideal world we would not even have a chapter with this title—we would be calling it something like "How to Speed Up the Routing Process." The problem is that Cisco is under pressure from other vendors who call *their* offerings layer 3 switching, and so the myth continues to be propagated. And as long as Cisco exams are going to have questions on this topic, we have to use the same language. The term means little enough, but once you start building boxes with IOS that have the capability to perform both switching *and* routing, all this business of switch-router intercommunications disappears inside the proprietary architecture, and you can't see it anymore. So the early switches didn't do layer 3 switching at all, the (dying) range of CatOS-based switches do it in a complex fashion (as in the first part of this chapter), and the new IOS-based switches do it wonderfully, but it's a secret!

CEF, then, is not a first-generation attempt to speed up the forwarding process, but is the most recent mechanism to be tested. I think that it would assist us in placing CEF in the proper context if we looked at how we got here, so I propose to first consider the actual forwarding mechanisms that have traditionally been used by Cisco routers.

Legacy Routing and Layer 3 Switching

Over the years, as Cisco routers have matured from the early days of the IGS and AGS platforms, faster processors have been employed to make the forwarding decisions more quickly. Nonetheless, it is not only the processor power that determines the latency of a switch. Right up there with processing delay is the time taken to forward packets around inside the router, hence the move toward ever faster router architectures.

Designers soon realized that even with faster buses, there were still some delays associated with internal packet forwarding that might benefit from other techniques, and this gave rise to the different switching modes employable in modern routers. Because the 3550 and Supervisor IV–equipped 4000 are really routers as well as switches, these processes suddenly became relevant to those engineers studying switches.

In order to really see the progression here from legacy routing to layer 3 switching, let's look at some of the history, specifically that of process switching (which you could easily call legacy routing), fast switching, and optimum switching (both cache-based methods for speeding up the forwarding process). Finally, we'll look properly at CEF.

Process Switching

When packets are process-switched, the complete packet is forwarded across the internal architecture to the route processor. This is the "heart" of the router, and is a busy place to be! Often accessed via two buses—the Cbus and the systems bus—it involves a long trip through the router and out to the forwarding interface for the whole packet. At the route processor, the forwarding interface and the MAC header rewrite information is applied. Delay is considerable, but there are some advantages: If the routing table holds multiple paths of equal cost to the destination, then load balancing can be carried out on a per-packet basis.

The routing process is shown in Figure 18.9. This diagram illustrates the linear nature of process-switching, where a packet travels right through the "heart" of the router, resulting in slow forwarding.

FIGURE 18.9 Process switching flow

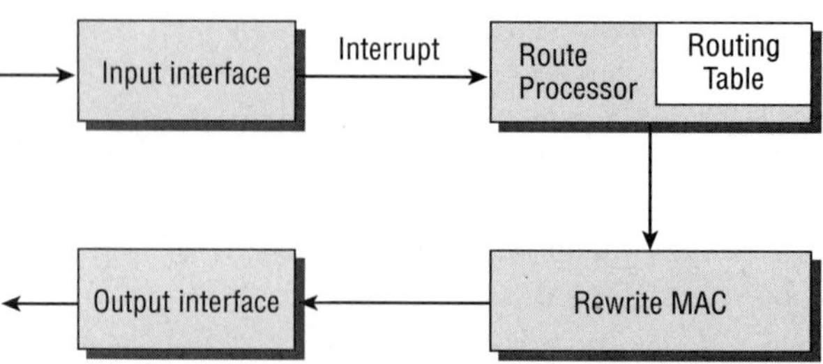

Fast Switching

Like process switching, fast switching has been available on all Cisco platforms for many years, including the ubiquitous 2500 series. Fast switching involves the use of a cache on the route processor where forwarding information is maintained. The first packet in a conversation is passed to the route processor, matched against routes, and process switched. The fast switching cache is updated, and subsequent packets have only the header matched in the cache. The result is that the rest of the conversation is forwarded without being passed to the route processor.

Forwarding information is stored in the form of a binary tree, which allows bit-by-bit decision making to be carried out regarding the next hop. This binary tree may require up to 32 levels of comparison to fully match a route, but the decision is often reached much more quickly, and is considered to be a very efficient lookup mechanism.

Entries in the fast cache are created at the beginning of a conversation, and therefore suffer the perennial problems of caches—how do updates to other information, such as the ARP cache, affect the cached information? And the answer is that they don't, leaving the possibility that changes in the ARP cache may leave the fast cache with out-of-date and incorrect information. In that case, the cache must be recreated. The second problem with fast switching is that the cache can construct only a single route to a destination, so any load sharing must be on a conversation-by-conversation basis (sometimes caller per-destination load sharing) with a cache entry for each conversation.

Nonetheless, fast switching is perhaps 10 times faster than process switching and is widely used.

The fast switching tree is shown in Figure 18.10. Each bit in the destination address is compared with the table, and because each possibility is either a 1 or a 0, a single match is gained with every pass.

Optimum Switching

Optimum switching also relies on a caching mechanism, but there are important differences from fast switching. The first difference is in the operation of the tree. Instead of a binary tree, with each level being a single comparison (1 or 0 in the binary string), optimum switching employs a 256-way multi-way tree (mtree). Each level allows selection of a single octet in the destination address, resulting in a maximum of four lookup probes to find any target.

FIGURE 18.10 Fast switching tree

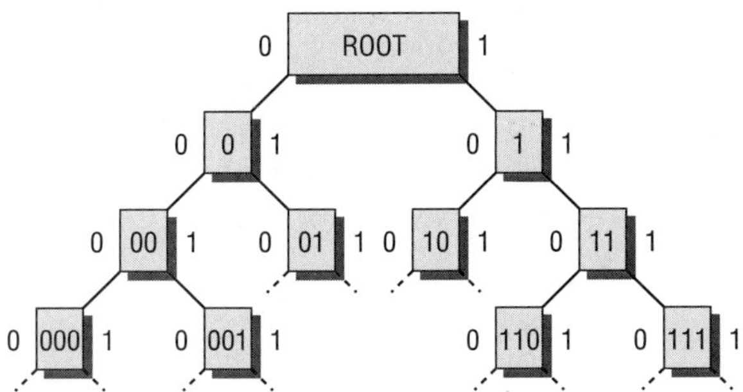

Optimum switching is very fast, but still suffers from the same problems of cache invalidation and therefore needs to be aged out regularly, interrupting the optimum flow while caches are rebuilt from requests to the route processor again.

The optimum switching tree is shown in Figure 18.11. Each octet in the 32-bit dotted-decimal address is matched individually, resulting in a far faster lookup process.

FIGURE 18.11 Optimum switching tree

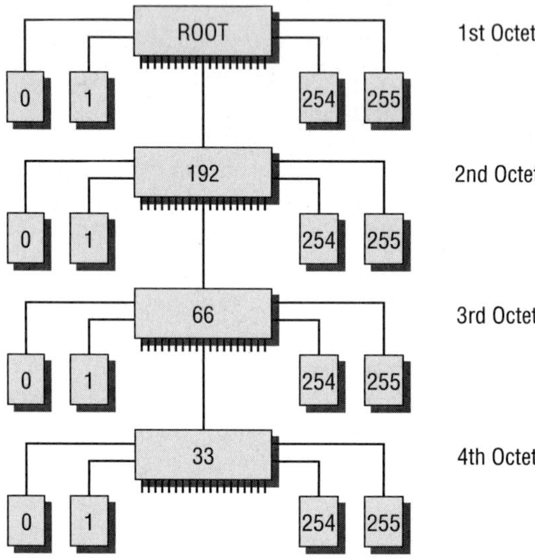

The CEF Forwarding Process

At last we come to CEF. CEF maintains two separate but related tables: the forwarding table and the adjacency table. The forwarding table contains routing information, and the adjacency table contains layer 2 next-hop addressing. CEF uses a trie instead of a tree. No, that's not a misprint. A *trie* is a pointer used with a data structure, where the data structure does not actually contain the data.

The separation in the data structure means that the lookup process can be recursive, allowing different routes to be selected for successive packets, thus enabling per-packet load sharing. Also, if information in a cache changes because the lookup is performed individually each time, the most up-to-date information is always used.

The CEF forwarding process is illustrated in Figure 18.12. This simple diagram illustrates that the lookup is much swifter because the 256-way data structure is the most efficient of all lookup methods, and is directly associated with the adjacency table.

The result of CEF forwarding is a much higher throughput. True, a lot of this increased speed is due to proprietary architecture inside the switch or router, including the increased use of ASICs and specialized buses and memory arrangements. But it's also true that packets no longer need to be forwarded across internal buses to the busy route processor, which is where most of the router latency is introduced. And there are other benefits to CEF, such as the ability to support packet-by-packet load sharing, which cannot be achieved using cached entries as in fast or optimum switching.

FIGURE 18.12 CEF forwarding process

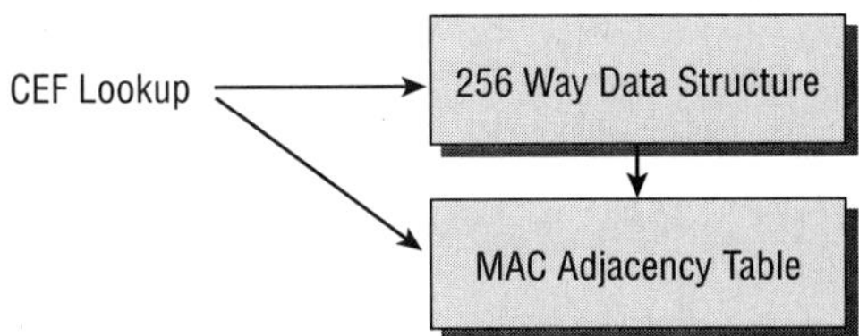

Configuring CEF

To configure CEF on a 3550 switch, you first have to enable IP routing. Remember that because this is a multilayer switch, only the layer 2 switching processes are enabled by default, to maintain the plug-and-play nature of all switches. Use the global command `ip routing` to enable ip routing, and use the global command `ip cef` to enable CEF, as follows:

```
Terry_3550#
Terry_3550#conf t
Enter configuration commands, one per line.  End with CNTL/Z.
Terry_3550(config)#ip routing
Terry_3550(config)#ip cef ?
  accounting          Enable CEF accounting
  load-sharing        Load sharing
  table               Set CEF forwarding table characteristics
  traffic-statistics  Enable collection of traffic statistics
  <cr>
```

Next, you have to convert the layer 2 interface to layer 3. To do this, use the interface command `no switchport`. Enable IP on the interface using the standard command, and then enable CEF on the interface using the `ip route-cache cef` interface command, as in this example:

```
Terry_3550#
Terry_3550#
Terry_3550#conf t
Enter configuration commands, one per line.  End with CNTL/Z.
Terry_3550(config)#int fa 0/1
Terry_3550(config-if)#no switchport
Terry_3550(config-if)#ip address 192.168.1.1 255.255.255.0
Terry_3550(config-if)#no shut
Terry_3550(config-if)#ip route-cache cef
Terry_3550(config-if)#^Z
```

Finally, you can confirm that CEF is running on the interface by using the `show ip interface` command:

```
Terry_3550#show ip int fa 0/1
FastEthernet0/1 is down, line protocol is down
  Internet address is 192.168.1.1/24
  Broadcast address is 255.255.255.255

[output cut]

  IP fast switching is enabled
  IP fast switching on the same interface is disabled
  IP Flow switching is disabled
  IP CEF switching is enabled
  IP CEF Fast switching turbo vector
  IP multicast fast switching is enabled

[output cut]

Terry_3550#
```

Any entries in the CEF table will be displayed in the following format, using the `show ip cef` command:

```
Terry_3550#sho ip cef fastEthernet 0/1
Prefix              Next Hop             Interface
Terry_3550#
```

Summary

The helpful thing about VLANs is that you can place users into the broadcast domain that suits them. This is great if your network works like the old 80:20 rule, because that's where most of their data will remain—inside their own VLAN. But that may not be the case, and you may need to transfer a lot of packets between VLANs.

In itself, transferring packets between VLANs is not a problem. Routers are very capable when moving data between subnets. The problem is that routers are traditionally a lot slower than switches, because they have to interrogate more of the packet, which naturally takes more time. Hence the development of MLS.

Given that there are different definitions of MLS, it's no surprise that MLS behaves differently on different platforms, employing different components. The 6500, for example, runs "classic" MLS, in that the first packet is routed, subsequent packets are frame-switched, and the whole process can be cleanly seen because the routing and switching functions are not terribly well integrated, even with the use of an internal route processor. This requires you to understand the flow process intimately and to be able to configure MLS on both routers and switches.

More modern switches, on the other hand, running an IOS that fully integrates the switching and routing processes, carry out the same process (route once, switch many), but do so internally, and therefore make a much better job of it. In fact, most of the process is automatic, transparent, and hard to examine.

Integrated switch-routers can forward data at incredible speeds due to the fast architecture employed. Is the routing (layer 3 switching) process much slower? Well, hardly, when you consider that the boxes all operate in a store-and-forward mode. Lots of time (comparatively speaking) is available during standard packet arrival latency for fast processes such as CEF to make up their minds how to forward packets or frames.

Exam Essentials

Know the components of MLS. Multilayer switching (MLS) is made of three components. The first is the MLS-SE, the switch. The second is the MLS-RP, the router that makes the changes to the initial packet. The third is MLSP, the communication protocol that is used between the router and any switches.

Understand what a flow is and how a switch uses them. A flow is nothing more than a conversation, a stream of packets between two devices. A switch caches information about the conversation and information about how the packets are supposed to be manipulated. When a packet arrives that matches a packet stream that the switch has already seen, the switch makes the necessary changes.

Know what information a switch can use to identify flows. A switch can use various pieces of information to identify flows, but only three broad configurations are allowed. The first configuration tells the switch to identify flows based only on the destination IP address. The second configuration says to use both source and destination IP addresses. The third configuration uses the protocol as well as the source and destination IP addresses and ports.

Understand how access control lists on the router affect MLS. Outbound access control lists have always been supported and are the primary way of telling the switch what information to use to identify the flow. Inbound access control lists are supported with additional configuration. Reflexive lists and IP security on the interface disable the MLS process for that interface.

Understanding and Configuring Multicast Operation

THE CCNP EXAM TOPICS COVERED IN THIS CHAPTER INCLUDE THE FOLLOWING:

- ✓ Describe the functionality of CGMP.
- ✓ Describe how switches facilitate multicast traffic.
- ✓ Translate multicast addresses into MAC addresses.
- ✓ Enable CGMP on the distribution layer devices.
- ✓ Describe how IP multicast operates on a multilayer switched network, including IGMP versions 1, 2, and 3 and CGMP.
- ✓ Understand how IP multicast operates on a routed network, including PIM in both sparse and dense modes.

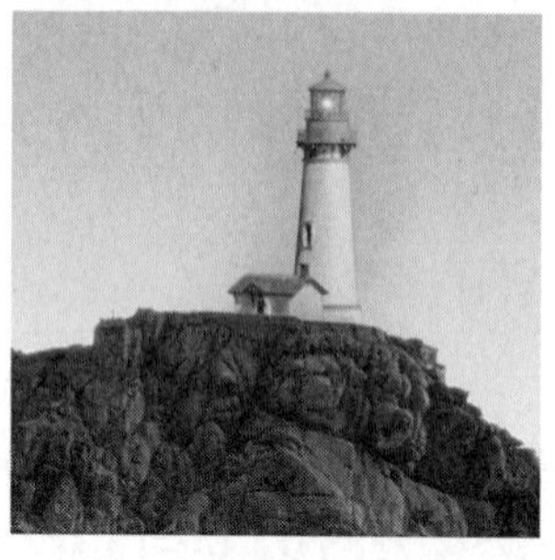

Today's web and enterprise applications are directed to larger audiences on the network than ever before, causing increased bandwidth requirements. This increased demand on bandwidth can be accommodated with as little cost increase as possible by using multicast. For example, voice and video are being sourced for larger and larger audiences, and one-on-one communications can overwhelm both servers and network resources. Unlike unicast and broadcast, however, multicast services can eliminate these problems.

This chapter helps you understand the differences in unicast, broadcast, and multicast communication methods and when each should be used. Unicast is an excellent method of point-to-point communication, whereas broadcast traffic is imperative for many systems and protocols to work on a network. Multicast comes in as a bridge between these two communication extremes by efficiently allowing point-to-multipoint data forwarding. It is essential that you understand how multicast addressing spans both layer 3 and layer 2 of the OSI model. You will also learn about the protocols and tools used to implement and control multicast traffic on your network. As with any service that runs on your network, you must understand the resources needed and the potential implications of enabling multicast forwarding.

You will also learn the steps and syntax for configuring IP multicast on Cisco routers and switches. You will see several new commands in this chapter. By the time you finish this chapter, and its review questions and lab (found on the accompanying CD), you will be thoroughly familiar with multicast and its implementation. Pay attention to small details that might usually seem unimportant. They are often the key to a successful implementation of an IP multicast network.

You will learn how to deploy an IP multicast network, and after you have a plan in place, you will move on to configuring equipment. Not only do the routers have to be IP multicast enabled, but you must enable a multicast protocol on every interface through which you want to be able to forward multicast traffic.

An IP multicast network can result in traffic flows that are very hard to predict. One way of preventing this problem is to try and force traffic along specific paths, and using specified routers as rendezvous points (RPs) to assist in this process is quite common, so you have to configure them as well. Then, to keep your multicast local to the enterprise network, you need to configure the time to live (TTL) thresholds on your external interfaces.

After the routers have been configured, you can concentrate on the hosts. Of course, we won't discuss host configuration in this chapter, but we will enable Cisco Group Management Protocol (CGMP) on the routers and switches, so that after the hosts are configured, the network will be available.

Multicast Overview

Just as blue, yellow, and red are different and each has its own place within the spectrum of visible light, unicast, broadcast, and multicast are different in that each is used to achieve a specific purpose or fulfill requirements of a specific part of the communication spectrum. It is important to know where each falls within the spectrum as well as the potential applications for each.

RFC 1112 discusses multicast and goes into great detail about host extensions and multicast groups. In addition to address assignment for multicast applications and hosts, protocol methods and procedures are discussed. For example, it covers the methods by which hosts join and leave multicast groups, and it also covers group advertisements and multicast forwarding.

Unicast

Unicast is used for direct host-to-host communication. When the layer 3 protocol data unit (PDU, or packet) is formed, two layer 3 IP addresses are added to the IP header. These are the source and destination IP addresses. They specify a particular originating and receiving host. After the layer 3 PDU is formed, it is passed to layer 2 to create the layer 2 PDU, or frame. The frame consists of all the previous layers' headers in addition to the layer 2 header. With an Ethernet frame, for example, the two 48-bit source and destination MAC addresses are specified in the layer 2 header. Other protocols such as IEEE 802.5 (Token Ring) and FDDI also have headers that contain specific host source and destination addresses.

Unicast communication is used when two hosts need to exchange data with only each other and are not concerned with sharing the data with everyone. A MAC address must *uniquely* identify a host. No two MAC addresses on a single network can be the same. Therefore, unicast capitalizes on the unique MAC address of each host. With the specific address, any source host should be able to contact the destination host without confusion.

One of the caveats with unicast communication is that the source host must know or be able to learn what every destination MAC address is for every station it wishes to communicate with. In order to figure out which MAC address the source should send frames to, it uses an ARP request, as explained in the following section. The normal operation is that the host has a default gateway assigned for use when the logical destination address does not reside on the same subnet as the source host. Figure 19.1 depicts how unicast traffic works on the same subnet.

Of course, unicast traffic may differ inside an internetwork interconnected by routers. In those circumstances, you will remember that the transmitting client needs to know the IP (and MAC) addresses of the default gateway.

FIGURE 19.1 Unicast communication

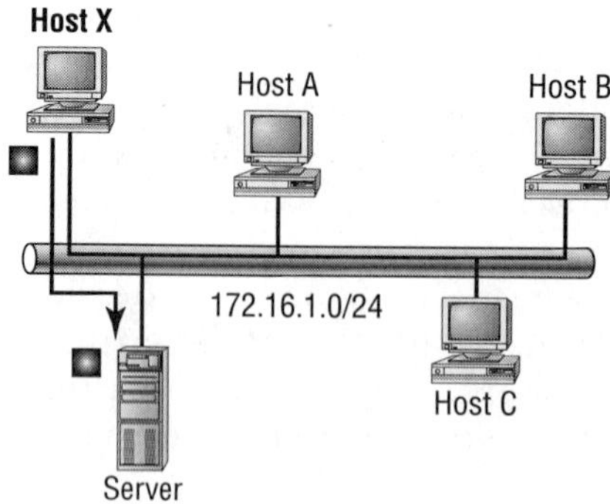

The unicast process occurs between two hosts only. A single destination address is used to ensure that data is sent to only one host. This could be client-to-server, server-to-client, or peer-to-peer. It doesn't matter, so long as the frames are addressed to a unicast address. So when one host wants to send data to multiple hosts or to all the hosts on the same network segment, things have to change. That is where multicast and broadcast communication comes in.

Broadcast

Now that you have a good understanding of unicast, we can discuss the principle of broadcast communication on networks. Whereas unicast messages target a single host on a network (unicast communication can be compared to sending an e-mail to a friend; the mail is addressed to the friend, and it is sent from you), *broadcast* messages are meant to reach all hosts on a broadcast domain (such as when you shout out to everyone in the room, "Who wants an ice cream?"). Figure 19.2 depicts a broadcast message sent from Host X to all machines within the same broadcast domain.

FIGURE 19.2 Broadcast message on a network

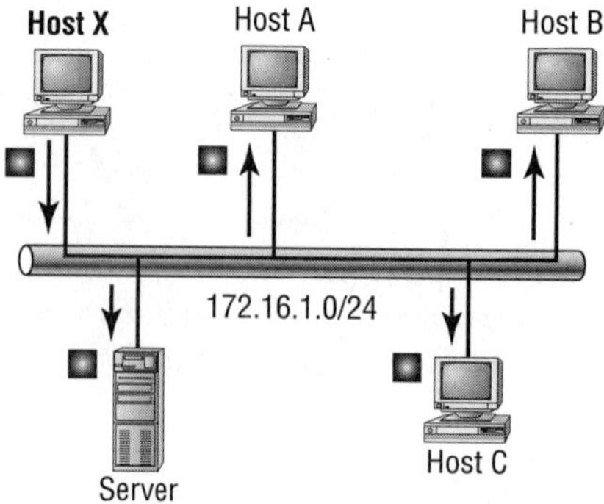

A good example of a broadcast message is an Address Resolution Protocol (ARP) request. When a host has a packet, it knows the logical address of the destination. To get the packet to the destination, the host needs to forward the packet to a default gateway if the destination resides on a different IP network. If the destination is on the local network, the source will forward the packet directly to the destination. Because the source doesn't have the MAC address it needs to forward the frame to, it sends out a broadcast, something that every device in the local broadcast domain will listen to. This broadcast says, in essence, "If you are the owner of IP address 192.168.2.3, please forward your MAC address to the source address of this frame." Each device will answer a request for its own IP address, but a correctly configured router can serve as a proxy as well, with the process of Proxy ARP.

This brings up another good point: Broadcasts can cause problems on networks. Because the broadcast frame is addressed to include every host, every host must process the frame. CPU interruption occurs so that the frame can be processed. This interruption affects other applications that are running on the host. When unicast frames are seen by a router, a quick check is made to identify whether the frame is intended for the host. If it isn't, the frame is discarded.

Multicast

Multicast is a different beast entirely. At first glance, it appears to be a hybrid of unicast and broadcast communication, but that isn't quite accurate. Multicast does allow point-to-multipoint communication, which is similar to broadcasts, but it happens in a different manner. The crux of *multicast* is that it enables multiple recipients to receive messages without flooding the messages to all hosts on a broadcast domain.

Multicast works by sending messages or data to IP *multicast group* addresses. Routers then forward copies of the packet out every interface that has hosts *subscribed* to that group address. This is where multicast differs from broadcast messages. With multicast communication, copies of packets are sent only to subscribed hosts.

The difference between multicast and unicast is comparable to the difference between mailing lists and spam. You subscribe to a mailing list when you want to receive mail from a specific group regarding specific information—for example, a Cisco User Group mailing list. You expect to get messages only from other members of the group regarding topics related to the user group. In contrast, spam is unsolicited mail that arrives in your inbox. You aren't expecting it from the sender, nor are you likely to be interested in the content.

Multicast works in much the same way as a mailing list. You (as a user) or an application will subscribe to a specific IP multicast group to become a member. After you become a member of the group, IP multicast packets containing the group address in the destination field of the header arrive at your host and are processed. If the host isn't subscribed to the group, it will not process packets addressed to that group. Refer to Figure 19.3 for a reference on how multicast works.

Broadcast and multicast traffic can occur at different layers of the OSI model. Each is characterized by the fact that they are addressed to a wide group of hosts and are not usually acknowledged. At the Data Link layer, broadcasts manage useful concepts such as ARP. At the Network layer, they may be responsible for routing updates or server requests. At the Application layer, they may be misused. E-mail broadcasts are often referred to as spam.

FIGURE 19.3 Multicast communication

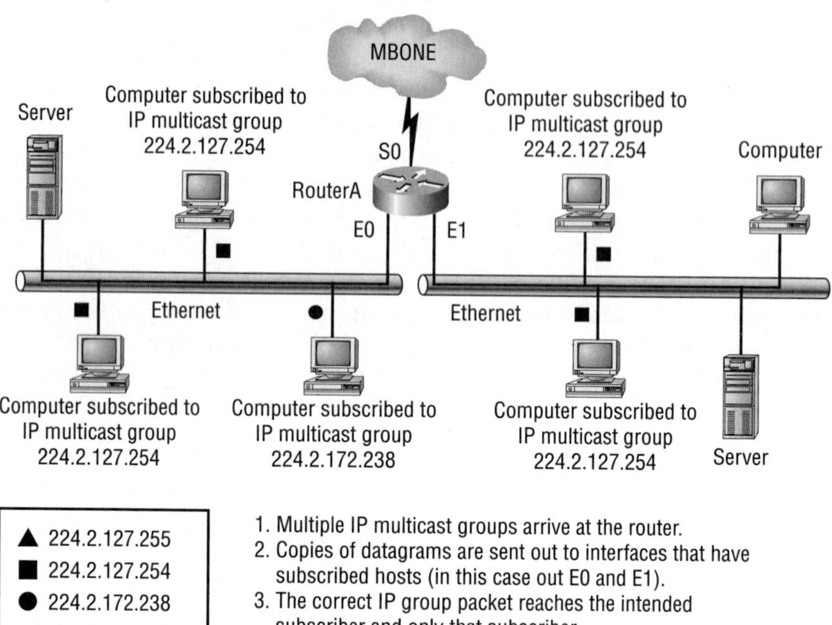

The key to multicast is the addressing structure. This is key because all communication is based on addressing. In unicast communication, there is a unique address for every host on a network. In broadcast communication, a global address that all hosts will respond to is used. Multicast uses addressing that only some hosts will respond to. The next section covers multicast addressing in detail.

Using Multicast Addressing

Just as with mailing lists, there are several different groups that users or applications can subscribe to. The range of multicast addresses starts with 224.0.0.0 and goes through 239.255.255.255. As you can see, this range of addresses falls within IP Class D address space based on classful IP assignment. This is denoted by the first four bits in the first octet being set to 1110. Just as with regular IP addresses, there are some addresses that can be assigned and there are ranges of reserved addresses.

It is important to recognize that the reserved addresses are categorized. Table 19.1 depicts some of the reserved addresses and their corresponding categories. For a full listing of these assignments, you can go to `www.iana.org/assignments/multicast-addresses`.

TABLE 19.1 IP Multicast Reserved Addresses

Address	Purpose	Reserved Category
224.0.0.0–224.0.0.18	Use by network protocols	Local-link
224.0.0.1	All hosts	Local-link
224.0.0.2	All routers	Local-link
224.0.0.19–224.0.0.255	Unassigned	Local-link
224.0.1.0–224.0.1.255	Multicast applications	Misc. applications
224.0.1.1	NTP	Misc. applications
224.0.1.8	NIS+	Misc. applications
224.0.1.39	Cisco-RP-Announce	Misc. applications
224.0.1.40	Cisco-RP-Discovery	Misc. applications
224.0.1.80–224.0.1.255	Unassigned	Misc. applications
224.0.0.10	EIGRP	Local-link
239.0.0.0–239.255.255.255	Private multicast domain	Administratively scoped

Each address range is managed by the Internet Address Number Authority (IANA). Due to the limited number of multicast addresses, there are very strict requirements for new assignments within this address space. The 239.0.0.0–239.255.255.255 range is equivalent in purpose to the private networks defined by RFC 1918.

The difference between the IP multicast ranges of 224.0.0.0–224.0.0.255 and 224.0.1.0–224.0.1.255 is that addresses in the first range will not be forwarded by an IP router. Both ranges of addresses are used by applications and network protocols. The first group, classified as local-link, is meant to remain local to the subnet or broadcast domain on which the system resides. The second group is a global address that can be routed and forwarded across multiple IP routers.

Mapping IP Multicast to Ethernet

Multicast addressing began on MAC addresses. Growth needs required that there be a way to use multicast across routers instead of limiting it to the physical segment where hosts were located. In regular unicast, MAC addresses are layer 2 addresses, and in order for the local host to reach remote hosts, layer 3 logical IP addresses are used to route data to the destination. After the packet reaches the remote subnet, the ARP is used to find the MAC address of the host. By using an existing ARP table, or via an ARP request, the MAC address that is associated to the layer 3 IP address is found and the packet is forwarded to the destination host.

IP multicast generates a MAC address based on the layer 3 IP multicast address. The MAC frame has a standard prefix of 24 bits. This prefix, 01-00-5e, is used for all Ethernet multicast addresses. This leaves another 24 bits for use in creating the multicast MAC address. When the MAC address is generated, the 25th bit (or high order bit) is set to 0 and then the last 23 bits of the IP address are mapped to the remaining 23 bits of the MAC address. Figure 19.4 depicts how this looks.

MAC addresses are made up of two sets of addresses, each with 24 bits. The first set is an address reserved for a particular manufacturer. The second set identifies a particular device by that manufacturer. This is why Cisco devices always seem to have one of a small number of "first halves." Multicast MAC addresses use 01-00-5E for the vendor code, with the device code based on the IP address.

Let's look at some examples of mapping layer 3 multicast addresses to layer 2 multicast addresses. A local IP multicast address is 224.0.0.1. Refer to Figure 19.5 to see how this is mapped. The conversion from binary to hexadecimal reveals the MAC multicast address. The prefix was 01-00-5e. The last 23 bits, including the high order bit, give you 00-00-01. Put them together and you get 01-00-5e-00-00-01 as the MAC address.

Now let's try one a little bit harder. Suppose, for example, you have the IP multicast address of 225.1.25.2 (follow along in Figure 19.6). Part of the 225 octet falls within the Class D mask. However, there is one bit that is not masked. By looking carefully at the location of the bit, you see that it is part of five lost bits and is not mapped to the layer 2 MAC multicast address.

FIGURE 19.4 IP multicast mapped to MAC multicast

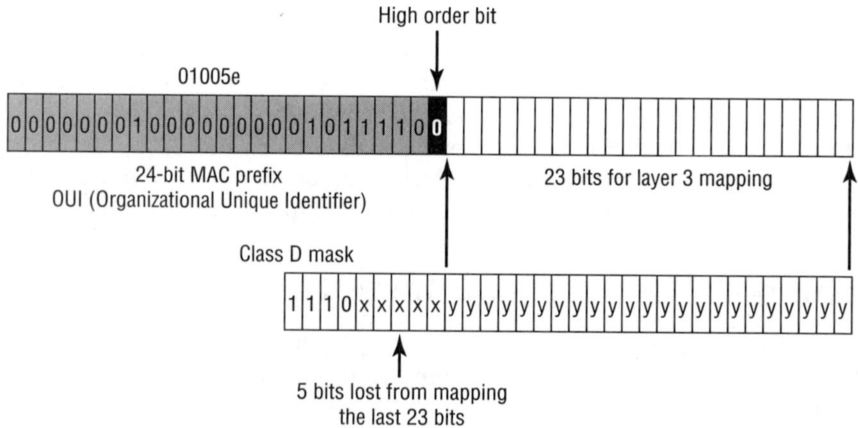

FIGURE 19.5 Example 1 for mapping IP multicast to MAC multicast addresses

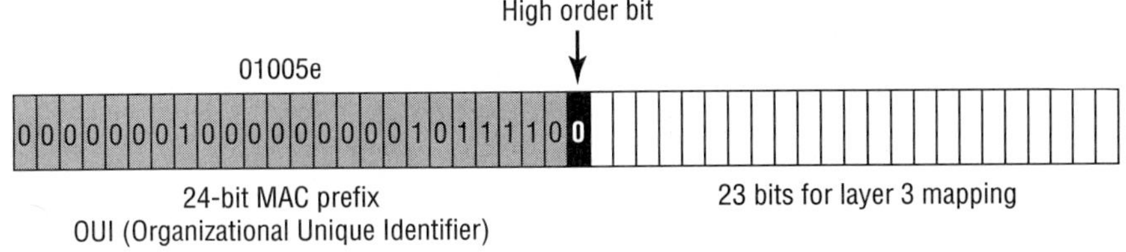

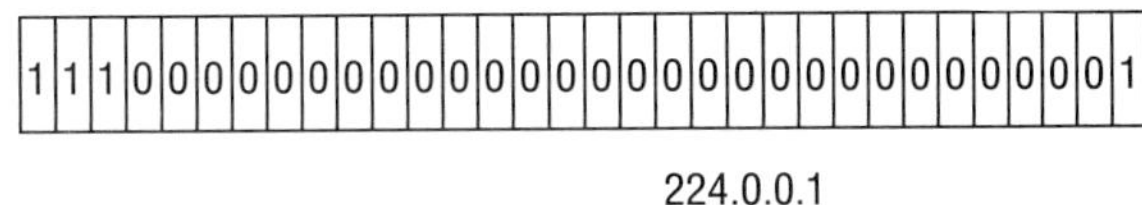

Final MAC
multicast address

01-00-5e-00-00-01

Convert the octets from decimal into binary so you can get a clear picture of what the last 23 bits are. Here you would see the following address (the last 23 bits are indicated in bold font): 11100001.**00000001.00011001.00000010**. Also, as you can see, Figure 19.6 depicts the last 23 bits that are mapped to the free spaces of the multicast MAC address. After the mapping has occurred in binary, convert the binary value to hex and you have the new MAC multicast address.

After you do the math and map the last 23 bits, the MAC address becomes 01-00-5e-01-19-02. The easiest way to map layer 3 to layer 2 manually is to do the math and make the binary conversion so you can see what the last 23 bits of the layer 3 IP address are. After you have that number, all you have to do is insert it into the MAC address and then calculate the remaining 3 hex octet values. The first three octets are always the same: 01-00-5e.

It is important that you spend time studying this procedure and the steps needed to convert a layer 3 IP multicast address to a layer 2 MAC multicast address.

There is one last method of determining the last 23 bits, but this method works only on some addresses. Keep in mind that the highest value you can get in the second octet is 127 and still have it be included in the 23 bits that will map to the MAC address. You know that the last two octets (3 and 4) will map no matter what. So you have 7 bits from the second octet, and 16 bits from the last two octets, for a total of 23 bits. After your value goes above 127 in the second octet, you have to break down the octet into binary so you can see the values of the first seven fields.

FIGURE 19.6 Example 2 for mapping IP multicast to MAC multicast addresses

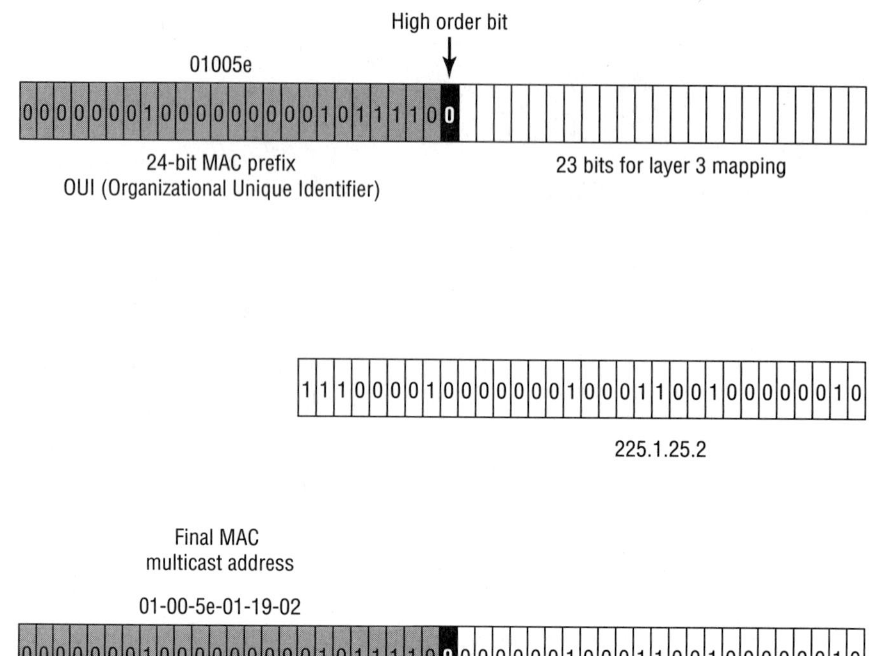

Layer 3 to Layer 2 Overlap

By the time you've done a few of these conversions, you'll notice that there is a problem with this conversion scheme. By not using all available bits for a Class D address, you cannot get an accurate map of layer 3 to layer 2 addresses. If you look at properties of a Class D address, you will see that the high order bit lies in the first octet and is in the 16s value position. This leaves 28 bits for host specification. However, by using only 23 bits of the layer 3 IP address, you leave five bits out of the mapping. This causes an overlap of 2^5, or 32 layer 3 addresses for every one layer 2 address. With a ratio of 32:1, you can expect to see a significant amount of address ambiguity. It is safe to say that any IP addresses that have the same values in the last 23 bits will map to the same MAC multicast address.

For example, 224.0.1.1 and 225.128.1.1 map to the same MAC address. Figure 19.7 shows why this is true. You can see that the bits that differ between 224.0.1.1 and 225.128.1.1 are all within the lost five bits. The last 23 bits are equivalent.

The impact of this overlap can be significant. The overlap creates a window for multiple multicast groups' data to be forwarded to and processed by machines that didn't intentionally subscribe to the multiple groups. To give another example, a machine that subscribes to multicast group 224.2.127.254 would be given a MAC address of 01-00-5e-02-7f-fe. This host also processes packets that come from multicast group 225.2.127.254 because the layer 2 MAC address is identical.

FIGURE 19.7 Multicast addressing overlap

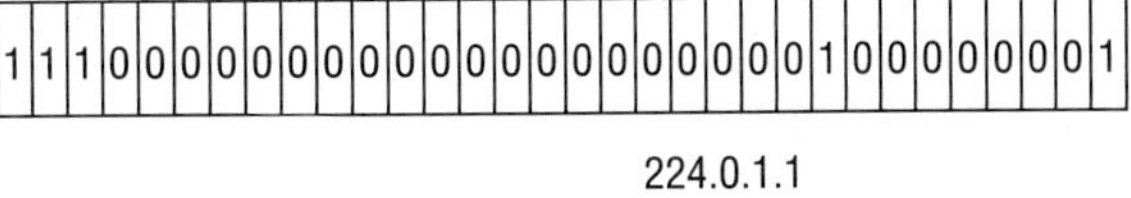

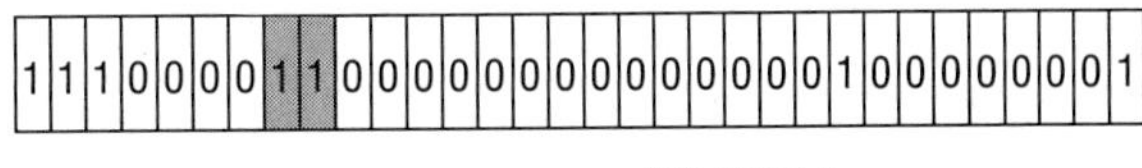

Final MAC multicast address

01-00-5e-00-01-01

The problem this creates is that the end host must now process packets from both multicast groups even though it is interested only in data from 224.2.127.254. This causes unwanted overhead and processor interrupts on the host machine.

Managing Multicast in an Internetwork

As a user on the network, you can understand that spam is not something that is managed by a systems administrator, whereas valid mailing lists require maintenance to keep a current list of valid subscribers. The same can be said of multicast. As we said earlier, one of the major differences between broadcast and multicast communication is that broadcast traffic goes to all hosts on a subnet, whereas multicast traffic goes only to the hosts that request it. The distinguishing factor that puts multicast traffic so far ahead of broadcast traffic in utility is the ability to specify which multiple hosts will receive the transmission.

This isn't done magically; routers and switches don't know who and where the recipients are just because it's multicast traffic. As with any application, protocols are needed to make things happen. Multicast works on the basis of host subscription to groups.

Several methods and protocols have been developed and implemented to facilitate multicast functionality within the internetwork:

- Subscribing groups
- Maintaining groups
- Joining groups
- Leaving groups

Each of these protocols and methods is used for specific tasks or to achieve specific results within the multicast environment. More importantly, each device in the network must know its role regarding multicasting; otherwise, you are left with nothing except a broadcast.

We will now look at these protocols and learn just where they fit in and what they are needed for. We begin with the most important—subscription and group maintenance—and then move on to enhancements for multicast deployment and distribution.

Subscribing and Maintaining Groups

For multicast traffic to reach a host, that host must be running an application that sends a request to a multicast-enabled router informing the router that it wishes to receive data belonging to the specified multicast group. If this request were never to take place, the router wouldn't be aware that the host was waiting for data from the specified group.

Consider this overview: A multicast-enabled router receives all group advertisements and routes. It listens on all interfaces, waiting for a request from a host to forward multicast group traffic. After a host on an interface makes a request to become a member of a group, the interface activates the requested group on itself and only on itself. While the host is a member, multicast data is forwarded to that interface, and any host subscribed to the group receives the data.

That was a simple overview. Now let's look at how this is accomplished in more detail. We start by discussing five major host subscription protocols:

- IGMPv1
- IGMPv2
- IGMPv3
- CGMP
- IGMP Snooping

The differences among them will become apparent as we get further into the discussion.

Internet Group Management Protocol Version 1 (IGMPv1)

As the name indicates, *Internet Group Management Protocol version 1 (IGMPv1)* was the first version of the protocol. It was a result of RFC 1112. The purpose of this protocol is to enable hosts to subscribe to or join specified multicast groups. By subscribing to groups, the hosts are thereby enabled to receive multicast data forwarded from the router.

IGMP has several processes that it executes to manage multicast group subscription and maintenance. We will discuss them in greater detail so you can get an understanding of what happens.

Three processes are employed by version 1 of IGMP:

- Query
- Join
- Leave

These processes are the means by which multicast group membership is maintained. The first two processes are functional processes, whereas the Leave process is more of a timeout than a formal request. Each process is defined in detail next.

Membership Query Process

One important process is the *IGMP Query process*, which is kindred to a keepalive procedure. Because the router needs to keep tabs on which multicast groups need to remain active, or be made active or inactive, it sends a Membership Query out each interface. The query is directed to the reserved address of 224.0.0.1, to which all multicast hosts will answer.

After the request is received, the hosts report back with their group subscription information. After a specific group has been reported to the router, subsequent reports for the same group coming from different hosts are suppressed. This is done because only one host on a subnet/VLAN needs to request membership for the router to activate that group on the interface. Once active on the router interface, any host on that segment wanting to receive data for that specific group will receive it. Figure 19.8 depicts how this process works.

You can follow the numbers indicated in this figure. First, the query to 224.0.0.1 is sent, and subsequently, the hosts begin to report back. The first host to respond (#2a) is Host B, requesting data for the multicast group 224.2.127.254. Host D responds next (#3a) with a request for the group 224.2.168.242. The next host to reply is Host A (#4a). However, because the report from Host D was already multicast to the 224.2.168.242 group, Host A heard the report and suppressed its own report to the group.

FIGURE 19.8 IGMPv1 Query process

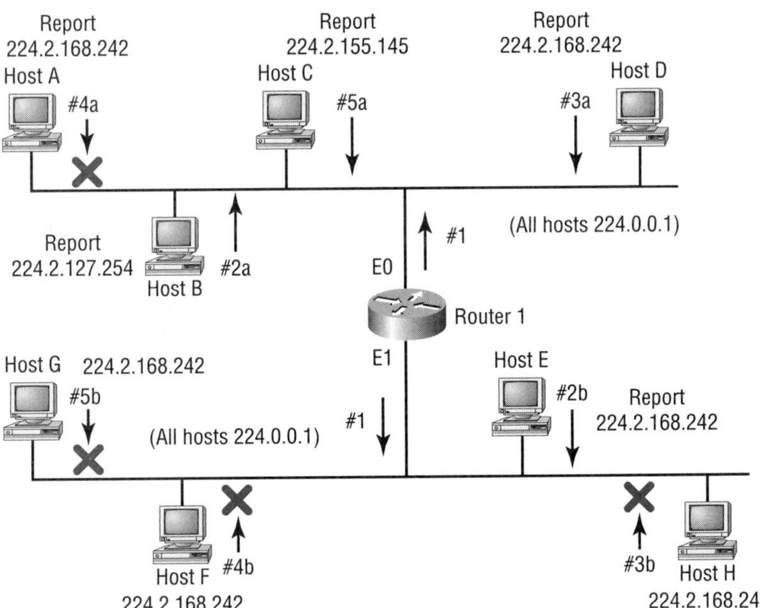

The protocol is "smart" enough to understand that after one host has reported, more hosts don't need to report as well. This helps prevent unwanted and unnecessary bandwidth and processor utilization. To accomplish this, when a query is sent, each participating device sets a random countdown timer. The first device whose timer runs out will respond; the others will reset their timers.

Host C (#5a) responds with a different group number, 224.2.155.145. After all the hosts have responded to the query, Router 1 can maintain activity for these groups on interface E0.

Notice that this description applies to interface E0 on Router 1. Simultaneously, a multicast flood to 224.0.0.1 was sent out interface E1 as well. The first host to respond on this segment is Host E (#2b), and it is reporting membership to 224.2.168.242. Notice that this report was not suppressed, even though Host D had already multicast a report to this group, because it occurred on a different interface. The router queries the local All Hosts address 224.0.0.1, which is not forwarded by the router. That is why the same query is sent out all interfaces on the router. Now that Host E has multicast to the group for that segment, none of the other hosts on the E1 segment will report because they are all members of the 224.2.168.242 group.

Join Process

The other processes are joining and leaving multicast groups. Both of these processes are quite simple and straightforward. You understand how interfaces are maintained in an active state through Membership Queries. The query process runs only every 60 seconds. If a host wants to join a multicast group outside the Membership Query interval, it can simply send an unsolicited report to the multicast router stating that it wants to receive data for the specified multicast group. Figure 19.9 depicts how this occurs. This is known as the *IGMP Join process.*

FIGURE 19.9 Unsolicited join requests

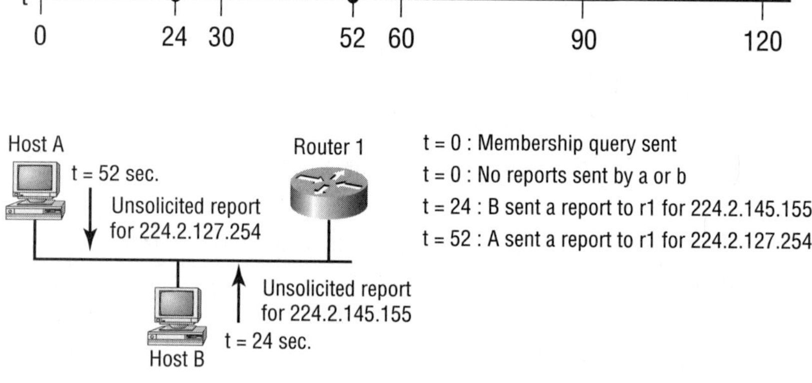

Leave Process

Withdrawal from a group is not initiated by the host, as one would imagine. The router hosts a timer that is reset every time a response is received from a host on the subnet. The timer runs for three minutes, which is equivalent to three Membership Query cycles (a cycle lasts 60 seconds). If the timer expires and no response is received from the hosts on the interface, the router disables multicast forwarding on that interface. If the router was forwarding for a specific group and doesn't get responses for that group but continues to get responses for other groups, it stops forwarding only for the group that no longer has hosts listening.

Internet Group Management Protocol Version 2 (IGMPv2)

As with any software revision, features are made better. Defined by RFC 2236, *Internet Group Management Protocol version 2 (IGMPv2)* provides the same functionality as version 1 did, but with a few enhancements:

- The Leave process in version 2 was included to avoid long timeouts that are experienced in version 1.
- There are two Query forms: General and Group-Specific.
- Network traffic is less bursty due to new timing mechanisms.

In this section, these enhancements are discussed.

It is important to be aware of issues when both versions of IGMP are present on the network. Version 2 provides backward compatibility with version 1, but the functionality of version 2 is lost when it's operating with version 1 devices. A version 2 host has to use version 1 frame formats when talking with a version 1 router. The same applies when a version 2 router tries to communicate with a version 1 host—it must use the version 1 format.

General and Group-Specific Query Processes

One enhancement that was made to IGMPv2 processes was the creation of a new query type. The Membership Query, as it was called in IGMPv1, was renamed General Queries, and the new type is Group-Specific Query. The new query type is used to query a specific multicast group (kind of obvious from the name). The overall procedure is the same as it is in IGMPv1.

When multiple IGMPv1 routers existed on the same segment, a multicast routing protocol made the decision as to which of all the multicast routers would perform the Membership Queries. Now, the decision is made by using a feature added to IGMPv2. This feature is known as the Querier Election Process.

The frame for the query was changed to enable a maximum response time that allows the hosts on the segment more time to respond to the query. This reduces the bursty traffic on the network.

IGMPv2 Leave Process

IGMPv2 implemented the capability for hosts to remove themselves from the multicast group immediately (in a matter of seconds) instead of the router having to wait up to three minutes. The process is known as the *IGMP Leave process*. The two new additions of the Leave and

Group-Specific messages work together to enable a host to remove itself from the multicast group immediately without interrupting the state of the interface on the multicast router.

Figure 19.10 depicts how the IGMPv2 Leave process works. First, Host A sends a Leave message to the all multicast routers address (224.0.0.2), expressing the intent to withdraw from the multicast group. Because Router 1 doesn't know how many hosts on the segment belong to group 224.2.155.145, it must send a Group-Specific Query to see whether any hosts remain members of the group. If no responses are received, the router disables multicast forwarding out of the interface for the 224.2.155.145 group. If any hosts respond to the query, the router leaves the interface status quo. In the figure, you can see that Host B responds because it is still participating in the group 224.2.155.145. Hence, the interface is left active for that group.

FIGURE 19.10 IGMPv2 Leave process

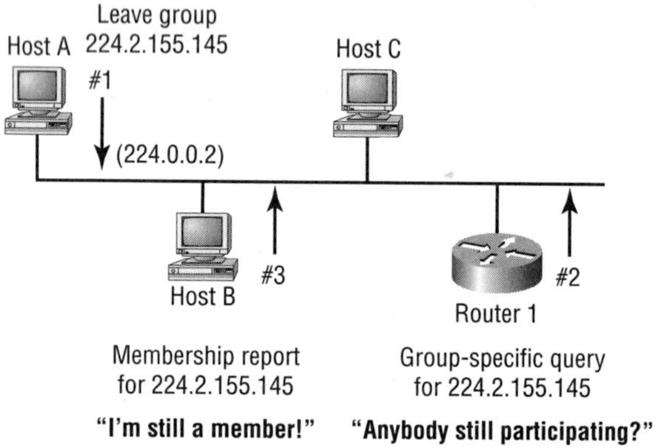

Internet Group Management Protocol Version 3 (IGMPv3)

Multicasting is a rapidly evolving world of multicast traffic flows. No surprise, then, that version 2 of IGMP is not without its own flaws.

Known problems with IGMPv2 (which were not obvious in the past) include

- The possibility of two multicast applications being "live" at the same time with the same multicast address
- The lack of knowledge about the multicast server source address causing routing tree instability
- The ease with which multicast groups can be subjected to denial-of-service attacks (or even simple spamming)

Internet Group Management Protocol version 3 (IGMPv3) addresses these problems specifically by allowing hosts to specify the list of hosts from whom they want to receive traffic, blocking traffic from other hosts transmitting the same stream, and allowing hosts to block packets that come from sources sending unwanted traffic.

Only two types of message exist in IGMPv3: Membership Query and Membership Report.

Membership Query

The Query message is used to determine if there are any extant members in a particular group. Two types of query exist: Group-Specific Queries and Group-and-Source-Specific Queries.

Group-Specific Queries If a host receives an IGMPv3 Group-Specific Query in its source-specific range, it must respond with a report.

Group-and-Source-Specific Queries An IGMPv3 router will query any source-specific channel that a host has requested to leave with a Group-and-Source-Specific Query. Hosts must respond to any Group-and-Source-Specific Query for which both the group and source match any channel to which they are subscribed.

Membership Report

IGMPv3 receivers signal their membership to a multicast host group in one of two possible modes: Include and Exclude.

Include When operating in Include mode, the receiver announces its membership to a host group and provides a list of IP addresses (referred to as the include list) from which it wants to receive traffic.

Exclude When operating in Exclude mode, the receiver announces membership to a host group and provides a list of IP addresses (referred to as the exclude list) from which it does not want to receive traffic. Obviously, this indicates that the host will only receive traffic from other sources whose IP addresses are not listed in the exclude list.

To receive traffic from all sources, a host transmits an empty exclude list.

Cisco Group Management Protocol (CGMP)

We have discussed IGMPv1, IGMPv2, and IGMPv3, which are open standard protocols for host membership of multicast groups. When running multicast at layer 2, things get a little complicated for the switch. It doesn't know which packets are membership report messages or which are actual multicast group data packets because all of them have the same MAC address. *Cisco Group Management Protocol (CGMP)* was implemented to fill this void. It runs on both routers and switches.

The key feature of CGMP is that it uses two MAC addresses:

Group Destination Address (GDA) The GDA is the multicast group address mapped to the MAC multicast address.

Unicast Source Address (USA) The USA is the unicast MAC address of the host. USA enables the host to send multicast membership reports to the multicast router—the multicast router can also be a Route Switch Module (RSM) or Multilayer Switch Feature Card (MSFC)—and still tell the switch which port needs to receive the multicast data.

In addition to being able to make port assignments on the switch, CGMP also handles the interface assignment on the router. If a switch doesn't have any ports that need to receive multicast data, CGMP informs the router that it doesn't need to forward multicast group data out the router interface.

Real World Scenario

Multicast Design

If the router interface is connected to a hub or a switch that doesn't understand multicasting, when the router forwards the multicast, the stream acts like a broadcast. In other words, every device gets a copy. In IGMPv1, the router would keep forwarding the multicast stream out to the hub, which forwards it to every connected client. Multicast routers work well because they can forward a broadcast from one router to the next, something that doesn't happen with true broadcasts. The problem is that clients on a multicast segment get the stream whether they want it or not.

This type of scenario is fine when the CEO wants to give a speech to every desktop, but what about video that is only for a specific division, department, or business unit? If the packets need to go to five different locations, and after you get past the routers all you have are switches, everyone will receive the multicast stream. This doesn't reduce bandwidth utilization!

So far, corporate multicasting with IGMP, either version, works well at the router level. Too bad most clients aren't connected directly to router ports. Because IGMP is essentially nothing more than intelligent broadcast propagation, Cisco created something that would enable switches to participate as well: CGMP.

CGMP uses many of the same processes IGMP uses. The main difference is that CGMP is used between the router and switch. When switches are involved, the IGMP requests must be translated to CGMP and passed on to the switch. These processes include the following:

- CGMP Join process
- Switch host management
- CGMP Leave process

CGMP Join

Hosts do not use CGMP; only the switches and routers that the host connects to use it. When a host sends an IGMP report (Membership Report) advertising membership of a multicast group, the message is forwarded to the router (that is, an actual multicast router, an RSM, or an MSFC) for processing. The router sees the request and processes it accordingly. The multicast group is set up, and the two MAC addresses are generated. The router then gives the switch the CGMP message. With the CGMP message, the switch can assign the multicast group to the port of the requesting host. You can see the entire process in Figure 19.11.

FIGURE 19.11 CGMP Join process

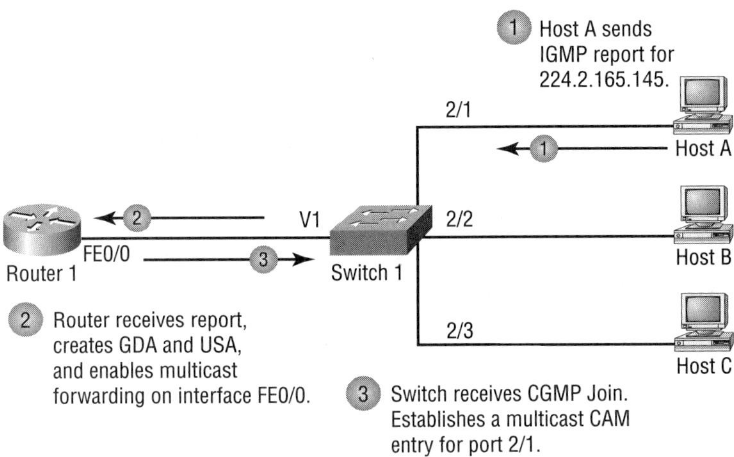

Host Management

Host management is performed by the router. The router continues to receive IGMP messages from the host. Then the router converts the message into a CGMP message and forwards it to the switch. The switch then performs the port maintenance as directed by the router. This process is followed for the multiple types of messages that the host can generate. The router forwards three critical pieces of information to the switch in the CGMP message:

- Request type
- MAC address of the requesting host
- Multicast group the request is for

The CGMP Leave process is done in the same manner. The router receives the request and then informs the switch that the multicast group address needs to be removed from the Content Addressable Memory (CAM) table for the host's port.

IGMP Snooping

While CGMP is a Cisco proprietary protocol to enable switches and routers to communicate regarding multicast traffic patterns, *IGMP Snooping* is referenced in IGMPv3 and does that same thing. Several vendors have created implementations of IGMP Snooping that don't quite play well with each other.

IGMP Snooping doesn't require any sort of translation into a different protocol at the switch. IGMP is used from the client to the router. The switch monitors, or sniffs, the IGMP packets as they pass through and records the MAC addresses and the port that requested to be a part of the process.

Because the switch becomes an integral part of the process of IGMP, the router forwards status messages to the switch and the switch forwards them out the appropriate ports. This is the process of Fast-Leave and is done on both CGMP and IGMP Snooping:

- Client A is listening to a multicast stream and decides to stop listening. The client sends an IGMP Leave message to the switch.
- The switch responds with an IGMP Query to find out whether other clients exist that still want that multicast stream.
- If a client exists out that port, the switch makes no changes.
- If there is no reply out that port but other ports are receiving the stream, the switch does nothing.
- If there is no reply to the Query and there are no other ports participating, the switch forwards the Leave message to the router.

Real World Scenario

Multicast and Spanning Tree

It might seem that CGMP and IGMP Snooping are the way to go. That is true—if you have a very stable network. Remember that STP is used to allow for redundancy but that it disables the redundant links until they are needed. If you have a switched network with redundant connections and a link drops, spanning tree takes over and figures out the next best topology. Unfortunately, the spanning tree process doesn't tell the multicasting process that this is happening. The switch will still forward the multicast message out the port that it was using. This can cause delays and dropped connections. Eventually it settles down, unless the topology changes are always going on.

Routing Multicast Traffic

Up to this point, we have been discussing the host side of multicast. You have learned how hosts interact with switches and routers to join multicast groups and receive the traffic. It is now time to move on to discuss how multicast traffic travels across the Internet (or intranet) from a source on a remote network to a local router and host.

Unicast data uses routing protocols to accomplish the task of getting data to and from remote destinations. Multicast does the same, but it goes about it in a somewhat different manner. Unicast relies on routing tables. Multicast uses a sort of spanning tree system to distribute its data. This section describes the tree structures that can be implemented to enable multicast routing. In addition to trees, several different protocol methods can be used to achieve the desired implementation of multicast.

Distribution Trees

Two types of trees exist in multicast:

Source trees *Source trees* use the architecture of the source of the multicast traffic as the root of the tree.

Shared trees *Shared trees* use an architecture in which multiple sources share a common rendezvous point.

Each of these methods is effective and enables sourced multicast data to reach an arbitrary number of recipients of the multicast group. Let's discuss each of them in detail.

Source Trees

Source trees use special notation. This notation is used in what becomes a multicast route table. Unicast route tables use the destination address and next-hop information to establish a topology for forwarding information. Here is a sample from a unicast routing table:

```
B     210.70.150.0/24 [20/0] via 208.124.237.10, 3d08h
B     192.5.192.0/24 [20/0] via 208.124.237.10, 2w1d
B     193.219.28.0/24 [20/0] via 208.124.237.10, 1d03h
B     136.142.0.0/16 [20/0] via 208.124.237.10, 3d07h
B     202.213.23.0/24 [20/0] via 208.124.237.10, 1w2d
      202.246.53.0/24 is variably subnetted, 2 subnets, 2 masks
B        202.246.53.0/24 [20/0] via 208.124.237.10, 1w2d
B        202.246.53.60/32 [20/0] via 208.124.237.10, 1w2d
```

Multicast route tables are somewhat different. A sample of a multicast table follows. Notice that the notation is different. Instead of having the destination address listed and then the next hop to get to the destination, source tree uses the notation (S, G). This notation specifies the source host's IP address and the multicast group address for which it is sourcing information. Let's take the first one, for example. This is seen as (198.32.163.74, 224.2.243.55), which means that the source host is 198.32.163.74 and it is sourcing traffic for the multicast group 224.2.243.55:

```
(198.32.163.74, 224.2.243.55), 00:01:04/00:01:55, flags: PT
  Incoming interface: POS1/0/0, RPF nbr 208.124.237.10, Mbgp
  Outgoing interface list: Null
(198.32.163.74, 224.2.213.101), 00:02:06/00:00:53, flags: PT
  Incoming interface: POS1/0/0, RPF nbr 208.124.237.10, Mbgp
  Outgoing interface list: Null
(195.134.100.102, 224.2.127.254), 00:00:28/00:02:31, flags: CLM
  Incoming interface: POS1/0/0, RPF nbr 208.124.237.10, Mbgp
  Outgoing interface list:
    FastEthernet4/0/0, Forward/Sparse, 00:00:28/00:02:54
```

```
    FastEthernet4/1/0, Forward/Sparse, 00:00:28/00:02:31
(207.98.103.221, 224.2.127.254), 00:00:40/00:02:19, flags: CLM
  Incoming interface: POS1/0/0, RPF nbr 208.124.237.10, Mbgp
  Outgoing interface list:
    FastEthernet4/0/0, Forward/Sparse, 00:00:41/00:02:53
    FastEthernet4/1/0, Forward/Sparse, 00:00:41/00:02:19
(128.39.2.23, 224.2.127.254), 00:04:43/00:02:06, flags: CLMT
  Incoming interface: POS1/0/0, RPF nbr 208.124.237.10, Mbgp
  Outgoing interface list:
    FastEthernet4/0/0, Forward/Sparse, 00:04:43/00:02:43
    FastEthernet4/1/0, Forward/Sparse, 00:04:43/00:03:07
(129.237.25.152, 224.2.177.155), 00:17:58/00:03:29, flags: MT
  Incoming interface: POS1/0/0, RPF nbr 208.124.237.10, Mbgp
  Outgoing interface list:
    FastEthernet4/0/0, Forward/Sparse, 00:17:58/00:02:44
```

Figure 19.12 gives you a good picture of how source trees work.

FIGURE 19.12 Source tree forwarding

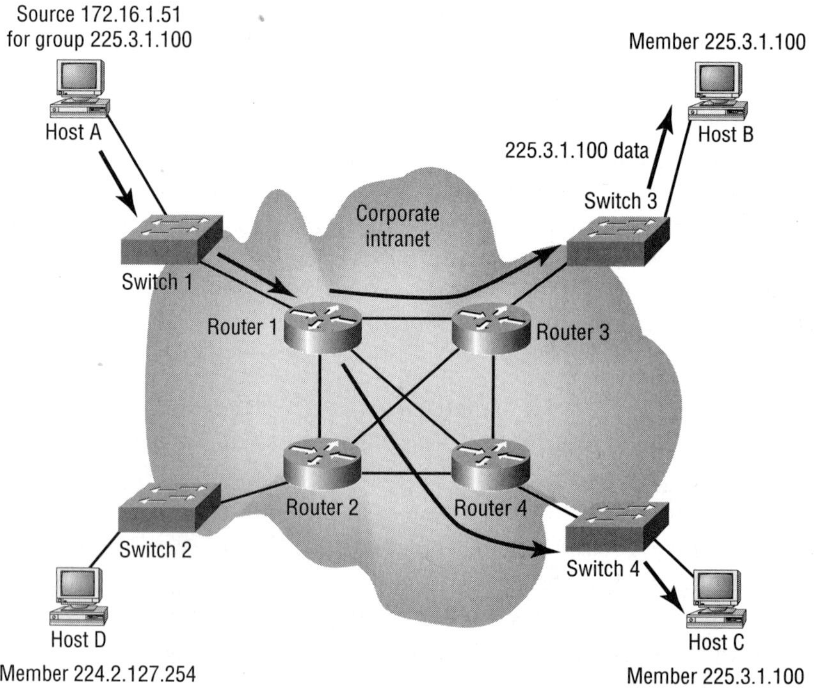

Also notice in this figure that the shortest path to the receivers was chosen. This is known as choosing the shortest path tree (SPT). You can see from the preceding output that there are three sources for the same group of 224.2.127.254. This indicates that there are three SPT groups shown here: (195.134.100.102, 224.2.127.254), (207.98.103.221, 224.2.127.254), and (128.39.2.23, 224.2.127.254). Each of these sources has its own shortest path tree to the receivers.

Shared Trees

There are two types of shared tree distribution:

- Unidirectional
- Bidirectional

Both of them work a little differently from source tree distribution. Shared tree architecture lies in the possibility that there might be multiple sources for one multicast group. Instead of each individual source creating its own SPT and distributing the data apart from the other sources, a shared root is designated. Multiple sources for a multicast group forward their data to a shared root or to a rendezvous point (RP). The rendezvous point then follows SPT to forward the data to the members of the group. Figure 19.13 depicts how the shared tree distribution works.

FIGURE 19.13 Shared tree forwarding

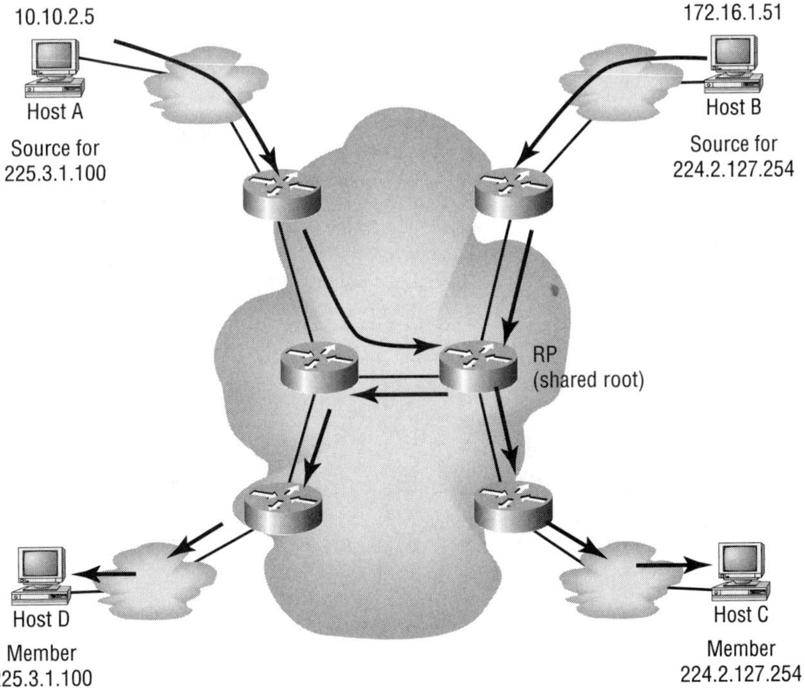

Unidirectional Shared Tree Distribution

Unidirectional shared tree distribution operates as shown in Figure 19.13. All recipients of a multicast group receive the data from an RP no matter where they are located in the network. This is very inefficient if subscribers are close to the source because they need to get the multicast stream from the RP.

Bidirectional Shared Tree Distribution

Bidirectional shared tree distribution operates somewhat differently. If a receiver lives upstream from the RP, it can receive data directly from the upstream source. Figure 19.14 depicts how this works. As you can see, Host A is a source for group 224.2.127.254, and Host B is a receiver of that same group. In a bidirectional shared tree, data goes directly from Host A to Host B without having to come from the RP.

FIGURE 19.14 Bidirectional shared tree

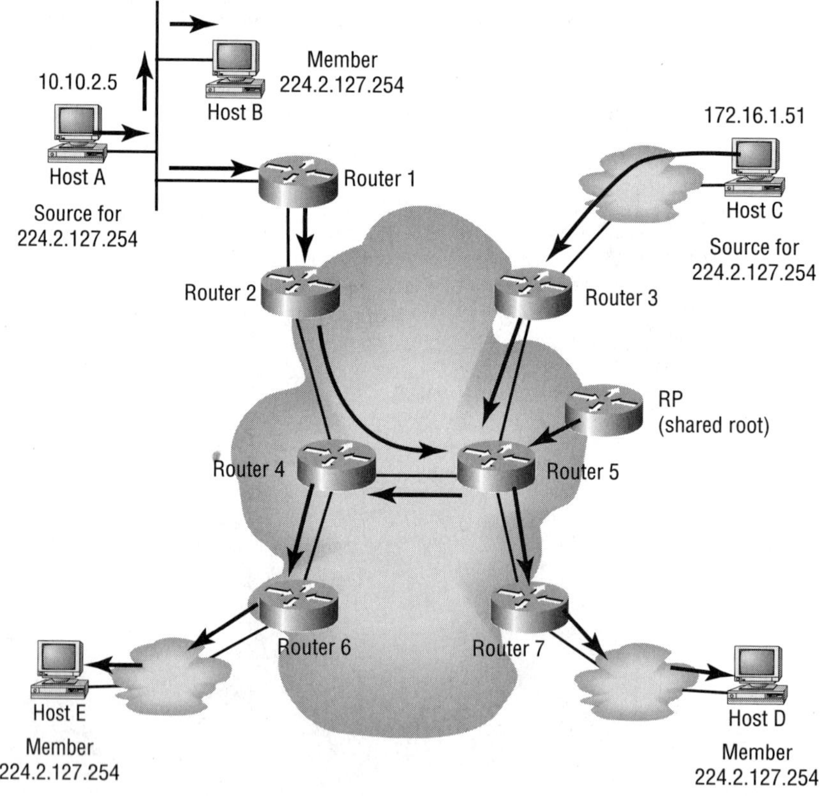

Managing Multicast Delivery

The tree distributions explain how source information is managed; now we must discuss how the actual data delivery is managed. There are several methods of making sure that delivery is as efficient as possible. The following techniques are discussed here:

- Reverse Path Forwarding (RPF)
- Time to live (TTL) attributes
- Routing protocols

Reverse Path Forwarding (RPF)

RPF works in tandem with the routing protocols, but it is described briefly here. As you have seen in Figures 19.13 and 19.14, the traffic goes only to the multicast group receivers. We also indicated that bidirectional distribution eliminates the need to forward data upstream. You might ask, "How do you define upstream?" It is easy to clarify. By means of the routing protocols, routers are aware of which interface leads to the source(s) of the multicast group. That interface is considered *upstream*.

The Reverse Path Forwarding process is based on the upstream information. After receiving an incoming multicast packet, the router verifies that the packet came in on an interface that leads back to the source. The router forwards the packet if the verification is positive; otherwise, the packet is discarded. This check stops potential loops. To avoid increased overhead on the router's processor, a multicast forwarding cache is implemented for the RPF lookups.

Time to Live (TTL)

You can also control the delivery of IP multicast packets through the TTL counter and TTL thresholds. The TTL counter is decremented by one every time the packet hops a router. After the TTL counter is set to zero, the packet is discarded.

Thresholds are used to achieve higher granularity and greater control within one's own network. Thresholds are applied to specified interfaces of multicast-enabled routers. The router compares the threshold value of the multicast packet to the value specified in the interface configuration. If the TTL value of the packet is greater than or equal to the TTL threshold configured for the interface, the packet is forwarded through that interface.

TTL thresholds enable network administrators to bound their network and limit the distribution of multicast packets beyond the boundaries. This is accomplished by setting high values for outbound external interfaces. The maximum value for the TTL threshold is 255. Refer to Figure 19.15 to see how network boundaries can be set to limit distribution of multicast traffic.

FIGURE 19.15 TTL threshold utilization

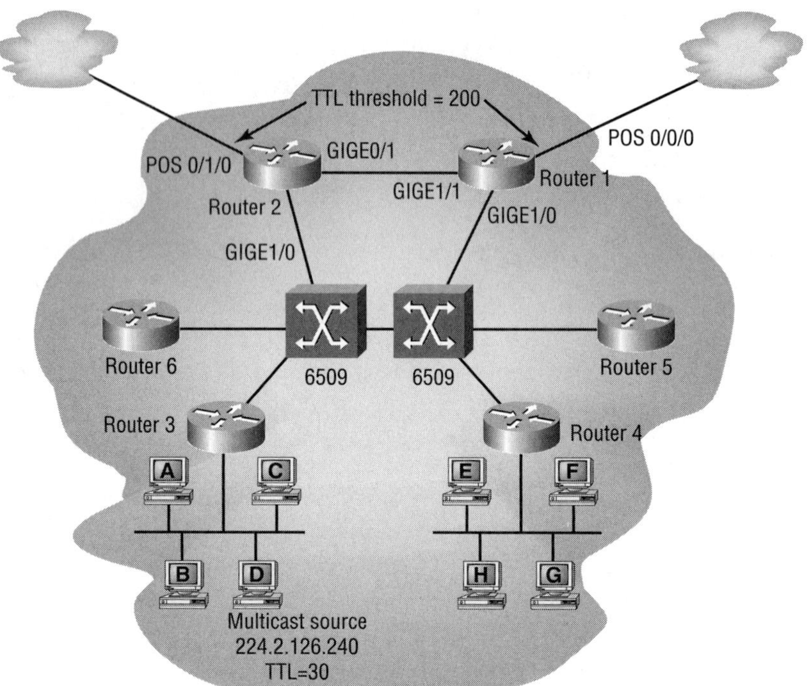

The multicast source initially sets the TTL value for the multicast packet and then forwards it on throughout the network. In this scenario, the TTL threshold values have been set to 200 on both of the exiting Packet over Sonet (POS) interfaces. The initial TTL value has been set to 30 by the application. There are three to four router hops to get out of the campus network. Router 3 will decrement by one, leaving a TTL value of 29; the Catalyst 6509's MSFC will decrement by one as well, leaving the value set to 28. After the packet reaches Router 2 or Router 1, the value will be 27 or 26, respectively. Both of these values are less than the TTL threshold of 200, which means that Router 1 and Router 2 will drop any outbound multicast packets.

Routing Protocols

Unicast has several routing protocols that build route tables enabling layer 3 devices such as routers and some switches to forward unicast data to the next hop toward its final destination. We have also discussed some of the methods that multicast, in general, uses to distribute multicast data. Similar to unicast, multicast has a variety of routing protocols, including distance vector and link-state protocols.

Protocols are used to enhance the efficiency by which multicast application data is distributed and to optimize the use of existing network resources. This section covers Distance Vector Multicast Routing Protocol (DVMRP), Multicast Open Shortest Path First (MOSPF), and Protocol Independent Multicast dense mode (PIM DM).

Distance Vector Multicast Routing Protocol (DVMRP)

Distance Vector Multicast Routing Protocol (DVMRP) has achieved widespread use in the multicast world. A few years ago, you might have often heard the term "DVMRP tunnel" used when discussing the implementation of multicast feeds from an ISP or a feed from the multicast backbone (MBONE). As the name indicates, this protocol uses a distance-vector algorithm. It uses several of the features that other distance-vector protocols (such as Routing Information Protocol, RIP) implement. Some of these features are a 32 max hop count, poison reverse, and 60-second route updates. It also allows for IP classless masking of addresses.

Just as with other routing protocols, DVMRP-enabled routers must establish adjacencies in order to share route information. After the adjacency is established, the DVMRP route table is created. Route information is exchanged via route reports. It is important to remember that the DVMRP route table is stored separately from the unicast routing table. The DVMRP route table is more like a unicast route table than the multicast route table that was shown earlier in this chapter. A DVMRP table contains the layer 3 IP network of the multicast source and the next hop toward the source.

Because the DVMRP table has this form, it works perfectly with source tree distribution, as discussed earlier. Using the information in the DVMRP table, the tree for the source can be established. In addition, the router uses this information to perform the Reverse Path Forwarding check to verify that the multicast data coming into the interface is coming in an interface that leads back to the source of the data. DVMRP uses SPT for its multicast forwarding.

Figure 19.16 shows how DVMRP works. You can see that not every router in the network is a DVMRP router. Notice also that the adjacencies are established over tunnel interfaces. DVMRP information is tunneled through an IP network. On either end of the tunnel, information is learned and exchanged to build a multicast forwarding database or route table.

FIGURE 19.16 DVMRP tunnels

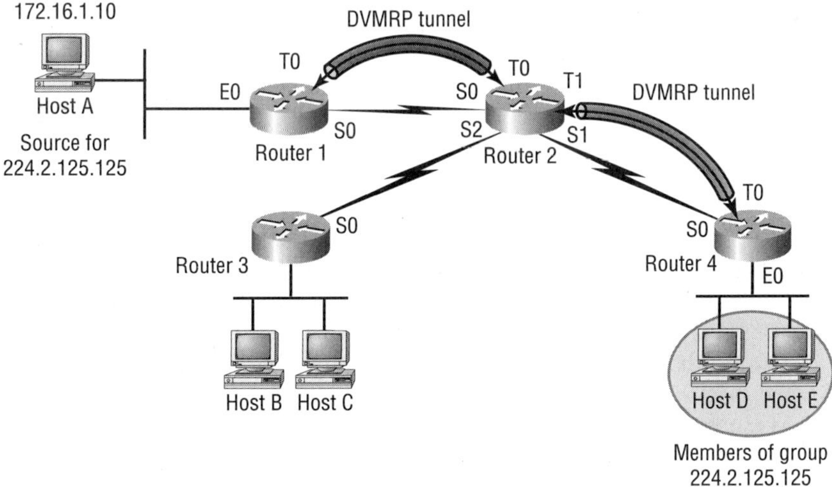

Multicast Open Shortest Path First (MOSPF)

Multicast Open Shortest Path First (MOSPF) is a link-state protocol. OSPFv2 includes some changes that allow multicast to be enabled on OSPF-enabled routers. This eliminates the need for tunnels such as those used for DVMRP.

To completely understand the full functionality of MOSPF, you must have a thorough understanding of OSPF itself. Here we cover only the basic functionality of MOSPF, so you should be fine with just a basic understanding of OSPF.

For more on OSPF, see Chapter 5, "OSPF Operation in a Single Area."

MOSPF's basic functionality lies within a single OSPF area. Design gets more complicated as you route multicast traffic to other areas (inter-area routing) or to other autonomous systems (inter-AS routing). This additional complication requires more knowledge of OSPF routing. We briefly discuss how this is accomplished in MOSPF, but most of the details will be regarding MOSPF intra-area routing.

Intra-Area MOSPF

OSPF route information is shared via different link-state advertisement (LSA) types. LSAs are flooded throughout an area to give all OSPF-enabled routers a logical image of the network topology. When changes are made to the topology, new LSAs are flooded to propagate the change.

In addition to the unicast-routing LSA types, in OSPFv2 there is a special multicast LSA for flooding multicast group information throughout the area. This additional LSA type required some modification to the OSPF frame format.

Here is where you need to understand a little about OSPF. Multicast LSA flooding is done by the designated router (DR) when multiple routers are connected to a multi-access media, such as Ethernet. On point-to-point connections, there are no DR and backup designated router (BDR). Look at the following code from a Cisco router running OSPF over point-to-point circuits:

```
Neighbor ID     Pri   State        Dead Time   Address         Interface
172.16.1.2        1   FULL/  -     00:00:31    172.16.1.2      Serial3/0
192.168.1.2       1   FULL/  -     00:00:39    192.168.1.2     Serial3/1
```

On a multi-access network, the DR must be multicast enabled—that is, running MOSPF. If any non-MOSPF routers are on the same network, their OSPF priority must be lowered so that none of them becomes the DR. If a non-MOSPF router were to become the DR, it would not be able to forward the multicast LSA to the other routers on the segment.

Inside the OSPF area, updates are sent describing which links have active multicast members on them so that the multicast data can be forwarded to those interfaces. MOSPF also uses (S, G) notation and calculates the SPT by using Dijkstra's algorithm. You must also understand that an SPT is created for each source in the network.

Intra-Area and Inter-Area MOSPF

When discussing the difference between intra-area and inter-area MOSPF, you must remember that all areas connect through Area 0, the backbone. In large networks, having full multicast tables in addition to all the unicast tables flow across Area 0 would cause a great deal of overhead and possibly latency.

Unicast OSPF uses a Summary LSA to inform the routers in Area 0 about the networks and topology in an adjacent area. This task is performed by the area's area border router (ABR). The ABR summarizes all the information about the area and then passes it on to the backbone (Area 0) routers in a summary LSA. The same is done for the multicast topology. The ABR summarizes which multicast groups are active and which groups have sources within the area. This information is then sent to the backbone routers.

In addition to summarizing multicast group information, the ABR is responsible for the actual forwarding of multicast group traffic into and out of the area. Each area has an ABR that performs these two functions within an OSPF network.

OSPF implements autonomous system border routers to be the bridges between different autonomous systems. These routers perform much the same as an ABR, but they must be able to communicate with non-OSPF-speaking devices. Multicast group information and data is forwarded and received by the multicast autonomous system border router (MASBR). Because MOSPF runs natively within OSPF, there must be a method or protocol by which the multicast information can be taken from MOSPF and communicated to the external AS. Historically, DVRMP has provided this bridge.

PIM DM

There are three types of *Protocol Independent Multicast (PIM)*: sparse mode, dense mode, and a combination of the two. Although *PIM dense mode (PIM DM)* maintains several functions, the ones that are discussed here are flooding, pruning, and grafting. We'll talk about sparse mode later in this chapter.

PIM is considered "protocol independent" because it actually uses the unicast route table for RPF and multicast forwarding. PIM DM understands classless subnet masking and uses it when the router is running an IP classless unicast protocol.

PIM DM routers establish neighbor relationships with other routers running PIM DM. It uses these neighbors to establish an SPT and forward multicast data throughout the network. The SPT created by PIM DM is based on source tree distribution.

PIM, either sparse mode or dense mode, is the method that Cisco recommends for multicast routing on their routers.

Flooding When a multicast source begins to transmit data, PIM runs the RPF, using the unicast route table to verify that the interface leads toward the source. It then forwards the data to all PIM neighbors. Those PIM neighbors then forward the data to their PIM neighbors. This happens throughout the network, whether there are group members on the router or not. Every multicast-enabled router participates; that is why it is considered *flooding* and is where the term "dense mode" comes from.

When multiple, equal-cost links exist, the router with the highest IP address is elected to be the incoming interface (used for RPF). Every router runs the RPF when it receives the multicast data.

Figure 19.17 depicts the initial multicast flooding in a PIM DM network. You can see that the data is forwarded to every PIM neighbor throughout the network. After a PIM neighbor does the RPF calculation, the router then forwards the data to interfaces that have active members of the group.

Pruning After the initial flooding through the PIM neighbors, pruning starts. *Pruning* is the act of trimming down the SPT. Because the data has been forwarded to every router, regardless of group membership, the routers must now prune back the distribution of the multicast data to routers that actually have active group members connected.

Figure 19.18 shows the pruning action that occurs for the PIM DM routers that don't have active group members. Router 5 does not have any active group members, so it sends a prune message to Router 3. Even though Router 4 has a network that does not have members, it has an interface that does, so it will not send a prune message.

Four criteria merit a prune message being sent by a router:

- The incoming interface fails the RPF check.
- There are no directly connected active group members and no PIM neighbors. (This is considered a leaf router because it has no downstream PIM neighbors.)
- A point-to-point non-leaf router receives a prune request from a neighbor.
- A LAN non-leaf router receives a prune request from another router, and no other router on the segment overrides the prune request.

If any of these criteria are met, a prune request is sent to the PIM neighbor and the SPT is pruned back.

FIGURE 19.17 PIM DM flooding

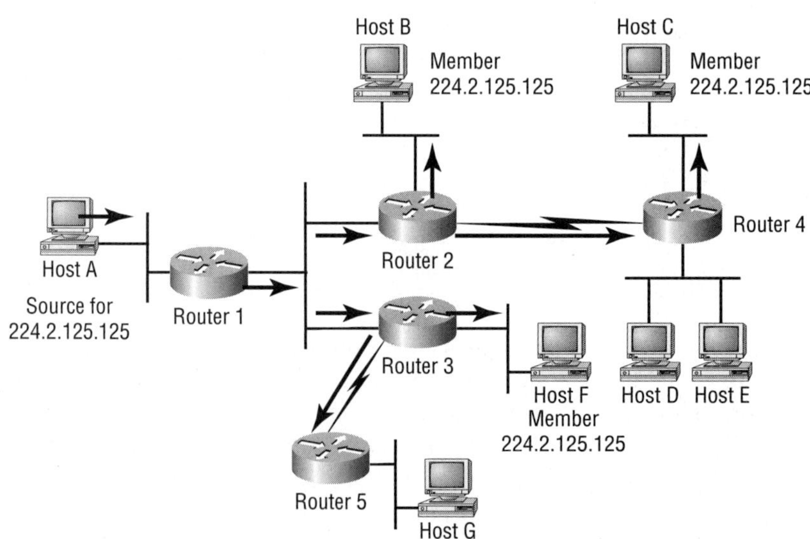

FIGURE 19.18 PIM DM pruning

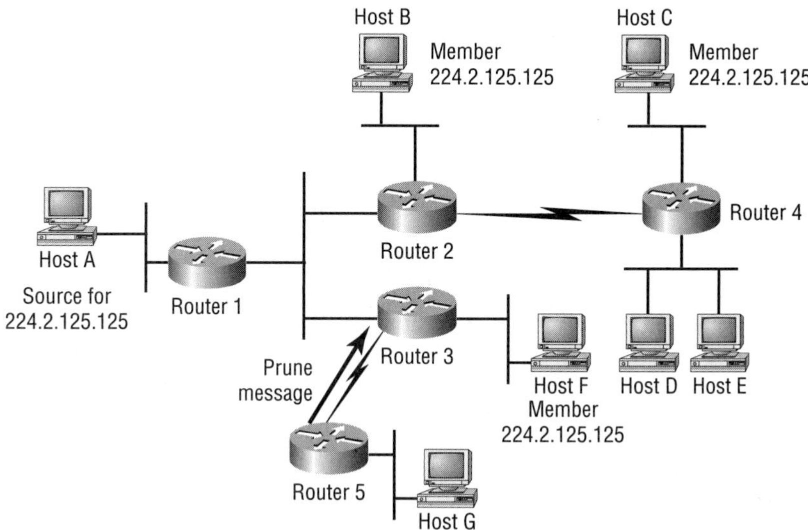

Grafting PIM DM is also ready to forward multicast data after a previously inactive interface becomes active. This is done through the process of *grafting*. When a host sends an IGMP group membership report to the router, the router then sends a graft message to the nearest upstream PIM neighbor. After this message is acknowledged, multicast data begins to be forwarded to the router and on to the host. Figure 19.19 depicts the grafting process.

Sparse Mode Routing Protocols

Sparse mode protocols use shared tree distribution as their forwarding methods. This is done to create a more efficient method of multicast distribution. Two sparse mode protocols are discussed in this section:

- Core-based trees (CBT)
- Protocol Independent Multicast sparse mode (PIM SM)

Core-Based Trees

When we discussed shared trees, you learned that there were two types: unidirectional and bidirectional. CBT utilizes the bidirectional method for its multicast data distribution. Because CBT uses a shared tree system, it designates a core router that is used as the root of the tree, enabling data to flow up or down the tree.

Data forwarding in a CBT multicast system is similar to the shared tree distribution we described earlier. If a source to a multicast group sends multicast data to the CBT-enabled router, the router then forwards the data out all interfaces that are included in the tree, not just the interface that leads to the core router. In this manner, data flows up and down the tree. After the data gets to the core router, the core router then forwards the information to the other routers that are in the tree. Figure 19.20 depicts this process.

FIGURE 19.19 PIM DM grafting

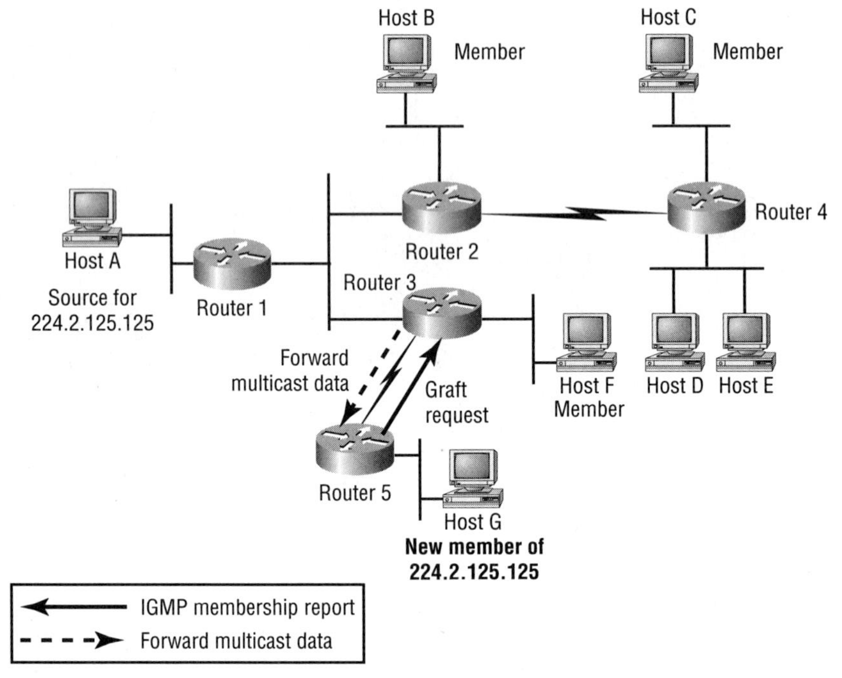

FIGURE 19.20 CBT data distribution

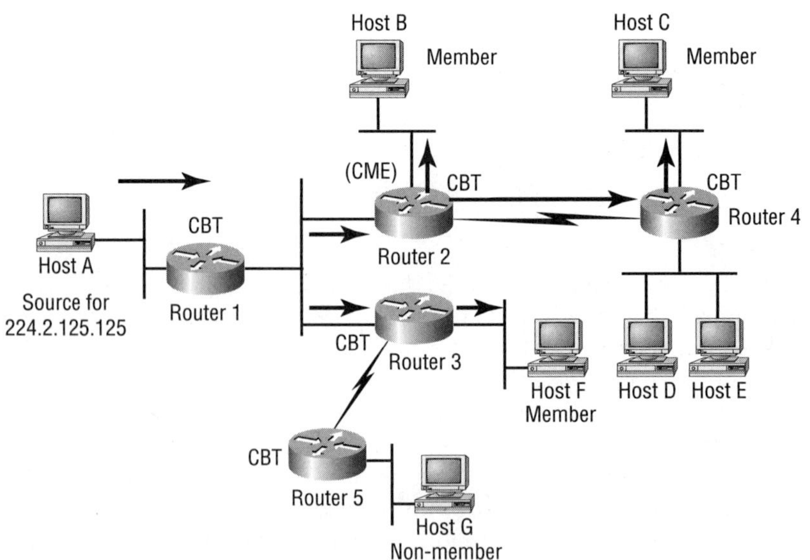

It is important to see the difference between this sparse mode method and the dense mode method. In sparse mode operation, routers are members of the tree only if they have active members directly connected. Notice in Figure 19.20 that Router 5 is not participating. Dense mode operates on the initial premise that all PIM neighbors have active members directly connected. The tree changes when the directly connected routers request to be pruned from the tree.

A CBT router might become part of the tree after a host sends an IGMP Membership Record to the directly connected router. The router then sends a join tree request to the *core* router. If the request reaches a CBT tree member first, that router will add the *leaf* router to the tree and begin forwarding multicast data.

Pruning the tree is done much the same way. When there are no more active members on a router's interfaces, the router sends a prune request to the upstream router. The answering router removes the interface from the forwarding cache if it is on a point-to-point circuit, or it waits for a timer to expire it if is on a shared access network. The timer gives enough time for other CBT routers on the segment to override the prune request.

PIM SM

PIM sparse mode (PIM SM) also uses the architecture of shared tree distribution. There is an RP router that acts as the root of the shared tree. Unlike CBT, however, PIM SM uses the unidirectional shared tree distribution mechanism. Because PIM SM uses the unidirectional method, all multicast sources for any group must register with the RP of the shared tree. This enables the RP and other routers to establish the RPT, or RP tree (synonymous with SPT in source tree distribution).

Just as with CBT, PIM SM routers join the shared tree when they are notified via IGMP that a host requests membership of a multicast group. If the existing group entry (*, G) does not already exist in the router's table, it is created and the join tree request is sent to the next hop toward the RP. The next router receives the request. Depending on whether it has an existing entry for (*, G), two things can happen:

- If an entry for (*, G) exists, the router simply adds the interface to the shared tree and no further join requests are sent toward the RP.
- If an entry for (*, G) does not exist, the router creates an entry for the (*, G) group and adds the link to the forwarding cache. In addition to doing this, the router sends its own join request toward the RP.

This happens until the join request reaches a router that already has the (*, G) entry or a join request reaches the RP.

The next facet of PIM SM is the shared tree pruning. With PIM SM, pruning turns out to be just the opposite of the explicit Join mechanism used to construct the shared tree.

When a member leaves a group, it does so via IGMP. When it happens to be the last member on a segment, the router removes the interface from the forwarding cache entry and then sends a prune request toward the RP of the shared tree. If there is another router with active members connected to the router requesting the prune, it is removed from the outgoing interface list and no additional prune messages are sent to the RP. See Figure 19.21 for a visual description.

FIGURE 19.21 PIM SM pruning

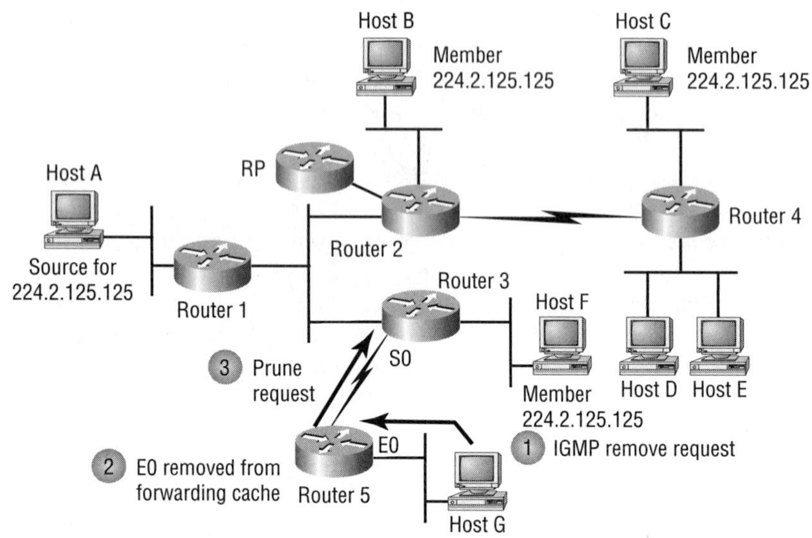

Router 5 receives an IGMP message requesting the removal of Host G from the group. Because Host G was the last active member of the group, the (*, G) entry is set to null 0 and a prune request is sent by Router 5 to Router 3. When Router 3 receives the request, it removes the link for interface S0 from the forwarding table. Because Host F is a directly connected active member of the group, the entry for (*, G) is not null 0, so no prune request is sent to Router 2 (the RP for this example).

If Host F were not active, the entry for (*, G) would have been set to null 0 also and a prune request would have been sent to the RP.

Multicast Source Discovery Protocol (MSDP)

In PIM sparse mode, the routers closest to the sources and receivers register with the RP, so the RP knows about all the sources and receivers for any group. But it is possible that several RPs may need to be created, resulting in several PIM SM domains. Naturally, the RPs don't know about multicast sources in other domains. *Multicast Source Discovery Protocol (MSDP)* was developed to address this issue.

ISPs offering multicast routes to their customers faced a dilemma. Naturally, they didn't want to have to rely on an RP maintained by another ISP, but they needed to access multicast traffic coming from the Internet. MSDP allows them to each run their own RP. RPs peer together using a TCP-based connection that allows them to share information about active sources inside their own domains.

ISPs have the option of which sources they will forward to other MSDP peers, or which sources they will accept, using filtering configurations. PIM SM is used to forward traffic between the RP domains.

ISPs have no problem with this peering relationship. ISP border routers already establish peering relationships with neighboring ISPs, running *Border Gateway Protocol (BGP)* version 4 to exchange routing information as part of the Internet architecture. ISPs with such peering relationships have regular meetings, and their inter-ISP links are part of their commercial raison d'etre. MSDP peering is simply an addition to the agenda.

Source-Specific Multicasting (SSM)

Within any multicast group, it is possible for two sources to exist. Therefore, as multiple listeners join the group, they all receive multicast streams from both sources. This can be filtered out, but possibly not until the last router is reached, in which case considerable unnecessary traffic will have been transmitted. *Source-Specific Multicasting (SSM)* is an extension to the PIM protocol that removes that problem without having to resort to MSDP source discovery. SSM requires the network be running IGMPv3.

In SSM multicast networks, the router closest to the receiver receives a request from that receiver to join to a multicast source. The receiver application uses the Include option to specify the required source. Once the multicast router knows the specific source of the multicast stream, it no longer needs to communicate via the RP, but can instead forward data to the receiver directly, using a source-based share tree distribution system.

Planning and Preparing for Using IP Multicast

You now know that multicast networks behave differently from unicast networks. It is important to keep this in mind when planning the deployment of an IP multicast network. You should take several factors into consideration, including bandwidth implications, use of multicast applications, application requirements, user requirements, the location of the recipients, required equipment, cost, and, most importantly, what multicast source(s) will be used.

All these factors require attention and planning for a successful deployment of IP multicast throughout the network. You must also think upside down when thinking about multicast routing. As discussed in the preceding chapter, distribution trees are built based on the position of the root (source) of the tree. Therefore, when planning the routing for the multicast network, you must know where your sources or RPs will be located.

By taking the time to plan and prepare for a multicast deployment, you will avoid headaches later. You must become familiar with the customer's requirements as well as the effects that multicast will have on the existing network.

There are many methods of implementing multicast on a network. Commonly, institutions will want to connect with the multicast backbone (MBONE) multicast sessions; therefore, they must implement multicast through a Distance Vector Multicast Routing Protocol (DVMRP) tunnel or with Multicast Border Gateway Protocol (MBGP). If the multicast source is within the network and meant to stay within the confines of the network, other design issues come into play. It is important that you understand what each multicast routing protocol brings to the table when it comes to operational functionality.

By better understanding the many protocols and possible implementations of multicast, you will be able to better plan and prepare for its deployment. With so many options, there is bound to be a solution for almost any requirement. Through understanding requirements and through preparing and planning, you can successfully implement an IP multicast network.

End-to-End IP Multicast

Part of deploying multicast is the determination of how much of the network should be multicast enabled. This is an important decision because it directly affects many aspects of multicast implementation. To strategically place the RPs, you must know where all the multicast leaf routers will be. Knowing the approximate number of potential multicast subscribers can have an effect on which protocols are run in the network to allow efficient multicast forwarding and routing.

The decision to use end-to-end deployment can be based on the applications that will be used or the intent of the multicast implementation. If you are enabling multicast for a corporate application, you would need to enable multicast on every interface on every router throughout the enterprise. However, if you need to provide access to only the MBONE for the engineering department, or some other department within the organization, perhaps the most efficient method would not include end-to-end configuration and deployment.

It is important to keep in mind that the state of technology is dynamic. Today, you might receive a request from a single department for multicast access. Before jumping on the project and planning for just that department, consider that in the near future, it is likely that other departments will also request access. Applications that require end-to-end multicast capability might be purchased or integrated into the enterprise. It is far better to plan an end-to-end deployment and initially activate only the routers and interfaces that are needed than to plan your implementation on a limited initial activation. It is easier to "build it right the first time" than to try to come back and work around or rebuild a poor IP multicast deployment.

Configuring IP Multicast Routing

When configuring multicast, keep in mind that many options and protocols can be configured. This is why it is so important that you have previously prepared and planned for the actual configuration. It isn't something that you can just sit down and throw together (not without a lot of problems, anyway).

Configuring routers for IP multicast is different from enabling CGMP on switches. You must also remember that switches do not understand Internet Group Management Protocol (IGMP) by default, and that you need to enable multicasting on switches and routers for hosts to be able to subscribe to a multicast group.

This section of the chapter covers the basics of configuring multicast on routers and switches. It also covers the configuration of rendezvous points. This is a very important task because without a rendezvous point, you will not be able to send or receive multicast packets across a network. We also cover the individual interface configurations on routers. CGMP processes are discussed in a little more detail than in the preceding chapter. Later, we will describe the multicast settings that can be made on a multicast-enabled router (and switches). The following sections "Enabling IP Multicast Routing" and "Enabling PIM on an Interface" describe required configuration, whereas the configuration described in the rest of this section is optional.

It is best to prepare a configuration task list before setting out to configure a group of routers. The configuration list should be specific to the device that will be configured. That fact makes it hard to present a set list of configuration tasks that would apply to all scenarios. However, two items definitely must be configured on a router in order for multicast to even begin working: enabling multicast routing and enabling PIM on the interfaces that will carry multicast traffic.

Enabling IP Multicast Routing

As we have said, multicast routing must be enabled on the router. This step is very straightforward, but without it, multicast will not work. Let's look at a configuration of a router that does not have multicast enabled:

```
Current configuration:
!
version 12.0
service timestamps debug uptime
service timestamps log uptime
no service password-encryption
!
hostname Terry_3640
!
aaa new-model
aaa authentication login default tacacs+ line
aaa authentication login oldstyle line
aaa accounting exec default start-stop tacacs+
enable secret 5 $1$G7Dq$em.LpM4Huem9uqjZDHLe4.
!
!
!
ip subnet-zero
ip telnet source-interface FastEthernet3/0
[output truncated]
```

Notice that no multicast information is running on this machine. If we were to try to execute a multicast-related command, we wouldn't get any information returned. For example, look at what happens when the `show ip mroute` command is issued:

```
Terry_3640#sho ip mroute
IP Multicast Routing Table
Flags: D - Dense, S - Sparse, C - Connected, L - Local,
P - Pruned R - RP-bit set, F - Register flag,
 T - SPT-bit set,J - Join SPT, M - MSDP created entry,
X - Proxy Join Timer Running
       A - Advertised via MSDP
Timers: Uptime/Expires
Interface state: Interface, Next-Hop or VCD, State/Mode

Terry_3640#
```

The command is `ip multicast-routing`, and an example of the execution follows:

```
Terry_3640#configure terminal
Enter configuration commands, one per line.  End with CNTL/Z.
Terry_3640(config)#ip multicast-routing
Terry_3640(config)#^Z
Terry_3640#
```

This enables the multicast on the router. Notice that it was executed while in global configuration mode. However, the router still cannot exchange multicast information with any neighbors because none of the interfaces have been enabled. This step is next.

Enabling PIM on an Interface

PIM is one of the required elements for multicast configuration. It enables IGMP on the router and enables it to receive and forward traffic on the specified interface. PIM must be enabled on every interface that is to participate in the multicast network.

PIM interface configuration has many options. Take a look at the available options in IOS 12.0(10)S1, shown in Table 19.2. Most of these options are for advanced multicast configuration that won't be addressed in detail here. The options that are discussed are `dense-mode`, `sparse-mode`, and `sparse-dense-mode`.

IP PIM Dense Mode

PIM dense mode functions by using the source root shared tree. It also assumes that all PIM neighbors have active multicast members directly connected, and therefore, it initially forwards multicast group data out all PIM-enabled interfaces.

TABLE 19.2 IP PIM Configuration Options

IP PIM Options	Description
bsr-border	Specifies the border of the PIM domain.
dense-mode	Enables PIM dense-mode operation.
nbma-mode	Specifies the use of non-broadcast multi-access (NBMA) mode on the interface.
neighbor-filter	Specifies the PIM peering filter.
query-interval	Specifies the PIM router query interval.
sparse-dense-mode	Enables PIM sparse-dense-mode operation.
sparse-mode	Enables PIM sparse-mode operation.
version	Displays the PIM version.

This command is simple: `ip pim dense-mode`. An example of placing an interface in PIM dense mode follows:

```
Terry_3640#configure terminal
Enter configuration commands, one per line.  End with CNTL/Z.
Terry_3640(config)#interface FastEthernet3/0
Terry_3640(config-if)#ip pim dense-mode
Terry_3640(config-if)#^Z
Terry_3640#
```

This is what the interface configuration looks like now:

```
!
interface FastEthernet3/0
 ip address 172.16.21.4 255.255.255.0
 no ip directed-broadcast
 ip pim dense-mode
!
```

IP PIM Sparse Mode

Sparse mode was developed to use shared root source tree distribution and relies on the knowledge of an RP. If an RP cannot be found, the router is unable to forward multicast information, strictly because it does not know the source of the multicast traffic. If it can't determine where the traffic is supposed to be coming from, the Reverse Path Forwarding (RPF) check fails and no interfaces are added to the multicast forwarding table.

Configuration of PIM sparse mode is just as simple as it is for IP dense mode. The command for enabling IP PIM sparse mode is `ip pim sparse-mode`. Sparse mode PIM also activates IGMP on the interface, allowing the interface to listen for IGMP membership reports. Here is an example of enabling IP PIM sparse mode multicast on an interface:

```
Terry_3640#configure terminal
Enter configuration commands, one per line.  End with CNTL/Z.
Terry_3640(config)#interface FastEthernet3/0
Terry_3640(config-if)#ip pim sparse-mode
Terry_3640(config-if)#^Z
Terry_3640#
```

Here is a look at the interface configuration after the preceding execution:

```
!
interface FastEthernet3/0
 ip address 172.16.21.4 255.255.255.0
 no ip directed-broadcast
 ip pim sparse-mode
!
```

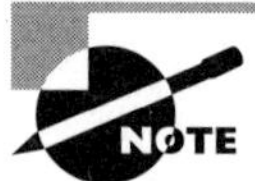

All forms of sparse mode also require a rendezvous point to be configured.

IP PIM Sparse-Dense Mode

The name of this command gives an indication of the functionality it provides. Due to the increasing use of multicast and the variety of applications available today, it is best to configure an interface to be able to use both sparse mode and dense mode. With the previous commands, the interface was assigned the operating mode, and the interface could not change between modes depending on the need at the time.

PIM sparse-dense mode configuration now enables the interface to use whichever forwarding method is needed by the application or multicast group. The interface uses the multicast group notation to decide which mode it needs to operate in. If the interface sees something with the notation (S, G), it operates in dense mode. If the interface sees a notation similar to (*, G), the interface operates in sparse mode.

An added benefit of implementing sparse-dense mode on the interfaces is the elimination of the need to hard-configure the RP at every leaf router. The Auto-RP information is sent out across the network by using dense mode forwarding.

IP PIM sparse-dense mode is enabled by using `ip pim sparse-dense-mode` on the interface command line. Here is an example:

```
Terry_3640#configure terminal
Enter configuration commands, one per line.  End with CNTL/Z.
Terry_3640(config)#interface FastEthernet3/0
Terry_3640(config-if)#ip pim sparse-dense-mode
Terry_3640(config-if)#^Z
Terry_3640#
```

Again, here is what the interface looks like after the preceding lines have been executed:

```
!
interface FastEthernet3/0
 ip address 172.16.21.4 255.255.255.0
 no ip directed-broadcast
 ip pim sparse-dense-mode
!
```

In summary, when using the sparse-dense mode configuration on an interface, you need to understand that three criteria will activate the interface and place it into the multicast forwarding table. The first criterion applies to either sparse or dense mode; the others cause the interface to operate specifically for sparse or dense mode. Table 19.3 provides the details.

TABLE 19.3 Interface Activation Criteria for Sparse-Dense-Mode Interfaces

Criteria	Mode of Operation
Directly connected group members or DVMRP neighbors	Sparse and dense
Non-pruned PIM neighbors	Dense
Join request received	Sparse

Configuring a Rendezvous Point

If you are using PIM DM throughout the multicast network, configuring a rendezvous point is an optional task. There are two ways of configuring a rendezvous point for a router. Notice that we did not say "configuring a router *to be*" a rendezvous point. You can manually specify the IP address of the RP on a router, or you can enable Auto-RP. Both are described in this section.

Manual RP Configuration

The syntax for the manual RP configuration command is simple: `ip pim rp-address` *`ip_address group_access_list_number`* `[override]`. The *`ip_address`* is the IP address of the router that is the RP. The `access_list_number` is for a standard IP access list (1–99) or an expanded range from 1300 to 1999. These lists are used to define which multicast groups can or cannot use this RP. If no access list is specified, all multicast groups will use the configured RP. Finally, the `override` option can be used to override any RP information that might be learned via an Auto-RP update. The static RP takes precedence over any Auto-RP-learned RP. Here is a sample configuration for manual RP configuration:

```
Terry_3640#configure terminal
Enter configuration commands, one per line.  End with CNTL/Z.
Terry_3640(config)#ip pim rp-address 172.16.1.253 50 override
Terry_3640(config)#^Z
Terry_3640#
```

Here is a look at the router after the execution. Notice that the command is a global command. Following the global configuration, you will see `access-list 50`. The list allows only groups within the range of 224.0.0.0 to 224.255.255.255 to use 172.16.1.253 as the RP. Other groups need Auto-RP information or another statically configured RP in order to work properly:

```
!
no ip classless
ip route 0.0.0.0 0.0.0.0 172.16.22.2
ip pim rp-address 172.16.1.253 50 override
!
access-list 50 permit 224.0.0.0 0.255.255.255
access-list 50 deny   any
!
```

Auto-RP Configuration

Because multiple RPs can exist in a multicast network, the *Auto-RP* function aids by distributing the RP information across a multicast network. Different multicast groups can use different RPs, so this feature keeps track of which groups are using which RP. It will also fine-tune the leaf router's RP by choosing the RP nearest to the leaf. If you don't like to use static routes in a unicast network, you probably don't want to statically configure multicast RPs either.

There are also two procedures that can be used to enable Auto-RP; which one you use depends on the state of your multicast network. If you are beginning a new deployment, it isn't necessary to create a default RP. If you are modifying an existing multicast network, you need to designate a default RP router in the network.

Here is a list of configuration tasks that must be completed to successfully implement Auto-RP in a multicast network:

- Designate a default RP (only when modifying an existing multicast network).
- Advertise each RP and the multicast groups associated with the RP.
- Enable an RP Mapping Agent.

As you can see, the list is short and simple. Now that you know what has to be done, let's discuss each step individually.

Designating a Default RP

This step is somewhat tricky, not so much because the configuration is tricky, but because of the decision regarding when to execute the step. The only time you need to designate a default RP is when you are running sparse mode only on any of your interfaces in an existing multicast network. If you are using sparse-dense mode, as suggested, you do not need to execute this step.

This step is executed as described in the "Manual RP Configuration" section earlier in this chapter. The default RP becomes the statically mapped RP on all the leaf routers. The default RP should serve all global multicast groups. That is all that has to be done.

Advertising RP Group Assignments

From each RP, a statement needs to be added that assigns and advertises multicast groups to that RP. The multicast groups are then advertised so the RP Mapping Agent can keep track of which RP hosts which multicast groups and resolve conflicts when necessary.

The syntax for the command is `ip pim send-rp-announce` *`type number scope ttl group_list access_list_number`*. The command is entered in global configuration mode. The first two options, *`type`* and *`number`*, are the interface type and number that indicate the RP IP address. *`scope`* defines the boundary of the RP advertisement by using a high TTL value that will be effectively blocked by interfaces with the TTL threshold set. The *`group_list`* uses the specified access list to determine which multicast group ranges the RP is allowed to announce.

Here is an example of the command as well as a valid access list:

```
Terry_3640#configure terminal
Enter configuration commands, one per line.  End with CNTL/Z.
Terry_3640(config)#access-list 5 permit 224.0.0.0 0.0.255.255
Terry_3640(config)#ip pim send-rp-announce fastethernet4/0 scope 230
  ➥group-list 5
Terry_3640(config)#^Z
Terry_3640#

Terry_3640#write terminal
. . .
!
ip pim send-rp-announce FastEthernet4/0 scope 230  group-list 5
!
access-list 5 permit 224.0.0.0 0.0.255.255
!
. . .
```

Configuring the RP Mapping Agent

This router is in charge of learning all the rendezvous point routers in the network, along with the multicast group assignments that each RP advertises. The Mapping Agent then tells all the routers within the multicast network which RP should be used for their source.

This is done with the `ip pim send-rp-discovery scope ttl` command. As you can see, this command is similar to the command in the preceding section. The scope defines the TTL value for the discovery. After the TTL is reached, the discovery packets are dropped. Here is an example:

```
Terry_3640#configure terminal
Enter configuration commands, one per line.  End with CNTL/Z.
Terry_3640(config)#ip pim send-rp-discovery scope 23
Terry_3640(config)#^Z
Terry_3640
```

In this example, you can see that the TTL value was set to 23. This means that after 23 hops, the discovery has expired. This command actually assigns to the router the role of RP Mapping Agent.

This concludes the tasks for configuring a rendezvous point in a multicast network. Keep in mind that the RP Mapping Agent can be an RP, although it doesn't have to be. The Mapping Agent's role is to learn of all the deployed rendezvous points throughout the network and then advertise which groups are available via the closest RP for all multicast-enabled routers in the network.

Configuring TTL

TTL threshold configuration is done to limit the boundary of scope of the IP multicast network. As you learned earlier in this chapter, limiting the scope of a multicast network is based on the TTL value in the multicast packet. Because this command is used to create a boundary, it must be executed on each border interface.

The default value for the TTL threshold is zero. The value can be changed with the `ip multicast ttl-threshold ttl` command. The syntax is straightforward, and the *ttl* value that is used is up to the discretion of the network administrator. The range of valid values for this option is between 0 and 255. However, the value should be high enough to stop multicast packets from exiting the interface. Here is an example:

```
Terry_3640#configure terminal
Enter configuration commands, one per line.  End with CNTL/Z.
Terry_3640(config)#interface FastEthernet0/0
Terry_3640(config-if)#ip multicast ttl-threshold 230
Terry_3640(config-if)#^Z
Terry_3640#

!
interface FastEthernet0/0
 ip address 172.16.5.1 255.255.255.0
 no ip directed-broadcast
 ip pim sparse-dense-mode
 ip multicast ttl-threshold 230
 no ip route-cache
```

```
 no ip mroute-cache
 full-duplex
!
```

Joining a Multicast Group

After the main configuration is done on the router to enable multicast, PIM, rendezvous points, and RP Mapping Agents, the only other major task is enabling hosts to join multicast groups.

Within Cisco IOS, the network administrator has the opportunity to verify functionality and connectivity before users use the multicast system and applications. You can configure a router to join any number of IP multicast groups and thus verify functionality.

This is achieved through the `ip igmp join-group` *`group_address`* command. The *`group_address`* is the multicast address of the group you want the router to join. An example follows:

```
Terry_3640(config)#interface FastEthernet4/0
Terry_3640(config-if)#ip igmp join-group 224.2.127.254
Terry_3640(config-if)#^Z
Terry_3640#
```

This tells the router to become a member of the 224.2.127.254 multicast group. Joining a group facilitates troubleshooting multicast connectivity issues as well.

Troubleshooting IP Multicast Connectivity

Multicast can be a difficult protocol to troubleshoot. However, a few basic tools (mostly `show` commands) can provide enough information for you to verify that connectivity is active or to determine whether other steps, such as debugging, are needed to troubleshoot the problem.

If you do need to debug a multicast-enabled interface, you must first disable the multicast fast switching on the interface. This is done so that the debug messages can be logged. The command to disable fast switching is `no ip mroute-cache`. The standard unicast fast (or other forms of) switching can be left enabled.

You are familiar with the troubleshooting tools for unicast connectivity, Ping and Traceroute. Well, these tools are also available for troubleshooting multicast connectivity. There is one minor difference, though: multicast requires a special version of traceroute—called mtrace, or "multicast-traceroute."

Ping After a device on the network becomes a member of a group, it can be identified by its layer 3 multicast address as well as the layer 2 MAC address. Because the device has an active address on its interface, it can respond to ICMP request packets. Here is an example:

```
Terry_3640#ping
Protocol [ip]:
Target IP address: 224.2.143.55
Repeat count [1]: 5
Datagram size [100]:
```

```
Timeout in seconds [2]:
Extended commands [n]:
Sweep range of sizes [n]:
Type escape sequence to abort.
Sending 5, 100-byte ICMP Echos to 224.2.143.55, timeout is  2 seconds:
.!!!!
Terry_3640#
```

This tool can be used to verify connectivity among RPs or other multicast routers.

mtrace Cisco also provides a multicast Traceroute tool. The multicast version of Traceroute is somewhat different from the unicast version. The complete syntax for mtrace is `mtrace` *`source_ip destination_ip group`*. The *`source_ip`* is the unicast IP address for the source of the multicast group. The *`destination_ip`* is used when following the forwarding path established by the source or shared tree distribution toward a unicast destination. The *`group`* option is used to establish the tree for the specified group. If no destination or group options are specified, the mtrace will work from the incoming multicast interfaces back toward the multicast source. Here are a few samples of the command and its output:

```
Jack_3640#mtrace 198.32.163.74
Type escape sequence to abort.
Mtrace from 198.32.163.74 to 172.16.25.9 via RPF
From source (blaster.oregon-gigapop.net) to destination  (?)
Querying full reverse path...
 0  172.16.25.9
-1  172.16.25.9 PIM/MBGP  [198.32.163.0/24]
-2  172.16.25.10 PIM/MBGP  [198.32.163.0/24]
-3  ogig-den.oregon-gigapop.net (198.32.163.13) [AS 4600]
 PIM  [198.32.163.64/26]
-4  Ocar-Ogw.oregon-gigapop.net (198.32.163.26) [AS 4600]
 PIM  [198.32.163.64/26]
-5  blaster.oregon-gigapop.net (198.32.163.74)
Jack_3640#

Jack_3640#mtrace 198.32.163.74 224.2.243.55
Type escape sequence to abort.
Mtrace from 198.32.163.74 to 172.16.25.9 via group  224.2.243.55
From source (blaster.oregon-gigapop.net) to destination  (?)
Querying full reverse path...
 0  172.16.25.9
-1  172.16.25.9 PIM/MBGP Reached RP/Core [198.32.163.0/24]
-2  172.16.25.10 PIM/MBGP Reached RP/Core [198.32.163.0/24]
-3  ogig-den.oregon-gigapop.net (198.32.163.13) [AS 4600]
```

```
 PIM Reached RP/Core [198.32.163.64/26]
-4  0car-0gw.oregon-gigapop.net (198.32.163.26) [AS 4600]
 PIM  [198.32.163.64/26]
Jack_3640#
```

As you can see, the outputs differ very little, but it is important to see how the paths are established. From the first sample output, no group or destination was specified, so the router strictly used RPF to calculate the path from the source to the router. In the other output, a group address was specified. This caused the router to specifically use the existing forwarding tree for group 224.2.243.55 to get back to the router.

These tools can be useful to determine connectivity as well as the effectiveness of the placement of RPs and multicast sources. There are other `show` commands that can aid you as well, but they are not related to the topic of this chapter.

Changing the IGMP Version

Several settings can be tweaked in the router to enhance or change performance. The majority of them are beyond the scope of this chapter. However, in this section, we discuss one important feature: changing the IGMP version. It is important that you understand and know how to perform this change because of the compatibility issues between IGMP versions.

To put it simply, the IGMP version that runs on the hosts must also run on the router. Cisco routers use IGMPv2 by default and do not auto-detect the IGMP version that the host is using. The command to change from IGMPv2 to IGMPv1, or vice versa, is `ip igmp version (2 | 1)`. Because the IGMP version needs to match only on the subnet, the command must be entered on the interface that connects to the subnet housing the IGMPv1 hosts. The other interfaces on the router can remain on IGMPv2.

Enabling CGMP and IGMP Snooping

When hosts connect to a router via a Catalyst switch, either CGMP or IGMP Snooping can be used to enable the switch to learn appropriate information. Catalysts run both so they can manage multicast membership reports from the router accordingly and so they can manage multicast ports on the switch. The router is the device that listens for the IGMP membership report; it then tells the switch which port needs to be activated. CGMP or IGMP Snooping must be activated on both the router and the switch.

CGMP Router Configuration

The router configuration syntax is simple. It must be applied to the interface connected to the Catalyst switch. The command is `ip cgmp` *`proxy`*. The *`proxy`* option is used for routers that are not CGMP capable. It enables them to use the proxy router for CGMP. Here is a sample configuration:

```
Terry_3640#configure terminal
Enter configuration commands, one per line.  End with CNTL/Z.
```

```
Terry_3640(config)#interface FastEthernet4/0
Terry_3640(config-if)#ip cgmp
Terry_3640(config-if)#^Z
Terry_3640#
```

Use the command `show running-config` to see whether CGMP is enabled or disabled on a particular router interface, as shown here:

```
!
interface FastEthernet4/0
 ip address 172.16.10.1 255.255.255.0
 no ip directed-broadcast
 ip pim sparse-dense-mode
 no ip route-cache
 ip igmp join-group 224.2.127.254
 ip cgmp
!
```

Catalyst Switch Configuration

The Catalyst syntax is just as simple as the syntax for the router configuration, if not simpler. By default, CGMP is turned off on the switch. If you want multicast to work properly, you must enable CGMP or IGMP Snooping on the switch. Enabling CGMP is done by using the command `set cgmp enable`. Here is an example:

```
Terry_4000> (enable) set cgmp enable
CGMP support for IP multicast enabled.
Terry_4000> (enable)
Terry_4000> (enable) show cgmp statistics
CGMP enabled

CGMP statistics for vlan 1:
valid rx pkts received          6
invalid rx pkts received        0
valid cgmp joins received       6
valid cgmp leaves received      0
valid igmp leaves received      0
valid igmp queries received     0
igmp gs queries transmitted     0
igmp leaves transmitted         0
failures to add GDA to EARL     0
topology notifications received 0
number of packets dropped       0
Terry_4000> (enable)
```

After CGMP is enabled, you can look at statistics by using the `show cgmp statistics` command. This is all that is needed to enable CGMP on the switch so that it can communicate with the router.

A CGMP-enabled switch can also be configured to detect IGMPv2 Leave messages generated by clients. To do this, simply use the command `set cgmp leave enable`. This command takes place globally on the switch.

The switch collects multicast group MAC addresses for each group address. To see what multicast groups your switch knows about, use the command `show multicast group cgmp`.

IGMP Snooping

IGMP Snooping can be configured to enable the switch to learn multicast information by examining the frames as they pass through the switch. The switch doesn't depend wholly on information received from the multicast router.

To configure IGMP Snooping on the switch, use the command `set igmp enable`. You cannot have CGMP and IGMP Snooping enabled on the same switch at the same time. To enable IGMP Snooping on the router, use the command `ip igmp snooping` while in global configuration mode.

Fast-Leave processing is a new feature that works only with IGMP Snooping and is one of the main reasons for its use. Fast-Leave processing enables a switch to receive an IGMP Leave message and immediately remove the interface from the table that lists which ports receive the multicast stream. Thus, if a client on port 2/5 generates a Leave message, the switch immediately removes port 2/5 from the list of ports receiving the multicast stream. To enable Fast-Leave processing on the switch, use the command `set igmp fastleave enable`.

Just as with CGMP, IGMP Snooping has a way of displaying the configuration and statistics. Using the command `show igmp statistics` will display the status of IGMP Snooping on the switch as well as the amount of traffic that has been processed.

Real World Scenario

The Fast-Leave Trap

Fast-Leave is a great tool in an organization that uses quite a bit of multicasting. There can be a problem though, when using it in a network where spanning tree changes frequently.

When a switch configured for Fast-Leave receives a Leave message, the switch will remove the port at which the message arrived from the forwarding table for the particular stream. What happens if this occurs on a core switch, on the port going out to a closet switch or stack? The core switch will remove all entries associated with that port. If several clients were listening to the stream and one leaves, the core switch will remove them all.

Whenever possible, only enable Fast-Leave processing on switches that have clients terminating at individual ports. Turn this feature on at the closets, but think twice before doing so at the core and distribution layer switches.

It is early to be too definite about this, but it would seem that Cisco is moving away from CGMP toward IGMP Snooping as a preference. With pressure on all the giant companies moving them toward a standards-based intercommunications approach, this would make sense, as would the fact that IGMP Snooping supports the Fast-Leave process. Readers should note that IGMP Snooping is enabled by default on both the 2950 and 3550 switches.

Summary

Multicast forwarding is relatively new. Until the growth of applications that required multicast delivery, it was used by service protocols such as "all OSPF routers." Now, many multimedia applications—such as video—and wide distribution applications—such as market data feeds—all require multicast delivery.

We have therefore given a lot of time to understanding the many facets of IP multicast. We started with an overview of multicast and compared it to unicast and broadcast communication, and then discussed how IP addresses were designated as multicast addresses. These layer 3 addresses must be converted to layer 2 MAC addresses using a standard mapping process.

Of course, theoretical knowledge needs to be backed up with an understanding of how to configure multicast on both Cisco routers and switches, because the routers carry the multicast traffic over the internetwork and the switches deliver it to the multicast hosts. The syntax of the commands is straightforward, but you need to ensure that the network is properly planned before starting the implementation. Care needs to be taken when considering the IGMP version to be used, for example.

When considering the multicast distribution, you need to select between PIM DM, PIM SM, and CBT. All three are independent protocols that use tree distribution to manage multicast data delivery in a network, but all three affect the network operation in different ways and require different configurations.

Exam Essentials

Know the difference between IGMP and IGMPv2 and IGMPv3. IGMPv1 and IGMPv2 are very similar. The major difference is that IGMPv2 has a message that the client sends when it doesn't want to receive the multicast stream anymore. The result of this small difference is that they don't work well together, and it makes sense for you to have only one version running. IGMPv3 is better still and supports extras such as SSM, but because it is very new, you have to make sure that all the hosts in your network support the Leave message

The Catalyst switch can listen for client Leave messages with both CGMP and IGMP Snooping. A switch configured for CGMP can listen for IGMPv2 and v3 Leave messages by being configured with the command `set cgmp leave enable`. A switch configured for IGMP Snooping can be configured for IGMP Fast-Leave processing with the command `set igmp fastleave enable`.

Know the difference between CGMP and IGMP Snooping. Although both CGMP and IGMP Snooping allow a switch to get involved in a multicast stream, they are very different protocols. CGMP is a Cisco proprietary protocol communication based on communication between a router and any attached switches. Routers receiving IGMP packets from other routers forward specific information to appropriate switches containing information on multicast memberships.

IGMP Snooping enables the switch to learn information from watching IGMP packets go through the switch. IGMP is an Internet standard. Snooping is being considered by the IETF as a standard and is currently in draft. Remember that snooping can't be enabled if CGMP is enabled, so you first need to make sure that CGMP is turned off. Next, enable IGMP Snooping with the `ip igmp snooping` command.

Know the difference between the multicast routing protocols. There are several options for routing multicast traffic. DVMRP is a distance-vector-based routing protocol, and MOSPF uses OSPF, but neither is the recommended method of doing multicast routing with Cisco equipment. Cisco recommends that PIM be used to route multicast streams because it learns from the pre-existing routing protocol. This means that EIGRP can be used to route multicast information.

PIM has two broad modes: sparse and dense. In dense-mode PIM, each router is automatically included in the multicast table and has to prune itself off if no clients need the stream. Sparse mode assumes no routers wish to participate. Routers are added as connected clients request access to the multicast streams, and a special router is used as the base for the entire tree. This router—a rendezvous point—needs to be referenced in each multicast router's configuration. Use the command `rp pim ip-address` *`ip_address`* to define the IP address of the rendezvous point.

Know how to troubleshoot your multicast setup. There are many `show` commands that can be done on the router and switch to show communication, but you still need to test the transport. You can use the `ping` command to reach out and touch a particular multicast IP address. If you want to do a traceroute, use the command `mtrace`.

Quality of Service (QoS)

THE CCNP EXAM TOPICS COVERED IN THIS CHAPTER INCLUDE THE FOLLOWING:

- ✓ Describe the needs of isochronous voice traffic on a switched data network.
- ✓ Understand QoS solutions to voice quality issues such as jitter and delay.
- ✓ Configure QoS features on multilayer switched networks.
- ✓ Describe the general design models for switched networks requiring integrated IP telephony.
- ✓ Plan the implementation of QoS features in a multilayer switched network.
- ✓ Configure router redundancy using HSRP and VRRP, and verify operation.
- ✓ Explain how both hardware and software redundancy is achieved in a multilayer switched network.
- ✓ Understand the general design models for switched networks requiring integrated IP telephony.
- ✓ Understand transparent LAN services and explain their use in service provider networks.
- ✓ Configure load balancing using GLBP and SLB, and verify operation.
- ✓ Implement QoS features in a multilayer switched network.

Quality of service (QoS) is a largely new concept to bring into the world of LANs. Traditional Ethernet networks have been constructed on base protocols that allow for best efforts delivery and little else. Legacy switched networks—if you will pardon the term—have been designed and built using the same principles. After all, Ethernet suffers from collisions, broadcasts are LAN-wide random events, and frame sizes are unpredictable. All of this pretty much guarantees that quality of service will also have some random aspects, doesn't it?

Well, maybe not. Over the last few years, considerable effort has been applied to the development of techniques designed to provide the Internet Protocol (IP) with some added bells and whistles. Many of these are associated with providing quality of service beyond the traditional best efforts capabilities of IP in order to make the Internet a better place for the transport of time-sensitive traffic such as voice, video, and multimedia applications.

Once these developments started to bear fruit, much of the effort shifted away from IP toward the edges of the networks. The idea is that if we can somehow create QoS-based switched networks in the campus, then it might be possible to create end-to-end QoS provision from LAN to LAN across the Internet.

This chapter deals primarily with the QoS options currently available on Cisco switches. We will have to start, however, with some detail about the QoS options in IP, so we can see how they may also be employed in multilayer switched networks and how the layer 3 and layer 2 QoS options map together at the campus edge.

The last section of this chapter, "Redundancy in Switched Networks," looks at redundancy in several of its implementations, including router redundancy and server redundancy. Although these techniques may not normally be considered QoS protocol, they do nonetheless add to the general availability of network services. The chapter ends with a brief discussion of one of the more interesting technologies to emerge from the new-look Ethernet—transparent Ethernet.

Understanding Application Needs

Understanding the needs of different applications is the key to developing an understanding of the many factors contributing to the selection of the most appropriate QoS options. Obviously, there are an enormous number of applications in use, but we can use some basic categories to define their needs and expectations in general terms.

One method is to define applications using some sort of classification and then apply QoS based on specific classes. I have selected three applications to illustrate this principle—e-mail, World Wide Web traffic, and voice over Ethernet—each of which possesses different characteristics.

E-mail

A number of different e-mail packages exist on the market today, and all have idiosyncrasies of some sort. Nonetheless, the basic method of operation (from the perspective of the bottom layers of the OSI model) is very similar in all cases.

E-mail uses a store-and-forward transfer mechanism, gaining its reliability from the TCP protocol. Data is formatted by the application and by TCP and IP into a reliable sequence of datagrams (packets) that are individually transmitted to the server or e-mail client. Little in the way of QoS needs to be applied to e-mail, largely because the users and the application both agree that this is not an instantaneous protocol.

Figure 20.1 shows e-mail packets traversing a network, comprising an e-mail message traveling from host Terry to host Stephanie. The message is fragmented into packets that are sent across the intervening internetwork and then are reassembled at the destination by the application. Because e-mail is designed from the top down to be a store-and-forward (rather than real-time) application, greater emphasis was placed on guaranteed delivery than on delay, and so each packet will be of the maximum size permitted by the media.

FIGURE 20.1 E-mail application fragments

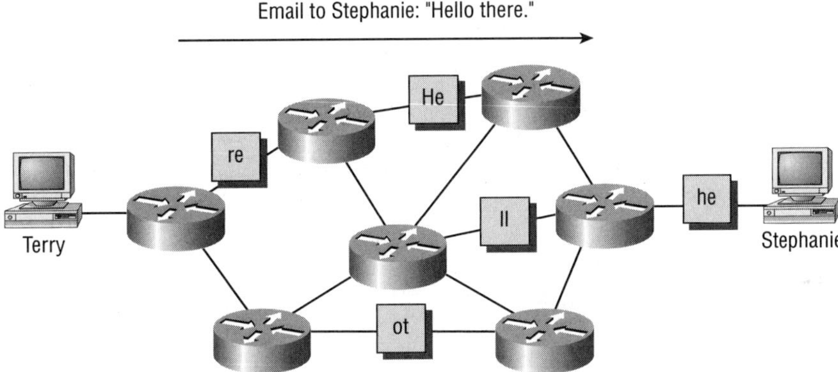

Obviously, if the delay in packet delivery became so large that users complained and the system became unusable, then something would have to be done, but given the reliability of TCP, this would generally only occur if network utilization was excessive.

WWW Traffic

All WWW traffic starts from somewhere, so assuming that you are connecting to the Web via your LAN, that's the first place where problems can affect the connection and the upload or download speed.This is just a small part of the story, however. The weakest link in a chain always sets the strength for the whole chain, and the same is true of networks. So as far as transfer speed is concerned, we need to spend most of our time working on the narrowest bandwidth (generally the lowest speed). And that is unlikely to be the switched Ethernet LAN.

After all, your LAN is probably running 100BaseT, switched, possibly with duplex links to important machines. The connection to the Internet is probably through the company firewall (a packet-filtering engine introducing its own delay), and the Internet speed itself available to your PC is probably be a fraction of an E-1 or T-1 at best!

Obviously, if the service runs too slowly to be of use, and if you can identify the switched Ethernet LAN that you are connected to as the choke point, then you need to do something about it. But for the moment, let's leave the problems with WWW to the WAN guys.

What is important to us is that the size of each WWW packet may be different. Even though we tend to equate being connected to a website as having a single flow, that is rarely true. The construction of modern websites and the surfing behavior of Internet users means that TCP sessions are being opened and closed all the time, and the download of different format content ensures that the service is very patchy (see Figure 20.2).

FIGURE 20.2 HTTP application fragments

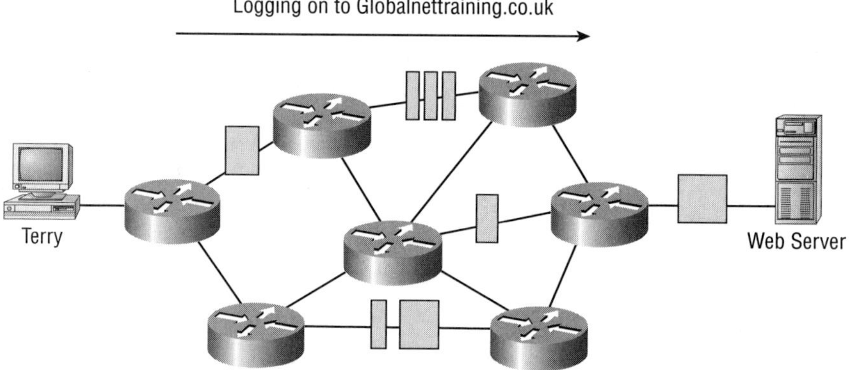

Voice over Ethernet

Now, at last, something that we can really get our teeth into! Voice traffic is very unusual, in that it presents an entirely different set of demands to an Ethernet LAN. We are all used to the usual pressures from applications—namely bandwidth and delay—but jitter is a new problem for us. In short, jitter is the variation in the delay experienced by successive packets in a flow.

Voice is a streaming protocol. As the analog signal is encoded and broken down into packets, each packet is transmitted across the network as a unique entity, and the whole is reassembled into a stream at the receiving end. Obviously, humans don't speak in packets, and we take pauses and breaks at random moments, uttering words when we need to. If the packets received at the end of the link are delayed too long, or if the delay is too variable for the decoder, then the voice stream cannot be properly reconstructed.

There is a name for this transmission type: *isochronous*. Derived from the Greek words for "equal" and "time," it describes processes that require timing to be coordinated. In other words, isochronous traffic requires that data flow continuously and at a steady rate in close timing with the ability of the display mechanism to receive and display the image data. Figure 20.3 demonstrates how jitter can affect the output of the playback buffers.

As you can see, the possibility exists for the playback buffer to be empty, full, or half-full. If the buffer is half-full, then a smoothly created output audio signal will result in good quality voice reception.

If the buffer is empty, then no audio signal output can be created; this is not a problem if the reason for the empty buffer is a genuine lack of transmitted data. But if the buffer is full, then there may be a problem. First, any new arriving packets will be dropped, and time is insufficient for them to be retransmitted, so they are lost forever. This, however, may not be the largest problem, because if the reason for the buffer alternating between full and empty is a variability in the arrival rate of voice-encapsulated data packets, then the output stream will be of poor quality.

Jitter is probably of greater significance than simple delay in voice networks, because (up to a certain limit) delay just means that the receiver has to wait a short time for the words. But jitter results in poor quality voice reception that may be unacceptable to the listener. Figure 20.4 illustrates a general design model for multimedia traffic, showing how voice will be integrated into the IP infrastructure. Obviously, we're focusing on the campus network, but you can see clearly that as IP datagrams carry voice into the IP cloud, inconsistencies start to appear in the delivery process.

FIGURE 20.3 Voice playback buffers

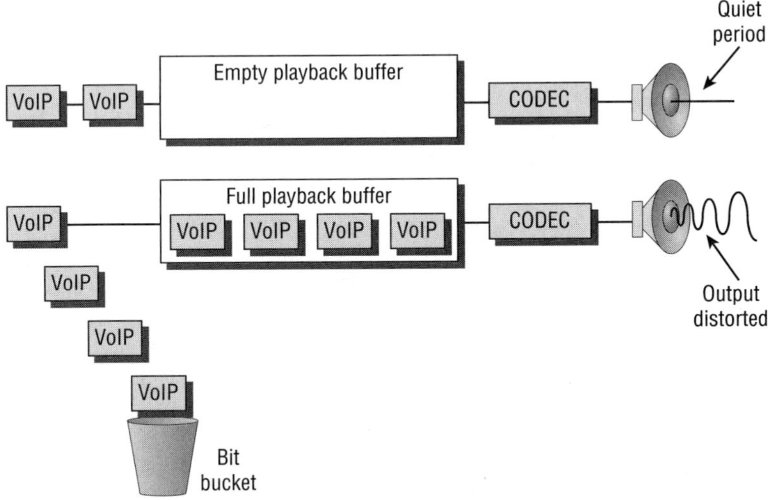

FIGURE 20.4 Voice design model

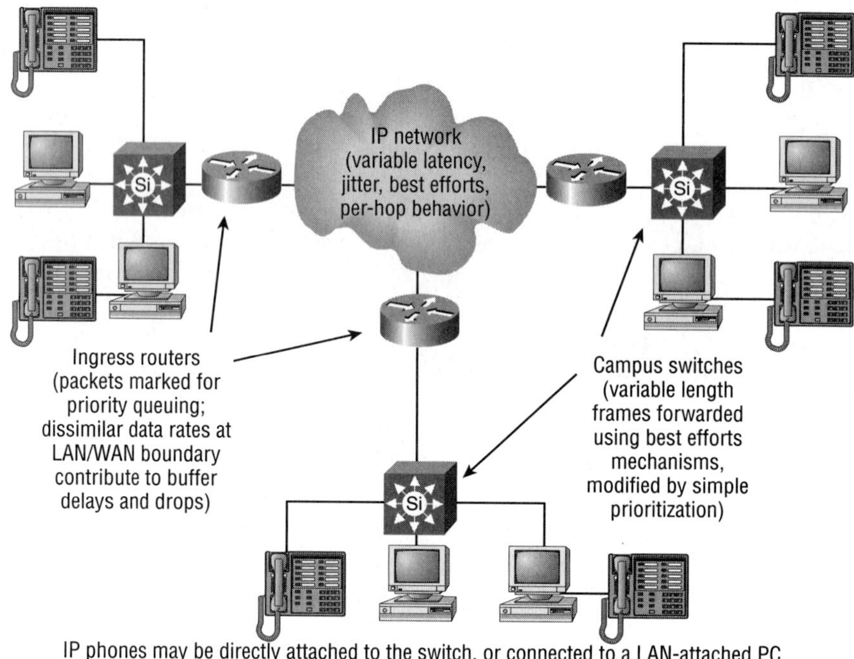

Understanding the Fundamentals of QoS

In order to fully understand QoS, there are a few changes we need to apply to our common mindset regarding network traffic. We need to consider the mechanisms behind our existing traffic forwarding, usually comprising a combination of connectionless and connection-oriented delivery, per-hop router/switch forwarding, and FIFO (first in, first out) queuing. We need to review what we know about networks where no QoS features are added to the basic protocol activity. These networks are called best efforts networks.

Best Efforts Networks

In a *best efforts network*, as illustrated in Figure 20.5, data is transmitted in the hope (an expectation) that it will be delivered. It's similar to the mail system. You write your letter, address it, and put it in the mailbox. And that's it. You hope (and expect) that it will be delivered, but it's out of your control. If something goes wrong with the system, your mail is undelivered. And you may not even know that it failed to get through!

FIGURE 20.5 Best efforts packets

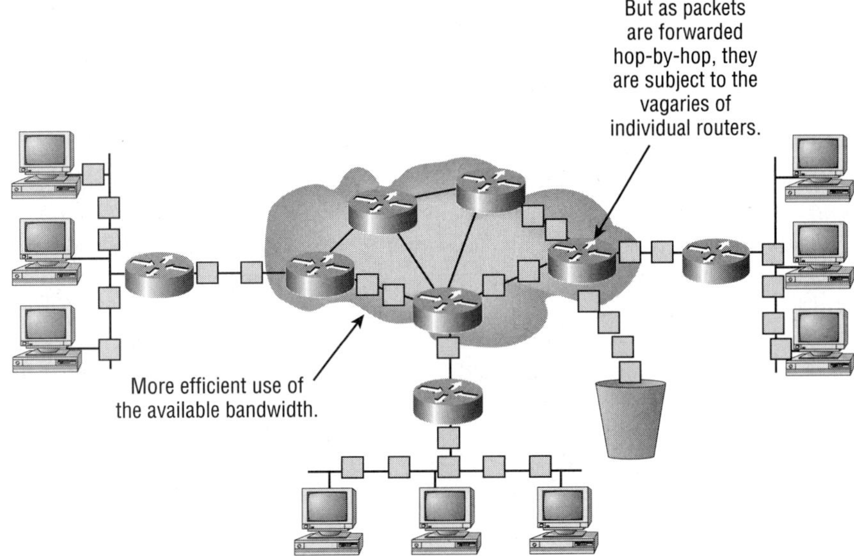

Of course, if the mail system were truly unreliable, you would complain loudly and eventually stop using it, so it can't be all that bad or it wouldn't still exist. But because there is no reliability built in, we refer to it as unreliable.

Under these circumstances, there are two choices open to us. We can either live with the unreliability, or try to do something about it.

Connection-Oriented Transport

One thing we could do is ask for a receipt to be signed at the far end so that we know it got through. This would make our system more reliable, but obviously the service would not be free, because there is greater overhead and therefore greater cost. In IP networks, we use TCP (Transport Control Protocol) to handle that receipting process for us, and we call those receipts acknowledgments. And it isn't free, because we have to wait for a packet to be acknowledged before we can send the next one, and that slows down the data throughput.

So in order to work properly, both the sequence number and the acknowledgment numbers must be synchronized at the start of the data transfer. In fact, other additional parameters also need to be set at this time, and so TCP has a complex process to initiate the data transfer, called the *connection sequence*.

In a way, this puts us on the road to QoS-based networks, because we have at least guaranteed that our data will be delivered. Now we have to deal with all of the other issues surrounding how it will be delivered.

Connectionless Transport

Sometimes the need for reliable data transfer is overridden by another, more pressing requirement. If the protocol in question uses broadcasts to deliver its data, then we cannot reasonably expect acknowledgments. It's bad enough that every station on the segment is interrupted by the original broadcast, without compounding the felony! Protocols such as RIP (Routing Information Protocol), the ubiquitous routing protocol) operate like this, resending their data at regular intervals to ensure that data gets through.

Another family of protocols that remain connectionless are the multicasts. Multicast traffic (as we know from Chapter 19, "Understanding and Configuring Multicast Operation") is delivered to stations that have joined a particular multicast group. Once again, it would be unreasonable to expect acknowledgments from such a potentially large receiver group, but there are additional factors.

Multicast streams often contain either time-sensitive or streaming information. In either case, the delays associated with acknowledgments would be unacceptable, interfering with the flow of the data.

Streaming Transport

There is one other option. Multicast traffic may not be acknowledged, but that is no reason for us to abandon all efforts to deliver the data in the sequence in which it was transmitted.

Real-Time Protocol (RTP) is one option to assist us here. RTP runs over UDP and provides both sequence information and a timestamp for each datagram. Although this in itself doesn't provide any service guarantees, it does mean that the receiver can make adjustments by changing the order of packet arrival to restore simple out-of-sequence deliveries, and packets arriving too late for insertion into the stream decoders can be ignored.

Common Problems in Best Efforts Networks

Best efforts networks attempt to deliver packets, but they are characterized by a variety of conditions that interfere in some way with forwarding data.

Simple Delay

Simple delay causes packets to arrive later than might be expected. There are several contributing factors to simple delay:

Laws of physics delay The *laws of physics delay* is caused by the fact that data cannot be propagated through either copper or fiber instantaneously, or even at anything like the speed of light. In fact, about 60 percent of light speed in copper, and not much faster in fiber, is the norm. The good news is that this delay is standard.

Data traveling across copper for a distance of 100 meters takes about 0.5 microseconds to arrive. This might seem very small, almost insignificant. But for data traveling at 100Mbits/second, this is a delay of about 50 bits!

Serialization delay *Serialization delay* is caused by store-and-forward devices such as switches and routers having to place data onto an outgoing interface. The greater the interface speed, the less time it takes to place the bits on the interface. So, the higher the speeds, the less serialization delay. This is obviously unpredictable, because varying frame/packet sizes will result in different delays.

Processing delay *Processing delay* is caused by the router or switch having to make a forwarding decision. This is again variable and unpredictable, because it may depend upon the processing overhead on that device at the moment of search, the internal buffer architecture and load, internal bus load, and the searching algorithm in use. There may be some statistically measurable average, but that's no good for individual packets.

Output buffer priorities *Output buffer priorities* are the final stage of the delay. Should a buffer become full, then the mechanism for discarding may be simple tail-drop, or something more complex such as Random Early Discard. And if the queuing method is FIFO, then that favors larger frames/packets, whereas if we implement sophisticated queuing, we must always remember that putting one data stream at the front of the queue is bound to result in another stream being at the back.

There are other components contributing to the total delay, but for the purposes of the BCMSN exam, they can be ignored. A quick search for "serialization delay" on the Web, however, reveals several educational sites with further information for the adventurous reader.

Jitter

Jitter is what happens when packets arrive either earlier or later than expected, outside established parameters for simple delay. The effect is to interfere with the smooth playback of certain types of streaming traffic (voice, video, and so on), because the playback buffers are unable to cope with the irregular arrival of successive packets. Jitter is caused by variations in delay, such as the following:

Serialization delay Serialization delay can cause jitter, with subsequent packets being of different sizes. One technique that might be used to standardize this delay would be to make all frames the same size, irrespective of their data content. This is the method used by Frame Relay using the FRF.11 (for voice) recommendation, and by ATM. This solution is good for voice but bad for data, because of the overhead created by increasing the number of frames per packet.

Serialization delay is simple to calculate using the formula bits in the packet or the frame/data rate of the interface. Thus, a 1518-byte frame transmitted out of a 10Mbits/second Ethernet interface takes 1.2 milliseconds. Just for the record, I have also heard serialization delay referred to as insertion delay.

Queue disposition *Queue disposition* can affect delay, because while packets at the front of the queue may have constancy of delay, packets further back are behind an unknown number of frames/packets at the front, giving rise to variability. Cisco provides a number of different queuing options, allowing the most appropriate to be selected on a case-by-case basis.

Per-hop routing *Per-hop routing* behavior can affect delay variably, because subsequent packets may travel to the same destination via different paths due to routing changes.

Packet Loss

Packet loss may seem to be the most important issue, but that is often not the case. If packet loss occurs in connection-oriented services, then the lost packet will be requested and retransmitted. This may be annoying if it slows down the data transfer too much, but connection-oriented applications are built to manage this problem. Nonetheless, this is seen by ISPs as being a large problem, because it results in packets being retransmitted with smaller TCP windows, thus causing a positive feedback circuit.

In a connectionless network, once lost, the data is gone forever. If the loss exceeds certain parameters (which are different for each application), then the application will be deemed unusable and terminated either by the user (quality too poor) or by the application itself. This may not be a problem at lower values—voice, for example, may just sound less clear, as in a noisy analog circuit. In either case, the user and application are exposed to the poor quality with the resulting dissatisfaction regarding the network. Packet loss can occur in a number of places, with each location introducing loss in a different way:

Line loss *Line loss* is usually caused by data corruption on unacknowledged links. Corrupted packets may fail a checksum and are discarded, but are not scheduled for retransmission. In a well-designed Ethernet network, this should be a rare occurrence.

Buffer overflows *Buffer overflows* occur when network devices are too busy internally, or when the output network is congested. The key to managing buffer overflows lies in early detection of the problem and careful application throttling.

Discard eligible *Discard eligible* packets are flagged to be deliberately dropped when congestion occurs on Frame Relay and ATM networks. There is no exactly comparable process with Ethernet LANs, but if we establish traffic classes in order to create priorities, then it follows that those frames in the lowest priority traffic streams run the risk of being dropped more frequently as network congestion occurs.

QoS Options

Obviously, the ultimate quality of service would be if we were able to guarantee that every packet/frame on the network were delivered reliably, in the correct sequence, and with zero delay. Well, guess what? That's not going to happen! But a variety of techniques can be applied to try to get close enough to the end of the rainbow to allow the applications to manage the rest themselves.

The following parameters are considered essential for measuring and providing any QoS:

- Service availability
- Frame loss
- Frame order
- Frame duplication
- Transit delay experienced by frames
- Frame lifetime
- Undetected frame error rate
- Maximum service data unit size supported
- User priority
- Throughput

Two main mechanisms exist for dealing with end-to-end QoS: *Differentiated Services* and *Integrated Services*. Both are contenders for the ultimate solution, but we will focus on Differentiated Services because that's what Cisco uses with Ethernet.

The Integrated Services model involves setting up an end-to-end connection across an internetwork of RSVP-enabled routers using a new IP-based signaling protocol called Resource Reservation Setup Protocol (RSVP). RSVP routers request and reserve bandwidth across an internetwork and release it back to the internetwork after the connection is terminated.

The Differentiated Services Model

The QoS implementation in Catalyst switches is based on the Differentiated Services (DiffServe) architecture. This reference model states that packets are marked (classified) at the entry point into the network, and that every subsequent router or switch, implementing hop-by-hop forwarding, uses the *classification* to try to match the forwarding process to the classification. This is achieved by each DiffServe router in the path having a locally configured queuing priority for forwarding marked packets. Non-DiffServe-enabled routers will simply forward packets based upon default queues. Figure 20.6 shows the DiffServe architecture, with routers in the end-to-end path either being in the domain or without. The entry point to the domain is called the ingress, and the exit point is called the egress.

At layer 3, this classification and marking is established by setting bits in the IP Type of Service (TOS) field to differing values. At layer 2, however, this is a little more difficult, because there are no fields inside legacy Ethernet available for this purpose. Even so, there are some clever mechanisms that allow us to map layer 2 priorities to layer 3.

The basic QoS model underlying all efforts is closely related to the DiffServe architecture. Shown in Figure 20.7, it consists of a series of discrete stages. First, the packets are classified and tested to see if they conform to the configured classification. This stage is called *policing*.

FIGURE 20.6 Differentiated Services model

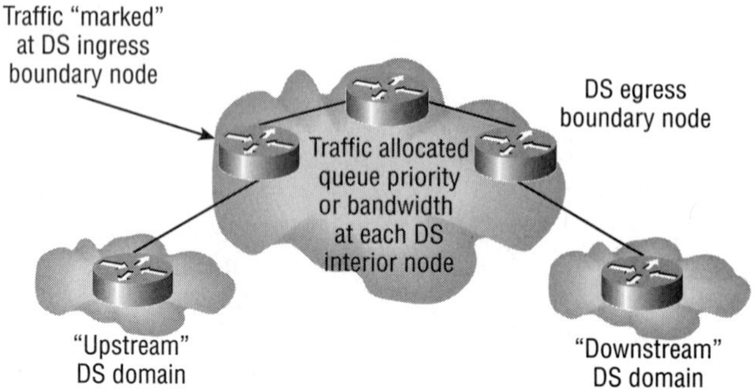

Next, the packet is marked and forwarded to the DiffServe network, where the marking will be used to set priorities in queues and establish any other forwarding rules before reaching the egress point. The last router or switch in the path forwards the data to the target client according to locally configured rules.

It is not a condition of basic IP that routers understand the TOS or DS fields. Non-DiffServe routers in a path will treat the IP datagram in the same way as all other datagrams, forwarding it in a best efforts fashion. This is quite useful, because it means that DiffServe is easy to implement in phases on a network.

DiffServe uses some specific bits in the IP header to mark the service class required. All DiffServe routers understand these settings, and administrators are responsible for configuring router queues in such a way as to best meet the needs of the specific traffic class. The DiffServe field is part of the IP header, which is extended and changed slightly from the original TOS field.

The original IPv4 TOS field was defined years ago in RFC 791, when nobody had any idea how the Internet and its applications would pan out. This single octet has three bits of Precedence configurable as a group, providing seven levels of Precedence. In addition, a further four, individually configurable, bits are available to request one of four types of service, with one bit unused (which must be zero):

- Minimize delay
- Maximize throughput
- Maximize reliability
- Minimize monetary

A replacement header field, called the DS field, is defined in RFC 2474, which is intended to supersede the existing definition. Six bits of the DS field are used as a Differentiated Services Code Point (DSCP) to select the Per-Hop Behavior (PHB) a packet experiences at each node. A two-bit currently unused (CU) field is reserved. All six bits must be tested by DiffServe-compliant routers.

FIGURE 20.7 Basic QoS model

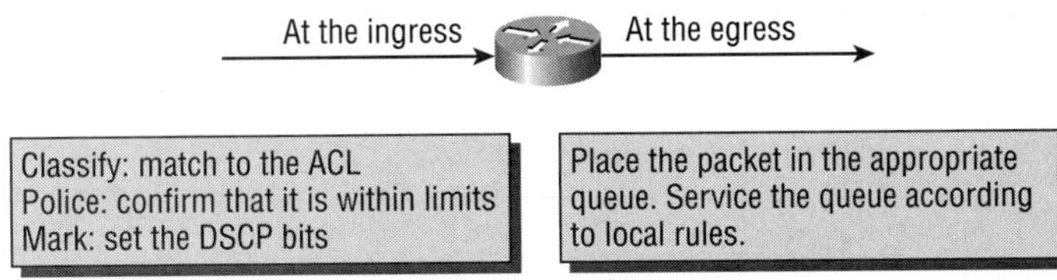

There is no backward compatibility with the TOS fields, but the implementation of one does not prevent implementation of the other. In either case, the actual forwarding mechanism applied by each router in the path is established by local configuration of queues and priorities and is likely to be proprietary, so routers could forward along planned paths according to either TOS or DS bits.

In order to classify packets, we need to determine some traffic types to use as templates. Table 20.1 defines traffic types.

TABLE 20.1 Differentiated Services Traffic Types

Traffic Type	Characteristics of Traffic Needs
Network control	High requirement to get through to maintain and support the network infrastructure
Voice	Less than 10 milliseconds delay
Video	Less than 100 milliseconds delay
Controlled load	Important applications
Excellent effort	Best efforts for important users
Best effort	Ordinary LAN priority
Background	Bulk transfers, games, and so on

IEEE 802.1p

The *IEEE 802.1p* standard defines important methods for traffic class expediting and dynamic multicast filtering, thus providing QoS at the MAC level. This standard may be considered an extension to the 802.1Q standard discussed in Chapter 14, "VLANs, Trunks, and VTP." Three bits are allocated inside the 802.1Q insert that were unspecified at the time, but have been allocated by 802.1p.

802.1p establishes eight levels of priority that are conceptually similar to the three bits specified by IP Precedence. Layer 2 switches can prioritize data in their output buffers according to these priority bits, and many layer 3 switches are capable of "mapping" the 802.1p Precedence to the TOS or DiffServe fields inside IP so as to achieve end-to-end QoS across integrated switched and routed internetworks.

Applying the QoS Model

The first stage in determining how the switches and routers in the network will prioritize traffic is the classification process. Essentially, the idea is to somehow mark traffic with an indication that it should be treated differently from packets with dissimilar marking.

The second stage is traffic policing. This is the process whereby a switch/router determines whether the frame/packet matches the preconfigured profiles. Packets that exceed specified limits are considered to be nonconforming. The policing process specifies the action to take for packets by either setting bandwidth limits for conforming traffic, or by dropping or remarking nonconforming traffic.

The third stage is to actually mark the frame/packet. Data can be marked at layer 2 (in the 802.1p header) or at layer 3 (inside the IP header), depending upon the device. Switches that operate at layer 3 are able to mark at either layer, but switches operating purely at layer 2 are able to mark only the frame.

So if the switch is a layer 3 switch, we have the option of forwarding a packet with QoS. Then, using the general principles of traffic types, we need to "map" the traffic type to a TOS or DiffServe number. After the packet has been through the classification, policing, and marking processes, it is assigned to the appropriate queue before exiting the switch. If the switch has received the packet inside an 802.3 frame with 802.1p priority specified, this process may be automated. If not, then we must map it manually.

Finally, the packet must be forwarded out of a shared output buffer onto the media toward the next hop. This is usually accomplished by establishing a queuing process and placing traffic into different queues according the policies defined earlier.

Prioritizing Traffic Classes

Traffic marking is normally carried out using mapping commands. There is a wide range of mapping commands in the Cisco IOS, including route-maps (for manipulating route parameters), crypto-maps (for establishing encryption parameters), and others. The ones we are most interested in are the policy-maps and the class-maps.

All IOS maps have some things in common. Maps begin with a `match` command, which unambiguously identifies some form of traffic, at the frame, packet, or even application layers. This would involve the additional use of an access list. Class-maps allow for the matching of an IP address, a protocol, or an incoming interface.

Once traffic has been matched, then the map (sometimes the same map, sometimes a "sister" map, as in the case of policy-maps and class-maps) is used to "set" an attribute. A wide variety of attributes can often be associated with matched traffic in this way, but the policy-map allows only for the setting of the DSCP code point. Figure 20.8 shows where the marking takes place in both the Data Link and Network protocol data units (PDUs).

FIGURE 20.8 Frame and packet marking

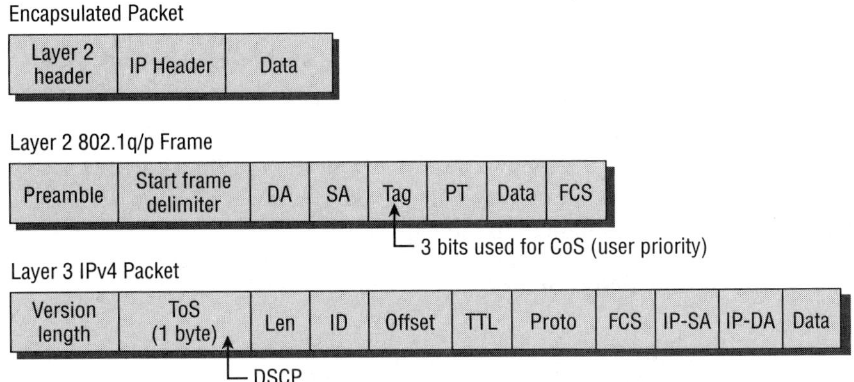

Queuing Mechanisms

A number of different queuing mechanisms exist on Cisco layer 2 and layer 3 switches. The reason for this is that across the globe, different network managers require different prioritization for different networks running a wide variety of legacy, common, and emerging applications. No single queuing mechanism could support these diverse needs, so several mechanisms exist. It is up to the intelligent network administrator to apply the method available for their network that best suits their needs. Here is a short list of the most prevalent methods available across the spectrum of Cisco layer 2 and layer 3 switches:

First in, first out queuing *First in, first out (FIFO)* queuing transmits frames/packets according to the timed arrival of the first bits in the frame/packet at the input interface. This is often the default method.

Weighed fair queuing *Weighed fair queuing (WFQ)* places data into different queues according to a conversation index associated with each packet. The conversation index is a term applied to different applications, whose packets are then marked with a number inside the switch or router. The selection of the data type and queue is internal and proprietary, but results in low-volume interactive traffic (voice) being granted higher priority than high-volume non-interactive traffic (FTP).

Custom queuing *Custom queuing* allows administrators to create up to 16 queues, each with configurable sizes and forwarding thresholds. Data is placed in queues according to access lists, and queues are emptied on a round-robin basis.

Priority queuing *Priority queuing* allows the administrator to create a number of queues and configure the size of each. Data is placed into queues according to access lists, and queues are emptied on a strict priority basis. Packets in the highest priority queue are always transmitted first, and packets in lower priority queues are not transmitted until the queues higher up are emptied.

Weighted round-robin queuing *Weighted round-robin (WRR) queuing* is a simplified version of custom queuing. A fixed number of queues are serviced in round-robin fashion, each being configurable only as to the size of the queue.

Multistage queuing *Multistage queuing* can be implemented on some platforms, and involves the creation of multiple queuing processes in a dependency fashion. For example, a mixture of priority and WFQ could be used.

Figure 20.9 shows how packets arriving at three interfaces at the same time need to be sorted into an output queue to be transmitted serially. Of course, it is in the output queue that we can influence packet delay by arranging how the queue works.

FIGURE 20.9 Queuing overview

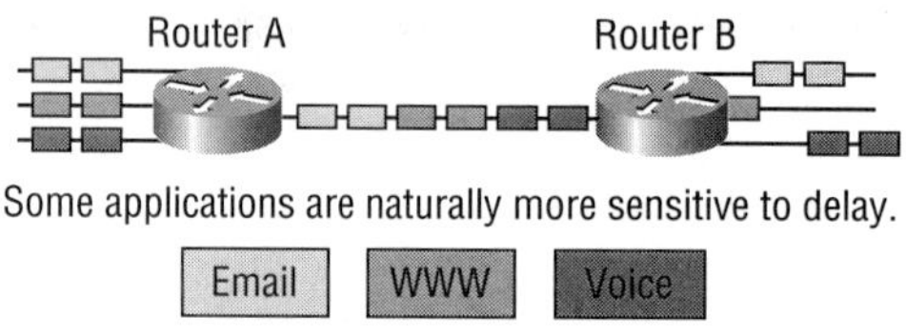
Router A
Router B
Some applications are naturally more sensitive to delay.
Email
WWW
Voice
It makes sense to give those a higher priority in the queues.

Auto-QoS

Obviously, implementing QoS can be an administrative headache. Some configurations have the potential to affect application delivery across a wide spectrum of the network, and without practical skills and experience it's easy to make mistakes. To help administrators build QoS-based networks with the minimum of effort, Cisco has created something called auto-QoS.

Auto-QoS can be used to simplify the deployment of QoS features. Auto-QoS makes certain assumptions about the network design, allowing the switch to prioritize different traffic flows and use the output queues appropriately instead of just using the default QoS behavior of best efforts service from a single queue. Auto-QoS uses the input packet label and traffic type to automatically classify traffic. The switch then uses this classification to place traffic in the appropriate output queue.

One of the main features of auto-QoS is the ability of the switch to identify ports that have IP telephones attached to them and allocate sufficient buffer space to afford the VoIP (Voice over IP) calls the correct QoS. This does not just apply to the ports with the IP phones connected, but also to uplinks that carry the VoIP calls to the next switch. This process is called *trust*.

Trust allows for ports that may carry VoIP traffic (but not actually have IP phones directly connected) to recognize that a packet marked as carrying such a service must be afforded the same QoS as if it were directly connected, and therefore proven to be VoIP. Trust is configured across a QoS domain. Packets are marked only at the ingress to the domain and trusted from there on, obviating the need to mark again at every switch or router.

Trust will be pretty important in the future, when all networks start to use QoS. Obviously, QoS is not going to be free, and ISPs will probably charge more for better QoS on the Internet. It follows that when an arriving packet demands a better QoS because of some bits set in an IP header, we should be certain that we are prepared to agree to those demands; otherwise the system would be open to abuse. Disreputable users would be able to manipulate the DSCP code bits to create higher priorities for web browsing, for example.

Configuring QoS on Cisco Switches

The Cisco range of switches is currently undergoing one of the largest series of changes I have ever seen. As you may know, Cisco became one of the largest switch vendors in the world, partly by buying up some of the best competition. Companies such as Kalpana, Grand Junction, and Catalyst all provided input to the range. The result has been a mixture of operating systems and command-line interfaces that Cisco engineers and technicians have had to learn.

As Cisco standardizes the range into IOS, we are also experiencing an emerging need for something better than best efforts data delivery on our computer networks. The combination of the newer operating systems, new switch architectures, and new application demands means that there is a lot more to learn. Because the process is ongoing, not every Cisco switch will support every QoS feature. And because the IOS now plays such a large part in all this, new versions of the IOS may offer enhancements over previous versions.

This section covers the main commands used in the three current operating system options, CatOS and the standard and enhanced IOS images. But you need to stay up-to-date on this, because a major new IOS revision will almost certainly cause some things to change.

2950 Series Switches

The 2950 switch transmits network traffic in the following fashion: Frames are classified by assigning priority-indexed class of service (CoS) values to them and giving preference to higher priority traffic such as telephone calls.

Each transmit port has a default normal-priority transmit queue and may be configured with up to four additional high-priority transmit queues. Frames in the high-priority queue are forwarded before frames in the normal-priority queue. Frames are forwarded to queues dependent upon the defined priority-to-queue mapping. Queues can be emptied using strict priority queuing or weighted round-robin queuing as desired.

If your 2950 switch is running the standard software image, there are some restrictions on what you can configure. In fact, you are limited to configuring the CoS priorities and the WRR settings. To do this, use the `wrr-queue cos-map` global command to establish the queues, and the `wrr-queue bandwidth` statement to set the queue thresholds if needed:

```
Terry_2950#conf t
Terry_2950(config)#wrr-queue ?
```

```
  bandwidth  Configure WRR bandwidth
  cos-map    Configure cos-map for a queue
Terry_2950(config)#wrr-queue cos-map ?
  <1-4>  enter cos-map queue id (1-4)
Terry_2950(config)#wrr-queue cos-map 1 ?
  <0-7>  cos values separated by spaces (up to 8 values total)
Terry_2950(config)#wrr-queue cos-map 1 0 1
Terry_2950(config)#wrr-queue cos-map 2 2 3
Terry_2950(config)#wrr-queue cos-map 3 4 5
Terry_2950(config)#wrr-queue cos-map 4 6 7
Terry_2950(config)#wrr-queue bandwidth 10 20 30 40
Terry_2950(config)#
Terry_2950#
```

If your switch has the enhanced image, you will be able to carry out classification and marking in addition to being able to perform DSCP mapping.

The following example will identify a particular traffic stream, identified by MAN address, and associate a DiffServe value with it. First, we need to establish the way that we will identify the traffic to be classified. Use the `class-maps` *name* global command to define the match criteria when classifying traffic:

```
Terry_2950(config)# class-map terry1
Terry_2950(config-cmap)# match access-group 701
Terry_2950(config-cmap)# exit
```

There is a selection of match options inside a class map:

```
Terry_2950(config-cmap)#match ?
  access-group      access group
  input-interface   Select an input interface to match
  mpls              Multi Protocol Label Switching values
  protocol          Protocol
  <cr>
```

In this example, we will use an access list in conjunction with the class-map to clearly identify the traffic to be classified:

```
Terry_2950(config)#access-list 701 permit 0011.2345.6789 00aa.1234.5678
```

Finally, we need to determine what the classification will be. Use the global configuration command `policy-map` *name* to determine the classification criteria to be set for incoming traffic:

```
Terry_2950(config)#policy-map macpolicy1
Terry_2950(config-pmap)#class terry1
```

```
Terry_2950(config-pmap-c)#set ip dscp 56
Terry_2950(config-pmap-c)#exit
Terry_2950(config)#int fa0/1
Terry_2950(config-if)#service-policy input macpolicy1
```

For a full explanation of the differences between the standard and enhanced images available on the 2950 switch range, see Chapter 21, "Catalyst Switch Technologies."

3550 Series Switches

The 3550 supports an entirely greater range of QoS options because of the layer 3 capability of the hardware and the IOS. There is, in fact, a good case for referring to the 3550 as a multiport router with layer 2 capabilities rather than a switch with layer 3 capabilities.

Essentially, the combined layer 2 and layer 3 QoS functionality means that the switch can classify traffic using sophisticated access lists, mark at both layers, forward using either DSCP or 802.1p priority bits, and even translate from one to the other. This combined functionality involves accepting the default mapping that places DSCP traffic into Ethernet frames with a closely related CoS (or maps the IP datagram inside an incoming Ethernet with CoS set to the IP datagram itself as a DSCP). If the defaults are not suitable for your network, you can use an `mls qos-map` command to establish your own translation values.

This large range of options means that we have to restrict ourselves a little, because the subject of QoS as applied by routers and other layer 3 devices is large enough to warrant a book all by itself. In fact, it is one of the core subjects of a new advanced Cisco certification, the CCIP (Cisco Certified Internetwork Professional). So, to stay on target, we will concentrate our efforts on those configurations that are likely to appear on the BCMSN exam.

Configured QoS

To configure QoS on a 3550 switch, first enable QoS globally with the `mls qos` command.

The use of class-maps and policy-maps to define the match and classification criteria for incoming traffic is very similar to the way they are used inside the 2950.

Class-maps can be configured using an extension allowing the matching of either all or any of the criteria specified in the map. To manage this feature, use either the `class-map match-all` or the `class-map match-any` global commands. In addition, the class-map supports matching against a VLAN or a group of up to 30 VLANs. To select this match option, use the `match vlan vlan-list` c-map command.

The following example shows traffic arriving at interface gigabitethernet0/1, sourced from VLAN 66 or being already marked with an IP Precedence of 1, having the DSCP set to 63 at the ingress:

```
Terry_3550(config)#mls qos
Terry_3550(config)#access-list 101 permit ip any any precedence 1
Terry_3550(config)#class-map match any terry2
```

```
Terry_3550(config-cmap)#match access-group 101
Terry_3550(config-cmap)#match vlan 66
Terry_3550(config-cmap)#exit
Terry_3550(config)#policy-map ip_or_VLAN66
Terry_3550(config-pmap)#class terry2
Terry_3550(config-pmap-c)#set ip dscp 63
Terry_3550(config-pmap-c)#exit
Terry_3550(config-pmap)#exit
Terry_3550(config)#interface gigabitethernet0/1
Terry_3550(config-if)#service-policy input ip_or_VLAN66
```

If you are configuring QoS inside a trusted domain and you do not use auto-QoS, then you have to decide what to do about trust. If you wish to trust incoming CoS values, use the interface command `mls qos trust cos` to ensure that the CoS value in received traffic is trusted, and use the `mls qos trust device cisco-phone` command to specify that the Cisco IP phone is a trusted device and ensure that a non-trusted device does not misuse the CoS available. Remember to enable CDP:

```
Terry_3550(config)#int fa0/1
Terry_3550(config-if)#cdp enable
Terry_3550(config-if)#mls qos trust ?
  cos           Classify by packet COS
  device        trusted device class
  dscp          Classify by packet DSCP
  ip-precedence Classify by packet IP precedence
  <cr>
Terry_3550(config-if)# mls qos trust cos
Terry_3550(config-if)# mls qos trust device cisco-phone
Terry_3550(config-if)#^c
```

Because trusted traffic will automatically gain access to the process whereby CoS is mapped to DSCP, there is an option to forward CoS values without changing the existing DSCP (and vice versa) through the switch. This is called pass-through and can be configured for either option:

```
Terry_3550(config-if)# mls qos trust cos pass-through dscp
```

or

```
Terry_3550(config-if)# mls qos trust dscp pass-through cos
```

Auto-QoS

The implementation of auto-QoS simplifies the configuration of switches inside a trusted domain. First, enable QoS in the usual way, with the `mls qos` command:

```
Terry_3550(config)#mls qos
```

Now you have a choice. If the interface has an IP phone directly connected, use the commands shown next:

```
Switch(config)#interface fastethernet0/1
Switch(config-if)#auto qos voip cisco-phone
```

If the interface is not directly connected to an IP phone but is a trusted device, then enter this alternative:

```
Switch(config)#interface gigabitethernet0/1
Switch(config-if)#auto qos voip trust
```

Note that up to release 12.1(14)EA1 of the IOS, auto-QoS configures only the switch for VoIP with Cisco IP phones.

4000 Series Switches

If your 4000 switch has been upgraded to run IOS, then the classification, marking, and forwarding of packets is the same as for the 3550. But when running the legacy CatOS operating system, the QoS options available for the 4000 series switches are relatively unsophisticated. This section describes the CatOS QoS options.

Each transmit port has three possible queues. There is one non-configurable queue, and there are two queues where some configuration is possible. The drop thresholds can be configured, but tail-drop occurs in all cases when the queue is full.

The switch has a default 802.1p CoS of 0 (zero), but this can be changed. In that case, all unmarked frames entering the switch are marked with the specified CoS value. Marked frames cannot be changed.

The default condition is for QoS to be disabled, so first you have to enable QoS on the switch. Take care that any configuration changes are carried out at an appropriate time, because some of them will reset ports, and possibly cause spanning tree instability if the network converges. You can turn on QoS using the `set qos enable` command.

The port type is defined by the number of transmit queues and the number of drop thresholds that are supported on the port. For example, the 2q1t port type supports two transmit queues each with a single configurable drop threshold.

Port types on the Catalyst 4000 are dependent upon the hardware. Use the `show port capabilities` command to find out what port type you are configuring.

To configure the CoS mapping and set the thresholds on a configurable port, use the `set qos map` *`port_type q# threshold# cos cos_list`*. The port type you will already know. You need to decide which threshold to apply to which queue, and the CoS values to map to the specified transmit queue. The following example shows the two queues on a 2q1t port being configured, one with CoS 2-4 and the other with CoS 5-7:

```
Terry_4000> (enable) set qos map 2q1t 1 1 cos 2-4
Terry_4000> (enable) set qos map 2q1t 2 1 cos 5-7
Qos tx priority queue and threshold mapped to cos successfully.
Terry_4000> (enable)
```

To view the QoS configuration, use the `show qos info config` command.

Queuing Mechanisms

In addition to setting the QoS parameters, it is common for devices operating at layer 3 to have to receive and transmit packets, applying simple queuing mechanisms to the forwarding process. The most common of the configurable queuing mechanisms are priority queuing and custom queuing.

Priority Queuing

With *priority queuing,* data is placed into one of four different queues, defined as high, medium, normal, and low. These queues are emptied on a strict priority basis. Packets in the highest priority queue are always transmitted first, and packets in lower priority queues are not transmitted until the queues with higher priorities are emptied.

Configuration options available to the administrator include how to define the traffic, what queue to place the traffic into, and how large each queue should be. To define the traffic for a particular priority queue, use the `priority-list` global command:

```
Terry_3550(config)#priority-list 1 ?
  default      Set priority queue for unspecified datagrams
  interface    Establish priorities for packets from a named interface
  protocol     priority queueing by protocol
  queue-limit  Set queue limits for priority queues

Terry_3550(config)#priority-list 1 protocol ?
  arp            IP ARP
  bridge         Bridging
  cdp            Cisco Discovery Protocol
  compressedtcp  Compressed TCP
  ip             IP

Terry_3550(config)#priority-list 1 protocol ip ?
  high
  medium
  normal
  low
```

```
Terry_3550(config)#priority-list 1 protocol ip high ?
  fragments  Prioritize fragmented IP packets
  gt         Prioritize packets greater than a specified size
  list       To specify an access list
  lt         Prioritize packets less than a specified size
  tcp        Prioritize TCP packets 'to' or 'from' the specified port
  udp        Prioritize UDP packets 'to' or 'from' the specified port
  <cr>

Terry_3550(config)#priority-list 1 prot ip high list ?
  <1-199>      IP access list
  <1300-2699>  IP expanded access list
Terry_3550(config)#^Z
Terry_3550#
```

To define the maximum queue size for a particular priority queue, use the `priority-list` *`priority-queue`* `queue-limit` global command:

```
Terry_3550(config)#priority-list 1 ?
  default      Set priority queue for unspecified datagrams
  interface    Establish priorities for packets from a named interface
  protocol     Priority queueing by protocol
  queue-limit  Set queue limits for priority queues

Terry_3550(config)#priority-list 1 queue-limit ?
  <0-32767>  High limit
Terry_3550(config)#priority-list 1 queue-limit 5000
Terry_3550(config)#^Z
Terry_3550#
```

Allocating the priority queue to a particular outgoing interface is achieved using the `priority-list` *`priority-queue`* interface command:

```
Terry_3550(config)#int fastEthernet 0/1
Terry_3550(config-if)#priority-group 1
Terry_3550(config)#^Z
Terry_3550#
```

It is common to make the queue sizes increasingly larger as the priority decreases. Naturally, packets in the lowest priority queue stand a statistically greater chance of spending more time in the queue, and it makes sense to allow the packets somewhere to wait.

The following configuration uses access list 101 to place Telnet traffic between any two hosts into the high-priority queue, uses access list 102 to place web traffic between any two hosts into the medium-priority queue, and places all other IP traffic into the normal-priority queue, while CDP traffic is placed into the low-priority queue. The list is applied to interface FastEthernet 0/24:

```
Terry_3550(config)#priority-list 1 prot ip high list 101
Terry_3550(config)#priority-list 1 prot ip medium list 102
Terry_3550(config)#priority-list 1 prot ip normal
Terry_3550(config)#priority-list 1 protocol cdp low
Terry_3550(config)#access-list 101 permit tcp any any eq telnet
Terry_3550(config)#access-list 102 permit tcp any any eq www
Terry_3550(config)#int fastEthernet 0/24
Terry_3550(config-if)#priority-group 1
Terry_3550(config)#^Z
Terry_3550#
```

Custom Queuing

With *custom queuing,* data is placed into one of up to 16 different queues, defined by queue number. These queues are emptied on a strict rotational basis. Once a queue's transmit threshold has been reached, the next queue is serviced, irrespective of whether the current queue still has packets in it.

Configuration options available to the administrator include how to define the traffic, what queue to place the traffic into, how large each queue should be, and how large each queue's service threshold should be.

To define the traffic for a particular custom queue, use the `queue-list` global command:

```
Terry_3550(config)#queue-list ?
  <1-16>  Queue list number

Terry_3550(config)#queue-list 1 ?
  default        Set custom queue for unspecified datagrams
  interface      Establish priorities for packets from a named interface
  lowest-custom  Set lowest number of queue to be treated as custom
  protocol       Priority queueing by protocol
  queue          Configure parameters for a particular queue
  stun           Establish priorities for stun packets

Terry_3550(config)#queue-l 1 interface ?
  Async              Async interface
  BVI                Bridge-Group Virtual Interface
  Dialer             Dialer interface
  FastEthernet       FastEthernet IEEE 802.3
```

```
  GigabitEthernet    GigabitEthernet IEEE 802.3z
  Group-Async        Async Group interface
  Lex                Lex interface
  Loopback           Loopback interface
  Multilink          Multilink-group interface
  Null               Null interface
  Port-channel       Ethernet Channel of interfaces
  Transparent        Transparent interface
  Tunnel             Tunnel interface
  Virtual-Template   Virtual Template interface
  Virtual-TokenRing  Virtual TokenRing
  Vlan               Catalyst Vlans
  fcpa               Fiber Channel

Terry_3550(config)#queue-l 1 interface fastEthernet 0/12 ?
  <0-16>  queue number

Terry_3550(config)#queue-l 1 interface fastEthernet 0/12 1
Terry_3550(config)#queue-l 1 interface fastEthernet 0/13 2
Terry_3550(config)#queue-l 1 interface fastEthernet 0/14 2
Terry_3550(config)#^Z
Terry_3550#
```

To define the maximum queue size for a particular custom queue, use the `queue-list queue-limit` *`queue-number byte-count`* global command:

```
Terry_3550(config)#queue-list 1 ?
  default        Set custom queue for unspecified datagrams
  interface      Establish priorities for packets from a named interface
  lowest-custom  Set lowest number of queue to be treated as custom
  protocol       Priority queueing by protocol
  queue          Configure parameters for a particular queue
  stun           Establish priorities for stun packets

Terry_3550(config)#queue-list 1 queue 1 ?
  byte-count  Specify size in bytes of a particular queue
  limit       Set queue entry limit of a particular queue

Terry_3550(config)#queue-list 1 queue 1 byte-count ?
  <1-16777215>  Size in bytes
```

```
Terry_3550(config)#queue-list 1 queue 1 byte-count 10000 ?
  limit  Set queue entry limit of a particular queue
  <cr>

Terry_3550(config)#queue-list 1 queue 1 byte-count 10000 limit ?
  <0-32767>  Number of queue entries
Terry_3550(config)#queue-list 1 queue 1 byte-count 10000 limit 10
Terry_3550(config)#^Z
Terry_3550#
```

Allocating the priority queue to a particular outgoing interface is achieved using the `custom-queue-list` *`custom-queue`* interface command:

```
Terry_3550(config)#int fastEthernet 0/1
Terry_3550(config-if)#custom-queue-list 1
Terry_3550(config)#^Z
Terry_3550#
```

The following configuration uses access list 101 to place Telnet traffic between any two hosts into queue 1, uses access list 102 to place web traffic between any two hosts into queue 2, and places all other IP traffic into queue 3, while CDP traffic is placed into queue 4. Changing the queue sizes has the effect of "fairly" allocating queue space to traffic:

```
Terry_3550(config)#queue-list 1 protocol ip 1 list 101
Terry_3550(config)#queue-list 1 protocol ip 2 list 102
Terry_3550(config)#queue-list 1 protocol ip 3
Terry_3550(config)#queue-list 1 protocol cdp 4
Terry_3550(config)#access-list 101 permit tcp any any eq telnet
Terry_3550(config)#access-list 102 permit tcp any any eq www
Terry_3550(config)#queue-list 1 queue 1 byte-count 2000 limit 25
Terry_3550(config)#queue-list 1 queue 2 byte-count 5000 limit 20
Terry_3550(config)#queue-list 1 queue 3 byte-count 10000 limit 10
Terry_3550(config)#queue-list 1 queue 4 byte-count 1000 limit 5
Terry_3550(config)#^Z
Terry_3550#
```

The 16 queues are all configurable, but you only need to configure as many as you need or want to. A separate 17th queue is created by the router for use by systems traffic. This queue is not configurable.

Redundancy in Switched Networks

Redundancy is the art of ensuring that even when a component or service fails, network availability remains. This is obviously difficult to achieve in areas of the network where a single point of failure exists. One of the most common single points of failure is the default gateway used by non-routing hosts.

Here is a reminder of the basic IP connection procedure. When an IP host needs to access a second IP host, it knows the three things: its own IP address and mask and the address of the target. Using its own mask, a host decodes the target IP address in what is colloquially known as a *test for adjacency*. If the target host is on the same network, the host ARPs the target IP address directly. If the test for adjacency fails—the target is on a different subnet—then the host must send the data to a router. The most common method used to identify the default gateway is a statically configured default gateway.

Under normal circumstances, if the default gateway is unavailable, the result would be that the host would not receive a reply to an ARP request, would not be able to create Ethernet frames addressed to the default gateway, and would be unable to send data outside the local subnet. Even if a second default gateway were configured on the host, there would be a delay while the host realized that the first default gateway was not going to reply.

There are other ways of allowing a host to find a router. Hosts could run passive RIP, which would allow them to listen to RIP routing updates from local routers and complete a proper routing table. This is common in some Unix implementations, but is slow to converge and can use a lot of memory for the routing tables. The Internet Router Discovery Protocol (IRDP) and IPv6 with its ICMP router discovery hello packets may also be suitable. But most Microsoft Windows machines use the static default gateway configuration.

Cisco's Hot Standby Routing Protocol was designed to provide a solution to this perennial problem.

Hot Standby Router Protocol

The principles behind the Hot Standby Routing Protocol are marvelously simple: Two or more routers are configured in such a way that they act as a sort of cluster, creating a single, virtual router. Hosts are configured to use the address of the virtual router as their default gateway, and the *Hot Standby Routing Protocol (HSRP)* manages the decision-making regarding which router acts as the real default gateway.

Figure 20.10 shows the general layout of an HSRP group, with two routers sharing a standby IP address, and hosts using that address as their default gateway.

Each member of the virtual router cluster can also act as a standard router, as long as all clients wishing to use the (non-virtual) router as their default gateway have the correct configuration—in other words, the standard IP address of the router interface.

FIGURE 20.10 HSRP virtual router

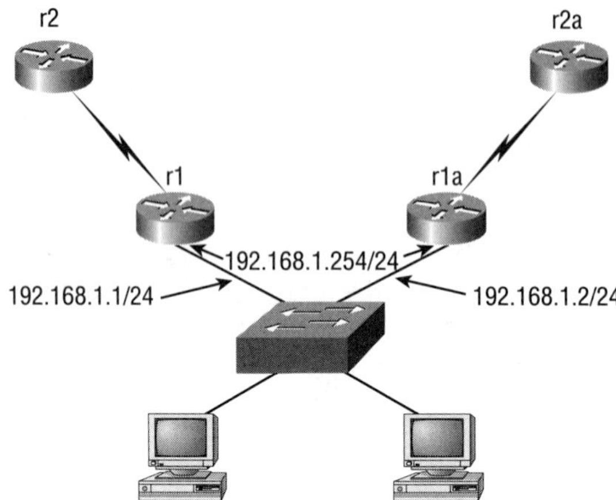

HSRP Operation

Routers assume membership of an HSRP group after being configured with a standby IP address on an Ethernet interface in addition to the regular IP address. All routers in a group are configured with the same standby IP address, and an internal process in each router creates a standby MAC address of 0000.0c07.ac**, where the two stars represent the HSRP group number. (It follows that up to 256 HSRP groups could be configured.)

HSRP routers send hello packets, based on a three-second default timer (configurable, of course), out of this interface, advertising the fact that they are now in a virtual router group. These hello packets contain the group ID of the HSRP group and the advertised priority of the router sending the hello.

Based on a priority system, one router assumes the role of the active router in the group. Other routers will adopt the standby condition. Active routers, on receipt of a packet that needs to be forwarded, will forward the packet. Standby routers will drop the packet, even though they also have a route.

This state remains static as long as the hello packets are continually received from the active router. Should these fail to arrive, then after the hold time has been exceeded, the next senior standby router assumes the active role and starts to forward packets. The default hold timer is 10 seconds, but is configurable.

Figure 20.11 shows the activity of the hello packets as they advertise their priorities on a specific standby group. The diagram shows router Terry sending hellos with a default priority of 100, and router Jack switched off. When router Jack is started, it sends out a hello with the configured priority of 105. Router Terry realizes that it is no longer the active router and now advertises that it is standby. Note that the hellos come from the "natural" Ethernet IP address.

FIGURE 20.11 HSRP hello process

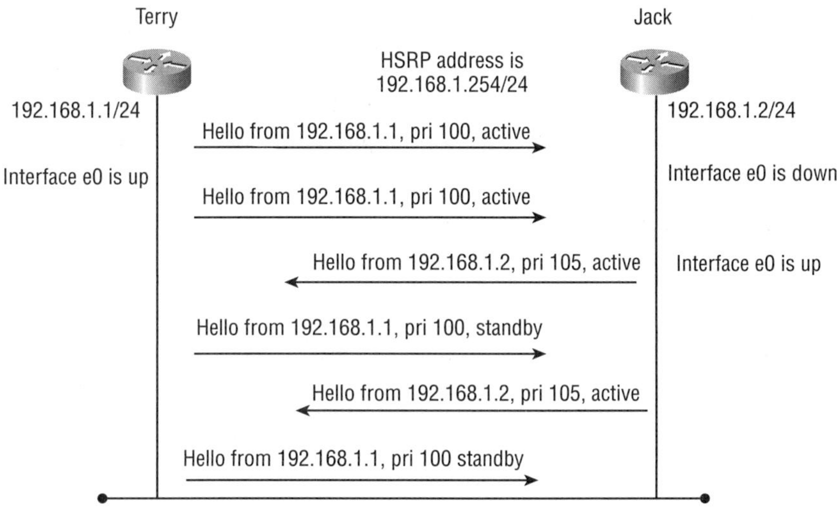

Preemption

Preemption is the process whereby the router with the highest configured priority becomes the active router. In the case of HSRP, the highest priority is the highest number in the range 0–255 (one octet).

The result is that if an active router fails and then comes back online, it is able to take over being the active router once again. Without the preemption process, the standby router that had become active would remain as the active router until a new election process was started.

Interface Tracking

One additional advantage of the preemption process is that it allows the selection of the active router at arbitrary moments on a network without having to wait for formal elections. Thus if a standby router receives a hello from the active router and the active router is lower than its own configured priority, it will preempt and become active itself. By the same process, if an active router receives a hello from a router with a higher priority; it will cease to remain active.

This leads to a rather clever situation where a router can be configured to track another interface, with a view to reducing the standby priority on the standby interface should the other interface fail. There is a default reduction of 10, but this is configurable, allowing for complex scenarios to be created.

Multiple HSRP Groups

Within a group of VLANs, there will be more than one default gateway specified. If the Cisco advice of a subnet per VLAN is followed, then there will be the same number of default gateways.

Redundancy is both expensive and necessary, but we need not create full redundancy by having each default gateway backed up by another physical device. We can use multiple HSRP groups to do this in a more cost-effective fashion. One router could be used to act as the standby router for several different groups.

Furthermore, it is possible to create two groups on a pair of routers, and make each router active in one group and standby in the other. In this way, each router would forward traffic for its own group while providing redundancy to the other, thus providing a kind of load sharing.

Given that this scenario can be expanded to a much larger implementation by creating up to 256 HSRP groups, it follows that some very complex configurations can be created to meet a variety of different needs.

Configuring HSRP

To configure HSRP on a Cisco router, use the `standby ip` *`ip_address`* command in interface configuration mode:

```
Terry_1#conf t
Terry_1(config)#
Terry_1(config)#int e0
Terry_1(config-if)#standby ?
  <0-255>         group number
  authentication  Authentication string
  ip              Enable hot standby protocol for IP
  mac-address     Specify virtual MAC address for the virtual router
  mac-refresh     Refresh MAC cache on switch by periodically sending packet
                  from virtual mac address
  name            Name string
  preempt         Overthrow lower priority designated routers
  priority        Priority level
  timers          Hot standby timers
  track           Priority tracks this interface state
  use-bia         Hot standby uses interface's burned in address

Terry_1(config-if)#standby ip 172.16.1.254
Terry_1(config)#^Z
Terry_1#

Terry_1#show standby
Ethernet0 - Group 0
  Local state is Active, priority 100
  Hellotime 3 holdtime 10
  Next hello sent in 00:00:00.358
  Hot standby IP address is 172.16.1.254 configured
  Active router is local
  Standby router is unknown expired
```

```
  Standby virtual mac address is 0000.0c07.ac00
  2 state changes, last state change 00:03:34
Terry_1#
```

Note that if no HSRP group is specified, the default group of 0 is used, resulting in a standby MAC address of 0000.0c07.ac00 being used.

To configure preemption, use the `standby preempt` command in interface configuration mode:

```
Terry_1#conf t
Terry_1(config)#int e0
Terry_1(config-if)#standby preempt ?
  delay     Wait before preempting
  priority  Priority level
  <cr>

Terry_1(config-if)#standby preempt
Terry_1(config-if)#
Terry_1#
```

Note the options with this command. The `delay` option allows you to specify minimum delay timers prior to a router preempting. The `priority` option allows you to select which router is going to become the active router. The default is 100, and the highest priority wins.

To configure interface tracking, use the `standby track` command in interface configuration mode:

```
Terry_1#conf t
Terry_1(config)#int e0
Terry_1(config-if)#standby track ?
  Async                 Async interface
  BRI                   ISDN Basic Rate Interface
  BVI                   Bridge-Group Virtual Interface
  Dialer                Dialer interface
  Ethernet              IEEE 802.3
  Lex                   Lex interface
  Loopback              Loopback interface
  Multilink             Multilink-group interface
  Serial                Serial
  Tunnel                Tunnel interface
  Virtual-Template      Virtual Template interface
  Virtual-TokenRing     Virtual TokenRing
  Vlan                  Catalyst Vlans
Terry_1(config-if)#
Terry_1#
```

Shown next is the configuration for an active HSRP router, with a priority of 105, tracking interface serial 0, with authentication and modified timers:

```
Terry_1#show run
Building configuration...
!
[output cut]
!
hostname Terry_1
!
interface Ethernet0
 ip address 172.16.1.1 255.255.255.0
 no ip redirects
 standby timers 1 4 advertise 2
 standby priority 105 preempt
 standby authentication globalnet
 standby ip 172.16.1.254
 standby track Serial0
!
interface Serial0
 ip address 172.16.2.1 255.255.255.252
!
[output cut]
!
end
```

The dynamic information on the HSRP group and interface can be seen using the `show standby` command:

```
Terry_1#sho stand
Ethernet0 - Group 0
  Local state is Active, priority 105, may preempt
  Hellotime 1 holdtime 4 configured hellotime 1 secholdtime 4 sec
     advertise 2 secs
  Next hello sent in 00:00:00.004
  Hot standby IP address is 172.16.1.254 configured
  Active router is local
  Standby router is 172.16.1.2 expires in 00:00:03
  Standby virtual mac address is 0000.0c07.ac00
  2 state changes, last state change 00:40:59
  Tracking interface states for 1 interface, 0 up:
    up Serial0
Terry_1#
```

Real World Scenario

HSRP in Action at the ISP Edge

Many Internet service providers (ISPs) use HSRP when providing dual-homed, resilient Internet connections. Border Gateway Protocol (BGP) is perfectly suitable for managing the flow of traffic to the client, and the ISP will certainly be running BGP in any case. But for the client end of the connection, where BGP may not be running and clients demand high-speed responses to link or topology failures, HSRP is a better bet.

An example would be where a customer is dual-homed to an ISP, with connections going from his site to different points of presence (POPs). It is possible to use a single router at the client site to connect both serial links to the client network, but that still leaves the router (in other words, the default gateway) as a single point of failure. Using more than one router makes the connection to the Internet more resilient, but would cause confusion among client PCs if multiple default gateway addresses were needed. HSRP allows the implementation of multiple routers with a common default gateway IP address and an automatic failover. The two HSRP routers would be configured with a common standby IP address as the default gateway, and prioritization used to select the active router and therefore the path taken out of the customer network. Symmetry (ensuring that return packets take the same path, whatever the active HSRP router) is achieved using BGP attribute manipulation. You can learn more about BGP in Part I of this book.

Server Load Balancing

The *Server Load Balancing (SLB)* protocol can be considered an extension to HSRP, which Cisco recommends should be already configured on the switches performing Server Load Balancing. The purpose of SLB is to share the load normally associated with multiple traffic streams terminating on a single server across several servers.

A virtual server represents a cluster of real servers. Clients connect to the virtual address and—according to a load-balancing algorithm—to a selected real server. Obviously, clients and servers need to be on separate LANs or VLANs for SLB to work, because packets have to traverse the SLB switch.

Two different methods of load sharing may be used: weighted round-robin (WRR) and weighted least connections (WLC). WRR specifies the next server to be connected to using a circular selection, modified by a weight that allows more clients to connect to particular servers prior to stepping to the next one. WLC connects to servers based on the number of existing active connections, weighting this with the server capacity, which can be specified.

It is also possible to use SLB to load-share between firewalls, in which case the real group of devices is called a firewalls farm.

Configuring SLB

To configure SLB redundancy on a switch, use the `ip slb serverfarm` *`serverfarm_name`* global command. This will create a new prompt during which you can start to configure the SLB options. You then need to specify the virtual IP address to be used by clients wishing to connect to the servers under SLB control using the `real` *`ip-address`* `[port_number]` command, plus any other options that you want to select. You can configure more servers, but each server entry must be followed by the `inservice` command to enable the preceding server.

The second part of the configuration requires you to enter the global command `ip slb vserver` *`virtual_server-name`*, which changes the prompt again to the mode required to create the virtual IP address. Now you can enter the command `virtual ip-address` *`[network-mask] {tcp | udp} [port-number | wsp | wsp-wtp | wsp-wtls | wsp-wtp-wtls] [service service-name]`* to establish the virtual server IP address. Once again, you need to enter the `inservice` command to enable the specified IP address. Collectively, these commands will create a name for the server farm, associate it with the real IP addresses of the servers, and enable the process.

A basic configuration, providing a virtual IP address of 10.1.1.1 for a group called vserver_one, serving two e-mail servers with real IP addresses of 192.168.1.1 and 192.168.1.2, is as follows:

```
Terry_4840#configure terminal
Enter configuration commands, one per line.  End with CNTL/Z.
Terry_4840#(config)ip slb serverfarm email
Terry_4840#(config-slb-sfarm)real 192.168.1.1
Terry_4840#(config-slb-sfarm)inservice
Terry_4840#(config-slb-sfarm)real 192.168.1.2
Terry_4840#(config-slb-sfarm)inservice
Terry_4840#(config-slb-sfarm)exit
Terry_4840#(config)ip slb vserver vserver_one
Terry_4840#(config-slb-vserver)virtual 10.1.1.1 tcp 25
Terry_4840#(config-slb-vserver)serverfarm email
Terry_4840#(config-slb-vserver)inservice
Terry_4840#(config-slb-vserver)exit
Terry_4840#(config)^z
Terry_4840#
```

SLB Stateful Backup

The most advanced configuration would be to implement SLB in a stateful backup mode. This involves configuring one virtual server group per VLAN, and using HSRP to determine which switch would act as the SLB active device. The configuration of more switches, each one acting as the default for a different VLAN (or VLANs), would mean that load-sharing could be on a per-VLAN basis, with a range of complex possibilities for full redundancy.

Virtual Router Redundancy Protocol

HSRP is a Cisco proprietary protocol, only usable on Cisco devices. Nonetheless, it is such a useful protocol that other vendors have wanted something similar in the open standards domain.

The *Virtual Router Redundancy Protocol (VRRP)* is an Internet standard, defined in RFC 2338. Specifically, VRRP specifies the protocol responsible for selecting one of a group of VRRP routers on a LAN to be the Master. Any of the virtual router IP addresses on the LAN may be used as the default router by hosts using a statically configured default gateway.

The Master VRRP router forwards packets sent to IP addresses associated with the VRRP group. As with HSRP, the election process has dynamic failover should the Master become unavailable.

There seems to be no obvious benefit to changing over to VRRP if you are already running HSRP in a satisfactory configuration. But if you intend to mix with some non-Cisco routers or have a bee in your bonnet about proprietary protocols, then a change may be required.

Gateway Load Balancing Protocol

As a grand generalization, the *Gateway Load-Balancing Protocol (GLBP)* can be regarded as an alternative to both HSRP and VRRP, in that GLBP also provides a virtual default gateway as the target for hosts on an Ethernet. The main difference between the protocols is that both HSRP and VRRP select an active router, and the standby routers are not used at all.

GLBP uses the same principle for the virtual IP address as the default gateway, but uses more than one virtual MAC address to bind this to. This has the impact of allowing hosts to select different routers as the default gateway while still using the virtual IP address that guarantees redundancy.

GLBP is very similar to HSRP, apart from the fact that more than one MAC address will be used to map to the virtual IP address. It may be hard to see why you should choose to use GLBP, given the fact that HSRP has such a large following. In fact, the load-sharing capacity of GLBP, while very useful, can almost be achieved by HSRP if you have several VLANs to support, as each VLAN can be configured with its own default gateway mapped to a unique HSRP group.

Nonetheless, when using HSRP in a single VLAN environment, and with a single default gateway address, it is true that only one router will be forwarding in the group. GLBP will change that.

The design of the GLBP group is very simple in basic networks, but in large networks where you require multiple groups, time must be taken to consider how different groups can interact.

Remember to plan your entire configuration beforehand, because this protocol starts running as soon as it is enabled.

Many of the commands that you have seen in HSRP have a parallel inside GLBP, so don't expect any surprises in the next sections.

Active Gateway Selection

The active gateway is selected using a similar mechanism to HSRP. GLBP routers are configured with a priority (the default is 100) and the one with the highest priority becomes the active router, called the *active virtual gateway (AVG)* on GLBP. As with HSRP, non-AVG routers in the same group provide router redundancy.

Once a router is elected to AVG, the clever part begins. The AVG now allocates virtual MAC addresses to other members of the group. All routers in the group forward packets, but each router is individually responsible for forwarding packets addressed to their assigned virtual MAC address.

Addressing

Up to four virtual MAC addresses are possible per GLBP group. The non-AVG routers are assigned MAC addresses in sequence by the AVG. A non-AVG router is referred to as an *active virtual forwarder (AVF)*.

AVF routers fall into two categories. Any one assigned a virtual MAC address by the AVG directly is known as a primary virtual forwarder. Group members arriving late do not know the real IP address of the AVG and use hellos to discover its identity. They are then allocated MAC addresses and are known as secondary virtual forwarders.

Prioritization, Redundancy, and Failover

If the AVG fails, then an election takes place to determine which AVF will take over and be responsible for allocating MAC addresses. This election uses the same principle as the initial election, and the remaining routers select a new AVG based on the (configurable) priorities of the remaining routers. The highest priority wins. To configure the priority on an interface in GLBP mode, use the `glbp` *`group priority level`* interface command.

As with HSRP, the ability for a higher priority router to become the AVG—and even the delay before the election is forced—can be configured. To do either of these things, use the interface command `glbp` *`group preempt [delay minimum seconds]`*.

Additionally, interfaces can be tracked (as in HSRP), with the result that failed interfaces cause the priority of a router to be reduced by a configurable amount. This has the effect of forcing a new election for the position of AVG. To track interfaces and change the priority based on an interface failure, use the interface command `glbp` *`group weighting track object-number [decrement-value]`*.

Load-Balancing

Up to 1024 separate GLBP groups can be established, each with its own AVG. Different user groups (VLANs, for example) can be configured with different group AVGs as their default gateways, thus sharing out the traffic loading.

Configuring GLBP

To configure GLBP on a Cisco router, use the `glbp` *`group ip [ip-address [secondary]]`* command in interface configuration mode:

```
Terry_1#conf t
Terry_1(config)#
Terry_1(config)#int fastethernet 0/0
```

```
Terry_1(config-if)#ip address 10.1.1.1
Terry_1(config-if)#glbp 99 ip 10.1.1.254
Terry_1(config-if)#glbp 99 priority 105
Terry_1(config-if)#glbp 99 preempt delay 10
Terry_1(config-if)#glbp 10 weighting track int S0 10
Terry_1(config)#^Z
Terry_1#
```

This configuration shows a router configured with a single GLBP group. The regular IP address is set to 10.1.1.1. The virtual address is 10.1.1.254 and the priority is set to 105, so in the absence of other routers having their default priority of 100 changed, this will be the AVG for group 10. In addition, interface serial 0 is being tracked, and if it fails, the priority drops to 95, allowing a router with a default 100 priority to take over as AVG. Also, if interface serial 0 comes up again, then this router will preempt and take back over the task of AVG.

To view the entered configuration, use the standard `show running-config` command:

```
interface fastethernet 0/0
 ip address 10.1.1.1 255.0.0.0
 glbp 99 ip 10.1.1.255
 glbp 99 preempt delay minimum 10
 glbp 99 priority 105
 glbp 99 weighting track interface S0 10
```

Transparent Ethernet

Ethernet has become a clear winner in the LAN environment, for all the reasons that we have considered in this book. Factors such as cost, simplicity of implementation, and scalability have been powerful reasons to select Ethernet. In this chapter, we have focused on how to provide reliable and QoS-driven Ethernet networks.

It's not too much of a step to consider that this very friendly protocol may have uses beyond the LAN—perhaps into the metropolitan area, and maybe, somehow, into the wide area. After all, with the end of shared media LANs and the advent of duplex connectivity, distance is not the same problem as it was. And with Ethernet data rates many times the data rates of traditional WAN services, replacing some MAN and WAN links with Ethernet seems very seductive.

Remember that the distance limitations imposed by legacy Ethernet are a direct result of the need to detect collisions. Without that need, the only limitations are attenuation and delay. Repeaters solve the attenuation problem, and delay is pretty small over a fiber link.

Many Cisco Ethernet switches now have special "metro" interfaces; sometimes even a particular switch is manufactured specifically to provide the correct interfaces needed to drive the signals much further. Services such as these are available in the 3550, 4000, and 6500 series switches.

New technologies are under development, including the ability to encapsulate Ethernet into either SONET or SDH frames, thus allowing Ethernet to be transported over unlimited distances.

SONET (Synchronous Optical Networks), widely used in the USA, and SDH (Synchronous Digital Hierarchy), used throughout the rest of the world, are ultra-high-speed technologies used to transport data over fiber-optic cables.

In fact, several technologies exist that allow Ethernet to be transported inside another protocol over unlimited distances, including the following:

- Long-distance Ethernet over fiber (EOF) using Cisco Catalyst switches
- Ethernet over SONET or SDH
- Ethernet over DWDM
- Ethernet inside IP using MPLS
- Ethernet tunneled over native IP using Layer 2 Tunneling Protocol version 3 (L2TPv3)

The benefit to the end user of these services is in the way that the network is perceived. Because the wide or metropolitan connection now behaves like a LAN, users can connect using standard broadcast protocols to servers and services that are large distances away. VLANs can be extended into other offices, and mobile users may be able to connect directly to their regular VLAN even when in a remote company site. Because the network would like Ethernet end-to-end, the term *transparent Ethernet* has been coined.

This is still new to service providers, and not all ISPs provide all services—in fact, some don't provide transparent Ethernet at all. But transparent Ethernet is still in its early stages, and as the Internet becomes more stable and the QoS that we have covered in this chapter becomes more widespread, we are likely to see transparent Ethernet cropping up in the strangest of places.

The IEEE is in the process of considering standards for running Ethernet in the metropolitan area network (MAN). This is called Ethernet in the First Mile (EFM) and the appropriate standard is IEEE 802.3ah. Consideration is being given to different subscriber topologies using point-to-point connections over the existing copper infrastructure.

Summary

Quality of service (QoS) is a broad descriptive term, and can be applied to a variety of different processes. Traditional network design is driven by throughput and reliability. Tomorrow's networks will be driven by the need to support multimedia, time-sensitive applications. Today's networks are somewhere in between.

When considering reliability, many factors need to be taken into account. All over the network, single points of failure abound, from the host PC right through to the Internet access router. We cannot hope to solve all of the problems in one go, and it may not be our responsibility to do so. But we can focus on the areas where we can have a large impact. HSRP is one of those areas, where a failure of the default gateway is such a critical factor that Cisco developed a proprietary protocol—HSRP—to manage the problem.

The second side to QoS is the approach taken to try to provide connection-oriented-like services over best efforts networks. This is a serious challenge, as both Ethernet (at the Data Link layer) and IP (at the Network layer) provide genuine best efforts connectivity, and without the addition of extra content, we would make no progress.

The result has been a spate of new protocol extensions developed by various standards bodies, from the IEEE to the IETF. In IP, we have the type of service (ToS) bits, and their new implementation, the Differentiated Services Code Points. In Ethernet, we have the class of service (CoS) extensions to 802.1Q, specified in 802.1p. Naturally, the DSCP is supported properly only in layer 3 switches, but there is some automatic mapping between the layers in the higher-specification switches.

Cisco switches at layer 2 and layer 3 support a variety of these new protocols, although they are somewhat limited as yet. This is partly because we in the networking community have yet to achieve consensus on what we want and how we will implement it. When we provide the lead, you can be sure the IOS will follow.

Exam Essentials

Understand what quality of service is. QoS is a combination of processes and procedures for trying to enhance the service usually allocated to a frame or packet delivered by a best efforts network. This involves identifying the data, marking it, and then using that marking as a key for how the data will be managed inside queues across a network.

Understand why some applications benefit from QoS. Not every application benefits greatly from applying priorities to its data. Many legacy applications are built to run as store-and-forward flows, and are satisfied with the simple reliability that they get from TCP. E-mail, FTP, and so on do not have the same urgency as mission-critical data with a delay limit. In addition, some applications place considerable demands across the network because although the bandwidth needs may be small, they cannot manage jitter. Defined as the variation in *latency* between successive frames or packets, jitter spells the death knell for multimedia applications.

Understand what QoS features Cisco switches can support. Not every Cisco switch can support every QoS feature. This is true largely because QoS can be applied at either layer 2 or layer 3. Some Cisco switches are simple layer 2 devices, whereas others have so much layer 3 capability that they could easily be called routers. Obviously, layer 2 switches cannot support layer 3 QoS. Layer 2 QoS is limited to setting and responding to the TOS bits inside the 802.1p extension to 802.1Q. Layer 3 QoS uses either the TOS bits from legacy IPv4, or the newer DSCP implementation of the same field. Both can be mapped to the layer 2 TOS at a device supporting both layers.

Understand how to configure QoS on Cisco switches. There are still different versions of operating systems on Cisco switches. From the 4000 and 6500 running CatOS, to the same switches running IOS, to the 3550 running a full IOS and the 2950 running IOS in either the standard or enhanced image options, many differences occur. Using the basic information regarding layer 2 and layer 3 QoS, you need to be able to configure any of these switches for QoS. Remember that the BCMSN exam has simulations and is new, so there may be more in the future. Simulations carry several extra marks, so make sure you are familiar with all the commands in this book.

Understand how redundancy is achieved using Cisco switches and routers. Redundancy can be applied to many places in the network, but this course, focusing as it does on the campus network, exposes the fact that most PCs use a default gateway to get off-LAN. This critical device can be a single point of failure. Cisco's HSRP and less commonly VRRP can be used to provide that redundancy. By creating a virtual router IP address and using that as the default gateway, we can configure more than one router to be prepared to forward data sent to the group, with options for prioritized selection and preempting of control. Both SLB and GLBP can be used to load-share the cross-router traffic.

Catalyst Switch Technologies

THE CCNP EXAM TOPICS COVERED IN THIS CHAPTER INCLUDE THE FOLLOWING:

- ✓ Identify the Cisco Route Switch processors and explain how they are implemented.
- ✓ Understand the function of the Content Addressable Memory (CAM) and Ternary CAM (TCAM) within a Catalyst switch.
- ✓ Describe how network analysis modules on Catalyst switches can be used to improve network traffic management.
- ✓ Be able to convert CatOS to native IOS on Catalyst switches and manage native IOS images using best practice methods.
- ✓ Describe the operation of both the Content Addressable Memory (CAM) and Ternary Content Addressable Memory (TCAM) as implemented in different Catalyst switches.

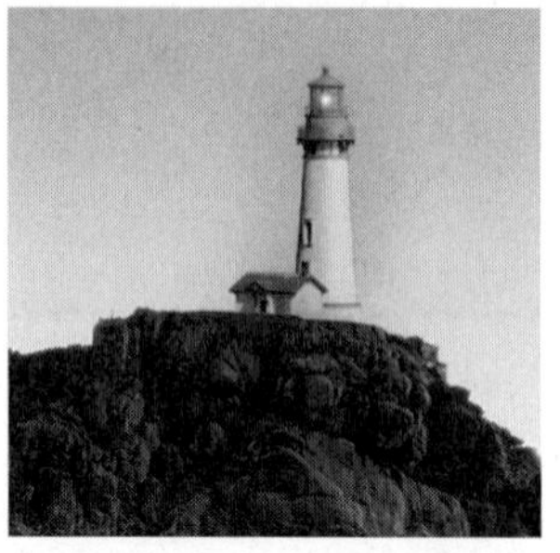

Cisco switches are at the forefront of modern technology, and comprise some of the most flexible devices on the market. But the changing nature of applications' demands upon switching is reflected in the variety in the range. Some of the older switches still use a bus technology on the backbone, whereas newer switches use a "shared memory" forwarding engine. The most modern switches employ a matrix fabric at the heart of the switch.

The reason for this is the continuing growth of multimedia applications. Voice and video place unique demands upon the network that can be satisfied only by a combination of high availability and configurable QoS. High availability means that the switches have to be non-blocking. In other words, we don't want them to get in the way!

In this chapter, you will learn what the different switch architectures are, and which type relates to which Cisco switch. I will explain how the switch memory functions, and how the bridging tables are stored and accessed. We will look at the different Cisco switches currently offered, and see how these technologies are implemented.

We end this chapter with a discussion of the techniques that can be used to manage and troubleshoot an integrated switch network.

The Switching Process

All of the descriptions of the switching process contain the same words and phrases. We hear people using terms such as "wire speed" and "low latency," but these expressions don't tell us what is going on inside the switch, only how long it takes to happen! If you are anything like me, you want to know what goes on inside. But the inside of a switch is not like the inside of the family auto—taking it to bits doesn't always let you see the interesting stuff. Let me explain.

When frames arrive at an ingress interface, they must be buffered. Unless the switch is operating in cut-through or fragment-free mode, the frame check sequence (FCS) needs to be calculated and tested against the arriving FCS. After the frame is confirmed as uncorrupted, it must be passed to a switching "fabric" of some sort, where it can go through the forwarding process to the egress interface.

This forwarding will be expedited by a table lookup process, which must be very quick if the frame is not to be delayed. Finally, there may be contention for the egress interface, and the frame will have to be held in a buffer until the output channel is clear. This complete process will involve a number of discrete steps taken by specific devices.

I am using the term *switching fabric* here for two reasons. First, you will hear the term used throughout the industry, often by people who are not quite sure what it means, but who will expect you to know. Second, because it is a broad descriptive term, without a single definition, and because I also intend to use it throughout this chapter. What I mean is the "heart" of the switch, where frames are redirected to an outgoing interface. It might be a crossbar, a bus, or shared memory. Read on and see what I mean.

Switch Architecture and Components

Switches come in a variety of shapes and sizes, as you would expect; after all, as long as the standards are complied with when stated, how you make that happen can be entirely proprietary. And Cisco, which has a range of switches in the portfolio—some designed in-house and others the result of canny purchases—has more than one type of switch.

Modern switches differ from bridges because they support micro-segmentation, and because they do everything very quickly. So they have to be both scalable and efficient, which means that the architecture needs to be designed for the job. You can't make a world-class switch by purchasing chips from the corner shop and soldering them together.

So modern switches have a number of key components designed for specific purposes, and an architecture that describes how they are connected together.

Non-blocking Switches

The term non-blocking comes from the telecommunications industry, specifically that section concerned with telephone exchange design. It means that the *non-blocking switch* must have sufficient capacity in the switching fabric to be able to avoid delaying the frame forwarding. Figure 21.1 shows a non-blocking switch architecture, with eight Gigabit Ethernet interfaces and a 4Gb fabric. This would be the minimum fabric to be truly non-blocking.

The comparison to telephone exchanges is worth following up, especially as we move toward VoIP. How often do you try to make a telephone call these days and get a tone that says "the exchange is busy"? Not very often, I'll bet. That is because modern telephone exchanges are non-blocking. But it wasn't always so. It has taken exchange and network designers some years to get to this advanced stage. And in the data communications industry, we're not there yet!

Now, it doesn't take too much effort to see that there are really only two ways to create this type of switch. You could use a *crossbar*, which has a cross-point for every possible interface pair in any given frame-forwarding action (crossbars are described fully in the next section), or you could have some sort of *shared memory* coupled to a multi-tasking operating system (also explained in the next section). Everything else will result at some time in a frame being queued because the fabric is busy. This has led to the rise of the term "essentially non-blocking."

FIGURE 21.1 Non-blocking switch fabric

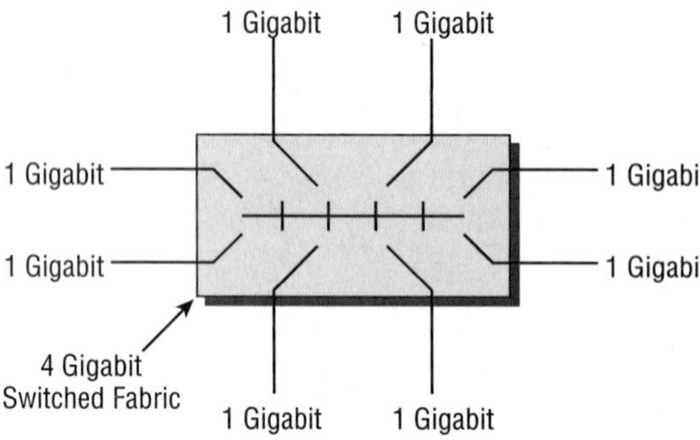

Switches that are essentially non-blocking are so described because the manufacturers deem that the chances of frames being delayed in the fabric, or of any delays being significant, are almost non-existent. This gives the designers of such switches more leeway, and opens the door for fabrics comprising bus architectures.

The term "essentially non-blocking" is statistically sound when applied to telephone networks, as it sometimes is. That's because we can predict with some accuracy the distribution of telephone calls throughout the network across the day. This is less predictable with data, and some forwarding delays will occur. You have to keep an eye on your switch port statistics to ensure that it's not a problem on your network.

Non-blocking switches are sometimes referred to as *wire speed* switches, in an attempt to explain that, in the absence of any other delays, the switch can forward data at the same rate as which it is received.

Switch Fabrics

There are three main switch fabrics in use today: bus, shared memory, and matrix. Each has its own advantages and disadvantages, and manufacturers select designs based upon the throughput demanded by the switch and the cost required to achieve it.

Bus Switching Fabric

A *bus fabric* involves a single frame being forwarded at a time. The first issue that this raises is one of contention. Although the frames could be forwarded on a first-come first-served basis, this is unlikely to prove "fair" to all ports, and so most bus fabrics have a contention process involving a second bus just used for contention and access. The most common approach is for an ingress buffer to make a request for access to the forwarding bus when there is a queued frame. The resulting permission from some central logic allows the buffer to forward the frame to the forwarding bus.

Of course, this forwarding bus need not be a simple serial affair, where bits are transmitted one after the other. Because the whole frame is already stored in a buffer prior to being forwarded, the bus could be parallel, allowing the frame to be forwarded much more quickly. For example, a 48-bit-wide bus clocked at only 25MHz would result in a possible throughput of 1.2Gbs/second.

Figure 21.2 shows four line cards connected to a shared bus switching fabric.

FIGURE 21.2 Bus switching fabric

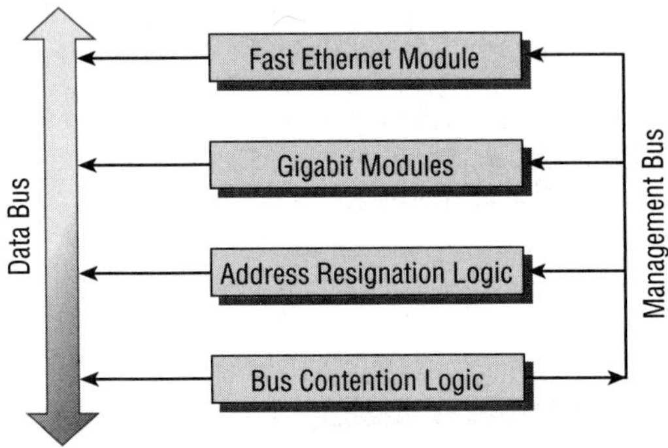

Shared Memory Switching Fabric

Shared memory fabrics pass the arriving frame directly into a large memory block, where all of the checking for corruption is carried out. Corrupted frames are discarded from here.

The header of the frame is checked against the bridging table on the processor, which has direct access to the shared memory. The forwarding decision results in the frame being forwarded to the egress port, and scheduling or prioritization will be managed as the frame leaves the shared memory.

One advantage of shared memory fabrics is that the frame may only have to be queued once as it passes through the switch. Under light loads, very high throughput can be achieved from such architecture. In addition, the line cards don't need to have the same level of intelligence as with bus architectures, because there is no requirement for a contention mechanism to access the fabric.

Figure 21.3 shows four line cards connected to a shared memory fabric.

FIGURE 21.3 Shared memory switching fabric

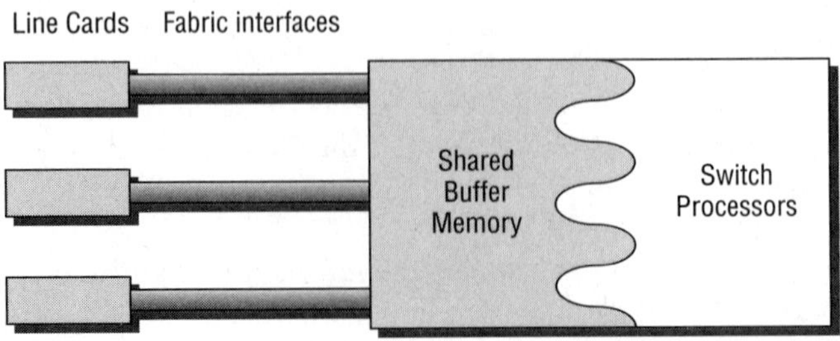

Crossbar Switching Fabric

Crossbar switching uses a fabric composed of a *matrix*. In other words, the core of the switch is a series of cross-points, where every input interface has direct access to the matrix, resulting in a truly non-blocking architecture. This design is at the heart of many telephone switches.

What is common, however, is to reduce the size of the matrix by not giving every port its own path to the matrix, but instead giving every line card direct access. Of course, some prioritization and contention management is needed on the line cards, but the system is still extremely fast. Add to this the additional availability created by a second matrix (with line cards attached to each), and you might rightly refer to it as "essentially non-blocking."

Figure 21.4 shows the basic arrangement for a group of line cards connected to a single crossbar switch.

FIGURE 21.4 Crossbar switching fabric

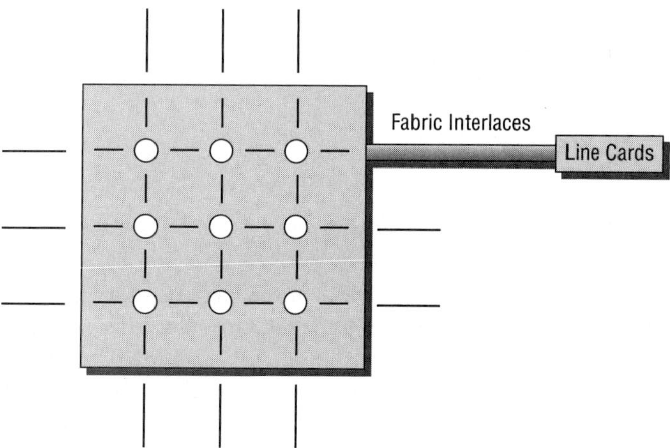

Bridging Table Operation

Naturally, the bridging table is one of the most important parts of a switch. There is little point in being able to forward data at wire speed if it takes ages to make a decision as to where to forward it. The main mechanisms for table lookup in use today are the *Content Addressable Memory (CAM)* and the *Ternary Content Addressable Memory (TCAM)*.

Content Addressable Memory (CAM)

CAM is not unique to Cisco, but is almost an industry-standard mechanism for how the lookup process for data operates in modern devices. CAM is not the same as a traditional indexing method. These older mechanisms use a pointer to identify the location in memory of specific information (such as an address/port match).

With CAM, a precise relationship exists between the information in the data and its location in the data store. This means that all data with similar characteristics will be found close

together in the store. CAM could therefore be defined as any kind of storage device that includes some comparison logic with each bit of data stored.

CAM is sometimes called *associative memory*.

Ternary Content Addressable Memory (TCAM)

In normal CAM lookups, all of the information is important—in other words, there is nothing you wish to ignore. This is a function of the fact that binary has just the two bits—1s and 0s. This is restricting, because time must be spent looking for a match for the whole data structure, 48 bits in a MAC address and 32 bits in an IP address.

Ternary mechanisms add a third option to the binary possibilities, that of "don't care," commonly shown as the letter X. This means that data can be searched for using a masking technique where we want to match 1s and 0s and ignores Xs.

For example, in a standard CAM, a lookup for the IP address 172.16.0.0 would require a match of 32 bits of 1s and 0s. But if we were trying to find a match on the network 172.16.0.0/16, then we really only need to match the first 16 bits. The result is a much faster lookup because we only have to search for the bits we want to match—extraneous bits would be flagged with a mask of Xs.

TCAMs are useful when there may be bits in a lookup that we can afford to ignore. Good examples are layer 2 and layer 3 forwarding tables and access control lists.

Memory

One of the most important aspects of a switch is the memory. Switches are often presented with interfaces running at different speeds. In fact, the differences are commonly factors of 10 (10/100/1000 Ethernet). Combined with this possible bandwidth mismatch between interfaces, the fact that switches move frames from one interface to another at very high speed means that buffer space can fill up very quickly. The result is that the science of data buffering is quite advanced, and the simple serial shift-register memory of the past is no longer suitable.

The reason for using fixed-size buffers in the first place is not necessarily intuitive. You might think that better use would be made of shared memory by just placing arriving frames/packets into the next free space and making an entry in a table, rather like the way your hard drive manages files. But the problems that arise from this are in fact very similar to the hard drive file storage mechanism. In short, how do we use space that has been released after data has been forwarded from memory?

Obviously, the space made available after a packet has left the memory block is likely to be the wrong size to exactly fit the next occupant. If the next packet is too small, space will be wasted. If it is too large, it won't fit, and we would need to fragment it. After a while, throughput would slow down and more and more packets would have to be chopped up for storage and reassembled for transmission. On our hard drive, we'd have to defragment our disk regularly. In shared memory, we'd just end up with smaller and smaller memory spaces, with the resulting loss of throughput.

Fixed size buffers allow us to control the way that memory is allocated.

Rings

In order for arriving packets to be placed into the shared memory buffers, it is common to use a buffer control structure called a ring. Shared memory devices usually have two rings, one to control the receive packet buffering and one to control transmit packet buffering.

Rings act effectively as a control plane (if you have a telecommunications background, think out-of-band signaling) that carries information about which frame may go where.

Contiguous Buffers

Contiguous buffers are fixed-size buffers where different units of data (frame, packet, and so on) are placed in separate buffers. This has the advantage of creating easily addressed blocks where data can quickly be both stored and accessed efficiently. In general, contiguous buffers are easy to manage. But there is also a disadvantage in that considerable space can be wasted if, for example, a 64-byte frame has to be placed into a 1500-byte buffer.

On Cisco switches (and routers) that use this method, the contiguous buffers are created in a variety of fixed sizes at startup of the switch. The size of the contiguous buffers is designed to be suitable for a variety of frames/packets of common sizes to be properly stored with the minimum of wasted space.

The contiguous buffering allocation can be most wasteful on routers, where the need to create buffers to support the maximum transmission unit (MTU) of all interfaces may mean that some buffers as large as 18 kilobytes may be reserved (FDDI or high-speed Token Ring, for example). Under these circumstances, very few frames or packets may demand a buffer this large, but once created, the memory is not available for other purposes. And the maximum memory on switches and routers may be quite limited.

Figure 21.5 shows the disadvantages of the contiguous buffering system. Despite the different-sized buffers that have been created, there is always going to be waste.

FIGURE 21.5 Contiguous buffering

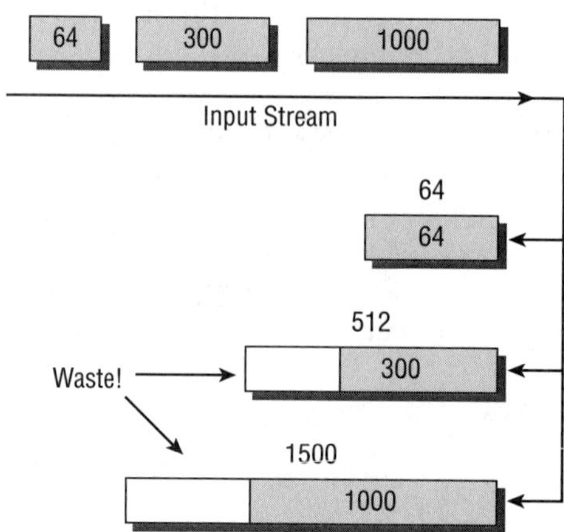

Shown next is the output of the `show buffers` command executed on a WS-C2950-24 switch. You can see the sizes of the system buffers and the default number that are created at startup by this particular switch.

```
Terry_2950#show buffers
Buffer elements:
     500 in free list (500 max allowed)
     58 hits, 0 misses, 0 created

Public buffer pools:
Small buffers, 104 bytes (total 52, permanent 25, peak 52 @ 00:16:09):
     52 in free list (20 min, 60 max allowed)
     50 hits, 9 misses, 0 trims, 27 created
     0 failures (0 no memory)
Middle buffers, 600 bytes (total 30, permanent 15, peak 39 @ 00:16:09):
     30 in free list (10 min, 30 max allowed)
     24 hits, 8 misses, 9 trims, 24 created
     0 failures (0 no memory)
Big buffers, 1524 bytes (total 5, permanent 5):
     5 in free list (5 min, 10 max allowed)
     4 hits, 0 misses, 0 trims, 0 created
     0 failures (0 no memory)
VeryBig buffers, 4520 bytes (total 0, permanent 0):
     0 in free list (0 min, 10 max allowed)
     0 hits, 0 misses, 0 trims, 0 created
     0 failures (0 no memory)
Large buffers, 5024 bytes (total 0, permanent 0):
     0 in free list (0 min, 5 max allowed)
     0 hits, 0 misses, 0 trims, 0 created
     0 failures (0 no memory)
Huge buffers, 18024 bytes (total 0, permanent 0):
     0 in free list (0 min, 2 max allowed)
     0 hits, 0 misses, 0 trims, 0 created
     0 failures (0 no memory)

Interface buffer pools:
Calhoun Packet Receive Pool buffers, 1560 bytes (total 512, permanent 512):
     480 in free list (0 min, 512 max allowed)
     56 hits, 0 misses

Terry_2950#
```

You can change the buffer allocations by using the `buffers` *buffer_size buffer_setting number* command, but this is a skilled task with considerable ramifications. If too much memory is allocated to buffers, performance will suffer. If you think you need to alter the default buffer allocations, either liaise with the Cisco TAC or, at the very least, model the impact on a non-production switch.

Particle Buffers

Particle buffers are a new mechanism designed to overcome the limitations of the contiguous buffering system. Instead of allocating a contiguous block, particle-based systems allocate small, discontiguous blocks of memory called particles, which are then linked together to form a logically contiguous packet buffer. These packet buffers are therefore spread across multiple physical particles in different locations.

The advantage of this method is that no buffers of specific sizes need to be allocated in advance; instead, buffers are created as needed, and of the optimum size (within the limits of the particle sizes, which are usually split into pools of 128 and/or 512 bytes).

Figure 21.6 shows how the use of particles may not completely eliminate waste, but sure cuts it down to a minimum!

Software

At the heart of the switch is the software. At the moment, a variety of different images appear in the range. This is partly because Cisco is in a transitional stage between the legacy operating systems of the older switches and the completion of the migration toward IOS-based switches. It is also partly because some switches do more than just layer 2 switching. The minute a switch operates at layer 3, it is, in effect, a router as well—which means a router-compliant IOS.

The two main issues that you must understand when considering software are

- On a 2950 switch, is the IOS *Standard Image (SI)* or *Enhanced Image (EI)*?
- On a 4000 or 6500 series switch, is the IOS a hybrid of CatOS and IOS, or is it true IOS?

FIGURE 21.6 Particle buffers

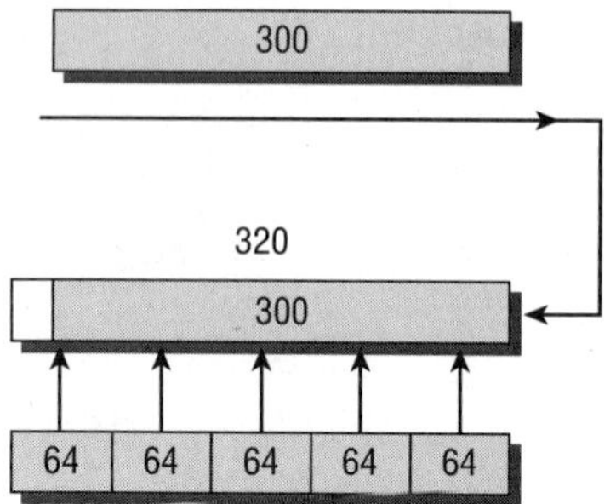

2950 Series Software

Taking the first subject first, Cisco produces the IOS for the 2950 in two versions: Standard Image and Enhanced Image. The images are platform-dependent, and when you buy a switch with SI installed, you cannot upgrade to EI.

Standard Image IOS

The SI is installed on the 2950SX-24, 2950-12, and 2950-24. The SI supports basic IOS functionality, and includes functionality to support basic data, video, and voice services at the access layer. In addition to basic layer 2 switching services, the SI supports

- IGMP snooping
- L2 CoS classification
- 255 multicast groups
- 8000 MAC addresses in up to 64 VLANs

Enhanced Image IOS

The EI is installed on the 2950G-12, 2950G-24, 2950G-48, 2950G-24-DC, 2950T-24, and 2950C-24. The EI supports all features of the SI, plus several additions, including enhanced availability, security, and quality of service (QoS). In addition to the services provided by the SI, the EI supports

- 8000 MAC addresses in up to 250 VLANs
- 802.1s Multiple Spanning Tree Protocol
- 802.1w Rapid Spanning Tree Protocol
- Gigabit EtherChannel
- Port-based access control lists
- DSCP support for up to 13 values
- Rate limiting on Gigabit Ethernet

A full breakdown of the components of both the SI and EI images is available at Cisco's website: `www.cisco.com/en/US/products/hw/switches/ps628/prod_bulletin09186a00800b3089.html`.

4000 and 6500 Series Software

The 6500 and 4000 series routers are the ones most exposed to the changing face of Cisco operating systems. Coming from a history of native CatOS, they have moved to a hybrid CatOS/IOS operating system, on the path to becoming fully IOS supported. These changes have brought with them increased functionality and faster throughput.

CatOS/IOS Hybrids

The native operating system on the two platforms has always been *CatOS*, with the familiar `set`, `show`, and `clear` commands used for almost all control aspects. The introduction of routing and layer 3 switching features on a separate module created the concept of two operating systems on a single switch.

By using an internal Telnet connection, or a separate console port on the front of the introduced module, access is gained to the IOS-based routing engine. The Catalyst 4000 4232-L3 module and the Catalyst 6000 Multilayer Switch Feature Card 1 (MSFC 1) and 2 (MSFC 2) fall into this category.

Native IOS

There are some limitations to running two operating systems, not including the most obvious one of having to understand and remember two different sets of commands. The CatOS was written before Cisco acquired the Catalyst company, and it represents a different configuration philosophy. It is cumbersome, unfriendly, and very limited when compared with the Cisco *IOS*, which is mature and flexible.

It makes sense to be able to integrate the complete layer 2 and layer 3 functionality available in the combined switching engines, and this can only be leveraged through the use of an operating system that understands everything. Enter IOS, ready to run in native format on the integrated platform.

Upgrading the IOS is a well-defined process involving a series of steps:

- Confirm that your platform will support the new IOS.
- Confirm that you have the correct IOS from Cisco.
- Establish a Trivial File Transfer Protocol (TFTP) server that your switch can access.
- Ensure that your switch has sufficient flash memory for the new image.
- Copy the new IOS into flash.
- Reload the switch with the new IOS running.

A reference document on the Cisco website contains detailed instructions for the step-by-step upgrade process on all platforms (including the old 5000 series switches). It can be found at `www.cisco.com/en/US/products/hw/switches/ps700/products_tech_note09186a00801347e2.shtml`.

Switches: The Current Range

The current Cisco range of switches represents the most powerful yet. Many of them have layer 3 switching capabilities in addition to layer 2, which means that they can almost be configured as a multi-port router. Many also run a version of the IOS as standard. The only two still running the set-based CatOS have an upgrade path to allow them to run IOS. Despite figuring in the current exam, CatOS is doomed.

This next section looks at the four main switch families in turn, and links together the technologies we have discussed so far in this chapter with the real world of Cisco products.

2950 Series Switches

The 2950 series comprises a number of fixed configuration switches that can be operated in a stand-alone fashion or joined together in a stack. There are two distinctly different IOS-based software images (which are platform dependent and not interchangeable), allowing users to purchase the most suitable system for their environment.

The Standard Image (SI) software offers IOS-based basic data, video, and voice services. The Enhanced Image (EI) software provides additional features such as advanced quality of service (QoS), rate limiting, and security filtering for more exposed locations in the topology.

All Catalyst 2950 and 2955 models have the Cisco Cluster Management Suite (CMS) software embedded in the operating system. (CMS is discussed later in this chapter.)

The basic architecture of the 2950 switches is shown in Figure 21.7.

FIGURE 21.7 2950 switch architecture

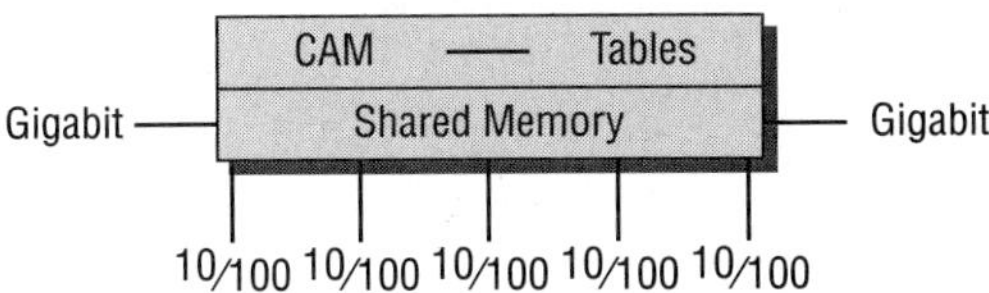

A wide range of switch configurations and port densities is available. You can determine the switch model and the version of the IOS by entering the `show version` command. Shown next is the output from the `show version` command executed on a WS-C2950-24 switch (the underlines are mine to highlight the image and switch model):

```
Terry_2950#show version
Cisco Internetwork Operating System Software
IOS (tm) C2950 Software (C2950-I6Q4L2-M), Version 12.1(11)EA1, RELEASE SOFTWARE
(fc1)
Copyright (c) 1986-2002 by cisco Systems, Inc.
Compiled Wed 28-Aug-02 10:25 by antonino
Image text-base: 0x80010000, data-base: 0x80528000
ROM: Bootstrap program is CALHOUN boot loader
Terry_2950 uptime is 19 minutes
System returned to ROM by power-on
System image file is "flash:/c2950-i6q4l2-mz.121-11.EA1.bin"
cisco WS-C2950-24 (RC32300) processor (revision G0) with 20402K bytes
  ➥of memory.
Processor board ID FOC0650W11A
Last reset from system-reset
Running Standard Image
24 FastEthernet/IEEE 802.3 interface(s)
```

```
32K bytes of flash-simulated non-volatile configuration memory.
Base ethernet MAC Address: 00:0B:BE:53:2C:00
Motherboard assembly number: 73-5781-11
Power supply part number: 34-0965-01
Motherboard serial number: FOC06500D9W
Power supply serial number: PHI06460AS1
Model revision number: G0
Motherboard revision number: A0
Model number: WS-C2950-24
System serial number: FOC0650W11A
Configuration register is 0xF

Terry_2950#
```

The 2950 series switches operate only at layer 2, and all use a CAM for address lookup and a shared memory switching fabric for forwarding frames. Shown next is the output from the `show mac-address-table` command executed on a WS-C2950-24 switch:

```
Terry_2950#show mac-address-table
          Mac Address Table
------------------------------------------

Vlan    Mac Address       Type        Ports
----    -----------       ----        -----
   1    00e0.b063.c196    DYNAMIC     Fa0/1
   1    00e0.b064.6ee5    DYNAMIC     Fa0/2
   2    0000.0c76.1f30    DYNAMIC     Fa0/3
   2    00e0.b063.c197    DYNAMIC     Fa0/4
Total Mac Addresses for this criterion: 4
Terry_2950#
```

The 2950 stores the VLAN information in a separate database file (`vlan.dat`) from the one used for the configuration files (`config.text`). Shown next is the output from the `show flash` command executed on a WS-C2950-24 switch:

```
Terry_2950#show flash

Directory of flash:/

    2  -rwx     2664051   Mar 01 1993 00:04:35  c2950-i6q4l2-mz.121-11.EA1.bin
    3  -rwx         269  Jan 01 1970 00:02:46  env_vars
    5  -rwx         676  Mar 01 1993 00:48:45  vlan.dat
    6  -rwx              Mar 03 1993 05:25:47  private-config.text
```

```
  7  drwx       704   Mar 01 1993 00:05:13  html
 19  -rwx       109   Mar 01 1993 00:05:14  info
 20  -rwx       109   Mar 01 1993 00:05:14  info.ver
 21  -rwx      1580   Mar 03 1993 05:25:47  config.text

7741440 bytes total (3778048 bytes free)
Terry_2950#
```

3550 Series Switches

The 3550 Series Intelligent Ethernet switch comprises a number of fixed configuration switches that can be operated in a stand-alone fashion or joined together in a stack. More powerful than the 2950 switches, they provide several enhancements to both security and quality of service (QoS), thanks in part to the additional layer 3 capability of the IOS.

All Catalyst 3550 models have the Cisco Cluster Management Suite (CMS) software embedded in the operating system. (CMS is discussed later in this chapter.)

The 3550 series switches operate using a distributed shared-memory switching fabric. The forwarding decisions, at layers 2, 3, and 4, as well as CEF, are taken by "satellite" ASICs located near the main shared memory. Figure 21.8 shows the relationship between the shared memory, the decision-making satellite ASICs, and the ring request mechanism.

FIGURE 21.8 3550 switch architecture

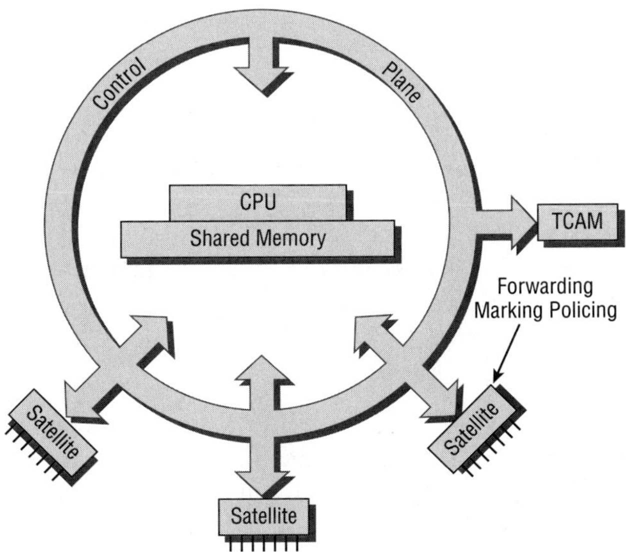

The 3550 switches operate at both layer 2 and layer 3, and use a CAM for address lookup at both layers for 10/100 Mbits/second interface traffic. All switches in the range use TCAM for faster switching because of the proliferation of Gigabit interfaces. You can tell which version of the switch you are connected to by using the `show version` command:

```
Terry_3550#show version
Cisco Internetwork Operating System Software
IOS (tm) C3550 Software (C3550-I5K2L2Q3-M),
   Version 12.1(13)EA1a, RELEASE SOFTWARE (fc1)
Copyright (c) 1986-2003 by cisco Systems, Inc.
Compiled Tue 25-Mar-03 23:56 by yenanh
Image text-base: 0x00003000, data-base: 0x008BA914

ROM: Bootstrap program is C3550 boot loader

Terry_3550 uptime is 4 days, 23 hours, 10 minutes
System returned to ROM by power-on
System image file is "flash:/c3550-i5k2l2q3-mz.121-13.EA1a.bin"

[output cut]

cisco WS-C3550-24-PWR (PowerPC) processor
   (revision B0) with 65526K/8192K bytes of memory.
Processor board ID CAT0709X07M
Last reset from warm-reset
Bridging software.
Running Layer2/3 Switching Image
Ethernet-controller 1 has 12 Fast Ethernet/IEEE 802.3 interfaces
Ethernet-controller 2 has 12 Fast Ethernet/IEEE 802.3 interfaces
Ethernet-controller 3 has 1 Gigabit Ethernet/IEEE 802.3 interface
Ethernet-controller 4 has 1 Gigabit Ethernet/IEEE 802.3 interface
24 FastEthernet/IEEE 802.3 interface(s)
2 Gigabit Ethernet/IEEE 802.3 interface(s)

Terry_3550#
```

Shown next is the output from the `show tcam` command executed on the same switch. Very few entries exist in this TCAM, but the command can be used to view the remaining TCAM capacity:

```
Terry_3550#show tcam ?
  inacl    Show Ingress ACL TCAM
```

```
  outacl  Show Egress ACL TCAM
  pbr     Show PBR TCAM
  qos     Show Ingress QoS TCAM

Terry_3550#show tcam qos ?
  <1-1>  TCAM ID

Terry_3550#show tcam qos 1 ?
  entries      Show entry information
  masks        Show mask information
  port-labels  Show port label information
  size         Show size
  statistics   Show statistics
  vlan-labels  Show vlan label information

Terry_3550#show tcam qos 1 statistics
QoS TCAM#1: Number of active labels: 0
QoS TCAM#1: Number of masks   allocated: 4,available:412
QoS TCAM#1: Number of entries allocated: 1,available:3327

Terry_3550#
```

4000 Series Switches

The Cisco Catalyst 4000 Series switches are modular in construction, and are based around the Catalyst 4003 and Catalyst 4006 chassis, both of which operate using a shared memory switching fabric. A range of line cards supporting different arrangements of port numbers and speeds is available and is compatible with both chassis. The Cisco Catalyst 4000/4500 Supervisor Engine IV is the current "heart" of the machine, comprising a fabric that Cisco defines as supporting, among other features:

- Integrated resiliency
- Cisco Express Forwarding (CEF)-based layer 2/3/4 switching
- Advanced quality of service (QoS)
- Non-blocking switch fabric forwarding at 48Mbps

(Other Cisco documentation defines the 4000 series switching as "layer 2 switching powered by a 24-Gbps, 18-Mbps engine and layer 3 switching powered by a scalable, 8-Gbps, 6-Mbps engine," thus allowing you calculate the 48Mbps by yourself.)

Cisco also offers a Catalyst 4500 Series Supervisor Engine II-Plus engine, running Cisco IOS software.

The basic architecture of the 4000 series switches is shown in Figure 21.9.

FIGURE 21.9 4000 switch architecture

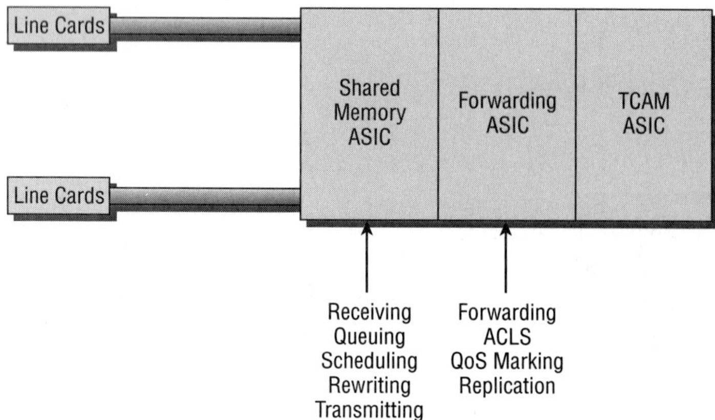

The model number of the 4000 series and details of the operating system are displayed using the `show version` command. The following shows the output when the command is executed on a WS-C4003 switch:

```
Terry_4003 (enable)show version
WS-C4003 Software, Version NmpSW: 4.5(2)
Copyright (c) 1995-1999 by Cisco Systems, Inc.
NMP S/W compiled on Jun 25 1999, 15:53:36
GSP S/W compiled on Jun 25 1999, 15:38:34

System Bootstrap Version: 5.4(1)

Hardware Version: 2.1  Model: WS-C4003  Serial #: JAE044001T8

Mod Port Model          Serial #         Versions
--- ---- ----------     ------------------------------
1   0    WS-X4012       JAE044001T8      Hw : 2.1
                                         Gsp: 4.5(2.0)
                                         Nmp: 4.5(2)
2   48   WS-X4148-RJ    JAE04271V1N      Hw : 2.3
3   34   WS-X4232-GB-RJ JAE043203CK      Hw : 2.3

       DRAM                    FLASH                   NVRAM
Module Total   Used    Free    Total   Used    Free    Total Used  Free
------ ------- ------- ------- ------- ------- ------- ----- ----- -----
1      65536K  17723K  47813K  12288K  3764K   8524K   480K  126K  354K
```

```
Uptime is 183 days, 3 hours, 32 minutes
Terry_4003 (enable)
```

The bridging table in a 4000 series switch is held in the CAM. While this is considered fast enough for the 10/100 interfaces, the Gigabit Ethernet interfaces need more speed, and so a TCAM is used for both layer 2 and layer 3 lookup when the faster interfaces are installed.

Shown next is the output from the `show cam` command executed on a WS-C4003 switch. Note that it is possible to see either dynamic or static entries, and also to have them displayed by VLAN:

```
Terry_4003 (enable) show cam
Usage: show cam [count] <dynamic|static|permanent|system> [vlan]
       show cam <dynamic|static|permanent|system> <mod_num/port_num>
       show cam <mac_addr> [vlan]
       show cam agingtime

Terry_4003 (enable) show cam dynamic
* = Static Entry. + = Permanent Entry. # = System Entry.
   R = Router Entry. X = Port Security Entry

VLAN  Dest MAC/Route Des  Destination Ports or VCs / [Protocol Type]
----  ------------------  ----------------------------------------
1     00-00-00-1d-f0-b6   2/26 [ALL]
1     00-00-85-07-7d-ba   2/25 [ALL]
1     00-02-a5-03-69-e0   2/23 [ALL]
1     00-02-a5-09-ef-08   2/31 [ALL]
1     00-02-a5-09-ef-14   2/43 [ALL]
1     00-02-a5-0c-ab-01   2/36 [ALL]
1     00-02-a5-0c-f9-c7   2/46 [ALL]
1     00-02-a5-22-8f-b4   2/24 [ALL]
1     00-02-a5-31-ac-d8   2/32 [ALL]

[output cut]
```

6500 Series Switches

The 6500 series switches use a crossbar switching fabric. This is good, because as the heart of the Cisco high-end range, they are widely used as core switches, and need to ensure non-blocking throughput at very high speeds.

The 6500 series switches have 8 usable slots, with 2 fabric channels per slot and 8 Gigabits/sec per fabric channel, providing an advertised 256 Gigabits/second (full-duplex) switching fabric.

A TCAM lookup mechanism is applied to the architecture for the fastest possible address-matching decision, and the actual forwarding mechanism is assisted by a distributed forwarding mechanism using the Distributed Forwarding Card. (This is similar to the satellite ASICs in the 3550 series.)

In addition, the 6500 series gains a large increase in throughput speed by using a process called Demand-Base Switching. This involves updating an ASIC-based cache with information from the first layer 3 packet forwarded at routing table speeds, and then switching the rest of the packets along the same path. The use of ASICs to manage this table increases the throughput by a factor of thousands. This is in addition to standard fast CEF table. The basic architecture of the 6500 switches is shown in Figure 21.10.

You can select the options you need in this modular architecture, taking into account both cost and requirements. For example, line cards can be installed with several configuration options, including the following:

- Classic line cards: bus connectivity only
- Fabric-enabled line cards: switch fabric and bus connectivity
- Fabric-only line cards: dual switch fabric, no bus connectivity
- Switch fabric: line cards that contain the actual 256 Gigabits fabric

For details of the full range of line cards available for the 6500 series, see the Cisco website for the most up-to-date details: `www.cisco.com/en/US/products/hw/switches/ps708/products_data_sheets_list.html`.

FIGURE 21.10 6500 switch architecture

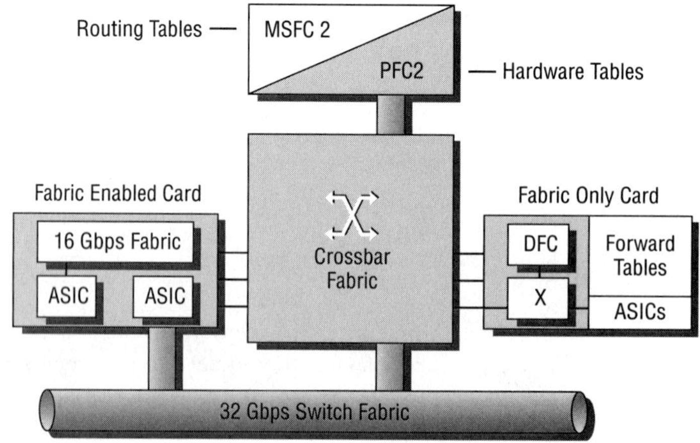

Debugging, Management, and System Testing

Modern switches are usually part of a large, possibly integrated network topology. As such, two different management techniques need to be established. First, administrators need to be able to view the complete network, taking a holistic approach to managing the environment. The second technique relates to managing individual switches.

For the first problem, Cisco designed the Cisco Cluster Management Suite, and all modern switches are enabled with the correct processes to support this centralized management. For the second problem, we have the regular range of `show` commands, supplemented by a process called debugging. Read on, MacDuff.

The Cisco Cluster Management Suite (CMS)

The Cisco Cluster Management Suite (CMS) represents the smallest of the management options supplied by Cisco. Larger offerings fall into the CiscoWorks range of SNMP-based management programs.

CMS supports the management of up to 16 distributed switches. Access is via a standard browser interface, providing a web-based interface for managing the IOS commands on a Cisco switch. CMS is used as an alternative to connecting to the console or establishing a Telnet session to a switch and using the standard command-line interface (CLI).

The use of a standard browser plus the enhancements made possible by customization of the interface mean that this is a simple-to-use application. CMS provides a topology map to enable you to identify the switch that you wish to configure simply by looking at the diagram. Built-in applets include report creation and alarm monitoring. CMS supports all of the advanced features found on the CLI, including MLS forwarding options and QoS for voice and video.

Debugging

Debugging may be new to you. It is available only on IOS-based switches, and there is no comparable feature in CatOS. Of course, debugging has been inside routers since time began, so those of you familiar with router IOS already know something about it. For those wanting to learn the complete story of debugging, I refer you to *CCNP: Cisco Internetwork Troubleshooting Study Guide*, by Arthur Pfund and Todd Lammle (Sybex, 2004).

Debugging is the process whereby you can gather information about specific activities going on in the switch as they happen. Bearing in mind that debugging commands often have several extensions allowing greater granularity of capture, you must remember that the context-sensitive help provides the best guide to what debugging commands you can use.

Real World Scenario

Debugging Danger!

Not too long ago, I was consulting for a large ISP, and we were working as a team making lots of changes to customer networks in the wee small hours of the morning. At one stage, one of the guys needed to debug some activity on the customer router, and he was a little worried about the effect. Because we had no time to run tests on the debug, I suggested that he set a reload timer on the router in question so that it would reboot in five minutes if everything went wrong. Well, things started off fine, but when he typed the `undebug all` command, he got a little confused and typed `debug all` instead.

The target router lasted about 30 seconds before it terminated his Telnet session and overloaded the memory and processor. Fortunately, it reloaded about two minutes later, and all was well. He bought the beers. The moral of this story is don't ever use the `debug all` command outside the lab or classroom!

Debugging is not free. Debugging takes place in the router processor at the heart of the switch, and uses system buffers to store debugging information. If you try to debug too much all at once, then you run the genuine risk of preventing the switch from functioning due to an overworked processor and overloaded memory. Debugging should therefore be used like a surgeon's scalpel, cutting finely into what you need to see. Don't use debugging like a club!

It is easy to forget precisely which debugging command you have entered, and therefore commands exist to disable all debugging activity. There are two choices; `no debug all` and `undebug all` work equally well.

```
Terry_2950#no debug all
All possible debugging has been turned off
Terry_2950#undebug all
All possible debugging has been turned off
Terry_2950#
```

System Testing

In addition to the sophisticated debugging option, a huge variety of `show` commands are available to allow you to take snapshot views of everything from the configuration to information about the frame flow on an interface. In the absence of a photographic memory, the context-sensitive help is the first step in determining which command you need. This can best be demonstrated by using the `show help` command.

```
Terry_3550#show ?
  access-expression  List access expression
```

```
  access-lists        List access lists
  accounting          Accounting data for active sessions
  adjacency           Adjacent nodes
  aliases             Display alias commands
  arp                 ARP table
  auto                Show Automation Template
  boot                show boot attributes
```

One command you may wish to familiarize yourself with is the `show processes` command. In addition to providing an (almost indecipherable) list of the processes running, it provides a very valuable snapshot of the processor overhead. (The underlines are mine.)

```
Terry_3550#show processes ?
  cpu      Show CPU use per process
  memory   Show memory use per process
  |        Output modifiers
  <cr>
Terry_3550#show processes cpu
CPU utilization for five seconds: 20%/20%; one minute: 16%; five minutes: 10%
 PID Runtime(ms)   Invoked      uSecs    5Sec    1Min    5Min TTY Process
   1           0         1          0   0.00%   0.00%   0.00%   0 Chunk Manager
   2           4    105887          0   0.00%   0.00%   0.00%   0 Load Meter
   3           0        72          0   0.00%   0.00%   0.00%   0 SpanTree Helper
   4           0         2          0   0.00%   0.00%   0.00%   0 IpSecMibTopN
   5      106752     53797       1984   0.00%   0.01%   0.00%   0 Check heaps
   6           4       477          8   0.00%   0.00%
[output cut]
```

One additional module that can be implemented with the 6500 series switches is the Network Analysis Module (NAM), which constitutes an integrated traffic monitoring solution, enabling network managers to gain "application-level visibility" into network traffic. The NAM supplies an embedded, web-based traffic analyzer, providing remote monitoring and troubleshooting through a browser. NAM's Main features include

- Integrated monitoring
- Real-time and historical data gathering
- Performance management
- Fault isolation
- QoS and VoIP monitoring
- Capacity planning

Summary

The architecture of modern switches does not conform to a single model. Vendors, in competition with each other, devise their own mechanisms to create faster, more scalable switches to suit every niche in the modern network. Cisco is no exception; in fact, they are probably among the world's greatest innovators.

New technologies such as the Content Addressable Memory (CAM) lookup system are used in the entry-level 2950 series switches, and CAM's big brother, the Ternary CAM (TCAM), is used in the 3550, 4000, and 6500 series. This provides the speedy lookup required for fast decision-making. In turn, this decision-making is itself speeded up by the use of processors external to the memory tables. In the 3550, these are satellite ASICs, and in the 6500 they are provided by the Distributed Forwarding Card.

All of this is bound together by the selection of the most appropriate switching fabric. Whether it is the shared memory of the 2950 and the 4000, the distributed shared memory of the 3550, or the crossbar of the 6500, each switch has a fabric that matches its needs and position in the network. In addition, a range of software options is currently available, with the biggest decisions centering around whether to purchase SI or EI for the 2950, and whether to use hybrid IOS or native IOS on the 4000 and 6500.

Finally, switch management has never been more difficult. With the range of newer technologies such as voice and video demanding newer QoS options, we find ourselves with an almost bewildering array of configuration options. To manage this environment, we have the legacy range of `show` and `debug` commands, although `debug` will be new to many of you without a router background. But we also have the Cisco Cluster Management Suite (CMS), which allows us to manage up to 16 switches using a single front end.

Exam Essentials

Understand what switching architecture is. Switches have come a long way in the last few years. From simple systems using shared buses and interrupt-driven access, we have arrived at the crossbar switch—a truly non-blocking architecture suitable for building the largest switches in the busiest environments. But the crossbar is expensive, and other mechanisms exist that are suitable for lesser needs. These include the shared memory and distributed shared memory fabrics. And you need to understand how they work, and remember which Cisco switch uses which.

Understand CAM and TCAM. Storing addressing information in memory is quite easy. The difficult part is referencing it and accessing it quickly. A number of different techniques have emerged in the past to carry out this task, including simple pointing and hash referencing, but all have been slow. A modern, more intelligent process is called a Content Addressable Memory (CAM). In the CAM, the location of the data in the memory block is somehow related to the type of data that is stored, making for a much faster lookup.

Even so, the CAM is limited by the fact that there are only two binary numbers, and that means checking every bit. By adding a third bit (the "don't care" bit) in a mask, the resulting Ternary CAM (TCAM) can provide even faster lookups by ignoring unnecessary bits of information.

Understand switch types. Cisco switches come in a variety of shapes and sizes. As the range changes and becomes more modern, some new switches have appeared. Some of them, such as the fixed-configuration 3550 series, are almost multi-port routers, running native IOS. Others, such as the 4000 and 6500 series, are modular, running updated versions of the IOS. You need to know which switches have which features, and know how to upgrade the CatOS to IOS.

Understand switch management. Switches need to be managed, and in an increasingly complex network topology, that task also becomes more complex. Cisco has the Cluster Management Suite (CMS) to help, and there is a range of `show` and `debug` commands that you need to learn, practice, and remember.

Building Cisco Remote Access Networks (BCRAN)

Cisco Solutions for Remote Access

THE CCNP EXAM TOPICS COVERED IN THIS CHAPTER INCLUDE THE FOLLOWING:

- ✓ Specify Cisco products that best meet the connection requirements for permanent or dial-up access WAN connections.
- ✓ Know the benefits and detriments of WAN connection types.
- ✓ Select appropriate WAN connection for specific site connection considerations.
- ✓ Choose Cisco equipment that addresses the specific needs of the WAN topology.
- ✓ Identify the components necessary for WAN connections such as Frame Relay and ISDN PRI from the central site to a branch office.
- ✓ Identify the requirements for ISDN connections.
- ✓ Understand the placement of cable modem and DSL technologies in Remote Access solutions.

As the computer industry has evolved, the number of access solutions available to the network designer has also increased. Modern networks require a substantial number of solutions to address the wide array of industry needs. Corporations, home office users, and mobile workers all require connectivity options that stress the divergent goals of cost control, bandwidth, and availability.

Cisco has greatly augmented its product line to address some of these needs. The material covered in this book focuses on your ability to apply Cisco-centric solutions to the production networks of today. Architects and designers should always evaluate all vendors' solutions for each problem that they face; however, there is some merit to coming up with a strategic solution that maintains consistency along vendor and product lines. Many problems can arise from the interoperability issues that can result from the use of multiple vendors.

This text focuses on two goals. As with other Study Guides, the ultimate goal is to provide a substantial foundation of knowledge so you can successfully pass the Remote Access exam. The second goal is to provide information that relates to the live production networks that you will be challenged by every day. The benefit of this approach is that the live network experience you will encounter while reading will help you attain certification, and the certification will in turn provide you with a foundation to get experience with a live network.

This chapter begins with an overview of the fundamentals of remote access. In the first section, you will learn about the various wide area network (WAN) connection types, WAN encapsulation protocols, and how to select a WAN protocol. In the next section, you will learn how to choose from among Cisco's remote connection products. And, in the final section, you will learn about WAN cabling and assembly issues. Developing a solid foundation in these topics is an extremely important part of your preparation for Cisco's Remote Access exam, because it provides a framework for the subsequent chapters and the exam, not to mention real-world applications.

What Is Remote Access?

The term *remote access* is broadly defined as those services used to connect offices over a wide geographical area. These services are typically encompassed under the guise of a *wide area network (WAN)*. Traditionally, a wide area network uses a telecommunications provider to link distant locations; however, this definition is undergoing substantial change. Many providers are starting to offer Ethernet technologies over significant distances, although Ethernet is typically a local area network (LAN) technology. Unlike LANs, WANs usually use the telecommunications infrastructure—a group of services that are leased from service providers and phone companies.

Historically, the most common remote access installations have provided connectivity between fixed locations and a corporation's headquarters. Such installations are relatively simple once a design has been selected, because the solution used for the first office is applicable to the hundredth. Designers need concern themselves only with scalability and availability—as long as the bandwidth needs of each office are comparable.

In the modern remote access design, the architect needs to focus on multiple solutions to address not only the branch office, but also the sales force (a typically mobile group) and telecommuters working from their homes. Residential installations usually have a different set of needs than office configurations, and T-1 and other high-speed access technologies are usually not available for home use.

With the deployment of digital subscriber line (DSL) technologies, designers can provide the equivalence of T-1 bandwidth, and more, to the residential user. Actual T-1s are generally not available in residential settings but have been installed when the expense was warranted. This chapter presents various remote access technologies, including ISDN, Frame Relay, and asynchronous dial-up.

WAN Connection Types

The Remote Access exam is concerned primarily with six types of WAN connections. These are predominantly older, more established technologies. The following are WAN connection types you can expect to see on the Remote Access exam:

- Asynchronous dial-up
- Integrated Services Digital Network (ISDN)
- Frame Relay
- Leased lines
- Digital subscriber line (DSL)
- Cable modems

Notably absent from this list are Asynchronous Transfer Mode (ATM), wireless, and cellular technologies. Although the Remote Access exam was revised in 2003, and cable modems and DSL were added to the topics addressed, these other remote access technologies remain absent.

Even though these newer technologies are not covered yet, it is important to know a bit about them. For instance, wireless technologies have greatly enhanced the options available to home users. The primary benefit of wireless services is little to no provisioning time, but roaming and cheaper deployment also can be found with these solutions, as discussed later in this chapter. *Asynchronous Transfer Mode (ATM)* is a cell-based system similar in many respects to Frame Relay, although the use of fixed-length cells can make ATM better suited to installations that integrate voice, video, and data. Wireless technologies include microwave, 802.11 LANs, and laser and satellite systems, which typically require a fixed transmitter and receiver, although major strides are being made to add mobility. Cellular systems are very mobile but do not provide substantial bandwidth; however, the technology is being improved and cellular can now provide ISDN-comparable data rates.

If you are a designer who is building a remote access solution, you will need to augment the technical material in this text in order to compose the best remote access solutions for your customers' needs.

Asynchronous Dial-Up

Asynchronous dial-up is traditional modem-based access over the public analog phone network. The primary advantage of asynchronous dial-up is that it is available virtually everywhere. Unfortunately, its greatest limitation is bandwidth, which is currently limited to less than 56 kilobits per second (Kbps). In addition, asynchronous dial-up connections require a negotiation period, during which time traffic must be buffered and the user experiences delay.

Because hotels, homes, and customer sites are already supplied with the traditional level of connectivity, dial-up connections are primarily suited to those members in the workforce who are mobile. Such connections are a substantial benefit when compared to the other remote access technologies, each of which must be predefined or preprovisioned.

Given the universal availability of analog circuits, most designers find that they still require dial-up installations to be a part of their remote access solution. Typically, ISDN installations lend themselves to a dual role—as an ISDN Primary Rate Interface (PRI) that can terminate 23 analog connections, or an assortment of ISDN B channels (user data bearer channels) and analog connections. This ability to service both ISDN digital connections and asynchronous dial-up connections can greatly ease facilities, configuration, and administration burdens.

Analog circuits are best suited for short-duration, low-bandwidth applications. Examples of this type of traffic include terminal emulation and e-mail services. Limited file-transfer and client/server-based application activity could also use this connection.

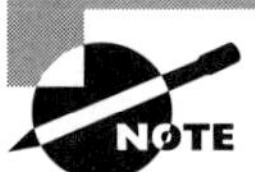

In this Study Guide, you will see the terms *asynchronous dial-up* and *analog* used synonymously.

X.25

X.25 is a reliable layer 2 and layer 3 protocol that can scale up to 2 megabits per second (Mbps), although most installations stop at 56Kbps. The X.25 protocol was intended to provide reliable data transfer over unreliable circuits. Currently, X.25 is typically used for terminal emulation and small file transfers. Due to its low bandwidth and high overhead, X.25 is losing favor as a remote access technology. Originally, it was designed to address the higher error rates that were experienced on analog circuits. This high degree of overhead makes the protocol very inefficient but well suited to less-advanced telecommunications infrastructure such as old carrier management systems.

Designers typically find that X.25 is one of the most widely available technologies on an international basis. This availability greatly adds to the desirability of the protocol. However, it is likely that demands for greater bandwidth and the proliferation of fiber-based networks will continue to erode X.25's market share. Although a migration to Ethernet has already begun, it is important to note that many telecommunications carriers continue to use X.25 for management of their switches and other systems.

Integrated Services Digital Network (ISDN)

Integrated Services Digital Network (ISDN) is the result of efforts to remove analog services from the telecommunications network. In the 1960s, the American phone company, AT&T, realized that their network would be more efficient with digital services throughout. This included the residence, where most ISDN BRI (explained next) is found. However, the model scaled beyond this, and included aggregation and other interfaces that allowed efficient *MUXing*, or the consolidation of multiple small links into one large one.

Two types of ISDN services are available. The first, ISDN *Basic Rate Interface (BRI)*, provides for two 64Kbps channels (the bearer, or B, channels) and one 16Kbps channel (the D channel), which can carry user data. The second type of ISDN service, called *Primary Rate Interface (PRI)*, provides 23 64Kbps B channels for user data and one 64Kbps channel (D channel) for signaling, based on the North American T-1 standard. The E-1 European standard provides 2.048Mbps worth of bandwidth and a corresponding increase to 30 in the number of B channels.

Please note that the 16Kbps channel in ISDN BRI is used for signaling; however, many providers permit the transit of user data using this bandwidth. This is frequently marketed as "always-on" ISDN. ISDN PRI uses a single 64Kbps channel for signaling.

Some ISDN BRI installations limit each B channel to 56Kbps.

The primary advantage of ISDN is its capability to provide faster access than would be available from traditional asynchronous dial-up connections. Unfortunately, the service is not as widely available as traditional analog services, and it tends to be more costly. ISDN is typically used in scenarios including low-bandwidth video, low-bandwidth data, and voice services. It is important to note that each of the two ISDN channels can provide the user with a traditional analog dial-up connection.

ISDN services are quickly being replaced in the United States by DSL services. Digital subscriber line connections are currently available at over 1Mbps, and some provide over three times this rate. However, substantial restrictions exist regarding the distance over which these connections can be set up (the maximum distance is 18,000 feet, or under 3 miles from the central office to the residence), and some sources predict that up to 40 percent of homes will be too far from the central office to receive the service. As of this writing, DSL still failed to compete with cable modem and ISDN installations in terms of number of deployments in the United States. In Europe, however, where more people live closer to their exchanges, ISDN is rapidly being killed off by ADSL.

ISDN is well suited for most applications, including file transfers. However, its high per-minute pricing (depending on service package) makes it impractical when it is needed for more than a couple hours per day. Frame Relay, which you will learn about next, is typically a better solution for higher bandwidth, long-duration connections.

Frame Relay

Frame Relay is a logical, low-overhead transport protocol that removes much of the overhead found in X.25. Frames are marked with a data link connection identifier (DLCI) that provides direction to the switch regarding frame forwarding. As such, frames in Frame Relay are layer 2 elements. In many companies, setting up Frame Relay services between central locations and remote offices is very popular. The primary benefit of Frame Relay is that it is traditionally tariffed to be distance insensitive; this means that a connection that crosses the United States will be comparable in cost to that of a connection across town. In addition, Frame Relay services are available internationally from many providers.

Frame Relay, in addition to DSL, is becoming more accepted in the telecommuter workspace. Telecommuters are finding that connections are required for more than a few hours per day—a threshold that makes ISDN more costly than the other options. In addition, ISDN is incapable of expanding beyond 128Kbps without using PRI services or bonding. Frame Relay is available in a myriad of bandwidths, up to and including DS3. New variations on Frame Relay are increasing this performance characteristic.

Note that ISDN cannot scale beyond 128Kbps in user data on a single pair of B channels. Just as two B channels can be bonded together into a single logical data conduit, it is possible to bond multiple ISDN BRI circuits into a single logical data stream. Chapter 24, "Point-to-Point Protocol," discusses PPP bonding in greater detail, and Chapter 26, "Integrated Services Digital Network (ISDN)," discusses ISDN bonding.

For the network designer, there are two factors to consider when deploying Frame Relay: Frame Relay is available with a *committed information rate (CIR)*, and Frame Relay enables multiple *permanent virtual circuits (PVCs)* to terminate at a single physical connection point on the router. A PVC is a previously defined logical path through the network. The DLCI is used to determine which PVC is to be used. *Switched virtual circuits (SVCs)* are alternatives to PVCs. SVCs are similar to PVCs, but they are not predefined and static, so before data can be transmitted by using SVCs, a path must be established dynamically through the network.

The CIR is best thought of as a guaranteed amount of bandwidth available on a PVC. This figure might be substantially lower than the capacity of the circuit itself. The corporation will pay for the bandwidth guaranteed by the CIR, and any traffic that exceeds the CIR will be handled on a best effort basis. Thus, a company can obtain better throughput than that for which it is being charged.

The capability of Frame Relay to enable multiple PVCs to terminate at a single physical connection point on the router is a powerful tool. This means that a designer need not purchase additional interfaces to accommodate multiple connections. In addition, there's a substantially lowered lead time for new connections, and such connections can be provisioned without a visit to the head-end location.

The Frame Relay protocol is primarily designed to encapsulate data on reliable, digital connections. Its benefits include low overhead when compared to X.25 (X.25 using protocol overhead for data reliability), lower costs when compared to point-to-point connections, and a single access point on the router that can terminate multiple virtual circuits (each of which can go to different destinations). This last benefit greatly reduces the costs associated with the router hardware. The Frame Relay protocol and its benefits are explored in more detail in Chapter 29, "Frame Relay."

Due to its relatively low cost and high bandwidth, Frame Relay is better suited for higher bandwidth demands than other access technologies, including ISDN.

Leased Lines

Leased lines are commonly referred to as dedicated connectivity options. This means that the connection between the two endpoints is permanent in nature and that 100 percent of the capacity is available to the end user. Leased lines are owned by the telecommunications carrier and are often provided in the form of a T-1. These connections are also called point-to-point links because the capacity of a leased line is dedicated to the corporation. Unfortunately, because bandwidths cannot be shared, this type of connection is more expensive than Frame Relay or ATM.

In addition, leased lines are also distance sensitive. Unlike Frame Relay, with leased lines, the telephone company will charge the end user for both the local loop and the transit network. For short distances, the differences in costs might be negligible, but for long distances, the costs increase dramatically. For example, a 200-mile Frame Relay connection might cost $200 a month, which would be the same as a 2,000-mile Frame Relay connection. The leased line installation might also cost $200 a month for 200 miles, but most likely, it would cost $3,000 a month for the 2,000-mile link.

The most common leased-line service available in the United States is called a T-1. This provides the corporation with 1.544Mbps of dedicated bandwidth. Older leased lines were digital data service (DDS) circuits and yielded up to 56Kbps of bandwidth. These connections were popular for mainframe connectivity at both the 9.6Kbps and 56Kbps levels.

Digital Subscriber Line

Digital subscriber line (DSL) technologies were developed to be the magic bullet of the telecommunications industry. Primarily designed to add bandwidth to the home without installing fiber-optics, the various DSL protocols, referred to in the generic as xDSL, have the potential to provide 52Mbps over already installed copper wire—a marked increase in performance. This feat is accomplished with special encoding of the digital signal.

At present, DSL technologies are being used as a replacement for ISDN and analog Internet service provider (ISP) connections. However, as DSL technologies are accepted into the home and office, they will likely be used for primary and backup data transfer and for high-demand services such as live video. DSL currently lags behind cable modem installations, but some vendors, including Next Level Communications (`www.nlc.com`), have equipment in production that demonstrates the long-term potential of this technology. The NLC-based systems can provide voice (plain old telephone system, or POTS, based), video, and high-speed Internet service over DSL technologies, and are priced competitively when compared to obtaining these services independently.

The different DSL standards provide for varying amounts of upstream and downstream bandwidth based on the equipment in use and the distances between this equipment. As a result of the distance sensitivity of xDSL, connections typically must terminate within three miles of the central office, but access technologies can be employed to extend the range. Access products connect a remote termination device to the central office via fiber-optics, which greatly extends the reach of xDSL. Figure 22.1 illustrates a typical installation of xDSL with and without an access product. As shown, a home four miles away cannot obtain xDSL access without an access product. Please note that most xDSL technologies support distances between 1,800 feet and 18,000 feet.

FIGURE 22.1 xDSL installations

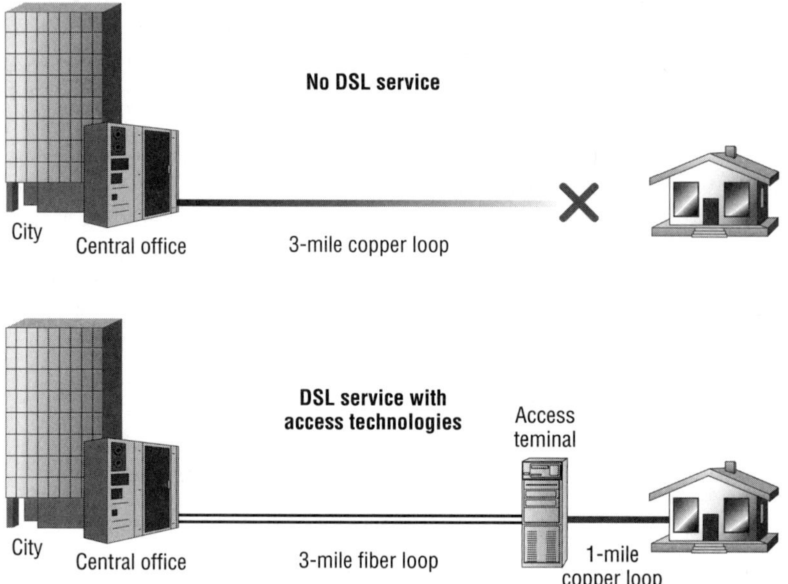

As of this writing, vendors are deploying DSL at fairly low speeds and as an Internet connectivity solution. Most vendors provide 1.544Mbps downstream bandwidth as viewed from the central office site, and 128Kbps to 384Kbps upstream. These bandwidths greatly surpass ISDN and analog offerings, but they cannot provide the multi-service goals of xDSL—primarily MPEG-2 video streaming. Table 22.1 shows the various xDSL technologies available.

Most vendors deploy one of the following two xDSL implementation models: ISP-based installation (layer 3) and remote LAN (RLAN, or layer 2). The traditional ISP-based installation simply substitutes ISDN or analog dial-up for xDSL. Because DSL is an always-on technology, there is no call setup or teardown process, and the connection to the digital subscriber line access multiplexer (DSLAM) is always active. There is a single link to the service provider, and all packets are routed to their destination. RLAN, on the other hand, places the DSL connection on par with Frame Relay or point-to-point links in the WAN. This provides more secure connectivity that can support nonroutable protocols. This solution is being deployed for telecommuters as opposed to

TABLE 22.1 The Various xDSL Technologies

Standard	Characteristics
Asymmetric DSL (ADSL)	There are a number of flavors to ADSL; the two most popular are G.lite and G.dmt (discrete multitone). The G.lite specification provides 1.5Mbps/384Kbps bandwidth and typically invokes lower capital costs. The G.dmt specification can provide 8Mbps downstream and 1.5Mbps upstream.
High bit-rate DSL (HDSL)	HDSL is similar to SDSL but uses double and triple pairs of copper wire. Most other DSL technologies operate over a single pair, which can simplify installation compared to HDSL. HDSL typically provides distances reaching 15,000 feet.
ISDN-based DSL (IDSL)	ISDN-based DSL typically allows the greatest distances but is limited to 144Kbps.
Symmetric DSL (SDSL)	Symmetric DSL provides 2Mbps bidirectional bandwidth over a single pair of copper wires. Distances are typically limited to 10,000 feet.
Very high bit-rate DSL (VDSL)	VDSL can provide up to 52Mbps downstream bandwidth, but its distance is limited to less than 4,500 feet. This is usually the shortest range DSL service.

interoffice connections. Ultimately, designers might find that the consumer level of support currently offered in DSL will be augmented, and the lower price for setup will encourage companies to replace Frame Relay and leased-line installations for interoffice traffic with DSL as well.

Both of these implementation methods can make a modern network design perform better. However, some caveats should be considered. At present, most DSL vendors offer a single PVC with DSL installations. This limits connectivity options and makes redundancy difficult. A second PVC could provide a link to another head end—perhaps a distribution layer aggregation point—and most vendors have multiple DSLAMs in the central office. An SVC-based solution would also make a fault-tolerant design more successful.

Another concern with current DSL installations is that most products do not offer security solutions. The RLAN model greatly reduces this risk because the links are isolated at layer 2, but all connectivity must be provided by the head end, including Internet connectivity. For Internet connections, the risk is significantly greater, especially when the bandwidth available for an attack and the use of static IP addresses or address pools are considered. A number of significant attacks have already occurred as a result of these issues, and although they should not deter the use of the technology, the risks should be addressed with firewall technology.

A third consideration in DSL is the installation delay compared to other technologies. Vendors are moving toward splitterless hardware so that the phone company does not have to install a splitter in the home. The splitter divides the traditional phone signals from the data stream and provides a jack for standard telephones—DSL transport data and voice over the same twisted-pair wiring used for standard analog phone service. At present, because the circuit to the home and the installation of the splitter need to be validated, installations may require weeks to complete.

DSL technologies are presented in greater detail in Chapter 27, "Remote Access with Digital Subscriber Line."

Cable Modems

It would be unfair to present the DSL technologies without providing some space to discuss the alternative: cable modems. *Cable modems* operate over the same cabling system that provides cable television service; in other words, they use the same coax cable that is already used in the homes with cable television. Most cable installations provide two cables—one for the television and one for the data converter—but the signaling and the system are the same. This is accomplished by allocating a television channel to data services. Bandwidth varies with each installation; however, many installations provide up to 2Mbps in the downstream direction and 128Kbps to 256Kbps in the upstream one. *Downstream* is a common term for traffic from the provider to the customer; *upstream* is return traffic. This type of asymmetric connection is sufficient for most Internet users, because these users typically pull more information (bits) to their machines than they send.

Detractors of cable modem technology are quick to point out that these installations are shared bandwidth, similar to Ethernet, which results in contention for the wire among neighbors. This shared bandwidth also introduces a security risk, in that network analysis is possible, although vendors have addressed this concern with switching and encryption technology. This issue does not exist in DSL because the local loop connection to the home is switched. In DSL, traffic is not integrated until it reaches the central office, and at that point, the switch will forward only traffic destined for the end station based on the Media Access Control (MAC) address. Basically, cable modems are a shared technology—hub-based Ethernet versus switched. Along the same lines, a cable modem is really a broadband Ethernet bridge to the cable.

There is a lot of confusion in the marketplace regarding oversubscription and performance in the residential DSL and cable modem markets. DSL is usually oversubscribed 10 to 1 at the central office; if a DS3 is used to link the DSLAM to the Internet, as many as 300 homes could be connected to the DSLAM. None of those users would be oversubscribed on their connection to the DSLAM. Cable modems typically share bandwidth before the head end. As a result, users contend for bandwidth both before and after the head end.

Network designers might wish to consider cable modems as part of a virtual private network (VPN) deployment because the technology will not lend itself to the RLAN-type designs available in DSL. Recall that an RLAN requires layer 2 isolation—a service not offered by cable modem providers at present. This might change in the future if channels can be isolated to specific users. This might be especially true in very remote rural areas, where cable is available and DSL is not.

Cable modem technology, including the features of Data over Cable Service Interface Specification (DOCSIS), is presented in Chapter 28, "Remote Access with Cable Modems and Virtual Private Networks."

New WAN Connection Technologies

As noted previously, there are many new technologies with which designers and administrators should be familiar, but they aren't covered on the current Remote Access exam. These include Asynchronous Transfer Mode (ATM), and wireless (802.11) and cellular services.

Asynchronous Transfer Mode (ATM)

ATM does not relate in any way to asynchronous dial-up connections. Rather, it refers to the transmission of fixed-length cells and the transport of data, voice, and video services. The majority of the public telephone network has already converted to this technology for the aggregation of phone lines. Cells are fixed in length, and therefore latency and delay can be determined and controlled accurately.

ATM is rarely used as a remote access technology in the context applied to the exam, and it would be best to think of it as a potential replacement for Frame Relay installations. Typically, residential ATM installations appear in the form of DSL—ATM being the underlying Data Link (layer 2) technology.

Wireless and Cellular

Wireless technologies, including cellular systems, provide a mobile access method. Typically, these technologies offer substantially lower bandwidth than wire line services.

For wireless solutions (wireless LAN), the current standard is based on IEEE 802.11, with interoperability between systems certified by the Wi-Fi committee. This technology is well suited for short-range deployments within a building or campus environment, and provides for bandwidths up to 54Mbps. Security, a long-time stumbling block for deployment (the original security provided by wireless LANs, Wired Equivalent Protocol (WEP), was relatively poor and subject to hacking), has been addressed by vendors and will be part of the 802.11i specification when ratified. Current solutions include Temporal Key Integrity Protocol (TKIP), and it is likely that 802.1*x* (an authentication model) and Advanced Encryption Standard (AES) will be found in both wireless LAN and wired solutions.

Three standards are available for wireless LAN installations, as described in Table 22.2.

Because wireless LAN is outside of the scope of the Remote Access exam, it is presented here only as an introduction. This technology could be deployed as part of remote access solutions in the future. For further information, we suggest that you consult the 802.11 Planet website at `www.80211-planet.com`.

Another area not addressed on the current Remote Access exam is cellular communications. Although historically used in voice communications, the latest Global System for Mobile Communications (GSM) and code division multiple access (CDMA) technologies provide sufficient bandwidth for lower demand applications. Although the technical characteristics and benefits

TABLE 22.2 802.11 Standards

Standard	Frequency Used	Bandwidth Available (Maximum Rated)	Range	Features
802.11b	2.4GHz	11Mbps	Longest	Original specification and most widely used today. Provides three non-overlapping channels of 11Mbps, but prone to interference from cordless phones and microwave ovens.
802.11a	5.0GHz	54Mbps	Shortest	Uses frequency space that is less prone to interference.
802.11g	2.4GHz	54Mbps (standard ratified at 22 Mbps)	Medium to long	Backward compatible with 802.11b.

of each technology are beyond the scope of this text, this technology is important for real-world application of remote access design. Not only will cellular-based systems provide for roaming and small form factor connectivity, but they will ultimately link small offices and other services while removing the last mile that is typically the most costly and time-consuming portion of a remote access link. The term *last mile* refers to the connection between the telecommunications providers and the end customer.

Summarizing WAN Connection Technologies

Table 22.3 summarizes the WAN connection technologies discussed in this chapter in order to provide comparisons among them.

TABLE 22.3 Summary of WAN Connection Technologies

Connection	Max Throughput	U.S. Availability	Relative Cost
Asynchronous dial-up 56Kbps/DDS	56Kbps	Widely available	Low
Leased line T-1/E-1	1.544Mbps/ 2.048Mbps	Widely available in the U.S.	Medium
Leased line DS3	44.736Mbps/ 34.368Mbps(E-3)	Widely available	High

TABLE 22.3 Summary of WAN Connection Technologies *(continued)*

Connection	Max Throughput	U.S. Availability	Relative Cost
ATM	10Gbps. However, it is virtually unlimited from a protocol perspective.	Moderately available	Very high
ISDN BRI	128Kbps for user, 16Kbps for control data, and 48Kbps for overhead	Moderately available	Low. However, per-minute tariffs can quickly alter this.
ISDN PRI	1.5Mbps T-1, and about 2Mbps E-1	Moderately available	Medium
DSL	128Kbps to 2Mbps (some installations up to 52Mbps)	Available in larger cities, becoming more available in rural areas	Low
Frame Relay	Wide range of speeds, from 56K over T-1 to DS3 (45Mbps)	Widely available	Low
Cable modem	From 128 Kbps to 3Mbps	Widely available	Low

WAN Encapsulation Protocols

There are many WAN encapsulation protocols that operate at layer 2 to provide consistent transport at the Data Link layer. It is important to note that some of these protocols extend into layer 3, especially X.25. These protocols include the Point-to-Point Protocol (PPP); the X.25 Link Access Procedure, Balanced (LAPB) protocol; and the Frame Relay protocol. Additional WAN encapsulation protocols include the Serial Line Internet Protocol (SLIP), the High-Level Data Link Control (HDLC) protocol, and Asynchronous Transfer Mode (ATM).

Again, the Remote Access exam omits many these protocols, both older and newer encapsulations. SLIP has been largely replaced by PPP, and ATM is quite common, but both are outside the scope of the exam. The omission of HDLC is significant if only because this protocol is the foundation for many other transports. In addition, it remains the default encapsulation for Cisco serial interfaces.

The encapsulations covered within the Remote Access exam include the following:

- Point-to-Point Protocol
- X.25
- Frame Relay

In later sections of this chapter and in other chapters, you will learn about each of these in greater detail.

The current Remote Access exam does not include ATM, HDLC, or SLIP. Here you will find brief descriptions of these three protocols for reference only.

Asynchronous Transfer Mode (ATM)

You might be asking what the difference is between the technology and the encapsulation type. ATM as a technology is different from the protocol itself. Unfortunately, it would be inappropriate to go into significant detail regarding ATM in this chapter—both because this chapter functions as an introduction and because this material is not on the exam. However, to understand ATM as an encapsulation type, you need to look at ATM adaptation layers (AAL) and cell header formats.

ATM is a cell-based service that breaks data into 53-byte packets. This fixed length enables processing to be handled in hardware, which reduces delay and provides for deterministic latency. ATM is primarily designed to integrate voice, data, and video services.

High-Level Data Link Control (HDLC)

High-Level Data Link Control (HDLC) is the encapsulation method used by serial links and is the default on Cisco serial interfaces. The protocol provides for a 32-bit checksum and three transfer modes: normal, asynchronous response, and asynchronous balanced. Many point-to-point connections using Cisco routers continue to make use of the HDLC protocol.

Serial Line Internet Protocol (SLIP)

The *Serial Line Internet Protocol (SLIP)* is designed for point-to-point serial connections using TCP/IP. The Point-to-Point Protocol (PPP), which you will learn about next, has effectively replaced SLIP. Some installations, however, still rely on SLIP because of its simplicity.

Point-to-Point Protocol (PPP)

The *Point-to-Point Protocol (PPP)* is a standard, efficient layer 2 technology designed for connections between two endpoints. As such, it doesn't include addressing functionality as Ethernet's MAC address does, but it can be augmented to operate in point-to-multipoint installations. The PPP has effectively replaced SLIP and is commonly found in lower-bandwidth applications, although it is also used as a ubiquitous protocol for a wide range of higher-bandwidth installations. One of the most innovative benefits of PPP is its support for multiple upper-layer protocols. This is accomplished by the use of the Network Control Protocol (NCP), which encapsulates the upper layers. The Link Control Protocol (LCP) is used to negotiate connections on the WAN data link, and in PPP, it provides for authentication and compression. Use of PPP permits the binding of connections, also called multilink PPP.

PPP is covered in more detail in Chapter 24.

The X.25 Protocol

The X.25 protocol really comprises many protocols, including LAPB and X.25 itself, which is a layer 3 protocol. X.25 also uses various standards, including X.121, X.75, and X.3, among others.

We have included information regarding X.25 in this text; however, it is very likely that this information will not be included in the exam as it is modified in the future. Readers can expect to see questions relating to the technology, and given its historical significance, learning about X.25 is not unwarranted.

LAPB operates at layer 2 of the Open System Interconnect (OSI) model and is responsible for providing reliability. Specifically, LAPB provides windowing functions and detects missed frames.

Readers who wish to review the OSI model should refer to *CCNA: Cisco Certified Network Associate Study Guide, 4th Edition*, by Todd Lammle (Sybex, 2004).

X.25 (which can be described as also belonging to layers 1 through 3) was designed to catch errors, because it was developed to operate on poor-quality telecommunications systems. At layer 3, X.25 describes the formation of data packets and the methods to be used for connectivity, in addition to addressing.

Some consider the X.25 standards to be recommendations from the International Telecommunications Union–Telecommunication (ITU-T) Standardization Sector. In practice, this can be accurate because private X.25 networks are free to operate over any methodology that works. However, the standards can simplify matters and become very important in public X.25 networking.

The X.25 addressing standard is X.121. X.121 addresses are composed of a Data Network Identification Code (DNIC) and a Network Terminal Number (NTN). These numbers work similarly to the way area codes and phone numbers work—the DNIC is akin to an area code that is defined on a country basis, and the NTN is a specific node identifier.

Frame Relay

The Frame Relay protocol is quite simple compared to X.25 because the error correction functions have been removed. This enables the protocol to scale up to 45Mbps in currently available offerings, although this is more a practical limit than a technology-based one. The greatest benefit of Frame Relay is its availability and its low cost over long distances at high bandwidths.

The protocol itself is used to define virtual circuits, which adds an additional benefit to Frame Relay: a single physical port can terminate numerous logical virtual circuits. This can greatly reduce the hardware costs associated with an installation. Each virtual circuit is defined with a DLCI.

Frame Relay is formally presented in Chapter 29, but in the context of this chapter, the protocols of this international standard should be noted. The specifics of the protocol are defined in the following standards:

- ANSI T1.617
- ITU-T Q.933
- ITU-T Q.922

To remember the function of each standard, look at the second digit of the ITU number. As could be inferred, Q.933 is a layer 3 (OSI model) protocol, whereas Q.922 operates at layer 2.

Selecting a WAN Protocol

You should consider the following factors when selecting a WAN type:

- Availability
- Bandwidth
- Cost
- Manageability
- Applications in use
- Quality of service
- Reliability
- Security

Many of these elements are common to any network design regardless of its WAN or LAN delineation. This section defines each of these factors and provides some guidance as to how they might apply to remote access deployments.

Availability

Unfortunately, not all of the WAN technologies introduced in this chapter are available in all locations. Although this is frequently true in more rural locations, it might also be true on a country-by-country basis. Distance, technology, and infrastructure all play a role in determining what services will be available in a particular location. Table 22.4 summarizes the technologies and general availability throughout the world.

Bandwidth

Applications might demand more bandwidth than is readily available with some WAN technologies. For example, an asynchronous dial-up connection is limited to 56Kbps. Should the application require the movement of more data than will fit in this constraint, the network architect will be required to select a different technology.

TABLE 22.4 Worldwide Availability of WAN Technologies

Technology	Availability
Asynchronous dial-up	Widely available
X.25	Widely available
ISDN	Moderately available
Frame Relay	Widely available
Leased lines	Widely available
DSL	Moderately available
Cable modem	Widely available (U.S.)

Frequently, selecting another technology will increase overall costs; for example, a T-1 circuit will cost substantially more than a standard analog connection at a remote location. Some technologies provide high levels of bandwidth for relatively low cost. Frame Relay is an example of one such technology.

Table 22.5 compares available bandwidth of common WAN technologies.

TABLE 22.5 Bandwidth Comparison of WAN Technologies

Technology	Bandwidth
Asynchronous dial-up	Low
X.25	Low
ISDN	Moderate
Frame Relay	High
Leased lines	High
DSL	Moderate
Cable modem	Moderate

Cost

Cost is almost always the single most important criteria in the network design. As such, network designers and architects are required to weigh the relative cost of a WAN technology against the services that it provides. Again, Frame Relay frequently reduces the costs of a WAN circuit compared to a point-to-point leased line. The network architect needs to weigh this cost differentiation against the other factors used in determining the appropriate WAN protocol to use.

Table 22.6 compares the costs of various WAN technologies.

TABLE 22.6 Cost Comparison of WAN Technologies

Technology	Cost
Asynchronous dial-up	Low. However, per-minute and distance charges can significantly increase total cost.
X.25	Low. However, per-minute and distance charges can significantly increase total cost.
ISDN	Low. However, per-minute and distance charges can significantly increase total cost.
Frame Relay	Low.
Leased lines	High.
DSL	Low.
Cable modem	Low.

Manageability

The best networks cannot hope to operate without being manageable. In local area networks, this is fairly simple because the administrator controls everything from the wall jack to the server or WAN router. In remote access, these advantages no longer exist because the ability to physically access the remote end has been removed. When the connection is down or disconnected (reflecting the potential differences between dedicated circuits and on-demand connections), it is not possible to logically connect to the remote equipment. Either of these limitations can greatly work against quick problem resolution.

For remote access manageability, the designer and administrator will frequently try to automate as many functions as possible. This can be accomplished with tools including Dynamic Host Configuration Protocol (DHCP), which automatically assigns IP addresses; and authentication servers, including Enhanced Terminal Access Controller Access Control System (TACACS+), which can centralize the user-authentication database. Administrators prefer centralization, instead of the alternative, which would require placing each user and password on every access resource manually. This centralizing of the security function will also make the network more secure; removing a single terminated employee will remove their access account from all entrances into the network.

Table 22.7 shows the difference in manageability of various WAN technologies.

TABLE 22.7 Manageability Comparison of WAN Technologies

Technology	Manageability
Asynchronous dial-up	Little.
X.25	Some, including congestion statistics.
ISDN	Some.
Frame Relay	High.
Leased lines	High.
DSL	Some.
Cable modem	Some. Very little controllable by the end user, but the carrier can perform some management functions on their behalf.

Real World Scenario

Remote Access in the Field: Manageability

The benefits of centralized access control cannot be overemphasized, but a certain amount of care must accompany this process. Many older security products would store the password file in cleartext, which could be read by anyone with access to the server. This, coupled with no requirement to change the passwords on a regular basis, made centralized security less secure than one that stores passwords in an encrypted form or one that uses tokens or other mechanisms than passwords.

Obviously, the trick is to make sure that the central access control database and server are secure. This again yields a benefit to the administrator because this can be accomplished easily when there are one or two security servers (remember, redundancy is an important consideration). Although the remote access devices will also demand a degree of security, it's far easier to protect a single resource than tens or hundreds—the basis for perimeter firewalls.

A note regarding forcing regular password changes: it can be taken too far. Consider an organization that requires monthly password changes. Our first guess at everyone's password would be some combination of month and year—jun00, for example. Incremented passwords, such as Tyler7, Tyler8, and so on, would also be common; of course, substitute the name of your child, pet, or significant other in the string.

Applications in Use

Network designers are concerned with two specific characteristics of the traffic when selecting a WAN protocol. The first consideration relates to the upper layer protocol that will be used. For example, it's not possible to use SLIP with any other upper layer protocol except IP. To use a different protocol, the administrator would have to select another lower level protocol (PPP, for example) to transport native Internetwork Packet Exchange (IPX) packets. The second consideration has to do with the acceptability of delay on the part of the upper layer protocol. Systems Network Architecture (SNA), a mainframe protocol, traditionally cannot accept a high level of delay.

Fortunately, most applications can use many transport protocols and most operate using IP. This enables the remote access solution to focus on supporting a single protocol in most cases, and it enables the use of a protocol that does not suffer significantly from the delay present in low-bandwidth and on-demand connections. Because of this, many vendors and designers will opt to use PPP as a transport protocol.

Quality of Service (QoS)

Unlike the marketing term "quality of service" that is based on traffic shaping and control, this *quality of service (QoS)* refers to the reliability of the connection and its capability to process non-data traffic. This simpler view is controlled less by configuration and software and is more reliant on the physical and logical characteristics of the standard.

There are two factors to consider when evaluating quality of service requirements on a WAN link. The first factor involves the type of application traffic that will traverse the link—whether data and voice traffic will both share the available bandwidth, for example. The second factor focuses more upon the reliability of the connection; for example, dial-up analog connections are frequently considered less reliable than a point-to-point link. As a result, designers might wish to incorporate backup technologies based on both the criticality of the data and the reliability of the selected WAN protocol. For instance, Frame Relay, though it is considered a reliable protocol, is frequently backed up with analog connections or ISDN.

Reliability

Reliability is a quality of service characteristic; however, it is relatively important and warrants separate consideration. As noted in the quality of service description, reliability is frequently a factor in determining whether a backup link is required. Some designers will use multiple PVCs to provide a greater level of reliability when problems are anticipated in the WAN cloud; this differs from those situations when the designer is concerned with reliability in the local loop or in the last portion of the circuit. In these situations, a separate connection is warranted.

The designer might also wish to use separate components in remote locations to further augment reliability. This migrates the objective into the category of redundancy. It would require disparate routers, circuits, data service unit/channel service unit (DSU/CSU) terminations, and electrical systems to become fully fault tolerant, although it might also require placing the equipment in two separate telephone closets with different building entrances to different service providers' offices. Different providers would further add to the redundancy of the design and its ultimate survivability, which is synonymous to reliability. See Table 22.8 for a comparison of various WAN technologies. Please note that this table refers to the technology's inherent capability to recover from data corruption, error, or topology change.

TABLE 22.8 Reliability Comparison of WAN Technologies

Technology	Reliability
Asynchronous dial-up	Low
X.25	High
ISDN	Moderate
Frame Relay	Moderate
Leased lines	Moderate
DSL	Moderate
Cable modem	Moderate

Examining this table further, it's important to consider each factor of reliability. Dial-up connections cannot recover errors within packets and cannot automatically find a new path through the network, except when the circuit is emulated over ATM or another technology within the carrier's cloud. X.25 is considered highly reliable by most—including Cisco—because the protocol provides for error correction and other mechanisms to protect data without relying on upper layer protocols.

The technologies rated with moderate reliability are typically quite robust and will work for most users without any problems. Historically, however, Cisco presented the position that these technologies were more prone to problems, including lower service guarantees. Although none of the technologies rated moderate provide for error correction as X.25 does, the quality of cables, equipment, and software makes errors very rare and easily addressed by the upper level protocols.

Carriers are turning to Multi-Protocol Label Switching (MPLS) for their voice and data clouds and IP datagrams for all services. This will eventually position each of these technologies as a last-mile service; the technology within the cloud will be transparent to the user and data. Table 22.8 focuses on the end-to-end use of the noted technologies.

Security

Security is an important consideration when selecting a WAN protocol—security relating to protection from corruption, theft, or misuse of digital transmissions. Some applications, such as financial ones, require a high level of security. For example, many designers in financial institutions will select private point-to-point connections over fiber-optic cable. In installations that require less security, the designer might opt for a public connection, which frequently has a substantially reduced cost.

Remote access solutions can alter the security model of a corporation substantially, because it is reasonable to assume that some business data will be stored remotely. This immediately causes a security concern because a lost or stolen notebook can quickly lead to the release of corporate data. The network designer will typically be more concerned with the security requirements that will prevent unauthorized access to the network. This, again, is a fairly simple model because the majority of the security configuration will be placed on the remote access servers.

Virtual Private Networks (VPNs)

In recent years, the use of *virtual private network (VPN)* technology has entered into the remote access landscape. VPNs allow secure connections over public networks—typically making use of the Internet. Data is encrypted for transport in a virtual tunnel between source and destination, and its costs are greatly reduced without a substantial decrease in security. As such, a VPN is a system of these tunnels used to create a logical system of conduits that transport user data.

Although most VPN software is very solid, it's important to note that most companies bristle at the thought of using only basic software to secure data. In addition, the processing demands required by some encryption technologies are high, and many implementations will likely require newer processors or co-processed implementations. Co-processors offload specific functions from the main processor; video adapters have used them for years to provide better graphics output. Encryption can benefit from this coprocessor design as well.

Two common VPN technologies are in use today: IPSec and SSL. The IP Security Protocol (IPSec) is an encapsulation mechanism that operates at layer 3 of the OSI model. It is useful in providing a virtual end-to-end connection between points regardless of the technology. In IPSec, the client is on the network and can use most software and applications. IPSec uses triple-DES (Data Encryption Standard) in most instances, but this will be replaced in the near future by the less demanding, and possibly more secure, AES, or Advanced Encryption Standard. Both technologies encrypt data so it cannot be modified or intercepted en route.

Secure Sockets Layer (SSL) is commonly used to secure web sessions and transactions; however, it is being used more and more by application emulators and remote access technologies. These installations provide a screen presence to the remote user—all the processing occurs at the central, hosting location. As networking evolves, it is quite likely that VPNs and technology independence will become common, and customers will use any physical connectivity technology—including Ethernet—to access remote locations.

Choosing Remote Connection Cisco Products

Cisco offers a wide range of router products available for use in remote access solutions. Most of these fall into one of two general categories: fixed interface or modular interface. Fixed-interface solutions are fairly common in remote deployments, whereas modular interfaces are found in central locations. This placement also relates well to their characteristics: Fixed-interface solutions are very limited and lack upgradeability. Modular routers are expandable and usually provide better performance.

In addition to the interface types, different software options are available in the Cisco product line. Many products take advantage of the Cisco Internetwork Operating System (IOS), which simplifies administration and training expenses because administrators need to learn only one operating system. Routers based on this software also support more features under most circumstances. Other Cisco routers make use of the Cisco Broadband Operating System (CBOS), which can be found on the 600 series products. The CBOS software is limited in functionality, and many of its commands differ from their IOS counterparts. However, the 600 series routers can reduce acquisition costs by more than half compared to an IOS-based platform—a substantial cost difference when magnified against the hundreds of routers that might be acquired in a large-scale remote access deployment.

Real World Scenario

Remote Access in the Field: Outsourcing Remote Access Solutions

Given the complexity of managing equipment in hundreds of locations internationally, many companies have elected to outsource their remote access solutions. This option provides a great deal of support flexibility because the outsourcing company can frequently provide technicians over a larger geographical area. As a result, outsourcing provides a great deal of benefit because it can provide faster response times and can free corporate support personnel from the responsibility of responding themselves.

Outsourcing solutions can also provide cost savings in the form of leasing options for remote access equipment. Although the final cost of leasing might be greater, many companies use this financing option as a means to reduce corporate taxes.

By no means should companies use outsourcing as a panacea. Significant down sides exist, including the real risk of outsourcing too many components of the network. Should the outsourcing company be unable to comply with service-level agreements or unable to provide a reasonable level of service, the remote users will suffer and the ultimate recourse will be to change outsourcing companies—a process that is time-consuming and costly.

Companies should seriously evaluate the benefits of outsourcing against their overall corporate strategy. Selective use of outsourcing, in addition to leasing, can greatly facilitate remote access solutions.

Fixed Interfaces

Early routers were little more than Unix workstations and PCs equipped with two Ethernet interfaces. The first fixed-purpose routers were typically fixed interface as well—there was no provision for adding an additional interface or a new type of interface. As router products evolved, the capability to add modularity to the products increased. A fixed-interface router cannot be expanded, so one with two Ethernet interfaces will always have only two Ethernet interfaces. When you need a third, you must replace the router or augment it with another.

Fixed-interface routers typically reduce the costs associated with acquisition, which directly relates to the initial capital expense. Many organizations try to reduce capital costs, even when this leads to ultimate replacement requirements. In addition, fixed-interface routers are simpler to install than modular routers, especially by less experienced staff and vendors. Fixed-interface equipment lacks an upgrade path, however. It is impossible to add features without requiring a complete replacement of the equipment. Replacing equipment can quickly offset the savings you made with the initial purchase. Therefore, designers should seriously evaluate the life span of the equipment and the growth potential for the environment before they make any irreversible decisions. Typically, sites with more than 30 users will quickly outgrow fixed-configuration routers, although different environments yield different thresholds.

Cisco offers two alternatives to the fixed router. The modular router enables network modules or port adapters to be installed by supplying the type and volume of interfaces needed; this is discussed in the next section. In addition, routers are also available for expansion with fixed interfaces and one or more modular ports. The Cisco 1600 is a good example of this hybrid router type and is discussed later in this chapter.

Modular Interfaces

The modular-interface remote access products provide the designer with a few benefits, including an upgrade path and, typically, higher densities that are unavailable in the fixed-interface models. This flexibility comes at a price; however, and the costs associated with the removal and replacement of network equipment easily offsets this initial cost difference.

The benefits of the modular router also lead to potential savings in the initial acquisition of the device. Sometimes the fixed-interface router provides interfaces that are not needed—Cisco still charges for the unused ports. Although port disparity is uncommon given the wide array of fixed-configuration routers in the Cisco product line, it is possible to find situations in which a high number of Ethernet ports also require a high number of serial ports on a fixed router, which greatly adds to the cost. Modular routers provide the following positives and negatives:

Pros	Cons
Defined upgrade path	Higher cost
Potentially lower total cost of ownership	More complex installation
	More difficult and costly to stock spare equipment

Again, it's usually best to select modular routers to avoid forklift upgrades in the future—ones that require the complete replacement of the chassis. However, the use of modular routers comes at higher initial and support costs.

Product Selection Tools

Most designers find that the best information regarding Cisco's product line comes from their sales representatives. The sales force, though, relies upon information on Cisco's website. Cisco has provided a product selection tool that enables the designer to define the features needed for their particular WAN project. As of this writing, this service is available at `www.cisco.com/pcgi-bin/front.x/corona/prodtool/select.pl`; however, Cisco does change its site from time to time.

The end of this chapter provides a high-level presentation of the major remote access platforms provided by Cisco.

Cabling and Assembling the WAN

The cabling of the WAN will vary depending on the technologies used and the equipment locations. For example, central sites typically use modular, high-capacity routers, whereas branch offices typically use modular or fixed-configuration routers. Usually telecommuter equipment entails fixed-configuration devices and attempts to place all components of the customer premises equipment (CPE) in a single chassis.

The cabling will also depend on the media to be used. For example, RJ-45 interfaces are typically used to terminate Ethernet connections, whereas serial connections are typically terminated with RS-232 or V.35 cables. Cisco also provides integrated data service units (DSUs) that can accept the T-1 connection or DS3's COAX connection directly—a serial port uses an external DSU and is the focus of the Remote Access certification.

This section supplies an overview of the cable connections used with different WAN types. You will learn about interfacing and terminating options for remote access equipment, identifying appropriate equipment, and verifying a network installation. Subsequent chapters will expand upon many of the concepts introduced here, including ISDN, X.25, Frame Relay, PPP, security, and the types of telecommuters and specific equipment in the Cisco product line.

Internetworking Overview and Remote Access Interface Options

Selecting interface types and determining their interoperability for the various cable connections are a couple of the most critical components used to construct an internetwork. Although it's possible to perform media conversion for some interfaces, it's far easier to maintain consistency throughout the design. For example, if a fiber connection is needed to link the router to the switch, it is generally preferred to use a fiber interface on the router, as opposed to using a copper interface and then using a copper-to-fiber converter upstream. This is also applicable for serial connectors—it's far easier to manage the network when all cables and interfaces are the same and relevant to that provided by the vendors. To successfully design this standardization, it is important to know the functionality of each connection and how it might be used to terminate network interfaces; each of these connections is presented next.

Asynchronous or Analog Connections

Standard telephone service typically terminates with an RJ-11 interface, which connects the modem to the telephone company's jack. External modems are attached to a Cisco router with an RS-232 cable. This is also referred to as an EIA/TIA-232 cable. The router end of this connection uses the Cisco DB-60 connector, a 60-pin termination specific to Cisco routers, and a DB-25 connector, which interfaces to the modem. The DB-25 connector is quite common in telecommunications equipment.

ISDN BRI

ISDN BRIs are common in branch and telecommuter installations in which higher than asynchronous bandwidth is needed. The BRI specification avails two 64Kbps bearer channels (B channels) for user traffic, and it uses a single 16Kbps D channel for management and signaling. It is important to remember that these connections are circuit switched and that the data link protocol on the D channel is Link Access Procedure, Data (LAPD).

This differs from the X.25 protocol, which uses LAPB. The ISDN B channel is similar to a standard voice channel in terms of bandwidth, and therefore most systems allow the use of a B channel for a traditional analog call. Although the single channel is encoded digitally from the ISDN device to the switch—unlike an analog connection from a phone to a phone switch—the overall mechanics between them are similar.

Some installations of ISDN allow only 56Kbps for each B channel. The reference to X.25 is incorporated in this section due to the comparison provided by the protocol. X.25 is a highly robust protocol, but is not commonly deployed and is no longer part of the exam.

The ISDN BRI is terminated with different connections, but the network (phone company) is usually terminated with an RJ-11 or RJ-45 interface. According to the specifications, the termination should always be accomplished with an RJ-45, which provides for additional signaling and visually distinguishes the ISDN interface from analog connections. However, the exterior pins (1, 2, 7, and 8) of the RJ-45 are frequently unused, so some providers use RJ-11 instead. If you can control this part of the installation, specify RJ-45 and use a specific color to differentiate it from Ethernet, T-1, and other connections.

ISDN PRI (North America)

In North America, ISDN PRIs are provisioned over T-1 standards. The T-1 standard, also called DS1, is capable of servicing 24 64Kbps channels—each channel being historically provisioned for a single voice connection. From this, 23 B channels are allocated, with the last 64Kbps channel used for D channel signaling.

The most important thing to note, in addition to the channels of ISDN PRI, is that ISDN PRI operates over *channelized T-1* connections. This means that at its core, each B channel is one time slot in the T-1 specification, although clearly, there is additional functionality. PRI requires only two pairs of copper wire (the same as T-1); however, all installations should use RJ-45, which has four pairs. This provides a visual variance to RJ-11 ports, and typically RJ-45 provides a better, cleaner connection.

ISDN PRI (Europe)

The European telecommunications standard comparable to T-1 services is called *E-1*, and it provides for 31 channels. (Time slot 0 is used for signaling and is not a channel in the ISDN framework.) The last channel (actually channel 16) is used as a D channel for signaling, yielding a total of 30 user bearer channels. As a significant aside, in Europe, the vendor typically provides the network termination, whereas in the U.S., the customer usually provides it.

It is important to understand the differences between the North American and European specifications. With either PRI or BRI, a U.S.-manufactured ISDN router will not function elsewhere in the world because the NT is built-in. As the service provider expects to provide the NT, the interfaces are incompatible. ISDN routers manufactured elsewhere will work in the U.S. if you add an external NT.

Consult with the vendor to determine the proper termination for E-1 PRI installations. These should differ little from American installations, but there might be small alterations, which could include, for example, providing the demarcation point on a wiring block. ISDN remains popular in Europe and is likely to continue as an access technology there for some time, but there is increasing evidence of DSL proliferation.

Chapter 26 addresses some of the differences in European ISDN specifications—as compared to North American installations—in greater detail. However, it's important to note that the middle channel of the E-1 circuit (16) is the D channel, contrasted with 24 in the T-1 specification. In addition, T-1 starts numbering at 0, and E-1 starts with 1. (As noted before, channel 0 is used for framing.)

Frame Relay

Using Frame Relay is a powerful way of getting remote access and WAN connectivity. As a packet-switched technology, Frame Relay operates at bandwidths up to 45Mbps, although older networks might limit this to 1.544 (DS3 versus T-1).

Please check with your vendor for the latest information regarding access loop capacity. Also remember that DS3 is sometimes—incorrectly—called T-3, but in normal conversation the two terms indicate the same amount of bandwidth.

Frame Relay is supported on Cisco routers with EIA/TIA-232, EIA/TIA-449, V.35, X.21, and EIA-530 signaling, but the DB-60 serial cable is almost always used. The network side of the DSU/CSU connection is RJ-45.

Identifying Company Site Equipment

One of the key challenges for the network designer is selecting the equipment that is appropriate to both the current and future demands of the network. This becomes even more difficult when cost constraints are taken into account.

Designers need to select equipment based primarily on the port type and density required for their application. *Port type* refers to the topology, interface, and protocol (T-1, PRI ISDN with an RJ-45 connector, for example). *Port density* is a simplified way of noting the number of ports that can be squeezed into a particular slot or chassis. Frequently changing connectors will allow greater density; however, a larger chassis can also increase the density. As a result, equipment purchased for the central site will frequently require larger and more modular platforms. Equipment for remote locations tends to be simpler and less expensive—primarily to simplify administrative costs.

Although the current version of the Remote Access exam is relatively new, some of Cisco's recommendations and questions might refer to end-of-life or end-of-sales equipment. Please consider this when deploying a production remote access solution, and consult the Cisco website, `www.cisco.com`, for the most current information.

Central Site

The central site has different requirements compared to the remote branch and telecommuter locations. Unlike those locations, the central site is an aggregation point for all of the other links, and, as such, it requires greater bandwidth, larger equipment, and additional administration.

As of this writing, Cisco suggests four high-end routers to meet the demands of the central site. Designers should consider protocols, interfaces, and scalability when selecting a piece of network equipment. The recommended platforms are as follows:

- Cisco 3600XM and 3700
- Cisco AS5x00
- Cisco 7000/7500

Note that each of these platforms is modular in nature. In addition, Cisco continually introduces new platforms into the product line and will most likely continue to do so as part of its AVVID initiative. *AVVID* stands for *Architecture for Voice, Video, and Integrated Data*, and although it's a marketing term, it will likely define an entire class of equipment for some time. Historically, remote access technologies have been centered on data transport, with support for voice—ISDN and the use of a B channel, for example. Demands will increase for video, voice integration, and data transport in the future; in fact, these demands are already surfacing today.

The following sections provide a more detailed overview of these platforms.

The Cisco 3600 Platform

The Cisco 3600 and 3600XM router platform is well suited to smaller aggregation point deployments and is currently available in the 3620, 3640, and 3660 models. The third digit in these numbers reflects the number of slots available for modules: 2, 4, and 6, respectively. The 3600 was originally designed to address high-bandwidth services and the integration of voice and video, along with traditional data services. Due to these characteristics, the platform is also well suited to the remote branch application.

Many production networks have deployed this system in the remote branch locations as well, when high-speed or multiple interfaces are required. The OC-3 ATM port adapter and the newer inverse multiplexing for ATM (IMA) adapter are benefits to the 3600 platform in remote branch installations. Prior to the release of the 3660, the 3600 series was limited to a single internal AC power supply, which reduced its acceptance in the data center or central site—the 3620 and 3640 routers were provisioned with only a single power supply. These boxes could, however, be outfitted with external DC-based redundant systems, but this solution was never clean from a wiring and simplifying perspective.

Many different types of equipment can be used in the central site, but Cisco recommends the 3600 platform overall. As one of the newest routers, the 3600 does provide a solid service offering for designers. The AS5x00 platform is also well suited to ISDN and dial-up terminations in the central site.

The Cisco 3700 Platform

The Cisco 3700 series is a newer version of the 3600, with significantly greater expandability options. As of this writing there are two versions of the platform: the 3725 and the 3745. The third digit in the model number relates to the number of Network Module (NM) slots in the chassis.

Both versions of the 3700 router provide two 10/100 Ethernet ports, two Advanced Integration Module slots (AIM) and three WAN Interface Card (WIC) slots. The platforms are well suited to branch installations, particularly when Voice over IP (VoIP) services might be installed. The platform supports switched Ethernet services with inline power as well.

The Cisco AS5x00 Platform

The Cisco AS5x00 access servers are designed to terminate ISDN and analog dial-up connections. These systems differ substantially from other router platforms in the central site. The primary benefit of these systems is that the routing, switching, channel services, and modems are all integrated into a single chassis, which reduces the number of external connections and space requirements in the rack. These devices can terminate hundreds of connections.

The Cisco 7000/7200/7500 Platforms

Prior to the release of the Gigabit Switch Router (GSR), or Cisco 12000 series, the 7000 series was the flagship of the Cisco router line. The 7000 series is still well suited to the task of remote access aggregation, which is typically less demanding than the high-speed ISP niche of the GSR.

The 7200 platform is most frequently used in new remote access installations. Cisco positions this box as a high-performance, high-density central site router for terminating LAN and WAN connections. Many companies use the 7500 (specifically the 7513) in their network cores, and the platform is still one of the most capable multiprotocol routers in production.

The GSR is beyond the scope of this text and is currently used in high-end data centers and ISP environments. It is designed to forward IP packets only.

Remote Branch

The concept of a remote branch is highly variable, depending upon the individual location and services needed. A branch office might contain two or a hundred users, and their demands might be substantial in terms of redundancy, bandwidth, and supportability.

Typically, a remote branch services a population of users rather than a single user. In addition, the level of technical expertise in the remote location is usually limited. Platforms typically recommended for the remote branch include the following:

- Cisco 1600 platform
- Cisco 1700 platform
- Cisco 1800 platform
- Cisco 2600XM platform

The Cisco 1600 Platform

The Cisco 1600 provides an ISDN BRI termination in addition to a WAN expansion slot. This enables the router to accept a WIC, which can be used for a serial connection or integrated T-1/fractional T-1 services. The WIC can also be used for Frame Relay terminations. The router is commonly deployed in remote branch facilities because it can link the Ethernet interface to a Frame Relay network with ISDN BRI backup. This configuration does not provide router redundancy but can greatly augment circuit fault tolerance.

As an IOS-based router, the 1600 can support most features, including Network Address Translation (NAT), access-list control, and multi-protocol support, including IP, IPX, and AppleTalk.

The 1600 series is now end-of-life, but it may remain in the exam for a little while yet. The replacement is the 1800 series.

The Cisco 1700 Platform

The Cisco 1700 series routers provide two modular card slots for WAN interfaces, in addition to VPN features. This platform can support Ethernet and FastEthernet LANs. Expansion cards are interchangeable with other platforms in the Cisco line, including the 3600.

The Cisco 1800 Platform

The 1800 series is designed to replace the 1600 platform and also act as an upgrade for the 1700 series. The architecture supports newer interfaces, especially the High-Speed WAN Interface Card (HWIC) range, which includes a 4-port Ethernet switch. Many of the 1700 series interface cards are also supported. Designed for small to medium sized enterprises, several new options for cards are also offered, such as VPN and security options.

The Cisco 2500 Platform

The Cisco 2500 series router is available in a wide array of fixed configurations, and depending on the model, it can support Ethernet, Token Ring, serial, and ISDN BRI connections. Some models include an integrated Ethernet hub.

Most of the 2500 series routers are end-of-sale and cannot be ordered. The 2600XM series provides the best replacement; however, some users might wish to review the 3700 series for more advanced branch and small office installations. Cisco continues to sell the 2509, 2511, AS2509, and AS2511 platforms, but prudence dictates review of newer platforms before ordering. But if you are buying routers yourself to practice on, consider buying some cheap 2500 series on eBay!

The Cisco 2600XM Platform

The Cisco 2600XM platform builds upon the 2500 series with the addition of two modular card slots for WAN interfaces, including T-1, ISDN PRI, and Frame Relay.

Telecommuter

In the real world, telecommuters fall into two distinct categories: remote users and telecommuters. The remote user requires access from multiple locations because they might be at home, at a customer's site, or in a hotel. Typically, these users use analog dial-up connections. However, wireless technologies are becoming increasingly popular with these users. Most remote users use a modem connected to (or built into) their PC.

Telecommuters operate from a home office or an otherwise fixed location. For telecommuters, the smaller, fixed-configuration routers are best suited to the task, and therefore, the technologies recommended by Cisco for remote access mesh well with their needs. These platforms include the following:

- Cisco 700 series
- Cisco 800 series
- Cisco 1000 series

The primary characteristics of these platforms include simple options and fixed configurations, both of which can lower the cost of these systems.

The 700 Series

The 700 series was designed for telecommuters and supports ISDN. Routing services are provided for IP and IPX, and this router uses the Cisco IOS-700 software as opposed to the standard IOS. This can add to the training requirements for a corporation because the differences in syntax can be substantial.

You might be confused that this section is devoted to the Cisco 700 series routers, as this platform has been removed from the product line. The 700 series also will likely be removed from the exam. However, you see a question or two regarding the platform, particularly as it relates to various connectivity options. Unfortunately, the Cisco certification exams do not always parallel the current level of technology being deployed and marketed.

The 700 series has three models. These are outlined in Table 22.9.

TABLE 22.9 Cisco 700 Series Platform Features

Platform	Cisco 761	Cisco 775	Cisco 776
ISDN interface	S/T	S/T	S/T and U
Analog ports	No	Yes, RJ-11	No
Ethernet	10-BaseT	Four-port 10-BaseT	10-BaseT

Cisco claims that each of the 700 series routers can support up to 30 users; however, in practice, the limitations of ISDN and the platform realistically place fewer than 10 users as a more reasonable population.

The 700 series also supports the following configuration features:

DHCP Relay This can forward DHCP client requests to an off-subnet DHCP server. DHCP provides automatic IP addressing, which can greatly reduce the administration overhead of manual addressing.

DHCP Server This feature enables the 700 series router to provide the DHCP Server function as opposed to forwarding DHCP requests to an external server. Although this feature might have some benefits, most large corporations prefer to use a centrally located and administered server and leave the routing function to the routers.

Port Address Translation (PAT) PAT is an interesting feature for the designer and administrator to consider. It can significantly conserve address space because all devices share a single IP address to the outside network. The router alters the port number and maintains a dynamic one-to-one relationship between the source IP address and port and the altered port assignment. Unfortunately, PAT and its associated feature Network Address Translation (NAT) do not function correctly with protocols that embed the IP address, including NetBIOS packets. This makes these features difficult to implement in Windows installations that rely on NetBIOS functions.

Compression The 700 series routers can compress data by using the Stacker compression algorithm when communicating with Cisco IOS-based routers. Compression is a method by which computing devices substitute longer strings of repeated sequences with token or symbolic notation; the net result is a reduction in the number of bits required to send data. There is a performance penalty because the routers must compress and decompress the data stream; however, this is negligible in lower bandwidth instances.

IPX and IP routing All 700 series routers support IPX and IP packet routing. Bridging is offered for support of other protocols. This is not a major issue for many corporations because IP is easily the dominant protocol. However, it does mean that Macintosh environments that have not migrated to IP will likely wish to select another platform. Stated another way, AppleTalk is not included in the 700 series and is not on the exam.

Bonding The Cisco 700 series routers support *Multilink Protocol (MP) bonding*, which allows for the aggregation of two or more channels into a single logical connection. Bonding can be used to improve the throughput when only low-bandwidth links are available.

Management Simple Network Management Protocol (SNMP) management is available with routers in the 700 series. This allows for pooling and trap alarm messages. Some organizations do not opt to manage their remote equipment (home-based) due to the volume of false error messages and the sheer number of devices.

Multinational support The 700 series routers support both North American and international applications, including most major ISDN switches. The platform is certified for use in more than 25 countries. Administrators should check with the Cisco website or their sales representative for a current listing of countries, and remember to verify power requirements for their installation.

Support for telephone services Specific models of the Cisco 700—including the 765, 766, 775, and 776—provide telephone services over ISDN, including call-waiting, call-hold, and call-retrieve. The telecommunications service provider must make these services available.

Snapshot routing The *Routing Information Protocol (RIP)* is a fairly chatty protocol, sending a full update every 30 seconds. *Snapshot routing* resolves the problems that result from using RIP on an ISDN circuit. Because ISDN is tariffed on a per-minute basis in most installations, it would not be cost-effective to have the circuit open all the time just for routing updates. Snapshot routing caches the dynamic routing information and maintains it in the router's route table even when the link is down.

Product Selection and Outsourcing

When recommending a router product, we generally steer away from platforms such as the 700 series. The limitations of the platform and the differences in command syntax generally add to the total cost of ownership, and the price difference, with discounts, is generally not that significant compared to IOS-based routers. Of course, when magnified over thousands of routers, a $200 difference per unit is suddenly $200,000 or more. Corporate budgets might bristle at that increase unless the consultant or designer can justify the extra expense with extra benefits.

One alternative that some companies choose is outsourcing their remote access platforms. This generally appears as a lease, which can be advantageous to the accountants and can offload the support and repair functions from the staff.

The 800 Series

Cisco's lowest price IOS-based routers are found in the 800 series. For remote access, these routers offer ISDN BRI terminations and basic telephone service ports. Recall that ISDN BRI can be used for two traditional analog services. As of this writing, the 800 series includes ADSL, Ethernet, HDSL, ISDN, and serial terminations, as noted in the following list:

- Cisco 837 ADSL Broadband Router
- Cisco 836 ADSL over ISDN Broadband Router
- Cisco 831 Ethernet Broadband Router
- Cisco 828 G.SHDSL Router
- Cisco 827 ADSL Router
- Cisco 827H ADSL Router
- Cisco 827-4V ADSL Router
- Cisco 826 ADSL Router
- Cisco 813 ISDN Router
- Cisco 811 ISDN Router
- Cisco 806 Broadband Router
- Cisco 805 Serial Router
- Cisco 804 ISDN Router
- Cisco 803 ISDN Router
- Cisco 802 ISDN Router
- Cisco 801 ISDN Router

In addition, Cisco has released the SOHO (small office, home office) 7X and 9X platforms. Their Linksys product line, recently acquired, is being offered as an independent series and is not included in the 800 series, but these systems do compete in many instances.

The latest information regarding the 800 series is available at `http://www.cisco.com/en/US/customer/products/hw/routers/ps380/index.html`.

Please be careful with this statement: The 800 series is currently the *lowest* cost *IOS*-based router. This does not make it the cheapest router mentioned. The 700 series is generally the *lowest* cost router.

The 1000 Series

The Cisco 1000 series routers are based on a fixed configuration; however, they provide for WAN options beyond ISDN. The Cisco 1005 router provides a traditional serial interface for expansion. Most corporations appear to be selecting other platforms than the 1000 series.

Verifying a Network Installation

Verification of the network installation is encompassed in three phases:

- Bit error rate tests and validation diagnostics
- Connection of customer premise equipment
- Configuration

The telephone company installer usually performs bit error rate tests and other validation diagnostics, the first component of verification. The second phase of verification typically requires connecting the customer premise equipment—the router or DSU. After the equipment is connected, the installer can use the LED information to provide a high-level overview of the usability of the link. The third phase of verification uses an actual configuration. For example, the installer or network architect might configure one of the PVCs to carry an upper layer protocol for simple connectivity tests. For the purposes of the exam, Cisco is primarily interested in the use of the LED indicators.

Verifying the Central Site

As explained previously, Cisco recommends using its 3600 series routers (XM) for the central site, although other platforms are also available. Therefore, the following text focuses on the verification steps for installation of the 3600 platform.

Figure 22.2 shows the front of the 3600 router (in this case, it is a 3640 router). As you will notice, the router is fairly limited in the amount of diagnostic information it can provide. LEDs are limited in the same way that idiot lights are more limited than gauges in an automobile: They can alert you when there is a problem, but full instrumentation (in a car this would include gauges and a tachometer) can provide details and advanced warning. However, it is a good place to start the process of troubleshooting, just as an oil warning light in the car helps you eliminate the brakes as a problem area.

FIGURE 22.2 The 3640 router front view

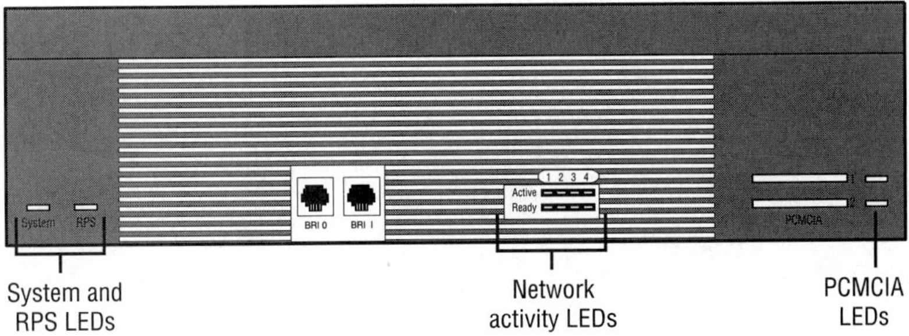

The front panel LEDs are presented as follows:

System The System LED is used to show both the system power and operation characteristics. When the System LED is off, the router is not receiving power; a solid green LED denotes proper, powered operation. An amber indicator shows that the router is not functioning correctly, but that power is connected. A blinking green light indicates that the router is powered and working properly, but it's in ROM monitor mode. Alternating amber and green show that the self-test is running. As indicated, a single LED can provide a great deal of information.

RPS The RPS LED denotes the status of the redundant power supply. On the 3640, only one power supply can be operational at a time. An off LED reflects that the RPS is not installed. A blinking green LED denotes that both the internal and redundant power supplies are operational; administrators should reconfigure the installation to run on one or the other system. A solid green LED denotes that the RPS is operational, and amber shows that the RPS is installed but not in operation.

Network Activity There are two sets of LEDs in the Network Activity section of the router. There are four LEDs per set, with one per slot. The Ready LEDs illuminate to show that a module is installed in the slot and operational. An off LED indicates that nothing is installed in the slot or that it is not functioning. The Active LEDs blink to indicate activity.

PCMCIA The PCMCIA (or PC Card) LEDs light up to show activity on that slot. This should serve as a warning to not remove the flash card when reading or writing data. Flash cards are also called PCMCIA memory cards and they store the router's flash image.

The module LEDs vary widely depending on the type of interface; however, most include at least a link or enable the LED to denote connectivity. Many LEDs also include activity indicators—the serial module, for example, also includes clocking indicators to show the presence or absence of synchronization.

Verifying the Remote Branch

As noted previously, Cisco recommends the 1600 series router for remote branch installations. This platform provides an IOS-based system with expandability. Figure 22.3 illustrates the front of the Cisco 1600 router.

FIGURE 22.3 The Cisco 1600 LEDs

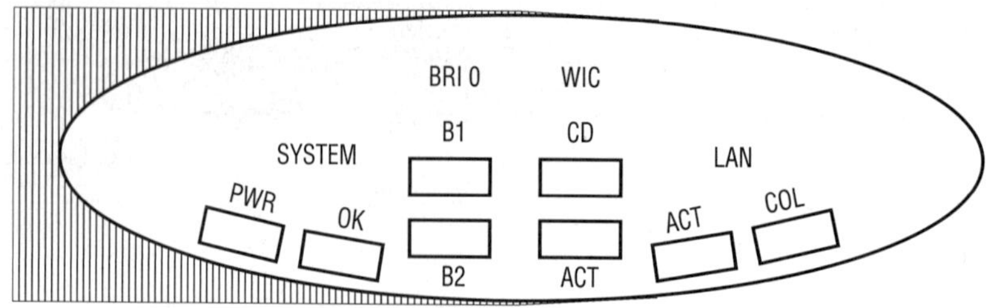

You should understand what each indicator means, as explained in the following list:

System PWR The green System power LED illuminates to show that the system is on and receiving power.

System OK The green System OK LED blinks during the boot cycle. After the boot cycle is complete, this LED is steady.

BRI0 B1 and BRI0 B2 These LEDs display active connections on the BRI0 B1 and B2 channels, respectively. BRI 0 is the first ISDN BRI interface on the router.

WIC CD This LED denotes a connection on the WAN Interface Card. This indication can be helpful when troubleshooting DSU/CSU issues.

WIC ACT The WAN Interface Card activity LED can be used to indicate circuit use, although it is helpful to use the command-line interface to see the direction and characteristics of the traffic itself.

LAN ACT The LAN activity LED is similar to the WIC activity LED, but it represents traffic on the Ethernet interface.

LAN COL The LAN collision LED indicates a collision on the Ethernet segment. It is yellow, unlike the other LEDs, which are all green.

Verifying the Telecommuter Installation

Cisco generally recommends the use of the Cisco 700 router in telecommuter installations. One example of this device is the 766 router. This device includes a substantial number of diagnostic LEDs, shown in Figure 22.4.

FIGURE 22.4 The Cisco 766 LEDs

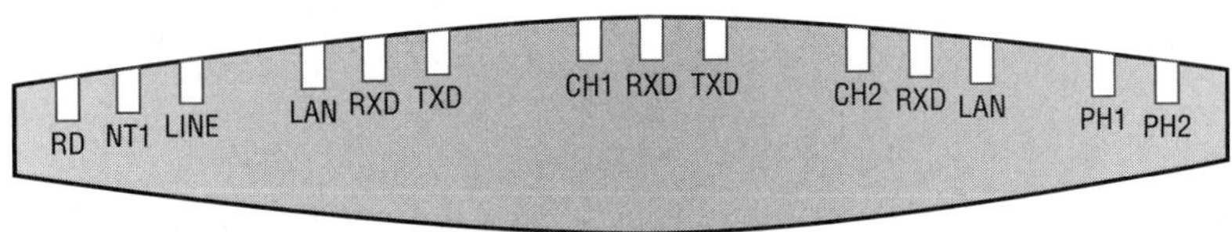

These LEDs are read as follows:

RD The ready LED is illuminated when the router is operating normally. You can use it to verify that a successful power-on self-test (POST) has been completed and that power is available to the device.

NT1 For routers with an internal ISDN NT1, this LED displays the status of the ISDN connection. When steady, the ISDN switch and the NT1 are synchronized; when it's blinking, the connection is attempting synchronization.

LINE The LINE LED indicates that framing between the router and the ISDN switch has been established.

LAN This light indicates that the Ethernet interface on the router is active and that a frame has been sent or received within the past 60 seconds. A link light on the back of the router denotes a valid connection.

LAN RXD The LAN received LED blinks upon receipt of a frame on the Ethernet interface.

LAN TXD The LAN transmitted LED blinks when frames are sent from the router onto the Ethernet link.

CH1 and CH2 These LEDs indicate the status of the two B channels on the ISDN BRI. They illuminate steadily when the connection is established and blink during the negotiation process.

CH1 RXD and CH2 RXD These LEDs reflect the receipt of packets on their respective ISDN BRI channels. Each packet generates a blink of the LED.

CH1 TXD and CH2 TXD These LEDs reflect the transmission of packets on the respective ISDN BRI channel. Each packet generates a blink of the LED.

PH1 and PH2 For routers so equipped, these LEDs provide information regarding the use of the POTS ports on the router. These ports can be used for telephone, fax, or analog modem services.

Remember the significance of each LED, including its color, for the exam. This information can be helpful in live troubleshooting as well.

Summary

As with most aspects of networking, the Physical layer provides the foundation for both LAN-based solutions and remote access ones. *Remote access* refers to the use of longer range solutions than the 100-meter Ethernet solutions commonly found in local area networks (LANs).

Remote access technologies include dial-up lines, ISDN BRI and PRI technologies, leased lines, Frame Relay, cable modem, and xDSL. Each of these solutions provides the designer with various benefits and detriments, including availability, cost, and complexity. For example, dial-up lines are widely available but are relatively expensive and of lower capacity than Frame Relay.

In addition to the physical circuits between remote locations, remote access solutions also require the physical termination equipment. This customer premises equipment (CPE) includes the router, a DSU/CSU where necessary, or a modem. ISDN also incorporates different types of terminations that the administrator needs to keep in mind.

Routers for remote access solutions vary widely within the Cisco product line. The Cisco 800 series routers are well suited to small offices and home users, whereas the Cisco 3600XM/3700 platform affords more expansion capabilities and performance.

The Remote Access exam materials might continue to focus on the older Cisco 700 series ISDN routers. Although these routers are no longer available, success on the Remote Access exam requires a high level of understanding of the platform and its characteristics. Specific attention should be paid to the interface types of the model, in addition to the fact that the 700 series does not run an IOS image.

It's also important to note that the materials in this chapter focus on the exam and the information needed for the exam, rather than the solutions necessary in modern remote access solutions. For example, the Remote Access exam fails to note ATM technologies, which are quite common in many networks today. This failure should be of concern to the reader and warrants further augmentation beyond the focus of this text.

Exam Essentials

Understand the ISDN terminations of the Cisco 700 series platforms. The Cisco 776 router includes both the S/T and the U type ISDN interfaces, for example, whereas the other 700 series platforms presented provide only the S/T interface. More information regarding these interfaces is included in Chapter 26.

Know which remote access platforms are best suited to small offices and home offices. Cisco recommends that users consider the Cisco 700, 800, 1000, and 1600 platforms for inexpensive remote connectivity to small user populations.

Be familiar with the WAN connection types. Readers should be comfortable with Frame Relay, ISDN, analog, leased-line, and X.25 connection options. As presented in this chapter, analog connections are the most common. They are highly available, but the bandwidth provided is quite limited and the costs associated with usage are quite high. X.25 is a reasonable option, particularly outside of the United States, and it is well suited to poor line conditions. Leased line and Frame Relay typically provide the highest bandwidth capabilities, with Frame Relay adding the benefit of distance-insensitive pricing.

Know the differences between ISDN BRI and PRI technologies. ISDN BRI services operate over a 144Kbps connection, divided into two 64Kbps channels (B, or bearer) and a single 16Kbps channel (D, or data). This is best used for the remote side of a remote access solution. The ISDN PRI technology uses a T-1 or E-1 connection for transport and can provide 23 or 30 B channels, respectively.

Understand the differences between North American and European standards. The ISDN Primary Rate Interface (PRI) in North America and Japan offers 23 B channels and one D channel for a total interface rate of 1.544Mbps. ISDN PRI in Europe, Australia, and other parts of the world provide 30 B channels plus one 64Kbps D channel.

Be familiar with the high-end router platforms for central office termination. Cisco recommends a wide variety of platforms for aggregation points, including the AS5300 series, the Cisco 7000 series routers, and the smaller 3600 systems. Admittedly there is some inconsistency in selecting these platforms; test takers would be advised to understand the platforms and select the best answer for each question.

Understand the router platforms' flexibility regarding configuration. Fixed-configuration routers are limited with regard to future enhancements. These platforms include the 700 and 800 series. Modular routers—including the 1600, 2600XM, and 3600/3700 series—allow for the addition or replacement of specific components, which can be used to add features without the need for a forklift upgrade.

Asynchronous Connections

THE CCNP EXAM TOPICS COVERED IN THIS CHAPTER INCLUDE THE FOLLOWING:

- ✓ Know the commands and procedures necessary to configure an access server for modem connectivity so telecommuters can access the central site.
- ✓ Know the commands and procedures to configure dial-out connections.
- ✓ Know the commands used for reverse Telnet.
- ✓ Understand how to configure the modem for basic asynchronous operations.
- ✓ Know the commands and procedures used for the modem autoconfiguration feature.

As noted in Chapter 22, "Cisco Solutions for Remote Access," asynchronous (analog) remote access solutions are extremely popular, primarily because little preparation is needed on the remote side of the connection. Unlike Frame Relay, ISDN, and X.25, *asynchronous connections* use standard phone lines and are available virtually everywhere. With cellular modems, these services are even available on a wireless basis. (This is different from the code division multiple access (CDMA) and Global System for Mobile Communications (GSM) data connections briefly noted in Chapter 22.) This wide availability provides a huge advantage over other remote access solutions and effectively mandates the inclusion of asynchronous connections in modern implementations. Unfortunately, analog-based modems suffer from low performance and relatively high cost per kilobyte.

With a digital connection at the service provider's side of the connection, it is possible to provide up to 56Kbps of theoretical bandwidth to remote users; however, the Federal Communications Commission (FCC) limits this to 53Kbps in the United States. Also, asynchronous connections require a lengthy call-setup time—sometimes more than one minute—which can substantially affect user and application performance.

Administrators frequently look for other technologies to replace asynchronous modems, or dial-up connections, in order to improve performance. Even with the proliferation of ISDN, DSL, cable modems, and other technologies, no system has yet successfully dethroned simple dial-up services.

Understanding Asynchronous Modems

Technically, *modems* are modulator/demodulators, but most people define them by their high-level function: modems connect devices to the telephone network. The modem connects the computer or router to the phone network and might incorporate a pass-through for an analog phone set. Although the phone cannot be used while the computer is connected to a remote location, this does afford a non-concurrent role for the installation—only the phone or the data connection can be used at any given time.

Modems are considered *data communications equipment (DCE)*, whereas computers and routers are *data terminal equipment (DTE)*. The connection between the modems, or DCEs, is *analog* in nature, meaning that bits are defined by an analog waveform that is continuous and variable. DTE connections are *digital* in nature; this means that each bit has a clear 0 or 1 value defined by voltage to denote the bit. It is important to remember that asynchronous refers to clocking and not a digital or analog transmission. *Clocking* is provided in asynchronous connections with start and stop bits, which typically results in 10 bits per byte of data—8 for the byte of data and 1 each for the start and stop markers.

Unlike asynchronous connections, synchronous connections have precise clocking to denote the data bits; in these connections, bytes can begin only on the downbeat of the synchronous drum, for example. There really isn't a drum in synchronous signaling. Rather, bits are sent in sync with the clocking pulse; it's similar to taking a dance step for every drumbeat, with the dance step being the data. For an asynchronous connection there are actually three distinct connections (DTE to DCE, DCE to DCE, and DCE to DTE), which are illustrated in Figure 23.1.

As you can see in Figure 23.1, the DTE-to-DCE bandwidth is uncompressed and is four times that of the modem connection, assuming optimum compression. Remember that this figure represents an optimal situation rather than a realistic one. Therefore, it is unlikely that either the DTE-to-DCE or DCE-to-DCE connections will normally see this level of performance. Some of this is attributable to the DCE-to-DCE limitations; however, limitations also exist in the serial interface from the PC to the modem.

The *Universal Asynchronous Receiver/Transmitter (UART)* is a chip that controls asynchronous communications to and from a device. It can buffer inbound and outbound data. Most UARTs are limited to the speed of 115.2Kbps, which is insufficient for 56Kbps connections, and the most capable UART provides for only a 56-byte receive buffer and a 64-byte transmit buffer. Even with these relatively large buffers this may be insufficient for maximum throughput.

In current computer designs, the UART is virtually disregarded as a component in the communications system. This is because most systems today provide sufficient buffering systems to address the volume of packets that come with 56Kbps asynchronous transmissions—specifically, the 16550 UART (16550 is a part number). In the early days of PCs, the most common chipset was the 8250 UART from National Semiconductor. It contained a single buffer of sorts—it could hold a single byte of data. Any transmission speed greater than 19,200Kbps was too fast for the UART to forward properly. This was a substantial cause of performance problems with the original deployments of 28.8Kbps modems.

Again, this issue is not of much consequence in modern communications systems. Unless you are installing a 386 or older computer (which by 2005 is very unlikely), you should find that 16550 UARTs (or better) were used for the serial ports. Please note that most internal modem cards include either the 16550 UART or a proprietary buffering system to alleviate these problems.

FIGURE 23.1 An asynchronous end-to-end connection

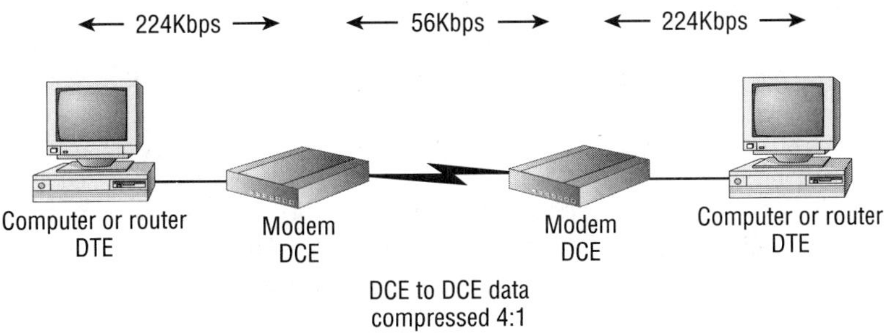

Real World Scenario

Remote Access with Modems

When discussing the limitations of serial signaling, it would be remiss not to discuss the limitations of the public phone system and the analog technology available today. As noted earlier in this chapter, asynchronous connections are limited to 56Kbps, or 53Kbps by FCC order. Distance and line quality further limit this amount of bandwidth, possibly reducing throughput to 28.8Kbps or less. (This was written in a Boston hotel room, where there was no reliable connection beyond 26Kbps.) In addition, connections might take up to a minute to establish and might be further impeded by load coils and analog-to-digital conversions between you and the central office (CO). Load coils are amplifiers used to accommodate longer distances than normal, and analog-to-digital conversions are often used in new housing developments to convert the copper pairs to fiber, again extending the length of the link. It is far cheaper to run a few pairs of fiber to an access terminal (a small cabinet that sits in the neighborhood and converts the fiber to copper) where the copper runs than it is to extend into the home.

You need to remember that the plain old telephone service (POTS) is exactly that—old. It was developed from the same technology that Alexander Graham Bell developed in his lab over a hundred years ago and was never intended to address the needs of video and data. That's the first problem with analog connections: they were never designed to allow millions of bits of data to flow from one point to another.

The second problem with analog connections is their inefficiency. Voice is a specific type of data and fits in a single 64Kbps channel. You might already be aware of the channels of voice aggregation, or T-1 circuits—where 24 voice signals (DS0, digital signal) fit into a T-1 or DS1. Data is unlike voice, however, which leads to inefficiency. Voice demands that the idle (or no data) points in the conversation be communicated as well, so there is always a constant flow of information. Data doesn't work that way; if no data is transmitted, there is little need for the bandwidth to be consumed. By using only the available bandwidth that is necessary, it is possible to service more connections with data than voice. You might have heard of convergence or time division multiplexing (TDM), two very different concepts that relate to this topic. *Convergence* is the concept of voice, video, and data all using the same network, whereas *TDM* is the old voice channel model—each channel always given the same amount of access to the network regardless of the need. Convergence will remove TDM from the network and place everything into packets that can then use only the required amount of bandwidth, as opposed to reserving more than is necessary.

However, convergence will also effectively eliminate the analog network (an event that has already occurred in the core of the telephone world). But before that comes to fruition, network administrators will need to contend with the problems of the current network, including long call-setup times, poor-quality connections, and low bandwidths.

These problems, just for the record, already have solutions in many cases. Although it is true that analog connections are the most prevalent in the world, the availability of DSL, cable, ISDN, Frame Relay, wireless, and Long Reach Ethernet (LRE) enables designers to incorporate alternatives into their installations and provides an indication of what will happen in the near future.

At the beginning of this sidebar, we noted problems with analog service and the phone network. While discussing these problems, we failed to address what is possibly the most important problem—cost. Readers of the *CCDP: Cisco Internetwork Design Study Guide* (Sybex, 2000) will recall the emphasis on business concerns when designing the network. Cost is frequently the single biggest business factor, period. Business managers who do not understand bits and protocols certainly understand the benefits of a $40-a-month fixed cost per employee compared to a variable bill that could surpass $100 a month.

One last item: virtual private networks. *Virtual private networks (VPNs)* are encrypted sessions between two devices over the public network, typically the Internet. These sessions are virtually private because the encrypted data is, conceptually, protected from snooping. Users, however, will still be affected by delay and bandwidth limitations that could be better controlled in private network installations.

VPNs provide remote access designers with two benefits. The first is low cost, which, as noted in the previous paragraph, is a powerful business case argument. The second benefit is universality—or the capability to allow access from different technologies. With VPNs, the administrator no longer cares what technology is used on the remote side of the connection. The remote side simply needs to connect to the Internet via any available transport, or in some cases, an internationally accessible single-vendor network (which can provide service-level agreements and other service guarantees). Once connected, the connection traverses the network and is decrypted at the corporate access point, typically a T-1 or DS3, depending on the bandwidth demands. For smaller support departments, this entire service might be outsourced so the maintenance of the VPN equipment and connections is not an additional burden on the team.

Signaling and Cabling

The cables used in various asynchronous connections differ depending on the end equipment plus the type and distance of the connection.

Modems typically use two types of connectors—one for the connection to the host and one for the connection to the phone network. An RS-232-C 25-pin connector typically provides the connection to the host; the RS-232-C connector is also called an EIA/TIA-232 connector. Both terms are still used today, although the EIA/TIA terminology is more current. A standard RJ-11 connector provides the connection to the phone network.

For the connection between the DTE and the DCE, individual wires are used in the serial cable. These wires and their functions are listed in Table 23.1.

TABLE 23.1 DTE-to-DCE Signaling

Wire	Function
TXD	Transmits data from the DTE to the DCE. All serial connections send their data one bit at a time over a single transmission path. This differs from parallel transmissions that have multiple paths. Printers, for example, send a full octet per signaling window. TX is on pin 2.
RXD	Receives data from the DCE to the DTE and is carried on pin 3. If there is a need to cross two serial ports together, as is the case in DTE-to-DTE connections, pin 2 is linked to 3 and vice versa.
GND	The electrical ground provides a baseline for voltage changes on the TX and RX wires. It is on pin 7.
RTS	Request to send. This signal is used when the DTE would like to send data.
CTS	The clear to send signal is used to inform the DTE that the DCE is ready to send data received from the DTE.
DTR	The data terminal ready wire is a modem control signaling wire, which signifies that the DTE can accept a call from the DCE.
CD	Carrier detection indicates that the local DCE has a connection to the remote DCE. It is also a modem control wire.
RI	The ring indication/indicator is used to signal the DTE device that an incoming call is ringing the phone. On nine pin interfaces, RI is on pin 9.

The information in Table 23.1 is important to understand from a troubleshooting perspective; however, it is also nice to know for an overview of wiring. In some instances, such as the extension of a serial connection, it might be necessary to serially link two devices by using Category 5 cable, for example. Hoods are available to make this link, and in fact, many Cisco connections use so few wires in serial connections that console ports are terminated with RJ-45 connections. (*Hood* is a slang term describing the plastic converter that covers the wiring as it changes from RJ to DB connections. Another term for this is *media converter*.)

Refer to the documentation that came with your router or switch regarding console connections. Cisco has been inconsistent with this implementation, sometimes requiring the use of rolled connection cables and at other times needing straight-through patch cords. A rolled connection places pin 1 on one end into the pin 8 position on the other end; thus, pin 2 falls into the pin 7 position, and so forth. Straight-through connections map 1 to 1 and 2 to 2, through to pin 8 connecting to pin 8.

Modulation Standards

Modulation defines the method used to encode the data stream between DCE devices. There are many modulation standards, including several proprietary methods. Modems will negotiate the modulation standard to be used during the connection. Modern modems will alter this negotiation during the connection, should line conditions permit. This can provide improved performance or prevent a connection from terminating, should the line condition degrade. Table 23.2 notes the common modem modulation standards.

TABLE 23.2 Modem Modulation Standards

Modulation	DCE to DCE Bandwidth	Status
V.22	1,200bps	ITU standard
V.22bis	2,400bps	ITU standard
V.32	9,600bps	ITU standard
V.32bis	14.4Kbps	ITU standard
V.32 terbo	19.2Kbps	Proprietary
V.34	28.8Kbps	ITU standard
V.fast	28.8Kbps	Proprietary
V.FC	28.8Kbps	Proprietary
V.34 annex 12	33.6Kbps	ITU standard
K56Flex	56Kbps	Proprietary
X2	56Kbps	Proprietary
V.90	56Kbps	ITU standard
V.92	56Kbps	ITU standard—adds faster call connection capabilities
V.61 or V.34Q	56Kbps	ITU standard—adds simultaneous voice and data capabilities

Most modems support all lower bandwidth ITU standards for backward compatibility, and many V.90 and V.92 modems also support either X2 or K56Flex. Modems that shipped with X2-only or K56Flex-only support—before the V.90 standard was ratified—can usually be upgraded in the field, frequently with software only. This might not be the case when upgrading from V.90 to V.92. You will have to consult your modem vendor for upgrade capabilities and cost.

The V.92 standard represents three significant modem enhancements:

- Quick Connect, which reduces the amount of time required for the modems to negotiate a connection. In some instances, a user might see a 50 percent reduction in connection time.
- The V.92 standard includes Modem on Hold, which enables a user to accept an incoming phone call without terminating their existing connection. For users with only one phone line in their home or office, Modem on Hold enables them to handle both data and voice calls over the same telephone line.
- V.92 supports PCM Upstream, which allows for faster uploading and sending of large e-mail messages, photos, and documents. With PCM Upstream, users gain faster upstream communication with speeds reaching up to 48,000 bits per second, as compared to 33,600 bits per second with V.90 technology.

The modulation standards also incorporate data compression and error correction specifications, which are detailed next.

Data Compression

Data compression substitutes repetitive data in a bit stream with fewer bits that will be interpreted, or uncompressed, on the other device. Later in this book, we will present a more detailed example of data compression; for this introduction, it is sufficient to know that compression will allow fewer bits of data to represent the total number of bits needed to reconstruct the message accurately. One of the more common compression systems today is V.42bis, which is based on the theoretical works of Professors Jacob Ziv and Abraham Lempel at Technion University in Israel. We visited Technion in 1984 and were extremely impressed with their facilities and the technical capabilities of their students. At that time, they had perfected systems that could convert English text to Hebrew text, and they could integrate both texts into a single document. To better understand how impressive this was, consider that this was happening the same year as the first Apple Macintosh release.

The work of Ziv and Lempel was used by Englishman Terry Welch to develop the *LZW algorithm*, named to honor the three men. The LZW process uses two steps to parse character sequences into a table of strings; these strings are then represented with one of 256 codes. The parsing process works by constantly trying to find longer sequences that aren't part of the current 256 values. This enables the compression process to substitute longer and longer strings, which subsequently increases the benefits of the compression.

V.44 is the latest compression standard approved by the ITU and is included with the V.92 standard. V.42bis was created about 10 years ago, so it wasn't designed with the Internet in mind. V.44 was, and it is therefore much more efficient at compressing web pages—up to 100 percent more efficient in some cases.

Error Correction

Error correction validates the integrity of the data and is frequently used with compression to verify that the compression process did not corrupt the data. The impact of a single-bit error can distort substantial amounts of compressed data—instead of just impacting a single bit, it might distort two or more bytes, which, in turn, might require the retransmission of even more data. When you consider the overhead of asynchronous communications—the start and stop bits require two extra bits per eight-bit byte, or 20 percent of the final bit stream data rate—the added overhead that would result from errors involving compressed data only serves to further reduce the actual throughput. Detection, and correction when applicable, of errors as quickly as possible can reduce the amount of data that needs to be retransmitted and, thus, improve total throughput.

The error correction process relies on a checksum value that validates the data. A simple example of this checksum looks like the following:

$$21 + 9 + 6 + 17 + 8 + 29 + 4 + 27 = 121$$

It is reasonably certain that the calculation on the left side of the equal sign is accurate because it does equal the value on the right side. However, it would also be possible for the 21 to be a 22 and for the 9 to be an 8, which also yields an answer of 121. Error correction works on the same premise as this equation; however, most error correction algorithms work to allow for multiple errors and other distortions. Many error correction processes block the binary data and divide that value by a fixed value. This value is then added to the block of data and is transmitted with the user data. On the opposite end of the transmission, the checksum is calculated against the binary value of the data and the division of the same fixed value. If they match the data block, the result is considered true and forwarded. If the values do not match, the data is discarded.

Configuring Asynchronous Modem Connections

Asynchronous connections, like other connections, require configuration before they can be used. In applications using Cisco routers, this configuration can be supplemented with automatic functions or it can be manual. As such, there are three possible configuration options:

- Manual configuration
- Autoconfigure
- Autodiscovery

Manual configuration requires knowledge of the commands required by the modem to establish the parameters that govern flow control, error control, compression, and the number of rings that will occur before the line is answered. Flow control is a function that uses the clear-to-send and ready-to-send pins on the serial cable to govern the bit stream, and it can be serviced by hardware or software.

The *autoconfigure* function is used to automatically configure a modem from a router that has been given the modem type. The configuration information is stored in a database on the router.

The *autodiscovery* function detects the modem type and then supplies the proper initialization string information. This process works by first negotiating the baud, or data rate, and then sending queries to the modem to learn its identity. This is accomplished with standard attention (AT) command sequences based on the router's database. If there is no match, the autodiscovery function will fail.

Stated another way, Cisco routers provide two methods for preparing the modem for operation. These are manual and automatic, and within automatic configuration there are two options: a completely automatic process that learns the type of modem in use and a hybrid that relies on the administrator to define the type of modem connected to the router. This alternative removes the need for a negotiation process; however, it is still considered an automatic process. The modem's configuration must match the router so that communications between the two devices are properly coordinated.

Automatic Configuration

Most modern modems provide the capability to identify their type and specifications, which a computer or router can use to assist in the configuration process. Obviously, the benefit of automatic configuration is that it reduces the number of administrative tasks required during installation; however, the learning process can delay modem availability and can fail. The delay is the result of the interrogation process, and failure can occur if the router fails to understand the responses from the modem. This can happen if the modem is not in the modemcap database, discussed later in this chapter.

Commands for Automatic Configuration

This section introduces the commands used for automatic configuration.

The *modem autoconfigure type* Command

The `modem autoconfigure type` *`modem-type`* command is used to instruct the router to automatically configure the modem attached to a port by using the commands in the modemcap database for the modem type specified. The *modemcap database* is a listing of modem configuration commands that provide basic information enabling the modem to operate with the router.

To show this database, use the `show modemcap` command. The output of this command is shown next. This output provides a list of the modem types that are defined in the database. This list is from a Cisco 2600 series router, and thus it reflects those modem types that are included with that router image:

```
Router_A#show modemcap
default
codex_3260
usr_courier
usr_sportster
hayes_optima
```

```
global_village
viva
telebit_t3000
microcom_hdms
microcom_server
nec_v34
nec_v110
nec_piafs
cisco_v110
mica
```

Each modem type has a related AT command-string sequence stored, which is shown with the `show modemcap` *`modem-type`* command. AT stands for *attention* and is the prefix for many modem commands. The output of this command, when used for the U.S. Robotics Courier, is as follows:

```
Router_A#show modemcap usr_courier
Modemcap values for usr_courier
Factory Defaults (FD):  &F
Autoanswer (AA):  S0=1
Carrier detect (CD):  &C1
Drop with DTR (DTR):  &D2
Hardware Flowcontrol (HFL):  &H1&R2
Lock DTE speed (SPD):  &B1
DTE locking speed (DTE):  [not set]
Best Error Control (BER):  &M4
Best Compression (BCP):  &K1
No Error Control (NER):  &M0
No Compression (NCP):  &K0
No Echo (NEC):  E0
No Result Codes (NRS):  Q1
Software Flowcontrol (SFL):  [not set]
Caller ID (CID):  [not set]
On-hook (ONH):  H0
Off-hook (OFH):  H1
Miscellaneous (MSC):  [not set]
Template entry (TPL):  default
Modem entry is built-in.
```

This output is similar to what would happen if you manually sent the modem the sequence AT&FS0=1&C1&D2&H1&R2&B1. This sequence would instruct a Courier to reset its configuration and then answer in one ring, using hardware flow control with DTR dropping and carrier detect.

As denoted, this modem entry is included in the router's operating system—it is built-in. Please note that the database entry must be complete and exact. As shown in the following output, the router will respond with an error message if the entry is abbreviated:

```
Router_A#show modemcap usr_cou
There is no record of modem usr_cou
```

In addition, the command `modemcap entry` *`modem-profile-name`* can be used to obtain an abbreviated version of the output, assuming that attributes are not set.

The *modemcap edit* Command

To add entries to the modemcap database, the administrator can use the `modemcap edit` command followed by the database name: `modemcap edit` *`modem-profile-name`*. Configurations provided with the router cannot be modified. Administrators should create a similar user-created entry with their modifications.

To create a user-defined profile by using an existing profile as a template, use the `modemcap edit` *`new-profile-name`* `template` *`existing-profile-name`* command with the template being the key parameter. This will create a profile with the name *`new-profile-name`* and copy all settings from the *`existing-profile-name`*.

Use care when removing modemcap entries. The `no modemcap edit` *`modem-profile-name`* command will delete the entire entry, not just a single line. To delete only one line from the profile, use `modemcap edit` *`modem-profile-name attribute`*.

It is generally recommended that administrators specify the type of modem that is connected to the router. This reduces the probability of error and hastens the configuration process.

The *modem autoconfigure discovery* Command

The command for discovering and automatically configuring the modem attached to a port is `modem autoconfigure discovery`. The discovery process will try to learn the make and model of the modem automatically. Automatic modem recognition is made possible by the modemcap database. The command is entered in line mode, as shown in the following output:

```
Router_A(config)#line 1
Router_A(config-line)#modem autoconfigure discovery
```

This sequence will instruct the router, or access server, to send an AT command sequence to line 1 at varying baud rates until it receives an acknowledgment from the modem. After it has determined the appropriate speed with which it should communicate to the modem, the router will attempt to determine the modem type with additional AT commands.

We need to define a term here: *baud*. *Baud* is a representation of the signaling speed, and it frequently corresponds to the bits-per-second capacity of the link. However, this assumes a modulation of one bit per signaling change—an inconsistent assumption given the wide variety of modulation protocols available in modern modems.

The modem entries in the modemcap database vary based on the version of IOS software and platform.

Automatic modem recognition can take up to five seconds. A default setting will be sent to the modem after a six-second timeout. This will occur if no match is found during the autodiscovery process, which means that a relevant entry was not found in the modemcap database. Specifying the type of modem and using the autoconfigure command should take less than two seconds for modem configuration.

Verifying and Troubleshooting the Automatic Configuration

Cisco provides many troubleshooting services to assist in the diagnostic process, and support for troubleshooting the automatic configuration service is no exception. However, before using the `debug` commands and other troubleshooting tools, it is best to review the status of the installation and the connections between the modem and the router. Make sure to check for the following:

- The modem is turned on and is receiving power.
- The cable is of the right type and is secured.
- The DIP switches or other physical options on the modem are set to known values or factory defaults. In this case, *known values* means settings that are known to work for this router and modem configuration in other installations; sometimes the factory defaults will not work. In addition, administrators might find that random guessing is required to find the proper settings.
- The modem is plugged into a phone jack and the dial tone is present.

After these steps have been completed, you need to *reverse Telnet* to communicate with the modem. For reverse Telnet to work, the line interface needs the `transport input all` and `modem inout` commands. These commands enable the port to accept input and transfer data to and from the modem. Note that reverse Telnet is not a command but a tool used to provide a connection to a reserved TCP port on the router, which maps to a physical asynchronous port. For example, the physical port on line 4 would map to TCP port 2004. The administrator can telnet to the router and, by altering the port number (the default TCP port for Telnet is 23), can be connected directly to the attached device, such as a modem. TCP ports starting with 2000 are used for Telnet, whereas 4000 is the start of the range for non-Telnet-specific TCP connections. Ports starting with 6000 are used for binary-mode Telnet. Of these, most administrators find it necessary to use ports only in the 2000 range.

Reverse Telnet is a powerful tool that has been required for practical demonstrations of Cisco expertise and certifications. Readers should be familiar with its functionality.

Manual Configuration

Manual configuration can eliminate the negotiation process required for automatic configuration, but it adds substantially to the configuration process. It requires router configuration changes if the modem is changed, possibly through an upgrade or replacement to a different vendor or model. Manual router configuration requires knowledge of the AT, or Hayes, command instructions.

The attention (AT) commands are used to configure the modem and, for most purposes, are used to create a standard configuration methodology for modems. There are differences from vendor to vendor in the function of each command, but for the most part they have been standardized. AT commands enable configuration and diagnostic services to become fairly advanced, including settings that report the modem's status, the quality of the network (phone company) connection, and the configuration of flow control and other modem functions. Software, including terminal software, will frequently provide these commands upon selection of a menu-driven function, which insulates the user from needing to learn and use the commands.

Please consult with the modem manufacturer regarding the appropriate codes for your modem.

Most modems have a number of commands in common, and many of these are quite useful for the administrator. These commands are listed in Table 23.3.

TABLE 23.3 Common AT Commands

Command	Function
&F	The AT&F command resets most modems to their factory defaults.
&C	This command configures the modem-for-modem control (C is for *Carrier Detect*). C1 instructs the modem to use CD to reflect the actual connection status.
S0=1	There are a number of S series commands, of which S0 is the first. S0 controls the number of rings before the modem answers; in this case the modem will answer on the first ring. A setting of at least 2 is suggested for caller ID installations; some secure installations use fairly high values—perhaps 10 rings or more. This is because most "war dialers" (or automatic dialers) assume the line is not terminated after eight or more rings.
&D	The &D command relates to DTR. With a setting of D3, the modem will hang up the line when the DTR drops. This is the normal configuration.
M0	This command turns off the audio output from the modem. This can provide a great benefit when you are not troubleshooting; the screeching of the modem connection sequence can be quite irritating.

TABLE 23.3 Common AT Commands *(continued)*

Command	Function
`L1`	The `L` commands control the volume on the modem speaker. `L3` would turn the volume to maximum. Note that modems with external volume controls, such as the U.S. Robotics Courier, will also require the physical knob to be turned.
`&Q6`	The `&Q6` command is significant because it results in the DTE speed being locked. This is discussed in greater detail in Chapter 25, "Using Microsoft Windows 95/98/2000/XP," but basically, this means that locking the DTE speed can improve performance on lower-quality circuits.

From the router's perspective, a number of commands are necessary to configure an asynchronous connection. These commands are described in Table 23.4.

TABLE 23.4 Asynchronous Router Commands

Command	Function
`line` *N*	Cisco routers refer to asynchronous ports as lines. *N* is equal to the number of the port and is used before the rest of the commands in this table to get into line configuration mode.
`login`	The `login` command is required to force authentication of a connection.
`password`	This command establishes the password to be used on the line.
`flowcontrol`	The `flowcontrol` command can be followed with `hardware` or `software` settings. Typically, hardware flow control provides greater control over the data flow and allows for higher communication speeds. Software flow control is not recommended.
`speed`	The `speed` command establishes the maximum speed to be used between the modem and access server or router. It defines the speed of both transmit and receive, and it is noted in bits per second (bps). Note that the modem and access server can negotiate a slower speed or data rate.
`transport input`	The `transport input` command defines the protocol to use in reverse Telnet connections. This may be LAT, MOP, NASI, PAD, RLOGIN, Telnet, or V120; however, administrators typically use the `all` keyword to allow all connection types. This is potentially less secure because a hacker could use one of these protocols to gain access or deny service to the router. For example, if there is no business need to use RLOGIN, why leave the access available to allow repeated access attempts from an outsider?

TABLE 23.4 Asynchronous Router Commands *(continued)*

Command	Function
`stopbits`	Stop bits are used in asynchronous communications to define the end of each byte. Typically, the `stopbits` value is set to 1 because there is little reason to send additional bits; however, values of 1.5 and 2 are also valid.
`modem`	The `modem` command is used to define the type of calls allowed. By default, the router allows dial-in, or incoming, calls only. However, to allow reverse Telnet or dial-out connections, in addition to dial-in, the administrator would use the `inout` keyword.

It is important to note that each line, or logical interface, (specified with the `line` command in Table 23.4) has an associated physical interface. This is defined by the router. There is also a line associated with the aux interface. The asynchronous, or async, interface is the physical representation of the interface, and configurations on async interfaces define the protocol characteristics of the connection. This would be used to define a protocol such as Point-to-Point Protocol (PPP) or the addressing mechanism to be used. An async interface can be a capable serial interface configured for asynchronous services with the `physical-layer async` command, or the aux (auxiliary) port on the router.

Configuration begins with the `line` command and the number of the interface. This is followed with the specific information that is needed—for example, the login capabilities and DTE-to-DCE speed. A typical configuration might appear as follows:

```
line 3
   modem inout
   stopbits 1
   databits 8
   parity none
   transport output all
   transport input all
   speed 56000
   flowcontrol hardware
   login
   password tplekprp
```

This configuration would allow calls in or out, with all protocols supported and login required. We've also configured the data rate to 56Kbps and added a common set of modem parameters (N, 8, 1) to the configuration. These last parameters define those communications characteristics and must match on both sides of the connection. Hardware flow control would be used. Flow control is used to prevent buffer overruns and maintain an efficient flow of data by signaling the sender that it should slow down or speed up.

If there is a problem with manual configuration, it will be first noted when the administrator attempts to use the modem. Reverse Telnet and use of the diagnostic commands associated with that modem are most likely the best tools available for troubleshooting.

Summary

Asynchronous, or analog, connections are widely available and extremely popular methods for providing remote access in today's networks, but they are not without their disadvantages. However, no other technology has come along to replace them entirely.

Modern modems provide a wide range of modulation types, which provides the user with many connection speed options. Connecting modems to an access server is straightforward due to the use of the universal EIA/TIA-232 (RS-232-C) serial connector.

Asynchronous modems provide a challenge for remote access connections, and configuration options include manual, automatic (autoconfigure), or autodiscovery. Each method has its own characteristics. For instance, manual configuration requires the knowledge of which AT commands to use to configure the modem for dial-in access. If using automatic configuration, the only knowledge needed is the type of modem used on the access server, and the router will try to apply the best match. When using autodiscovery, the administrator does not need to know what type of modem is connected to the access server; the router will query the modem to determine its type and then apply the best matching parameters.

Exam Essentials

Know how to identify the different connection types in analog communications. The DTE-to-DCE connection occurs between the router (DTE) and the modem (DCE). The DCE-to-DCE connection occurs between the two modems over the phone network.

Understand the different modulation types and their speeds. You should know the 14 modulation types and the data rates they provide as listed in Table 23.2. You should also understand that asynchronous connections are limited to 56Kbps, or 53Kbps by FCC order.

Understand the different signals carried in the communications cable. Make sure you know which signal does what when two devices are communicating over an EIA/TIA-232 (RS-232-C) connection:

- TXD is used for transmission of data.
- RXD is for reception of data.
- CD is used to signal that a connection exists between local and remote DCE.
- GND is used as a reference signal.
- RTS and CTS are used in hardware flow control.

Know the compression and correction standards. V.42bis is the most widely used data compression standard. V.44 is the more recent kid on the block and is significantly more efficient than V.42bis.

Understand the different IOS modem configuration modes. Cisco IOS has the capability to automatically configure a modem by using the information in the modemcap database. The router can also automatically discover the modem type and configure that modem for asynchronous communications. You can also manually supply the router with modem configuration commands.

Know the major attention (AT) commands used for manual modem configuration. You should understand what the `AT&F` command will do to most modems. Make sure you understand the other AT commands described in Table 23.3.

Know how to create a new modemcap database entry by using an existing database entry as a template. To create a new modemcap database entry, use the `modemcap edit` *`new-profilename`* `template` *`existing-profilename`* command with `template` being the key parameter.

Know which commands to use in line configuration mode and which to use in the logical interface configuration mode. The commands described in Table 23.4 are used in line configuration mode to specify the physical characteristics of the asynchronous connection. The commands used in interface configuration mode configure parameters such as encapsulation and addresses used on the asynchronous connection.

Point-to-Point Protocol

THE CCNP EXAM TOPICS COVERED IN THIS CHAPTER INCLUDE THE FOLLOWING:

- ✓ Know the commands and syntax used to configure PPP connections between the central site and branch offices.
- ✓ Understand the commands and syntax to configure PAP or CHAP authentication.
- ✓ Know how to configure multilink services.
- ✓ Be able to verify and troubleshoot PPP configurations.
- ✓ Know the commands and procedures to configure a PC for dial-up connections.

The Point-to-Point Protocol (PPP) is one of the serial encapsulations that administrators find useful for remote access solutions. PPP operates over a wide range of media and was designed to simplify the transport of multiple protocols (IP, IPX, AppleTalk, and so on) over serial links. Though the protocol does operate over other media, this chapter focuses solely on remote access solutions.

With the intense demand for connectivity by salespeople, remote staff, and telecommuters, it becomes clear that consistent remote access solutions are required. The benefits of using PPP are that it is universal and efficient. PPP on Windows should be able to communicate with PPP on any access server, and the configuration demands on the client side are extremely small, thus resulting in fewer support issues. Although HDLC, SLIP, and Frame Relay encapsulations are also somewhat standardized, the benefits of PPP and its low overhead, along with virtually universal media support, make it an excellent choice for remote access.

This chapter provides an overview of PPP and the commands and processes required to configure this protocol on Cisco access servers.

PPP Overview and Architecture

PPP is documented in RFC 1661 as a standard method for transporting multiple protocols over point-to-point links. PPP substantially improved upon the Serial Line Internet Protocol (SLIP). SLIP transports IP packets only across serial circuits.

Although beyond the scope of this Study Guide, PPP has evolved to operate over Ethernet (PPPoE), as specified in RFC 2516, and over ATM (PPPoA), as specified in RFC 2364. Packet over SONET (Synchronous Optical Network) also uses PPP-based encapsulations. One of these options may well be implemented in an ADSL (asymmetrical digital subscriber line) solution from some service providers.

PPP contains three main components:

- The encapsulation method used, and for PPP the default is an HDLC-like framing.
- *Link Control Protocol (LCP)* is used when establishing, configuring, and testing the data-link connection.
- A family of *Network Control Protocols (NCPs)*, which establishes and configures different Network layer protocols. PPP, LCP, and NCP are all considered layer 2 protocols.

RFCs for Remote Access Networks

There appear to be two schools of thought on *Request for Comments (RFCs)*—the documents that are used to establish and document standards in computer networking. Some believe that only geeks bother to memorize and recite the various RFC numbers, whereas others believe that such knowledge is critical to the proper design and administration of the network.

Regardless of your individual position, the RFCs that document PPP are worthy of your time and attention. The various protocols are well documented and invaluable in troubleshooting. Some of the RFCs that warrant specific attention include the following:

RFC 1334 includes the PPP authentication protocols.

RFC 1661 includes the current revision of the PPP protocol.

RFC 1990 includes the PPP Multilink protocol, which is discussed later in this chapter.

There are many RFCs that would augment this brief list, but their relevance is highly variable depending on the installation requirements. The Internet Engineering Task Force (IETF) website at `www.ietf.org` provides links to all RFCs; other sources are available as well.

The PPP protocol adds a minimal amount of overhead to the packet, as illustrated in Figure 24.1.

FIGURE 24.1 The PPP frame structure

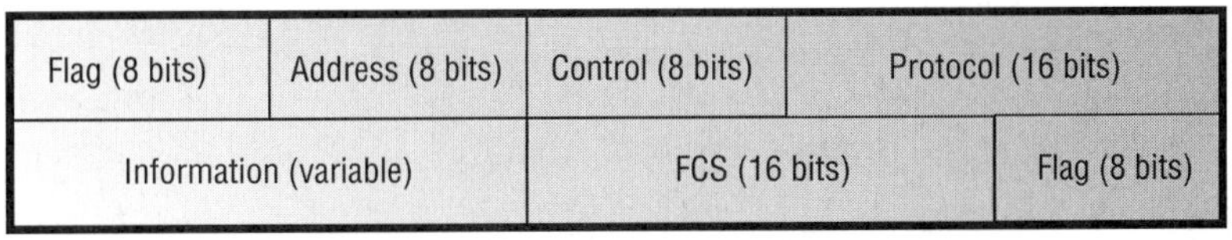

Flag (8 bits)	Address (8 bits)	Control (8 bits)	Protocol (16 bits)
Information (variable)		FCS (16 bits)	Flag (8 bits)

The remainder of this section describes each of the components found in the PPP frame.

The Flag Field

The *Flag field* is a single octet (eight bits) that indicates the beginning and end of each frame; it has a unique pattern of 01111110. Sometimes, a single flag ends one frame and begins the next. But, as can be seen in Figure 24.1, distinct start and end frames are also found. Both of these examples use the same pattern. *Bit stuffing* is used to make this pattern unique. Bit stuffing is a technique that alters patterns in the user data that appear the same as the frame delimiter or other framing information. For example, if the sequence 0101011111110100 appeared representing two characters, the protocol would interpret this as the start of a frame—01111110. Bit-stuffing will re-represent the characters by altering this flow so that the 01111110 pattern remains unique.

The Address Field

The *Address field* is a single octet (eight bits) with the binary sequence of 11111111 (0xff hexadecimal). This is known as the All-Station Address because PPP does not assign individual station addresses. The field is included to allow addressing; however, as inferred by the term *point-to-point*, the destination is always the opposite end of the link.

The Control Field

The *Control field* is a single octet (eight bits) and contains the binary sequence 00000011 (0x03 hexadecimal), which is the Unnumbered Information (UI) command. This signifies that the subsequent bits will provide information regarding the remaining data—as opposed to the data being part of the PPP protocol.

The Protocol Field

The *Protocol field* is two octets (16 bits) and identifies the upper layer protocol. An upper layer protocol would include IPCP, the IP Control Protocol. The more commonly assigned Protocol fields and their hexadecimal values are listed in Table 24.1. This list is beneficial for two reasons: First, it shows the wide diversity of PPP; second, the list will supplement troubleshooting.

TABLE 24.1 PPP Assigned Protocol Fields

Value (in hex)	Protocol Name
0001	Padding Protocol
0021	Internet Protocol
0023	OSI Network Layer
0025	Xerox NS IDP
0027	DECnet Phase IV
0029	AppleTalk
002b	Novell IPX
002d	Van Jacobson Compressed TCP/IP
002f	Van Jacobson Uncompressed TCP/IP

TABLE 24.1 PPP Assigned Protocol Fields *(continued)*

Value (in hex)	Protocol Name
0031	Bridging PDU
0035	Banyan VINES
0041	Cisco Systems
0201	802.1d Hello Packets
0203	IBM Source Routing BPDU
8021	Internet Protocol Control Protocol
8023	OSI Network Layer Control Protocol
8025	Xerox NS IDP Control Protocol
8027	DECnet Phase IV Control Protocol
8029	AppleTalk Control Protocol
802b	Novell IPX Control Protocol
803d	Multilink Control Protocol
80fd	Compression Control Protocol
c021	Link Control Protocol
c023	Password Authentication Protocol
c025	Link Quality Report
c223	Challenge Handshake Authentication Protocol

Notice that both Password Authentication Protocol (PAP) and Challenge Handshake Authentication Protocol (CHAP) are listed toward the bottom of this table. These two protocols are discussed later in this chapter; however, it is significant to note them here in the context of PPP's broad support for features. Authentication, multilink (the ability to bond different physical channels into a single logical connection), and compression are all supported in PPP and its associated upper layer protocols.

The Information Field

The *Information field* is also called the *Data field*. This field contains the data of the packet that has been encapsulated in PPP. The Information field's length is determined by the amount of user data offered, which can range from 0 to 1,500 octets. The maximum receive unit (MRU) establishes this upper limitation.

The Frame Check Sequence (FCS) Field

The *Frame Check Sequence field* is two octets (16 bits) and provides a cyclical redundancy check (CRC) value, and it is used to validate the packet's integrity. This is also called a *checksum*.

Configuring Access Servers

Although differences can exist in the configuration methodology needed for different platforms, most steps are consistent and similar. Stated another way, commands for a Cisco access server are different from those for a Shiva LanRover, but the functions are similar.

Router ports on remote access devices can terminate standard terminal emulation (exec session)—sometimes thought of as a terminal or VT100 terminal—or a wide array of protocols including PPP, SLIP, and ARAP (AppleTalk Remote Access Protocol). The type of protocol used can be predefined by the administrator or automatically selected by the router. This feature uses the `autoselect` command. When `autoselect` is not enabled, the router will start an exec session on the line.

If `autoselect` is not used, the user can still start a session by using one of the other protocols, but they will need to provide the command to start. With `autoselect`, the router can detect the protocol flag value—0x7E for PPP, 0x10 for ARAP, and 0xC0 for SLIP. A carriage return is interpreted as a request for an exec session.

For the remainder of this section, the PPP protocol will remain our focus.

Configuring PPP

There are a few choices for the administrator or designer to consider when deploying PPP. These choices are above and beyond those that would be used with any other technology such as IP addressing assignments (the actual addresses, not the method used) and the provisioning of routing protocols. This section focuses on some of the more common issues regarding PPP, including the selection of dedicated or interactive PPP and the implementation of layer 3 addressing. Later in this chapter we will introduce authentication protocols and multilink technologies.

Dedicated or Interactive PPP

To dedicate a line for use by SLIP or PPP, the administrator can use the `async mode dedicated` command. This command prevents the user from changing the encapsulation protocol and can augment security by restricting the method of access.

The interactive option, configured with the `async mode interactive` command, enables the user to select any encapsulation for the session by entering a command in exec mode.

The default for each interface is no `async mode`. As such, neither PPP nor SLIP is available.

Interface Addressing Options for Local Devices

PPP configuration also requires attention to layer 3 addressing. In this section, IP addressing considerations are presented due to both their complexity and frequency. These include static, IP unnumbered, and dynamic addressing options:

Static addressing Clearly, the use of static addresses is the most basic IP addressing technique. Static addresses are entered on each interface manually and require administration and documentation. The benefit of static addresses is supportability—troubleshooting is simplified with statics. However, there is a substantial amount of administration overhead. Static addresses are well suited to the central office remote access server.

IP unnumbered An alternative to static addressing is the use of IP unnumbered. This is not a dynamic solution, which will also be explained in this section, but rather a feature that Cisco provides to allow a point-to-point link to share an IP address from another interface. For example, the remote router might be configured with a static IP address on its Ethernet interface, whereas the serial interface could be configured with an unnumbered interface, effectively using the same IP address assigned to the Ethernet port. The down side of this solution is that the troubleshooting options are more limited. An alternative to using a physical interface is to use the loopback interface. Some argue that this interface is best used with IP unnumbered because, theoretically, it can never go down.

Cisco documentation presents the loopback interface as one that can never go down; however, administrative errors can disable the interface. Overall, it remains a better alternative than a physical interface.

Dynamic addressing Dynamic addressing is an excellent solution in a number of installations, especially those that use modem-attached workstations from a remote location. The administrator can configure a pool of addresses that are assigned on a per-call basis rather than manually assigning a single IP address for each user. This greatly reduces the number of addresses that must be assigned and simplifies the administrative tasks. These assignments typically use DHCP, Dynamic Host Configuration Protocol.

Configuring Dynamic Addressing

The commands to configure dynamic addressing depend on the method used. Although DHCP is one option (used as an example in the following text), there are other methods, including proprietary ones.

Before we discuss incorporating a dynamic addressing solution, it is best to acknowledge the option of manually addressing the client. In Windows 95/98, this is accomplished by using the Dial-Up Connection Properties menu to access the TCP/IP Settings dialog box. This dialog box is shown in Figure 24.2. Note that you must select Specify an IP Address to manually enter a selection.

Windows will provide a warning if you attempt to use Network Control Panel to configure the dial-up adapter, as shown in Figure 24.3. As shown, configuration parameters in properties will overwrite any custom parameters on the individual dial-up connection. Many users might connect to different locations, with each location requiring a different set of parameters. As such, the warning is well heeded and administrators will likely choose to configure all settings per connection.

If you are configuring a router to provide the dial-up connection between the client and remote access server, you should use the standard Ethernet configuration commands. These entries, shown in Figure 24.4, include the IP address, subnet mask, default gateway, and name servers. Please note that although a static configuration is shown, the administrator could use DHCP.

FIGURE 24.2 Manual IP address configuration in Windows 95/98

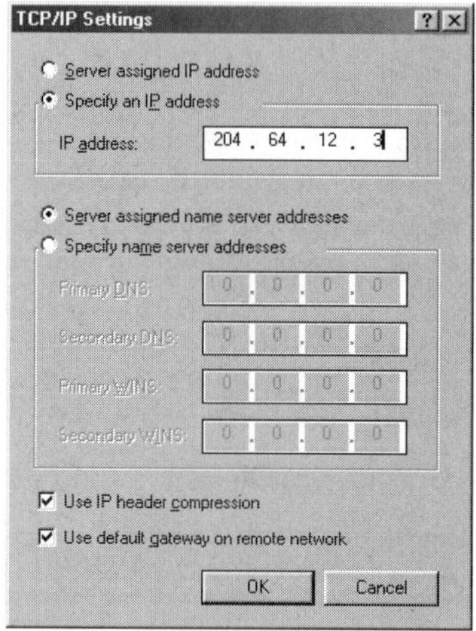

FIGURE 24.3 Configuring a dial-up adapter from Windows Control Panel

FIGURE 24.4 Ethernet-based manual IP address configuration in Windows 95/98

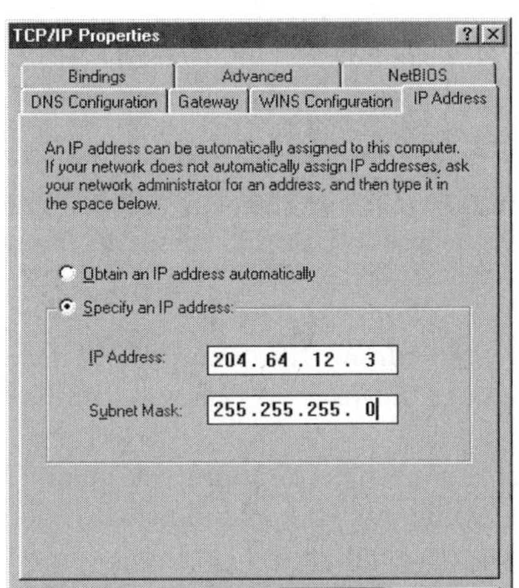

The configuration dialog box is accessed through Control Panel ➤ Network ➤ TCP/IP ➤ Adapter.

On the router, the configuration is straightforward, but it depends on the role of the router and the type of dynamic assignment desired. The `async dynamic address` command enables the client to provide its address, but the `peer default ip address [ip-address | dhcp | pool` *`poolname`*`]` command is used more often. This command enables the administrator to select manual, DHCP, or pool-based address selection.

When selecting the DHCP option, the administrator must also configure the router for one of three choices:

- IP helper address
- IP DHCP server
- DHCP server on router

The IP helper address option is often found in router configurations, but without additional configuration, this option will forward broadcast traffic to the helper address. The *helper address* is the address of the server or group of servers that provide the required service—DHCP, in this example.

A newer command is `ip dhcp-server`, which the administrator can use to specify the address of the DHCP server.

In addition, some routers might also provide DHCP server functionality. This should be considered for smaller installations only; routers are best suited to provide routing. However, this feature might be ideal for small office/home office installations.

It is important to remember that certain IP broadcast traffic will be forwarded to the helper address by default. This can be blocked to include only DHCP datagrams by using the no `ip forward-protocol udp` *udp-port-number* command. The following UDP (User Datagram Protocol) ports are enabled by default: 69 (TFTP), 53 (DNS), 37 (Time), 42 (name server), 49 (TACACS), 67 (BOOTP Client), 68 (BOOTP Server), 137 (NetBIOS WINS), and 138 (NetBIOS datagram). BOOTP (Bootstrap Protocol) was the predecessor to DHCP and shares the same UDP port numbers.

To configure DHCP services on the router, the administrator must first decide if they wish to use a DHCP database agent to help manage the lease process. Cisco calls this feature *conflict logging*.

If conflict logging is desired, the administrator must also configure an FTP or TFTP server, which is defined with the `ip dhcp database` command. If the administrator does not wish to implement conflict logging, the command `no ip dhcp conflict logging` must be used instead. Note that in some instances the administrator must exclude an address from the DHCP pool. To do this, they must use the `ip dhcp` *`excluded-address low-address`* `{`*`high-address`*`}` command.

An entire configuration file for DHCP services is shown here:

```
service dhcp
ip dhcp database ftp://dhcp:cisco@10.11.1.10/dhcp

ip dhcp pool 0
network 10.10.1.0 /24
default-router 10.10.1.1
domain-name foo.com
dns-server 10.2.20.51
netbios-name-server 10.2.20.51
```

The preceding configuration example uses an FTP server at 10.11.1.10 to capture information regarding the DHCP leases. The pool is for 10.10.1.0/24 and a default gateway of 10.10.1.1. The domain is `foo.com`, and DNS and WINS services are provided by 10.2.20.51. The `service dhcp` command used here is optional; the service is available by default. The FTP server username is `dhcp` with a password of `cisco` in the preceding output; however, this is not a very secure option.

Although this chapter focuses on Windows 95/98 configuration, readers should note that Windows NT and 2000 differ little in most regards. Figure 24.5 shows Windows 2000's Dial-Up Connection Properties dialog box.

How DHCP Works

DHCP is an open standard that is based partly on the BOOTP protocol specified in RFC 951 and RFC 1541. DHCP can be used by Unix, Macintosh, and Windows-based systems. However, the protocol did not attain mainstream corporate recognition until the service was incorporated into Windows NT.

FIGURE 24.5 Windows 2000 dial-up networking

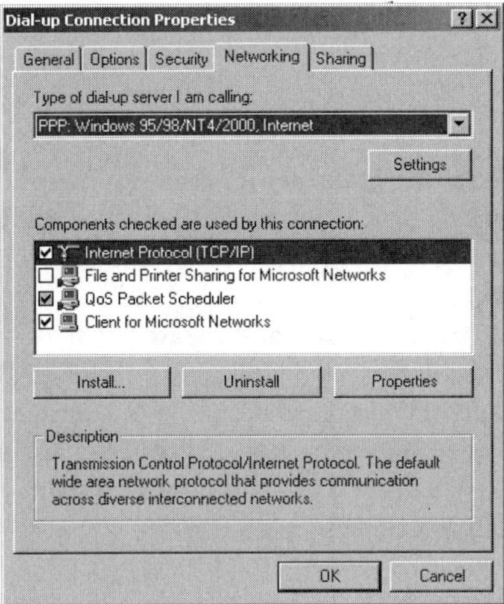

DHCP enables a host to learn its IP address dynamically. This process is termed a *lease* because the address assigned belongs to the host for an administratively defined time. On Windows implementations, this assignment is set for 72 hours by default.

DHCP leases are discussed in the following section.

From a router perspective, DHCP requires one of two components: a DHCP server on the local subnet or a method of forwarding the broadcast across the router. DHCP lease requests are broadcasts, so the network designer would need a DHCP server present on each segment in the network. This clearly would not scale well and is impractical in most network designs, but it would provide addressing information to the clients.

The alternative is to provide a little help to DHCP. This is accomplished with the IP helper address, a statically defined address on each router interface that is connected to the local segment that needs the help. This segment, with the help of the helper address, will be able to get to the DHCP server. Broadcast requests for addresses are sent to the helper address as unicasts, thus significantly reducing overall broadcast traffic.

Most DHCP implementations, including Microsoft's, can provide a great deal of information to the client as well, including time servers, default gateways, and other address-based services.

When using the router as a DHCP server, there is generally less of a motivation to provide redundancy; whenever more than a handful of networks require addressing services, it is generally better to add a dedicated server. If the router is unavailable, it is unlikely that users will be concerned about the loss of a DHCP lease. If there are multiple networks, the likelihood of a single router point of failure is reduced, but there is also an increased load on the router from the number of leases that must be managed. When designing for DHCP, most architects and administrators consider the DHCP lease length.

DHCP Lease Length

The length of the DHCP lease governs the amount of time a host "owns" the address. To continue using the address, the host must renew with the server before the lease expires. Designers must consider the overhead of this renewal traffic and the impact of failed or unavailable DHCP servers. In general, long leases are appropriate for fixed environments, and short leases are applicable in more dynamic installations.

Consider a fully functioning network with 100 workstations and a lease length of five minutes. This is an extreme example (that no self-respecting engineer would install) because DHCP will send a renewal request at an interval equal to one-half the lease period. The overhead for just IP address leases would be 2,400 requests per hour, not including any DNS queries and the multiple packets involved in each request (see Figure 24.6). This is a high amount of overhead for information that should not change under normal circumstances.

In addition, when a lease expires, the host must release its IP address. Without a DHCP server, it will be unable to communicate on the network because it has no IP address.

The alternative to a short lease is to make the lease very long. Consider the impact of a lease equal to 60 days. Should the hosts remain on a local subnet with very few changes, this would substantially reduce the volume of traffic.

However, this would not be appropriate for a hotelling installation. *Hotelling* is a concept introduced years ago in which notebook users would check into a cubicle for a day or even a week. DHCP is a great solution for such an installation because the MAC addresses are constantly changing, but a long lease time would be inappropriate here. Consider a scenario in which each visitor connects once per quarter, or every 90 days. And, for this example, presume that there are 800 users of the service, and the pool is a standard Class C network of 254 host addresses. If the lease were long—90 days for this example—only the first 254 users would be able to obtain an address. Clearly, this is not appropriate for this type of installation, which is an important consideration for the network designer.

As mentioned earlier, the default DHCP lease renewal interval (on Windows NT) is 72 hours. DHCP attempts to renew the lease after one-half the lease duration, or 36 hours in the case of default Windows NT.

The default lease on Cisco IOS-based DHCP servers is 24 hours.

For reference, the mechanism by which DHCP obtains an address is illustrated in Figure 24.6. Note that DHCP uses a system of discovery to locate the DHCP server—a phase that uses the helper function. After the DHCP server is found, the offer is returned to the workstation, and the request is positively or negatively acknowledged. One way to remember the DHCP process is with the mnemonic DORA, which stands for Discover, Offer, Request, and Acknowledgment.

FIGURE 24.6 The DHCP process

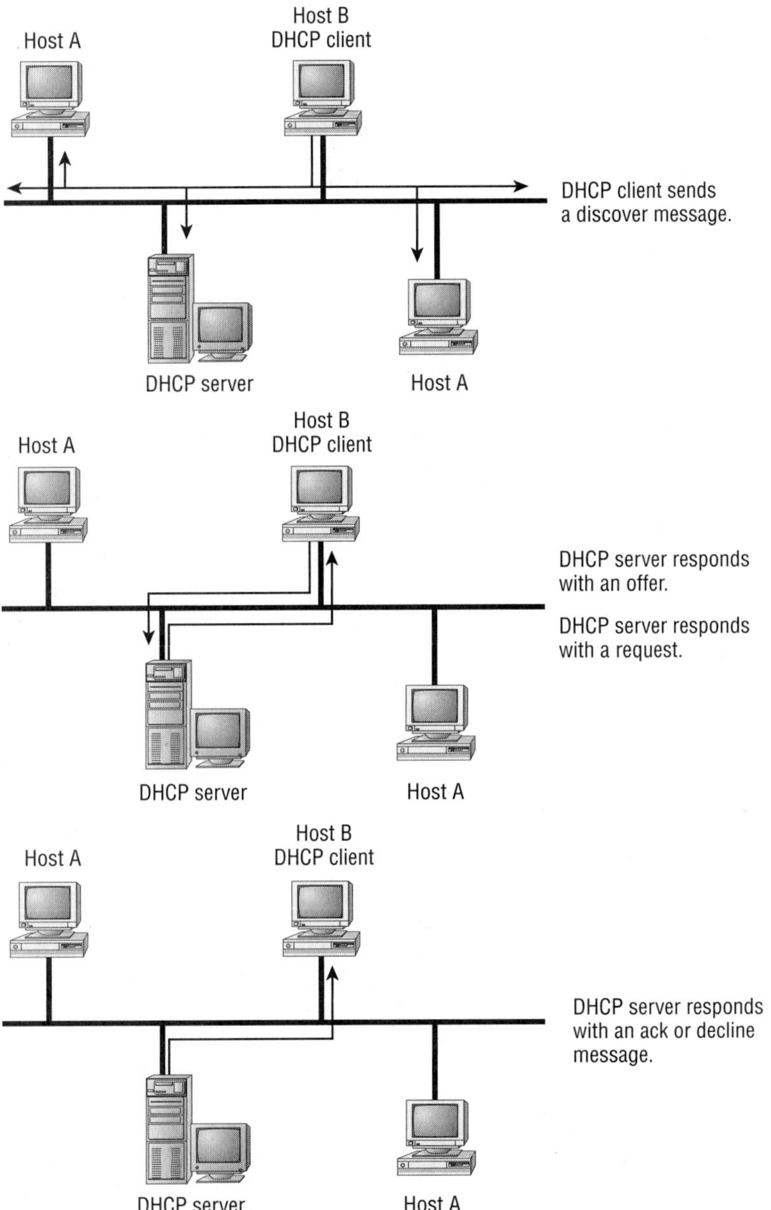

DHCP operates in similar fashion when served from the router: as noted previously, only the configuration process changes. While an interesting feature, the DHCP server on the router is not practical in most installations. The need to maintain a separate FTP server for the database usually leads the administrator to opt for a more scalable option that requires installing a dedicated server.

PAP and CHAP Authentication

One of the key benefits of PPP is the ability to add authentication services, which are provided by PAP or CHAP. Authentication adds substantially to the security of the network and should be used. Even though PAP is explained in this section, its use is discouraged and administrators should configure their networks for the more secure CHAP.

Password Authentication Protocol (PAP)

Password Authentication Protocol (PAP) provides basic security authentication for connections. The username and password information, however, are transmitted in cleartext, which can be intercepted by a hacker to compromise the network. Unfortunately, a few older systems support only PAP and not the more secure CHAP, which mandates PAP's usage in those cases.

PAP is defined in RFC 1334.

PAP operates by establishing a connection and then checking the username and password information. If the username and password information matches, an OK message is returned and the session is allowed to proceed. This is illustrated in Figure 24.7. Note that the username and password are transmitted in cleartext in PAP—a significant security risk.

PAP usernames and passwords are transmitted in cleartext, reducing the security benefits of the protocol. Use CHAP whenever possible.

FIGURE 24.7 PAP authentication

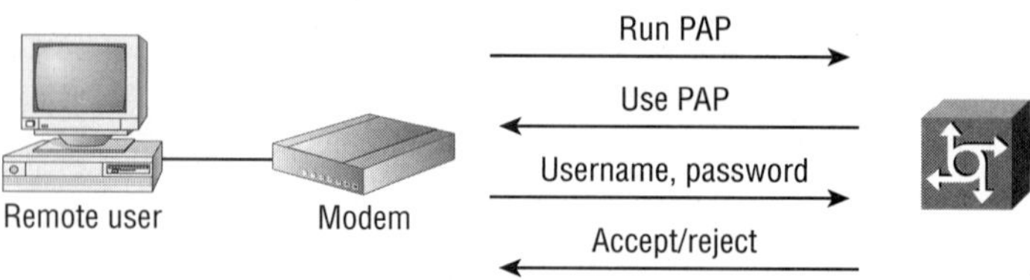

To configure PAP, the administrator needs to configure both the service and a database of usernames and passwords. The commands used to do this are shown here:

```
encapsulation ppp
ppp authentication {chap | chap pap | pap chap |
   pap} [if-needed] [list-name | default] [callin]
```

Usernames and passwords are added to the router with the `username` *`name`* `password` *`secret`* command.

There isn't much more to PAP—it works with a minimal amount of configuration, in large part due to its lack of security. Readers should be familiar with the existence of this protocol and understand that it should not be used in current designs.

Challenge Handshake Authentication Protocol (CHAP)

The *Challenge Handshake Authentication Protocol (CHAP)* is significantly more secure than PAP. This is because of the mechanism used to transfer the username and password: CHAP protects against playback hacking (resending the packet as part of an attack) by using a hash value that is valid only for that transaction. When the attacker captures the CHAP session and replays that dialog in an attempt to access the network, the hash method will prevent the connection. The password is also hidden from the attacker; it is never sent over the circuit.

The hash value used in CHAP is derived from the Message Digest type 5 (MD5) algorithm, which takes a message of arbitrary length and produces as output a 128-bit message digest of the input. The message digest's strength comes from being nonreversible, and it is computationally infeasible to produce two messages having the same message digest. The MD5 algorithm is defined in RFC 1321.

The MD5 hash shown in Figure 24.8 is valid for a relatively brief time, and no unencrypted information is sent over the link. This data might allow a hacker to impersonate the authentic user.

FIGURE 24.8 CHAP authentication

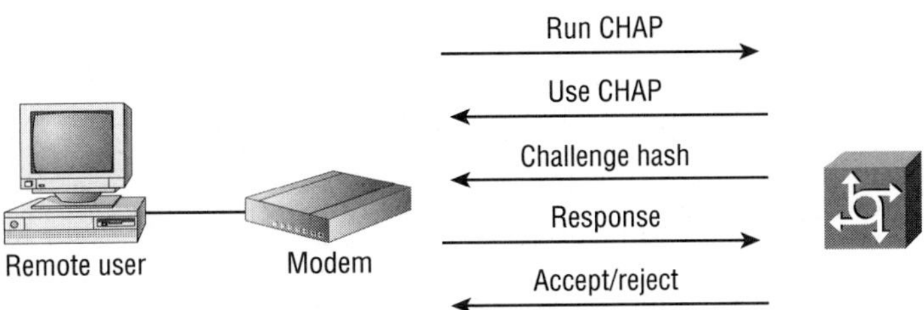

The commands to configure CHAP are similar to those for PAP. Instead of selecting `pap` in the `ppp authentication` command, the administrator uses the `chap` keyword. Notice, from the following configuration snippet, that two additional options are also available: `chap pap` and `pap chap`. These keywords provide the administrator with a means of selecting both protocols, and they are attempted in order; thus, `chap pap` tries to authenticate via the CHAP protocol first. Typically, this configuration option is used only during a transition because security would be compromised if PAP were permitted. The following commands are used to enable PPP, a requirement for CHAP, and to configure the router for CHAP authentication:

```
encapsulation ppp
ppp authentication {chap | chap pap | pap chap |
   pap} [if-needed] [list-name | default] [callin]
```

The additional commands that you see are used for external user authentication and one-way authentication. These are beyond the scope of this book, but they are included for completeness.

Usernames and passwords are added to the router with the `username` *`name`* `password` *`secret`* command.

In Windows networking, the administrator is given the choice of whether to require password encryption, as shown in Figure 24.9. Note that this Require Encrypted Password check box is not selected, meaning that the user or administrator has chosen not to require encrypted passwords.

FIGURE 24.9 Windows 95/98 password encryption

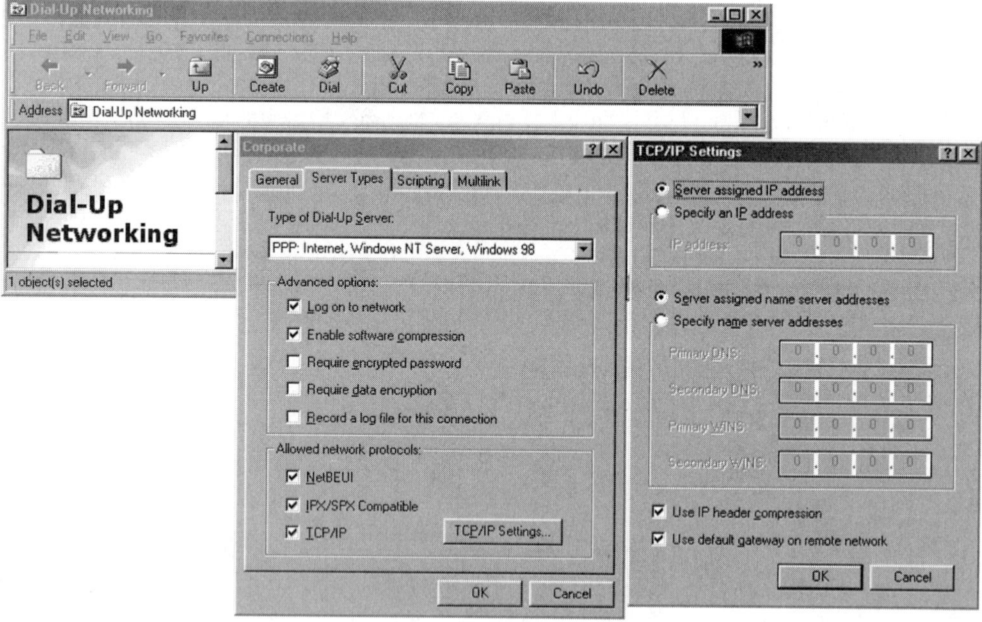

This configuration will work so long as PAP is not the only selected authentication method on the access server. The Windows client will attempt to connect with MS-CHAP, a Microsoft proprietary version of the CHAP protocol. If the check box is selected—meaning the password must be encrypted—either PAP or CHAP will be used, depending on the configuration of the server; if the server is not set to require CHAP, the client can fall back to a PAP, non-encrypted password.

PPP Callback

Security in PPP can be further augmented with the use of *PPP callback*, which instructs the access server to disconnect the incoming connection after successful authentication and re-establish the connection via an outbound call. This security feature requires that the caller be in a single physical location and diminishes the impact of a compromised username and password. The service can also be used to control costs because all connections appear to be from the remote access server—allowing volume-based discounts.

PPP callback is documented in RFC 1570.

Clearly, this solution is not well suited to mobile users; for example, callback to a hotel room would require repeated configuration and a mechanism to deal with extensions. Some callback solutions enable the remote user to enter the callback number—a solution that removes the physical location restrictions and enhances mobility.

Cisco's callback feature does not permit remote users to dynamically enter the callback number.

Consider the security provided by a callback configuration:

- The remote client (user) must connect into the remote access server.
- By using an authentication protocol such as CHAP, the user must authenticate.
- If authentication is successful, the session will terminate and the remote access server will call the remote client back. If the authentication fails, the connection will terminate.
- Upon callback, the client and server can again perform password verification.

Clearly, these extra steps could enhance security.

To configure callback, the administrator needs to use the `ppp callback accept` command on the router interface that receives the initial inbound call and the `ppp callback request` command on the interface that is making the initial outbound call.

PPP callback will not make repeated retries to establish a return connection. This means that a busy signal or other impediment will require the client side to re-request the session.

Real World Scenario

Configuring PPP Callback

For the following scenario, we set up a spoke router that needs to call into a hub router. The configuration must also allow the hub router to call the spoke router back on a predefined phone number after authentication. This situation has two benefits: One is added security, because the hub router calls Spoke1 back on a predefined number. The other benefit is that it is cheaper for the hub router to call Spoke1 because of discounts negotiated by the company for long-distance calls from the hub site.

As a backup, we configured a callback from a spoke router to the hub router, where each router is a Cisco 2600 series router and has a USR (US Robotics) modem attached to the aux port. We'll allow the Spoke1 router to call into the hub router, authenticate, and let the hub router call the Spoke1 router back on a predefined number.

Here are the relevant commands we used to get things started:

```
Hub#config title
Hub(config)#username Spoke1 password sybex
Hub(config)#chat script Dialout
  ➥ABORT ERROR ABORT BUSY "" "AT" OK "ATDT \T" TIMEOUT 45 CONNECT \c
Hub(config)#modemcap entry USR_MODEM:MSC=&F1S0=1
Hub(config)#dialer-list 1 protocol ip permit
Hub(config)#line aux 0
Hub(config-line)#modem inout
Hub(config-line)#modem autoconfigure type USR_MODEM
Hub(config-line)#script dialer Dialout
Hub(config-line)#speed 115200
Hub(config-line)#transport input all
Hub(config-line)#stopbits 1
Hub(config-line)#flowcontrol hardware
Hub(config-line)#exec-timeout 0 0
Hub(config-line)#exit
Hub(config)#interface async65
Hub(config-if)#ip address 192.168.190.1 255.255.255.0
Hub(config-if)#encapsulation ppp
Hub(config-if)#dialer in-band
Hub(config-if)#dialer-group 1
Hub(config-if)#async default routing
Hub(config-if)#async mode dedicated
```

```
Hub(config-if)#ppp authentication chap
Hub(config-if)#^Z
Hub#
Spoke1#config title
Spoke1(config)#username Hub password sybex
Spoke1(config)#chat script Dialout
  ➥ABORT ERROR ABORT BUSY "" "AT" OK "ATDT \T" TIMEOUT 45 CONNECT \c
Spoke1(config)#modemcap entry USR_MODEM:MSC=&F1S0=1
Spoke1(config)#dialer-list 1 protocol ip permit
Spoke1(config)#line aux 0
Spoke1(config-line)#modem inout
Spoke1(config-line)#modem autoconfigure type USR_MODEM
Spoke1(config-line)#script dialer Dialout
Spoke1(config-line)#speed 115200
Spoke1(config-line)#transport input all
Spoke1(config-line)#stopbits 1
Spoke1(config-line)#flowcontrol hardware
Spoke1(config-line)#exec-timeout 0 0
Spoke1(config-line)#exit
Spoke1(config)#interface async65
Spoke1(config-if)#ip address 192.168.190.2 255.255.255.0
Spoke1(config-if)#encapsulation ppp
Spoke1(config-if)#dialer in-band
Spoke1(config-if)#dialer-group 1
Spoke1(config-if)#async default routing
Spoke1(config-if)#async mode dedicated
Spoke1(config-if)#ppp authentication chap
Spoke1(config-if)#^Z
Spoke1#
```

There are some things we need to point out before continuing. We created a custom modemcap entry for our USR modem instead of using the built-in modemcap entry. We also omitted the `dialer map` statements, which we will discuss in greater detail later. Finally, because both sides need to dial out, we configured a chat script required to successfully dial out.

Next, we configured the routers—one as the client and one as the server—for callback. The configuration is slightly different between the client and server callback routers. The Spoke1 router will be the callback client, and the Hub router will be the callback server. We will use the `dialer map` command on the spoke router just as you might expect, but on the Hub router we need to add a `class` parameter to the `dialer map` command for callback purposes.

Please note that map-class configurations are beyond the scope of the exam and this book, and you need not be too concerned at this point about the minutia. However, the syntax is fairly straightforward. We recommend that you focus on the material for the exam at this point, and, after you've passed, refer to the Cisco website or practice in your lab environment with the following commands. Here is the configuration for each router:

```
Spoke1#config t
Spoke1(config)#interface async65
Spoke1(config-if)#dialer map ip 192.168.190.1 name Hub  broadcast 5551211
Spoke1(config-if)#ppp callback request
Spoke1(config-if)#^Z
Spoke1#
Hub#config t
Hub(config)#map-class dialer Spoke1_Auth
Hub(config-map-class)#dialer callback username
Hub(config-map-class)#exit
Hub(config)#interface async65
Hub(config-if)#dialer map ip 192.168.190.2
  ➥name Spoke1  broadcast 5551212 class Spoke1_Auth
Hub(config-if)#ppp callback accept
Hub(config-if)#^Z
Hub#
```

When the spoke initiates a call to the hub router, the hub router will authenticate the spoke router, and the spoke router will tell the hub router it would like to use callback. Then, the hub router will drop the line and call back the spoke router on the number specified in the `dialer map` command. When the spoke router gets the call, it will authenticate again before starting the PPP negotiation process.

Notice that we did not specify any dynamic routing protocols over this link. Doing so would make this configuration complex and is beyond the scope of this Study Guide. As noted before, map-class and chat scripts are also beyond the scope of this book, but we want to give you a taste of the possibilities when configuring Cisco IOS.

PPP Compression and Multilink

It seems that there is never enough bandwidth for current user demand. However, PPP compression and multilink can provide different mechanisms for increasing the throughput between different locations.

Compression uses representation to remove bytes from the data stream. For example, if the word *the* is represented by an @ sign, the protocol could save two characters per instance.

Repeated hundreds of times for different strings, it is possible to save substantial amounts of bandwidth, which will improve performance. The overhead incurred with most compression is minor compared to the resultant savings.

Multilink takes a different approach from compression. *Compression* uses the current connection and squeezes additional information across the link. *Multilink* takes the standard data stream and bonds multiple connections to increase the amount of bandwidth available to the application. With multilink, two or more circuits can be made to appear as a single large pipe. This is more expensive than compression because each location requires two or more analog phone lines or ISDN circuits. This option is better when more bandwidth is required, but higher bandwidth technologies are not available. Multilink ultimately improves throughput and reduces latency. Compression and multilink can be combined to further improve throughput.

Compression Configuration

Compression is available in the IOS software on virtually every Cisco router. However, despite its benefits, software-based compression places a significant load on the router's processor. Therefore, administrators must weigh the benefits of compression against the potential performance degradation that could result. In addition, monitoring the router's CPU is required, that is, ensuring that the utilization of the CPU does not exceed 65 percent. You can determine the CPU utilization by viewing it with the `show process cpu` command. This command will show you a one-minute and five-minute CPU utilization trend, as shown next, where the router is running consistently at three percent utilization:

```
Router1#show process cpu
CPU utilization for five seconds: 3%/3%; one minute: 3%; five minutes: 3%
```

To configure compression, use the following commands:

```
encapsulation ppp
compress [predictor | stac | mppc [ignore-pfc]]
```

Note that both sides of the serial link need to be configured for the same compression method; different compression protocols are not compatible with each other. Designers should also consider the type of data that will be used when configuring compression:

Predictor The predictor option provides a useful benefit in that compressed data will not be *recompressed*—a process that typically increases the transmitted size and adds substantial delay. This is a good choice for a mixture of compressed and uncompressed data that will traverse the link. Predictor can be more memory-intensive than other choices, but it does not burden the router's CPU substantially.

Stac Most significantly, the stac compression option is the only supported algorithm for the CBOS-based router platforms, including the Cisco 700 series. As with other compression mechanisms, stac substitutes repetitive data sequences with brief, summarized values, which are decoded on the other end. The specific compression algorithm is called LZW, or Lempel-Ziv-Welch, the names of the creators.

MPPC Microsoft Point-to-Point Compression (MPPC) is used when receiving compressed data from Windows clients. With this option, all data is compressed.

In addition, a fourth compression type is available to the designer: TCP header compression. Invoked with the `ip tcp header-compression` command, TCP header compression does exactly that—it compresses only the TCP header information (20 bytes). The specifics of TCP header compression, which is not unique to PPP, are documented in RFC 1144. This type of compression reduces the number of bytes required for each TCP packet and provides this reduction with a minimum amount of overhead. TCP header compression does not impact UDP or Internet Control Message Protocol (ICMP) packets.

Administrators wishing to offload the route processor from the burdens of compression computations might wish to use the Cisco 7500 series router with the compression service adapter. When this card is present, the router will use the hardware-based compression that is running on this card. If the router contains VIP2 cards, the compression process can be *distributed*, which will move the overhead of compression away from the central processor. Interface functions on the card will be affected, however. Without VIP2 technology or the compression service adapter, the router will default to software-based compression.

Other Cisco routers support the use of hardware-assisted compression. The 2600, 3700, and 3660 series routers support the use of a compression Advanced Integration Module (AIM) to offload compression duties from the CPU. Also, the 3620/40 routers support a network module that offloads PPP and Frame Relay (FRF.9) compression.

Compression is generally avoided beyond the 2Mbps level, and ideally, it is used only for links below 128Kbps. Review your requirements carefully before selecting the type of compression. If traffic is truly that high, it might be a short time before additional capacity is necessary anyway.

Multilink Configuration

Like compression, multilink is fairly easy to configure. Figure 24.10 illustrates the desired configuration. Users or administrators simply configure the modem to be used and the phone number to be dialed. Multilink services require two or more modems and two or more phone lines on the client side, which are bonded together into a single logical connection.

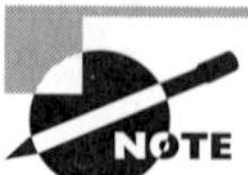

For further reference, the Multilink PPP (MPPP) RFC is 1990.

The commands for configuring asynchronous multilink or ISDN multilink differ little, and the primary commands need to include only the following:

```
encapsulation ppp
ppp multilink
```

FIGURE 24.10 Multilink installation

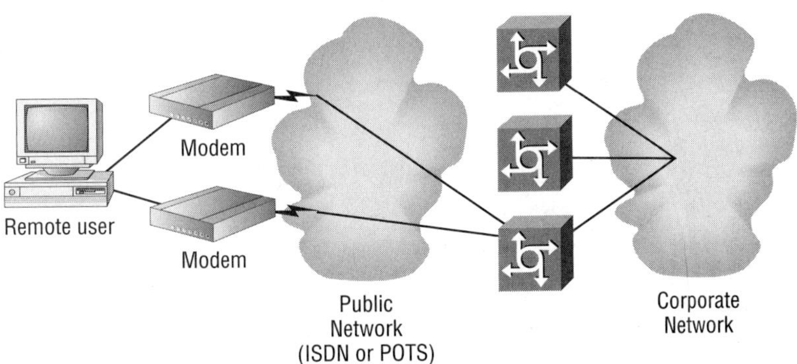

Without multilink support, each individual ISDN B channel per interface remains isolated. Modems (async connections) can also be used for multilink, and the Multilink Protocol (MP) standard is supported in Windows 95/98. The configuration is fairly straightforward; the user or administrator defines the second access number under the Multilink tab, as shown in Figure 24.11.

FIGURE 24.11 Windows 95/98 multilink

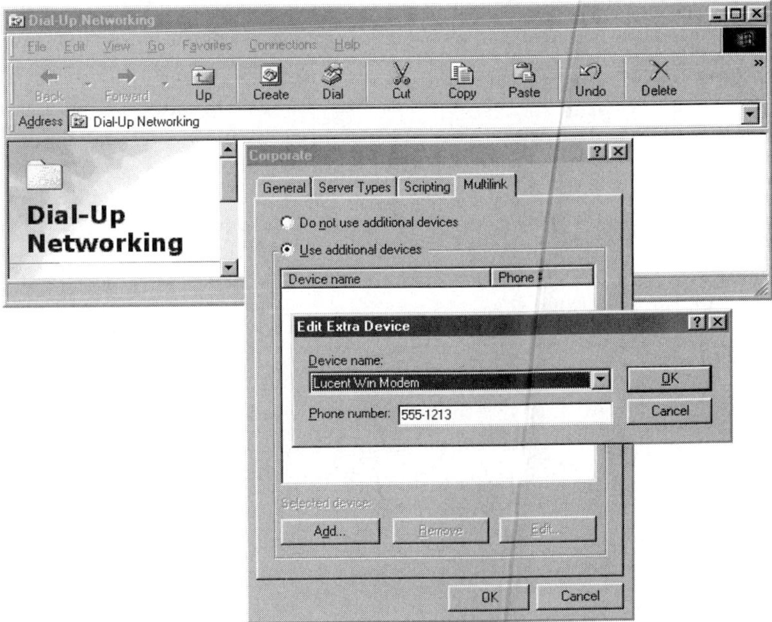

Another multilink option is available on Cisco routers and access servers: *Multichassis Multilink Protocol (MMP)*. This proprietary protocol enables the various bonded sessions to terminate on different access servers, as shown in Figure 24.12.

FIGURE 24.12 Multichassis Multilink Protocol

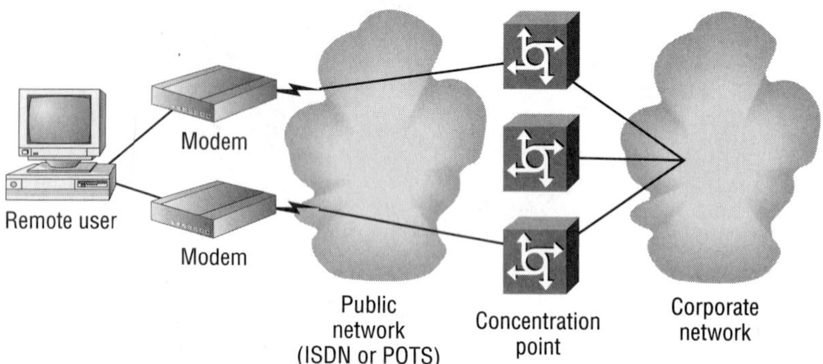

The benefit of this configuration is that single points of failure at the concentration point can be removed and port utilization can be optimized. MMP is an interesting subject but is beyond the scope of this Study Guide.

It is recommended that all PPP connections use authentication—PAP or CHAP. If authentication is not used, the telecommunications vendor will need to pass caller ID information for some services.

Verifying and Troubleshooting PPP

As with most troubleshooting on Cisco routers, administrators have a wide range of `show` and `debug` commands available to resolve problems that can occur with the Point-to-Point Protocol. Using standard troubleshooting methodologies, the administrator should be able to isolate physical problems quickly and then use these tools to locate and resolve logical issues.

Ideally, designers and administrators unfamiliar with PPP will need to implement a simple configuration before adding additional features such as authentication and multilink bonding. However, one or both of these services might be required as part of the initial installation. The `debug` and `show` commands will quickly help isolate the various issues.

This section focuses on the three most common `debug` commands:

- `debug ppp authentication`
- `debug ppp negotiation`
- `debug ppp packet`

The *debug ppp authentication* Command

Authentication failures can make a perfectly functional link appear faulty, and given the ease with which one can mis-enter a password or username, it is one of the most common issues. The `debug ppp authentication` command is useful for resolving these problems.

Examine the following output from the debug session. The ISDN BRI attempted to connect, but the challenge failed and the link was disconnected immediately. The second packet attempted to restore the link (`response id 8`) and also failed. This type of output points to either a username or password problem—in this case, the password was incorrect:

```
Router#debug ppp authentication
01:54:14: %LINK-3-UPDOWN: Interface BRI0:1, changed state to up.
01:54:14: BR0:1 PPP: Treating connection as a callout
01:54:14: BR0:1 PPP: Phase is AUTHENTICATING, by both
01:54:14: BR0:1 CHAP: O CHALLENGE id 7 len 27 from "Router"
01:54:14: BR0:1 CHAP: I CHALLENGE id 7 len 24 from "Top"
01:54:14: BR0:1 CHAP: O RESPONSE id 7 len 27 from "Router"
01:54:14: BR0:1 CHAP: I FAILURE id 7 len 25 msg is "MD/DES
compare failed"
01:54:15: %ISDN-6-DISCONNECT: Interface BRI0:1
disconnected from 18008358661 , call lasted 1 seconds
01:54:15: %LINK-3-UPDOWN: Interface BRI0:1, changed state to down.
01:54:18: %LINK-3-UPDOWN: Interface BRI0:1, changed state to up.
01:54:18: BR0:1 PPP: Treating connection as a callout
01:54:18: BR0:1 PPP: Phase is AUTHENTICATING, by both
01:54:18: BR0:1 CHAP: O CHALLENGE id 8 len 27 from "Router"
01:54:18: BR0:1 CHAP: I CHALLENGE id 8 len 24 from "Top"
01:54:18: BR0:1 CHAP: O RESPONSE id 8 len 27 from "Router"
01:54:18: BR0:1 CHAP: I FAILURE id 8 len 25 msg is "MD/DES
compare failed"
01:54:19: %ISDN-6-DISCONNECT: Interface BRI0:1 disconnected
from 18008358661 , call lasted 1 seconds
01:54:19: %LINK-3-UPDOWN: Interface BRI0:1, changed state to down.
01:54:22: %LINK-3-UPDOWN: Interface BRI0:1, changed state to up.
```

The `debug ppp authentication` command is most helpful in troubleshooting password problems. As shown in the preceding example, the message `I FAILURE id 8 len 25 msg is "MD/DEScompare failed"` is a clear indication that the administrator should look at the password settings.

The *debug ppp negotiation* Command

The `debug ppp negotiation` command is useful for two reasons. First, it can enhance the troubleshooting process on PPP links. Second, it provides a wonderful summary of how PPP works, including LCP and the higher protocols. The higher protocols consist of IPCP (IP) and CDPCP (CDP), among others.

The following output shows the messages that might appear when using the **debug ppp** `negotiation` command:

```
Router#debug ppp negotiation
PPP protocol negotiation debugging is on
Router#ping 10.1.1.1
Type escape sequence to abort.
Sending 5, 100-byte ICMP Echos to 10.1.1.1, timeout is 2 seconds:
00:22:28: %LINK-3-UPDOWN: Interface BRI0:1, changed state to up
00:22:28: BR0:1 PPP: Treating connection as a callout
00:22:28: BR0:1 PPP: Phase is ESTABLISHING, Active Open
00:22:28: BR0:1 LCP: O CONFREQ [Closed] id 3 len 10
00:22:28: BR0:1 LCP: MagicNumber 0x50239604
(0x050650239604)
00:22:28: BR0:1 LCP: I CONFREQ [REQsent] id 13 len 10
00:22:28: BR0:1 LCP: MagicNumber 0x5023961F
(0x05065023961F)
00:22:28: BR0:1 LCP: O CONFACK [REQsent] id 13 len 10
00:22:28: BR0:1 LCP: MagicNumber 0x5.023961F
(0x05065023961F)
00:22:28: BR0:1 LCP: I CONFACK [ACKsent] id 3 len 10
00:22:28: BR0:1 LCP: MagicNumber 0x50239604
(0x050650239604)
00:22:28: BR0:1 LCP: State is Open
00:22:28: BR0:1 PPP: Phase is UP
00:22:28: BR0:1 CDPCP: O CONFREQ [Closed] id 3 len 4
00:22:28: BR0:1 IPCP: O CONFREQ [Closed] id 3 len 10
00:22:28: BR0:1 IPCP: Address 10.1.1.2 (0x03060A010102)
00:22:28: BR0:1 CDPCP: I CONFREQ [REQsent] id 3 len 4
00:22:28: BR0:1 CDPCP: O CONFACK [REQsent] id 3 len 4
00:22:28: BR0:1 IPCP: I CONFREQ [REQsent] id 3 len 10
00:22:28: BR0:1 IPCP: Address 10.1.1.1 (0x03060A010101)
00:22:28: BR0:1 IPCP: O CONFACK [REQsent] id 3 len 10
00:22:28: BR0:1 IPCP: Address 10.1.1.1 (0x03060A010101)
00:22:28: BR0:1 CDPCP: I CONFACK [ACKsent] id 3 len 4
00:22:28: BR0:1 CDPCP: State is Open
00:22:28: BR0:1 IPCP: I CONFACK [ACKsent] id 3 len 10
00:22:28: BR0:1 IPCP: Address 10.1.1.2 (0x03060A010102)
00:22:28: BR0:1 IPCP: State is Open
00:22:28: BR0 IPCP: Install route to 10.1.1.1
```

```
Router#.!!!
Success rate is 60 percent (3/5), round-trip min/avg/max = 32/38/48 ms
00:22:29: %LINEPROTO-5-UPDOWN: Line protocol on Interface
BRI0:1, changed state to up
00:22:29: %LINK-3-UPDOWN: Interface BRI0:2, changed state to up
00:22:29: BR0:2 PPP: Treating connection as a callin
00:22:29: BR0:2 PPP: Phase is ESTABLISHING, Passive Open
00:22:29: BR0:2 LCP: State is Listen
00:22:30: BR0:2 LCP: I CONFREQ [Listen] id 3 len 10
00:22:30: BR0:2 LCP: MagicNumber 0x50239CC8
(0x050650239CC8)
00:22:30: BR0:2 LCP: O CONFREQ [Listen] id 3 len 10
00:22:30: BR0:2 LCP: MagicNumber 0x50239CDA
(0x050650239CDA)
00:22:30: BR0:2 LCP: O CONFACK [Listen] id 3 len 10
00:22:30: BR0:2 LCP: MagicNumber 0x50239CC8
(0x050650239CC8)
00:22:30: BR0:2 LCP: I CONFACK [ACKsent] id 3 len 10
00:22:30: BR0:2 LCP: MagicNumber 0x50239CDA
(0x050650239CDA) 00:22:30: BR0:2 LCP: State is Open
00:22:30: BR0:2 PPP: Phase is UP
00:22:30: BR0:2 CDPCP: O CONFREQ [Closed] id 3 len 4
00:22:30: BR0:2 IPCP: O CONFREQ [Closed] id 3 len 10
00:22:30: BR0:2 IPCP: Address 10.1.1.2 (0x03060A010102)
00:22:30: BR0:2 CDPCP: I CONFREQ [REQsent] id 3 len 4
00:22:30: BR0:2 CDPCP: O CONFACK [REQsent] id 3 len 4
00:22:30: BR0:2 IPCP: I CONFREQ [REQsent] id 3 len 10
00:22:30: BR0:2 IPCP: Address 10.1.1.1 (0x03060A010101)
00:22:30: BR0:2 IPCP: O CONFACK [REQsent] id 3 len 10
00:22:30: BR0:2 IPCP: Address 10.1.1.1 (0x03060A010101)
00:22:30: BR0:2 CDPCP: I CONFACK [ACKsent] id 3 len 4
00:22:30: BR0:2 CDPCP: State is Open
00:22:30: BR0:2 IPCP: I CONFACK [ACKsent] id 3 len 10
00:22:30: BR0:2 IPCP: Address 10.1.1.2 (0x03060A010102)
00:22:30: BR0:2 IPCP: State is Open
00:22:31: %LINEPROTO-5-UPDOWN: Line protocol on Interface BRI0:2, changed state
to up
00:22:32: BR0:1 LCP: O ECHOREQ [Open] id 12 len 12 magic
0x5020C645
00:22:32: BR0:1 LCP: echo_cnt 1, sent id 12, line up
00:22:32: BR0:1 PPP: I pkt type 0xC021, datagramsize 16
00:22:32: BR0:1 LCP: I ECHOREP [Open] id 12 len 12 magic
```

```
0x5020C654
00:22:32: BR0:1 LCP: Received id 12, sent id 12, line up
00:22:32: BR0:2 LCP: O ECHOREQ [Open] id 12 len 12 magic
0x5020CD1B
00:22:32: BR0:2 LCP: echo_cnt 1, sent id 12, line up
00:22:32: BR0:2 PPP: I pkt type 0xC021, datagramsize 16
00:22:32: BR0:2 LCP: I ECHOREP [Open] id 12 len 12 magic
0x5020CD0D
00:22:32: BR0:2 LCP: Received id 12, sent id 12, line up
00:22:33: BR0:1 PPP: I pkt type 0xC021, datagramsize 16
00:22:33: BR0:1 LCP: I ECHOREQ [Open] id 12 len 12 magic
0x5020C654
00:22:33: BR0:1 LCP: O ECHOREP [Open] id 12 len 12 magic
0x5020C64500:21:23: BR0:2 PPP: I pkt type 0xC021, datagramsize 16
00:22:33: BR0:2 LCP: I ECHOREQ [Open] id 12 len 12 magic
0x5020CD0D
00:22:33: BR0:2 LCP: O ECHOREP [Open] id 12 len 12 magic
0x5020CD1B
00:22:34: BR0:2 PPP: I pkt type 0x0207, datagramsize 15
00:22:35: BR0:2 PPP: I pkt type 0x0207, datagramsize 312
00:24:28: %ISDN-6-DISCONNECT: Interface BRI0:1 disconnected
from 18008358661 To p, call lasted 120 seconds
00:24:28: %LINK-3-UPDOWN: Interface BRI0:1, changed state to down
00:24:10: %ISDN-6-DISCONNECT: Interface BRI0:2 disconnected from 8358663, call
lasted 120 seconds
00:24:28: %LINK-3-UPDOWN: Interface BRI0:2, changed state to down
00:24:29: %LINEPROTO-5-UPDOWN: Line protocol on Interface
BRI0:1, changed state to down
00:24:29: %LINEPROTO-5-UPDOWN: Line protocol on Interface
BRI0:2, changed state to down
```

Notice that in this output, the first two ICMP packets (pings) failed due to the delay in bringing up the ISDN BRI. Although faster than asynchronous connections, ISDN still introduces connection delay, which can impact user applications. In addition, the output from the **debug ppp** `negotiation` command shows the process by which a PPP session is activated.

This output does not use CHAP, compression, or multilink. Instead, as you can see, PPP starts and then LCP is activated. After this occurs, the NCP negotiations begin, starting with CDPCP and followed by IPCP. *Cisco Discovery Protocol (CDP)* is a proprietary advertisement protocol that sends router and switch information between Cisco devices. It operates over any physical media that supports Subnetwork Access Protocol (SNAP) (except ATM) and is independent of IP. The IP Control Protocol (IPCP) was started to transport the ICMP pings that were sent from the router.

Remember that PPP sessions must undergo a negotiation process and that the **debug ppp negotiation** command will display upper level protocols such as IPCP, along with LCP and PPP.

The *debug ppp packet* Command

The **debug ppp packet** command reports real-time PPP packet flow, including the type of packet and the specific B channel used in the case of ISDN. Although this command generates a significant amount of output and could slow the access server, it is quite useful for locating errors that involve upper layer protocols.

As with other **debug** *protocol* **packet** commands, the **debug ppp packet** command records each packet that moves through the router using PPP. As such, the administrator can monitor traffic flows as if they had a protocol analyzer attached to the interface. This might be useful for troubleshooting Application layer problems, but a formal protocol analyzer is highly recommended. This output includes both CDP packets (shown with the CDPCP entries) and IP packets (showing proper configuration of IP on the link):

```
Router#debug ppp packet
PPP packet display debugging is on
Router#ping 10.1.1.1
Type escape sequence to abort.
Sending 5, 100-byte ICMP Echos to 10.1.1.1, timeout is 2 seconds:
00:24:49: %LINK-3-UPDOWN: Interface BRI0:1, changed state to up.
00:24:50: BR0:1 LCP: O CONFREQ [Closed] id 4 len 10
00:24:50: BR0:1 LCP: MagicNumber 0x5025BF23
(0x05065025BF23)
00:24:50: BR0:1 PPP: I pkt type 0xC021, datagramsize 14
00:24:50: BR0:1 PPP: I pkt type 0xC021, datagramsize 14
00:24:50: BR0:1 LCP: I CONFREQ [REQsent] id 14 len 10
00:24:50: BR0:1 LCP: MagicNumber 0x5025BF46
(0x05065025BF46)
00:24:50: BR0:1 LCP: O CONFACK [REQsent] id 14 len 10
00:24:50: BR0:1 LCP: MagicNumber 0x5025BF46
(0x05065025BF46)
00:24:50: BR0:1 LCP: I CONFACK [ACKsent] id 4 len 10
00:24:50: BR0:1 LCP: MagicNumber 0x5025BF23
(0x05065025BF23)
00:24:50: BR0:1 PPP: I pkt type 0x8207, datagramsize 8
00:24:50: BR0:1 PPP: I pkt type 0x8021, datagramsize 14
00:24:50: BR0:1 CDPCP: O CONFREQ [Closed] id 4 len 4
00:24:50: BR0:1 PPP: I pkt type 0x8207, datagramsize 8
00:24:50: BR0:1 IPCP: O CONFREQ [Closed] id 4 len 10
00:24:50: BR0:1 IPCP: Address 10.1.1.2 (0x03060A010102)
```

```
00:24:50: BR0:1 CDPCP: I CONFREQ [REQsent] id 4 len 4
00:24:50: BR0:1 CDPCP: O CONFACK [REQ.!!!
Success rate is 60 percent (3/5), round-trip min/avg/max = 36/41/52 ms
Router#sent] id 4 len 4
00:24:50: BR0:1 PPP: I pkt type 0x8021, datagramsize 14
00:24:50: BR0:1 IPCP: I CONFREQ [REQsent] id 4 len 10
00:24:50: BR0:1 IPCP: Address 10.1.1.1 (0x03060A010101)
00:24:50: BR0:1 IPCP: O CONFACK [REQsent] id 4 len 10
00:24:50: BR0:1 IPCP: Address 10.1.1.1 (0x03060A010101)
00:24:50: BR0:1 CDPCP: I CONFACK [ACKsent] id 4 len 4
00:24:50: BR0:1 IPCP: I CONFACK [ACKsent] id 4 len 10
00:24:50: BR0:1 IPCP: Address 10.1.1.2 (0x03060A010102)
00:24:51: BR0:1 PPP: O pkt type 0x0021, datagramsize 104
00:24:51: %LINEPROTO-5-UPDOWN: Line protocol on Interface
BRI0:1, changed state to up
00:24:51: BR0:1 PPP: O pkt type 0x0207, datagramsize 323
00:24:51: %LINK-3-UPDOWN: Interface BRI0:2, changed state to up
00:24:51: BR0:2 PPP: I pkt type 0xC021, datagramsize 14
00:24:51: BR0:2 LCP: I CONFREQ [Listen] id 4 len 10
00:24:51: BR0:2 LCP: MagicNumber 0x5025C5EF
(0x05065025C5EF)
00:24:51: BR0:2 LCP: O CONFREQ [Listen] id 4 len 10 00:24:51:
  ➥BR0:2 LCP: MagicNumber 0x5025C605
(0x05065025C605)
00:24:51: BR0:2 LCP: O CONFACK [Listen] id 4 len 10
00:24:51: BR0:2 LCP: MagicNumber 0x5025C5EF
(0x05065025C5EF)
00:24:51: BR0:2 PPP: I pkt type 0xC021, datagramsize 14
00:24:51: BR0:2 LCP: I CONFACK [ACKsent] id 4 len 10
00:24:51: BR0:2 LCP: MagicNumber 0x5025C605
(0x05065025C605)
00:24:51: BR0:2 PPP: I pkt type 0x8207, datagramsize 8
00:24:51: BR0:2 PPP: I pkt type 0x8021, datagramsize 14
00:24:51: BR0:2 CDPCP: O CONFREQ [Closed] id 4 len 4
00:24:51: BR0:2 IPCP: O CONFREQ [Closed] id 4 len 10
00:24:51: BR0:2 IPCP: Address 10.1.1.2 (0x03060A010102)
00:24:51: BR0:2 CDPCP: I CONFREQ [REQsent] id 4 len 4
00:24:51: BR0:2 CDPCP: O CONFACK [REQsent] id 4 len 4
00:24:51: BR0:2 PPP: I pkt type 0x8207, datagramsize 8
00:24:51: BR0:2 IPCP: I CONFREQ [REQsent] id 4 len 10
```

```
00:24:51: BR0:2 IPCP: Address 10.1.1.1 (0x03060A010101)
00:24:51: BR0:2 PPP: I pkt type 0x8021, datagramsize 14
00:24:51: BR0:2 IPCP: O CONFACK [REQsent] id 4 len 10
00:24:51: BR0:2 IPCP: Address 10.1.1.1 (0x03060A010101)
00:24:51: BR0:2 CDPCP: I CONFACK [ACKsent] id 4 len 4
00:24:51: BR0:2 IPCP: I CONFACK [ACKsent] id 4 len 10
00:24:51: BR0:2 IPCP: Address 10.1.1.2 (0x03060A010102)
00:24:52: BR0:1 LCP: O ECHOREQ [Open] id 1 len 12 magic
0x5025BF23
00:24:52: BR0:1 LCP: echo_cnt 1, sent id 1, line up
00:24:52: BR0:1 PPP: I pkt type 0xC021, datagramsize 16
00:24:52: BR0:1 LCP: I ECHOREP [Open] id 1 len 12 magic
0x5025BF46
00:24:52: BR0:1 LCP: Received id 1, sent id 1, line up
00:24:52: BR0:2 LCP: O ECHOREQ [Open] id 1 len 12 magic
0x5025C605
00:24:52: BR0:2 LCP: echo_cnt 1, sent id 1, line up
00:24:52: BR0:2 PPP: I pkt type 0xC021, datagramsize 16 00:24:52:
  ➥BR0:2 LCP: I ECHOREP [Open] id 1 len 12 magic
0x5025C5EF
00:24:52: BR0:2 LCP: Received id 1, sent id 1, line up
00:24:52: %LINEPROTO-5-UPDOWN: Line protocol on Interface
BRI0:2, changed state to up
00:24:52: BR0:1 PPP: O pkt type 0x0207, datagramsize 323
00:24:52: BR0:2 PPP: I pkt type 0x0207, datagramsize 312
00:24:53: BR0:1 PPP: O pkt type 0x0021, datagramsize 104
00:24:53: BR0:2 PPP: I pkt type 0x0021, datagramsize 104
00:24:53: BR0:1 PPP: O pkt type 0x0021, datagramsize 104
00:24:53: BR0:2 PPP: I pkt type 0x0021, datagramsize 104
00:24:53: BR0:1 PPP: O pkt type 0x0021, datagramsize 104
00:24:53: BR0:2 PPP: I pkt type 0x0021, datagramsize 104
00:24:53: BR0:1 PPP: I pkt type 0xC021, datagramsize 16
00:24:53: BR0:1 LCP: I ECHOREQ [Open] id 1 len 12 magic
0x5025BF46
00:24:53: BR0:1 LCP: O ECHOREP [Open] id 1 len 12 magic
0x5025BF23
00:24:53: BR0:2 PPP: I pkt type 0xC021, datagramsize 16
00:24:53: BR0:2 LCP: I ECHOREQ [Open] id 1 len 12 magic
0x5025C5EF
00:24:53: BR0:2 LCP: O ECHOREP [Open] id 1 len 12 magic
```

```
0x5025C605
Router#
00:25:02: BR0:1 LCP: O ECHOREQ [Open] id 2 len 12 magic
0x5025BF23
00:25:02: BR0:1 LCP: echo_cnt 1, sent id 2, line up
00:25:02: BR0:1 PPP: I pkt type 0xC021, datagramsize 16
00:25:02: BR0:1 LCP: I ECHOREP [Open] id 2 len 12 magic
0x5025BF46
00:25:02: BR0:1 LCP: Received id 2, sent id 2, line up
00:25:02: BR0:2 LCP: O ECHOREQ [Open] id 2 len 12 magic
0x5025C605
00:25:02: BR0:2 LCP: echo_cnt 1, sent id 2, line up
00:25:02: BR0:2 PPP: I pkt type 0xC021, datagramsize 16
00:25:02: BR0:2 LCP: I ECHOREP [Open] id 2 len 12 magic
0x5025C5EF
00:25:02: BR0:2 LCP: Received id 2, sent id 2, line up
00:25:03: BR0:1 PPP: I pkt type 0xC021, datagramsize 16
00:25:03: BR0:1 LCP: I ECHOREQ [Open] id 2 len 12 magic
0x5025BF46
00:25:03: BR0:1 LCP: O ECHOREP [Open] id 2 len 12 magic
0x5025BF23
00:25:03: BR0:2 PPP: I pkt type 0xC021, datagramsize 16
00:25:03: BR0:2 LCP: I ECHOREQ [Open] id 2 len 12 magic
0x5025C5EF
00:25:03: BR0:2 LCP: O ECHOREP [Open] id 2 len 12 magic
0x5025C605
```

The `debug ppp packet` command is most helpful in locating upper layer protocol errors. It filters out non-PPP output, resulting in a cleaner debug output than a regular `debug ip packet` command. Note that the magic numbers referred to in the previous output are used to thwart playback attacks by maintaining a form of state for the session.

Summary

PPP is a versatile protocol that provides a designer with many options when deploying it in the network. Through the use of interactive PPP, you can provide flexibility to dial-in users using asynchronous interfaces. If you are looking for a more secure dial-in environment, you can configure an asynchronous interface to run in dedicated PPP mode. Another option for the security conscious is to utilize PPP callback for enhanced security.

Addressing can be configured by using static IP addresses, but for greater flexibility we suggest using DHCP or address pools to automatically assign IP addressing. User authentication can be accomplished by using Password Authentication Protocol (PAP) or its more secure cousin, Challenge Handshake Authentication Protocol (CHAP).

Compression and multilink are two PPP options that a network designer can use to increase traffic flow on a connection. They can be used separately or together for even greater throughput.

When trouble occurs with an asynchronous connection, Cisco IOS offers a variety of troubleshooting commands to assist the administrator in narrowing down the problem. These commands can be used to show the PPP negotiation process, PPP authentication process, or each PPP packet as it traverses an interface.

Exam Essentials

Know how to set up PPP on an interface and know what LCP and NCP are used for. To configure PPP encapsulation on an interface, use the `encapsulation ppp` command. LCP is used for PPP link control, including circuit testing and authentication. NCP is used to negotiate which upper layer protocols will run over a connection and negotiates their addressing.

Understand how to set up an interface to allow multiple protocols and how to restrict the method of access to a single protocol. An interface can be set up with the command `async mode interactive` to enable a user to choose between SLIP and PPP encapsulation. The administrator can restrict the user from changing the encapsulation by using the `async mode dedicated` command. By using the `autoselect` command to sense the desired protocol, the router can automatically configure the interface.

Know the three methods to give an interface an IP address. You can use static IP addressing, which requires more administrator overhead; IP unnumbered, which has troubleshooting problems; or dynamic IP address allocation using DHCP or IP address pools.

Be able to give a general overview of how DHCP works. The DHCP client uses a broadcast packet to communicate with a DHCP server. A negotiation process determines an IP address lease. After half of the lease time has expired, the DHCP client will attempt to renew the lease.

Understand the differences between the two PPP authentication protocols and when to use them. You should understand how the PAP and CHAP protocols work and why CHAP is the better protocol to use. CHAP never sends the username and password over the link, whereas PAP sends both in cleartext. Security can be compromised with PAP, but sometimes legacy systems require its use.

Know the commands to use when configuring compression and Multilink PPP (MPPP). Use the `compress [predictor | stac | mppc [ignore-pfc]]` command to configure compression on a link, making sure to use the same method on each end of a connection. You can bond multiple channels into a single connection for greater speed by using the `ppp multilink` command. Compression and multilink can be used together or separately to enhance connection throughput.

Know the PPP troubleshooting commands and how to spot a problem. You can use the `debug ppp authentication`, `debug ppp negotiation`, and `debug ppp packet` commands to determine the cause of a remote access problem.

Using Microsoft Windows 95/98/2000/XP

THE CCNP EXAM TOPICS COVERED IN THIS CHAPTER INCLUDE THE FOLLOWING:

✓ **Connect to the central site with Microsoft Windows.**

We have elected to retain this chapter for this revision of the text because the exam might incorporate questions related to the material. Based on the most recent information, this is admittedly unlikely. You should be confident that cursory retention of the material in this chapter is all that might be needed for real-world and examination success. This chapter focuses on Windows 95/98 because of Cisco's focus on these versions. Please note that Windows 2000 and Windows XP incorporate processes and protocols that are similar to these earlier versions, and this chapter can provide benefit and understanding in that context.

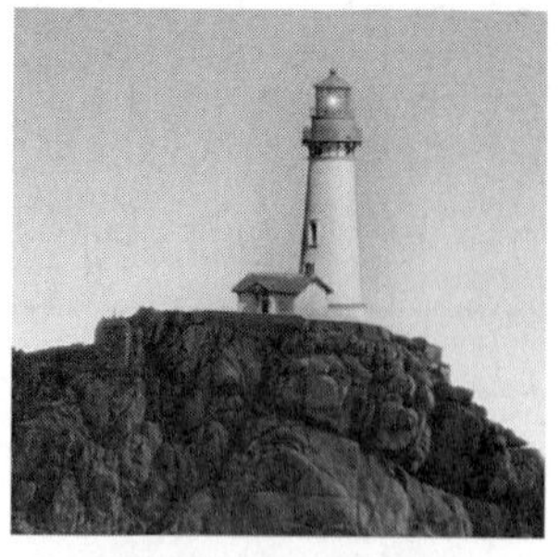

Any book on remote access would be remiss if it did not include a section on the world's most popular desktop operating system. It would be difficult to find a remote access solution that does not require support for Windows. You might question the dedication of an entire chapter in a present-day remote access book to the consumer-oriented platforms of Windows 95 and 98, especially when Microsoft no longer supports Windows 95 and retired Windows 98 in 2004. However, Cisco still requires an understanding of Windows dial-up networking. Fortunately, older versions parallel the modern versions of the operating system, and, as such, this chapter also provides a foundation for using Windows XP and 2000.

This chapter focuses on the configuration and support issues that surround this popular client software. Particular attention should be paid to the protocols that are supported and the configuration steps that are required on the client.

Reasons to Use Dial-Up Networking

Fortunately, not only is configuring and using dial-up networking in Windows 95/98 simple, but it also provides a broad base of services for remote users. These services include the following:

Automatic connection to websites Once configured, the operating system automatically establishes a dial-up connection to connect with a remote web server. If a user simply types a URL into Microsoft Internet Explorer, the modem will dial the Internet service provider (ISP) and request the web page.

E-mail Mobile clients can connect to Microsoft Exchange or another e-mail service in the office. This provides an efficient way to communicate with colleagues.

File synchronization Remote users can obtain file updates and post their files on a server in the office for local users. Although Microsoft provides the My Briefcase application for this purpose, Symantec's pcAnywhere and other such programs might be desired by more demanding users.

Remote control One alternative to high-bandwidth applications is remote control. Remote control software does exactly what it sounds like it does: keystrokes and mouse movements are sent to the host, and the host returns the image to the remote user, enabling the user to control the host. This solution enables only the screen images to be transferred, which can greatly reduce the required bandwidth for supporting the application.

Consider the following: A remote user on a dial-up connection needs to access a database, and this access results in 10MB of data being transferred. When using remote control, only the screen data will be sent for the session; with compression, this means that possibly less than 2MB of data will be sent. Clearly, this bandwidth savings can be substantial. Note that remote control solutions must be connected to access data—unlike remote node solutions, which use the remote user's processor for local applications and data and use the modem as a slower network link. Also, the bandwidth savings can differ significantly depending on the data demands of the application. In this context, remote control utilizes remote node solutions for transport, but the connection must be maintained for the duration of the remote control session. Windows XP includes a terminal server option.

Effectively, anything that a user can accomplish in the office is possible to accomplish remotely with dial-up networking. Unfortunately, the significantly lower bandwidth of dial-up connections can make this impractical, depending on the application.

Configuring Dial-Up Networking with Windows 95/98

Dial-up networking in Windows 95/98 is still popular, perhaps for no other reason than approximately 100 million clients worldwide have a Microsoft operating system installed. From a client's perspective, the cost and effort needed to connect to the office remotely requires little more than a phone line and modem.

As you will see in this chapter, configuring and administering a single Windows workstation for dial-up networking is very simple. Unfortunately, administering dial-up networking for thousands of remote users is not as simple, and there are few existing tools that make this task easier.

Microsoft Windows 95/98 supports remote dial-up networking with the protocols that provide transport for NetBIOS:

- NetBEUI
- IPX
- IP

Supporting these protocols is logical because of Windows networking's historical dependency upon the NetBIOS protocol and the name services that it provides. This changed in Windows 2000 and XP. It is possible to add other protocols with third-party transport, but most designers find IP support to be sufficient, and they configure the client for PPP services.

See Chapter 24, "Point-to-Point Protocol" for more information about the PPP.

Configuring a Dial-Up Connection Client

The configuration of a Windows client for dial-up networking is a relatively painless process, although many configuration options are available, and good planning will greatly simplify an enterprise-level deployment.

By default, the Windows 95/98 installation includes the basic files for installing and configuring a network connection. It's always a good idea, though, to have the original installation CD-ROM available because the setup program might need additional files to complete the installation. In addition, the latest service packs and updates should be installed—service packs contain many updates and problem fixes called *patches*. In general, the installation of patches is a benign event; however, before performing the upgrade, it is best to back up critical files and review the appropriateness of the patch. For multiple node upgrades, it's best to test the patch before you deploy it.

Check the Windows website at `www.microsoft.com` for the latest patches, service packs, and tips for configuring dial-up networking.

Although many tools are available for installing and configuring dial-up networking, this book focuses on the basic installation—PPP and TCP/IP protocols. However, multilink connections and scripting are also presented.

The screen captures in this chapter, unless otherwise noted, are from Windows 98 Second Edition. The screens from other versions of Windows might differ slightly.

Dial-Up Networking Application

To start configuring a dial-up connection, choose Start ➢ Programs ➢ Accessories ➢ Communications ➢ Dial-Up Networking. This opens a dialog box similar to the one shown in Figure 25.1.

On the system shown here, this is the first dial-up connection, so Windows provides only a Make New Connection icon. Clicking this icon brings up the Dial-Up Networking Wizard. If other connections were available, the user or administrator could select them to initiate a call or to go into an already established connection in order to reconfigure options.

Make New Connection Wizard

After you select the Make New Connection icon, Windows begins the Make New Connection Wizard. The first dialog box of this wizard is shown in Figure 25.2.

In this dialog box, you type a name for the connection and set the kind of modem that you will be using for the connection. If Windows did not detect and install a modem in the Select a Device box, you need to correct this before continuing.

FIGURE 25.1 The Windows Dial-Up Networking dialog box

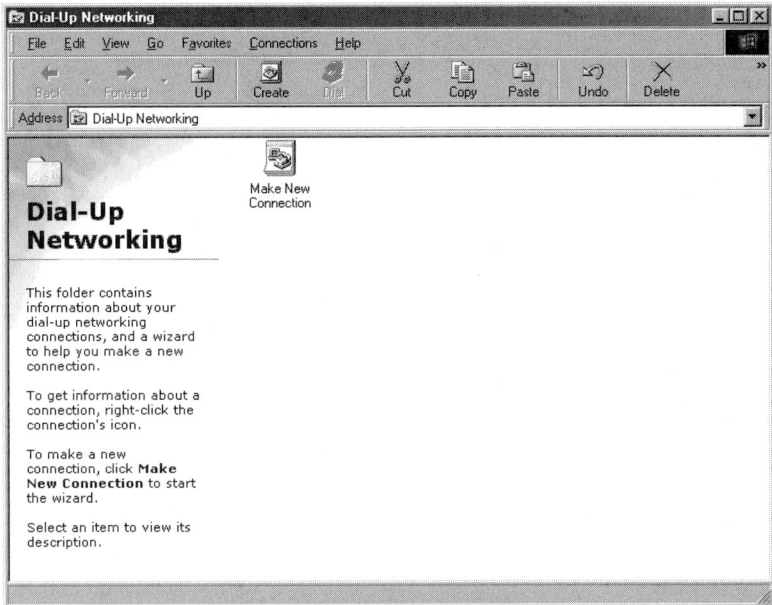

FIGURE 25.2 Making a new connection

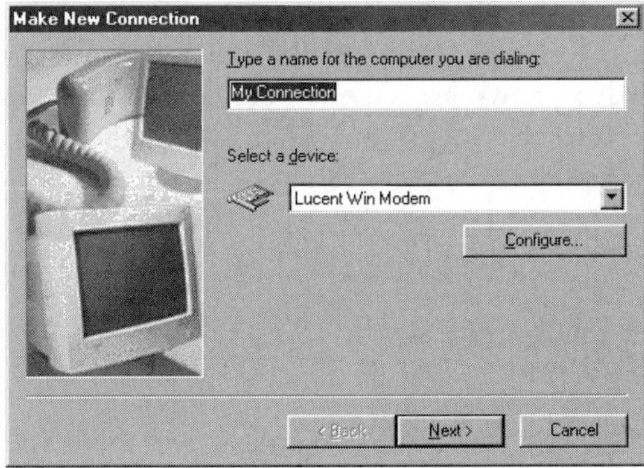

For instructions on installing a modem in Windows, please refer to the product documentation.

Note that in Figure 25.2, the Lucent Win Modem has been automatically selected, and the user has been prompted to provide a name for the connection.

Check the hardware compatibility list (HCL) to verify that your equipment is certified to operate in the Windows environment. This information is found on the Microsoft website, `www.microsoft.com/whdc/hcl/search.mspx`.

By default, Windows inserts the name My Connection; however, you should change this to a more descriptive name for the particular connection you are setting up. Figure 25.3 shows the Make New Connection dialog box.

FIGURE 25.3 Changing the dial-up name

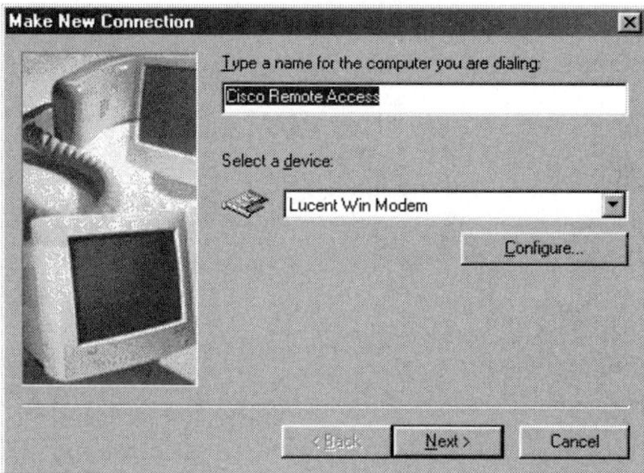

When you are finished renaming the connection and selecting the appropriate modem, click the Next button. The next dialog box (see Figure 25.4) enables you to define the phone number that will be called. The default area code is the area code defined when the modem was first installed. The Country or Region Code drop-down list is used to define what digits will precede the area code. For example, if you were making a call to somewhere in the United Kingdom, you would define it by selecting country code 44 for the connection.

FIGURE 25.4 Defining the phone number

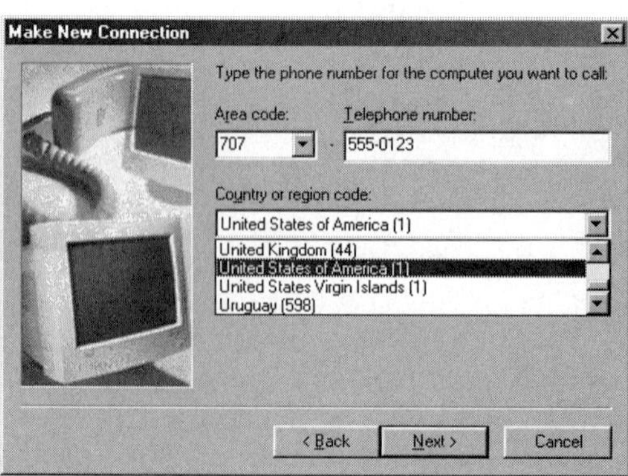

When you are finished, click Next. Windows then provides a confirmation similar to the one shown in Figure 25.5. An icon is placed in the Dial-Up Networking folder as well.

FIGURE 25.5 A successful connection defined

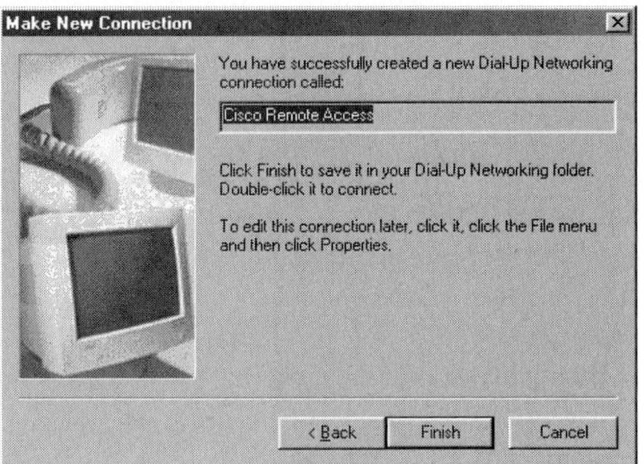

Connection Properties

After this initial phase is completed, you have the opportunity to select the icon and attempt a connection with the defaults, or you can right-click the icon to select the properties of the connection. Select the option you wish to edit, and the connection properties dialog box (shown in Figure 25.6) opens. Note that there are four tabs: General, Server Types, Scripting, and Multilink.

FIGURE 25.6 Connection properties dialog box

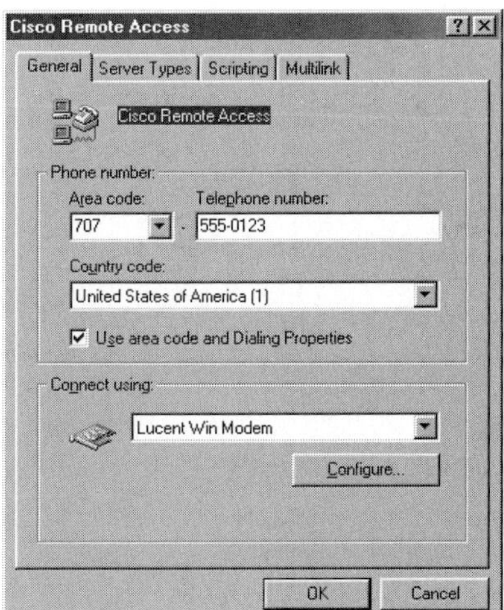

It's important to understand how to select and configure the properties on each of the four tabs.

General Tab

The General tab displays the initial configuration information, including the name, phone number, country code, and modem that will be used. This tab is shown in Figure 25.6.

Server Types Tab

You will find that the Server Types tab is the most important for remote access configuration. This tab addresses protocols, encapsulations, addressing, compression, and encryption. You need to match these settings to those on a Cisco remote access device in order to establish an efficient connection.

As shown in Figure 25.7, the first option asks you to specify the type of dial-up server. There are five options (although the drop-down list shown in this figure has room to show only four). The types of servers are as follows:

- CSLIP: Unix Connection with IP Header Compression
- NRN: NetWare Connect Version 1.0 and 1.1
- PPP: Internet, Windows NT Server, Windows 98
- SLIP: Unix Connection
- Windows for Workgroups and Windows NT 3.1

You will learn more about each of these server types next.

FIGURE 25.7 The Windows dial-up networking server types

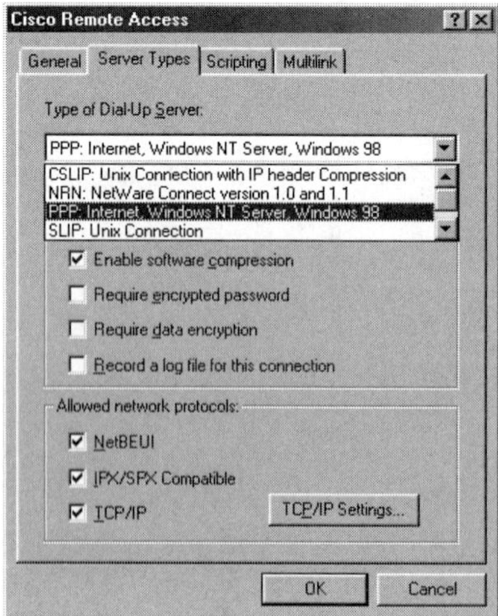

Note that the server types described here are not servers in the traditional sense; they are daemons or descriptions of protocols.

It's important to understand the distinctions between each of these server types:

CSLIP: Unix Connection with IP Header Compression This server type is seldom used for the reason indicated in Chapter 24: SLIP (Serial Line Internet Protocol) is rarely used due to its sole support for IP. Legacy Unix servers, however, might still require this option. CSLIP stands for Compressed Serial Line Internet Protocol. This option supports only IP and does not support software compression, encrypted passwords, or data compression.

NRN: NetWare Connection Version 1.0 and 1.1 Just as SLIP and CSLIP supports only IP, the NRN connection supports only IPX/SPX. This option is provided for legacy installations of NetWare, but most environments have migrated away from this platform.

PPP: Internet, Windows NT Server, Windows 98 PPP is not only the default dial-up server type, it is also the most recommended. As shown in Figure 25.7, it supports all protocols and features.

PPP is described in detail in Chapter 24.

SLIP: Unix Connection As with CSLIP, SLIP supports only IP connections and does not provide advanced features. Although PPP is both recommended and popular, a significant number of installations support only SLIP. Migration from SLIP to PPP is highly recommended because of PPP's multiprotocol support.

Windows for Workgroups and Windows NT 3.1 This server type supports only NetBEUI and its upper layer protocol, NetBIOS. NetBEUI does not support routing, however. It is a simple protocol and negates the need for addressing. NetBEUI might provide the best performance for a single connection, but it cannot scale and, given the demands on the network, it's probably best to use PPP.

The remainder of this section focuses on the rest of the options on the Server Types tab for a PPP server type.

Advanced Options

Microsoft considers optional functions to be advanced options. These options include settings to control compression and authentication protocols.

Under Advanced Options, five choices can be made by the user or administrator. Figure 25.8 shows the default configuration for a PPP connection with the NetBEUI and IPX/SPX options unselected.

FIGURE 25.8 Configuring PPP

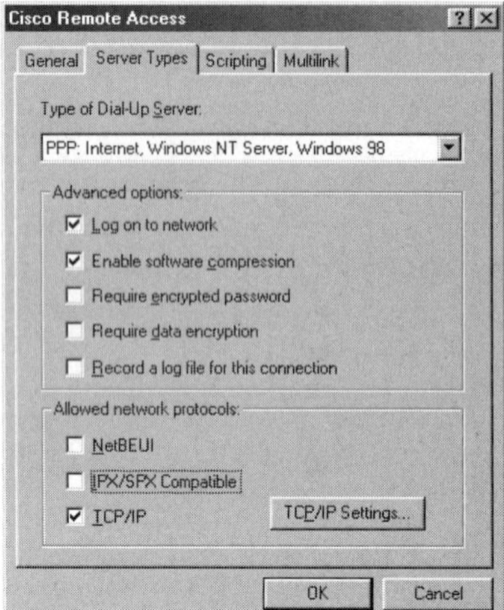

To improve performance, disable the NetBEUI and IPX/SPX Compatible network protocols unless they are required.

The five Advanced Option choices you can select are as follows:

Log On to Network If you are connecting to an NT domain, you use this option to establish a network connection and to attempt to log into the domain. Leave this option unselected to improve performance on networks where this service is not required.

Enable Software Compression Software-based compression is different from the modem-based compression features that were presented in Chapter 23, "Asynchronous Connections." By selecting this option, you can improve throughput by enabling compression, but this depends on the type of data and equipment you use. By compressing with software, you are substituting a repetitious series of characters to reduce the amount of bandwidth required. When decompressing, the compressed data stream is translated back into an uncompressed form.

Require Encrypted Password By selecting the Require Encrypted Password check box, you are precluding the use of cleartext authentication. Microsoft supports several encrypted password options, including Shiva Password Authentication Protocol (SPAP), Data Encryption Standard (DES), Challenge Handshake Authentication Protocol (CHAP), and MS-CHAP. MS-CHAP is based on Rivest-Shamir-Adleman (RSA) MD4 (Message Digest type 4). On Windows NT, this is enhanced to MD5 with Service Pack 3 or greater, and is standard in newer versions of Windows.

Remember when choosing your password that passwords are generally case sensitive.

Require Data Encryption By selecting this check box, you are making sure that information passing through your connection will be encrypted. Unlike data compression, encryption protects the contents of the data during transmission. Even though this option provides relatively weak encryption, you might want to use it when you are transmitting critical data. Note that your performance will suffer slightly with this option because the encryption is processed in software.

Record a Log File for This Connection When you select this check box, a log file will be recorded. You might find that log files are useful for troubleshooting purposes, but most administrators find the lack of information provided by this output frustrating. The log file might help to augment the diagnostic process, however. When used with caution, the Cisco `debug` commands provide substantially better troubleshooting output.

Viewing a Log File

The output shown next provides an example of the log output. Note that the software automatically recovered from an error condition found when hanging up the modem via hardware command by lowering DTR (data terminal ready).

The log is a standard text file that can be viewed by choosing Connection ➤ Advanced from the modem's properties dialog box and then clicking the View Log button in the Advanced Connection Settings dialog box that opens (see Figure 25.9).

FIGURE 25.9 The View Log option

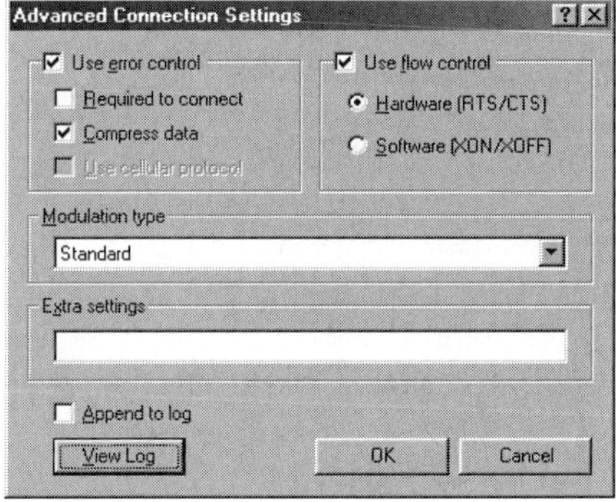

Following is a sample log file that shows the preliminary handshake with the modem. This identifies the information file (INF) that is used, in addition to the status of connections, error control, compression, and hang-up characteristics. Note that in this case, the modem did not respond to the lowering of DTR for the hang-up and was disconnected with software. This might indicate a configuration problem with the modem; however, it is benign in this case.

```
02-15-2000 22:36:33.15 - Lucent Win Modem in use.
02-15-2000 22:36:33.16 - Modem type: Lucent Win Modem
02-15-2000 22:36:33.16 - Modem inf path: LTMODEM.INF
02-15-2000 22:36:33.16 - Modem inf section: Modem_PNP_DSVD
```

```
02-15-2000 22:36:34.80 - 115200,N,8,1
02-15-2000 22:36:34.80 - 115200,N,8,1
02-15-2000 22:36:34.80 - Initializing modem.
02-15-2000 22:36:34.80 - Send: AT<cr>
02-15-2000 22:36:34.81 - Recv: AT<cr>
02-15-2000 22:36:34.81 - Recv: <cr><lf>OK<cr><lf>
02-15-2000 22:36:34.81 - Interpreted response: Ok
02-15-2000 22:36:34.81 - Send: AT &F E0 &C1 &D2 V1   S0=0\V1<cr>
02-15-2000 22:36:34.85 - Recv: AT &F E0 &C1 &D2 V1 S0=0\V1<cr>
02-15-2000 22:36:34.85 - Recv: <cr><lf>OK<cr><lf>
02-15-2000 22:36:34.85 - Interpreted response: Ok
02-15-2000 22:36:34.85 - Send: ATS7=60S30=0L0M1\N3%C1&K3B0B15B2N1\J1X4<cr>
02-15-2000 22:36:34.86 - Recv: <cr><lf>OK<cr><lf>
02-15-2000 22:36:34.86 - Interpreted response: Ok
02-15-2000 22:36:34.86 - Dialing.
02-15-2000 22:36:34.86 - Send: ATDT;<cr>
02-15-2000 22:36:37.38 - Recv: <cr><lf>OK<cr><lf>
02-15-2000 22:36:37.38 - Interpreted response: Ok
02-15-2000 22:36:37.38 - Dialing.
02-15-2000 22:36:37.38 - Send: ATDT#######<cr>
02-15-2000 22:37:10.81 - Recv: <cr><lf>CONNECT 26400 V42bis<cr><lf>
02-15-2000 22:37:10.81 - Interpreted response: Connect
02-15-2000 22:37:10.81 - Connection established at 26400bps.
02-15-2000 22:37:10.81 - Error-control on.
02-15-2000 22:37:10.81 - Data compression on.
02-15-2000 22:37:44.27 - Hanging up the modem.
02-15-2000 22:37:44.27 - Hardware hangup by lowering DTR.
02-15-2000 22:37:45.47 - WARNING: The modem did not respond to lowering
  ➥DTR.  Trying software hangup...
02-15-2000 22:37:45.47 - Send: +++
02-15-2000 22:37:45.55 - Recv: <cr><lf>OK<cr><lf>
02-15-2000 22:37:45.55 - Interpreted response: Ok
02-15-2000 22:37:45.55 - Send: ATH E1<cr>
02-15-2000 22:37:45.63 - Recv: <cr><lf>OK<cr><lf>
02-15-2000 22:37:45.63 - Interpreted response: Ok
02-15-2000 22:37:45.63 - 115200,N,8,1
02-15-2000 22:37:46.69 - Session Statistics:
02-15-2000 22:37:46.69 -                 Reads : 811 bytes
02-15-2000 22:37:46.69 -                 Writes: 2991 bytes
02-15-2000 22:37:46.69 - Lucent Win Modem closed.
```

Allowed Network Protocols

The Allowed Network Protocols section of the Server Types tab enables eligible protocols to be included or omitted from the dial-up networking connection. All three—NetBEUI, IPX, and IP—are allowed in Figure 25.8 because PPP was selected. The TCP/IP Settings button enables the user or administrator to choose DHCP-assigned IP address information (the default), or to enter static entries.

Scripting Tab

Scripts enable the administrator or user to automate functions, including login or program execution. A parallel of a script is a to-do list for getting ready in the morning—get up, brush teeth, get dressed, and so forth. Scripts should be approached with care because they are not stored in a secure manner and therefore can present a security risk.

To select a script, type the script name in the File Name text box (see Figure 25.10). The Step Through Script option (grayed out in this figure because a script file was not defined) can be useful for timing a script or for general debugging, and the Start Terminal Screen Minimized option can be used to hide the script's execution from being displayed to the user.

FIGURE 25.10 The Scripting tab

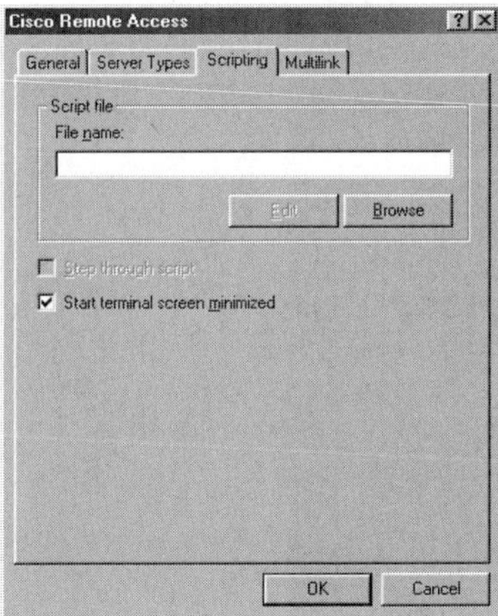

Multilink Tab

You learned about multilink services and the Multilink Protocol (MP) in Chapter 24. Multilink provides the ability to create a single logical connection through two or more physical modems, which can provide greater aggregate bandwidth for a remote user. Note that Microsoft's multilink feature does not support the Cisco proprietary Multilink Multipoint Protocol (MPP), only the standards-based MP. Users or administrators need to provide only the phone number to configure the service, as shown in Figure 25.11. The Edit Extra Device dialog box shown in Figure 25.11 opens when the user selects Use Additional Devices and clicks the Add button.

FIGURE 25.11 The Multilink tab

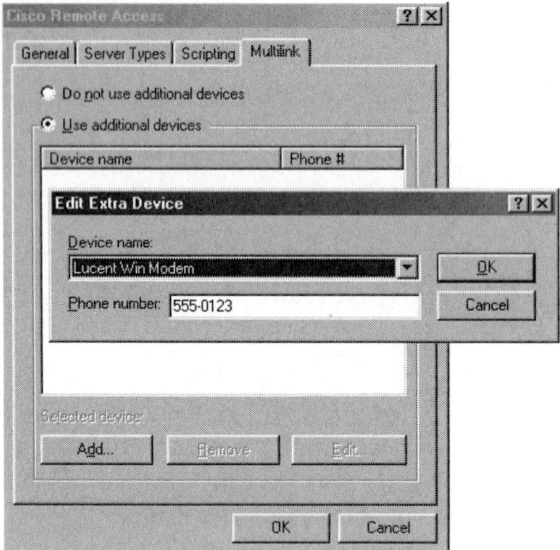

Figure 25.11 shows a Windows 98 screen. In Windows 2000, Microsoft changed the dialog boxes such that you must have installed and configured multiple modems for the option to appear.

Setting Additional Configuration Options

This section addresses two of the most common optional configurations that administrators and users select in dial-up networking:

- Lock DTE speed
- Launch terminal windows

The first option, locking DTE (data terminal equipment) speed, is predominantly used for troubleshooting or for improving performance on degraded circuits—circuits that are impaired due to line conditions. This option is becoming less significant as phone line quality and termination equipment improve.

The second option, launching terminal windows, is usually used for third-party authentication; however, it can also be used for manual control of the session.

Unlike the previous options, both of these selections are grouped with the modem controls as opposed to the networking configuration options. This is due to their relationship with the Physical and Data Link layers—both DTE speed and a terminal window are independent of the Network Layer protocol in use.

Locking DTE Speed

At times the user might want to lock the DTE speed to complete a connection. Locking the DTE speed can provide better performance on degraded lines if the speed is locked to a value lower than would otherwise be possible—a result of fewer retransmissions to cope with the errors. For most connections, this step is unnecessary.

To lock the DTE speed, select the Only Connect at This Speed box in the Modem Properties dialog box, as shown in Figure 25.12. Recall that this is DTE-to-DCE speed, and as such, it should relate to the capacity of the DCE device, as defined in Chapter 23.

FIGURE 25.12 Locking the DTE speed

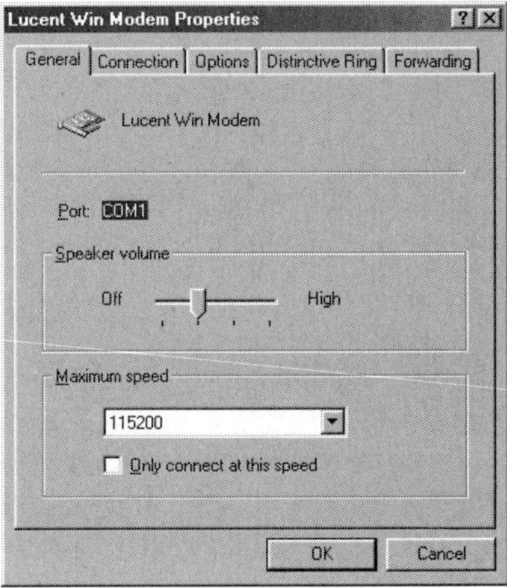

Launching Terminal Windows

On the Modem Properties Options tab, the user is offered the option of launching a terminal window either before or after the connection is made. The option of opening a terminal window after the connection is made is frequently necessary for hard authentication options such as SecureID. This tab is shown in Figure 25.13.

Typically, the terminal window is launched with a *challenge* sent from the SecureID or a similar third-party product. The challenge is a dynamically created value that is entered into a physical calculator programmed to generate the proper response. This response is valid only for the duration of the challenge—typically a minute—and it is a single-use password. These security solutions require physical possession of the token, or password generator, and the PIN that allows access. This security model is sometimes referred to as "something you have and something you know." Bank ATM cards use a similar principle.

FIGURE 25.13 Launching a terminal window

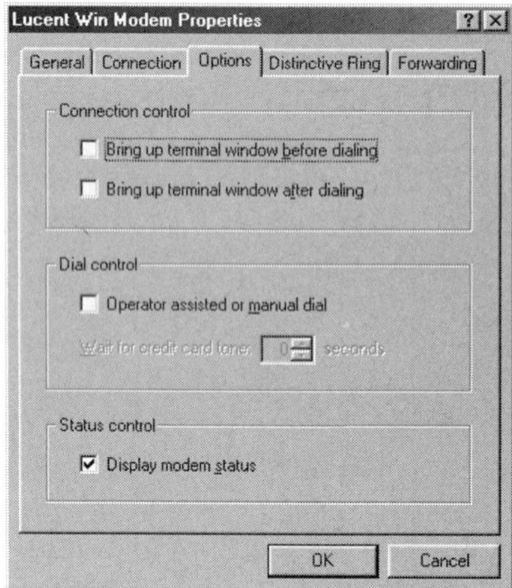

Verifying a Dial-Up Connection

Dial-up connections work without a significant amount of troubleshooting under most circumstances. When they don't, Windows generally provides an indication of the error and a recommended course of action, as shown in Figure 25.14. This screen shows error 680, which means that there was no dial tone.

On the access server, the administrator can choose to use the `show line` command to view the status of the connection. Unfortunately, this requires that much of the connection is already established—a presumption that does not always coincide with troubleshooting.

FIGURE 25.14 Dial-up networking error

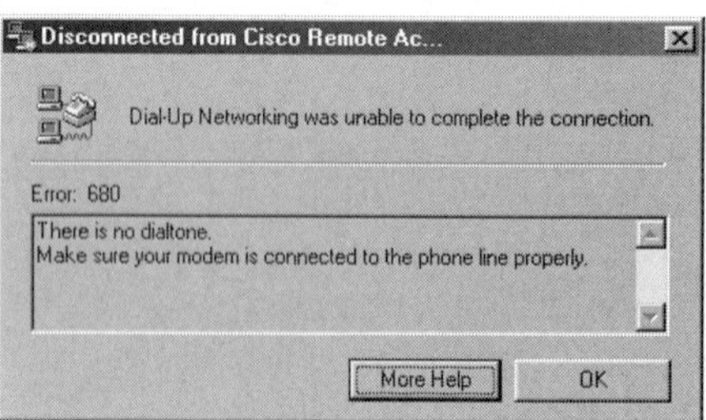

Summary

Remote access solutions provide connectivity beyond the local area network. In prior chapters, you read about solutions that use Cisco routers to communicate to other Cisco routers. This chapter differs in that it is completely focused on a non-Cisco technology—Microsoft Windows—the leading desktop operating system in use today. Although the current versions of Windows (XP and Windows 2000) are not covered in this chapter, the Cisco position to focus only on Windows 95/98 is not completely without merit. While outdated and no longer supported, Windows 95/98 shares many comparable traits with its offspring, and learning the old operating system can provide a solid foundation for newer implementations. Having said that, Cisco should update their exam materials to reflect shipping versions of software, and readers will need to augment this chapter's material, which focuses on the exam, with study and practice on newer versions in order to transition to real-world practical usage.

Windows dial-up networking interoperates with Cisco remote access solutions via each of the three layer 2 and layer 3 protocols offered by Microsoft. These are TCP/IP, which is actually IP; IPX, the Novell networking protocol; and NetBEUI. NetBEUI is a bridged protocol and technically operates at layer 2. The most common of these in production networks is IP.

At the Data Link layer, Microsoft installations are typically configured with PPP. This is the most common implementation with Cisco solutions and is the most important to understand.

For some reason, Cisco stresses knowing the method used in configuring the dial-up networking options within the Windows operating system. Microsoft places these options (unlike most other network settings) under the Accessories option, and not the Control Panel or Network icons. This is very important to know for successful implementation of the remote access solution; however, it would be fair to note that many users have already learned the quirks of Windows configuration and would therefore question Cisco's judgment in stressing a process that is more than seven years old. Suffice it to say that familiarity is important, and it would be prudent to focus on this if you are approaching the exam or practical usage without Microsoft experience.

There are other minor elements in Windows remote access that are valuable to know. Microsoft supports bonding and Multilink Protocol. Troubleshooting tools and terminal options are also available. Terminal windows are often used with third-party authentication solutions.

The use of Windows devices directly attaching to Cisco routers or AS5000 series aggregation routers can be an efficient way to provide remote connectivity. As a final point, readers are cautioned on using this model to provide new remote access solutions. Although outside the scope of this chapter due to Cisco's focus and objectives, modern solutions would likely take advantage of VPN, DSL, cable modem, and other more economical, secure, and scalable solutions.

Exam Essentials

Know which Cisco remote access protocols Windows 95 supports. Windows 95 supports IP, IPX, and NetBEUI protocols, which are also supported by Cisco remote access. The most common of these is IP.

Know the configuration settings location. The dial-up networking options are located under Start ➤ Programs ➤ Accessories ➤ Communications ➤ Dial-Up Networking.

Understand that the Windows Control Panel is not used to configure a dial-up networking session. These options are controlled under Programs.

Realize that each dial-up networking session is started by a specific icon. The dial-up networking icons are located in Start ➤ Programs ➤ Accessories ➤ Communications ➤ Dial-Up Networking, followed by the specific icon created for that connection.

Know how to use the terminal window option. Remember that the terminal window can be used to add parameters to a dial-up session or to integrate with enhanced authentication products.

Integrated Services Digital Network (ISDN)

THE CCNP EXAM TOPICS COVERED IN THIS CHAPTER INCLUDE THE FOLLOWING:

- ✓ Describe how different WAN technologies can be used to provide remote access to a network, including asynchronous dial-in, Frame Relay, ISDN, cable modem, and DSL.
- ✓ Explain the operation of remote network access control methods.
- ✓ Identify PPP components, and explain the use of PPP as an access and encapsulation method.
- ✓ Configure an ISDN solution for remote access.
- ✓ Plan a Cisco ISDN solution for remote access or primary link backup.
- ✓ Troubleshoot nonfunctional remote access systems.

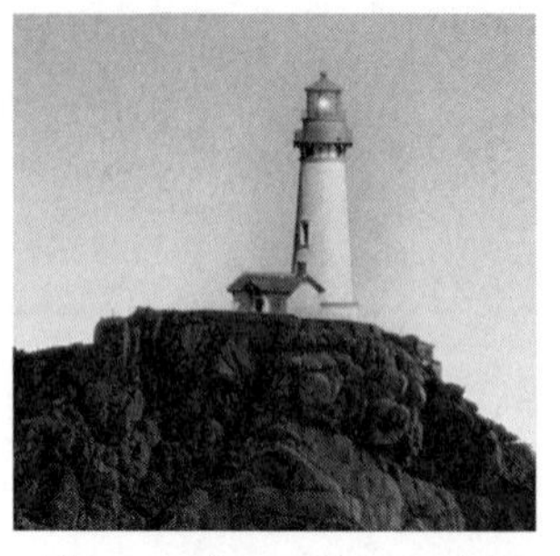

Integrated Services Digital Network (ISDN) has gained quite a following over the past few years. It offers a switched high-speed data connection that you can also use to support voice, video, or fax calls, making it an excellent choice for small office/home office (SOHO) users. However, digital subscriber line (DSL) will probably replace ISDN completely within the next few years because DSL is cheaper and faster—which means it must be better, right? Maybe. Just like ISDN, DSL can also provide data, voice, and fax services to end users. Cable modems have also been around for a few years. They provide a large amount of bandwidth for a neighborhood to access the Internet, but cable modems are really just composed of a large Thinnet network in which all your neighbors share the same bandwidth. Thinnet is the type of wiring used for 10Base2 Ethernet networks, which was popular before the 10BaseT standard. It runs over a thin coaxial cable similar to RG-6 wiring used by cable providers, hence the term *Thinnet network*.

Now, you might be thinking, "Hey, I thought this was an ISDN chapter; what's with DSL taking over the discussion?" It is an ISDN chapter, and you do need to know about the topic. ISDN won't be replaced overnight, and although DSL will probably replace it, it is possible that it won't. Remember about six or seven years ago when everyone was saying that ATM was going to take over the world? Pretty glad we didn't buy stock in that rumor. ATM is a contender, but the expense and difficult technical administration make it unpopular compared to Gigabit Ethernet for the LAN and to DSL for the WAN. In defense of ISDN, it does have a few benefits over DSL and cable modems that we will describe in this chapter.

ISDN is still a good choice for WAN services because of its high speed (Cisco calls ISDN high speed). It can run anywhere from 56K to T-1 speeds (1.544Mbps). 128Kbps is the most common, though. Although 128Kbps is not high speed to most people, compared to a 33Kbps dial-up analog modem, it is.

Outside of the U.S., the maximum speed of ISDN is 2.048 Mbps (E-1 standard).

Unlike a modem (which is analog), ISDN is digital from end to end. Analog modems translate from digital on the computer, to analog between modems, and then back to digital on the remote end. ISDN is more efficient and faster, and it also has a faster setup connection speed than an analog modem.

In this chapter, you will learn about ISDN, beginning with the Physical layer and working up. Topics covered in this chapter include ISDN device types, layer 2 (Q.921) and layer 3 (Q.931) specifications, ISDN reference points (R, S, T, U, and V), configuring dial backup and bandwidth on Demand configurations, and commonly used ISDN commands.

What Is Integrated Services Digital Network (ISDN)?

Integrated Services Digital Network (ISDN) has been under development for a couple of decades but has been hampered by the lack of applications that can use its speed. It wasn't until recently that telecommuting, video conferencing, and *small offices/home offices (SOHOs)* have needed the capabilities that ISDN offered. Another factor slowing the development of ISDN was that it was somewhat proprietary in nature. However, this ended when National ISDN-1 became available in 1992. National ISDN-1 is a standard switch type used by ISDN providers. This standard enabled vendors to interoperate among devices.

Different service providers adopted different standards, but on a national basis, so several different ISDN switch types are now "standard."

Before getting into what ISDN is and does, you first need to understand how our traditional, or *plain old telephone service (POTS)*, operates. Typically, you pick up the telephone receiver, you dial the number, and the party answers at the other end. Your voice—which is an analog wave—is converted into a digital signal through a process called *pulse code modulation (PCM)*. PCM samples your voice 8,000 times per second and converts the audio level into an 8-bit value. This 64Kbps channel, or *DS0*, is multiplexed with 23 other channels to form a T-1.

If you do the math, you'll notice that a T-1 is 1.544Mbps; however, 24 64Kbps is only 1.536Mbps. Where are the other 8Kbps? Before we answer that question, think of the purpose of a T-1. Each telephone call in the past required two copper wires to carry the voice traffic. A T-1 was originally designed to carry 24 individual voice calls on the same wire. Each voice call received its own channel. The underlying technique to carry all 24 channels on the same wire is called time division multiplexing (TDM). TDM breaks up the circuit into 24 separate channels and provides a distinct time slot for each.

Now back to the math. Each of the 24 channels is composed of 8 bits, for a total of 192 bits (8×24). According to the Nyquist theorem, we know that we need to sample at 8,000 times per second to replicate the human voice. Therefore, to produce all 24 channels, the entire 192 bits must be transmitted 8,000 times each second, for a subtotal of 1,536,000 bits per second, or 1.536Mbps ($8{,}000 \times 192$).

Specifically, Nyquist states that we should sample at twice the highest data rate of the sampled signal, and rounding the voice spectrum up to 4Kbps gives us the 8,000. The 8 bits for each channel comes from the 256 sampling *levels* used at each sample time.

Now for the missing 8Kbps. A single framing bit is added between each 24-channel frame. Therefore, an additional 8,000 framing bits are sent each second (remember the sampling rate for human voice), raising our total to 1,544,000 bits per second, or 1.544Mbps (1,536,000 + 8,000). This number is the bit rate of the line itself, and the one you commonly see with reference to a T-1 circuit. Because 8,000 of the bits sent each second are used for framing and not data, however, the maximum data you could theoretically put on the wire is the smaller number: 1.536Mbps.

ISDN differs from POTS in a couple of ways. First, ISDN data starts off as digital signaling, so there is no analog-to-digital conversion. Second, call setup and teardown is accomplished through a dedicated 16Kbps channel also known as a D (data) channel. By using "out of band" signaling, you have the entire 64Kbps for data. This leaves one or two B (bearer) channels for your data or voice traffic that does not have an intrusion on the line for clocking or error control. ISDN then provides unadulterated bandwidth to end users.

ISDN benefits include improved speed over an analog modem, fast call setup (one second or less, typically), and lower cost than a dedicated point-to-point circuit. DSLs and cable modems are replacing ISDN in some areas and will continue to do so as they fit the need for high-speed Internet access to the home. However, ISDN has some advantages over these newer, faster technologies. Here is a list of the advantages that ISDN can provide:

- Ability to dial into many locations simultaneously
- High-speed dial-up services for traveling telecommuters
- A fault-tolerant link for dedicated lines
- Remote SOHO connectivity
- Video conferencing

ISDN Line Options

ISDN is available in many configurations, or line options. In this section, you will learn about two of the most common: Basic Rate Interface (BRI) and Primary Rate Interface (PRI). These flavors of ISDN vary according to the type and number of channels that carry data. Each option has two or more DS0s, or *B (bearer) channels,* and a *D (data) channel.* ISDN is characterized by the presence of a D channel, which carries control and signaling information, freeing up the B channels exclusively for voice and data transport.

Each DS0 is capable of carrying 64,000 bits per second of either voice or data. Telephone companies (telcos) can provide ISDN on their current infrastructure with little additional work. Table 26.1 shows the relationship between the DS level, speed, designations, and number of DS0s per circuit. Only the DS1 level is associated with ISDN, which is the transport that a PRI circuit uses.

TABLE 26.1 North American Digital Hierarchy

Digital Signal Level	Speed	Designation	Channel(s)
DS0	64K	None	1
DS1	1.544Mbps	T-1	24

TABLE 26.1 North American Digital Hierarchy *(continued)*

Digital Signal Level	Speed	Designation	Channel(s)
DS2	6.312Mbps	T-2	96
DS3	44.736Mbps	T-3	672
DS4	274.176Mbps	T-4	4,032

Different standards, called Synchronous Optical Network (SONET) and Synchronous Digital Hierarchy (SDH), were developed for Fiber Optics Transmission Systems (FOTS). These standards are not covered in this book.

Another ISDN element is the *service profile identifier (SPID)*. A SPID identifies the characteristics of your ISDN line. SPIDs might or might not be needed, depending on the type of switch your service provider uses. ISDN National-1 and DMS-100 switches require a SPID for each B channel, whereas a SPID is optional with an AT&T 5ESS switch type. Please consult your ISDN provider if you are not sure whether you need a SPID. The format of a SPID is usually the 10-digit phone number, plus a prefix and possibly a suffix. For example, say that your telephone number is 949-555-1234. Now add a prefix of 01 and a suffix of 0100. This gives you a SPID of 0194955512340100.

SPIDs are only used in the U.S.

To place an ISDN call, you will also need a *directory number*, or DN. A DN is the actual number you would call to reach that B channel. In the example from the previous paragraph, the DN would be 9495551234 or 5551231. Knowing the SPID, switch type, and DN will speed up the configuration of your router. Your service provider should provide you with this information. Other than the directory number, the rest might be automatically detected.

Basic Rate Interface (BRI)

A *Basic Rate Interface (BRI)* uses a single pair of copper wires to provide up to 192Kbps of bandwidth for both voice and data calls A BRI uses two 64Kbps B channels and one 16Kbps D channel. An additional 48Kbps are used for framing and synchronization.

To review the math, each B channel is 64Kbps, so that totals 128Kbps. Add the 16Kbps D channel, and the usable bandwidth for ISDN BRI is now at 144Kbps. Finally, add the 48Kbps for framing and synchronization to get a total circuit speed of 192Kbps. Figure 26.1 shows the ISDN protocol layers.

FIGURE 26.1 ISDN protocol layers

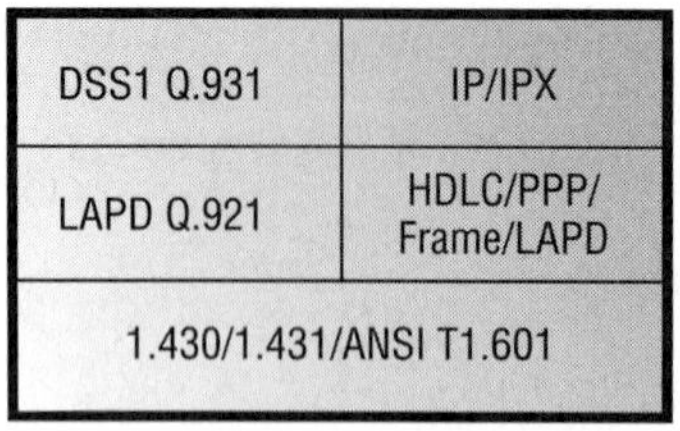

DSS1 Q.931	IP/IPX
LAPD Q.921	HDLC/PPP/ Frame/LAPD
1.430/1.431/ANSI T1.601	

Both the B and D channels share layer 1. Layers 2 and 3 operate over the D channel, but the B channel operates in either an HDLC or PPP encapsulation mode. This architecture is used to encapsulate the upper layer protocols instead of using layer 2 and layer 3 directly. LAPD is the framing protocol used for the D channel data. DSS1 (digital subscriber signaling system number 1) is the layer 3 protocol for the D channel where Q.931 is used. B channels are used by the IP or IPX protocols for data transfer, and the D channel is used by dial-on-demand routing (DDR), which builds the connection over ISDN.

BRI Switch Options

Several BRI switch options are available for configuring your router. These switch types vary according to geographic location. The available switch types are listed in Table 26.2.

TABLE 26.2 ISDN BRI Switch Types

Switch Type	Typically Used
BASIC-1TR6	1TR6 switch type for Germany
BASIC-5ESS	AT&T 5ESS switch type for the U.S.
BASIC-DMS100	Northern DMS-100 switch type for the U.S.
BASIC-NET3	NET3 switch type for the U.K. and most of Europe
BASIC-NI	National ISDN switch type for the U.S.
BASIC-TS013	TS013 switch type for Australia
NTT	NTT switch type for Japan
VN3	VN3 and VN4 switch types for France
EZ-ISDN	North American ISDN standard service package

A benefit to using a BRI is being able to make a voice call while maintaining your Internet connection. This is a great solution for SOHO deployments.

The D channel can also be used to transport packet-switched data communications such as X.25. In fact, Cisco has enabled this feature in version 12 of its IOS software. The feature is called Always On/Dynamic ISDN (AO/DI). Basically, it enables the low-bandwidth traffic to use the D channel and initiates a call by using one or two B channels if the traffic warrants. This feature will be most useful for point-of-sale applications but is not supported by all service providers.

Primary Rate Interface (PRI)

Most Internet service providers use *Primary Rate Interface (PRI)* ISDN to connect to the public switched telephone network (PTSN). A PRI enables service to analog modem users, digital modem users, and ISDN customers. The calls are routed to the appropriate modems after the access server receives the calling number's bearer capability. ISDN also provides a means to deliver calling line ID (CLID), as well as called number or automatic number identification (ANI). These features can be used to determine the correct authentication server for this customer.

PRIs have the following capacities:

- A T-1–based PRI has 23 64Kbps B channels and one 64Kbps D channel, which equals a bandwidth of 1.536Kbps. An 8Kbps channel for framing and synchronization is also used, resulting in a total bandwidth of 1.544Mbps for a U.S. T-1/PRI. The last T-1 channel is used as the D channel.
- An E-1–based PRI has 30 B channels and one 64Kbps D channel. An E-1 uses channel 15 for signaling (D channel). An E-1 has 2.048Mbps of total bandwidth.

PRI Switch Options

As with BRI, you have several switch types to select from. Check with your provider to configure the correct one. Otherwise, you might have to reboot your router for the switch type change to take effect.

Table 26.3 shows the typical available switch types used with PRI.

TABLE 26.3 PRI Switch Types

Switch Type	Typically Used
PRIMARY-5ESS	AT&T 5ESS switch type for the U.S.
PRIMARY-4ESS	AT&T 4ESS switch type for the U.S.
PRIMARY-DMS100	Northern DMS-100 switch type for the U.S.

TABLE 26.3 PRI Switch Types *(continued)*

Switch Type	Typically Used
PRIMARY-NET5	NET5 switch type for the U.K. and most of Europe
VN3	VN3 and VN4 switch types for France
PRIMARY-NTT	Japanese ISDN PRI switches
PRIMARY-NI	AT&T National ISDN switch type for the U.S.

T-1– and E-1–based PRIs use different line-coding and framing schemes. A T-1–based PRI uses binary eight-zero substitution (B8ZS) for encoding and Extended Super Frame (ESF) for framing. An E-1–based PRI uses high-density bipolar Order 3 (HDB3) for encoding and cyclic redundancy check, level 4 (CRC-4) for framing.

ISDN Function Groups

The ISDN function groups represent the devices in an ISDN environment such as terminals, terminal adapters, network-termination devices and line-termination equipment. It is important to understand the different function groups when you design and troubleshoot your ISDN network. Figure 26.2 shows the function groups and their placement in an ISDN network.

FIGURE 26.2 ISDN function groups

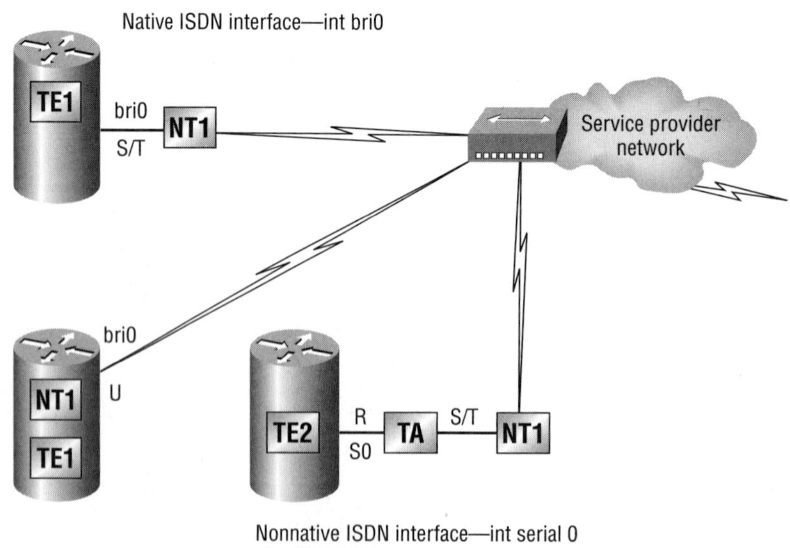

The following are definitions and examples of ISDN BRI function groups as they relate to Figure 26.2:

Terminal equipment 1 (TE1) A device that understands ISDN digital-signaling techniques. Examples of TE1 devices are digital telephones, routers with ISDN interfaces, and digital facsimile equipment. TE1 devices are 4-wire (2 pair) and need to be 2-wire (1 pair) to communicate with an ISDN network. A TE1 will connect into a network termination type 1 (NT1) to connect the 4-wire subscriber wiring to the 2-wire local loop facility.

Terminal equipment 2 (TE2) Equipment that does not understand ISDN signaling standards. Examples of TE2 devices are analog telephones, X.25 interfaces, and serial interfaces on a router. A TE2 device needs to be converted to ISDN signaling, which is provided by a terminal adapter (TA). After that, it still needs to be converted to a 2-wire network with an NT1 device.

Network termination type 1 (NT1) This device is used to convert a 4-wire ISDN connection to the 2-wire ISDN used by the local loop facility. This device is primarily used in the United States, because European service providers retain ownership of this functionality.

Network termination type 2 (NT2) This device is used to direct traffic from ISDN devices (TEs) to an NT1. This is probably the most intelligent device in the ISDN network; it provides switching and concentrating and can sometimes even be a private branch exchange (PBX).

Terminal adapter (TA) This device enables a TE2 device to communicate with the telco's network by providing any necessary protocol and interface conversion. In essence, a TA adapts the unipolar signal coming from a non-ISDN device into a bipolar signal used by the ISDN network.

Local termination (LT) This is the same device as an NT1, but located at the provider's site.

Exchange termination (ET) The connection to the ISDN switch, typically an ISDN line card. The ET forms the physical and logical boundary between the digital local loop and the carrier's switching office. It performs the same functions at the end office that the NT performs at the customer's premises. Both the LT and the ET together are typically referred to as the local exchange (LE).

ISDN Reference Points

A *reference point* defines a connection point between two functions; you can also refer to it as an interface, though it does not represent an actual physical interface. The reference point is where data is converted between device types. Figure 26.3 shows the reference points defined in an ISDN network.

The reference points shown in Figure 26.3 are described in detail in the following list:

R reference point The R reference point defines the point between non-ISDN equipment and a TA. It enables a non-ISDN device to appear on the network as an ISDN device. Unlike the others, this is a nonstandardized reference because it is dependent on the TE2 equipment's interface.

S reference point The S reference point is the point between the user terminals and NT2 or, in other words, between a TE1 or a TA and the network termination (which is either an NT1 or NT2).

FIGURE 26.3 ISDN reference points

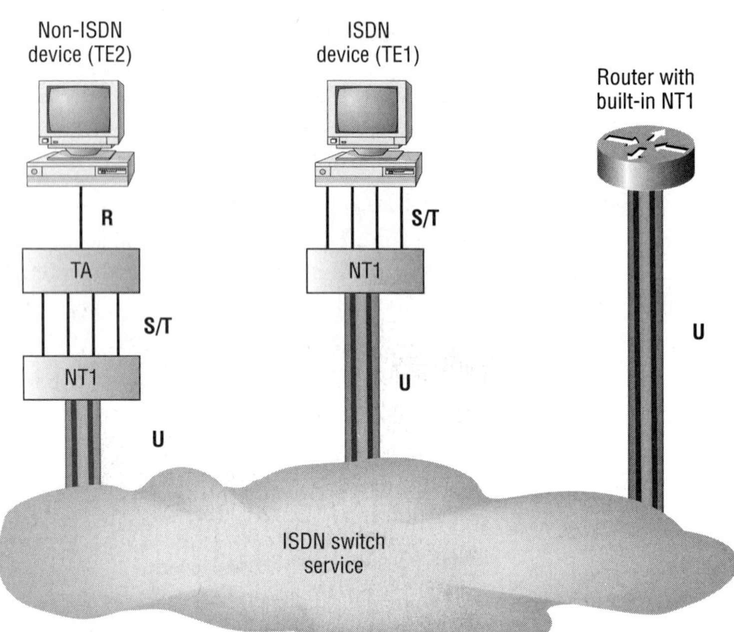

T reference point The T reference point defines the point between NT1 and NT2 devices.

S/T interface As the name implies, the S/T interface combines both the S and T interfaces. This interface is governed by the ITU I.430 standard, which defines the connection as a 4-wire connection. The S/T interface is typically an RJ-45, with 8-pin cables using pins 3 and 6 to receive data and pins 4 and 5 to transmit data. Service providers in Europe use this interface to deliver ISDN BRI service.

The International Telecommunications Union (ITU) is a United Nations–sponsored organization formed in 1865 to promote worldwide communication systems compatibility. It has two groups: ITU-T and ITU-R. ITU-T deals with telecommunications, and ITU-R is responsible for radio communications. You can visit their website at `www.itu.int` for more information.

U reference point The U reference point is also known as a U (user) interface. This is a 2-wire connection between the NT1 and the telephone company (LE). Cisco routers are marked with an *X* if the interface is a U and with a crossed-out *X* if the interface is an S/T. This is an ANSI standard used in the U.S. but not in Europe.

V reference point The V reference point is the interface point in an ISDN environment between the line termination and the exchange termination.

In practical terms, it may be important for you to remember that in the TE1 is part of the customer premises equipment (CPE) and is installed inside the route. Thus an American router presents a U interface to the world, whereas in the rest of the world, the TE1 is service provider–owned and the router presents an S/T interface. So you cannot use a U.S.-sourced router elsewhere in the world, but you can use an elsewhere-sourced router in the U.S. if you buy an external TE1.

ISDN Protocols

ISDN protocols define how information is transferred from one device to another in the network. The ITU-T has established three types of protocols to handle this information transfer:

- Protocols beginning with the letter *E* specify ISDN on the existing telephone network.
- Protocols beginning with the letter *I* specify concepts, terminology, and services.
- Protocols beginning with the letter *Q* specify switching and signaling. Two Q standards of interest are Q.921, which handles layer 2, and Q.931, which deals with layer 3 interfacing.

Spending some time reviewing the Q standards will help you use a couple of the IOS **debug** commands covered later in this chapter. As just stated, the ITU-T recommendations Q.921 and Q.931 handle switching and signaling. Q.921 uses *Link Access Procedure, Data (LAPD)* to communicate with other ISDN devices across the D channel. LAPD's primary purpose is to transport signaling information.

LAPD Frames

While the ISDN protocols define the transfer of information, layer 2 and 3 functions are handled with LAPD. Understanding the information contained in this frame will help you understand Q.921 and Q.931 debug outputs. Remember that LAPD is the framing protocol used for D channel data and that the D channel is used to build connections to an ISDN link.

An *LAPD frame* has six parts to it: Flag, Address, Control, Information, CRC, and a final Flag. Figure 26.4 shows the LAPD frame and the fields within the frame.

The following information describes the fields within the LAPD frame:

Flag This one-octet field starts and ends the frame with a value of 7E (0111 1110). The LAPD Flag and Control fields are identical to those of HDLC.

FIGURE 26.4 Link Access Procedure, Data frame

Flag	Address	Control	Information	CRC	Flag

Address This field is two octets long and contains some important information. This field identifies the TE using this link and has four parts: service access point identifier (SAPI), command/response (C/R), address extension 0 (AE0), and terminal endpoint identifier (TEI).

Service access point identifier (SAPI) This field is six bits long. Table 26.4 shows the SAPI values that can be used in an LAPD frame.

TABLE 26.4 SAPI Values

SAPI	Description
0	Call control procedures
1	Packet mode using Q.931 call procedures
16	Packet mode communications procedures
32–47	Reserved for national use
63	Management procedures
Others	Reserved for future use

Command/response (C/R) This field is one bit long. This bit identifies the frame as either a command or a response. The user side always sends commands with this bit set to 0 and responds with it set to 1. The network side is the exact opposite, sending a command with this bit set to 1, or a 0 if it is responding.

Address extension 0 (AE0 and AE1) These are one bit long. Their value indicates whether the associated octet is the last in the Address field. Setting the value to 1 in the last bit of an address octet (the AE field) indicates to the receiving device that this is the last octet in the Address field.

Terminal endpoint identifier (TEI) These values uniquely identify each TE on an ISDN S/T bus. A TEI can be either dynamically or statically assigned. Table 26.5 lists the values for this field.

TABLE 26.5 Terminal Endpoint Identifier (TEI) Values

TEI	Description
0–63	Fixed TEI assignments
64–126	Dynamically assigned (assigned by the switch)
127	Broadcast to all devices

Control This field has 11 available values, each one listed in Table 26.6, along with its application. You will see one of three types of information here: Information Transfer, Supervisory, or Unnumbered.

TABLE 26.6 Control Field Values

Format	Message Type	Control/Response
Information Transfer	I = Information	Control
Supervisory	RR = Receive Ready	Control/Response
Supervisory	RNR = Receive Not Ready	Control/Response
Supervisory	REJ = Reject	Control/Response
Unnumbered	SABME = Set Asynchronous Balanced Mode Extended	Control
Unnumbered	DM = Disconnected Mode	Response
Unnumbered	UI = Unnumbered Information	Control
Unnumbered	DISC = Disconnect	Control
Unnumbered	UA = Unnumbered Acknowledgment	Response
Unnumbered	FRMR = Frame Reject	Response
Unnumbered	XID = Exchange Identifier	Control/Response

Information This field carries the Q.931 protocol data. Figure 26.5 illustrates how it is laid out. This is where the user data is carried.

The following information describes the field format as shown in Figure 26.5:

Protocol discriminator One octet. Identifies the layer 3 protocol.

Length One octet. Indicates the length of the call reference value (CRV).

Call reference value (CRV) One or two octets. This value is assigned to each call at the beginning, is used to distinguish between other simultaneous calls, and is released after the call is torn down.

Message type One octet.

Mandatory and optional information elements (variable length) Options based on the message type.

CRC Contains the cyclic redundancy check derived value from the Address, Control, and Information fields. This is also known as the frame check sequence (FCS) field.

FIGURE 26.5 Q.921/Q.931 Information field format

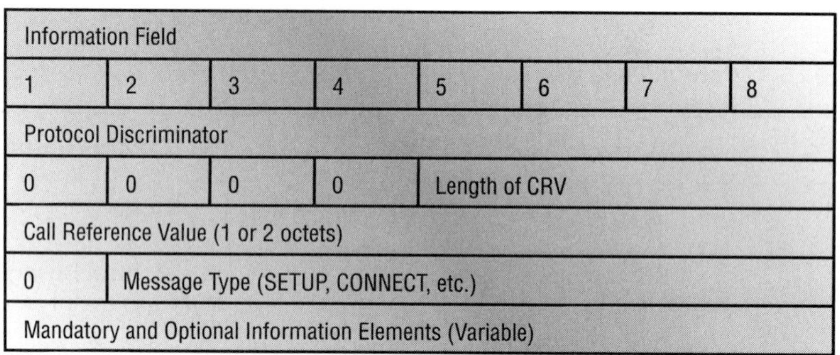

Layer 2 Negotiation

You need to have an understanding of the LAPD frame before you understand how layer 2 negotiates. This will help you identify where a potential or existing problem is occurring. One useful feature of Cisco equipment is that it includes good diagnostic tools for finding ISDN problems. Knowing which side of the ISDN connection does what will help you identify a problem and start corrective action.

The first part of the process is TEI assignment, which is accomplished by using this process:

1. The terminal endpoint (TE) and the network initially exchange Receive Ready (RR) frames, listening for an initiated connection.
2. The TE sends an Unnumbered Information (UI) frame with a SAPI of 63 (management procedure, query network) and TEI of 127 (broadcast).
3. The network assigns an available TEI (in the range 64–126).
4. The TE sends a Set Asynchronous Balanced Mode Extended (SABME) frame with a SAPI of 0 (call control, used to initiate a SETUP) and a TEI of the value assigned by the network.
5. The network responds with an Unnumbered Acknowledgment (UA); SAPI = 0, TEI = assigned.

As you examine this partial output from the command `debug isdn q921`, please refer to Table 26.7, which explains the meaning of the output.

```
ISDN BRO: TX -> SABMEp sapi = 0 tei = 77
ISDN BRO: RX <- IDCKRQ ri = 0 ai = 127
ISDN BRO: TX -> IDCKRP ri = 44602 ai = 77
ISDN BRO: TX -> IDCKRP ri = 37339 ai = 78
ISDN BRO: RX <- IDREM ri = 0 ai = 77
ISDN BRO: TX -> IDREQ ri = 44940 ai = 127
ISDN BRO: RX <- IDREM ri = 0 ai = 78
```

```
ISDN BR0: TX ->  IDREQ  ri = 43085  ai = 127
ISDN BR0: TX ->  IDREQ  ri = 11550  ai = 127
ISDN BR0: RX <-  IDASSN  ri = 11550  ai = 79
ISDN BR0: TX ->  SABMEp sapi = 0  tei = 79
ISDN BR0: TX ->  IDREQ  ri = 65279  ai = 127
ISDN BR0: RX <-  UAf sapi = 0  tei = 79
ISDN BR0: TX ->  INFOc sapi = 0  tei = 79  ns = 0
  ➥nr = 0  i = 0x08007B3A0A3038333538363631303l
ISDN BR0: RX <-  IDASSN  ri = 65279  ai = 80
ISDN BR0: TX ->  SABMEp sapi = 0  tei = 80
ISDN BR0: RX <-  INFOc sapi = 0  tei = 79  ns = 0  nr = 1  i =
  ➥0x08007B3B028181
ISDN BR0: TX ->  RRr sapi = 0  tei = 79  nr = 1
ISDN BR0: RX <-  UAf sapi = 0  tei = 80
ISDN BR0: TX ->  INFOc sapi = 0  tei = 80  ns = 0  _
nr = 0  i = 0x08007B3A0A30383335383636333031
ISDN BR0: RX <-  INFOc sapi = 0  tei = 80  ns = 0  nr = 1  i =
  ➥0x08007B3B028381
ISDN BR0: TX ->  RRr sapi = 0  tei = 80  nr = 1
```

TABLE 26.7 Debug ISDN Q.921 Details

Output	Meaning
`ISDN BR0:`	This is the interface.
`TX ->`	This router is sending this information.
`RX <-`	This router is receiving this information.
`SABME`	Indicates the Set Asynchronous Balanced Mode Extended command. This command places the recipient into modulo 128 multiple frame acknowledged operation. This command also indicates that all exception conditions have been cleared.
`sapi`	Identifies the service access point at which the Data-Link layer entity provides services to layer 3 or to the management layer. A SAPI with the value 0 indicates it is a call control procedure.
`IDCKRQ ri = 0  ai = 127`	Indicates the Identity Check Request message type sent from the ISDN service provider on the network to the local router during the TEI check procedure. This message is sent in a UI command frame. The `ri` field is always 0. The `ai` field for this message contains either a specific TEI value for the local router to check or 127, which indicates that the local router should check all TEI values.

TABLE 26.7 Debug ISDN Q.921 Details *(continued)*

Output	Meaning
`IDREM`	This indicates the Identity Remove message type sent from the network to the user-side layer management entity during the TEI removal procedure. This message is sent in a UI command frame. The message includes a reference number that is always 0, because it is not responding to a request from the local router. It is sent twice by the network to prevent a lost message.
`IDCKRP`	Indicates the Identity Check Response message type sent from the local router to the ISDN service provider on the network during the TEI check procedure. This message is sent in a UI command frame in response to the IDCKRQ message
`IDREQ`	This indicates an Identity Request message sent from the local router to the network during the automatic TEI assignment.
`UAf`	This confirms that the network side has accepted the `SABME` command previously sent by the local router. The final bit is set to 1.
`INFOc`	This is an information command. It is used to transfer sequentially numbered frames containing Information Fields cap provided by layer 3.
`IDASSN`	This indicates an Identity Assigned message type sent from the network's ISDN service provider to the local router during the automatic TEI assignment procedure.
`RRx`	This indicates Receive Ready. If *x* = `r`, it is responding to an `INFOc`. If *x* = `p`, the router is polling the network side. And *x* = `f` means the network side has responded to the poll and the final bit is set.

Now what does everything in Table 26.7 mean? According to the output, the router attempts to establish a connection with the switch, using legacy TEI information that it has left over:

```
ISDN BRO: TX ->  SABMEp sapi = 0  tei = 77
```

The service provider's switch disapproves of this and orders a check of the router's current TEIs with the `IDCKRQ` message. The `ai` of 127 (broadcast) simply tells the router that the switch would like for it to check all TEIs it currently has registered:

```
ISDN BRO: RX <-  IDCKRQ  ri = 0  ai = 127
```

The router promptly returns an IDCKRP message for each TEI it finds within itself. In this case, these are 77 and 78:

```
ISDN BRO: TX ->  IDCKRP  ri = 44602  ai = 77
ISDN BRO: TX ->  IDCKRP  ri = 37339  ai = 78
```

The switch does not want the router to continue using these TEIs, so it issues an IDREM message for each offending TEI. This tells the router to forget about these TEIs:

```
ISDN BRO: RX <-  IDREM  ri = 0  ai = 77
```

The router quickly throws itself at the mercy of the switch by sending the IDREQ message with an ai of 127. Notice that the router is looking for two TEIs, one for each logical B channel interface within BRI0, but it has to issue four IDREQs to overcome the timeouts:

```
ISDN BRO: TX ->  IDREQ  ri = 43085  ai = 127
ISDN BRO: TX ->  IDREQ  ri = 11550  ai = 127
```

As soon as an IDASSN returns that matches the ri of one of the IDREQs, as follows:

```
ISDN BRO: RX <-  IDASSN  ri = 11550  ai = 79
```

the router turns around and establishes service with a new SABME message, using the new TEI:

```
ISDN BRO: TX ->  SABMEp sapi = 0  tei = 79
ISDN BRO: TX ->  IDREQ  ri = 65279  ai = 127
```

Because the switch obviously approves of this TEI, it responds with the UA message the router was originally looking for.

```
ISDN BRO: RX <-  UAf sapi = 0  tei = 79
```

After the UAs come in, the whole INFO/RR exchange for layer 3 information begins for each TEI assigned:

```
ISDN BRO: TX ->  INFOc sapi = 0  tei = 79  ns = 0  nr = 0  i =
  ➥0x08007B3A0A30383335383636313031
ISDN BRO: TX ->  RRr sapi = 0  tei = 79  nr = 1
```

This occurs for both the 79 and 80 TEIs.

ISDN Call Setup and Teardown

ISDN uses ITU-T Q.931 to establish and tear down calls. Call control and signaling information is carried over the D channel. Figure 26.6 shows the Q.931 procedures.

FIGURE 26.6 ISDN call setup and teardown

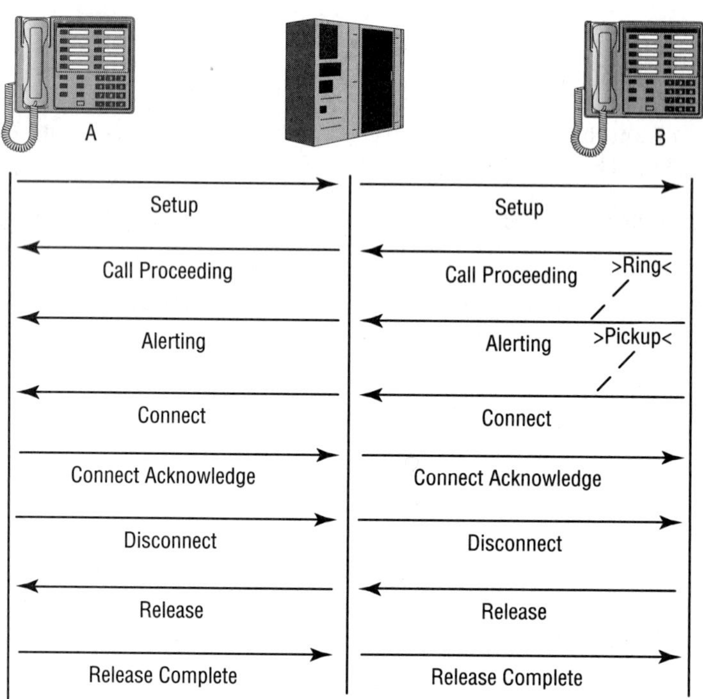

The process for ISDN call setup and teardown is as follows:

1. First, a SETUP message is sent from device A. The SETUP contains information necessary to make the call.
2. Next, the switch sends a CALL PROCEEDING back to device A.
3. An ALERTING message is sent back when device B is contacted. You might hear the phone ring at this point.
4. CONNECT and CONNECT ACKNOWLEDGE messages are sent to indicate that the call has been accepted.
5. Call teardown starts when one of the users hangs up. Here, device A hangs up, and a DISCONNECT message is sent to device B. The switch now disconnects B and sends a RELEASE to A. A RELEASE COMPLETE message confirms the process.

Using the `debug isdn q931` command, you get the following output.

```
ISDN BRO: TX ->  SETUP pd = 8  callref = 0x05 _
Bearer Capability i = 0x8890 Channel ID i = 0x83
        Keypad Facility i = '8358662'
ISDN BRO: RX <-  CALL_PROC pd = 8  callref = 0x85 _
```

```
Channel ID i = 0x89 Locking Shift to Codeset 5
        Codeset 5 IE 0x2A  i = 0x809402, '`=', 0x8307, _
'8358662', 0x8E0B, ' TELTONE 2 '
ISDN BR0: RX <-  CONNECT pd = 8  callref = 0x85
ISDN BR0: TX ->  CONNECT_ACK pd = 8  callref = 0x05
ISDN BR0: TX ->  DISCONNECT pd = 8  callref = 0x05 _
Cause i = 0x8090 - Normal call clearing
ISDN BR0: RX <-  RELEASE pd = 8  callref = 0x85
ISDN BR0: TX ->  RELEASE_COMP pd = 8  callref = 0x05
```

Table 26.8 describes the output from the Q.931 command.

TABLE 26.8 Debug ISDN Q.931 Details

Output	Meaning
`TX ->`	The message originating at the router.
`RX <-`	The message received from the network.
`SETUP`	Used to initiate a call. Either the network or the local router can send it.
`pd = 8`	Indicates the protocol discriminator. The protocol discriminator distinguishes messages for call control over the user-network ISDN interface from other ITU-T-defined messages, including other Q.931 messages.
`Callref = 0x05`	Indicates the number of calls the router has processed. It increments every time a call goes out or comes in.
`Bearer Capability i = 0x8890`	The bearer service requested by the router. 88 = ITU coding standard, unrestricted digital information 90 = Circuit mode, 64Kbps 21 = Layer 1, V.110/X.30 8F = Synchronous, no in-band negotiation, 56Kbps
`Channel ID i = 0x83`	The channel Identifier. It indicates which B channel to use. 83 = Use any channel. 89 = Use B1. 8A = Use B2.
`Keypad facility`	Also known as *called party number.*
`DISCONNECT pd = 8 callref = 0x05 Cause i = 0x8090 - Normal call clearing`	The router is sending a DISCONNECT message to the network. The reason for this disconnect is `Normal call clearing` 0x80. See "ISDN Switch Types, Codes, and Values" on Cisco Connection Online (CCO) at `www.cisco.com`.

ISDN Configuration

To configure ISDN, you need to understand that there are both simple and complex configurations. Although you certainly can make more money by understanding the complex configurations, the simple ones are just as important. In this section, you will look at some benefits and drawbacks of two ISDN configuration types: PRI and BRI. In this section you will learn about the differences between the PRI and BRI interface configurations. First, though, you need to understand how the old and new ways differ.

Real World Scenario

How to Order ISDN

Okay, we know this is a CCNP Study Guide and you are probably getting ready for the test, but after you are certified (or certifiable), you are the Cisco expert and should know the process of attaining as well as configuring the lines. Here's what you do:

Who Do I Call?

The first step to getting your ISDN service up and running is to contact your local telephone company (service provider). The telephone numbers and web addresses for ordering ISDN service are provided at `http://www.nationalisdncouncil.com`.

What Do I Need to Tell the Telephone Company?

Ordering ISDN can be as easy as requesting basic phone service from the telephone company; most of the questions that the telephone company will ask you are the same in both cases. For example, because ISDN was designed to work over the existing wire, which supports your current telephone service, you will probably not have to specify any unique wiring changes or additions. However, some specialized capabilities of ISDN will require you to provide additional information related to your ISDN equipment selection. The best way to provide this additional information is through an ISDN Ordering Code (IOC), or as Cisco calls them, the capabilities package ordering codes, which should be identified in your ISDN equipment documentation. This will give you a set of standardized BRI line features that simplify the process of configuring an ISDN line that is connected to an NI1 switch. An example is the package R, which provides circuit-switched data on both B channels (no voice capabilities). Data capabilities include calling number identification. Cisco recommends this NI1 capability package for Cisco 801 and Cisco 802 routers.

What Does the Phone Company Need to Tell Me?

Most ISDN connections in North America require the use of one or more service profile identifiers (SPIDs), which we discussed earlier in this chapter. SPIDs are numbers assigned only by

North American telephone service providers. SPIDS identify the ISDN B channels. As stated earlier, the SPID format is generally an ISDN telephone number with several numbers added to it, for example, 40855512340101. Depending on the switch type that supports your ISDN BRI line, your ISDN line could be assigned none, one, or two SPIDs.

And that's it. The configuration of and use of this information is covered in the context of this chapter.

Some of you might have grown up in a router world, where you used `dialer map` statements to configure a dial session. But the times they are a-changin', and actually for the better. By using a dialer profile, the basic configuration for a physical interface is entered under the actual interface, but the detailed configuration is placed under a virtual dialer interface. This is a really good feature if you have a PRI that receives and makes calls to and from different locations (with different subnets).

Using a Legacy Interface

To get your feet wet, let's start with a simple BRI configuration:

```
hostname R1
isdn switch-type basic-ni
!
interface BRI0
 ip address 10.1.1.3 255.255.255.0
 encapsulation ppp
 isdn spid1 91955512120100 5551212
 dialer map ip 10.1.1.1 name R2 555-1212
```

As you can see, the first statement defines the switch type. The BRI0 interface binds an IP address and sets up PPP as the encapsulation type. The last two lines identify the SPID and the `dialer map` command. These set the protocol with a next-hop address of 10./1.1.1, identify the remote host as R2, and indicate that the dial string (telephone number) should be sent to the dialing device when it the device recognizes packets that have specified addresses matching the configured access lists.

Under the old legacy way, you could have a main IP address under the physical interface, along with several secondary addresses. This worked fine, but you ran into problems if you were using a routing protocol, because the physical interface always uses its primary address when sending out packets.

Here's an example of a configuration using the old way. Notice the `dialer map` statements. This enabled an administrator to tell the router which number to dial based on the destination IP address in packets it received on one of the router's incoming interfaces. See for yourself:

```
hostname R1
!
interface Serial 0/0:23
 encapsulation ppp
 ip address 192.168.250.1 255.255.255.0
 ip address 192.168.251.1 255.255.255.0 secondary
 dialer map ip 192.168.250.2 name R2 555-1212
 dialer map ip 192.168.251.2 name R3 555-1234
router ospf 100
 network 192.168.250.1 0.0.0.0 area 0
 network 192.168.251.1 0.0.0.0 area 0
!
end

hostname R2
!
interface BRI0
 ip address 192.168.250.2 255.255.255.0
 encapsulation ppp
 isdn spid1 91955512120100 5551212
 isdn spid2 91955512130100 5551213
 dialer map ip 192.168.250.1 name R1 5551900
router ospf 100
 network 192.168.250.2 0.0.0.0 area 0
!
end

hostname R3
!
interface BRI0
 ip address 192.168.251.2 255.255.255.0
 encapsulation ppp
 isdn spid1 91955512230100 5551234
 isdn spid2 91955512350100 5551235
 dialer map ip 192.168.251.1 name R1 5551900
router ospf 100
 network 192.168.251.2 0.0.0.0 area 0
!
end
```

You need to look at several points in this configuration. Host R1 is using a PRI ISDN interface on Serial 0/0. The `secondary` command enables you to have a second route on the same interface. We cover the `Serial 0/0:23` command later in this chapter, but a quick explanation is that for ISDN, the D channel time slot is equivalent to the :23 channel for channelized T-1. And finally, we are using the dialer map to bind an IP address to an ISDN DN.

In these router configurations, both routers R2 and R3 will call into R1, but Open Shortest Path First (OSPF) will work only between R1 and R2, because R2 uses the primary address on R1, whereas R3 uses the secondary. This source IP address issue can be a real problem, but only if you're not aware of it. What is the solution to the primary IP address issue? Dialer interfaces.

Using a Dialer Interface

Using a dialer interface solves the primary IP address/secondary IP address problem because each interface can be assigned its own primary address. The `dialer map` command does not have to be used because each interface has its own IP address and dial number configured by using the `dialer string` command.

A virtual interface must be associated with a dialer pool. The dialer pool is a group of one or more physical interfaces in charge of placing calls. Here's an example of a configuration using dialer interfaces:

```
hostname R1
!
isdn switch-type basic-5ess
!
interface Ethernet0
 ip address 192.168.1.1 255.255.255.0
!
interface Serial0/0:23
 no ip address
 encapsulation ppp
 dialer pool-member 1 priority 100
!
interface Dialer1
 ip address 192.168.250.1 255.255.255.0
 encapsulation ppp
 dialer remote-name R2
 dialer idle-timeout 300
 dialer string 5551212
 dialer load-threshold 50 either
 dialer pool 1
 dialer-group 1
!
```

```
interface Dialer2
 ip address 192.168.251.1 255.255.255.0
 encapsulation ppp
 dialer remote-name R3
 dialer string 5551234
 dialer load-threshold 150 either
 dialer pool 1
 dialer-group 1
!
router ospf 100
 network 192.168.250.1 0.0.0.0 area 0
 network 192.168.251.1 0.0.0.0 area 0
!
dialer-list 1 protocol ip permit
!
end
```

Notice how the interface Dialer1 creates a virtual interface with the correct configuration—`ip address`, `encapsulation`, and `dialer string`—the same items that were bound to the physical interface BRI0 in the first example. The interface Dialer carries a 1 as its index. The virtual Dialer interface is then bound to a dialer string that references the ISDN DN. The dialer pool 1 is then bound to the virtual Dialer to point to the physical interface that will be carrying out the dialing. The index of the dialer pool 1 maps to the `dialer pool-member 1`—the physical interface of Serial 0/0. The last configuration command worthy of noting is the `dialer-list 1 protocol ip permit`, which tells the router what traffic is interesting and to bring the connection up when interesting traffic is identified.

OSPF will work properly because the source address on both sides of the link matches the network statement. The source address of a packet originating at a router is the primary address on the outgoing interface. Dialer interfaces are easy to configure. Consider the following example:

```
router#config t
router(config)#interface dialer 2
router(config-if)#
```

Now the network administrator can create the configuration as you would under a physical interface. The physical PRI interface—Serial0/0:23—is designated as a member of a dialer pool using the `dialer pool-member` command.

Authentication

If you are using PPP encapsulation, you can also use authentication. *Authentication* enables you to verify who is connected to a service. Note that this is optional and not required in any ISDN configurations.

The two authentication choices are *Password Authentication Protocol (PAP)* and *Challenge Handshake Authentication Protocol (CHAP)*. CHAP is preferred over PAP because of its superior security features. CHAP and PAP are covered in greater detail in Chapter 24, "Point-to-Point Protocol," of this book.

Password Authentication Protocol (PAP)

PAP uses a two-way handshake to establish the identity of the remote peer. This simple authentication protocol does not encrypt the username or password, making it somewhat insecure and subject to a playback attack. Because of this security problem, it is recommended that you use CHAP authentication instead.

After the PPP link establishment, the optional Authentication-Protocol Configuration Option packet is sent. An Authentication-Protocol Configuration Option packet for PAP has three fields: Type, Length, and Authentication-Protocol. The Type field is 8 bits long with a value of 3, Length is 8 bits long with a value of 4, and Authentication-Protocol is 16 bits long with a value of c023.

PAP Packets

A PAP packet has four fields carried one at a time in the PPP Information field: Code, Identifier, Length, and Data.

The Code field is 8 bits long and can have one of three values:

- Authenticate-Request
- Authenticate-Ack
- Authenticate-Nak

The Identifier field is also 8 bits long and is used for matching authentication requests and replies. It changes every time an Authenticate-Request is sent.

Length is a 16-bit field indicating the packet's length.

The Data field varies in length and format, depending on the packet type: Request, Ack, or Nak.

Authenticate-Request Packets

An Authenticate-Request packet is sent by the calling party to the called party. The Data field has four fields:

Peer-ID length Eight bits long; indicates the length of the Peer-ID.

Peer-ID Zero or more octets long; contains the username.

Passwd-length Eight bits long; indicates the length of the password.

Password Zero or more octets long; contains the cleartext password.

The called end will respond with either an Authenticate-Ack (Type 2) or Authenticate-Nak (Type 3) packet. Both packets have two fields as data. One is Msg-Length (8 bits), and the other is Message (one or more octets).

The following output is from a `debug ppp authentication` command on a router that is authenticating by using PAP with PPP:

```
BRO/0:1 PPP: Phase is AUTHENTICATING, by the peer
BRO/0:1 PAP: O AUTH-REQ id 3 len 14 from "r3"
BRO/0:1 PAP: I AUTH-ACK id 3 len 5
```

You can follow this debug PPP authentication router output by referring to Figure 26.7.

FIGURE 26.7 PAP authentication

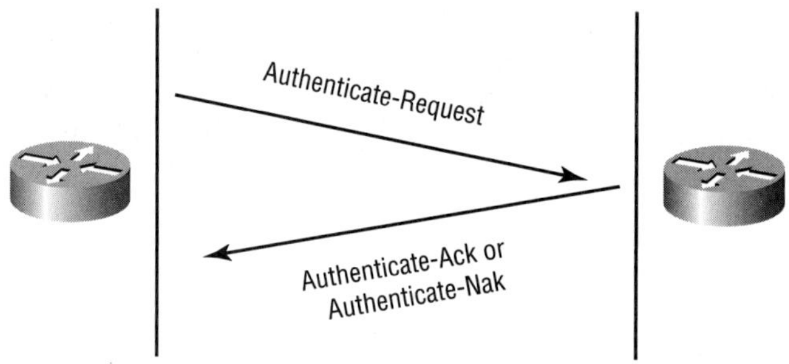

Configuring PAP authentication is a pretty straightforward process. Here's an example:

```
Router#config t
Router(config)#username todd password cisco
Router(config)#interface bri0
Router(config-if)#encapsulation ppp
Router(config-if)#ppp authentication pap
Router(config-if)#^Z
Router#
```

Challenge Handshake Authentication Protocol (CHAP)

CHAP is used to periodically verify the identity of the remote peer by using a three-way handshake. Normally this occurs immediately after the initial link establishment and before proceeding to the Network layer phase. CHAP can also send a new challenge periodically to verify the remote node. All PPP authentications are optional. Both ends must be configured with the same authentication type if you are using authentication.

One CHAP packet is encapsulated in the Information field of a PPP packet, with the Type field set to 3, the Length field to 5, the Authentication-Protocol field to c223, and the algorithm to 5 (MD5). A CHAP Challenge packet is illustrated in Figure 26.8.

FIGURE 26.8 CHAP Challenge packet

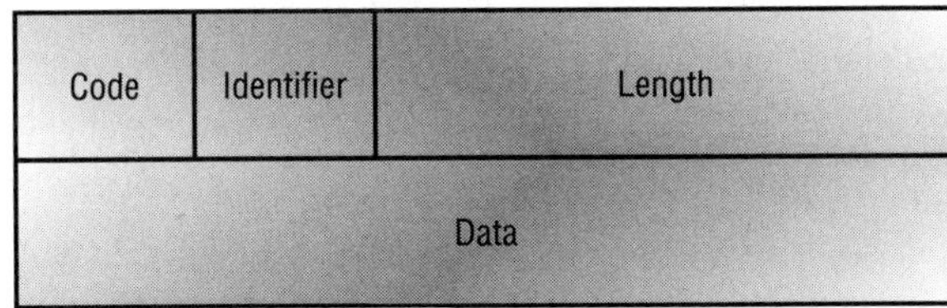

A CHAP packet consists of an 8-bit Code field, an 8-bit Identifier field, a 16-bit Length field, and a variable-length Data field. The Code field identifies the type of CHAP packet; there are four type options:

- Challenge
- Response
- Success
- Failure

The *Identifier* field contains an incrementally changing identifier, which the remote end copies into the response packet. Frequently changing the identifier provides protection against a playback attack. The *Length* field is 16 bits long and indicates the length of the CHAP packet, including the Code, Identifier, Length, and Data fields. Octets outside the range will be ignored. The *Data* field is zero or more octets and is determined by the Code field.

Configuring CHAP authentication is a pretty straightforward process. Here's an example:

```
Router#config t
Router(config)#username todd password cisco
Router(config)#interface bri0
Router(config-if)#encapsulation ppp
Router(config-if)#ppp authentication chap
Router(config-if)#^Z
Router#
```

The `username` *`name`* `password` *`password`* command is used to configure authentication between two routers. The username is the host name of the router you want to connect to. The passwords must be the same on each side for this to work. For example, if you had a corporate router with a host name of Acmecorporate and a remote router with a host name of Acmeremote, the configuration of the corporate router would look like this:

```
Acmecorporate(config)#username Acmeremote password sameone
```

The remote router's configuration would be this:

```
Acmeremote(config)#username Acmecorporate password sameone
```

The CHAP Authentication Process

The authentication process between two routers occurs as follows:

1. Challenger sends a Challenge (Type 1) packet to the remote end.
2. The remote end copies the identifier into a new packet and into a Response (Type 2) packet along with the hashed secret. The secret (the password) isn't transmitted, only the hashed value.
3. The Challenger receives the Response packet and checks the hashed secret against its hashed secret. If they match, it sends a Success (Type 3) packet back. Otherwise, it'll send a Failure (Type 4) packet back.

Challenge and Response packets have the following fields:

Code Eight bits; value of 1 for Challenge, or 2 for Response.

Identifier Eight bits; must be changed every time a challenge is sent.

Value-Size Eight bits; indicates the length of the Value field.

Value Variable (eight-bit minimum). The field is quite different depending on a Challenge or Response. The Challenge value contains the challenge and is a variable stream of octets. The Challenge value *must* be changed each time a Challenge is sent. The length of the Challenge value depends on the method used to generate the octets and is independent of the hash algorithm used.

The Response value is the one-way hashed response calculated over a stream of octets consisting of the Identifier, followed by (concatenated with) the "secret," followed by (concatenated with) the Challenge value. The length of the Response value depends on the hash algorithm used (16 octets for MD5).

Name Variable (eight-bit minimum); identifies the system transmitting the packet.

Success (3) and Failure (4) packets have these fields:

- CodeIdentifier (which is copied from Response)
- Length
- Message

The Message field is one or more octets long and contains information that is readable by humans. By using the `debug ppp authentication` command, you can see each step that is taken with the CHAP Challenge and Response fields:

```
BRO:1 PPP: Treating connection as a callout
BRO:1 PPP: Phase is AUTHENTICATING, by both
BRO:1 CHAP: O CHALLENGE id 1 len 23 from "r2"
BRO:1 CHAP: I CHALLENGE id 1 len 23 from "r3"
BRO:1 CHAP: O RESPONSE id 1 len 23 from "r2"
BRO:1 CHAP: I SUCCESS id 1 len 4
BRO:1 CHAP: I RESPONSE id 1 len 23 from "r3"
BRO:1 CHAP: O SUCCESS id 1 len 4
```

Figure 26.9 shows the CHAP authentication process.

FIGURE 26.9 CHAP authentication

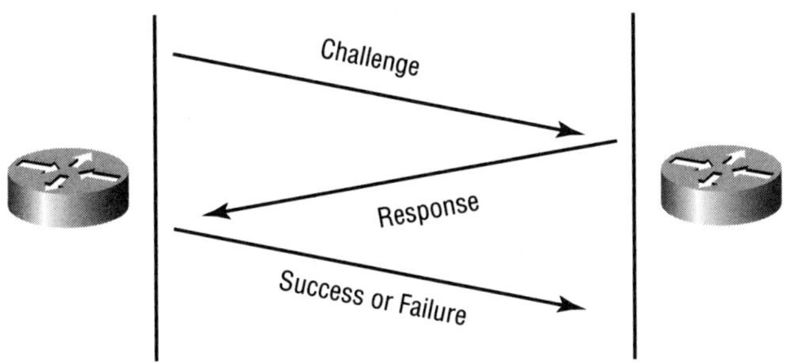

Dial-on-Demand Routing (DDR)

Dial-on-demand routing (DDR) enables two Cisco routers to use a dial-up connection on an as-needed basis and is usually used as a backup solution in case of WAN circuit failure. DDR is used only for low-volume, periodic network connections using either a PSTN asynchronous or ISDN link. This was designed to reduce WAN costs if you have to pay on a per-minute or per-packet basis.

Other terms you will undoubtedly run into are *Legacy DDR Spoke configuration* and *Legacy DDR Hub configuration*. These terms are pretty simple to understand. A spoke interface is any interface that calls or receives calls from exactly one other router. A hub, on the other hand, calls or receives calls from more than one other router. Both configurations are similar in theory, except that the hub is configured to call multiple locations.

DDR works when a packet received on an interface meets the requirements of an administrator-defined access list, which defines interesting traffic. The following seven steps give a basic description of how DDR works when an interesting packet is received in a router interface:

1. The route to the destination network is determined.
2. Interesting packets dictate a DDR call.
3. Dialer information is looked up.
4. The call is placed.
5. The connection is established.
6. Traffic is transmitted.
7. The call is terminated when no more interesting traffic is being transmitted over a link and the idle-timeout period ends.

Configuring DDR

To configure legacy DDR, you need to perform three tasks:

- Define static routes, which define how to get to the remote networks and which interface to use to get there.
- Specify the traffic that is considered interesting to the router.
- Configure the dialer information that will be used to dial the interface to get to the remote network.

Configuring the Static Routes

To forward traffic across the ISDN link, you configure static routes in each of the routers. The suggested routing method is static routes. Keep the following in mind when creating static routes:

- All participating routers must have static routes defining all routes of known networks.
- Default routing can be used if the network is a stub network.

An example of static routing with ISDN follows:

```
RouterA(config)#ip route 172.16.50.0 255.255.255.0 172.16.60.2
RouterA(config)#ip route 172.16.60.2 255.255.255.255 bri0
```

What this does is tell the router how to get to network 172.16.50.0, which is through 172.16.60.2. The second line tells the router how to get to host address 172.16.60.2 and to send traffic out the BRI0 interface.

Specifying Interesting Traffic

After setting the route tables in each router, you need to configure the router to determine what brings up the ISDN line. An administrator uses the `dialer-list` global configuration command to define what is interesting traffic.

The command to configure all IP traffic as interesting is as follows:

```
804A(config)#dialer-list 1 protocol ip permit
804A(config)#interface bri0
804A(config-if)#dialer-group 1
```

The `dialer-group` command associates a dialer list to the BRI interface. Extended access lists can be used with the `dialer-list` command to define exactly which traffic is interesting. We'll cover that in a minute.

Configuring the Dialer Information

There are five steps in the configuration of dialer information:

1. Choose the interface.
2. Set the IP address.

3. Configure the encapsulation type.
4. Link interesting traffic to the interface.
5. Configure the number or numbers to dial.

Here is an example of how to configure the five steps:

```
804A#config t
804A(config)#interface bri0
804A(config-if)#ip address 172.16.60.1 255.255.255.0
804A(config-if)#no shutdown
804A(config-if)#encapsulation ppp
804A(config-if)#dialer-group 1
804A(config-if)#dialer string 8358662
```

Instead of the `dialer string` command, you can use a `dialer map` command, which provides more security:

```
804A(config-if)#dialer map ip 172.16.60.2 name 804B 8358662
```

The `dialer map` command is used to configure the IP address of the next hop router, the name of the remote router for authentication, and the number to dial to get there. The name is usually the host name of the remote router, but it must be the name used by the remote router to identify itself.

Take a look at the following configuration of an 804 router:

```
804B#show run
Building configuration...
Current configuration:
!
version 12.0
no service pad
service timestamps debug uptime
service timestamps log uptime
no service password-encryption
!
hostname 804B
!
ip subnet-zero
!
isdn switch-type basic-ni
!
interface Ethernet0
 ip address 172.16.50.10 255.255.255.0
```

```
 no ip directed-broadcast
!
interface BRI0
 ip address 172.16.60.2 255.255.255.0
 no ip directed-broadcast
 encapsulation ppp
 dialer idle-timeout 300
 dialer string 8358661
 dialer load-threshold 2 either
 dialer-group 1
 isdn switch-type basic-ni
 isdn spid1 0835866201 8358662
 isdn spid2 0835866401 8358664
 dialer hold-queue 75
 ppp multilink
!
ip classless
ip route 172.16.30.0 255.255.255.0 172.16.60.1
ip route 172.16.60.1 255.255.255.255 BRI0
!
dialer-list 1 protocol ip permit
!
```

The BRI interface is running the PPP encapsulation and has a timeout value of 300 seconds, which is discussed in the next section. The `load-threshold` command makes both BRI channels come up immediately (if you are paying for both, you want them both up all the time) and is used with multilink, which we will discuss later in this section. The one thing you should really notice is the number in the `dialer-group 1` command. That number must match the number in the `dialer-list` command, which is used to define what is interesting traffic. The `dialer hold-queue 75` command tells the router that when it receives an interesting packet, it should queue up to 75 packets while it is waiting for the BRI to come up. If more than 75 packets are queued before the link comes up, the packets beyond the 75 will be dropped.

Using Optional Commands

You should configure two other commands on your BRI interface: `dialer load-threshold` and `dialer idle-timeout`. The `dialer load-threshold` command is used in conjunction with the `ppp multilink` command for multilink PPP (MPPP).

The `dialer load-threshold` command tells the BRI interface when to bring up the second B channel. The value specified is from 1–255, where 255 tells the BRI to bring up the second B channel only when the first channel is 100 percent loaded. The second option for that command is `in`, `out`, or `either`. This calculates the actual load on the interface either on outbound traffic, inbound traffic, or either inbound or outbound traffic. The default is outbound.

The `dialer idle-timeout` command specifies the number of seconds to wait for interesting traffic before a call is disconnected. The default is 120 seconds.

```
RouterA(config-if)#dialer load-threshold 127 either
RouterA(config-if)#dialer idle-timeout 180
```

The `dialer load-threshold 127` command tells the BRI interface to bring up the second B channel if either the inbound or outbound traffic load is 50 percent. The `dialer idle-timeout 180` command changes the default disconnect time from 120 to 180 seconds.

MPPP allows load-balancing between two or more B channels on a BRI or PRI interface. It is non-vendor-specific and provides packet fragmentation and reassembly, along with sequencing and load-calculating. Cisco's MPPP is based on RFC 1990, which is referred to as PPP Multilink Protocol (MP). The configuration would then look like this:

```
RouterA(config)#int BRI0
RouterA(config-if)#dialer load-threshold 127 either
RouterA(config-if)#dialer idle-timeout 180
RouterA(config-if)#ppp multilink
```

Not a tough configuration, but you should use it nonetheless. The `ppp multilink` command will fragment packets and send them over both lines, which provides a load-balancing effect on the data being sent over the link. You can verify that the Multilink Protocol is working by using the `show ppp multilink` command.

Using DDR with Access Lists

You can use access lists to be more specific about what is interesting traffic. In the preceding examples, we set the dialer list to allow any IP traffic to bring up the line and keep it up. That's great if you are testing, but it can defeat the purpose of why you use a DDR line in the first place. You can use extended access lists to set the restriction, for example, to only e-mail or Telnet.

Here is an example of how you define the dialer list to use an extended access list:

```
804A(config)#dialer-list 1 protocol ip list 110
804A(config)#access-list 110 permit tcp any any eq smtp
804A(config)#access-list 110 permit tcp any any eq telnet
804A(config)#int bri0
804A(config-if)#dialer-group 1
```

In the previous example, you configure the `dialer-list` command to look at an IP extended access list. This doesn't have to be IP; it can be used with any protocol. Create your dialer list and then apply it to the BRI interface with the `dialer-group` command.

Verifying the ISDN Operation

The following commands can be used to verify legacy DDR and ISDN:

ping* and *telnet These are great IP tools for any network. However, your interesting traffic must dictate that `ping` and `telnet` are acceptable as interesting traffic to bring up a link. After a link is up, you can ping or telnet to your remote router regardless of your interesting traffic lists.

show dialer This command gives good diagnostic information about your dialer and shows the number of times the dialer string has been successfully connected, the idle-timeout values of each B channel, the length of the call, and the name of the router to which the interface is connected.

show isdn active This command shows the number called and whether a call is in progress.

show isdn status A good command to use before you try to dial, this shows whether your SPIDs are valid and whether you are connected and communicating with layers 1 through 3 to the provider's switch.

show ip route A popular Cisco diagnostics command, this shows all routes that the router currently knows about.

debug isdn q921 This command is used to see layer 2 information only between the router and the service provider's ISDN switch.

debug isdn q931 This command is like `debug isdn q921` but is used to see layer 3 information, including call setup and teardown between the access server and the provider's ISDN switch.

debug dialer This command gives you call setup and teardown activity from the dialer's standpoint.

isdn disconnect interface bri0 This clears the interface and drops the current connection if one exists. Performing a shutdown on the interface can give you the same results.

Dial Backup

Dial backup, dial-on-demand routing (DDR), and Bandwidth on Demand (BoD) all use the same basic interface configuration. Dial backup and BoD use the interface backup commands to determine if, when, and how long an interface is to be activated. DDR is used for a temporary dial-up connection from a branch or home office.

Time to do some design work: Using Figure 26.10, you'll design and configure both legacy and dialer interfaces. For the sake of this project, you'll assign some addresses to the interfaces on R2 and R3 in the figure. Add any additional configuration required to complete the project. The following list of addresses will give you a starting point. Here is a list of the addresses you'll use.

R2 - To0	172.16.2.0/24
R3 - E0/0	192.168.252.0/24
ISDN cloud	192.168.254.0/24
Frame cloud	192.168.123.0/24

FIGURE 26.10 Network diagram

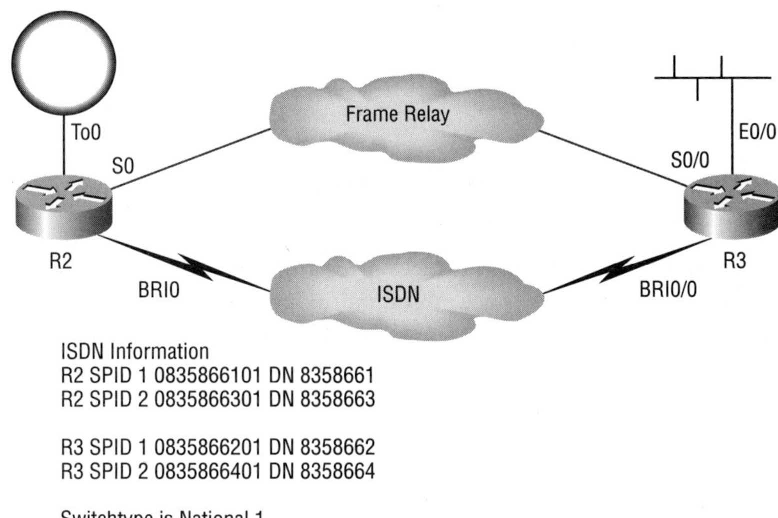

Setting Up Dial Backup

Your first project is setting up dial backup on the routers. You'll keep this fairly basic. R2 will call R3 when serial 0.202 goes down. The interesting traffic you'll designate is all IP. You will not use a routing protocol, so you'll have to use a floating static route. Typically, floating static routes are used with DDR because they can be set to a higher administrative distance than the routing protocol being used. This enables the router to automatically bring up the BRI line if the main serial line were to drop.

In the following configuration, you'll issue a `show isdn status` command on Router 2 to verify that the interface configuration is working correctly:

```
r2#show isdn status
The current ISDN Switchtype = basic-ni
ISDN BRI0 interface
    Layer 1 Status:
        ACTIVE
```

```
    Layer 2 Status:
        TEI = 100, State = MULTIPLE_FRAME_ESTABLISHED
        TEI = 101, State = MULTIPLE_FRAME_ESTABLISHED
    Spid Status:
        TEI 100, ces = 1, state = 5(init)
            spid1 configured, spid1 sent, spid1 valid
            Endpoint ID Info: epsf = 0, usid = 1, tid = 1
        TEI 101, ces = 2, state = 5(init)
            spid2 configured, spid2 sent, spid2 valid
            Endpoint ID Info: epsf = 0, usid = 3, tid = 1
    Layer 3 Status:
        0 Active Layer 3 Call(s)
    Activated dsl 0 CCBs = 1
        CCB: callid=0x0, sapi=0, ces=1, B-chan=0
    Total Allocated ISDN CCBs = 1
```

As you can see, layers 1 and 2 are up, you are using TEI 100 and 101, and the SPIDs and dialed numbers (DNs) are valid. This is one of the most important commands you can use. If the SPIDs are invalid or the configuration is wrong, you will see it in the `show isdn status` command.

Now you'll issue the `backup interface bri0` command under serial 0.202. This tells the interface s0.202 to use interface BRI0 if the serial interface loses DCD (data carrier detect), which means the link is down:

```
r2(config)#interface serial0.202
r2(config-subif)#backup interface bri0
r2(config-subif)#
%ISDN-6-LAYER2DOWN: Layer 2 for Interface BRI0, TEI 100 changed to down
%ISDN-6-LAYER2DOWN: Layer 2 for Interface BRI0, TEI 101 changed to down
%LINK-5-CHANGED: Interface BRI0, changed state to standby mode
%LINK-3-UPDOWN: Interface BRI0:1, changed state to down
%LINK-3-UPDOWN: Interface BRI0:2, changed state to down
```

As you can see, this command places the main interface in Standby mode, effectively turning the interface down. This deactivates layer 1 on the BRI0 interface. This can be verified by issuing a `show ISDN status` command at the router prompt:

```
r2#show ISDN status

The current ISDN Switchtype = basic-ni
ISDN BRI0 interface
    Layer 1 Status:
        DEACTIVATED
    Layer 2 Status:
        Layer 2 NOT Activated
```

```
Spid Status:
    TEI Not Assigned,ces = 1, state = 1(terminal
    down)
        spid1 configured,spid1 NOT sent,spid1 NOT
        valid
    TEI Not Assigned,ces = 2, state = 1(terminal
    down)
        spid2 configured,spid2 NOT sent,spid2 NOT
        valid
Layer 3 Status:
    0 Active Layer 3 Call(s)
Activated dsl 0 CCBs = 0
Total Allocated ISDN CCBs = 0
```

Using the physical BRI interface as a backup can cause problems because the BRI interface appears to be disconnected to the service provider. There is no way to verify that the ISDN BRI circuit is in proper working order unless you remove it as a backup interface. This is why it's best to use a dialer interface as the backup and not the physical ISDN BRI interface, which is illustrated later in this chapter.

Testing the Backup

After the configuration, it's important to test your backup link. You don't want to wait for an actual outage before discovering you have made a configuration mistake. You'll test the backup by disabling the connected serial interface on R2.

When the test is performed, it takes 11 seconds for the backup line to come out of Standby mode and another four seconds for layers 1 and 2 to come up. The following router output shows this. Why would using a dialer interface save you four seconds in this scenario?

```
00:46:22: %LINEPROTO-5-UPDOWN: Line protocol on Interface Serial0, _
  ➥changed    state to down
00:46:23: %LINK-3-UPDOWN: Interface Serial0, changed state to down
00:46:23: %FR-5-DLCICHANGE: Interface Serial0 - DLCI 202 state changed_
  ➥to    DELETED
00:46:23: %FR-5-DLCICHANGE: Interface Serial0 - DLCI 100 state changed
  ➥_to    DELETED
00:46:23: %FR-5-DLCICHANGE: Interface Serial0 - DLCI 200 state changed
  ➥_to    DELETED
00:46:23: %LINEPROTO-5-UPDOWN: Line protocol on Interface Serial0.202,
  ➥_ changed    state to down
00:46:34: %LINK-3-UPDOWN: Interface BRI0:1, changed state to down
00:46:34: %LINK-3-UPDOWN: Interface BRI0:2, changed state to down
00:46:34: %LINK-3-UPDOWN: Interface BRI0, changed state to up
```

```
00:46:38: %ISDN-6-LAYER2UP: Layer 2 for Interface BR0, TEI 107 changed to up
00:46:38: %ISDN-6-LAYER2UP: Layer 2 for Interface BR0, TEI 108 changed to up
00:46:59: %LINK-3-UPDOWN: Interface BRI0:1, changed state to up
00:47:00: %LINEPROTO-5-UPDOWN: Line protocol on Interface BRI0:1, _
  ➥changed    state to up
00:47:06: %ISDN-6-CONNECT: Interface BRI0:1 is now connected to 8358662
00:47:23: %LINEPROTO-5-UPDOWN: Line protocol on Interface Serial0, _
  ➥changed    state to up
00:47:24: %LINK-3-UPDOWN: Interface Serial0, changed state to up
00:47:24: %FR-5-DLCICHANGE: Interface Serial0 - DLCI 202 state changed_
  ➥to    ACTIVE
00:47:24: %LINEPROTO-5-UPDOWN: Line protocol on Interface Serial0.202, _
  ➥changed    state to up
00:48:24: %LINK-3-UPDOWN: Interface BRI0:1, changed state to down
00:48:24: %ISDN-6-DISCONNECT: Interface BRI0:1  disconnected from_
  ➥unknown, call    lasted 85 seconds
00:48:24: %ISDN-6-LAYER2DOWN: Layer 2 for Interface BRI0, TEI 107_
  ➥changed to    down
00:48:24: %ISDN-6-LAYER2DOWN: Layer 2 for Interface BRI0, TEI 108_
  ➥changed to    down
00:48:24: %LINK-5-CHANGED: Interface BRI0, changed state to standby mode
00:48:24: %LINK-3-UPDOWN: Interface BRI0:1, changed state to down
00:48:24: %LINK-3-UPDOWN: Interface BRI0:2, changed state to down
00:48:25: %LINEPROTO-5-UPDOWN: Line protocol on Interface BRI0:1, _
  ➥changed    state to down
```

You should also note in the preceding router output that the backup line dropped one minute after the primary link came up. Changing the delay between primary failure and activation of the backup line plus delay between primary recovery and deactivation of the backup line can be modified by using the `backup delay 10 60` command. The first number (10) is how many seconds to wait before activating the backup interface, and the second number (60) is how many seconds to stay up once the primary line recovers.

As we stated earlier, it is best to use a *dialer profile,* or dialer interface, as the backup interface, so we will show you how this is done. Setting up a dialer profile requires two steps: configuring the primary interface and configuring the dialer interface. The primary interface needs only some basic information; for example, take a look at this configuration:

```
interface BRI0
 no ip address
 encapsulation ppp
 isdn spid1 0835866101 8358661
 isdn spid2 0835866301 8358663
 dialer pool-member 1
!
```

Basically, all we did was set up ISDN layers 1 and 2, enable PPP encapsulation, and assign this interface to dialer pool 1—pretty simple so far.

The next step involves the dialer interface. A dialer interface is *virtual*, meaning it is not a physical interface, and you add it by using the global command `interface dialer 1`. The connection-specific configuration commands are placed under this interface, including creation of the dialer pool, phone number to dial, remote device name, interesting traffic, authentication, and IP address information. Again, it's not that difficult. Take a look at this configuration:

```
interface Dialer1
 ip address 192.168.254.2 255.255.255.0
 encapsulation ppp
 dialer remote-name r3
 dialer string 8358662
 dialer pool 1
 dialer-group 1
 ppp authentication chap callin
```

Note that the `callin` option on the `ppp authentication` command indicates authentication on incoming (received) calls only.

You will notice that the dialer interface goes into Standby but the BRI interface doesn't. You can verify this by using the `show ISDN status` command:

```
r2#show isdn status
The current ISDN Switchtype = basic-ni
ISDN BRI0 interface
    Layer 1 Status:
        ACTIVE
    Layer 2 Status:
        TEI = 109, State = MULTIPLE_FRAME_ESTABLISHED
        TEI = 110, State = MULTIPLE_FRAME_ESTABLISHED
    Spid Status:
        TEI 109, ces = 1, state = 5(init)
            spid1 configured, spid1 sent, spid1 valid
            Endpoint ID Info: epsf = 0, usid = 1, tid = 1
        TEI 110, ces = 2, state = 5(init)
            spid2 configured, spid2 sent, spid2 valid
            Endpoint ID Info: epsf = 0, usid = 3, tid = 1
    Layer 3 Status:
        0 Active Layer 3 Call(s)
    Activated dsl 0 CCBs = 1
        CCB: callid=0x0, sapi=0, ces=1, B-chan=0
    Total Allocated ISDN CCBs = 1
```

The BRI interface is still active and not in Standby. This makes it easy to tell when there is a problem with the BRI circuit.

We will introduce a useful diagnostic command here: `show dialer`. This output gives you a lot of information such as dial reason (what was the source and destination address of the packet that caused the call to be placed), whom you called or who called you, how long the interface has been up, how long it has been since it has seen interesting traffic, and how much more time remains until it hangs up.

```
r2#show dialer

BRI0 - dialer type = ISDN

Dial String      Successes   Failures    Last called   Last status
0 incoming call(s) have been screened.

BRI0:1 - dialer type = ISDN
Idle timer (120 secs), Fast idle timer (20 secs)
Wait for carrier (30 secs), Re-enable (15 secs)
Dialer state is data link layer up
Dial reason: ip (s=192.168.254.2, d=192.168.252.3)
Interface bound to profile Dialer1
Time until disconnect 105 secs
Current call connected 00:00:16
Connected to 8358662

Dialer1 - dialer type = DIALER PROFILE
Idle timer (120 secs), Fast idle timer (20 secs)
Wait for carrier (30 secs), Re-enable (15 secs)
Dialer state is data link layer up

Dial String  Successes Failures Last called   Last status
8358662      18         0        00:00:19      successful
```

The final configuration is shown next. R2 is set up to use a dialer interface; R3 is using the legacy configuration:

```
r2#show run
Building configuration...

Current configuration:
!
version 12.0
```

```
service timestamps log uptime
no service password-encryption
no service udp-small-servers
no service tcp-small-servers
!
hostname r2
!
enable password cisco
!
username r3 password 0 cisco
isdn switch-type basic-ni
!
interface Serial0
 no ip address
 encapsulation frame-relay
 no fair-queue
!
interface Serial0.202 point-to-point
 backup delay 10 60
 backup interface Dialer1
 ip address 172.16.34.2 255.255.255.0
 frame-relay interface-dlci 202
!
interface BRI0
 no ip address
 encapsulation ppp
 isdn switch-type basic-ni
 isdn spid1 0835866101 8358661
 isdn spid2 0835866301 8358663
 dialer pool-member 1
!
interface Dialer1
 ip address 192.168.254.2 255.255.255.0
 encapsulation ppp
 dialer remote-name r3
 dialer string 8358662
 dialer pool 1
 dialer-group 1
 ppp authentication chap
!
```

```
ip classless
ip route 0.0.0.0 0.0.0.0 172.16.34.3
ip route 0.0.0.0 0.0.0.0 192.168.254.3 210
!
dialer-list 1 protocol ip permit
!
end

r2#

r3#show run
Building configuration...

Current configuration:
!
version 12.0
service timestamps debug uptime
service timestamps log uptime
no service password-encryption
!
hostname r3
!
enable password cisco
!
username r2 password 0 cisco
ip subnet-zero
!
isdn switch-type basic-ni
!
interface FastEthernet0/0
 ip address 192.168.252.3 255.255.255.255
 no ip directed-broadcast
!
interface Serial0/0
 no ip address
 no ip directed-broadcast
 encapsulation frame-relay
 no ip mroute-cache
 frame-relay lmi-type cisco
!
```

```
interface Serial0/0.203 point-to-point
 ip address 172.16.34.3 255.255.255.0
 no ip directed-broadcast
 frame-relay interface-dlci 203
!
interface BRI0/0
 ip address 192.168.254.3 255.255.255.0
 no ip directed-broadcast
 encapsulation ppp
 dialer map ip 192.168.254.2 8358661
 dialer-group 1
 isdn switch-type basic-ni
 isdn spid1 0835866201 8358662
 isdn spid2 0835866401 8358664
 ppp authentication chap
 dialer hold-queue 75
!
ip classless
ip route 172.16.2.0 255.255.255.0 172.16.34.2
ip route 172.16.2.0 255.255.255.0 192.168.254.2 210
!
dialer-list 1 protocol ip permit
!
end
```

As you can see, the configuration is not that complex. Having a good working knowledge of this will help you solve many dial backup scenarios. Of course, you can make this as complex as you'd like; we kept this example fairly simple as an illustration.

The command `dialer-list` creates the interesting traffic. The command `dialer-group` assigns the dialer list to an interface. The numbers must match. In the previous example, both the dialer list and the dialer group are 1. The `dialer hold-queue` command creates a buffer for incoming interesting traffic that is waiting for the BRI to be dialed. The 75 means is that *if 75 interesting* packets arrive on queue before the interface comes up, the 76th and subsequent will be dropped until the line comes up and the queue gets some relief.

Bandwidth on Demand

What do you do if you have more traffic than bandwidth? Wouldn't it be great if you could pull your magic router wand out and make the traffic go faster? You can approximate this magic by using Bandwidth on Demand.

Bandwidth on Demand (BoD) is an interface-only command, meaning you cannot apply it to a subinterface. Here is the syntax to assign a backup load to an interface:

```
backup load {enable-threshold | never} {disable-load | never}
```

The enable threshold load is the percentage of interface load where you want the additional bandwidth dialed up. The disable load is the percentage of interface load where you want the extra bandwidth dropped. At what point is the circuit congested enough to need extra bandwidth? Some people say 75 percent; yet others say queuing is needed. You will probably have to figure this out based on corporate policy, cost, sensitivity to slow responsiveness, and so on. Because BoD is a dial-up feature, you might incur additional long-distance costs, so be careful about setting your thresholds.

Configuring BoD is almost the same as configuring dial backup, except you're replacing the amount of backup delay with the amount of backup threshold. Here is an example:

```
Router#config t
Enter configuration commands, one per line.  End with CNTL/Z.
Router(config)#interface serial0
Router(config-if)#backup interface BRI0
```

This configuration sets the interface serial0 to use interface BRI0 as a backup as the main interface goes down. The following configuration shows how to configure the backup delay and the backup load:

```
Router(config-if)#backup ?
  delay      Delays before backup line up or down transitions
  interface  Configure an interface as a backup
  load       Load thresholds for line up or down transitions

Router(config-if)#backup delay ?
  <0-4294967294>  Seconds
  never           Never activate the backup line

Router(config-if)#backup delay 10 ?
  <0-4294967294>  Seconds
  never           Never deactivate the backup line

Router(config-if)#backup delay 10 60
```

The previous configuration sets the backup delay to 10 seconds and 60 seconds. This means that the backup interface will not dial until serial0 is down for 10 seconds, and it will drop the link after the serial link is back up for 60 seconds. The `backup load` command syntax is as follows:

```
Router(config-if)#backup load ?
  <0-100>  Percentage
```

```
  never     Never activate the backup line

Router(config-if)#backup load 75 ?
  <0-100>  Percentage
  never     Never deactivate the backup line

Router(config-if)#backup load 75 35
Router(config-if)#^Z
Router#
```

This command sets the router to dial the ISDN BRI0 interface if the bandwidth reaches a maximum of 75 percent and then to drop the link after the bandwidth is back at 35 percent.

The interface configuration is shown next:

```
Router#show run
[output cut]
interface Serial0
 backup delay 10 60
 backup interface BRI0
 backup load 75 35
 ip address 10.53.69.69 255.255.255.0
 no ip directed-broadcast
 --More–
```

Channelized T-1/E-1 (PRI)

Large businesses typically use point-to-point connections with DSU/CSUs to connect two sites. In turn, these are connected to low- and high-speed serial interfaces on routers—usually Cisco routers. The router backplane and the number of interfaces the router can handle determine how well it supports WAN connections. The Cisco 7000 series of routers supports the Fast Serial Interface Processor (FSIP), which provides either four or eight serial ports, permitting the four or eight point-to-point connections to remote offices. Other Cisco routers support the Multichannel Interface Processor (MIP), which furnishes support for two full T-1/E-1 ports in the 7000 series and one port in the 4000 series.

ISDN T-1s, which are called Primary Rate Interfaces (PRIs), run at 1.544Mbps. These use 24 channels in contrast to E-1s, which use 31 channels and run at 2.048Mbps. E-1 is mainly used in Europe, and both T-1 and E-1 are considered wide-area digital transmission schemes.

Each port in the MIP can support 24 DS0 channels of 64Kbps each when using a T-1 interface, and 31 DS0 channels when using an E-1 interface. The MIP refers to each serial interface as a channel group; this enables each channel or DS0 to be configured individually. Each channel has the same characteristics and options as regular serial interfaces.

Configuring ISDN PRI

The serial links connect into either a private data network or a service provider's network. Both the line encoding and the framing must match the service provider's equipment. To configure a PRI on a serial link, you must supply the following information:

Channel type Either T-1 or E-1.

Frame type When using a T-1, this can be either D4, sometimes referred to as Super Frame, or Extended Super Frame (ESF). D4 is the original T-1 frame format and comprises one framing bit and a DS0 time slot for each channel on the line. ESF comprises 24 D4 frames. As each D4 frame contains a framing bit, an ESF has 24 framing bits that it uses for synchronization (6 bits), error checking (6-bit cyclic redundancy check), and diagnostic data channel (12 bits).

Linecode This will be either alternate mark inversion (AMI) or binary 8-zero substitution (B8ZS). B8ZS is typically used in the U.S.; however, most legacy phone systems still use AMI.

Dynamic Multiple Encapsulation Back in the old days, prior to Cisco IOS 12.1, the interface encapsulation that we used in the previous example—PPP and others such as Frame Relay, High-Level Data Link Control (HDLC), Link Access Procedure (LAP), and X.25—could support only one ISDN B channel connection over the entire link, or as in the case of HDLC and PPP, the entire link needed to use the same encapsulation method. With the Dynamic Multiple Encapsulation feature, the ISDN B channel becomes a forwarding device, and the D channel is ignored, thereby allowing different encapsulation types and per-user configuration.

Which T-1 time slots to use By using the `pri-group` command on your PRI interface, you can define which time slots will be controlled by the D channel (subchannel 23). You can also specify dedicated time slots on the same interface with the `channel-group` *`number`* `time slot` *`range`* command. This will assign the time slots in the *`range`* specified, to the subchannel group of *`number`*.

In the following example, we chose to configure slot 1, port 0 of the MIP card in a 7000 router, and we opted for ESF framing, with B8ZS line coding. Remember not to get confused with the channel group and time slot numbering; the channel group numbers range from 0 to 23, whereas the time slot values range from 1 to 24. Also remember that channel 15 on the E-1 and channel 23 on the T-1 are for the D channels. The command `pri-group timeslots 12-24` indicates that the D channel will control time slots 11 through 23 on the PRI circuit. Channel group 1 has six time slots running at 64Kbps. We could choose up to 24 DS0s but purchased only six from our provider, with 12 through 24 being controlled with the PRI D channel. Here's the output:

```
Router#config t
Enter configuration commands, one per line.   End with CNTL/Z.
Router(config)#controller T1 1/0
Router(config-if)#framing esf
Router(config-if)#linecode b8zs
Router(config-if)#pri-group timeslots 12-24
Router(config-if)#channel-group 1 timeslots 1-6 speed 64
Router(config-if)#^Z
```

An IP address and the serial encapsulation method (HDLC is the default) then needs to be assigned to each interface, as shown in the following example:

```
Router#config t
Enter configuration commands, one per line. End with CNTL/Z.
Router(config)#interface serial1/0:23
Router(config-if)#encapsulation ppp
Router(config-if)#ip address 172.16.30.5 255.255.255.252
Router(config)#interface serial1/0:1
Router(config-if)#encapsulation hdlc
Router(config-if)#ip address 172.16.30.5 255.255.255.252
```

Output for the five other B channels (serial/0-2-6) has been omitted to save space.

```
Router(config-if)#^Z
Router#
```

When connecting two MIP cards back-to-back, you must specify the clocking on one controller. This is done with the `clock source internal` command.

Configuring E-1

The E-1 configuration is similar to the T-1 configuration but has a few different parameters:

Framing The E-1 framing types available are crc4 and no-crc4, with australia as an option. The default is crc4, and it specifies CRC error checking, with no-crc4 specifying that CRC checking is (surprise!) disabled. The australia framing method is used when configuring an E-1 in (another surprise!) Australia.

Linecode This is either AMI or HDB3 when configuring an E-1, with HDB3 as the default.

In the following example, we specified slot 0, port 1 on our MIP card, using the crc4 framing type. The provider has defined HDB3 as the linecode (HDB3 is the default) to match the carrier's equipment. For an E-1 PRI circuit, the D channel is 15 so the command `pri-group time-slots 1-16` will specify that channels 1 through 15 will be controlled by the D channel (subchannel 15). Again, remember not to get confused with the channel group and time slot numbering; the channel group numbers range from 0 to 30, whereas the time slot values range from 1 to 31. Also remember that channel 15 on the E-1 and channel 23 on the T-1 are for the D channels. However, time slots 17 to 30 are for a dedicated connection with up to 30 available if purchased:

```
Router#config t
Enter configuration commands, one per line. End with CNTL/Z.
```

```
Router(config)#controller E1 1/0
Router(config-if)#framing crc4
Router(config-if)#linecode hdb3
Router(config-if)#pri-group timeslots 1-16
Router(config-if)#channel-group 1 timeslots 17-30 speed 64
Router(config-if)#^Z
Router#
```

You then need to specify the IP address and encapsulation methods used, just as in the T-1 example:

```
Router#config t
Enter configuration commands, one per line. End with CNTL/Z.
Router(config)#interface serial1/0:15
Router(config-if)#encapsulation ppp
Router(config-if)#ip address 172.16.30.5 255.255.255.252
Router(config)#interface serial1/0:1
Router(config-if)#encapsulation hdlc
Router(config-if)#ip address 172.16.30.5 255.255.255.252
Router(config-if)#^Z
Router#
```

Summary

ISDN is an old but still very viable networking standard that supports voice, data, and video. It is slowly being replaced by DSL and cable modems. Layer 2 is negotiated by using the ITU-T Q.921 standard, and layer 3 is negotiated by using the Q.931 standard. The ISDN reference model is set up with function groups and reference points. The function groups classify each device in the ISDN network, and the reference points identify the connections and electrical characteristics between each function group. Many IOS `debug` and `show` commands are available to help you understand and troubleshoot ISDN connections.

The types of connections include dial backup, dial-on-demand routing (DDR), and Bandwidth on Demand (BoD). There are many ways to set up a connection from one device to another by using ISDN and analog links. The legacy method uses the physical interface to specify IP address, dialing properties, and authentication. Dialer profiles provide more flexibility when using dial backup and other dial-up connections. When using PPP authentication, both Password Authentication Protocol (PAP) and Challenge Handshake Authentication Protocol (CHAP) can be used. Some IOS `debug` and `show` commands are associated with PPP negotiation and authentication.

Exam Essentials

Know the types of ISDN. ISDN comes in two flavors: BRI and PRI. The BRI is a standard that runs over a 192Kbps circuit, whereas a PRI can run over a T-1 (1.544Mbps) or E-1 (2.048Mbps) circuit. Know when to use a BRI and when to use a PRI. There are many PRI and BRI ISDN switch types supported, and you should know which ones require SPIDs and which do not.

Understand the ISDN function groups. You need to know what function the groups NT1, NT2, TA, LT, ET, TE1, and TE2 provide in the ISDN network.

Know the ISDN reference points. Identify the ISDN reference points of R, S, T, and U. Know where these reference points are in the ISDN network and between which function groups they are found.

Understand the two ITU-T Q standards used by ISDN. The Q.921 standard is used to set up layer 2 between the router and local switch, and the Q.931 standard is used to set up layer 3. You need to know what these protocols' structures look like and what happens when a call is set up and when it is torn down. You should also be familiar with the `debug isdn q921` and `debug isdn q931` commands and what to look for in troubleshooting a problem.

Know how to set up dial-on-demand routing (DDR), dial backup, and Bandwidth on Demand (BoD) by using both legacy and dialer profiles. Dialer profiles are used when you need to set up a routing protocol over a dial-up connection; the legacy setup is used when a simple point-to-point connection is needed between two sites. You should know how to set up authentication and callback when security is needed on a dial-up connection. Multilink is also available when more bandwidth is needed on a connection.

Know how to set up a channelized interface. You should know how to set up a T-1 or E-1 controller for channelized operation. You need to know the different framing and linecoding options. The `pri-group` command is used when setting up a channelized interface to become an ISDN PRI. The `channel-group` command is used when an interface or a portion of the interface is used for dedicated access.

Remote Access with Digital Subscriber Line

THE CCNP EXAM TOPICS COVERED IN THIS CHAPTER INCLUDE THE FOLLOWING:

- ✓ Understand digital subscriber line technologies.
- ✓ Know the differences in digital subscriber line technologies.
- ✓ Know how to configure digital subscriber line technologies.
- ✓ Understand how to troubleshoot digital subscriber line technologies.

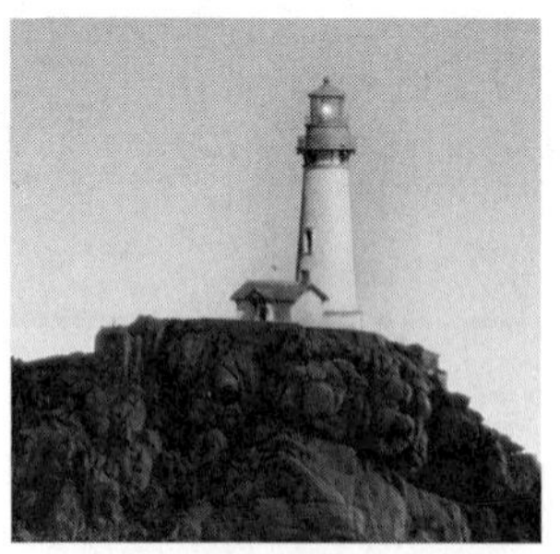

In this chapter we will examine the remote access technologies encompassed in digital subscriber line (DSL) services. This set of newer remote connectivity access methods provides residential and business locations with high-speed, low-cost connections that can surpass T-1 in some instances. In addition to the basics of DSL, we will also compare the different flavors of the technology and the troubleshooting methodologies employed.

What Is Digital Subscriber Line?

Digital subscriber line (DSL) is the result of demand for cheaper and higher bandwidth services over the already existing copper phone-line network. As with ISDN, there was, and is, a great deal of installed and widely available sub-Category 3 cable that, with a new encoding method, could provide high-bandwidth services.

Within this chapter the terms *DSL* and *xDSL* are used. By convention, both mean the same thing, although *xDSL* is a generic term that means all DSL technologies, including ADSL and HDSL. These variants of DSL are described later in this chapter. *DSL* is typically used to describe the base technology.

However, this existing cable currently supports analog voice services, so the new technology, again like ISDN, needs to support legacy voice services in addition to providing the new data service. So DSL is a voice and data service that supports multi-megabit data rates over the same cable that previously supported only voice.

The *digital subscriber line access multiplexer (DSLAM)* provides the cornerstone of the DSL infrastructure. This device provides two important functions in the DSL network: First, it separates voice and data traffic from each line, and, second, it terminates each connection to the residence or business. Figure 27.1 illustrates a typical DSL residential installation with an access terminal (DSLAM) extending the link from the central office. Note that a remote access terminal is not required and that a one-mile copper connection could extend directly from a central-office-located DSLAM.

As an overview, DSL provides the following benefits:

- Voice and data services over the same copper pair
- Significantly greater bandwidth than ISDN or analog services over comparable physical media

Unfortunately, DSL also has some negatives, including these:

- Significant distance limitations at higher data rates
- Low tolerance for low-quality copper wiring

FIGURE 27.1 xDSL installation

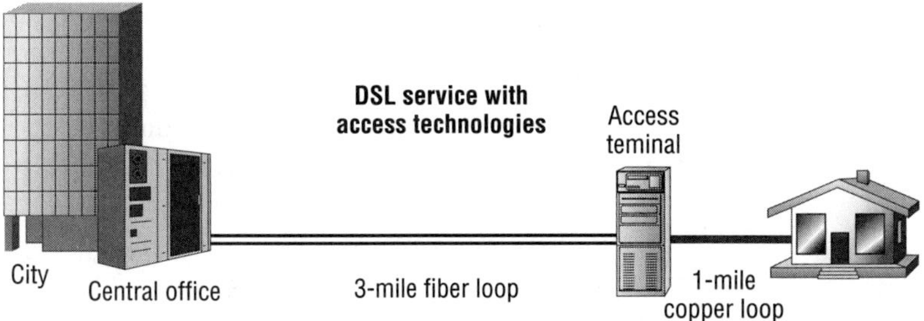

- Complex, labor-consuming installation procedures for some versions
- An inability to work with legacy line-conditioning equipment, including load coils

This chapter covers the flavors of DSL that are available to the administrator for remote access solutions, in addition to covering configuration and troubleshooting of this technology.

The Different Flavors of DSL

You learned in Chapter 26, "Integrated Services Digital Network (ISDN)," that there are a couple of different flavors to that technology—specifically BRI and PRI. We will discuss six different flavors of DSL in this chapter, although there are many more. These include:

- Asymmetric digital subscriber line
- G.lite
- High bit-rate DSL
- Symmetric DSL
- ISDN DSL
- Very-high data rate DSL

The different flavors of DSL typically alter the bandwidth available and the range—or distance—between the DSLAM and the end point. There can be other differences as well, such as the need for a *splitter* to separate voice traffic from the circuit.

Asymmetric Digital Subscriber Line

The most common DSL variant is *asymmetric digital subscriber line (ADSL)*, and this is often used for home and business users. It is called *asymmetric* because the bandwidth is not equal in the upstream and downstream directions. Upstream traffic is sent from the user, and downstream traffic is sent from the direction of the DSLAM.

When discussing a DSL circuit without specifying the type of DSL being used, it is common to refer to xDSL.

This unequal traffic flow is well suited to Internet surfing and centralized data storage, as would be found in many tele-worker applications. For example, many users download graphics, documents, and other large files from the remote network, while only sending small e-mail messages or requests for information. As such, the network needs to provide only a small amount of bandwidth to service these smaller datagrams from the user, and it's preferable to provide larger amounts of bandwidth to support the greater volume of data from the network.

ADSL requires the use of a splitter to isolate the voice traffic from the data stream on the copper pair.

Real World Scenario

Oversubscription and Bandwidth Contention

A discussion of consumer DSL, of which ADSL is a common offering, necessitates a discussion of vendor claims regarding oversubscription and bandwidth contention. As you might know, oversubscription occurs when the network is provisioned with greater potential demand than could be serviced at any one time, under the reasonable assumption that use patterns and the quantity of bandwidth demanded will never be 100 percent.

This assumption is very reasonable in many networks. Consider your network for a moment. You might have 100 workstations connected to a switch with a single 100Mbps uplink to the core. If each of the 100 workstations is connected at 100Mbps, the network would be oversubscribed 100:1. Consumer DSL network vendors commonly oversubscribe at ratios between 3 and 10 to 1, or 10:1.

Let's suspend discussion of oversubscription for a moment and consider bandwidth contention. DSL providers quickly point out that cable modem networks provide shared bandwidth from the head end to a population of users. Think of this as shared Ethernet. They then add that their DSL technology is more akin to switched Ethernet, where each user has no contention for bandwidth from their router to the DSLAM.

On the surface it would appear that DSL is the superior technology, as many networkers have migrated from the old shared network model to the superior switched network in Ethernet. The marketing folks for DSL providers enjoy that analogy and relish in users choosing the dedicated technology.

However, all is not as it appears. Although it is true that DSL dedicates bandwidth from the end user to the head end at the Physical layer, we must return to oversubscription. I might have a dedicated 100Mbps Ethernet connection to my workstation, and Piper might have 100Mbps to her workstation, but if we have a single 100Mbps uplink from the switch to our resource, we could expect only 50 percent, or 50Mbps in this example, of throughput. So long as we have that consideration, shared bandwidth is always a factor, even if the hop from my router to the head end is dedicated. As such, cable modem's shared technology (presented further in Chapter 28, "Remote Access with Cable Modems and Virtual Private Networks") is less of a concern than DSL providers would like.

Cisco contends that ADSL is best suited to video on demand and video conferencing; however, in practice we would recommend against this generalization. The asymmetric nature of ADSL is such that quality upstream video conferencing is unlikely if there is concurrent load. Because video conferencing is typically a bidirectional experience, it would be overgeneralizing to conclude that ADSL is the best solution. We justify their answer by simplifying the scope and comparing ADSL to ISDN, analog (POTS), and other remote access technologies. In this light, ADSL is the best solution. However, HDSL and other DSL flavors, discussed later, might be better for your installation.

G.lite

G.lite, which is sometimes called *splitterless DSL*, is quickly dethroning ADSL for the most common DSL variant, although technically it is only a subspecification of ADSL itself. As the *splitterless* nickname infers, this technology does not require a splitter to be installed at the customer location. In this splitterless installation, the provider isolates voice from data in the central office by controlling the frequency of the voice channel.

The advantage to this type of installation is significant. In a splitter (ADSL) type of deployment, the provider needs to visit the customer location and install a splitter on the line in addition to a second jack—one jack is for the DSL router, and the other jack is for the telephone. The cost of this is very high compared to the alternative of encoding the data and voice so the end equipment can isolate the voice traffic where no splitter installation is required. G.lite installations can be completed at the central office, and the user can simply plug their router into the jack as they would a telephone.

G.lite is further described in ITU-T standard G.992.2.

High Bit-Rate DSL

High bit-rate DSL (HDSL) requires two pairs of copper for service, unlike most other DSL offerings. In exchange, it provides a T-1-like presence of 1.544Mbps in each direction. It's important to note that this service does not support analog voice.

Symmetric DSL

Symmetric DSL (SDSL) is a variant of HDSL; however, it runs over a single copper pair. HDSL requires two pairs of copper. The data rate is 1.544Mbps in each direction.

ISDN DSL

ISDN DSL (IDSL) provides up to 144Kbps of bandwidth—which is equal to the two B channels and one D channel of ISDN BRI—by employing the same line coding (2B1Q) as ISDN. It is important to note that this flavor of DSL does not support analog voice service.

The primary reason for offering IDSL is that the range can be extended to cover virtually any existing copper path that is devoid of amplifiers or load coils—both of which can be used in very long analog connections. With repeaters, IDSL can extend to 45,000 feet.

Very-High Data Rate DSL

Very-high data rate DSL (VDSL), sometimes also called *very-high bit-rate DSL*, is exactly that—a high-bandwidth variant of DSL. Most implementations are capable of downstream bandwidths in excess of 50Mbps. Consider for a moment that most VDSL deployments are in residential settings and that the service provides in essence a DS-3 worth of capacity, and you begin to appreciate the "very-high" aspects indeed.

There are a few installations of VDSL available in large markets, including Denver and Phoenix in the United States. These services leverage VDSL to provide video, data, and voice services over the DSL circuit. With over 50Mbps, it's possible to provide four broadcast-quality video streams over the connection, while also supporting an always-available Internet data path and analog voice services—a road to the fully converged network if you will.

Of course, you can't get something for nothing, and VDSL is no exception. The significant downside to the technology is its limited range. Stated another way, ADSL technologies can frequently extend to over 18,000 feet, whereas VDSL is limited to 4,500 feet. The highest data rates are attainable at only 1,000 feet in most real-world settings.

The DSL types described in this chapter are summarized in Table 27.1.

TABLE 27.1 DSL Types

Type	Analog Support	Downstream Bandwidth	Upstream Bandwidth	Range
ADSL	Yes	Up to 9Mbps	Up to 640Kbps	Up to 18,000 feet
G.lite	Yes	Up to 1.5Mbps	Up to 512Kbps	Up to 18,000 feet
HDSL	No	1.544Mbps	1.544Mbps	Up to 12,000 feet
SDSL	No	1.544Mbps	1.544Mbps	Up to 10,000 feet
IDSL	No	144Kbps	144Kbps	Up to 45,000 feet
VDSL	Yes	Up to 52Mbps	Up to 2.3Mbps	Up to 4,500 feet

You might find that different vendors and sources document range and bandwidth figures that are not the same as those in Table 27.1. We have used the Cisco figures, which are sometimes over or under the values included in other specifications. The variances should not have a significant impact on the test or real-world deployment—for example, HDSL might have a range of 15,000 feet or 12,000 maximum, but wire condition, interference, and other factors can greatly influence this, and a real-world installation might operate correctly at only 7,000 feet. This chapter covers only DSL basics consistent with the examination.

Cisco DSL Routers

Cisco's product line for supporting DSL services is comprised of three classifications of equipment. The first is the focus of the Remote Access examination, which is primarily made up of the Cisco 800 series of routers and the SOHO (small office, home office) 70 series. The second is comprised of the xDSL modules for the branch and office routers, including the 2600 and 3600 series. And the third is the head-end DSLAM switches, including the Cisco 6260 IP DSL switch.

There could be a fourth Cisco DSL product category in their Linksys acquisition. The Linksys product line includes a wide range of solutions for the SOHO market and frequently integrates other functions such as print services and wireless networking.

For the SOHO environment and small remote office, Cisco provides their SOHO line of DSL routers in addition to the Cisco 800 series. Here is a list of the various DSL platforms in this category:

- Cisco 837 ADSL Broadband Router
- Cisco 836 ADSL over ISDN Broadband Router
- Cisco 828 G.SHDSL Router
- Cisco 827 ADSL Router
- Cisco 827-4V ADSL Router
- Cisco 826 ADSL Router
- Cisco SOHO 78 G.SHDSL Router
- Cisco SOHO 77 ADSL Router
- Cisco SOHO 77 H ADSL Router
- Cisco SOHO 76 ADSL Router

There is not much to focus on in this list, other than noting the diversity within the Cisco 827 product line, which includes the 827-4V. This platform provides four voice ports in addition to ADSL support. The H variant of the 827 provides a four-port hub in addition to DSL termination.

For larger offices, Cisco provides DSL support on the 1700, 2600XM, and 3600 series routers via a WAN Interface Card (WIC). This allows for the installation of other services, including network modules (NMs) for content delivery. Voice Interface Cards (VICs) can also terminate voice services on these platforms.

At the head end, Cisco provides the following switches for terminating DSL connections:

- Cisco 6260 IP DSL Switch
- Cisco 6160 IP DSL Switch
- Cisco 6015 IP DSL Switch

These solutions are targeted toward servicing multi-tenant buildings, telecommunications service providers, and ISPs. The specifics of these platforms are well beyond the scope of the Remote Access examination.

Configuring DSL

The specific configuration settings for a DSL installation will depend on the type of router used and the features desired, but there are common elements.

The key element of a DSL installation is that the technology is fundamentally a physical transport of ATM cells. As such, we will configure a Cisco 3810 router to terminate multiple DSL connections (ADSL, in this case). The head end is a T-1 ATM connection. You might realize that the T-1 is a poor termination choice for ADSL services; however, for this application it is an appropriate solution. A DS-3 or other ATM connection could provide the termination just as well.

Configuration of the DSLAM is beyond the scope of the test and this book, but functionally it is PVC configuration and other parameters. Stated another way, it is not complicated.

In addition to the typical configuration parameters you might include (such as routing, logging, security, and management), the DSL configuration requires very little additional configuration. In this excerpt, we configure the T-1 physical interface with Extended Super Frame and B8ZS encoding, in addition to setting it for ATM cells. The ATM interface has no configuration, but is subinterfaced for multiple connections. (Recall that this is a head-end, non-DSLAM connection.) We configure a PVC with unspecified bit rate (UBR) ATM, and, as an extra service, we configure Operation, Administration, and Maintenance (OAM) cells to the PVC. OAM provides link monitoring; if any part of the PVC fails, OAM will detect it and shut down the interface until corrected.

The following configuration also specifies AAL5SNAP, or AAL5 with SNAP headers, for the encapsulation type. So long as this matches on each side, there is no issue in most cases. For those not familiar with PVC configurations, interface ATM0.1 has a VPI (virtual path identifier) of 5 and a VCI (virtual circuit identifier) of 51.

```
!
controller T1 0
 framing esf
 linecode b8zs
 mode atm
 fdl both
 description T1 to DSL Cloud
!
interface ATM0
 description DSL Headend
 no ip address
 no ip directed-broadcast
!
```

```
interface ATM0.1 point-to-point
 description DSL link to Gryffendor
 ip address 10.1.1.25 255.255.255.252
 no ip directed-broadcast
 pvc 5/51
  ubr 1500
  oam-pvc manage
  oam retry 3 5 1
  encapsulation aal5snap
!
interface ATM0.2 point-to-point
 description DSL Link to Ravenclaw
 ip address 10.1.1.33 255.255.255.252
 no ip directed-broadcast
 pvc 4/51
  ubr 1500
  oam-pvc manage
  oam retry 3 5 1
  encapsulation aal5snap
 !
```

If there were only one PVC for this circuit, it would be acceptable to use the major interface and not a subinterface. However, if an installation *might* use more than one PVC in the future, then the use of a subinterface is recommended.

Other routers might limit various options. The Cisco 827, for example, uses a Bridge Group Virtual Interface (BVI), which is part of Integrated Routing and Bridging (IRB) services for connectivity instead of routing in most installations. This bridging solution negates layer 3 and leverages Network Address Translation (NAT) for those services that are layer 3. The configuration is not DSL-specific however, because the use of IRB is primarily used to negate the need for remote configuration. A standard router configuration file can service all end points because DHCP and NAT hide the Ethernet network, and the DSL side is assigned its address dynamically.

IRB, BVI, NAT, and DHCP in this context are beyond the scope of this chapter and of the exam. Chapter 31, "Network Address Translation (NAT) and Port Address Translation (PAT)," provides information regarding NAT, and Chapter 25, "Using Microsoft Windows 95/98/2000/XP," describes DHCP. If you are interested in learning more about the 827 router (a common remote DSL platform) and IRB/BVI, please refer to Cisco's documentation at `www.cisco.com/en/US/customer/products/hw/routers/ps380/prod_release_note09186a008007e1fe.html`.

Troubleshooting DSL

DSL is an ATM technology at its core, so troubleshooting DSL connections requires an understanding of ATM in addition to generic troubleshooting. Generic troubleshooting includes examination of the various layers, including physical connectivity, data-link connectivity, and protocol configuration.

In the following example, the DSL interface has received 1,714 frames with CRC errors, while the interface itself has reset three times. The IP address is confirmed to be correct, and the load does not appear to be problematic. Although the problem could be the ATM PVC configuration under different circumstances, in this case there is likely a line problem or an issue with the physical interface at the transmission end. Remember that ATM is a cell-based technology, and although beyond our scope here, each cell is 53 bytes long. Of this, with ATM adaptation layer 5, 48 bytes are for user data and 5 bytes of each cell are used for header information. A CRC error could occur if any one of the cells that made up a particular frame were damaged. With an average frame size of just over 100 bytes (159,780 bytes in 1,512 frames), it's apparent that the average frame is sent via three cells:

```
Router#show int atm0
ATM0 is up, line protocol is up
  Hardware is PQUICC_SAR (with Alcatel ADSL Module)
  Internet address is 10.1.1.1/24
  MTU 1500 bytes, sub MTU 1500, BW 640 Kbit, DLY 80 usec,
     reliability 40/255, txload 2/255, rxload 2/255
  Encapsulation ATM, loopback not set
  Keepalive not supported
  Encapsulation(s):AAL5, PVC mode
  10 maximum active VCs, 1 current VCCs
  VC idle disconnect time:300 seconds
  Last input 00:16:39, output 00:16:39, output hang never
  Last clearing of "show interface" counters never
  Input queue:0/75/0 (size/max/drops); Total output drops:0
  Queueing strategy:Per VC Queueing
  5 minute input rate 0 bits/sec, 0 packets/sec
  5 minute output rate 0 bits/sec, 0 packets/sec
     1512 packets input, 159780 bytes, 0 no buffer
     Received 0 broadcasts, 0 runts, 0 giants, 0 throttles
     0 input errors, 1714 CRC, 0 frame, 0 overrun, 0 ignored, 0 abort
     1426 packets output, 146282 bytes, 0 underruns
     0 output errors, 0 collisions, 3 interface resets
     0 output buffer failures, 0 output buffers swapped out
```

Summary

In this chapter, you learned that digital subscriber line (DSL) technology was developed to add functionality to the large existing copper cable plant installed for the analog phone system. The service is built around ATM technology and provides a wide variety of flavors to offer different data rates and service distances. DSL variants range in bandwidth from 144Kbps to over 50Mbps.

Unlike other WAN technologies, many DSL flavors are asymmetric; that is, they provide different bandwidths in upstream and downstream directions.

We described the configuration and troubleshooting elements of DSL, while noting that from the transport point-of-view, DSL is examined the same as ATM. We also noted that DSL sometimes uses complex bridging and routing solutions to simplify larger deployments. DSL is a consumer service in many installations, and with over 28 million installations (as of late 2003), simple, repeatable deployments are crucial. To that end, we described the primary feature of G.lite, or splitterless DSL.

Exam Essentials

Understand how DSL can fit into your remote access solutions. DSL is well suited to remote workers and small branch offices for remote connectivity. It offers many of the same bandwidths as T-1 at lower prices, and, in some cases, its asymmetric offerings are perfect for high-demand users.

Know the differences in the various flavors of DSL. The DSL service offerings are best considered in terms of bandwidth and analog voice support. G.lite is a splitterless offering that provides for analog voice without a splitter in the line. HDSL and SDSL provide symmetric bandwidth.

Be able to compare DSL to other remote access technologies. HDSL and SDSL both provide bandwidths comparable to T-1 services. This can be very important for the administrator—for example, T-1 might not be available but HDSL is, and, ironically, HDSL might be cheaper. Other xDSL services can be replacements for Frame Relay or other access methods.

Understand the configuration of DSL services. The key to configuring DSL services is to understand their relationship to ATM in the networking model. DSL commonly uses the same PVC configuration and other logical constructs.

Remote Access with Cable Modems and Virtual Private Networks

THE CCNP EXAM TOPICS COVERED IN THIS CHAPTER INCLUDE THE FOLLOWING:

- ✓ Understand cable modem technologies.
- ✓ Know how to configure cable modem technologies.
- ✓ Understand how to troubleshoot cable modem technologies.
- ✓ Understand VPN technologies including IPSec.
- ✓ Know how to configure VPN technologies.

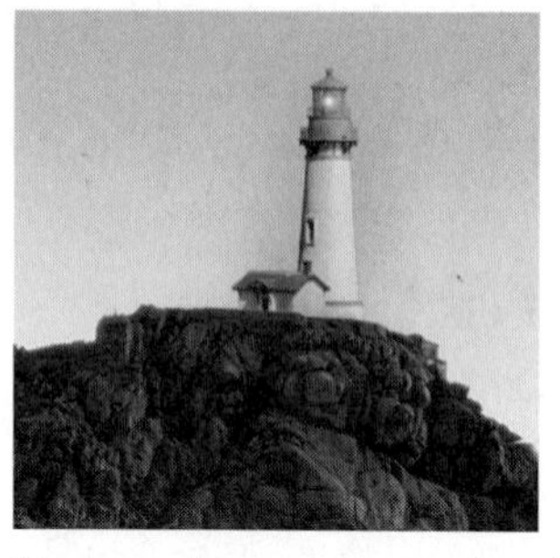

In this chapter, we discuss two increasingly important technologies in remote access: cable modems and virtual private networks (VPNs). Although Cisco has finally added these topics to the Remote Access exam, they have not attained the prominence that one might expect compared to legacy technologies such as ISDN. Cable modems, like DSL, provide high data rates at low cost, and don't suffer from the call setup and bonding issues that ISDN includes. In addition to providing an overview of cable modem and VPN technologies, this chapter also covers the configuration of IPSec, one of the most common VPN technologies.

What Is a Cable Modem?

The *cable modem* is the industry's response to DSL and other broadband network services from competitors. It provides remote access connectivity by establishing a shared data channel across the existing cable television network. In fact, it's apt to call it a channel—the bandwidth provided to customers is actually taken from one of the 6MHz channels that would normally be used for a video feed such as CNN or ESPN.

This 6MHz channel (NTSC—the North American standard from the National Television System Committee) can provide up to 40Mbps of downstream (to the user) bandwidth and 12Mbps of upstream bandwidth. This bandwidth, as noted in Chapter 27, "Remote Access with Digital Subscriber Line," is shared by all the customers within a specific area. As such, due to the normal installation and design model, in addition to bandwidth rate limiting by the provider, a typical user should expect less than 2Mbps downstream and 128Kbps to 256Kbps upstream. The typical cable modem installation is illustrated in Figure 28.1.

As shown in this figure, each home is connected to the coax (coaxial cable) that is running through the neighborhood and providing video services. At the head end, or cable service provider, this cable is connected to a hybrid fiber-coax (HFC) device that might also provide the cable modem termination system (CMTS). This device is connected to the router that links to the Internet and to the video streams (greatly simplified in this figure). The CMTS is the electronic engine that processes cable modem feeds comparable to the digital subscriber line access multiplexer (DSLAM) in DSL.

The installation at the home requires the installation of a filter to service all the televisions on the premises. An unfiltered connection is provided to the cable modem itself. Note that for customers without cable modems, the filter is typically placed in the street. In residences with cable data services, the filter can be installed anywhere between the head end and the televisions that will be using the cable signal. Many customers, as a result, never have to concern themselves with the filter, but it does complicate the installation of a cable modem, just as the splitter complicates DSL installations.

FIGURE 28.1 A cable modem installation

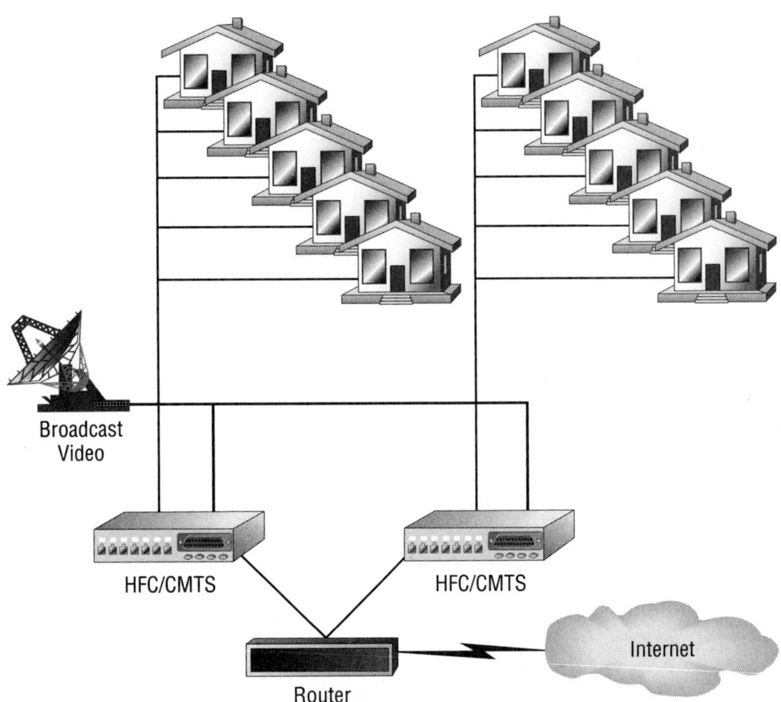

Note that cable modems have a perceived disadvantage of shared bandwidth for all users on a particular link—there are two distinct shared domains shown in Figure 28.1. As noted in Chapter 27, this is not a significant issue from a bandwidth perspective. It could be a security concern however, as data from one home is viewable from all other homes within that domain. This is addressed by the *Data Over Cable Service Interface Specification (DOCSIS)* ratified by CableLabs, a nonprofit organization composed of cable service providers in the Americas. DOCSIS is described in the following section; it provides customer data protection over the shared medium.

The biggest advantage to cable modems is their capability to provide high per-user bandwidth over long distances, often significantly greater than DSL. Although the cable is capable of providing up to 40Mbps of downstream bandwidth, the network is provisioned so that each user can obtain only a predefined rate—typically less than 2Mbps. For consumer installations, this is sufficient and leads to a very economical solution. However, the provider could easily increase the bandwidth to an individual user, although they would need to have a dedicated coax connection to attain the full capacity.

DOCSIS

The primary purpose of DOCSIS was to ensure interoperability between vendors' equipment. Different versions provide standards for security, encapsulation, management, QoS, and services. There are three versions of the DOCSIS specification, as outlined in Table 28.1.

TABLE 28.1 DOCSIS Specifications

Version	Features
DOCSIS 1.0	This was the original specification and provided for standardization between vendors.
DOCSIS 1.1	This version of DOCSIS is commonly used today and provides basic quality of service and security functions. This is very important for most users, and cable networks leverage these features to protect user traffic in transit from being intercepted. Please note that this does not protect user machines from attack; the specifications are not firewalls, but rather a switched emulation over the shared infrastructure. The specification is backward compatible. DOCSIS 1.1 adds voice and streaming services. This version also takes steps to prevent theft of service from the provider. In previous specifications, a user with cable service could remove the filter in the street and have data service for free.
DOCSIS 2.0	This new standard will provide six times the upstream capacity of DOCSIS 1.0 (three times the capacity of 1.1). The channel is increased to 6.4MHz for greater capacity and efficiency. It is also backward compatible.

DOCSIS specifies the connection between only the CMTS and the cable modem or cable modem router. The PC, network router(s), and other network elements are not involved. Readers wanting to study the DOCSIS 2.0 standard should visit `www.cisco.com/en/US/netsol/ns469/networking_solutions_event_and_seminar_home.html`, where a number of DOCSIS white papers are available.

Cisco's Cable Modem Product Line

As with the DSL product line, Cisco caters to the head end and the remote installation. At the central office, Cisco provides the uBR10012 and uBR7100/7200 series Universal Broadband routers. The uBR10012 product combines the Cisco 10000 Edge Services Router with the uBR7200 product, which can support up to 8,000 terminations.

For remote installations, the product line contains two products: the uBR905 and the uBR925. Both support VPN tunnels (IPSec) and firewall services in addition to routing, but the uBR925 adds support for voice over the cable network and a USB port.

Unlike the DSL product line, Cisco does not currently support a cable modem interface for the higher end routers, including the 1700, 2600XM, and the 3600 series. This will likely change in the future, but administrators should note that cable television is not as prevalent in business parks and commercial buildings as compared to residential settings.

Cisco Cable Manager

To help customers configure and monitor large cable modem infrastructures, Cisco has developed Cisco Cable Manager (CCM). This Solaris-based product is beyond the scope of the exam, but it provides a centralized interface for managing up to 100,000 devices, and it provides auto-topology and polling features.

Virtual Private Networks

You might be questioning the inclusion of a section on virtual private network (VPN) technologies in a chapter presenting cable modems. It is true that VPN is technology agnostic and will operate over DSL, Frame Relay, or any other transport. However, cable modems and VPNs are both covered briefly on the Remote Access exam, and neither seems to warrant a chapter on its own. In addition, many cable modem installations for business customers leverage VPN tunnels to provide connectivity.

A *virtual private network* is a logical tunnel across a physical topology. This physical layer could be the Internet, or it could be a corporate network or other private network. The tunnel need not be encrypted to be private, but this is a method of providing privacy. In reality, however, so long as the data is not visible to non-recipients, the tunnel has a certain degree of protection. As such, VPNs are commonly thought of as IPSec, L2TP (Layer 2 Tunneling Protocol), SSL-VPN, and MPLS constructions, but Frame Relay and ATM PVCs, in addition to 802.1Q and GRE (generic routing encapsulation) can also be considered VPNs. This is discussed in greater detail later in this chapter.

By far the most common VPN technology deployed today is IPSec, or IP Security Protocol. Quickly gaining momentum is an alternative technology that has been used for years for web-based security, Secure Sockets Layer (SSL).

IPSec

IPSec is a generic description of a set of protocols that establish the parameters and encryption for a tunnel between two end points, but IPSec itself provides none of these functions. The standard is defined in RFCs 2401 through 2411 and in RFC 2451; this is recommended reading for anyone supporting or installing a large-scale IPSec VPN. The elements that comprise many IPSec functions are outlined in Table 28.2.

Many configurations of IPSec have difficulties with Network Address Translation (NAT), described in Chapter 32, "Centralized Security in Remote Access Networks." A new feature—IPSec NAT Transparency—has been introduced with IOS version 12.2(13)T and should be evaluated for installations that require NAT and IPSec support.

TABLE 28.2 Components of IPSec

Protocol or Function	Description
IKE	*Internet Key Exchange* is a general term used to define how keys are exchanged and tunnels are authenticated. It is defined in RFC 2409, which is recommended reading for anyone deploying IPSec VPNs.
3DES	Triple Data Encryption Standard performs three DES hash processes with three keys in sequence to encrypt data. DES (Data Encryption Standard) performs a single hash process.
AES	Advanced Encryption Standard will likely replace DES and 3DES because the processing power required for AES is significantly lower than that for 3DES.
AH	The *Authentication Header* option ensures authenticity and data integrity, but it does not encrypt the payload—thus the name reference to "authenticating the header." It is defined in RFC 2402.
Tunnel mode	*Tunnel mode* protects the entire IP packet—including the original header—and appends a new 20-byte IP header. Tunnel mode must be used for VPN applications involving hosts behind the IPSec peers, which is the most common configuration.
Transport mode	*Transport mode* protects only the IP payload via encryption, and the original header information is left unencrypted.
ESP	*Encapsulating Security Payload* protects the data within the datagram, but does nothing to the header. It is defined in RFC 2406 and is best remembered via the term *payload* in its title.

Because IPSec is the leading VPN technology, we will spend a moment discussing the configuration of this technology; however, please note that the current exam does not include configuration in scope.

The primary functions of IPSec address four key areas of concern for most data transmissions:

- The confidential transmission of the data. This is provided by the encryption of the payload as it crosses the network and is important to prevent confidential data compromises.
- The integrity of the data. Receivers in IPSec can validate that the payload has not been altered in transmission.
- The authentication of the transmission source. IPSec receivers can authenticate the source of the packets to validate that they are from a trusted source.
- Protection from replay. The IPSec functions can support detection and rejection of packets that are replayed. This function is useful in preventing the retransmission of a packet containing a password for later authentication.

IPSec Configuration

Cisco could have made configuration of IPSec a little easier than they did, but unfortunately they didn't. This section defines a common IPSec configuration and illustrates some of the options available to the administrator, including the use of Data Encryption Standard (DES) or 3DES. The code sample in Table 28.3 is the basis for our configuration.

TABLE 28.3 Commands Used for IPSec

Command	Function
`crypto isakmp policy 10`	This command creates an IKE process on the router. You must have an IOS version that supports the IPSec feature set. The priority number can be anything from 1 to 10,000, and 1 is the highest priority. As with other elements such as route maps, the convention is to start with 10 and increment by 10 to allow for future changes. You are now in ISAKMP policy configuration command mode.
`hash md 5`	This command specifies that you will use a preshared key and the MD5 hash algorithm for packet authentication. It is possible to configure a key dynamically using RSA public key signatures, but that requires a certificate server and other infrastructure.
`group 2`	This parameter is generally set to 2 to reflect the Diffie-Hellman group number to use for key negotiation. Group 1 uses a 768-bit key exchange, and group 2 uses 1,024 bits. A complete list of the group numbers and their related parameters is available at `www.cisco.com/en/US/customer/products/hw/vpndevc/ps2286/products_user_guide_chapter09186a008015d00c.html`.
`lifetime 3600`	The `lifetime` parameter defines how long a security association will last. It is defined in seconds and can range from one minute to one day. A value of 3,600 seconds is equal to one hour. Longer lifetimes might compromise security but can reduce overhead.
`crypto isakmp key tyler address 10.1.1.1`	This configuration command defines the key to be used and the IP address of the far-end Ethernet segment that services as the termination of the tunnel. In this instance, the key is tyler and the IP address is 10.1.1.1. This key will be defined on both routers, is case-sensitive, and can be up to 128 characters long. Security can be enhanced by using longer keys with alphanumeric characters.

TABLE 28.3 Commands Used for IPSec *(continued)*

Command	Function
`crypto IPSec transform-set tunnel-A ah-md5-hmac esp-des`	This command defines the transforms that will be used. This command defines AH (MD5) and ESP (56-des), but other combinations might include specifying triple DES or LZS compression. Depending on the choices selected, the administrator can select up to three transforms. IOS will prevent incompatible values.
`crypto map map-A local-address Ethernet0`	Here we define a crypto-map called map-A. It is bound to the Ethernet 0 interface; recall that we are going to create a tunnel from one Ethernet interface to another.
`crypto map map-A 10 ipsec-isakmp`	This command enters crypto-map configuration mode with a map numbered 10. Again, this is a definable value.
`set peer 10.1.1.1`	Here we set the peer by again defining the IP address of the remote. This is for the map and not the key, but it would be nice if Cisco would simplify this relationship.
`set transform-set tunnel-A`	This command links the map to the transform set previously defined.
`match address 110`	This defines the ACL to be used in determining what traffic is encrypted. Please note that ACLs 100 through 102 are reserved for use by the DOCSIS configuration file and should not be used with cable modems.
`interface Ethernet0`	This selects the Ethernet interface.
`ip address 10.1.2.1 255.255.255.0`	This defines the local IP address of 10.1.2.1/24.
`interface cable-modem0`	This selects the cable modem interface.
`crypto map map-A`	This defines that crypto-map map-A is to be used.
`access-list 110 permit ip 10.1.2.0 0.0.0.255 10.1.1.0 0.0.0.255`	This defines access list 110, which was assigned to tunnel-A. This defines that all traffic destined for 10.1.1/24 from 10.1.2/24 should be encrypted. Remember that this uses wildcard mask rules.

That's it. Of course, a real configuration would also need routing and other parameters to be defined. The cable modem would also require an IP address. The opposing router would require a comparable configuration as well to establish the tunnel.

Other VPN Technologies

As noted in the introduction to this chapter, VPNs can be composed of any tunneling technology to varying degrees. Some other VPN technologies include those listed in Table 28.4.

TABLE 28.4 VPN Technologies

Technology	Description
Generic router encapsulation (GRE)	GRE is not really a private technology because the data is not encrypted, but it is a tunneling technology, and the data contained within is somewhat transparent to the overall network. One common use of GRE is to tunnel IPX or other non-IP traffic over an IP-only backbone.
Virtual circuit (VC)	VCs can be permanent or switched, and are found in Frame Relay and ATM. Traffic within a VC is not encrypted, but could be considered a tunnel and can be marketed as a virtual private network.
802.1Q in Q	802.1Q in Q also lacks privacy because the data is not encrypted, but, like a virtual circuit, data that is tagged in one logical VLAN is private from other VLANs. The technology for Q in Q is the same as 802.1Q itself, except for a second .Q header being added. This second header is controlled by the service provider. One advantage to this model is that the original customer tag is not changed. For those familiar with ATM, an analogy is the virtual path identifier.
L2TP	Layer 2 Tunneling Protocol is an extension to PPP, discussed in Chapter 24, "Point-to-Point Protocol." L2TP allows for the tunneling of packets independent of layer 3.
Multi-Protocol Label Switching (MPLS)	MPLS is quickly gaining as the standard service tagging model. Many service providers are converting their data networks to MPLS, which is simply a dynamic tag added to the front of the packet. Again, the data is not encrypted, but vendors are selling the service as a managed VPN. In reality, it has little functional difference when compared to other technologies, except for the significant benefit that it is transport agnostic. Most other technologies require a specific set of physical layer technologies. MPLS can also provide rapid fault detection and correction compared to other technologies.
IPSec	IP Security is a set of protocols that encrypt and authenticate the integrity of the data between two points.

TABLE 28.4 VPN Technologies *(continued)*

Technology	Description
SSL	Secure Sockets Layer is a popular encryption technology used for many HTTP business transactions (HTTPS). However, the protocol is not limited to HTTP/HTTPS and is now used for remote control and other remote access functions, and the protocol can be used for other services. The most significant advantage of SSL is that the client requires no preconfiguration and the network is transparent to the entire flow. Each end station is responsible for encryption and decryption, and only the payload is protected.
Frame Relay and ATM	These PVC-based technologies can create private paths across the public network. Although not typically thought of in VPN concepts, they are rightfully included in this list.

Summary

This chapter examined cable modem technology and presented VPN services, including IPSec. Cable modems offer the administrator an alternative low-cost technology for remote access, and they can provide longer-range connections than DSL. Although cable modems use a shared medium, the overall performance is comparable to the switched DSL in real-world deployments. The key to cable modem services is DOCSIS and the incorporated security and other services that this standard provides.

Most remote access users will map IPSec tunnels over the cable modem network to allow for corporate access. Although not the only VPN technology, IPSec is currently the most popular and provides for encrypted tunneling of IP data between locations. We also briefly noted a number of other tunneling technologies that provide solutions for remote access.

Exam Essentials

Understand how cable modems can be used as part of a remote access solution. Be able to compare cable modem technologies to other remote access methods, including DSL. Also understand the internal characteristics of cable modem, including DOCSIS.

Understand VPN technologies such as IPSec. Know the differences in various VPN technologies, including the modes of IPSec and its encryption benefits.

Know how to configure cable modems and IPSec. Understand the protocols and relationships between IPSec components, including AH, ESP, and tunnel and transport mode. Knowing how to configure IPSec can help this, but is not required for the exam.

Frame Relay

THE CCNP EXAM TOPICS COVERED IN THIS CHAPTER INCLUDE THE FOLLOWING:

✓ Describe how different WAN technologies can be used to provide remote access to a network, including asynchronous dial-in, Frame Relay, ISDN, cable modem, and DSL.

✓ Describe traffic control methods used to manage traffic flow on WAN links.

✓ Explain the operation of remote network access control methods.

✓ Identify PPP components, and explain the use of PPP as an access and encapsulation method.

✓ Configure Frame Relay operation and traffic control on WAN links.

✓ Design a Cisco Frame Relay infrastructure to provide access between remote network components.

✓ Troubleshoot nonfunctional remote access systems.

The use of *packet-switching* protocols has become the most popular method for moving traffic across a wide area network (WAN). One particular packet-switching protocol—Frame Relay—has become the dominant player in the packet-switching market. Other methods of passing data between routers across the WAN include dedicated lines, time division multiplexing (TDM), ATM, ISDN, DSL, and others.

Because DSL is so much cheaper and faster than Frame Relay, it could eventually replace Frame Relay and ISDN as the dominant player in the WAN markets. As network sizes increase, you should pay particular attention to how DSL is playing a larger role in network deployment. However, DSL presently has too many distance limitations to completely replace Frame Relay anytime soon.

Understanding the theory and function of Frame Relay is important for numerous reasons. Not only is it still tested on Cisco's Remote Access exam, but when you get a Cisco-related job, you will most likely see quite a few networks that depend on Frame Relay. Mastery of the information covered in this chapter will enable you to gain an in-depth understanding of how and why you would implement Frame Relay on your internetwork. This chapter goes over what Frame Relay is, the components of Frame Relay, Frame Relay configuration, and how to verify that Frame Relay is running properly.

Understanding Frame Relay

Before we dive right into Frame Relay we need to have a better understanding of what Frame Relay is, how it is used, and how it came about.

What Is Frame Relay?

Frame Relay is a telecommunications service designed for cost-efficient data transmission across a WAN. Frame Relay puts data in a variable-size unit called a *frame* and leaves any necessary error correction up to the end points. This provides for a high-speed, low-overhead, efficient network.

Frame Relay is a layer 2 (Data Link layer) connection-oriented protocol that creates virtual circuits (VCs)—usually permanent virtual circuits (PVCs)—between two end devices such as routers, through a Frame Relay network. A Frame Relay *bearer service* was defined as a network service within the framework of ISDN. It was designed to be more efficient and faster than X.25. The major difference between Frame Relay and traditional ISDN is that in Frame Relay, the control information needed to keep the link synchronized is not in a separate channel as it is in ISDN, but instead is included with the data. This single stream of data provides for flow control, congestion control, and frame routing. Frame Relay is a form of packet switching, whereas ISDN is still considered circuit switching.

You should understand that the error and congestion control works only at the Data Link layer and that Frame Relay also relies on upper layer protocols and applications for error correction.

A Brief History of Frame Relay

Currently, Frame Relay is the most prevalent type of packet switching used in North America; however, Frame Relay's origin is very humble. Initially, Frame Relay was not even a standard unto itself; instead, it was an extension of the Integrated Services Digital Network (ISDN) standard. The International Telecommunications Union-Telecommunications, or ITU-T, (formerly known as the *Comité Consultatif International de Téléphonique et Télégraphique*, or CCITT) was the first to define the Frame Relay standard.

Many companies that saw the value of this technology quickly adopted the ITU-T standard for Frame Relay. After these companies showed interest, ITU-T and other organizations proceeded to develop the standard, but very slowly. Several corporations saw a need for a more rapid development and implementation of a Frame Relay standard. Four companies—Digital Equipment Corporation (DEC), Northern Telecom (Nortel), Cisco, and StrataCom—bound together to form the *Group of Four*. This group began developing Frame Relay technology more quickly, which enabled Frame Relay to work on disparate devices. In September 1990, the Group of Four published *Frame Relay Specifications with Extensions*. This group eventually became what is currently known as the *Frame Relay Forum*.

Frame Relay Virtual Circuits

As mentioned earlier, Frame Relay is a layer 2 (Data Link layer) connection-oriented protocol. After a connection has been established, end devices can transmit data across the network. This layer 2 connection across the packet-switched network is called a *virtual circuit*.

The end devices (in this case, routers) will act as data terminal equipment (DTE), and the Frame Relay switch will be the data communications equipment (DCE). The difference between the two is that the DCE device will most likely be responsible for the clocking of the line and also initiates LMI messages, which we will discuss later in this chapter.

Two quick terms you will encounter later: *ingress* refers to Frame Relay frames from an access device toward the Frame Relay network, and *egress* refers to Frame Relay frames leaving a Frame Relay network toward the destination device.

From the point-of-view of the router, the virtual circuit is somewhat transparent. This means that the router sees the virtual circuit, but only up to the Frame Relay switch, which is where the term *locally significant* originates with regard to the DLCI. In other words, the router speaks LMI and understands what a DLCI is. This isn't all that transparent. The transparency comes in when you consider that the router uses the DLCI like a MAC address for the remote router to bind the virtual circuit to the protocol address. The previous statement, however, is not a pure Frame Relay function. In pure Frame Relay terms, the router still has to know how to recognize the existence of the ingress Frame Relay switch. Even though the circuit might traverse many switches en route to its destination, the router simply sees its connection to the local Frame Relay switch, which again is part of the VC.

Figure 29.1 shows how routers see the Frame Relay network. In the figure, notice that Frame Relay is configured between the routers and the switching office.

FIGURE 29.1 Frame Relay operation

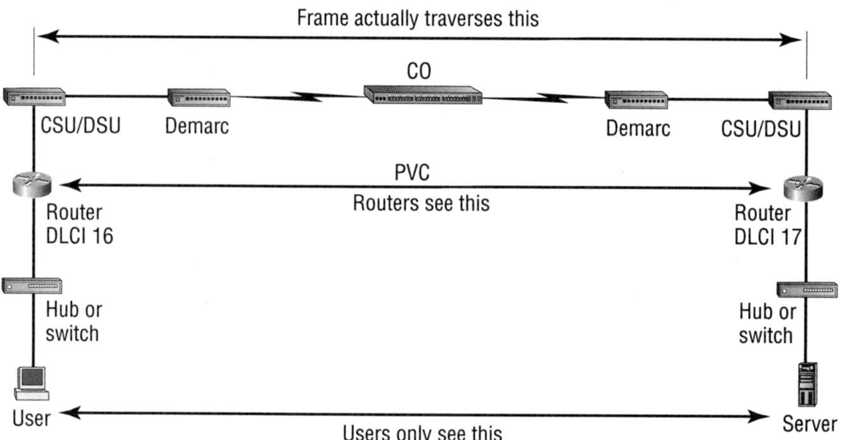

There are two ways for Frame Relay to establish this connectivity. Either you can set up a circuit that is enabled only when needed by using a switched virtual circuit, or you can set up a dedicated circuit between the local router and remote router by using a permanent virtual circuit (PVC). Each of these is discussed in more detail next.

Switched Virtual Circuits

Switched virtual circuits (SVCs) provide an economical way to connect to a Frame Relay network. An SVC is a type of circuit that is brought up only when there is data to send. These circuits provide temporary connectivity to the network on an as-needed basis. Switched virtual circuits are used with many technologies—for example, a standard telephone call.

It is rare to find a Frame Relay SVC connection, and indeed, you might never see one. Typically, PVCs are the only connections used with Frame Relay, although Cisco routers do support Frame Relay with SVCs.

Because they are rarely used, SVCs are not covered further in this book and are not on the Remote Access exam.

Permanent Virtual Circuits

Permanent virtual circuits (PVCs) are dedicated virtual paths through the Frame Relay network that are up and running 100 percent of the time (well, at least in theory!). Unlike an SVC, a PVC does not require the call establishment and call teardown phases. However, when the circuit initially comes up, some parameter negotiations do pass over the wire; these communications should occur only when the dedicated circuit goes down.

The two phases for PVCs are as follows:

Data exchange Data is transmitted between two devices, and each device can transmit data as needed because it doesn't need to wait for a call to be established to do so. The data exchange can happen at any time because the virtual connection is permanent and always available.

Idle The connection is still active, but data is not being transmitted. The idle time can be indefinite: the circuits will not time out. The idle time keeps the VC up and keeps the line from timing out when no data is present. This is done by the transmission of idle frames, the sole purpose of which is to keep line synchronization in the absence of data.

PVCs have gained in popularity as the price for dedicated lines has decreased. They are the types of links that we will configure later in this chapter.

Data Link Connection Identifier (DLCI)

Frame Relay provides statistical time division multiplexing (Stat-TDM). Time division multiplexing (TDM) is like going to Disneyland. It's true. Remember how you have to stand in line to get into Space Mountain? Well, after you get to the loading area, you're placed in a section with rails that separate you from the other passengers. You can then get into only the one car that is in front of you and only when it is empty. Think of the holding area as the interface buffers of a router; the cars are the time slots on the circuit. When a time slot drives up, you can get in, but not before that, and not if someone is already in that slot.

Now Stat-TDM is an improvement over straight TDM. Stat-TDM enables you to jump into a different line if it is not in use and to get into any car. This is a first-come, first-served technology. Stat-TDM is used with Frame Relay to allow multiple logical data connections (virtual circuits) over a single physical link. Basically, these circuits give time slots to first-come, first-served and priority-based frames over the physical link. Going back to our analogy, you can think of Frame Relay as the capability to send multiple cars through space on one train, each car holding a different person.

So, how is each person (data) identified in the car (time slot)? How does the frame switch know where to send each frame? The answer to this is a *data link connection identifier (DLCI)*. Because Frame Relay is based on virtual circuits instead of physical ones, DLCIs are used to identify a virtual circuit and tie it to a physical circuit. This means each frame can be identified as it traverses the Frame Relay switch and is then sent to the routers at the remote ends.

DLCIs are considered only locally significant, which means that they see the entire virtual circuit but only up to the point of the Frame Relay switch. The provider is responsible for assigning DLCIs and their significance to the network.

DLCIs identify the logical virtual circuit between the customer premises equipment (CPE) and the Frame Relay switch. The switch then maps the DLCIs between each pair of routers in order to create the PVC. The Frame Relay switch keeps a mapping table of DLCI numbers to outgoing ports; it uses this table to forward frames out ports on the switch. (More information about mapping follows in the next section, "DLCI Mapping.")

When configuring your Cisco router to participate in a Frame Relay network, you must configure a DLCI number for each connection. The Frame Relay provider supplies the DLCI numbers for your router. If a DLCI is not defined on the link, the switch will discard the frame.

Figure 29.2 shows an example of how DLCIs are assigned to offices in Chicago and Miami. The Chicago office will communicate through the Frame Relay switch to Miami by using DLCI 17. Miami will communicate to Chicago by using DLCI 16. Remember that the valid range of DLCIs is from 16 to 991.

FIGURE 29.2 Frame Relay PVC configuration

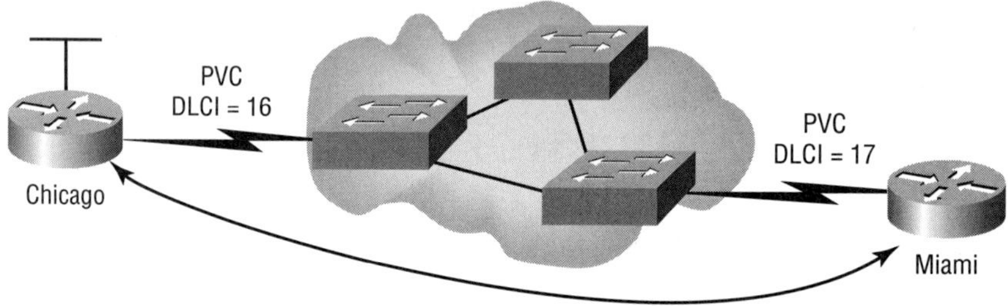

Some providers assign a DLCI in such a way that it appears that the DLCI is globally significant. For example, all circuits that terminate in Miami could be assigned the local DLCI 17 at each site. But remember that even though all of these DLCIs have the same number, they are not the same because DLCIs are typically only locally significant.

DCLI Mapping

There needs to be a way to link the layer 2 identifiers (DLCI) to layer 3 (Network layer) addresses. *Mapping* provides a mechanism to link one or more network addresses to a DLCI. Remember that

Frame Relay works only at the Data Link layer (layer 2 of the OSI model) and does not understand IP addressing. In fact, to communicate via IP (because it could just as easily be IPX and AppleTalk instead of IP), you need to convert the destination IP address to a destination DLCI (PVC) number. The frame switch uses only DLCI numbers to communicate, not IP addresses.

Mappings can be done either statically by an administrator or dynamically via the router. If you are mapping a static Network layer address to a DLCI number, you use the `frame-relay map` command. It is necessary to create static mappings when the remote router does not support dynamic addressing or when you're using OSPF in some network configurations. It's also necessary even if you want to control broadcasts over your Frame Relay network.

To understand how to use static mappings, look at Figure 29.3. Figure 29.3 shows a corporate office in Chicago connected to two other sites—one in Miami and one in New York. The IP address of the serial interface in New York is 172.16.1.2/24, and the IP address of the Miami serial interface is 172.16.1.3/24. It's important to note that the Miami location is a Cisco router, and the New York location is a non-Cisco router. A static mapping would have to be used for different Frame Relay encapsulation methods to run under the same physical serial interface, unless all routers used an open encapsulation type for interoperability, resulting in the ability to use dynamic mapping.

FIGURE 29.3 Configuring Frame Relay static mappings

The following router output shows an example of how you would create static Frame Relay mappings on the Chicago router:

```
Router(config)#interface serial 0
Router(config-if)#ip address 172.16.1.1 255.255.255.248
Router(config-if)#frame-relay map ip 172.16.1.2 20 broadcast ietf
Router(config-if)#frame-relay map ip 172.16.1.3 16 broadcast
Router(config-if)#exit
```

The `frame-relay map` command maps the IP address of the remote location to a specific PVC or DLCI. The first map statement tells the Chicago router that if it has an IP packet with a destination IP address of 172.16.1.2, it should use PVC 20 to get there. Also, because the New York office is not a Cisco router (can you imagine that?), it should use the standard Internet Engineering Task Force (IETF) encapsulation method. We'll talk about encapsulation methods used with Frame Relay in a minute.

Because Miami is a Cisco router, no specification of encapsulation is necessary because Cisco is the default encapsulation method. The broadcast parameter at the end of each line specifies that broadcasts should be forwarded over the PVC because they are not forwarded by default. The `frame-relay map` command supports many Network layer protocols, including IP, Connectionless Network Services (CLNS), Digital Equipment Corporation's Networking architecture (DECnet), Xerox Network Services (XNS), and Virtual Integrated Network Service (VINES).

Dynamic addressing is turned on by default. It automatically maps Network layer addresses to DLCI addresses rather well. *Inverse ARP (IARP)* is used to automatically map a DLCI to a network address (IP, IPX, and so on) without any user configuration. It provides Network layer-to-DCLI-number translation and creates an entry in the DLCI mapping table. This table is used by the router to correctly route outgoing traffic. No map configuration is necessary for IARP to work.

Frame Relay Local Management Interface (LMI)

In 1990, the Group of Four developed extensions to the Frame Relay standard to help ease the management and configuration burden. One of these extensions was the *Local Management Interface (LMI)*. LMI provides for virtual circuit status messages and multicasting.

Cisco routers support three versions of the LMI standard: Cisco, ANSI, and ITU-T (Q.933a). LMI autosense, the automatic detection of the LMI type, was introduced in IOS version 11.2. LMI autosense determines the LMI type by rapidly trying each of them in order: ANSI, ITU-T (Q.933a), and then Cisco. If it cannot determine the LMI type within 60 seconds, it will terminate the autosense process and revert to the Cisco LMI type.

After LMI is established between the router and the switch, the next stage is DLCI determination and IARP. The router will query the switch, asking what the DLCI(s) is/are for this circuit. The router will configure itself with that DLCI(s) and query the switch to determine the status of the circuit.

This query is the first stage of discovery. The query that is sent includes the local router's network information. The remote router will record the network information and reply in kind. The local router will map the DLCI it learned from static or dynamic addressing to other network addresses it discovered from queries.

When an IARP is made, the router updates its map table with one of three possible LMI connection states:

Active The connection is active, and the routers can exchange data through the PVC.

Inactive The local connection to the Frame Relay switch is working, but the remote end of the PVC is not communicating to the Frame Relay switch.

Deleted No LMI keepalive information from the switch to the router is being received for this PVC. This could be because no LMI is actually being exchanged or because the DLCI is not configured on the ingress switch.

Figure 29.4 shows that the Chicago office PVC to Miami is deleted because the Miami office is not receiving keepalives from the Frame Relay switch. Neither this inactive state nor this deleted state affect the other connections (PVCs) that Chicago might have to other locations.

FIGURE 29.4 LMI connection states

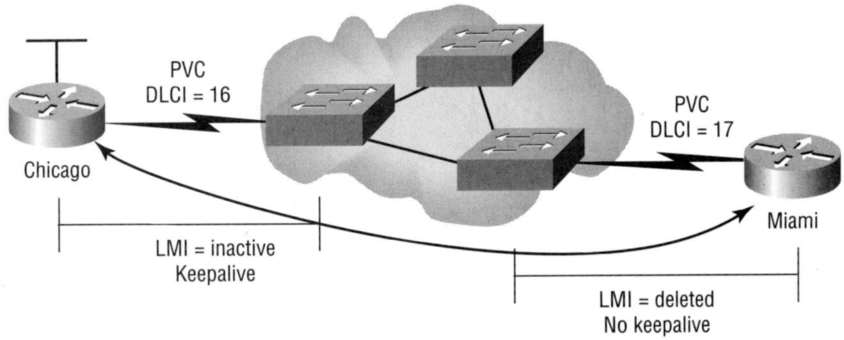

Configuring Frame Relay

The first step in configuring Frame Relay is to select the interface and then enable the Frame Relay encapsulation on the serial interface. You do this with the `encapsulation frame-relay` command. As you will notice in the following router configuration commands, there are two options: `cisco` and `ietf`.

```
Router#config t
Router(config)#interface serial 0
Router(config-if)#encapsulation frame-relay [cisco or ietf]
```

Cisco is the default encapsulation, which means that you have another Cisco router on the remote end with which your router will communicate. You will use the IETF encapsulation when communicating with a remote router that is not a Cisco device.

After you configure the encapsulation to the serial interface, you then need to add the Network layer address, DLCI number, and LMI type. Cisco's capability to autosense the LMI type has greatly simplified configuration. The following router configuration shows the process of specifying the IP address and DLCI number, but not the LMI type because it is automatically detected:

```
Router(config-if)#ip address 172.16.10.1 255.255.255.0
Router(config-if)#frame-relay interface-dlci 16
Router(config-if)#no shutdown
```

Frame Relay Congestion Control

Frame Relay is optimized for speed and contains little error control. Frame Relay will discard errored frames and will not attempt to recover from the error either through retransmission or repair. Ideally, users can send as much data as they want across the network without interference. However, because user requests for bandwidth often outstrip the network's capability to provide bandwidth, a mechanism is needed to handle congestion in the frame switch.

In this section, you will learn about the factors that affect network performance, as well as methods for handling Frame Relay congestion. The two primary methods of congestion handling use Frame Relay switches and routers.

Factors Affecting Performance

Network performance at the router level is affected by three primary factors:

- Access rate
- Committed information rate (CIR)
- Bursting

Each of these has an effect on Frame Relay.

Access Rate

Access rate is the maximum speed at which data can be transferred to the Frame Relay network. This number denotes the actual line speed of the connection to the provider. In a dedicated circuit, you would consider this the actual data rate. However, in a Frame Relay network, this is considered the maximum data rate.

Committed Information Rate (CIR)

The committed information rate (CIR) is the rate at which the provider guarantees to deliver network traffic. The CIR is always less than or equal to the access rate. The CIR is advertised in Kbps and is actually averaged over a specified time period, referred to as *committed rate measurement interval (Tc)*. This is what the cost of the Frame Relay connection is normally based upon.

Bursting

Bursting is one of the features that has made Frame Relay so popular. Bursting enables a user to transmit data faster than the CIR for a short period of time. Figure 29.5 shows the difference between the CIR and the access rate and how the burst traffic rate can increase beyond the CIR. The network controls this bursting capability, and it usually does not result in any additional fees on the user. There is a catch, though. Some burst traffic has the *Discard Eligibility (DE) bit* turned on, indicating excess traffic above CIR. If a Frame Relay switch becomes congested, traffic with the DE bit set (excess burst traffic) is the first to be dropped.

FIGURE 29.5 Frame Relay rates

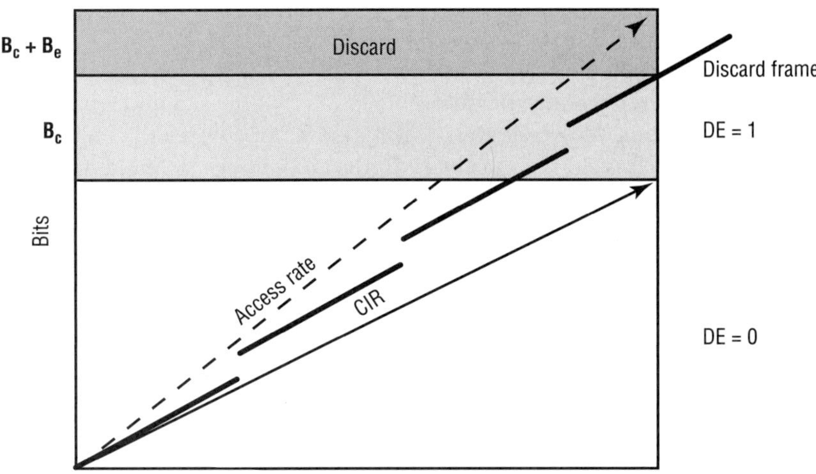

In Figure 29.5, you will see the following symbols: B_c, B_e, and T_c. Committed burst size (B_c) and excess burst size (B_e) are the two types of burst sizes. Each of these sizes is measured over the committed rate measurement interval (T_c). B_c is the maximum amount of data that the network can guarantee will be delivered during the time T_c. B_e is the amount of traffic by which the user can exceed the committed burst size.

For example, take a user who buys a Frame Relay circuit with the following characteristics:

- 1,544Kbps access rate
- 256Kbps committed information rate
- Four-second committed time interval

The user is guaranteed a CIR of 256Kbps over a four-second period. The user could transmit 256Kbps for four seconds, and the network would ensure delivery. The user could alternately send 1,024Kbps for one second, representing the committed burst. However, for the remaining three seconds, there would be no guarantee of delivery for the excess burst traffic.

Congestion Handling by Frame Relay Switches

A Frame Relay switch has a simple job: It forwards all the data that it can. If there is more data than bandwidth, the switch will first drop the data with the DE bit set and will then drop committed data if needed. In addition, the Frame Relay switch will also send out messages that congestion is occurring.

Backward explicit congestion notification (BECN) and *forward explicit congestion notification (FECN)* are the primary notification mechanisms used for handling congestion on the Frame Relay switching internetwork. BECNs and FECNs both send notices that congestion is occurring. A BECN is transmitted in the direction from which the traffic came, and an FECN is transmitted in the direction in which the traffic is going.

Under normal circumstances, only Frame Relay switches send BECN and FECN messages.

The end devices receive these notifications indicating that they should reduce the amount of traffic that they are sending. A Frame Relay switch does not enforce the reduction; it simply notifies the end devices. It is the responsibility of the end devices to reduce the traffic.

The congestion mechanisms are important to understand because congestion occurs frequently on Frame Relay networks. As providers attempt to maximize the use of their lines, they sell more bandwidth than they can actually provide. This is called *oversubscription*. Oversubscription is a growing trend, so you must be aware of the implications and effects of the resulting congestion.

Some providers will attempt to sell you a zero CIR. Although inexpensive, you have no guarantee that mission-critical data (or any data, for that matter!) will get through.

Congestion Handling by Routers

The router can also play a part in determining which traffic is more or less important on the Frame Relay network. The Discard Eligibility list (`frame-relay de-list` global command) and Discard Eligibility group (`frame-relay de-group` interface command) give the router the capability to set the Discard Eligibility bit on a frame.

Consider a company that notices an increased number of dropped frames on the Frame Relay network. They determine that the primary cause is an increase in the amount of AppleTalk traffic across the Frame Relay network. The additional traffic has impaired the performance of mission-critical traffic.

To have the router turn on the DE bit for AppleTalk traffic, thereby dropping the noncritical AppleTalk traffic before any other traffic, use the `frame-relay de-list` command. Here is an example of how to configure a router to do this:

```
RouterA#config t
RouterA(config)#frame-relay de-list 1 protocol appletalk
RouterA(config)#interface serial0
RouterA(config-if)#frame-relay de-group 1 100
```

In this example, the `frame-relay de-list` command uses a list number of 1 and a protocol of AppleTalk. The list number of 1 is then applied to the interface connected to the Frame Relay network with the `frame-relay de-group` command for a specified DLCI, in this case 100.

You could also use an AppleTalk access list (600–699) to define which AppleTalk traffic is set with the DE bit.

The modified router configuration looks like this:

```
RouterA#show running-config
Building configuration...

Current configuration:
!
version 11.2
!
hostname RouterA
!
appletalk routing
frame-relay de-list 1 protocol appletalk
!
interface Serial0
 ip address 192.168.1.1 255.255.255.0
 encapsulation frame-relay
 appletalk address 8.202
 appletalk zone Sybex
 frame-relay de-group 1 100
 frame-relay map appletalk 8.201 100 broadcast
 frame-relay map ip 192.168.1.2 100 broadcast
!
end
RouterA#
```

The Frame Relay DE list will match AppleTalk frames. The `frame-relay de-group` command binds the DE list to the interface. In the event of congestion, these two packet types are much more likely to be dropped than mission-critical traffic. The 100 at the end of the `frame-relay de-group` command specifies to use the list on DLCI 100.

Point-to-Point and Multipoint Interfaces

At times, it is useful to have a multipoint network, such as Frame Relay, behave as if each connection were a point-to-point link. The network example in Figure 29.6 has two connections from one location (multipoint); this type of setup can lead to network problems if not thoroughly understood. This multipoint configuration experiences problems primarily because of the way it handles routing updates. In distance-vector routing protocols, there is a mechanism known as *split horizon*. Split horizon states that it is never advantageous to send routing information back out on the interface through which that information was learned. Or, simply put, "Don't tell me what I told you." This is used to stop possible routing loop problems. Consider the split-horizon implication of Figure 29.6.

FIGURE 29.6 Split-horizon issues with Frame Relay

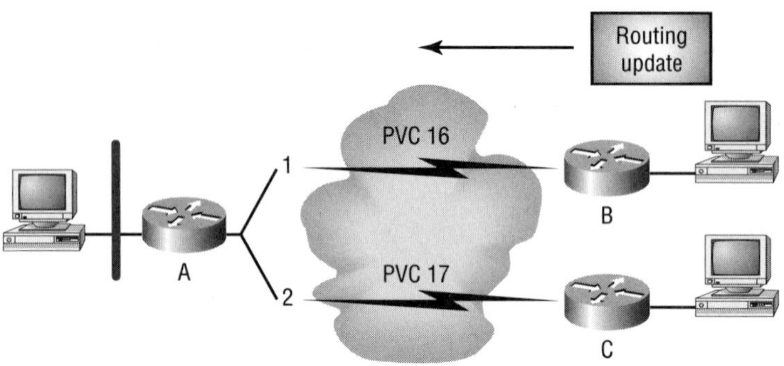

In this figure, Router B sends a routing update to Router A, telling it about its directly connected networks. Router A receives the routing information on its serial 0 interface and modifies its routing table. Router A does not send the routing information back out serial 0 because of split horizon. Because the routing information cannot be sent back out serial 0, Router C never learns the networks off Router B. The networks are unreachable from Router C because Router C has not heard of Router B's directly connected networks.

The problem in Figure 29.6 is that there is only one physical interface and there are two virtual circuits. The solution is to create a logical interface for each circuit, which solves the split horizon issues. A *subinterface* is a logical interface within the router that is mapped to a particular DLCI. When you set up subinterfaces, the interface previously configured for multipoint will now appear as two point-to-point interfaces to the router. This would change the previous example, as shown in Figure 29.7.

In this figure, Router A learns of Router B's networks on the Serial 0.1 subinterface. Without violating the split-horizon rule, Router A can send all the network information out on subinterface Serial 0.2 to Router C.

To configure a subinterface on an interface, use the `interface` *`type`*`.subinterface-number [point-to-point | multipoint]` command. For illustration purposes, configure Router A with a subinterface. (The router commands are shown next.) Both types of subinterfaces that can be configured appear in this example: point-to-point and multipoint. Point-to-point is used when each PVC is a separate subnet. Multipoint is used when all PVCs use the same subnet.

FIGURE 29.7 Split-horizon issues with subinterfaces

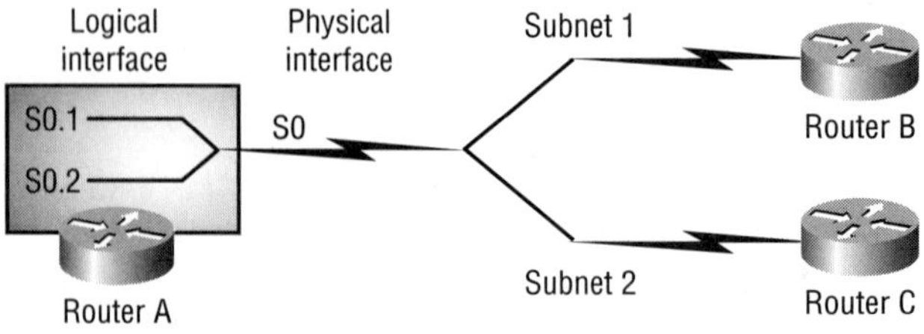

Also notice in the following configuration that you can use any subinterface number, but for administration purposes the DLCI number can be used. The subinterface number is only locally significant:

```
RouterA(config)#interface serial0.?
  <0-4294967295>  Serial interface number
RouterA(config)#interface serial0.16 ?
  multipoint      Treat as a multipoint link
  point-to-point  Treat as a point-to-point link
RouterA(config)#interface serial0.16 point-to-point
RouterA(config-subif)#ip address 192.168.1.1 255.255.255.0
RouterA(config-subif)#frame-relay interface-dlci 16
RouterA(config-subif)#exit
RouterA(config)#interface serial0.17 multipoint
RouterA(config-subif)#ip address 192.168.2.2 255.255.255.0
RouterA(config-subif)#frame-relay map ip 192.168.2.1 17 broadcast
```

The configuration of Router A will now look like this:

```
RouterA#show running-config
Building configuration...
Current configuration:
!
version 11.3
!
hostname RouterA
!
interface Serial0
 no ip address
 encapsulation frame-relay
!
interface Serial0.16 point-to-point
 ip address 192.168.1.1 255.255.255.0
 frame-relay interface-dlci 16
!
interface Serial0.17 multipoint
 ip address 192.168.2.2 255.255.255.0
 frame-relay map ip 192.168.2.1 17 broadcast
!
end
RouterA#
```

This configuration specifies which DLCI is associated with which subinterface. This is necessary because the router has no way of determining which particular DLCI should be associated with which subinterface.

Many people find the point-to-point subinterface configuration easier and less prone to routing errors than a physical multipoint configuration.

Verifying Frame Relay

It is just as important to be able to verify Frame Relay as it is to be able to understand how to configure it. In this section, you will learn about the various commands used to verify Frame Relay. These include the following:

- `show interface`
- `show frame-relay pvc`
- `show frame-relay map`
- `clear frame-relay-inarp`
- `show frame-relay lmi`
- `debug frame-relay lmi`

The *show interface* Command

The `show interface` command can be used with interface parameters, for example, **`show interface serial 0`**. This provides information pertaining to just serial 0. By itself, the `show interface` command provides information about all interfaces on the router.

The `show interface` command displays information regarding the encapsulation, layer 1 and layer 2 status, and the LMI DLCI. In the following code, the **`show interface serial 0`** command is used. Notice the encapsulation is Frame Relay. The LMI information is shown as well.

```
Router#show interface serial0
Serial0 is up, line protocol is up
  Hardware is HD64570
  MTU 1500 bytes, BW 1544 Kbit,DLY 20000 usec,rely 255/255,load 1/255
  Encapsulation FRAME-RELAY,loopback not set,keepalive set(10 sec)
  LMI enq sent  0, LMI stat recvd 0, LMI upd recvd 0, DTE LMI down
  LMI enq recvd 0, LMI stat sent  0, LMI upd sent  0
  LMI DLCI 1023  LMI type is CISCO  frame relay DTE
  FR SVC disabled, LAPF state down
  Broadcast queue 0/64, broadcasts sent/dropped 0/0, interface broadcasts 0
  Last input never, output never, output hang never
```

```
  Last clearing of "show interface" counters never
  Queueing strategy: fifo
  Output queue 0/40, 0 drops; input queue 0/75, 0 drops
  5 minute input rate 0 bits/sec, 0 packets/sec
  5 minute output rate 0 bits/sec, 0 packets/sec
     0 packets input, 0 bytes, 0 no buffer
     Received 0 broadcasts, 0 runts, 0 giants, 0 throttles
     0 input errors, 0 CRC, 0 frame, 0 overrun, 0 ignored, 0 abort
     0 packets output, 0 bytes, 0 underruns
     0 output errors, 0 collisions, 19 interface resets
     0 output buffer failures, 0 output buffers swapped out
     0 carrier transitions
     DCD=down  DSR=down  DTR=down  RTS=down  CTS=down
Router#
```

Notice that the LMI counter information is shown, as well as the LMI type, which is Cisco by default. As you can see, this output shows both errors for the interface and the time that the interface counters were last cleared.

The *show frame-relay pvc* Command

The `show frame-relay pvc` command displays the status of each configured connection as well as traffic statistics. As you'll notice in the following router output, if you type the `show frame-relay pvc` command, you'll see all the PVCs that are configured on your router and their status. You can also use a specific PVC number at the end of the command to see only that particular PVC information:

```
Router_A#show frame-relay pvc

PVC Statistics for interface Serial0 (Frame Relay DTE)

DLCI = 160, DLCI USAGE = LOCAL, PVC STATUS = ACTIVE, INTERFACE = Serial0

  input pkts 7      output pkts 13        in bytes 2252
  out bytes 1886    dropped pkts 0        in FECN pkts 0
  in BECN pkts 0    out FECN pkts 0       out BECN pkts 0
  in DE pkts 0      out DE pkts 0
  out bcast pkts 8 out bcast bytes 1366
  pvc create time 00:06:54, last time pvc status changed 00:03:17

DLCI = 17, DLCI USAGE = LOCAL, PVC STATUS = ACTIVE, INTERFACE = Serial0

  input pkts 1      output pkts 7         in bytes 30
```

```
  out bytes 832     dropped pkts 0          in FECN pkts 0
  in BECN pkts 0    out FECN pkts 0         out BECN pkts 0
  in DE pkts 0      out DE pkts 0
  out bcast pkts 7 out bcast bytes 832
  pvc create time 00:01:59, last time pvc status changed 00:00:49
Router_A#
```

As you can see, the `show frame-relay pvc` command also shows you the number of BECN and FECN packets received on the router. Please note that the BECN and FECN statistics are per PVC, not across the entire router.

The *show frame-relay map* Command

You can see the current map entries and information about the connections by using the `show frame-relay map` command. This command shows the Network-layer-to-DLCI mappings table in the router. An example output of this command is given here:

```
Router_A#show frame-relay map
Serial0 (up): ip 172.16.1.2 dlci 500(0x64,0x1840), dynamic,
              broadcast, status defined, active
Router_A#
```

LMI used IARP to determine the address of the remote router and created this dynamic mapping.

If you want to clear the Network layer-to-DLCI mappings on a router, you can use the command `clear frame-relay-inarp`, which clears dynamically created maps on the router.

The *show frame-relay lmi* Command

The `show frame-relay lmi` command shows you the LMI statistics for an interface, as in the following example:

```
Router#show frame lmi
LMI Statistics for interface Serial0 (Frame Relay DTE) LMI TYPE = CISCO
  Invalid Unnumbered info 0           Invalid Prot Disc 0
  Invalid dummy Call Ref 0            Invalid Msg Type 0
  Invalid Status Message 0            Invalid Lock Shift 0
  Invalid Information ID 0            Invalid Report IE Len 0
  Invalid Report Request 0            Invalid Keep IE Len 0
  Num Status Enq. Sent 109087         Num Status msgs Rcvd 109087
  Num Update Status Rcvd 0            Num Status Timeouts 0
Router#
```

The important statistics to notice are the number of inquiries sent and received. This indicates the number of LMI status messages sent by the DTE device. The DCE sends a status message in return. Noticing this statistic enables you to see whether data is passing between the two devices.

The *debug frame-relay lmi* Command

The `debug frame-relay lmi` command is used to help you troubleshoot and verify Frame Relay connections. As you'll see in the router output shown next, the `out` parameter is an LMI status inquiry sent out from the router, and the `(in)` parameter is a reply from the Frame Relay switch:

```
Router#debug frame-relay lmi
Serial0(in): Status, myseq 128
RT IE 1, length 1, type 0
KA IE 3, length 2, yourseq 128, myseq 128
PVC IE 0x7, length 0x6, dlci 16, status 0x2, bw 0
Serial0(out): StEnq, myseq 128, yourseen 214, DTE up
datagramstart = 0x1959DF4, datagramsize = 13
FR encap = 0xFCF10309
00 75 01 01 01 03 02 C6 E5

Serial0(in): Status, myseq 129
RT IE 1, length 1, type 1
KA IE 3, length 2, yourseq 129, myseq 129
Serial0(out): StEnq, myseq 130, yourseen 129, DTE up
datagramstart = 0x1959DF4, datagramsize = 13
FR encap = 0xFCF10309
00 74 01 01 01 03 02 C9 E3
```

The `type 1` is an LMI keepalive from the router to the Frame Relay switch every 10 seconds. This tells the router that the switch is still active and vice versa. The `type 0` is an IARP exchanged between routers every 60 seconds. Now notice that when the type is 0, you have a full status message on your hands. When the type is 1, it is the standard status message, which is the keepalive mentioned earlier (sometimes called the heartbeat).

Remember that the DLCI is known. There is no IP address in this output. Therefore, this would be a poor excuse for an InARP reply (notice the *in* designation, corresponding to a reply). Furthermore, Status and StEnq messages go between the DTE and DCE only. These messages do not traverse the cloud, meaning they couldn't possibly have anything to do with InARP. Full status messages from the switch include all PVCs known by the switch. In this case, there's only one—DLCI = 16. The type 1 message will always have three lines, whereas the type 0 message will have four or more, assuming PVCs exist. You would see InARP messages coming in the exact same way you would see any other non-LMI frames coming in (such as ICMP pings), by using the `debug frame-relay packet` command. Status indicators are pretty straightforward and adhere to the following rules:

0x0 (no bits turned on) means "inactive."

0x2 (second bit turned on) means "active."

0x3 means that the active DLCI cannot accept any more traffic without drops occurring—sort of a flow-control code. (Active bit [2nd] is on, but the first bit is also on as sort of a Receive Not Ready (RNR) bit because Cisco uses this bit even though the ITU-T indicates the first bit is reserved.)

0x4 (third bit turned on) means "deleted."

Looking at our status, the DLCI 16, status 0x2 means the DLCI is active.

Frame Relay Switching

Routers are typically edge devices that connect your LANs to the Frame Relay network. However, you can use a router as part of the Frame Relay cloud or you can use it to create your own Frame Relay network. *Frame Relay switching* is the forwarding of Frame Relay frames based upon their DLCI assignments. You have seen how to configure a Frame Relay DTE device; now, let's look at how to configure a Frame Relay DCE switch. Routers are DTE devices by default; however, by changing the Frame Relay interface type to a DCE, you can provide switching of frames.

Compare Figure 29.8 to Figure 29.9. Both of these diagrams represent the same network. In Figure 29.8, you see the Frame Relay cloud without any detail. Each router on the right side will send traffic to the router on the left by using DLCI 100. Keep in mind that the DLCI is an identifier and that the DLCIs in this diagram could be the same or different and still communicate. The router on the left will use DLCIs 101 and 300 to reach each router on the right. This is the normal way that you should think about the frame cloud. It is typically not your concern what happens within the Frame Relay network. Figure 29.9 shows that this particular Frame Relay cloud is a single router configured as a switch.

FIGURE 29.8 Logical Frame Relay network

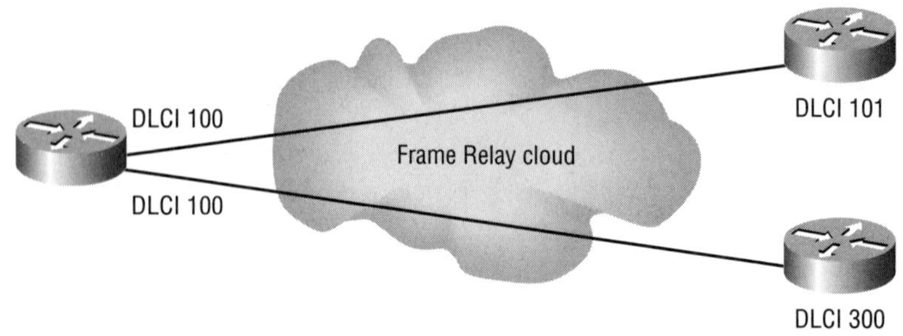

FIGURE 29.9 Physical Frame Relay network

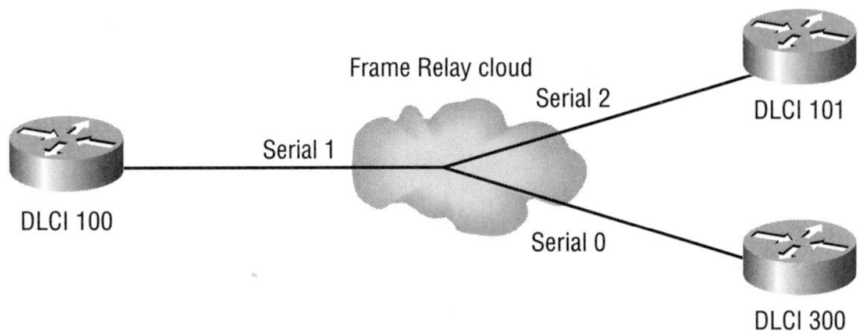

Frame Relay Switching Commands

The command used to enable Frame Relay switching on a Cisco router is as follows:

```
Router_A#config t
Router_A(config)#frame-relay switching
```

This command must come before any of the other Frame Relay switching–related commands can be executed, or these commands won't be allowed. When Frame Relay encapsulation is enabled on an interface, it defaults to DTE, so you will need to change it to DCE for Frame Relay switching. For a Frame Relay serial connection to function, you must have a DTE at one end and a DCE at the other. You first configure the router with the following command:

```
Router_A(config)#interface serial0
Router_A(config-if)#frame-relay intf-type dce
```

The clocking on a serial link is provided by the DCE device, which is determined by the type of cable connected to the serial interface. For a Frame Relay connection, the DCE status is configured, whereas serial DCE status is cabled. For Frame Relay, the DCE device is the one that provides LMI.

Because this interface is now functioning as the Frame Relay DCE device, you can change the LMI type from the default of Cisco with the following command:

```
Router_A(config-if)#frame-relay lmi-type ?
  cisco
  ansi
  q933a
Router_A(config-if)#frame-relay lmi-type
```

The next step in the configuration process is to create the proper DLCI forwarding rules. These rules dictate that when a frame enters a particular interface on a certain DLCI, it will be forwarded to another interface and DLCI. Let's look at such an example on interface serial 1:

```
Router_A#config t
Router_A(config)#interface serial 1
Router_A(config-if)#frame-relay route 100 interface Serial2 101
```

This command states that any frame received on interface serial 1, with DLCI 100, shall be forwarded to interface serial 2, with DLCI 101. You can view all the frame routing information with the `show frame-relay route` command. The following router output shows the settings of Router A:

```
Router_A#show frame-relay route
Input Intf    Input Dlci    Output Intf   Output Dlci   Status
Serial0       300           Serial1       200           active
Serial1       100           Serial2       101           active
Serial1       200           Serial0       300           active
Serial2       101           Serial1       100           active
Router_A#
```

The configuration of a router as a Frame Relay switch can be useful for a lab environment or even as part of a production network.

Now, let's look at the configuration of the Frame Relay switch:

```
Router_A#show running-config
Building configuration...
Current configuration:
!
version 11.2
!
hostname Router_A
!
frame-relay switching
!
interface Serial0
 no ip address
 encapsulation frame-relay
 clockrate 56000
 frame-relay intf-type dce
 frame-relay route 300 interface Serial1 200
!
interface Serial1
```

```
 no ip address
 encapsulation frame-relay
 clockrate 56000
 frame-relay intf-type dce
 frame-relay route 100 interface Serial2 101
 frame-relay route 200 interface Serial0 300
!
interface Serial2
 no ip address
 encapsulation frame-relay
 clockrate 56000
 frame-relay intf-type dce
 frame-relay route 101 interface Serial1 100
!
end
Router_A#
```

Notice the global command `frame-relay switching` is at the top of the configuration. Also notice that both interfaces are configured with `frame-relay intf-type dce` commands. On the serial interfaces, you'll also see that the `clock rate` command is used to provide clocking for the line because the router serving as the Frame Relay switch is a DCE device on the physical interface.

Frame Relay Traffic Shaping

Traffic shaping on Frame Relay provides different capabilities, and because this information might be covered on the exam, it is important that you can describe each one. On production networks, this information can help you understand whether switch problems are occurring.

In this section, you will learn about traffic-shaping techniques and when to use them. You'll then learn how to configure traffic shaping.

Using Traffic-Shaping Techniques

The following list outlines the traffic-shaping techniques used with Frame Relay:

- To control the access rate transmitted on a Cisco router, you can configure a peak rate to limit outbound traffic to either the CIR or excess information rate (EIR).
- You can configure BECN support on a per-VC basis, which will enable the router to then monitor BECNs and throttle traffic based on BECN-designated packets.
- Queuing can be used for support at the VC level. Priority, custom, and weighted fair queuing (WFQ) can be used. This gives you more control over traffic flow on individual VCs.

It's also important to understand when you would use traffic shaping with Frame Relay. The following list explains this:

- Use traffic shaping when one site, such as the corporate office, has a higher speed line (for example, a T1), and the remote branches have slower lines (for example, 56Kbps). This connection would cause bottlenecks on each VC and would result in poor response times for time-sensitive traffic such as SNA and Telnet. This can cause packets to be dropped. By using traffic shaping at the corporate office, you can improve response on each VC.
- Traffic shaping is also helpful on a router with many subinterfaces. Because these subinterfaces will use traffic as fast as the physical link allows, you can use rate enforcement on the subinterface to match the CIR of the VC. This means you can preallocate bandwidth to each VC.
- Traffic shaping can be used to throttle back transmission on a Frame Relay network that is constantly congested. This can help prevent packet loss and is done on a per-VC basis.
- Traffic shaping is used effectively if you have multiple Network layer protocols and want to queue each protocol to allocate bandwidth effectively. Since IOS version 11.2, queuing can be performed at the VC level.

Configuring Traffic Shaping

To configure Frame Relay traffic shaping, you must first enter the map class configuration mode so you can define a map class. You enter the map class with the global configuration command `map-class frame-relay name`. The *name* parameter is the name you use to apply the map class to the VC where you want traffic shaping performed. The command looks like the following:

```
RouterA#config t
RouterA(config)#map-class frame-relay scott
RouterA(config-map-class)#
```

Notice that the `map-class frame-relay scott` command changes the prompt to `config-map-class`. This enables you to configure the parameters for your map class.

The map class is used to define the average and peak rates allowed in each VC associated with the map class. The map class mechanism enables you to specify that the router can dynamically fluctuate the rate at which it sends traffic, depending on the BECNs received. It also enables you to configure queuing on a per-VC basis.

To define the average and peak rate for links that are faster than the receiving link can handle, use the following command:

```
RouterA(config-map-class)#frame-relay traffic-rate average [peak]
```

The average parameter sets the average rate in bits per second, which is your CIR. Now, how do you calculate the peak value? First, start with the EIR. The EIR is the average rate over which bits will be marked with DE and is given by the formula EIR = B_e/T_c, with B_e being excessive burst and T_c representing the committed rate measurement interval. The peak value is then calculated by taking the CIR plus EIR, or peak = CIR + EIR.

The peak parameter is optional. An example of a line is as follows:

```
RouterA(config-map-class)#frame-relay traffic-rate 9600 18000
```

To specify that the router should dynamically fluctuate the rate at which it is sending traffic depending on the number of BECNs received, use the following command:

```
RouterA(config-map-class)#frame-relay adaptive-shaping becn
```

To set bandwidth usage for protocols, you can configure traffic shaping to use queuing on a per-VC basis. To perform this function, use the following commands:

```
RouterA(config-map-class)#frame-relay custom-queue-list number
RouterA(config-map-class)#frame-relay priority-group number
```

You can use either command, depending on the type of queuing you are using. The *number* parameter at the end of the command is the queue list number. A detailed discussion of queuing is presented in the next chapter.

After the map class parameters are completed, you then need to configure the traffic shaping on the interface you want. The following commands are used to perform traffic shaping on an interface and to apply the map class and its parameters to a subinterface and, by association, its corresponding VC:

```
RouterA#config t
RouterA(config)#interface serial0
RouterA(config-if)#frame-relay traffic-shaping
RouterA(config-if)#interface serial0.16 point-to-point
RouterA(config-subif#frame-relay class scott
RouterA(config-subif)#frame-relay interface-dlci 16
```

You first must enable traffic shaping and per-VC queuing on the interface with the `frame-relay traffic-shaping` command. You can then go to the interface or subinterface and assign the map class by using the `frame-relay class` *name* command. The example just shown uses the name `scott` because that is the name of the map class defined in the earlier example.

After you have completed the configuration, use the `show running-config` and the `show frame-relay pvc` commands to verify the configuration.

Summary

Frame Relay is one of the most popular WAN protocols in the world. This technology will become even more critical as corporations stretch their networks globally and the Internet becomes more pervasive.

Real World Scenario

The Lowdown on Committed Information Rate (CIR)

We've talked formally about CIR—we even presented a calculation—but what does it really mean? As we have said, the acronym itself stands for committed information rate, which really doesn't seem that difficult to understand. But there seems to be widespread misinterpretation of this concept, especially by some service providers, so let's attempt to figure the whole thing out.

We've discussed terms such as *burst rate* and phrases such as *bursting above your CIR*, but these terms can be misleading. They were devised by network engineers who assumed—you know what that leads to—that we wouldn't understand hardcore network-engineering concepts, so they tried to put them in layman's terms and botched the whole thing up. In reality, you're always "bursting" to your line speed because Frame Relay is an HDLC protocol and there's no other way to make it work.

HDLC is a synchronous protocol (which means that the data is synchronized to a clock) that sends data with a standardized framing and checksum technique. When a frame is transmitted, the data must be contiguous; that is, there cannot be any holes or spaces between bytes of data. So if you're transmitting 500 bytes of data, you can't send 250 and then wait for a while and then send the rest. It has to go out as one big chunk. The Frame Relay expression *bursting over your CIR* comes into play because there is no way to slow down the data or to change the length of the chunk after you start transmitting; you just send until you are finished. If you happen to send too much data because your data chunk is larger than the allotment, you've bursted over your CIR.

So what is the big deal about CIR, then? And why, when you buy Frame Relay from a company like Qwest, do they quote you a CIR? CIR is the "worst-case" throughput that the Frame Relay network provider attempts to guarantee. It's like a restaurant guaranteeing that you'll always be able to eat a certain amount of food from its buffet. Like the restaurant, the Frame Relay network provider can't guarantee that you'll always be able to transmit at the CIR (take the case when everyone on the network happens to be transmitting at once), but they can guarantee it over a reasonable time span (usually over a span of seconds). Basically, the network backbone is engineered to handle reasonable loads—just like the number of lanes in a highway. Given a certain amount of traffic, the data should flow through the backbone without delay. At times, when unusually heavy traffic exists, you have what is called congestion.

To become a successful CCNP, you need to understand the Frame Relay protocol. This technology makes up the majority of the world's non-dedicated circuits, and its importance cannot be underestimated.

Frame Relay is the distant cousin to X.25, without some of X.25's overhead. It does provide congestion notification, which can be used with traffic shaping to help traffic response. Like X.25, Frame Relay provides for permanent and switched virtual circuits.

LMI is an extension to the Frame Relay protocol developed by the Frame Relay Forum and is used to provide management for virtual circuits. This makes the management of DLCI information easier for the network administrator.

Cisco provides for a mechanism to enable a multipoint interface such as Frame Relay to look like multiple virtual point-to-point or multipoint interfaces called subinterfaces. Point-to-point subinterfaces can be used to solve problems caused by distance-vector routing protocols running over multipoint interfaces.

Setting up a Cisco router as a Frame Relay switch is not something that you would do often, but it is a useful feature when you are working in a lab environment. There are many troubleshooting commands that can be used to verify the configuration of Frame Relay on a Cisco router. They can be used to see the DLCI-to-Network-layer-address mapping and the current state of LMI on the router. Frame Relay is a technology used in many networks, and mastering its configuration and operation will take you far in your networking career.

Exam Essentials

Understand Frame Relay and its history. Frame Relay is a streamlined version of X.25 without the windowing and retransmission capabilities. Frame Relay is a layer 2 protocol that was defined as a network service for ISDN by the CCITT (now ITU-T). The Group of Four extended Frame Relay in 1990 to allow for a Local Management Interface (LMI) to assist in PVC management.

Understand the two types of virtual circuits (VCs). Know what a switched virtual circuit (SVC) is used for and what a permanent virtual circuit (PVC) is used for. Understand why you would use one type over another.

Know what a DLCI is and how it is mapped to Network layer protocols. The data link connection identifier (DLCI) is used to identify a PVC in a Frame Relay network. The DLCI-to-Network-layer mapping can be statically configured by an administrator using the `frame-relay map` command or can be dynamically set by using Inverse ARP (IARP).

Understand the Local Management Interface (LMI). LMI was an extension to Frame Relay to manage the virtual circuits on a connection. LMI virtual circuit status messages provide communication and DLCI synchronization between Frame Relay DTE and DCE devices.

Know how to configure Frame Relay and what it uses for congestion control. The `encapsulation frame-relay` command is used to configure an interface for Frame Relay operation. The `frame-relay intf-type dce` command is used to configure an interface for DCE operation, but by default, the Frame Relay interface type is DTE. Frame Relay uses backward explicit congestion notification (BECN) and forward explicit congestion notification (FECN) messages to control congestion on a Frame Relay switch.

Understand the options for traffic shaping on a Frame Relay interface. There are many options for traffic shaping to enable a Frame Relay network to operate more efficiently. You can have the router slow traffic on a VC in response to BECNs received. You can set up queuing on a per-VC basis and limit traffic going out of a VC. You need to know what the committed information rate (CIR) and excess information rate (EIR) are.

Know what Cisco IOS commands are used to verify and troubleshoot a Frame Relay connection. The commands `show interface`, `show frame-relay pvc`, `show frame-relay map`, `show frame-relay lmi`, and `debug frame-relay lmi` are all used to see and verify the operation of Frame Relay. The command `clear frame-relay-inarp` is used to delete the dynamic PVC-to-Network-Layer addressing entries.

Queuing and Compression

THE CCNP EXAM TOPICS COVERED IN THIS CHAPTER INCLUDE THE FOLLOWING:

- ✓ Determine why queuing is enabled, identify alternative queuing protocols that Cisco products support, and determine the best queuing method to implement.
- ✓ Specify the commands to configure queuing.
- ✓ Specify the commands and procedures used to verify proper queuing configuration.
- ✓ Specify the commands and procedures used to effectively select and implement compression.
- ✓ Describe traffic control methods used to manage traffic flow on WAN links.
- ✓ Plan traffic shaping to meet required quality of service on access links.
- ✓ Troubleshoot traffic control problems on a WAN link.

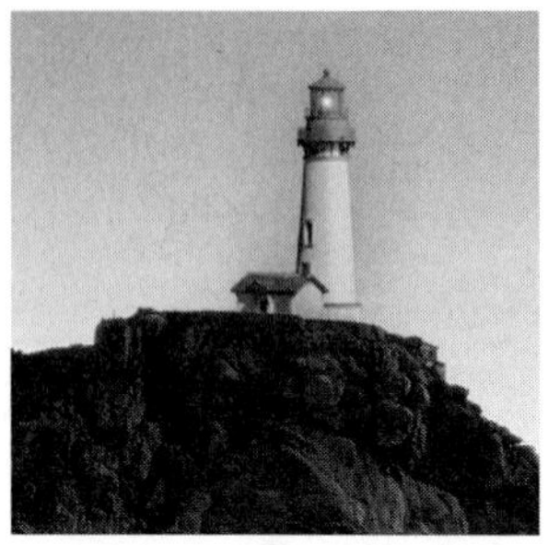

This chapter teaches you how to use both queuing and compression to help maintain a healthy network, which is important because user data consists of many types of data packets roaming the internetwork, hungering for and consuming bandwidth. *Queuing* is the act of sequencing packets for servicing—similar to a line at an amusement park with a FastPass or "go to the front" ability. Compression is the ability to communicate a piece of information with fewer bits, typically by removing repetitions within the data.

As a network administrator, you can help save precious bandwidth on WAN links, the largest bottlenecks in today's networks. With Gigabit Ethernet running the core backbones and 10-gigabit Ethernet networks just now being deployed, a 1.544Mbps T-1 link is painfully slow. By implementing both queuing and compression techniques, you can help save bandwidth and get the most for your money.

In addition, this chapter teaches you the three *queuing* techniques available on the Cisco router: weighted fair queuing (WFQ), priority queuing, and custom queuing. You will learn when to use each type, as well as how to configure each type on your router. We also present an overview of newer queuing and policing technologies, including low latency queuing (LLQ), class-based weighted fair queuing (CBWFQ), and committed access rate (CAR).

Finally, this chapter provides the information you need to both understand and configure the types of compression on Cisco routers. The types of compression techniques covered in this chapter include header, payload, and link compression.

Queuing

When a packet arrives on a router's interface, a protocol-independent switching process handles it. The router then switches the traffic to the outgoing interface buffer. An example of a protocol-independent switching process is first-in, first-out (FIFO), which is the original algorithm for packet transmission. FIFO was the default for all routers until weighted fair queuing (WFQ) was developed. The problem with FIFO is that transmission occurs in the same order as messages are received. If an application such as Voice over IP (VoIP) required traffic to be reordered, the network engineer needed to establish a queuing policy other than FIFO queuing.

Cisco IOS software offers three queuing options as an alternative to FIFO queuing:

- Weighted fair queuing (WFQ) prioritizes interactive traffic over file transfers to ensure satisfactory response time for common user applications.
- Priority queuing ensures timely delivery of a specific protocol or type of traffic that is transmitted before all others.
- Custom queuing establishes bandwidth allocations for each type of traffic.

We will discuss these three queuing options in detail in the "IOS Queuing Options" section later in this chapter.

Traffic Prioritization

Packet prioritization has become more important because many types of data traffic need to share a data path through the network, often congesting WAN links. If the WAN link is not congested, you don't need to implement traffic prioritization, although it might be appropriate to add more bandwidth in certain situations.

Prioritization of traffic will be required on your network if you have, for example, a mixture of file transfer, transaction-based, and desktop video conferencing. Prioritization is most effective on WAN links where the combination of bursty traffic and relatively lower data rates can cause temporary congestion. This is typically necessary only on WAN links slower than T-1/E-1. However, prioritization can also be used across OC (optical carrier)-12 and OC-48 links, because at times, tests can be run to saturate these links, but you might still want voice and video to have a priority.

Queuing Policy

Queuing policies help network managers provide users with a high level of service across a WAN link, as well as control WAN costs. Typically, the corporate goal is to deploy and maintain a single enterprise network, even though the network supports disparate applications, organizations, technologies, and user expectations. Consequently, network managers are concerned about providing all users with an appropriate level of service while continuing to support mission-critical applications and having the ability to integrate new technologies at the same time.

Figure 30.1 shows a serial interface that is congested and needs queuing implemented. It's important to remember that you need to implement queuing only on interfaces that experience congestion.

The network administrator should understand the delicate balance between meeting the business requirements of users and controlling WAN costs. Queuing enables network administrators to effectively manage network resources.

FIGURE 30.1 Queuing policy

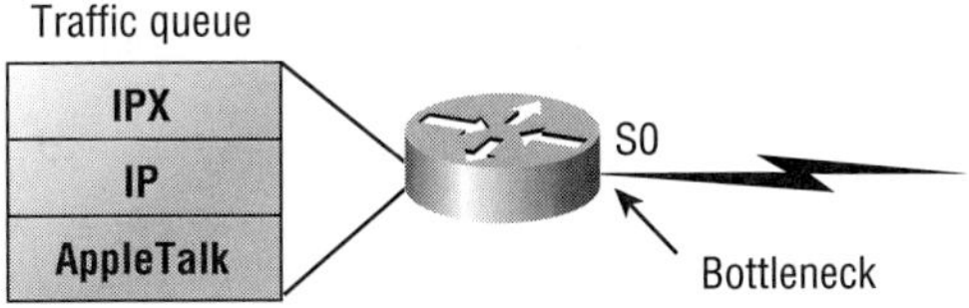

IOS Queuing Options

As we've said, if your serial links are not congested, you do not need to implement queuing. However, if the load exceeds the transmission rate for small periods of time, you can use a Cisco IOS queuing option to help the congestion on a serial link.

To effectively configure queuing on a serial link, you must understand the types of queuing available. If you choose the wrong type of queuing, you can do more harm on the link than help. Also, this is not a one-time analysis of traffic patterns. You must constantly repeat your analysis of your serial link congestion to make sure you have implemented the queuing strategy correctly.

Figure 30.2 shows the queuing options available from Cisco.

FIGURE 30.2 Queuing options

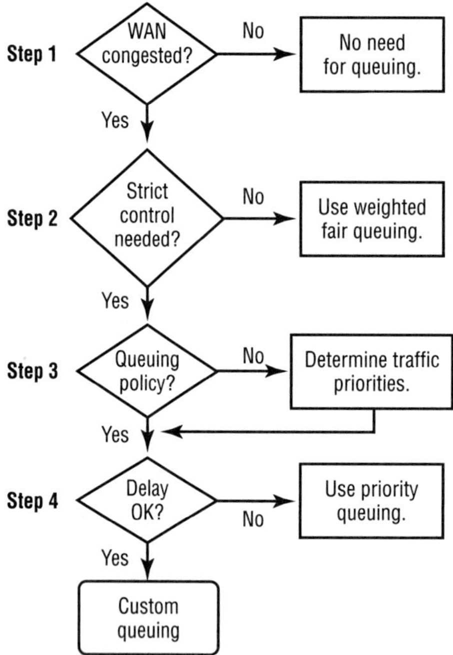

The following steps and Figure 30.2 describe the analysis you should make when deciding on a queuing policy:

1. Determine whether the WAN is congested.
2. Decide whether strict control over traffic prioritization is necessary and whether automatic configuration is acceptable.
3. Establish a queuing policy.
4. Determine whether any of the traffic types you identified in your traffic pattern analysis can tolerate a delay.

Weighted Fair Queuing

Weighted fair queuing (WFQ) provides equal amounts of bandwidth to each conversation that traverses the interface. WFQ uses a process that refers to the timestamp found on the last bit of a packet as it enters the queue.

Assigning Priorities

WFQ assigns a high priority to all low-volume traffic. Figure 30.3 demonstrates how the timing mechanism for priority assignment occurs. The algorithm determines which frames belong to either a high-volume or low-volume conversation and forwards the low-volume packets from the queue first. Through this timing convention, remaining packets can be assigned an exiting priority.

In Figure 30.3, packets are labeled A through F. As depicted in this figure, Packet A will be forwarded first because it's part of a low-volume conversation, even though the last bit of session B will arrive before the last bit of the packets associated with Packet A did. The remaining packets are divided between the two high-traffic conversations, with their timestamps determining the order in which they will exit the queue.

FIGURE 30.3 Priority assignment using WFQ

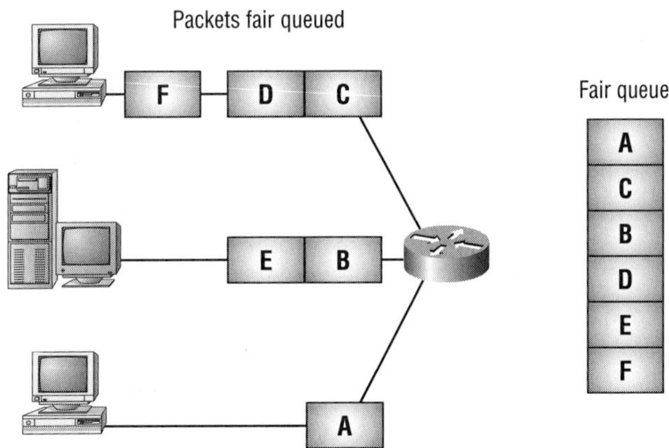

Assigning Conversations

We've discussed how priority is assigned to a packet or conversation, but it's also important to understand the type of information that the processor needs to associate a group of packets with an established conversation.

The most common elements used to establish a conversation are as follows:

- Source and destination IP addresses
- MAC addresses

- Port numbers
- Type of service
- DLCI number assigned to an interface

Say a router has two active conversations, one a large FTP transfer and the other an HTTP session. The router, using some or all of the factors just listed to determine which conversation a packet belongs to, allocates equal amounts of bandwidth to each conversation. Each of the two conversations receives half of the available bandwidth.

Configuring Weighted Fair Queuing

You're now ready to learn how to configure WFQ. For all interfaces having a line speed equal to or lower than 2.048Mbps (E-1 speed), WFQ is on by default. Here's an example of how WFQ is configured on an interface. You can use the `fair-queue` command to alter the default settings:

```
Router_C#config t
Enter configuration commands, one per line. End with CNTL/Z.
Router_C(config)#interface serial0
Router_C(config-if)#fair-queue 96
Router_C(config-if)#^Z
Router_C#
```

To understand what was configured, look at the syntax of the command:

```
fair-queue [congestive-discard-threshold [dynamic-queues [reservable-queues]]]
```

congestive-discard-threshold This value specifies the number of messages allowed in each queue. The default is 64 messages, with a range 16–4,096. When a conversation reaches this threshold, new message packets will be dropped.

dynamic-queues Dynamic queues are exactly that—queues established dynamically to handle conversations that don't have special requirements. The valid values for this parameter are 16, 32, 64, 128, 256, 512, 1024, 2048, and 4096, with the default value being 256; ISDN BRI has a default of 16.

reservable-queues This parameter defines the number of queues established to handle special conversations. The available range is from 0 to 1,000. The default is 0. These queues are for interfaces that use Resource Reservation Protocol (RSVP).

Verifying Weighted Fair Queuing

Now that WFQ is configured on the router's serial 0 interface, let's see what it's doing. To verify the configuration and operation of the queuing system, you can issue the following two commands:

```
show queueing [fair | priority | custom]
show queue [interface-type interface-number]
```

When you use the show commands, note that *queuing* is misspelled. It has that extra *e*.

Results from these commands on Router C can be seen next. Since WFQ is the only type of queuing that's been enabled on this router, it isn't necessary to issue the optional commands of `fair`, `custom`, or `priority`.

```
Router_C#show queueing
Current fair queue configuration:

 Interface  Discard      Dynamic      Reserved
           threshold    queue count  queue count
 Serial0      96           256           0
 Serial1      64           256           0

Current priority queue configuration:
Current custom queue configuration:
Current RED queue configuration:
Router_C#
```

This command shows that WFQ is enabled on both serial interfaces and that the discard threshold for serial 0 was changed from 64 to 96. There's a maximum of 256 dynamic queues for both interfaces—the default value. The lines following the interface information are empty because their corresponding queuing algorithms haven't been configured yet.

The next command displays more detailed information pertaining to the specified interface:

```
Router_C#show queue serial0
 Input queue: 0/75/0 (size/max/drops); Total output drops: 0
 Queueing strategy: weighted fair
 Output queue: 0/1000/96/0 (size/max total/threshold/drops)
   Conversations 0/1/256 (active/max active/max total)
   Reserved Conversations 0/0 (allocated/max allocated)
```

This command displays the input queue information, which is the current size of the queue, the maximum size of the queue, and the number of conversations that have been dropped. The queuing strategy is defined as `weighted fair`, or WFQ. The output queue (usually the one with the most activity) defines the current size, the maximum total number of output queue entries, the number of conversations per queue, and the number of conversations dropped. The conversations section represents the number of conversations in the queue. The `active` number describes the number of current active conversations. The `max active` keeps a record of the maximum number of active conversations at any one time, and `max total` gives the total number of all conversations possible within the queue. Reserved queues are also displayed with the current number allocated and maximum number of allocated queues.

Priority Queuing

Unlike weighted fair queuing, which occurs on a session basis, *priority queuing* occurs on a packet-by-packet basis and is ideal in network environments that carry time-sensitive traffic. When congestion occurs on low-speed interfaces, priority queuing guarantees that traffic assigned a high priority will be sent first. On the negative side, if the queue for high-priority traffic is always full and monopolizing bandwidth, packets in the other queues will be severely delayed or dropped.

Assigning Priorities

Priority queuing uses the packet header information consisting of either the TCP port or the protocol as a classification mechanism. When a packet enters the router, it's compared against a list that will assign a priority to it and forward it to the corresponding queue.

Priority queuing can assign a packet to one of four priorities—high, medium, normal, and low—with a separate dispatching algorithm to manage the traffic in all four. Figure 30.4 shows how these queues are serviced. You can see that the algorithm starts with the high-priority queue processing all the data there. When that queue is empty, the dispatching algorithm moves down to the medium-priority queue, and so on down the priority chain, performing a cascade check of each queue before moving on. So if the algorithm finds packets in a higher priority queue, it will process them first before moving on. This is where problems can develop; packets in the lower priority queues could be totally neglected in favor of the higher priority ones if they're continually busy with the arrival of new packets.

FIGURE 30.4 Using priority queuing

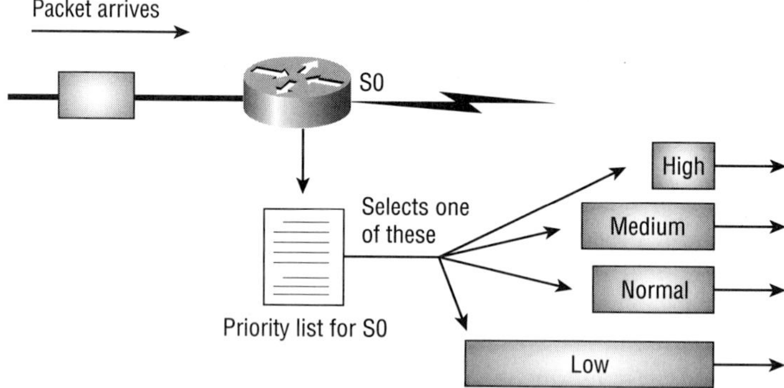

Configuring Priority Queuing

Implementing priority queuing on an interface requires three steps:

1. Create a priority list that the processor will use to determine packet priority.
2. Adjust the size of the queues if desired.
3. Apply the priority list to the desired interfaces.

Let's go over how to build a priority list by using the following commands:

```
priority-list list-number protocol protocol-name] {high | medium | normal | low}
queue-keyword keyword-value
priority-list list-number interface interface-type {high | medium | normal | low}
```

The `list-number` parameter identifies the specific priority list, and the valid values are 1 through 16. The `protocol` parameter directs the router to assign packets to the appropriate queue based on the protocol, and `protocol-name` defines which protocol to match. The `queue-keyword` and `keyword-value` parameters enable packets to be classified by their byte count, access list, protocol port number, or name and fragmentation. With the `interface` parameter, any traffic coming from the interface is assigned to the specified queue. Next, after specifying the protocol or interface, the type of queue needs to be defined—`high`, `medium`, `normal`, or `low`.

```
priority-list list-number default queue-number
```

The same `priority-list` command can be used to configure a default queue for traffic that doesn't match the protocols or interfaces defined in the priority list.

```
priority-list list-number queue-limit [high-limit [medium-limit [normal-limit
[low-limit]]]]
```

The `queue-limit` parameter is used to specify the maximum number of packets allowed in each of the priority queues. The configuration of the queue size must be handled carefully, because if a packet is forwarded to the appropriate queue but the queue is full, the packet will be discarded—even if bandwidth is available. This means that enabling priority queuing on an interface can be useless (even destructive) if queues aren't accurately configured to respond to actual network needs. It's important to make the queues large enough to accommodate congestion so that the influx of packets can be accepted and stored until they can be forwarded.

After creating the priority list, you can apply that list to an interface in interface configuration mode with the following command:

```
priority-group list
```

The `list` parameter is the priority list number, from 1 to 16, to use on this interface. After the list is applied to the interface, it is implicitly applied to outbound traffic. All packets will be checked against the priority list before entering their corresponding queue. The ones that don't match will be placed in the default queue. Here's an example:

```
Router_C#config t
Enter configuration commands, one per line. End with CNTL/Z.
Router_C(config)#priority-list 1 protocol ip high gt 1000
Router_C(config)#priority-list 1 protocol ip low lt 256
Router_C(config)#priority-list 1 protocol ip normal
Router_C(config)#priority-list 1 interface serial 1 normal
Router_C(config)#priority-list 1 interface ethernet 0 high
Router_C(config)#priority-list 1 default normal
```

```
Router_C(config)#priority-list 1 queue-limit 40 80 120 160
Router_C(config)#interface serial 0
Router_C(config-if)#priority-group 1
Router_C(config-if)#^Z
Router_C#
```

The first line of the priority list assigns high priority to all IP traffic with a packet size greater than (`gt`) 1,000 bytes. The second line assigns low priority to IP traffic with a packet size less than (`lt`) 256 bytes. The third line assigns all remaining IP traffic to the normal queue. The fourth line assigns all incoming traffic on serial 1 to the normal queue also. All incoming traffic on Ethernet 0 is assigned a high priority, and any remaining traffic will be assigned normal priority. The size of each queue is defined by the `queue-limit` parameter, and the numbers follow the order of high, medium, normal, and low queue sizes.

Following is an example of what the interface configuration looks like. The priority list has been assigned to the interface with the `priority-group` command. You can see the final form of the applied priority list in the following configuration snippet:

```
!
interface Serial0
 ip address 172.16.40.6 255.255.255.252
 priority-group 1
!
priority-list 1 protocol ip high gt 1000
priority-list 1 protocol ip low lt 256
priority-list 1 protocol ip normal
priority-list 1 interface Serial1 normal
priority-list 1 interface Ethernet0 high
priority-list 1 queue-limit 40 80 120 160
```

As with access control lists, the order of a matching packet is important. A 1,500-byte packet on Serial 0 would match the first and fourth lines, but would only be queued by the first instruction, placing it in the high-priority queue.

Verifying Priority Queuing

To make sure the queuing configuration is working and configured properly, you can use the same command used to verify WFQ with the added option for priority queuing.

The following command output summarizes the preceding configured priority list:

```
Router_C#show queueing priority
Current priority queue configuration:

List  Queue Args
1   high  protocol ip gt 1000
1   low  protocol ip lt 256
1   normal protocol ip
```

```
1   normal interface Serial1
1   high interface Ethernet0
1   high limit 40
1   medium limit 80
1   normal limit 120
1   low limit 160
Router_C#
```

Custom Queuing

Custom queuing functions on the concept of sharing bandwidth among traffic types. Instead of assigning a priority classification to a specific traffic or packet type, custom queuing forwards traffic in the different queues by using the FIFO method within each queue. Custom queuing offers the ability to customize the amount of actual bandwidth that a specified traffic type uses.

While remaining within the limits of the physical line's capacity, virtual pipes are configured through the custom queuing option. Varying amounts of the total bandwidth are reserved for various specific traffic types, and if the bandwidth isn't being fully utilized by its assigned traffic type, other types can borrow its bandwidth. The configured limits go into effect during high levels of utilization or when congestion on the line causes different traffic types to compete for bandwidth.

Figure 30.5 shows each queue being processed, one after the other. After this begins, the algorithm checks the first queue, processes the data within it, and then moves to the next—if it comes across an empty one, it will simply move on to the next one without hesitating. Each queue's byte count specifies the amount of data that will be forwarded from that queue, which directs the algorithm to move to the next queue after it has been reached. Custom queuing permits a maximum of 16 configurable queues. The system queue is for network specific traffic, including system datagrams such as SNMP and routing updates.

FIGURE 30.5 Custom queuing algorithm

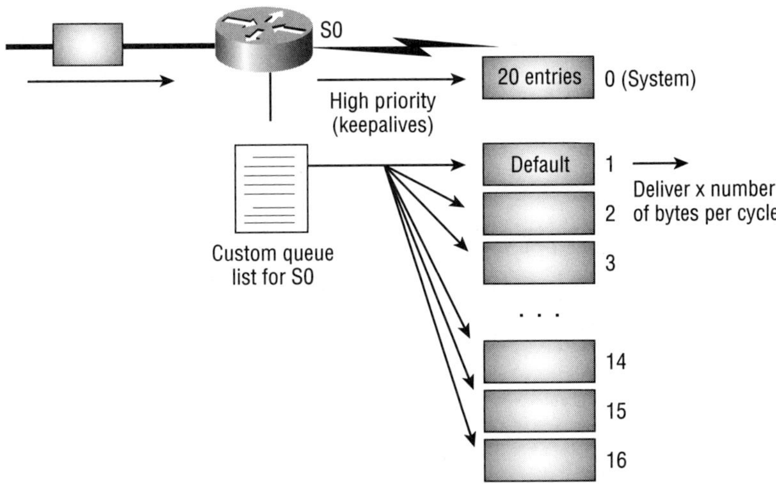

Figure 30.6 shows how the bandwidth allocation via custom queuing looks relative to the physical connection. Using the frame size of the protocols and configuring the byte count for each queue will configure appropriate bandwidth allocations for each traffic type. In other words, when a particular queue is being processed, packets are sent until the number of bytes sent exceeds the queue byte count defined.

FIGURE 30.6 Bandwidth allocation using custom queuing

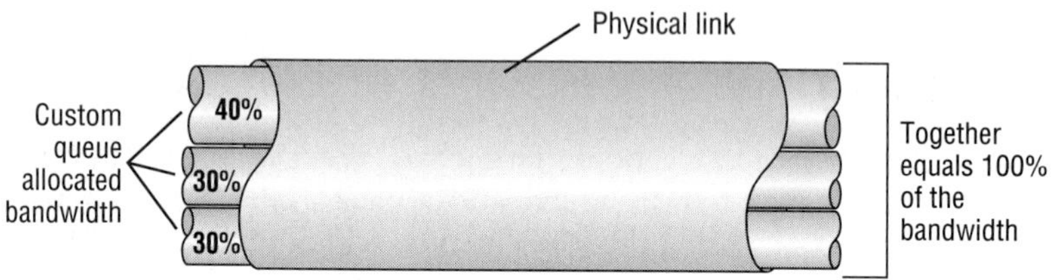

Configuring Custom Queuing

Configuring custom queuing is similar to configuring priority queuing, but instead of completing three tasks, you must complete five. As with priority queuing, you have to configure a list to separate types of incoming traffic into their desired queues. After that, you must configure a default queue for the traffic that will be unassigned to any of the other queues. After the specific and default queues are defined, you can adjust the capacity or size of each queue or just stick with the default settings.

When that's complete, specify the transfer rate, or byte count, for each queue. This is important—the byte count determines the percentage of bandwidth reserved for a specified queue, with a default of 1,500 bytes as the denominator. After these parameters are set, apply them to an interface.

The commands used to configure the queuing list, default queue, queue size, and transmit rate follow:

```
queue-list list-number default queue-number
queue-list list-number interface interface-type interface-number queue-number
queue-list list-number lowest-custom queue-number
queue-list list-number protocol protocol-name queue-number queue-keyword
keyword-value
queue-list list-number queue [queue-number byte-count byte-count-number | limit
limit-number]
queue-list list-number stun [queue-number | address STUN-group-number]
```

The syntax can be presented in many ways to configure the desired command. The *list-number* is a value from 1 to 16 and associates the list with the given number. The following are available options:

default The `default` option designates a custom queue for packets that do not match another `queue-list`.

interface The `interface` option assigns incoming packets on the specified interface to a custom queue. When the `interface` option is specified, you must supply the *`interface-type`* and *`interface-number`* as well. The *`interface-type`* is the type of physical interface, and *`interface-number`* is the interface's physical port.

lowest-custom The `lowest-custom` option specifies the lowest queue number considered a custom queue.

protocol The `protocol` option indicates that the packets are to be sent to the custom queue if they are of the protocol specified. The `protocol` option also requires additional information. Obviously, the *`protocol-name`* must be specified. In Table 30.1, a sample of available protocol names is listed, but available protocols are dependent upon the feature set and version of IOS. After the *`protocol-name`*, you might supply the *`keyword-value`* to refine the protocols and port numbers used for filtering.

queue The `queue` option allows for specific queue parameters to be configured. The parameters for the queue are discussed later in this section.

stun The `stun` option establishes queuing priority for STUN packets.

TABLE 30.1 Sample of Available Protocol Names

Protocol Name	Description
`aarp`	AppleTalk ARP
`apollo`	Apollo
`appletalk`	AppleTalk
`arp`	IP ARP
`bridge`	Bridging
`bstun`	Block Serial Tunnel
`cdp`	Cisco Discovery Protocol
`compressedtcp`	Compressed TCP
`decnet`	DECnet
`decnet_node`	DECnet Node
`decnet_router-l1`	DECnet Router L1
`decnet_router-l2`	DECnet Router L2

TABLE 30.1 Sample of Available Protocol Names *(continued)*

Protocol Name	Description
`dlsw`	DLSw+
`ip`	IP
`llc2`	LLC2

Table 30.2 lists the available keyword values.

TABLE 30.2 Available Keyword Values

Keyword Value	Description
`fragments`	Prioritize IP fragments
`gt`	Greater than specified value
`list`	Access list
`lt`	Less than specified value
`tcp`	TCP packets
`udp`	UDP packets

To define the operational parameters for the custom queues, you use the `queue` option. After specifying the *`queue-number`*, you're given two parameters to configure:

limit The `limit` parameter enables you to change the number of packets allowed in the queue. The range is from 0 to 32,767, with the default being 20.

byte-count The `byte-count` parameter specifies the average number of bytes forwarded from each queue during a queue cycle.

Configuring Byte Count

Configure the byte-count queues carefully, because if the setting is too high, the algorithm will take longer than necessary to move from one queue to the next. This is not a problem while the processor empties the queue, but if it takes the processor too long to get back to other queues, they could fill up and start to drop packets.

This is why it's important to understand how to configure the bandwidth percentage relationship by using the `byte-count` command. Because frame sizes vary from protocol to protocol, you'll need to know the average frame sizes of the protocols using the custom queued interface to define the byte count efficiently. You can do this by using simple math.

Suppose you have a router that uses IP, IPX, and SNA as its protocols. Let's arbitrarily assign frame sizes, realizing that the values aren't the real ones. Assign a frame size of 800 bytes to IP, 1,000 bytes to IPX, and 1,500 bytes to SNA. You calculate a simple ratio by taking the highest frame value and dividing it by the frame size of each protocol:

IP = 1,500 ÷ 800 = 1.875

IPX = 1,500 ÷ 1,000 = 1.5

SNA = 1,500 ÷ 1,500 = 1.0

These values equal your frame size ratios. To assign correct bandwidth percentages, multiply each ratio by the bandwidth percentage you want to assign to that protocol. For example, assign 40 percent to IP, 30 percent to IPX, and 30 percent to SNA:

IP = 1.875 × (0.4) = 0.75

IPX = 1.5 × (0.3) = 0.45

SNA = 1 × (0.3) = 0.30

These values now need to be normalized by dividing the results by the smallest value:

IP = 0.75 ÷ 0.3 = 2.5

IPX = 0.45 ÷ 0.3 = 1.5

SNA = 0.3 ÷ 0.3 = 1

Custom queuing will send only complete frames. Because the ratios are fractions, you must round them up to the nearest integer values that maintain the same ratio. To arrive at the nearest integer value, multiply the original ratios by a common number that will cause the ratios to become integers. In this case, you can multiply everything by 2 and get the resulting ratio of 5:3:2. What does this mean? Well, five frames of IP, three frames of IPX, and two frames of SNA will be sent. Because of the protocols' varying frame size, the bandwidth percentage works out just the way you calculated:

IP = 5 frames × 800 bytes = 4,000 bytes
IPX = 3 frames × 1,000 bytes = 3,000 bytes
SNA = 2 frames × 1,500 bytes = 3,000 bytes

Total bandwidth is 10,000 bytes. Percentages are verified by dividing the protocol rate by the total. After doing the math, you verify that IP = 40 percent, IPX = 30 percent, and SNA = 30 percent.

Now that the byte count has been calculated (4,000, 3,000, and 3,000), you can apply the results in the `queue-list` command. The custom queuing algorithm will forward 4,000 bytes worth of IP packets, move to the IPX queue and forward 3,000 bytes, and then go to the SNA queue and forward 3,000 bytes.

The following queue list does not follow the IP, IPX, and SNA example we've been discussing.

See the following example on how to configure and apply custom queuing lists:

```
Router_B#config t
Enter configuration commands, one per line. End with CNTL/Z.
Router_B(config)#queue-list 1 interface Ethernet0 1
Router_B(config)#queue-list 1 protocol ip 2 tcp 23
Router_B(config)#queue-list 1 protocol ip 3 tcp 80
Router_B(config)#queue-list 1 protocol ip 4 udp snmp
Router_B(config)#queue-list 1 protocol ip 5
Router_B(config)#queue-list 1 default 6
Router_B(config)#queue-list 1 queue 1 limit 40
Router_B(config)#queue-list 1 queue 5 byte-count 4000
Router_B(config)#queue-list 1 queue 4 byte-count 500
Router_B(config)#queue-list 1 queue 3 byte-count 4000
Router_B(config)#queue-list 1 queue 2 byte-count 1000
Router_B(config)#interface serial0
Router_B(config-if)#custom-queue-list 1
Router_B(config-if)#^Z
Router_B#
```

After analyzing the list, you can see that six queues were configured. The first one was configured to handle incoming traffic from interface Ethernet 0, and the second is reserved for Telnet traffic. Queue number 3 is configured for WWW traffic, and the fourth is configured to handle SNMP traffic. The fifth queue will handle all other IP traffic, while queue number 6 is set up as the default queue where all unspecified traffic will go. A limit of 40 packets was placed on queue 1 (from the default of 20), and the byte count was changed from the default value of 1,500 for queues 2, 3, 4, and 5. Finally, after the queue list was created, it was applied to interface serial 0.

Here is what the configuration looks like:

```
!
interface Serial0
 ip address 10.1.1.1
 255.255.255.0
 custom-queue-list 1
!
queue-list 1 protocol ip 2 tcp telnet
queue-list 1 protocol ip 3 tcp www
queue-list 1 protocol ip 4 udp snmp
queue-list 1 protocol ip 5
queue-list 1 default 6
queue-list 1 interface Ethernet0 1
queue-list 1 queue 1 limit 40
```

```
queue-list 1 queue 2 byte-count 1000
queue-list 1 queue 3 byte-count 4000
queue-list 1 queue 4 byte-count 500
queue-list 1 queue 5 byte-count 4000
```

As with the other queuing algorithms, you need to verify both the configuration and the status of custom queuing. Issuing the same command as before, except this time substituting `custom` for `priority`, produces the following output:

```
Router_B#show queueing custom
Current custom queue configuration:

List  Queue Args
1   6   default
1   1   interface Ethernet0
1   2   protocol ip      tcp port telnet
1   3   protocol ip      tcp port www
1   4   protocol ip      udp port snmp
1   5   protocol ip
1   1   limit 40
1   2   byte-count 1000
1   3   byte-count 4000
1   4   byte-count 500
1   5   byte-count 4000
Router_B#
```

This output information gives you a breakdown of the custom queue lists configured on the device, detailing queue assignments and any limits or byte counts assigned to each custom queue.

The Real Use of Queuing

As with most things in networking, queuing is a trade-off technology that can provide significant benefit or detriment to the administrator. As a result, when coupled with the implementation and management overhead involved, most networks forgo queuing and quality of service (QoS) in favor of other techniques. The most common of these is bandwidth.

The reality is that bandwidth can be used as a QoS mechanism; however, it will not prioritize a filled queue, which is the point where queuing takes over. This can greatly degrade voice services (VoIP), but it can also be a factor when the link is presented with a significant amount of additional data. This can occur under parallel link failure, wherein two paths are reduced to one, presumably with a resulting 50 percent loss of total bandwidth.

QoS and queuing can provide a mechanism to protect traffic under this model, and might be a good augmentation to bandwidth services in your network. The challenge is how to categorize and prioritize traffic—identification of traffic flows, the amount of bandwidth required, the amount available, the benefit to the firm, and the ability to categorize are all considerations for the designer to evaluate. NetFlow, a Cisco IOS feature that can audit network traffic, and Network-Based Application Recognition (NBAR) can help in this process, but NetFlow requires a good amount of storage and manual evaluation, and NBAR is not recommended for high-capacity links because of its processor demands.

In addition, you will likely find infighting as a result of your decisions; a group with its traffic prioritized as bronze will commonly buck and question why an application was rated above it at gold. Obtaining early sign-off can greatly reduce this contention.

Another queuing option available to the administrator is in-band prioritization. This does not help user traffic, but can insulate the network from large-scale denial of service attacks. In this model, queue priority is given to Telnet, Secure Shell (SSH), and TFTP (Trivial FTP) so that these ports are available to the network administrator when the network is under heavy load. This load might be due to user traffic or an attack such as Code Red or Nimda. The caution is that processor load and other factors might be saturated to negate this protection, and, of course, users will still lose their applications under attack.

Cisco's Newer Queuing Technologies

Because of their notable absence in the topics covered by the Remote Access examination, we only briefly cover some of the newer queuing management technologies in this section. Queue control has become a more important issue in remote access networking with the proliferation of voice services and other real-time protocols. As these protocols suffer from congestion and low bandwidth, they are strong candidates for quality of service (QoS), of which queuing is a part.

Remember that queuing is intended to manage the transmission of packets held in the router's buffer. Unlike voice, data networks buffer packets during periods of congestion.

Although we could discuss a wide number of queuing options, three key methods are gaining prominence in the market: low latency queuing, class-based weighted fair queuing, and committed access rate.

Low Latency Queuing

Low latency queuing (LLQ) is actually a strict priority queue within class-based weighted fair queuing (CBWFQ), discussed in the next section. LLQ is Cisco's solution for voice and other very small packets that require real-time processing. LLQ operates by prioritizing key packets to the front of the queue. Because these packets are small by nature, there is little risk of queue starvation or other problems. However, administrators should evaluate the demands of other traffic within the network.

Class-Based Weighted Fair Queuing

Class-based weighted fair queuing (CBWFQ) builds upon WFQ by adding the concept of traffic classes. Classes can be defined by a tag within the frame such as type of service (ToS) or differentiated services code point (DSCP). These tags are added by the end station or the access router and are used to forward packets through the network core without each router re-examining the packet to determine that datagram's priority. We are not defining the methodology used but simply explaining the fact that you can use this information for CBWFQ.

Common implementations of CBWFQ establish three or four classes of application services, typically described as gold, silver, bronze, and other. This categorization does not include network traffic such as routing updates, which should always have priority over user application traffic. Although some users will take exception to their traffic being described as a low priority, the network administrator needs to constrain the total number of classes to keep administration manageable and negate a situation in which bandwidth is being managed to the bit via QoS policy.

One of the strongest benefits to CBWFQ is the ability to define a specific amount of bandwidth to an application. For example, Financial Information Exchange (FIX) is a common financial systems protocol that might warrant special attention. Perhaps this application requires a guaranteed 256Kbps to prevent application failure on a T-1 link. CBWFQ can provide this guarantee, and, perhaps more importantly, will allow the application to use more than the 256Kbps if bandwidth is available. This is different from CAR, discussed in the next section, which establishes a hard limit on the bandwidth available to a specific protocol. Please note that by default you cannot allocate more than 75 percent of the link's total bandwidth for management by CBWFQ.

With regard to traffic classes, the model is fairly straightforward. When congestion occurs, the queue will process packets in the gold class before those in the silver class within the constraints of WFQ. As such, the administrator is defining that the queue should be fair to all applications, but that gold traffic is the most important. This will lead to the managed unfairness that is the basis for all QoS policies; under congestion, the network will have to discard something to stay within the available resources.

ToS and DSCP are not commonly accepted from end nodes because many applications and some operating systems will automatically tag all packets for the highest priority. It is recommended that you configure your edge routers to ignore the end station and tag based on address or port information.

Committed Access Rate

Committed access rate (CAR) is an older bandwidth and policing system; however, it is commonly used in concert with bandwidth management. As noted before, like CBWFQ, committed access rate can specify a bandwidth guarantee to an application. However, CAR also specifies a hard upper limit to that application as well. This can be very useful when wanting to reserve bandwidth for bursty applications. One example of this would be file transfer with Common Internet File System (CIFS) and other protocols on a circuit with web traffic. An administrator might wish to use CAR to allocate 128Kbps for HTTP/web traffic, which would have the same impact as saying all traffic on a T-1 except HTTP/web has over 1,400Kbps available. The advantage is that an administrator need not define each of the other applications to implement this solution.

CAR has some benefits. However, in many enterprises with a QoS strategy, CBWFQ is leading the way, and administrators are opting to protect important applications with the newer technique. You should evaluate CAR and CBWFQ for your specific environment.

Compression

The Cisco IOS provides congestion control on WAN links by adding compression on serial interfaces. This can ease the WAN bandwidth bottleneck problems by using less bandwidth on the link. Along with using the different queuing methods discussed earlier in this chapter, one of the more effective methods of WAN optimization is compression of the data traveling across the WAN link.

Software compression can significantly affect router CPU performance, and the Cisco rule of thumb is that the router's CPU load must not exceed 65 percent when running software compression. If it does exceed this limit, it would be better to disable any compression running.

Cisco equipment supports the following types of compression:

- TCP header compression
- Payload compression
- Link compression
- Microsoft Point-to-Point Compression (MPPC)

By default, Cisco routers transmit data across serial links in an uncompressed format, but by using Cisco serial compression techniques, you can make more efficient use of your available bandwidth. It's true that any compression method will cause overhead on the router's CPU, but the benefits of compression on slower links can outweigh that disadvantage.

Figure 30.7 shows the three types of compression used in a Cisco internetworking environment.

FIGURE 30.7 Cisco serial compression methods

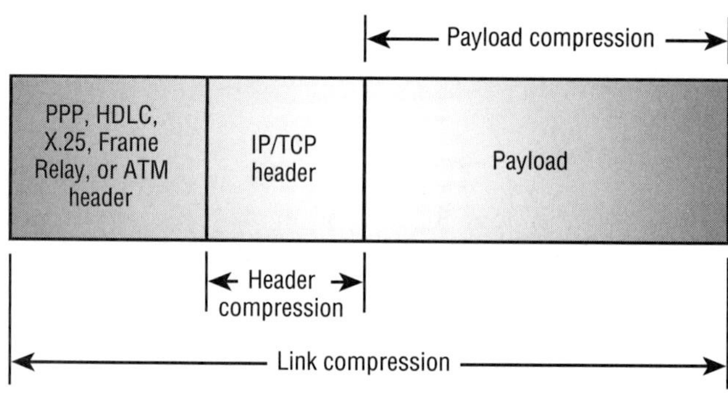

The compression methods are as follows:

TCP header compression Cisco uses the Van Jacobson algorithm to compress the headers of IP packets before sending them out onto WAN links.

Payload compression This approach compresses the data but leaves the header intact. Because the packet's header isn't changed, it can be switched through a network. This method is the one generally used for switching services such as X.25, Switched Multimegabit Data Service (SMDS), Frame Relay, and ATM.

Link compression This method is a combination of both header and payload compression, and the data will be encapsulated in either PPP or LAPB. Because of this encapsulation, link compression allows for transport protocol independence.

Microsoft Point-to-Point Compression (MPPC) protocol This is defined in RFC 2118 and enables Cisco routers to exchange compressed data with Microsoft clients. You would configure MPPC when exchanging data with a host using MPPC across a WAN link. The MPPC is not discussed further in this section.

The Cisco compression methods are discussed in more detail next.

TCP Header Compression

TCP header compression as defined in RFC 1144 compresses only the protocol headers, not the packet data. TCP header compression lowers the overhead generated by the disproportionately large TCP/IP headers as they are transmitted across the WAN.

It is important to realize that the layer 2 header is not touched, and only the headers at layers 3 and 4 are compressed. This enables the layer 2 header to direct that packet across a WAN link.

You would use the header compression on a network with small packets and a few bytes of data such as Telnet. Cisco's header compression supports X.25, Frame Relay, and dial-on-demand WAN link protocols. Because of processing overhead, header compression is generally used at lower speeds such as 64Kbps links.

TCP header compression is achieved by using the `ip tcp header-compression` command:

```
Router(config)#interface serial0
Router(config-if)#ip tcp ?
  compression-connections  Maximum number of compressed connections
  header-compression       Enable TCP header compression
Router(config-if)#ip tcp header-compression ?
  passive  Compress only for destinations which send compressed headers
```

The `passive` parameter is optional and is used to instruct the router to compress the headers of outbound TCP traffic if the other side is also sending compressed TCP headers. If you don't include the `passive` argument, all TCP traffic will use compressed TCP headers.

Payload Compression

Payload compression, also known as *per-virtual-circuit compression*, compresses only the payload, or data portion, of the packet. The header of the packet is not touched.

Link Compression

Link compression, also known as *per-interface compression*, compresses both the header and payload section of a data stream. Unlike header compression, link compression is protocol independent.

The link compression algorithm uses *Stac* or *Predictor* to compress the traffic in another link layer such as PPP or LAPB, ensuring error correction and packet sequencing. Cisco proprietary HDLC protocol is capable of using Stac compression only.

Predictor Use this approach to solve bottleneck problems caused by a heavy load on the router. The Predictor algorithm learns data patterns and "predicts" the next character by using an index to look up a sequence in a compression dictionary. This is sometimes referred to as *lossless* because no data will be lost during the compression and decompression process.

Stac This method is best used when bottlenecks are related to bandwidth issues. The Stac method searches the input data stream for redundant strings and replaces them with a token that is shorter than the original redundant data string.

If the data flow traverses a point-to-point connection, use link compression. In a link compression environment, the complete packet is compressed and the switching information in the header is not available for WAN switching networks. Typical examples are leased lines or ISDN.

If you use payload compression, you should not use header compression. This is redundant, and you should configure payload compression only.

In the following example, we turned on LAPB encapsulation with Predictor compression and set the maximum transmission unit (MTU) and the LAPB N1 parameters:

```
Router#config t
Enter configuration commands, one per line. End with CNTL/Z.
Router(config)#interface serial0
Router(config-if)#encapsulation lapb
Router(config-if)#compress ?
predictor  predictor compression type
stac       stac compression algorithm
Router(config-if)#compress predictor
Router(config-if)#mtu 1510
Router(config-if)#lapb n1 12096
```

The LAPB N1 represents the number of bits in an LAPB frame, which holds an X.25 packet. It is set to eight times the MTU size, plus any overhead when using LAPB over leased lines. For instance, the N1 is specified at 12,080 (that is, 1,510 × 8) plus 16 bits for protocol overhead. The LAPB N1 parameter can cause major problems if it's not configured correctly, and most often it should be left at its default value. Even so, it can be really valuable if you need to set the MTU size.

Compression Considerations

You need to keep a few considerations in mind when selecting and implementing a compression method:

Modem compression Modems can compress data up to four times smaller than its original size. There are different types of modem compression techniques, so make sure you understand that modem compression and router software compression are not compatible. However, the modems at both ends of the connection will try to negotiate the best compression method to use. If compression is being done at the modem, do not configure the router to also run compression.

Encrypted data Compression happens at the Data Link layer (layer 2), and encryption functions at the Network layer (layer 3), although the payload is also encrypted, which includes layer 7. After the application encrypts the data, the data is then sent to the router, which provides compression. The problem is that encrypted data typically does not have repetitive patterns, so the data will not compress. The router will spend a lot a processor time to determine the traffic is not compressible. So, if data is encrypted, do not attempt to compress it by using a layer 2 compression algorithm.

CPU cycles versus memory The amount of memory that a router must have varies according to the protocol being compressed, the compression algorithm, and the number of configured interfaces on the router. Memory requirements will be higher for Predictor than for Stac, but Stac is typically more processor intensive.

Viewing Compression Information

To view information about the status of compression on the router, use the `show compress` command. The following is a sample of the output from this command:

```
Router2#show compress
 Serial1
  uncompressed bytes xmt/rcv 82951/85400
  1 min avg ratio xmt/rcv 0.798/0.827
  5 min avg ratio xmt/rcv 0.789/0.834
  10 min avg ratio xmt/rcv 0.779/0.847
  no bufs xmt 0 no bufs rcv 0
  restarts 0
      Additional Stacker Stats:
      Transmit bytes: Uncompressed = 27044 Compressed =           66749
      Received bytes: Compressed = 76758 Uncompressed = 0
```

This command shows the uncompressed byte count of compressed data transmitted and received as well as the ratio of data throughput gained or lost in the compression routine in the last 1, 5, and 10 minutes. If the restarts are more than 0, the compression routine detected that the dictionaries were out of sync and restarted building the compression dictionary. Using this command, you will be able to see if compression is making a difference for the type of traffic being compressed.

Summary

Queuing is an important technology when using WAN links. As the speed of LAN interfaces increases more and more, data will be expected to traverse WAN links. Congestion is inevitable, so to ensure that important data gets through, a queuing mechanism is necessary. There are many queuing options available when using Cisco IOS.

Weighted fair queuing (WFQ) is the default technique when using interfaces of 2.048Mbps or slower. WFQ will track conversations and enable lower bandwidth conversations to take priority over higher bandwidth conversations. This feature can be tuned to allow tracking of more conversations.

Priority queuing is used to classify traffic into four queues of high, medium, normal, and low. Each queue is serviced sequentially, and the traffic is forwarded from the higher level queues before the router services the lower level queues. The lower level queues might not be serviced for quite some time if there is a large amount of higher priority traffic.

Custom queuing can allocate a certain percentage of the total bandwidth available on the interface. There are 16 queues available, which can hold a certain type of traffic, and each queue can be allocated a specific amount of bandwidth. Custom queuing does not suffer from queue starvation as priority queuing can.

To alleviate congestion on WAN links, compression can be configured on the interface. The types of compression algorithms are Stac, Predictor, and MPPC. MPPC is used primarily for Windows clients, whereas Stac and Predictor can be used on many types of WAN technologies. TCP header compression is the simplest compression technique. Payload compression compresses the payload portion of the packet and does not alter the layer 2 or layer 3 header information. The link compression algorithm uses Stac or Predictor to compress the traffic and then encapsulates the compressed traffic in another link layer such as PPP or LAPB to ensure error correction and packet sequencing.

Various techniques can ensure that the queuing and compression technologies are working correctly. The `show queue` command is used to see queuing on the interface, and the `show queueing [priority | custom | fair]` command is used to display the queuing technique configured on the router. For compression, the `show compress` command is used to see how well the compression process is compressing traffic and whether problems might occur with the compression process.

Exam Essentials

Understand the queuing technologies available in Cisco IOS. You should know that there is weighted fair queuing (WFQ), priority queuing, and custom queuing. Each has its strengths and weaknesses, but WFQ is the default technique used for 2.048Mbps or slower interfaces. WFQ can be tuned with the `fair-queue` command to enable more conversations to be tracked per interface.

Know how to configure priority queuing and when it is best used. Picking the proper queuing mechanism is very important, and priority queuing is ideal if you want to ensure that certain traffic gets priority over other traffic. A priority queue is set up with the `priority-list` command and is applied to the interface with the `priority-group` command.

Know how to configure custom queuing and when it is best used. Custom queuing is a technique that enables the WAN designer to allocate a certain amount of bandwidth to different traffic types. There are 16 queues that can be set up to contain certain types of traffic, and each of these queues can be allocated a specific amount of bandwidth. A custom queue is configured with the `queue-list` command and is applied to the interface with the `custom-queue-list` command.

Understand compression techniques and algorithms and when to use them. You should know that the compression techniques are TCP header compression, payload compression, link compression, and MPPC compression. TCP header compression is used on point-to-point links and when smaller TCP packets, such as Telnet traffic, are being sent over the link. Payload compression can be used on links other than point-to-point and is used to compress the data portion of the packet; it will not alter the layer 2 and layer 3 headers. Link compression is used only on point-to-point links but is protocol independent. It will compress the whole packet and encapsulate that packet in another protocol to ensure reliability and sequencing. MPPC is used when the Cisco device needs to talk to Windows-based clients.

Know the troubleshooting commands used for queuing and compression. The commands to show queuing are `show queue` and `show queueing [fair | priority | custom]`. These can be used to display queuing on the device and the counters involved. The compression troubleshooting command is `show compress`, which can be used to view the compression efficiency and status.

Network Address Translation and Port Address Translation

THE CCNP EXAM TOPICS COVERED IN THIS CHAPTER INCLUDE THE FOLLOWING:

- ✓ Describe the process of Network Address Translation (NAT).
- ✓ Configure Network Address Translation (NAT).
- ✓ Troubleshoot nonfunctional remote access systems.

As the Internet grows and individuals increasingly need more than one IP address to use for Internet access from their home and office PCs, their phones (Voice over IP, VOIP), their office's network printers, and many other network devices, the number of available IP addresses is diminishing. To add insult to injury, the early designers of TCP/IP—back when the Internet project was being created by the Advanced Research Projects Agency (ARPA)—never anticipated the explosion of users from private industry that has occurred.

ARPA's goal was to design a protocol that could connect all the United States Defense Department's major data systems and enable them to talk to one another. The ARPA designers created not only a protocol that would enable all the Defense Department's data systems to communicate with one another, but one that the entire world now relies on to communicate over the Internet.

Unfortunately, because of the unexpected popularity of this protocol, the distribution of IP addresses was inadequately planned. As a result, many IP addresses are unusable, and many are placed in networks that will never use all the addresses assigned to them. For example, every organization with a Class A network, which provides 16,777,214 addresses per Class A assignment, would find it difficult to use more than half of the addresses available, and those that are not used are wasted.

All the Class A and Class B addresses are already assigned to organizations. There are 65,534 Class B addresses available in each Class B address range. If a new organization needs more than one Class C address range, which provides only 254 addresses, they must get another Class C address range.

IP version 6 will eventually alleviate IP addressing problems because it increases the address space from 32 bits to 128 bits, but its adoption has been slow because of the problems associated with infrastructure and application support. Outside the United States, IPv6 is being paid more attention because less IPv4 address space is available. Specifically, Japan has implemented a large-scale IPv6 network because of the number of addresses needed and the availability of IPv6 address space.

This chapter introduces you to Network Address Translation (NAT) and Port Address Translation (PAT). Cisco routers and internal route processors use these two protocols to allow the use of a limited number of registered IP addresses by a large number of users and devices. As you progress through the chapter, you will learn the differences between NAT and PAT, as well as their operational boundaries, how to configure them, and how to troubleshoot problems associated with these two protocols.

Understanding Network Address Translation (NAT)

Before exploring the details of *Network Address Translation (NAT)* operations, configuration, and troubleshooting, it's important to thoroughly understand what it is, the terminology associated with it, its advantages and disadvantages, and the traffic types it supports. NAT is a protocol that maps an inside IP address used in the local, or inside, network environment to the outside network environment and vice versa. There are many reasons for using NAT in your network environment. Some of the benefits you will receive from NAT include the following:

- Enabling a private IP network to use unregistered IP addresses to access an outside network such as the Internet
- Providing the ability to reuse assigned IP addresses that are already in use on the Internet
- Providing Internet connectivity in networks where there are not enough individual Internet-registered IP addresses
- Appropriately translating the addresses in two merged intranets such as two merged companies
- Translating internal IP addresses assigned by old Internet service providers (ISPs) to a new ISP's newly assigned addresses without manually configuring the local network interfaces

NAT Terminology

Before continuing with this chapter, you should be familiar with the following Cisco terms:

Inside network The *inside network* is the set of network addresses that is subject to translation. The IP addresses used within the network are invalid on an outside network such as the Internet or the network's ISP. Often, the IP addresses used in the inside network are obsolete, or an IP address is allocated in a range specified by RFC 1918 or RFC 3330 (which reserves certain IP addresses for internal use only) and is not Internet routable.

Outside network The *outside network* is not affiliated with or owned by the inside network organization. (Keep in mind we are referring to a network—not network addresses.) This can be the network of another company when two companies merge, but typically is the network of an ISP. The addresses used on this network are legally registered and Internet-routable IP addresses.

Inside local IP address The *inside local IP address* is the IP address assigned to an interface in the inside network. This address can be illegal to use on the Internet, or it can be an address defined by RFC 1918 as unusable on the Internet. In both cases, this address is not globally routable. If the address is globally routable, it can be assigned to another organization and cannot be used on the Internet.

Inside global IP address The *inside global IP address* is the IP address of an inside host as it appears to the outside network. This is the "translated IP address." Addresses can be allocated from a globally unique address space, typically provided by the ISP (if the enterprise is connected to the global Internet).

Outside local IP address The *outside local IP address* is the IP address of an outside host as it appears to the inside network. These addresses can be allocated from the RFC 1918 space if desired.

Outside global IP address The *outside global IP address* is the configured IP address assigned to a host in the outside network.

Simple translation entry A *simple translation entry* is an entry in the NAT table that results when the NAT router matches an illegal inside IP address to a globally routable IP address that is legally registered for Internet use.

Extended translation entry An *extended translation entry* is a translation entry that maps one IP address and port pair to another.

How NAT Works

NAT is configured on the router or route processor closest to the border of a stub domain (a LAN that uses IP addresses—either registered or unregistered for internal use) between the inside network (local network) and the outside network (public network such as an ISP or the Internet). The outside network can also be another company, such as when two networks merge after an acquisition.

An illustration of NAT is shown in Figure 31.1. You should note that the router separates the inside and outside networks. NAT translates the inside local addresses into the globally unique inside global IP address, enabling data to flow into the outside network.

FIGURE 31.1 The NAT router on the border of an inside network and an outside network such as the Internet

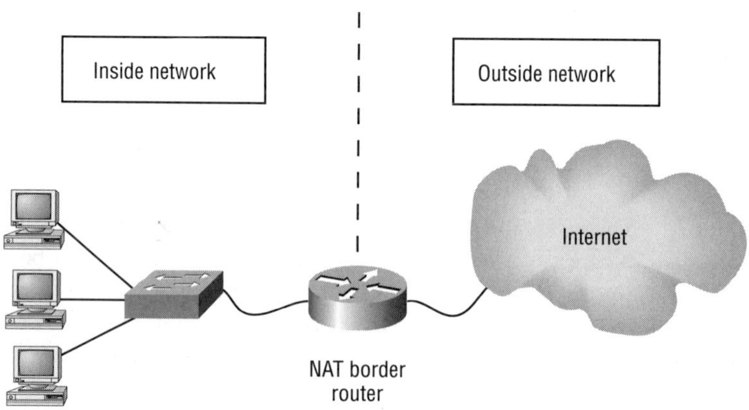

NAT takes advantage of there being relatively few network users using the outside network at any given time. NAT does this by using process switching to change the source address on the outbound packets, directing them to the appropriate router. This enables fewer IP addresses to be used than the number of hosts in the inside network. Before the implementation of NAT on all Cisco enterprise routers, the only way to implement these features was to use pass-through firewall gateways.

NAT was first implemented in Cisco's IOS release 11.2 and spelled out in RFC 1631.

Advantages of NAT

There are many advantages of using NAT. Some of the more important benefits include the following:

- NAT enables you to incrementally increase or decrease registered IP addresses without changes to hosts, switches, or routers within the network. (The exception to this is the NAT border routers that connect the inside and outside networks.)
- NAT can be used either statically or dynamically:
  - Static translation occurs when you manually configure an address translation table with IP addresses. A specific address on the inside of the network uses a specific outside IP address—manually configured by the network administrator—to access the outside network. The network administrator can also translate an inside IP address and port pair to an outside IP address and port pair.
  - Dynamic mappings enable the administrator to configure one or more pools of outside IP addresses on the NAT border router. The addresses in the pools can be used by nodes on the inside network to access nodes on the outside network. This enables multiple internal hosts to utilize a single pool of IP addresses.
- NAT can allow the sharing of packet processing among multiple servers by using the Transmission Control Protocol (TCP) load distribution feature. NAT load distribution can be accomplished by using one individual global address mapped to multiple local server addresses. This round-robin approach is used on the router distributing incoming connections across the servers.

There is no limit to the number of NAT sessions that can be used on a router or route processor. The limit is placed on the amount of DRAM the router contains. The DRAM must store the configurable NAT pools and handle each translation. Each NAT translation uses approximately 160 bytes, which translates into about 1.53MB for 10,000 translations. This is far more translations than the average router needs to provide.

- If your internal addresses must change because you have changed your ISP or have merged with another company that is using the same address space, you can use NAT to translate the addresses from one network to the other.

Disadvantages of NAT

Now that you know about the advantages of using NAT, you should learn about the disadvantages as well. The following is a list of some of the disadvantages of using NAT compared to using individually configured, registered IP addresses on each network host:

- NAT increases latency (delay). Delays are introduced into the switching path due to the processor overhead needed to translate each IP address contained in the packet headers. The router's CPU must be used to process every packet to decide whether the router needs to translate and change the IP header. Some Application layer protocols supported, such as DNS, have IP addresses in their payload that must be translated also. This adds to the increased delay.
- NAT hides end-to-end IP addresses that render some applications unusable. Some applications that use the host IP address inside the payload of the packet will break when NAT translates the IP addresses across the NAT border router.
- Because NAT changes the IP address, there is a loss of IP end-to-end traceability. The multiple packet-address changes confuse IP tracing utilities. This provides one advantage from a security standpoint: It eliminates some of a hacker's ability to identify a packet's source.
- NAT also makes troubleshooting or tracking down where malicious traffic is coming from more troublesome. Because the traffic could be coming from a single user who is using different IP addresses depending on when the traffic passes through the NAT router, accountability becomes much more difficult.

NAT Traffic Types

NAT supports many traffic types. The Remote Access exam includes questions on both the supported and unsupported types. Let's take a look at these types now.

Supported Traffic Types

NAT supports the following traffic types:

- TCP traffic that does not carry source and destination addresses in an application stream
- UDP traffic that does not carry source and destination addresses in an application stream
- Hypertext Transfer Protocol (HTTP)
- Trivial File Transfer Protocol (TFTP)
- File Transfer Protocol (FTP `PORT` and `PASV` commands)
- Archie, which provides lists of anonymous FTP archives
- Finger, a software tool for determining whether a person has an account at a particular Internet site
- Network Time Protocol (NTP)

- Network File System (NFS)
- `rlogin`, `rsh`, `rcp` (TCP, Telnet, and Unix entities to ensure the reliable delivery of data)

NAT-supported protocols that carry the IP address in the application stream include:

- Internet Control Message Protocol (ICMP)
- NetBIOS over TCP (datagram, name, and session services)
- Progressive Networks's RealAudio
- CUseeMe Networks CUseeMe
- Xing Technology's StreamWorks
- DNS "A" and "PTR" queries
- H.323 in IOS versions 12.0(1)/12.0(1)T or later
- Microsoft's NetMeeting (IOS versions 12.0(1)/12.0(1)T or later)
- VDOnet's VDOLive – IOS versions 11.3(4)/11.3(4)T or later
- Microsoft's VXtreme – IOS versions 11.3(4)/11.3(4)T or later
- IP Multicast – IOS version 12.0(1)T or later, source address translation only
- Point-to-Point Tunneling Protocol (PPTP) support with Port Address Translation (IOS version 12.1(2)T or later)
- Skinny Client Control Protocol, IP Phone to Cisco CallManager (IOS version 12.1(5)T or later)

Unsupported Traffic Types

NAT does not support some traffic types, including the following:

- Routing table updates
- DNS zone transfers
- BOOTP and DHCP
- Talk
- Ntalk
- Simple Network Management Protocol (SNMP)
- NetShow

Performing NAT Operations

Understanding how NAT functions when it is configured a certain way will aid you in your configuration decisions. This section covers NAT's operations when NAT is configured to provide the following functions:

- Translating inside local addresses
- Overloading inside global addresses

- Using TCP load distribution
- Overlapping networks

Translating Inside Local Addresses

NAT operates on a router and usually connects two networks. NAT translates the local non-unique IP addresses into legal, registered Internet addresses before forwarding packets from the local network to the Internet or another outside network. To do this, NAT uses a six-step process, as shown in Figure 31.2.

The six-step process, as Figure 31.2 illustrates, is as follows:

1. User 10.1.2.25 sends a packet and attempts to open a connection to 206.100.29.1.
2. When the first packet arrives at the NAT border router, the router checks to see whether there is an entry for the local address that matches a global address in the NAT table.
3. If a match is found in the NAT table, the process continues to step 4. If a match is not found, the NAT router uses what is called a simple entry from its pool of global addresses. A simple entry occurs when the NAT router matches a local IP address (such as the one currently being used) to a global IP address. In this example, the NAT router will match the address of 10.1.2.25 to 200.1.1.25.
4. The NAT border router then replaces the local address of 10.1.2.25 (listed as the packet's source address) with 200.1.1.25. This makes the destination host believe that the sending device's IP address is 200.1.1.25.

FIGURE 31.2 The process of translating inside local addresses

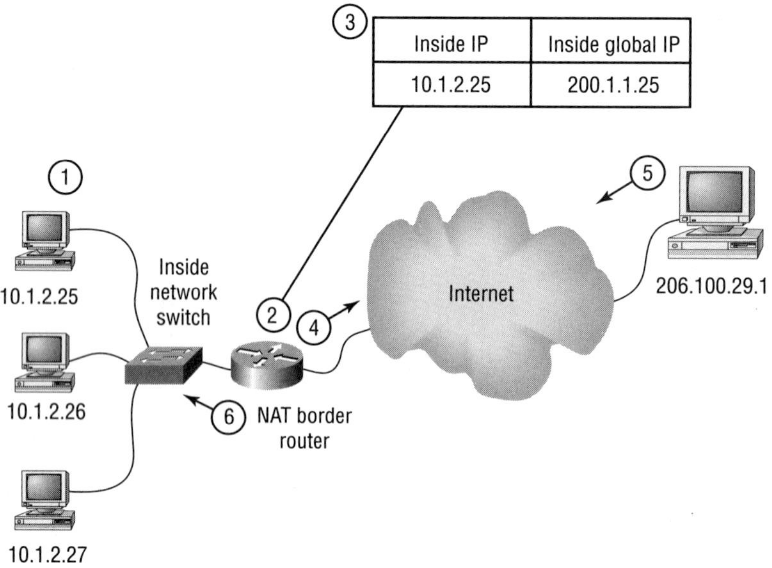

5. When the host on the Internet using the IP address 206.100.29.1 replies, it uses the NAT router–assigned IP address of 200.1.1.25 as the destination address.
6. When the NAT border router receives the reply from 206.100.29.1 with the packet destined for 200.1.1.25, the NAT border router checks its NAT table again. The NAT table shows that the local address of 10.1.2.25 should receive the packet destined for 200.1.1.25 and replaces the destination address with the internal interface's IP address.

Steps 2 through 6 are repeated for each individual packet.

Overloading Inside Global Addresses

You can conserve addresses in the inside global address pool by enabling the router to use one global address for many local addresses. When NAT overloading is enabled, the router maintains higher level (layer 4) protocol information in the NAT table for TCP and UDP port numbers to translate the global address back to the correct inside local address. When multiple local addresses map to one global address, NAT uses the TCP or UDP port number of each inside host to make unique, distinguishable outside network addresses.

Figure 31.3 shows the NAT operation when one inside global address represents multiple inside local addresses. The TCP port number is the portion of the global IP network address that differentiates between the two inside local addresses on the network.

When the router processes multiple nonroutable inside IP addresses to one globally routable global IP address, it performs the following steps to overload inside global addresses:

1. The host at the inside IP address of 10.1.2.25 opens a connection to a host at IP address 205.1.1.25 on an outside network.

FIGURE 31.3 NAT overloading inside global addresses

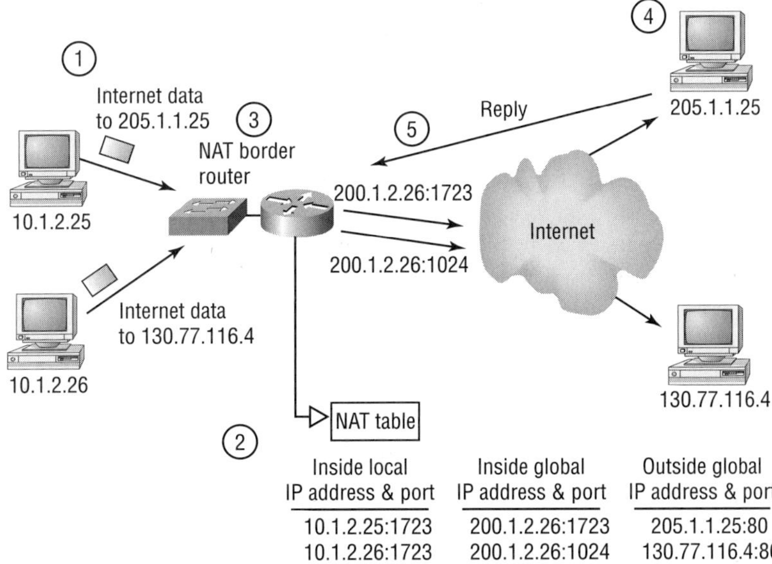

2. The first packet that the NAT border router receives from the host at 10.1.2.25 causes the router to check its NAT table. Because no translation entry exists, the router determines that address 10.1.2.25 must be translated and configures a translation to the inside global address of 200.1.2.25. If overloading is enabled and another translation is active, the router reuses the global IP address from that translation and saves enough information to translate returning packets back. This type of entry is called an extended entry.
3. The router replaces the inside local source address of 10.1.2.25 with the selected globally routable address and a unique port number and forwards the packet. In this example, the source address is now shown as 200.1.2.26:1723 in the NAT table.
4. The host at 205.1.1.25 receives the packet and responds to the host at 10.1.2.25 by using the inside global IP address and port in the source address field of the packet received (200.1.2.26:1723).
5. The NAT border router receives the packet from 205.1.1.25. It then performs a NAT table lookup, using the inside global address and port, with the outside address and outside port number. The router then translates the address back to the destination address of 10.1.2.25. The NAT border router then forwards the packet to the host using the IP address of 10.1.2.25 on the inside network.

Steps 2 through 5 are continued for all subsequent communications until the connection is closed.

Both the host at IP address 205.1.1.25 and the host at IP address 130.77.116.4 think they are talking to a single host at IP address 200.1.2.26. They are actually talking to different hosts, with the port number being the difference that the NAT border router uses to forward the packets to the correct host on the local inside network. In fact, with the port addressing scheme, you use could allow approximately 4,000 hosts to share the same inside global IP address by using the many available TCP and UDP port numbers.

Using TCP Load Distribution

TCP load distribution is a dynamic form of destination IP address translation that can be configured for certain outside network traffic to be mapped to a valid inside network for IP traffic destined for more than one node. After a mapping scheme is created, destination IP addresses matching an access list are replaced with an address from a rotary pool on a round-robin basis.

When a new connection is established from the outside network to the inside network, all non-TCP traffic will be passed without being translated, unless another translation type is applied to the interfaces. Figure 31.4 illustrates TCP load distribution, which is explained in further detail next.

Let's look at the process NAT uses to map one virtual host to several real hosts:

1. In Figure 31.4, the PC using global IP address 206.2.2.25 opens a TCP connection to a virtual host at 200.1.1.25.
2. The NAT border router receives this new connection request and creates a new translation, which allocates the next real host of 10.1.2.25 for the inside local IP address and adds this information to the NAT table.

FIGURE 31.4 TCP load distribution steps

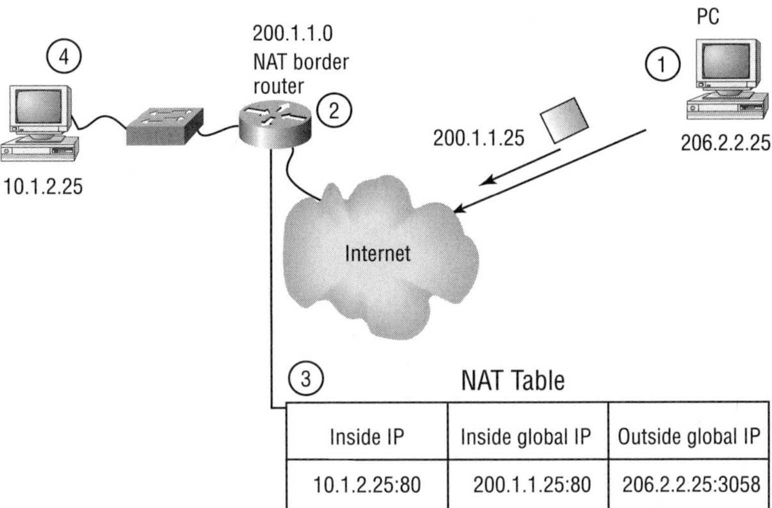

3. The NAT border router replaces the destination IP address with the selected real host IP address and then forwards the packet.
4. The real host at IP address 10.1.2.25 receives the packet and responds.
5. The NAT border router receives the packet and performs another NAT table lookup by using the inside local IP address and port number and the outside IP address and port number as the key. The NAT border router then translates the source address to the virtual host's address and forwards the packet.
6. The next connection request to that inside global IP address causes the NAT border router to allocate 10.1.2.26 for the inside local address.

Overlapping Networks

Let's say your network uses an IP addressing scheme that is valid and globally usable, but another company is using it or you are no longer authorized to use it. Now imagine your ISP thinks it has you locked in because it's providing your IP address scheme, and it suddenly doubles your prices. Rather than pay the higher prices, you shop for a new ISP with a different IP address range.

You finally find this terrific new ISP that is going to supply you with terrific Internet speeds at a third of the cost of your other ISP. Unfortunately, it's also going to supply you with a terrific new IP address scheme that you must apply to your network. Even in a mid-sized network, you would spend many hours changing your IP address scheme—and waiting for this would affect your users tremendously. The solution is to implement a *NAT overlapping address translation.*

In this section, you will learn how to translate IP addresses that are not legally usable on an outside network such as the Internet into the new officially assigned IP addresses from your ISP.

For now, we will cover only the steps NAT uses to translate overlapping addresses. We will cover configuring overlapping address translation later in this chapter, in the section "Configuring NAT to Perform Overlapping Address Translation."

The following steps are used when translating overlapping addresses:

1. The host on the inside network tries to open a connection to a host on the outside network by using a fully qualified domain name (FQDN) by requesting a name-to-address lookup from an Internet Domain Name Server (DNS).
2. The NAT border router intercepts the Internet DNS's reply and begins the translation process with the returned address if there is an overlapping address that is residing illegally in the inside network.
3. To translate the returned address, the NAT border router creates a simple translation entry. This entry maps the overlapping legal outside address to an address from an outside local address pool of addresses legally usable on the outside network
4. The NAT border router replaces the source address with the new inside global address, replaces the destination address with the outside global address, and forwards the packet. This translation is for new outgoing traffic to the newly DNS-Learned IP Address.
5. The host on the outside network receives the packet and continues the conversation.
6. For each packet sent from the outside to the inside host, the router will perform a NAT table lookup, replace the inside global destination address with the inside local address, and replace the outside global source address with the outside local address. Conversely, for each packet sent from the inside to the outside host, the router will perform a NAT table lookup, replace the outside local destination address with the outside global address, and replace the inside local source address with the inside global address.

Configuring NAT

In this section, you will learn how to configure NAT for the following situations:

- Static NAT
- Dynamic NAT
- Inside global address overloading
- TCP load distributing
- Translating of overlapping addresses
- Verifying NAT's configuration
- Troubleshooting NAT
- Clearing NAT translation entries

Configuring Static NAT

Static NAT maps an illegal inside IP address to a legal global IP address so that the data can be sent through the Internet. Before trying to configure static NAT, IP routing should be enabled on your router, and the appropriate IP addresses and subnet masks should be configured on each interface.

Let's start the configuration process in global configuration mode, assuming that you have only one interface on the router connected to your inside network. In this example, the PC using the illegal inside IP address of 10.1.2.25 needs to access data on the Internet. When the NAT border router receives a packet going to the outside network from the IP address of 10.1.2.25, you will configure it to translate the source address to a legally usable address of 200.1.1.25. Do this by using the following command:

```
BorderRouter(config)#ip nat inside source static 10.1.2.25 200.1.1.25
```

To enable NAT, you must first select the interface that connects your inside network to the router or internal route processor. There is at least one interface on the router connected to the inside network and at least one interface connected to the outside network. You need to identify each and enable NAT on both with different commands. In this example, the router's inside network interface is Ethernet 0, and the outside interface is serial 0. To configure Ethernet 0 as a NAT inside interface, use the following steps from global configuration mode:

1. Enter the interface configuration mode, enable NAT, and identify whether you would like NAT to translate inside or outside addresses. In this example, you will have NAT translate inside addresses to outside addresses:

   ```
   BorderRouter(config)#interface ethernet0
   BorderRouter(config-if)#ip nat inside
   BorderRouter(config-if)#
   ```

2. Next, you need to configure serial 0 as the interface connected to your outside network. From global configuration mode, use the following commands:

   ```
   BorderRouter(config)#interface serial0
   BorderRouter(config-if)#ip nat outside
   BorderRouter(config-if)#
   ```

3. You should see the following when displaying the router configuration. The IP addresses of 10.1.2.254 and 200.1.1.1 are the IP addresses configured on the physical interfaces on the router:

   ```
   !
   interface Ethernet0
     ip address 10.1.2.254 255.255.0.0
     ip nat inside
   !
   interface Serial0
     ip address 200.1.1.1 255.255.0.0
     ip nat outside
   ```

Configuring Dynamic NAT, Inside Global Address Overloading, and TCP Load Distribution

This section explains how to configure *dynamic NAT* using inside global address overloading as well as TCP load distribution.

Dynamic NAT maps an illegal inside IP address to any legally registered, globally routable IP address from an identified pool of addresses. Before trying to configure dynamic NAT, you should enable IP routing on your router and configure the appropriate IP addresses and subnet masks on each interface.

Again, let's start the configuration process in global configuration mode, assuming you have only one interface on the router connected to your inside network and one connected to your outside network. In this example, a PC using the illegal inside IP address of 10.1.2.25 needs to access data on the Internet. When the NAT border router receives a packet going to the outside network from IP address 10.1.2.25, the NAT border router will choose an available globally routable IP address from the address pool and translate the source IP address to the legally usable address of 200.1.1.26. Do this by following these steps:

1. NAT translations from the inside local network to the inside global network take place after routing. Therefore, any access lists or policy routing will have been applied before the translation occurs. You will create an access list to specify the IP addresses to translate. In this example, you have a rather large network using the 10.1.0.0/16 IP address range, so the following command will be used to create a standard IP access list that contains a wildcard mask for the last two octets:

   ```
   BorderRouter(config)#access-list 2 permit 10.1.0.0 0.0.255.255
   ```

2. Now that you have an access list, which defines that packets coming from 10.1.2.25 will be translated, you need to define the actual pool of addresses that are routable on the Internet. This is the range of legal IP addresses that your ISP allocated to you for your use. You might have been given only 254 IP addresses for your 1,000 PCs and servers in the network, but because all your PCs aren't on the Internet at any given time, this might be enough. If it isn't, you need to use another solution, such as configuring inside global address overloading. Before you begin configuring your pool of addresses, you need to decide on a name. In this case, you will call your address pool `InternetIPPool`. To define the 254 IP addresses your ISP gave you (200.1.1.1 to 200.1.1.254 with the subnet mask 255.255.255.0), use the following command:

   ```
   BorderRouter(config)# ip nat pool InternetIPPool 200.1.1.1 200.1.1.254
    ➥netmask 255.255.255.0
   ```

To configure the router to utilize individual TCP ports, thus enabling an IP address to be used more than once, add the parameter `overload` after the NAT pool name.

Additional Options of *ip nat pool*

The command `ip nat pool` has two other options. First, instead of using the `netmask` syntax, you can use the `prefix-length` command followed by the number of bits in the mask, which indicates how many bits are ones. In this case, `24` indicates your netmask. You can also use `type rotary` after the netmask to enable TCP load distribution. This indicates that the IP addresses in the pool are real inside hosts that can be used for TCP load distribution. Second, you can use the parameter `match-host`, which attempts to match the host portion of the IP address to be translated to the same host number in the translated IP address. This is useful for quickly finding which internal host a translated IP address belongs to, but you must have at least a one-to-one relationship between local and global addresses.

3. At this point, you need to associate access list 2 (which you created in step 1) with the IP NAT pool `InternetIPPool` you created in step 2. To do this, use the following command:

```
BorderRouter(config)#ip nat inside source list 2 pool InternetIPPool
```

4. To enable NAT, you must first select the interface that connects your inside network to the router or internal route processor. To configure Ethernet 0 as a NAT inside interface, use the following commands from global configuration mode:

```
BorderRouter(config)#interface ethernet0
BorderRouter(config-if)#ip nat inside
BorderRouter(config-if)#
```

5. Next, you need to configure serial 0 as the NAT interface connected to your outside network. From global configuration mode, use the following commands:

```
BorderRouter(config)#interface serial0
BorderRouter(config-if)#ip nat outside
BorderRouter(config-if)#
```

There is another option when configuring dynamic NAT. You can use an interface instead of a pool of IP addresses. This is useful when you might not know the IP address of the outside interface—for example, when using DHCP on the outside interface. You still configure an access list that defines the traffic to NAT and defines which interfaces are inside and outside, but there is no `ip nat pool` command. In addition, the command to configure the NAT is slightly different: `ip nat inside source list` *`list-number interface outside-interface`* `overload`. The `overload` parameter is not required but is highly recommended because many inside hosts will be using the outside interfaces' IP address for their link to the outside network.

Configuring NAT to Perform Overlapping Address Translation

Configuring NAT to perform overlapping address translation is similar to configuring dynamic NAT. The difference is that you must identify and apply a pool of addresses for the NAT border router interface connecting to the inside network interface, as well as a pool to allow for connection to the outside network.

You will start the NAT configuration process in global configuration mode. The pool of addresses used in the inside network is 10.1.2.1 to 10.1.2.254. On the outside interface, you will configure a smaller pool of addresses that are globally routable on the Internet, assuming not all 100 of your PCs will need to access the outside network at the same time. The pool of addresses you will configure will be 200.1.1.1 to 200.1.1.50. It is assumed that the NAT border router is configured with routing, and the interfaces are configured with the proper IP addresses. Again, assume that your inside network is connected to the Ethernet 0 interface on the router, and the serial 0 interface connects your NAT border router to the outside network.

To configure the NAT router to perform overlapping address translation, complete the following steps:

1. Define a standard IP access list for the IP addresses on the inside network, as discussed earlier in the "Configuring Dynamic NAT, Inside Global Address Overloading, and TCP Load Distribution" section. The access list needs to be configured to permit traffic on the inside network that needs to be translated by NAT:

   ```
   BorderRouter(config)#access-list 2 permit 10.1.2.0 0.0.0.255
   ```

2. Define an IP NAT pool for the inside network addresses. The pool name will be called `outsidepool`, and the range of addresses is 192.168.1.1 to 192.168.1.253. The final syntax indicates the number of bits for the subnet mask. You can also use the command `netmask 255.255.255.0` as shown in step 3, which also identifies a 24-bit subnet mask. The pool does not include address 192.168.1.254 because that is the NAT border router's inside interface IP address:

   ```
   BorderRouter(config)#ip nat pool outsidepool  192.168.1.1 192.168.1.253
     ➥prefix-length 24
   ```

3. Define an IP NAT pool for the inside local network addresses. The pool name will be called `insidepool`, and the range of addresses is 200.1.1.1 to 200.1.1.50:

   ```
   BorderRouter(config)#ip nat pool insidepool 200.1.1.1 200.1.1.50 netmask
     ➥255.255.255.0
   ```

4. Next, associate the previously created access list to the previously created inside NAT pool with the following command:

   ```
   BorderRouter(config)#ip nat inside source list 2 pool insidepool
   ```

Again, you can use the `overload` command after the NAT pool name to reuse IP addresses in the pool.

5. Also, associate the same access list used in the previous command to the outside NAT pool with the following command:

```
BorderRouter(config)# ip nat outside source list 2 pool
  ➥outsidepool
```

6. For NAT to work, you must first configure the interface that connects your inside network to the router. To configure Ethernet 0 as the inside NAT interface, use the following commands from global configuration mode:

```
BorderRouter(config)#interface e0
BorderRouter(config-if)#ip nat inside
BorderRouter(config-if)#
```

7. Next, you need to enable NAT on the serial 0 interface connected to your outside network. From global configuration mode, use the following commands:

```
BorderRouter(config)#interface s0
BorderRouter(config-if)#ip nat outside
BorderRouter(config-if)#
```

The finished NAT router configuration follows:

```
ip nat pool insidepool200.1.1.1 200.1.1.50 netmask 255.255.255.0
ip nat pool outsidepool 192.168.1.1 192.168.1.253prefix-length 24
ip nat outside source list 2 pool outsidepool
ip nat inside source list 2 pool insidepool!
interface Serial0
 ip address 200.1.1.51 255.255.255.0
 ip nat outside
!
interface Ethernet0
 ip address 10.1.2.254 255.255.255.0
 ip nat inside
!
access-list 2 permit 10.1.2.0 0.0.0.255
```

Verifying NAT Configuration

To aid in verifying the configuration of NAT, you can use two specific commands. The `show ip nat translation` command shows the translations in the NAT table and the output in the following simple example:

```
BorderRouter(config)#show ip nat translations
Pro Inside global Inside local Outside local Outside global
--- 200.1.1.25    10.1.1.25    ---           ---
--- 200.1.1.26    10.1.1.26    ---           ---
```

You can use the same command with an additional parameter to get more information about each NAT table entry. The `show ip nat translation verbose` command displays more information about each NAT table entry, such as the time left until the entry in the NAT table expires, as shown here:

```
BorderRouter(config)#show ip nat translations verbose
Pro Inside global   Inside local Outside local    Outside global
--- 200.1.1.25     10.1.1.25     ---           ---
  create 00:05:01, use 00:00:00, left 23:12:40, flags: none
--- 200.1.1.26     10.1.1.26     ---           ---
  create 00:04:29, use 00:00:00, left 23:13:10, flags: none
```

The second command is used to display statistics and configuration information about NAT running on the router. The `show ip nat statistics` command displays information about the NAT table, as shown here:

```
BorderRouter(config)# show ip nat statistics
Total active translations:2(0 static, 2 dynamic,0 extended)
Outside interfaces: Loopback 0, Serial1
Inside interface: Serial0
Hits: 243 Misses: 2
Expired translations: 0
Dynamic mappings:
-- Inside Source
access-list 2 pool insidepool refcount 1
  pool insidepool: netmask 255.255.255.0
   start 200.1.1.1 end 200.1.1.4
   type generic,total address 5,allocated 2 (50%),misses 0
```

Troubleshooting NAT

Using the `debug ip nat` command can assist you when troubleshooting NAT problems. In the following output, you will notice that the source address 10.1.2.5 is sending a packet to the destination address 206.1.2.5. An arrow (->) indicates that a packet's source address was translated. An asterisk (*) indicates that a packet is traveling through the *fast path* or the hardware processing path. A packet in a conversation with another node will always first travel through a process-switched *slow path* or the software processing path. Additional packets used in that flow will go through the fast path if there is a cache entry for the source and destination address. Here is the output from the described scenario:

```
BorderRouter#debug ip nat
NAT: s=10.1.2.5->200.1.2.25, d=206.1.2.5 [0]
NAT: s=206.1.2.5, d=200.1.2.25->10.1.2.5 [0]
```

```
NAT: s=10.1.2.5->200.1.2.25, d=206.1.2.5 [1]
NAT: s=10.1.2.5->200.1.2.25, d=206.1.2.5 [2]
NAT: s=10.1.2.5->200.1.2.25, d=206.1.2.5 [3]
NAT*: s=206.1.2.5, d=200.1.2.25->10.1.2.5 [1]
NAT: s=206.1.2.5, d=200.1.2.25->10.1.2.5 [1]
NAT: s=10.1.2.5->200.1.2.25, d=206.1.2.5 [4]
NAT: s=10.1.2.5->200.1.2.25, d=206.1.2.5 [5]
NAT: s=10.1.2.5->200.1.2.25, d=206.1.2.5 [6]
NAT*: s=206.1.2.5, d=200.1.2.25->10.1.2.5 [2]
```

Two parameters can be used with the debug `ip` nat command: `list` and `detailed`. The value in brackets is the IP identification number. This information enables you to correlate these trace packets with other packet traces from sniffers used for troubleshooting in the network. (*Sniffers* are devices that can be used to look at the traffic flowing through the network.)

Clearing NAT Translation Entries

Occasionally, NAT is properly configured but translations are not occurring. Most of the time, clearing the NAT translations resolves the problem. Table 31.1 shows the available commands for clearing the NAT table.

TABLE 31.1 Commands Available to Clear the NAT Table

Command	Meaning
`clear ip nat translation *`	Clears all NAT table entries.
`clear ip nat translation inside` *`global-ip`*	Clears all inside NAT table simple translation entries.
`clear ip nat translation outside` *`local-ip`*	Clears all outside NAT table simple translation entries.
`clear ip nat translation` *`protocol inside global-ip global-port local-ip local-port`* [*`outside local-ip local-port global-ip global-port`*]	Clears all NAT table extended entries.

Using Port Address Translation (PAT)

If you wish to enable address translation on the 700 series router, you use *Port Address Translation (PAT)*. PAT is a subset of NAT and is the only address translation feature on the Cisco 700 series of routers. PAT uses TCP ports to enable an entire network to use only one globally routable IP address in the network. PAT is similar to overloading with traditional NAT.

The Cisco 700 series routers with release 4 software and higher support PAT, which enables local hosts on an inside IP network to communicate to an outside IP network such as the Internet. Traffic destined for an outside IP address on the other side of a border router will have its source IP address translated before the packet is forwarded to the outside network. IP packets returning to the inside network will have their destination IP addresses translated back to the original source IP addresses on the inside network.

PAT conserves network addresses by enabling a single Internet-routable IP address to be assigned to an entire LAN. All WAN traffic is usually mapped to a single IP address, which is the ISDN-side IP address of the Cisco 700 series router. Because all the traffic on the outside network appears to come from the Cisco 700, the inside network appears invisible to the outside network or Internet.

You should configure a static IP address and port if remote users need to access a specific server on the inside network. PAT will allow packets with a specific well-known port number to get through, such as FTP or Telnet. This feature is known as a default port handler.

PAT is also sometimes referred to as NAT overload.

Disadvantages of PAT

Using PAT has some disadvantages because it takes away end-to-end reachability. These disadvantages are as follows:

- You cannot use Ping from an outside host to a host in the private network.
- Telnet from an outside host to an inside host is not forwarded unless the Telnet port handler is configured.
- Only one FTP server and one Telnet server are supported on the inside network.
- Packets destined for the router itself and not an inside network IP address, such as DHCP, SNMP, PING, or TFTP, are not rejected or filtered by PAT.
- Because the 700 series is a low-end solution, if more than 12 PCs try to boot up simultaneously on the inside, one or more might get an error message about not being able to access the server.
- The PAT table is limited to 400 entries for the inside machines to share. If TCP translations are set up and the TCP timeouts are kept alive, no more than 400 machines can get to the outside world at any one time.

- The Cisco 700 series router with PAT enabled does not handle any fragmented FTP packets; this needs to be noted when troubleshooting.
- Some well-known ports cannot have port handlers defined. They include the following:
  - DHCP client ports used by the router for getting DHCP server responses
  - WINS NetBIOS ports used by the inside network clients operating Windows 95 PCs to get WINS information

Configuring PAT

The PAT feature enables local hosts with designated private IP addresses to communicate with the outside world. Basically, the router translates the source address of the IP header into a global, unique IP address before the packet is forwarded to the outside network. Likewise, IP packets returning will go through address translations again to the designated private IP addresses where the communication originated.

When PAT is enabled, RIP packet transmission is automatically disabled to prevent leaking private IP addresses to the outside network.

To enable PAT, the two commands that you need are as follows:

set ip pat on This command enables PAT and must be configured before the `set ip pat porthandler` command can be used.

set ip pat porthandler The port handler translates a public TCP or UDP port to a private IP address and port. When a packet is received from the outside, the router compares the port number with an internally configured port handler list of up to 15 entries. If a port handler is defined for this port, it routes the packet to the appropriate port handler (internal IP address). If a default port handler is defined, it routes the packet there. The possible parameters are as follows:

> *default* enables the port handler for all well-known ports, except ports specifically assigned a handler.
>
> *telnet* enables the port handler for the Telnet protocol on port 23.
>
> *ftp* enables the port handler for File Transport Protocol (FTP) and uses TCP protocol port 21.
>
> *smtp* enables the port handler for Simple Mail Transfer Protocol (SMTP) and uses TCP protocol port 25.
>
> *wins* enables the port handler for NetBIOS session service on port 139.
>
> *http* enables the port handler for World Wide Web–HTTP service and secure-HTTP port 80 or 443.
>
> *off* disables a certain port handler.
>
> *port* configures a custom port handler for a port not normally considered a well-known port. Remember that only 15 port handlers can be configured at once.

All parameters are followed by the appropriate IP address.

Real World Scenario

Configuring a Typical Office with a 700 Series Router for Internet Access

Company XYZ has decided it's time to get into this Internet thingy. The company has determined that their employees need to have Internet access to do research and send e-mail to their suppliers and customers. There is an internal web server that outside clients and employees will need to access from the Internet. They have contracted with you to set up a low-cost solution that will enable them to have access to the Internet from an ISDN line.

You have come up with the following configuration, which enables IP unnumbered across the WAN connection, enables DHCP server functionality, creates a port handler for the internal web server at IP address 10.1.2.21, and enables PAT on a Cisco 765 router. It will set the IP address on the router to 10.1.2.1 and then create a username—XYZ—that was supplied by the ISP. The following lists the entire configuration on a 765 router. The underlined commands are those discussed in the previous section:

```
>set systemname XYZ
XYZ> set switch ni-1
XYZ> set 1 spid 80155511110101
XYZ> set 2 spid 80155522220101
XYZ> set 1 directory 5551111
XYZ> set 2 directory 5552222
XYZ> set dhcp server
XYZ> set dhcp address 10.1.2.2 100
XYZ> set dhcp netmask 255.255.255.0
XYZ> set dhcp gateway primary 10.1.2.1
XYZ> set dhcp dns primary 200.1.1.48
XYZ> set dhcp wins primary 200.1.1.49
XYZ> set dhcp domain mydomain
XYZ> cd lan
XYZ:LAN> set bridging off
XYZ:LAN> set ip routing on
XYZ:LAN> set ip address 10.1.2.1
XYZ:LAN> set ip netmask 255.255.255.0
XYZ:LAN> cd
XYZ> set user ISP
XYZ:ISP> set ppp clientname XYZ
XYZ:ISP> set ppp secret client
Enter new Password: sybex1
Re-Type new Password: sybex1
XYZ:ISP> set ppp password client
Enter new Password: sybex1
```

```
Re-Type new Password: sybex1
XYZ:ISP> set bridging off
XYZ:ISP> set ip routing on
XYZ:ISP> set ip rip update off
XYZ:ISP> set ip route destination 0.0.0.0/0 gateway 0.0.0.0
XYZ:ISP> set 1 number 18015553333
XYZ:ISP> set 2 number 18015553333
XYZ:ISP> set ip pat on
XYZ:ISP> set ip pat porthandler http 10.1.2.21
XYZ:ISP> set ppp address negotiation local on
XYZ:ISP> set ppp authentication outgoing none
XYZ:ISP> set timeout 300
XYZ:ISP> set active
```

With this configuration, a router in XYZ's office will be able to dial up to the ISP and place their office on the Internet by using PAT through a single IP address. This will also allow outside clients and employees access to their web server by using the HTTP port handler.

Monitoring PAT

To monitor PAT and view the configuration settings, use the `show ip pat` command. When monitoring PAT, you can view the number of packets dropped, the timeouts, and the service or IP address using each individual TCP port. When you configure a Cisco 765 with the configuration shown in the real-world scenario, you should see output similar to the following example using the `show ip pat` command:

```
765:user1>show ip pat
Dropped - icmp 0, udp 0, tcp 0, map 0, frag 0
Timeout - udp 5 minutes, tcp 30 minutes
Port handlers [no default]:

Port     Handler          Service
-------------------------------------
21       Router           FTP
23       Router           TELNET
67       Router           DHCP Server
68       Router           DHCP Client
69       Router           TFTP
80       10.1.2.21        HTTP
161      Router           SNMP
162      Router           SNMP-TRAP
520      Router           RIP
```

Summary

As the Internet grows and companies need more and more IP addresses, the number of available IP addresses diminishes. This is one of the main reasons for the implementation of NAT and PAT—technologies that are critical to overcoming the shortage of IP addresses. You need to understand how NAT and PAT operate and how to configure each of them.

These two protocols, which allow for specifically defined address translations, provide some other interesting uses as well. For instance, NAT and PAT enable private IP networks to use unregistered IP addresses to access outside networks such as the Internet. They also provide the ability to reuse assigned IP addresses already in use on the Internet. In addition, they appropriately translate the addresses in two merged intranets, such as those of two merged companies. Finally, NAT and PAT translate internal IP addresses assigned by an old Internet service provider (ISP) to a new ISP's newly assigned addresses without manual configuration of all the local network interfaces.

There are some disadvantages to using NAT and PAT in a network. Specifically, they don't allow for a full end-to-end communication between two hosts. Some protocols carry IP address information in the payload of the packet that might not get translated by the border NAT router.

There are many IOS commands used specifically for troubleshooting NAT problems. The `show ip nat translations` command is one of the most useful, in addition to the `debug ip nat` feature. PAT also has its own troubleshooting commands; the `show ip pat` command is the most important.

Exam Essentials

Understand what NAT and PAT are and how to use them. NAT is a technology, specified in RFC 1631, that is used to hide network addresses behind a single IP address or multiple IP addresses. A company can use IP addresses set aside by RFC 1918 on their internal networks and use single or multiple Internet-routable IP addresses to connect their company to the network. PAT is like using NAT through a single IP address.

Know the advantages of NAT and PAT. The advantages of NAT and PAT are that they enable an entire network to hide behind IP addresses. They provide a certain level of security and enable a company to change ISPs quickly and painlessly. They also provide a primitive load-balancing mechanism between multiple hosts performing the same function.

Know the disadvantages of NAT and PAT. One disadvantage of using NAT and PAT is that some protocols will not work because they carry IP address information in the payload of the packet. In addition, NAT and PAT do not provide end-to-end significance for the IP address. Cisco IOS will correct some of these problems with the most popular protocols, but it cannot cover them all. Finally, a significant delay occurs in translating IP addresses, which introduces latency in the communication path.

Understand how to configure NAT and PAT on a Cisco router. One option when configuring NAT is to use dynamic NAT using a pool of IP addresses or through an interface. You can also reuse those IP addresses with the `overload` parameter. PAT uses only a single IP address. Another option is to configure a static translation from an outside IP address to an internal IP address. PAT can also be configured with static translations, but they are based on TCP and UDP port numbers and not on IP addresses only.

Know the troubleshooting techniques for NAT and PAT. The commands used to troubleshoot NAT are `show ip nat translation` with the optional `verbose` parameter, and `debug ip nat`, which logs NAT events as they occur on the router. For PAT, the only command used to show troubleshooting information is the `show ip pat` command on the 700 series router.

Centralized Security in Remote Access Networks

THE CCNP EXAM TOPICS COVERED IN THIS CHAPTER INCLUDE THE FOLLOWING:

- ✓ Know the security features of CiscoSecure and the operation of a CiscoSecure server.
- ✓ Understand the commands and procedures used to configure routers to access a CiscoSecure server and to use AAA.
- ✓ Know the commands used to configure AAA on a router to control access from remote access clients.

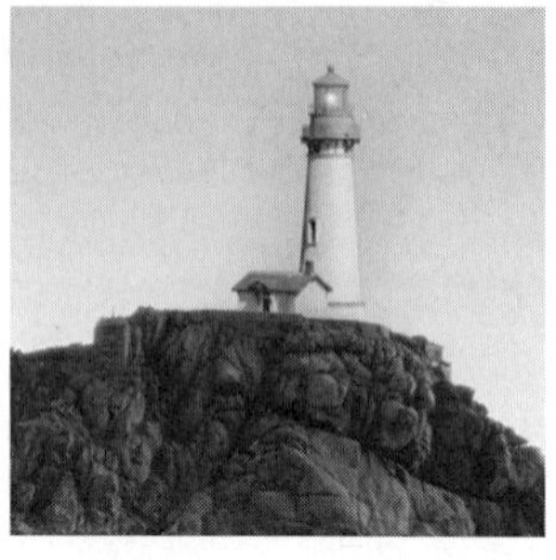

Remote access encompasses two elements:

- The communications channel between two points, or the connection
- Access control, or determining who or what can access the network and its data

These concepts are known as *authentication, authorization, and accounting (AAA).* AAA is Cisco's way of explaining the access control components and processes, and it is the topic of this chapter.

This book has covered many of the fundamental elements of authentication and authorization—particularly in the context of Challenge Handshake Authentication Protocol, or CHAP (see Chapter 24, "Point-to-Point Protocol"). This chapter explores these concepts further, but the discussion focuses more on the theoretical concepts of security and Cisco's preferred implementation of each of these concepts. AAA services are essential to providing centralized access control services, which is a recurrent theme in this chapter and most Cisco security implementations.

Security Terminology

Many of the terms presented in the other chapters of this book are familiar or easily interpreted from the context. This chapter's terms differ slightly because they might not be as familiar. Treat this list as a high-level introduction to these security components, but realize that more detail will be provided throughout the chapter:

Authentication The *authentication* function answers the fundamental question: Who is the user? By performing this function, you ensure that unwanted intruders will be denied access to the network while other users will be permitted. The user's identity can then be used to determine access permissions and to provide an audit trail of activity.

Authorization The *authorization* function often works in concert with authentication. It provides a means for defining which network services will be available to the authenticated user.

Accounting *Accounting* is an optional function in AAA; however, it is responsible for the auditing process, which can greatly enhance the security of the network. Accounting can also log the activities of the user, including the time that they start and stop their connection.

RADIUS *Remote Access Dial-In User Service (RADIUS)* is a protocol that is used to communicate between the remote access device and an authentication server. Sometimes an authentication server running RADIUS will be called a *RADIUS server.*

TACACS+ *Enhanced Terminal Access Controller Access Control System (TACACS+* is a protocol similar to RADIUS. Sometimes the server is called a *T-plus* or *T+ server*.

Security server A *security server* runs the protocol—TACACS+ or RADIUS—that is used to provide AAA services. It should be secured and redundant, especially if it provides business-critical access control. CiscoSecure is Cisco's version of this type of server and is available on Windows NT and Unix.

Cisco Access Control Solutions

Consider your home or apartment for a moment. It contains all your property, and theoretically, it's a private space for you and your family. Most likely, the door has a lock of some kind that restricts entry, and, with the use of a key, only you and other authorized persons are able to enter.

In this example, the door is very much like the remote access device in the network. It provides a gateway between the outside world and the home—in this case, the corporate network. The electronic door also has a key of sorts—frequently a username and password. *Access control* defines the manner in which these metaphorical keys are allocated and used; also, it defines what each person who enters the system can do.

Cisco access control solutions are used to implement the security policies of the network—specifically, the remote access connectivity. These solutions are targeted for a wide variety of platforms and functions. You will find Cisco access solutions for several platforms, including Windows NT and Unix.

Consider the following components used in remote access:

Clients In Cisco access control, a client is typically a remote user using a dial-in connection like the one that would be found on an asynchronous or an ISDN connection. These clients can use different forms of security and authentication, including CHAP and PAP (discussed in Chapter 24), or they can use remote client software, such as CiscoRemote. In addition, hardware-based tokens can be used to increase security—the tokens do this by calculating the proper response to a one-time challenge from the access server.

RADIUS and token-based authentication usually require the use of PAP, which passes the password in cleartext and is less secure than CHAP.

Access servers Clients connect to *access servers*, which provide the far end of a connection as viewed from the remote user's perspective. Stated another way, the access server is the front door to the network for remote users. The Cisco IOS and other software, including Cisco Broadband Operating System (CBOS), can provide varying degrees of security, including dialer profiles, access control lists (ACLs), and encryption.

To communicate between security servers and access servers, new protocols were developed, including TACACS+, RADIUS, and Kerberos.

Security servers Security servers provide a centralized means of controlling policy and storing account information. This can greatly simplify administration—similar to the way that Domain Name Server (DNS) eases name-to-address resolution. Recall that before DNS, each workstation was populated with a hosts file, which had to be modified for each change. DNS enabled hosts to query a single server for the resolution. Security servers operate in much the same manner—rather than storing usernames and passwords on each router, they can be stored on the server and queried by the network device when needed. Cisco's security server offering is called CiscoSecure, and it operates on Unix and Windows NT platforms. CiscoSecure is discussed in the next section.

Protocols for centralized authentication CHAP and PAP were designed for use on serial connections, making them unsuitable for Ethernet and other LAN technologies.

CiscoSecure

The CiscoSecure product is Cisco's security server solution. This product incorporates many services, including TACACS+ and RADIUS servers, as well as logging functionality.

CiscoSecure uses web-based interfaces and Java to provide multiple administrators with access to the server. Though the product supports both Internet Explorer and Netscape, it ships with a Netscape FastTrack Server, and some administrators find it to be more reliable with the Netscape client. CiscoSecure also relies on a relational database to manage accounts and store information—currently it supports the Oracle and Sybase database platforms.

For enhanced security, administrators can choose to use *one-time challenge tokens*. These tokens provide for the use of a different password for each login—a tactic that prevents session replay and other techniques that would otherwise compromise security. Token cards from CRYPTOCard, Enigma Logic, and Security Dynamics Technologies are supported with CiscoSecure.

Authentication, Authorization, and Accounting

Regarded as distinct elements, authentication, authorization, and accounting (AAA) all work cooperatively to establish and enforce a security model. This model is the result of a *security policy*, which should define an overall set of standards that will be used by the organization to secure and protect its assets. This policy can include definitions of access rights that will be assigned to different groups and the protocols that will be used for various functions. For example, one policy statement might include that TACACS+ is the sole protocol used and that SSH, a secure tool used for administration, is preferred over Telnet.

Real World Scenario

CiscoSecure's Response to Brute Force and Denial-of-Service Attacks

The CiscoSecure product, like other such products, has the capability to disable accounts automatically in response to brute force attacks. This is accomplished by *intruder detection*, in which the software assumes that the party is an intruder after a certain number of failed logins. A *brute force attack* is one in which the attacker bombards the system with login attempts. Ultimately, such an attack can lead to access—especially when passwords and account information are relatively simple. By detecting such an attack, products can disable the account before it is compromised. Frequently, such logic is limited to the number of attempts per unit of time, however. For example, a brute force rule might allow five bad login attempts per hour before locking the account for a day, or it might detect three bad passwords and then lock the account until the administrator releases it.

Unfortunately, most solutions to a brute force attack lead to another type of attack: denial-of-service. A *denial-of-service attack* usually does not lead to the access of private information; rather, as the name suggests, it prevents legitimate users from obtaining that data or using the resource. Administrators must balance the impact of brute force compromises against the potential of blocking access to legitimate users as a result of this protection. As with most products, including CiscoSecure and others, the responsibility to balance access control with access is placed on the administrator.

It is important to understand how authentication, authorization, and accounting work together to promote and support a security model. In this chapter, you will learn about how AAA works, as well as how AAA functions in Cisco's router access modes. AAA services are the basic tenet of Cisco remote access solutions, and, although their presentation has been left to the end of the book, you should find that the Physical and Network layers supplement these concepts well. This includes physical security, the use of access lists, static or authenticated IP routing, and other security techniques.

How AAA Works

It is important to remember that AAA is simply a grouping of three security functions—authentication, authorization, and accounting. Most texts examine each component as an isolated process, and although this is perhaps more accurate, here they have been placed into a three-step process to better communicate the interactions between each service. For example, it is perfectly valid to use only authentication and authorization while omitting accounting, but if you do so, administrators will lose the auditing benefits that are provided by the auditing service.

Step 1: Authentication

Authentication is the first facet of the three security elements, and it provides a basis for the remaining two components. Authentication provides the "who" in the AAA model. Like journalists who ask themselves the questions they must answer to make their story good (Who?, What?, Where?, When?, and How?), administrators need to ask who is involved in their system; it is one of the fundamental pieces of information they need to set up their system. Unfortunately, in computing, as in non-computing situations, it can be fairly simple to lie about one's identity.

To facilitate the authentication process, most systems require both a username and a password—it is hoped the password will be maintained in confidence in order to preclude the potential of compromise. By requiring two elements of identity, the computer-based system doubles the likelihood that the user is accurately identified.

However, it is possible to obtain, lie about, or guess both pieces of information. The likelihood of accurate authentication is stronger if a physical element is added. In non-computing situations, this might include a passport or driver's license; in the computer world, it might include a token-based device. As presented in the CiscoSecure section of this chapter, there are many products that can provide this service as a software receiver of the physical code card data.

Step 2: Authorization

After the identity of the user has been established, a decision must be made regarding what rights that user can exercise. This is called *authorization*, and is assigned by the administrator based on the requirements and business policies of the organization. An example of authorization would include permissions to access a remote access device or the ability to print a file. Because authentication and authorization are so involved and dependent on each other, they are regarded as a single security component in most environments.

Step 3: Accounting

Whereas authentication and authorization work to prevent unauthorized access, *accounting* provides a means of verifying that only authorized users obtain access. In addition, accounting is used to audit the actions of an authorized user.

An accounting record relies on the authenticity of the authentication process—a fraudulent user might provide a valid login, but the accounting feature provides the audit trail required to assess the damage. This log provides a record of when an activity occurred and what action was performed—connecting to a router, for example.

Router Access Modes

A Cisco router can be accessed by using one of two access modes. These are broadly categorized as character mode and packet mode. In essence, the difference between these modes can be best understood by looking at the commands that configure character and packet modes. You should understand the difference in the modes and use this section as an introduction to the configuration command syntax.

Character-Mode Connections

Character-mode connections describe character-based access, including access via the VTY, TTY, AUX (auxiliary), and CON (console) ports. Although such access might be through a packet-based network—Telnet, for example—the connection is still viewed as being character based. The AAA commands that configure character-mode access are as follows:

- `login`
- `exec`
- `nasi`
- `connection`
- `arap`
- `enable`
- `command`

Character-mode access usually includes connections only to the router or network device. Table 32.1 includes explanations of these commands.

TABLE 32.1 Character-Mode Authentication and Authorization Commands

Command	Description
`aaa authentication enable default tacacs+ enable`	Uses TACACS+ to determine whether the user can access enabled mode. If TACACS+ is unavailable, the local enable password will be used.
`aaa authorization exec tacacs+ local`	Determines whether the user is allowed access to the EXEC shell. This example provides for TACACS+ authentication, and should TACACS+ fail, it permits authorization via the local database. The local database is populated with the `username` command.
`aaa authorization command` *n* `tacacs+ local`	Runs authorization for all commands at privilege level *n* (a number between 0 and 15). Every line entered by a user can be controlled and authorized by TACACS+, although performance can suffer.
`username` *user* `password` *password*	Creates or adds to the local database with a username of *user* and the password of *password*. This database is stored in the router's configuration file in NVRAM (nonvolatile random access memory), and it can be accessed upon authentication failure depending on configuration.

Packet-Mode Connections

Packet-mode connections include most dial-up connections, including the following:

- `async`
- `group-async`

- serial
- ISDN BRI
- ISDN PRI

Packet-mode connections typically secure connections that pass traffic through the network device. You use the ppp, network, and arap AAA commands to control packet-mode connections. Table 32.2 offers a list with explanations of these commands.

These sections do not provide a complete breakdown of all possible commands, but instead they introduce the more common commands. Please refer to the documentation specific to your version of the IOS for a current listing of all commands and options or use the incorporated Help function.

TABLE 32.2 Packet-Mode Authentication Commands

Command	Description
`aaa authentication ppp user if-needed tacacs+`	AAA is used for PPP packet-mode challenges. The list user is used first, and if unsuccessful, TACACS+ will be used.
`aaa authorization network tacacs+ if-authenticated`	TACACS+ is used to determine whether the user is permitted to make packet-mode connections if the user is authenticated.
`interface async16 ppp authentication chap user`	This is a new command for this chapter in that it associates an AAA function with an interface. Specifically, line async16 is instructed to use the list user for CHAP authentication. Note that an AAA server (RADIUS, and so on) is not used.

AAA Configuration

Although AAA was designed to centralize access control, it still requires configuration on each and every network device. Fortunately, after AAA is configured, there are few instances when the administrator will need to alter its configuration—for example, when the encryption key is changed. Aside from such minor alterations, all changes—including those for user accounts—are invoked at the security server. This configuration process lets the router or access device know about the type of security to be used, the location of the security server, and the passwords or other information needed to facilitate communications.

In addition to these configuration commands, the administrator must establish network-level connectivity between the access device and the security server. This might require access list modification or route entries.

Table 32.3 outlines some of the AAA commands, including those for authentication and accounting. The configurations that relate to these commands are shown later in this section.

TABLE 32.3 Overview of AAA Commands and Configuration

Command	Description
`aaa new-model`	Enables AAA services on the router. `new-model` reflects changes from the initial implementation, which is no longer supported. In the absence of other AAA commands, the local database will be used for username and password. If no database is present and no other AAA method is specified, this command will lock out the router.
`aaa authentication login default tacacs+ enable`	Configures TACACS+ to be the default method used for login-level access. If TACACS+ is unavailable, use the local enable password.
`aaa authentication enable default tacacs+ enable`	Configures TACACS+ to be the default method used for enable-level access. If TACACS+ is unavailable, use the local enable password.
`aaa accounting exec start-stop tacacs+`	Configures the accounting process, logging the start and stop times of each exec session access.
`tacacs-server host` *`10.1.98.36`*	Specifies the IP address of the TACACS+ server. The `single-connection` parameter can be used to improve performance by maintaining a single TCP session as opposed to starting a separate session for each authentication.
`tacacs-server key` *`tjelkprp`*	Specifies the encryption key to be used for communications between the router and TACACS+ server.

Authentication Configuration

Authentication is configured differently on Cisco routers and switches; however, the general parameters are similar. In broad terms, the administrator must first instruct the device to use an authentication protocol and then provide the IP address for communications to the security server.

Router Configuration

The following is extracted from the full configuration file of the router to highlight the commands used for AAA configuration:

```
aaa new-model
aaa authentication login default tacacs+ enable
aaa authentication enable default tacacs+ enable
aaa accounting exec start-stop tacacs+
```

```
tacacs-server host 10.1.98.36
tacacs-server host 10.1.5.36
tacacs-server key tjelkprp
```

The preceding output is an example of a typical router configuration. This output starts the AAA service, establishes authentication services for both the login and enable processes, and audits the start and end times of each access. The two TACACS+ servers noted here are defined, and the preshared key is assigned.

In this example (which uses TACACS+), the `aaa authentication` command is used to define the type of authentication protocol. The `enable` keyword at the end of the two authentication commands allows the local enable secret password (use of the enable password would be used if the secret is not defined, but this is not recommended from a security perspective) to be used if network connectivity is lost between the security server and router; however, this also can be considered a security risk. This risk is minor, considering that the attacker would have to physically access the router or compromise the internal network sufficiently to change routes or block packets. Here, the `tacacs-server` command is being used to define the IP address of each TACACS+ server. In this example, the server key is being used to provide basic security over the communications link to the security server. Note that this configuration includes an `aaa accounting` command, which instructs the router to log the start and stop times of an exec session to the TACACS+ server.

Each of these commands is documented at the end of this chapter.

Catalyst Switch Configuration

On the Cisco Catalyst series switch platform running Catalyst Operating System (CatOS), the authentication commands present themselves differently, but the resulting behavior is the same. The following configuration, like the router configuration, uses TACACS+ for login and enable (privileged) mode:

```
#tacacs+
set tacacs server 10.1.98.36 primary
set tacacs server 10.1.5.36
set tacacs attempts 3
set tacacs directedrequest disable
set tacacs key tjelkprp
set tacacs timeout 5
set authentication login tacacs enable
set authentication login local enable
set authentication enable tacacs enable
set authentication enable local enable
```

Again, this configuration file is an excerpt from the Catalyst switch configuration file—displayed with the `show config` command. There are two TACACS+ servers defined; however, notice that one is defined as primary. On the router, the first server listed is defaulted to primary, but the switch allows for the primary's configuration by using the `primary` keyword. Don't be too concerned with understanding the switch configuration—the test focuses only on the router-based commands. The configuration is provided here so readers who have not previously experienced Catalyst commands can become familiar with them. The remainder of this chapter focuses only on the router commands.

The switch commands in this chapter are based on version 4.5.5 of the Catalyst code. There might be minor differences with other versions. `show config` or `write terminal` are often used to show the configuration information.

Authorization Configuration

Authorization defines the network services that are available to an individual or group. It provides an easy means of allowing privileged-mode (enable-mode) access while restricting the commands that can be executed. For example, you might want to isolate most enable commands to a single administrator or manager, while allowing operators to perform limited diagnostic functions. More experienced operators would be granted higher levels of authorization—for example, they might be permitted to shut down an interface. The unrestricted enable-mode administrator would be required for additional functions.

Use care in restricting administrative rights to the router. Although this is a helpful option when allocating rights to vendors and other parties, too restrictive a policy will lead to the distribution of the unrestricted account information, which can create a larger security risk.

A Sample TACACS+ Configuration File

The easiest way to understand the authorization function is to examine a configuration file that controls authorized services. Look at the following sample configuration file that controls authorized services:

```
#TACACS+ V2.1 configuration file
#created 5/14/03
#edited 8/26/03
#
#If user doesn't appear in the config file user/etc/password
default authentication = file /etc/passwd
accounting file = /home1/logs/tacacs+.accounting
```

```
#Must be same as router IOS "tacacs-server key"
key = tjelkprp
#
user=netops {
   member=operator
   login=cleartext dilbert
}
user=rpadjen {
   # Robert Padjen
   default service=permit
   login=cleartext yummy
}
group=operator {
   name="Network Operator"
   cmd=debug {
      permit .*
   }
   cmd=write {
      permit terminal
   }
   cmd=clear {
      permit .*
   }
   cmd=show {
   #permit show commands
   permit .*
   }
}

user=shayna {
   # Shayna Padjen
   member=operator_plus
   login=cleartext flatshoe
}
group=operator_plus {
   name="Network Operator Plus"
   cmd=debug {
      permit .*
   }
   cmd=write {
      permit terminal
```

```
   }
   cmd=clear {
      permit .*
   }
      #permit show commands
   cmd=show {
      permit .*
   }
   cmd=configure {
      permit terminal
   }
   cmd=interface {
      permit .*
   }
   cmd=shutdown {
      permit .*
   }
   cmd=no {
      permit shutdown
   }
}
```

This file establishes a number of user accounts and authorization rights. The first group, `operator`, is provided with basic diagnostic and administrative functions, while the `operator_plus` group is enhanced with `shutdown`, `interface`, and `configure` commands. All commands are available to one administrator. Note that Shayna is a member of `operator_plus`, and Rob is allowed full access.

Pay particular attention to a few additional items about this specific configuration file. First, the passwords are in cleartext, meaning that anyone with access to the server can obtain them. Most configuration files are encrypted. Second, observe that restrictions can be quite granular and could include functions such as Ping while blocking extended ping.

Please refer to the documentation that accompanies your server for syntax and configuration instructions specific to your installation.

Authorization Commands

Recall that authorization is the AAA process responsible for granting permission to access particular components in the network. The administrator will need to define these permissions based on corporate policy and user privileges. It is important to note that although a TACACS+ file was included in the previous section to illustrate authentication, the actual authorization controls were not included.

The commands associated with authorization include parameters for the protocols that are to be used and the method used for authorization. These commands are used after the authentication phase of AAA, and they are described in Table 32.4.

TABLE 32.4 AAA Authorization Commands

Command	Description
`aaa authorization network` *method*	Performs authorization security on all network services—including SLIP, PPP, and ARAP—using the method specified by the *method* parameter. The method could be TACACS+, RADIUS, local, and so on.
`aaa authorization exec` *method*	Authorizes the EXEC process with the specified AAA method.
`aaa authorization commands level 15` *method*	Authorizes all EXEC commands used at the specified level (0–15) by using the specified method. In this example, this is level 15, which is regarded as full authorization and normally associated with enable mode.
`aaa authorization config-commands`	Uses AAA authorization for configuration mode commands.
`aaa authorization reverse-access` *method*	Uses AAA authorization specified by the *method* parameter for reverse Telnet connections.
`aaa authorization function` *if-authenticated*	Permits the user to use the requested function only if the user is authenticated.
`aaa authorization function` *local*	Uses the local database for authorization for the specified function. This database is stored on the router's configuration in NVRAM.
`aaa authorization function` *radius*	Uses RADIUS for authorization of the specified function.
`aaa authorization function` *tacacs+*	Uses TACACS+ for authorization of the specified function.

Accounting Configuration

The accounting function records who did what and for how long. Because of this, it relies upon the authentication process to provide part of the audit trail. For this reason, it is recommended that accounts be established with easily identified usernames—typically a last-name, first-initial configuration. This information is coupled with six accounting types, as described in Table 32.5.

TABLE 32.5 AAA Accounting Types

Accounting Type	Function
Command	Documents the commands submitted by the user and the privilege level associated with them.
Connection	Provides auditing of all outbound connections.
EXEC	Logs user EXEC terminal sessions.
Network	Audits all PPP, SLIP, and ARAP session traffic counts, including number of packets and total bytes.
System	Records system-level events.
Resource	Provides information regarding connections that have failed, enabling the administrator to evaluate user attempts.

The configuration of accounting is fairly simple, but there are a few choices that should be considered. Table 32.6 provides a subset of the more common commands. Administrators will need to balance the desire to obtain complete accounting records against the overhead incurred. In Table 32.6, there is a function that is being accounted for that includes commands, connections, system events, and so on. There is a method used to account for those functions that includes start-stop, stop-only, and wait-start, and the server type to send this information to.

TABLE 32.6 AAA Accounting Commands

Command	Description
`aaa accounting command` *`level method server`*	Audits all commands at a specified level by using the specified method. (The options are start-stop, stop-only, and wait-start.) Sends this information to the server type (TACACS+ or RADIUS) specified.
`aaa accounting connection` *`method server`*	Audits all outbound connections (including Telnet and rlogin) to the specified server type by using the specified method.
`aaa accounting exec` *`method server`*	Audits the EXEC process with the specified method to the specified server type.
`aaa accounting network` *`method server`*	Audits network service requests (including SLIP, PPP, and ARAP requests) to the specified server type by using the specified method.

TABLE 32.6 AAA Accounting Commands *(continued)*

Command	Description
`aaa accounting system` *`method server`*	Audits system-level events by using the specified method to the specified server type. This includes reload, for example. Because a router reload is one of the ultimate denial-of-service attacks, it would be useful to know what user identification was used to issue the command.
`aaa accounting` *`function`* `start-stop` *`server`*	Documents the start and stop of a particular type of session specified by the `function` parameter to the specified server type. Audit information is sent in the background, negating any delay for the user.
`aaa accounting` *`function`* `stop-only` *`server`*	Sends a stop accounting notice at the end of a user process specified by the `function` parameter to the specified server type.
`aaa accounting` *`function`* `wait-start` *`server`*	Similar to `aaa accounting start-stop`, this command documents the start of a particular type of session specified by the `function` parameter to the specified server type. However, the user is not permitted to continue until the accounting server acknowledges the log entry. This can delay user access.
`aaa accounting` *`function`* `method {tacacs+ | radius}`	Enables accounting information to be sent to the TACACS+ or RADIUS accounting server for the specified `function` by using the specified method.

One area in which accounting transcends security is charge-back. If accurate start and stop times are recorded, a company could charge users for their time on the system to offset the cost. Internet service providers (ISPs) have long considered this as an alternative to the flat-rate model currently found in the United States.

Virtual Profiles

Virtual profiles and virtual templates provide ways to apply centralized, user-specific parameters to multiple access servers and their physical interfaces. This can greatly reduce the impact of changes to widely distributed access points.

As suggested by the name, there is a difference between a virtual profile and the element it replaces—the dialer profile. Dialer profiles maintain information on a single access server for specific users. The virtual profile adds the following:

- User-specific configurations served from the AAA server
- An open methodology for defining both standards-based and vendor-specific parameters

After the user authenticates the system, a virtual template is applied to the virtual access interface. User parameters are then obtained from the AAA server (security server) and applied to the virtual access interface. This solution allows for better scalability and easier administration than would be allowed with standard dialer profiles. As a result, the virtual profile is actually a combination of the physical interface, generic information stored in a virtual template on the access server, and user-specific parameters stored on the security server.

If you want to expand your understanding of virtual profiles and their usage, refer to the Cisco website (`www.cisco.com`).

Summary

To have a complete security policy in place, authorization, authentication, and accounting (AAA) must be implemented on a network. AAA not only allows full control over dial-up connections, but login and exec access to devices. Tracking and auditing is accomplished through the accounting services in AAA.

CiscoSecure is software that allows for centralized control over access to every device in your network. It will run on Windows NT and Unix and provides RADIUS as well as TACACS+ authentication, authorization, and accounting services.

The two access modes, which are controlled by AAA, are character-mode and packet-mode connections. Character-mode connections usually terminate at the access server or router, and packet-mode connections are those that pass traffic through an access server or router.

Configuration of AAA services for Cisco devices has many facets. The administrator must first configure how to authenticate users and then define which services those users will be allowed to access. The optional accounting feature can be used to audit the user's activity on the system.

The use of a virtual template is a technology that enables the security server to supply the access server with user-specific dialer profile information. Instead of each access server containing user-specific dialer profile information, this information is kept on the security server and downloaded to the access server when the user is authenticated.

Exam Essentials

Understand the components of AAA. You should know that AAA is the acronym for authentication, authorization, and accounting. Authentication is used to verify a user's authenticity, usually with a username and password. Authorization is used to determine which services are available to a verified user. Accounting is used to audit the user's activity on the system to provide tracking.

Know the services provided by CiscoSecure. The CiscoSecure software runs on Windows NT and Unix and provides a Java-based web client for configuration. The software provides RADIUS and TACACS+ services for authentication, authorization, and accounting. The software can store and retrieve user information with outside databases, including Oracle and Sybase.

Understand the functions provided by each AAA component, including the six accounting types. In addition to the AAA functions of authorizing and authenticating a user for access to various functions in the router, the accounting function can audit commands, connections, EXEC, network, system, and resources.

Know how to configure AAA services for Cisco IOS. AAA has been updated since its initial inception; the command `aaa new-model` is used so the user can utilize the new AAA commands. There are many AAA commands used to configure authentication, authorization, and accounting on a Cisco device. Each service command begins with the `aaa` prefix. You don't need to know the AAA commands for Cisco Catalyst series switches, but they are included in this chapter for completeness.

Understand the differences between packet-mode and character-mode services. Packet-mode services are typically dial-up connections, including asynchronous and ISDN access. Character-based services are connections such as login, exec, NASI, and commands. Most of these services terminate at the access device, which is typical of character-mode services.

Know that *aaa new-model* requires additional commands to configure correctly. Invoking the `aaa new-model` command with no other parameters will lock the administrator out of the router.

Cisco Internetwork Troubleshooting (CIT)

PART IV

Troubleshooting Methodology

THE CCNP EXAM TOPICS COVERED IN THIS CHAPTER INCLUDE THE FOLLOWING:

✓ Know troubleshooting methodologies.

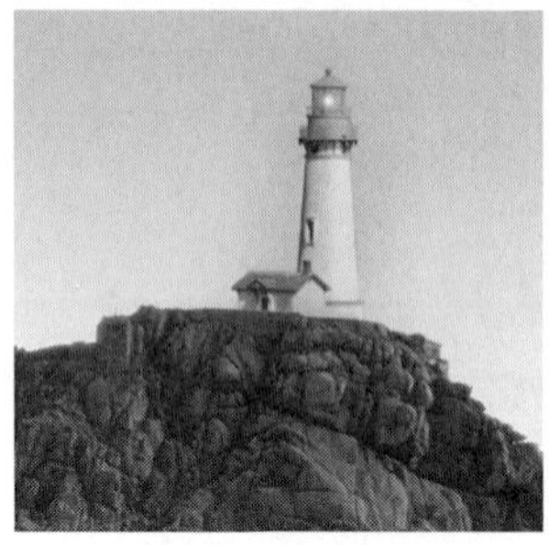

Troubleshooting is a skill that takes time and experience to fully develop. To be successful when diagnosing and repairing network failures, a good set of troubleshooting tools and skills is essential.

The information presented here is the foundation for the rest of the information covered on the exam. This chapter emphasizes the importance of following a specific set of troubleshooting steps when you try to diagnose and solve network problems. An effective troubleshooting methodology is needed because of the complexity of today's network environments. As a Cisco Certified Network Professional (CCNP), you need to understand and know how to apply an efficient and systematic troubleshooting methodology. Otherwise, you would be required to have a very intimate understanding of the network you are troubleshooting. It is imperative that you learn troubleshooting skills and understand the information available to you while solving network problems.

The Complexity of Internetworks

When a network failure occurs, time is of the essence. When a production network goes down, several things are affected. The most important of these is the bottom line—network failures cost money.

A good example is a call-center network. The company relies on the network to be available for its employees so that they can take phone orders, answer inquiries, or perform other business transactions that generate income. A failure in this environment needs to be diagnosed and repaired in a timely manner. The longer the network is down, the more money the company loses.

To minimize monetary and productivity losses, network failures must be resolved quickly. Troubleshooting is an integral part of getting this done. Intimate knowledge of a network also facilitates rapid resolution. Armed with a few troubleshooting skills and intimate knowledge of your network, you can solve most problems rather quickly, thus saving money.

Hold on a minute. What if you're new on the job and you don't yet have an intimate knowledge of the network? You can probably get up to speed quickly enough, right? Although that may have been the case in the past, getting up to speed becomes an overwhelming challenge in today's complex networks. These networks consist of many facets of routing, dial-up, switching, video, WAN (ISDN, Frame Relay, ATM, and others), LAN, and VLAN technologies.

Figure 33.1 gives you an idea of how these technologies intertwine. Notice that ATM, Frame Relay, Token Ring, Ethernet, and FDDI all are present. Each technology has its own properties and commands to allow for troubleshooting. Various protocols are used for each of these technologies. In addition, different applications require specific network resources. (At least the seven-layer OSI model, which you will review in Chapter 36, "Protocol Attributes," is used to maintain a common template when designing new technologies and protocols.) It would take you a long time to master all of the technologies implemented in the network and to be able to solve network problems based on your knowledge of the network alone. All of these factors contribute to today's complex network environments.

There must be an easier, more logical way to efficiently and successfully troubleshoot without having to become intimately familiar with every network environment. Well, you'll be happy to know that there is an easier option—following a troubleshooting model, which is discussed in detail in this chapter. By following a troubleshooting model, the need for intimate knowledge of the network is reduced. A troubleshooting model should be adopted to help resolve network malfunctions and reduce downtime.

Let's move on to discuss Cisco's model in detail.

FIGURE 33.1 Today's complex enterprise network

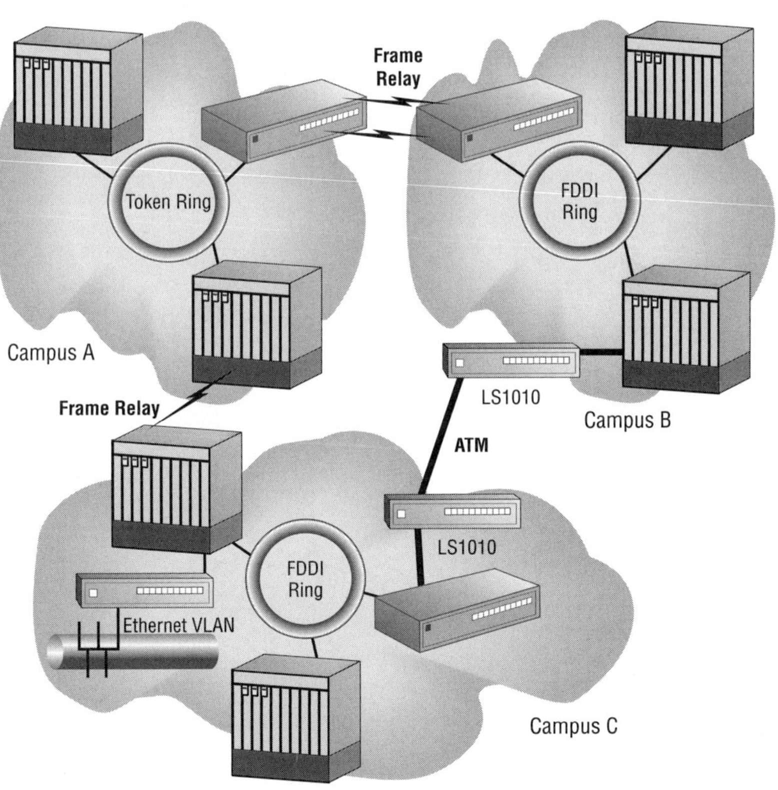

Cisco Troubleshooting Model

Imagine trying to solve a network failure by using a different approach every time. With today's complex networks, the possible scenarios would be innumerable. Because so many different things can go wrong within a network, it's possible to start from many different points. Not only is this an ineffective method of troubleshooting, but it's also time-consuming, and time is very valuable in a "network down" situation.

Cisco has designed an effective *troubleshooting model* that contains three steps. A troubleshooting model is a list of troubleshooting steps or processes that can be followed to provide an efficient manner of resolving network problems. The headings in this section contain information specific to each step of the troubleshooting model. After the three steps are completed and the problem is resolved, a few more actions follow, such as documenting the problem-solving events.

To be effective when troubleshooting and to achieve faster resolution times, follow the model outlined in Figure 33.2. This flow chart shows the three steps.

FIGURE 33.2 Cisco's troubleshooting model

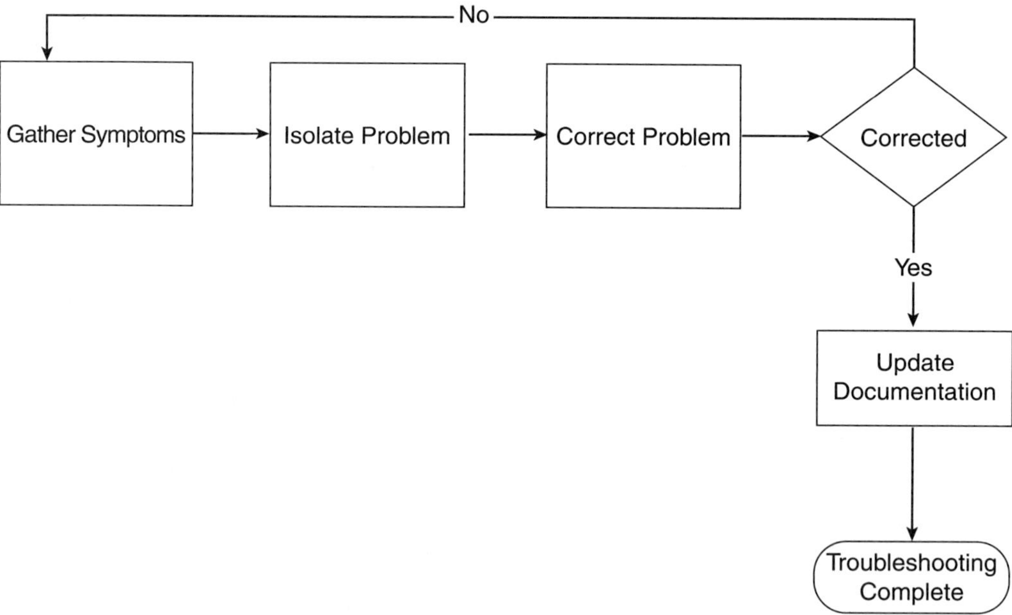

The troubleshooting process begins when a network failure is reported to you. The following are brief descriptions of the steps to take:

1. **Gather symptoms.** At this point in the process, it is important gather and document the symptoms of the problem that is being experienced.
2. **Isolate the problem.** After identifying the symptoms, the administrator looks for commonalities in the symptoms and tries to determine at what layer of the OSI model the problem is occurring. During this phase, it may be necessary to go back and gather more symptoms.

3. **Correct the problem.** Based on the information that was gathered and the determinations that were made in the previous two steps, the network administrator now makes the changes necessary to correct the problem. Once the corrective steps have been taken, the administrator observes the results of the changes to ensure that the problem was corrected. If the problem was not corrected, then the changes made should be backed out and the administrator should start the troubleshooting process over with the gather symptoms stage. If the changes do correct the problem, then the administrator should update the necessary documentation. The final item of importance when correcting the problem is to make sure that you make only one change at a time. This will ensure that you do not make unnecessary changes, which could introduce new problems.

The best way to understand how Cisco's model works and how you should use it is by looking at an example. For this example, assume you are in charge of operational support of the network pictured in Figure 33.3. There are two campus networks, connected via a Frame Relay cloud. Within each network, VLANs are connected to a Catalyst 6500 switch and then to a core router that has a connection to the Frame Relay cloud in one way or another.

FIGURE 33.3 Example campus network

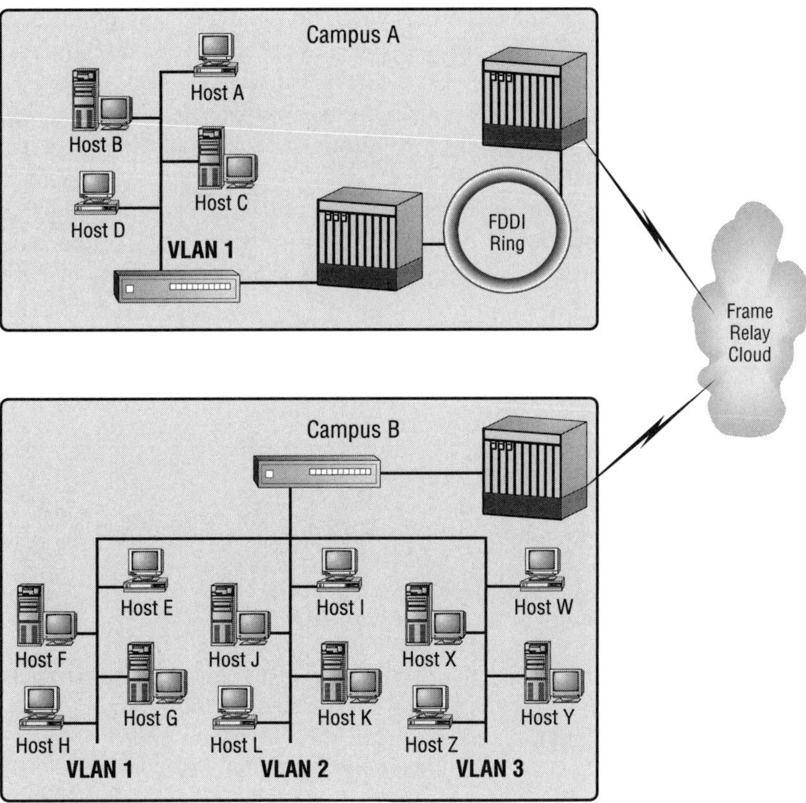

The fun begins when you get a call from a user who "can't get to Host Z." Based on this information, let's apply Cisco's troubleshooting model to solve the user's difficulty and fix the problem in the network.

Step 1: Gather Symptoms

As you can see, the user's problem is vague; you need more information if you are to solve the problem any time soon. This is where the first step comes in. Gathering symptoms is the step in the troubleshooting model when details about the problem are gathered from as many sources as is practical. These symptoms can come from a number of sources, including but not limited to the network devices, users, monitoring tools, and console messages.

Now, while you still have the user on the line, the first step is to ask him what he means when he says he can't "get to" Host Z. The user then defines the situation by telling you that he can't ftp to Host Z. Ask the user if he experiences any other difficulties or if this is the only one. Verify where the user is currently located. After these preliminary questions, you'll have a basic idea of what is and isn't working. Unfortunately, you can't simply assume that FTP is broken, because there are many other pieces of the network that can contribute to this problem.

At this point, the problem is still pretty vague and needs more definition. Additional information should include data that excludes other possibilities and helps pinpoint the actual problem. An example in the case we're discussing is to verify whether you can ping, traceroute, or telnet to Host Z, thus reducing the number of possible causes.

Depending on the user and situation, you may or may not be able to get more detailed information. It is up to you as a network engineer or administrator to solve the problem, which means that you may have to get the information yourself.

It is important that you gain as much information as possible to actually define the problem correctly. Without a proper and specific definition of the problem, it will be much harder to isolate and resolve. Information that is useful for gathering symptoms is listed in Table 33.1.

TABLE 33.1 Useful Information for Gathering Symptoms

Information	Example
Symptoms	Can't telnet, ftp, or get to the WWW.
Reproducibility	Is this a one-time occurrence, or does it always happen?
Timeline	When did it start? How long did it last? How often does it occur? Has the current configuration ever worked properly?
Scope	What are you able to access successfully via Telnet or FTP? Which WWW sites can you reach, if any? Who else does this affect?
Baseline Info	Were any recent changes made to the network configurations?

All of this information can be used to guide you to the actual problem and to create the problem statement. Use your network topology diagram and check each item in Table 33.1. Once you are done talking to the user, you need to define what is working and what isn't.

Figure 33.4 is a picture of your network. Although the large X on the Frame Relay cloud represents that there is an FTP connectivity issue, it does not indicate the location of the failure. Right now, all you know is that a single user cannot ftp to Host Z.

FIGURE 33.4 Host A cannot ftp to Host Z.

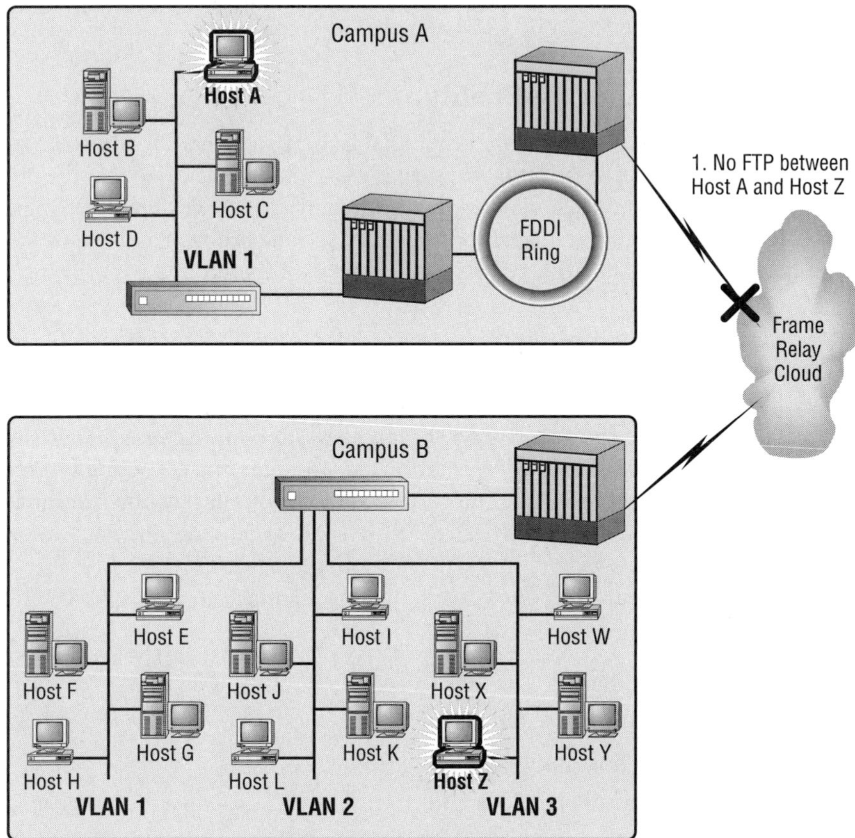

Reproduce the Problem

Before spending time and effort trying to solve this problem, verify that it is still a problem. Troubleshooting is a waste of time and resources if the problem can't be reproduced. It's just like a dog chasing its tail. If the issue is intermittent, further steps should be taken to capture as much information as possible about the event the next time it does occur. This will help narrow down the scope of items you will look at.

Understand the Timeline

In addition to verifying whether the problem is reproducible, it is important to investigate the frequency of the problem. For instance, maybe it happens only once or twice a day. By establishing a timeframe you can more readily identify any possible causes. In addition, you need to know whether this is the first time the user has attempted this function. There is a different set of variables involved with an item that worked yesterday but not today than there is with something that fails during first-time use. Obviously, if it worked yesterday, you can look at what changed overnight and look for something that is broken. If the user has never used this feature before, there may be an existing access list or other security device that has only now been activated by the user's initial use of this application.

Determine the Scope of a Problem

Next, you need to find out whether anyone else is unable to ftp to Host Z. If others can ftp to Host Z (for the sake of this example, assume that they can), you can be pretty sure that the problem is specific to the user, either on their station or on the destination host. This step determines the scope of the problem and helps to differentiate between a user-specific problem and a more widely spread problem. Figure 33.5 shows that other hosts can ftp to Host Z without any problems.

Step 2: Isolate the Problem

This step within the troubleshooting model is used to contemplate the possible causes of the failure. Obviously, it is quite easy to create a very long list of possible causes. That's why it's so important to gather as much relevant information as you can in the gathering symptoms phase. By defining the problem and assigning the corresponding boundaries, the resulting list of possible causes diminishes because the entries in the list will be focused on the actual problem and not on "possible" problems.

First, review what you know about your sample problem:

- Host A can't ftp to Host Z.
- Host A can't ftp to any host on Campus B.
- Host A can't ping to anywhere outside its own network.
- Host A can ftp to any host on its own network.
- All other hosts on Host A's network can ftp to Host Z, as well as to other hosts.

Based on what you know, you now need to list possible causes. These possible causes are as follows:

- No default gateway is configured on Host A.
- The wrong subnet mask is configured.
- There is a misconfigured access list on the router connected to the switch on Campus A.

If you had not gathered such specific information in step 1, this list could have included all possible problems with any piece of equipment between Host A and Host Z. That would have been a long list, and it would take a lot of time to eliminate all of the possible causes.

FIGURE 33.5 Other hosts can ftp to Host Z.

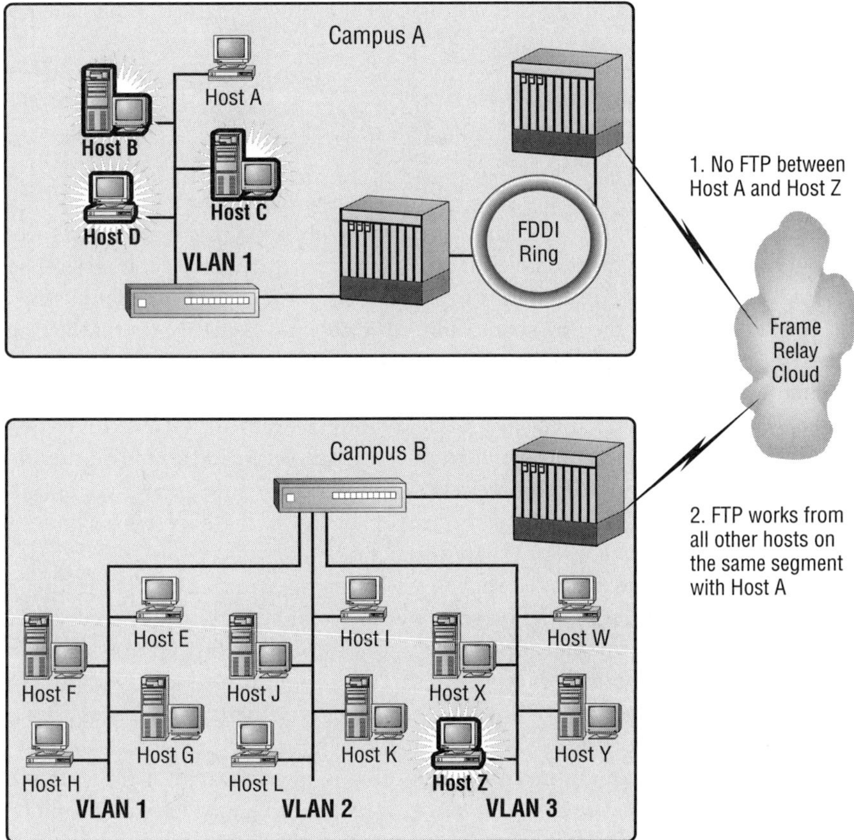

Remember that because these are only *possible* causes, you still have to choose the most likely option, implement it, and observe to see whether the changes made were effective. When the list of possible problems is long, it may require more iterations of the problem-solving steps to actually solve the problem. In this example, you have only three possible causes, so this is a much more manageable list. Although there may be other possible causes that you can think of (and it's great that you can do that), for this example and in the interest of simplicity, only these three are listed.

Here's where it gets interesting. You now have to check each of these possibilities and fix them if they are the cause of the problem.

Step 3: Correct the Problem

The investigation gave you three leads about the source of the problem. Now it's a matter of checking out each possibility and determining which one is most likely the source of the issue.

The majority of the possibilities point directly at the host machine, so start there. The first two causes are host configuration issues. Now, assume that you've checked the TCP/IP configuration on the host and everything is configured properly. You can eliminate the host machine as the culprit.

You then move on to the remaining possible cause, which is an access list on the router. While looking at the configuration on the router, you see that an access list is applied to the Ethernet interface directly connected to the host segment. After reviewing the syntax of the access list, you determine that it is the cause of the failure.

Great—you've found the problem. Now what? Once you find the problem, you must decide what is needed to fix it. In this case, it is an access-list problem, so there are some special considerations about how to restore functionality. You must be careful in your actions here, because that access list may contain other entries that provide security or other network administrative functionality. You can't just remove the list—you could cause new problems as you fix the original one.

The best thing to do in this situation is to make a copy of the access list in a text editor, and then make changes that are specific to your problem. When editing the access list, change its number. After all of the changes are made in your text editor, ensure that you have a current backup of the configuration on the router in case you need to restore the original configuration. Then paste the modified access list back into the router. Finally, go to the interface and apply the new access list. By following this procedure, the access list is never removed from the interface.

Obviously, you have now changed the access-list number that is applied to the interface, so any documentation that refers to the original number will need to be updated. If the access list that was causing the problem was applied only to Ethernet 0, you can now safely remove the old list, update this list with the corrections to address your problem, and put it back on the router. Then reapply this list to Ethernet 0. As was the case before, the access list is never removed from the interface.

When you are going through the troubleshooting methodology, it is important that you don't fix one problem and cause another. Before implementing any changes, think it through or discuss it with coworkers to pick it apart, and make sure that your solution will fix the problem without doing anything to create adverse side effects.

Another good practice when implementing changes is to change only one thing at a time, if possible. If multiple changes must be made, it is best to make the changes in small sets. This way it is easier to keep track of what was done, what worked, and what didn't. Observing the effects of a change becomes much more effective if only a single change is made at a time. There is nothing worse than troubleshooting your self-induced errors in addition to the original difficulties!

To summarize, follow these practices and guidelines to making changes:

- Make one change or a set of related changes at a time, and then observe the results.
- Make non-impacting changes—this means trying not to cause other problems while implementing the changes. The more transparent the change, the better.
- Do not create security holes when changing access lists, TACACS+, RADIUS, or other security-oriented configurations.
- Most importantly, make sure you can revert to the original configuration if unforeseen problems occur as a result of the change. Always have a backup or copy of the configuration.

In the preceding paragraphs, there were references to observing the results of the changes. Observing results consists of using the exact same methods and commands that were used to obtain information to gather symptoms—to see whether the changes you implemented had the results you want. By making a change and then testing its effectiveness, you move toward the correct solution.

It may take one or more changes to fix the problem, but you should observe each change separately to monitor progress and to make sure that the alteration doesn't create any adverse effects. After the first change is made, you should be able to gather enough information to learn whether or not the modification was effective, even if it doesn't entirely solve the problem.

Real World Scenario

Looks Can Be Deceiving

One common mistake when observing the results of a change is seeing symptoms go away and assuming that the problem has been solved. For example, assume that users are complaining about slow response time while accessing the Internet. In the course of troubleshooting, you find and correct some non-optimally-configured interface settings on the router on the users' segment. You then go back to the user who originally reported the problem. She reports that everything is running fine now. However, she neglects to mention the fact that there was a shift change, and now only two people are connecting to the Internet where there used to be 50. The next day, when all of the users are back online, the problem repeats itself. If an analysis of the observations had been done, it would have demonstrated that the traffic flow to the Internet had dropped off and that this could be a contributing factor to the improvement in response times.

As is demonstrated in this example, failure to analyze your observations creates the risk that important information can be overlooked and the problem will recur. To avoid this possibility, make sure to look at the entire scope of the problem. Use your network management tools to help you determine whether the problem is really resolved. You can also look at your network baseline information to find out what the "normal" traffic pattern looks like. In this example, it should show a sharp drop-off in utilization when the shift changes. This would tell you that the improvement in connection speed may not be due to the interface changes you've made, but rather due to a lower volume of traffic. More verification may be needed.

If the changes made have corrected the problem, move on and document the modifications that were made to the network. If the changes did not work, you need to go back and either gather more information or try another one of the potential issues that you identified while isolating the problem.

Iterations—repetitions of certain steps within the troubleshooting model—are simply ways of whittling away at a larger problem. By implementing changes and monitoring the results, you can move toward solving the overall problem.

Iterations of the troubleshooting process allow you to focus with more and more detail on the possible causes of the failure. The result of focusing on the problem is your ability to identify more specific possibilities for the failure.

The iteration process has its own set of steps: While working through the process, you might get more ideas of possible sources of the trouble. Write them down; if the current changes do not work, you have notes about some other options. If you feel that you have exhausted all of the possible causes, you should probably go back and gather more information. You will probably find additional clues.

This is also the time to undo any changes that had adverse effects or that did not fix the problem. Make sure to document what was done, so it will be easier to undo the any configuration modifications.

Document the Changes

The network problem has been officially resolved after you've implemented a change, observed that the symptoms have disappeared, and can successfully execute the tests that were used to aid in gathering information about the problem. In this example, the way to verify that the problem is solved is for Host A to try to ftp to Host Z. If this test is successful, then the problem is resolved.

In the previous sections, we have emphasized that documentation is an integral part of troubleshooting. When you keep track of the alterations that were made, the routers, switches, or hosts that were changed, and when the changes occurred, you have valuable information for future reference. There is always the possibility that something you changed might have affected something else and you didn't notice it. If this happens, you will have documentation to refer to, so you can undo the changes. Or if a similar problem occurs in the future, you can refer to these documents to resolve the new problem, based on what was done the last time. Later chapters in this book will give you more information about documentation and establishing baseline information.

Troubleshooting by Layer

The earlier sections of this chapter explained a general troubleshooting methodology. When going through this methodology, it is often helpful to approach the problem in a logical manner that leverages the OSI model. Therefore, Cisco has started backing a model of troubleshooting that does just that. This model has three distinct approaches: bottom-up, top-down, and divide-and-conquer.

Bottom-Up Troubleshooting Approach

As the name implies, when you use the *bottom-up troubleshooting* approach, you start with the bottom—the Physical layer of the OSI model—and work your way up to the top—the Application layer. This approach is used when you suspect the problem is at the Physical layer, or when you are troubleshooting a complex network problem. In these situations, ensuring that the core components required for networking are in place can go a long way toward isolating the problem.

The downside to bottom-up troubleshooting is that it can require the checking of each interface along the path to see if errors are occurring there. Depending on the length of the path from the end points of the problem, this process can be very time-consuming. In these cases, determining the most likely culprit based on the symptoms of the trouble can save a lot of time.

Top-Down Troubleshooting Approach

If you suspect that the problem lies in a piece of software, then *top-down troubleshooting* should be used. You start by testing the application and work down the OSI layers to find the source of the problem. The challenge to this type of troubleshooting is that you need to check all the user's network applications in order to find the one that is causing the errors. This is a potentially time-consuming troubleshooting method if there are a large number of applications that could be the source of the trouble.

Divide-and-Conquer Troubleshooting Approach

The *divide-and-conquer troubleshooting* approach allows you to select the specific layer (Data Link, Network, or Transport) of the OSI model in which to begin troubleshooting. You make your selection based on experience with similar problems in the past, along with the specific symptoms of the current trouble. After selecting the layer you wish to start with, the next task is to determine the direction of the problem by determining whether the problem exists at, above, or below this layer. Most commonly this is done by studying output from the IOS commands on the router or through analysis of the output of network management tools. Once the direction of the problem is determined, you continue troubleshooting through the OSI model in that direction until you isolate the difficulty.

Often you can check the first four layers (Physical through Transport) by using the `traceroute` command.

Summary

With the complexity of today's networks, it is important to adhere to a troubleshooting model to aid in efficiently and effectively isolating and resolving network problems.

Various methods of problem isolation and the troubleshooting method itself help administrators pinpoint problem areas and foresee future trouble. Troubleshooting skills are gained through experience. It is unreasonable to expect that you can jump in on your first network failure and be able to solve it quickly. Experience is the best teacher. Following a problem-solving model helps you to reach a timely solution to network failures. It helps to know your network, but the "shooting-from-the-hip" style of troubleshooting is nowhere near as effective as a methodical and logical process.

Using the three steps of the Cisco troubleshooting model in order is a clear, calculated, and logical way to make a network run more smoothly. The three methods of problem isolation (bottom-up, top-down, and divide-and-conquer) are more subjective, and it is up to each individual to use the appropriate method for the problem that they are facing. It is important to document changes so you have a trail of what was done on the network. Finally, it's important to reverse any network alterations that did not correct the problem.

Exam Essentials

Know the three steps to the Cisco troubleshooting model and the function that each step performs. The three steps to the Cisco troubleshooting model are gather symptoms, isolate the problem, correct the problem, and repeat if necessary. Once a problem is resolved, documentation should be updated.

Know the troubleshooting methodologies and how to use them. These troubleshooting methodologies are bottom-up, top-down, and divide-and-conquer. In addition to understanding them, know when it is most appropriate to use each method.

Be able to apply the Cisco troubleshooting methodology to example situations. Know how to apply each step of the troubleshooting model in real-life scenarios. You should be able to determine what step in a troubleshooting scenario is next in the series, and understand how to correlate a task with the correct step in the process.

Network Documentation

THE CCNP EXAM TOPICS COVERED IN THIS CHAPTER INCLUDE THE FOLLOWING:

- ✓ Understand the document control process and documentation standards.
- ✓ Establish a baseline indicative of optimal network performance.
- ✓ Create system topology documentation and diagrams.

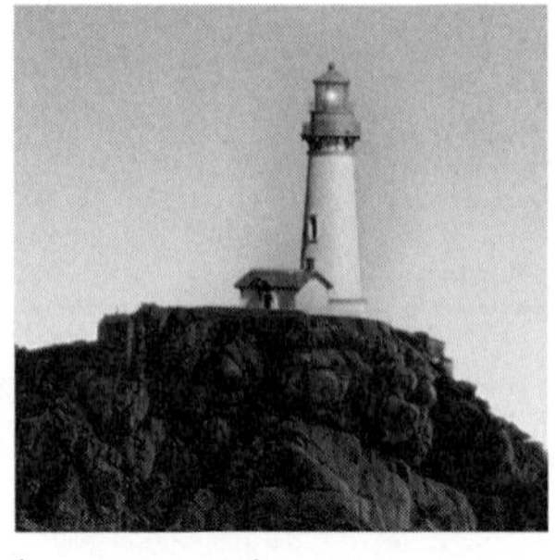

When the network is down, one of your most important troubleshooting tools can be your network documentation. Accurate and up-to-date network documentation can make the difference between a short outage and an extended one.

In this chapter, we will focus on the network documentation that you need to have available and how to create this documentation. We will first study a network baseline; then we'll look at the network configuration table and the network topology diagram. The documents created in this and the following chapter will allow you to effectively troubleshoot a network problem even if you are new to the network itself.

The Network Baseline

The easiest way to solve network problems is to be able to compare current configurations against previous configurations. This sounds easy enough, but it requires a lot of effort to get a system established for keeping a historical *baseline* of your network. A historical baseline is simply a collection of network settings and configurations that are maintained over time. This baseline makes it easy to locate changes and identify the differences between a current configuration and a previous one.

A network baseline is sometimes referred to as a baseline network model.

Baseline information is actually a composite of various network and end-system documentation. This collection includes

- Network configuration table
- Network topology diagram
- End-system network configuration table
- End-system network topology diagram

The first two items—the network configuration table and the network topology diagram—are covered in this chapter. The latter two items—the end-system network configuration table and the end-system network topology diagram—are discussed in Chapter 35, "End-System Documentation and Troubleshooting."

When creating any documentation of this sort, there are several things to keep in mind:

- First, before you start, determine the scope of what the documentation should cover. Without clearly understanding what is inside and outside of the scope of the documentation effort, you could end up taking on more than you bargained for.
- The second rule is to be consistent. If you do not collect the same information for all the devices in the network, the documentation may have holes that will come back to haunt you later.
- Third, know your objective. When you are collecting your information, be certain you understand what the documentation will be used for, and include all relevant pieces.
- Be sure to use the documentation and ensure that it is accessible in the event of an emergency. This information was not put together just as an exercise; it is meant to be useful.
- Finally, after putting together your baseline information, you must maintain it. If the baseline is out-of-date, troubleshooting will be much more difficult.

After you your start using the documentation, if you are finding that you are consistently going back to the network devices to find a particular bit of information, it may be a good idea to include that information on your baseline. Likewise, if you notice that you are never using certain information, it may be best to remove that data from the baseline documentation to prevent clutter.

Network Configuration Table

The general purpose of a *network configuration table* is to give a listing of the hardware and software components used in the network. This information will be used in the course of troubleshooting to ensure that the functioning of the network is well understood. At a minimum, a network configuration table should include the name of the network device, the layer 2 addresses and implemented feature sets, and the layer 3 addresses and implemented features. In addition to these items, you should include any additional information about layers 4 through 7 that is deemed important (for instance, extended access lists and application flow details). Finally, all of the specifics about the physical devices should be recorded (their location in the computer room, their UPS circuit information, and so forth).

One of the most common ways to determine the specific items that will go into your network configuration table is to divide the types of information being observed into groups corresponding to the layers of the OSI model. Some items, such as name of the device, do not necessarily fall in a particular layer, but these can be incorporated as part of the Physical layer or placed in a separate column. A sample list of items that can be included in a network configuration table is shown in Table 34.1.

TABLE 34.1 Sample List of Network Configuration Table Items

Classification	Items
Miscellaneous Information	Device name, device model, CPU type, flash memory, DRAM, interface description
Layer 1	Media type, speed, interface numbers, connecting jack or port
Layer 2	MAC address, Spanning Tree Protocol (STP) state, STP root bridge, portfast information, VLAN(s), EtherChannel configuration, encapsulation, trunking status, interface type, port security, VTP state, VTP mode
Layer 3	IP address, IPX address, secondary IP address, Hot Standby Routing Protocol (HSRP) address, subnet, subnet mask, routing protocol(s), access lists, tunneling information, loopback interfaces

Cisco technically considers the list of items under miscellaneous information as layer 1 items.

Once you have identified the information that you will put in your network configuration table, the next step is organizing this information in a logical and repeatable sequence. When planning the organization of this information, you must take into account all the device types that are in the network as well as the needs of each of these devices. Due to the variation in the requirements for different types of network devices such as switches and routers, in many cases you will need a different table structure for each major classification of device. For example, in most instances, there will be one set of information gathered for routers and a separate set of information for switches. This separation prevents a lot of unnecessary fields that are left empty because they do not apply. By separating these information groups, you can simplify the overall network documentation.

If you do decide to separate switches from routers in your network documentation, be sure to have a plan for how to account for devices that do *both* routing and switching. You might create both a routing and a switching document for such devices. Alternately, you could create a third set of documentation specifically for these types of devices.

In most cases, the preferred manner to store this information is in a spreadsheet or database. For smaller networks, a spreadsheet is usually the preferred method due to its low cost and ease of use. For large networks, a database is the preferred arrangement because of its flexibility, and it lets you better manage large volumes of data. For both of these means of storage, hard copies of the information should be maintained in addition to the electronic versions. This paper documentation may be critical during a network outage, when the information contained in the network configuration table will be most useful and you may not be able to access the online version.

Router Network Configuration Table

Now that we have discussed the basis for what goes into a network configuration table, let's go through a couple of examples. We will first create the template for what we are looking for, and then step through the gathering of the necessary information. For these examples, we will first create a separate network configuration table for routers and one for switches. The network itself in this example is a small one, containing fewer than 15 routers and 20 switches.

Based on this information, we have decided to include the following list of items in our router network configuration table:

- Device Name
- Model #
- Location
- Flash
- DRAM
- IOS Version
- Interface Name
- MAC Address
- Subnet
- Subnet Mask
- IP Address
- Routing Protocol

The start of the router network configuration table is shown in Figure 34.1. As you can see in the figure, part of the information has already been entered for our example. This information was gathered through a series of `show` commands run on each router. Specifically, the commands used were

- `show version`
- `show ip interface brief`
- `show interface`
- `show ip protocols`
- `show ip interface`

FIGURE 34.1 Sample network configuration table for routers

Device Name, Model	Location	Flash	DRAM	IOS	Interface	MAC Address	Subnet/ Subnet Mask	IP Address	Routing Protocol
Salmon, 2610	Seattle	16	48	12.0(2)	E0/0	0004.4d65.b9c0	10.254.254.0/24	10.254.254.1	EIGRP 200
					S0/0	NA	10.10.10.0/30	10.10.10.1	EIGRP 200
Marlin, 3640	Miami	16	48	12.1(2)	FA0/0	0060.837b.b880	10.20.20.0/24	10.20.20.1	OSPF 21
					S1/0	NA	10.10.10.0/30	10.1.10.2	EIGRP 200

Though the information in the first two columns of the sample network configuration table can be obtained through some `show` commands (assuming the `location` or `snmp location` options are set in the router), in our example, as well as in most real-world scenarios, they are already known by the network administrator doing the work. The next three columns in our example—Flash, DRAM, and IOS—are all obtained by using the `show version` command:

```
salmon>show version
Cisco Internetwork Operating System Software
IOS (tm) C2600 Software (C2600-JS-M), Version 12.0(12), RELEASE SOFTWARE (fc1)
Copyright (c) 1986-2000 by cisco Systems, Inc.
Compiled Tue 11-Jul-00 10:09 by htseng
Image text-base: 0x80008088, data-base: 0x80B1468C
ROM: System Bootstrap, Version 11.3(2)XA4, RELEASE SOFTWARE (fc1)
salmon uptime is 3 days, 20 hours, 48 minutes
System restarted power on
System image file is "flash:c2600-js-mz.120-12.bin"
cisco 2610 (MPC860) processor (revision 0x203) with 39936K/9216K bytes
  ➥of memory.
Processor board ID JAD04430NYN (832809334)
M860 processor: part number 0, mask 49
Bridging software.
X.25 software, Version 3.0.0.
SuperLAT software (copyright 1990 by Meridian Technology Corp).
TN3270 Emulation software.
Basic Rate ISDN software, Version 1.1.
1 Ethernet/IEEE 802.3 interface(s)
2 Serial(sync/async) network interface(s)
1 ISDN Basic Rate interface(s)
32K bytes of non-volatile configuration memory.
16384K bytes of processor board System flash (Read/Write)

Configuration register is 0x2102
```

The flash information is shown at the bottom of the `show version` output, the DRAM is in the middle, and the IOS is at the top. One item to note is that because the 2610 is a shared memory router, the DRAM information here is divided into two categories, separated by a slash character. The first number represents the local memory on the router, and the number on the right-hand side of the slash represents the I/O memory on the router. The local memory is used for items such as holding the running IOS, whereas the I/O memory is used for buffers and similar input and output functions.

To obtain the interfaces that are active on the router, as well as the IP addresses that are assigned to these interfaces, the `show ip interface brief` command is used:

```
salmon#show ip interface brief
Interface    IP-Address    OK? Method Status                Protocol
Ethernet0/0 10.254.254.1  YES NVRAM  up                    up
Serial0/0    10.10.10.1    YES NVRAM  up                    up
Serial0/1    unassigned    YES unset  administratively down down
```

Once you have determined which interfaces are used on the router, you can execute the `show interface` command to get the MAC addresses of the interfaces and the subnet information:

```
salmon#show interface e0/0
Ethernet0/0 is up, line protocol is up
 Hardware is AmdP2, address is 0004.4d65.b9c0 (bia 0004.4d65.b9c0)
 Internet address is 10.254.254.1/24
 MTU 1500 bytes, BW 10000 Kbit, DLY 1000 usec, rely 255/255, load 1/255
 Encapsulation ARPA, loopback not set, keepalive set (10 sec)
 ARP type: ARPA, ARP Timeout 04:00:00
 Last input 00:00:00, output 00:00:00, output hang never
 Last clearing of "show interface" counters never
 Queueing strategy: fifo
 Output queue 0/40, 0 drops; input queue 0/75, 0 drops
 5 minute input rate 0 bits/sec, 0 packets/sec
 5 minute output rate 0 bits/sec, 0 packets/sec
   27067 packets input, 3624228 bytes, 0 no buffer
   Received 27067 broadcasts, 0 runts, 0 giants, 0 throttles
   0 input errors, 0 CRC, 0 frame, 0 overrun, 0 ignored, 0 abort
   0 input packets with dribble condition detected
   39804 packets output, 3815083 bytes, 0 underruns
   0 output errors, 0 collisions, 0 interface resets
   0 babbles, 0 late collision, 0 deferred
   0 lost carrier, 0 no carrier
   0 output buffer failures, 0 output buffers swapped out
```

In looking at the output of the show interface command, notice that following the MAC address is the output (bia 0004.4d65.b9c0). The bia stands for burned-in address and is the MAC address that was assigned by Cisco to the interface. The BIA is usually, but not always, the MAC address that is used on the interface. Specifically, by using the interface-level mac-address command, a network administrator can set the MAC address used to any value considered appropriate.

The final command we'll examine that is used to populate the network configuration table is show ip protocols:

```
salmon#show ip protocols
Routing Protocol is "eigrp 200"
 Outgoing update filter list for all interfaces is
 Incoming update filter list for all interfaces is
 Default networks flagged in outgoing updates
 Default networks accepted from incoming updates
 EIGRP metric weight K1=1, K2=0, K3=1, K4=0, K5=0
 EIGRP maximum hopcount 100
 EIGRP maximum metric variance 1
 Redistributing: eigrp 200
 Automatic network summarization is in effect
 Routing for Networks:
  10.0.0.0
 Routing Information Sources:
  Gateway      Distance   Last Update
 Distance: internal 90 external 170
```

The preceding command tells you the routing protocol that is active on the router, as well as the networks this routing protocol is used for.

One command that was not demonstrated in our example is often used in creation of network configuration tables: the show ip interface command. In addition to the standard IP address information, this command provides a wealth of other information such as whether or not access lists are applied to the interface, the switching methodology of the interface, and whether or not there is a helper address assigned. Here is a sample output of the show ip interface command:

```
salmon#show ip interface e0/0
Ethernet0/0 is up, line protocol is up
 Internet address is 10.254.254.1/24
 Broadcast address is 255.255.255.255
 Address determined by non-volatile memory
 MTU is 1500 bytes
 Helper address is not set
 Directed broadcast forwarding is disabled
```

```
Multicast reserved groups joined: 224.0.0.10
Outgoing access list is not set
Inbound access list is not set
Proxy ARP is enabled
Security level is default
Split horizon is enabled
ICMP redirects are always sent
ICMP unreachables are always sent
ICMP mask replies are never sent
IP fast switching is enabled
IP fast switching on the same interface is disabled
IP Flow switching is disabled
IP Fast switching turbo vector
IP multicast fast switching is enabled
IP multicast distributed fast switching is disabled
IP route-cache flags are Fast
Router Discovery is disabled
IP output packet accounting is disabled
IP access violation accounting is disabled
TCP/IP header compression is disabled
RTP/IP header compression is disabled
Probe proxy name replies are disabled
Policy routing is disabled
Network address translation is disabled
Web Cache Redirect is disabled
BGP Policy Mapping is disabled
```

Switch Network Configuration Table

Now that the router network configuration table is complete, let's move on to the switch version of this table. More information on switches and switch commands is provided in Chapter 41, "Troubleshooting Switched Ethernet." As stated in the preceding section, in this example we are assuming that there are about 20 switches in the network for which we are creating documentation. In addition, we are working with switches that have only layer 2 functionality. Based on this arrangement, we have decided to include the following list of items in our switch network configuration table:

- Device Name
- Model #
- Location
- Flash

- DRAM
- CatOS Version
- Management Address
- VTP Domain
- VTP Mode
- Port Number
- Port Speed
- Port Duplex
- VLAN
- Spanning Tree Protocol (STP) State
- Portfast Status
- Trunk Status

The beginning of the switch network configuration table is shown in Figure 34.2.

As was the case with the network configuration table for routers, just a few commands are needed to populate the table produced for the switches. Specifically, these commands are

- `show version`
- `show interface`
- `show vtp domain`, `show port`
- `show trunk`
- `show spantree` *`vlan`*

Note that the preceding are CatOS commands. The IOS equivalents of these commands are `show version`, `show interface`, `show vtp status`, `show interface`, `show interfaces trunk`, and `show spanning-tree` *`vlan`*, respectively. More information about the differences between CatOS and IOS are covered in Chapter 41.

FIGURE 34.2 Sample network configuration table for switches

Device Name, Model	Location	Flash	DRAM	CATOS	Mgmt IP	VTP Domain	VTP Mode	Port	Speed	Duplex	VLAN(s)	STP State (Fwd/Block)	Portfast (Yes/No)	Trunk (Yes/No
core_switch, 6509	Dover, DE	16	64	6.4(3)	10.40.40.2	dover_core	Transparent	1/1	1000	Full	1,2,45,46	Fwd	No	Yes
								1/2	1000	Full	1,2,45,46	Block	No	Yes
								3/1	100	Full	45	Fwd	Yes	No
								3/2	10	Half	45	Fwd	Yes	No
								3/3	A-100	A-Full	45	Fwd	Yes	No

The first of these commands, `show version`, operates similarly to the same command in the router. It produces a number of the elements that are needed in order to populate the switch network configuration table:

```
core_switch> (enable) show version
WS-C6509 Software, Version NmpSW: 6.4(3)
Copyright (c) 1995-2003 by Cisco Systems
NMP S/W compiled on Apr 10 2003, 17:33:25

System Bootstrap Version: 5.3(1)

Hardware Version: 2.0 Model: WS-C6509 Serial #: SCA123456F

PS1 Module: WS-CAC-1300W  Serial #: SON01234564
PS2 Module: WS-CAC-1300W  Serial #: SON01234569

Mod Port Model               Serial #    Versions
--- ---- ------------------- ----------- ---------------------------
1    2   WS-X6K-SUP1A-2GE    SAD05430RPV Hw : 3.2
                                         Fw : 5.3(1)
                                         Fw1: 5.1(1)CSX
                                         Sw : 6.4(3)
                                         Sw1: 6.4(3)
         WS-F6K-PFC          SAD05430LYJ Hw : 1.1
3   48   WS-X6248-RJ-45      SAD04330N7Z Hw : 1.2
                                         Fw : 5.1(1)CSX
                                         Sw : 6.4(3)
7   24   WS-X6324-100FX-MM  SAD0234523C  Hw : 1.3
                                         Fw : 5.4(2)
                                         Sw : 6.4(3)
8   8    WS-X6408A-GBIC   SAL43566W9J    Hw : 2.0
                                         Fw : 5.4(2)
                                         Sw : 6.4(3)


                DRAM                    FLASH                   NVRAM
Module Total    Used    Free    Total   Used    Free    Total Used  Free
------ ------- ------- ------- ------- ------- ------- ----- ----- ----
1       65408K  48425K 16983K  16384K  9568K   6816K    512K  310K 202K

Uptime is 55 days, 11 hours, 28 minutes
```

As you can see in the underlined output, the `show version` command provides the CatOS level of the switch, as well as the flash and DRAM information.

The next command, `show vtp domain`, reports both the VTP domain and the VTP mode of the switch. (VTP [VLAN Trunk Protocol] is covered in more detail in Chapter 41.)

```
core_switch> (enable) show vtp domain
Domain Name                Domain Index VTP Version Local Mode   Password
----------------------- ------------ ----------- ----------- ----------
dover_core                    1            2       Transparent      -

Vlan-count Max-vlan-storage Config Revision Notifications
---------- ---------------- --------------- -------------
13             1023               0            enabled

Last Updater    V2 Mode  Pruning   PruneEligible on Vlans
--------------- -------- -------- -------------------------
10.40.40.2      disabled disabled           2-1000
```

Once you have obtained the VTP data, the next piece of information needed is the management interface IP address. This address is included as part of the output from the `show interface` command. Notice that on a switch, the command displays far less information than for routers and focuses only on the management interfaces, not on the user ports.

```
core_switch> (enable) show interface
sl0: flags=51<UP,POINTOPOINT,RUNNING>
  slip 0.0.0.0 dest 0.0.0.0
sc0: flags=63<UP,BROADCAST,RUNNING>
  vlan 2 inet 10.40.40.2 netmask 255.255.255.252 broadcast 10.40.40.3
```

By using a separate VLAN for the management VLAN, we ensure that management traffic to or from the switch will not be directly affected by user traffic, and vice versa. For further protection, a separate uplink instead of a common trunk can be used for the management VLAN, as is shown in this example.

The next command that is used to populate the switch network configuration table is the `show port` command, which provides a substantial amount of fairly concise information about each port on the switch. Be aware, however, that the output can get very lengthy if there are a large number of ports on the switch. For the purpose of the switch network configuration table, the port numbers, VLAN (for nontrunked ports), duplex, and speed information can be obtained from this output:

```
core_switch> (enable) show port
Port  Name               Status     Vlan       Duplex Speed Type
----- ------------------ ---------- ---------- ------ ----- -----------
 1/1  core_switch_2      connected  trunk      full   1000  1000BaseSX
```

```
1/2    core_switch_2    connected  trunk      full   1000  1000BaseSX
3/1    server1          connected  45         full   100   10/100BaseTX
3/2    mgmt_tool1       connected  45         half   10    10/100BaseTX
3/3    server3          connected  45         a-full a-100 10/100BaseTX
3/4                     notconnect 45         auto  auto   10/100BaseTX
3/5                     notconnect 45         auto  auto   10/100BaseTX
3/6                     notconnect 45         auto  auto   10/100BaseTX
...
...
<Output removed>
```

The output removed from the foregoing show port command includes more than just additional port numbers, names, status, VLAN, duplex, speed, and type. It contains packet statistics, error rates, security parameters, and much more. This information was not shown here because it does not directly relate to the switch network configuration table.

Because the VLAN information is not included in the output of a `show port` command for a trunked port, we need to get this data in another manner. There are a couple of ways to get this information, but the usual method is via the `show trunk` command:

```
core_switch> show trunk
* - indicates vtp domain mismatch
Port     Mode         Encapsulation  Status       Native vlan
-------- ----------- ------------- ------------ -----------
 1/1     nonegotiate     dot1q       trunking        45
 1/2     nonegotiate     dot1q       trunking        45

Port     Vlans allowed on trunk
-------- ---------------------------------------------------------------
 1/1     1-2,45-46
 1/2     1-2,45-46

Port     Vlans allowed and active in management domain
-------- ---------------------------------------------------------------
 1/1     1-2,45-46
 1/2     1-2,45-46

Port     Vlans in spanning tree forwarding state and not pruned
-------- ---------------------------------------------------------------
 1/1     1-2,45-46
 1/2     1-2,45-46
```

The VLANs that traverse the trunk are shown in the `Vlans allowed on trunk` section of this output. If a VLAN is not listed in this section, then it will not be permitted on the trunk.

The final command necessary to complete the information in the switch network configuration table is the `show spantree` *`vlan`* command. In our case, we need information regarding VLAN 45, the VLAN in which our servers reside.

```
core_switch> show spantree 45
VLAN 45
Spanning tree mode      PVST+
Spanning tree type      ieee
Spanning tree enabled

Designated Root            00-d0-f6-bc-aa-aa
Designated Root Priority   49152
Designated Root Cost       3004
Designated Root Port       1/1
Root Max Age   20 sec  Hello Time 2 sec  Forward Delay 15 sec

Bridge ID MAC ADDR         00-d0-f6-bc-7e-00
Bridge ID Priority         49152
Bridge Max Age 20 sec  Hello Time 2 sec  Forward Delay 15 sec

Port             Vlan Port-State    Cost      Prio Portfast Channel_id
---------------- ---- ------------- --------- ---- -------- ----------
 1/1               45  forwarding       4       32  disabled    0
 1/2               45  blocking         4       32  disabled    0
 3/1               45  forwarding      19       32  enabled     0
 3/2               45  forwarding     100       32  enabled     0
 3/3               45  forwarding      19       32  enabled     0
 3/4               45  not-connected   19       32  disabled    0
 3/5               45  not-connected   19       32  disabled    0
 3/6               45  not-connected   19       32  disabled    0
 ...
 ...
 <Output removed>
```

Notice that this command provides the necessary information to complete the STP State and the Portfast configuration columns of the table.

When both the router and switch network configuration tables are complete, we can move on to creating the network topology diagrams.

Network Topology Diagrams

Network configuration tables are great building blocks for your network documentation, but they are not sufficient for getting a clear picture of how devices connect and interact within the network. This is where the *network topology diagram* comes in. Simply put, a network topology diagram is nothing more than a graphical representation of the network, allowing you to easily see how components in the network are connected and how they interact. Arguably, it is the most heavily utilized piece of documentation used in network troubleshooting and maintenance.

Components of a Network Topology Diagram

Like the network configuration table, the network topology diagram can contain a number of items; its scope will depend on the complexity of the network involved. In its simplest form, a network topology diagram will only include the devices and the connections between them. However, in most cases, the diagram will contain much more information. Some common items are as follows:

- Device Name
- Connections Between Devices (which can also include circuit numbers on WAN links)
- Device Type
- Interface Name
- Speed
- Media Type
- MAC Address
- VLANs
- Trunk
- Encapsulation
- IP Address
- Subnet
- Subnet Mask
- Routing Protocols

Unlike the network configuration tables, it is quite common for the network topology diagram to depict a combination of layer 2 and layer 3 devices. This allows for a more complete view of the interactions in the network and a better overall view of network connectivity. Just as you do with network configuration tables, however, you need to be careful to incorporate enough information into the topology diagram without adding too much. These are working documents; if they become too overloaded with information, their maintenance will be more difficult. On the other side, you don't want to be hunting down information in the middle of an emergency. There is a delicate balance between too much and not enough information.

Another point of note: Unless your network is small, you are not going to be able to fit it into a single network topology diagram. Typically, you will need to make multiple topology diagrams that cover separate aspects of the network. Depending on the drawing program you are using to create the diagrams, you can also link each of these separate topology diagrams together. In this manner, you can double-click a particular area to see more- or less-detailed information or move to another segment of the network.

Consistency and Simplicity Are the Keys

When creating network documentation, one goal that is frequently overlooked is the need to make the documentation consistent and easy to read. Make an effort to apply the same structure and methodology consistently to all the documentation. In this chapter we have discussed the need for consistency when gathering the information and setting up a document, but it is also important to maintain this uniformity from one document to the next.

One of the main purposes of your network documentation is its role in a troubleshooting effort when the network is down. Because you can't schedule when a problem will occur, it is quite possible that you will be using your documentation to solve a problem in the middle of the night, when you are not completely rested and are not operating at your peak effectiveness. At such a time, you do not want to be saddled with documents that are incompatible or so cluttered with information that they are difficult to read. Keep in mind when and how the network documentation is going to be used, and take some simple steps to make it easy to comprehend.

One of the first things you should do is ensure that the symbols used on all the diagrams mean the same thing on each one. Do not use one symbol to signify a router on one diagram and a different symbol to represent the same router on another.

Next, create a template for all your network configuration tables and topology diagrams. Earlier in this chapter we discussed the template for a network configuration table, but templates for network topology diagrams can be even more useful. For example, if you have multiple branch locations, use an identical format and device-placement scheme on all the topology diagrams so that similar information is always in the same spot on each diagram. This will save you time in locating the facts you need.

Besides maintaining consistency, it is also important to avoid too much complexity. If the network documentation contains extraneous information, that can make it difficult to find the specifics that you need for your troubleshooting. The documentation should have enough information to help you understand how things are connected and what the baseline of the network is, without overwhelming you with data that may or may not be relevant.

Creating a Network Topology Diagram

Now that we have explained the purpose and suggested components for a network topology diagram, let's go through the steps to create one.

We will begin with an examination of the standard set of symbols used in such diagrams. By now, most of you will have already seen and know these symbols; they are illustrated in Figure 34.3. Employing a standard set of symbols for device types helps to ensure that any new network administrators coming into the environment will be able to easily understand the documentation.

FIGURE 34.3 Networking symbols

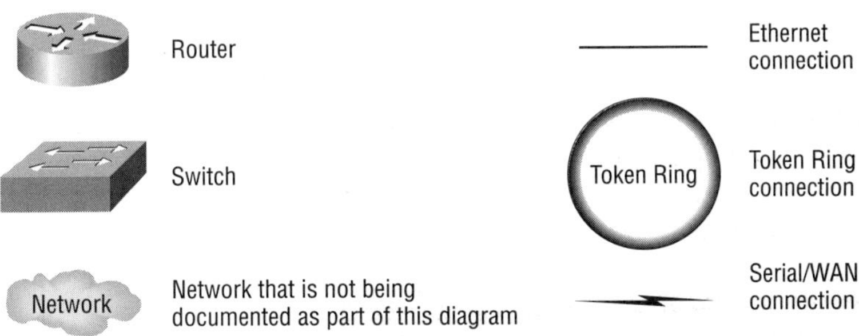

In most cases, a network topology diagram is created after the network configuration tables are set up, because the topology diagram uses much of the information contained in the configuration tables. Figure 34.4 illustrates a sample network topology diagram and its relationship to some of the information used from the router configuration table.

Similarly, there is also a direct correlation between items on the topology diagram and the switch network configuration table, as illustrated in Figure 34.5.

Because most of the information that is on the network topology diagram has already been retrieved and placed in the network configuration tables, relatively few commands are needed to generate the diagram itself. One command of great assistance is `show cdp neighbors`. The Cisco Discovery Protocol (CDP) is a proprietary protocol that identifies directly attached Cisco devices. This discovery is done at layer 2, so there is no need to have IP connectivity to see the neighbors. The `show cdp neighbor` command shows the neighbors that have been learned via CDP and gives their summary information. More detailed information can be found by using the `show cdp neighbors detail` command.

FIGURE 34.4 Items from the router configuration table

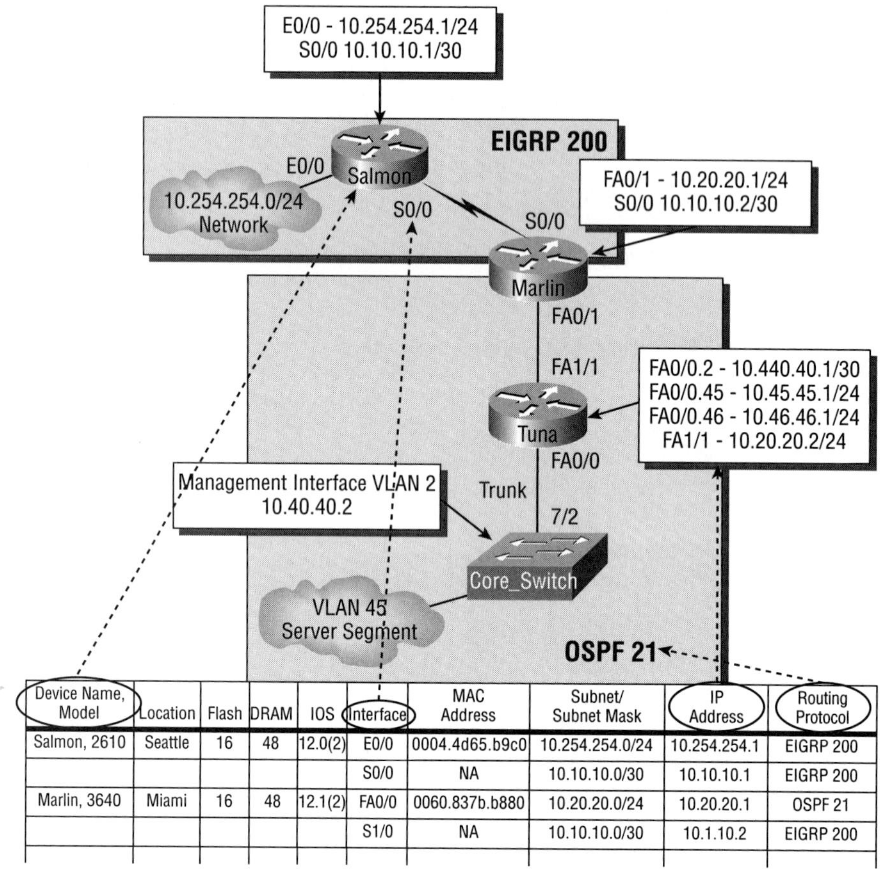

Device Name, Model	Location	Flash	DRAM	IOS	Interface	MAC Address	Subnet/ Subnet Mask	IP Address	Routing Protocol
Salmon, 2610	Seattle	16	48	12.0(2)	E0/0	0004.4d65.b9c0	10.254.254.0/24	10.254.254.1	EIGRP 200
					S0/0	NA	10.10.10.0/30	10.10.10.1	EIGRP 200
Marlin, 3640	Miami	16	48	12.1(2)	FA0/0	0060.837b.b880	10.20.20.0/24	10.20.20.1	OSPF 21
					S1/0	NA	10.10.10.0/30	10.1.10.2	EIGRP 200

FIGURE 34.5 Items from the switch configuration table

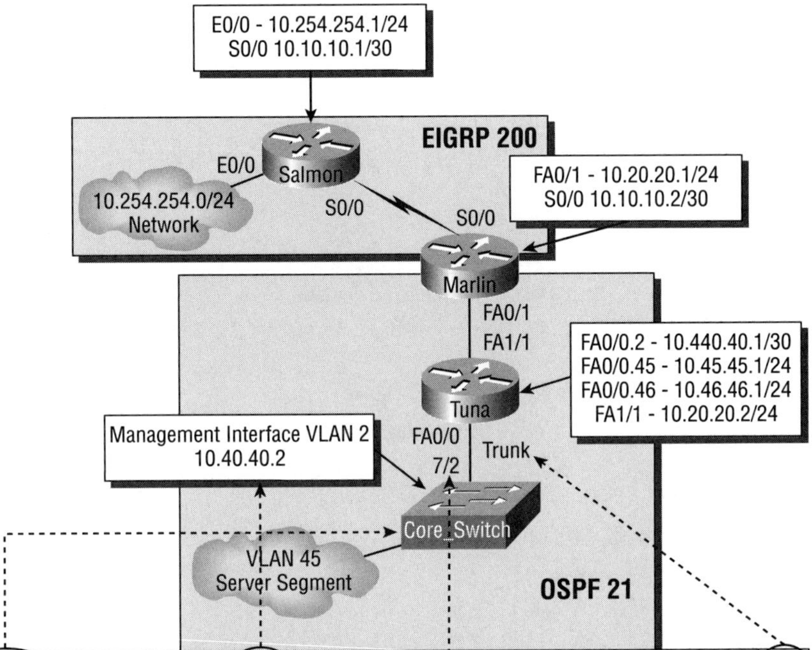

Device Name, Model	Location	Flash	DRAM	CATOS	Mgmt IP	VTP Domain	VTP Mode	Port	Speed	Duplex	VLAN(s)	STP State (Fwd/Block)	Portfast (Yes/No)	Trunk (Yes/No)
core_switch, 6509	Dover, DE	16	64	6.4(3)	10.40.40.2	dover_core	Transparent	1/1	1000	Full	1,2,45,46	Fwd	No	Yes
								1/2	1000	Full	1,2,45,46	Block	No	Yes
								3/1	100	Full	45	Fwd	Yes	No
								3/2	10	Half	45	Fwd	Yes	No
								3/3	A-100	A-Full	45	Fwd	Yes	No

The following are examples of the output of each command:

```
salmon#show cdp neighbors
Capability Codes: R - Router, T - Trans Bridge, B - Source Route Bridge
        S - Switch, H - Host, I - IGMP, r - Repeater

Device ID            Local Intrfce Holdtme  Capability Platform Port ID
marlin               Ser 0/0        172         R        3640    Ser 0/0
069017443(switch_a)  Eth 0/0        141       T B S     WS-C5500 2/13
```

```
salmon#show cdp neighbors detail
-------------------------
Device ID: marlin
Entry address(es):
 IP address: 10.10.10.2
Platform: cisco 3640, Capabilities: Router
Interface: Serial0/0, Port ID (outgoing port): Serial0/0
Holdtime : 160 sec

Version :
 Cisco Internetwork Operating System Software
 IOS (tm) 3600 Software (C3640-JS56I-M), Version 12.1(2), RELEASE
  SOFTWARE (fc2)
 Copyright (c) 1986-2000 by cisco Systems, Inc.
 Compiled Thu 08-Dec-00 04:50 by phanguye

-------------------------
Device ID: 069017443(switch_a)
Entry address(es):
 IP address: 10.254.254.102
Platform: WS-C5500, Capabilities: Trans-Bridge Source-Route-Bridge
Switch
Interface: Ethernet0/0, Port ID (outgoing port): 2/13
Holdtime : 130 sec

Version :
WS-C5500 Software, Version McpSW: 4.5(5) NmpSW: 4.5(5)
Copyright (c) 1995-1999 by Cisco Systems
```

Because these commands are available in both routers and switches, you can effectively move across the network one device at a time, documenting each neighbor along the way.

One final recommendation: Accuracy is the key to any successful documentation strategy. As things change in the network, your documents must be updated to reflect these changes. It is usually best to get in the habit of changing your documents as a normal part of changing the network, not as an afterthought. (This applies to scheduled changes as well as after troubleshooting!) In this manner, you are less likely to get involved in other tasks and forget to update the documentation.

Summary

Documentation is essential in today's increasingly complex networks. It provides vital information that can greatly reduce network downtime. It also provides verification that the network is operating correctly.

Baseline information on a network is information about the normal operating conditions of a network. This baseline is used to determine whether a network configuration is set up in the manner expected and whether it is operating normally. Some of the specific components of the network baseline are the network configuration tables, the network topology diagrams, the end-system configuration tables, and the end-system topology diagrams.

Network configuration tables show the key configuration parameters that are in place on the network devices. Some typical items included in a network configuration table are device name, flash memory DRAM, IOS/CatOS, interface number, MAC address, speed, duplex, VLANs, trunking, IP address, subnet, subnet mask, and routing protocol. Although these are some of the standard items in a network configuration table, each table will vary based on a device's type and on the design of the particular network. In most cases this information is stored in a spreadsheet or database format, but hard copies should be regularly printed so that information will always be available in the event of a problem or failure.

Network topology diagrams are graphical representations of the network components, and in most cases they contain a subset of the data maintained in the network configuration tables. The topology diagrams are meant to make the network administrator better able to visualize the path across the network. Some standard items that go into a network topology are device name, connections between devices, interface name, VLANs, trunking, IP address, subnet mask, and routing protocols. As is true for the network configuration tables, hard copies of network topology diagrams should be regularly printed to ensure that information is always available when the network goes down.

Exam Essentials

Know what a network baseline is and the major components that go into making it. A baseline is a set of documentation that establishes normal operating conditions on the network. Some of the key components of a baseline are the network configuration tables, the network topology diagrams, the end-system configuration tables, and the end-system topology diagrams.

Know what network configuration tables are and the information they contain. Network configuration tables are used to record key settings of network devices, as well as other related information. Some common items included in a network configuration table are device name, flash information, DRAM, IOS/CatOS, interface number, MAC address, speed, duplex, VLANs, trunking, IP address, subnet, subnet mask, and routing protocol.

Know what network topology diagrams are and the information they contain. Network topology diagrams are graphical representations of the network; they are usually built from many of the same components as the network configuration tables. Some common components of network topology diagrams are device name, connections between devices, interface name, VLANs, trunking, IP address, subnet mask, and routing protocols.

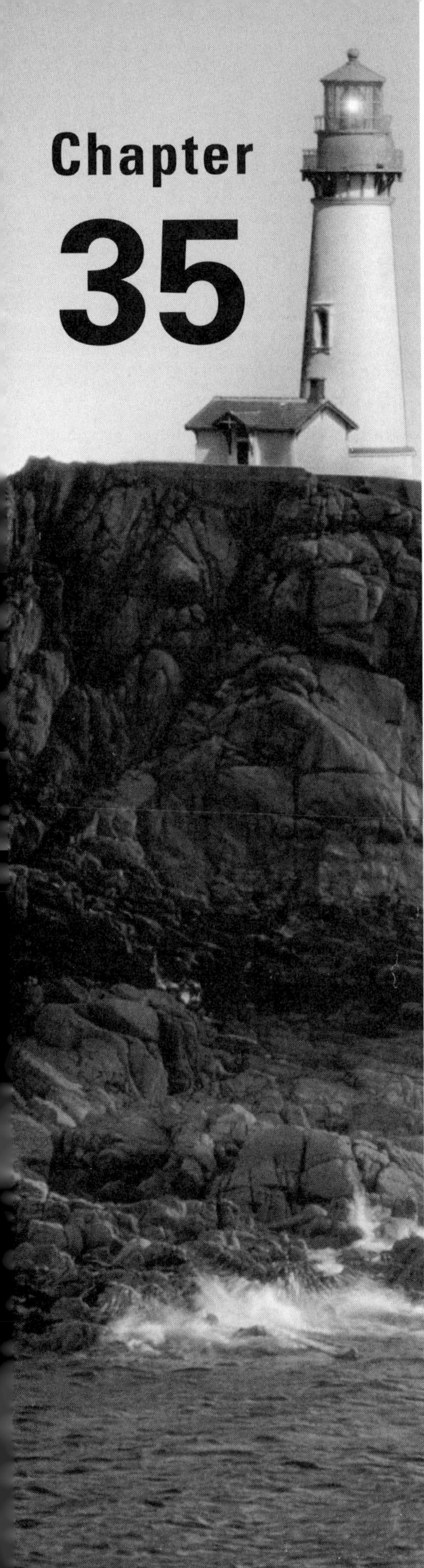

End-System Documentation and Troubleshooting

THE CCNP EXAM TOPICS COVERED IN THIS CHAPTER INCLUDE THE FOLLOWING:

- ✓ Create end-system documentation.
- ✓ Know troubleshooting methodologies.
- ✓ Verify network connectivity.
- ✓ Use the optimal troubleshooting approach in resolving network problems.
- ✓ Develop a network documentation system.
- ✓ Work with end users to diagnose and resolve network problems.
- ✓ Understand the document control process and documentation standards.
- ✓ Establish a baseline indicative of optimal network performance.
- ✓ Create a baseline monitoring methodology.

You learned in Chapter 34, "Network Documentation," that detailed network information can be an invaluable tool in troubleshooting network problems. However, many network problems are a result of the end systems on the network, not the network itself. The purpose of this chapter is to examine the documentation for these end systems so that you can effectively address network problems in these areas. This chapter will also explore a new troubleshooting approach based on the OSI model. Finally, this chapter will end with an overview of some of the commands that can be used on end systems to assist in troubleshooting network problems.

End-System Network Configuration Table

The general purpose of an *end-system network configuration table*, also referred to as an end-system configuration table, is to give a listing of the hardware and software components on the end systems in the network. Much like the network configuration table was a listing of network devices, the end-system network configuration table is a listing of the end systems in the environment and key features about them. Depending on the size of your network, an end-system network configuration table may contain all devices or just the servers and network management stations.

Though it was mentioned in Chapter 34, it is worth repeating that there are five steps to ensuring that you have good, effective documentation:

- Determine the scope.
- Know your objective.
- Be consistent.
- Keep the documents accessible.
- Maintain the documentation.

These actions directly apply to the end-system documentation as well, so be sure to keep them in mind as you are planning for and implementing your documentation strategy.

The specific items included in your end-system network configuration table will vary depending on the purpose of the table. There will be vastly different information included if the table is going to be used only for inventory purposes, as compared with the type of table maintained as a troubleshooting tool. Therefore, in order to determine what you need to include in your end-system configuration table, you need to start by defining the role of the table and choosing items for the table that will achieve this goal. Some common items included in end-system configuration tables are listed in Table 35.1.

TABLE 35.1 Sample List of Network Configuration Table Items for End Systems

Classification	Items
Miscellaneous information	System name, system manufacturer/model, CPU speed, RAM, storage, system purpose
Layers 1 and 2	Media type, interface speed, VLAN, network jack
Layer 3	IP address, default gateway, subnet mask, WINS, DNS
Layer 7	Operating system (including version), network-based applications, high-bandwidth applications, and low-latency applications, special considerations

One of the items you will immediately notice when looking at the table is the information that is included on layer 7, the Application layer. Because one of the primary roles for servers is to service applications, it is imperative that layer 7 information be captured somewhere. For example, say you get a call from a user who cannot get to the XYZ database, but everything else on their system is working fine. By looking at the end-system configuration table you can see that the XYZ database exists on a single server. You have now greatly narrowed the scope of the problem and can more effectively begin the troubleshooting process.

The end-system configuration table is typically compiled in either a spreadsheet or database application. In addition to this electronic version, regular hardcopies of the end-system configuration table must be made to ensure that the information is accessible in the event of a network problem.

Now that we have defined what an end-system network configuration table is, the next section will walk you through the process of creating one.

Creating an End-System Network Configuration Table

The easiest way to explain how to create an end-system network configuration table is to study an example. In this example, we will look at creating the table for some servers. These servers are used companywide for such processes as e-mail, system backup, and streaming video. All of the servers are located in the Miami office of this company.

Based on this information, we have decided to include the following list of items in our end-system network configuration table:

- System Name
- System Purpose
- Operating System
- VLAN
- IP Address
- Subnet Mask

- Default Gateway
- DNS Servers
- WINS Server
- Network Applications
- High-Bandwidth Network Applications
- Low-Latency Network Applications

The start of the end-system network configuration table is shown in Figure 35.1, which shows part of the information already entered for our example.

FIGURE 35.1 Sample end-system network configuration table

System Name/Purpose	OS	IP Address/Mask	Default Gateway	DNS	WINS	Network Applications	High Bandwidth Apps	Low Latency Apps
streamer/(Live Streaming Video)	Win 2000 SP4	10.45.45.8/24	10.45.45.1	10.3.3.3, 10.4.4.3	10.5.5.3, 10.6.6.3	http, iptv,ftp	NA	iptv
backup1/(Backup Server)	Unix Solaris 7	10.45.45.12/24	10.45.45.1	10.3.3.3, 10.4.4.3	NA	Backup Pro, ftp, telnet, smtp	Backup Pro	NA
web1/Web Server	LINUX Redhat Ent AS 2.1	10.45.45.25/24	10.45.45.1	10.3.3.3, 10.4.4.3	NA	http, ftp, telnet, smtp	NA	NA

Unless you have an inventory management tool that can gather this information for you, a lot of it will have to be collected manually. Depending on the system type, there are a number of commands available to gather this information. As you will see in the "End-System Troubleshooting Commands" section later in this chapter, many of these same commands can also be used in troubleshooting when there is a problem in the network. Specifically, the commands that we will examine are as follows:

- For the Windows platforms: `ping`, `arp`, `telnet`, `ipconfig`, and `winipcfg`.
- For Unix, Linux, and Mac OS X systems: `ping`, `ifconfig`, and `cat /etc/resolv.conf`.

Most people are already familiar with the very useful `ping` command. This command is used to send an ICMP echo and receive an ICMP echo reply over the network. The end-system implementation of the `ping` command is very similar to that on Cisco routers and switches. Run in a command window on an NT/2000/XP station, four Ping packets are sent out by default any time the command is executed. Though it is primarily used for troubleshooting, `ping` can be used in the discovery phase of documentation to verify which IP addresses on the network are in use.

The options of the `ping` command can be seen by executing the command `ping /?`, as shown here:

```
C:\>ping /?

Usage: ping [-t] [-a] [-n count] [-l size] [-f] [-i TTL] [-v TOS]
            [-r count] [-s count] [[-j host-list] | [-k host-list]]
            [-w timeout] target_name
```

```
Options:
    -t             Ping the specified host until stopped.
                   To see statistics and continue - type Control-Break;
                   To stop - type Control-C.
    -a             Resolve addresses to hostnames.
    -n count       Number of echo requests to send.
    -l size        Send buffer size.
    -f             Set Don't Fragment flag in packet.
    -i TTL         Time To Live.
    -v TOS         Type Of Service.
    -r count       Record route for count hops.
    -s count       Timestamp for count hops.
    -j host-list   Loose source route along host-list.
    -k host-list   Strict source route along host-list.
    -w timeout     Timeout in milliseconds to wait for each reply.
```

In the following output, the `ping` command in Windows NT/2000/XP shows not only the results of the ping but a summary of the results, as well:

```
C:\>ping 10.10.10.1

Pinging 10.10.10.1 with 32 bytes of data:

Reply from 10.10.10.1: bytes=32 time=136ms TTL=120
Reply from 10.10.10.1: bytes=32 time=136ms TTL=120
Reply from 10.10.10.1: bytes=32 time=138ms TTL=120
Reply from 10.10.10.1: bytes=32 time=137ms TTL=120

Ping statistics for 10.10.10.1:
    Packets: Sent = 4, Received = 4, Lost = 0 (0% loss),
Approximate round trip times in milli-seconds:
    Minimum = 136ms, Maximum = 138ms, Average = 136ms
```

From a Unix, Linux, or MacOS X end system, the default values vary somewhat, but the general concept is the same as a Windows end system. For example, from a Sun Solaris end system, the options for `ping` are:

```
unix1% ping
usage: ping host [timeout]
usage: ping -s[drvRlLn] [-I interval] [-t ttl] [-i interface] host
[data size] [npackets]
```

The output of the ping command can also vary based on the particular end system that is being used. For example, the output could be four Ping packets as was the case with Windows, or just a simple message stating the end system is alive, as is the case here:

```
unix1% ping 10.10.10.1
10.10.10.1 is alive
unix1%
```

The help files in Unix are called man (short for manual) pages. These files can be accessed by typing **man command**. So, to get more information on the ping command, you would type **man ping**.

The arp command is used to show the current MAC-address-to-IP-address mappings on the end system. These mappings can be used to determine which other end systems were recently contacted. This can provide clues as to what applications are interdependent. The downside to the arp command is that, because it is dependent on layer 2 information, it will only show the IP address of other end systems on the same subnet. If network communication is with a device on another subnet, the arp table will just show the IP address and MAC address of the default gateway.

Like the ping command, options for the arp command are displayed by adding a /? at the end of the command.

```
C:\>arp /?

Displays and modifies the IP-to-Physical address translation tables
  used by address resolution protocol (ARP).

ARP -s inet_addr eth_addr [if_addr]
ARP -d inet_addr [if_addr]
ARP -a [inet_addr] [-N if_addr]

  -a            Displays current ARP entries by interrogating the current
                protocol data.  If inet_addr is specified, the IP and Physical
                addresses for only the specified computer are displayed.
                If more than one network interface uses ARP, entries for
                each ARP table are displayed.
  -g            Same as -a.
  inet_addr     Specifies an internet address.
  -N if_addr    Displays the ARP entries for the network interface specified
                by if_addr.
  -d            Deletes the host specified by inet_addr. inet_addr may be
                wildcarded with * to delete all hosts.
```

```
  -s            Adds the host and associates the Internet address inet_addr
                with the Physical address eth_addr.  The Physical address
                is given as 6 hexadecimal bytes separated by hyphens. The
                entry is permanent.
  eth_addr      Specifies a physical address.
  if_addr       If present, this specifies the Internet address of the
                interface whose address translation table should be modified.
                If not present, the first applicable interface will be used.
Example:
  > arp -s 157.55.85.212   00-aa-00-62-c6-09  Adds a static entry.
  > arp -a                                    Displays the arp table.
```

And here is a sample output of the arp command using the -a option to list the current translations:

```
C:\>arp -a

Interface: 10.9.9.9 --- 0x2
  Internet Address      Physical Address      Type
  10.9.9.1              00-06-22-fd-06-01     dynamic
  10.9.9.100            00-e0-18-19-a8-19     dynamic
  10.9.9.222            00-a0-cc-cb-64-c5     dynamic
```

The telnet command is used for the discovery of end systems in two different ways. First, telnet can be used by the network administrator to log in to some of the end systems on the network remotely. This functionality is enabled by default on most Unix and Linux servers but is not by default available on Windows NT/2000/XP. Secondly, telnet can be used to verify that an end system is indeed listening on a particular TCP port. For example, you can telnet to a web server on TCP port 80. You will not see any meaningful data, but if a connection is established, you have verified not only that the server is listening on port 80 but also that port 80 traffic is getting through the network to the server.

Use caution when telnetting to a port. Though it is usually not a problem, some custom applications do not respond well to these types of connections.

The options for Telnet on Windows NT/2000/XP are shown in the following command output:

```
C:\>telnet /?

telnet [-a][-e escape char][-f log file][-l user][-t term][host [port]]
 -a     Attempt automatic logon. Same as -l option except uses the currently
        logged on user's name.
 -e     Escape character to enter telnet client prompt.
 -f     File name for client side logging
```

```
 -l       Specifies the user name to log in with on the remote system. Requires
          that the remote system support the TELNET ENVIRON option.
  -t      Specifies terminal type.  Supported term types are vt100, vt52,
          ansi and vtnt only.
 host     Specifies the hostname or IP address of the remote computer to connect
          to.
 port     Specifies a port number or service name.
```

The ipconfig command is the first command in the series discussed here that will go a long way toward getting the data you need in order to complete the end-system network configuration table. This command shows detailed information on the IP address, DNS servers, and WINS servers that are configured on the Windows NT/2000/XP workstation. As is the case for all the commands covered in this section, ipconfig is run from the command prompt on the Windows NT/2000/XP end system. Some of the other command options will be explained in the "End-System Troubleshooting Commands" section later in this chapter, but for the documentation process, the /all option is what is primarily used. The entire list of options for ipconfig are shown here:

```
C:\>ipconfig /?

USAGE:
    ipconfig [/? | /all | /renew [adapter] | /release [adapter] |
              /flushdns | /displaydns | /registerdns |
              /showclassid adapter |
              /setclassid adapter [classid] ]
where
    adapter         Connection name
                   (wildcard characters * and ? allowed, see examples)

    Options:
       /?           Display this help message
       /all         Display full configuration information.
       /release     Release the IP address for the specified adapter.
       /renew       Renew the IP address for the specified adapter.
       /flushdns    Purges the DNS Resolver cache.
       /registerdns Refreshes all DHCP leases and re-registers DNS names
       /displaydns  Display the contents of the DNS Resolver Cache.
       /showclassid Displays all the dhcp class IDs allowed for adapter.
       /setclassid  Modifies the dhcp class id.

The default is to display only the IP address, subnet mask and default gateway
for each adapter bound to TCP/IP.

For Release and Renew, if no adapter name is specified, then the IP address
```

```
leases for all adapters bound to TCP/IP will be released or renewed.

For Setclassid, if no ClassId is specified, then the ClassId is removed.

Examples:
    > ipconfig                   ... Show information.
    > ipconfig /all              ... Show detailed information
    > ipconfig /renew            ... renew all adapters
    > ipconfig /renew EL*        ... renew any connection that has its
                                     name starting with EL
    > ipconfig /release *Con*    ... release all matching connections,
                                     eg. "Local Area Connection 1" or
                                         "Local Area Connection 2"
```

The following is the output of the `ipconfig /all` command. The IP address, subnet, gateway, DNS servers, and WINS servers are underlined:

```
C:\>ipconfig /all

Windows IP Configuration

        Host Name . . . . . . . . . . . . : Server1
        Primary Dns Suffix  . . . . . . . : fla.somecompany.com
        Node Type . . . . . . . . . . . . : Hybrid
        IP Routing Enabled. . . . . . . . : No
        WINS Proxy Enabled. . . . . . . . : No
        DNS Suffix Search List. . . . . . : fla.somecompany.com
                                            somecompany.com

Ethernet adapter Local Area Connection 4:

        Connection-specific DNS Suffix  . :
        Description . . . . . . . . . . . : NVIDIA nForce MCP
    Networking Adapter
        Physical Address. . . . . . . . . : 00-cc-47-49-F4-32
        Dhcp Enabled. . . . . . . . . . . : No
        IP Address. . . . . . . . . . . . : 10.9.9.9
        Subnet Mask . . . . . . . . . . . : 255.255.255.0
        Default Gateway . . . . . . . . . : 10.9.9.1
        DNS Servers . . . . . . . . . . . : 10.3.3.3
                                            10.4.4.3
        Primary WINS Server . . . . . . . : 10.5.5.3
        Secondary WINS Server . . . . . . : 10.6.6.3
```

If the end system you are working on is Windows 9*x* or Windows ME, a different methodology is used to discover this information. On these machines, there is a GUI tool that replaces the `ipconfig` command-line command. The executable to start this tool is `winipcfg.exe`. This utility shows all the same information as `ipconfig`, but it does so via the GUI instead of the command line.

Both `ipconfig` and `winipcfg` are available in Windows 98.

To get the IP information from a Unix, Linux, or MacOS X system, you use the `ifconfig -a` command. This prints out the address information for each interface on the box. Here's a sample output:

```
unix1% ifconfig -a
lo0: flags=849<UP,LOOPBACK,RUNNING,MULTICAST> mtu 8232
        inet 127.0.0.1 netmask ff000000
hme0: flags=863<UP,BROADCAST,NOTRAILERS,RUNNING,MULTICAST> mtu 1500
        inet 10.7.7.58 netmask ffffff00 broadcast 10.7.7.255
```

As is the case in many routers, the loopback interface is an internal virtual interface. Because the loopback is addressed with 127.0.0.1, it is only used for internal communication inside the box. The hme0 interface is the interface that is connected to the network and is the one that goes into the end-system network configuration table.

Because Unix, Linux, and MacOS X end systems do not use WINS, the only remaining bit of IP information that you need to get from the end system is the DNS servers' names. This is stored in the `resolv.conf` file, which is most often found in the `/etc` directory on the system. To see the DNS servers that are defined, all you need to do is to list the contents of the `resolv.conf` file using the `cat` command, as shown here:

```
unix1% cat /etc/resolv.conf
domain fla.somecompany.com
search fla.somecompany.com somecompany.com
nameserver      10.3.3.3
nameserver      10.4.4.3
```

For the remaining information in the end-system configuration table such as the applications on the system and which of these applications are high- and low-bandwidth and/or low-latency applications, it is best to talk with the server administrators. They will have the best idea of what is on each server and how it is used.

End-System Network Topology Diagram

Now that the end-system network configuration table is complete, we will focus on the end-system network topology diagram. Like the topology diagram for the network, the end-system diagram is designed to give a graphical representation of the end-systems in the network, giving you a better view of traffic flow and interdependencies. This view also allows for easier identification of potential bottlenecks or significant points of failure. For example, you can easily see on the end-system network topology diagram whether your users will need to cross a slow serial connection to get to new servers that are being put in. You can also see if there is only one path available from these users to the servers, and, if redundancy is required, alter the location of the servers or add another path.

In most cases, the end-system network topology diagram is just an extension of the network topology diagram, with the information gathered for the end-system network configuration table added. Because of the amount of information included in these diagrams, it is necessary to ensure that only pertinent data is added. Adding too much data can quickly clutter up the diagram and make it difficult to use.

Typical items in an end-system topology diagram are as follows:

- System Name
- Connection to the Network
- System Purpose
- VLAN
- IP Address
- Subnet Mask
- Network Applications

At a minimum, the system name and connection to the network are needed on the topology diagram. The exception to this rule is when you are including a large number of like-configured end systems that serve a common purpose and exist on the same subnet. In this arrangement, where it is impractical to include each separate machine in the diagram, they can be grouped together and represented by descriptive text. An example of this grouping is shown in Figure 35.2 in the next section.

Real World Scenario

Windows Name Resolution

When working with Windows systems, it is important to know the process by which names are associated to IP addresses. In a Unix system, this resolution is relatively straightforward and usually involves the use of cached entries, a `HOSTS` file, or DNS. In a Windows environment, however, there are a few other options available. All the options that are available are as follows:

- Internal cache of recently used entries
- Broadcast message to the local network
- Local `LMHOSTS` file
- Local `HOSTS` file

- WINS server
- DNS server

In addition to the local cache, the HOSTS file, and DNS are three other options: broadcast, LMHOSTS, and WINS. The order in which these items are checked in a Windows system varies based on a number of factors, but in general, the internal cache and broadcast message are the first items used to try to resolve a name into an IP address.

Following this, the LMHOSTS and HOSTS files are used. Both these files are usually located in the `%SystemRoot%\System32\Drivers\Etc` directory of each Windows end system. They are text-based files that can be edited to provide static name-to-IP-address translation.

Next in the series is the Windows Internet Name Service (WINS) server, which is Microsoft's version of a NetBIOS name server. It dynamically updates the names of other Windows clients that are on the network. The server can then be queried in much the same manner as a DNS server for name-to-IP-address resolution.

The final item used by a Windows end system is a DNS server. As is the case with any station using DNS, a Windows station sends a query to the DNS server, and the server responds with the IP address or a notification saying it does not know the address.

Creating an End-System Network Topology Diagram

Now that an end-system network topology diagram has been explained, let's go through the steps to create one. Because most end-system network topology diagrams are built on the network topology diagrams, the standard symbols set that was used in the network diagrams will also be used here in the end-system network topology diagram. In addition, there will be symbols to indicate servers, workstations, and other network attached end systems.

The other information added to the end-system network topology diagram is a subset of the data in the end-system network configuration table. Figure 35.2 shows how this data maps to the topology diagram.

As you can see in Figure 35.2, the servers entered in the network configuration are shown in their appropriate place in the network. Only the key information on the servers was transferred to the topology diagram to keep it from becoming too cluttered. Also, as mentioned earlier in this discussion, notice in the upper-left of the diagram that a grouping of computers was used instead of showing all 12 of the Seattle users' computers. This simplifies the drawing without sacrificing too much detail. If more detail is needed, specifically on the Seattle office, a new end-system network topology diagram could be created specifically for that office.

Well, after what seems like an eternity, you have completed your network configuration tables, network topology diagrams, end-system network configuration tables, and end-system network topology diagrams! Now you just have to make sure that you keep them accessible and update them any time there's a change in the network. Also, remember to print hardcopies regularly, so that you will still have your documentation if the network is down.

FIGURE 35.2 Sample end-system network topology diagram

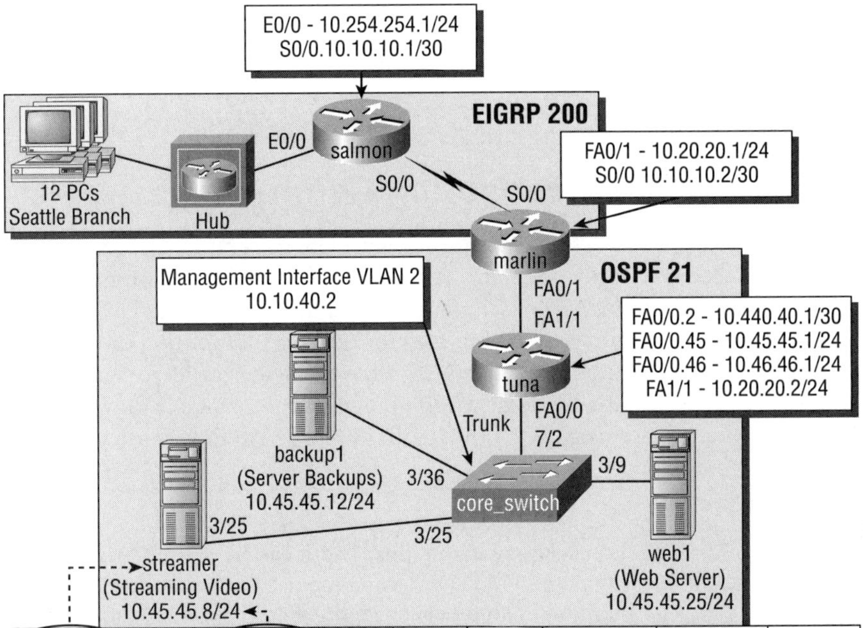

System Name/Purpose	OS	IP Address/Mask	Default Gateway	DNS	WINS	Network Applications	High Bandwidth Apps	Low Latency Apps
streamer/(Live Streaming Video)	Win 2000 SP4	10.45.45.8/24	10.45.45.1	10.3.3.3, 10.4.4.3	10.5.5.3, 10.6.6.3	http, iptv,ftp	NA	iptv
backup1/(Backup Server)	Unix Solaris 7	10.45.45.12/24	10.45.45.1	10.3.3.3, 10.4.4.3	NA	Backup Pro, ftp, telnet, smtp	Backup Pro	NA
web1/Web Server	LINUX Redhat Ent AS 2.1	10.45.45.25/24	10.45.45.1	10.3.3.3, 10.4.4.3	NA	http, ftp, telnet, smtp	NA	NA

Troubleshooting End-System Problems

In a perfect world, network administrators would be free to work solely on the network components of the system, and the end systems would be taken care of by someone else. The reality is that we do not live in such a place, so network administrators frequently must help troubleshoot problems on the end systems. The assistance provided may be simply checking connectivity, or it may involve the complete rebuilding of the end system! We are not going to get into the rebuilding of a Windows server from scratch. In this section, you will see how to diagnose what is happening on an end system, and how to take some simple corrective actions when they are needed.

In addition to running these commands directly, you can also have the end user run many of these commands for you and tell you the results. This can be very helpful, especially when the users are located in a remote location.

Some of the commands examined in this section are variations of the ones used in creating the end-system documentation; others are new. But before we look at how to identify and correct problems, we will spend a little more time on how to approach the problem.

End-System Troubleshooting Commands

As you learned earlier in this chapter in the section "Creating an End-System Network Configuration Table," there are many occasions when you need to execute commands on the end system in order to get a clear picture of what is going on in the network. This is true not only for the discovery of network information but also for the troubleshooting of network behavior. Because the basic commands used for discovery were discussed earlier in the chapter, here in this section we will focus specifically on the troubleshooting commands. You will notice that many of the same commands are used for both troubleshooting and discovery.

In this section, the Unix versions of the commands are used for the Unix, Linux, and MacOS X end-system types. There can be slight variations between the Unix and the Linux/MacOS X versions of the commands. However, most are very similar and in some cases identical to their Unix counterparts.

Ping

The `ping` command was covered in some detail earlier in this chapter, so you can refer back to the section "Creating an End-System Network Configuration Table" for the `ping` basics. Here we will focus on some of the options available under the `ping` command that are helpful in your troubleshooting activities.

One of the most common `ping` options is the continuous ping. These pings send a continuous stream of packets to the destination address. Setting up a continuous ping to an end system that is having connectivity problems is a good way to see when the end system is once again reachable over the network. In Windows systems, the flag to send a continuous ping is `-t`, and in the Unix environment the flag is `-s`.

Another frequently used `ping` option used for troubleshooting is the record route option. This records the path the packet is taking through the network and stores this information in the IP header of the ping packet.

The record route option does require that the intervening routers and the end station retain this information in the packet, and the hop count is limited to nine.

In a Windows station, record route can be enabled with the `-r` *`#_of_hops_to_record`* option. In the following example, the route will be recorded for up to nine hops, which is the maximum value allowed:

```
C:\>ping -r 9 10.5.5.5

Pinging 10.5.5.5 with 32 bytes of data:

Reply from 10.5.5.5: bytes=32 time=86ms TTL=251
    Route: 10.45.45.1 ->
           10.10.10.66 ->
           10.5.5.1 ->
           10.5.5.5 ->
           10.16.16.18 ->
           10.10.9.56 ->
           10.10.7.23 ->
           10.56.21.3
Reply from 10.5.5.5: bytes=32 time=86ms TTL=251
    Route: 10.45.45.1 ->
           10.10.10.66 ->
           10.5.5.1 ->
           10.5.5.5 ->
           10.16.16.18 ->
           10.10.9.56 ->
           10.10.7.23 ->
           10.56.21.3
Reply from 10.5.5.5: bytes=32 time=85ms TTL=251
    Route: 10.45.45.1 ->
           10.10.10.66 ->
           10.5.5.1 ->
           10.5.5.5 ->
           10.16.16.18 ->
           10.10.9.56 ->
           10.10.7.23 ->
           10.56.21.3
Reply from 10.5.5.5: bytes=32 time=83ms TTL=251
    Route: 10.45.45.1 ->
           10.10.10.66 ->
           10.5.5.1 ->
           10.5.5.5 ->
           10.16.16.18 ->
```

```
          10.10.9.56 ->
          10.10.7.23 ->
          10.56.21.3

Ping statistics for 10.5.5.5:
    Packets: Sent = 4, Received = 4, Lost = 0 (0% loss),
Approximate round trip times in milli-seconds:
    Minimum = 83ms, Maximum = 86ms, Average = 85ms
```

In Unix, the similar command option for record route is as follows:

```
unix1% ping -s -nRv 10.5.5.5
PING 10.5.5.5 (10.5.5.5): 56 data bytes
64 bytes from 10.5.5.5: icmp_seq=0. time=123. ms
  IP options:  <record route> 10.45.45.1, 10.10.10.66, 10.5.5.1,
   10.5.5.5, 10.16.16.18, 10.10.9.56, 10.10.7.23,
10.56.21.3
```

Traceroute

Similar to the record route option of the ping command, the traceroute command is used to determine the path that the packet is taking through the network. However, traceroute uses a different approach than the `ping` command. Specifically, the traceroute command starts by sending out a packet with a time to live (TTL) of 1. The TTL of this packet will expire at the first router, and therefore this device will send back a TTL expiration message. The address from which the TTL expiration comes is then recorded, and a second packet is sent out with a TTL of 2. The second-hop router then replies back with a TTL expiration message. This process continues until the destination is reached.

The traceroute command operates in the Unix and Windows environment in the same manner as the `trace` command in the Cisco router.

Though the functionality is the same, it is worthy of note that in the Cisco and the Unix versions of traceroute, a UDP packet on port 33434 is used for the tracing, whereas Windows stations use an ICMP echo instead.

In Windows, the syntax for the traceroute command is `tracert`. The options for the command are shown in the following output, which is followed by a sample trace:

```
C:\>tracert /?

Usage: tracert [-d] [-h maximum_hops] [-j host-list] [-w timeout] target_name
```

```
Options:
    -d                  Do not resolve addresses to hostnames.
    -h maximum_hops     Maximum number of hops to search for target.
    -j host-list        Loose source route along host-list.
    -w timeout          Wait timeout milliseconds for each reply.


C:\>tracert 10.5.5.5

Tracing route to 10.5.5.5 over a maximum of 30 hops

  1     7 ms     1 ms     1 ms  10.21.2.1
  2    84 ms    83 ms    84 ms  10.45.45.3
  3    88 ms    85 ms    83 ms  10.10.10.67
  4    87 ms    86 ms    88 ms  10.5.5.5

Trace complete.
```

When looking at the preceding trace, there are a couple things to note. First, Windows by default sends out three traces for each TTL value. The times listed to the left of the IP address are the times for each of the TTL expiration messages from these packets to return.

Also, when comparing the output from a recorded ping to the output of the traceroute command, be aware of a couple of noteworthy differences. Ping records the exiting interface on the router, whereas traceroute in general records the interface on which you enter. Another difference is that when using a traceroute, you only get the path taken to the end device; you do not see the return path.

As is the case with many of the commands discussed here, there are some subtle differences between Unix and Windows in terms of both syntax and output. Here are the Unix command options and a sample output:

```
unix1% traceroute
Usage: traceroute [-dFInvx] [-f first_ttl] [-g gateway | -r] [-i iface]
        [-m max_ttl] [-p port] [-q nqueries] [-s src_addr] [-t tos]
        [-w waittime] host [packetlen]
unix1% traceroute 10.5.5.5
traceroute to 10.5.5.5 (10.5.5.5), 30 hops max, 40 byte packets
 1  10.21.2.1 (10.21.2.1)  1.046 ms  1.878 ms  1.880 ms
 2  10.45.45.3 (10.45.45.3)  82.487 ms  84.850 ms  83.378 ms
 3  10.10.10.67 (10.10.10.67)  84.196 ms  86.057 ms  84.105 ms
 4  10.5.5.5 (10.5.5.5)  89.133 ms  88.664 ms  88.597 ms
unix1%
```

The *arp* Command

Although the arp command was covered in the earlier discovery section, it is being repeated here because it can be a very meaningful part of the troubleshooting process. As is the case on the routers, sometimes it is necessary to verify that the layer-2-to-layer-3 translation is working as expected on the end system. In both Unix and Windows NT/2000/XP systems, the command to display this information is arp -a. The command options and sample output from an XP box are as follows:

```
C:\>arp /?

Displays and modifies the IP-to-Physical address translation tables
used by address resolution protocol (ARP).

ARP -s inet_addr eth_addr [if_addr]
ARP -d inet_addr [if_addr]
ARP -a [inet_addr] [-N if_addr]

  -a            Displays current ARP entries by interrogating the current
                protocol data.  If inet_addr is specified, the IP and Physical
                addresses for only the specified computer are displayed.  If
                more than one network interface uses ARP, entries for each ARP
                table are displayed.
  -g            Same as -a.
  inet_addr     Specifies an internet address.
  -N if_addr    Displays the ARP entries for the network interface specified
                by if_addr.
  -d            Deletes the host specified by inet_addr. inet_addr may be
                wildcarded with * to delete all hosts.
  -s            Adds the host and associates the Internet address inet_addr
                with the Physical address eth_addr.  The Physical address
                address is given as 6 hexadecimal bytes separated by hyphens.
                The entry is permanent.
  eth_addr      Specifies a physical address.
  if_addr       If present, this specifies the Internet address of the
                interface whose address translation table should be modified.
                If not present, the first applicable interface will be used.
Example:
  > arp -s 157.55.85.212   00-aa-00-62-c6-09  .... Adds a static entry.
  > arp -a                                    .... Displays the arp table.

C:\>arp -a
```

```
Interface: 10.12.1.11 --- 0x2
  Internet Address      Physical Address      Type
  10.12.1.1             00-06-5a-23-06-f9     dynamic
```

Similar output from a Unix machine is shown next.

```
unix1% arp
Usage: arp hostname
       arp -a
       arp -d hostname
       arp -s hostname ether_addr [temp] [pub] [trail]
       arp -f filename

unix1% arp -a
Net to Media Table
Device   IP Address               Mask      Flags   Phys Addr
------ -------------------- --------------- ----- ---------------
hme0   10.12.1.1            255.255.255.255       00:06:5a:23:06:f9
hme0   10.12.1.68           255.255.255.255       00:04:f2:cd:65:1f
hme0   224.0.0.0            240.0.0.0       SM    01:00:5e:00:00:00
```

In addition to displaying information about the translation from layer 2 to layer 3, the `arp` command can also be used to add and delete entries to the ARP table.

The *route* Command

If an end station has multiple interfaces, it can be useful to know which of these interfaces is being used for particular destinations. In theses cases, for both Windows NT/2000/XP stations and Unix stations, you can use the `route` command. The following are the options and the syntax for displaying the routing table for Windows NT/2000/XP:

```
C:\>route /?

Manipulates network routing tables.

ROUTE [-f] [-p] [command [destination] [MASK netmask]  [gateway]
[METRIC metric]  [IF interface]

  -f           Clears the routing tables of all gateway entries.  If this is
               used in conjunction with one of the commands, the tables are
               cleared prior to running the command.
  -p           When used with the ADD command, makes a route persistent across
               boots of the system. By default, routes are not preserved when
```

```
              the system is restarted. Ignored for all other commands, which
              always affect the appropriate persistent routes. This option
              is not supported in Windows 95.
command       One of these:
                PRINT     Prints  a route
                ADD       Adds    a route
                DELETE    Deletes a route
                CHANGE    Modifies an existing route
destination   Specifies the host.
MASK          Specifies that the next parameter is the 'netmask' value.
netmask       Specifies a subnet mask value for this route entry. If not
              specified, it defaults to 255.255.255.255.
gateway       Specifies gateway.
interface     The interface number for the specified route.
METRIC        Specifies the metric, ie. cost for the destination.

All symbolic names used for destination are looked up in the network Database
file NETWORKS. The symbolic names for gateway are looked up in the host name
database file HOSTS.

If the command is PRINT or DELETE. Destination or gateway can be a wildcard,
(wildcard is specified as a star '*'), or the gateway argument may be omitted.

If Dest contains a * or ?, it is treated as a shell pattern, and only matching
destination routes are printed. The '*' matches any string, and '?' matches
any one char. Examples: 157.*.1, 157.*, 127.*, *224*.
Diagnostic Notes:
    Invalid MASK generates an error, that is when (DEST & MASK) !=
DEST.
    Example> route ADD 157.0.0.0 MASK 155.0.0.0 157.55.80.1 IF 1
            The route addition failed: The specified mask parameter is
 invalid.
 (Destination & Mask) != Destination.

Examples:

    > route PRINT
    > route ADD 157.0.0.0 MASK 255.0.0.0  157.55.80.1 METRIC 3 IF 2
           destination^      ^mask      ^gateway     metric^    ^
                                                      Interface^
```

```
     If IF is not given, it tries to find the best interface for a
given gateway.
    > route PRINT
    > route PRINT 157*          .... Only prints those matching 157*
    > route CHANGE 157.0.0.0 MASK 255.0.0.0 157.55.80.5 METRIC 2 IF 2
      CHANGE is used to modify gateway and/or metric only.
    > route PRINT
    > route DELETE 157.0.0.0
    > route PRINT
```

```
C:\>route print
===========================================================================
Interface List
0x1 ........................... MS TCP Loopback interface
0x2 ... 00 04 f2 cd 65 1f...... NVIDIA nForce MCP Networking Adapter -
  ➥Packet Scheduler Miniport
===========================================================================
===========================================================================
Active Routes:
Network Destination        Netmask          Gateway       Interface  Metric
        0.0.0.0          0.0.0.0        10.12.1.1     10.12.1.11       20
      127.0.0.0        255.0.0.0        127.0.0.1      127.0.0.1        1
      10.12.1.0    255.255.255.0       10.12.1.11     10.12.1.11       20
     10.12.1.11  255.255.255.255        127.0.0.1      127.0.0.1       20
    10.12.1.255  255.255.255.255       10.12.1.11     10.12.1.11       20
      224.0.0.0        240.0.0.0       10.12.1.11     10.12.1.11       20
255.255.255.255  255.255.255.255       10.12.1.11     10.12.1.11        1
Default Gateway:        10.12.1.1
===========================================================================
Persistent Routes:
  None
```

For the Unix side of things, the options and sample printout are as follows:

```
unix1% route
usage: route [ -fnqv ] cmd [[ -<qualifers> ] args ]
unix1% route -n
Kernel IP routing table
Destination     Gateway         Genmask         Flags Metric Ref    Use Iface
10.12.1.0       0.0.0.0         255.255.255.0   U     0      0        0 hme0
127.0.0.0       0.0.0.0         255.0.0.0       U     0      0        0 lo
0.0.0.0         10.12.1.1       0.0.0.0         UG    0      0        0 hme0
```

In addition to printing out the routing table, the `route` command can also be used to add or delete static routes if they are needed.

The *netstat* Command

The `netstat` command is used to display current connections to the end system. This can be useful in a troubleshooting scenario to assist in the verification of connectivity. In addition to the IP addresses of the connections, the `netstat` command also shows the port the connections are using. The Windows NT/2000/XP options and sample output of the command are shown here:

```
C:\>netstat /?

Displays protocol statistics and current TCP/IP network connections.

NETSTAT [-a] [-e] [-n] [-o] [-s] [-p proto] [-r] [interval]

  -a            Displays all connections and listening ports.
  -e            Displays Ethernet statistics. This may be combined with the -s
                option.
  -n            Displays addresses and port numbers in numerical form.
  -o            Displays the owning process ID associated with each connection.
  -p proto      Shows connections for the protocol specified by proto; proto
                may be any of: TCP, UDP, TCPv6, or UDPv6.  If used with the -s
                option to display per-protocol statistics, proto may be any of:
                IP, IPv6, ICMP, ICMPv6, TCP, TCPv6, UDP, or UDPv6.
  -r            Displays the routing table.
  -s            Displays per-protocol statistics.  By default, statistics
                are shown for IP, IPv6, ICMP, ICMPv6, TCP, TCPv6, UDP, and
                UDPv6; the -p option may be used to specify a subset of the
                default.
  interval      Redisplays selected statistics, pausing interval seconds
                between each display.  Press CTRL+C to stop redisplaying
                statistics.  If omitted, netstat will print the current
                configuration information once.

C:\>netstat -n

Active Connections

  Proto  Local Address          Foreign Address        State
  TCP    10.12.1.11:3718        10.215.198.192:80      ESTABLISHED
  TCP    10.12.1.11:3719        10.215.198.153:80      ESTABLISHED
```

```
TCP    10.12.1.11:3722        10.215.198.6:80        ESTABLISHED
TCP    10.12.1.11:3724        10.12.1.100:139        ESTABLISHED
TCP    10.12.1.11:3726        10.255.37.1:23         ESTABLISHED
```

The Unix version of the command is very similar to the Windows version. Its options and sample output are as follows:

```
unix1% netstat -help
usage: netstat [-adgimnprsDMv] [-I interface] [interval]
unix1% netstat -n

TCP
   Local Address      Remote Address    Swind Send-Q Rwind Recv-Q State
----------------- -----------------    ----- ------ ----- ------ ------
10.4.132.58.32891  10.4.132.58.162      57344      0 57344      0 ESTAB
10.4.132.58.162    10.4.132.58.32891    57344      0 57344      0 ESTAB
10.4.132.58.53074  10.4.128.10.1960     24820      0  8760      0 ESTAB
10.4.132.58.38090  10.104.108.13.1960   62780      0  8760      0 ESTAB
...
...
<output removed>
```

The *ipconfig* Command

The "Creating an End-System Network Configuration Table" section earlier in this chapter introduced the `ipconfig` command used with the `/all` option. While this option is useful for gathering information on a system, other options in the `ipconfig` command are helpful for troubleshooting purposes.

The first of these options are the `/release` and `/renew` options, which are used to release and renew DHCP addresses. Here are two examples:

```
C:\>ipconfig /release

Windows IP Configuration


Ethernet adapter Local Area Connection:

        Connection-specific DNS Suffix  . :
        IP Address. . . . . . . . . . . . : 0.0.0.0
        Subnet Mask . . . . . . . . . . . : 0.0.0.0
        Default Gateway . . . . . . . . . :
```

```
C:\WINDOWS\system32>ipconfig /renew

Windows IP Configuration


Ethernet adapter Local Area Connection:

        Connection-specific DNS Suffix  . :
        IP Address. . . . . . . . . . . . : 10.22.5.3
        Subnet Mask . . . . . . . . . . . : 255.255.255.0
        Default Gateway . . . . . . . . . : 10.22.5.1
```

The next option useful in troubleshooting is the `/displaydns` option. It allows you to see the DNS-name-to-IP-address cache that is on the workstation. The following output is from an XP machine right after pinging `www.cisco.com`:

```
C:\>ipconfig /displaydns


Windows IP Configuration

         ns1.cisco.com
         ----------------------------------------
         Record Name . . . . . : ns1.cisco.com
         Record Type . . . . . : 1
         Time To Live  . . . . : 86227
         Data Length . . . . . : 4
         Section . . . . . . . : Answer
         A (Host) Record . . . : 128.107.241.185


         1.0.0.127.in-addr.arpa
         ----------------------------------------
         Record Name . . . . . : 1.0.0.127.in-addr.arpa.
         Record Type . . . . . : 12
         Time To Live  . . . . : 0
         Data Length . . . . . : 4
         Section . . . . . . . : Answer
         PTR Record  . . . . . : localhost
```

```
ns2.cisco.com
----------------------------------------
Record Name . . . . . : ns2.cisco.com
Record Type . . . . . : 1
Time To Live  . . . . : 86227
Data Length . . . . . : 4
Section . . . . . . . : Answer
A (Host) Record . . . : 192.135.250.69


www.cisco.com
----------------------------------------
Record Name . . . . . : www.cisco.com
Record Type . . . . . : 1
Time To Live  . . . . : 86227
Data Length . . . . . : 4
Section . . . . . . . : Answer
A (Host) Record . . . : 198.133.219.25


Record Name . . . . . : ns1.cisco.com
Record Type . . . . . : 1
Time To Live  . . . . : 86227
Data Length . . . . . : 4
Section . . . . . . . : Additional
A (Host) Record . . . : 128.107.241.185


Record Name . . . . . : ns2.cisco.com
Record Type . . . . . : 1
Time To Live  . . . . : 86227
Data Length . . . . . : 4
Section . . . . . . . : Additional
A (Host) Record . . . : 192.135.250.69


localhost
----------------------------------------
Record Name . . . . . : localhost
Record Type . . . . . : 1
```

```
Time To Live . . . . : 0
Data Length . . . . . : 4
Section . . . . . . . : Answer
A (Host) Record . . . : 127.0.0.1
```

In addition to the local DNS cache on the machine, Internet Explorer (IE) keeps its own name resolution cache. By default, names are cached in Internet Explorer versions 4.0 or higher for 30 minutes, and for 24 hours in IE versions below 4.0. Shutting down Internet Explorer and restarting it will refresh this cache.

The final option for the `ipconfig` command that we will discuss is `/flushdns`, which is complementary to the `/displaydns` option. The `/flushdns` option clears out all entries in the DNS cache on the workstation. This works out well for troubleshooting stale DNS entries. The output of the command is shown here:

```
C:\>ipconfig /flushdns

Windows IP Configuration

Successfully flushed the DNS Resolver Cache.

C:\>
```

The *nbtstat* Command

As was touched on earlier, Windows systems can also use WINS (NetBIOS) to resolve names into IP addresses. In these cases the `ipconfig /displaydns` command will not show these associations. In order to view this information you need to use the `nbtstat` command. The options that are available for this command are listed in the following example:

```
C:\>nbtstat /?

Displays protocol statistics and current TCP/IP connections using NBT
(NetBIOS over TCP/IP).

NBTSTAT [ [-a RemoteName] [-A IP address] [-c] [-n]
        [-r] [-R] [-RR] [-s] [-S] [interval] ]

  -a   (adapter status) Lists the remote machine's name table given its name
  -A   (Adapter status) Lists the remote machine's name table given its IP
                        address.
```

```
-c   (cache)          Lists NBT's cache of remote [machine] names and their
                      IP addresses
-n   (names)          Lists local NetBIOS names.
-r   (resolved)       Lists names resolved by broadcast and via WINS
-R   (Reload)         Purges and reloads the remote cache name table
-S   (Sessions)       Lists sessions table with the destination IP addresses
-s   (sessions)       Lists sessions table converting destination IP
                      addresses to computer NETBIOS names.
-RR  (ReleaseRefresh) Sends Name Release packets to WINS and then, starts
                      Refresh
RemoteName   Remote host machine name.
IP address   Dotted decimal representation of the IP address.
interval     Redisplays selected statistics, pausing interval seconds between
             each display. Press Ctrl+C to stop redisplaying statistics.
```

The two options that you will most likely use in a troubleshooting situation are the -c and -R options. The -c option is used to display the current name resolution cache, and the -R option is used to clear this cache. Sample output from both of these commands is displayed here:

```
C:\>nbtstat -c

Local Area Connection:
Node IpAddress: [10.1.1.1] Scope Id: []

                  NetBIOS Remote Cache Name Table

        Name              Type       Host Address    Life [sec]
    ------------------------------------------------------------
    MICHELE        <20>  UNIQUE      10.2.2.2            570
    NERMAL         <20>  UNIQUE      10.100.100.100      580
    NERMAL         <00>  UNIQUE      10.100.100.100      575
    PICASO         <42>  UNIQUE      10.8.8.8            415
    ALEX           <20>  UNIQUE      10.9.9.9            582
    LEAH           <20>  UNIQUE      10.10.10.10         492

\Device\NetBT_Tcpip_{D84EDBA9-F40F-4AFF-8409-24613C6A325B}:
C:\> nbtstat -R
    Successful purge and preload of the NBT Remote Cache Name Table.
```

Summary

End-system documentation is just as important as the network documentation in terms of the overall documentation strategy. The two main components that make up end-system documentation are the end-system network configuration table and the end-system network topology table.

End-system network configuration tables are documents that show the key configuration parameters in place on the end systems in the network. Some of the common items in an end-system network configuration table are the system name, system manufacturer/model, CPU speed, RAM, storage, system purpose, media type, interface speed, VLAN, IP address, default gateway, subnet mask, WINS, DNS, operating system (including version), network-based applications, high-bandwidth applications, and low-latency applications. The specific items included on the end-system network configuration table depend on the purpose of the documentation. In most cases, the end-system table is kept in a spreadsheet or database format. As is the case with all the documentation covered in this book, be sure to keep hardcopies of the documents to use in the event of a network outage.

End-system network topology diagrams are graphical representations of the end systems in the network. In many cases, they are just additions to the network topology diagram; however, they can be their own entity. The data included in an end-system network topology diagram is usually a small subset of that maintained in the end-system network configuration tables. The topology diagrams are meant to make the network administrator better able to visualize the path across the network. Some of the standard items that go into an end-system network topology are system name, connection to the network, system purpose, VLAN, IP address, subnet mask, and network applications.

Finally, in this chapter we covered a number of commands that can be used to effectively troubleshoot problems on end systems. These commands include `ping` and its record route option, `traceroute`, `arp`, `route`, `nbtstat`, `netstat`, and `ipconfig`. All of these commands have Windows NT/2000/XP and Unix equivalents, and most have a direct relationship to a Cisco IOS command.

Exam Essentials

Know what end-system network configuration tables are and the information they contain. End-system network configuration tables are used to record key settings of end systems in the network. Items commonly included in an end-system network configuration table are system name, system manufacturer/model, CPU speed, RAM, storage, system purpose, media type, interface speed, VLAN, IP address, default gateway, subnet mask, WINS, DNS, operating system (including version), network-based applications, high-bandwidth applications, and low-latency applications.

Know what end-system network topology diagrams are and the information they contain. End-system network topology diagrams are graphical representations of the network and are usually built with many of the same components as the end-system network configuration tables. Some common components of the end-system network topology diagram are system name, connection to the network, system purpose, VLAN, IP address, subnet mask, and network applications.

Know the commands to discover information and troubleshoot end systems. There are Unix and Windows versions of the discovery and troubleshooting commands, and many of them correlate directly to Cisco IOS commands. Some of these commands are `arp`, `ifconfig`, `ipconfig`, `netstat`, `ping`, `route`, `telnet`, and `traceroute`.

Protocol Attributes

THE CCNP EXAM TOPICS COVERED IN THIS CHAPTER INCLUDE THE FOLLOWING:

- ✓ Verify network connectivity.
- ✓ Use the optimal troubleshooting approach in resolving network problems.
- ✓ Minimize downtime during troubleshooting.
- ✓ Use Cisco IOS commands to identify problems.
- ✓ Determine the layer or layers on which a problem is occurring.

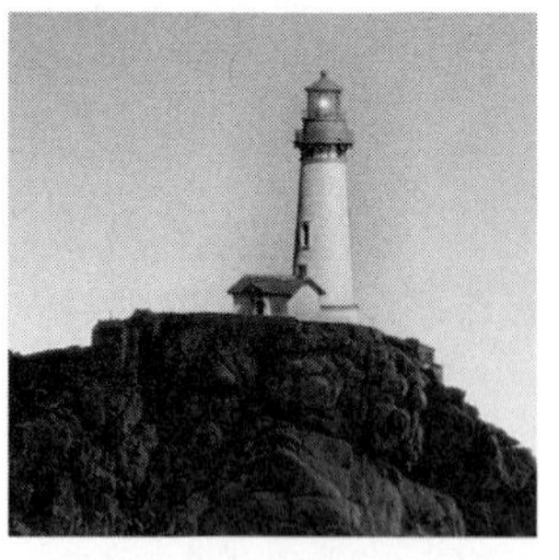

As you know, to successfully troubleshoot network problems, it is important to have a good understanding of how network components, including PCs and servers, communicate with each other. Without this basic knowledge, troubleshooting a network problem is like trying to read a book in a foreign language. The information is there, but it just isn't comprehensible. Although the troubleshooting model discussed in Chapter 33, "Troubleshooting Methodology," provides the method of retrieving all the necessary information, the data is useless without an understanding of the information presented.

This chapter is a review of the protocols used by layers 2, 3, and 4 of the OSI model. We briefly review the seven layers of the OSI model, and then discuss how they communicate with one another. We then discuss layer 2 and layer 3 protocols. More specific information on some of the material covered here can be found in later chapters and is cross-referenced here where appropriate.

The OSI Reference Model

This section is a review of the OSI model, which was originally discussed in *CCNA: Cisco Certified Network Associate Study Guide, 4th ed.*, by Todd Lammle (Sybex, 2004). The *OSI model* (the Open Systems Interconnection reference model) is the template used to design applications or protocols that allow nonhomogenous computers or networks to communicate with one another. The ISO (International Organization for Standardization) developed the OSI model.

The OSI model consists of seven layers. Each layer communicates directly with its adjacent layers, as well as with the corresponding layer of the destination system (depicted in Figure 36.1). Communication between layers facilitates the transfer of data up and down the OSI model. Communication between the corresponding layers of the source system and the destination system enables two heterogeneous networks or computers to understand each other.

The OSI template defines the services and roles that each layer is to provide. Because each layer provides different services and functions, the layers need to communicate so that the data can be transmitted up and down the seven layers and onto the destination system. The following list summarizes the responsibility of each of the seven layers, starting from the Physical layer and working up to the Application layer:

Physical This layer sends and receives bits with values of 1s and 0s. The Physical layer is in charge of determining how it sends these values. If the physical connection between two machines is fiber-optic, then the Physical layer has to use light to transmit the 1s and 0s. If the connection is electrical, then electrical signals are sent to represent the 1s and 0s.

FIGURE 36.1 OSI layer communication scheme

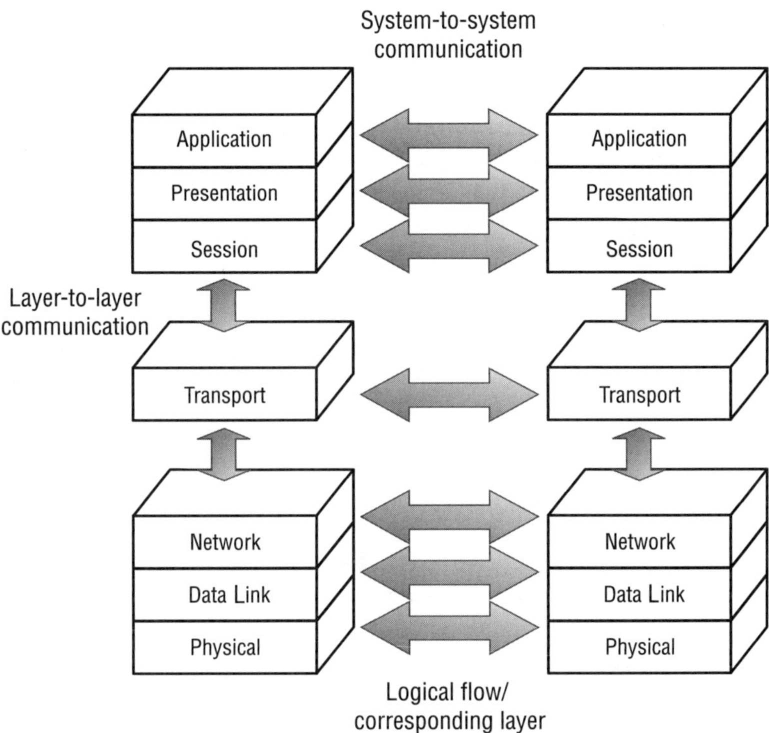

Data Link This layer takes all the data that is accumulated as packets are handed from one layer to the next and then packages it into frames. The Data Link layer equates the Network layer address (IP address) to a data link address, or MAC address, of the next hop. Once the physical address is known, the frame is sent to that address. The receiving interface uses the Data Link layer to extract the packet from the frame, discards the frame, and then sends the packet up to the Network layer.

Network This layer defines the topology of the network through the use of logical addressing. Routing protocols use this information to route packets.

Transport This layer takes care of end-to-end communications. It is responsible for the connection to the destination system, as well as for packet segmentation and assembly. The Transport layer includes both connection-oriented and connectionless protocols (for example, TCP and UDP).

Session This layer is responsible for coordinating communication among applications, which it does through dialog-control methods.

Presentation This layer negotiates syntax, so it is responsible for the proper method of presenting the data to the Application layer. Some of the Presentation layer functions are compression/decompression and encryption/decryption of data.

Application This is the user and application interface. The Application layer is responsible for data exchange and job management. It also handles file, print, message, database, and application services.

You saw how the logical data flow of the OSI model works, but look at Figure 36.2, in which you can see the actual data flow. This figure depicts data that is handed from the Application layer all the way down to the Physical layer. At that point, the data is transmitted across any variety of physical media to the next hop, or destination system. Once the 1s and 0s arrive at the Physical layer of the destination system, the information is sent to layer 2 (the Data Link layer). This layer discards the frame, and then the extracted packet is handed up to the Network layer. The network packet header is stripped off, and the resulting packet is handed up to the Transport layer. This process is repeated for each layer until it arrives at the Application layer.

Now that each layer of the OSI reference model has been explained briefly, you need to focus on the functions of each layer in detail. This detail provides the necessary background and information to effectively troubleshoot network problems that occur within specific layers of the OSI model.

FIGURE 36.2 Data flow through the OSI model

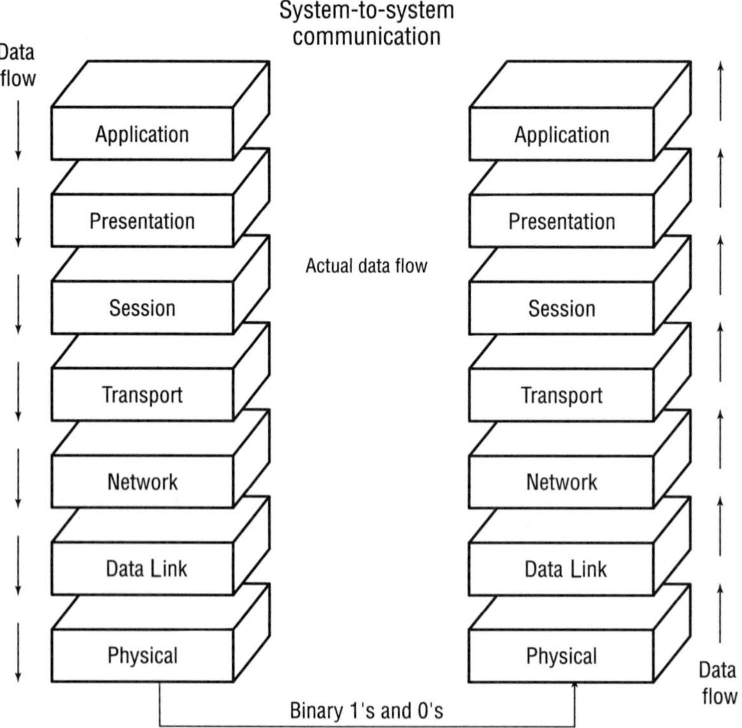

Global Protocol Classifications

As mentioned, each layer of the OSI model utilizes specific protocols that enable the layer to perform the necessary functions and communicate with adjacent layers. Each protocol has specific properties based on the functions that it needs to accomplish. Throughout all seven layers, there are two major protocol classifications: connection-oriented and connectionless.

Connection-Oriented Protocols

Connection-oriented protocols contain inherent functions that control the connection as well as data transfer. These functions are very detailed in the procedures that are followed to enable reliable and error-free data transfer. When a source open system needs to transfer data to a destination open system, the connection-oriented protocols actually establish a communication pipe. The *pipe,* as it is called here, is nothing more than a logical connection between two open systems. A great deal of information is used to establish this communication pipe, however.

In order to establish a connection, the two open systems must share certain information that allows them to negotiate terms and finally establish a link. The information includes the common protocol that will be used, required resources, and available resources. Look at Figure 36.3. This figure shows the steps taken as communication is established between two open systems when using TCP, a connection-oriented protocol.

FIGURE 36.3 Link establishment and data transfer using a connection-oriented protocol

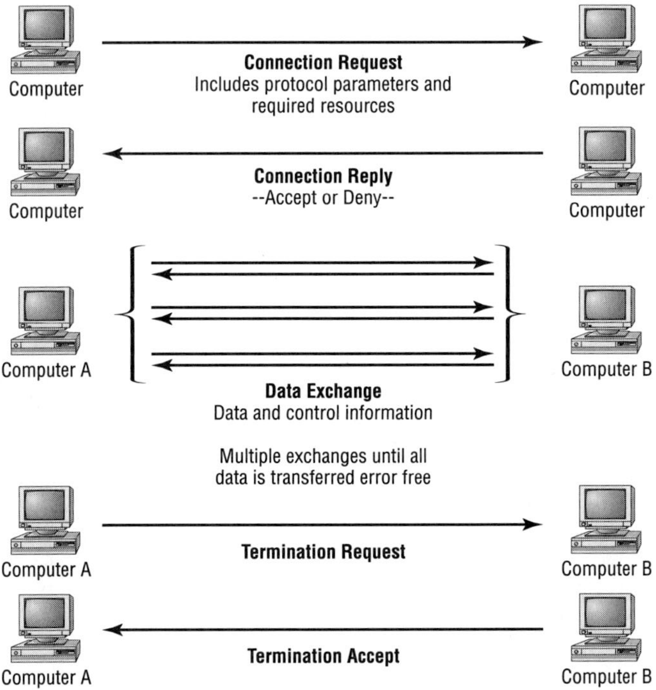

The originating system first sends a connection request to the destination system. This request contains information that the two systems need to agree upon before the connection can be established. Some of the information includes the common protocol, protocol parameters, and required resources. *Protocol parameters* are the window sizes and other possible parameters. The *window size* is the amount of data that a station can transmit before needing an acknowledgment from the destination system that all the data was received without error, or that errors existed and part of the data will need to be retransmitted. *Required resources* can include necessary bandwidth, specific port numbers, and other network resources.

The destination system receives this connection request; if it can accommodate the common protocol, protocol attributes, and required resources, it replies with a connection accept. If, for some reason, the destination system cannot accommodate any of the requirements sent by the originating system, the destination system responds with a connection deny. A denied connection can result from a blocked port on the destination system, insufficient bandwidth between the systems, or other unavailable requested resources.

Assuming that a connection is established between the two systems, data and control information is exchanged during the life of the connection. This data exchange can be considered a *dialog*. First, the originating system sends data until the window size is reached. That system then waits for a response from the destination system. The destination system sends control information that informs the originating system what needs to happen next. The transmission can be an acknowledgment that all data in the transmission was received without error and that the originating system can send the next batch of data. In addition, the destination system can send a message informing the originating system that some of the data was missing, corrupted, or had other errors that require the data to be retransmitted.

The foregoing procedure can be summarized with the description of three processes. You will learn more about each of these processes in the following sections:

Sequenced data transfer Each packet of a session is assigned a sequence number.

Flow control Acknowledgments are required after a specified amount of data has been sent.

Error control Verification of contiguous and nonerroneous packets.

Sequenced Data Transfer

Systems send protocol data units (PDUs) to one another, and each level of the OSI model has its own type of PDU. Figure 36.4 shows the PDU names for all seven OSI layers. For example, the Application layer's PDU name is layer 7 PDU. Although this convention can be used for all layers, some layers use other names as well. For instance, a layer 3 PDU is called a *packet* and a layer 2 PDU is called a *frame*. When a system sends data to another system, the data has to be fragmented so that it fits the MTU (maximum transmission unit). Therefore, several frames may be needed to transfer the original data. Connection-oriented protocols assign a sequence number to each outgoing and incoming PDU. This is *sequenced data transfer*.

Figure 36.5 shows you how sequencing works. There is a possibility that the destination system will receive the PDUs out of order. If this happens, the protocol on the destination system uses the sequence numbers to put the PDUs back into the correct order so that the original data is obtained.

FIGURE 36.4 OSI layer PDU names

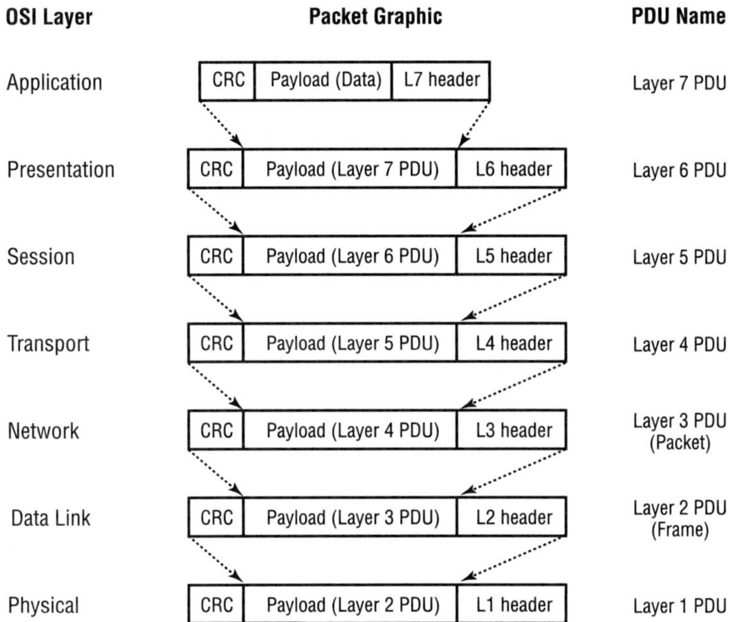

FIGURE 36.5 Connection-oriented PDU sequencing

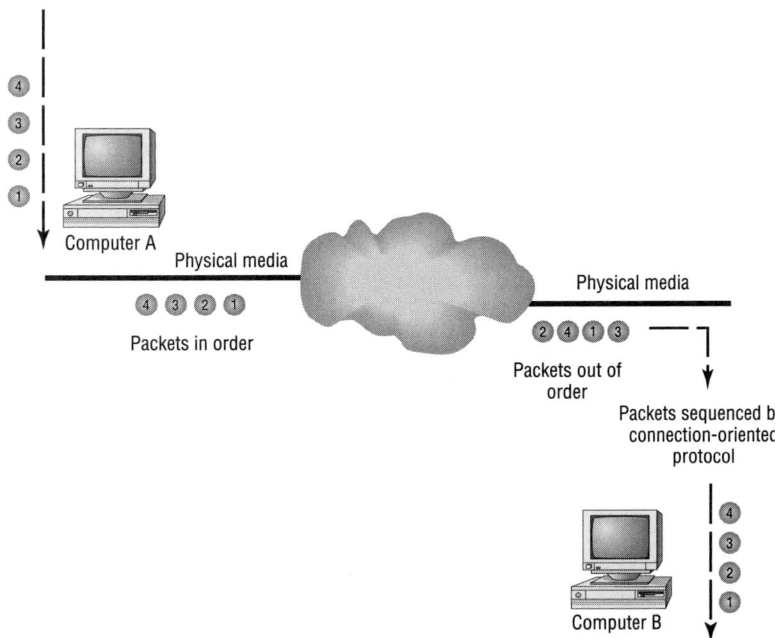

Flow Control

Although flow control was briefly described earlier, this section contains more detail. *Flow control* is responsible for ensuring that the transmitting station does not send data faster than the receiving station can process it. This is done by establishing a window size for the transmission.

Look at Figure 36.6 to see how windowing works. Notice that the originating system sends out a specified number of PDUs. Once that number is reached, the originating system waits for a response from the destination system. After the response is received, the system continues to transmit data.

Error Control

Error control is responsible for checking each transmission and verifying that all of the PDUs are contiguous and not erroneous. If there are missing or damaged PDUs, the destination will not send an ACK packet for the previous transmission. (Refer to Figure 36.6.)

FIGURE 36.6 Flow control and error control

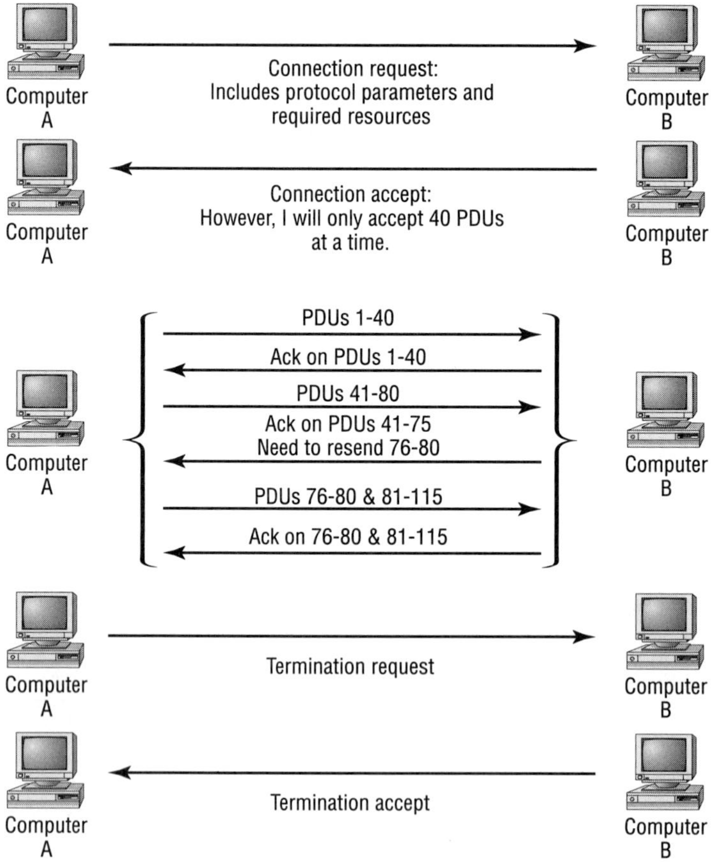

Once all of the data is transferred without errors, the originating system sends a termination request, which tells the destination system that no more data needs to be transmitted. The destination system then responds with a termination acknowledgment.

As you can see, both systems do a lot of communicating, aside from the exchange of data. From the connection request to the termination acknowledgment, every exchange is accompanied with control information that keeps the data transfer reliable and error free. Table 36.1 gives examples of several connection-oriented protocols.

TABLE 36.1 Connection-Oriented Protocols

Protocol Name	Protocol Description
ATM	ATM (Asynchronous Transfer Mode) uses virtual circuits from one node to another. The permanent virtual circuits (PVCs) are established by using connection-oriented procedures.
TCP	TCP (Transmission Control Protocol) was developed to overcome reliability problems. It uses flow control and error control extensively.
Novell SPX	Novell SPX (Sequenced Packet Exchange) is Novell's implementation of a network protocol that provides error-free and reliable data transport.
AppleTalk ATP	Apple uses ATP (AppleTalk Transaction Protocol) to provide connectivity between two socket clients. It is based on the request/response interaction of the two clients.

Connectionless Protocols

Now that connection-oriented protocols have been discussed, we'll move on to connectionless protocols. *Connectionless protocols* differ from connection-oriented protocols because they do not provide for flow control.

Figure 36.7 shows you how connectionless protocols work. This figure looks somewhat like Figure 36.3, except that there are no steps that involve a connection setup or termination. It is also missing the flow control and error control information sent by the receiving system.

Connectionless protocols do not send data relative to any other data units. The data included in the PDU must contain enough information for the PDU to get to its destination and for the receiving system to properly process it. Because there is no established connection, flow and error control cannot be implemented. Without flow and error control, the originating system has no way of knowing whether all of the transmitted data was received by the destination system without errors. Table 36.2 shows examples of connectionless protocols.

FIGURE 36.7 Connectionless data transfer

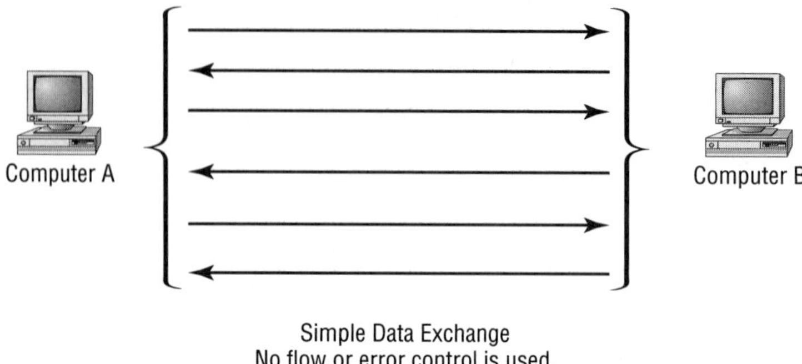

In this section, you learned the difference between connection-oriented and connectionless protocols. These protocol characteristics may be found at any level of the OSI model. The Transport layer, layer 4 of the OSI model, is most notably known for the functions it provides by using connection-oriented or connectionless protocols. Some of the Transport layer's responsibilities are session establishment, flow control and error control, and session teardown.

TABLE 36.2 Connectionless Protocols

Protocol Name	Protocol Description
UDP	UDP (User Datagram Protocol) is a connectionless protocol used by IP (Internet Protocol).
AppleTalk DDP	DDP (Datagram Delivery Protocol) is a connectionless network protocol used for service between two network sockets.
Novell IPX	Novell IPX (Internetwork Packet Exchange) is Novell's layer 3 protocol.

The following sections begin discussions of protocols that are specific to the Data Link and Network layers, respectively.

Layer 2: Data Link Layer Protocols and Applications

This section is dedicated to layer 2 protocols and applications. It is a very important section because it provides specific information on how the layer 2 protocols work. What better way to be able to troubleshoot a problem than by understanding the intricacies of the protocol in question?

This section covers the following layer 2 protocols:

- Ethernet/IEEE 802.3
- PPP
- SDLC
- Frame Relay
- ISDN

Ethernet/IEEE 802.3

These two terms actually refer to different things: *Ethernet* is a communication technology and *IEEE802.3* is a variety of Ethernet. Ethernet, in the more specific sense, is a *carrier sense, multiple access/collision detection (CSMA/CD)* local area network. An Ethernet network uses these attributes—carrier sense, multiple access, and collision detection—to enhance communication. This definitely does *not* mean that Ethernet is the only technology that uses these attributes. In today's technical jargon, however, the term *Ethernet* is getting closer to meaning *all* CSMA/CD technologies.

Both Ethernet and IEEE 802.3 are broadcast networks. All frames that cross a given segment can be heard by all machines populating that segment. Because all machines on the segment have equal access to the physical media, each station tries to wait for a quiet spot before it transmits its data. If two machines talk at the same time, a collision occurs.

Ethernet services both the Physical and Data Link layers, whereas IEEE 802.3 is more concerned with the Physical layer and how it talks to the Data Link layer. Several IEEE 802.3 protocols exist; each one has a distinct name that describes how it is different from other IEEE 802.3 protocols. Table 36.3 summarizes these differences.

TABLE 36.3 IEEE 802.3 Characteristics

802.3 Values	Data Rate (Mbps)	Signaling Method	Maximum Segment Length (m)	Media	Topology
10Base5	10	Baseband	500	50 Ohm coax	Bus
10Base2	10	Baseband	185	50 Ohm coax	Bus
1Base5	1	Baseband	185	Unshielded twisted pair	Star
10BaseT	10	Baseband	100	Unshielded twisted pair	Star
100BaseT	100	Baseband	100	Unshielded twisted pair	Star
10Broad36	10	Broadband	1800	75 Ohm coax	Bus
1000BaseT	1000	Baseband	100	Unshielded twisted pair	Star

Table 36.3 is an excerpt from Cisco documentation; for the full document, please see www.cisco.com/univercd/cc/td/doc/cisintwk/ito_doc/ethernet.htm.

In Table 36.3, you will notice that the terms baseband and broadband are used to describe the signaling type. In a baseband transmission, only a single frequency is used for sending data, and therefore only a single signal can be sent over the same media. A broadband signal multiplexes multiple signals of different frequencies together on the same physical media.

Though not specifically called out in the table, there are four different IP encapsulation types supported by Cisco for Ethernet: ARPA, SNAP, Novell-Ether, and SAP. Of these, ARPA is the default encapsulation type used.

Frame Structure

Frame formats are similar between Ethernet and IEEE 802.3. Figure 36.8 depicts the similarities and differences between the two. The frame structures are read from right to left. Starting at the right, you see that both frames begin with a preamble. The `Preamble` is a seven-byte field. (Notice that we have moved from bits to bytes to specify field lengths.) The preamble consists of alternating 1s and 0s.

The next field is the `SOF`, the start-of-frame delimiter. It is used to synchronize the frame-reception portions of all the machines on the segment. This field is only one byte long.

The two fields following the SOF are six bytes each; they are the `Destination` and `Source` MAC addresses of the receiving and sending stations. Each MAC address is unique.

Up to this point, the frames are exactly the same. Starting with the next field, they are different. The next field is a two-byte field in both frame structures. Ethernet defines the field as a `Type` field; IEEE 802.3 defines it as a `Length` field. Ethernet uses this field to specify which upper layer protocol will receive the packet. IEEE 802.3 uses the field to define the number of bytes in the payload (802.2 header and data) field. One easy method of observing the difference between an Ethernet and 802.3 frame is to look at the `Type/Length` field. If this value is 1500 (0x05DC) or less, then it is an IEEE 802.3 frame. If it is greater than 1500, it is an Ethernet frame.

FIGURE 36.8 Ethernet vs. IEEE 802.3 frames

Next is the Data field, in both Ethernet and 802.3 formats. The only difference between the two versions of this field is that Ethernet uses a variable byte size, between 46 and 1500 bytes, for data. This data is what will be handed to the upper layer protocols. IEEE 802.3 uses a 46–1500 variable byte size, as well, but the information here contains the 802.2 header and the encapsulated data that will eventually be passed to an upper layer protocol that is defined within the Data field.

Finally, the last field is the Frame Check sequence (FCS) field. It is four bytes and stores information that will be used for calculating the CRC after the data has been sent or received.

Point-to-Point Protocol (PPP)

Point-to-Point Protocol (PPP) is used to transfer data over serial point-to-point links. It accomplishes this by using a layer 2 serial encapsulation called *High-Level Data Link Control (HDLC)*. HDLC is used for frame encapsulation on synchronous serial lines. It uses a link control protocol (LCP) to manage the serial connection. Network control protocols (NCPs) are used to allow PPP to use other protocols from layer 3, thus enabling PPP to assign IP addresses dynamically.

PPP uses the same frame structure as HDLC. Figure 36.9 gives you a picture of what the frame looks like. As always, we move from right to left.

FIGURE 36.9 PPP packet structure

2 or 4 bytes	Variable	5	3	2	1	0
FCS	Data	Protocol	Control	Address	Flag	

First, we have the Flag field, which uses one byte to specify the beginning or ending of a frame. Then there is another byte that is used in the Address field to hold a broadcast address of 11111111.

The Address field is followed by the one-byte Control field, which requests a transmission of user data. The two-byte Protocol field follows the Control field. This field indicates the encapsulated data's protocol.

The Data field contains the information that will be handed to the upper layer protocols. It is a variable-length field. After that is the FCS. Like the other protocols, it is used for CRC calculation.

Synchronous Data Link Control (SDLC)

Synchronous Data Link Control (SDLC) is based on a synchronous, more-efficient, faster, and flexible bit-oriented format. SDLC has several derivatives that perform similar functions with some enhancements: HDLC, LAPB (Link Access Procedure, Balanced), and IEEE 802.2, just to name a few. HDLC is the default encapsulation type on most Cisco router serial interfaces.

SDLC is used for many link types. Two node types exist within SDLC: *primary nodes* and *secondary nodes*. Primary nodes are responsible for the control of secondary stations and for link management operations such as link setup and teardown. Secondary nodes talk only to the primary node when fulfilling two requirements. First, they have permission from the primary node; second, they have data to transmit. Even if a secondary node has data to send, it cannot send the data if it does not have permission from the primary node.

Primary and secondary stations can be configured together in four different topologies:

Point-to-point This topology requires only two nodes—a primary and a secondary.

Multipoint This configuration uses one primary station and multiple secondary stations.

Loop This configuration uses one primary and multiple secondary stations. The difference between the loop and multipoint setups is that in a loop, the primary station is connected between two secondary stations, which makes two directly connected secondary stations. When more secondary stations are added, they must connect to the other secondary stations that are currently in the loop. When one of these stations wants to send information to the primary node, it must transit to the other secondary stations before it reaches the primary.

Hub go-ahead This configuration also uses one primary and multiple secondary stations, but it uses a different communication topology. The primary station has an outbound channel. This channel is used to communicate with each of the secondary stations. An inbound channel is shared among the secondary stations and has a single connection into the primary station.

Frame Structure

SDLC uses three different frame structures: information, supervisory, and unnumbered. Overall, the structure of the frames is similar among all three, except for the Control frame. The Control frame is varied to distinguish the type of SDLC frame that is being used. Figure 36.10 gives the structure for the different SDLC frames. Pay close attention to the bit values next to the send sequence number within the Control frame.

First, let's talk about the frame fields that are common among all three frame types. As you can see, all three frames depicted in Figure 36.10 start with a `Flag` field that is followed by an `Address` field. The `Address` field of SDLC frames is different from other frame structures because only the address of the secondary node is used, rather than a destination and source address. The secondary address is used because all communication is either originated or received by the primary node; thus, it is not necessary to specify its address within the frame.

The Control frame follows the `Address` field. Information contained within the Control frame defines the SDLC frame type. The Control frame begins with a receive sequence number. This sequence number is used to tell the protocol the number of the next frame to be received.

The `P/F` or `Poll Final` number following the receive sequence number is used differently by primary and secondary nodes. Primary nodes use the information to communicate to the secondary node that an immediate response is required. The secondary node uses the information to tell the primary node that the frame is the last one in the current dialog.

FIGURE 36.10 SDLC frame structures

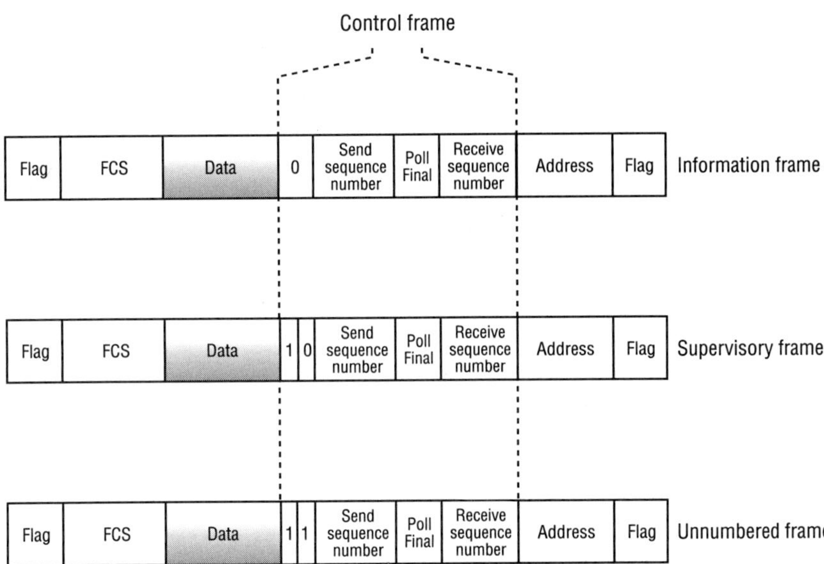

After the P/F bit, the Send Sequence Number is used to identify the current frame's sequence number. Following that, one or two bits are used to define the frame type. Table 36.4 specifies the bit values and the corresponding frame type.

TABLE 36.4 SDLC Frame Types

Bit Value	Frame Type
0	Information
0 1	Supervisory
1 1	Unnumbered

The Data field follows the Control frame. As with other frame types, the FCS field comes next and is used to calculate the CRC. SDLC frames differ again with the last field, which is another Flag field like one at the beginning of the frame.

Now that we have discussed the frame structure, let's examine the three different frame types. Information frames carry exactly that—information destined for the upper layer protocols. Supervisory frames control SDLC communications; they are responsible for flow control and error control for I-frame (information). Unnumbered frames provide the initialization of secondary nodes, as well as other managerial functions.

Frame Relay

Frame Relay was developed as a digital packet-switching technology, whereas older technologies such as X.25 were analog-based technologies. The technology used in Frame Relay allows it to multiplex several different data flows over the same physical media. More information on Frame Relay is presented in Chapter 39, "Troubleshooting Serial Line and Frame Relay Connectivity."

Frame Relay also uses permanent and switched virtual circuits between the data terminal equipment (DTE) (customer connection) and the data communication equipment (DCE) (service provider's frame relay switch). These virtual circuits have unique identifiers that allow the Frame Relay to keep track of each logical data flow. The identifier is known as a *DLCI* (data link connection identifier). The DLCI number is used to create a logical circuit within a physical circuit. Multiple logical circuits can be created within one physical circuit.

Look at the following router configuration excerpt:

```
interface Serial1/5
 description Physical Circuit
 no ip address
 no ip directed-broadcast
 encapsulation frame-relay
!
interface Serial1/5.1 point-to-point
 description To Building A
 ip address 172.16.1.17 255.255.255.252
 no ip directed-broadcast
 frame-relay interface-dlci 17 IETF
!
interface Serial1/5.2 point-to-point
 description To Building B
 ip address 172.16.1.25 255.255.255.252
 no ip directed-broadcast
 frame-relay interface-dlci 22 IETF
```

From this configuration, you can see that two logical circuits have been defined to communicate over one physical circuit. Notice that each subinterface or logical circuit has a unique DLCI. Each DLCI maps to another DLCI within the Frame Relay cloud. This mapping continues throughout the Frame Relay cloud until it maps to another DTE on the destination side of the virtual circuit.

Frame Structure

Frame Relay does not provide any information on flow and error control. As a result, no space is reserved within the frame for this information. These functions are left to the upper layer protocols. Frame Relay *does* provide congestion detection and can notify the upper layers of possible problems; however, Frame Relay is primarily concerned only with the transmission and reception of data.

As a mechanism for data circuit identification, Frame Relay uses a DLCI number. Ten bits of the two-byte `Address` field are used to define the DLCI. To a Frame Relay frame, the DLCI is the most significant address in the header. Figure 36.11 depicts a Frame Relay frame.

FIGURE 36.11 Frame Relay frame structure

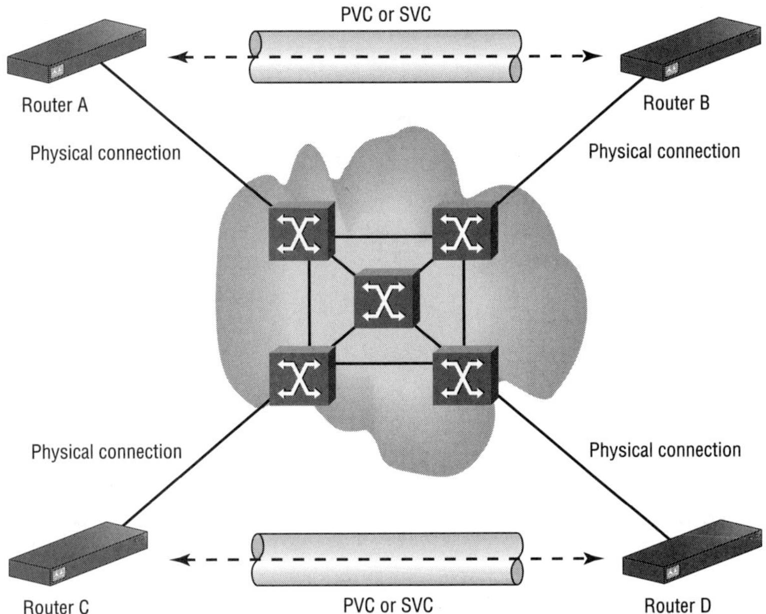

Integrated Services Digital Network (ISDN)

Integrated Services Digital Network (ISDN) is a service that allows telephone networks to carry data, voice, and other digital traffic. There are two types of ISDN interfaces: *Basic Rate Interface (BRI)* and *Primary Rate Interface (PRI)*. BRI uses two B channels and one D channel. Each of the two B channels operates at 64Kbps bidirectionally; the D channel operates at 16Kbps. The B channels are used for transmitting and receiving data. The D channel is used for protocol communications and signaling.

In contrast, PRI uses 23 B channels and 1 D channel. All 23 B channels are added to a rotary group, as well. The D channel runs at the same line speed as the B channels—64Kbps. Because of the D channel's additional line speed, PRI has the equivalent line speed of a T-1 circuit (1.544Mbps). In Europe, PRI offers 30 B channels and 1 D channel, making it the equivalent of an E-1 circuit.

Just as there are two types of ISDN interfaces, there are two terminal equipment types. Type 1 (TE1) is equipment that was built specifically for use on ISDN. Type 2 (TE2) is equipment that was made before the ISDN specifications, and it requires a terminal adapter to actually interface with ISDN. Terminal equipment, which is comparable to DTE as described in the "Frame Relay" section earlier in this chapter, includes computers or routers.

In order for terminal equipment to work, it must be able to connect to a network termination. There are three types of ISDN network terminations, known as NT devices. Type 1 (NT1) devices are treated as customer premises equipment. Type 2 (NT2) devices are more intelligent devices than NT1 and can perform concentration and switching functions. The last type is a combination of Types 1 and 2. It is known as a Type 1/2 or NT1/2.

More information about troubleshooting ISDN is covered in Chapter 40, "Troubleshooting ISDN."

Frame Structure

Look at Figure 36.12 to get a picture of the ISDN frame. As you can see, this frame is similar to the HDLC frame that you studied earlier (Figure 36.11). ISDN uses LAP (Link Access Procedure) on the D channel for layer 2 functions. Unlike the HDLC frame, the ISDN frame is bounded by `Flag` fields.

FIGURE 36.12 ISDN frame format

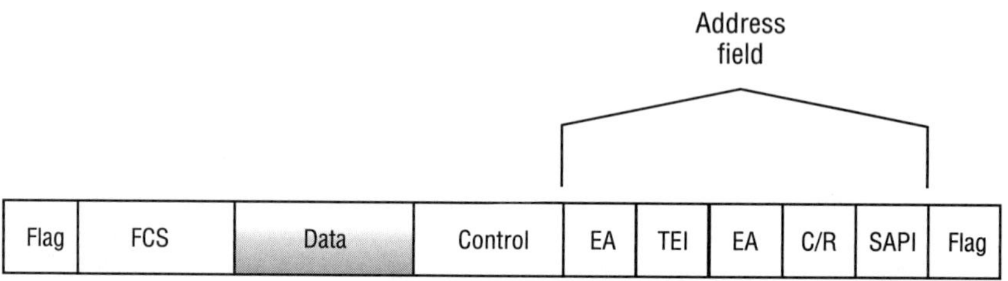

After the `Flag` field, again going from right to left, we see the `Address` field. The `Address` field contains several bits of key information:

SAPI This field is the service access point identifier. It defines which services are provided to layer 3.

C/R This field designates the frame as a command or a response.

EA This is the last bit of the first byte of the `Address` field. This bit defines the `Address` field as one or two bytes. If it is set to one byte, this is the last field within the `Address` field. If it is set to two bytes, then one more field follows, ending with another `EA` bit.

TEI This is the terminal end point identifier, the layer 2 address used to identify individual devices connecting to an ISDN network.

Layers 3 and 4: IP Routed Protocols

The Network layer is used by the Transport layer to provide the best end-to-end services and path for PDU delivery. This means that the Network layer also uses protocols to accomplish this task. This section discusses protocols that are used within layer 3 of the OSI model. Some of these protocols use other protocols within them for finer granularity of certain functions.

There is a significant difference between *routing* protocols and *routed* protocols. Routing protocols are used to exchange route information and to create a network topology, thus enabling routing decisions to be made. The routed protocols, on the other hand, contain information regarding the end systems, how communication is established, and other information relevant to the transfer of data. The routing protocols will be covered in Chapter 38, "TCP/IP Routing Protocol Troubleshooting."

Internet Protocol (IP)

It is important to distinguish between the Internet Protocol suite and the actual Internet Protocol that is used in the Network layer of the OSI model.

The IP suite consists of several discrete protocols that are implemented at different levels of the OSI model.

The *Internet Protocol (IP)* is a Network layer protocol of the IP suite. It is used to allow routing among internetworks and heterogeneous systems. IP is a connectionless protocol, even though it can provide error reporting, and it performs the segmentation and reassembly of PDUs.

IP Packet Structure

Now that you know what IP is, let's look at the actual packet structure in more detail. The following is an IP packet that was broken down by EtherPeek, a network analyzer. The entire header has six layers, and each layer consists of 32 bits. Look at each section of the header and get an explanation for each:

```
IP Header - Internet Protocol Datagram
  Version:               4
  Header Length:         5
  Precedence:            0
  Type of Service:       %000
  Unused:                %00
  Total Length:          60
  Identifier:            0
  Fragmentation Flags:   %000
  Fragment Offset:       0
  Time To Live:          2
  IP Type:               0x58  EIGRP
  Header Checksum:       0x10dc
  Source IP Address:     205.124.250.7
  Dest. IP Address:      224.0.0.10
  No Internet Datagram Options
```

At this point, we will define the key fields that appear in this listing. As you can see, the packet IP header starts out with the `Version` field. Right now, the standard is IPv4. The version parameter uses four of the 32 bits available.

The next field is the IP `Header Length`, or IHL. This field also uses another four bits, and it specifies the datagram header length in 32-bit words.

The `Type of Service` (TOS field) follows the IHL. This field uses eight bits and indicates datagram priority and how other OSI layers are to handle the datagram once they receive it.

Following the TOS field is the `Total Length` parameter. This field indicates how long the packet is, including header and payload or data. The length is in units of bytes. The field itself uses 16 bits, which brings the total for these fields to 32 bits or four bytes.

The second field begins with the `Identifier` or `Identification` field. The `Identifier` is a 16-bit field that contains an integer value that identifies the packet. It is like a sequencing number that is used when reassembling datagram fragments.

The `Fragmentation Flags` field follows, using only three bits. This field is used to control fragmentation of a datagram. If the datagram can be fragmented, the first bit has a value of 0; otherwise, a value of 1 is assigned to the first bit if the datagram is not to be fragmented. The second bit is used to indicate the last fragment of a fragmented datagram. The third bit is an undefined bit and is set to 0.

`Fragment Offset` follows the Flags field. This value uses 13 bits and specifies the fragment's position in the original datagram. The position is measured from the beginning of the datagram and marked off in 64-bit increments. This again brings you to 32 bits, so you must move down to the next layer in the IP packet.

The third field begins with the `Time-to-Live` (TTL) field, which is a counter whose units are measured in hops. A starting value is given, and it counts decrements by 1 as it passes through each hop or router. Once the value of this field is 0, the packet is discarded. This field uses eight bits.

The protocol field (`IP Type`) follows the TTL parameter. This field tells layer 3 which upper layer protocol is supposed to receive the packet. It uses a decimal value to specify the protocol. This field uses eight bits.

The `Header Checksum` field finishes the third layer. The checksum is used to help verify the integrity of the IP header. This field uses 16 bits.

The next two fields are the `Source IP Address` and `Dest. IP Address` respectively. Both of these fields are 32 bits long.

An `Options` field occupies the final field of the header. The field needs to be 32 bits long, so any additional empty bits are padded.

Figure 36.13 gives a good visual representation of the IP packet structure.

IP Addressing Review

No review of TCP/IP networking would be complete without a review of IP addressing. In this section we will not explain the basics of IP addressing; rather, we will focus more on the application of *variable-length subnet masking (VLSM)* and the calculation of networks as it pertains to troubleshooting in an IP environment. If you need a more detailed discussion, see *CCNA: Cisco Certified Network Associate Study Guide, 4th ed.*, by Todd Lammle (Sybex, 2004).

FIGURE 36.13 The IP packet structure

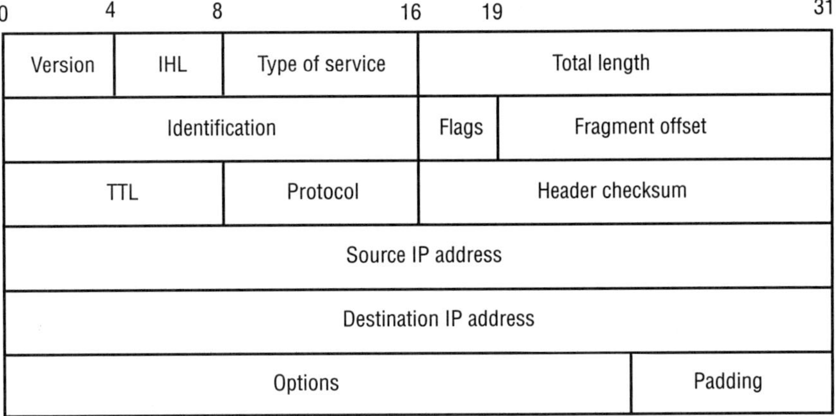

As internetworks grew and address space became more scarce, several methodologies were devised to extend the address space availability. One of these methodologies was VLSM. In older routing protocols, if you wanted to subnet a major network, you had to make all the subnets the same size. This was because the routing protocols passed only network information and did not include subnet mask information. Newer routing protocols pass subnet information along with the individual routes, allowing for the use of VLSM. This enables better use of address space because network administrators can size the subnets based on the need. For example, a point-to-point connection has only two nodes on it, and as such only needs two host addresses. Without VLSM, if your standard subnet mask was 255.255.255.0, a /24 subnet, then 256 "addresses" would be used on this point-to-point connection (though 256 addresses are used, only 254 are usable by hosts). With VLSM, this same connection could use a 255.255.255.252 mask, /30, using only four addresses—two for the hosts, one for the subnet, and one for the broadcast address. For reference, Table 36.5 shows various subnet mask information.

TABLE 36.5 Subnet Mask Information

Subnet	Mask	Total # of Addresses per Subnet	# of Usable Addresses per Subnet
/32	255.255.255.255	1	0
/31	255.255.255.254	2	0
/30	255.255.255.252	4	2
/29	255.255.255.248	8	6
/28	255.255.255.240	16	14

TABLE 36.5 Subnet Mask Information *(continued)*

Subnet	Mask	Total # of Addresses per Subnet	# of Usable Addresses per Subnet
/27	255.255.255.224	32	30
/26	255.255.255.192	64	62
/25	255.255.255.128	128	126
/24	255.255.255.0	256	254
/23	255.255.254.0	512	510
/22	255.255.252.0	1,024	1,022
/21	255.255.248.0	2,048	2,046
/20	255.255.240.0	4,096	4,094
/19	255.255.224.0	8,192	8,190
/18	255.255.192.0	16,384	16,382
/17	255.255.128.0	32,768	32,766
/16	255.255.0.0	65,536	65,534
/15	255.254.0.0	131,072	131,070
/14	255.252.0.0	262,144	262,142
/13	255.248.0.0	524,288	524,286
/12	255.240.0.0	1,048,576	1,048,574
/11	255.224.0.0	2,097,152	2,097,150
/10	255.192.0.0	4,194,304	4,194,302
/9	255.128.0.0	8,388,608	8,388,606
/8	255.0.0.0	16,777,216	16,777,214
/7	254.0.0.0	33,554,432	33,554,430

TABLE 36.5 Subnet Mask Information *(continued)*

Subnet	Mask	Total # of Addresses per Subnet	# of Usable Addresses per Subnet
/6	252.0.0.0	67,108,864	67,108,862
/5	248.0.0.0	134,217,728	134,217,726
/4	224.0.0.0	268,435,456	268,435,454
/3	192.0.0.0	536,870,912	536,870,910
/2	128.0.0.0	1,073,741,824	1,073,741,822
/1	0.0.0.0	2,147,483,648	2,147,483,646

One drawback to VLSM is the complexity that it adds to the network. When there was only one mask used in an environment, the network administrators could easily memorize the subnet information. With VLSM, however, subnet information needs to be calculated based on the individual situation. Miscalculation of the subnets can lead to communication problems if machines are assigned outside a subnet boundary or on a subnet or broadcast address.

Tips for Successfully Using VLSM in a Network

As is the case with many elements of networking, planning is the key to successfully using VLSM in a network. This is especially true of VLSM implementations being put in place on existing networks. Without proper planning, a VLSM implementation can provoke serious support problems. There are numerous ways to implement VLSM; here we will only focus on two.

Divide up a single /24 network. This implementation strategy is best designed for smaller remote sites connecting to one or two central locations. A single /24 network can be divided up and used for the remote sites. In this manner, summarization and problem tracking are made easier. For example, assume that the standard remote location has 60 IP-enabled devices on a single segment, two routers, one switch, and two point-to-point Frame Relay links, and is assigned the 10.1.1.0 /24 subnet. Using the small-site VLSM strategy, you can take this /24 and divide it up into the following:

10.1.1.0 /25 for the user segment

10.1.1.244 /30 for Frame Relay link 2

10.1.1.248 /30 for Frame Relay link 1

10.1.1.253 /32 for router 2 loopback

10.1.1.254 /32 for router 1 loopback

As you can see, /32 subnets are being used for the router loopback addresses. This does not conform to the rules of IP addressing, but it is supported by Cisco routers. Also, though it is true that with only 60 IP-enabled devices a /26 mask could have been used, that would leave no room for future growth. The suggested arrangement, on the other hand, allows for effective use of the address range and permits some future expansion. Notice also that /30 masks were used for the Frame Relay links. In the event that these links might become point-to-multipoint links, however, a different mask should be used.

Use one mask size per service. The second tip for implementing VLSM is to try to use the same mask size for the same service type. For example, use a /32 mask for all loopback interfaces, a /30 mask for all point-to point links, a /26 mask for all server segments, and a /24 mask for all user segments. In this manner you can easily identify the general purpose of a subnet just by looking at the mask.

As stated, there are various ways to implement VLSM successfully; it just takes some planning up front. This planning must take into account the current IP addressing scheme. In addition, make sure that the final implementation is consistently applied and will be scalable and adaptable as the network requirements change.

Internet Control Message Protocol (ICMP)

The *Internet Control Message Protocol (ICMP)* is used throughout IP networks. ICMP was designed to provide routing-failure information to the source system. This protocol provides four types of feedback that are used to make the IP routing environment more efficient:

Reachability This is determined by using ICMP echo and reply messages.

Redirects These messages tell hosts to redirect traffic or choose alternative routes.

Timeouts These messages indicate that a packet's designated TTL is expired.

Router Discovery These messages discover directly connected routers' IP addresses. Router discovery actually uses the ICMP Router Discovery Protocol to do this. This passive method gathers directly connected IP addresses without having to understand specific routing protocols.

Here is a look at a couple of ICMP packets (echo request and reply):

```
ICMP - Internet Control Messages Protocol
  ICMP Type:              8  Echo Request
  Code:                   0
  Checksum:               0x495c
  Identifier:             0x0200
```

```
  Sequence Number:      512
  ICMP Data Area:
  abcdefghijklmnop   61 62 63 64 65 66 67 68 69 6a 6b 6c    6d 6e 6f 70
  qrstuvwabcdefghi   71 72 73 74 75 76 77 61 62 63 64 65    66 67 68 69
Frame Check Sequence:  0x342e3235
ICMP - Internet Control Messages Protocol
  ICMP Type:            0  Echo Reply
  Code:                 0
  Checksum:             0x515c
  Identifier:           0x0200
  Sequence Number:      512
  ICMP Data Area:
  abcdefghijklmnop   61 62 63 64 65 66 67 68 69 6a 6b 6c    6d 6e 6f 70
  qrstuvwabcdefghi   71 72 73 74 75 76 77 61 62 63 64 65    66 67 68 69
Frame Check Sequence:  0x342e3235
```

The ICMP structure is similar to the IP structure in that it has a type, checksum, identifier, and sequence number. The field names differ a little but have the same functionality.

Transmission Control Protocol (TCP)

The *Transmission Control Protocol (TCP)*, a connection-oriented protocol on the Transport layer that provides reliable delivery of data, is an integral part of the IP suite. Look at the structure of the TCP packet. The following EtherPeek frame was taken during a POP3 transaction:

```
TCP - Transmission Control Protocol
  Source Port:       110   POP3
  Destination Port: 1097
  Sequence Number:  997270908
  Ack Number:        7149472
  Offset:            5
  Reserved:          %000000
  Code:              %010000
            Ack is valid
  Window:            8760
  Checksum:          0x8064
  Urgent Pointer:    0
  No TCP Options
  No More POP Command or Reply Data
Extra bytes (Padding):
  UUUUUU              55 55 55 55 55 55
Frame Check Sequence:  0x04020000
```

This structure is similar to the IP packet structure. The TCP header is 32 bits long and has a minimum length of five fields, but can be six fields deep when options are specified. The first layer starts with the `Source Port` and `Destination Port` fields. Each of these fields is 16 bits long.

A `Sequence Number` field occupies the entire second layer, meaning that it is 32 bits long. TCP is a connection-oriented protocol, and this field is used to keep track of the various requests that have been sent.

The third layer is a 32-bit length field containing the acknowledgment sequence number that is used to track responses.

The fourth layer begins with the `Offset` field, which is four bits and specifies the number of 32-bit words present in the header. Six bits are reserved for future use (this is called the `Reserved` field). This field follows the `Offset` field.

The next field, called the `Flag` or `Code` field, is also a six-bit field, and it contains control information. Look at Table 36.6 for an explanation of the six bits within the `Flag` field.

The `Window` field specifies the buffer size for incoming data. Once the buffer is filled, the sending system must wait for a response from the receiving system. This field is 16 bits long.

Layer 5 of the TCP header begins with the `Checksum` parameter, which also occupies 16 bits. It is used to verify the integrity of the transmitted data.

The `Urgent Pointer` field references the last byte of data, so the receiver knows how much urgent data it will receive. This is also a 16-bit field.

Finally, there is the `Option` field, which must also be 32 bits long. If the options do not occupy 32 bits, padding is added to reach the correct length.

TABLE 36.6 Flag Bit Assignments

Bit Number (right to left)	Control Information	Definition
1	URG	Urgent pointer is significant.
2	ACK	Acknowledgment pointer is significant.
3	PSH	Push function.
4	RST	Reset connection.
5	SYN	Synchronize sequence numbers.
6	FIN	No more data to transfer.

User Datagram Protocol (UDP)

The *User Datagram Protocol (UDP)* is a connectionless protocol on the Transport layer of the OSI model. The overall structure of UDP is simpler than TCP, because UDP is connectionless and therefore does not have overhead to maintain connection information. UDP is commonly used for real-time applications such as video and voice. In these time-sensitive applications, when a packet is lost or corrupted there is not enough time for the applications to recognize that a packet is missing and request that it be resent, and for this retransmitted packet to arrive. Therefore, the overhead that comes with TCP is not warranted for this type of data transfer.

The following frame snippet was taken using EtherPeek and is of a DNS request:

```
UDP - User Datagram Protocol
   Source Port:       1213
   Destination Port:  53 domain
   Length:            38
   Checksum:          0xBFBA
```

As you can see, all of the overhead that is associated with the connection-oriented nature of the TCP frame, such as sequence and acknowledgment number, has been removed in UDP. As a result, the UDP packet is condensed down to four fields.

The first two of these fields, `Source Port` and `Destination Port`, are both 16 bits long. The `Destination Port` field must be filled in with the destination port of the service that is being requested; however, the `Source Port` field only needs a value when the sending station needs a reply from the receiver. When the conversation is unidirectional and the source port is not used, this field should be set to 0. When a reply is needed, the receiving station will reply to the sender on the port indicated in the original packet's source field.

The last two fields in a UDP header are `Length` and `Checksum`. Like the source and destination port information, the length and checksum are both 16 bits long. The `Length` field shows the total number of bytes in the UDP packet, including the UDP header and user data. `Checksum`, though optional, allows the receiving station to verify the integrity of the UDP header as well as the data that is contained in the packet. If `Checksum` is not used, it should be set to a value of 0.

Summary

A great deal of information is covered in this chapter, with the focus on Network and Data Link layer protocols. It is important to understand this information in order to facilitate your troubleshooting efforts. If you do not sufficiently understand the protocols present in layers 2 and 3 of the OSI model, you should study them in depth. The majority of networking problems occur in these two layers.

Many encapsulation types are available at the second layer of the OSI model. The ones discussed in this chapter were Ethernet, PPP, SDLC, Frame Relay, and ISDN. Each has its own strengths and weaknesses that make it better suited for a particular installation.

There are two major protocol classifications: connection-oriented and connectionless. Connection-oriented protocols allow for sequenced data transfer, flow control, and error control. Examples of connection-oriented protocols include ATM and TCP. Connectionless protocols require less overhead; however, they do so at the expense of the sequenced data transfer and the error and flow control offered by connection-oriented protocols. The connectionless protocol discussed in this chapter is UDP.

Exam Essentials

Know the differences between connectionless and connection-oriented protocols. Connection-oriented protocols have flow-control and error-checking methodologies that are not present in connectionless protocols. Connectionless protocols offer better performance characteristics for real-time voice and video applications.

Know the Data Link protocols and technologies. The major technologies covered in this section include Ethernet, PPP, SDLC (HDLC), Frame Relay, and ISDN.

Know how to calculate subnet masks. Understand how VLSM functions, and know how to determine an appropriate address and subnet mask combination.

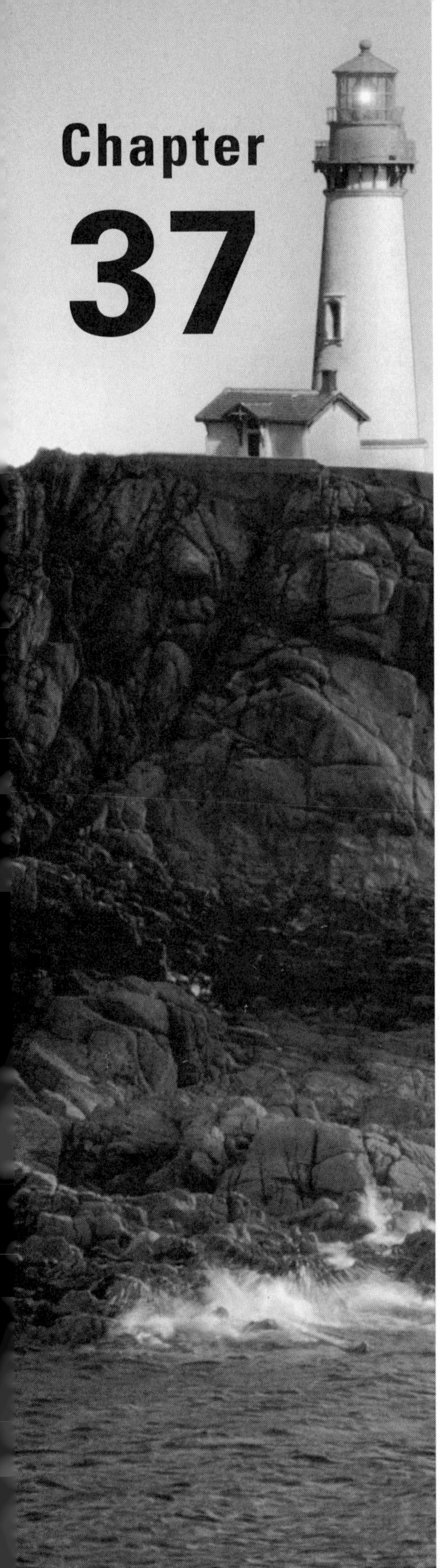

Cisco Diagnostic Commands and TCP/IP Troubleshooting

THE CCNP EXAM TOPICS COVERED IN THIS CHAPTER INCLUDE THE FOLLOWING:

- ✓ Verify network connectivity.
- ✓ Use the optimal troubleshooting approach in resolving network problems.
- ✓ Minimize downtime during troubleshooting.
- ✓ Use Cisco IOS commands to identify problems.
- ✓ Rectify suboptimal performance issues at layers 2 through 7.

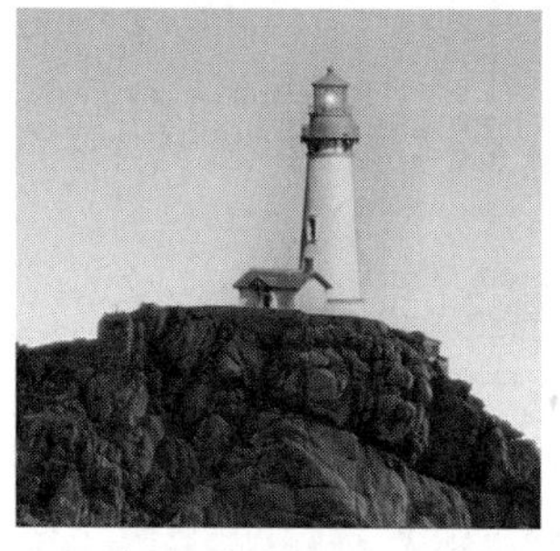

The next two chapters are focused primarily on essential TCP/IP troubleshooting skills and tools. Here in this chapter, we will explain `show` and `debug` commands. In addition, generic commands such as `ping` and `traceroute` will be applied to network problems. Problem isolation techniques that are used in troubleshooting LANs will be outlined and implemented. Finally, the use and kinds of access lists will be examined.

The next chapter, Chapter 38, "TCP/IP Routing Protocol Troubleshooting," focuses on the IP routing protocols, including RIP, IGRP, EIGRP, OSPF, and BGP. In addition to an explanation of these routing protocols, the `show` and `debug` commands used specifically for them will be examined. The final part of Chapter 38 explores redistribution issues and solutions.

Many of the `show` and `debug` commands are not protocol-specific. Though these commands do not deal exclusively with the TCP/IP protocol, they are used in troubleshooting many TCP/IP problems and therefore are included in this chapter for completeness. As is the case with the `show` and `debug` commands, logging and core dumps are not limited to the TCP/IP but can be used to contribute to troubleshooting TCP/IP problems and are also included in this chapter for completeness.

In addition to all the detailed problem-solving techniques presented in these two chapters, quick reference summary charts are located at the end of Chapter 38. These tables help to quickly associate a cause to many TCP/IP symptoms.

Troubleshooting Commands

We will cover several troubleshooting tools in this chapter, each of which is part of the Cisco IOS. There are many `show` commands that are supported by the router. In addition to `show` commands, a tool called debug is used to see specific information regarding packet transfer and exchange.

Part of effectively using these tools is using them without adversely affecting the router and its many processes. Here you will learn the specifics of several troubleshooting commands, along with the information needed in order to use them without causing additional problems on your network.

We start with non-intrusive, Cisco-specific `show` commands. After discussing the `show` commands, we move on to the debug tool. To finalize this section, we discuss some non-Cisco-specific troubleshooting tools: `ping` and `traceroute`.

show Commands

A large number of `show` commands are supported by Cisco IOS. Explaining them all is beyond the scope of this book. The most effective and useful `show` commands are described in the following sections, and Table 37.1 lists the ones most frequently used. To get an idea of all of the `show` commands, execute the `show ?` command from the router prompt.

TABLE 37.1 Frequently Used *show* Commands

show Command	Information Produced
`access-lists`	List of access lists
`accounting`	Accounting data for active sessions
`adjacency`	Adjacent nodes
`buffers`	Buffer pool statistics
`cdp`	Cisco Discovery Protocol (CDP) information
`cef`	Cisco Express Forwarding (CEF)
`configuration`	Contents of the NVRAM
`controllers`	Interface controller status
`debugging`	State of each debugging option
`environment`	Environmental monitor statistics
`extended`	Extended interface information
`frame-relay`	Frame Relay information
`interfaces`	Interface status and configuration
`ip`	IP information
`line`	TTY line information
`logging`	Contents of logging buffers
`memory`	Memory statistics
`ppp`	PPP parameters and statistics
`processes`	Active process statistics
`protocols`	Active network routing protocols
`queue`	Queue contents
`queueing`	Queuing configuration

TABLE 37.1 Frequently Used *show* Commands *(continued)*

show Command	Information Produced
`running-config`	Current operating configuration
`stacks`	Process stack utilization
`startup-config`	Contents of startup configuration
`tcp`	Status of TCP connections
`tech-support`	System information for Tech Support
`version`	System hardware and software version and status

The following sections describe the `show` commands grouped into four categories: global, interface-related, process-related, and protocol-related. Depending on the problem you are troubleshooting, you can focus on the problem by using the appropriate commands. For example, if you are troubleshooting a protocol-related problem, then you will probably use the protocol family of `show` commands. If you notice problems on a circuit, you can use the interface family of `show` commands to obtain detailed information about the interface.

Global Commands

Global commands deal with global router settings. Information that does not relate to interfaces or protocols, yet has overall router information, is considered to be subject to a global `show` command. Table 37.2 shows the useful global `show` commands. A detailed description of these commands as well as sample output is included after the table. (Logging is covered in its own section at the end of the chapter.)

TABLE 37.2 Global *show* Commands

Global *show* Command	Information Produced
`version`	System hardware and software status
`running-config`	Current operating configuration
`startup-config`	Contents of startup configuration
`logging`	Contents of logging buffers
`buffers`	Buffer pool statistics

TABLE 37.2 Global *show* Commands *(continued)*

Global *show* Command	Information Produced
`stacks`	Process stack utilization
`tech-support`	System information for Tech Support
`access-lists`	List of access lists
`memory`	Memory statistics

show version

This command is used to display the system hardware and software versions. It also provides information about how long the router was running and the reason it was last restarted. Review the following output of the `show version` command:

```
Router_B>show version
Cisco Internetwork Operating System Software
IOS (tm) RSP Software (RSP-JSV-M), Version 12.1(16), RELEASE SOFTWARE (fc1)
Copyright (c) 1986-2002 by cisco Systems, Inc.
Compiled Tue 09-Jul-02 07:36 by kellythw
Image text-base: 0x60010958, data-base: 0x614C4000

ROM: System Bootstrap, Version 11.1(8)CA1, EARLY DEPLOYMENT RELEASE
 SOFTWARE (fc1)
BOOTLDR: RSP Software (RSP-BOOT-M), Version 12.1(16), RELEASE SOFTWARE (fc1)

Router_B uptime is 35 weeks, 1 day, 6 hours, 18 minutes
System returned to ROM by reload at 00:12:02 EST Tue Oct 8 2002
System restarted at 23:52:37 EST Mon Oct 7 2002
System image file is "slot0:rsp-jsv-mz.121-16.bin"

cisco RSP4 (R5000) processor with 131072K/2072K bytes of memory.
R5000 CPU at 200Mhz, Implementation 35, Rev 2.1, 512KB L2 Cache
Last reset from power-on
G.703/E1 software, Version 1.0.
G.703/JT2 software, Version 1.0.
X.25 software, Version 3.0.0.
SuperLAT software (copyright 1990 by Meridian Technology Corp).
Bridging software.
```

```
TN3270 Emulation software.
Chassis Interface.
5 VIP2 controllers (2 FastEthernet)(6 HSSI)(1 ATM).
1 VIP2 R5K controller (8 Serial).
2 FastEthernet/IEEE 802.3 interface(s)
8 Serial network interface(s)
6 HSSI network interface(s)
1 ATM network interface(s)
123K bytes of non-volatile configuration memory.

20480K bytes of Flash PCMCIA card at slot 0 (Sector size 128K).
8192K bytes of Flash internal SIMM (Sector size 256K).
No slave installed in slot 7.
Configuration register is 0x102

Router_B>
```

As you can see, the output contains a great deal of information. We'll move through it field by field.

The first field indicates the revision of software that is actively running on the router. In this case, it is Cisco IOS 12.1(16).

The next field is the bootstrap version, which indicates the Cisco IOS that is used in case the IOS isn't found. This IOS is stored on the PROMs or flash memory of the router. The router boots by using 11.1(8)CA. This allows the router to actually boot so that you can fix software problems.

Current router status information is located in the field following the bootstrap information. This output tells you the length of time the router has been up and the last date it was reloaded. If an error caused the router to reload, the error message is included in this field. Finally, the file that was used while booting is listed.

Directly after this section is a line that tells the type of processor used and the amount of DRAM present. The DRAM is displayed in the format `value1/value2 bytes of memory`. `value1` is the amount of local memory present; `value2` is the amount of I/O memory present. The total DRAM in the router is the sum of these two values.

The final section describes the route processor and amount of RAM. At the end of the section, all interface processors are listed, followed by the number of interfaces. The last three lines indicate the different amounts and types of memory.

show startup-config and *running-config*

These two commands are used to view the syntax of the router's configuration. The `show startup-config` command displays the contents of the configuration that was written to NVRAM. The `show running-config`, `show config`, and `write term` commands are all equivalent. The results of these commands display the configuration that was loaded into memory and is running on the router.

Although you should already be familiar with these two commands, here is a very good troubleshooting tip: Compare the two configurations when working on network problems. It is always possible that configuration changes were made to the running configuration but not copied to the startup configuration. There may be extra or missing commands in the configuration versions. You may be able to solve the problem of missing commands in the running configuration quickly by copying the `startup-config` to the `running-config`.

These commands provide you with global, protocol, and interface information. You can analyze them for proper configuration and then make changes, if needed. Many problems can be isolated by viewing the configuration. What usually happens is that you will see something that wasn't there before, see something that shouldn't be there, or notice that something is missing that needs to be there. For this technique to work, you must be familiar with the router and its configuration. If backups are made of the configurations, you can compare them to the `running-config` to look for differences.

show buffers

The buffers come configured with default settings. They can be modified, if necessary, but if you do this it's usually a good idea to have a Cisco TAC engineer look at the memory allocation and suggest the new buffer settings. Following is an example of the buffer settings:

```
Router_B>show buffers
Buffer elements:
     999 in free list (500 max allowed)
     2594679003 hits, 0 misses, 500 created

Public buffer pools:
Small buffers, 104 bytes (total 480, permanent 480):
     455 in free list (20 min, 1000 max allowed)
     243410950 hits, 0 misses, 0 trims, 0 created
     0 failures (0 no memory)
Middle buffers, 600 bytes (total 360, permanent 360):
     357 in free list (20 min, 800 max allowed)
     374760214 hits, 8298 misses, 5776 trims, 5776 created
     2275 failures (0 no memory)
Big buffers, 1524 bytes (total 360, permanent 360):
     358 in free list (10 min, 1200 max allowed)
     274949626 hits, 0 misses, 0 trims, 0 created
     0 failures (0 no memory)
VeryBig buffers, 4520 bytes (total 40, permanent 40):
     40 in free list (5 min, 1200 max allowed)
     12900991 hits, 173 misses, 519 trims, 519 created
     0 failures (0 no memory)
Large buffers, 5024 bytes (total 40, permanent 40):
```

```
     40 in free list (3 min, 120 max allowed)
     0 hits, 0 misses, 0 trims, 0 created
     0 failures (0 no memory)
Huge buffers, 18024 bytes (total 4, permanent 0):
     3 in free list (3 min, 52 max allowed)
     2459 hits, 2 misses, 8716 trims, 8720 created
     0 failures (0 no memory)

Interface buffer pools:
IPC buffers, 4096 bytes (total 312, permanent 312):
     312 in free list (104 min, 1040 max allowed)
     696006349 hits, 0 fallbacks, 0 trims, 0 created
     0 failures (0 no memory)

Header pools:
```

You can view six buffer distinctions in this output: small, middle, big, very big, large, and huge. Each division is allocated a particular amount of buffer space. These allocations are determined at router bootup and vary by interface type. The `show buffers` output details the buffer name and size, with the buffer size following immediately after its name. The `(total 120, permanent 120)` for the small pool specifies that there are a total of 120 spaces allocated to the small pool. The `permanent` means that the 120 buffer spaces are permanently assigned to the small buffer pool. When a buffer's space is permanent, it cannot be deallocated and given back to the system memory for other uses.

In the next field, you can see the number of free buffer spaces that are open to accepting a packet. Each pool maintains a minimum and maximum threshold, which the pool uses to decide whether more buffer space needs to be allocated to it. This is seen in the `min` and `max allowed` indicators.

The last two lines of information given for each pool describe the activity happening there. This information, which includes all hits, misses, trims, created spaces, and failures, is described in the following list:

Hits The number of times the pool was used successfully.

Misses The number of times a packet tried to find a space within a pool but found no available spaces. In this case, the packet is not discarded; rather, a space is created for it.

Trims The number of spaces removed from the pool because the amount exceeded the number of allowed buffer spaces. This value is only meaningful on dynamically allocated buffer pools; static pools cannot be trimmed.

Created The number of spaces created to accommodate requests for space when there wasn't enough at the time the request was made or if there were fewer than the `min` of a certain type of buffer available. Once the space is no longer needed, it will be trimmed.

Failures The number of times a buffer pool tried unsuccessfully to create space. When a failure occurs, the requesting packet is dropped.

The last field is the `no memory` field, which records the number of failures that occurred due to the lack of sufficient system memory required to create additional buffer space.

If you observe a significant increase in the number of misses while monitoring buffers with the `show buffers` command, the pool can be tuned by assigning different values to the `max-free`, `min-free`, and `permanent` parameters. Increasing the values for these parameters overrides the system defaults—instead of having to create additional spaces on demand within a pool, the spaces can be statically allocated and assigned. This helps you avoid racking up missed and failed packet statuses.

You can adjust these parameters with the following command:

```
buffers {small | middle | big | verybig | large | huge |   type number}
 {permanent | max-free | min-free |   initial} number
```

The `type` represents interface type, and `number` is the number to be assigned to the specified parameter.

Table 37.3 depicts the sizes of the buffer space within a pool. When a packet needs to be stored in a buffer, it requests space from the pool in proportion to its size requirement. For example, a full-size Ethernet packet at a 1500MTU requires one buffer space from the big buffer pool.

TABLE 37.3 Sizes of the Buffer within a Pool

Pool Name	Buffer Size (in Bytes)
Small	104
Middle	600
Big	1524
Very Big	4520
Large	5024
Huge	18,024

show stack

The `show stack` command is not very useful to you, but it is invaluable information for the Cisco TAC. An example of output from the command appears in this section. As you can see, it won't make a lot of sense to the user. The information is sent to Cisco, and Cisco runs it through a stack decode that provides the information relevant to system problems.

Stacks are used to provide information on the router's processes and processor utilization. The output displayed is from a healthy router. If the router were to crash, the latest stack information is saved so it can be captured once the router comes back up. The data contains information regarding the reason for the reload and any errors that are attributed to the crash.

```
Router_A#show stack
Minimum process stacks:
 Free/Size   Name
10288/12000  Init
 5196/6000   Router Init
 9672/12000  Virtual Exec

Interrupt level stacks:
Level    Called Unused/Size  Name
  1       49917   8200/9000  Network Interrupt
  2           2   8372/9000  Network Status Interrupt
  3           0   9000/9000  OIR interrupt
  4           0   9000/9000  PCMCIA Interrupt
  5        2561   8652/9000  Console Uart
  6           0   9000/9000  Error Interrupt
  7    27140712   8608/9000  NMI Interrupt Handler
Router_A#
```

show tech-support

The show tech-support command is a compilation of several show commands (version, running-config, controllers, stacks, interfaces, diagbus, buffers, process memory, process cpu, context, boot, flash bootflash, ip traffic, and controllers cbus). It should be noted that, although these are the typical commands issued by show tech-support, the commands can vary depending on hardware and software levels. You can get most of the information you need by issuing the show tech-support command, instead of issuing all of the commands separately.

The show tech-support command does not allow you to scroll through its output on the router because of the enormous amount of information that is displayed. To capture the output, you need a terminal with a large line-buffer setting, or you can log the output directly to a terminal.

show access-lists

The show access-lists command is useful to view the access list configuration without sorting through the running or start-up configuration. In addition to displaying the line entries of the access list, the command uses the access list number to define what type of access list is being displayed. The output from the show access-lists command follows:

```
Router_B#show access-lists
Extended IP access-list 105
    permit ip 172.16.0.0 0.0.255.255 any (97160 matches)
    permit ip 10.0.0.0 0.255.255.255 any
    deny   ip any any (102463 matches)
```

```
Novell access-list 801
    permit 606E3000 (3245 matches)
    permit 506E3074
    permit B06F2E00 (655 matches)
    permit D06F2EFE
    permit 717B012C
    permit E06F2E67
    permit F9BE0714 (5038 matches)
    permit A054AB00
    permit 617B07C4
    permit 017B1900
```

This information gives you a summary of each access list on the router. The access list type is defined, and the number assigned to it is shown. Each line of the list is displayed individually. The list also specifies matchups between networks and wildcard masks.

show memory

The `show memory` command is helpful for diagnosing memory problems such as allocation failures, low amounts of free memory, and so on. In the following output, you can see that the first field has the memory divided between processor memory and fast memory. The fields are self-explanatory; they describe the total, used, and free amounts of memory. As you will see in the "Process Commands" section later, the output here is very similar to the `show processes memory` command.

```
Router_C>show memory
      Head        Total(b)    Used(b)    Free(b)     Lowest(b)  Largest(b)
Proc  60DC38E0    52676384    34896328   17780056    15823612   14764584
Fast  60DA38E0    131072      128344     2728        27282684
Processor memory
Address   Bytes Prev.     Next     Ref PrevF NextF Alloc PC   What
60DC38E0  1056  0         60DC3D2C  1               601342A4  List Elements
60DC3D2C  2656  60DC38E0 60DC47B8  1               601342A4  List Headers
60DC47B8  9000  60DC3D2C 60DC6B0C  1               60135498  Interrupt Stack
60DC6B0C  9000  60DC47B8 60DC8E60  1               60135498  Interrupt Stack
```

Interface Commands

Interface commands deal with detailed interface settings and configurations. Because each type of interface uses particular protocols and technologies, the `show interface` command is capable of displaying all data related to a specified interface. Table 37.4 lists the useful interface-related `show` commands. Here in this section, we will focus on the `show interface` and `show ip interface` commands.

TABLE 37.4 *show interface* Commands

show interface Command	Information Produced
queuing/queue	Queuing configuration and contents
interface *interface-type interface-number*	Interface status and configuration
ip interface	Information specifically related to IP interfaces

show queueing and *show queue*

To verify the configuration and operation of the queuing system, you can issue the following two commands:

```
show queueing [fair | priority | custom]
show queue [interface-type interface-number]
```

Following are the results from these commands on Router C. Because weighted fair queuing is the only type of queuing that has been enabled on this router, it wasn't necessary to issue the optional command options `fair`, `custom`, or `priority`.

```
Router_C#show queueing
Current fair queue configuration:
Interface  Discard      Dynamic       Reserved
           threshold     queue count  queue count
 Serial0      96           256           0
 Serial1      64           256           0
Current priority queue configuration:
Current custom queue configuration:
Current RED queue configuration:
Router_C#
```

This command output shows that weighted fair queuing is enabled on both serial interfaces, and that the discard threshold for Serial 0 was changed from 64 to 96. There's a maximum of 256 dynamic queues for both interfaces—the default value. The lines following the interface information are empty because their corresponding queuing algorithms aren't configured yet.

The next command, `show queue`, displays more detailed information pertaining to the specified interface:

```
Router_C#show queue serial0
 Input queue: 0/75/0 (size/max/drops); Total output drops: 0
 Queueing strategy: weighted fair
```

```
 Output queue: 0/1000/96/0 (size/max total/threshold/ drops)
   Conversations 0/1/256 (active/max active/max total)
   Reserved Conversations 0/0 (allocated/max allocated)
Router_C#
```

show interface

As mentioned, the `show interface` command has many derivatives. Table 37.5 lists many of the options that are available with this command.

It is important to recognize that the interface processors listed are there because they are present on the router. For example, you won't see a Token Ring interface listed unless there is a Token Ring interface on the router.

TABLE 37.5 *show interface* Command Options

show interface **Command Option**	**Information Produced**
atm *interface-type*	ATM interface
ethernet *interface-type*	IEEE 802.3
serial *interface-type*	Serial
hssi *interface-type*	High-Speed Serial Interface (HSSI)
accounting	Interface accounting
fair-queue	Interface Weighted Fair Queueing (WFQ) info
rate-limit	Interface rate-limit info
mac-accounting	Interface MAC accounting info

Now look at sample outputs from an Ethernet and a serial interface. After each sample, we will go through a detailed explanation:

```
Router_A#show interface Ethernet 5/4
Ethernet5/4 is up, line protocol is up
  Hardware is cxBus Ethernet, address is 009a.822e.51b6 (bia 90.323f.acdb)
  Description: Connection to Router_B
  Internet address is 172.16.1.1/24
```

```
  MTU 1500 bytes, BW 10000 Kbit, DLY 1000 usec, rely 255/
    255, load 33/255
  Encapsulation ARPA, loopback not set, keepalive set (10
    sec)
  ARP type: ARPA, ARP Timeout 04:00:00
  Last input 00:00:00, output 00:00:00, output hang never
  Last clearing of "show interface" counters never
  Queueing strategy: fifo
  Output queue 0/40, 101553 drops; input queue 0/75, 1327
    drops
  5 minute input rate 247000 bits/sec, 196 packets/sec
  5 minute output rate 1329000 bits/sec, 333 packets/sec
     421895792 packets input, 2524672293 bytes, 1 no
     buffer
     Received 453382 broadcasts, 0 runts, 0 giants
     6 input errors, 1 CRC, 5 frame, 0 overrun, 494
     ignored,       0 abort
     0 input packets with dribble condition detected
     618578101 packets output, 977287695 bytes, 0
     underruns
     0 output errors, 30979588 collisions, 1 interface
    resets
     0 babbles, 0 late collision, 0 deferred
     0 lost carrier, 0 no carrier
     0 output buffers copied, 0 interrupts, 0 failures
Router_A#
```

This output starts with the most pertinent information—the physical interface and line protocol status. In this case, both are up. There is much argument as to what constitutes an "up" interface. It is very simple—the controller sends a signal that there are electrons flowing through the physical interface. So, just doing a `no shut` on an interface brings it into an "up" status, even if nothing is plugged into the interface. `Line protocol is up` means that the interface is able to send itself a frame and receive it back.

The next fields contain the layer 2 MAC address, the interface description, and the layer 3 IP address. Below the interface address information, you'll find the line settings for the interface; MTU, bandwidth, delay, reliability, and load are listed. These values are used to calculate a distance-vector protocol route metric.

Default Ethernet encapsulation for Cisco is ARPA. You can see that this is true and that the keep-alive is the default at 10 seconds. This line is very important when troubleshooting Ethernet problems. If the encapsulation type is not compatible with other machines on the network, you will have communication problems. In order to better demonstrate this, let's examine the example given in the following paragraph.

When the router broadcasts from an interface, it uses the encapsulation that is configured. Look at Figure 37.1. In this case, an ARPA frame (#1) is sent. If the hosts on the network do not understand ARPA, they do not respond to the broadcast. On the other hand, if a host broadcast uses a SNAP frame (#2), the router is designed to understand any incoming frame encapsulation and can respond to the broadcast. Another bit of useful information that the router adds to the ARP table is the encapsulation type of that host. Then, the next time that the router wants to speak with the given host, it uses the documented frame type instead of the type configured on the interface. Here's a look at the ARP table (notice that the `Type` field is SNAP):

```
Router_C>show arp
Protocol  Address        Age (min)  Hardware Addr   Type  Interface
Internet  172.16.1.1     -          0010.296a.a820  ARPA  Ethernet5/0
Internet  172.16.1.22    62         0010.29d1.68a0  SNAP  Ethernet5/0
Router_C>
```

Continuing on with the output from the `show interface` command, you can see a great deal of statistical information. The counters for the interface have not been cleared since the router booted. Queuing type for the interface is first in, first out (FIFO). You should be familiar with the next few fields, because the input and output queue were previously discussed in the sections describing the `show queueing` and `show queue` commands. Here, you have statistical information that displays the number of drops. The interface traffic statistics follow.

FIGURE 37.1 Ethernet frame encapsulation compatibility

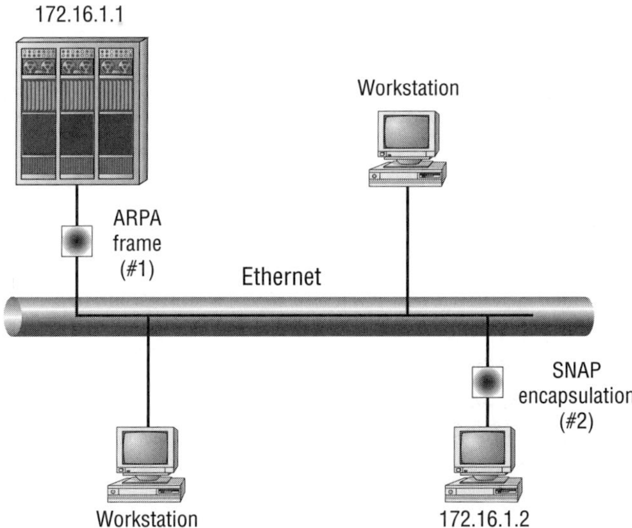

Statistical information includes the number of packets that travel across the interface and the bandwidth utilization. The following fields are dedicated to Ethernet troubleshooting. The `cyclic redundancy check` field counts the number of frames that were received that do not pass the CRC test. Next are `frame errors` and `overruns`. Overruns occur when the receiver on the interface receives frames faster than it can move them to the hardware buffer on the interface. The ignore signal is sent if there are buffer problems.

Output errors consist of underruns and collisions. The other fields are counters for the physical interface: `resets`, `lost carrier`, and `no carrier`. These are followed by more buffer error counters.

Now let's review the output from a serial interface:

```
Router_D#sho int s1/0
Serial1/0 is up, line protocol is up
  Hardware is cxBus Serial
  Description: Connection to frame-relay cloud
  MTU 1500 bytes, BW 1544 Kbit, DLY 20000 usec, rely 255/
  255, load 1/255
  Encapsulation FRAME-RELAY, loopback not set, keepalive
  set     (10 sec)
  LMI enq sent  195167, LMI stat recvd 195165, LMI upd
  recvd     10, DTE LMI up
  LMI enq recvd 0, LMI stat sent  0, LMI upd sent  0
  LMI DLCI 1023  LMI type is CISCO  frame relay DTE
  Broadcast queue 0/64, broadcasts sent/dropped 0/0,
  interface broadcasts 908350
  Last input 00:00:00, output 00:00:00, output hang never
  Last clearing of "show interface" counters never
  Input queue: 0/75/4 (size/max/drops); Total output
  drops:     22795
  Queueing strategy: weighted fair
  Output queue: 0/64/22795 (size/threshold/drops)
     Conversations  0/59 (active/max active)
     Reserved Conversations 0/0 (allocated/max allocated)
  5 minute input rate 7000 bits/sec, 9 packets/sec
  5 minute output rate 9000 bits/sec, 8 packets/sec
     55695166 packets input, 3680326698 bytes, 1 no buffer
     Received 0 broadcasts, 0 runts, 0 giants
     1 input errors, 0 CRC, 0 frame, 0 overrun, 0 ignored,
     1 abort
     56424159 packets output, 569801054 bytes, 0 underruns
     0 output errors, 0 collisions, 2 interface resets
     8656902 output buffers copied, 0 interrupts, 0
```

```
    failures
    3 carrier transitions
    RTS up, CTS up, DTR up, DCD up, DSR up
Router_D#
```

This output has a lot of Frame Relay information that we will discuss in Chapter 39, "Troubleshooting Serial Line and Frame Relay Connectivity." For now, we'll just review the fields of information that are available by using this command. You can see that the first line is the interface status line. The metric values are also listed. Following the Frame Relay information, you see the interface traffic statistics. At the bottom of the output are the buffer error fields, as well as the physical interface counters. A carrier transition is counted any time the carrier status change occurs. (We will explore this output in Chapter 39.)

show ip interface

The `show ip interface` command provides information specific to the TCP/IP configuration of the specified interface. Information regarding the interface status, IP address, subnet mask, broadcast address, and applied access lists is all contained in the `show ip interface` command output. In addition, the command also provides information on proxy ARP, which will be explained in further detail later in this chapter; helper addresses, which are used for DHCP configurations; the status of Network Address Translation (NAT); and many other items. The amount of output from the `show ip interface` command for a particular interface is second only to that of the `show interface` command. Here is an example:

```
Router_B#show ip interface serial 0
Serial0 is up, line protocol is up
  Internet address is 172.16.30.6/30
  Broadcast address is 255.255.255.255
  Address determined by non-volatile memory
  MTU is 1500 bytes
  Helper address is not set
  Directed broadcast forwarding is enabled
  Multicast reserved groups joined: 224.0.0.10
  Outgoing access list is not set
  Inbound  access list is not set
  Proxy ARP is enabled
  Security level is default
  Split horizon is enabled
  ICMP redirects are always sent
  ICMP unreachables are always sent
  ICMP mask replies are never sent
  IP fast switching is enabled
  IP fast switching on the same interface is enabled
  IP multicast fast switching is enabled
```

```
  Router Discovery is disabled
  IP output packet accounting is disabled
  IP access violation accounting is disabled
  TCP/IP header compression is disabled
  Probe proxy name replies are disabled
  Gateway Discovery is disabled
  Policy routing is disabled
  Network address translation is disabled
Router_B#
```

Process Commands

Process commands deal directly with the processes running on the router. If the standard `show processes` command is issued, you get a result similar to a `ps -ef` executed on a Unix box. The output details each process, including process ID number (PID), time running, and stack information. This output is too general to be used effectively while troubleshooting, but there are two very important process command options that can be executed to refine this output.

The two options available with the `show processes` command are `cpu` and `memory`, as described in Table 37.6. Each of these options refines the processes' output and makes it more useful and user-friendly.

TABLE 37.6 *show processes* Commands

***show processes* Command**	**Information Produced**
cpu	Amount of CPU time being spent on each process
memory	Memory statistics

show processes cpu

The output from this command, shown later in this section, relates the router's processes and CPU utilization. The first line of the output displays the router's CPU utilization over three periods. In addition, you will notice that the CPU utilization for the five-second interval has two percentages: 15 percent and 6 percent. The first number is the average CPU utilization for all processes on the router over the last five seconds. The second number is the percentage of the CPU spent on interrupt-driven processes. In general, interrupt-driven tasks are core to the router's ability to route packets. Examples of these tasks include fast- or process-switched packets, input from the console or auxiliary ports, and corrections of memory-alignment issues. Items such as maintaining VTY sessions and responding to SNMP queries are non-interrupt-driven processes that would only show up in the first percentage.

Underneath the CPU utilization line, you can see the processes running on the router. Starting from the left, you can see the PID, followed by the runtime and other data. The three columns that deal with CPU utilization detail the percentage of CPU cycles used by the specified process. The process description is found in the far-right column:

```
Router_C>show processes cpu
CPU utilization for five seconds: 15%/6%; one minute: 7%;    five minutes: 7%
 PID  Runtime(ms)  Invoked  uSecs    5Sec    1Min    5Min    TTY  Process
   1          76   1564143      0   0.00%  0.00%  0.00%    0 Load Meter
   2           0         1      0   0.00%  0.00%  0.00%    0 LAPF Input
   3     3638844    872510   4170   0.00%  0.04%  0.00%    0 Check heaps
   4           4        28    142   0.00%  0.00%  0.00%    0 Pool Manager
   5           0         2      0   0.00%  0.00%  0.00%    0 Timers


 . . . [output removed] . . .
```

When the overall CPU utilization gets high, you can identify which process is using the most CPU cycles, and then focus your attention on that process. For example, if the IP-EIGRP CPU utilization runs high, you can determine that there is a problem within EIGRP, perhaps a routing loop or some other instability.

show processes memory

The second helpful option for the `show processes` command is `memory`, which is used to associate memory utilization with the router's processes. Here is a sample output:

```
Router_D>show processes memory
Total: 52503792, Used: 45141524, Free: 7362268
 PID  TTY  Allocated      Freed    Holding    Getbufs      Retbufs Process
   0    0      54400        304    8898364          0      0 *Init*
   0    0        632 3906083084        632          0      0 *Sched*
   0    0  700723436  729437084     472484    1091352      0 *Dead*
   1    0         96          0       6876          0      0 SSCOP Input
   2    0          0          0       6780          0      0 Check heaps
   3    0   17262036     152680       6916     12351248  260336 Pool Manager

. . . [output removed] . . .
```

The first line details the total, used, and free amounts of system memory. Following that, you see the PID, allocated, freed, and holding memory. This means that the processor has allocated a given amount of memory to the process; if the process does not need all of that memory, it frees some of it and retains the rest.

TCP/IP Protocol Commands

We will discuss the major TCP/IP protocol commands in this section. In addition to the TCP/IP-related commands listed here, other protocol-related commands are covered later in this book. These cover protocols including HDLC, Frame Relay, X.25, and ISDN.

Table 37.7 lists the frequently used IP options for the show command.

TABLE 37.7 Frequently Used *show IP* Command Options

show ip Command Option	Information Produced
access-lists	IP access lists
accounting	The active IP accounting database
arp	Information regarding the IP ARP entries in the ARP cache
interface	IP interface status and configuration
protocols	Information regarding the IP routing protocols running on a router
route	IP routing table
traffic	IP protocol statistics

show ip access-list

This command provides information regarding a specified access list, or all access lists that fall within the 1–199 range. When various access lists are configured on the router, the show ip access-list command shows named IP access lists only. (Named access lists are explained later in this chapter.) From the following sample output, you can see that it lists both standard and extended lists:

```
Standard IP access list 5
    permit 172.16.14.2
    permit 172.16.91.140
    permit 172.16.10.51
    permit 172.16.1.7
    permit 172.16.155.0, wildcard bits 0.0.0.255
Extended IP access list 152
    deny ip any 172.16.91.0 0.0.0.63 log (268436 matches)
    deny ip any host 172.16.91.66 log (81058 matches)
    permit tcp any any established (8809 matches)
    permit ip host 172.16.2.55 any
    permit ip host 172.60.22.10 any (2194226 matches)
    permit ip host 172.140.64.8 any (7930443 matches)
    permit ip 172.16.10.0 0.0.255.255 any (9076 matches)
```

show ip arp

This command provides information contained in the router's ARP cache, including the IP address, MAC address, encapsulation type, and interface from which the MAC was learned. Here is a sample:

```
Router_C#show ip arp
Protocol  Address          Age (min)  Hardware Addr   Type  Interface
Internet  172.16.60.1              -  0010.7bd9.2881  ARPA  Ethernet0/1
Internet  172.16.50.2              -  0010.7bd9.2880  ARPA  Ethernet0/0
Internet  172.16.50.1              6  0000.0c09.99cc  ARPA  Ethernet0/0
Router_C#
```

show ip protocols

This command provides information about the IP routing protocols that run on the router. The sample output shown here includes only EIGRP information, because that is all that is being run on the router. As you can see, global filters are not applied. Metric values are displayed for each individual routing protocol. Route redistribution information is also provided:

```
Router_B#show ip protocols
Routing Protocol is "eigrp 100"
  Outgoing update filter list for all interfaces is not
  set
  Incoming update filter list for all interfaces is not
  set
  Default networks flagged in outgoing updates
  Default networks accepted from incoming updates
  EIGRP metric weight K1=1, K2=0, K3=1, K4=0, K5=0
  EIGRP maximum hopcount 100
  EIGRP maximum metric variance 1
  Redistributing: eigrp 100
  Automatic network summarization is not in effect
  Routing for Networks:
    172.16.0.0
  Routing Information Sources:
    Gateway         Distance      Last Update
  Distance: internal 90 external 170
Router_B#
```

show ip route

This command returns information stored in the IP route table. The command can be issued as a general command, and all IP routes and corresponding information will be displayed. Additionally, you can specify a given network, and the command will return information regarding that network only.

This section contains two examples of the show ip route command. Notice that the two outputs are different. The general command provides summary information for every IP route in the route table. However, when a network is specified, the results are much more detailed. Items such as the exact routing protocol responsible for learning the route, the source interface, and the next-hop router's IP address are all included:

```
Router_A>show ip route
Codes: C - connected, S - static, I - IGRP, R - RIP, M - mobile, B - BGP
    D - EIGRP, EX - EIGRP external, O - OSPF, IA - OSPF
    inter area
    N1 - OSPF NSSA external type 1, N2 - OSPF NSSA
    external type 2
    E1 - OSPF external type 1, E2 - OSPF external type 2,
    E - EGP
     i - IS-IS, L1 - IS-IS level-1, L2 - IS-IS level-2, *
     - candidate default
U - per-user static route, o - ODR

Gateway of last resort is not set

     172.16.0.0/16 is variably subnetted, 2 subnets, 2    masks
D       172.16.50.0/24 [90/2195456] via 172.16.30.6, 00:00:19, Serial1
C       172.16.30.4/30 is directly connected, Serial1
Router_A>

Router_A>show ip route 172.16.50.0
Routing entry for 172.16.50.0/24
  Known via "eigrp 100", distance 90, metric 2195456, type  internal
  Redistributing via eigrp 100
  Last update from 172.16.30.6 on Serial1, 00:02:03 ago
  Routing Descriptor Blocks:
  * 172.16.30.6, from 172.16.30.6, 00:02:03 ago, via
  Serial1
      Route metric is 2195456, traffic share count is 1
      Total delay is 21000 microseconds, minimum bandwidth
      is 1544 Kbit
      Reliability 128/255, minimum MTU 1500 bytes
      Loading 1/255, Hops 1

Router_A>
```

show ip traffic

This command returns information pertaining to IP traffic statistics. When the command is issued, the output is organized according to the IP protocol. Here is a sample:

```
Router_B#show ip traffic
IP statistics:
  Rcvd:  400 total, 400 local destination
         0 format errors, 0 checksum errors,
         0 bad hop count
         0 unknown protocol, 0 not a gateway
         0 security failures, 0 bad options,
         0 with options
  Opts:  0 end, 0 nop, 0 basic security,
         0 loose source  route
         0 timestamp, 0 extended security, 0 record route
         0 stream ID, 0 strict source route, 0 alert,
         0 cipso
         0 other
  Frags: 0 reassembled, 0 timeouts, 0 couldn't reassemble
         0 fragmented, 0 couldn't fragment
  Bcast: 0 received, 0 sent
  Mcast: 398 received, 401 sent
  Sent:  404 generated, 0 forwarded
         0 encapsulation failed, 0 no route

ICMP statistics:
  Rcvd: 0 format errors, 0 checksum errors, 0 redirects, 0
  unreachable
        0 echo, 0 echo reply, 0 mask requests, 0 mask
        replies, 0 quench
        0 parameter, 0 timestamp, 0 info request, 0 other
        0 irdp solicitations, 0 irdp advertisements
  Sent: 0 redirects, 0 unreachable, 0 echo, 0 echo reply
        0 mask requests, 0 mask replies, 0 quench, 0
        timestamp
        0 info reply, 0 time exceeded, 0 parameter problem
        0 irdp solicitations, 0 irdp advertisements

UDP statistics:
  Rcvd: 0 total, 0 checksum errors, 0 no port
  Sent: 0 total, 0 forwarded broadcasts
```

```
TCP statistics:
  Rcvd: 0 total, 0 checksum errors, 0 no port
  Sent: 0 total

Probe statistics:
  Rcvd: 0 address requests, 0 address replies
        0 proxy name requests, 0 where-is requests, 0
        other
  Sent: 0 address requests, 0 address replies (0 proxy)
        0 proxy name replies, 0 where-is replies

EGP statistics:
  Rcvd: 0 total, 0 format errors, 0 checksum errors, 0 no
  listener
  Sent: 0 total

IGRP statistics:
  Rcvd: 0 total, 0 checksum errors
  Sent: 0 total

OSPF statistics:
  Rcvd: 0 total, 0 checksum errors
        0 Hello, 0 database desc, 0 link state req
        0 link state updates, 0 link state acks

  Sent: 0 total

IP-IGRP2 statistics:
  Rcvd: 402 total
  Sent: 406 total

PIMv2 statistics: Sent/Received
  Total: 0/0, 0 checksum errors, 0 format errors
  Registers: 0/0, Register Stops: 0/0

IGMP statistics: Sent/Received
  Total: 0/0, Format errors: 0/0, Checksum errors: 0/0
  Host Queries: 0/0, Host Reports: 0/0, Host Leaves: 00
  DVMRP: 0/0, PIM: 0/0
```

```
ARP statistics:
  Rcvd: 0 requests, 0 replies, 0 reverse, 0 other
  Sent: 1 requests, 5 replies (0 proxy), 0 reverse
Router_B#
```

debug Commands

The `debug` commands and options are very powerful tools. The messages produced by the debugging process give detailed information and provide insight into what is happening on a very low level.

This power does not come free of charge. In most cases, debugging requires every packet to be process-switched, meaning that the route processor has to look at every packet entering the router in order for valid information to be obtained. In addition, the router must run and manage many other processes. Debugging can cause a great deal of additional overhead on a router. Therefore, it is important to use the tool with discretion. Use it to provide additional information on an existing problem, not to monitor a router. As a rule of thumb, `debug` commands should not be run on a router that already has a CPU utilization greater than 50 percent.

Because most problems are reported while a network is in production, the last thing you want to do is crash a router or cause unnecessary overhead by using the debug tool. By focusing the application of the `debug` command by using various command options and access lists, you can effectively troubleshoot problems without causing additional ones.

Always remember to turn the debugging function off after you obtain the necessary data. If left on, it can cause another network problem.

There are two tricks to successfully using the debug tool. First, make sure that your router is configured to apply timestamps to all messages. This is done with the following commands:

```
Router_A(config)#service timestamps debug datetime msec localtime
Router_A(config)#service timestamps log datetime msec localtime
```

Next, make sure that you see these messages. By default, error and debug messages are sent only to the console. If you are telnetted to the router, you will not see the debug or log messages unless you issue the following command:

```
Router_A#terminal monitor
```

You can turn the messages off again by issuing the `no` form of the command:

```
Router_A#terminal no monitor
```

If the output messages from the debug become excessive, it becomes difficult, if not impossible, to enter commands. Should this happen, there are two commands that you can issue to stop the messages. The first one was already mentioned (`terminal no monitor`, or `term no mon` for short). In this case, you type, but you don't see anything echo back. It can get confusing. Remember that the text messages that echo to the screen are not entered on the command line of the router. You can safely type **term no mon** and press Enter, even with hundreds of messages scrolling past you on the screen. The router eventually recognizes and processes the command. That stops the messages from scrolling down the screen, but it does not stop the processor from looking at every packet.

To stop the debug process altogether, the easiest way is to type the shorthand form of `undebug all`, like this:

```
Router_A#un all
```

It is short and sweet, yet effective. It works especially well when the router seems to be having a runaway. This command stops all debug processes and all associated messages. It can be entered safely while messages are scrolling wildly down the screen. It may take the router a few CPU cycles to accept the command and actually stop the debug process, so don't panic.

As an alternative, you can also have the `un all` command ready to go if you allow multiple telnet sessions to the same router. In this instance, you would telnet to the router twice. In one of the telnet sessions, set up the `terminal monitor` command so that you would receive the debug output. In the other window, type in the `undebug all` command but do not press Enter. Then return to your first telnet session and execute the `debug` command you need. If the output is overwhelming, go back to your other telnet session and hit Enter. As was the case before, it may take several seconds for the router to process the command and the messages to stop appearing on the screen.

Limiting Debug Output

Because of the potential impact to the router, you should take precautions whenever you use `debug` commands. Be as specific as possible when entering the `debug` commands so that you look only at information relevant to your issue. In addition to the commands themselves, you can apply access lists to the `debug` commands to further limit the information you are examining.

For example, if you wanted to see ping (ICMP) packets going between stations with IP addresses of 10.20.20.20 and 10.30.30.30, you could create an access list like this:

```
access-list 100 permit icmp host 10.20.20.20 host 10.30.30.30
```

Then apply this access list to the `debug` command as shown here:

```
Router_C#debug ip packet detail 100
IP packet debugging is on (detailed) for access list 100
Router_C#
IP: s=10.20.20.20 (Serial0), d=10.30.30.30 (Serial1), g=10.5.30.30, len
 100, forward ICMP type=8, code=0
```

In this manner, only ICMP packets going from 10.20.20.20 to 10.30.30.30 are shown in the debug output, rather than all of the packets going through the router.

As with the show commands, there are global-, interface-, and protocol-related debugging options. Because these tools and commands are used and discussed often in upcoming chapters, they are only summarized here according to usage.

Real World Scenario

Verify the Packet Flow without Using Debug

One question that frequently arises during troubleshooting is whether a particular packet is making it all the way through or even to a particular router. One way to verify this is by using debugging commands. The usual warning applies: Debugging commands can have a severe impact on the overall functionality of the router. Therefore, alternate solutions should be examined. In this case, one alternate solution is to use the log feature of an access list.

Assume that you want to verify that pings from 10.20.20.20 and destined to 10.30.30.30 are getting to the router. To do this, we first create an access list with two lines:

```
access-list 100 permit icmp host 10.20.20.20 host 10.30.30.30 log
access-list 100 permit ip any any
```

Notice the `log` at the end of the first line of the access list. This will put an entry in the log any time a packet meeting the criteria specified in the line is seen by the router. Also notice the `permit ip any any` at the end of the second line. This line ensures that other traffic on the interface will not be affected.

At this point, make sure you are on the console or have your Telnet session set up as a terminal monitor, and apply the access list inbound on the interface to be used by the packets to enter the router. These commands look like this:

```
Router_A(config)#interface serial0
Router_A(config-if)#ip access-group 100 in
%SEC-6-IPACCESSLOGDP: list 100 permitted icmp 10.20.20.20 -> 10.30.30.30 (0/0),
  ➥1 packet
```

By using access lists in this manner, you are able to verify that particular traffic is flowing over this router.

Although potentially safer than using debug, the `log` option on access lists can also create a large amount of data if substantial traffic meets the selection criteria specified in the access list. In addition, if an access list is already in place on a particular interface, modifications to accommodate this list will need to be part of the implementation. Even with these caveats, this trick can save you time and aggravation over using the debug commands.

Global Debugging

Some global **debug** commands are listed in Table 37.8. The table is not comprehensive; it is just a list of commonly used global **debug** commands. To obtain a comprehensive list, issue the following command:

```
Router_A#debug ?
```

TABLE 37.8 Common Global *debug* Commands

Global *debug* Command	Description
aaa	Enable AAA Authentication, Authorization, and Accounting debugging options.
adjacency	Enable adjacency debugging options.
all	Enable all debugging options.
cbus	Enable debug options dealing with ciscoBus events.
cdp	Enable debugging on CDP information.
chat	Enable chat scripts activity debugging.
dhcp	Enable debugging on DHCP client activity.
dialer	Enable debugging on Dial-on-Demand events.
domain	Enable debugging on Domain Name System (DNS) events.
entry	Enable debugging on incoming queue entries.
snmp	Enable SNMP debugging.
tacacs	Enable TACACS authentication and authorization event debugging.
tbridge	Enable debugging on transparent bridging.

Interface Debugging

Interface debugging is used to obtain information that is specific to interfaces, interface signaling, and interface processes. The same caution applies to interface-related **debug** commands as it does to the global commands: The more focused the debug through the use of options, the easier it is to isolate the problem.

Interface-oriented commands are listed in Table 37.9. Again, each of these commands has additional options available. To see the related options, use the commands listed, followed by a question mark. Most of these commands will be described and applied in later chapters.

TABLE 37.9 Interface-Related *debug* Commands

debug **Command**	**Description**
`atm`	Enable debugging on ATM interface events.
`channel`	Enable debugging on the channel interface information.
`ethernet-interface`	Enable debugging on Ethernet interface events.
`fastethernet`	Enable debugging on FastEthernet interface events.
`serial`	Enable debugging on serial interface events.
`token`	Enable debugging on Token Ring interface events.
`tunnel`	Enable debugging on the functioning of a tunnel interface.

Protocol Debugging

There are two protocol classes that can be debugged: desktop (or routed) protocols and routing protocols. Several debug options exist for protocol information, and each protocol has its own associated debug options. These options can be obtained by using the command-line help on the router.

Table 37.10 lists the protocol-related `debug` commands available.

TABLE 37.10 Protocol-Related *debug* Commands

debug **Command**	**Description**
`apple`	Enable debugging on AppleTalk events.
`arp`	Enable debugging on IP ARP and HP probe transactions.
`atm`	Enable debugging on ATM signaling.
`broadcast`	Enable debugging on broadcast packets.
`dlsw`	Enable debugging on Data Link Switching (DLSw) events.
`eigrp`	Enable debugging on the EIGRP routing protocol.

TABLE 37.10 Protocol-Related *debug* Commands *(continued)*

debug Command	Description
frame-relay	Enable debugging on Frame Relay events.
ip	Enable debugging on IP-specific information.
ipx	Enable debugging on Novell/IPX-specific information.
isis	Enable debugging on the IS-IS routing protocol.
ppp	Enable debugging on PPP (Point-to-Point Protocol) events.
spanning	Enable debugging on spanning tree information.
telnet	Enable debugging on incoming Telnet connections.
translate	Enable debugging on protocol translation events.
vlan	Enable VLAN-related debugging.

IP Debugging

Just like the show commands, numerous **debug** commands and options exist specifically for IP. The problem being analyzed will dictate which IP **debug** commands need to be used. Table 37.11 lists many of the available **debug** commands and options within IP. Note that the first command, arp, is not an IP-specific command, yet it provides valuable IP information.

TABLE 37.11 IP-Related *debug* Commands and Options

Command	Description
arp	Enable debugging of IP ARP and HP Probe transactions.
bgp	Enable debugging of the BGP routing protocol.
cache	Enable debugging of IP cache operations.
cef	Enable debugging of IP CEF operations.
cgmp	Enable debugging of the CGMP protocol activity.
eigrp	Enable debugging of the IP EIGRP routing protocol information.

TABLE 37.11 IP-Related *debug* Commands and Options *(continued)*

Command	Description
`error`	Enable debugging of IP errors.
`ftp`	Enable debugging of FTP events.
`http`	Enable debugging of HTTP connections.
`icmp`	Enable debugging of ICMP transactions.
`igmp`	Enable debugging of IGMP protocol activity.
`igrp`	Enable debugging of IGRP information.
`mbgp`	Enable debugging of the MBGP routing protocol.
`mcache`	Enable debugging of IP multicast cache operations.
`mds`	Enable debugging of IP distributed multicast information.
`mobile`	Enable debugging of mobile IP protocols.
`mpacket`	Enable debugging of IP multicast packets.
`mrouting`	Enable debugging of IP multicast routing events.
`msdp`	Enable debugging of Multicast Source Discovery Protocol (MSDP) events.
`mtag`	Enable debugging of IP multicast tag-switching activity
`nat`	Enable debugging of NAT events.
`ospf`	Enable debugging of OSPF routing protocol information.
`packet`	Enable IP packet debugging and IPSO security transactions.
`peer`	Enable debugging of IP peer address activity.
`pim`	Enable PIM protocol activity debugging.
`policy`	Enable debugging of policy routing events.
`rip`	Enable IP RIP routing protocol debugging.

TABLE 37.11 IP-Related *debug* Commands and Options *(continued)*

Command	Description
routing	Enable routing table event.
rsvp	Enable debugging on the RSVP protocol.
security	Enable debugging of the IP security options.
tcp	Enable debugging of TCP-based transactions.
udp	Enable debugging of UDP-based transactions.

The `debug ip packets` command contains an option to provide an access list, which narrows the scope of the debug even more. There are some prerequisites, though. In order to properly use `debug ip packets`, the packets must be process-switched, which means that all switching types must be turned off. Fast, optimum, and other switching types do not provide the necessary information regarding the IP transactions.

By looking at the output of these commands, you can get a sense of what is going on at each layer of the OSI model. They allow you to identify where a problem is occurring and let you focus in on that layer. Though not the first place to start in troubleshooting, debugging can be a valuable tool in the overall process.

logging Commands

The last set of commands examined here are the `logging` commands. `Logging` commands allow you to save errors and other messages for later review. This information can be sent to the console, to a terminal, to an internal buffer on the router, and/or to a Syslog server.

You can view the logging information on a router by executing the `show logging` command that was referenced in the "`show` Commands" section (see Table 37.2). Here's a sample output of this command:

```
Router_B>show logging
Syslog logging: enabled (6519 messages dropped, 0 flushes, 0 overruns)
    Console logging: level debugging, 9047 messages logged
    Monitor logging: level debugging, 1256 messages logged
    Buffer logging: level debugging, 9047 messages logged
    Trap logging: level notifications, 3276 message lines logged
        Logging to 10.20.20.20, 3276 message lines logged

Log Buffer (65536 bytes):
```

```
Feb 11 01:00:45: %CLEAR-5-COUNTERS: Clear counter on all interfaces by
 user1 on vty0 (10.20.20.20)
Feb 11 19:40:26: %SYS-4-SNMP_WRITENET: SNMP WriteNet request. Writing
current configuration to 10.30.30.30
Feb 12 07:40:39: %DUAL-5-NBRCHANGE: IP-EIGRP 64700: Neighbor
10.40.40.40 (Serial1/1/1.30) is down: holding time expired
```

As you can see, the four different logging locations available—console, monitor, buffer, and trap (Syslog server)—are referenced in the output. In addition to the locations, there are some logging "levels" indicated as well.

Cisco routers have eight possible logging levels. These levels or values range from 0 to 7 and are described in Table 37.12. The logging level, indicated after each of the locations in the `show logging` command, represents the level of severity that is required for a message to be logged. Any message with a severity equal to or less than the logging level will be recorded. For example, the trap level in the foregoing output was set to notifications, or 5. This means that all messages with a level of 5 or less (in other words, notifications, warnings, errors, critical, alerts, and emergencies) will be sent to the Syslog server. In contrast, the console has its level set to debugging. Because debugging is the highest level, all messages, no matter what level, will be sent to the console.

TABLE 37.12 Logging Levels

Logging Level	Name	Description
0	Emergencies	System unusable messages
1	Alerts	Take immediate action
2	Critical	Critical condition
3	Errors	Error message
4	Warnings	Warning messages
5	Notifications	Normal but significant condition
6	Informational	Information messages
7	Debugging	Debug messages

The next logical question is, "How do I know what level of debugging I need?" By default, the console, monitor, and buffer logging are set to the debugging level, and the trap logging is set to informational. If you want to modify these values, you can gauge the value you want to use by looking at the messages that have already been logged. Most messages include the logging level as part of the entry. For instance, in the preceding example, -5- in the middle of CLEAR COUNTERS indicates a level 5 notification; and -4- between SYS and SNMP indicates a level 4 warning. Also, if you look at the earlier Real World Scenario sidebar, "Verify the Packet Flow without Using Debug," you will note the -6- in the log output from the access list. This message would be treated as a level 6 informational message.

Finally, it should be noted that the process of message logging does consume router CPU cycles. As with the debug tool, care must be taken with logging. If too many messages are being logged and the router is already busy, performance issues can result. In most cases, the messages that are being logged are being generated by a debug command. Therefore, if you know you are going to run a debug command that will generate a large amount of output, you can turn off some of the logging to help minimize the performance impact of this debug. However, not all of the logging types are created equal when it comes to load on the router. The logging options are as follows, from most load to least load: console, monitor, trap, and buffer. So if you are doing a debug that will produce abundant messages, you can minimize the load on the router by ensuring that only the buffer logging is enabled.

The commands used with the logging options are described in Table 37.13.

TABLE 37.13 Logging-Related Commands

logging Command	Description
Buffered	Sets buffer size, as well as the logging level for the buffer. The no form of this command disables the logging buffer.
clear logging	Clears the logging buffer.
Console	Sets the logging level for the console. The no form of this command disables logging to the console.
Monitor	Sets the logging level for the monitor. The no form of this command disables logging to the monitor.
Trap	Sets the logging level for the Syslog server. The no form of this command disables logging to the Syslog server.

Executing a Router Core Dump

The information contained in a core dump can be useful for diagnosing router problems. A core dump contains an exact copy of the information that currently resides in system memory. Depending on the amount of RAM and the memory utilization, the core dump file can be very large. The information provided is normally used only by Cisco engineers.

There are two general methods for capturing the information contained in memory. In the first method, a router is configured to execute a core dump when the router crashes. The second method is to use a user-privileged exec command from the command line.

exception Command

The `exception` command allows you to configure a router to execute a core dump if the router crashes. An integral part of the `exception` command is the TFTP, FTP, or RCP server. Here is a sample configuration:

```
Router_A#conf t
Enter configuration commands, one per line. End with CNTL/Z.
Router_A(config)#exception dump 172.16.10.10
Router_A(config)#^Z
Router_A#
```

The IP address in the command is the IP address of the TFTP, FTP, or RCP server. The router needs this address so it knows where to download the core dump. It uses any of these three protocols (TFTP, FTP, or RCP).

Configuration varies, depending on which type of server is used. TFTP does not require any additional configuration than the preceding example. FTP and RCP, however, require additional commands in order to support the file transfer. Here is an example:

```
Router_A#conf t
Enter configuration commands, one per line. End with CNTL/Z.
Router_A(config)#exception dump 172.16.10.11
Router_A(config)#ip ftp username kevin
Router_A(config)#ip ftp password aloha
Router_A(config)#ip ftp source-interface e0
Router_A(config)#exception protocol ftp
Router_A(config)#^Z
Router_A#
```

Because FTP servers require some type of username and password combination to allow access to the file system, this information must be specified on the router. You can map the FTP server to the exiting interface on the router by using the `source-interface` command. This is just like a static route. If the route table did not have the route in its table, it would still know how to get to the FTP server. You must also specify which protocol is going to be used.

RCP requires configuration on the RCP server by editing the `.rhosts` files, as well as the router configuration. Here is a sample:

```
Router_A#conf t
Enter configuration commands, one per line. End with CNTL/Z.
Router_A(config)#exception protocol rcp
Router_A(config)#exception dump 172.16.10.12
Router_A(config)#ip rcmd remote-username kevin
Router_A(config)#ip rcmd rcp-enable
Router_A(config)#ip rcmd rsh-enable
```

```
Router_A(config)#ip rcmd remote-host kevin 172.16.10.12 kevin
Router_A(config)#^Z
Router_A#
```

The `remote-host` command is configured by providing the local username, followed by the IP address for the RCP server and the remote username for the RCP server. This allows the router to log in on the RCP server and commence transferring the core dump.

write core Command

The `write core` command allows the user to execute a core dump without crashing the router.

It is not advisable to use this command unless it is requested by Cisco TAC. Because it is copying the contents of memory via TFTP, it could have an adverse effect on the router.

Here is a sample of the `write core` command:

```
Router_A#write core
Remote host? 172.16.10.10
Name of core file to write [Router_A-core]?
Write file Router_A-core on host 172.16.10.10? [confirm]
Writing Router_A-core !!!!! [OK]
Router_A#
```

The router output has been truncated in this example. You will see exclamation marks until the file is completely transferred. The more memory that needs to be copied, the longer it will take.

Again, this information will only be useful to Cisco engineers for diagnosing and resolving router problems. Be aware that this command does have limitations. In a real router crash, it is quite possible that routing will be affected and, as a result, the router will not know how to get to the exception server. Therefore, if the exception server is not on a directly connected segment, then setting up a default gateway (`ip default-gateway`) will correct this issue.

ping Commands

The tools discussed thus far are in-depth tools used for problems that require troubleshooting with a high level of granularity. These tools are used to provide very detailed and specific information at a very low-level view. The `ping` command, on the other hand is a high-level simple tool. It is used to test for reachability and connectivity throughout a network.

Ping can be used to effectively isolate network problems. If certain hosts on a network respond to the pings when others do not, this directs your efforts to focus more on the individual hosts that are not responding.

Cisco provides two implementations of the `ping` command: the user and privileged levels. On both levels, `ping` works for the following protocols:

- IP
- IPX
- AppleTalk
- CLNS
- Apollo
- VINES
- DECnet
- XNS
- VRF (now in 12.*x*)

For this study guide, we will specifically focus on the IP `ping` command.

User EXEC Mode

The user mode for `ping` is restricted. Only the non-verbose method is allowed for the user level. IP `ping` uses ICMP as the protocol to provide connectivity and reachability messages. It works on a simple principle: An ICMP echo message is sent to the specified IP address. If the address is reachable, the receiving station sends an ICMP echo-reply message back to the sending station.

It is important to be able to decipher the symbols that are echoed to the screen while a ping is taking place. By default and for user mode, five ICMP echo messages are sent. Here are a few samples:

```
Router_A>ping 172.16.1.10
Type escape sequence to abort.
Sending 5, 100-byte ICMP Echoes to 172.16.1.10, timeout is 2 seconds:
!!!!!
Success rate is 100 percent (5/5), round-trip min/avg/max = 1/2/4 ms
Router_A>
Router_A>ping 172.16.2.130
Type escape sequence to abort.
Sending 5, 100-byte ICMP Echoes to 172.16.2.130, timeout is    2 seconds:
.....
Success rate is 0 percent (0/5)
Router_A>
```

It looks good so far, but what do the different characters mean? Table 37.14 defines the two that we have just seen as well as the other possible outputs.

TABLE 37.14 *ping* Character Map

Character	Explanation
!	Received an echo-reply message
.	Timeout
U / H	Destination unreachable
N	Network unreachable
P	Protocol unreachable
Q	Source quench
M	Unable to fragment
A	Administratively denied
?	Unknown packet type

Now that the characters are defined, you can analyze the sample outputs. In the first ping, all five packets received echo-reply messages, which indicates that the host is reachable. Notice that the output gives a success percentage based on the five requests that were sent. It also gives the minimum, average, and maximum response times.

The second ping doesn't look so good. All five requests timed out. This means that each request waited two seconds for a response. When no response was received, a . character was echoed to the screen. It is possible that a request was received, but it was after the two-second waiting period. Either way, the host cannot be considered reachable.

Privileged EXEC Mode

The privileged mode for ping is known as an *extended ping*. This mode allows many options to aid in providing additional detailed information. The functionality of the `ping` command is based on the same technology as for user mode. The extended ping offers options to change some of the ping settings.

The best way to understand it is to see it:

```
Router_B #ping
Protocol [ip]:
Target IP address: 172.16.12.93
Repeat count [5]:
Datagram size [100]:
Timeout in seconds [2]:
Extended commands [n]: y
Source address or interface: 172.16.1.2
```

```
Type of service [0]:
Set DF bit in IP header? [no]:
Validate reply data? [no]:
Data pattern [0xABCD]:
Loose, Strict, Record, Timestamp, Verbose[none]: r
Number of hops [ 9 ]:
Loose, Strict, Record, Timestamp, Verbose[RV]:
Sweep range of sizes [n]:
Type escape sequence to abort.
Sending 5, 100-byte ICMP Echoes to 172.16.12.93, timeout is 2 seconds:
Packet has IP options:  Total option bytes= 39, padded    length=40
 Record route: <*> 0.0.0.0 0.0.0.0 0.0.0.0 0.0.0.0
         0.0.0.0 0.0.0.0 0.0.0.0 0.0.0.0 0.0.0.0
Reply to request 0 (1 ms). Received packet has options
 Total option bytes= 40, padded length=40
 Record route: 172.16.1.2 172.16.0.13 172.16.12.1172.16.12.93
 172.16.0.14 172.16.0.21 172.16.1.2 <*> 0.0.0.0 0.0.0.0
 End of list
Reply to request 1 (4 ms). Received packet has options
 Total option bytes= 40, padded length=40
 Record route: 172.16.1.2 172.16.0.13 172.16.12.1172.16.12.93
 172.16.0.14 172.16.0.21 172.16.1.2 <*> 0.0.0.0 0.0.0.0
 End of list
Reply to request 2 (4 ms). Received packet has options
 Total option bytes= 40, padded length=40
 Record route: 172.16.1.2 172.16.0.13 172.16.12.1 172.16.12.93
 172.16.0.14 172.16.0.21 172.16.1.2 <*> 0.0.0.0 0.0.0.0
End of list
Reply to request 3 (1 ms). Received packet has options
 Total option bytes= 40, padded length=40
 Record route: 172.16.1.2 172.16.0.13 172.16.12.1 172.16.12.93
172.16.0.14 172.16.0.21 172.16.1.2 <*> 0.0.0.0 0.0.0.0
 End of list
Reply to request 4 (1 ms). Received packet has options
 Total option bytes= 40, padded length=40
 Record route: 172.16.1.2 172.16.0.13 172.16.12.1 172.16.12.93 172.16.0.14
➥172.16.0.21 172.16.1.2 <*> 0.0.0.0 0.0.0.0
 End of list
Success rate is 100 percent (5/5), round-trip min/avg/max = 1/2/4 ms
Router_B#
```

If present, the character echoes have the same meaning as listed for the user mode of the `ping` command. In addition, the summary information provided at the end of the extended ping is the same as that of the user mode ping. However, the dialog used in the extended ping is slightly different from that of the user ping. The extended ping mode is accessed by just typing the word `ping`. The default protocol is IP. The next field is the target IP address. The default values are located within the brackets of each dialog question. The repeat count is five ICMP requests. The next field is the datagram size, followed by the timeout.

Additional commands are available by answering **yes** to the extended commands prompt. Extended options include the source IP address (it must be an IP address that is present on the router), type of service, don't fragment bit, data pattern, and header options.

Header options enable the route processor to analyze the packet header. There are five header options:

- Loose
- Strict
- Record
- Timestamp
- Verbose

The Record option records the ICMP packet's route to the destination address; it records up to nine hops. You can see the results of using the Record packet header option in the previous output. The IP addresses are the addresses of the exiting interface. If you follow the route, you can see the packet leave the router and finally get to the destination on the fourth hop. But wait a minute—there are still more addresses. Yes, they are the addresses of the path back to the router. The path is recorded for both directions, not just to the destination.

The final option in the extended ping command allows the router to increment the packet size between 76 bytes and 18,024 bytes. Because it is an Ethernet interface, it does not exceed 1500 bytes.

traceroute Command

The `traceroute` command is used for displaying the packet's path toward its destination. The functionality of the traceroute utility works on error messages that are generated by expired TTL values in the IP packet header. When the TTL value in an IP header reaches 0, the entire packet is discarded. At the same time, the IP host responsible for discarding the packet sends an error message to the source IP address in the header, informing the source that the packet was dropped. The TTL value is decremented by 1 every time the packet transits a router or IP host.

Traceroute capitalizes on this message exchange. When the traceroute function is used, the TTL in the IP header is set to a value of 1. It then sends the packet to the specified destination. Because the next hop decrements the TTL counter to 0, the packet is discarded and a message is sent back to the source address. The traceroute utility records the IP address from the error message and echoes it to the screen. An `nslookup` is performed on the IP address; if a result is received, the DNS name is displayed in addition to the IP address.

The TTL is then incremented to 2 and sent out. The packet transverses the first hop, the TTL is decremented to 1, and the packet is forwarded on to the next hop. When the second hop receives the packet, the TTL is decremented to 0, and the error message is sent to the source address.

This process is followed until the destination host responds or until the TTL is exceeded. By default, the maximum TTL is 30. This means that if the destination host does not respond, the traceroute utility will attempt 30 times. Multiple requests are sent at each attempt, which results in three RTT responses. In addition to the TTL error messages, Port Unreachable (P) messages provide sufficient information for a path to the destination.

Table 37.15 lists the explanation for the response characters available within the traceroute utility.

TABLE 37.15 *traceroute* Response Meanings

Character	Explanation
`xx msec`	The RTT for each packet
`*`	Timeout
`H`	Host unreachable
`U`	Port unreachable
`N`	Network unreachable
`P`	Protocol unreachable
`A`	Administratively denied
`Q`	Source quench
`?`	Unknown packet type

Successful functionality of the `traceroute` command depends on the IP configuration on each host along the path to the destination. It is possible that the IP configuration will not send error messages when the TTL expires, when TTL is not decremented, or when no port unreachable messages are sent. If any of these problems exists, you'll probably get timeout responses.

In addition, it is important to note that not all trace utilities use the same protocol. Cisco routers and some Linux stations use a UDP packet as the probe packet, whereas many Unix and Windows stations use an ICMP packet to probe. Therefore, if you are blocking UDP in a firewall but allowing ICMP, it is possible that a trace from a Cisco device will be blocked, while one from an NT station will get through without difficulty.

User EXEC Mode

The user mode of the `traceroute` command allows only the default options when using the command. Here is a sample output:

```
Router_B>traceroute www.netscape.com
Translating "www.netscape.com"...domain server (172.16.4.2)    [OK]
Type escape sequence to abort.
Tracing the route to www-ld1.netscape.com (207.200.75.200)
1 172.16.2.1 0 msec 0 msec 0 msec
```

```
2 172.16.4.53 [AS 209] 12 msec 8 msec 8 msec
   3 den-core-02.inet.qwest.net (205.171.16.137) [AS 209]     12 msec
     12 msec 8 msec
   4 sfo-core-02.inet.qwest.net (205.171.4.1) [AS 209]     32 msec
     36 msec 36 msec
   5 sjo-core-01.inet.qwest.net (205.171.4.101) [AS 209]     36 msec
     36 msec 40 msec
   6 sjo-core-03.inet.qwest.net (205.171.22.6) [AS 209]     36 msec
     36 msec 36 msec
   7 sjo-edge-05.inet.qwest.net (205.171.22.50) [AS 209]     36 msec
     40 msec 36 msec
   8 205.171.48.154 [AS 209] 36 msec 36 msec 36 msec
   9 h-207-200-69-241.netscape.com (207.200.69.241)  [AS 6992] 40 msec
     40 msec 36 msec
  10 www-ld1.netscape.com (207.200.75.200) [AS 6992] 36 msec     36 msec 36 msec
Router_B>
```

As you can see, the `nslookup` for the first two hops failed. The RTTs for the three probes follow. The times increment as the packet moves closer to the destination address. In addition to the DNS entry, IP address, and RTT, the AS number is also listed.

Here is another sample that includes timeouts and administratively denied probes:

```
Router_B>traceroute www.novell.com
Translating "www.novell.com"...domain server (172.16.4.2)     [OK]
Type escape sequence to abort.
Tracing the route to www.novell.com (137.65.2.5)
1 172.16.1.13 0 msec 0 msec 0 msec
   2 205.171.48.53 [AS 209] 8 msec 8 msec 12 msec
   3 den-core-01.inet.qwest.net (205.171.16.109) [AS 209]
 12 msec 8 msec 12 msec
   4 den-brdr-01.inet.qwest.net (205.171.16.114) [AS 209]
 8 msec 12 msec 12 msec
 5 s2-0-0.den-bb1.cerf.net (134.24.112.77) [AS 1740] 8
 msec     16 msec 12 msec
   6 s10-0-0.slc-bb1.cerf.net (134.24.46.98) [AS 1740]
 88 msec 84 msec 84 msec
   7 novell-gw.slc-bb1.cerf.net (134.24.116.54) [AS 1740]
 84 msec 84 msec 84 msec
   8 134.24.116.58 [AS 1740] 84 msec 84 msec 84 msec
   9  *  *  !A
Router_B>
```

Here, the probe made it to the destination address, but instead of receiving a TTL Expired or Port Unreachable message, we get an Administratively Denied message.

Privileged EXEC Mode

The privileged mode has options that are similar to the ping privileged mode. The dialog contains several prompts that change the traceroute settings. The default settings are listed in the brackets. They can be selected by pressing Enter, or changed by substituting a new value. We'll now look at the privileged dialog, and then we can explain each of the prompts:

```
Router_B#traceroute
Protocol [ip]:
Target IP address: 137.65.2.11
Source address: 172.16.2.9
Numeric display [n]:
Timeout in seconds [3]:
Probe count [3]:
Minimum Time to Live [1]:
Maximum Time to Live [30]:
Port Number [33434]:
Loose, Strict, Record, Timestamp, Verbose[none]:
Type escape sequence to abort.
Tracing the route to www.novell.com (137.65.2.11)
1 172.16.0.1 0 msec 0 msec 0 msec
   2 205.171.48.53 [AS 209] 8 msec 8 msec 12 msec
   3 den-core-02.inet.qwest.net (205.171.16.137) [AS 209]
  12 msec 8 msec 12 msec
   4 den-brdr-01.inet.qwest.net (205.171.16.142) [AS 209]
  8 msec 12 msec 12 msec
   5 s2-0-0.den-bb1.cerf.net (134.24.112.77) [AS 1740]
  12 msec 12 msec 12 msec
   6 s10-0-0.slc-bb1.cerf.net (134.24.46.98) [AS 1740]
  84 msec 84 msec 88 msec
   7 novell-gw.slc-bb1.cerf.net (134.24.116.54) [AS 1740]
  84 msec 84 msec 84 msec
   8 134.24.116.58 [AS 1740] 84 msec 88 msec 84 msec
   9 134.24.116.58 [AS 1740] !A  *  *
Router_B#
```

Here's what the prompts mean:

Target IP address The IP address of the destination host.

Source address The IP address present on the router. This is used to select an address that is not directly connected to the next hop.

Numeric display Disables `nslookup` on the IP address. Consequently, if this option is chosen, only the IP address is displayed.

Timeout The threshold for response times for the returning error message.

Probe count The number of probes sent at each TTL level.

Minimum TTL The numerical value for the first TTL level.

Maximum TTL The maximum TTL value; an equivalent of 30 hops is the default and is the highest value possible.

Port number The port number used by UDP that creates a Port Unreachable error message.

Loose source routing Specifies nodes that must be included in the path to the destination.

Strict source routing Specifies the only nodes allowed in the path to the destination.

Record Specifies the number of hops for the verbose path to display.

Timestamp Specifies the number of timestamps to display.

Verbose Automatically selected if any of the previous options are selected.

LAN Connectivity Problems

Troubleshooting LAN connectivity was covered in part through the discussion of troubleshooting Ethernet problems in Chapter 36, "Protocol Attributes." Those are LAN technologies. This section deals with host connectivity in relation to Cisco routers.

Obtaining an IP Address

Hosts can obtain an IP address in one of two ways: statically or dynamically. Once an IP address is configured on a host, it is assigned to that host until the administrator removes it. If the address, mask, and gateway were configured correctly, and it is not a duplicate IP address, the host will not have any problems connecting to the LAN that could be attributed to its IP address and configuration.

Two protocols are used to allow hosts to obtain their IP address dynamically: *Bootstrap Protocol (BootP)* and *Dynamic Host Configuration Protocol (DHCP)*.

DHCP

DHCP is a superset of the Bootstrap Protocol (BootP). This means that it uses the same protocol structure as BootP, but it has enhancements added. Both of these protocols use servers that dynamically configure clients when requested. The two major enhancements are address pools and lease times.

The process for DHCP differs somewhat from BootP. DHCP clients broadcast a Discover message that contains the MAC address, host name, and other options. The broadcast is sent from UDP port 67 to UDP port 68. Servers respond by sending from UDP port 68 destined to UDP port 67. When the server sends the response, it is called an Offer. The Offer includes the information sent in the client's Discover request, IP configuration information, and lease information. If the client chooses to accept the offer, it sends a Request that includes the Offer information as well as the original Discover information. If the DHCP server is still able to grant the Offer configuration, it will send an acknowledgment to the client. If it cannot grant the Offer, it sends a Decline message to the client. Figure 37.2 gives a clearer picture of these transactions.

FIGURE 37.2 DHCP client/server sequence

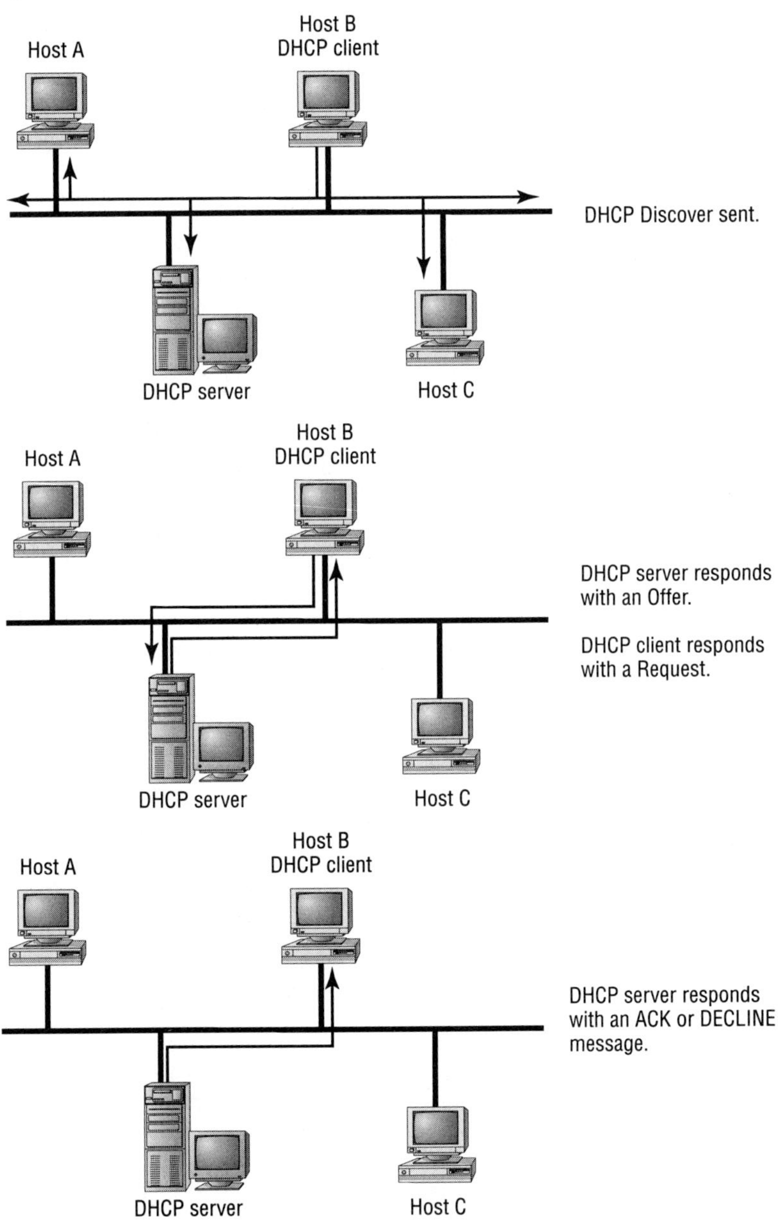

Lease information is one of the enhancements of DHCP. It allows an IP address to be assigned for a preconfigured amount of time. When the lease expires, the IP address is added back to the available address pool. Each host tries to renew the lease when the time is half-expired.

BootP

The BootP process is much simpler. When a host tries to obtain an IP address, it sends a bootrequest, which contains the client's MAC address. When the BootP server receives the request, it checks its database for the MAC address. If it finds an entry, then a bootreply, which contains the IP address and other configuration settings, is sent. If the BootP server does not find the client's MAC address in its database, it does not respond.

Helper Addresses

As mentioned, DHCP and BootP messages are broadcast messages. Therefore, by default, the router will not forward them. In small environments, the solution to this is to have a DHCP or BootP server on each segment. However, this solution does not scale well as the size of a network grows. In these situations, you can use the `ip helper-address` *`address`* command on the router. The IP address referenced in the command is the address of the centralized DHCP or BootP server.

By adding this command to each interface on which you have DHCP or BootP clients, all DHCP and BootP broadcasts will be forwarded via unicast to the DHCP or BootP server. This server then responds to the requesting station via the router in the form of a unicast packet. In addition, if there are redundant DHCP or BootP servers, the command could be put on the interface multiple times, once for each server. In this manner, if one of the servers goes down, the others are still available to handle requests.

One downside to the `ip helper-address` *`address`* command is that after it is enabled, by default, it not only forwards DHCP/BootP UDP broadcasts, it also forwards UDP broadcasts destined for the following ports:

- Time service (port 37)
- IEN-116 Name Service (port 42)
- TACACS service (port 49)
- Domain Name System (port 53)
- Trivial File Transfer Protocol (TFTP) (port 69)
- NetBIOS Name Server (port 137)
- NetBIOS Datagram Server (port 138)

In order to only forward DHCP/BootP broadcasts, you can use the global configuration command `no ip forward-protocol udp` *`port`* for each of the services in the preceding list.

DHCP Services on a Router

Beginning with IOS 12.0(1) T, you can also configure a router as a DHCP server. In contrast to the helper address, which forwards requests to an external DHCP server, configuring a router as a DHCP server allows the router to service DHCP requests locally. The router becomes a full-featured DHCP server and can provide DHCP addresses, from separate IP address pools to any device on a connected interface.

Troubleshooting DHCP and BootP

Because these protocols are dynamic, there may be times when they fail or when an end user is unable to connect to the network. If you have a protocol analyzer, you could capture the DHCP and BootP sequences to make sure that the clients and servers are talking.

You can also use the show commands available to aid in troubleshooting DHCP on Cisco routers, as follows:

```
Router_C#show dhcp server
DHCP Proxy Client Status:
   DHCP server: ANY (255.255.255.255)
    Leases:   0
    Offers:   0       Requests: 0     Acks: 0     Naks: 0
    Declines: 0       Releases: 0     Bad:  0
Router_C#
```

If the router is configured to use DHCP, you can also get information regarding the lease by issuing the show dhcp lease command.

ARP

Address Resolution Protocol (ARP) maps layer 2 MAC addresses to layer 3 IP addresses. An ARP table is built on the router through the exchange of ARP requests and replies. Here is a sample ARP table:

```
Router_C>show arp
Protocol  Address       Age (min)  Hardware Addr   Type   Interface
Internet  172.16.60.1     -        0010.7bd9.2881  ARPA   Ethernet0/1
Internet  172.16.50.2     -        0010.7bd9.2880  ARPA   Ethernet0/0
Internet  172.16.50.1   108        0000.0c09.99cc  ARPA   Ethernet0/0
Router_C>
```

Notice the Age field in the ARP table. ARP entries are stored or cached for future use. This allows a router to look up the MAC address instead of having to send a broadcast to learn it again. However, the ARP entry does not stay in the table indefinitely.

Several problems could occur if a MAC address were permanently mapped to an IP address. You learned that DHCP can assign a given IP address to any requesting host, if it is available. In this scenario, the IP address could be assigned to different MAC addresses. If this were to happen, any existing entry in an ARP table would be invalidated. If an NIC is replaced on a host, the MAC address is changed as well. If the ARP cache was not cleared and updated, the IP address would still be mapped to the old MAC address. You get the picture. These mappings are not permanent, so the cache entries cannot be permanent, either.

Sometimes difficulties occur within a network because of ARP problems. The best way to troubleshoot these issues is by looking at the ARP table on the router with the `show arp` command and (if necessary) using the `debug arp` tool. Problems can fixed by simply clearing the ARP cache and allowing the router to rebuild the table.

It is also worthy of note that the last ARP reply that is received is the one that is entered in the ARP cache. Therefore, if you are looking at an ARP entry that is changing values, it could indicate a duplicate address conflict, or possibly signals that someone is trying to hack into your system by spoofing an address!

Proxy ARP

By default, Cisco router interfaces have *proxy ARP* enabled. Proxy ARP, defined in RFC 1027, aids in routing packets from workstations that have no default gateway set or that have misconfigured subnet information. Specifically, a Cisco router will reply to an ARP request with its own MAC address if the following conditions are met:

- Proxy ARP is enabled on the interface on which the ARP was seen.
- The ARP request is for an address not on the local subnet.
- The router has a route for that subnet in its routing table.
- All routes in the routing table for the requested address are out an interface other than the interface on which the ARP was seen.

The host that originated the ARP request will then send packets destined for this address to the router, which will then forward them on to their destination. If you want to disable proxy ARP on an interface, you can use the `no ip proxy-arp` command.

Though there are a couple uses for proxy ARP, most are to overcome the requirement of "standard" network configurations. For example, proxy ARP allows low for mismatched router/workstation subnet masking that may be required for the routing protocol you are using. Or it can be used as a safeguard to enable functionality to users not well versed in the world of networking.

Sample TCP Connection

In order to properly troubleshoot a connection issue, it is important to clearly understand how this connection is set up from the start. TCP is a connection-oriented protocol. As such, before data can be exchanged, a connection needs to be established. This connection is established by the *TCP three-way handshake*. To better explain exactly how this works, we'll give you an example. Figure 37.3 has a graphical representation of this example.

Assume that two computers on the same segment—Computer A and B—have just been powered on. A user on Computer A wants to initiate a Telnet session to Computer B. Computer A has an IP address of 192.168.1.100 and B has an address of 192.168.1.101. To keep things simple for this example, assume that the user is telnetting to computer B by its IP address, not its name.

When the user presses Enter on the Telnet request, Computer A first looks at its ARP cache and sees if it has a MAC address associated with the IP address of B, 192.168.1.101. Because this computer was just powered on, it does not. Computer A now checks to verify that Computer B is on the subnet. Since it is, Computer A sends out an ARP request for the MAC address of 192.168.1.101. If Computer B were on a different subnet, Computer A would have sent out an ARP request for the default gateway instead.

FIGURE 37.3 Sample connection scenario

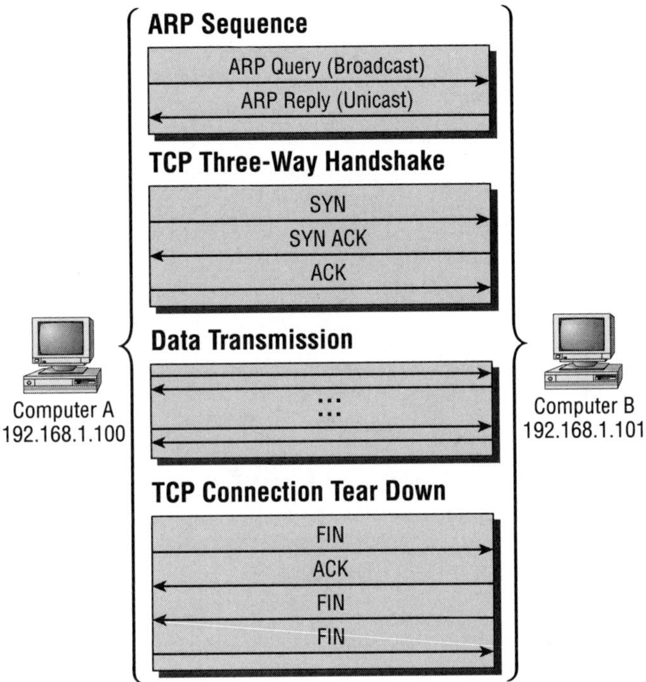

ARP requests are layer 2 broadcasts, so all computers connected to the subnet, including Computer B, receive this ARP request. Computer B sees that the ARP is for its IP address and responds directly to Computer A with its MAC address. Computer B also gleaned Computer A's IP address and MAC information from the ARP request and added this information to its own ARP cache.

Now that Computer A has the IP and MAC information, the TCP three-way handshake can begin. The start of this process is Computer A sending a SYN (synchronize) packet to Computer B on TCP port 23, letting Computer B know that Computer A wants to set up a connection. Computer B then responds with a SYN ACK (synchronize and acknowledgment) packet. Computer A responds to the SYN ACK message from B with an ACK (acknowledgment) packet.

At this point, the TCP session is set up and the Telnet session data can flow normally between A and B. Once the user is done with the Telnet session, the connection needs to be torn down. In order to do this, Computer A sends a FIN (Finished or Finalize) packet to Computer B, and B responds with an ACK packet. Communication from A to B has now been torn down. However, B also needs to indicate that it has finished with the connection as well. Computer B sends a FIN packet to Computer A to do this. Computer A responds with an ACK packet, and the connection is terminated.

IP Access Lists

Troubleshooting access lists is a very simple task when you understand how they are written and when you are familiar with the protocols that can be managed by using extended access lists.

Standard Access Lists

A *standard access list* is a sequential list of Permit or Deny statements that are based on the source IP address of a packet. When a packet reaches a router, the packet has to follow a particular procedure based on whether the packet is trying to enter or leave an interface. If there is an access list on the interface, the packet must go through every line in it until the packet matches the specified criteria. If the packet goes through the entire list without a match, it is dropped. For the packet to be forwarded, there has to be a Permit statement at the end of the list allowing that, or else the packet will simply be dropped.

In Cisco IOS, there's an implied Deny statement at the end of the access list, so if the purpose of your access list is to deny a few criteria but forward everything else, you must include a Permit statement as the final line of the access list. However, you do not have to end the access list with a Deny statement if the list's purpose is to permit only certain criteria and drop the rest—this is automatically understood.

Figure 37.4 shows a flowchart that describes the steps taken when a packet enters or leaves an interface.

FIGURE 37.4 Flowchart process of a standard access list

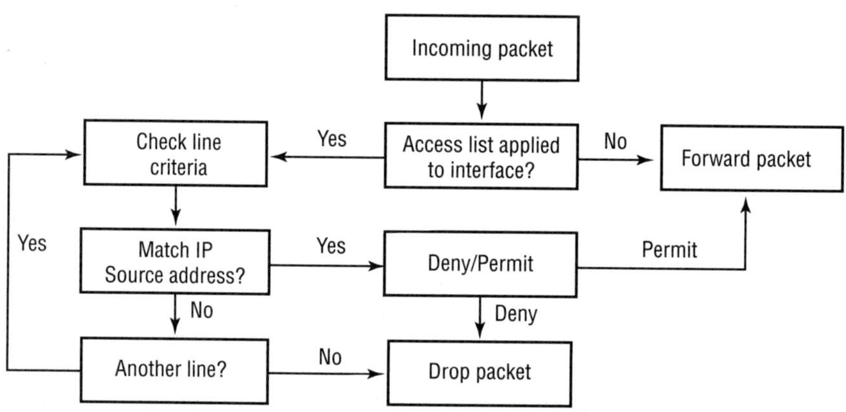

Stepping through the flowchart, you can see that the packet arrives at the specific interface through which it must enter or leave. The router's first step is to check whether there is an access list applied to the interface. If so, router steps through each line of the access list until the packet's source address matches one of the source addresses listed. If a packet's information matches multiple lines in the access list, the first match will be the one used, whether that line is a Permit or a Deny. If the packet fails to match any of the source addresses, it is denied. However, if the packet's source address does find a match in the list, the packet is then subjected to any condition applied on that line of the access list. The two conditional possibilities are to deny the packet or permit it. When a packet is denied, it is dropped; when it is permitted, it is forwarded to the next hop.

Exiting packets are first routed to the exiting interface and then verified by the access list, which determines whether the packet will be dropped or forwarded through the interface. Incoming packets arrive from the forwarding machine or router and are then checked against the access list. If the packet is permitted by the list, the packet is accepted through the interface and forwarded to the exit interface. This is important information to understand when troubleshooting any access list. The situation depends on whether the packet is incoming or outgoing, so you can tell which interfaces to look at and analyze access lists for.

Troubleshooting standard access lists is very simple because they are based on only one criterion—the source IP address. The basic method of troubleshooting an access list is to read it line by line and analyze it to determine whether any lines are out of order or typed incorrectly.

If, after analyzing the access list, you cannot see any problems but the problem is still occurring, you can temporarily remove the access list from the interface to see what effect this has on the problem. If the problem disappears after the access list is removed, something is wrong with the access list and it needs to be fixed. If the problem does not go away with the removal of the access list from the interface, you can eliminate the access list as a possible cause.

The commands used to view IP access lists are `show running-config`, `show startup-config`, and `show ip access-list` *`access-list number`*. These commands provide the information regarding each line of the access list. In addition to these commands, you can issue the `show ip interface` command, which provides you with information about which access lists are applied to the interface. Here is a sample output from the `show ip interface` command:

```
Router_B>show ip interface
Ethernet0 is up, line protocol is up
  Internet address is 172.16.50.1/24
  Broadcast address is 255.255.255.255
  Address determined by non-volatile memory
  MTU is 1500 bytes
  Helper address is not set
  Directed broadcast forwarding is disabled
  Multicast reserved groups joined: 224.0.0.10
  Outgoing access list is not set
  Inbound  access list is not set
  Proxy ARP is enabled
  Security level is default
  Split horizon is enabled
  ICMP redirects are always sent
  ICMP unreachables are always sent
  ICMP mask replies are never sent
  IP fast switching is enabled
  IP fast switching on the same interface is disabled
  IP multicast fast switching is disabled
```

```
Router Discovery is disabled
IP output packet accounting is disabled
IP access violation accounting is disabled
TCP/IP header compression is disabled
Probe proxy name replies are disabled
Gateway Discovery is disabled
Policy routing is disabled
```

As you can see from this output, interface Ethernet0 does not have any access lists applied to it.

Extended Access Lists

Extended access lists offer filtering on port numbers, session layer protocols, and destination addresses, in addition to filtering by source address. Although these extended filtering features make this kind of access list much more powerful, they can also make the list more difficult to troubleshoot because of the potential complexity.

A packet must follow the same basic process when arriving at an interface with an extended access list applied to it as it does when confronting an interface with an applied standard list. Figure 37.5 illustrates the procedure that a packet follows when being compared against an extended list—the only difference is the much greater scope of criteria that are specifiable.

FIGURE 37.5 Packet processing through an extended access list

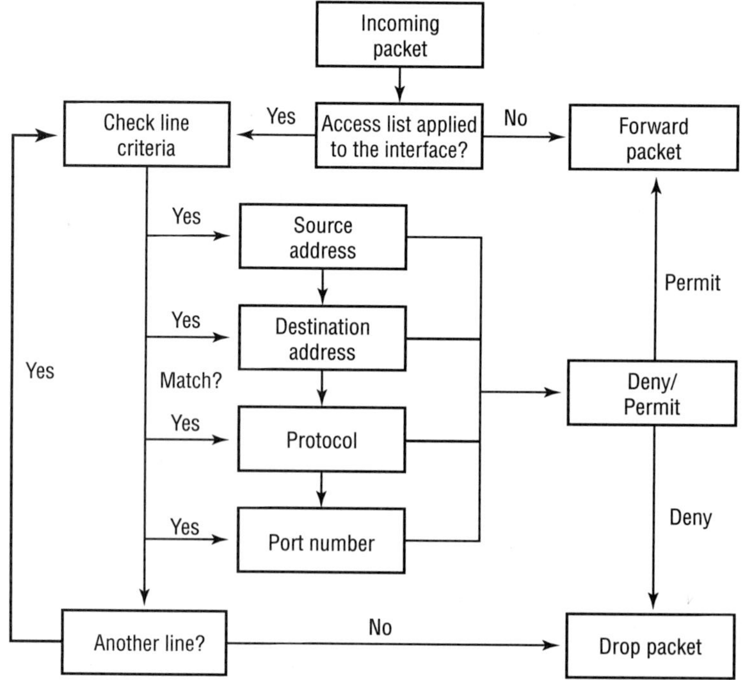

In addition to correctly analyzing the lines of the access list, you must know which way the list is applied to the interface. By conceptualizing the packet flow through an interface and the subsequent access list, you will be successful in troubleshooting access list–related problems. Here is a sample extended access list:

```
access-list 101 deny   tcp any any eq chargen
access-list 101 deny   tcp any any eq daytime
access-list 101 deny   tcp any any eq discard
access-list 101 deny   tcp any any eq echo
access-list 101 deny   tcp any any eq finger
access-list 101 deny   tcp any any eq kshell
access-list 101 deny   tcp any any eq klogin
access-list 101 deny   tcp any any eq 37
access-list 101 deny   tcp any any eq uucp
access-list 101 deny   udp any any eq biff
access-list 101 deny   udp any any eq bootpc
access-list 101 deny   udp any any eq bootps
access-list 101 deny   udp any any eq discard
access-list 101 deny   udp any any eq netbios-dgm
access-list 101 deny   udp any any eq netbios-ns
access-list 101 permit udp host 172.16.10.2 any eq snmp
access-list 101 deny   udp any any eq snmp
access-list 101 permit udp host 172.16.10.2 any eq
   snmptrap
access-list 101 deny   udp any any eq snmptrap
access-list 101 deny   udp any any eq who
access-list 101 permit udp 172.16.50.0 0.0.0.255 any eq
   xdmcp
access-list 101 deny   udp any any eq xdmcp
access-list 101 permit tcp any any
access-list 101 permit udp any any
access-list 101 permit icmp any any
access-list 101 permit igmp any any
access-list 101 permit eigrp any any
```

As you can see, there are many line options that need to be understood when troubleshooting extended access lists. Not only do you have to understand the significance of the line, but you have to be familiar with the protocol you are troubleshooting. If necessary, debug options can be used in conjunction with access lists to isolate and diagnose network failures.

Named Access Lists

Beginning with IOS 11.2, in addition to the numbered standard and extended access lists, you can also use *named access lists*. Named access lists can be either standard or extended. Though the fundamental concepts of named and numbered access lists are the same, there are a couple major differences between the two.

The first is that a named access list has a logical name, not an arbitrary number like its numbered counterpart. In addition, if you want to remove a single line from a named access list, you can. To accomplish this same function with a numbered access list, you must remove and reapply the entire list. Finally, a named access list does not have the access list name at the beginning of each line, thus making it slightly easier to read. Instead, the name is shown at the top of the access list, and then the individual Permit/Deny statements follow. For example, if the access list from the preceding "Extended Access List" section were converted to a named list, it would look like the following:

```
ip access-list extended ENGINEERING-DEPT-IN
 deny   tcp any any eq chargen
 deny   tcp any any eq daytime
 deny   tcp any any eq discard
 deny   tcp any any eq echo
 deny   tcp any any eq finger
 deny   tcp any any eq kshell
 deny   tcp any any eq klogin
 deny   tcp any any eq 37
 deny   tcp any any eq uucp
 deny   udp any any eq biff
 deny   udp any any eq bootpc
 deny   udp any any eq bootps
 deny   udp any any eq discard
 deny   udp any any eq netbios-dgm
 deny   udp any any eq netbios-ns
 permit udp host 172.16.10.2 any eq snmp
 deny   udp any any eq snmp
 permit udp host 172.16.10.2 any eq snmptrap
 deny   udp any any eq snmptrap
 deny   udp any any eq who
 permit udp 172.16.50.0 0.0.0.255 any eq xdmcp
 deny   udp any any eq xdmcp
 permit tcp any any
 permit udp any any
 permit icmp any any
 permit igmp any any
 permit eigrp any any
```

Note the keyword `extended` in the first line of the access list. This denotes the list as an extended access list. If it were a standard access list, this keyword would have been `standard`.

Although there are some differences between named and numbered access lists, the overall functionality remains the same. If a named list is a standard access list, the flowchart in Figure 37.4 applies to the logical flow of data. If it is an extended access list, refer to Figure 37.5. As such, the restriction on standard access lists' filtering only on source address still applies to a named list. Another important difference between a named and numbered access list is that individual lines of a named list can be removed for editing; to edit a line in a numbered list, however, the whole list needs to be removed and readded.

Summary

When used properly, the `show` and `debug` commands are powerful tools for troubleshooting a problem or just for researching the performance of a router. However, these commands—especially the `debug` commands—should be used with care, as they can substantially increase the load on the router. Therefore, when debugging, it is advisable to use access lists to limit the information that is being debugged.

In addition to the `show` and `debug` commands, logging is another method to determine whether there is a problem on the router. Logging information can be sent to the console, the terminal monitor, an internal buffer on the router, and/or an external Syslog server. In addition to the various locations that can be used to view logging information, the logging messages can also be viewed based on the severity of the problem.

Other troubleshooting commands, such as core dumps, `ping`, and `traceroute`, can be used to further define an issue. The `exception dump` command causes the router to write to a file the information that is in the memory at the time of a crash. This file can later be used by TAC to help isolate the cause of the problem. The `ping` and `traceroute` commands can be used to verify the reachability of hosts as well as the path taken to get to the hosts.

In order to effectively troubleshoot network problems, an engineer needs to understand how the protocols in the network work. This includes the ARP protocol, the TCP connection and teardown sequence, as well as the functions of DHCP and BootP.

IP access lists come in multiple varieties—named, numbered, standard, and extended—and all use the same basic structure and have the same basic function. Primarily used for protecting networks from unwanted traffic, the access list is read from the top down. If at any point the packet matches a line in the list, whether this line is a Permit or a Deny, the list is exited and the associated function is performed on the packet. In addition to looking at packet flow, access lists are also used for many other tasks such as restricting routing updates, limiting access to telnet sessions to the router, and limiting SNMP access to the router.

Exam Essentials

Know the *show* and *debug* commands that are available and how to interpret the output. The CCNP Support exam covers several `show` and `debug` commands. In addition to knowing the commands, you should also know how to limit the output of the `debug` command using access lists.

Know and understand the logging levels on a router. The logging levels are debugging, informational, notifications, warnings, errors, critical, alerts, and emergencies. You should be able to determine the logging levels for each logging destination on a router.

Know how to use the *ping* and *traceroute* commands. The `ping` command is used to test for reachability and connectivity throughout a network. The `traceroute` command is used for displaying the packet's path toward its destination. Knowing how to use the commands includes knowing the extended `ping` and `traceroute` options available under privileged mode.

Understand how DHCP and BootP function. DHCP and BootP are broadcast messages; DHCP is a superset of BootP. Know the specific functions of each and understand the similarities and differences between the two. Also, be familiar with the function of a helper address on a router.

Understand what an ARP broadcast is and how it is used in networking. ARP stands for Address Resolution Protocol. ARP provides a table of information that the router can look up, instead of having to broadcast for information. Be sure you also understand the proxy ARP protocol.

Understand the TCP three-way handshake. TCP uses the three-way handshake—SYN, SYN ACK, ACK—to establish a connection. To tear down a connection, the packet sequence is FIN, ACK, FIN ACK.

Know the different types of access lists and their functions. The two types of IP access lists are standard and extended. Both types can be used as either named or numbered lists.

TCP/IP Routing Protocol Troubleshooting

THE CCNP EXAM TOPICS COVERED IN THIS CHAPTER INCLUDE THE FOLLOWING:

- ✓ Verify network connectivity.
- ✓ Use the optimal troubleshooting approach in resolving network problems.
- ✓ Minimize downtime during troubleshooting.

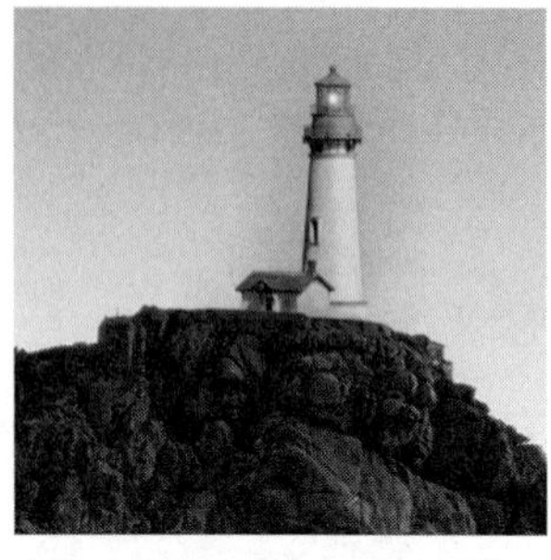

This chapter is dedicated to covering essential skills and tools for TCP/IP routing protocol troubleshooting. Starting with a description of default gateways and the difference between static and dynamic routing, specifics on troubleshooting the different routing protocols will be discussed. These routing protocols include RIP, IGRP, EIGRP, OSPF, and BGP. In addition to examining the routing protocols themselves, we will review the subject of redistribution and how to filter information being passed from one protocol to another.

In addition to covering detailed problem-solving techniques, we have included quick-reference summary charts at the end of the chapter that summarize information provided in both this chapter and Chapter 37, "Cisco Diagnostic Commands and TCP/IP Troubleshooting." These tables help to quickly associate a cause with many TCP/IP symptoms.

Default Gateways

The capability of a router to route or forward data depends on its knowledge of the world around it. This knowledge comes in the form of a route table. The route table is populated by the router's own networks, as well as by advertisements received from neighboring routers. This will be covered in detail in the upcoming section on static and dynamic routing.

What happens if a router doesn't have a route to a destination? There are two possibilities. If the router is configured to do so, it will send the packet to a neighboring router that is considered the default gateway, with the hope that the default gateway will know where to send the packet. If the router is not configured to take this action, it will simply drop the packet.

How do you configure a router to send packets to a neighbor without a route? That's where the gateway of last resort comes in. A gateway of last resort tells the router that if it doesn't have a route to a given network, it should send the packet out the specified interface, or default gateway.

The purpose of a default gateway is somewhat of a last-ditch effort to forward a packet. Look at Figure 38.1. In this example, Router A receives from Host A a packet that is destined for network 10.1.2.0. The problem is that Router A does not have a route for 10.1.2.0. The only chance of getting the packet forwarded to network 10.1.2.0 is to send it to Router B and hope that Router B has a route to network 10.1.2.0. Router A considers Router B as its default gateway and so sends the packet to Router B. For this example, assume that Router B does have the route and sends the packet on its way.

TCP/IP hosts also have default gateways set. If the default gateway for a router or a host is configured improperly, data will not be routed. Default gateways are used on TCP/IP hosts so that they don't have to keep individual route tables. All hosts need to point to a router on the same network in order to be used as the default gateway.

FIGURE 38.1 Default gateways

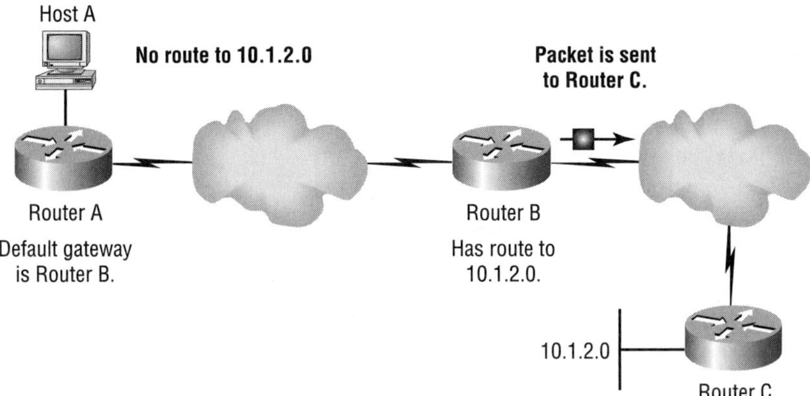

When the default gateway is not working properly, whether it is on a host or on a router, the problem is likely caused by incorrect configuration. As you remember from Chapter 35, "End-System Documentation and Troubleshooting," to check for proper configuration on Windows, issue the `ipconfig /all` command from a DOS prompt. As a refresher, here is a sample output from that command:

```
1 Ethernet adapter :

        Description . . . . . . . . : ELPC3R Ethernet Adapter
        Physical Address. . . . . . : 00-A0-24-A5-06-57
        DHCP Enabled. . . . . . . . : No
        IP Address. . . . . . . . . : 172.16.50.130
        Subnet Mask . . . . . . . . : 255.255.255.0
        Default Gateway . . . . . . : 172.16.50.1
        Primary WINS Server . . . . :
        Secondary WINS Server . . . :
        Lease Obtained. . . . . . . :
        Lease Expires . . . . . . . :

C:\WINDOWS>
```

The way to check for a default gateway on a Cisco router is to use the `show ip route` command. The output follows:

```
Router_C#show ip route
Codes: C - connected, S - static, I - IGRP, R - RIP, M -    mobile, B - BGP
    D - EIGRP, EX - EIGRP external, O - OSPF, IA - OSPF
    inter area
```

```
    E1 - OSPF external type 1, E2 - OSPF external type 2,
    E - EGP
    i - IS-IS, L1 - IS-IS level-1, L2 - IS-IS level-2, *
    - candidate default
       U - per-user static route

Gateway of last resort is 172.16.50.2 to network 10.1.2.0

     172.16.0.0/16 is variably subnetted, 2 subnets, 2
     masks
C       172.16.50.0/24 is directly connected, Ethernet0/0
D       172.16.30.4/30 [90/2195456] via 172.16.50.1, 00:00:18, Ethernet0/0
Router_C#

Router_B#show ip route
Codes: C - connected, S - static, I - IGRP, R - RIP, M - mobile, B - BGP
    D - EIGRP, EX - EIGRP external, O - OSPF, IA - OSPF
       inter area
    N1 - OSPF NSSA external type 1, N2 - OSPF NSSA
    external type 2
     E1 - OSPF external type 1, E2 - OSPF external type 2,
    E - EGP
     i - IS-IS, L1 - IS-IS level-1, L2 - IS-IS level-2, *
    - candidate default
       U - per-user static route, o - ODR

Gateway of last resort is 172.16.50.2 to network 0.0.0.0

     172.16.0.0/16 is variably subnetted, 2 subnets, 2 masks
C       172.16.50.0/24 is directly connected, Ethernet0
C       172.16.30.4/30 is directly connected, Serial0
S*   0.0.0.0/0 [1/0] via 172.16.50.2
Router_B#
```

The difference between these two examples is that one was dynamically set by using the `ip default-network` command and the other is set by using a static route. Both methods end with the same results. If Router B does not have a route for a requested destination, it forwards the packet to the next hop of 172.16.50.2.

As stated earlier, having a default gateway configured is very important. The `ping` and `traceroute` commands can be used to isolate default gateway problems. When the router uses a dynamic method of selecting a default gateway, there's a greater possibility that it may fail.

Static and Dynamic Routing

Static routing depends solely on the manual input of routes. If you do not want to enable a routing protocol on the router, you can manually enter all the routes that you believe will be necessary; for everything else, the default gateway is used. This is a very cumbersome and poor way to configure a router. Static routes are only used locally and are not advertised to neighboring routers unless they are redistributed into a routing protocol session.

Dynamic routing is based on active routing protocols that share route information with one another. When a destination is no longer reachable, the route is removed from the routing table and the change is propagated throughout the network. If a new destination becomes available, the router adds the information into the route table and propagates the change throughout the network.

This dynamic approach is much better than static routes. When there is failure of a host that has been entered in the route table via a static route, the route can remain in the route table. If this static route is redistributed, other routers would still learn the route and send traffic there. The result is that packets reaching the router with the static address are dropped.

By issuing the `show ip route` command, you can tell which routes are learned dynamically and which are learned statically. Here is an example:

```
Router_B>show ip route
Codes:  C-  connected, S- static, I- IGRP, R - RIP, M -    mobile, B - BGP
    D - EIGRP, EX - EIGRP external, O - OSPF, IA - OSPF
    inter area
    N1 - OSPF NSSA external type 1, N2 - OSPF NSSA
    external type 2
       E1 - OSPF external type 1, E2 - OSPF external type
       2, E - EGP
       i - IS-IS, L1 - IS-IS level-1, L2 - IS-IS level-2,
       *    - candidate default
       U - per-user static route, o - ODR

Gateway of last resort is 172.16.50.2 to network 0.0.0.0

     172.16.0.0/16 is variably subnetted, 3 subnets, 2
     masks
C       172.16.50.0/24 is directly connected, Ethernet0
D       172.16.60.0/24 [90/2195456] via 172.16.50.2, 00:31:39, Ethernet0
C       172.16.30.4/30 is directly connected, Serial0
S*      0.0.0.0/0 [1/0] via 172.16.50.2
Router_B>
```

The S indicates that the route is a static route. The other routes are either directly connected or learned via a routing protocol—in this case, EIGRP.

Troubleshooting RIP

Routing Information Protocol (RIP) was first designed for Xerox. The protocol, known as *routed*, was later used in Unix. Thereafter, RIP was implemented as a TCP/IP routing protocol. RIP is used by most versions of Novell NetWare for routing. Other protocols have been derived from RIP.

RIP is a distance-vector routing protocol. The metric used by RIP is the *hop count*, which specifies the number of steps or nodes that a packet must transit in order to reach the destination host.

RIP's major drawback is that it has a hop-count limit: the packet can travel a maximum of 15 hops. If the route to the destination exceeds 15 hops, the destination is tagged as unreachable. This is good for small networks because it helps prevent the count-to-infinity in a routing loop, but it is inefficient for today's Internet.

Now that you know a little about how RIP works, look at the packet structure in Figure 38.2. The packet is 24 bytes long. RIP uses five parameters to define packet information. The packet is divided into nine fields, and zeros are used to pad the packet to the full 24 bytes.

FIGURE 38.2 RIP packet structure

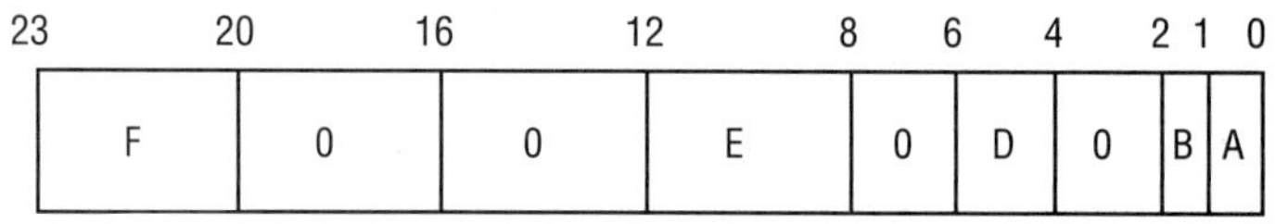

23 20 16 12 8 6 4 2 1 0

F	0	0	E	0	D	0	B	A

Table 38.1 shows a legend of the five parameters used within the RIP packet. As you can see in Figure 38.2, some of the fields are empty; they are just padded with zeros.

TABLE 38.1 RIP Parameters

Parameter Key	Parameter	Description
A	Command	Identifies the packet as a request (value = 1) or a response (value = 2). Requests tell the receiving router to send its route table information. Response packets include the route table information.
B	Version number	Specifies the version of RIP being used.
D	Address family identifier	Address family type. This means which protocol is carrying the RIP packet.
E	Address	The 32-bit IP address.
F	Metric	The hop count to the destination system.

RIP version 1 is a classful protocol, which means it doesn't include any subnet information about the network with route information. However, RIP version 2 is classless, allowing it to function in environments using variable-length subnet masking (VLSM).

RIP-1 and RIP-2

The original version of RIP (RIP-1) had several limitations that restricted its use and scalability. Problems such as the frequent routing updates and limited hop count needed to be overcome. RIP uses UDP broadcasts to flood route updates. Every router floods the network with its update. RIP also features split horizon and poison reverse updates to prevent routing loops. RIP updates every 30 seconds and has a hop-count limit of 16 hops.

RIP-2 functions in much the same way as RIP-1, but with a few enhancements. RIP-2 supports classless routing (CIDR), route summarization, and variable-length subnet masks (VLSM). Other key enhancements in RIP-2 are that it uses a multicast (to address 224.0.0.9), instead of a broadcast for updates. In addition, RIP-2 can do triggered updates and also has the capability to use authentication if desired.

show Commands

The `show` commands that are useful for troubleshooting RIP-1 and RIP-2 are listed in Table 38.2.

TABLE 38.2 RIP-Related *show* Commands

Command	Description
`show ip route rip`	Displays the RIP route table.
`show ip route`	Displays the IP route table.
`show ip interface`	Displays IP interface configuration.
`show running-config`	Displays the running configuration.

debug Commands

As was mentioned in previous chapters, the `debug` command should always be used with caution and, in many circumstances, as a last resort. If the `show` commands described in the preceding section do not provide you with enough information to isolate and resolve the RIP problem, you can enable the debug tool.

The syntax for the debug mode in RIP is `debug ip rip events`. If you need even more general RIP information, use the global form of the command, `debug ip rip`. This command provides you with all possible RIP protocol information.

Typical RIP Problems

Because RIP uses UDP broadcasts by default, it can cause network congestion or broadcast storms if the protocol is not configured correctly. The way to avoid this problem is to configure RIP to allow unicast updates. This is done with the *neighbor* statement from within the RIP protocol configuration mode. In addition to using the `neighbor` statement, specified interfaces can be made passive by using the `passive-interface` command. This command stops routing updates from being sent out to the specified interfaces. Even if neighbor statements are used, too-frequent routing updates can also cause network congestion. This can be controlled or remedied by adjusting the various RIP timers.

Problems can also occur due to RIP version mismatches. By default, Cisco routers can understand both versions, but they advertise and forward data using RIP-1. It is possible to configure interfaces to send and receive only one version. The problem occurs when the RIP- versions on the two connected interfaces do not match.

For example, if Router A's interfaces are configured to send and receive only RIP-2, and Router B's interfaces are configured to listen to and speak RIP-1, the two routers won't be able to share RIP information. This problem can be resolved by analyzing the interface configuration on both routers and changing them so they match.

Troubleshooting IGRP

The *Interior Gateway Routing Protocol (IGRP)* is a Cisco proprietary routing protocol that uses a distance-vector algorithm because it uses a vector (a one-dimensional array) of information to calculate the best path. This vector or metric can consist of five elements:

- Bandwidth
- Delay
- Load
- Reliability
- MTU

By default, only two of the elements are used in the calculation of the metric: bandwidth and delay. Bandwidth is the minimum bandwidth over the path, and delay is the cumulative delay over the path. IGRP is intended to replace RIP and create a stable, quickly converging protocol that will scale with increased network growth.

IGRP Features and Operation

IGRP has several features included in the algorithm—these features and brief descriptions can be found in Table 38.3. The features were added to make IGRP more stable, and a few were created to deal with routing updates and make network convergence happen faster. Note also that IGRP is a classful routing protocol.

Updates in IGRP are sent out as broadcasts to everyone on the segment, much like what occurs in RIP-1. However, unlike RIP, which uses a UDP packet on port 520, Cisco decided against using TCP or UDP for IGRP and instead uses an IP datagram with protocol ID 9. This allows them to start the IGRP header information directly after the IP header, thus reducing overhead.

TABLE 38.3 IGRP Features

Feature	Description
Configurable metrics	Metrics involved in the algorithm responsible for calculating route information. They may be configured by the user.
Flash update	Updates are sent out before the default time setting. This occurs when the metrics change for a route.
Poison reverse updates	Implemented to prevent routing loops. These updates place a route in *holddown*. Holddown means that the router will not accept any new route information on a given route for a certain period.
Unequal-cost load balancing	Allows packets to be shared/distributed across multiple paths.

show Commands

The `show` commands that are useful for troubleshooting IGRP are listed in Table 38.4.

TABLE 38.4 IGRP-Related *show* Commands

Command	Description
`show running-config`	Displays the current configuration.
`show ip route igrp`	Displays IGRP routes only.
`show ip route`	Displays the entire route table.

debug Commands

IGRP events—as well as the protocol itself—can be analyzed by the debug tool. To watch IGRP events and protocol communications, you can enter the following **debug** commands:

- `debug ip igrp events`
- `debug ip igrp transactions`

Depending on the problem or the activity within IP, these commands can produce a great number of messages being logged to the console and the router's logging buffer.

Typical IGRP Problems

Because IGRP is a distance-vector protocol, you will not encounter problems with neighbor relationships or the different databases used by link-state protocols.

For IGRP, the most typical problems are caused by access lists, improper configuration, or the line to an adjacent router being down. The easiest way to tell if the router is receiving and sending IGRP information is to use the two debugging tools.

The primary symptom of a problem with IGRP is the lack of IGRP learned routes. This can be verified through the use of the `show` commands listed earlier in Table 38.4.

Troubleshooting EIGRP

Enhanced IGRP (EIGRP) is a hybrid link-state and distance-vector routing protocol that was created to resolve some of the difficulties encountered with IGRP. For example, in IGRP the entire route table is sent when changes are made in the network, and there is a lack of formal neighbor relationships with connected routers. Like IGRP, EIGRP is also a proprietary Cisco routing protocol. EIGRP is a hybrid of both link-state and distance-vector routing algorithms, which brings the best of both worlds together.

EIGRP's specific features are listed in Table 38.5. The features offered by EIGRP make it a stable and scalable protocol. Just as IGRP is proprietary to Cisco, so is EIGRP. However, unlike IRGP, EIGRP uses a multicast for communication. This multicast address, 224.0.0.10, is used for all EIGRP packets.

TABLE 38.5 EIGRP Features

Feature	Description
Route tagging	Distinguishes routes learned via different EIGRP sessions.
Formal neighbor relationships	Uses the Hello protocol to establish peering.
Incremental routing updates	Only changes are advertised, rather than the entire route table.
Classless routing	EIGRP supports subnet and VLSM information.
Configurable metrics	Metric information can be set through configuration commands.
Equal-cost load balancing	Allows traffic to be sent equally across multiple connections.

To aid in calculating the best route and in load sharing, EIGRP utilizes several databases of information:

- The route database, where the best routes are stored
- The topology database, where all route information resides
- A neighbor table, which is used to house information concerning other EIGRP neighbors

Neighbor Formation

The manner in which EIGRP establishes and maintains *neighbor relationships* is derived from its link-state properties. EIGRP uses the Hello protocol (similar to OSPF) to establish and maintain peering relationships with directly connected routers. Hello packets are sent between EIGRP routers to determine the state of their connection. Once the neighbor relation is established via the Hello protocol, the routers can exchange route information.

Each router establishes a *neighbor table*, in which it stores important information regarding the neighbors that are directly connected. The information consists of the neighbor's IP address, holdtime interval, smooth round-trip timer (SRTT), and queue information. These data are used to help determine when the link state changes.

When two routers initialize communication, their entire route tables are shared. Thereafter, only changes to the route table are propagated. These changes are shared with all directly connected EIGRP-speaking routers. Here is a summary of these steps:

1. Hello packets are multicast out all of the router's interfaces.
2. Replies to the Hello packets include all routes in the neighbor router's topology database, including the metrics. Routes that are learned from the originating router are not included in the reply.
3. The originating router acknowledges the update to each neighbor via an ACK packet.
4. The topology database is then updated with the newly received information.
5. Once the topology database is updated, the originating router then advertises its entire table to all the new neighbors.
6. Neighbor routers acknowledge the receipt of the route information from the originating router by sending back an ACK packet.

These steps are used in the initialization of EIGRP neighbors and change only slightly when updates are sent to existing neighbors.

Route Calculation and Updates

Because EIGRP uses distance-vector and link-state information when calculating routes by using the DUAL algorithm, convergence is much faster than with IGRP. The trick behind the convergence speed is that EIGRP calculates new routes only when a change in the network directly affects the routes contained in its route table.

Like IGRP, EIGRP's metric can be based on bandwidth, delay, load, reliability, and/or MTU. By default, only bandwidth and delay together are used; however, the user has the option to use the remaining items if they wish. To make that a little clearer, look at Figure 38.3, in which you see three routers meshed, *and* each router has an Ethernet segment connected as well.

FIGURE 38.3 Route updating versus calculation of new route

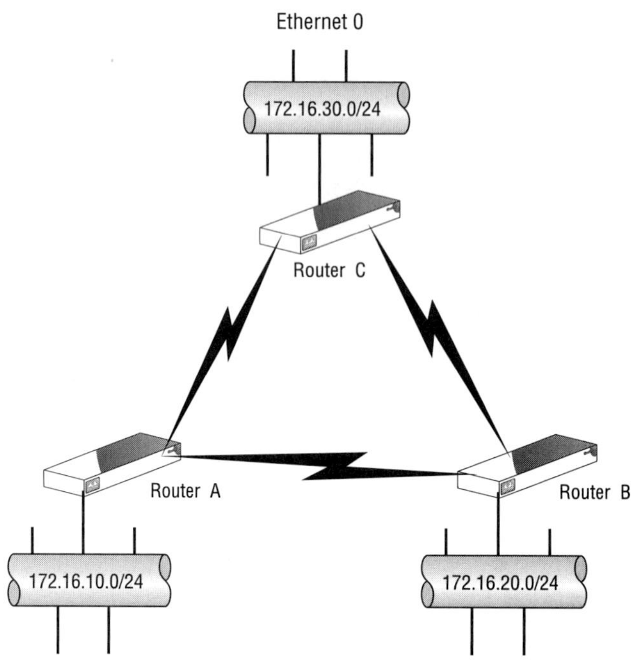

It is important to understand the difference between *accepting* a routing update and *calculating* a new route. If a change occurs to a network that is directly connected to a router, all of the relevant information is used to calculate a new metric and route entry for it. After the router calculates the new route, it is advertised to the neighbors.

Using Figure 38.3 as the example, assume that Ethernet 0 on Router C is very congested because of high traffic volumes. Also assume that load has been added to the metric calculation for all routers in this mesh. Router C then uses the distance and link information to calculate a new metric for network 172.16.30.0. With the new metric in place, the change is propagated to Routers A and B. To understand completely, you need to recognize that the other routers don't do any calculation—they just receive the update. Routers A and B don't need to calculate a new route for network 172.16.30.0 because they learn it from Router C.

On the other hand, if the link between Router A and Router C becomes congested, both routers have to calculate a new route metric. The change is then advertised to Router B by both Routers A and C.

Topology and Route State Information

The topology database stores all routes and metrics known via adjacent routers. By default, six routes can be stored for each destination network. If there are multiple routes to the destination, the router chooses the route with the best (lowest) metric and installs this into the routing table. It is possible for multiple routes to a destination to have the same metric. In these cases, assuming these routes have the best metric, they all will be installed in the routing table, and traffic destined to this network will be load-shared across them. The remaining routes will then serve as backups for the primary route if they meet the feasibility condition. While the best route is being chosen for a destination, the route is considered to be in an active state. After the route is chosen, the route status changes to passive.

The information list in Table 38.6 represents closely, though not exactly, that contained in an actual topology table. The Status field shows whether a new route is being calculated or whether a primary route has been selected. In our example, the route is in passive state because it has already selected the primary route.

TABLE 38.6 Topology Table Information

Status	P
Route—Adjacent Router's Address (Metrics)	10.10.10.0/24 via 10.1.2.6 (*3611648*/3609600) via 10.5.6.6 (4121600/3609600) via 10.6.7.6 (5031234/3609600)
Number of Successors	1 (Router C)
Feasible Distance	3611648

Updates and Changes

EIGRP also has link-state properties. One of these properties is that it propagates only changes in the route table instead of sending an entire new route table to its neighbors. When changes occur in the network, a regular distance-vector protocol sends the entire route table to neighbors. By avoiding sending the entire route table, less bandwidth is consumed. Neighboring routers don't have to reinitialize the entire route table, which would cause convergence issues. The neighbors just have to insert the new route changes. This is one of the principal enhancements over IGRP.

Updates can follow two paths. If a route update contains a better metric or a new route, the routers simply exchange the information. If the update contains information that a network is unavailable or if the metric is worse than before, an alternate path must be found. The flowchart in Figure 38.4 describes the steps that must be taken to choose a new route.

The router first searches the topology database for feasible successors. If no feasible successors are found, a multicast request is sent to all adjacent routers. Each router then responds to the query. Depending on how the router answers, different paths are taken. After the intermediate steps are taken, two final actions can occur. If route information is eventually found, the route is added to the route table and an update is sent. If the responses from the adjacent routers do not contain any route information, the route is removed from the topology and route tables. After the route table is updated, the new information is sent to all adjacent routers via a multicast.

FIGURE 38.4 Handling route changes

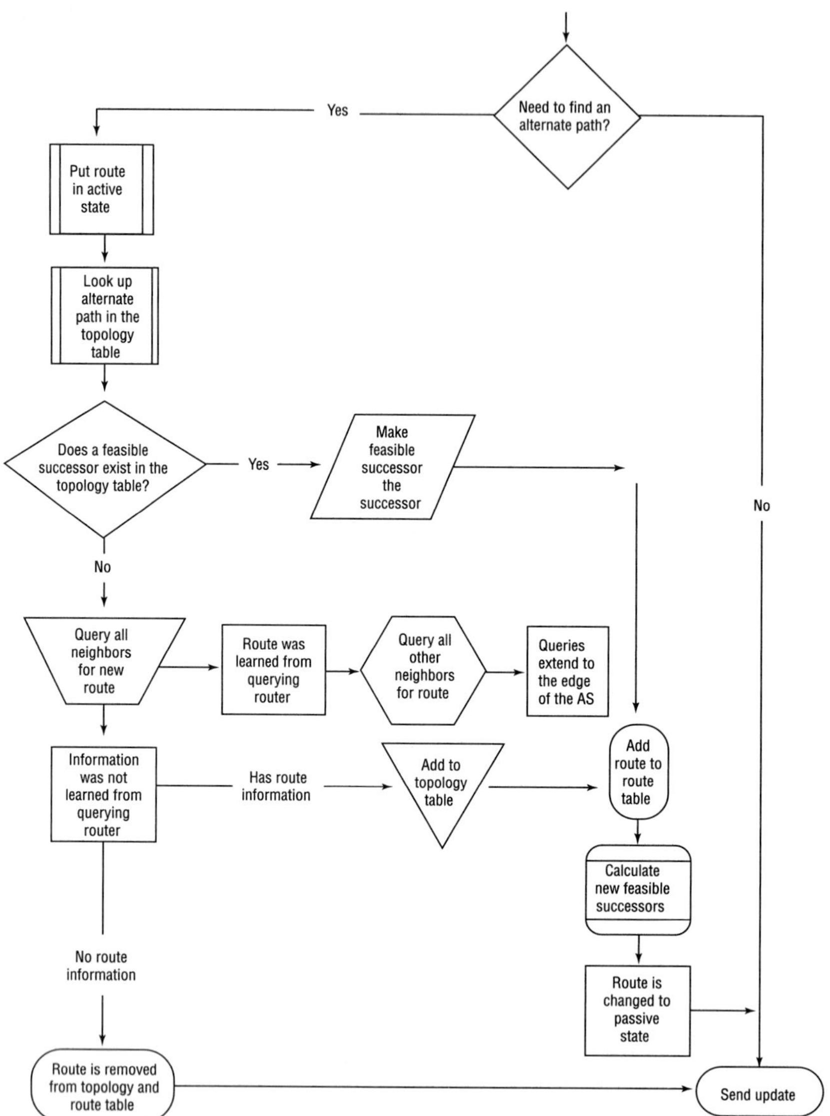

show Commands

Due to the complexity of EIGRP, there are several more show commands available to aid in troubleshooting EIGRP problems. The majority of these commands are listed in Table 38.7.

TABLE 38.7 EIGRP-Related *show* Commands

Command	Description/Output
`show running-config`	Displays the current configuration.
`show ip route`	Displays the full IP route table.
`show ip route eigrp`	Displays the EIGRP routes.
`show ip eigrp interfaces`	Displays EIGRP peer information for that interface.
`show ip eigrp neighbors`	Displays all EIGRP neighbors, along with summary information about each neighbor.
`show ip eigrp topology`	Displays the contents of the EIGRP topology table.
`show ip eigrp traffic`	Displays a summary of EIGRP routing statistics, such as the number of Hellos and routing updates.
`show ip eigrp events`	Displays a log of the most recent EIGRP protocol events. This information includes the insertion and removal of routes from the route table, updates, and neighbor status.

debug Commands

Several debug commands within EIGRP allow you to specify what processes you want to debug:

- `debug ip eigrp` *AS_number*
- `debug ip eigrp neighbor`
- `debug ip eigrp notifications`
- `debug ip eigrp summary`
- `debug ip eigrp`

Here is a sample of the information that can be obtained by using these commands:

```
Router_C#debug ip eigrp
IP-EIGRP Route Events debugging is on
IP-EIGRP: Processing incoming QUERY packet
IP-EIGRP: Int 172.16.30.4/30 M 4294967295 - 0 4294967295 SM
   4294967295 - 0 4294967295
```

```
IP-EIGRP: 172.16.30.4/30 routing table not updated
IP-EIGRP: 172.16.30.4/30, - do advertise out Ethernet0/0
IP-EIGRP: Int 172.16.30.4/30 metric 4294967295 - 1657856 4294967295
IP-EIGRP: Processing incoming UPDATE packet
IP-EIGRP: Int 172.16.30.4/30 M 2195456 - 1657856 537600 SM
   2169856 - 1657856 512000
IP-EIGRP: Int 172.16.30.4/30 metric 2195456 - 1657856 537600
IP-EIGRP: Processing incoming QUERY packet
IP-EIGRP: Int 172.16.30.4/30 M 4294967295 - 0 4294967295 SM
   4294967295 - 0 4294967295
IP-EIGRP: 172.16.30.4/30 routing table not updated
IP-EIGRP: 172.16.30.4/30, - do advertise out Ethernet0/0
IP-EIGRP: Int 172.16.30.4/30 metric 4294967295 - 1657856 4294967295
IP-EIGRP: Processing incoming UPDATE packet
IP-EIGRP: Int 172.16.30.4/30 M 2195456 - 1657856 537600 SM
   2169856 - 1657856 512000
IP-EIGRP: Int 172.16.30.4/30 metric 2195456 - 1657856 537600
```

You can see in this information when routes are removed from the route table and no longer advertised. Once the route is advertised to the router, it inserts the route back into the route table and commences advertisement.

Typical EIGRP Problems

Some of the typical problems with EIGRP are the loss of neighbor adjacencies, lost routes in earlier versions of IOS, stuck in active, and lost default gateways.

Neighbor failures can be attributed to link failures just as much as they can be attributed to software problems. If a neighbor relation has problems establishing, use the proper `debug` command to see what is occurring between both routers.

When troubleshooting an EIGRP problem, it's always a good idea to get a picture of the network. The most relevant picture is provided by the `show ip eigrp neighbors` command. This command shows all adjacent routers that share route information within a given autonomous system. If neighbors are missing, check the configuration and link status on both routers to verify that the protocol has been configured correctly.

If all neighbors are present, verify the routes learned. By executing the `show ip route eigrp` command, you gain a quick picture of the routes in the route table. If the route does not appear in the route table, verify the source of the route. If the source is functioning properly, check the topology table.

The topology table is displayed by using the `show ip eigrp topology` command. If the route is in the topology table, it's safe to assume that there is a problem between the topology database and the route table. You need to find the reason why the topology database is not injecting the route into the route table.

Other commands, such as `show ip eigrp traffic`, can be used to see whether updates are being sent. If the counters for EIGRP input and output packets don't increase, no EIGRP information is being sent between peers.

The `show ip eigrp events` command is an undocumented command. It displays a log of every EIGRP event—when routes are injected and removed from the route table and when EIGRP adjacencies reset or fail. This information can be used to see whether there are routing instabilities in the network.

Stuck in Active

Another problem that you will see quite often in larger EIGRP implementations is routers that are stuck in active (SIA). In EIGRP, when a route is removed, the router sends a query to each neighbor for new route. If the neighbor doesn't have the route, they in turn send a query to all their neighbors (except the one that sent them the initial query.) This process then continues until the edge of the EIGRP network is reached, or until a summary boundary is reached (summary boundaries are explained in more detail later in this section). A route becomes stuck in active when a router does not receive a reply to all of the queries it sent out within a set time interval (three minutes by default). This occurs most often in larger networks as queries traverse from one side of the network to the other and then replies to queries must be sent back. This all happens one router at a time, and any single router in the network can cause the problem.

One of the most common ways to address the SIA problem is to limit the size of your EIGRP query domain. This can be done through the use of another routing protocol to create a query boundary, which is self-explanatory. Or, more commonly, you can use summaries. Let's see how this works.

If EIGRP receives a query for a route that is an exact match for a route in its routing table, EIGRP will send a query to all of its EIGRP neighbors asking about this route. However, if a query is received for a route *not* in the routing table, EIGRP sends a negative response to the query but does not send a query to its neighbors. Because a summary restricts the more specific routes from being advertised and causes EIGRP to only send the summary route, the more specific routes are never in the routing table of any router past the point of summarization. Therefore, when routers past this point get a query for one of the specific routes, they look for it in their routing table. Finding only the summary route, they send a negative response to the query and do not send a query to their neighbors, thus creating a query boundary and lessening the probability of having a SIA problem.

Troubleshooting OSPF

Open Shortest Path First (OSPF) differs from IGRP and Enhanced IGRP because it is a pure link-state routing technology. Also, it is an open standard routing protocol, which means that it was not developed solely by Cisco. OSPF was designed and developed by the IETF to provide a scalable, quickly converging, and efficient routing protocol that can be used by all routing equipment. Complete details for OSPF are found in RFC 2178.

Areas are used within OSPF to define a group of routers and networks belonging to the same OSPF session. Links connect routers, and the information about each link is defined by its link state. On each broadcast or multi-access network segment, two routers must be assigned the responsibilities of designated router (DR) and backup designated router (BDR).

Like EIGRP, OSPF maintains three databases: adjacency, topology, and route. The adjacency database is similar to the neighbor database used by EIGRP. It contains all information about OSPF neighbors and the links connecting them. The topology database maintains all route information. The best routes from the topology database are placed in the route database, or route table.

Neighbor and Adjacency Formation

The Hello protocol is used to establish peering sessions among routers. Hello packets are multicast out every interface. The information that is multicast includes the router ID, timing intervals, existing neighbors, area identification, router priority, designated and backup router information, authentication password, and stub area information. All this information is used when establishing new peers. Descriptions of each element can be found in Table 38.8.

TABLE 38.8 OSPF Multicast Information

Information	Description
Router ID	Highest active IP address on the router.
Time intervals	Intervals between Hello packets, and the allowed dead time interval.
Existing neighbors	Addresses for any existing OSPF neighbors.
Area identification	OSPF area number and link information, which must be the same for a peering session to be established.
Router priority	Value assigned to a router and used when choosing the DR and BDR.
DR and BDR	If these routers have already been chosen, their router ID and address are contained in the Hello packet.
Authentication password	All peers must have the same authentication password if authentication is enabled.
Stub area flag	This is a special area—two routers must share the same stub information. This information is not necessary to initiate a regular peering session with another OSPF router.

Figure 38.5 is a flowchart that depicts each step of the initialization process. The process starts by sending out Hello packets. Every listening router then adds the originating router to the adjacency database. The responding routers reply with all of their Hello information so that the originating router can add them to its adjacency table.

After adjacencies are established, the DR and BDR must be chosen before route information and link-state information can be exchanged. Once the DR and BDR are chosen, route information is exchanged, and the OSPF peers continue to multicast Hello packets every 10 seconds to determine whether neighbors are still reachable.

Before we go any further with peer initialization, we need to discuss several terms specific to OSPF. These terms are key to your understanding of OSPF and how it functions.

FIGURE 38.5 OSPF peer initialization

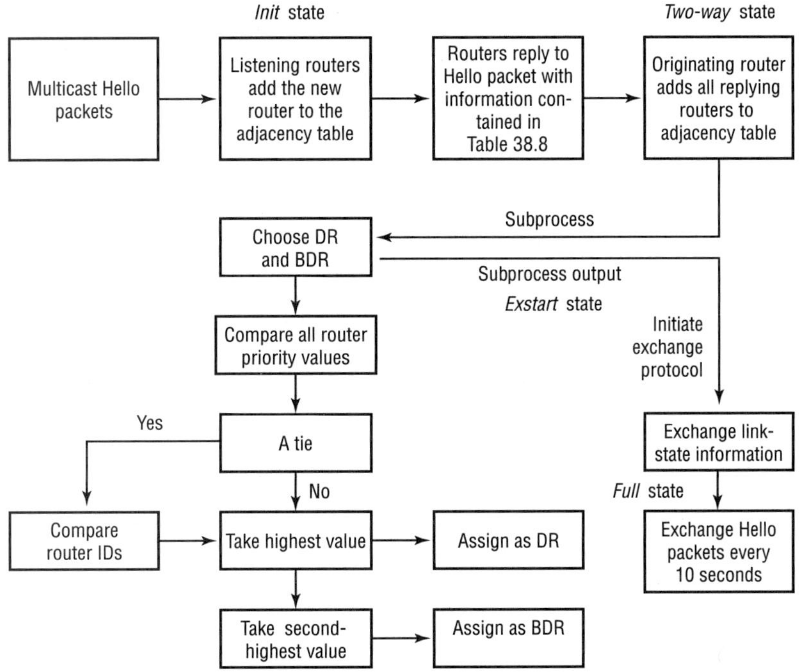

OSPF Area Types

The easiest way to understand OSPF areas is to build from what you already know about EIGRP. You learned that EIGRP uses autonomous system numbers to specify routing processes and the routing process to which individual routers belong. OSPF uses areas in place of an autonomous system. An OSPF area consists of a group of routers or interfaces on a router that is assigned to a common area. When deploying OSPF, there must be a backbone area. Standard and stub areas connect to the backbone area. Following are brief descriptions of each router type:

Backbone This area accepts all link-state advertisements (LSAs) and is used to connect multiple areas.

Stub This area does not accept any external routing update, but it accepts summary LSAs.

Totally Stub These areas are closed off from accepting external or summary advertisements.

Standard This is the normal area that accepts internal and external LSAs, and summary information.

Not So Stubby This type of area is similar to a stub area except that Type 5 LSAs (see Table 38.9) are not flooded into the area from the core. The not so stubby area (NSSA) can import external AS routes into the area.

Move on now to learn the different types of link-state advertisements. LSAs are the heart of OSPF's information exchange. Each type of LSA represents a particular type of route information. All of the defined and used LSA types are summarized in Table 38.9.

TABLE 38.9 OSPF LSA Types

LSA Type	Description
1 - Router link entry	This LSA is broadcast only within its defined area. The LSA contains all the default link-state information.
2 - Network entry	This LSA is multicast to all area routers by the DR. This update contains network-specific information.
3 and 4 - Summary entries	Type 3 LSAs contain route information for internal networks and are sent to backbone routers. Type 4 LSAs contain information about autonomous system border routers (ASBRs). Summary information is multicast by the area border router (ABR), and the information reaches all backbone routers (see Table 38.10).
5 - Autonomous system entry	Originating from the ASBR, these packets contain information about external networks.
7 - Not so stubby area	Not so stubby area (NSSA) permits Type 7 AS external routes to be imported inside the NSSA area by redistribution.

The LSA types represent the types of route being advertised and assist in restricting the number and type of routes that are accepted by a given area. As is shown in Table 38.9, an LSA of Type 5 is sent only by the autonomous system border router (ASBR). This brings you to the point where you need to understand the router types that belong to the various OSPF areas.

Multiple router types can exist within an OSPF area. Table 38.10 lists all of the OSPF router types and the role that each plays within the area.

TABLE 38.10 OSPF Router Types

Router Type	Responsibility
Internal	All interfaces are defined on the same area. All internal routers have an identical link-state database.
Backbone	Has at least one interface assigned to area 0.
Area border router (ABR)	Interfaces are connected to multiple OSPF areas. Information specific to each area is stored on this type of router.
Autonomous system boundary router (ASBR)	This type of router has an interface connected to an external network or to a different AS.

In addition to the responsibilities explained previously, a router can also be assigned other responsibilities. These additions are assumed when a router is assigned the role of DR or BDR.

show Commands

Because of the complexity of OSPF, several `show` commands are available to provide information regarding the configuration and functionality of OSPF on a router. Table 38.11 lists most of the available OSPF-related `show` commands. These commands provide you with substantial information valuable for troubleshooting OSPF routing problems.

TABLE 38.11 OSPF-Related *show* Commands

Command	Description / Output
`show running-config`	Displays the current router configuration.
`show ip route`	Displays the entire IP route table.
`show ip route ospf`	Displays OSPF routes.
`show ip ospf`	Displays information for OSPF.
`show ip ospf` *process-id*	Displays information relevant to the specified process ID.

TABLE 38.11 OSPF-Related *show* Commands *(continued)*

Command	Description / Output
`show ip ospf border-routers`	Displays the routers that join different areas, or border routers.
`show ip ospf database`	Provides an OSPF database summary.
`show ip ospf interface`	Displays OSPF information on an interface.
`show ip ospf neighbor`	Displays OSPF neighbor information.
`show ip ospf request-list`	Displays the link-state request list.
`show ip ospf retransmission list`	Displays the link-state retransmission list.
`show ip ospf summary-address`	Displays summary-address redistribution information.
`show ip ospf virtual-links`	Displays virtual link information.
`show ip interface`	Displays IP interface settings.

debug Commands

OSPF runs many processes to maintain all its databases, routing updates, and peering connections. Most of these processes use link-state advertisements (LSAs) to share information. LSAs are the heart of OSPF's information exchange. These types were highlighted in Table 38.9.

Here are the available debug options for OSPF:

debug ip ospf adj Provides debug information about events concerning adjacency relationships with other OSPF routers.

debug ip ospf events Provides debug information for all OSPF events.

debug ip ospf flood Provides information about OSPF flooding. Flooding is the way that an OSPF router sends updates. It broadcasts a change in its route table, and all other members of the OSPF area receive the update.

debug ip ospf lsa-generation Gives detailed information regarding the generation of LSA messages.

debug ip ospf packet Gives detailed information regarding OSPF packets.

debug ip ospf retransmission If OSPF has to retransmit information, it triggers a retransmission event that `debug` captures and echoes to the console.

debug ip ospf spf Provides debug information for all SPF transactions. By enabling SPF debugging, OSPF events debugging is also turned on.

debug ip ospf tree Provides information for the OSPF database tree.

Following is a `debug ip ospf` trace. Notice that OSPF event debugging was turned on as well (second and third lines of the output). SPF is an algorithm used to select the best route to each destination:

```
Router_A#debug ip ospf spf
OSPF spf intra events debugging is on
OSPF spf inter events debugging is on
OSPF spf external events debugging is on
Router_A#
%LINEPROTO-5-UPDOWN: Line protocol on Interface Serial1, changed state to down
%LINK-3-UPDOWN: Interface Serial1, changed state to down
OSPF: running SPF for area 0
OSPF: Initializing to run spf
 It is a router LSA 172.16.40.1. Link Count 1
  Processing link 0, id 172.16.30.4, link data 255.255.255.252, type 3
   Add better path to LSA ID 172.16.30.7, gateway 172.16.30.4, dist 64
   Add path fails: no output interface to 172.16.30.4,
   next hop 0.0.0.0
OSPF: Adding Stub nets
OSPF: Path left undeleted to 172.16.30.4
OSPF: Entered old delete routine
OSPF: No ndb for STUB NET old route 172.16.60.0, mask /24, next hop 172.16.30.6
OSPF: No ndb for STUB NET old route 172.16.30.4, mask /30, next hop 172.16.30.5
OSPF: No ndb for NET old route 172.16.50.0, mask /24, next hop 172.16.30.6
OSPF: delete lsa id 172.16.60.255, type 0, adv rtr 172.16.60.1 from delete list
OSPF: delete lsa id 172.16.30.7, type 0, adv rtr 172.16.40.1 from delete list
OSPF: delete lsa id 172.16.50.1, type 2, adv rtr 172.16.50.1 from delete list
OSPF: running spf for summaries area 0
OSPF: sum_delete_old_routes area 0
OSPF: Started Building Type 5 External Routes
OSPF: ex_delete_old_routes
OSPF: Started Building Type 7 External Routes
OSPF: ex_delete_old_routes
%LINK-3-UPDOWN: Interface Serial1, changed state to up
%LINEPROTO-5-UPDOWN: Line protocol on Interface Serial1, changed state to up
OSPF: running SPF for area 0
OSPF: Initializing to run spf
```

```
 It is a router LSA 172.16.40.1. Link Count 1
  Processing link 0, id 172.16.30.4, link data 255.255.255.252, type 3
   Add better path to LSA ID 172.16.30.7, gateway 172.16.30.4, dist 64
   Add path: next-hop 172.16.30.5, interface Serial1
OSPF: Adding Stub nets
OSPF: insert route list LS ID 172.16.30.7, type 0, adv rtr 172.16.40.1
OSPF: Entered old delete routine
OSPF: running spf for summaries area 0
OSPF: sum_delete_old_routes area 0
OSPF: Started Building Type 5 External Routes
OSPF: ex_delete_old_routes
OSPF: Started Building Type 7 External Routes
OSPF: ex_delete_old_routes
```

This is a lot of information over a very short period. You can get an idea of what the CPU goes through when there is a link-state change in an OSPF network.

Typical OSPF Problems

Because of the great number of processes and calculations that must be made by the CPU when changes occur in an OSPF network, the router can become overwhelmed with all the processing that has to be done. The bigger the OSPF network, the more calculations that occur, not to mention the greater probability of changes that are propagated throughout the network.

A general rule of thumb is to not add more than 100 routers per area, and to not have more than 700 routers throughout the network. It is possible to have smaller or larger networks, but the numbers here are given simply as a guideline. As links are added to a network, the likelihood of instability also increases. When a large network experiences instability, the routers have to spend a great deal of time and CPU cycles processing link and route updates. Proper route summarization can go a long way to correcting the issues noted in this chapter.

Another problem common to OSPF is wrongly configured wildcard masks in the OSPF network statements. OSPF uses wildcard bits to specify the networks that should be advertised, instead of using multiple network statements. Both approaches work, but be aware of potential problems with the wildcard mask.

It is not always convenient for all areas to connect back to area 0. Therefore, in many cases virtual links are used. A virtual link allows for a remote area to connect to area 0 by "tunneling" through another area. Though this will allow for OSPF to function, there can be issues with this configuration if the virtual connection takes an unreliable path, causing flapping of the area. Consequently, virtual links should be used sparingly.

At times, the most difficult challenge with OSPF is just getting the neighbors to come up. A common issue in getting a neighbor relationship up is the occurrence of a mismatch in OSPF settings (Hello interval, dead interval, authentication, and so on). If all of these are configured correctly, make sure that the OSPF interface network types match. These interface network types are broadcast, point-to-point, NBMA, point-to-multipoint, and virtual link.

Troubleshooting BGP

You are now familiar with several IGPs (Interior Gateway Protocols), including IGRP, EIGRP, and OSPF. For enterprise networks to communicate with other autonomous systems or ISPs, the IGP information has to be injected into BGP, which is used by all network entities that compose the Internet.

Border Gateway Protocol (BGP) is an open-standard protocol that was developed and defined in several RFCs: 1163, 1267, 1654, and 1655, to name a few. The two types of BGP are iBGP and eBGP. There are several differences between the two. Primarily, iBGP (internal BGP) is used to share BGP information with routers within the same AS, whereas eBGP (external BGP) is used to share route information between two separate autonomous systems. More details will be given as we discuss each type separately.

Neighbor Relationship

The key to BGP configuration is the neighbor relationship. Unlike many of the previously discussed protocols, BGP uses TCP to establish neighbor relationships. Specifically, a TCP connection on port 179 is set up when the neighbor relationship is formed, and remains up as long as the relationship exists. This connection is used to send routing updates, notifications, and keepalives between the routers.

BGP is an Exterior Gateway Protocol (EGP), and as such, its design assumes it will be used to connect many different companies with varying configurations and levels of trust. Because of this design assumption, there are numerous configuration options for each neighbor relationship. You can set up BGP to

- Prefer one neighbor's routes over another (all the time or only some of the time).
- Update the next-hop information to one neighbor but not another.
- Advertise a route only if another route is in the routing table.
- Update the path information for some but not all routes from a neighbor.
- Perform many other manipulations on the routes that are entered into the routing table.

In addition, most of these attributes can be assigned based on groups of neighbors as well as on an individual neighbor-by-neighbor basis.

The cost of this flexibility is complexity. A simple BGP configuration, with a couple of neighbors and little or no manipulation of the routes, is no harder to manage and maintain than any IGP such as OSPF or EIGRP. However, if significant route manipulation and neighbor relationship management is needed in your implementation, troubleshooting any issue can become a major undertaking. Therefore, whenever possible, create groups for neighbors and simplify any route manipulation to adjust a minimum number of terms.

eBGP versus iBGP

The distinguishing characteristic between an iBGP neighbor and an eBGP neighbor is that an iBGP neighbor is in the same autonomous system and an eBGP neighbor is in a different autonomous system. Treatment of iBGP and eBGP peers differs greatly. In general, eBGP neighbors share a common subnet, while iBGP neighbors can be anywhere within the same AS. In addition, an eBGP route has an administrative distance of 20 by default, compared with 200 for an iBGP route.

It is not a requirement for eBGP neighbors to share a common subnet. If they do not—for example, if you are using loopbacks—the path to the neighbor's loopback must be known by a means other than BGP, such as a static route, and be no more than 255 hops away. Once this is complete, add a `neighbor ip` *address* `ebgp-multihop` command for that neighbor into the BGP configuration.

In iBGP, route information learned from one iBGP peer is not advertised to another iBGP peer. Therefore, per the RFCs, all routers connected via iBGP should be in a logical mesh. This avoids inconsistent route information and routing loops. By default, when routes are exchanged between iBGP peers, the "next-hop" attribute is not updated. This goes back to the assumption that there is a logical mesh of all iBGP peers. With this mesh, it is assumed that every device in the mesh knows how to get to all the same networks, and therefore the next hop does not need to be updated because the iBGP peers should know about it. As is the case with most things in BGP, this behavior can be changed if your needs dictate.

The purpose of eBGP is to inject routes owned by the enterprise network into another AS. Two prerequisites must be met in order for internal routes to be propagated via BGP:

- The route to be advertised must be present in the router's IGP route table. You can fulfill this condition by injecting the routes into a router's route table via one of these three methods: an IGP, a static route, or directly connected networks. BGP has a synchronization option that requires BGP and the IGP routes to synchronize before BGP will advertise IGP-learned networks. The `no synchronization` command indicates that BGP and the IGP do not have to synchronize before BGP advertises the routes.
- BGP must learn the route. You also have three ways to accomplish this second prerequisite. BGP learns of networks that it needs to advertise through other BGP advertisements, network statements, and redistribution of an IGP into BGP.

show Commands

There are numerous `show` commands available for BGP. Many are similar to ones that were issued for other routing protocols. Table 38.12 describes the principal `show` commands for BGP.

debug Commands

Despite the overall complexity of BGP, there are relatively few `debug` commands. Those that do exist are very focused as to the information that they show. This does mean you need to know specifically what you are looking for, but it also makes the `debug` commands less of a burden on the router to run. Therefore, the `debug` commands that are available are usable in most real-life installations.

TABLE 38.12 BGP-Related *show* Commands

Command	Description
`show ip bgp`	Shows information about BGP learned routes, including indicating which ones will be in the routing table.
`show ip bgp` *network*	Shows BGP information on a specific network.
`show ip bgp neighbors`	Shows information on BGP neighbors.
`show ip bgp neighbors` *ip_address advertised-routes*	Shows all routes being advertised to a particular neighbor.
`show ip bgp neighbors` *ip_address received-routes*	Shows all routes being received from a particular neighbor.
`show ip bgp peer-group`	Shows information about BGP peer groups.
`show ip bgp summary`	Shows a summary of all BGP connections.
`show ip route bgp`	Displays the BGP route table.
`show ip route`	Displays the IP route table.
`show ip interface`	Displays IP interface configuration.
`show running-config`	Displays the running configuration.

As with all debug commands, you need to take care when using the BGP debug options. Even though they are focused, significant load can be placed on the processor if there are a large number of routes in the routing table. Some of the frequently used commands are as follows:

- `debug ip bgp` *ipaddress* `updates`
- `debug ip bgp dampening`
- `debug ip bgp events`
- `debug ip bgp keepalives`
- `debug ip bgp updates`

Here is an example of the output from `debug ip bgp` *ip_address* `updates`:

```
Router_B#debug ip bgp 172.16.20.6 updates
BGP updates debugging is on for neighbor 172.16.20.6
BGP: 172.16.20.6 computing updates, neighbor version 0, table
   version 2, starting at 0.0.0.0
```

```
BGP: 172.16.20.6 send UPDATE 10.0.0.0/8, next 172.16.20.5, metric 0, path 100
BGP: 172.16.20.6 1 updates enqueued (average=50, maximum=50)
BGP: 172.16.20.6 update run completed, ran for 0ms, neighbor version 0,
   start version 2, throttled to 2, check point net 0.0.0.0
BGP: 172.16.20.6 rcv UPDATE w/ attr: nexthop 172.16.20.6, origin ?,
   metric 0, path 200
BGP: 172.16.20.6 rcv UPDATE about 19.0.0.0/8
BGP: 172.16.20.6 rcv UPDATE about 100.100.0.0/16
BGP: 172.16.20.6 rcv UPDATE about 100.200.0.0/14
BGP: 172.16.20.6 rcv UPDATE about 199.199.0.0/16
BGP: 172.16.20.6 rcv UPDATE about 200.200.1.0/24
BGP: 172.16.20.6 rcv UPDATE about 200.200.64.0/18
BGP: 172.16.20.6 computing updates, neighbor version 2, table
   version 8, starting at 0.0.0.0
BGP: 172.16.20.6 update run completed, ran for 0ms, neighbor version 2,
   start version 8, throttled to 8, check point net 0.0.0.0
Router_B#
```

Typical BGP Problems

Most problems with BGP are a result of the complexity of the implementation. These problems will most likely occur during the implementation itself. Once BGP is set up and running, it is a very stable protocol that can effectively manage the routing table for the entire Internet.

Many of the typical problems that occur in BGP affect the areas in which BGP differs from other routing protocols. For example, in other routing protocols, when a route is learned from a neighbor and there is no other route in the routing table for this network, the route is installed in the network. In BGP, certain other conditions may need to be met before this occurs. In addition, BGP's network statements work differently from other routing protocols'. For example, in EIGRP, a `network 10.0.0.0` command would tell EIGRP to route out any network between 10.0.0.0 and 10.255.255.255. In BGP, this same statement means to send the 10.0.0.0 /8 network if it is in the routing table. If the 10.2.2.0 /24 network is in the table, in BGP this will not be sent (assuming the auto-summary feature of BGP has been disabled).

Another common BGP difficulty concerns the default manner in which iBGP distributes routes. Because iBGP is built on the concept that all iBGP neighbors have the same routes in their routing table, the next-hop attribute of a route is left as the address of the eBGP peer and is not updated when routes are sent to iBGP peers. If an iBGP peer's routing table does not contain the external peer's address, traffic for this destination will be dropped. To overcome this, the `next-hop-self` command can be used to tell the router to advertise itself rather than the external peer as the next hop.

Redistribution of Routing Protocols

When multiple routing protocols are used within a network and they need to be redistributed into one another, it is important that it be done correctly by assigning the proper metrics through the redistribution. If protocols are redistributed without metric adjustment, many networking problems can occur.

Although redistribution allows multiple protocols to share routing information, it can result in routing loops, slow convergence, and inconsistent route information. This is caused by the differing algorithms and methods used by each protocol. It is not good practice to redistribute bidirectionally (if, for example, you have both IGRP 100 and RIP routing sessions running on your router). Bidirectional redistribution occurs if you enter redistribution commands under each protocol session. Here is an example:

```
Router_A#config t
Enter configuration commands, one per line. End with CNTL/Z.
Router_A(config)#router igrp 100
Router_A(config-router)#redistribute RIP
Router_A(config-router)#router RIP
Router_A(config-router)#redistribute igrp 100
Router_A(config-router)#^Z
Router_A#
```

When a route from RIP, IGRP, or OSPF is injected into another routing protocol, the route loses its identity and its metrics are converted from the original format to the other protocol's format. This can cause confusion within the router. Ensuring that the metric is converted properly is done through metric commands. In most cases, the specific command used is `default-metric`.

Dealing with Routing Metrics

The router in which multiple protocols or sessions meet is called the *autonomous system boundary router (ASBR)*. When routes from one protocol or session are injected or redistributed into another protocol or session, the routes are tagged as external routes. Following is a simple example of a route table that has external routes:

```
Router_X#show ip route eigrp
     172.16.0.0/16 is variably subnetted, 301 subnets, 10
     masks
D EX    172.16.27.230/32
           [170/24827392] via 172.16.131.82, 02:33:32,
           ATM6/0/0.3114
D EX    172.16.237.16/29
```

```
           [170/40542208] via 172.16.131.82, 23:40:32,
           ATM6/0/0.3114
           [170/40542208] via 172.16.131.74, 23:40:32,
           ATM6/0/0.3113
D EX    172.16.237.24/29
           [170/40542208] via 172.16.131.82, 23:40:32,
           ATM6/0/0.3114
           [170/40542208] via 172.16.131.74, 23:40:32,
           ATM6/0/0.3113
D EX    172.16.52.192/26
           [170/2202112] via 172.16.131.82, 23:40:27,
           ATM6/0/0.3114
D EX    172.16.41.216/29
           [170/46232832] via 172.16.131.82, 23:40:28,
           ATM6/0/0.3114
D EX    172.16.38.200/30
           [170/2176512] via 172.16.131.82, 23:40:27,
           ATM6/0/0.3114
D EX    172.16.237.0/29
           [170/40542208] via 172.16.131.82, 23:40:32,
           ATM6/0/0.3114
           [170/40542208] via 172.16.131.74, 23:40:32,
           ATM6/0/0.3113
D       172.16.236.0/24
           [90/311808] via 172.16.131.82, 23:40:32,
           ATM6/0/0.3114
           [90/311808] via 172.16.131.74, 23:40:32,
           ATM6/0/0.3113
D       172.16.235.0/24
           [90/311808] via 172.16.131.82, 23:40:32,
           ATM6/0/0.3114
```

Most of the information in this example is self-explanatory, but there are a couple of points that need discussion. As you can see, in this route table, all of the routes are prefaced with a `D`, meaning that they are EIGRP routes. Routes that originated outside EIGRP and were redistributed into it are denoted with the EX (external) tag. The numbers inside the brackets (for instance, `[90/311808]`) represent the administrative distance/metric of the route, respectively. In this case, the router is using the default administrative distances of 90 for internal and 170 for external EIGRP routes.

IGRP and EIGRP Metrics

Each protocol has its own method of route redistribution. You must be familiar with each protocol's implementation of route redistribution and default-metric settings.

IGRP and EIGRP use the same command to adjust metrics: the `default-metric` command. Here is an example:

```
default-metric bandwidth delay reliability load MTU
```

This command takes the metrics for the protocol being injected into IGRP or EIGRP and converts them directly to values that IGRP or EIGRP can use. The *bandwidth* is the capacity of the link; *delay* is the time in microseconds; *reliability* and *load* are values from 1 to 255; and *MTU* is the maximum transmission unit in bytes. If you are looking for some possible values for the default metric, you can just examine the output of a `show interface` command.

Finally, you can also change the distance values that are assigned to EIGRP (90 internal; 170 external). The administrative distance value tells the router which protocol to believe. The lower the distance value, the more believable the protocol. The administrative distance values for EIGRP are changed with the following command from within the EIGRP session:

```
distance eigrp internal-distance external-distance
```

Internal-distance and *external-distance* both have a range of values from 1 to 255.

Remember that a value of 255 tells the router to ignore the route. So, unless you want the routes from the protocol to be ignored, never use the value of 255.

You may find the distance setting to be a source of trouble when you're troubleshooting routing problems. If multiple protocols advertise the same routes, it's possible that differences in the administrative distance may cause the route to be learned by the wrong protocol, and thus it is not propagated correctly throughout the network.

Metrics used by EIGRP are essentially equal to 256 times the IGRP metrics. As with IGRP, metrics decide how the routes are selected. The higher the metric associated with a route, the less desirable the route is.

The specific formula for determining the EIGRP metric is the following:

$\text{Metric} = 256 \times [K1 \times Bandwidth + (K2 \times Bandwidth) \div (256 - load) + K3 \times Delay] \times [K5 \div (reliability + K4)]$

where the values $K1$ through $K5$ are configurable constants. By default, $K2$, $K4$, and $K5$ are set equal to 0, and $K1$ and $K3$ are set equal to 1. If $K5$ is set to 0, the last section of the formula $(K5 \div (reliability + K4))$ is not used. Because $K2$, $K4$, and $K5$ are set to 0 by default, the default formula reduces down to

$\text{Metric} = 256 \times [Bandwidth + Delay]$

Remember that the *Bandwidth* as referred to in the formula is the minimum bandwidth on the network path and the *Delay* is actually the sum of the delays on the network path.

OSPF Metrics

The metrics associated with OSPF are different from those associated with IGRP and EIGRP. OSPF uses bandwidth as the main metric in selecting a route. The cost is calculated by using the bandwidth for the link. The equation is 100,000,000 (10 to the 8th power) divided by the bandwidth. You can change bandwidth on the individual interface.

The cost is manipulated by changing the value to a number within the range of 1 to 65,535. Because the cost is assigned to each link, the value must be changed on each interface. The command to do this is `ip ospf` *`cost`*.

Cisco bases link cost on bandwidth. Other vendors may use other metrics to calculate the link's cost. When connecting links between routers from different vendors, you may have to adjust the cost to match the other router. Both routers must assign the same cost to the link for OSPF to work.

You can configure the OSPF distance with the following command:

```
distance ospf [external | Intra-area | Inter-area] distance
```

This command allows the distance metric to be defined for external OSPF, and intra-area and inter-area routes. As the names imply, intra-area routes are routes that exist in a particular OSPF area, and inter-area routes are routes that come from other OSPF areas. Distance values range from 1 to 255—and the lower the distance, the better.

Other values important to OSPF's operation are not actually metrics, but can be configured as well. Values such as the router ID and router priority are important in router initialization and for DR and BDR selection. You can change these values with some minor configuration changes.

To change the router priority, use the following command on the desired interface:

```
ip ospf priority number
```

The *`number`* can range from 0 to 255—a higher value indicates a higher priority when choosing the DR and BDR for the area.

Just as with EIGRP, new metrics must be assigned to route information that is injected into the OSPF session. The command in this case is much simpler than the command used when assigning metrics for EIGRP or IGRP—it is almost the same, but only one metric is assigned. The value of the metric is the cost for the route:

```
default-metric cost
```

Distribute Lists

Distribute lists are access lists applied to an interface from within a routing protocol. The purpose of a distribute list is to control which routes are advertised to adjacent routers. As of IOS 12.0(3)T, you can also use a *prefix list* in place of the access list. A prefix list, specified by the `ip prefix-list` command, allows greater flexibility in specifying the networks that should be allowed. For example, with a prefix list, you can tell the routing protocol to accept all routes as long as the mask length for the route is between /8 and /24, as in the following command:

```
ip prefix-list MASK-SIZE permit 0.0.0.0/0 ge 8 le 24
```

Problems can occur if distribute lists are missing or improperly configured. Figure 38.6 shows three meshed routers. Here, undesired routing can occur if the advertised routes are not controlled through the use of distribute lists.

FIGURE 38.6 Distribute lists to prevent routing loops

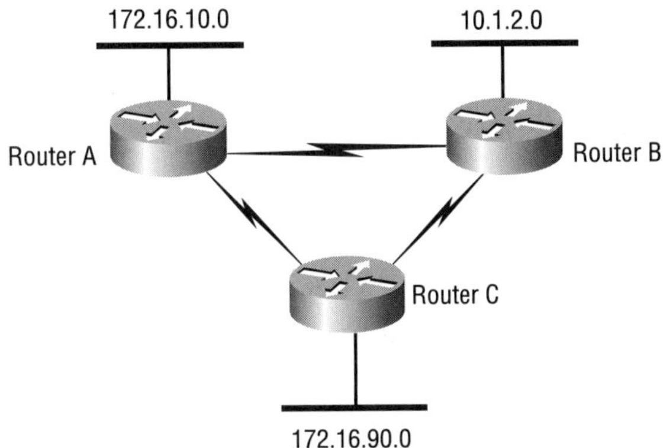

Routers A and B are core-level routers. Router C is a small access router. The potential problem is that Router A could learn about network 10.1.2.0 via Router C instead of Router B, if no distribute lists are used to control what routes are advertised from Router C.

If all of Router A's traffic destined for 10.1.2.0 were routed through Router C, it could easily overwhelm the small router. In this scenario, you'd only want Router C to have redundant links to the core, and not let the core transit an access router to reach another core router.

The problem can be solved or avoided by configuring an access list that permits only networks connected to Router C. The access list would be applied outbound to the interfaces connecting Routers A and B with the `distribute-list` command. The command is issued from within the routing protocol configuration mode.

Distribute lists can solve problems as well as cause them. When the downstream routers are configured to learn their default gateway dynamically, the router must have the default network in the route table. If the route is not present, the router will lose the gateway of last resort. When a distribute list is applied, you must verify that it allows route advertisement of the default network, as well as any other crucial routes.

Route Maps

Route maps are used to manipulate routing. They are small scripts that can contain multiple instances and multiple conditions for each instance. Route maps are somewhat like access lists if you specify that the packet must match an access list. In addition to the capability of permitting or denying the packet, you can define what is done before the packet is forwarded.

Route maps can be used to set metrics for route updates, to set a command to its default value, and so on. Table 38.13 gives a list of what a route map can do.

TABLE 38.13 Route Map Configuration Commands

Command	Description
`default`	Sets a command to its defaults.
`exit`	Exits from route-map configuration mode.
`help`	Describes the interactive help system.
`match`	Matches values from routing table.
`no`	Negates a command or sets its defaults.
`set`	Sets values in destination routing protocol.

Here is a sample route map:

```
route-map test permit 10
 match ip address 1
 set metric-type type-2
!
route-map test permit 20
 match ip address 2
 set metric-type type-1
!
route-map test permit 30
 set metric 100
```

The router runs through this route map, just as it runs through an access list. The only difference is that the router performs some commands instead of simply forwarding or dropping the packet. In this example, any packet matching the addresses listed in the IP access list 1 has its metric set as an OSPF type-2 metric. Any packet matching the addresses specified in access list 2 has its OSPF metric set to type-1. The final instance of the route map "test" is to set the metric of the route update to 100.

Real World Scenario

Managing Access Lists and Route Maps

This chapter discusses how access lists and route maps are used to assist in route control. As is the case with many router control elements, managing these items in a smaller environment is not a problem. However, as the environment gets larger and more components are added, an effective management plan can save administrative overhead and potentially eliminate some problems before they occur. The first item that needs attention in this plan is *naming*.

Whenever possible, use named access lists. Some commands, such as `snmp-server community` and `access-class`, accept only numbered lists; however, in most instances you can use the named lists. By using named lists, you will be able to easily determine the use of the access list as well as, potentially, the direction in which it is applied.

When naming your access lists and route maps, be sure to use descriptive names. Also, if the access list will be used to filter traffic on an interface, indicate in the name of the list whether it will be applied inbound or outbound on the interface. If they are to be used in a route map, name the route map and access list similarly. All of these naming suggestions will allow for easier correlation during troubleshooting. Because the named access list and route map are case-sensitive, it's a good practice to use either all capital or all lowercase letters. This makes it easier to spot whether a letter is out of place.

For example, if your naming standard used all capital letters for named access lists, the access list that would be applied inbound on the interface connecting to the engineering department could be ENGINEERING-DEPT-IN.

If you are running a code level above 12.0(2)T, you can also use remarks to assist in documenting the role for a particular access list line. Following are examples of the remark command for both named and numbered lists:

Numbered List:

```
access-list 100 remark Do not allow Sales Dept subnet to telnet out
access-list 100 deny tcp 10.30.30.0 0.0.0.255 any eq telnet
```

Named List:

```
ip access-list extended SALES-DEPT-IN
 remark Do not allow Sales Dept subnet to telnet out
 deny tcp 10.30.30.0 0.0.0.255 any eq telnet
```

One final suggestion: If the same access list or route map is used on multiple routers, be sure to name them the same on all the routers. This will avoid confusion and allow for easier documentation and updating. For example, if you have a standard numbered access list that is used to limit SNMP read-only traffic on the routers, always use the same number on every router. By using these simple procedures, life with access lists and route maps will be that much more bearable.

TCP/IP Symptoms and Problems: Summary Sheet

Table 38.14 lists several common TCP/IP symptoms and their probable causes.

TABLE 38.14 TCP/IP Symptoms and Causes

Symptom	Problems
Local host cannot communicate with a remote host	(a) DNS not working properly (b) No route to remote host (c) Missing default gateway (d) Administrative denial (access lists)
Certain applications won't work properly	(a) Administrative denial (access lists) (b) Network not configured to handle the application
Booting failures	(a) BootP server did not have an entry for the MAC address (b) Missing IP helper address (c) Access lists (d) Change in the NIC or MAC address (e) Duplicate IP address (f) Improper IP configuration
Can't ping a remote station	(a) Access lists (b) No route to host (c) No default gateway set (d) Remote host down
Missing routes	(a) Improper routing protocol configuration (b) Distribute lists (c) Passive interface (doesn't receive updates) (d) Neighbor not advertising routes (e) Protocol version mismatch (f) Neighbor relation not established
Adjacencies not forming	(a) Improper routing protocol configuration (b) Improper IP configuration (c) Misconfigured network or neighbor statements (d) Mismatched Hello timers (e) Mismatched area ID
High CPU utilization	(a) Several routing updates due to instabilities (b) Debug wasn't turned off (c) A process gone amok

TABLE 38.14 TCP/IP Symptoms and Causes *(continued)*

Symptom	Problems
Route stuck in active mode	(a) Misconfigured timers (b) Hardware problems (c) Unstable link

TCP/IP Problems and Action Plans: Summary Sheet

Table 38.15 contains action plans for each of the problems outlined listed in the table.

TABLE 38.15 Action Plans for Common TCP/IP Problems

Problem	Action Plan
DNS not working properly	Check the DNS configuration on host and DNS server. May use the `nslookup` utility to verify functionality of the DNS server.
No route to remote host	This can be caused by several different things: 1. Check the default gateway using the `ipconfig /all` or `winipcfg` command if you are on a Windows machine. 2. Using the `show ip route` command, check to see whether the router has a route. 3. If the router doesn't have a route, use the `show ip route` command to see whether a gateway of last resort is set. 4. If there is a gateway, check the next hop in the path toward the destination. If there is no gateway, fix the problem or investigate why the router does not have a route.
Access lists	If you isolate the problem to an access list, you must analyze the list, rewrite it correctly, and then apply the new access list.
Network not configured to handle the application	When applications use NetBIOS, NetBEUI, IPX, or other non-IP applications, verify that the routers involved are configured to properly handle the applications by using transparent bridging, SRB, tunneling, and so on.

TABLE 38.15 Action Plans for Common TCP/IP Problems *(continued)*

Problem	Action Plan
Booting failures	1. Check the DHCP or BootP server, and verify that it has an entry for the MAC address of the problem station. 2. Use `debug ip udp` to verify that packets are being received from the host. 3. Verify that the helper addresses are correctly configured. 4. Check for access lists that might be denying the packets. 5. Make the necessary changes.
Missing routes	1. Look on the first router to see what routes are being learned. Issue the `show ip route` command. 2. Depending on the routing protocol, verify that adjacencies have been formed with neighboring routers. 3. Using the `show running-config` command, look at the router's configuration and verify that the routing protocol has the proper network or neighbor statements. 4. When troubleshooting OSPF, verify that the wildcard mask permits the correct routes. 5. Check the distribute lists that are applied to the interfaces. Analyze the inbound filters. 6. Verify that both neighbors have the correct IP configuration. 7. If routes are being redistributed, verify the metric. 8. Verify that the routes are being redistributed properly.
Adjacencies not forming	1. Perform a `show ip` *`protocol`* `neighbors` command to list the adjacencies that have formed. 2. Look at the protocol configuration to confirm which adjacencies have not formed. 3. Check the network statements in the protocol configuration. 4. Show the `ip` *`protocol`* interface to obtain interface-specific information such as Hello timers. 5. Once you have isolated the problem, make the necessary changes.

Summary

Before the advent of the routing protocol, the only way to get packets from point A to point B was to use static routes. As internetworks grew in size, it became impractical to keep adding new routes manually. Engineers began creating and using dynamic routing protocols. One of the first of these—RIP—provided dynamic updates as well as automatic fail over in the event of a failure. However, RIP did not have many of the other features common in routing protocols today. As new routing protocols were created, they offered more features and capabilities. With each generation, engineers gained more flexibility in determining how packets were routed through the network.

Today, a number of protocols can be used to route TCP/IP traffic. These include the ones studied in this chapter—RIP, IGRP, EIGRP, OSPF, and BGP. Each of these protocols has its own strengths and weaknesses and is best suited for particular environments. Problems can arise, however, when one routing domain must redistribute its routes into another. This redistribution can cause suboptimal routing or routing loops.

To prevent these issues, special steps should be taken at the redistribution points. Specifically, distribute lists, prefix lists, and/or route maps should be used. These tools allow for the filtering of the routes being redistributed, as well as the filtering of the routes that are sent to or received from a neighbor. In addition to the distribution lists, prefix lists, and/or route maps, engineers also can employ a wide array of `show` and `debug` commands to determine exactly what a routing protocol is doing. These commands vary in granularity. Some show information about the general routing characteristics on a router; others show detailed information about a singular route learned from a particular protocol. By using these commands together, you can effectively troubleshoot routing problems of any type and severity.

Exam Essentials

Know the concept of the default gateway and how it is used. The default gateway can be either dynamically learned or statically defined. In either case, the default gateway is used as the destination path for any packet for which there is no specific route in the routing table.

Know the difference between static and dynamic routing. Static routing allows the administrator to define routes on a router-by-router basis. However, the cost of this flexibility is a high amount of overhead any time there is a change in the network. Dynamic routing, using one of the routing protocols mentioned in this chapter, automatically distributes routing tables to all participating routers. Dynamic routing also allows automatic updates to all routers when there is a change in the network.

Know the routing protocols and the *show* and *debug* commands that can be used with them. The routing protocols covered in this chapter are RIP, IGRP, EIGRP, OSPF, and BGP. Be sure to review the tables showing the `show` and `debug` commands available for each protocol.

Know the issues surrounding the redistribution of one routing protocol into another. Redistribution, if not done properly, can cause routing loops. Special care is needed when bidirectional redistribution takes place. In addition to routing loops, using multiple routing protocols with different administrative distances can cause suboptimal routing.

Know how to use distribute lists, prefix lists, and route maps to filter routing information. Distribute lists, prefix lists, and route maps can be used to filter and manipulate routing updates in various ways. Though all three are similar in function, distribute lists are really nothing more than access lists that are applied to routing updates. Prefix lists add the ability to filter based on the address as well as on the subnet mask of the route. Route maps allow for the manipulation as well as the filtering of routing updates.

Troubleshooting Serial Line and Frame Relay Connectivity

THE CCNP EXAM TOPICS COVERED IN THIS CHAPTER INCLUDE THE FOLLOWING:

- ✓ Verify network connectivity.
- ✓ Use the optimal troubleshooting approach in resolving network problems.
- ✓ Minimize downtime during troubleshooting.
- ✓ Use Cisco IOS commands to identify problems.
- ✓ Work with external providers to diagnose and resolve network problems.

Many of the commands that are available to troubleshoot serial and Frame Relay problems are similar. This chapter first discusses topics relating to troubleshooting serial lines. After those topics have been covered in detail, the **show** and **debug** commands relating to Frame Relay are discussed.

Summaries of troubleshooting symptoms and solutions are provided at the end of each section. These summaries will be valuable as quick-reference guides when you are isolating and diagnosing problems on serial lines and Frame Relay interfaces.

Troubleshooting Serial Lines

There are numerous commands available to aid in troubleshooting serial lines. Some of them are **show** commands; others are **debug** commands. Here is a list of the commands that are discussed in this section, along with advice about the information they provide for troubleshooting:

- `clear counters serial`
- `show interface serial`
- `show controllers serial`
- `show buffers`
- `debug serial interface`

An integral part of serial connections is the hardware involved. Look at Figure 39.1. In this graphic, you see Router A connected to a channel service unit/digital service unit (CSU/DSU), through a serial cable that is connected to another CSU/DSU, and then connected to Router B. Please refer to this figure as you go through the rest of the discussion.

FIGURE 39.1 Serial line setup

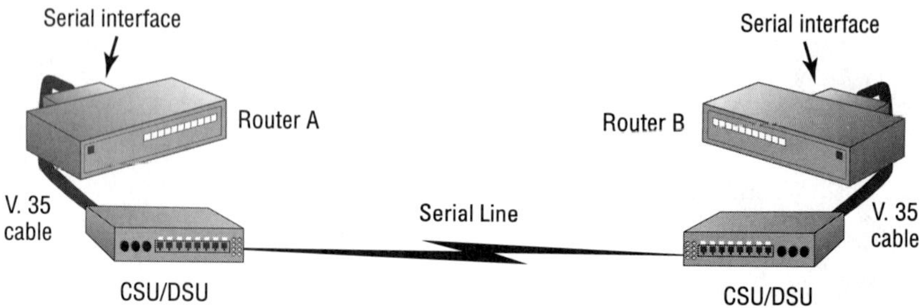

HDLC Encapsulation

High-Level Data Link Control (HDLC) is an encapsulation method used by serial links. HDLC provides a 32-bit checksum and three different transfer modes: normal, asynchronous response, and asynchronous balanced.

HDLC is used by default on Cisco serial interfaces. The first important point of troubleshooting serial line problems is to verify that both sides of the link are using the same encapsulation type. Here is a look at a serial interface from a Cisco 2501. Notice that the encapsulation type is HDLC:

```
Router_A>show interface serial0
Serial0 is administratively down, line protocol is down
  Hardware is HD64570
  Internet address is 172.16.20.6/30
  MTU 1500 bytes, BW 1544 Kbit, DLY 20000 usec, rely 255/
  255, load 1/255
  Encapsulation HDLC, loopback not set, keepalive set (10
  sec)
  Last input never, output never, output hang never
  Last clearing of "show interface" counters never
  Input queue: 0/75/0 (size/max/drops); Total output
  drops: 0
  Queueing strategy: weighted fair
  Output queue: 0/1000/64/0 (size/max total/threshold/
drops)
     Conversations  0/0/256 (active/max active/max total)
     Reserved Conversations 0/0 (allocated/max allocated)
  5 minute input rate 0 bits/sec, 0 packets/sec
  5 minute output rate 0 bits/sec, 0 packets/sec
     0 packets input, 0 bytes, 0 no buffer
     Received 0 broadcasts, 0 runts, 0 giants, 0 throttles
     0 input errors, 0 CRC, 0 frame, 0 overrun, 0 ignored,
     0 abort
     0 packets output, 0 bytes, 0 underruns
     0 output errors, 0 collisions, 1 interface resets
     0 output buffer failures, 0 output buffers swapped
     out
     0 carrier transitions
     DCD=down  DSR=down  DTR=down  RTS=down  CTS=down
Router_A>
```

Other encapsulations may be used on serial interfaces, but HDLC is used for synchronous data link control. In addition Cisco's version of HDLC is slightly different from that of "generic" HDLC.

show interface serial Command

The show interface serial commands provide you with a great deal of helpful information when you troubleshoot problems related to serial lines and other serial interfaces such as Frame Relay. However, in order to get correct information, you should first clear the counters for the interface of interest.

Before you do so, look at the output of the show interface serial 1 command:

```
Router_A>show interface serial 1
Serial1 is up, line protocol is up
  Hardware is HD64570
  Internet address is 172.16.30.5/30
  MTU 1500 bytes, BW 1544 Kbit, DLY 20000 usec, rely 255/  255, load 1/255
  Encapsulation HDLC, loopback not set, keepalive set (10  sec)
  Last input 00:00:08, output 00:00:07, output hang never
  Last clearing of "show interface" counters never
  Input queue: 0/75/0 (size/max/drops);
Total output drops: 0
  Queueing strategy: weighted fair
  Output queue: 0/1000/64/0 (size/max total/threshold/drops)
     Conversations  0/1/256 (active/max active/max total)
     Reserved Conversations 0/0 (allocated/max allocated)
  5 minute input rate 0 bits/sec, 0 packets/sec
  5 minute output rate 0 bits/sec, 0 packets/sec
     1307 packets input, 85380 bytes, 0 no buffer
     Received 695 broadcasts, 0 runts, 0 giants, 0 throttles
     0 input errors, 0 CRC, 0 frame, 0 overrun, 0 ignored,
     0 abort
     1308 packets output, 85652 bytes, 0 underruns
     0 output errors, 0 collisions, 116 interface resets
     0 output buffer failures, 0 output buffers swapped
     out
     238 carrier transitions
     DCD=up  DSR=up  DTR=up  RTS=up  CTS=up
Router_A>
```

First note that the output tells you the interface is up and the line protocol is also up. The information contained in the `show interface serial` command will be discussed in more detail in just a moment. For now, it's important to recognize that many of the counters have elevated numbers. Also, notice that the seventh line of the output declares that the counters were never cleared.

You cannot effectively troubleshoot if you do not have accurate data returned through the many diagnostic commands. One way to ensure that the data you are analyzing is accurate and directly applies to the problem at hand is to perform the `clear counters serial` *`number`* command, which resets the interface counters to zero. This ensures that the data retrieved from the `interface` command is representative of what is happening at that moment on the network.

Here's how it is done and what the interface looks like after the command has been issued:

Line numbers have been added to the output below for ease of reading.

```
Router_A#clear counters serial 1
Clear "show interface" counters on this interface [confirm]
%CLEAR-5-COUNTERS: Clear counter on interface Serial1 by console
Router_A#show interface serial 1
 1. Serial1 is up, line protocol is up
 2.  Hardware is HD64570
 3.  Internet address is 172.16.30.5/30
 4.  MTU 1500 bytes, BW 1544 Kbit, DLY 20000 usec, rely 255/255, load
 5.  51/255
 6.  Encapsulation HDLC, loopback not set,
 7.  keepalive set (10  sec)
 8.  Last input 00:00:00, output 00:00:00, output hang never
 9.  Last clearing of "show interface" counters 00:28:48
10.  Input queue: 1/75/0 (size/max/drops);
11. Total output drops: 0
12. Queueing strategy: weighted fair
13.  Output queue: 0/1000/64/0 (size/max total/threshold/drops)
14.     Conversations  0/2/256 (active/max active/max total)
15.     Reserved Conversations 0/0 (allocated/max allocated)
16.  5 minute input rate 321000 bits/sec, 48 packets/sec
17.  5 minute output rate 320000 bits/sec, 48 packets/sec
18.     12439 packets input, 13257786 bytes, 0 no buffer
19.     Received 202 broadcasts, 0 runts, 0 giants, 0 throttles
20.     0 input errors, 0 CRC, 0 frame, 0 overrun, 0 ignored,
21.     0 abort
22.     12438 packets output, 13256434 bytes, 0 underruns
23.     0 output errors, 0 collisions, 0 interface resets
```

```
24.      0 output buffer failures, 0 output buffers swapped
25.      out
26.      0 carrier transitions
27.      DCD=up  DSR=up  DTR=up  RTS=up  CTS=up
Router_A#
```

Notice the ninth line of the output. It says that the counters were cleared 28 minutes before. Once the counters are cleared, you can associate any new data with current network events. If you try to associate current network events with inaccurate data, you will never find the problem. In addition to clearing the individual interface, you can execute the `clear counters` command without specifying an interface to clear all the counters on the router.

Now we'll go through the available data provided by the `show interface serial` command. Refer to the preceding output, line 1.

The first line provides information regarding the status of the interface and the line protocol:

```
Serial1 is up, line protocol is up
```

In this case, both are up and functional. If the interface is down, the line protocol must also be down.

Cabling problems, carrier problems, or hardware problems can all be reasons for a serial interface to report as down. These problems can be addressed by verifying proper cable connectivity, replacing hardware (including cables), and checking the CSU/DSU for carrier signal. If you cannot resolve the problem by using these techniques, you can and should contact the local carrier, who can verify the carrier service.

Another possibility for the interface status is that the interface is up but the line protocol is down. When this happens, it can be due to one or more of a variety of problems, as follows:

- Failed CSU/DSU
- Router interface problems
- Mismatched timing on CSU/DSU or carrier network
- Misconfigured interface
- Keepalive signals not received from the remote router
- Carrier problem

You should verify that the local interface and the remote interface are properly configured. *Loopback tests* can be performed. These tests will be discussed in the CSU/DSU section of this chapter.

Continuing with the description of the output of the `show interface serial` command, notice that the second line of the output displays the hardware type of the interface:

```
Hardware is HD64570
```

The third line shows the layer 3 IP address with the associated subnet mask:

```
Internet address is 172.16.30.5/30
```

Lines 4 and 5 contain all of the information needed to create a route metric for the interface. The data includes MTU, bandwidth, delay, reliability, and load. Note that the load and reliability values are in fractional form (out of 255):

```
MTU 1500 bytes, BW 1544 Kbit, DLY 20000 usec, rely 255/255, load 51/255
```

Lines 6 and 7 indicate the type of encapsulation that is being used on the line, as well as loopback and keepalive information:

```
Encapsulation HDLC, loopback not set, keepalive set (10 sec)
```

The eighth line displays the last time the interface saw any traffic:

```
Last input 00:00:00, output 00:00:00, output hang never
```

Again, the ninth line shows the time that transpired since the last time the interface counters were cleared:

```
Last clearing of "show interface" counters 00:28:48
```

Lines 10 through 15 contain information regarding the queuing on the interface:

```
Input queue: 1/75/0 (size/max/drops);
Total output drops: 0
  Queueing strategy: weighted fair
  Output queue: 0/1000/64/0 (size/max total/threshold/
  drops)
     Conversations  0/2/256 (active/max active/max total)
     Reserved Conversations 0/0 (allocated/max allocated)
```

Lines 16 and 17 display the five-minute average for input and output bits per second, and packets per second on the interface:

```
5 minute input rate 321000 bits/sec, 48 packets/sec
5 minute output rate 320000 bits/sec, 48 packets/sec
```

Beginning with line 18 and until line 21, the output displays interface input information. The first line is a counter that keeps track of the number of incoming packets on the interface. The next line displays information for broadcast, runt, giant, and throttled packets. The last lines (lines 20 and 21) display any input, CRC, frame, overrun, ignored, or abort errors:

```
12439 packets input, 13257786 bytes, 0 no buffer
     Received 202 broadcasts, 0 runts, 0 giants,
     0 throttles
     0 input errors, 0 CRC, 0 frame, 0 overrun, 0 ignored,
     0 abort
```

The output interface statistics begin with line 22 and end on line 26. This data reflects the number of output packets, underruns, output errors, collisions, interface resets, output buffer failures, swapped output buffers, and carrier transitions:

```
12438 packets output, 13256434 bytes, 0 underruns
     0 output errors, 0 collisions, 0 interface resets
     0 output buffer failures,
     0 output buffers swapped out
     0 carrier transitions
```

Input and output information contain 32-bit counters for the packet and byte counts. As soon as each count increments over roughly 4.2 billion, the counter resets at zero.

Interface resets should be considered warning flags. If you see a large number of interface resets after clearing the counter, you should be concerned. Interface resets are caused by the following:

- Queued packets not sent for several seconds
- Problems with hardware (for example, router interface, cable, or CSU/DSU)
- Mismatched clocking signals
- Looped interface
- Interface shut down
- Line protocol down and the interface resetting periodically

The next warning flag to note is the carrier transitions statistic. This counts the number of times that the DCD (data carrier detect) signal changes state. If the carrier keeps fluctuating, you do not have a stable circuit. This is often a carrier problem, and the local carrier must be contacted.

The final line of the `show interface serial` command displays carrier-specific information:

```
DCD=up  DSR=up  DTR=up  RTS=up  CTS=up
```

show controllers Command

The `show controllers` command is used to display interface status and tells you whether a cable is connected to the interface. Following are a couple of different outputs from the `show controllers` command.

The first output is from interface serial 0. There is no cable attached to the interface:

```
Router_A#show controllers serial 0
HD unit 0, idb = 0x94AEC, driver structure at 0x99870
buffer size 1524  HD unit 0, No cable, clockrate 4000000
cpb = 0x41, eda = 0x4940, cda = 0x4800
RX ring with 16 entries at 0x414800
```

```
.
.  {some output omitted}
.
TX ring with 2 entries at 0x415000
.
.  {some output omitted}
.
0 missed datagrams, 0 overruns
0 bad datagram encapsulations, 0 memory errors
0 transmitter underruns
0 residual bit errors

Router_A#
```

The second output is from interface serial 1, which does have a cable connected, V.35 DCE, and is functioning properly:

```
Router_A#show controllers serial 1
HD unit 1, idb = 0x9D4E0, driver structure at 0xA2260
buffer size 1524  HD unit 1, V.35 DCE cable, clockrate 4000000
cpb = 0x42, eda = 0x3104, cda = 0x3118
RX ring with 16 entries at 0x423000
.
.  {some output omitted}
.
TX ring with 2 entries at 0x423800
.
.  {some output omitted}
.
0 missed datagrams, 0 overruns
0 bad datagram encapsulations, 0 memory errors
0 transmitter underruns
0 residual bit errors

Router_A#
```

The basic information provided by this command is the interface status regarding missed datagrams, overruns, bad encapsulation, memory errors, underruns, and bit errors. In addition, it indicates the interface clock rate, as well as the type of cable connected to the interface.

If you don't see a cable connected to the interface, verifying that a cable is properly connected is a good item to include in a troubleshooting action plan. Excessive errors on the interface can be an indication of faulty hardware.

show buffers Command

The show buffers command can be used to look at system buffer pools, but it also provides information regarding interface buffers. Look at the sample output from a 2514 router:

```
Router_B>show buffers
Buffer elements:
     500 in free list (500 max allowed)
     52587626 hits, 0 misses, 0 created

Public buffer pools:
Small buffers, 104 bytes (total 50, permanent 50):
     50 in free list (20 min, 150 max allowed)
     7709985 hits, 0 misses, 0 trims, 0 created
     0 failures (0 no memory)
Middle buffers, 600 bytes (total 25, permanent 25):
     24 in free list (10 min, 150 max allowed)
     2045756 hits, 0 misses, 0 trims, 0 created
     0 failures (0 no memory)
Big buffers, 1524 bytes (total 50, permanent 50):
     50 in free list (5 min, 150 max allowed)
     2541768 hits, 774 misses, 217 trims, 217 created
     24 failures (0 no memory)
VeryBig buffers, 4520 bytes (total 10, permanent 10):
     10 in free list (0 min, 100 max allowed)
     52464 hits, 0 misses, 0 trims, 0 created
     0 failures (0 no memory)
Large buffers, 5024 bytes (total 0, permanent 0):
     0 in free list (0 min, 10 max allowed)
     0 hits, 0 misses, 0 trims, 0 created
     0 failures (0 no memory)
Huge buffers, 18024 bytes (total 0, permanent 0):
     0 in free list (0 min, 4 max allowed)
     0 hits, 0 misses, 0 trims, 0 created
     0 failures (0 no memory)

Interface buffer pools:
Ethernet0 buffers, 1524 bytes (total 32, permanent 32):
     5 in free list (0 min, 32 max allowed)
     255684 hits, 64696 fallbacks
     8 max cache size, 5 in cache
```

```
Ethernet1 buffers, 1524 bytes (total 32, permanent 32):
     0 in free list (0 min, 32 max allowed)
     300993 hits, 1024384 fallbacks
     8 max cache size, 6 in cache
Serial0 buffers, 1524 bytes (total 32, permanent 32):
     7 in free list (0 min, 32 max allowed)
     25 hits, 0 fallbacks
     8 max cache size, 8 in cache
Serial1 buffers, 1524 bytes (total 32, permanent 32):
     7 in free list (0 min, 32 max allowed)
     25 hits, 0 fallbacks
     8 max cache size, 8 in cache
```

Notice that the interface buffers are listed at the end of the output. This information can be useful to troubleshoot serial interface problems. It is important to look at the number of free buffers. These numbers indicate the memory that is available on the interface for buffering incoming and outgoing packets.

debug serial interface Command

As always with debug tools, you must exercise caution. When executing a serial debug or Frame Relay debug, the router can generate large amounts of data that can encumber the router. Make sure that the specific command is used when possible. You can use **debug** in conjunction with access lists to focus the application of the debug tool.

The debug of a serial interface displays HDLC or Frame Relay communication messages. A sample follows that includes Frame Relay information. It is important to understand that the output of this command varies with the encapsulation type used on the interface:

```
Router_A#debug serial interface
Serial network interface debugging is on
Serial0(out): StEnq, myseq 135, yourseen 134, DTE up
Serial0(in): Status, myseq 135
Serial1(out): StEnq, myseq 2, yourseen 8, DTE up
Serial1(in): Status, myseq 2
Serial2(out): StEnq, myseq 247, yourseen 247, DTE up
Serial2(in): Status, myseq 247
Serial3(out): StEnq, myseq 30, yourseen 28, DTE up
Serial3(in): Status, myseq 30
Serial0(out): StEnq, myseq 136, yourseen 135, DTE up
Serial0(in): Status, myseq 136
Serial1(out): StEnq, myseq 3, yourseen 9, DTE up
Serial1(in): Status, myseq 3
```

```
Serial2(out): StEnq, myseq 248, yourseen 248, DTE up
Serial2(in): Status, myseq 248
Serial3(out): StEnq, myseq 31, yourseen 29, DTE up
Serial3(in): Status, myseq 31
Serial0(out): StEnq, myseq 137, yourseen 136, DTE up
Serial0(in): Status, myseq 137
Serial1(out): StEnq, myseq 4, yourseen 10, DTE up
Serial1(in): Status, myseq 4
Serial2(out): StEnq, myseq 249, yourseen 249, DTE up
Serial2(in): Status, myseq 249
Serial3(out): StEnq, myseq 32, yourseen 30, DTE up
Serial3(in): Status, myseq 32
```

This sample includes output from many interfaces. The underlined type is used to highlight the data for interface serial 0. Here are definitions of what you see:

StEnq An LMI (Local Management Interface) status inquiry sent from the router to the Frame Relay switch. (LMIs are discussed further in the sections on troubleshooting Frame Relay later in this chapter.)

Status Reply sent to the router from the Frame Relay switch.

myseq The local keepalive number. The value is the sequence identifier.

yourseen The keepalive sent by the other side of the serial connection. This value is the actual sequence number last received, incremented by 1. It indicates expectation of the next sequence number to be sent.

DTE The data termination equipment status. In this example, it is up.

The `in` and `out` specify the directions in which the packets are sent. Outbound packets are keepalives sent by the local side; inbound packets are the keepalives sent from the other end.

If the sequence numbers for a given interface don't increment, then there is probably a timing or line problem at one or the other end of the connection. The line will reset if two out of six consecutive keepalive packets fail to increment. Although the layer 3 protocol considers the line protocol to be down, the layer 2 protocol continues to send keepalive messages.

Here is a sample of HDLC communication:

```
Router_A#debug serial interface
Serial network interface debugging is on
Serial0: HDLC myseq 172188, mineseen 172188*, yourseen 172326, line up
Serial0: HDLC myseq 172189, mineseen 172189*, yourseen 172327, line up
Serial0: HDLC myseq 172190, mineseen 172190*, yourseen 172328, line up
Serial0: HDLC myseq 172191, mineseen 172191*, yourseen 172329, line up
Router_A#
```

The field values are very similar to the field values in the Frame Relay output. Here are the field definitions:

myseq The local keepalive number. The value is the sequence identifier.

yourseen The keepalive sent by the other side of the serial connection, incremented by 1.

mineseen This is the other side's sent `yourseen`, or the expectation of what will be sent next. If everything is working properly, this should equal the `myseq`.

CSU/DSU Loopback Tests

Loopback tests aid in physically isolating serial line and Frame Relay problems. Four different loopback tests can be performed to troubleshoot the circuit. You can perform two of them, and the local provider has access to perform the other two. Here is a list of the four loopback tests:

- Local loopback on the local CSU/DSU
- Local loopback on the remote CSU/DSU
- Remote loopback from the local NIU to the remote CSU/DSU
- Remote loopback from the remote NIU to the local CSU/DSU

Though it is possible to perform a subset of these loopback commands on certain interface types on a router, they are more commonly performed on the CSU/DSU. Therefore, it is the CSU/DSU variation of the loopbacks that this chapter focuses on.

Look at Figure 39.2 to see how the tests are performed.

The tests that you can perform are the two local loopback tests. You can perform these tests because you have access to the equipment. The local provider has to perform the remote loopback tests because it has access to the equipment within the cloud.

FIGURE 39.2 CSU/DSU loopback tests

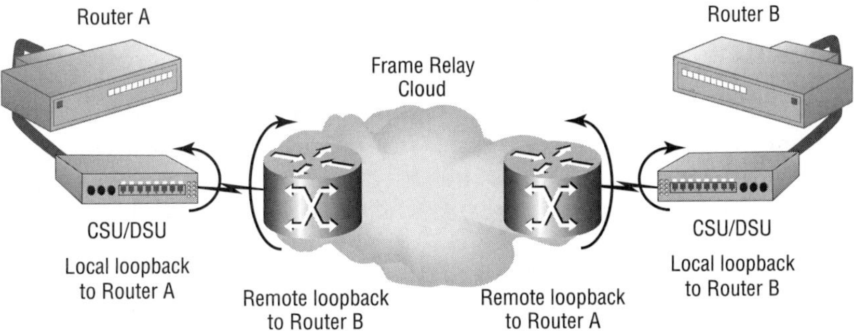

When using loopback tests for troubleshooting, you should follow these steps:

1. Perform the local loopback test for the local router (Router A in the example in Figure 39.2).
2. Verify the line status. This means to check for LMI status when using Frame Relay on the interface.
3. Perform the local loopback test for the remote router, Router B.
4. Verify the line status. This means to check for LMI status when using Frame Relay on the interface.
5. If you see LMI but cannot get remote connectivity, contact your local service provider, which can run the remote loopback tests.

Remember that LMI stands for Local Management Interface. See the section "Troubleshooting Frame Relay" later in this chapter for more on LMIs.

When you see LMI up on a router interface during a loopback test, it means that the protocol is working locally, but not necessarily remotely. By putting a CSU/DSU into loopback, the signal is sent back to the interface, so the line protocol shows up. For end-to-end connectivity, both end sites must have LMI up status. In addition, all of the Frame Relay switches that participate in the permanent virtual circuit (PVC) must be working properly. Remote loopback tests confirm the functionality of the circuit.

Serial Line Summary

Several encapsulations and protocols may be used over serial lines. Because of this variety, many different problems can occur. Again here, it is important to realize that the output of show commands may differ depending on the interface configuration.

To aid you in diagnosing and resolving serial line problems, this section includes two quick reference tables: one with symptoms and problems, and one with suggested action plans.

Real World Scenario

Troubleshooting Red, Yellow, and Blue

When troubleshooting a serial connection, many times you need the assistance of your local telephone company or carrier in order to resolve the problem. Though it is tempting to call and open a ticket with them at the first sign of trouble, I have found that in many cases you can assist them in finding the problem—or solve it yourself—with some testing on your own.

The first thing that I do when a circuit is down is to perform the loopback tests described in this chapter to ensure that my router, in-house wiring, and CSU/DSU are working correctly. Assuming that these items test correctly, I put a DS-1/DS-3 test on the circuit and look at the signal coming to and from the carrier. In most cases I will get either a red, yellow, or blue alarm coming from them.

If I get a red alarm on the signal from the carrier, this means I am not receiving any signal on the link. I may or may not be transmitting information correctly. If I see a yellow alarm, it means the far-end device is not receiving any information. However, because I am receiving the yellow alarm signal that it is sending, I know that my receive path is fine, and therefore the problem lies on the transmitting path somewhere between my current location and the destination device. Finally, a blue alarm is an all-ones signal. This usually is generated by one of the carrier's systems that needs to be reset or reconfigured.

With this information in hand, I then can open a trouble ticket with the carrier and help them isolate where to start looking for the problem, thus decreasing the time it takes to correct the problem.

Symptoms and Problems

Table 39.1 lists several common serial line conditions and their related possible problems.

TABLE 39.1 Serial Line Symptoms and Problems

Symptom or Condition	Associated Problems
Interface is administratively down; line protocol is down.	(a) The interface has been placed in shutdown via a configuration command. (b) Duplicate IP addresses are not allowed, and one of the two interfaces with the same IP address will be shut down.
Interface is down; line protocol is down.	(a) Improper cabling. (b) No carrier signal from local provider. (c) Hardware failure (interface or CSU/DSU; cabling). (d) Clocking (or lack thereof).
Interface is up; line protocol is down.	(a) Misconfigured interface, local or remote. (b) Local provider problem. (c) Keepalive sequencing not incrementing. (d) Hardware failures (local or remote interfaces and CSU/DSU). (e) Noisy line. (f) Timing mismatches. (g) L2 issues such as LMI.
Interface is up; line protocol is up (looped).	The circuit is in loopback somewhere.
Incrementing carrier transition counter	(a) Unstable signaling coming from the local provider. (b) Faulty cabling. (c) Failing hardware (for example, interface or CSU/DSU).
Incrementing interface resets	(a) Faulty cabling, causing the loss of the CD signal. (b) Hardware failure. (c) Line congestion.

TABLE 39.1 Serial Line Symptoms and Problems *(continued)*

Symptom or Condition	Associated Problems
Input drops, errors, CRC, and framing errors	(a) Line speed oversubscribes the router interface capacity. (b) Local provider problem. (c) Noisy line. (d) Faulty cabling. (e) Improper cabling. (f) Failing hardware.
Output drops.	The interface is capable of transmitting at higher than line speed.

Problems and Action Plans

Now that you have seen the list of symptoms with their associated problems, you need a quick reference for resolving the problems. Table 39.2 provides summary action plans for handling the listed serial line problems.

TABLE 39.2 Action Plans for Common Serial Line Problems

Problem	Resolution Action Plan
Local provider problems	1. Check the CSU/DSU for a CD signal. Check for other signals, such as RX and TX clocking, to see if the circuit is transmitting and receiving information. 2. If you do not get a CD signal or have other problems, contact the local service provider to troubleshoot and fix the problem.
Improper or faulty cabling	1. Make sure you are using the proper cable for the equipment being used. 2. Use a breakout box to check the control leads. 3. Swap faulty cables.
Misconfigured interface	1. View the interface configuration using the `show running-config` command. 2. Make sure that the same encapsulation type is used at both ends of the circuit by using the `show interface` command.
Keepalive problems	1. Verify that keepalives are being sent. You can check this via the router configuration or by using the `show interface` command. 2. If the configuration says that keepalives are being sent, you may want to enable debug `serial interface` for the interface. 3. Verify that the sequence numbers are incrementing. 4. If the sequences don't increment, run loopback tests on the local and remote sites. 5. If the sequences don't increment even when the CSU/DSU is in loopback, you have a hardware problem. Replace faulty hardware.

TABLE 39.2 Action Plans for Common Serial Line Problems *(continued)*

Problem	Resolution Action Plan
Hardware failure	Replace the hardware.
Interface is in loopback mode.	1. Check the interface configuration. 2. If there is a loopback entry in the interface configuration, remove it with the no form of the command. 3. If the interface configuration is clean, check the CSU/DSU to see if it is placed in loopback. 4. If the CSU/DSU is in loopback, remove it from loopback mode. 5. If the CSU/DSU is not in loopback mode, contact the local provider; it may have placed the circuit in loopback.
Interface is administratively down.	1. Check the configuration. Verify that the IP address is not a duplicate. 2. Enter the configuration mode and issue the `no shutdown` command within the interface.
Line speed is larger than the interface capacity.	1. Reduce input queue size by using the `hold-queue in` command. 2. Increase output queues on exiting interfaces.
Interface speed is larger than the line speed.	1. Reduce broadcast traffic. 2. Increase output queue. 3. Implement queuing algorithms, if necessary.

Troubleshooting Frame Relay

Frame Relay is a popular WAN solution in many networks. Frame Relay supports PVCs and switched virtual circuits (SVCs). These virtual circuits are built by using *DLCI numbers*. A *data link connection identifier (DLCI)* is used to identify the virtual circuits in a Frame Relay cloud. Figure 39.3 depicts a Frame Relay network. Notice the DLCI numbers assigned to the interfaces throughout the network.

It is important to remember that the DLCI is significant only locally. The DLCI maps to layer 3 IP addresses, as shown in Figure 39.3. The IP addresses given on the diagram suggest the PVCs that exist through the Frame Relay cloud.

When Frame Relay problems occur, follow this troubleshooting checklist:

1. Check layer 1—the Physical layer—for any cabling or interface problems.
2. Check the interface encapsulation.
3. Check the LMI type.
4. Verify the DLCI-to-IP address mapping.

FIGURE 39.3 Frame Relay network

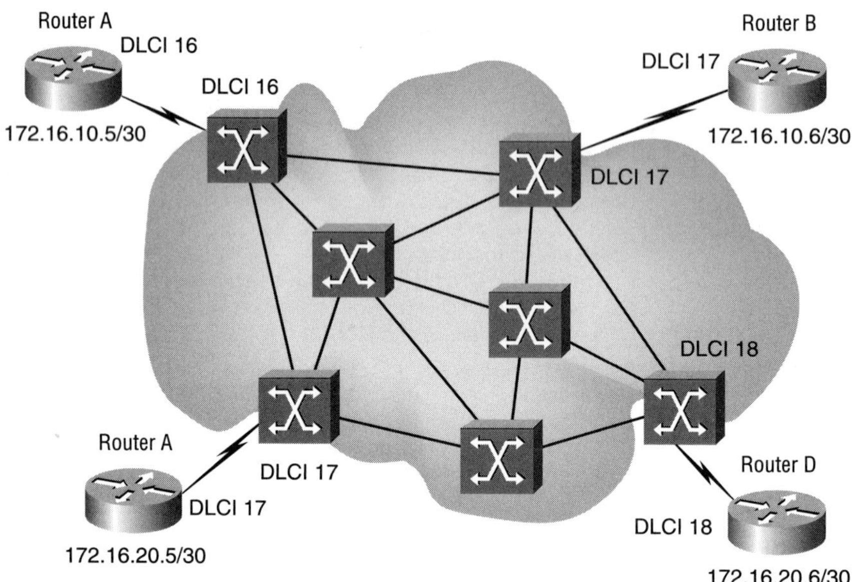

5. Verify the Frame Relay PVCs.
6. Verify the Frame Relay LMI.
7. Verify the Frame Relay map.
8. Verify the loopback tests, as described in the "CSU/DSU Loopback Tests" section earlier in the chapter.

The following sections describe the commands to execute each of these steps.

Frame Relay *show* Commands

The following `show` commands are covered in this section:

- `show interface`
- `show frame-relay lmi`
- `show frame-relay pvc`
- `show frame-relay map`

Notice that the second command listed here contains the term *LMI (Local Management Interface)*. LMI provides support for keepalive devices to verify data flow. As mentioned in the earlier sections on serial line troubleshooting, this part of the chapter includes many references to LMI. You will see this term a great deal when dealing with Frame Relay troubleshooting.

show interface

The `show interface` command is used to provide information on serial lines. In addition to normal serial line information, Frame Relay information is included in the output if the interface is configured for Frame Relay.

Line-by-line detail has already been given in this chapter for a normal serial interface. Only the fields relating to Frame Relay are listed here. Following is a sample of a Frame Relay interface output:

```
Router_A#show interface serial0
Serial0 is up, line protocol is up
  Hardware is HD64570
  MTU 1500 bytes, BW 1544 Kbit, DLY 20000 usec, rely 255/255, load 1/255
  Encapsulation FRAME-RELAY, loopback not set, keepalive set (10 sec)
  LMI enq sent  823406, LMI stat recvd 823403, LMI upd recvd 507, DTE LMI up
  LMI enq recvd 0, LMI stat sent  0, LMI upd sent  0
  LMI DLCI 1023  LMI type is CISCO  frame relay DTE
  Broadcast queue 0/64, broadcasts sent/dropped 0/0, interface broadcasts
  ➥36752578
  Last input 00:00:00, output 00:00:00, output hang never
  Last clearing of "show interface" counters never
  Input queue: 0/75/0 (size/max/drops); Total output drops: 0
  Queueing strategy: weighted fair
  Output queue: 0/64/0 (size/threshold/drops)
     Conversations  0/20 (active/max active)
     Reserved Conversations 0/0 (allocated/max allocated)
  5 minute input rate 5000 bits/sec, 6 packets/sec
  5 minute output rate 5000 bits/sec, 6 packets/sec
     134880248 packets input, 102288228 bytes, 0 no buffer
     Received 823910 broadcasts, 0 runts, 0 giants
     1 input errors, 1 CRC, 0 frame, 0 overrun, 0 ignored,
     1 abort
     136835759 packets output, 3397101778 bytes, 0 underruns
     0 output errors, 0 collisions, 14 interface resets
     0 output buffer failures, 0 output buffers swapped
     out
     2 carrier transitions
     DCD=up  DSR=up  DTR=up  RTS=up  CTS=up
Router_A#show interface serial 0.2
Serial0.2 is up, line protocol is up
  Hardware is HD64570
  Internet address is 172.16.30.6/30
```

```
  MTU 1500 bytes, BW 1544 Kbit, DLY 20000 usec, rely 255/  255, load 1/255
  Encapsulation FRAME-RELAY
Router_A#
```

Here are the relevant Frame Relay terms:

Encapsulation The Frame Relay encapsulation type used; either Cisco (default) or IETF.

LMI enq sent The number of LMI enquiries (alternative spelling of *inquiries*) sent.

LMI stat recvd The number of LMI status packets received.

LMI upd recvd The number of LMI updates received.

DTE LMI The status of the DTE (data termination equipment) Local Management Interface.

LMI enq recvd The number of LMI enquiries received.

LMI stat sent The number of LMI status packets sent.

LMI upd sent The number of LMI updates sent.

LMI DLCI The DLCI number used for LMI. Cisco LMI type uses DLCI 1023. When ANSI is used, the LMI DLCI is 0.

LMI type The LMI type used by the interface. The default is Cisco; the other two types are ANSI and ITU-T (aka Q933a). The LMI types on the router and the Frame Relay switch must match. Simply put, LMI type must match on the DTE and DCE equipment.

show frame-relay lmi

The `show frame-relay lmi` command displays LMI-relevant information. The following output contains the LMI type, inquiry, update, and status information:

```
Router_B#show frame-relay lmi
LMI Statistics for interface Serial0 (Frame Relay DTE) LMI TYPE = CISCO
  Invalid Unnumbered info 0   Invalid Prot Disc 0
  Invalid dummy Call Ref 0   Invalid Msg Type 0
  Invalid Status Message 0   Invalid Lock Shift 0
  Invalid Information ID 0   Invalid Report IE Len 0
  Invalid Report Request 0   Invalid Keep IE Len 0
  Num Status Enq. Sent 823406   Num Status msgs Rcvd 823403
  Num Update Status Rcvd 507   Num Status Timeouts 3
```

show frame-relay pvc

When you issue the `show frame-relay pvc` command, you get output that contains the LMI status of every DLCI on the router, or you may be more specific and enter a command to check only certain PVCs.

There are two types of DLCI usage: local DTE and switched. Things to check for in the output of the command include dropped frames, congestion notifications, and discard-eligible packets.

Here is a sample output. The data provided includes PVC information. It has the input and output packets for the interface, as well as FECN and BECN packet information. These statistics are available for every PVC on the router. Here, only two PVCs are shown:

```
Router_A#show frame-relay pvc

PVC Statistics for interface Serial0 (Frame Relay DTE)

DLCI = 18, DLCI USAGE = LOCAL, PVC STATUS = ACTIVE, INTERFACE = Serial0.4

input pkts 37515875 output pkts 38589330 in bytes 4113557032
out bytes 2755391175 dropped pkts 16 in FECN pkts 0
in BECN pkts 0 out FECN pkts 0 out BECN pkts 0
in DE pkts 315420 out DE pkts 0
pvc create time 13w4d, last time pvc status changed 06:40:12

DLCI = 19, DLCI USAGE = UNUSED, PVC STATUS = ACTIVE, INTERFACE = Serial0

input pkts 38 output pkts 0 in bytes 8372
out bytes 0 dropped pkts 0 in FECN pkts 0
in BECN pkts 0 out FECN pkts 0 out BECN pkts 0
in DE pkts 0 out DE pkts 0
pvc create time 13w4d, last time pvc status changed 7w4d
Num Pkts Switched 0
```

Problems can be detected by watching the number of FECN or BECN packets increase, which indicates line congestion. If these values are increasing rapidly compared to the overall number of frames going across the network, there could be an issue. Forward explicit congestion notification (FECN) notifies the receiving station (DTE) that congestion was experienced en route to the destination. Backward explicit congestion notification (BECN) notifies the sending station that congestion was experienced. FECN messages are sent in the direction of the congestion, and BECN messages are sent in the opposite direction of the congestion.

show frame-relay map

The `show frame-relay map` command provides information about the DLCI numbers and the encapsulation of all Frame Relay interfaces. The status of the interface is indicated with the up or down state found within the parentheses. The next field indicates the type of interface: point-to-point or multipoint. The DLCI for the interface and the encapsulation type are also included in the output.

Here is a sample:

```
Router_B#show frame-relay map
Serial0.10 (down): point-to-point dlci, dlci 24(0x18,0x480), broadcast,
```

```
 IETF, BW = 1024000 status defined, inactive
Serial0.7 (down): point-to-point dlci, dlci 21(0x15,0x450), broadcast,
 IETF, BW = 1024000 status defined, inactive
Serial0.5 (up): point-to-point dlci, dlci 20(0x14,0x440), broadcast,
 IETF, BW = 1024000 status defined, active
Serial0.6 (up): point-to-point dlci, dlci 30(0x1E,0x4E0), broadcast,
 IETF, BW = 48000 status defined, active
Serial0.4 (up): point-to-point dlci, dlci 18(0x12,0x420), broadcast,
 IETF, BW = 1024000 status defined, active
Serial0.2 (up): point-to-point dlci, dlci 27(0x1B,0x4B0), broadcast,
 IETF, BW = 48000 status defined, active
Serial0.11 (up): point-to-point dlci, dlci 31(0x1F,0x4F0), broadcast,
 IETF, BW = 48000 status defined, active
Serial0.9 (up): point-to-point dlci, dlci 29(0x1D,0x4D0), broadcast,
 IETF, BW = 48000 status defined, active
Serial0.12 (up): point-to-point dlci, dlci 32(0x20,0x800), broadcast,
 IETF, BW = 48000 status defined, active
Serial0.8 (up): point-to-point dlci, dlci 28(0x1C,0x4C0), broadcast,
 IETF, BW = 48000 status defined, active
Serial1.1 (up): point-to-point dlci, dlci 16(0x10,0x400), broadcast,
 IETF, BW = 1024000 status defined, active
```

Frame Relay *debug* Commands

As always, you must exercise caution when using **debug** commands, due to the amount of output they can generate. The more traffic that exists on an interface, the more output will be generated on the router. The commands discussed in this section are:

- `debug frame-relay lmi`
- `debug frame-relay events`

debug frame-relay lmi

An LMI Frame Relay debug displays LMI exchange information. The exchange consists of LMI status inquiries and responses, including sequencing numbers. Here is a sample:

```
Router_B#debug frame-relay lmi
Frame Relay LMI debugging is on
Displaying all Frame Relay LMI data
Serial0(out): StEnq, myseq 142, yourseen 141, DTE up
datagramstart = 0x40081DA0, datagramsize = 13
FR encap = 0xFCF10309
```

```
00 75 01 01 01 03 02 8E 8D
Serial0(in): Status, myseq 142
RT IE 1, length 1, type 1
KA IE 3, length 2, yourseq 142, myseq 142
Serial1(out): StEnq, myseq 9, yourseen 15, DTE up
datagramstart = 0x40000528, datagramsize = 13
FR encap = 0xFCF10309
00 75 01 01 01 03 02 09 0F

Serial1(in): Status, myseq 9
RT IE 1, length 1, type 1
KA IE 3, length 2, yourseq 16, myseq 9
Serial2(out): StEnq, myseq 254, yourseen 254, DTE up
datagramstart = 0x40000528, datagramsize = 13
FR encap = 0xFCF10309
00 75 01 01 01 03 02 FE FE
```

The `StEnq`, `myseq`, and `yourseen` data are similar to the data provided by the `serial debug` command, explained earlier. Following are definitions of the fields introduced here:

RT IE Report Type Information Element

KA IE Keepalive Information Element

This `debug` command does not generate a great deal of output, as you can see. Therefore, it can be used even during high-traffic times. Some outputs will include more information than the sample displayed previously. Additional information includes clocking, PVC, and committed information rate (CIR) detail.

debug frame-relay events

Data provided by this command is useful because it gives details about protocols and applications using the DLCI. A sample follows. The `(i)` and `(o)` specify inbound and outbound traffic:

```
Router_A#debug frame-relay events
Serial3(i): dlci 1023(0xFCF1), pkt type 0x309, datagramsize 13
Serial3.6(o): dlci 1023(0xFCF1), pkt type 0x309, datagramsize 13
Serial3(i): dlci 1023(0xFCF1), pkt type 0x309, datagramsize 13
Serial3.6(o): dlci 1023(0xFCF1), pkt type 0x309, datagramsize 13
Serial0.2(o): dlci 1023(0xFCF1), pkt type 0x309, datagramsize 13
Serial3(i): dlci 1023(0xFCF1), pkt type 0x309, datagramsize 13
```

The `pkt type` is used to distinguish the packet type that transits the DLCI. The packet type tells you which applications are on the circuit. Several different packet types may appear in the `pkt type` field.

Frame Relay Summary

This summary section includes tables that can be used for quick reference when you are diagnosing, isolating, and resolving Frame Relay problems.

Symptoms and Problems

Table 39.3 includes Frame Relay symptoms and their related problems.

TABLE 39.3 Frame Relay Symptoms and Problems

Symptom or Condition	Associated Problem(s)
Frame Relay link is down.	(a) Faulty cabling (b) Faulty hardware (c) Local service provider problem (d) LMI type mismatch (e) Keepalives not being sent (f) Encapsulation type (g) DLCI mismatch
Cannot ping remote host across a Frame Relay network.	(a) DLCI assigned to wrong subinterface (b) Encapsulation mismatch (c) Access list problem (d) Interface misconfiguration

Problems and Action Plans

Table 39.4 includes the resolution action plans for the problems listed in Table 39.3.

TABLE 39.4 Action Plans for Common Frame Relay Problems

Problem	Resolution Action Plan
Faulty cabling	1. Check the cabling and use a breakout box to test the control leads. 2. Replace cabling as needed.
Faulty hardware	1. Isolate hardware problems by performing loopback tests. 2. Change the cable to a new interface on the router and configure the new interface to match the configuration of the old interface. If the link comes up, you know that you must replace the hardware.
Local service provider problem	If loopback tests bring the LMI state up, but you cannot connect to the remote site, contact the local carrier. Problems can include carrier problems as well as Frame Relay misconfiguration such as DLCI mismatch or encapsulation mismatch.

TABLE 39.4 Action Plans for Common Frame Relay Problems *(continued)*

Problem	Resolution Action Plan
LMI type mismatch	1. Verify that the LMI type on the router matches the LMI type for every device in the PVC. 2. If you're using a public provider network, you won't have access to the LMI information; contact the carrier.
Keepalive problems	1. Use the `show interface` command to see whether keepalives are disabled or to verify that they are configured properly. 2. If the keepalive is not set, enter the configuration mode and specify the keepalive interval on the proper interface.
Encapsulation type	1. Verify that the encapsulation type is the same on both routers. If non-Cisco equipment is used, the encapsulation must be set for IETF. You can display this information by using the `show frame-relay map` command. 2. To change the encapsulation, use the `encapsulation frame-relay ietf` command.
DLCI mismatch	1. Use the `show running-config` command to display the DLCI number assigned to the proper interface. The `show frame-relay pvc` command can also display the DLCI assigned to the interface. 2. If the correct DLCI number is configured on the proper interface, contact the local carrier to verify that it has the same DLCI configured on the Frame Relay switch.
Access list problem	1. Use the `show ip interface` command to display the access list applied to the interface. 2. Analyze the access list, and then remove and modify it, if necessary.

Summary

Though the protocols involved are different, troubleshooting WAN connectivity uses the same basic problem-solving techniques that were used to troubleshoot LAN connectivity issues earlier in this book. These techniques will continue to be applied, as well, for functions explained through the rest of this book.

Although there are several different types of interfaces, some form of a serial interface will most often be used to create the WAN connection. This serial interface may or may not have a built-in CSU/DSU. In either case, there are numerous `show` and `debug` commands for examining the health of this interface as well as the connection or connections it supports. Many of these same commands, such as `show interface` and `show controllers`, are used to examine LAN interfaces as well. In addition to the `show` and `debug` commands, loopbacks can also be set up on the Cisco routers, or more commonly, on the CSU/DSU used in the circuit path.

Various encapsulation types can be used on a WAN circuit. By default, a Cisco serial interface uses High-Level Data Link Control (HDLC) as the encapsulation type. This encapsulation type is used for synchronous data link control. Another common encapsulation type is Frame Relay. Frame Relay allows for multiple locations to be connected on a single physical interface. This is done through the use of virtual circuits, either permanent or switched, and via data link connection identifiers (DLCIs).

Exam Essentials

Know how to determine the encapsulation type of an interface. By looking at the output of a `show interface` command, you can determine the encapsulation type of an interface. You should also know the major characteristics of the encapsulation used and how to identify these characteristics.

Know the *show* and *debug* commands that are used to troubleshoot serial line problems. Among the `show` and `debug` commands that can be used to troubleshoot serial line problems are `show interface serial`, `debug serial interface`, and `debug serial packet`. You should know the `show` and `debug` commands for the interfaces as well as the protocol being used. Also, you need to understand the buffer information that is displayed as part of the output from some of these commands.

Know how HDLC functions and how to troubleshoot issues. HDLC is a point-to-point protocol. It is also the default protocol used on Cisco router serial interfaces. The `show interface` command as well as the `serial debug` command provides detailed information about the functioning of HDLC.

Know how Frame Relay functions and how to troubleshoot issues. Frame Relay can be used as a point-to-point, point-to-multipoint, or multipoint-to-multipoint protocol. It provides this functionality through the use of one or multiple virtual circuits (VCs) per physical circuit. The commands `show frame-relay pvc`, `show frame-relay map`, `show frame-relay lmi`, `show interface`, `debug frame-relay lmi`, and `debug frame-relay events` can be used to diagnose Frame Relay issues.

Understand DLCI and LMI information and how these interfaces are used in Frame Relay. DLCIs are only significant locally and represent the VC, either switched or permanent. LMI is used for management of the Frame Relay link.

Know the purposes of loopbacks and how they can be applied. Loopbacks are used to help isolate a problem to a specific section of the circuit. They are most often applied on the local or remote CSU/DSU.

Troubleshooting ISDN

THE CCNP EXAM TOPICS COVERED IN THIS CHAPTER INCLUDE THE FOLLOWING:

- ✓ **Verify network connectivity.**
- ✓ **Use Cisco IOS commands to identify problems.**
- ✓ **Determine the layer or layers on which a problem is occurring.**
- ✓ **Rectify sub-optimal performance issues at layers 2 through 7.**
- ✓ **Work with external vendors to diagnose and resolve network problems.**

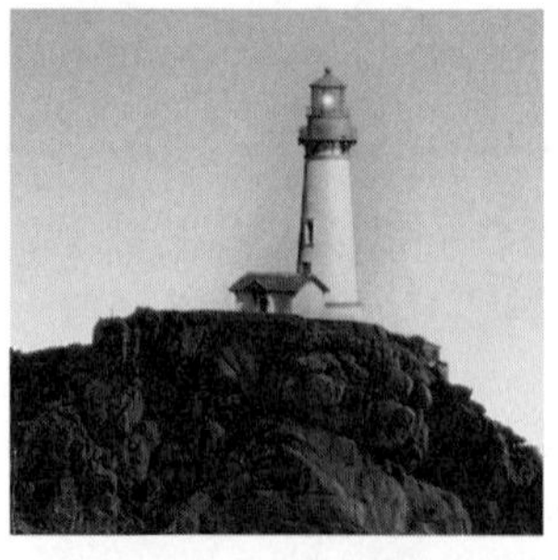

"It Still Does Nothing."

"Yes, this is the phone company. May I please speak with Mr. Isdn?"

The jokes and stories about ISDNs (Integrated Services Digital Networks) have been merciless and, in some cases, more prevalent than the service itself.

Although it is true that ISDN is difficult to order and configure, ISDN is an important option for administrators to consider when designing networks. Frame Relay and xDSL are strong contenders, but ISDN's availability and cost advantages in certain situations are difficult to ignore. In addition, the configuration challenges have been removed to a large degree as the service becomes better known.

This chapter covers the basics of how ISDN operates and how to troubleshoot common problems. Specifically, ISDN switch types are covered, along with PPP, and features such as dialer lists and restricting traffic over an ISDN interface. This chapter finishes up by discussing the debugging options that are available for ISDN.

Some of the commands listed in this chapter are unavailable on certain Cisco routers because of hardware and software considerations. The Cisco 804 router with internal ISDN BRI was used to provide the screen output for this chapter.

ISDN Fundamentals

ISDN was developed in large part from the phone company's conversion to digital networks from analog switches. This conversion, which started in the 1960s, resulted in the following features:

- Clearer, cleaner signals
- Compressible voice, resulting in better trunk utilization
- Longer distances between switching devices
- Value-added features, including caller ID and three-way calling
- Greater bandwidth—a single connection to the phone company can service more than one phone number
- Elimination of load coils and amplifiers in the network

The concept of ISDN was originally conceived as a means to move the digital network into the home, where a single ISDN connection would provide two standard phone lines and digital services for data. This migration from the analog phone would continue to use the existing copper wire plant, while adding services that would ultimately increase revenues.

Unfortunately, users failed to accept ISDN in the numbers desired. This was especially true in the United States, where installation problems, service availability, and high pricing all conspired to hinder acceptance.

In the late 1990s, ISDN was finding a new marketplace. Always On ISDN uses the D channel to replace legacy X.25 networks, especially in point-of-sale transactions. (A description of the B and D channels is included in the section "Physical Layer Connections" later in this chapter.) Standard ISDN service is popular for videoconferencing and as a residential connection to the Internet. However, cable modems and DSL technologies have replaced much of this market in today's environment.

Common ISDN Problems

Like problems that affect other protocols and networking devices, ISDN difficulties occur in certain common areas. Some frequently encountered problems are presented in this section for administrators to consider when evaluating real-world issues. Later in this chapter, the commands that are appropriate for troubleshooting these problems with Cisco routers will be described.

ISDN problems can be divided into three general categories: misconfigured routers, physical wiring and ISDN protocol issues, and misconfigured switches.

Misconfigured Routers

The router configuration is one of many areas that can require attention when researching ISDN problems. Misconfiguration issues can happen due to a variety of reasons, including typographical errors, erroneous information from service providers, and failure to correctly configure the router itself. The following sections discuss several aspects of router configuration that often contribute to router misbehavior, with suggestions for troubleshooting those problems.

Service Profile Identifiers (SPIDs)

The *service profile identifiers (SPIDs)* can be compared to phone numbers in the analog phone environment. The SPID numbers usually include the telephone number with area code and, occasionally, extra digits used by the switch. So a SPID like this one, 41555512340101, corresponds to phone number 415-555-1234, with additional parameters of 0101. The local service provider should document these numbers for the administrator.

SPIDs are used only in North America, and the integration of the phone number into the SPID is most applicable for public ISDN installations.

In some cases, the service provider will also assign a local directory number (LDN). The LDN is not required to make outgoing calls, but if it's not present and is required by the service provider, its absence can create problems for connecting on both B channels.

ISDN is unique in that the local device must learn its identifying number. This is in contrast to analog phones, which remain unaware of their actual phone number, relying on a switch to trigger the ringer. If this does not happen or if the SPIDs or LDNs are misconfigured, you can have problems with your ISDN connection.

It is surprisingly common for administrators to assign IP addresses within two different subnets on ISDN interfaces that connect to each other. It is important to consider each end of an ISDN DDR connection to be part of a single subnet. From a layer 3 perspective, they are the same as any other point-to-point WAN connection.

Challenge Handshake Authentication Protocol (CHAP)

ISDN provides the capability to control access by requiring authentication, which helps to make public network usage more acceptable from a business/security perspective.

The inner workings of the *Challenge Handshake Authentication Protocol (CHAP)* are beyond the scope of this chapter; basically, CHAP is used to provide a layer of security on inbound connections. When troubleshooting, it is important to confirm that the CHAP configurations on both routers match. As noted in the `ppp` command output that follows, Cisco also supports the Microsoft CHAP and Password Authentication Protocol (PAP) protocols. MS-CHAP was added in IOS 12.0.

CHAP authentication requires the point-to-point protocol (PPP). This is enabled on the interface with the command `encapsulation ppp`.

```
Top(config-if)#ppp auth ?
  chap      Challenge Handshake Authentication Protocol      (CHAP)
  ms-chap   Microsoft Challenge Handshake Authentication     Protocol (MS-CHAP)
  pap       Password Authentication Protocol (PAP)
```

When troubleshooting, remember that it is quite common for the username parameters that define the passwords to be set incorrectly, by including a typo in the password itself or omitting a username. With encrypted passwords, this is more difficult to research. If a password problem is suspected, an administrator should enable the `debug ppp authentication` function. As shown in the output that follows (the lines that are underlined), the authentication failed due to an incorrect password.

```
Bottom#debug ppp authentication
PPP authentication debugging is on
Bottom#ping 10.1.1.1
Type escape sequence to abort.
```

```
Sending 5, 100-byte ICMP Echos to 10.1.1.1, timeout is 2   seconds:
01:54:14: %LINK-3-UPDOWN: Interface BRI0:1, changed state   to up.
01:54:14: BR0:1 PPP: Treating connection as a callout
01:54:14: BR0:1 PPP: Phase is AUTHENTICATING, by both
01:54:14: BR0:1 CHAP: O CHALLENGE id 7 len 27 from   "Bottom"
01:54:14: BR0:1 CHAP: I CHALLENGE id 7 len 24 from "Top"
01:54:14: BR0:1 CHAP: O RESPONSE id 7 len 27 from "Bottom"
01:54:14: BR0:1 CHAP: I FAILURE id 7 len 25 msg is "MD/DES compare failed"
01:54:15: %ISDN-6-DISCONNECT: Interface BRI0:1 disconnected from
 18008358661 , call lasted 1 seconds
01:54:15: %LINK-3-UPDOWN: Interface BRI0:1, changed state to down.
01:54:18: %LINK-3-UPDOWN: Interface BRI0:1, changed state to up.
01:54:18: BR0:1 PPP: Treating connection as a callout
01:54:18: BR0:1 PPP: Phase is AUTHENTICATING, by both
01:54:18: BR0:1 CHAP: O CHALLENGE id 8 len 27 from   "Bottom"
01:54:18: BR0:1 CHAP: I CHALLENGE id 8 len 24 from "Top"
01:54:18: BR0:1 CHAP: O RESPONSE id 8 len 27 from "Bottom"
01:54:18: BR0:1 CHAP: I FAILURE id 8 len 25 msg is "MD/DES compare failed"
01:54:19: %ISDN-6-DISCONNECT: Interface BRI0:1 disconnected from
 18008358661 , call lasted   1 seconds
01:54:19: %LINK-3-UPDOWN: Interface BRI0:1, changed state to down.
01:54:22: %LINK-3-UPDOWN: Interface BRI0:1, changed state to up.
```

In PPP, both the username and password are case-sensitive, so be careful when entering both of these values.

Dialer Map Entries

Dialer map statements relate upper layer addresses to their associated phone numbers. Therefore, it is critical that dialer map entries contain valid IP addresses and numbers. If they are not valid, you could cause the ISDN line to come up when it is not supposed to, or worse yet, not come up at all. Note that an individual dialer map statement is needed for each protocol, as follows:

```
dialer map ip 10.11.3.20 name Top broadcast 18005551212
dialer map appletalk 310.10 name Top broadcast 18005551212
```

In certain cases you can run dial-on-demand routing (DDR) without using dialer maps. But for ease of troubleshooting and consistency, maps should be used whenever possible.

Real World Scenario

One-Way Chap Authentication

In many businesses today, ISDN lines no longer fill just one specific role. They are being used to connect remote locations back to the corporate network; they are being used for dial-backup, for connecting to the Internet, and in many more scenarios. I have also seen the same line being used for multiple purposes simultaneously.

When all of these connections are made within like company devices, bidirectional CHAP does not create a problem, because all of the devices can be configured to use this authentication methodology. However, when using the same router for incoming calls and to connect to an ISP or an ISDN device made by a company other than Cisco, CHAP can become an issue. In many of these instances, CHAP is not configured on the called device. In other cases, the far-end device does not support CHAP challenges from the calling device. However, you still want to use CHAP authentication when your router is called.

In these problematic situations, the simplest solution that I have found is to use the Cisco IOS command `ppp authentication chap callin` to enable *one-way* CHAP authentication. This command is used at the interface level and will send a CHAP challenge only when the router is called, not when it calls out. This allows you to connect to devices that don't support bidirectional CHAP authentication or are not configured for CHAP, without giving up the security that CHAP provides when you receive an incoming call.

Note, too, that a similar command also exists for PAP if you are running PAP in your environment. As is the case with CHAP, this configuration goes on the calling router.

Some ISDN switches require the area code and escape character, even when the phone numbers are in the same area code.

Access Lists

Access lists are commonly used in ISDN connections to prevent certain types of traffic from triggering a connection and to bring up the link only when "interesting traffic" is seen. Most frequently, this is done to save money, because ISDN is often tariffed on a per-minute, per-B-channel basis. However, Frame Relay and other technologies commonly provide the same or greater bandwidth at lower cost. This is usually true after approximately 40 hours per month of utilization on the B channels. The xDSL technologies are quickly gaining market share at an unlimited usage tariff, as well.

To control usage, administrators frequently configure an access list based on permitted functions only, and all other services are denied. This sometimes causes problems when a new service is added to the system without being explicitly added to the access list. Troubleshooting any

ISDN configuration that worked in the past should include a thorough review of all access lists, including the dialer lists:

```
Bottom(config)#dialer-list 1 protocol ip ?
  deny     Deny specified protocol
  list     Add access list to dialer list
  permit   Permit specified protocol
```

A dialer list to provide IP, IPX, and AppleTalk services is as follows:

```
dialer-list 1 protocol ip permit
dialer-list 1 protocol appletalk permit
dialer-list 1 protocol ipx permit
```

The preceding list is just a sample of a dialer list. As written, it will cause the ISDN line to be brought up for any IP, IPX, or AppleTalk traffic. Although this is useful for demonstrations and in the lab, a more restrictive list is more appropriate for real-world installations.

Point-to-Point Protocol

Although the Point-to-Point Protocol (PPP) is recommended for ISDN connectivity, there are other options available, including the default HDLC. PPP is recommended in large part to provide security via CHAP, as described previously in this section.

For troubleshooting, PPP provides additional information regarding the connection, including the protocol type. This information rarely presents itself in a manner that is usable to administrators, however. Often more helpful to the administrator will be an understanding of the protocol and its capability to provide useful functions, including CHAP. Note that the PPP protocol is the same for analog or ISDN connections, so the configuration of PPP on a workstation using an analog modem requires PPP encapsulation on an ISDN host router. PPP also supports compression.

PPP contains protocol field values that document the upper layer information included in the datagram. Table 40.1 provides a list of some protocol field values.

TABLE 40.1 Point-to-Point Protocol Field Values

Hex Value of Field	Protocol
0021	IP
0029	AppleTalk
002B	IPX
003D	Multilink

TABLE 40.1 Point-to-Point Protocol Field Values *(continued)*

Hex Value of Field	Protocol
0201	802.1d Hellos
0203	Source route bridging bridge protocol data units (BPDUs)
8021	IPCP
8029	ATCP
802B	IPXCP
C223	CHAP
C023	PAP

Physical Layer Connections

It is important to consider the Physical layer when troubleshooting ISDN, especially in new installations. Wiring is particularly important when connecting ISDN videoconferencing equipment to internal PBX equipment. Some administrators use Category 5 wiring for internal ISDN connections, although Category 3 is acceptable. This chapter focuses on the Basic Rate Interface (BRI), which operates over standard copper pairs.

The Basic Rate Interface

Most installations of ISDN in the field are BRI. This differs from the available Primary Rate Interface (PRI), which uses a T1 as the conduit. The primary rate of telecommunications connections is usually measured in DS-1 increments. A DS-1, or T1, is equivalent to 24 T1 voice channels. The basic rate for a voice connection is referred to as a DS-0, or a single 64Kbit channel of the T1. In ISDN, this refers to the single B channel capacity of the circuit. The formal description of BRI is specified in I.430; the I.431 specification addresses PRI ISDN.

ISDN BRI was designed to provide digital services over existing pairs of copper. The service is used for videoconferencing, voice services, data, and out-of-band management. In addition, in many cases, the D channel function of BRI is used for replacement of legacy X.25 networks.

The ISDN BRI Channels

ISDN BRI is a 192Kbps circuit that is divided into three distinct channels. The two primary data channels are the B channels. Each B channel provides 64Kbps. The third channel provides 16Kbps of bandwidth for commands and signaling and is referred to as the D channel. The remaining bandwidth of 48Kbps is overhead.

The physical frame in ISDN BRI is 48 bits, and the circuit sends 4000 frames per second.

The Local Loop

Although the majority of administrators troubleshoot only the local side of the ISDN circuit, there is a remote side that is critical to the successful operation of ISDN.

The *local loop* refers to the circuit between the customer premises and the central office (CO). This may include an access layer, referred to as an RT, which permits digital connections to be greater distances from the central office. The local loop interconnects the ISDN device to an ISDN switch—a DMS-100, for example. Note that all digital services are sensitive to the distance between the switch and end device.

The Physical Layer

In order to properly troubleshoot ISDN, it is very important that you have a good understanding of its technology, terminology, architecture, and functionality. Figure 40.1 shows the ISDN components and where these components' points fit into the ISDN installation. In addition to the components, the illustration also shows the reference points that are commonly used in troubleshooting ISDN issues. Following are descriptions of the components and reference points in Figure 40.1.

LT/ET The line termination and exchange termination points are called *LT* and *ET* respectively. They handle the termination of the local loop and switching functions.

NT1 The *NT1* is the network termination point. It is often the demarcation point (demarc) where the provider terminates their portion of the circuit. It connects the four-wire subscriber line to the two-wire local loop and acts as an entry point for the ISDN circuit. In North America, the NT1 is provided by the customer and is considered customer premises equipment (CPE). However, in most other parts of the world this device is provided and managed by the carrier.

FIGURE 40.1 ISDN components and reference points

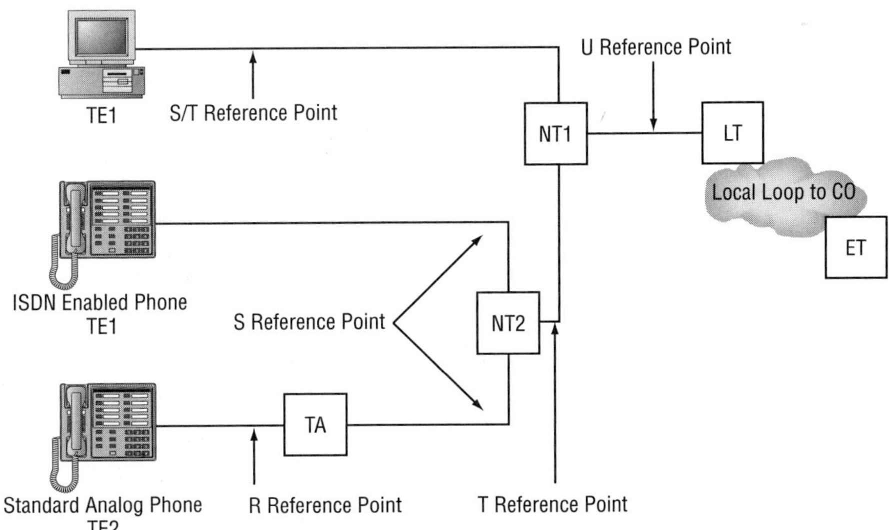

NT2 The *NT2* is primarily seen only in larger companies that are using PBXs. The NT2 is used to perform layer 2 and layer 3 protocol functions and as a concentration point.

TA The *TA* is the terminal adapter. This device is used to connect non-ISDN-enabled devices—TE2—to the ISDN network. A TA may be added to the device itself or may be a stand-alone unit.

TE1 A device with a four-wire, twisted-pair digital interface is referred to as *terminal equipment type one* (*TE1*). Most modern ISDN devices are of this type.

TE2 *Terminal equipment type two* (*TE2*) devices do not contain ISDN interfaces. A TA is required.

R reference point Devices without internal ISDN functions are called TE2s and require a connection to a TA for operation in ISDN networks. There is no standard connection between these devices, however—the connection is referred to as the *R reference point.*

S reference point The *S reference point* is the interface between the ISDN router (or other user equipment) and the NT2 or NT1. Note that the user equipment is referred to as the TE1 or TA.

S/T reference point If no NT2 is installed, the connection between the NT1 and either the TA or the TE1, depending on which is installed, is the *S/T reference point.* Because NT2 devices are rarely installed, most ISDN installations will have an S/T reference point.

T reference point The interface between the NT1, or the local loop termination point, and the NT2, or customer-site switching equipment, is referred to as the *T reference point.* This point, along with the S reference point, is within the customer premises, and faulty wiring may be the cause of a problem within this context.

U reference point The *U reference point* is between the NT1 and the LT. It is normally serviced on a single pair to reduce costs and simplify installations.

Layer 1 S/T interface The *layer 1 S/T interface* connection uses a physical connector of RJ-45, as defined in ISO 8877. A straight-through pin configuration connects the TE to the network termination (NT). Table 40.2 reflects the specific pinning.

Some installers use RJ-11 or RJ-14 connections for ISDN terminations. Although these connections work, RJ-45 is the recommended connection in all circumstances. Wires 1, 2, 7, and 8 may be used for alternate mark inversion (AMI) encoding, and RJ-45 connections provide a visual variance from standard phone jacks.

TABLE 40.2 The RJ-45 ISDN S/T Interface

Pin	Terminal End-Point (TE)	Network Termination (NT)
1	Power +	Power +
2	Power –	Power –

TABLE 40.2 The RJ-45 ISDN S/T Interface *(continued)*

Pin	Terminal End-Point (TE)	Network Termination (NT)
3	Transmit +	Receive +
4	Receive +	Transmit +
5	Receive –	Transmit –
6	Transmit –	Receive –
7	Power –	Power –
8	Power +	Power +

Misconfigured Phone Switches

Administrators must consider the possibility that the service provider failed to properly configure the ISDN switch. Although this is a very rare occurrence, the possibility exists and should be considered, especially in new installations.

An understanding of ISDN as it relates to the OSI model can greatly assist the network troubleshooter in locating causes of problems with the phone switches. In addition, administrators must be aware of the ISDN switch types and their impact on connectivity.

Troubleshooting Layer 2

There are two layer 2 troubleshooting targets that should be identified and analyzed when working on ISDN networks: the q.921 protocol and PPP.

q.921

ISDN maps well with the OSI reference model. Layer 2 is defined in *q.921*.

The q.921 signaling is carried over the D channel by using *Link Access Procedure on the D channel (LAPD)*. This connection between the central office switch (the Teltone ILS-2000 in the test network discussed here) and the router must occur and complete before connections are possible.

Troubleshooting q.921 problems is most frequently handled with the `debug isdn q921` command. Often, problems are related to the *terminal endpoint identifier (TEI)*. This value uniquely identifies each terminal in the network, and a TEI of 127 represents a broadcast. TEIs 64 through 126 are reserved for assignment during the activation of a layer 2 ISDN connection. This assignment is dynamic.

TEI has a variety of message types that allow the engineer to identify what type of information is being exchanged, thus identifying any failures in the TEI process. Refer to Table 40.3 for descriptions of these types. By using these references, you will be able to understand the exchanges during the TEI process.

TABLE 40.3 TEI Message Types

TEI Message Type	Type Description
1	ID Request
2	ID Assigned
3	ID Denied
4	ID Check Request
5	ID Check Response
6	ID Remove
7	ID Verify

Administrators may also need to review the *service access point identifier (SAPI)*. This field may include a SAPI of 0, which represents that layer 3 signaling is present. Such signaling is provided by the q.931 protocol (see the section "Troubleshooting Layer 3" later in this chapter). Other values may include 63, which is a management SAPI for the assignment of the TEI values, and 64, which is used for call control.

One last target to check while troubleshooting the q.921 with the `debug isdn q.921` command is the SABME (Set Asynchronous Balanced Mode Extended) message. The SABME is exchanged along with the ID verify messages. If the SABME fails and sends a disconnect response, no further link establishment will occur, and you should investigate the reason for the SABME failure. If the SABME succeeds, an acknowledgment is sent and the layer 2 connection is complete, and the TE will begin to send INFO frames.

Sample outputs for the `show interface` and `debug isdn q921` commands are discussed later in this chapter. The outputs are long and cover multiple pages. However, you should look through the output carefully and try to follow what is happening using the information you have learned thus far.

PPP

Troubleshooting targets within the PPP protocol is also important when trying to isolate and resolve ISDN BRI problems. *Link Control Protocol (LCP)* is the protocol used by PPP to set up and maintain links. It also assists in setting the PPP options. Before getting into the sequence used to set up PPP, let's look at some of the LCP options. The primary ones are listed in Table 40.4.

TABLE 40.4 LCP Type Options

LCP Type Number	LCP Type	Description
0	Reserved	Not used.
1	Maximum receive unit (MRU)	Sets the maximum packet size. Default is 1500 bytes.
3	Authentication protocol	Sets the authentication protocol to be used (CHAP or PAP).
4	Quality protocol	Sets the protocol to use for Link Quality Monitoring, which is disabled by default.
5	Magic number	Used to detect loopback links and other layer 2 issues.
7	Protocol field compression	Used to negotiate compression of the PPP Protocol field.
8	Address and control field compression	Used to negotiate compression of the Data Link layer address and control fields.

In addition to LCP for link control, PPP also uses *Network Control Protocol (NCP)* for configuring and establishing Network layer protocols. Administrators also need to review the steps in PPP and CHAP negotiation. Let's look at the steps taken by PPP to establish a link:

1. LCP at the router (TE) sends a configuration request known as a CONFREQ. Options are specified by the requesting router.
2. The request is either accepted or denied. If it is accepted, an acknowledgment—CONFACK—is returned to the TE. If the request is denied, a negative CONFACK is returned. The difference between a normal and a negative CONFACK is the acceptance or denial of the request. If the CONFREQ was not recognized by the remote TE, a configuration reject message—CONFREJ—is sent to the requesting TE.
3. If the CONFREQ was recognized and accepted and CHAP is being used for authentication, the process continues with the three-way handshake.
    A. Challenge is sent to the remote TE.
    B. The remote TE responds.
    C. If the values match, authentication is given.

The troubleshooting targets in this process are the request/response sequence between the peers, as well as all of the CHAP targets.

Troubleshooting Layer 3

The third layer of ISDN is addressed in the ITU-T I.451 specification, also called *q.931*. (An easy way to remember the difference between q.921 and q.931 is to look at the tens digit of the number. q.921 corresponds to layer 2, and q.931 corresponds to layer 3.) The q.931 protocol includes several message commands, which are viewed with the `debug isdn q931` command. These commands include `call setup`, `connect`, `release`, `cancel`, `status`, `disconnect`, and `user information`.

The output of the `show` and `debug` commands will be covered later in this chapter.

It is important to identify the troubleshooting targets that exist in layer 3 for ISDN BRI. Understand that the layer 3 connection is between the local router (TE) and the remote ISDN switch (ET). Just as the q.931 operates on the D channel, so does all debugging. Troubleshooting targets include the call reference flag, message types, and information elements. Tables 40.5, 40.6, and 40.7 provide summaries for the messages and their meaning.

TABLE 40.5 Call Reference Flag Definitions

Field Value	Definition
0	From call originator
1	To call originator

TABLE 40.6 q.931 Message Types

Field Value	Definition
0x05	Setup
0x45	Disconnect
0x7d	Status

TABLE 40.7 q.931 Information Elements

Field Value	Definition
0x04	Bearer capability
0x2c	Keypad facility
0x6c	Calling party number
0x70	Called party number
0x3a	SPID

Again, all of this information is provided by the debug isdn q931 command. A sample output is provided in the "Debugging ISDN" section later in this chapter. The easiest way to keep track of the various calls is with the call reference number indicated in the output of the debug command. This way, you will be able to follow the same call all the way through the process.

Note that these messages are carried on the D channel and are not end-to-end. Rather, they are for connections and setup between the central office switch and the router. The B channel is then available for data transfer.

ISDN calls are established between the router and the local switch over the D channel. The local switch establishes a separate connection to the remote switch, which is responsible for the call setup to the remote router or other ISDN device.

Now let's discuss the call setup on layer 3 via q.931. It will aid you in troubleshooting and isolating ISDN BRI network problems. This is the process that must be followed. You can use the output of the debug isdn q931 command to verify that the process is happening correctly.

1. SETUP: The SETUP process sends information elements; this occurs between the local TE and the remote TE.
2. CALL_PROC: The call proceeding signal is given; this occurs between the ET and the TE.
3. ALERT: The remote TE alerts the local TE via a ring-back.
4. CONNECT: The remote TE answers, thus stopping the local ring-back.
5. CONNECT_ACK: A message from the remote ET to the remote TE is sent, acknowledging that the setup is complete.

Switch Types

Recall that ISDN is a connection between the ISDN router and the phone company's central office switch. Therefore, it is important to define the type of switch in use to the router. This is configured with the isdn switch-type command. The isdn switch ? command reports the available switch types and their usual country or continent for the Cisco router:

```
Top(config)#isdn switch-type ?
  basic-1tr6     1TR6 switch type for Germany
  basic-5ess     AT&T 5ESS switch type for the U.S.
  basic-dms100   Northern DMS-100 switch type
  basic-net3     NET3 switch type for UK and Europe
  basic-ni       National ISDN switch type
  basic-ts013    TS013 switch type for Australia
  ntt            NTT switch type for Japan
  vn3            VN3 and VN4 switch types for France
```

In North America, if the switch type is unknown, an administrator may wish to use the auto-configuration command; this command is `isdn autodetect`. If the SPID is unknown, the command `isdn spidn 0` can be used. Some administrators prefer to specify the switch type and SPID information manually. Please be advised that these auto-configuration options are not available on many routers; however, it is available on the Cisco 804 router, and it may be helpful in new installations. It is likely that Cisco will add this function to new products.

It is important to note that the switch type is specific to the local loop switch, and not to the remote connection or entire connection. For example, when connecting a router in North America to use for connections to Europe, the North American router is likely to be set to `basic-dms100`. The European router is set to `basic-net3`.

ISDN Troubleshooting Commands

The Cisco IOS provides a broad range of troubleshooting commands to assist administrators in the deployment and configuration of ISDN, including the common problems noted in the foregoing sections. Although many of these troubleshooting commands are common to other topologies and protocols (`ping`, for example), other commands are specific to ISDN, including `debug isdn q931`.

Figure 40.2 diagrams the network used for this chapter.

Some switch types and configurations may set each B channel at 56Kbps, instead of the potentially available 64Kbps, due to constraints in the carrier's networks. Failure to match speeds causes connectivity problems.

FIGURE 40.2 ISDN Troubleshooting network design

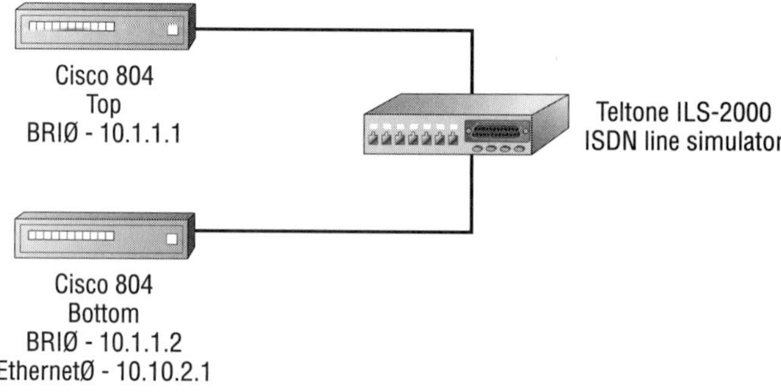

ping

As with non-dial-on-demand (DDR) connections, the `ping` command is one of the most useful troubleshooting tools. `ping` verifies routes and other connections; in DDR, the command triggers a call:

```
Bottom#ping 10.1.1.1
Type escape sequence to abort.
Sending 5, 100-byte ICMP Echos to 10.1.1.1, timeout is    2 seconds:
.
00:37:12: %LINK-3-UPDOWN: Interface BRI0:1, changed state   to up
00:37:13: %LINEPROTO-5-UPDOWN: Line protocol on Interface BRI0:1
  ➥changed state to up.!!!
Success rate is 60 percent (3/5), round-trip min/avg/max =      32/38/48 ms
Bottom#
00:37:14: %LINK-3-UPDOWN: Interface BRI0:2, changed state   to up
00:37:15: %LINEPROTO-5-UPDOWN: Line protocol on Interface BRI0:2,
 changed state to up
```

Notice that the five pings generated by the router completed before the second B channel came up.

It is quite common for up to the first three pings to fail in DDR ISDN connections. This is due to the two- to three-second delay in establishing the connection. It is usually not an indication of a problem. Also, be sure to ensure that ICMP is defined as "interesting traffic" for this interface, or the link will not come up at all.

clear interface bri n

The `clear interface bri` *n* command resets the various counters that are available on the interface and terminates a connection on the interface. The *n* value should equal the port, or the port and slot, of the interface. This command is most useful for clearing a call that was activated by a dialer map or other catalyst, which may be desired when configuring and testing new access lists and other call triggers:

```
Bottom#clear int bri0
Bottom#
00:26:158913789951: %ISDN-6-DISCONNECT: Interface BRI0:2
     disconnected from 8358663 , call lasted 104 seconds
00:26:154624128828: %LINK-3-UPDOWN: Interface BRI0:2,
   changed state to down
00:26:36: %ISDN-6-LAYER2UP: Layer 2 for Interface BR0, TEI
   92 changed to up
```

```
00:26:36: %ISDN-6-LAYER2UP: Layer 2 for Interface BRO, TEI
   93 changed to up
00:26:37: %LINEPROTO-5-UPDOWN: Line protocol on Interface
   BRIO:2, changed state to down
```

show interface bri n

Information regarding the ISDN BRI D channel is available with the `show interface bri` *n* command:

```
Bottom#show int bri0
BRI0 is up, line protocol is up (spoofing)
  Hardware is BRI with U interface and POTS
  Internet address is 10.1.1.2/24
  MTU 1500 bytes, BW 64Kbit, DLY 20000 usec,
     reliability 255/255, txload 1/255, rxload 1/255
  Encapsulation HDLC, loopback not set
  Last input 00:00:05, output 00:00:05, output hang never
  Last clearing of "show interface" counters never
  Input queue: 0/75/0 (size/max/drops); Total output   drops: 0
  Queueing strategy: weighted fair
  Output queue: 0/1000/64/0 (size/max total/threshold/   drops)
     Conversations  0/1/256 (active/max active/max total)
     Reserved Conversations 0/0 (allocated/max allocated)
  5 minute input rate 0 bits/sec, 0 packets/sec
  5 minute output rate 0 bits/sec, 0 packets/sec
     85 packets input, 791 bytes, 0 no buffer
     Received 4 broadcasts, 0 runts, 0 giants, 0 throttles
     0 input errors, 0 CRC, 0 frame, 0 overrun, 0 ignored,    0 abort
     92 packets output, 701 bytes, 0 underruns
     0 output errors, 0 collisions, 4 interface resets
     0 output buffer failures, 0 output buffers swapped    out
     1 carrier transitions
```

Note in the preceding output that the command reports the D channel's status, as well as spoofing on the interface. This is due to the dynamic nature of DDR connections—they are up only when necessary. In addition, note that the interface was not configured for Point-to-Point Protocol (PPP) but is using the default encapsulation of HDLC.

It is important for administrators to review the output of the `show interface` command, especially when researching user reports of slow performance. For example, the `txload` and `rxload` parameters provide a strong indication of bandwidth loads. Observe the `(spoofing)` tag in the preceding output as well. This indicates that the router is maintaining the link as though it was always active, even though ISDN is dynamic.

show interface bri n *1 2*

The show interface bri *n* 1 2 command is used to display a single B channel of the BRI interface. In this example, the circuit is down:

```
Bottom#show interface bri0 1
BRI0:1 is down, line protocol is down
  Hardware is BRI with U interface and POTS
  MTU 1500 bytes, BW 64Kbit, DLY 20000 usec,
     reliablility 255/255, txload 1/255, rxload 1/255
  Encapsulation PPP, loopback not set, keepalive set (10       sec)
  LCP Closed, multilink Closed
  Closed: BACP, CDPCP, IPCP
  Last input 00:02:09, output 00:02:09, output hang never
  Last clearing of "show interface" counters never
  Queueing strategy: fifo
  Output queue 0/40, 0 drops; input queue 0/75, 0 drops
  5 minute input rate 0 bits/sec, 0 packets/sec
  5 minute output rate 0 bits/sec, 0 packets/sec
     219 packets input, 3320 bytes, 0 no buffer
     Received 219 broadcasts, 0 runts, 0 giants, 0   throttles
     146 input errors, 9 CRC, 59 frame, 0 overrun, 0 ignored, 78 abort
     279 packets output, 16195 bytes, 0 underruns
     0 output errors, 0 collisions, 0 interface resets
     0 output buffer failures, 0 output buffers swapped   out
     15 carrier transitions
```

Although the show interface bri *n* 1 2 command can be important when isolating an individual B channel problem, the show interface bri *n* command usually suffices for the majority of troubleshooting processes.

show controller bri

The interface hardware controller information is displayed with the show controller bri command. This command is most useful for troubleshooting with Cisco's TAC, but some information can assist the administrator as well. Most importantly, the status of the interface—in this case a U type connection—is available in this show command:

```
Bottom#show controller bri
BRI unit 0:BRI unit 0 with U interface and POTS:
Layer 1 internal state is ACTIVATED
Layer 1 U interface is ACTIVATED.
ISDN Line Information:
    Current EOC commands:
```

```
        RTN - Return to normal
    Received overhead bits:
       AIB=1, UOA=1, SCO=1, DEA=1, ACT=1, M50=1,    M51=1, M60=1, FEBE=1
    Errors:  [FEBE]=0, [NEBE]=0
    Errors:  [Superframe Sync Loss]=0, [IDL2 Data       Transparency Loss]=0
             [M4 ACT 1 -> 0]=0
BRI U MLT Timers:  [TPULSE]=0, [T75S]=0
. . . some output omitted . . .
  0 missed datagrams, 0 overruns
  0 bad datagram encapsulations, 0 memory errors
  0 transmitter underruns
```

show isdn status

The `show isdn status` command is one of the more significant troubleshooting commands, because the output reports not only the status of the interface, but a breakdown of each layer. As shown in the first output example, the router has established a connection at layer 1, but layer 2 either remains in a negotiation mode or has failed to negotiate due to an improperly set switch or router:

```
Top#show isdn status
Global ISDN Switchtype = basic-ni
ISDN BRI0 interface
dsl 0, interface ISDN Switchtype = basic-ni
    Layer 1 Status:
ACTIVE
    Layer 2 Status:
TEI = 79, Ces = 1, SAPI = 0, State = MULTIPLE_FRAME_ESTABLISHED Spid Status:
TEI 79, ces = 1, state = 8(established)
    spid1 configured, no LDN, spid1 NOT sent, spid1 NOT      valid
TEI Not Assigned, ces = 2, state = 1(terminal down)
    spid2 configured, no LDN, spid2 NOT sent, spid2 NOT      valid
    Layer 3 Status:
0 Active Layer 3 Call(s)
    Activated dsl 0 CCBs = 1
CCB:callid=0x0, sapi=0x0, ces=0x1, B-chan=0 calltype =      INTERNAL
Total Allocated ISDN CCBs = 1
```

The following display reports a correctly configured router and switch. Note that the SPIDs are confirmed and all layers are active on both B channels:

```
Top#show isdn status
Global ISDN Switchtype = basic-ni
```

```
ISDN BRI0 interface
dsl 0, interface ISDN Switchtype = basic-ni
    Layer 1 Status:
ACTIVE
    Layer 2 Status:
TEI = 83, Ces = 1, SAPI = 0, State = MULTIPLE_FRAME_     ESTABLISHED
TEI = 84, Ces = 2, SAPI = 0, State = MULTIPLE_FRAME_     ESTABLISHED
    Spid Status:
TEI 83, ces = 1, state = 5(init)
    spid1 configured, no LDN, spid1 sent, spid1 valid
    Endpoint ID Info: epsf = 0, usid = 1, tid = 1
TEI 84, ces = 2, state = 5(init)
    spid2 configured, no LDN, spid2 sent, spid2 valid
    Endpoint ID Info: epsf = 0, usid = 3, tid = 1
    Layer 3 Status:
0 Active Layer 3 Call(s)
    Activated dsl 0 CCBs = 0
Total Allocated ISDN CCBs = 0
```

Although `show isdn status` is most frequently used for new installations, field installations and SOHO (small office, home office) installations frequently find the ISDN device turned off when not in use. This is usually because the router has been plugged into a power strip attached to a PC.

When the router is disconnected from the ISDN circuit, the D channel (which is always "on") suddenly disconnects. Some phone companies view this as an error and disconnect the circuit on the central office switch. When the user returns power to the circuit, connectivity doesn't occur and the switch no longer expects a connection. The `show isdn status` command provides an indication of problems that require contacting the phone company. If there is a problem with an ISDN connection and the user has disconnected the power or the ISDN phone cable, one potential problem could be that the phone company has disabled the circuit. To help prevent this problem, it is recommended that administrators instruct users that the cable or power is never to be disconnected.

show dialer

The `show dialer` command reports information regarding the DDR connections, including the number dialed, the success of the connection, the idle timers that control the duration of a DDR connection without data packets, and the number of calls that were screened or rejected due to administrative policy.

This command is useful for verifying a previous connection or checking the number called. Note that dialer map statements, which link network addresses to ISDN numbers, can be implemented incorrectly—for example, IP address 1 might be linked to number B instead of A. Although the router dials and the ISDN connection may succeed, the router cannot pass packets due to layer 3 mismatches. Notice the `Idle timer (120 secs)` notation, which reflects the default idle timer of two minutes for each B channel. The idle timer shuts down the connection when no "interesting" packets have traversed the link.

```
Bottom#show dialer
BRI0 - dialer type = ISDN
Dial String       Successes    Failures    Last called  Last status
18008358661               2           0    00:02:49     successful
0 incoming call(s) have been screened.
0 incoming call(s) rejected for callback.
BRI0:1 - dialer type = ISDN
Idle timer (120 secs), Fast idle timer (20 secs)
Wait for carrier (30 secs), Re-enable (15 secs)
Dialer state is idle
BRI0:2 - dialer type = ISDN
Idle timer (120 secs), Fast idle timer (20 secs)
Wait for carrier (30 secs), Re-enable (15 secs)
Dialer state is idle
```

show ppp multilink

Multilink is an extended portion of the Point-to-Point Protocol. As shown in italic in the following output, the service is configured with the `ppp multilink` bap and ppp bap commands. PPP multilink allows for the combining of both B channels in a connection to allow 128Kbps of throughput.

```
interface BRI0
 ip address 10.1.1.2 255.255.255.0
 no ip directed-broadcast
 encapsulation ppp
 dialer map ip 10.1.1.1 name Top broadcast 18008358661
 dialer-group 1
 isdn switch-type basic-ni
 isdn spid1 0835866201
 isdn spid2 0835866401
 ppp multilink
 dialer load-threshold 128 either
 hold-queue 75 in
```

Debugging ISDN

The debug commands in ISDN are extremely helpful for researching problem causes and resolving them. This section addresses the commands and provides some useful methods for employing them. In addition, scenarios are described in which such commands may be needed.

The debug command is assigned a high CPU priority and can generate a high processor load. Always use caution when using a debug command. The resulting processor load and output can degrade router performance or render the system unusable.

It is recommended that routers be configured with timestamps for debug and log output. To provide debug time information, use the command `service timestamps debug datetime msec and show-timezone localtime`.

debug bri

The `debug bri` command gives you information about the B channels of the BRI. An example of the command's output is provided here; note that bandwidth information is included.

The B channels of the BRI are the data-carrying channels; therefore, an error in the activation of a B channel prevents data flow. It is also possible for the router to command one B channel to connect while the other B channel fails, which may be due to a misconfigured SPID or configuration error. The `debug bri` command provides some insight into this potential problem:

```
Bottom#debug bri
Basic Rate network interface debugging is on
Bottom#ping 10.1.1.1
Type escape sequence to abort.
Sending 5, 100-byte ICMP Echos to 10.1.1.1, timeout is 2     seconds:
00:29:48: BRI: enable channel B1
00:29:48: BRI0:MC145572 state handler current state 3
  actions 1 next state 3
00:29:48: BRI0:Starting activation
00:29:48: %LINK-3-UPDOWN: Interface BRI0:1, changed state   to up.
00:29:49: BRI 0 B1: Set bandwidth to 64Kb
00:29:50: %LINEPROTO-5-UPDOWN: Line protocol on Interface
  BRI0:1, changed state to up
00:29:50: BRI 0 B2: Set bandwidth to 64Kb
00:29:50: BRI: enable channel B2
00:29:50: BRI0:MC145572 state handler current state 3
  actions 1 next state 3
00:29:50: BRI0:Starting activation
00:29:50: %LINK-3-UPDOWN: Interface BRI0:2, changed state   to up.!!!
Success rate is 60 percent (3/5), round-trip min/avg/max =     36/41/52 ms
00:29:50: BRI: enable channel B2
```

```
00:29:50: BRI0:MC145572 state handler current state 3
  actions 1 next state 3
00:29:50: BRI0:Starting activation
00:29:50: BRI 0 B2: Set bandwidth to 64Kb
00:29:51: %LINEPROTO-5-UPDOWN: Line protocol on Interface
  BRI0:2, changed state to up
```

debug isdn q921

The q.921 protocol addresses layer 2 of the OSI model and its relationship to ISDN. Information regarding the D channel interface is available via the `debug isdn q921` command.

The D channel is always connected in ISDN, and the channel is used for signaling between the switch and local ISDN device. Connections over the B channels cannot occur without signaling commands on the D channel. Administrators should use the `debug isdn q921` command to monitor the proper flow of messages when calls do not connect. It is recommended that a baseline debug be performed and recorded to compare against the suspected problem debug output.

```
Bottom#debug isdn q921
ISDN Q921 packets debugging is on
00:19:15: ISDN BR0: TX ->  RRp sapi = 0  tei = 92 nr = 12
00:19:64424550400: ISDN BR0: RX <-  RRf sapi = 0  tei = 92       nr = 12
Bottom#ping 10.1.1.1
Type escape sequence to abort.
Sending 5, 100-byte ICMP Echos to 10.1.1.1, timeout is 2      seconds:
.
00:19:23: ISDN BR0: TX ->  INFOc sapi = 0  tei = 92   ns = 12
  nr = 12   i = 0x080
10305040288901801832C0B31383030383335383636 31
00:19:98789554100: ISDN BR0: RX <-  INFOc sapi = 0   tei = 92
  ns = 12  nr = 13
i =   0x08018302180189952A1B809402603D8307383335383636318E0B2
   054454C544F4F45203120
00:19:23: ISDN BR0: TX ->  RRr sapi = 0  tei = 92  nr = 13
00:19:103079256064: ISDN BR0: RX <-  INFOc sapi = 0   tei = 92  ns = 13
  nr = 13
 i = 0x08018307
00:19:24: ISDN BR0: TX ->  RRr sapi = 0  tei = 92  nr = 14
00:19:24: %LINK-3-UPDOWN: Interface BRI0:1, changed state   to up
00:19:24: ISDN BR0: TX ->  INFOc sapi = 0  tei = 92   ns = 13  nr = 14
  i = 0x080
1030F
00:19:103079215104: ISDN BR0: RX <-  RRr sapi = 0   tei = 92     nr = 14
```

```
00:19:25: %LINEPROTO-5-UPDOWN: Line protocol on Interface
  BRI0:1, changed state to up
00:19:107379488692: ISDN BR0: RX <-  UI sapi = 0   tei = 127
  i = 0x08010A05040288
9018018A3401403B0282816C0941813833353836363337008C138333538   36   3632
00:19:25: %LINK-3-UPDOWN: Interface BRI0:2, changed state      to up.!!!
Success rate is 60 percent (3/5), round-trip min/avg/max =      32/38/48 ms
00:19:25: ISDN BR0: TX ->  INFOc sapi = 0  tei = 92   ns = 14
  nr = 14  i = 0x080
18A0718018A
00:19:107374223360: ISDN BR0: RX <- INFOc sapi = 0  tei = 92 ns = 14  nr = 15
 i = 0x08010A0F
00:19:25: ISDN BR0: TX ->  RRr sapi = 0  tei = 92  nr = 15
00:19:27: %LINEPROTO-5-UPDOWN: Line protocol on Interface
  BRI0:2, changed state to up
00:19:36: ISDN BR0: TX ->  RRp sapi = 0  tei = 93 nr = 0
00:19:154618822656: ISDN BR0: RX <-  RRf sapi = 0   tei = 93     nr = 0
```

debug dialer

The `debug dialer` command tells you about the cause of a dialing connection and the status of the connection. Note in the following output that an IP packet caused the dial to occur. This information can provide assistance for tuning connections. Administrators frequently do this to limit the use of an ISDN circuit when charged on distance and per-minute tariffs.

```
Bottom#debug dialer
Dial on demand events debugging is on
Bottom#ping 10.1.1.1
Type escape sequence to abort.
Sending 5, 100-byte ICMP Echos to 10.1.1.1, timeout is 2    seconds:
00:27:26: BRI0: Dialing cause ip (s=10.1.1.2, d=10.1.1.1)
00:27:26: BRI0: Attempting to dial 18008358661
00:27:27: %LINK-3-UPDOWN: Interface BRI0:1, changed state   to up.
00:27:27: dialer Protocol up for BR0:1
00:27:28: %LINEPROTO-5-UPDOWN: Line protocol on Interface
 BRI0:1, changed state to up
00:27:29: %LINK-3-UPDOWN: Interface BRI0:2, changed state   to up.!!!
Success rate is 60 percent (3/5), round-trip min/avg/max =      32/37/48 ms
Bottom#
00:27:29: dialer Protocol up for BR0:2
00:27:30: %LINEPROTO-5-UPDOWN: Line protocol on Interface
  BRI0:2, changed state to up
```

debug isdn q931

The q.931 specification addresses layer 3 of the OSI model for ISDN. Events occurring at Layer 3 can be monitored with the `debug isdn q931` command. In the following output, the two B channels are disconnected.

The output from this command is best compared to a baseline debug captured on a working connection. However, administrators can use the output to verify acknowledgments and messages without a complete understanding of the protocol. There is a great deal of information provided by the following command. Among other valuable uses, this abundance of information can be used to verify the Layer 3 (q.931) setup:

```
Bottom#debug isdn q931
ISDN Q931 packets debugging is on
00:15:184683593728: ISDN BRO: RX <-  STATUS_ENQ pd = 8       callref = 0x82
00:15:43: ISDN BRO: TX ->  STATUS pd = 8  callref = 0x02
00:15:43:          Cause i = 0x809E - Response to STATUS
  ENQUIRY or number unassigned
00:15:43:          Call State i = 0x0A
00:15:188978601984: ISDN BRO: RX <-  STATUS_ENQ pd = 8       callref = 0x06
00:15:44: ISDN BRO: TX ->  STATUS pd = 8  callref = 0x86
00:15:44:          Cause i = 0x809E - Response to STATUS
  ENQUIRY or number unassigned
00:15:44:          Call State i = 0x0A
00:16:55834615808: ISDN BRO: RX <-  STATUS_ENQ pd = 8    callref = 0x82
00:16:13: ISDN BRO: TX ->  STATUS pd = 8  callref = 0x02
00:16:13:          Cause i = 0x809E - Response to STATUS
  ENQUIRY or number unassigned
00:16:13:          Call State i = 0x0A
00:16:60129583104: ISDN BRO: RX <-  STATUS_ENQ pd = 8       callref = 0x06
00:16:14: ISDN BRO: TX ->  STATUS pd = 8  callref = 0x86
00:16:14:          Cause i = 0x809E - Response to STATUS
  ENQUIRY or number unassigned
00:16:14:          Call State i = 0x0A
00:16:188978601984: ISDN BRO: RX <-  DISCONNECT pd = 8      callref = 0x82
00:16:188978561024:          Cause i = 0x8290 - Normal call      clearing
00:16:188978601984:          Signal i = 0x3F - Tones off
00:16:44: %ISDN-6-DISCONNECT: Interface BRIO:1    disconnected    from
 18008358661 To p, call lasted 120   seconds
00:16:44: %LINK-3-UPDOWN: Interface BRIO:1, changed state   to down
```

```
00:16:44: ISDN BR0: TX ->  RELEASE pd = 8  callref = 0x02
00:16:188978601984: ISDN BR0: RX <-  RELEASE_COMP pd = 8      callref = 0x82
00:16:188978561024: %ISDN-6-DISCONNECT: Interface BRI0:2
      disconnected from 8358 663 , call lasted 120 seconds
00:16:44: ISDN BR0: TX ->  DISCONNECT pd = 8  callref =   0x86
00:16:44:          Cause i = 0x8090 - Normal call clearing
00:16:188978561024: ISDN BR0: RX <-  RELEASE pd = 8    callref = 0x06
00:16:44: %LINK-3-UPDOWN: Interface BRI0:2, changed state   to down
00:16:44: ISDN BR0: TX ->  RELEASE_COMP pd = 8  callref =     0x86
00:16:45: %LINEPROTO-5-UPDOWN: Line protocol on Interface
  BRI0:1, changed state to down
00:16:45: %LINEPROTO-5-UPDOWN: Line protocol on Interface
  BRI0:2, changed state to down
```

debug ppp negotiation

When the router is configured for point-to-point protocol, the `debug ppp negotiation` command provides real-time information about the establishment of a session. This is useful if connections are possible with the HDLC protocol, but failures are occurring with the PPP protocol.

Substantial information is produced by the following command. Apart from that, it can be used to verify the PPP negotiation described earlier in the chapter. You should use this output to verify the troubleshooting targets in PPP negotiation:

```
Bottom#debug ppp negotiation
PPP protocol negotiation debugging is on
Bottom#ping 10.1.1.1
Type escape sequence to abort.
Sending 5, 100-byte ICMP Echos to 10.1.1.1, timeout is 2     seconds:
00:22:28: %LINK-3-UPDOWN: Interface BRI0:1, changed state   to up
00:22:28: BR0:1 PPP: Treating connection as a callout
00:22:28: BR0:1 PPP: Phase is ESTABLISHING, Active Open
00:22:28: BR0:1 LCP: O CONFREQ [Closed] id 3 len 10
00:22:28: BR0:1 LCP:    MagicNumber 0x50239604      (0x050650239604)
00:22:28: BR0:1 LCP: I CONFREQ [REQsent] id 13 len 10
00:22:28: BR0:1 LCP:    MagicNumber 0x5023961F      (0x05065023961F)
00:22:28: BR0:1 LCP: O CONFACK [REQsent] id 13 len 10
00:22:28: BR0:1 LCP:    MagicNumber 0x5.023961F      (0x05065023961F)
00:22:28: BR0:1 LCP: I CONFACK [ACKsent] id 3 len 10
00:22:28: BR0:1 LCP:    MagicNumber 0x50239604      (0x050650239604)
```

```
00:22:28: BR0:1 LCP: State is Open
00:22:28: BR0:1 PPP: Phase is UP
00:22:28: BR0:1 CDPCP: O CONFREQ [Closed] id 3 len 4
00:22:28: BR0:1 IPCP: O CONFREQ [Closed] id 3 len 10
00:22:28: BR0:1 IPCP:    Address 10.1.1.2 (0x03060A010102)
00:22:28: BR0:1 CDPCP: I CONFREQ [REQsent] id 3 len 4
00:22:28: BR0:1 CDPCP: O CONFACK [REQsent] id 3 len 4
00:22:28: BR0:1 IPCP: I CONFREQ [REQsent] id 3 len 10
00:22:28: BR0:1 IPCP:    Address 10.1.1.1 (0x03060A010101)
00:22:28: BR0:1 IPCP: O CONFACK [REQsent] id 3 len 10
00:22:28: BR0:1 IPCP:    Address 10.1.1.1 (0x03060A010101)
00:22:28: BR0:1 CDPCP: I CONFACK [ACKsent] id 3 len 4
00:22:28: BR0:1 CDPCP: State is Open
00:22:28: BR0:1 IPCP: I CONFACK [ACKsent] id 3 len 10
00:22:28: BR0:1 IPCP:    Address 10.1.1.2 (0x03060A010102)
00:22:28: BR0:1 IPCP: State is Open
00:22:28: BR0 IPCP: Install route to 10.1.1.1
00:22:2.!!!
Success rate is 60 percent (3/5), round-trip min/avg/max =      32/38/48 ms
Bottom#9: %LINEPROTO-5-UPDOWN: Line protocol on Interface
  BRI0:1, changed state to up
00:22:29: %LINK-3-UPDOWN: Interface BRI0:2, changed state   to up
00:22:29: BR0:2 PPP: Treating connection as a callin
00:22:29: BR0:2 PPP: Phase is ESTABLISHING, Passive Open
00:22:29: BR0:2 LCP: State is Listen
00:22:30: BR0:2 LCP: I CONFREQ [Listen] id 3 len 10
00:22:30: BR0:2 LCP:    MagicNumber 0x50239CC8      (0x050650239CC8)
00:22:30: BR0:2 LCP: O CONFREQ [Listen] id 3 len 10
00:22:30: BR0:2 LCP:    MagicNumber 0x50239CDA      (0x050650239CDA)
00:22:30: BR0:2 LCP: O CONFACK [Listen] id 3 len 10
00:22:30: BR0:2 LCP:    MagicNumber 0x50239CC8      (0x050650239CC8)
00:22:30: BR0:2 LCP: I CONFACK [ACKsent] id 3 len 10
00:22:30: BR0:2 LCP:    MagicNumber 0x50239CDA      (0x050650239CDA)
00:22:30: BR0:2 LCP: State is Open
00:22:30: BR0:2 PPP: Phase is UP
00:22:30: BR0:2 CDPCP: O CONFREQ [Closed] id 3 len 4
00:22:30: BR0:2 IPCP: O CONFREQ [Closed] id 3 len 10
00:22:30: BR0:2 IPCP:    Address 10.1.1.2 (0x03060A010102)
00:22:30: BR0:2 CDPCP: I CONFREQ [REQsent] id 3 len 4
00:22:30: BR0:2 CDPCP: O CONFACK [REQsent] id 3 len 4
```

```
00:22:30: BR0:2 IPCP: I CONFREQ [REQsent] id 3 len 10
00:22:30: BR0:2 IPCP:    Address 10.1.1.1 (0x03060A010101)
00:22:30: BR0:2 IPCP: O CONFACK [REQsent] id 3 len 10
00:22:30: BR0:2 IPCP:    Address 10.1.1.1 (0x03060A010101)
00:22:30: BR0:2 CDPCP: I CONFACK [ACKsent] id 3 len 4
00:22:30: BR0:2 CDPCP: State is Open
00:22:30: BR0:2 IPCP: I CONFACK [ACKsent] id 3 len 10
00:22:30: BR0:2 IPCP:    Address 10.1.1.2 (0x03060A010102)
00:22:30: BR0:2 IPCP: State is Open
00:22:31: %LINEPROTO-5-UPDOWN: Line protocol on Interface
  BRI0:2, changed state to up
00:21:22: BR0:1 LCP: O ECHOREQ [Open] id 12 len 12 magic      0x5020C645
00:21:22: BR0:1 LCP: echo_cnt 1, sent id 12, line up
00:21:22: BR0:1 PPP: I pkt type 0xC021, datagramsize 16
00:21:22: BR0:1 LCP: I ECHOREP [Open] id 12 len 12 magic      0x5020C654
00:21:22: BR0:1 LCP: Received id 12, sent id 12, line up
00:21:22: BR0:2 LCP: O ECHOREQ [Open] id 12 len 12 magic      0x5020CD1B
00:21:22: BR0:2 LCP: echo_cnt 1, sent id 12, line up
00:21:22: BR0:2 PPP: I pkt type 0xC021, datagramsize 16
00:21:22: BR0:2 LCP: I ECHOREP [Open] id 12 len 12 magic      0x5020CD0D
00:21:22: BR0:2 LCP: Received id 12, sent id 12, line up
00:21:23: BR0:1 PPP: I pkt type 0xC021, datagramsize 16
00:21:23: BR0:1 LCP: I ECHOREQ [Open] id 12 len 12 magic      0x5020C654
00:21:23: BR0:1 LCP: O ECHOREP [Open] id 12 len 12 magic      0x5020C645
00:21:23: BR0:2 PPP: I pkt type 0xC021, datagramsize 16
00:21:23: BR0:2 LCP: I ECHOREQ [Open] id 12 len 12 magic      0x5020CD0D
00:21:23: BR0:2 LCP: O ECHOREP [Open] id 12 len 12 magic      0x5020CD1B
00:21:24: BR0:2 PPP: I pkt type 0x0207, datagramsize 15
00:21:25: BR0:2 PPP: I pkt type 0x0207, datagramsize 312
00:21:25: %ISDN-6-DISCONNECT: Interface BRI0:1    disconnected from
  18008358661 To p, call lasted 120   seconds
00:21:25: %LINK-3-UPDOWN: Interface BRI0:1, changed state   to down
00:21:107379488949: %ISDN-6-DISCONNECT: Interface BRI0:2
    disconnected from 8358 663 , call lasted 120 seconds
00:21:25: %LINK-3-UPDOWN: Interface BRI0:2, changed state   to down
00:21:26: %LINEPROTO-5-UPDOWN: Line protocol on Interface
  BRI0:1, changed state to down
00:21:26: %LINEPROTO-5-UPDOWN: Line protocol on Interface
  BRI0:2, changed state to down
```

debug ppp packet

The debug ppp packet command reports real-time PPP packet flow, including the type of packet and the specific B channel used. Although this command generates a significant amount of output, it is quite useful for locating errors that involve upper layer protocols.

As with other debug packet commands, debug ppp packet records each packet that moves through the router using PPP. The administrator can thus monitor traffic flows as if a protocol analyzer were attached to the interface. This can be useful for troubleshooting Application layer problems, but a formal protocol analyzer is highly recommended.

```
Bottom#debug ppp packet
PPP packet display debugging is on
Bottom#ping 10.1.1.1
Type escape sequence to abort.
Sending 5, 100-byte ICMP Echos to 10.1.1.1, timeout is 2     seconds:
00:24:49: %LINK-3-UPDOWN: Interface BRI0:1, changed state   to up.
00:24:50: BR0:1 LCP: O CONFREQ [Closed] id 4 len 10
00:24:50: BR0:1 LCP:    MagicNumber 0x5025BF23      (0x05065025BF23)
00:24:50: BR0:1 PPP: I pkt type 0xC021, datagramsize 14
00:24:50: BR0:1 PPP: I pkt type 0xC021, datagramsize 14
00:24:50: BR0:1 LCP: I CONFREQ [REQsent] id 14 len 10
00:24:50: BR0:1 LCP:    MagicNumber 0x5025BF46      (0x05065025BF46)
00:24:50: BR0:1 LCP: O CONFACK [REQsent] id 14 len 10
00:24:50: BR0:1 LCP:    MagicNumber 0x5025BF46      (0x05065025BF46)
00:24:50: BR0:1 LCP: I CONFACK [ACKsent] id 4 len 10
00:24:50: BR0:1 LCP:    MagicNumber 0x5025BF23      (0x05065025BF23)
00:24:50: BR0:1 PPP: I pkt type 0x8207, datagramsize 8
00:24:50: BR0:1 PPP: I pkt type 0x8021, datagramsize 14
00:24:50: BR0:1 CDPCP: O CONFREQ [Closed] id 4 len 4
00:24:50: BR0:1 PPP: I pkt type 0x8207, datagramsize 8
00:24:50: BR0:1 IPCP: O CONFREQ [Closed] id 4 len 10
00:24:50: BR0:1 IPCP:    Address 10.1.1.2 (0x03060A010102)
00:24:50: BR0:1 CDPCP: I CONFREQ [REQsent] id 4 len 4
00:24:50: BR0:1 CDPCP: O CONFACK [REQ.!!!
Success rate is 60 percent (3/5), round-trip min/avg/max =      36/41/52 ms
. . . some output omitted . . .
00:25:03: BR0:2 LCP: O ECHOREP [Open] id 2 len 12 magic
      0x5025C605undebug all
All possible debugging has been turned off
Bottom#
```

Summary

Though originally designed to bring digital networking to the home environment, ISDN has evolved into a commonly used business tool. It allows small offices to connect to multiple disparate locations without the need for a dedicated circuit. This connectivity includes connecting back to the corporate office, to other businesses, to an ISP, and to many other locations. In addition, ISDN has also been used to provide backup services when a primary link fails.

Numerous component and connection types are used in ISDN. Acronyms have been assigned and used to better describe how each major component interacts with the other major ISDN components. Commonly used connections between major components were given abbreviations called reference points. The specific component acronyms and reference points are detailed in Figure 40.1 and textually explained in the section that follows this figure.

An ISDN BRI channel is made up of two 64Kbps B channels used for carrying traffic and a single 16Kbps D channel used for signaling. The signaling that is used over the D channel for call setup is q.921 for layer 2, and q.931 for layer 3. In addition, the most common protocol used for encapsulation on an ISDN link is PPP. With negotiation occurring over the B channels, PPP supports multiple layer 3 protocols such as IP, IPX, and AppleTalk. PPP also supports CHAP and PAP security.

When troubleshooting ISDN, numerous `show` and `debug` commands can be used. These commands allow for detailed analysis of the interface, q.921, q.931, and PPP. Some common commands are `show interface`, `show ISDN status`, `show dialer`, `debug isdn q921`, `debug ISDN q931`, and `debug ppp authentication`.

Exam Essentials

Know the basics of how ISDN operates. Understand that ISDN is a digital service. Also know the number and size of B channels and D channels and the use of SPIDs.

Know the ISDN components. The components used in ISDN are TE1, TE2, TA, NT2, NT1, LT, and ET. In North America, the NT1 is the last component that is considered customer premises equipment (CPE), whereas in most other locations the NT1 is carrier provided and maintained.

Know the ISDN reference points. The reference points used in an ISDN connection are R, S, T, and U. If no NT2 is used, the S and T reference points combine to make an S/T reference point.

Understand how ISDN calls are set up. Access lists are used in conjunction with dialer maps to define the traffic type that will bring up a link, as well as to specify the number that is dialed. In addition, authentication can be set up to ensure the validity of an incoming call.

Know the function of q.921. The q.921 protocol in combination with LAPD is used to set up the layer 2 connection over the D channel. The `debug ISDN q921` command allows for the debugging of specific q.921 information.

Know the function of q.931. The q.931 protocol is used to set up the layer 3 connection over the D channel. The `debug ISDN q931` command allows for the debugging of specific q.931 information.

Know how PPP is used and how it is set up. LCP is used as the layer 2 protocol for link establishment and maintenance. NCP performs similar functions for layer 3 protocols. PPP also has the capability to use authentication. The `debug ppp negotiation` command can be used to look specifically at the PPP setup.

Know the function of CHAP and PAP. CHAP and PAP are both authentication protocols used with PPP. These protocols allow for verification of both the calling and called devices. The `debug ppp authentication` command can be used to look at the CHAP or PAP authentication process.

Troubleshooting Switched Ethernet

THE CCNP EXAM TOPICS COVERED IN THIS CHAPTER INCLUDE THE FOLLOWING:

- ✓ Use Cisco IOS commands to identify problems.
- ✓ Rectify suboptimal performance issues at layers 2 through 7.
- ✓ Rectify layer 1 connectivity problems.
- ✓ Restore services back to baseline conditions.

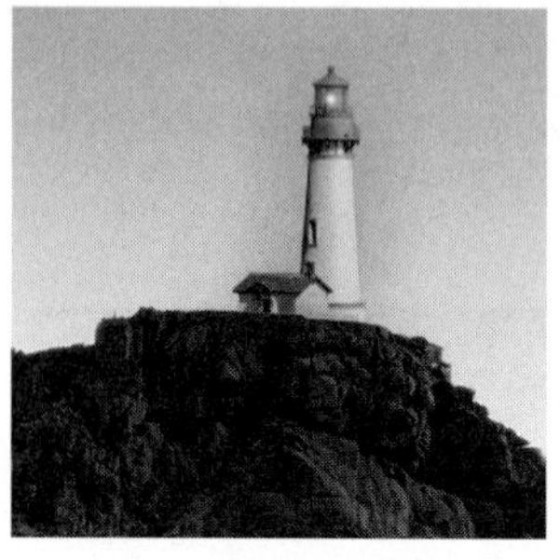

Switching and virtual networking became the Holy Grail of manufacturers and customers alike in the 1990s. High-speed, low-latency bridging at layer 2 provided the first inducement for administrators to purchase and install switches. By the late 1990s, switches were no longer restricted to layer 2, and route- and port-based switching at layers 3 and 4 were becoming commonplace.

Switching provides many significant advantages, including greater aggregate bandwidth at lower cost with collision (full-duplex) control. The downside of switching frequently includes a forklift upgrade in the wiring closet and slightly modified troubleshooting procedures. For example, it is not possible to simply plug a protocol analyzer into a port and see all traffic on the segment.

The Cisco Catalyst product line includes Ethernet, FDDI, Token Ring, and ATM switching. Although this section focuses primarily on the Catalyst 6500 product line, other Catalyst products are available and possibly better suited for some implementations.

Switches, Bridges, and Hubs

An understanding of switches and their functions requires an understanding of the differences between broadcast and collision domains.

The *broadcast domain* defines the scope of broadcasts within the network. Usually this is equal to the diameter of the subnet, because most upper layer protocols rely on broadcasts to function. As such, the broadcast domain is usually controlled by routers.

Collision domains are defined by the scope of impact that a collision may have. With hubs, this scope is equal to all stations connected to the shared media; as the number of nodes and traffic load increases, collisions become a more significant problem for administrators and designers. Switches reduce this scope to two stations: the switch port and the end node. By using full-duplex Ethernet, which is an option available on most switches and newer NICs, collisions are no longer a factor.

On an Ethernet hub, the collision domain and the broadcast domain are the same—all ports receive all frames, and the receivers are required to analyze the destination address. If the frame is a broadcast or a unicast to the station (omitting multicasts), the frame will be processed further. The negative to this is unnecessary processing at all the workstations for which the frames were not intended. The collision domain on a hub is inclusive of all ports and stations on that hub. The broadcast domain on a hub is identical to the collision domain, although this assumes that a single hub represents the entire network or that a single hub is the only device connected to the router port. Technically, routers contain the broadcast domain. All other stations will hear any frame sent from a station on the hub.

The collision domain on a switch is limited to the individual port on the switch and its directly connected resource (workstation or other device). This greatly reduces workstation overhead because the frames received by the workstation should be intended for that station. In addition, the switch can provide a dedicated pipe to the workstation. Thus, a 10Mb network interface card can provide 10Mb, rather than sharing that bandwidth with all other stations. A small 12-port Ethernet switch provides a theoretical 120Mb of bandwidth, compared to the 10Mb provided by a standard Ethernet hub or the 20 Mb provided by a two-port bridge.

Table 41.1 compares the differences between switches and hubs.

TABLE 41.1 Comparison of Switches and Hubs

Type	Switch	Hub
Unicasts	Sent only to destination port.	Sent to all ports.
Broadcasts	Sent to all ports defined to the same VLAN.	Sent to all ports.
Aggregate bandwidth	Equal to bandwidth of each port times number of ports. A 12-port Ethernet switch is capable of providing a total bandwidth of 120Mbit. (Note that backplane, processor, and other factors may change this simplification.)	Equal to speed of medium—an Ethernet hub would provide a total of 10Mbit.
Full/half-duplex	Full-duplex connections available.	Half-duplex only.
Support for mixed media: Token Ring, Ethernet, FDDI, and so on	Depending on the switch, translations may occur between frame types or physical media.	Supports single media.

Table 41.2 contrasts the differences between switches and bridges.

TABLE 41.2 Comparison of Switches and Bridges

Specification	Switches	Bridges
Support for mixed media	Usually	Depends on bridge configuration.
Processing of frames	Hardware (ASIC)	Software or generic hardware.
Number of ports	From 4 to over 100	Usually under 16; sometimes only two.
Frame type translation	Usually	Depends on bridge configuration.

Catalyst Troubleshooting Tools

The Catalyst system provides significant diagnostic and administrative tools in the CLI (command-line interface). Troubleshooting switched networks frequently includes correlating layer 2 addressing to layer 3, and researching Physical layer problems. Although this section focuses primarily on the tools and commands themselves, a review of standards and typical problems will be presented later in this chapter.

Catalyst Command-Line Interfaces

Many administrators prefer the command-line interface (CLI), especially if they are already experienced with the Cisco IOS. Although the GUI applications can simplify many functions, and (in some cases) address functions not available from the CLI, they fail to provide the speed and simplicity of CLI.

In the case of Cisco switches, you may encounter two different CLI types, depending on the switch and the code running on the switch. These two variations of code that are available to run on the switch are called *Native* mode and *Hybrid* mode. Native mode syntax very closely resembles router configuration commands that have been covered up to this point in this study guide. This variation of command syntax is the only one available on switches such as the 1900 series, 3550 series, and 2950 series. On switches in the 4500 and 6500 series, there is an option to run in either Native mode or Hybrid mode.

One major difference between running in Native mode and Hybrid mode is in how layer 3 functionality, if present, is handled in the switch. In Native mode, the configuration for items such as the MSFC (Multilayer Switch Feature Card) in a 6500 is combined with that of the layer 2 capabilities of the switch. In this manner, any configuration that is done on the switch, regardless of the layer, can be done via the same CLI. In Hybrid mode, layer 2 switching functionality is controlled by one CLI, and the routing functionality is controlled by a separate CLI. The switching CLI of the Hybrid mode is also referred to as `set`-based because many of the configuration statements begin with the word `set`.

Though the focus of this chapter is on the Hybrid-mode switching CLI, you'll find a table, Table 41.6, at the end of this chapter that shows the Native mode equivalents to some common Hybrid mode commands.

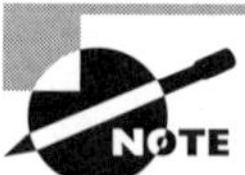

To avoid confusion, and unless specifically stated otherwise, the term *CLI* in this chapter refers to the Hybrid-mode switching CLI.

Hybrid Mode Catalyst CLI

The CLI provides a wealth of configuration and diagnostic tools for the administrator. Commands include the `set` and `clear` options that are used to configure the switch, and the `show` commands to monitor the current settings.

The show commands, displayed in enable mode with the `show ? command`, include the following:

```
accounting              Show accounting information
alias                   Show aliases for commands
arp                     Show ARP table
authentication          Show authentication information
authorization           Show authorization information
banner                  Show system banner
boot                    Show booting environment variables
cam                     Show CAM table
cdp                     Show Cisco Discovery Protocol Information
channel                 Show channel information
config                  Show system configuration
cops                    Show COPS information
counters                Show port counters
default                 Show default status
dot1q-all-tagged        Show dot1q tag status
dot1x                   Show dot1x port capability & version
dvlan                   Show dynamic vlan statistics
environment             Show environment information
errdisable-timeout      Show err-disable timeout config
errordetection          Show errordetection settings
fabric                  Show fabric information
file                    Show contents of file
flash                   Show file information on flash device
garp                    Show GARP information
gmrp                    Show GMRP information
gvrp                    Show GVRP information
ifindex                 Show information for this Ifindex
igmp                    Show IGMP information
imagemib                Show image mib information
interface               Show network interfaces
ip                      Show IP Information
kerberos                Show kerberos configuration information
lcperroraction          Show action on lcp errors
log                     Show log information
logging                 Show system logging information
mac                     Show MAC information
microcode               Show microcode versions
mls                     Show multilayer switching information
```

```
module              Show module info
msfcautostate       Show MSFC derived interface state enabled/disabled
msmautostate        Show MSM derived interface state enabled/disabled
multicast           Show multicast information
netstat             Show network statistics
ntp                 Show ntp statistics
pbf                 Show PBF information
port                Show port information
proc                Show cpu and processes utilization
protocolfilter      Show protocolfilter information
pvlan               Show Private Vlan Information
qos                 Show QOS information
radius              Show RADIUS information
rcp                 Show rcp information
reset               Show schedule reset information
rgmp                Show RGMP information
rspan               Show remote switch port analyzer information
running-config      Show system runtime configuration
security            Show Security ACL information
snmp                Show SNMP information
span                Show switch port analyzer information
spantree            Show spantree information
startup-config      Show system startup configuration
summertime          Show state of summertime information
system              Show system information
tacacs              Show TACACS information
tech-support        Show system information for Tech-Support
test                Show results of diagnostic tests
time                Show time of day
timezone            Show the current timezone offset
top                 Show TopN report
traffic             Show Traffic information
trunk               Show trunk ports
udld                Show Uni-directional Link Detection information
users               Show active Admin sessions
version             Show version information
vlan                Show Virtual LAN information
vmps                Show VMPS information
vtp                 Show VTP Information
```

show system

The `show system` command provides high-level summary information regarding the switch, including the status of power supplies, uptime and administrative settings, and the percentage of traffic on the backplane.

```
Switch_A> (enable) show system
PS1-Status PS2-Status
---------- ----------
ok         ok

Fan-Status Temp-Alarm Sys-Status Uptime d,h:m:s Logout
---------- ---------- ---------- -------------- ---------
ok         off         ok        331,09:58:18   20 min

PS1-Type             PS2-Type
-------------------- --------------------
WS-CAC-1300W         WS-CAC-1300W

Modem   Baud  Backplane-Traffic Peak Peak-Time
------- ----- ----------------- ---- -------------------------
disable  9600   0%                11% Thu Jul 10 2003, 01:30:06

PS1 Capacity: 1153.32 Watts (27.46 Amps @42V)
PS2 Capacity: 1153.32 Watts (27.46 Amps @42V)
PS Configuration : PS1 and PS2 in Redundant Configuration.

System Name              System Location          System Contact           CC
------------------------ ------------------------ ------------------------ ---
Switch_A                Dover, DE               Network Support

No active fabric module in the system.

Core Dump                Core File
------------------------ -----------------------
disabled                 slot0:crashinfo

Switch_A-> (enable)
```

show port

The show port commands give you specific information about ports or all ports on a module. This includes commands that are available from other show commands, including show mac, for example.

```
Switch_A> (enable) show port ?
Usage: show port
       show port <mod_num>
       show port <mod_num/port_num>
Show port commands:
show port broadcast       Show port broadcast information
show port cdp             Show port CDP information
show port channel         Show port channel information
show port counters        Show port counters
show port fddi            Show port FDDI information
show port filter          Show Token Ring port filtering
                            information
show port help            Show this message
show port mac             Show port MAC counters
show port multicast       Show port multicast information
show port security        Show port security information
show port spantree        Show port spantree information
show port status          Show port status
show port trap            Show port trap information
show port trunk           Show port trunk information
```

The show port command output appears as follows. Note that VLAN membership, port speed and configuration, and error statistics are available.

```
Switch_A-> (enable) show port 3/3
Port  Name                 Status     Vlan       Duplex Speed Type
----- -------------------- ---------- ---------- ------ ----- ------------
 3/3  Switch_B 2/7 MxC   connected  980          full  1000 1000-LX/LH


Port  Security Violation Shutdown-Time Age-Time Max-Addr Trap     IfIndex
----- -------- --------- ------------- -------- -------- -------- -----
 3/3  disabled  shutdown             0        0        1 disabled      13

Port  Num-Addr Secure-Src-Addr   Age-Left Last-Src-Addr     Shutdown/Time-Left
----- -------- ----------------- -------- ----------------- -----------
 3/3         0                 -        -                 -        -        -
```

```
Port     Broadcast-Limit Multicast Unicast Total-Drop
-------- --------------- --------- ------- --------------------
 3/3                   -         -       -                    0

Port  Send FlowControl  Receive FlowControl   RxPause    TxPause
      admin    oper     admin     oper
----- -------- -------- --------- ---------   ---------- ----------
 3/3  desired  off      off       off          0          0

Port  Status     Channel              Admin Ch
                 Mode                 Group Id
----- ---------- -------------------- ----- -----
 3/3  connected  auto silent              7     0

Port  Align-Err  FCS-Err    Xmit-Err   Rcv-Err    UnderSize
----- ---------- ---------- ---------- ---------- ---------
 3/3           0          0          0          0         0

Port  Single-Col Multi-Coll Late-Coll  Excess-Col Carri-Sen Runts     Giants
----- ---------- ---------- ---------- ---------- --------- --------- --------
 3/3           0          0          0          0         0         0        0

Port  Last-Time-Cleared
----- --------------------------
 3/3  Mon Jul 7 2003, 05:56:31
```

show log

The `show log` command does not report events the same way that a Cisco router does. The command reports significant events, including reboots of all modules, traps, and power supply failures. Note that the following output reports power supply failures, along with module reset information in the period that may be useful information for the administrator if users report intermittent connectivity problems.

```
Switch_A-> (enable) show log

Network Management Processor (ACTIVE NMP) Log:
  Reset count:   13
  Re-boot History:   Aug 17 2002 04:11:13 0, Aug 16 2002 16:59:51 0
                     Aug 16 2002 16:56:42 0, Aug 16 2002 12:54:29 0
                     Aug 13 2002 19:37:45 0, Jun 13 2002 10:46:28 0
                     Jun 12 2002 16:06:00 0, Jun 12 2002 16:03:16 0
                     Jun 12 2002 15:58:29 0, Jun 12 2002 15:40:03 0
```

```
  Bootrom Checksum Failures:      0  UART Failures:                 0
  Flash Checksum Failures:        0  Flash Program Failures:        0
  Power Supply 1 Failures:        1  Power Supply 2 Failures:       0
  Swapped to CLKA:                0  Swapped to CLKB:               0
  Swapped to Processor 1:         0  Swapped to Processor 2:        0
  DRAM Failures:                  0

  Exceptions:                     0

  Loaded NMP version:            6.3(5)
  Reload same NMP version count: 10

  Last software reset by user: 8/16/2002,16:59:30

  EOBC Exceptions/Hang:            0

Heap Memory Log:
Corrupted Block = none

NVRAM log:

Module 3 Log:
  Reset Count:   2
  Reset History: Sat Aug 17 2002, 04:13:04
                 Tue Aug 13 2002, 19:39:37


Module 4 Log:
  Reset Count:   2
  Reset History: Sat Aug 17 2002, 04:13:10
                 Tue Aug 13 2002, 19:39:42


Module 15 Log:
  Reset Count:   15
  Reset History: Sat Aug 17 2002, 04:12:25
                 Fri Aug 16 2002, 17:01:01
                 Fri Aug 16 2002, 16:57:52
                 Fri Aug 16 2002, 12:55:39
```

show logging buffer

The equivalent to the `show log` command on a router is the `show logging buffer` command on a switch. Depending on the logging level, `show logging buffer` can report on port up, port down, or spanning tree issues as well as just about anything else that is happening on the switch. The output of this command is as follows:

```
Switch_A> show logging buffer
2002 May 04 13:42:55 EST -04:00 %MLS-5-ROUTERADD:Route Processor
  ➥10.4.0.254 added
2002 May 04 13:44:32 EST -04:00 %SNMP-5-MODULETRAP:Module 2 [Down] Trap
2002 May 04 13:44:32 EST -04:00 %SPANTREE-5-PORTDEL_FAILNOTFOUND:2/1 in
vlan 1 not found (RedundantTask)
2002 May 04 13:44:32 EST -04:00 %SPANTREE-5-PORTDEL_FAILNOTFOUND:2/2 in
 vlan 1 not found (RedundantTask)
2002 May 04 13:44:34 EST -04:00 %SYS-5-SUP_MODSBY:Module 2 is in standby mode
2002 May 04 13:44:34 EST -04:00 %SNMP-5-MODULETRAP:Module 2 [Up] Trap
2002 May 04 13:45:01 EST -04:00 %SYS-5-SUP_IMGSYNCSTART:Active
 supervisor is synchronizing the NMP image
2002 May 04 13:45:09 EST -04:00 %SYS-5-SUP_IMGSYNCFINISH:Active
 supervisor has synchronized the NMP image
```

show interface

The `show interface` command reports the IP configuration of the Supervisor module. Although the SLIP (Serial Line Internet Protocol) connection is configured on `sl0`, most installations use the in-band `sc0` connection. As shown here, it belongs to VLAN 1, which always exists on the switch:

```
Switch_A> (enable) show interface
sl0: flags=51<UP,POINTOPOINT,RUNNING>
        slip 0.0.0.0 dest 0.0.0.0
sc0: flags=63<UP,BROADCAST,RUNNING>
        vlan 1 inet 10.11.10.1 netmask 255.255.255.0 broadcast 10.11.10.255
```

show cdp

Cisco Discovery Protocol (CDP) is an extraordinarily powerful troubleshooting tool. Available on all Cisco routers and switches, the protocol operates between Cisco devices on media that support SNAP. CDP has been available since IOS 10.3.

CDP packets are sent as a multicast and are not forwarded by the router or switch. Specifically, they are sent to the destination MAC address of 01:00:0c:cc:cc:cc.

Following is a sample of the CDP report on a Catalyst 6506 switch with three neighbors:

```
Switch_A> (enable) show cdp neighbor detail
Device-ID: Router_A.domain.com
Device Addresses:
  IP Address: 10.1.1.1
Holdtime: 142 sec
Capabilities: ROUTER
Version:
  Cisco Internetwork Operating System Software
  IOS (tm) 4500 Software (C4500-J-M), Version 11.2(15a)P, P RELEASE
    SOFTWARE (fc1)
  Copyright (c) 1986-1998 by cisco Systems, Inc.
Platform: cisco 4700
Port-ID (Port on Device): FastEthernet0
Port (Our Port): 2/1
____________________________________________________________
Device-ID: Router_B.domain.com
Device Addresses:
  IP Address: 10.1.2.1
Holdtime: 130 sec
Capabilities: ROUTER
Version:
  Cisco Internetwork Operating System Software
  IOS (tm) 4500 Software (C4500-J-M), Version 11.2(15a)P, P
     RELEASE SOFTWARE (fc1)
  Copyright (c) 1986-1998 by cisco Systems, Inc.
Platform: cisco 4700
Port-ID (Port on Device): FastEthernet0
Port (Our Port): 2/2
____________________________________________________________
Device-ID: Router_C.domain.com
Device Addresses:
  IP Address: 10.10.1.1
Holdtime: 177 sec
Capabilities: ROUTER SR_BRIDGE
Version:
  Cisco Internetwork Operating System Software
  IOS (tm) C2600 Software (C2600-JS-M), Version 12.0(2a), RELEASE
   SOFTWARE (fc1)
  Copyright (c) 1986-1999 by cisco Systems, Inc.
```

```
Platform: cisco 2612
Port-ID (Port on Device): Ethernet1/0
Port (Our Port): 2/17
```

A CDP datagram decodes with EtherPeek, as follows:

```
Packet 3 captured at 05/22/2003 09:08:57 AM; Packet size is    302(0x12e)bytes
      Relative time: 000:00:01.473
      Delta time: 0.042.868
Ethernet Protocol
      Address: 00-00-0C-1B-63-97 --->01-00-0C-CC-CC-CC
      Length: 288
Logical Link Control
      SSAP Address: 0xAA, CR bit = 0 (Command)
      DSAP Address: 0xAA, IG bit = 0 (Individual address)
      Unnumbered frame: UI
SubNetwork Access Protocol
      Organization code: 0x00000c
      Type: Custom Defined
Flags:          0x80  802.3
  Status:         0x00
  Packet Length:339
  Timestamp:      16:40:23.689000 03/16/2002
802.3 Header
  Destination:  01:00:0c:cc:cc:cc
  Source:         00:00:0c:17:b6:f2
  LLC Length:   321
802.2 Logical Link Control (LLC) Header
  Dest. SAP:      0xaa  SNAP
  Source SAP:     0xaa  SNAP
  Command:        0x03  Unnumbered Information
  Protocol:       00-00-0c-20-00
  Packet Data:
  . _'....Router_A  01 b4 9e 27 00 01 00 0c 52 6f 75 74 65 72 5f 41
  ...6............  00 02 00 36 00 00 00 03 01 01 cc 00 04 0a 02 01
  ...  ...._7.....  01 02 08 aa aa 03 00 00 00 81 37 00 0a 00 00 00
  ..... ...  ...._  0b 00 00 0c 17 b6 f2 02 08 aa aa 03 00 00 00 80
   ....o....Ethern  9b 00 03 00 02 6f 00 03 00 0d 45 74 68 65 72 6e
  et1.......... C   65 74 31 00 04 00 08 00 00 00 01 00 05 00 d0 43
  isco Internetwor  69 73 63 6f 20 49 6e 74 65 72 6e 65 74 77 6f 72
```

```
  k Operating Syst  6b 20 4f 70 65 72 61 74 69 6e 67 20 53 79 73 74
  em Software .IOS  65 6d 20 53 6f 66 74 77 61 72 65 20 0a 49 4f 53
   (tm) 4000 Softw  20 28 74 6d 29 20 34 30 30 30 20 53 6f 66 74 77
  are (XX-J-M), Ve  61 72 65 20 28 58 58 2d 4a 2d 4d 29 2c 20 56 65
  rsion 11.0(17),   72 73 69 6f 6e 20 31 31 2e 30 28 31 37 29 2c 20
  RELEASE SOFTWARE  52 45 4c 45 41 53 45 20 53 4f 46 54 57 41 52 45
   (fc1).Copyright  20 28 66 63 31 29 0a 43 6f 70 79 72 69 67 68 74
   (c) 1986-1997 b  20 28 63 29 20 31 39 38 36 2d 31 39 39 37 20 62
  y cisco Systems,  79 20 63 69 73 63 6f 20 53 79 73 74 65 6d 73 2c
   Inc..Compiled T  20 49 6e 63 2e 0a 43 6f 6d 70 69 6c 65 64 20 54
  hu 04-Sep-97 14:  68 75 20 30 34 2d 53 65 70 2d 39 37 20 31 34 3a
  44 by richv....c  34 34 20 62 79 20 72 69 63 68 76 00 06 00 0e 63
  isco 4000         69 73 63 6f 20 34 30 30 30
Frame Check Sequence:  0x00000000
```

show config

The `show config` command is similar to the `show running-config` command on Cisco routers. This command provides all configuration settings on the switch for all modules, with a few exceptions for certain modules such as the MSFC. One difference is that `show config` only shows the non-default configuration. If you want to see the entire configuration on a switch, execute the command `show config all`.

Here is the output of `show config`:

```
Switch_A-> (enable) show config
This command shows non-default configurations only.
Use 'show config all' to show both default and non-default configurations.
..............
..................
..................
....................
..

begin
!
# ***** NON-DEFAULT CONFIGURATION *****
!
!
#time: Mon Jul 14 2003, 08:28:01 EST
!
#version 6.3(5)
!
```

```
set password Dsasdf84nsmth;dHRkt@#sdf.sdfgg
set enablepass $safgP$PO921asfdgIOUPIUKLJKJh1
set prompt Switch_A->
set banner motd ^C

                           NOTICE:

Legal warning - Only use for legitimate purposes.

^C

!
#system
set system name  Switch_A
set system location Dover, DE
set system contact  Net Support
!
#!
#snmp
set snmp community read-only      public
set snmp community read-write     private
set snmp community read-write-all secret
set snmp rmon enable
set snmp trap enable  module
set snmp trap enable  chassis
set snmp trap enable  repeater
set snmp trap enable  vtp
set snmp trap enable  auth
set snmp trap enable  ippermit
set snmp trap 10.1.1.1 snmp port 162 owner CLI index 1
set snmp trap 10.2.2.2 snmp port 162 owner CLI index 2
!
#tacacs+
set tacacs server 10.8.8.8 primary
set tacacs server 10.9.9.9
set tacacs key good_key
!
#authentication
set authentication login tacacs enable console primary
set authentication login tacacs enable telnet primary
```

```
set authentication login tacacs enable http primary
set authentication enable tacacs enable console primary
set authentication enable tacacs enable telnet primary
set authentication enable tacacs enable http primary
!
#vtp
set vtp domain Switches_1
set vtp mode transparent
set vlan 1 name default type ethernet mtu 1500 said 100001 state active
set vlan 222 name Management type ethernet mtu 1500 said 10
0222 state active
set vlan 300 name Segment1 type ethernet mtu 1500 said 1009
66 state active
set vlan 301 name Crossconnect2 type ethernet mtu 1500 said 1009
68 state active
set vlan 302 name Accounting type ethernet mtu 1500 said 1009
70 state active
set vlan 303 name Travel type ethernet mtu 1500 said 1
00303 state active
set vlan 304 name Manufacturing1 type ethernet mtu 1500 said 1
00304 state active
set vlan 305 name Manufacturing2 type ethernet mtu 1500 said 1
00305 state active
set vlan 306 name Manufacturing3 type ethernet mtu 1500 said 1
00306 state active
set vlan 307 name Backoffice type ethernet mtu 1500 said 1009
80 state active
set vlan 308 name Network Support type ethernet mtu 1500 said 1009
83 state active
set vlan 309 name Finance type ethernet mtu 1500 said 1009
84 state active
set vlan 310 name Customer_Service type ethernet mtu 1500 said 1009
86 state active
set vlan 311 name Customer_Service2 type ethernet mtu 1500 said 1009
88 state active
set vlan 312 name Customer_Service3 type ethernet mtu 1500 said 100311
state active
set vlan 1002 name fddi-default type fddi mtu 1500 said 101002 state active
set vlan 1004 name fddinet-default type fddinet mtu 1500 said 101004
state active stp ieee
```

```
set vlan 1005 name trnet-default type trbrf mtu 1500 said 101005 state
active stp ibm
set vlan 1003 name token-ring-default type trcrf mtu 1500 said 101003
state active mode srb aremaxhop 7 stemaxhop 7 backupcrf off
!
#ip
set interface sc0 222 10.10.10.10/255.255.255.0 10.10.10.255

set ip route 0.0.0.0/0.0.0.0         10.10.10.1
!
#dns
set ip dns server 10.3.3.3 primary
set ip dns server 10.4.4.4
set ip dns server 10.5.5.5
set ip dns enable
set ip dns domain test.test-ap.com
!
#spantree
#vlan                        <VlanId>
set spantree fwddelay 15     1003
set spantree maxage   20     1003
set spantree disable  1005
set spantree fwddelay 15     1005
set spantree maxage   20     1005
!
#syslog
set logging server enable
set logging server 10.1.1.1
set logging server 10.2.2.2
set logging level cdp 5 default
set logging level earl 5 default
set logging level ip 5 default
set logging level pruning 5 default
set logging level snmp 5 default
set logging level spantree 5 default
set logging level tac 5 default
set logging level tcp 5 default
set logging level telnet 5 default
set logging level tftp 5 default
set logging level vtp 5 default
```

```
set logging level ld 2 default
set logging level privatevlan 2 default
!
#ntp
set ntp client enable
set ntp server 10.1.1.1
set ntp server 10.2.2.2
set timezone EST -5 0
set summertime enable EST
!
#set boot command
set boot config-register 0x102
set boot system flash bootflash:cat6000-sup2_6-3-5.bin
!
#cdp
set cdp version v1
!
#port channel
set port channel 1/2 5
set port channel 1/1 49
!
# default port status is enable
!
!
#module 1 : 2-port 1000BaseX Supervisor
set module name    1
set vlan 301  1/2
set vlan 302  1/1
set port name       1/1  Switch_A0 p1/1
set port name       1/2  Router_4 2/1
set trunk 1/1  off negotiate 1-1005,1025-4094
set trunk 1/2  off negotiate 1-1005,1025-4094
set port channel 1/1-2 mode off
!
#module 2 empty
!
#module 3 : 8-port 1000BaseX Ethernet
set module name    3
set vlan 300  3/7
set vlan 303  3/5
```

```
set vlan 304  3/6
set vlan 305  3/2
set vlan 306  3/1
set vlan 307  3/3
set vlan 308  3/4
set vlan 309  3/8
set port name       3/1  Switch_D Port 3/1
set port name       3/2  Switch_C Port 3/2
set port name       3/3  Switch_B 2/7 MxC
set port name       3/4  Switch_E 2/8 MxC
set port name       3/5  Router_1 Port 3/1
set port name       3/6  Router_2 Port 3/1
set port name       3/7  Router_3 2/1
set port name       3/8  Test_Net
set trunk 3/1  off negotiate 1-1005,1025-4094
set trunk 3/2  off negotiate 1-1005,1025-4094
set trunk 3/3  off negotiate 1-1005,1025-4094
set trunk 3/4  off negotiate 1-1005,1025-4094
set trunk 3/5  off negotiate 1-1005,1025-4094
set trunk 3/6  off negotiate 1-1005,1025-4094
set trunk 3/7  off negotiate 1-1005,1025-4094
set trunk 3/8  off negotiate 1-1005,1025-4094
set port channel 3/7 mode off
!
#module 4 empty
!
#module 5 empty
!
#module 6 empty
!
#module 7 empty
!
#module 8 empty
!
#module 9 empty
!
#module 15 : 1-port Multilayer Switch Feature Card
!
#module 16 empty
!
```

```
#cam
set cam agingtime 1    20000
set cam agingtime 222  20000
set cam agingtime 302  20000

end
```

show test

The status of the switch, including interface cards, power supplies, and memory, is available by using the `show test` command.

Observe that the first `show test` output reports only the status of the Supervisor module and no information specific to the other modules.

```
Switch_A-> (enable) show test

Diagnostic mode: minimal   (mode at next reset: minimal)

Environmental Status (. = Pass, F = Fail, U = Unknown, N = Not Present)
  PS1: .     PS2: .     PS1 Fan: .     PS2 Fan: .
  Chassis-Ser-EEPROM: .     Fan: .
  Clock(A/B): A          Clock A: .     Clock B: .
  VTT1: .    VTT2: .    VTT3: .

Module 1 : 2-port 1000BaseX Supervisor
Network Management Processor (NMP) Status: (. = Pass, F = Fail, U = Unknown)
  ROM:  .   Flash-EEPROM: .   Ser-EEPROM: .   NVRAM: .   EOBC Comm: .

Line Card Status for Module 1 : PASS

Port Status :
  Ports 1  2
  -----------
        .  .

Line Card Diag Status for Module 1  (. = Pass, F = Fail, N = N/A)

 Module 1
  Earl VI Status :
        NewLearnTest:           .
        IndexLearnTest:         .
```

```
        DontForwardTest:          .
        DontLearnTest:            .
        ConditionalLearnTest:     .
        BadBpduTest:              .
        TrapTest:                 .
        MatchTest:                .
        Ingress/EgressSpanTest:   .
        CaptureTest:              .
        ProtocolMatchTest:        .
        ChannelTest:              .
        IpFibScTest:              .
        IpxFibScTest:             .
        L3DontScTest:             .
        L3Capture2Test:           .
        L3VlanMetTest:            .
        AclPermitTest:            .
        AclDenyTest:              .
        InbandEditTest:           .
        ForwardingEngineTest:     .

    Loopback Status [Reported by Module 1] :
     Ports 1  2
     -----------
           .  .

    InlineRewrite Status :
           InlineRewrite Test skipped as Minimal diagnostics selected
```

The following output provides the test results from module 3 of a Catalyst 6509. The module has eight ports providing 1000Mbit Ethernet. As a result of the `show test 3` command, the switch reports the test results of the entire card.

```
Switch_A-> (enable) show test 3

Diagnostic mode: minimal   (mode at next reset: minimal)


Module 3 : 8-port 1000BaseX Ethernet


Line Card Status for Module 3 : PASS


Port Status :
```

```
  Ports 1  2  3  4  5  6  7  8
  ----------------------------
        .  .  .  .  .  .  .  .

Line Card Diag Status for Module 3  (. = Pass, F = Fail, N = N/A)

 Loopback Status [Reported by Module 1] :
  Ports 1  2  3  4  5  6  7  8
  ----------------------------
        .  .  .  .  .  .  .  .

 InlineRewrite Status :
        InlineRewrite Test skipped as Minimal diagnostics selected
```

show mac

The following output is from the `show mac` command. Because it is quite long, it was truncated from the original capture. For highly populated switches, this command requires a capturing program for later analysis.

Note that numerous counters are maintained in normal operation, including the frame traffic per port; the total number of incoming frames, including discards; and the total number of transmits and aborts due to excessive deferral or MTU violations. Broadcast counters are also maintained in addition to discards.

In some cases, an administrator may find the `show port` command more helpful in troubleshooting. Also, don't confuse this command with the `show cam` command explained later in this chapter. The `show cam` command shows the MAC to ports relationships on the switch, whereas, the `show mac` command provides port statistics.

The following output has been slightly modified for space considerations. `RCV-M` is representative of `RCV-Multi`. `Xmit-M` is used in place of `Xmit-Multi`, and `Dcrd` is used for `Discard`.

```
Switch_A> (enable) show mac
MAC Rcv-Frms Xmit-Frms Rcv-M Xmit-M Rcv-Broad Xmit-Broad
1/1        0         0     0      0         0          0
1/2        0         0     0      0         0          0
2/1     1840      1997    53    136         8         91
2/2      941      1026    56    133         4         95
2/3     6001      6489     0    187        26         73
2/4      776      1179     0    187         1         98
2/5     4951      6115     0    187         0         99
2/6        0         0     0      0         0          0
```

```
2/7        26        301     0   187          1         98
2/8       246        524     0   187          0         99
2/9         0          0     0     0          0          0
. . . some output omitted . . .
MAC  Dely-Exced MTU-Exced In-Dcrd Lrn-Dcrd In-Lost OutLost
1/1           0         0       0        0       0       0
1/2           0         0       0        0       0       0
2/1           0         0       0        0       0       0
2/2           0         0       0        0       0       0
2/3           0         0       0        0       0       0
2/4           0         0       0        0       0       0
2/5           0         0       0        0       0       0
2/6           0         0       0        0       0       0
2/7           0         0       0        0       0       0
2/8           0         0       0        0       0       0
2/9           0         0       0        0       0       0
. . . some output omitted . . .
Port     Rcv-unicast       Rcv-Multicast      Rcv-Broadcast
1/1                0                   0                  0
1/2                0                   0                  0
2/1             1814                  56                  8
2/2              882                  58                  8
2/3             5996                   0                 26
2/4              793                   0                  2
2/5             5099                   0                  0
2/6                0                   0                  0
2/7               26                   0                  1
2/8              252                   0                  0
2/9                0                   0                  0
. . . some output omitted . . .
Port   Xmit-Unicast      Xmit-Multicast      Xmit-Broadcast
1/1                0                   0                  0
1/2                0                   0                  0
2/1             1819                 141                 97
2/2              798                 140                101
2/3             6260                 195                 83
2/4              921                 195                107
2/5             6104                 195                109
2/6                0                   0                  0
2/7               16                 195                 08
2/8              242                 195                109
```

```
2/9                0                 0                 0
. . . some output omitted . . .
Port                    Rcv-Octet              Xmit-Octet
 1/1                            0                       0
 1/2                            0                       0
 2/1                       445231                  405059
 2/2                       208680                  300413
 2/3                      2935182                 2876636
 2/4                        61427                  114408
 2/5                       716265                  601719
 2/6                            0                       0
 2/7                         3125                   53564
 2/8                        36993                   96826
 2/9                            0                       0
. . . some output omitted . . .

Last-Time-Cleared
--------------------------
Fri Jul 11 2003, 12:14:38
```

show vtp domain

The VLAN Trunk Protocol (VTP) is designed to simplify the introduction of VLANs in multi-switch networks. Within the management domain, a new VLAN is only specified once, and the configuration is propagated throughout the network. The configuration information includes the parameters needed for differing topologies within the switched network.

The `show vtp domain` command provides the following status information. Note that VTP updates are sent over VLAN 1 when troubleshooting VTP issues.

```
Switch_A> (enable)  show vtp domain
Domain Name                    Domain Index VTP Version Local Mode   Password
------------------------------ ------------ ----------- ------------ --------
Global                         1            2           Transparent  -

Vlan-count Max-vlan-storage Config Revision Notifications
---------- ---------------- --------------- -------------
5          1023             0               enabled

Last Updater    V2 Mode  Pruning  PruneEligible on Vlans
--------------- -------- -------- -------------------------
10.1.2.20       disabled disabled 2-1000
```

show cam

Switches operate at layer 2 of the OSI model, so MAC addresses are the basis for forwarding decisions. Although VLANs are typically assigned on layer 3 boundaries, the switch directs unicast frames in the same manner as a bridge.

The `show cam` command reports the MAC address associated with the ports of the switch, as follows. Note the specifications that must be included with the command in the first output, followed by the actual MAC list in the second:

```
Switch_A> (enable) show cam
Usage: show cam [count] <dynamic|static|permanent|system> [vlan]
       show cam <dynamic|static|permanent> <mod_num/port_num>
       show cam <mac_addr> [vlan]
       show cam agingtime

Switch_A> (enable) show cam dynamic 1
VLAN  Dest MAC/Route Des  Destination Ports or VCs
1     00-80-2f-9f-54-5f   2/3
1     00-08-27-ca-c9-cd   3/18
1     00-08-27-ca-cd-da   3/23
1     00-08-27-ca-d1-20   3/27
1     00-08-27-29-89-80   3/44
1     00-08-27-29-88-a7   4/41
1     00-08-27-d2-ce-43   4/1
1     00-08-27-9a-0e-e9   3/13
1     00-08-27-ca-db-5e   4/38
1     00-08-27-ca-db-70   4/30
1     00-08-27-29-82-5d   2/22
1     00-08-27-8c-fd-e5   3/7
1     00-08-27-8c-fc-c0   3/32
1     00-08-27-d2-f8-10   4/43
1     00-08-27-ca-e0-47   4/29
1     00-08-27-ca-e0-6c   2/20
1     00-08-27-d2-fd-ab   3/2
1     00-08-27-d2-fe-4a   4/36
1     00-08-27-d2-fe-f5   2/24
1     00-08-27-d2-ff-c7   2/23
1     00-08-27-d2-ff-dd   4/45
1     00-08-27-d2-f1-87   2/8
Total Matching CAM Entries Displayed = 21
```

Duplicate MAC Addresses

Some network devices may be configured with the same MAC address on each interface, including certain dual-homed Unix workstations. This is a common event that can create substantial problems in the network. The `show cam` command is one of the best methods for finding this issue, although prevention via communication and change control can be more beneficial. If the administration of workstations and network services is divided in an administrator's organization, it is recommended that this issue be reviewed and that duplicate MAC addresses be used only when required. Documentation of the installation should accompany such a decision.

show spantree

Although the spanning tree process is covered later in this chapter, the use of spanning trees is crucial to the successful running of switched networks where loops may occur. The `show spantree` command reports the status of the spanning tree process for each VLAN, when enabled as follows:

```
Switch_A> (enable) show spantree
VLAN 1
Spanning tree enabled
Spanning tree type          ieee

Designated Root             00-90-86-fc-48-00
Designated Root Priority    32768
Designated Root Cost        0
Designated Root Port        1/0
Root Max Age   20 sec    Hello Time 2  sec   Forward Delay  15 sec

Bridge ID MAC ADDR          00-90-86-fc-48-00
Bridge ID Priority          32768
Bridge Max Age 20 sec    Hello Time 2  sec   Forward Delay  15 sec

Port      Vlan  Port-State     Cost  Priority  Fast-Start  Group-method
--------- ----  -------------  ----- --------  ----------  -----------
 1/1      1     not-connected    19        32   disabled
 1/2      1     not-connected    19        32   disabled
 2/1      1     forwarding       19        32   disabled
 2/2      1     forwarding       19        32   disabled
 2/3      1     forwarding       19        32   disabled
 2/4      1     forwarding       19        32   disabled
 2/5      1     forwarding       19        32   disabled
 2/6      1     not-connected    19        32   disabled
 2/7      1     forwarding       19        32   disabled
 2/8      1     forwarding       19        32   disabled
 2/9      1     not-connected   100        32   disabled
. . . some output omitted . . .
```

show version

The `show version` command provides hardware and software version numbers, in addition to memory and system uptime statistics. The output of the command appears as follows:

```
Switch_A-> (enable) show version
WS-C6509 Software, Version NmpSW: 6.3(5)
Copyright (c) 1995-2002 by Cisco Systems
NMP S/W compiled on Feb  7 2002, 19:33:49

System Bootstrap Version: 7.1(1)

Hardware Version: 2.0  Model: WS-C6509  Serial #: SCA041603LL

PS1  Module: WS-CAC-1300W    Serial #: ACP04060383
PS2  Module: WS-CAC-1300W    Serial #: ACP04081148

Mod Port Model               Serial #    Versions
--- ---- ------------------- ----------- ------------------------------
1   2    WS-X6K-S2U-MSFC2    SAD061503TJ Hw : 3.5
                                         Fw : 7.1(1)
                                         Fw1: 6.1(3)
                                         Sw : 6.3(5)
                                         Sw1: 6.3(5)
         WS-F6K-PFC2         SAD061506DS Hw : 3.2
3   8    WS-X6408-GBIC       SAD041009YA Hw : 2.4
                                         Fw : 5.1(1)CSX
                                         Sw : 6.3(5)
15  1    WS-F6K-MSFC2        SAD061505U8 Hw : 2.2
                                         Fw : 12.1(2)
                                         Sw : 12.1(2)

       DRAM                    FLASH                   NVRAM
Module Total   Used    Free    Total   Used    Free    Total Used  Free
------ ------- ------- ------- ------- ------- ------- ----- ----- -----
1      262016K  69444K 192572K  32768K   7136K  25632K  512K  270K  242K

Uptime is 331 days, 10 hours, 44 minutes
```

RMON

Modern network devices provide greater visibility into the functioning of the network. Simple Network Management Protocol (SNMP) and *Remote Monitoring (RMON)* provide much of this visibility. RMON is another method for obtaining environmental and statistical information from devices. Much of the RMON technology implementation is based on the deployment of RMON probes that gather the information from the circuit (physical media) because the router or switch may not support all levels of RMON information.

Catalyst 6500 series switches provide internal support for four of the nine RMON groups defined in RFC 1757. These groups include port utilization and error statistics, historical statistics, alarm notification, and event logging. Additional monitoring may use the Switched Port Analyzer (SPAN) function, which is also referred to as *port mirroring*. Cisco's SwitchProbe product line can provide access to the other five layers of RMON in addition to the RMON2 groups. Examples of the commands used to configure a SPAN port appear later in this chapter.

Indicator Lights

In addition to what is supplied by the CLI, the Catalyst switch provides diagnostic information via LEDs on the line modules and the Supervisor engine.

The Supervisor engine includes load LEDs that indicate the current utilization of the switch. A high load (over 60 percent) may indicate a network problem, including a broadcast storm or the need for review of the network design. This set of lights is useful when troubleshooting in the main equipment room or wiring closet.

Following startup, during which the LEDs will flash, the LEDs should appear steady green. An orange LED may indicate a problem; a red LED may indicate a failure.

Controlling Recurring Paths with Spanning Tree

Although there are differences, switches share many common positives and negatives with bridges. For example, bridges frequently hide larger network problems and are invisible to the administrator. This differs significantly from routers, which are visible through increments in hop counters and MAC address changes in each frame. Bridges do not modify the frame in any way, so a frame may traverse multiple bridges with no changes to the frame. A changing frame provides indications that facilitate troubleshooting.

One common problem in bridged networks involves loops, or a situation in which a single frame can continuously traverse the network. Note again that a bridge does not increment a counter—specifically, a time-to-live (TTL) value—in the packet to differentiate frame A from frame A the seventh time crossing the bridge. Such recurring paths can and should be controlled. The most typical method of control is called *spanning tree*. The spanning tree algorithm is defined in 802.1D and is used to control recurring paths among multiple switches, thus avoiding loops in the network.

Should switches fail to prevent multiple forwardings of the same packet, and an administrator interconnects multiple switches (or bridges) between two segments, a loop can occur. This loop could theoretically take a single broadcast packet, which a bridge would automatically forward and resend it hundreds of times, as illustrated in Figure 41.1.

FIGURE 41.1 A simple bridge/switch loop configuration

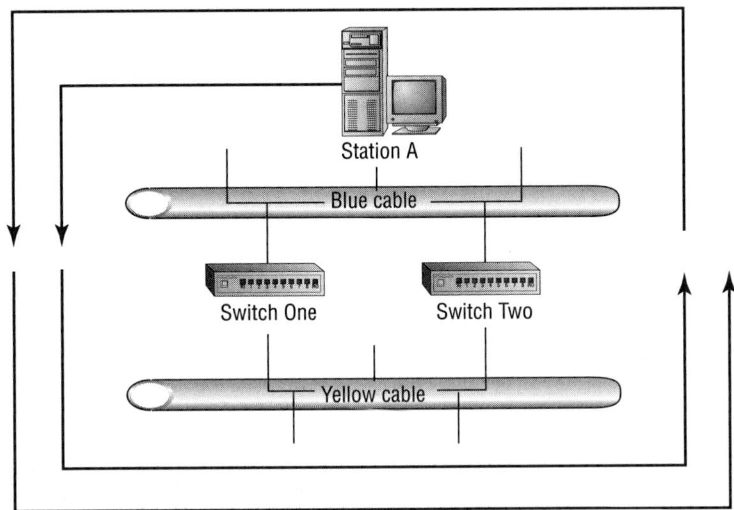

Station A sends a broadcast, Switch One forwards the packet to the yellow cable, and Switch Two sends the broadcast back to the blue cable. Switch One then receives a forwarded broadcast packet that is in turn forwarded to the yellow cable. This continues infinitely without some type of intervention or control built into the software on the switch.

Notice that Figure 41.1 denotes a single flow of packets that move counterclockwise; however, in a real loop, the initial broadcast is also forwarded clockwise. Although different cable colors have been used in this example, both cables are within the same VLAN.

Although Figure 41.1 reflects shared media connected to switches, a switch/bridge loop can occur in an all-switched network. This diagram simplifies the physical connections involved by moving them "outside the box."

Logically, an administrator could avoid the entire loop issue by removing one of the two bridges/switches. Because only one path would exist, no loop is created. However, there are advantages to installing multiple switches or bridges. With multiple switches/bridges, the network can incorporate some degree of fault tolerance.

Troubleshooting Spanning Tree Problems

There are several troubleshooting targets for isolating and resolving problems relating to the Spanning Tree Protocol (STP) in a switched network. The most essential aspect of troubleshooting spanning tree problems is to understand the protocol itself. It is also important to pay attention to indicators that there may be loops in the network. One simple indicator is the LED on the Supervisor engine: If the LED shows around 60% load, this may be a signal that loops are occurring.

Proper spanning tree functionality requires that there is only one unique bridge ID for each VLAN. You must also be aware that trunk ports on the Catalyst 6500 may belong to multiple spanning trees. This can cause the problem that if loops occur on one, the other spanning trees may be adversely affected. The `show spantree` command will display this information.

Spanning tree has many more implementation options than are listed here. If you would like more detailed information on spanning tree, please see Part II of this Study Guide.

When the Cisco portfast and uplinkfast modes are enabled on ports, some of the transitions of the spanning tree algorithm are skipped. This could add to the potential of loops in the network. The `show spantree` command also reports whether the fast-start option has been enabled on a port-by-port basis.

Real World Scenario

Eliminating Bootup Errors in a Switched Environment

Though the controls put in place to prevent spanning tree loops are necessary in order to ensure a stable network, they can have unintended side effects. If an operating system manufacturer has optimized its operating system to immediately start using the network connection, the length of delay caused by the spanning tree loop-detection process, usually around 35 seconds, can generate an error. These errors can manifest as "No Domain Controller Found" messages in an NT environment, or even a "No DHCP Server Available."

To avoid these problems, we have found it best to set up user and server ports on the switch differently from the setup for ports that connect to other routers, switches, and hubs. Specifically, on user and server ports, we enable spantree portfast, and disable EtherChannel negotiation and trunk negotiation. In addition, we also hard-code the speed and duplex settings on the port. In this manner, the switch port starts forwarding any packets seen from this port immediately after a link is detected. This effectively eliminates the errors caused by detection delays.

There are a couple of drawbacks to this arrangement. The first and most obvious is that more manual configuration is required any time there is a move, add, or change in the environment. The second drawback is that ports are not checked when they come up to see if there is a spanning tree loop. Note that spanning tree is still running on the port even with spantree portfast enabled. Therefore, a loop will be detected if it's there, and the appropriate port will be put into blocking mode. However, this loop will not be detected before traffic from the port is allowed through. Thus there is potential for a broadcast storm after the port is brought up but before the Spanning Tree Protocol detects and eliminates the loop. Even with these drawbacks, I have found that the overall benefit to configuring user and server ports in this manner outweighs the risks.

Virtual LANs

In their simplest form, *virtual LANs* (or *VLANs*) are no different from traditional LANs. The virtual component comes from the capability to define memberships based on individual ports, as administered by either a physical port or a dynamic relationship to the MAC address.

VLANs can potentially reduce the costs associated with moves, adds, and changes, in addition to reducing the costs for unused ports on non-VLAN hubs and switches. However, VLAN technology adds to the initial costs and may require additional training. It is not uncommon to find a single switch serving more than one subnetwork. This logical segmentation of ports can create its own set of troubleshooting issues. However, the VLAN's increased port utilization and other cost savings will more than offset these issues.

Administrators unaccustomed to segmented switches may find VLANs confusing. With hubs, all ports are part of the same network, and most networks are configured with a separate hub for each subnet—even if that subnet contains as few as two devices. Switches with VLAN capabilities, with their higher port cost and necessary management systems, may have three or four subnets connected into the same chassis. In troubleshooting, it is important to have an accurate understanding of the current switch configuration and of VLAN definitions, and—more importantly—to have verification that the end nodes match those definitions. It is not uncommon for a port to be defined to VLAN 1, where the workstation is configured with an IP address and default gateway matching VLAN 5. Under such circumstances, the workstation support staff will incorrectly believe that the configuration is correct, and the network administrator will document that the port is correct. In addition to the `show port` command, it is important to have valid documentation of all VLANs and the associated network configurations for each VLAN.

Inter-Switch Link (ISL)

It is not possible for a switch to forward datagrams from one VLAN to another without a router or routing function. Recall that switches operate at layer 2 of the OSI model, and although switches are available with routing engines and even layer 4 processors, this section will retain a definition limited to layer 2.

Inter-Switch Link (ISL) is a Cisco proprietary method of interconnecting two devices that support VLANs. These connections provide the administrator with a cost-effective option in deploying switches and VLANs in the network. For example, a normal switch installation requires that a single port in each VLAN be connected to the corresponding router interface, assuming a typical installation in which each VLAN is a logical extension of a subnet. This requires *n* ports on the router, in addition to the same number of ports on the switch.

Although this solution is easy to install and provides each VLAN with a dedicated 10Mb or 100Mb port on the router, it also greatly increases the costs and fails to account for differences in local and remote traffic. Recall that networks were historically designed with 80 percent of the traffic remaining on the local subnet. Although the percentage of local traffic is significantly lower today, it is still unlikely that you would find all traffic leaving the subnet.

What would happen if *n* VLANs on the switch could share a single 100Mb connection to the router? The number of ports used for connectivity would equal two, as opposed to (n*2), and the available number of ports for servers and workstations would increase substantially.

In this section, the use of ISL was defined with a switch-to-router connection. ISL should also be considered when the administrator wishes to connect multiple switches that are members of the same VLAN.

Administrators must keep the following issues in mind when considering ISL:

- ISL is available only on products that support ISL. Although a number of other vendors have licensed ISL technology (including Intel), the standard is proprietary to Cisco, and fewer vendors support the ISL standard compared to IEEE 802.1Q. In addition, with the release of 802.1Q and gigabit interfaces, Cisco has altered the default trunk encapsulation in favor of 802.1Q. Gigabit EtherChannel trunk links default to 802.1Q, whereas non-EtherChannel gigabit ports negotiate ISL or 802.1Q. FastEthernet ports, as of this writing, continue to default to ISL.
- ISL links must be point-to-point.
- ISL should only be used on 100Mb full-duplex or greater connections. Although it is possible to use ISL on 10Mb links, the limited bandwidth and other considerations make such a plan impractical.
- ISL may require an upgrade of the IOS or memory on the router.
- ISL can encapsulate Token Ring. This is referred to as ISL+.
- ISL adds 30 octets to the original frame (26 bytes in the header and an additional 4 byte CRC), which is encapsulated without modification.
- ISL includes a CRC value at the end of the frame.

Because ISL is an encapsulation of the original frame, an administrator must consider the overhead generated to support the encapsulation. Frequently, the available bandwidth is more than sufficient to cover this additional load. ISL adds 30 octets to the length of the original frame. In the case of Ethernet, this results in a frame 1548 octets long.

The ISL frame is shown in Figure 41.2.

FIGURE 41.2 The ISL encapsulation

8	16	24	32
ISL multicast			
Address	Type code, User bits	Source	
Address			
Length		Binary	
Expression	Organization ID		
VLAN ID and Bridge bit		Index	
Reserved		Original frame (up to 24,575 octets)	
ISL CRC			

Figure 41.2 is indexed in Table 41.3.

TABLE 41.3 Key for Figure 41.2

Figure Symbol	Definition
ISL multicast address	The ISL multicast address of 01:00:0C:00:00. *Note that this is a 40-bit value.*
Type code	The encapsulated frame's type code. For Ethernet, this is 0000. Token Ring frames are defined with 0001, and FDDI is marked with 0010. Type code 0011 is reserved for ATM.
User bits	The user-defined bits are used to mark the encapsulated frame's priority. Frames marked 0000 are processed as normal priority; 0011 marks the frame as high priority.
Source address	This is the 48-bit MAC address of the source port.
Length	The length field defines the length of the ISL frame minus the multicast address, the type and user-defined bits, and the source address of the ISL packet. The length field also omits its own length and the CRC from the 16-bit value. Thus, the length is always equal to the length of the ISL frame minus 18 octets.
Binary expression	ISL frames use SNAP LLC, and the binary expression decodes to AA:AA:03, which is the same as the SNAP header.
Organization ID	The organization ID bits provide the unique organization identifier of the source address. This is equal to the first three octets of the MAC address.
VLAN ID; Bridge bit	The VLAN identifier is a 15-bit value that identifies the VLAN membership of the frame. Cisco uses only 10 bits in this header to support up to 1024 virtual LANs. The bridge bit is set for all encapsulated bridge protocol frames, including spanning tree updates, in addition to Cisco's CDP and VTP packets.
Index	Useful for troubleshooting and contains the source port value of the frame.
Reserved	The reserved bits are set to 0 for Ethernet frames. However, when ISL encapsulates Token Ring, the access control (AC) and frame information (FC) octets are duplicated here. When encapsulating FDDI, the frame control octet is prefixed with 0x00 and copied in this field.
Original frame	This field may be 24,575 octets long and includes Ethernet, Token Ring, or FDDI frames—along with the original CRC value for the encapsulated frame.
ISL CRC	This field is a new 32-bit CRC that is calculated for the entire ISL frame. It is calculated using the entire ISL frame, including the original frame.

802.1Q Trunking

Although the *IEEE 802.1Q* standard is similar to the Cisco proprietary ISL protocol in terms of function, as a standard it may be used to connect non-Cisco trunks to Cisco equipment. Note that the 802.1Q encapsulation is accessed with the command `encapsulation dot1Q`, which is available in IOS versions 12.0.1(t) and higher on routers and in CatOS 4.1 on the Catalyst 6500 switches.

ISL provides additional functions, when compared with 802.1Q. For example, spanning trees are handled somewhat better in ISL. Nevertheless, 802.1Q should be recommended in any network that does not adhere to a strict Cisco-only policy, given the proprietary concerns.

From a troubleshooting perspective, 802.1Q requires the same understanding of the VLAN's relationships to the subnets that are beneficial in all switching diagnostics. The 802.1Q header differs from the ISL header, in that only 4 octets are added to the frame, as compared to the 30 added in ISL. Also, the 802.1Q information is not wrapped around the original packet—the VLAN information is inserted into the frame, following the destination and source addresses in the original packet. This lack of overhead is another benefit of 802.1Q.

Most protocol analyzers provide decode filters for 802.1Q in their current releases, but administrators should check with their vendor to ensure this functionality is supported. It is rare that the problem is directly related to the tag information itself (although administrators should consider this in researching trunk problems). Rather, most trunking problems—along with 802.1Q—result from misconfiguration of the VLANs or mismatches between two sides of the trunk. Though they serve similar functions, ISL cannot connect to 802.1Q on the same link.

VLAN Trunking Protocol (VTP)

The *VLAN Trunking Protocol (VTP)* uses multicast messages to inform all other switches in the VTP domain about the VLANs within the domain. This domain is a management domain that allows control of the VTP multicast updates. A switch can be configured with three different VTP settings:

VTP server The server maintains the VLAN information for the VTP domain. If you are operating with a VTP server to which clients are connecting, all VLAN modifications, additions, and deletions must be done on the VTP server. These changes will then be propagated down to all the VTP clients in the domain. Trunk ports are then reconfigured to allow traffic from the new VLAN.

VTP client The client also maintains a copy of the VLAN information for the domain and will transmit any changes received from the VTP server to other VTP clients in the same domain that are connected to the client. When a change is detected, the trunk ports are then reconfigured to allow traffic from the new VLAN.

VTP transparent When a switch is in transparent mode, changes made on the VTP server do not affect VLANs on this switch. The switch does, however, continue to forward VTP advertisements if you are running VTP version 2. If you need to modify, add, or delete VLAN from a switch in transparent mode, it must be done on the switch itself.

Cabling Issues

Today's networks operate at higher speeds than ever before. Bandwidth is measured in gigabits, with individual workstations accessing 100Mb connections or faster. Only recently it was still common to find a hundred stations sharing a 10Mb segment.

Higher speeds bring added complexity at the Physical layer of the network. Installations must adhere to strict tolerances regarding distance, cable type, and installation to permit proper operation. This creates new troubleshooting issues for the administrator.

Frequently, an administrator will convert a workstation to 100Mb (Fast)Ethernet, and will find an excessive number of errors that degrade performance so much that the link becomes unusable. The type of cable or the distance between the switch and workstation may cause this. For example, perhaps the original installation used Category 3 cable. Although satisfactory for 10Mb Ethernet, 100Mb Ethernet requires the higher capacity Category 5. Also, though the distance for both 10Mb and 100Mb Ethernet on copper media is 100 meters, it is possible to use longer lengths for 10Mb without degradation. When converting to 100Mb, problems may become evident. Consideration of the Physical layer is imperative when troubleshooting switched networks. Table 41.4 presents the Physical layer limitations.

TABLE 41.4 Physical Layer Standards

Cable	10Mb	100Mb
Distance with Category 3 copper	100 meters	Not available, per 100BaseTX standard
Distance with Category 5 copper	100 meters	100 meters
Distance with multimode fiber	2000 meters	2000 meters
Distance with single-mode fiber	Up to 100 km	Up to 100 km

Half-duplex FastEthernet implementations limit the multimode fiber distance to 400 meters to allow for the round-trip time of the packet transmission.

Cable Problems

Cable problems may appear as intermittent issues or as a single failure. Clearly, the intermittent issues provide greater challenges, especially if the problem is of very short duration. An intermittent cable problem may appear as slow performance or failure of the workstation. In most cases, the port to which the workstation is attached will show an increasing number of interface errors. These could be in the form of runts, CRCs (cyclic redundancy checks), and/or FCS (frame check sequence) errors. In addition, cabling runs that are longer than allowed by Ethernet specifications can also cause late collisions. However, it should be noted that these errors could be caused by a misconfigured or malfunctioning NIC as well.

An analyzer may be the best method for finding cable problems, and administrators should be familiar with the operation of an available cable tester, time domain reflectometer (TDR), or handheld analyzer. Even when certified by the cable installer, cables can break or develop problems during subsequent activity in the conduit or at the jack. In addition to a tester, it is a good idea to have spare cables on hand and a crimp set to quickly reterminate circuits when troubleshooting.

Multimeters and Cable Testers

There is a large variety of physical media testing equipment. The most basic tools are multimeters and cable testers.

Both *volt-ohm meters* and *multimeters* measure voltage (AC and DC), resistance, and current. In addition, these devices can also be used to verify the continuity of a cable run from end to end. As alluded to previously, these devices deal with electrical signals. Therefore, they can only be used to test copper (or other electrically based) wiring, and cannot be used to test any fiber-optic wiring.

Cable testers can be very general or they can be made for a specific type of cable. Some cable testers have adapters that allow them to test a wide range of cables such as unshielded twisted-pair (UTP), shielded twisted-pair (STP), or coaxial (coax) cable. Cable testers are made for electrical and optical cable.

Different from multimeters, cable testers can give the user much more information regarding the cable being tested. Cable testers come in varieties that can test both electrical and optical cables. Here are some examples of the attributes that are reported by an electrical cable tester:

- Electrical connectivity
- Open pairs
- Crossed pairs
- Out-of-distance specification
- Cross talk
- Attenuation
- Noise/interference
- Wiring maps
- MAC information
- Line utilization

Optical cable testers verify the same sort of information as electrical; however, they obviously use optical signals in place of electrical. In general, there are three different wavelengths that are predominantly used by optical cable testers: 850 nm, 1300 nm, and 1550 nm. Through the use of these wavelengths and by transmitting at a known power level, optical cable testers are able to measure attenuation and return loss on the fiber.

It is important to realize that not all cable testers provide all of this information. A given tester may provide only some of these attributes.

Time Domain Reflectometers (TDRs) and Optical TDRs (OTDRs)

Time domain reflectometers (TDRs) are complex cable testers. They are used to locate physical problems in a cable. They can detect where an open circuit, short circuit, crimped wire, or other abnormality is located in a cable.

TDRs and optical TDRs (OTDRs) work on the same principle: A signal is sent down the cable and the unit waits for the reflected signal to come back. Different abnormalities in cabling cause this signal to be reflected at different signal strengths, or amplitudes. Based on the amplitude, the meter distinguishes between opens, shorts, crimps, or other failures in the cable. These meters measure the time between the sending of the signal and the arrival of the reflected signal at the unit. This time interval is used to calculate where the failure is occurring in the cable. OTDRs can also provide information on conditions such as signal attenuation, fiber breaks, and losses through connectors.

Crossover Cables

A surprising number of network administrators have not used crossover cables, particularly when their previous experience is from the workstation installation and configuration segments of Information Services or other Information Technology departments. In other companies, such cables are used only when absolutely necessary and with a great deal of documentation, including highly recommended color-coding.

Normally, a workstation is connected to a hub that does not require the crossover of the transmit and receive pairs in the wire. However, there are times when a connection is needed and the pairs must be crossed. This occurs when connecting two 10BaseT workstations together without a hub, or when connecting two network devices. Note that some devices provide a button or other administrator-selectable setting to enable or disable the function. Small hubs frequently provide this with an "uplink" port.

Connectivity problems can occur when the wrong type of cable is installed or when a selectable port is set incorrectly. This error may be masked by link lights and other indications that the connection is correct. The only way to isolate this problem is to look at the colors in the cube (the RJ-45 connector) and verify that they are correct.

Figure 41.3 shows the appropriate pinout for an Ethernet crossover cable. It may be appropriate when troubleshooting to swap the original cable for another of the opposite type. This provides a quick check of the cable, and substituting a straight-through cable for a crossover cable may lead to evidence of equipment that is mislabeled or misconfigured. Note that Ethernet uses wires 1, 2, 3, and 6, while T-1 circuits on RJ-45 use wires 1, 2, 4, and 5. Swapping crossover cables will also lead to problems—for example, if a T-1 crossover is used for an Ethernet connection.

FIGURE 41.3 Ethernet crossover pinout

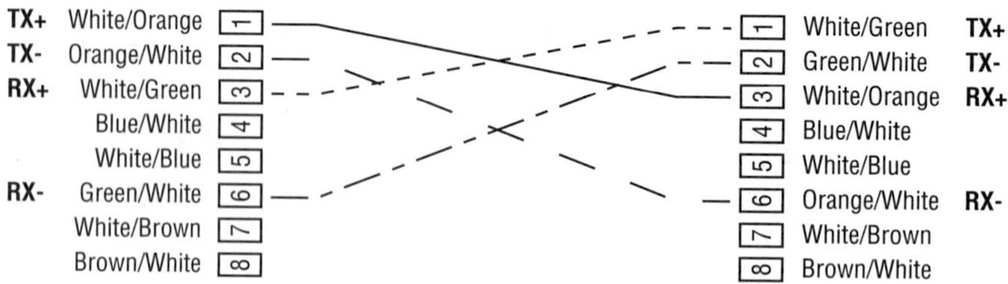

Troubleshooting Switched Connections

Switched networks incorporate a number of unique problems for administrators, including the use of port mirroring for protocol analysis, and routing and trunking. Routing and trunking within the Catalyst system may include an MSFC for routing. Trunking may incorporate one of many protocols, including ISL, 802.10, 802.1Q, and ATM LANE. The effect of trunking is the same, however. A single physical medium can be used to connect multiple VLANs (or ELANs) between switches and routers.

One of the most frequently occurring problems occurring on a switched network is a mismatch in speed or duplex settings between the switch port and the end-system NIC. If the speed of a port is set wrong, no traffic will be successfully sent; this problem is therefore relatively easy to identify and correct. However, mismatched duplex settings can be tougher to find. This is because the resulting problems will occur intermittently and most often during times of heavy load. When a duplex mismatch does occur, the user will often report slow response time and intermittent applications failures. In addition, on the side of the connection that is configured as half-duplex, there will be a steady increase in the number of late collisions reported.

The Switched Port Analyzer

This chapter previously noted that one of the difficulties in troubleshooting switched networks is the port isolation inherent in switches. Such isolation prevents the use of a protocol analyzer in a switched environment, without connecting directly to the wire between the switch and workstation. Also, such a connection cannot be full-duplex, as a general rule.

Cisco addresses this problem with the *Switched Port Analyzer (SPAN)*. You may also see this referred to as *port mirroring*. Effectively, the switch is commanded to copy all packets that would be sent to the workstation interface to another port as well. This port is not assigned a VLAN—it takes on the identity of the original port.

To configure the switch for SPAN, use the following commands:

```
set span enable|disable
set span <src_module/src_port> <dest_module/dest_port>      [rx|tx|both]
set span <src_VLAN> <dest_module/dest_port> [rx|tx|both]
```

Note that traffic may be monitored on the receive or transmit channels, or both. The administrator may select to mirror a single port within the VLAN or have all traffic within the VLAN copied onto the mirroring port. It is important for the administrator to understand the isolation problem's scope and the network topology before attempting to troubleshoot the SPAN function.

The Multilayer Switch Feature Card and Catalyst Routing

The MSFC is a Cisco router on a daughter card within the Catalyst chassis. This card is physically attached to the Supervisor module and therefore does not take an extra slot in the chassis. The MSFC can be configured to provide routing between VLANs. With an external router, companies often incur additional expense and complexity—the MSFC virtually attaches to VLANs and as such, does not occupy a port as would an ISL or 802.1Q-linked external router. Of course, there are times when an external router is required. The performance of the MSFC is faster than a 7513, and with the advent of the FlexWAN module, many of the same interface types are now supported on the 6500 series platform and the 7200 series routers.

Configuration of the MSFC is very similar to that of the Cisco router platform. As shown in the following output, the router module supports IOS features, including password encryption and HSRP. Note that the interfaces are defined as VLAN1 and VLAN2. Unlike the router, the MSFC is virtually connected to the VLANs via the backplane, which speeds up the overall router throughput.

To connect to the MSFC, administrators typically connect to the Supervisor engine CLI and then use the `session` command to attach to the MSFC. Because the MSFC does not occupy a slot in the chassis to itself, it is always shown in slot 15. For example, if the MSFC card were in slot 15, the command would read `session 15`.

If there is a redundant Supervisor/MSFC combination, the redundant MSFC would show in slot 16. You can see this, by using the `show module` command.

Following is the output from a `show running-config` command executed on the MSFC:

```
Building configuration...



Current configuration:

!
```

```
version 12.1
service timestamps debug uptime
service timestamps log uptime
no service password-encryption

!

hostname MSFC_A
!
interface Vlan1
 description Admin VLAN
 ip address 10.1.1.3 255.255.255.0
 no ip redirects
 standby 1 timers 5 15
 standby 1 priority 10
 standby 1 preempt
 standby 1 ip 10.1.1.1
!
interface Vlan2
 description User VLAN
 ip address 10.1.2.1 255.255.255.0
! ...output omitted...
```

The `show port` command provides the following information regarding the MSFC:

```
15/1 MSFC_A connected  trunk        full  1000 Route Switch
```

As noted previously, an external router may be used to connect VLANs on the Catalyst switch. This usually occurs through a single connection configured for ISL or another trunking protocol. FastEthernet and Gigabit Ethernet connections are common for this configuration.

When configuring the router for this type of connection, each VLAN must be defined to a subinterface, and the main interface must be configured without a configuration. This usually appears as follows:

```
interface fastethernet 0/0
no ip address
full-duplex
interface fastethernet 0/0.1
description vlan1
ip address 10.1.1.1 255.255.255.0
encapsulation isl 1
```

The `encapsulation isl 1` command specifies that VLAN1 is using this physical interface and is trunked via ISL. This command is placed on each subinterface. Use the `set trunk` and `clear trunk` commands on the switch to configure the switch side of the connection.

VLANs across Routers and Switches

So far in this chapter, VLAN implementation has been described on Catalyst switches and Catalyst switches with MSFCs. One VLAN implementation is left: using a router and a switch.

The router plays many important roles in the implementation of VLANs throughout a network. The overall role of a router is to provide communication among VLANs. Also, routers are able to perform many functions that add to the flexibility and scalability of VLAN deployment. Primary among these functions are

- Broadcast management
- Routing, policy control
- VLAN switching
- VLAN translation

Other functions include

- QoS management
- Redundancy
- Hierarchical design
- Traffic shaping and management

Broadcast Management

Simply put, routers will not forward broadcasts. Switches also control broadcasts by forwarding only to ports that are members of the source VLAN. This property allows routers to lower broadcast traffic on the network backbone.

Policy Control

Switches do not have the capability to apply policy control to individual ports or VLANs on the switch. Use of a router provides the means to implement security and policy control to and from connected VLANs. Access lists can be written and applied to the VLAN subinterface on the router to provide this capability.

VLAN Switching

VLAN switching occurs when a packet destined for the same VLAN on a different interface crosses the router. The header remains intact, and the frame is switched at layer 2 to the destination interface where the VLAN resides.

VLAN Translation

Translation must occur in two scenarios. The first scenario occurs when VLAN A uses a different VLAN protocol than VLAN B. For example, VLAN A uses ISL for its VLAN protocol, whereas VLAN B uses 802.1Q. In order for communication to take place between end systems on these VLANs, the router must perform protocol translation. This occurs at layer 2; the frame headers are changed to accommodate the change in protocol.

The second scenario is when a VLAN protocol must be translated into a non-VLAN layer 2 protocol. An example of this is when VLAN A (using ISL or 802.1Q) needs to communicate with a layer 2 destination that does not use any VLAN protocol. The router then translates the VLAN header into a header such as 802.10 so the two can communicate.

Routing

To enable communication between different VLANs or non-VLAN networks (layer 3), routing must occur. The router maintains routes for the subnets/networks that belong to each VLAN. When VLAN A needs to reach VLAN B, a route lookup is performed and the packets are routed on layer 3.

When a machine on a VLAN wants to communicate to a host on any other destination not on a local VLAN, routing is performed as well. It is important to realize that there is a difference between translation and routing. Routing is a layer 3 function, whereas translation occurs at layer 2.

Troubleshooting VLANs on Routers

Some commands are similar across the IOS for the routers and the software running on the switches. It is important, however, to know which commands provide unique output and should be executed on a router rather than on a switch.

From the router, the following commands provide additional information regarding the VLANs. The `debug` commands provide debug information with respect to VLAN packets and the Spanning Tree Protocol:

- `show vlans`
- `show arp`
- `show interface`
- `show cdp neighbor`
- `debug vlan packet`
- `debug spantree`

Some of these commands have been covered in previous chapters and will not be repeated here. The commands that have not been discussed are described in the following sections.

show vlans

This command is executed from the router; it displays the details about the VLANs configured on the router. The detail includes the VLAN name, the interface, and the IP address used. It also includes the VLAN protocol (encapsulation) and the interface protocol, such as IP or IPX. Here is a sample:

```
Router_A#show vlans

Virtual LAN ID:  1 (Inter Switch Link Encapsulation)

   vLAN Trunk Interface:   FastEthernet1/0.1
```

```
   Protocols Configured:   Address:          Received:    Transmitted:
           IP              172.16.1.1        4236441842   854332923

Virtual LAN ID:  2 (Inter Switch Link Encapsulation)

   vLAN Trunk Interface:   FastEthernet1/0.2

   Protocols Configured:   Address:        Received:        Transmitted:
           IP              172.16.2.1      3002644583       2325942305

Router_A#
```

debug vlan packet

This debug command can be useful in determining which VLANs are being sent over a trunk to a router. When `debug vlan packet` is enabled and a packet comes in for a VLAN that is not defined on the router, the router will note the VLAN and the interface on which the packet was seen. As with all debug commands, be careful when using this command, because it can place a load on the router if there are a lot of packets coming in the interface for an unknown VLAN.

```
Router_A#debug vlan packet

Virtual LAN packet information debugging is on

Router_A #
vLAN: ISL packet received bearing colour ID 10 on  FastEthernet1/0
 which has no subinterface configured  to route or bridge ID 10.
vLAN: ISL packet received bearing colour ID 102 on  FastEthernet1/0
 which has no subinterface configured  to route or bridge ID 102.
vLAN: ISL packet received bearing colour ID 23 on  FastEthernet1/0
 which has no subinterface configured  to route or bridge ID 23.
vLAN: ISL packet received bearing colour ID 10 on  FastEthernet1/0
which has no subinterface configured  to route or bridge ID 10.
```

VLAN Design Issues and Troubleshooting

Although VLANs must adhere to most of the basic network design rules, there are a number of new issues for administrators to consider with Catalyst switches.

First, the network diameter should be less than eight switches. This limitation is mostly related to spanning tree concerns; however, it is also a good rule of thumb for manageability.

Second, VLANs must be numbered within certain limitations, and each VLAN needs to adhere to MTU considerations. Although a large MTU is desirable for FDDI and Token Ring, the Ethernet MTU limitation of 1500 is recommended for all interfaces. This is partly due to the Catalyst backplane and the conversions that are needed between different Physical layers.

The default configuration of the switch includes the VLANs shown in Table 41.5.

TABLE 41.5 The Default Switch VLAN Configuration

VLAN Name	Type of VLAN	MTU	ISL VLAN ID	802.1Q VLAN ID (SAID)
Default	ethernet	1500	0001	100001
FDDI-default	fddi	1500	1002	101002
Token Ring default	token-ring	4472	1003	101003
FDDInet-default	fddi-net	1500	1004	101004
Trnet-default	tr-net	4472	1005	101005

When troubleshooting switches and routers, administrators should consider each element in the network by using a layered approach. For example, configuring a bridge to link two ISL trunks could cause spanning tree problems. In addition, there are two spanning tree protocols available on the switch: IEEE and DEC. Failure to use the same protocol will again cause spanning tree issues.

General routing rules apply to VLANs and the MSFC. For instance, a default router is still required on all devices, and all VLANs must have a router to go from one VLAN to another.

As an example, to display the physical interfaces, the administrator would use `show port` on the switch, as opposed to `show interface`, which is used on the router. The `show interface` command on the switch is used to check the SL0 and SC0 interfaces.

Remember that most troubleshooting is actually an exercise in isolation. View the network from each layer and work through the system. For example, is there a link light denoting layer 1 connectivity? Is the port configured for the same speed and duplex on each end? These basic questions, along with the Cisco debug and show commands, frequently provide the proper clues to isolate problems.

Although they are available, the use of automatic speed and duplex configuration settings is not recommended. Most administrators prefer the control and manageability that is available from manually configuring these settings. Administrators should familiarize themselves with the proper commands on various platforms. For example, Windows NT usually permits the modification of this setting from the network control panel, but some installations may require registry modification. On Solaris, the `/kernel/drv/hme.conf` file is modified when using that type of NIC.

Hybrid/Native Command Conversion

As was discussed at the beginning of the chapter, similar switch-related commands for the Hybrid and Native modes have a somewhat different syntax. Table 41.6 compares some of the common Hybrid commands to their Native mode equivalents. As is the case with configuring routers, the `show` commands are entered in user/exec mode and the configuration commands are entered in either global configuration mode or interface-level configuration mode.

TABLE 41.6 Hybrid/Native Mode Command Comparison

Hybrid Command	Native Command	Explanation
`clear vlan`	`no vlan`	Removes a VLAN from the configuration.
`set cam agingtime`	`mac-address-table aging-time`	Sets the timeout values for retaining MAC address information.
`set port dulex`	`duplex`	Interface command that sets the duplex on a particular port.
`set port name`	`description`	Interface command that sets the name on a port.
`set port speed`	`speed`	Interface command that sets the speed of a given port.
`set span`	`monitor session`	Sets up a SPAN port.
`set spantree`	`spanning-tree`	Sets Spanning Tree Protocol information.
`set vlan`	`switchport access vlan`	Assigns a particular interface to a given VLAN.
`show cam dynamic`	`show mac-address-table dynamic`	Shows the MAC address to port relationships. This information is stored in the CAM table.
`show port`	`show interface`	Shows port information.
`show span`	`show monitor`	Shows the span port.
`show test`	`show diagnostic`	Shows bootup test results.

TABLE 41.6 Hybrid/Native Mode Command Comparison *(continued)*

Hybrid Command	Native Command	Explanation
`show version`	`show version`	Shows IOS version information for the switch.
`show vlan`	`show vlan`	Shows VLAN information.
`show vtp domain`	`show vtp status`	Shows VTP information.

Summary

In today's network environment, switching has become an integral component. It allows for greater throughput, and it better utilizes existing hardware. In the Cisco switching offering, one of the main switches used is the Catalyst 6500 series. Thanks to the number of different modules available in this series, they are versatile enough to be used in almost any network.

Like the Cisco routers that were examined earlier, the Cisco switches also come with a fully featured command-line interface (CLI) that allows for configuration as well as verification of the current functionality of the switch. For the switches, this CLI comes in two different formats—`set`-based Hybrid mode or router-like Native mode. Although each has its strength, we focused on the `set`-based Hybrid mode commands in this chapter. Central to both CLIs is the `show` command. This command, along with the keywords available for use with it, allows for the display of nearly all the switch's characteristics.

Another important aspect of a switched environment is loop detection and elimination. This is done through the Spanning Tree Protocol. Spanning tree sends probing packets to all neighboring devices and uses these packets to determine whether there is a loop in the network. If a loop is detected, all except one of the paths that made the loop are put in blocking mode. Once a port is placed in blocking mode, it will not forward user data. By doing this, spanning tree ensures that there is only one path to a destination at a time. If that path were to go down or be removed, then one of the "blocked" paths would be unblocked, or changed to a forwarding state, and used for user data.

One of the largest advantages of switches over the typical hub is the ability of the switch to create VLANs. A switch can have multiple VLANs defined, and each port can be put in a separate VLAN. Because of this capability, there is no longer a need for specific hardware to separate subnets. All of the subnets can be created on a single device and logically separated into VLANs.

Any new software feature needs a method for controlling and configuring it. For VLANs this is VTP, or VLAN Trunking Protocol. VTP allows VLAN configuration information to be changed in one location—a VTP server—and for this information to propagate automatically to all of the VTP clients in the VTP domain, thus easing the administrative overhead of a switched environment. If there is a concern about one change taking down the entire switched area, discrete VTP domains can be set up, or switches can be set to transparent mode. In transparent mode, each switch must be manually configured any time there is a change in the VLAN structure.

To better take advantage of the switches' ability to use VLANs, Cisco has manufactured a routing card for the 6500 series switches. Called the Multilayer Switch Feature Card (MSFC), this card provides full routing functionality to the switch. Because this card is connected to the switch's backplane, it has immediate access to any of the VLANs created on the switch. Alternatively, you can also uplink to an external router to get this functionality. This uplink can be done for a specific VLAN or for a range of VLANs if trunking is used.

One of the items that can be easily overlooked in the network is the cabling. As 100Mb Ethernet is now the standard for most new Ethernet installations, many of the Cat 3 cable plants that were installed for 10Mb Ethernet need to be replaced with Cat 5 or better cabling. In addition, as switching allows for larger layer 2 domains and layer 3 functionality is added to the switches, it is becoming more common to use the crossover cable to connect two switches directly.

Exam Essentials

Know the differences among switches, bridges, and hubs. A hub can only run in half-duplex mode and has a broadcast-and-collision domain that includes all ports. Bridges do not generally have hardware ASICs and have a lower port density. Switches can operate in full- or half-duplex mode and have a collision domain of a single port and a broadcast domain of a single VLAN.

Know the *show* commands available for a switch. Switch `show` commands include but are not limited to `show cdp`, `show config`, `show flash`, `show log`, `show mac`, `show port`, `show span`, `show system`, `show test`, and `show version`.

Know how spanning tree is used in a switch. Spanning tree controls loops in a layer 2 environment. The switch does this automatically.

Understand the function of a VLAN. A VLAN is used to logically separate traffic on a switch. This allows a switch to have multiple individual subnets terminating on it.

Understand trunking and how it works. Trunking on a Cisco switch can be done by using either ISL or 802.1Q. It allows for multiple VLANs to share the same uplink.

Understand how VTP works. VLAN Trunking Protocol allows for easy administration of VLANs in a large switched environment. VLAN changes performed on a VTP server are automatically updated on all the VTP clients in the VTP domain. If a switch is in transparent mode, it will pass along any VTP changes sent by the server but will not make any modifications to its own VLANs.

Know how to troubleshoot cabling problems and when to use a crossover cable. A crossover cable is used anytime like network devices are directly connected together (e.g., router to router, switch to switch, or workstation to workstation). A straight-through cable is used to connect workstations or routers to switches. Cable testers and time domain reflectometers (TDRs) are among the tools that are available for testing physical cabling issues.

Chapter 42

Applying Cisco's Diagnostic Tools

THE CCNP EXAM TOPICS COVERED IN THIS CHAPTER INCLUDE THE FOLLOWING:

- ✓ Verify network connectivity.
- ✓ Use Cisco IOS commands to identify problems.
- ✓ Rectify layer 1 connectivity problems.
- ✓ Rectify sub-optimal performance issues at layers 2 through 7.
- ✓ Restore services back to baseline conditions.

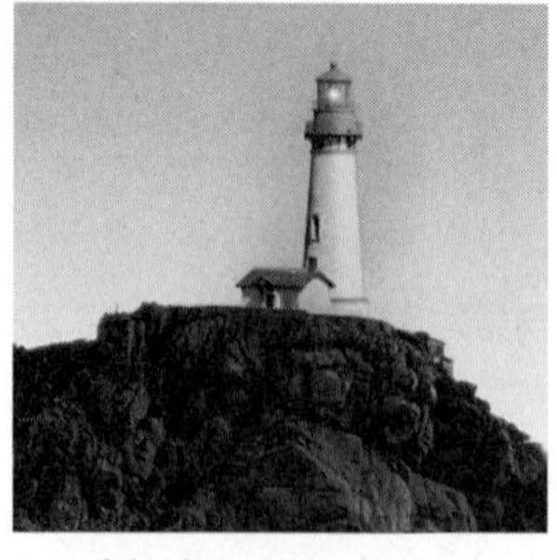

In the previous chapters, you learned a great deal about layer 2 and layer 3 technologies and protocols. With this knowledge, you'll be able to better interpret the information provided by the troubleshooting tools and commands.

The time has come to implement all that you've learned, including applying the troubleshooting methodology from Chapter 33, "Troubleshooting Methodology." Once you have the technical knowledge base, you must apply it by using a troubleshooting template if you are to efficiently and successfully troubleshoot network problems.

This chapter's format will be different from what you have seen up to now. Different types of network problems will be outlined in detail, and each will then be solved. The intent is for you to take the provided information and do the troubleshooting. You'll see substantial router output and packet decodes from a protocol analyzer. The information is there for your reference and at times may not have a great deal of explanation. You must look at the output carefully in order to determine what is happening on the router or network.

For each scenario, follow the steps outlined in Chapter 33 by gathering symptoms, isolating the problem, and correcting the problem. Because this book cannot be interactive, the scenarios are intended to help you get accustomed to using the methodology, but you'll not go so far as to actually verify that the proposed solution solved the network problem. Let's begin.

Identifying and Resolving Generic Router Problems

This section deals with Cisco routers and some simple generic problems that can be remedied easily, once they are identified. Each scenario is accompanied by outputs from relevant diagnostic tools. The focus is on the router itself, because many other scenarios involve additional network equipment.

Scenario #1

You are installing a Cisco 2600 series router that was sent to you after company headquarters entered the preliminary configuration.

Gathering Symptoms

You are connected to the console port. You power on the router, and this is what you see as the router boots:

```
System Bootstrap, Version 11.3(2)XA3, PLATFORM SPECIFIC   RELEASE
  SOFTWARE (fc1)
Copyright (c) 1998 by cisco Systems, Inc.
TAC:Home:SW:IOS:Specials for info
C2600 platform with 24576 Kbytes of main memory
program load complete, entry point: 0x80008000, size:   0x37b090
Self decompressing the image :
#######################################################################
#######################################################################
#######################################################################
#######################################################################
#################################### [OK]
Restricted Rights Legend
Use, duplication, or disclosure by the Government is
subject to restrictions as set forth in subparagraph
(c) of the Commercial Computer Software - Restricted
Rights clause at FAR sec. 52.227-19 and subparagraph
(c) (1) (ii) of the Rights in Technical Data and Computer
Software clause at DFARS sec. 252.227-7013.

           cisco Systems, Inc.
           170 West Tasman Drive
           San Jose, California 95134-1706
Cisco Internetwork Operating System Software
IOS (tm) C2600 Software (C2600-D-M), Version 11.3(4)T1,    RELEASE
 SOFTWARE (fc1)
Copyright (c) 1986-1998 by cisco Systems, Inc.
Compiled Wed 01-Jul-98 11:42 by phanguye
Image text-base: 0x80008084, data-base: 0x8066A278

Cisco 2611 (MPC860) processor (revision 0x202) with   18432K/6144K
              bytes of memory.
Processor board ID JAB023601NE (1537311773)
M860 processor: part number 0, mask 32
Bridging software.
X.25 software, Version 3.0.0.
2 Ethernet/IEEE 802.3 interface(s)
```

```
1 Serial network interface(s)
32K bytes of non-volatile configuration memory.
8192K bytes of processor board System flash (Read/Write)



Press RETURN to get started!


%LINK-3-UPDOWN: Interface Ethernet0/0, changed state to down
%LINK-3-UPDOWN: Interface Ethernet0/1, changed state to up
%LINK-3-UPDOWN: Interface Serial0/0, changed state to down
Cisco Internetwork Operating System Software
IOS (tm) C2600 Software (C2600-D-M), Version 11.3(4)T1,    RELEASE
  SOFTWARE (fc1)
Copyright (c) 1986-1998 by cisco Systems, Inc.
Compiled Wed 01-Jul-98 11:42 by phanguye

%LINK-5-CHANGED: Interface Serial0/0, changed state to  administratively down
%FR-5-DLCICHANGE: Interface Serial0/0 - DLCI 324 state   changed to DELETED
```

Well, it looks like two interfaces on the router are down—so much for the preconfigured router. You change to the privileged level by entering the enable password. Here is where you need to start gathering symptoms. The first symptom is that two of the interfaces on the router are down.

Before you look at the configuration or `show` commands, you check the cabling connections. Assuming that the connections check out, you should check the lights in the back of the router. Figure 42.1 shows the back of a 2611 router. The router comes with two Ethernet ports, a console port, an aux port, and a serial port. Each of the network interface ports (both Ethernet ports and the serial port) has a light next to it that indicates whether there is a physical connection. If any of these lights is not lit, there's a connectivity problem. In this example, assume that two of the three lights are lit. The light next to Ethernet 0/0 is not lit.

Now that you've observed the connectivity, you need to gather more information about the router's configuration. Go back to the console. You know that the problem involves two interfaces, Ethernet 0/0 and Serial 0/0. For this example, don't use `show running-config` or `show startup-config`. Instead, use the interface-specific `show` commands.

FIGURE 42.1 Rear view of a Cisco 2611

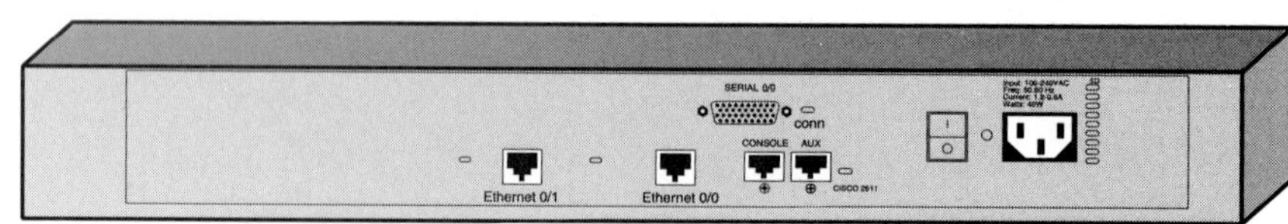

The first command issued is show interface ethernet 0/0. Here are the results:

```
Router_A#show interface ethernet 0/0
Ethernet0/0 is down, line protocol is down
  Hardware is AmdP2, address is 0010.7bd9.2880 (bia 0010.7bd9.2880)
  MTU 1500 bytes, BW 10000 Kbit, DLY 1000 usec, rely 255/255, load 1/255
  Encapsulation ARPA, loopback not set, keepalive set (10 sec)
  ARP type: ARPA, ARP Timeout 04:00:00
  Last input never, output never, output hang never
  Last clearing of "show interface" counters never
  Queueing strategy: fifo
  Output queue 0/40, 0 drops; input queue 0/75, 0 drops
  5 minute input rate 0 bits/sec, 0 packets/sec
  5 minute output rate 0 bits/sec, 0 packets/sec
     0 packets input, 0 bytes, 0 no buffer
     Received 0 broadcasts, 0 runts, 0 giants, 0 throttles
     0 input errors, 0 CRC, 0 frame, 0 overrun, 0 ignored,
        0 abort
     0 input packets with dribble condition detected
     0 packets output, 0 bytes, 0 underruns
     0 output errors, 0 collisions, 0 interface resets
     0 babbles, 0 late collision, 0 deferred
     0 lost carrier, 0 no carrier
     0 output buffer failures, 0 output buffers swapped out
Router_A#
```

The following outputs are from the show interface Ethernet 0/1 and show interface Serial 0/0 commands, respectively:

```
Ethernet0/1 is up, line protocol is up
  Hardware is AmdP2, address is 0010.7bd9.2881 (bia 0010.7bd9.2881)
  Internet address is 172.16.20.5/24
  MTU 1500 bytes, BW 10000 Kbit, DLY 1000 usec, rely 255/255, load 1/255
  Encapsulation ARPA, loopback not set, keepalive set (10 sec)
  ARP type: ARPA, ARP Timeout 04:00:00
  Last input never, output 00:00:02, output hang never
  Last clearing of "show interface" counters never
  Queueing strategy: fifo
  Output queue 0/40, 0 drops; input queue 0/75, 0 drops
  5 minute input rate 983450 bits/sec, 875 packets/sec
  5 minute output rate 435097 bits/sec, 357 packets/sec
     0 packets input, 0 bytes, 0 no buffer
```

```
     Received 0 broadcasts, 0 runts, 0 giants, 0 throttles
     0 input errors, 0 CRC, 0 frame, 0 overrun, 0 ignored,
        0 abort
     0 input packets with dribble condition detected
     274 packets output, 17062 bytes, 0 underruns
     0 output errors, 0 collisions, 11 interface resets
     0 babbles, 0 late collision, 0 deferred
     0 lost carrier, 0 no carrier
     0 output buffer failures, 0 output buffers swapped out
Router_A# show interface serial 0/0
Serial0/0 is administratively down, line protocol is down
  Hardware is PowerQUICC Serial
  Internet address is 172.16.20.5/30
  MTU 1500 bytes, BW 1544 Kbit, DLY 20000 usec, rely 255/255, load 1/255
  Encapsulation FRAME-RELAY, loopback not set, keepalive set (10 sec)
  LMI enq sent  0, LMI stat recvd 0, LMI upd recvd 0, DTE LMI down
  LMI enq recvd 0, LMI stat sent  0, LMI upd sent  0
  LMI DLCI 1023  LMI type is CISCO  frame relay DTE
  FR SVC disabled, LAPF state down
  Broadcast queue 0/64, broadcasts sent/dropped 0/0, interface broadcasts 0
  Last input never, output never, output hang never
  Last clearing of "show interface" counters never
  Input queue: 0/75/0 (size/max/drops); Total output drops: 0
  Queueing strategy: weighted fair
  Output queue: 0/1000/64/0 (size/max total/threshold/drops)
     Conversations  0/1/256 (active/max active/max total)
     Reserved Conversations 0/0 (allocated/max allocated)
  5 minute input rate 0 bits/sec, 0 packets/sec
  5 minute output rate 0 bits/sec, 0 packets/sec
     0 packets input, 0 bytes, 0 no buffer
     Received 0 broadcasts, 0 runts, 0 giants, 0 throttles
     0 input errors, 0 CRC, 0 frame, 0 overrun, 0 ignored, 0 abort
     0 packets output, 0 bytes, 0 underruns
     0 output errors, 0 collisions, 0 interface resets
     0 output buffer failures, 0 output buffers swapped out
     0 carrier transitions
     DCD=up  DSR=up  DTR=down  RTS=down  CTS=up
Router_A#
```

Isolating the Problem

What are your observations? Check your list against the following:

- No IP address is configured on Ethernet 0/0.
- No indicator light is lit for Ethernet 0/0.
- The number of lost carrier errors is the same as the number of output errors.
- Serial 0/0 is administratively shut down.
- DLCI 324 on Serial 0/0 is in a deleted state.
- Serial 0/0 is a Frame Relay link.
- Ethernet 0/1 is up and up.

In other situations, this list can contain more information regarding the interfaces such as encapsulation types and so on. For clarity and simplicity, only the observations relevant to this scenario are listed here.

After you are done gathering symptoms, it's time to isolate the problem. Initially, from what you saw while the router booted, the problem description was vague. It could have been written something like this: "Interfaces Ethernet 0/0 and Serial 0/0 are down."

In this first scenario, there appear to be a few problems that need resolution, and they all probably have simple solutions:

- Check the cable for the Ethernet port for a possible physical problem.
- Configure an IP address on Ethernet 0/0.
- Turn up interface Serial 0/0.

Correcting the Problem

With the proposed solutions, the only thing left is to implement them and see if they work. You replace the cable going to Ethernet 0/0, and modify the configuration of the router as follows:

```
Router_A#conf t
Enter configuration commands, one per line. End with CNTL/Z.
Router_A(config)#interface ethernet 0/0
Router_A(config-if)#ip address 172.16.10.1 255.255.255.0
Router_A(config-if)#interface serial 0/0
Router_A(config-if)#no shut
172.16.20.5 overlaps with Ethernet0/1
Serial0/0: incorrect IP address assignment
Router_A(config-if)#^Z
Router_A#
```

Gathering Symptoms—Take 2

Now check the interface status:

```
Ethernet0/0 is up, line protocol is up
Hardware is AmdP2, address is 0010.7bd9.2880 (bia 0010.7bd9.2880)
  MTU 1500 bytes, BW 10000 Kbit, DLY 1000 usec, rely 255/255, load 1/255
  Encapsulation ARPA, loopback not set, keepalive set (10 sec)
  ARP type: ARPA, ARP Timeout 04:00:00
  Last input never, output 00:00:05, output hang never
  Last clearing of "show interface" counters never
  Queueing strategy: fifo
  Output queue 0/40, 0 drops; input queue 0/75, 0 drops
  5 minute input rate 509000 bits/sec, 215 packets/sec
  5 minute output rate 1167000 bits/sec, 315 packets/sec
     12900 packets input, 10324500 bytes, 0 no buffer
     Received 235 broadcasts, 0 runts, 0 giants, 0 throttles
      0 input errors, 0 CRC, 0 frame, 0 overrun, 0 ignored,
         0 abort
     0 input packets with dribble condition detected
     18903 packets output, 15198309 bytes, 0 underruns
     0 output errors, 0 collisions, 1 interface resets
     0 babbles, 0 late collision, 0 deferred
     0 lost carrier, 0 no carrier
     0 output buffer failures, 0 output buffers swapped out
```

What happened to Serial 0/0? The console message stated that there was an address overlap with interface Ethernet 0/1, which means a duplicate IP address. The IP address on Ethernet 0/1 overlaps with the IP address on Serial 0/0. Look at the interface settings once more:

```
Router_A#show interface serial 0/0
Serial0/0 is administratively down, line protocol is down
  Hardware is PowerQUICC Serial
  Internet address is 172.16.20.5/30
  MTU 1500 bytes, BW 1544 Kbit, DLY 20000 usec, rely 255/255, load 1/255
  Encapsulation FRAME-RELAY, loopback not set, keepalive set (10 sec)
  LMI enq sent  0, LMI stat recvd 0, LMI upd recvd 0, DTE   LMI down
  LMI enq recvd 0, LMI stat sent  0, LMI upd sent  0
  LMI DLCI 1023  LMI type is CISCO  frame relay DTE
  FR SVC disabled, LAPF state down
  Broadcast queue 0/64, broadcasts sent/dropped 0/0, interface broadcasts 0
  Last input never, output never, output hang never
  Last clearing of "show interface" counters never
```

```
  Input queue: 0/75/0 (size/max/drops); Total output drops: 0
  Queueing strategy: weighted fair
  Output queue: 0/1000/64/0 (size/max total/threshold/ drops)
     Conversations  0/1/256 (active/max active/max total)
     Reserved Conversations 0/0 (allocated/max allocated)
  5 minute input rate 0 bits/sec, 0 packets/sec
  5 minute output rate 0 bits/sec, 0 packets/sec
     0 packets input, 0 bytes, 0 no buffer
     Received 0 broadcasts, 0 runts, 0 giants, 0 throttles
     0 input errors, 0 CRC, 0 frame, 0 overrun, 0 ignored, 0 abort
     0 packets output, 0 bytes, 0 underruns
     0 output errors, 0 collisions, 0 interface resets
     0 output buffer failures, 0 output buffers swapped out
     0 carrier transitions
     DCD=up  DSR=up  DTR=down  RTS=down  CTS=up
Router_A#
```

This output indicates that the interface is still administratively down. You saw the `no shut` command issued in the previous series of configuration commands, so why is it still in shutdown? Here's the answer: If an interface has a configuration conflict with another interface, it will not initialize. In this case, because the serial interface was configured with a duplicate IP address, it wouldn't initialize. It remains in its previous state—shutdown. In order to activate the serial link you must do some more analysis.

Isolating the Problem—Take 2

Referring to the `show interface` results for Ethernet 0/1, you see that it does have the same address as Serial 0/0. This problem can easily be resolved, as long as you know which interface should have the 172.16.20.5 address. In this scenario, you'll assume that Ethernet 0/1 has the incorrect IP address.

In essence, you've made these additional observations:

- Serial 0/0 is configured with IP address 172.16.20.5/30.
- Ethernet 0/1 is configured with IP address 172.16.20.5/24.
- You cannot change the administrative state for Serial 0/0 because of the IP address overlap with Ethernet 0/1.

Now, with these additional observations, new solutions must be proposed. Once the decision is made as to which IP address should be assigned to each interface, the problem should be resolved. The action plan is as follows:

- Leave IP address 172.16.20.5/30 assigned to interface Serial 0/0.
- Assign IP address 172.16.30.1/24 to interface Ethernet 0/1.
- Remove the administrative shutdown from interface Serial 0/0.

Correcting the Problem—Take 2

Here is the configuration. Following the configuration, you see the `show interface` output for each interface. This is done to verify that all the changes to the router have fixed the problems that were observed:

```
Router_A#conf t
Enter configuration commands, one per line. End with CNTL/Z.
Router_A(config-if)#interface ethernet 0/1
Router_A(config-if)#ip address 172.16.30.1 255.255.255.0
Router_A(config)#interface serial 0/0
Router_A(config-if)#no shutdown
Router_A(config-if)#^Z
%LINK-3-UPDOWN: Interface Serial0/0, changed state to up
%FR-5-DLCICHANGE: Interface Serial0/0 - DLCI 324 state changed to ACTIVE
%FR-5-DLCICHANGE: Interface Serial0/0 - DLCI 368 state changed to ACTIVE
%FR-5-DLCICHANGE: Interface Serial0/0 - DLCI 324 state changed to DELETED
%LINEPROTO-5-UPDOWN: Line protocol on Interface Serial0/0, changed state to up
Router_A#
Router_A#show interface ethernet 0/0
Ethernet0/0 is up, line protocol is up
  Hardware is AmdP2, address is 0010.7bd9.2880    (bia 0010.7bd9.2880)
  Internet address is 172.16.10.1/24
  MTU 1500 bytes, BW 10000 Kbit, DLY 1000 usec, rely 255/255, load 29/255
  Encapsulation ARPA, loopback not set, keepalive set (10  sec)
  ARP type: ARPA, ARP Timeout 04:00:00
  Last input 00:00:00, output 00:00:00, output hang never
  Last clearing of "show interface" counters never
  Queueing strategy: fifo
  Output queue 0/40, 0 drops; input queue 1/75, 0 drops
  5 minute input rate 509000 bits/sec, 215 packets/sec
  5 minute output rate 1167000 bits/sec, 315 packets/sec
     25800 packets input, 20685400 bytes, 0 no buffer
     Received 3235 broadcasts, 0 runts, 0 giants
     6 input errors, 1 CRC, 5 frame, 0 overrun, 640 ignored, 0 abort
     0 input packets with dribble condition detected
     37800 packets output, 30249800 bytes, 0 underruns
     283 output errors, 4 collisions, 2 interface resets
     0 babbles, 0 late collision, 0 deferred
     283 lost carrier, 0 no carrier
     0 output buffers copied, 0 interrupts, 0 failures
Router_A#show interface serial 0/0
```

```
Serial0/0 is up, line protocol is up
  Hardware is PowerQUICC Serial
  Internet address is 172.16.20.5/30
  MTU 1500 bytes, BW 1544 Kbit, DLY 20000 usec, rely 255/255, load 1/255
  Encapsulation FRAME-RELAY, loopback not set, keepalive set (10 sec)
  LMI enq sent  5, LMI stat recvd 6, LMI upd recvd 0, DTE LMI up
  LMI enq recvd 0, LMI stat sent  0, LMI upd sent  0
  LMI DLCI 1023  LMI type is CISCO  frame relay DTE
  FR SVC disabled, LAPF state down
  Broadcast queue 0/64, broadcasts sent/dropped 0/0, interface broadcasts 1
  Last input 00:00:03, output 00:00:03, output hang never
  Last clearing of "show interface" counters never
  Input queue: 0/75/0 (size/max/drops); Total output   drops: 0
  Queueing strategy: weighted fair
  Output queue: 0/1000/64/0 (size/max total/threshold/   drops)
     Conversations  0/1/256 (active/max active/max total)
     Reserved Conversations 0/0 (allocated/max allocated)
  5 minute input rate 0 bits/sec, 0 packets/sec
  5 minute output rate 0 bits/sec, 0 packets/sec
     6 packets input, 94 bytes, 0 no buffer
     Received 0 broadcasts, 0 runts, 0 giants, 0 throttles
     0 input errors, 0 CRC, 0 frame, 0 overrun, 0 ignored, 0 abort
     9 packets output, 129 bytes, 0 underruns
     0 output errors, 0 collisions, 3 interface resets
     0 output buffer failures, 0 output buffers swapped out
     0 carrier transitions
     DCD=up  DSR=up  DTR=up  RTS=up  CTS=up
Router_A#show interface ethernet 0/1
Ethernet0/1 is up, line protocol is up
  Hardware is AmdP2, address is 0010.7bd9.2881 (bia 0010.7bd9.2881)
  Internet address is 172.16.30.1/24
  MTU 1500 bytes, BW 10000 Kbit, DLY 1000 usec, rely 128/255, load 1/255
  Encapsulation ARPA, loopback not set, keepalive set (10 sec)
  ARP type: ARPA, ARP Timeout 04:00:00
  Last input never, output 00:00:07, output hang never
  Last clearing of "show interface" counters never
  Queueing strategy: fifo
  Output queue 0/40, 0 drops; input queue 0/75, 0 drops
5 minute input rate 488000 bits/sec, 164 packets/sec
5 minute output rate 1473000 bits/sec, 297 packets/sec
```

```
     9840 packets input, 7815720 bytes, 0 no buffer
     Received 0 broadcasts, 0 runts, 0 giants, 0 throttles
     0 input errors, 0 CRC, 0 frame, 0 overrun, 0 ignored,
        0 abort
     0 input packets with dribble condition detected
     17820 packets output, 14352560 bytes, 0 underruns
     0 output errors, 0 collisions, 0 interface resets
     0 babbles, 0 late collision, 0 deferred
     0 lost carrier, 0 no carrier
     0 output buffer failures, 0 output buffers swapped out
Router_A#
```

Gathering Symptoms—Take 3

From what you can see in the interface outputs, it appears that all interfaces are working properly. However, there are three messages of concern regarding the DLCI information in messages that were displayed after the Serial 0/0 interface was brought up. To be on the safe side, try to ping the router at the headquarters location:

```
Router_A#ping 172.16.20.6

Type escape sequence to abort.
Sending 5, 100-byte ICMP Echos to 172.16.20.6, timeout is 2 seconds:
.....
Success rate is 0 percent (0/5)
Router_A#
```

As suspected, there is still another issue that needs to be resolved. From the `show interface` command you can see that the router is receiving LMI messages and that the circuit itself appears fine. Take a look at the PVCs and the Frame Relay mappings that are on the router:

```
Router_A#show frame-relay pvc

PVC Statistics for interface Serial0/0 (Frame Relay DTE)

DLCI = 324, DLCI USAGE = LOCAL, PVC STATUS = DELETED,   INTERFACE = Serial0/0

  input pkts 0            output pkts 0            in bytes 0
  out bytes 0             dropped pkts 0           in FECN pkts 0
  in BECN pkts 0          out FECN pkts 0          out BECN pkts 0
  in DE pkts 0            out DE pkts 0
  out bcast pkts 0        out bcast bytes 0
  pvc create time 00:31:25, last time pvc status changed 00:31:25
```

```
DLCI = 368, DLCI USAGE = UNUSED, PVC STATUS = ACTIVE, INTERFACE = Serial0/0

  input pkts 0            output pkts 0           in bytes 0
  out bytes 0             dropped pkts 0          in FECN pkts 0
  in BECN pkts 0          out FECN pkts 0         out BECN pkts 0
  in DE pkts 0            out DE pkts 0
  out bcast pkts 0        out bcast bytes 0          Num Pkts Switched 0
  pvc create time 00:31:25, last time pvc status changed 00:31:25
Router_A#show frame-relay map
Serial0/0 (up): ip 172.16.20.6 dlci 324(0x144,0x5040),
  static,broadcast, CISCO, status deleted
Router_A#
```

Based on this output, there are two PVCs that are known to the router. One, 324, is in a deleted state and the other, 368, is in an active state. In addition, according to the `show frame-relay map` command, the IP address of the Headquarters router is statically mapped to the deleted DLCI 324.

Isolating the Problem—Take 3

With this information in hand, restate what's occurring at this point:

- Ethernet 0/0 and Ethernet 0/1 are working fine.
- Serial 0/0 is up and running without errors.
- Pinging the Headquarters router is unsuccessful.
- LMI is being sent and received successfully on Serial 0/0.
- There are two PVCs known by the router: 324 and 368.
- Only one PVC will be used at this location.
- The IP address of the headquarters router is statically mapped to DLCI 324.

Based on this new information, the most likely scenario is that when the router was preconfigured, the IP address was mapped to the incorrect DLCI. When a static IP-to-DLCI mapping is made, an entry for that DLCI is put in the router's PVC table. If the router doesn't receive an LMI message indicating that the frame switch knows about that DLCI, or if the interface on which this DLCI is assigned is down, the DLCI will go into a deleted state. In addition, when a router actively receives updates for a DLCI via LMI, the router will add this DLCI to its table in an active state. This appears to be what has occurred with DLCI 368. Therefore, you're assuming that DLCI 368 is the correct DLCI for this location.

Correcting the Problem—Take 3

Based on this information, your plan is to change the DLCI-to-IP mappings and map 172.16.20.6 to DLCI 368. It looks like this:

```
Router_A#conf t
Enter configuration commands, one per line. End with CNTL/Z.
```

```
Router_A(config)#interface serial 0/0
Router_A(config-if)#no frame-relay map ip 172.16.20.6 324 broadcast
Router_A(config-if)#frame-relay map ip 172.16.20.6 368 broadcast
Router_A(config-if)#^Z
Router_A#
Router_A#show frame-relay map
Serial0/0 (up): ip 172.16.20.6 dlci 368(0x170,0x5C00), static,
  broadcast, CISCO, status defined, active
Router_A#
Router_A#ping 172.16.20.6

Type escape sequence to abort.
Sending 5, 100-byte ICMP Echos to 172.16.20.6, timeout is   2 seconds:
!!!!!
Success rate is 100 percent (5/5), round-trip min/avg/max   = 28/30/32 ms
Router_A#
```

The changes made were effective, and they did not cause other network problems.

The final step is to document what was done:

- You added 172.16.10.1/24 to Ethernet 0/0.
- You left 172.16.20.5/30 on Serial 0/0.
- You changed administrative status for interface Serial 0/0 with the `no shutdown` command.
- You changed the DLCI used for the Frame Relay connection.
- You changed the IP address for interface Ethernet 0/1 from 172.16.20.5/30 to 172.16.30.1/24.

All of the necessary troubleshooting steps were taken to solve the problems. The first step was to gather symptoms. Then from these symptoms, the problem was isolated. After the first changes were made, interface Ethernet 0/0 came up. You saw that the router would not allow Serial 0/0 to be removed from administrative shutdown because of the duplicate IP address. The address conflicted with an IP address assigned to Ethernet 0/1. A new address was assigned to Ethernet 0/1, and Serial 0/0 was changed to an active state. After this, the DLCI used for the Frame Relay connection was changed, and complete connectivity was achieved.

Scenario #2

This next scenario is a little more challenging. Look at Figure 42.2 to get a picture of the network that you'll troubleshoot.

What's happening is that Host Z is trying to ftp a file to Host A, but Host Z is unable to do so. Let's move through the troubleshooting method to solve this problem. Start by listing your observations.

FIGURE 42.2 Network diagram for Scenario #2

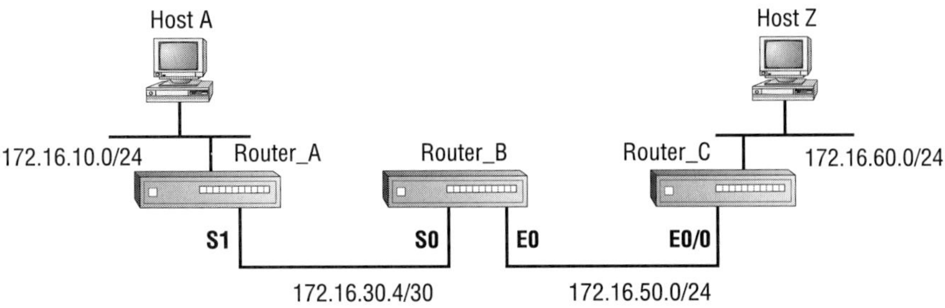

Frame Relay and Subinterfaces

In the Scenario #1 example with the Cisco 2600 router, the entire Frame Relay configuration was done on the main interface, and Frame Relay inverse ARP was turned off. This was done in order to make this example more interesting in terms of troubleshooting. Under this configuration, the interface would stay in an up/up state as long as it received LMI messages from the Frame Relay switch.

Although there are reasons to configure an interface in this manner (e.g., point-to-multipoint, multipoint-to-multipoint, consistency of configuration), using subinterfaces and the `frame-relay interface-dlci` command may have been more appropriate in this instance. Suppose that in this scenario, a subinterface (Serial 0/0.1, for example) had been configured specifically for the connection back to Headquarters. That would have made troubleshooting the DLCI problem easier. In that case, the main interface—Serial 0/0—would still have been in an up/up state, but the subinterface—Serial 0/0.1—would have been down/down until the DLCI issue was corrected. This correction would involve changing the `frame-relay interface-dlci` command to refer to DLCI 368 rather than to the originally configured value of 324. Using subinterfaces would have made it easier to spot the DLCI issue, as well as to verify when the problem had been corrected.

Gathering Symptoms

The first test is an actual ftp attempt, the results of which are shown in Figure 42.3. The software gives you a `host unreachable` error message, which is an ICMP response. EtherPeek was used to capture packets in this exchange. The first packet decode is Host Z sending an ftp connection request.

FIGURE 42.3 An FTP attempt failure

```
connecting to 172.16.10.2:21
! Connection failed 172.16.10.2 - host unreachable
! Connection failed 172.16.10.2
```

```
  Flags:          0x00
  Status:         0x00
  Packet Length:66
  Timestamp:      22:11:39.486000 04/18/2003
Ethernet Header
  Destination:    00:10:7b:d9:28:81  [0-5]
  Source:         00:a0:24:a5:06:57  [6-11]
  Protocol Type:08-00  IP  [12-13]
IP Header - Internet Protocol Datagram
  Version:                4  [14 Mask 0xf0]
  Header Length:          5  [14 Mask 0xf]
  Precedence:             0  [15 Mask 0xe0]
  Type of Service:        %000  [15 Mask 0x1c]
  Unused:                 %00  [15 Mask 0x3]
  Total Length:           48  [16-17]
  Identifier:             17152  [18-19]
  Fragmentation Flags:    %010  Do Not Fragment   [20  Mask 0xe0]
  Fragment Offset:        0  [20-22 Mask 0x1fffff]
  Time To Live:           128
  IP Type:                0x06  TCP  [23]
  Header Checksum:        0x1923  [24-25]
  Source IP Address:      172.16.60.130  [26-29]
  Dest. IP Address:       172.16.10.2  [30-33]
  No Internet Datagram Options
  TCP - Transport Control Protocol
  Source Port:       1038  [34-35]
  Destination Port: 21  FTP Control - File Transfer    Protocol  [36-37]
  Sequence Number:   6198340  [38-41]
  Ack Number:        0  [42-45]
  Offset:            7  [46 Mask 0xf0]
  Reserved:          %000000  [46 Mask 0xfc0]
  Code:              %000010  [47 Mask 0x3f]
           Synch Sequence
  Window:            8192  [48-49]
  Checksum:          0x2bb5  [50-51]
```

```
  Urgent Pointer:    0  [52-53]
  TCP Options:  [54]
    Option Type:     2  Maximum Segment Size  [55]
        Length:      4
        MSS:         1460  [56-58]
    Option Type:     1  No Operation  [59]
    Option Type:     1  No Operation  [60]
    Option Type:     4  [61]
        Length:      2
  No More FTP Command or Reply Data
Frame Check Sequence:  0x00000000
```

Everything looks fine with this packet. Now, look at the ICMP message received:

```
Flags:        0x00
  Status:        0x00
  Packet Length:74
  Timestamp:     22:11:39.489000 04/18/2003
Ethernet Header
  Destination:   00:a0:24:a5:06:57  [0-5]
  Source:        00:10:7b:d9:28:81  [6-11]
  Protocol Type:08-00  IP  [12-13]
IP Header - Internet Protocol Datagram
  Version:               4  [14 Mask 0xf0]
  Header Length:         5  [14 Mask 0xf]
  Precedence:            0  [15 Mask 0xe0]
  Type of Service:       %000  [15 Mask 0x1c]
  Unused:                %00  [15 Mask 0x3]
  Total Length:          56  [16-17]
  Identifier:            2815  [18-19]
  Fragmentation Flags:   %000  [20 Mask 0xe0]
  Fragment Offset:       0  [20-22 Mask 0x1fffff]
  Time To Live:          255
  IP Type:               0x01  ICMP  [23]
  Header Checksum:       0xe021  [24-25]
  Source IP Address:     172.16.60.1  [26-29]
  Dest. IP Address:      172.16.60.130  [30-33]
  No Internet Datagram Options
ICMP - Internet Control Messages Protocol  [34]
  ICMP Type:             3  Destination Unreachable  [35]
  Code:                  1  Host Unreachable
  Checksum:              0x6439  [36-37]
  Unused (must be zero):0x00000000  [38-41]
```

Notice that the source IP address in the ICMP packet is from 172.16.60.1. That's the gateway address for Host Z. Here is the header of the packet that caused the error:

```
IP Header - Internet Protocol Datagram
  Version:               4  [42 Mask 0xf0]
  Header Length:         5  [42 Mask 0xf]
  Precedence:            0  [43 Mask 0xe0]
  Type of Service:       %000  [43 Mask 0x1c]
  Unused:                %00  [43 Mask 0x3]
  Total Length:          48  [44-45]
  Identifier:            17152  [46-47]
  Fragmentation Flags:   %010  Do Not Fragment   [48 Mask     0xe0]
  Fragment Offset:       0  [48-50 Mask 0x1fffff]
  Time To Live:          127
  IP Type:               0x06  TCP  [51]
  Header Checksum:       0x1a23  [52-53]
  Source IP Address:     172.16.60.130  [54-57]
  Dest. IP Address:      172.16.10.2  [58-61]
  No Internet Datagram Options
TCP - Transport Control Protocol
  Source Port:       1038  [62-63]
  Destination Port:  21  FTP Control - File Transfer   Protocol     [64-65]
  Sequence Number:   6198340  [66-69]
  Ack Number:        0
```

The key information for your observation is provided under the ICMP header section. Notice the ICMP type of 3, Destination Unreachable—the code specifies that the host is not reachable. You might issue the `ping` command at this point, but it will render the same information—host unreachable.

There are a couple of different directions that may be taken. One method is to try to ftp a file to hosts that don't reside on the 172.16.10.0/24 network. Another option is to run a traceroute to see where the path to Host A is failing.

Try the latter. Following are the results of a traceroute to Host A:

```
C:\WINDOWS>tracert 172.16.10.2
Tracing route to 172.16.10.2 over a maximum of 30 hops
1     5 ms     2 ms     4 ms  172.16.60.1
2  172.16.60.1  reports: Destination host unreachable.
Trace complete.
```

These results indicate that Router C does not have a route to Host A. This allows you to determine that the problem appears to be between Router C and Router B.

Isolating the Problem

To further troubleshoot this problem, diagnostics must be executed from Router C. Bring up a console on Router C. The first command that should be issued is a `show ip route`. The results are as follows:

```
Router_C#show ip route
Codes: C - connected, S - static, I - IGRP, R - RIP, M - mobile, B -
 BGP D - EIGRP, EX - EIGRP external, O - OSPF, IA - OSPF inter area N1
 - OSPF NSSA external type 1, N2 - OSPF NSSA external type 2 E1 - OSPF
 external type 1, E2 - OSPF external type 2, E - EGPi - IS-IS, L1 - IS-
 IS level-1, L2 - IS-IS level-2, * - candidate default U - per-user
 static route, o - ODR
Gateway of last resort is not set
172.16.0.0/24 is subnetted, 2 subnets
C       172.16.60.0 is directly connected, Ethernet0/1
C       172.16.50.0 is directly connected, Ethernet0/0
Router_C#
```

Router C knows only routes for networks that are directly connected. This points to problems with routing updates or routing protocols between Routers B and C. Take a look at the configuration on both routers:

```
Router_C#show running-config
Building configuration...
Current configuration:
!
version 11.3
no service password-encryption
!
hostname Router_C
!
enable password aloha
!
interface Ethernet0/0
 ip address 172.16.50.2 255.255.255.0
!
interface Serial0/0
 no ip address
 shutdown
!
interface Ethernet0/1
 ip address 172.16.60.1 255.255.255.0
!
```

```
router eigrp 100
 network 172.16.0.0
 no auto-summary
!
ip classless
!
line con 0
line aux 0
line vty 0 4
 password aloha
 login
!
end
Router_C#
```

The show interface results should be reviewed before the configuration of Router B is displayed. The only interface of concern here is the one that connects the two routers—interface Ethernet 0/0. In the following results, notice that interface Ethernet 0/0 is up and functioning. This is proved by using the ping command:

```
Router_C>show interface ethernet0/0
Ethernet0/0 is up, line protocol is up
  Hardware is AmdP2, address is 0010.7bd9.2880 (bia 0010.7bd9.2880)
  Internet address is 172.16.50.2/24
  MTU 1500 bytes, BW 10000 Kbit, DLY 1000 usec, rely 255/255, load 1/255
  Encapsulation ARPA, loopback not set, keepalive set (10 sec)
  ARP type: ARPA, ARP Timeout 04:00:00
  Last input 02:54:40, output 00:00:00, output hang never
  Last clearing of "show interface" counters never
  Queueing strategy: fifo
  Output queue 0/40, 0 drops; input queue 0/75, 0 drops
  5 minute input rate 0 bits/sec, 0 packets/sec
  5 minute output rate 0 bits/sec, 0 packets/sec
     1006 packets input, 90611 bytes, 0 no buffer
     Received 990 broadcasts, 0 runts, 0 giants, 0 throttles
     0 input errors, 0 CRC, 0 frame, 0 overrun, 0 ignored,
        0 abort
     0 input packets with dribble condition detected
     4935 packets output, 402703 bytes, 0 underruns
     0 output errors, 0 collisions, 2 interface resets
     0 babbles, 0 late collision, 0 deferred
     0 lost carrier, 0 no carrier
     0 output buffer failures, 0 output buffers swapped out
```

```
Router_C>ping 172.16.50.1
Type escape sequence to abort.
Sending 5, 100-byte ICMP Echos to 172.16.50.1, timeout is  2  seconds:
.!!!!
Success rate is 80 percent (4/5), round-trip min/avg/max =    1/3/4 ms
Router_C>ping 172.16.50.1
Type escape sequence to abort.
Sending 5, 100-byte ICMP Echos to 172.16.50.1, timeout is  2  seconds:
!!!!!
Success rate is 100 percent (5/5), round-trip min/avg/max  =  4/4/4 ms
Router_C>
```

This output reveals that the routers are not sharing routing information. Something is causing the routing protocol to fail, but it's not because the interface is down. Before moving on, review your information and make sure that the correct path is being followed:

- Host Z cannot ftp to Host A.
- Host Z cannot ping to Host A.
- Host Z cannot traceroute to Host A.
- ICMP Destination Unreachable responses were returned from the FTP request.
- Router C does not have a route to the destination network.
- Ethernet 0/0 is up and functioning.
- There is capability to ping Router B.

The next step is to telnet to Router B:

```
Router_C>172.16.50.1
Trying 172.16.50.1 ... Open
User Access Verification
Password:
Router_B(boot)>
```

Something looks wrong. Instead of coming up with the normal prompt, the router is in boot mode, which explains why no routing is taking place. When a router is in boot mode, routing protocols do not work. This is the last key observation needed, and it allows you to define the problem.

You know that the router is in boot mode, but what's causing this? There are two simple reasons for a router's being in boot mode: There is a lack of IOS on the system flash, or the router is not looking in the right location for the IOS.

Look at the contents of Router B's flash, and then look at the router's version information:

```
Router_B(boot)#show flash
System flash directory:
File  Length   Name/status
  1   4287696  c2500-i-l.112-15.bin
```

```
[4287760 bytes used, 4100848 available, 8388608 total]
8192K bytes of processor board System flash (Read/Write)
Router_B(boot)#
```

This shows one IOS image on the system flash. Now, you need to determine which version of IOS is running on the router:

```
Router_B(boot)#show version
Cisco Internetwork Operating System Software
IOS (tm) 3000 Bootstrap Software (IGS-BOOT-R), Version 11.0(10c)XB1,
 PLATFORM SPECIFIC RELEASE SOFTWARE (fc1)
Copyright (c) 1986-1996 by cisco Systems, Inc.
Compiled Wed 10-Sep-97 13:06 by phester
Image text-base: 0x01010000, data-base: 0x00001000
ROM: System Bootstrap, Version 11.0(10c)XB1, PLATFORM SPECIFIC
 RELEASE SOFTWARE
(fc1)
Router_B uptime is 3 hours, 11 minutes
System restarted by reload
Running default software
cisco 2500 (68030) processor (revision A) with 4096K/2048K bytes of memory.
Processor board ID 01229726, with hardware revision 00000000
X.25 software, Version 2.0, NET2, BFE and GOSIP compliant.
Cisco-ET Extended Temperature platform.
1 Ethernet/IEEE 802.3 interface.
2 Serial network interfaces.
32K bytes of non-volatile configuration memory.
8192K bytes of processor board System flash (Read/Write)
Configuration register is 0x2101
Router_B(boot)#
```

The response displayed in the first few fields is that it is running a bootstrap version of IOS. Now, from these two outputs on Router B, it can be deduced that the IOS contained in flash memory was not used to boot the router.

As previously mentioned, reasons for a router's being in boot mode are that the IOS image could be corrupt, or the router is looking for the IOS in the wrong place. The router uses a configuration register to point to the location of the IOS image that it should load during the boot process.

The `config-register` is a 16-bit number that controls the router's boot sequence. The lowest four bits indicate the location from where the system image—or IOS—will be loaded. If the value is 0000, then the router enters into ROM monitor mode. If the register is set to 0001, then the IOS will be loaded from the boot ROM. (For a full description of `config-register` settings, refer to CCO.)

In this case, the configuration register was set to the hex value of 0x2101, which tells the router to look for the system image on the boot ROM. Remember that only the first four bits indicate the system image location.

Correcting the Problem

The plan for this scenario is to change the configuration register on Router B to load the image from system flash. The configuration changes are as follows. After the router reloads, a quick check can be made by issuing a `show version` command:

```
Router_B(boot)#conf t
Enter configuration commands, one per line. End with CNTL/Z.
Router_B(boot)(config)#config
Router_B(boot)(config)#config-register 0x2102
Router_B(boot)(config)#^Z
Router_B(boot)#
Router_B(boot)#reload
Proceed with reload? [confirm]
 [Connection to 172.16.50.1 closed by foreign host]
Router_C>172.16.50.1
Trying 172.16.50.1 ... Open
User Access Verification
Password:
Router_B>enable
Password:
Router_B#show version
Cisco Internetwork Operating System Software
IOS (tm) 2500 Software (C2500-I-L), Version 11.2(15), RELEASE SOFTWARE (fc1)
Copyright (c) 1986-1998 by cisco Systems, Inc.
Compiled Tue 07-Jul-98 21:51 by tmullins
Image text-base: 0x03022F80, data-base: 0x00001000
ROM: System Bootstrap, Version 11.0(10c)XB1, PLATFORM SPECIFIC
 RELEASE SOFTWARE(fc1)
BOOTFLASH: 3000 Bootstrap Software (IGS-BOOT-R), Version
 11.0(10c)XB1, PLATFORM
SPECIFIC RELEASE SOFTWARE (fc1)
Router_B uptime is 2 minutes
System restarted by reload
System image file is "flash:c2500-i-l.112-15.bin", booted via flash
cisco 2500 (68030) processor (revision A) with 4096K/2048K bytes of memory.
Processor board ID 01229726, with hardware revision 00000000
Bridging software.
X.25 software, Version 2.0, NET2, BFE and GOSIP compliant.
```

```
Cisco-ET Extended Temperature platform.
1 Ethernet/IEEE 802.3 interface(s)
2 Serial network interface(s)
32K bytes of non-volatile configuration memory.
8192K bytes of processor board System flash (Read ONLY)
Configuration register is 0x2102
Router_B#
```

This time, the system image file is `flash:c2500-i-l.112-15.bin` booted from flash. This means it is running the proper IOS. Now look at the route table:

```
Router_B#show ip route
Codes: C - connected, S - static, I - IGRP, R - RIP, M - mobile, B -
 BGP, D - EIGRP, EX - EIGRP external, O - OSPF, IA - OSPF inter area N1
 - OSPF NSSA external type 1, N2 - OSPF NSSA external type 2 E1 - OSPF
 external type 1, E2 - OSPF external type 2, E - EGPi - IS-IS, L1 - IS-
 IS level-1, L2 - IS-IS level-2, * - candidate default
 U - per-user static route, o - ODR
Gateway of last resort is not set
172.16.0.0/16 is variably subnetted, 2 subnets, 2 masks
D       172.16.60.0/24 [90/307200] via 172.16.50.2, 00:00:16, Ethernet0
D       172.16.10.0/24 [90/300200] via 172.16.30.5, 00:00:19, Serial0
C       172.16.50.0/24 is directly connected, Ethernet0
C       172.16.30.4/30 is directly connected, Serial0
Router_B#
```

Now the route to 172.16.10.0/24 is present in the route table. The next step is to look at the route table on Router C:

```
Router_C>show ip route
Codes: C - connected, S - static, I - IGRP, R - RIP, M - mobile, B -
 BGP, D - EIGRP, EX - EIGRP external, O - OSPF, IA - OSPF inter area N1
 - OSPF NSSA external type 1, N2 - OSPF NSSA external type 2 E1 - OSPF
 external type 1, E2 - OSPF external type 2, E - EGPi - IS-IS, L1 - IS-
 IS level-1, L2 - IS-IS level-2, * - candidate defaultU - per-user
 static route, o - ODR
Gateway of last resort is not set
172.16.0.0/16 is variably subnetted, 3 subnets, 2 masks
C       172.16.60.0/24 is directly connected, Ethernet0/1
C       172.16.50.0/24 is directly connected, Ethernet0/0
D       172.16.30.4/30 [90/2195456] via 172.16.50.1,   00:02:59, Ethernet0/0
D       172.16.10.0/24 [90/3295676] via 172.16.50.1,   00:02:59, Ethernet0/0
Router_C>
```

Everything looks to be in place, but the ultimate test is to ftp from Host Z to Host A. The connection is successful:

```
C:\WINDOWS>ftp 172.16.10.2
> ftp: connect :10061
ftp>
```

Let's review the steps taken. The initial symptom was that Host Z could not ftp to Host A. The problem was isolated by using the `ping` and `traceroute` commands. The problem was that Router B was in boot mode. This happened because the IOS image was loaded from the ROM instead of flash. The problem was remedied by changing the configuration register to indicate that the image should be loaded from the system flash.

The effect of the configuration changes was validated by showing the routes present on each router, as well as establishing an FTP session with Host A.

Scenario #3

The final general scenario in this chapter involves WAN connectivity problems but is slightly different from Scenario #1. In this situation, a facility has been moved, just yesterday afternoon, and the existing network equipment was reconfigured and reused in the new location. This move was also used as an opportunity to clean up the location's assigned IP address ranges to match the current addressing standard. Following the move, everything was verified and the users at the new site were able to get to internal and external resources successfully.

Overnight, however, there was a power outage at the new site, and this morning the users cannot get to any internal or external resources other than ones on their own segment. To make matters worse, there is no network administrator on site—the installation had been considered successful and the network administrator who did the installation has already left.

Figure 42.4 shows the network topology for this troubleshooting scenario.

FIGURE 42.4 Network diagram for Scenario #3

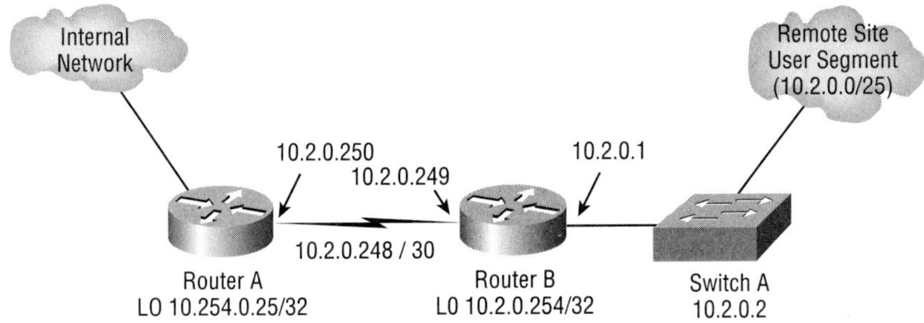

Gathering Symptoms

The first thing that you can do is ensure that Router B is reachable by pinging both the loopback interface and the other side of the serial connection:

```
Router_A#ping 10.2.0.254
Type escape sequence to abort.
Sending 5, 100-byte ICMP Echos to 10.2.0.254, timeout is 2 seconds:
.....
Success rate is 0 percent (0/5)
Router_A#ping 10.2.0.249
Type escape sequence to abort.
Sending 5, 100-byte ICMP Echos to 10.2.0.249, timeout is 2 seconds:
.....
Success rate is 0 percent (0/5)
Router_A#
```

Because the ping tests failed, you need to look deeper into the connectivity between Router A and Router B:

```
Router_A#show interface s0/0
Serial0/0 is up, line protocol is up
  Hardware is QUICC with integrated T1 CSU/DSU
  Internet address is 10.2.0.250/30
  MTU 1500 bytes, BW 1544 Kbit, DLY 20000 usec, rely 255/255, load 1/255
  Encapsulation HDLC, loopback not set, keepalive set (10 sec)
  Last input 00:00:02, output 00:00:00, output hang never
  Last clearing of "show interface" counters never
  Queueing strategy: fifo
  Output queue 0/40, 0 drops; input queue 0/75, 0 drops
  5 minute input rate 0 bits/sec, 0 packets/sec
  5 minute output rate 0 bits/sec, 0 packets/sec
     354 packets input, 31947 bytes, 0 no buffer
     Received 145 broadcasts, 0 runts, 0 giants, 0 throttles
     0 input errors, 0 CRC, 0 frame, 0 overrun, 0 ignored, 0 abort
     369 packets output, 27286 bytes, 0 underruns
     0 output errors, 0 collisions, 8 interface resets
     0 output buffer failures, 0 output buffers swapped out
     5 carrier transitions
     DCD=up  DSR=up  DTR=up  RTS=up  CTS=up

Router_A#
```

You observe that the interface is in an up/up state and that some traffic appears to be going across the interface. So at this point, layers 1 and 2 appear to be okay. Let's see if there is anything in Router A's log that could be of some assistance:

```
Router_A#show logging
Syslog logging: enabled (0 messages dropped, 0 flushes, 0 overruns)
    Console logging: disabled
    Monitor logging: level debugging, 0 messages logged
    Buffer logging: level debugging, 97 messages logged
    Trap logging: level informational, 32 message lines logged

Log Buffer (4096 bytes):
Jul 20 06:37:05.995: IP-EIGRP: Neighbor 10.100.0.249 not on common
 subnet for Serial0/0
Jul 20 06:37:19.603: IP-EIGRP: Neighbor 10.100.0.249 not on common
 subnet for Serial0/0
Jul 20 06:37:34.215: IP-EIGRP: Neighbor 10.100.0.249 not on common
 subnet for Serial0/0
Jul 20 06:37:48.439: IP-EIGRP: Neighbor 10.100.0.249 not on common
 subnet for Serial0/0
...
...
<output removed>
...
...
Jul 20 06:46:36.875: IP-EIGRP: Neighbor 10.100.0.249 not on common
 subnet for Serial0/0
Jul 20 06:46:50.015: IP-EIGRP: Neighbor 10.100.0.249 not on common
 subnet for Serial0/0
Jul 20 06:47:03.651: IP-EIGRP: Neighbor 10.100.0.249 not on common
 subnet for Serial0/0
Jul 20 06:47:17.791: IP-EIGRP: Neighbor 10.100.0.249 not on common
 subnet for Serial0/0
Jul 20 06:47:31.799: IP-EIGRP: Neighbor 10.100.0.249 not on common
 subnet for Serial0/0
Router_A#
```

The log indicates that the neighbor on Serial 0 is not on the same subnet and is using the IP address 10.100.0.249. See if you can confirm this by checking the CDP information:

```
Router_A#show cdp neighbors serial0/0 detail
-------------------------
Device ID: Router_B
```

```
Entry address(es):
  IP address: 10.100.0.249
Platform: cisco 3640,  Capabilities: Router
Interface: Serial0/0,  Port ID (outgoing port): Serial0/0
Holdtime : 179 sec
Version :
Cisco Internetwork Operating System Software
IOS (tm) 3600 Software (C3640-JS56I-M), Version 12.0(7)T,  RELEASE
  SOFTWARE (fc2)
Copyright (c) 1986-1999 by cisco Systems, Inc.
Compiled Wed 08-Dec-99 04:50 by phanguye

Router_A#
```

A `show CDP neighbors` *`xx`* *`detail`* confirms that Router B is using 10.100.0.249 as its IP address. In looking at your old documentation, you see that this is the address the router had when it was in the old location. Let's list the symptoms that you have gathered up to this point:

- Users in the remote location can only get to resources on their directly attached segment.
- Router A cannot ping the serial or loopback interface of Router B.
- Interface Serial 0/0 is up and the line protocol is up.
- There are EIGRP error messages in Router A's log, indicating a neighbor on an incorrect subnet.
- According to CDP, Router B is using the address 10.100.0.249 on its serial interface.
- 10.100.0.249 was the address that was used on Router B's serial interface in the old location.

Isolating the Problem

Based on the data so far, the possible reasons for an incorrect address on the interface are as follows:

- The configuration was changed.
- The new configuration was never saved to NVRAM, and the old configuration was brought up when the router was reloaded.

The second possibility is the most likely because it would also explain why users are not able to get to any services outside their subnet.

Correcting the Problem

Unfortunately, since Router B is remote and there is no one at the location who can assist, the change to the IP address must be done remotely if at all possible. To do this, you'll change the IP address of Router A's Serial 0/0 to be on the same subnet as Router B's. This will allow you to connect to Router B and correct its configuration.

Because you know that the IP address space has not yet been reassigned, in this particular scenario, you don't have to worry about creating another problem by accidentally duplicating IP addresses in the network. In your network, however, always be sure to verify that the IP address space you're using has not already been assigned elsewhere.

```
Router_A#configure terminal
Enter configuration commands, one per line.  End with CNTL/Z.
Router_A(config)#interface Serial0/0
Router_A(config-if)#ip address 10.100.0.250 255.255.255.252
```

Next, make sure you can ping the other side and see the EIGRP neighbor:

```
Router_A#ping 10.100.0.249
Type escape sequence to abort.
Sending 5, 100-byte ICMP Echos to 10.100.0.249, timeout is 2 seconds:
!!!!!
Success rate is 100 percent (5/5), round-trip min/avg/max = 1/3/4 ms
Router_A#
Router_A#show ip eigrp neighbors serial0/0
IP-EIGRP neighbors for process 3
H   Address             Interface   Hold Uptime   SRTT   RTO  Q  Seq
                                    (sec)         (ms)       Cnt Num
0   10.100.0.249          Se0/0        14 00:02:11 1018  5000  0  2
Router_A#
```

You can now telnet over to Router B and see how the interfaces are configured:

```
Router_B#show ip interface brief
Interface       IP-Address      OK? Method      Status          Protocol
Ethernet0/0      unassigned     YES NVRAM  administratively down   down
Serial0/0        10.100.0.249   YES NVRAM  up                      up
Serial0/1        unassigned     YES NVRAM  administratively down   down
FastEthernet1/0 10.100.0.1      YES NVRAM  up                      up
Ethernet2/0      unassigned     YES NVRAM  administratively down   down
TokenRing2/0     unassigned     YES NVRAM  administratively down   down
Loopback0        10.100.0.254   YES NVRAM  up                      up
Router_B#
```

In looking at the interfaces, you can see that all of them are set to their old values. Therefore, you need to update these values to the new correct ones:

```
Router_B#configure terminal
Enter configuration commands, one per line.  End with CNTL/Z.
```

```
Router_B(config)#interface loopback0
Router_B(config-if)#ip address 10.2.0.254 255.255.255.255
Router_B(config-if)#interface FastEthernet1/0
Router_B(config-if)#ip address 10.2.0.1 255.255.255.128
Router_B(config-if)#interface Serial0/0
Router_B(config-if)#ip address 10.2.0.249 255.255.255.252
```

Since the address you connected to the router is on Serial 0/0, when this address is changed, your Telnet session will be dropped. To reconnect, you will need to change the address on Serial 0/0 on Router A back to the correct value. This is done as follows:

```
Router_A#configure terminal
Enter configuration commands, one per line.  End with CNTL/Z.
Router_A(config)#interface Serial0/0
Router_A(config-if)#ip address 10.2.0.250 255.255.255.252
```

With Serial 0/0 correctly set up on both routers, you are once again able to telnet to Router B normally. From Router A, you need to verify connectivity to the loopback and serial addresses of Router B:

```
Router_A#ping 10.2.0.249
Type escape sequence to abort.
Sending 5, 100-byte ICMP Echos to 10.2.0.249, timeout is 2 seconds:
!!!!!
Success rate is 100 percent (5/5), round-trip min/avg/max = 1/3/4 ms
Router_A#ping 10.2.0.254
Type escape sequence to abort.
Sending 5, 100-byte ICMP Echos to 10.2.0.254, timeout is 2 seconds:
!!!!!
Success rate is 100 percent (5/5), round-trip min/avg/max = 1/3/4 ms
Router_A#
```

After this you need to verify with the users that they are able to connect to their resources. And finally, you execute a `copy running-config startup-config` command on Router B so that this problem does not happen again.

Troubleshooting Ethernet Problems

This section presents troubleshooting scenarios for Ethernet-related dysfunction. The examples are simple, and you need to use only Ethernet-related commands to solve these problems.

Real World Scenario

Using *reload* during Remote Configuration

It's not uncommon that a network administrator will need to work on a remote router. In many of these cases, a wrong step can sever network connectivity to the remote site, creating the need for someone to go out to the location and correct the problem. This is where the `reload` command can come in handy.

Before you start your work at the remote site, ensure that the current configuration is saved to NVRAM by executing the `copy running-config startup-config` command. Following this, assuming you only have minor alterations to make, execute the `reload in 15` command and begin your changes. This command tells the router to reload in 15 minutes. If your changes do cause the router to lose connectivity, in 15 minutes it will reset to the last saved configuration before the change started, allowing access once again. While you're doing the modifications, you can monitor the amount of time remaining before the reload by executing the `show reload` command. And, after your change is successful and everything is working as expected, you can execute the `reload cancel` command, which will cancel the scheduled reload.

Scenario #1

The difficulty in this first scenario is that Host A cannot telnet to Host Z. Figure 42.5 depicts the network you're working with. You know that the problem exists between Router C and Host Z. Because this is an Ethernet environment, you know what to look for.

FIGURE 42.5 Network diagram for Ethernet Scenario #1

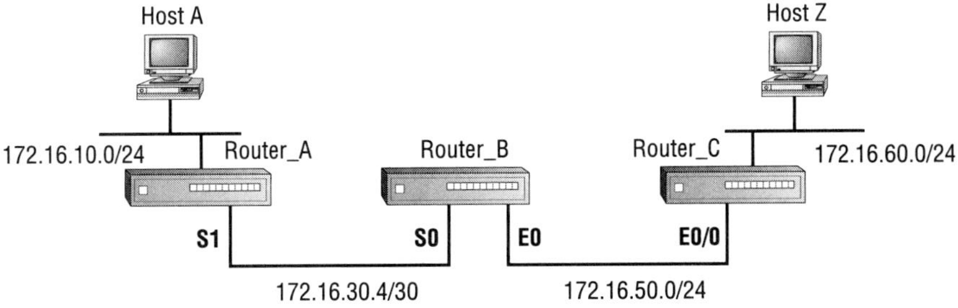

Gathering Symptoms

The first thing to do is verify that Host Z is still unreachable. Look at the results of a ping test:

```
Router_C#ping 172.16.60.130
Type escape sequence to abort.
```

```
Sending 5, 100-byte ICMP Echos to 172.16.60.130, timeout is 2 seconds:
.....
Success rate is 0 percent (0/5)
Router_C#
```

Because the ping test failed, the cause needs to be isolated. Let's look at the interface:

```
Router_C#show interface ethernet0/1
Ethernet0/1 is up, line protocol is up
  Hardware is AmdP2, address is 0010.7bd9.2881 (bia 0010.7bd9.2881)
  Internet address is 172.16.60.1/24
  MTU 1500 bytes, BW 10000 Kbit, DLY 1000 usec, rely 255/255, load 1/255
  Encapsulation ARPA, loopback not set, keepalive set (10 sec)
  ARP type: ARPA, ARP Timeout 04:00:00
  Last input 00:41:42, output 00:00:00, output hang never
  Last clearing of "show interface" counters never
  Queueing strategy: fifo
  Output queue 0/40, 0 drops; input queue 0/75, 0 drops
  5 minute input rate 0 bits/sec, 0 packets/sec
  5 minute output rate 0 bits/sec, 0 packets/sec
     147 packets input, 9568 bytes, 0 no buffer
     Received 5 broadcasts, 0 runts, 0 giants, 0 throttles
     0 input errors, 0 CRC, 0 frame, 0 overrun, 0 ignored, 0 abort
     0 input packets with dribble condition detected
     2009 packets output, 162455 bytes, 0 underruns
     0 output errors, 0 collisions, 2 interface resets
     0 babbles, 0 late collision, 0 deferred
     0 lost carrier, 0 no carrier
     0 output buffer failures, 0 output buffers swapped out
Router_C#
```

Everything looks good, except for the fact that no traffic is being sent across the interface. That can be another indication that there's a problem between the router and Host Z. Now, examine the ARP table:

```
Router_C>show arp
Protocol  Address      Age (min) Hardware Addr Type Interface
Internet  172.16.60.1  -     0010.7bd9.2881 ARPA  Ethernet0/1
Internet  172.16.50.2  -     0010.7bd9.2880 ARPA  Ethernet0/0
Internet  172.16.50.1   0    0000.0c09.99cc ARPA  Ethernet0/0
Router_C>
```

The address of interest is not listed in the ARP table, which means that Router C does not know where to send the layer 2 PDU. A trace using EtherPeek shows the router sending out an ARP broadcast:

```
Flags:         0x00
  Status:        0x00
  Packet Length:64
  Timestamp:     11:30:42.713000 04/19/2003
Ethernet Header
  Destination:  ff:ff:ff:ff:ff:ff Ethernet Brdcast  [0-5]
  Source:       00:10:7b:d9:28:81  [6-11]
  Protocol Type:08-06  IP ARP  [12-13]
ARP - Address Resolution Protocol
  Hardware:                  1  Ethernet (10Mb)  [14-15]
  Protocol:                  08-00  IP  [16-18]
  Hardware Address Length:   6  [19]
  Protocol Address Length:   4
  Operation:                 1  ARP Request  [20-21]
  Sender Hardware Address:   00:10:7b:d9:28:81  [22-27]
  Sender Internet Address:   172.16.60.1  [28-31]
  Target Hardware Address:   00:00:00:00:00:00  (ignored) [32-37]
  Target Internet Address:   172.16.60.130  [38-41]
Extra bytes (Padding):
  ................  00 00 00 00 00 00 00 00 00 00 00 00 00   00 00 00   [42-57]
  ..                00 00   [58-59]
Frame Check Sequence:  0x00000000
```

No response was received from this broadcast. List the symptoms that you have gathered:

- Router C cannot ping Host Z.
- Interface Ethernet 0/1 is up and line protocol is up.
- There are no collisions on the Ethernet interface.
- No traffic is transiting the Ethernet 0/1 interface.
- There is no listing for Host Z in the ARP table.
- An ARP broadcast was sent out Ethernet 0/1, but no response was received from Host Z.

Isolating the Problem

Focusing on the ARP table makes it simpler to decide the possible causes. What possible reasons are there for Host Z not to be listed in the ARP table? Here are some candidates:

- Failed host
- Cabling failures

- Bad Ethernet NIC on Host Z
- Mismatching frame encapsulation type

You verified that the host is not down. No traffic is transiting the Ethernet interface on the router. This indicates that the Ethernet card is not starting to fail, but could have completely failed. Cabling is probably not the issue because you would see interface resets or carrier transitions, and none of those symptoms are indicated on the interface. This leaves you with mismatching encapsulation type as the probable culprit.

The easiest way to test it is to ping Router C from Host Z:

```
C:\WINDOWS>ping 172.16.60.1
Pinging 172.16.60.1 with 32 bytes of data:
Reply from 172.16.60.1: bytes=32 time=7ms TTL=255
Reply from 172.16.60.1: bytes=32 time=1ms TTL=255
Reply from 172.16.60.1: bytes=32 time=2ms TTL=255
Reply from 172.16.60.1: bytes=32 time=4ms TTL=255
Ping statistics for 172.16.60.1:
    Packets: Sent = 4, Received = 4, Lost = 0 (0% loss),
Approximate round trip times in milli-seconds:
    Minimum = 1ms, Maximum =  7ms, Average =  3ms
C:\WINDOWS>
```

The ping was successful. Why is it that Router C can ping Host Z, but Host Z cannot ping Router C? Go back to the router. Look at the ARP table now:

```
Router_C>show arp
Protocol  Address  Age (min) Hardware Addr  Type  Interface
Internet  172.16.60.130 1   00a0.24a5.0657 SNAP  Ethernet0/1
Internet  172.16.60.1   -   0010.7bd9.2881 ARPA  Ethernet0/1
Internet  172.16.50.2   -   0010.7bd9.2880 ARPA  Ethernet0/0
Internet  172.16.50.1  111  0000.0c09.99cc ARPA  Ethernet0/0
Router_C>
```

Wait a minute! Host Z is listed in the table now. How did that happen? You must remember that although Cisco understands several different encapsulation types, its default is ARPA. When the router sent the ARP request, it was sent using ARPA. Host Z does not understand ARPA, and so it did not respond to the ARP request.

The process works differently on a Cisco router, however. When Host Z sent an ARP broadcast, it was sent with SNAP encapsulation. The difference is that the router understood the broadcast, recorded the encapsulation type, and entered it into the router's ARP table. The type allows the router to override the default encapsulation. Now, when the router needs to send a frame to Host Z, it uses SNAP encapsulation. Let's test it:

```
Router_C#ping 172.16.60.130
Type escape sequence to abort.
```

```
Sending 5, 100-byte ICMP Echos to 172.16.60.130, timeout   is 2 seconds:
!!!!!
Success rate is 100 percent (5/5), round-trip min/avg/max   = 4/4/8 ms
Router_C#
```

It worked just fine because the router now knows which encapsulation type must be used when communicating with Host Z.

This problem has been resolved temporarily. To solve it permanently, you must manually change the encapsulation type used for the interface to which Host Z connects, or create a static ARP entry. Now let's move on to the next scenario.

Scenario #2

This is another simple Ethernet problem. Using the example network depicted in Figure 42.6, you will attempt to solve a less tangible network misbehavior.

The user at Host A complains of very slow throughput to Host Z. He is able to ping and traceroute to the destination, but file transfers are experiencing very slow transfer times.

FIGURE 42.6 Network diagram for Ethernet Scenario #2

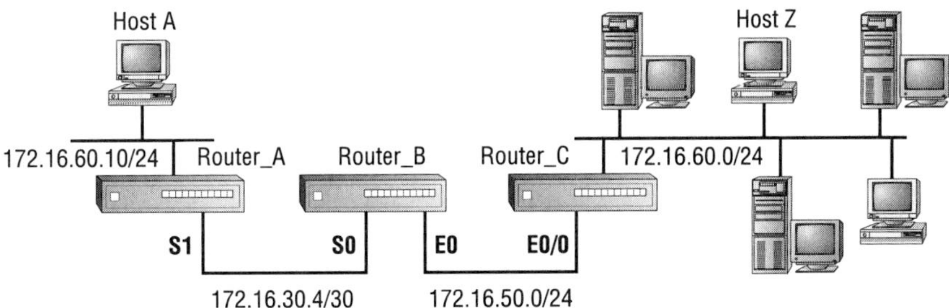

Gathering Symptoms

The user in this case was able to provide you with the following symptoms:

- Long transfer times
- Slow throughput
- Can ping and traceroute to host

The fact that ping and traceroute work indicates that the routing between Host A and Host Z is intact. Something else is causing latency somewhere along the line. Again, start at the far end of the problem.

The following are several `show interface` outputs of the same interface over an extended period of time. Look at them all and see if you can spot the problem:

```
Router_C#show int ethernet 0/1
Ethernet0/1 is up, line protocol is up
```

```
  Hardware is Lance, address is 0000.0c47.abea (bia 0000.0c47.abea)
  Internet address is 172.16.60.1/24
  MTU 1500 bytes, BW 10000 Kbit, DLY 1000 usec, rely 255/255, load 46/255
  Encapsulation ARPA, loopback not set, keepalive set (10 sec)
  ARP type: ARPA, ARP Timeout 04:00:00
  Last input 00:00:00, output 00:00:00, output hang never
  Last clearing of "show interface" counters 00:00:05
  Queueing strategy: fifo
  Output queue 0/40, 0 drops; input queue 0/75, 0 drops
  5 minute input rate 1259000 bits/sec, 629 packets/sec
  5 minute output rate 1822000 bits/sec, 486 packets/sec
     3476 packets input, 455808 bytes, 0 no buffer
     Received 2 broadcasts, 0 runts, 0 giants
     0 input errors, 0 CRC, 0 frame, 0 overrun, 0 ignored,
        0 abort
     0 input packets with dribble condition detected
     1165 packets output, 1667097 bytes, 0 underruns
     0 output errors, 175 collisions, 0 interface resets
     0 babbles, 0 late collision, 182 deferred
     0 lost carrier, 0 no carrier
     0 output buffer failures, 0 output buffers swapped out
Router_C#show int ethernet 0/1
Ethernet0/1 is up, line protocol is up
  Hardware is Lance, address is 0000.0c47.abea (bia 0000.0c47.abea)
  Internet address is 172.16.60.1/24
  MTU 1500 bytes, BW 10000 Kbit, DLY 1000 usec, rely 255/255, load 46/255
  Encapsulation ARPA, loopback not set, keepalive set (10 sec)
  ARP type: ARPA, ARP Timeout 04:00:00
  Last input 00:00:00, output 00:00:00, output hang never
  Last clearing of "show interface" counters 00:00:16
  Queueing strategy: fifo
  Output queue 0/40, 0 drops; input queue 0/75, 0 drops
  5 minute input rate 1243000 bits/sec, 627 packets/sec
  5 minute output rate 1826000 bits/sec, 484 packets/sec
     9872 packets input, 1760499 bytes, 0 no buffer
     Received 4 broadcasts, 0 runts, 0 giants
     0 input errors, 0 CRC, 0 frame, 0 overrun, 0 ignored,
        0 abort
     0 input packets with dribble condition detected
     2858 packets output, 3943213 bytes, 0 underruns
```

```
     0 output errors, 443 collisions, 0 interface resets
     0 babbles, 0 late collision, 471 deferred
     0 lost carrier, 0 no carrier
     0 output buffer failures, 0 output buffers swapped out
Router_C#show int ethernet 0/1
Ethernet0/1 is up, line protocol is up
  Hardware is Lance, address is 0000.0c47.abea (bia 0000.0c47.abea)
  Internet address is 172.16.60.1/24
  MTU 1500 bytes, BW 10000 Kbit, DLY 1000 usec, rely 255/255, load 46/255
  Encapsulation ARPA, loopback not set, keepalive set (10 sec)
  ARP type: ARPA, ARP Timeout 04:00:00
  Last input 00:00:00, output 00:00:00, output hang never
  Last clearing of "show interface" counters 00:00:37
  Queueing strategy: fifo
  Output queue 0/40, 0 drops; input queue 0/75, 0 drops
  5 minute input rate 1209000 bits/sec, 620 packets/sec
  5 minute output rate 1819000 bits/sec, 477 packets/sec
     21386 packets input, 3979009 bytes, 0 no buffer
     Received 9 broadcasts, 0 runts, 0 giants
     0 input errors, 0 CRC, 0 frame, 0 overrun, 0 ignored, 0 abort
     0 input packets with dribble condition detected
     5590 packets output, 8237684 bytes, 0 underruns
     0 output errors, 889 collisions, 0 interface resets
     0 babbles, 0 late collision, 1006 deferred
     0 lost carrier, 0 no carrier
     0 output buffer failures, 0 output buffers swapped out
Router_C#show int ethernet 0/1
Ethernet0/1 is up, line protocol is up
  Hardware is Lance, address is 0000.0c47.abea (bia 0000.0c47.abea)
  Internet address is 172.16.60.1/24
  MTU 1500 bytes, BW 10000 Kbit, DLY 1000 usec, rely 255/255, load 46/255
  Encapsulation ARPA, loopback not set, keepalive set (10 sec)
  ARP type: ARPA, ARP Timeout 04:00:00
  Last input 00:00:00, output 00:00:00, output hang never
  Last clearing of "show interface" counters 00:00:50
  Queueing strategy: fifo
  Output queue 0/40, 0 drops; input queue 0/75, 0 drops
  5 minute input rate 1209000 bits/sec, 620 packets/sec
  5 minute output rate 1819000 bits/sec, 477 packets/sec
     21386 packets input, 3979009 bytes, 0 no buffer
```

```
Received 9 broadcasts, 0 runts, 0 giants
0 input errors, 0 CRC, 0 frame, 0 overrun, 0 ignored, 0 abort
0 input packets with dribble condition detected
6000 packets output, 8237684 bytes, 0 underruns
0 output errors, 1020 collisions, 0 interface resets
0 babbles, 0 late collision, 1006 deferred
0 lost carrier, 0 no carrier
0 output buffer failures, 0 output buffers swapped out
```

So, what do you think? This exercise was designed specifically to educate you about Ethernet capabilities. The principal observation that you should have made was the increasing number of collisions on the interface.

Collisions are a normal occurrence for CSMA/CD protocols. The fact that a connection is not full-duplex creates the opportunity for collisions. Although collisions are normal, excessive collisions can be detrimental to a network. Though there is some debate over the exact value, when collisions exceed five to eight percent of the output packets, the interface becomes very ineffective. The higher the collision rate, the more packets have to be retransmitted.

Isolating the Problem

The output queue for the Ethernet interface doesn't stop filling up just because of collisions on the line. Therefore, not only does the interface have to transmit the normal queue of packets, it has to retransmit all the frames that were lost due to collisions. The number of packets that must be transmitted can grow exponentially. Calculate the collision percentage for the four `show interface` outputs you've just examined:

- 175 collisions / 1165 output packets = 15.02% collisions
- 443 collisions / 2858 output packets = 15.5% collisions
- 889 collisions / 5590 output packets = 15.9% collisions
- 1020 collisions / 6000 output packets = 17.0% collisions

All of these values are well in excess of five to eight percent. It looks like a key observation has been made, and now the problem statement can be written: "The collision percentage on Ethernet 0/1 exceeds healthy values and can be blamed for causing slow network throughput."

The hard part now is to determine what is causing the collisions. In this scenario, you will consider solutions from layer 1 up to layer 2. Following are possible solutions:

- Replace a faulty cable.
- Replace a faulty transceiver.
- Replace a faulty interface by changing the router.

First you'll test the cable. If the cable passes, then you'll change the transceiver. If that doesn't help, you'll assume that the interface on the router has gone bad. If the latter is the problem, you may be able to solve it by moving the connection to another interface on the same router or to a different interface on a different router.

Correcting the Problem

Figure 42.7 depicts the physical hardware involved in this scenario. The cable connects to the hub and to a transceiver that is connected to the router's AUI interface.

FIGURE 42.7 Ethernet physical hardware

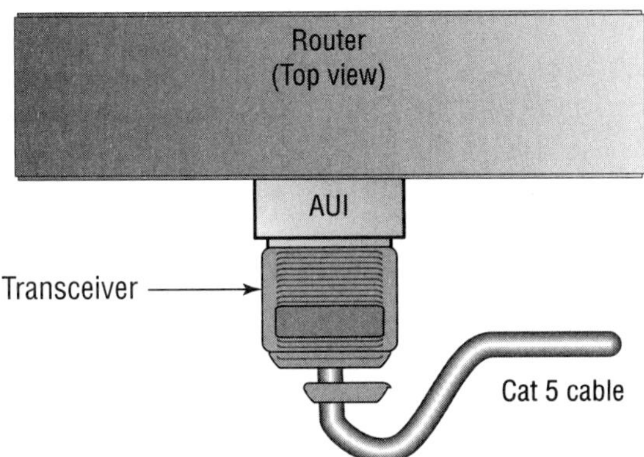

You tested the cable and it passed, so you then change transceivers, execute a `clear counters` command to reset the interface counters, and look at the interface status again:

```
Router_C#show interface ethernet 0/1
Ethernet0/1 is up, line protocol is up
  Hardware is Lance, address is 0000.0c47.abea (bia 0000.0c47.abea)
  Internet address is 172.16.60.1/24
  MTU 1500 bytes, BW 10000 Kbit, DLY 1000 usec, rely 255/255, load 28/255
  Encapsulation ARPA, loopback not set, keepalive set (10 sec)
  ARP type: ARPA, ARP Timeout 04:00:00
  Last input 00:00:00, output 00:00:00, output hang never
  Last clearing of "show interface" counters 00:00:11
  Queueing strategy: fifo
  Output queue 0/40, 0 drops; input queue 0/75, 0 drops
  5 minute input rate 1381000 bits/sec, 723 packets/sec
  5 minute output rate 1126000 bits/sec, 418 packets/sec
     8291 packets input, 1933415 bytes, 0 no buffer
     Received 3 broadcasts, 0 runts, 0 giants
     0 input errors, 0 CRC, 0 frame, 0 overrun, 0 ignored,
        0 abort
     0 input packets with dribble condition detected
     7172 packets output, 1446188 bytes, 0 underruns
     0 output errors, 251 collisions, 0 interface resets
```

```
     0 babbles, 0 late collision, 265 deferred
     0 lost carrier, 0 no carrier
     0 output buffer failures, 0 output buffers swapped out
Router_C#
Router_C#show interface ethernet 0/1
Ethernet0/1 is up, line protocol is up
  Hardware is Lance, address is 0000.0c47.abea (bia 0000.0c47.abea)
  Internet address is 172.16.60.1/24
  MTU 1500 bytes, BW 10000 Kbit, DLY 1000 usec, rely 255/255, load 28/255
  Encapsulation ARPA, loopback not set, keepalive set (10 sec)
  ARP type: ARPA, ARP Timeout 04:00:00
  Last input 00:00:00, output 00:00:00, output hang never
  Last clearing of "show interface" counters 00:00:49
  Queueing strategy: fifo
  Output queue 0/40, 0 drops; input queue 0/75, 0 drops
  5 minute input rate 1392000 bits/sec, 735 packets/sec
  5 minute output rate 1114000 bits/sec, 425 packets/sec
     39411 packets input, 8957876 bytes, 0 no buffer
     Received 14 broadcasts, 0 runts, 0 giants
     0 input errors, 0 CRC, 0 frame, 0 overrun, 0 ignored,
        0 abort
     0 input packets with dribble condition detected
     38944 packets output, 6409017 bytes, 0 underruns
     0 output errors, 1556 collisions, 0 interface resets
     0 babbles, 0 late collision, 1368 deferred
     0 lost carrier, 0 no carrier
     0 output buffer failures, 0 output buffers swapped out
Router_C#
Router_C#show interface ethernet 0/1
Ethernet0/1 is up, line protocol is up
  Hardware is Lance, address is 0000.0c47.abea (bia 0000.0c47.abea)
  Internet address is 172.16.60.1/24
  MTU 1500 bytes, BW 10000 Kbit, DLY 1000 usec, rely 255/255, load 28/255
  Encapsulation ARPA, loopback not set, keepalive set (10  sec)
  ARP type: ARPA, ARP Timeout 04:00:00
  Last input 00:00:00, output 00:00:00, output hang never
  Last clearing of "show interface" counters 00:01:16
  Queueing strategy: fifo
  Output queue 0/40, 0 drops; input queue 0/75, 0 drops
  5 minute input rate 1396000 bits/sec, 742 packets/sec
```

```
  5 minute output rate 1110000 bits/sec, 434 packets/sec
     60752 packets input, 13691996 bytes, 0 no buffer
     Received 22 broadcasts, 0 runts, 0 giants
     0 input errors, 0 CRC, 0 frame, 0 overrun, 0 ignored,
        0 abort
     0 input packets with dribble condition detected
     65212 packets output, 10035669 bytes, 0 underruns
     0 output errors, 2466 collisions, 0 interface resets
     0 babbles, 0 late collision, 2163 deferred
     0 lost carrier, 0 no carrier
     0 output buffer failures, 0 output buffers swapped out
Router_C#
Router_C#show interface ethernet 0/1
Ethernet0/1 is up, line protocol is up
  Hardware is Lance, address is 0000.0c47.abea (bia 0000.0c47.abea)
  Description: 10BaseT to Core3
  Internet address is 172.16.60.1/24
  MTU 1500 bytes, BW 10000 Kbit, DLY 1000 usec, rely 255/255, load 28/255
  Encapsulation ARPA, loopback not set, keepalive set (10 sec)
  ARP type: ARPA, ARP Timeout 04:00:00
  Last input 00:00:00, output 00:00:00, output hang never
  Last clearing of "show interface" counters 00:01:42
  Queueing strategy: fifo
  Output queue 0/40, 0 drops; input queue 0/75, 0 drops
  5 minute input rate 1415000 bits/sec, 753 packets/sec
  5 minute output rate 1135000 bits/sec, 442 packets/sec
     81784 packets input, 18845458 bytes, 0 no buffer
     Received 29 broadcasts, 0 runts, 0 giants
     0 input errors, 0 CRC, 0 frame, 0 overrun, 0 ignored,
        0 abort
     0 input packets with dribble condition detected
     97408 packets output, 14297058 bytes, 0 underruns
     0 output errors, 3498 collisions, 0 interface resets
     0 babbles, 0 late collision, 2986 deferred
     0 lost carrier, 0 no carrier
     0 output buffer failures, 0 output buffers swapped out
Router_C#
```

Collision percentage calculations result in an average of 3.72 percent collisions. This is much better than the 15 percent you saw previously. In this scenario, a bad transceiver was to blame for the excessive collisions. In addition to the transmitting and receiving of data on the LAN, the transceiver is also responsible for collision detection.

Opening a Case with the Technical Assistance Center

No matter how good your troubleshooting skills, if you work with Cisco routers long enough, at some point you're going to need to open a case with the Cisco Technical Assistance Center (TAC). This can be done either online at `www.cisco.com`, or via the telephone. In the United States, the number is (800) 553-2447. For overseas numbers, please see the Cisco web page.

Regardless of how the case is opened, you should be prepared to provide the following five items to the TAC when the case is opened:

- Service and Support Contract number, and the serial number of the product for which the case is being opened
- Network topology and explanation
- Output from a `show tech-support` command as well as any other relevant output
- Description of problem
- Software versions and types of equipment involved in the problem

Summary

You will encounter several common problems with routers in general, as well as more-specific issues with the Ethernet protocol when you are troubleshooting network issues. Most of these problems are found to be on layer 2 and layer 1, and occasionally layer 3. Often these typical misbehaviors have simple solutions. For instance, you may be able to solve a problem by verifying that the correct IP address is assigned, that the correct DLCI is used, or that the Frame Relay DLCI-to-IP address mapping is correct, or by removing the administrative shutdown on an interface.

The boot mode on a router contains no routing functionality. Therefore, when a router comes up in boot mode, either by error or due to a problem, you need to take steps to return it to normal operation. Specifically, make sure you have the correct image in flash, change the configuration register to indicate that the system image should be loaded from flash, and then reload the router.

A couple of problems are common in the Ethernet environment. An encapsulation mismatch on a segment will preclude the mismatched devices from communicating with each other. When there is an Ethernet frame encapsulation mismatch, an easy way to determine the host's encapsulation type is to allow the host machine to ARP for the router. The router then records the frame type in the ARP table. Another issue in Ethernet is a high number of collisions. When this occurs on a segment that is not being heavily utilized, a hardware problem is usually the culprit. In many of these cases, replacing the transceiver will correct the situation. Note that collisions are not excessive until they are over five to eight percent.

At some point, almost every network administrator will need to open a case with Cisco TAC. This can be accomplished via the website or by phone. Cisco requires certain information when opening a case, including contract number, network topology, output of a `show tech-support` command, and the version numbers of the hardware and software involved in the problem.

Exam Essentials

Know the *show* commands and how to interpret the output. Specifically in this chapter, we focused on `show arp`, `show cdp neighbors`, `show flash`, `show frame-relay pvc`, `show frame-relay map`, `show interface`, `show ip eigrp neighbors`, `show logging`, and `show version`.

Know the three steps to the Cisco troubleshooting model and the function that each performs. The Cisco troubleshooting steps are: gather symptoms, isolate the problem, correct the problem and repeat if necessary. These steps define an effective step-by-step methodology for troubleshooting any problem.

Be able to apply the Cisco troubleshooting methodology to example situations. You should know how to apply each step of the model in real-life scenarios. You should be able to determine what step in a troubleshooting scenario is next in the series, and to correlate a task with the correct step in the process.

Know how to use the *ping* and *traceroute* commands. This includes the extended ping and traceroute options available under privileged mode.

Know the general steps required to identify and rectify a Physical layer issue. Using the output of `show` commands, know what symptoms are characteristic of a physical dysfunction and what possible components can be causing the problem.

Know what information is required to open a Cisco TAC case. To open a TAC case you need the contract number, network topology, output of a `show tech-support` command, and the version numbers of the hardware and software involved in the problem.

Index

Note to the reader: Throughout this index **boldfaced** page numbers indicate primary discussions of a topic. *Italicized* page numbers indicate illustrations.

Numbers

A

B

C

E

F

G

H

I

J

K

L

M

N

O

P

Q

R

S

T

U

V

W

X

Z

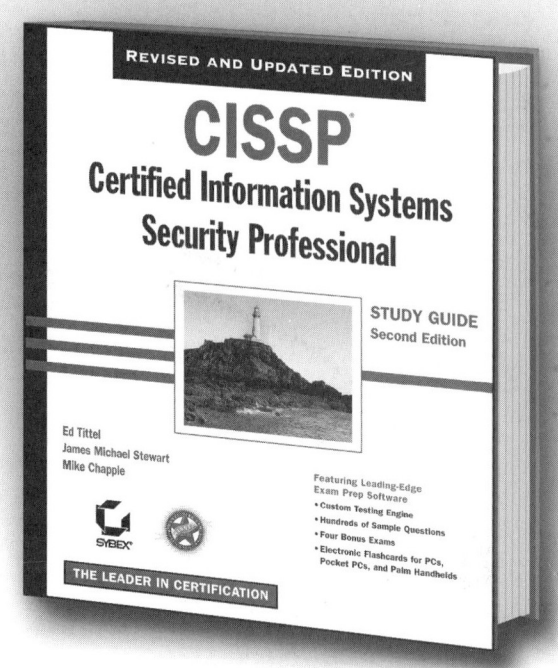

TELL US WHAT YOU THINK!

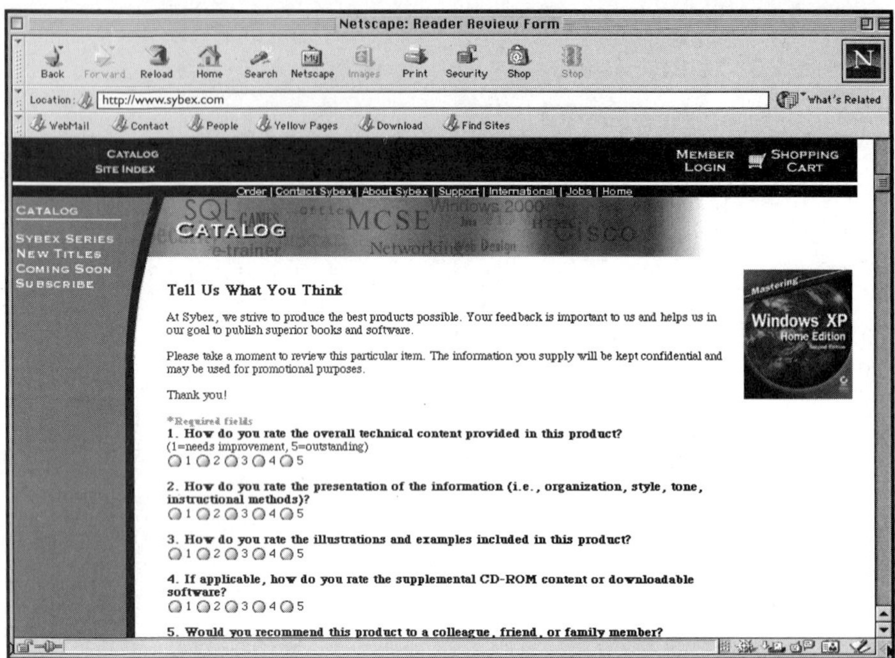

Your feedback is critical to our efforts to provide you with the best books and software on the market. Tell us what you think about the products you've purchased. It's simple:

1. Go to the Sybex website.
2. Find your book by typing the ISBN or title into the Search field.
3. Click on the book title when it appears.
4. Click **Submit a Review.**
5. Fill out the questionnaire and comments.
6. Click **Submit.**

With your feedback, we can continue to publish the highest quality computer books and software products that today's busy IT professionals deserve.

www.sybex.com

SYBEX Inc. • 1151 Marina Village Parkway, Alameda, CA 94501 • 510-523-8233

SYBEX®